Is America Necessary?

Conservative, Liberal &
Socialist Perspectives
of United States Political
Institutions

Written and Edited by

HENRY ETZKOWITZ · PETER SCHWAB

State University of New York at Purchase

WEST PUBLISHING CO. | St. Paul · New York · Boston
Los Angeles · San Francisco

Library of Congress Cataloging in Publication Data

Main entry under title:

Is America necessary?

    Bibliography: p.
    Includes index.
    1. United States—Politics and government—Addresses,
essays, lectures. 2. Right and left (Political science)
—Addresses, essays, lectures. I. Etzkowitz, Henry,
1940-   II. Schwab, Peter, 1940-
JK21.I8   320.9'73   75-45037
ISBN 0-8299-0090-X

In memory of C. Wright Mills who provided the intellectual and political inspiration for our analysis.

There was a strike in Pittsburgh. At the Homestead steel plant of Mr. Carnegie. And Mr. Carnegie decided to break the union. So he ran off for a European vacation and had his chief toady, that infamous piece of scum Henry Clay Frick, do the job. Frick imported an army of Pinkertons. The workers were on strike to protest the cutting of wages. The plant is on the Monongahela River and Frick towed his Pinkertons up the river and landed them at the plant from the river. There was a pitched battle. It was a war. When it was over ten were dead and dozens and dozens were wounded.

E. L. Doctorow
Ragtime

Acknowledgments

Bell, Daniel
"The Revolution of Rising Entitlements"

From *Fortune,* April 1975, pp. 98–103 ff.

Nadel, Mark V
"The Hidden Dimension of Public Policy: Private Governments and the Policy-Making Process"

From *The Journal of Politics* 37, no. 1 (February 1975), pp. 2–34.

Domhoff, William
"State and Ruling Class in Corporate America"

From *The Insurgent Sociologist* IV, no. 3 (Spring 1974), pp. 3–16.

Perlmutter, Amos.
"The Presidential Political Center and Foreign Policy: A Critique of the Revisionist and Bureaucratic Political Orientations"

From *World Politics* XXVII, no. 1. Copyright © 1974 by Princeton University Press. Reprinted by permission of Princeton University Press.

Reedy, George E.
"The American Monarchy"

From *The Twilight of the Presidency*, by George E. Reedy. Copyright © 1970 by George E. Reedy. Reprinted by arrangement with The New American Library, Inc., New York, N.Y.

Kolko, Gabriel
"The Men of Power"

From *The Roots of American Foreign Policy* (Boston: Beacon Press, 1969), pp. 3–26 ff. Copyright © 1969 by Gabriel Kolko. Reprinted by permission of Beacon Press.

Kissinger, Henry A.
"Force and Diplomacy in the Nuclear Age"

Reprinted by permission from *Foreign Affairs,* April 1956. Copyright 1956 by Council on Foreign Relations, Inc.

Mankoff, Milton, and Majka, Linda
"Economic Sources of American Imperialism"

Published by permission of Transaction, Inc., from SOCIETY, Volume 12, #4. Copyright © 1975, by Transaction, Inc.

Melman, Seymour
"The State-Management"

From PENTAGON CAPITALISM by Seymour Melman: Copyright © 1970 by Seymour Melman. Used with permission of McGraw-Hill Book Company.

"Summary of: Report to the President by the (Rockefeller) Commission on CIA Activities within the United States". (June 10, 1975).

Barnet, Richard J.
"Dirty Tricks and the Intelligence Underworld"

Published by permission of Transaction, Inc., from SOCIETY, Volume 12, #3. Copyright © 1975, by Transaction, Inc.

Wolfe, Alan
"Repression through Political Intelligence"

Copyright © 1973 by the David McKay Company Inc. From the book THE SEAMY SIDE OF DEMOCRACY, by Alan Wolfe. Reprinted with permission of the publisher.

Dexter, Lewis Anthony
"Influence...
Information...
Intelligence"

From HOW ORGANIZATIONS ARE REPRESENT-ED IN WASHINGTON by Lewis Anthony Dexter, copyright © 1969 by The Bobbs-Merrill Company, Inc., reprinted by permission of the publisher.

Domhoff, G. William
"How the Power Elite Make
Foreign Policy"

From THE HIGHER CIRCLES, by G. William Domhoff. Copyright © 1970 by G. William Domhoff. Reprinted by permission of Random House, Inc.

Mills, C. Wright
"Metropolitan 400"

From The Power Elite by C. Wright Mills. Copyright © 1959 by Oxford University Press. Reprinted by permission.

Diebold, John
"Why Be Scared of Them?"

From FOREIGN POLICY 12. Copyright 1973 by National Affairs, Inc.

Barnet, Richard J., and
Miller, Ronald
"The LatinAmericanization
of the United States"

From Global Reach: The Power of the Multinational Corporations. Copyright © 1974, by Richard J. Barnet and Ronald E. Miller. Reprinted by permission of Simon & Schuster, Inc.

O'Connor, James
"International Corporations
and Economic
Underdevelopment"

Reprinted from Science and Society XXXIV, no. 1 (Spring 1970), pp. 42–60.

Hawkins, Gordon
"God and the Mafia"

From THE PUBLIC INTEREST, Number 14 (Winter 1969, pp. 24–32. Copyright © 1969 by National Affairs, Inc.

Moynihan, Daniel P.
"The Private Government of
Crime"

Copyright 1961, The Reporter Magazine Co.

Gage, Nicholas
"Meyer-Lansky—
Underworld Genius"

From THE MAFIA IS NOT AN EQUAL OPPORTUNITY EMPLOYER by Nicholas Gage. Copyright © 1971 by Nicholas Gage. Used with permission of McGraw-Hill Book Company.

Polsby, Nelson W.
"Policy Analysis and
Congress"

From Public Policy XVIII, no. 1 (Fall 1969), pp. 61–74.

Harrington, Michael J.
"The Politics of Gun
Control"

From The Nation, January 12, 1974, pp. 41–5.

Green, Mark J.,
Fallows, James M.,
and Zwick, David R.
"Who Owns Congress?"

From WHO RUNS CONGRESS? by Mark J. Green, James M. Fallows, and David R. Zwick, Ralph Nader Congress Project. Copyright © 1972 by Ralph Nader. Reprinted by permission of Grossman Publishers.

Dahl, Robert A.
"Decision-Making in a
Democracy: The Supreme
Court as a National Policy-
Maker"

Reprinted with permission of the Emory Law Journal of Emory University School of Law.

Tench, Richard
"Whose Side Are Lawyers
On?"

Copyright © 1975 by The Antioch Review, Inc. First published by The Antioch Review, vol. 33, no. 1; reprinted by permission of the editors.

Lefcourt, Robert
"Law Against the People"

From LAW AGAINST THE PEOPLE: ESSAYS TO DEMYSTIFY LAW, ORDER, AND THE COURTS, edited by Robert Lefcourt. Copyright © 1971 by Robert Lefcourt. Reprinted by permission of Random House, Inc.

Wilson, James Q.
"The Dead Hand of
Regulation"

From THE PUBLIC INTEREST, Number 25 (Fall 1971), pp. 39–58. Copyright © 1971 by National Affairs, Inc.

Long, Norton E.
"Power and
Administration"

From *Public Administration Review* 9, no. 4 (1949), pp. 257–67.

Schaflander, Gerald M.
"The Balanced Liberal
Ideology at the FTC: A
Due-Process Radical
Alternative"

Copyright by Gerald M. Schaflander.

Dahl, Robert A.
"Political Parties:
Contributions to
Democracy"

Robert A. Dahl, PLURALIST DEMOCRACY IN THE UNITED STATES: CONFLICT AND CONSENT, First Edition, © 1967 by Rand McNally & Company, Chicago, pp. 243–57. Reprinted by permission of Rand McNally College Publishing Company.

Lowi, Theodore J.
"A 'Critical' Election
Misfires"

From *The Nation*, December 18, 1972, pp. 616–20.

Lerner, Michael P.
"How to Put Socialism on
the Agenda"

From *Socialist Revolution*, nos. 21–22 (July–December 1974), pp. 107–24.

Lambright, W. Henry, and
Henry, Laurin L.
"Using Universities: The
NASA Experience"

From *Public Policy* XX (Winter 1972), pp. 61–82.

Denhardt, Robert B.
"Exploring Political
Alternatives"

Reprinted from *Teaching Political Science* 2, no. 2 (January 1975), pp. 212–226, by permission of the Publisher, Sage Publications, Inc.

Wolfe, Alan
"The Professional
Mystique"

Chapter 10, "The Professional Mystique," by Alan Wolfe from AN END TO POLITICAL SCIENCE: The Caucus Papers, edited by Marvin Surkin and Alan Wolfe, © 1970 by Basic Books, Inc., Publishers, New York.

Weaver, Paul H.
"The New Journalism and
the Old—Thoughts After
Watergate"

From THE PUBLIC INTEREST, Number 35 (Spring 1974), pp. 67–88. Copyright © 1974 by National Affairs, Inc.

Wenglinsky, Martin
"Television News: A New
Slant"

From *The Columbia Forum* III, no. 4 (1974), pp. 2–9.

Parenti, Michael
"The Mass Media: By the
Few, For the Many"

From *Democracy for the Few* (New York: St. Martin's Press, Inc., 1974), pp. 167–78.

"The Great Banking
Retreat"

From *Business Week,* April 21, 1975, pp. 46–50.

Mayer, Martin
"How Banks Destroy the
Economy"

From *Harper's* Magazine, January 1975, pp. 49–52 ff.

Sweezy, Paul, and
Magdoff, Harry
"Banks: Skating on Thin Ice"

From *Monthly Review, Inc.*, (February, 1975), pp. 1–21. Copyright © 1975 by Monthly Review, Inc. Reprinted by permission of Monthly Review Press.

Schrank, Robert
"The Young Workers: Their
Influence on the
Workplace"

From *The Urban Review* 5–6 (June 1972), pp. 12–16.

Whalen, Eileen
"Working Women"

From *Up From Under* I, no. 5 (1973), pp. 31–5.

Georgakas, Dan, and
Surkin, Marvin
"Niggermation in Auto:
Company Policy and the
Rise of Black Caucuses"

From *Radical America* 9, no. 1 (January/February 1975), pp. 31–56. Used with permission of St. Martin's Press, Inc., © 1975, *Detroit: I Do Mind Dying*.

Rohatyn, Felix G.
"A New R.F.C. Is Proposed
for Business"

© 1974 by The New York Times Company. Reprinted by permission.

Ginsburg, Helen
"The Strategy of Misery"

From *The Nation*, February 1, 1975, pp. 114–17.

Sweezy, Paul, and
Magdoff, Harry
"The Economic Crisis in
Historical Perspective—
Part II"

Copyright © 1975 by Monthly Review, Inc. Reprinted by permission of Monthly Review Press.

Banks, Louis
"The Mission of Our
Business Society"

From *Harvard Business Review*, May/June 1975, pp. 57–65. © 1975 by The President and Fellows of Harvard College; all rights reserved.

Gardner, John W.
"Citizen Action"

Reprinted from COMMON CAUSE, by John Gardner. By permission of W.W. Norton & Company, Inc. Copyright © 1972 by W.W. Norton & Company, Inc.

Nader, Ralph, and
Ross, Donald
"Toward an Initiatory
Democracy"

From ACTION FOR A CHANGE by Ralph Nader and Donald Ross, Revised Edition. Copyright © 1971, 1972 by Ralph Nader. Reprinted by permission of Grossman Publishers.

Aronowitz, Stanley
"On Organization: A Good
Party Is Hard to Find"

From *Liberation* 18, no. 4 (December 1973), pp. 30–7.

Domhoff, G. William
"Blueprints for a New
Society"

From *Ramparts*, February 1974, pp. 13–16.

"Against The Common
Enemy"

From *Prairie Fire: The Politics of Revolutionary Anti-Imperialism*, pp. 139–146. Copyright © 1974 by Communications Co.

Harris, Fred R.
"Up with Those Who're
Down"

From *The New Populism* by Fred R. Harris. Copyright © 1973 by Fred R. Harris. Reprinted by permission of the publishers, Saturday Review Press/E.P. Dutton & Co., Inc.

Preface

Both of us are grateful for the help we have received from librarians at the State University of New York at Purchase and the New School for Social Research. Particularly, we wish to thank Paula Hane, research librarian at Purchase. The resources of New York City—libraries, universities, book stores, organizations—have greatly facilitated the collection of materials for *Is America Necessary?*

There are four groups of people whose support has personally helped the authors. (1) Our colleagues in the Social Science Division at Purchase have provided intellectual stimulation and challenged our thoughts. We are personally and intellectually grateful to Mary Edwards, Joe Fashing, John Howard, Esther Newton, and Susan Rennie. (2) From our own education the special influence in developing this work has come from Donald Meiklejohn of the University of Chicago, and Adamantia Pollis of the Graduate Faculty of the New School for Social Research. (3) Those associates who have had a political and intellectual impact upon us certainly deserve recognition. They are: Bogdan Denitch, Mary Howard, Dave McReynolds, Stanley Millet, Gerald Schaflander, and Marvin Surkin. (4) Henry Etzkowitz would like to especially thank his Men's Group for its friendship and support, and his brothers and sisters in the East Coast Conference of Socialist Sociologists, in particular, Blanka Eckstein, Marty Oppenheimer, and Peter Stein. He would also like to thank Sally Akan and Roger Mack. Peter Schwab is grateful for the friendship and support of Bobbi and Dan Kurland, Ruth Messinger and the 87th Street Collective, Addie Pollis, and Connie and Lee Shneidman. Both of us would like to thank our editors at West. Finally, Henry Etzkowitz would like to express his love and appreciation to Judy Richman.

Henry Etzkowitz
Peter Schwab

New York City
November 27, 1975

*

Contents

†

In this introduction we will treat the following questions:

(1) How does this book differ from other American Government readers?

(2) How does the question of whether there can be a value free political science relate to the study of political institutions?

(3) How do the three political traditions of conservatism, liberalism, and socialism influence the analysis of political institutions?

(4) How can the political position of an analysis of a political institution be discerned when it is not openly stated? In other words how are students to read what academic authors write?

These questions lead to an analysis of political institutions from a political approach. A political social science[1] asks the following questions about the analysis of political institutions:

(1) Is political analysis affected by the political/economic arrangements within which it develops?

(2) How does the analysis relate to the proponent's class perspective?

(3) What self-interest does the proponent of an idea have in it?

(4) Which groups stand to gain or lose if the idea is accepted or rejected?

(5) Is political science a science or an ideology? Or both?

Question 1.   How does this book differ from other American Government readers?

By comparing several analyses of the same issue, each presented from different and perhaps contrasting points of view, one can begin to see divergent issues at stake and to explore the world of conflict. Each of the fourteen political institutions dealt with in this book is discussed by three writers having a different political perspective. This method will show not only that there is more than one way of defining the role of each institution, but also that each position produces an analysis very different in kind.

Our belief that articles on political institutions are inevitably written from political perspectives is the organizing principle for this book. Political

Political ideologies and institutions

scientists, in our view, discuss political institutions and their role from three basic political approaches: conservative, liberal, socialist.2

This book of readings analyzes a number of political institutions from three perspectives. Most such books deal with a few institutions, or with one area in political science from one political perspective. This approach is usually chosen for three major reasons: (1) an editor has a specific theoretical framework in mind which has been deliberately chosen as the organizing principle of the book; (2) an editor may simply be looking for the *best* writing in the field. In this case articles will usually reflect a consistent but unstated underlying political perspective; (3) an editor *needs* a book to achieve status or tenure at his/her university. Here an editor will select articles on one political problem which may or may not have an underlying theoretical framework, because the topic is suddenly "in the news," relevant articles are easy to come by, and a book can be added to the curriculum vitae. Good and useful books can and do result from these approaches.

This text is different. It is the only text we know of that deals with a large number of political institutions from conservative, liberal, and socialist perspectives. In deliberately offering opposing perspectives it presents a different format. *Is America Necessary?* can be used as the main text for an American Government course, or in conjunction with a single-perspective book to introduce additional viewpoints to the course. It may also be used as a companion book in courses dealing with the institutions studied in this book.

In addition, if the instructor uses only the socialist article from each chapter, the result would be a socialist reader; or the instructor may opt for the liberal or conservative perspective, drawing on as many or as few observations from other perspectives as are necessary or useful. Of course the student may read any selection, whether assigned by the instructor or not. Access to literature must always remain free, but instruction is most meaningful if it propounds a perspective.

This book is designed to encourage students to use the conflicts and contradictions they encounter by their exposure to more than one analysis of a particular political institution. The aim of this reader is to provoke class discussions of political institutions, their effectiveness, and goals. We hope that *Is America Necessary?* will contribute towards making these discussions more informed and purposeful than before.

Question 2.   How does the question of whether there can be a value free political science relate to the study of political institutions?

To say either that something should be different from the way it is or that things are satisfactory the way they are is to make a value judgment. To praise or condemn a political institution is also making a value judgment. Value judgments say that something is "good" or "bad" or, perhaps, "important."

Marvin Surkin, in his essay "Sense and Non-Sense in Politics" argues that the so-called value-free social science is non-sense, because those who take this position are, whether they know it or not, taking a stand. According to Surkin, those who hold this value-free position are supporters of the politically conservative status-quo.

In effect, intellectual detachment and the disinterested quest for truth— the professed essence of the value-free, neutral social scientist—are replaced by the new elite role of the masters of knowledge whose knowledge is placed at the disposal of the "benevolent" political interests of the masters of power. Accordingly, social scientists become, in essence, "house-ideologues for those in power."[3]

Opposed to this thesis is Max Weber's essay on the relationship between values and social research. Weber argues that every research effort has its starting point in a value position, but that values apply only to the choosing of the research topic. Thereafter, the research process, including the questions posed and the methodologies used to obtain answers, does not involve questions of value. Therefore, although the choice of a topic is necessarily subjective, its implementation as a scholarly idea must be objective in nature.[4]

Often students come to the study of political science with the expectation that the discipline will provide them with a single agreed-upon set of answers to the problems of American society, that the empirical method applied to any issue will result in a specific answer indisputable by anyone who accepts the norms of science. This parallels the empirical school of thought in political science which holds that politics can be viewed neutrally and objectively.[5]

Everyone who enters into the discipline of political science must face up to the question of the place of value judgments. There has been for a number of years a debate in political science over this very issue. It has been expressed at association meetings, departmental meetings, and in academic journals. This has begun to have an effect on the organization of the discipline. For example, many political science departments, in order to come to grips with the issue, have changed their name from "political science department" to "political studies department." This is only a minor example of a controversy which has not yet been resolved. One of the purposes of this book is to address the implications of the value judgment issue.

The very act of defining some part of political existence as problematic necessarily involves using a value perspective; that is, it says that something is good or bad, worthwhile or worthless. Making this judgment is as inevitable in everyday life as it is in the practice of political science, if one does not totally ignore the world. To admit to making such judgments is not to say that political scientists discard the scientific method in their scholarly work. Rather, political scientists use it when examining political society, but the goals he/she desires will reflect his or her own perspective.

Whether they know it or not, political scientists in particular hold differing political perspectives and these color their scientific work. In fact, most of us take stands all the time. We say that the Presidency is too strong or too weak, that there is or is not a military-industrial complex. We sometimes think of our opinions as matters of fact that any sensible person would agree with. At other times we see our opinions as one side of a controversy to which there is at least one other arguable approach. Similarly, in political science, some writers recognize that there is an opposing analysis to the one they have set forth. At the other extreme, some political scientists assume that because they have conducted an empirical study only one answer to a particular political question is possible.

We believe that to questions and issues people care strongly about, different answers and perspectives are likely and even inevitable, for they are usually based on different assumptions. These are not random positions. Rather, they are usually consistent approaches—explicit or implicit—which connect to long-standing political traditions.

Question 3.　How do the three political traditions of conservatism, liberalism, and socialism influence the analysis of political institutions?

It is our objective to explicate three major trends—conservative, liberal, socialist—with respect to the study of political institutions. Conservatism, liberalism, and socialism, may be viewed as points on a spectrum moving from Right to Left, with many possible combinations and intermediate positions available. Each of these approaches to the study of political institutions contains within it a different perspective of the institution and a different analysis of its workability. Adherents of conservative, liberal, and socialist philosophies decide what is or is not problematic in political institutions based on the values of each of their schools of thought as Michael Parenti says:

The presumption that there is a scientifically discoverable "correct" solution to problems overlooks the fact that social problems involve conflicting ends and often irreconcilable value distributions; thus one man's "solution" is often another man's disaster. Unlike mathematical problems which might be resolved by procedures exogenous to the life subjectivities of various mathematicians, the solutions to social problems cannot be treated except in the context of vested and conflicting interests which give vested and conflicting definitions to the problem.[6]

Our objective here is not only to analyze American political institutions, but also to offer the reader an opportunity to try out certain intellectual tools of political analysis. In so doing the reader can better understand how political analyses of political institutions are developed and how they relate to his or her own political position, whether it be conservative, liberal, or socialist.

The political traditions of conservatism, liberalism, and socialism have many variations. Rather than offer an account of either their historical development or their contemporary complexities, it is more useful for our purpose to describe the typical features of each political value position. Thus, conservatism, liberalism, and socialism will not be presented in their fullest form. The following discussion will concentrate on the special features of the traditions so that the reader will have them at hand in ideal-typical form as an outline of essential characteristics. These positions represent our analysis of contemporary definitions of conservatism, liberalism, and socialism. These definitions may be used both to relate one's own political perspectives to these three traditions and to clarify the politics of the ideas presented in the articles.

What is conservatism?

Contemporary American conservatism views the business corporation as the paradigm for modern American society. It is therefore in relation to this fundamental institution as producer of goods and services that the foremost political goal of conservatism—*stability under hierarchical control*—must be achieved, both within the corporation and in the relationships between the corporation and other political institutions.

A fundamental goal of the corporation as a political institution is the expansion of the economy. The achievement of profits through bureaucratically controlled technological development is assumed as the chief aim of each citizen as well as of the state. Thus, every individual and governmental activity may be judged by the criterion of benefit to private enterprise. If one assumes that all individuals and institutions share this basic premise, the achievement of a harmonious society based on conservative principles becomes possible.

Many conservatives openly express their belief that there are of necessity a few individuals in any society eminently qualified to conduct the political affairs of that society. For them the principle political problem is to insure a means by which these few people will be encouraged and enabled to rule. Political science from this perspective will be an analysis of the people who fill roles in the generally and officially recognized major institutions. Other institutions, which may be as important, are not recognized by conservatives as political institutions. Nor will conservatives focus on social movements by large numbers of people except insofar as they may disrupt the workings of official institutions.

Conservatives thus believe that tradition, order, and stability are pre-eminently desirable political goals, but often they hold this belief only when they are in power. If others hold power, or if conservatives' continuance in power is threatened, they may well be willing to use drastic means and to create disorder and instability in order to maintain a condition of order and stability that is under their control. Sophisticated conservatives, to avoid such extreme possibilities, are willing to sponsor programs for specific and limited social innovations in order to maintain the basic outline of the American status quo. To this end conservatives will sometimes utilize the theory of pluralism—the thesis which argues that competing interest groups play a role in influencing the direction of American society. That is, pluralist theory is used by conservatives when necessary, even though they believe in hierarchical control in which the role of political elites is primary. From this conservative perspective, most political problems are viewed as open to amelioration through those very structures of capitalism, the corporation and its allied institutions, which socialists would view as the prime cause of the problem.

From this viewpoint the inclusion of ever greater numbers of people in the corporate system is its most certain insurance for future survival. Since social and political change for conservatives must be both minimal and beneficial to themselves, an expanding technology, and government involvement with that technology only when directed by corporate values, is the sole engine they see as consistent with their view of "progress." As Daniel Bell says:

We have a lot to learn about the possibilities of the market mechanism as a means to achieve social ends. In many public-policy discussions, it is assumed that our choices are either administrative regulation to achieve those ends—or abandoning the ends. But the market can often be used to achieve them efficiently. The market provides for self-adjustment and self-regulation, within a framework of rules. Thus, in dealing with pollution, a system of effluent charges, with the cost element becoming the lever of compliance, would be preferable to a system of administrative regulation.[7]

Thus, the corporation is the proper means used to achieve necessary social change.

In examining a political scientist's position to determine whether it is conservative, one might ask four possible questions: (1) Does the author, overtly or covertly, believe in rule by elites? (2) Is the author arguing in favor of continuing a political structure as it presently exists? In other words does he/she call for the maintenance of the status quo? (3) Is the author calling for the maintenance of the political order and stability as opposed to other more possible or even desirable goals? (4) Does the author consider the acquisition of private property as a major social/political goal and interference with that goal—especially by the state—an evil? Elite rule, stability, order, the maintenance of the status quo, tradition, and the attainment of private property may be seen as the principle components of most conservative arguments about the nature of political society. Conservatives sometimes accept govenment intervention, but only when that intervention is directed by the corporate controllers of society. Their political analyses are not always set forth within an obvious capitalist framework, but the framework is always inherently accepted.

Liberals believe that all good ends are the result of good means—and "good" means that orderly process is not violated. Due process is observed—a person is entitled to proceedings which are not arbitrary or capricious, but which follow a known and open procedure guaranteed to that person legally under the Constitution. This is an official model held by lawyers to be sacrosanct and presented as the way society is supposed to operate. A liberal holds to the principle that all ideas must be allowed to be heard. That the individual has inalienable rights, such as freedom of speech, is the heart of contemporary liberal political theory.

A basic assumption of liberal theory is the taken-for-granted existence of a capitalistic economic system. This economic system, as well as its allied political institutions, is seen to consist of a number of competing groups. This Madisonian concept of pluralism is predicated on the philosophy that no one group will be able to exert a permanent dominating power over another. According to this doctrine of James Madison, if a large number of "factions," or groups, exist in society, no one group will be able to "concert and carry into effect schemes of oppression." (This was written by Madison in Federalist Paper No. 10, prior to the ratification of the American Constitution. It is still the core of pluralist theory today.) The exercise of one's rights in the pluralist competition for power takes place in accordance with the established rules of law. In case of unresolvable disagreement between individuals or groups, recourse may be had to the primary interpreters of these rules, the courts. All sides are expected to accept the validity of the rules as well as the decision that is handed down from a source assumed by definition to be impartial regarding the dispute at hand.

In liberal theory, conflict can thus be handled within the limits of the existing structures of society. Although these structures are not believed to be immutable, change in the direction of fulfilling liberal values, such as equality of opportunity, is held to be attained at a relatively slow pace, gaining a little at a time through compromise with opponents. Liberals do not hold out for all they want. They take what they can get, now; then they work for more. Contemporary liberals believe that social improvement will occur gradually through the exercise of state power on behalf of those who are poor and oppressed. The contradiction liberals face, however, is that often individual rights conflict with states' rights, and individual rights must lose. When issues such as this arise, students may often find it difficult to differentiate between liberal and conservative. Liberals have accepted the Oliver W. Holmes doctrine of "clear and present danger"—when the state finds there is a clear and present danger to its existence it may limit individual rights since these rights are held not to be absolute. Supreme Court Justice Holmes declared this doctrine in 1919 in *Schenck v. United States,* in which he stated that individual rights were not violated by the draft, since the nation, in 1917, was at war and faced a "clear and present danger." In this decision, Holmes stated that freedom of speech, guaranteed in the First Amendment, was not absolute. Since the nation was in peril, Schenck did not have the right to attempt to obstruct the draft, and thus freedom of speech could be limited at certain times. This philosophy narrowed the rights of individuals into a legal frame that deals with means, not ends, thus submerging the individual to political forms. In this framework, discussion of ends can be considered only as related to means. This legal conceptualization allows new ends to be imported under the guise of already accepted means. For example, abortion has been nationally prohibited since it was seen to violate a fetus' Fourteenth Amendment right to life without due process. To argue against this position in a legal framework, an alternate principle must be used. A woman's right to control her own body is held under the Fourteenth Amendment's right-to-life principle to be superior law since a fetus is defined to be without life for its first six months. When an issue such as the above is decided there must be a constitutional practice that the decision follows legal precedent. This is really a game of legitimation in which each side attempts to subsume the other side's legal arguments.

The role of social science, according to liberal practice, is to provide legitimated information for advances toward liberal political goals. Such information may be used to persuade policy makers of the wisdom of implementing a political reform. It may be data which show that the public is ready to accept a political reform. It may be a theoretical framework showing that activities heretofore considered radical are actually in accord with liberal values if viewed in the proper light. It may be information brought into court to support legal arguments. Thus, in the 1954 *Brown v. Board of Education* Supreme Court case, social science data were used to support arguments that separate but equal educational facilities had negative effects on individuals subject to those facilities.

Liberals generally accept the basic conservative principle of the necessity of elites, but they try to limit and control possible arbitrary and harmful actions that elites might take. Thus, they are attentive to proper procedure and due process. Liberals also think it is of great importance to get better people into elite positions. A typical liberal goal is to elect a compassionate fair judge, or a president who will be wise and just. The potential for the good individual to act effectively to advance liberal goals is held to be greater than the ability of an often intractable system to absorb and nullify attempts at change. Liberal reform is sometimes seen as an endless effort to put good people in office who will later have to be replaced by other good people. This occurs since elected leaders must often compromise and liberals feel betrayed by such actions.

In her analysis of the Women's Liberation Movement, Jo Freeman takes the liberal approach. According to her:

Movements that hold steadfast to their radical goals and disdain political participation of any kind in an "evil" system often find themselves isolated in splendid ideological purity which gains nothing for anyone. They are

paralyzed by their own fear of cooptation; and such paralysis is, in turn, the ultimate cooptation as inactive revolutionaries are a good deal more innocuous than active "reformists." Thus a successful movement must not only maintain a balance between personal and political change, but also a creative tension between its "politics" and its "vision." It must keep well in mind where it wants to go while accepting the necessity of often following a twisted and tortured road in order to get there.

The continuing centralization of power in the central government means that it is the national feminist organizations that will have the greatest impact on policy.... NOW and the other older branch organizations are thriving at this point because they have been able to use the institutional tools which our society provides for social and political change.[8]

In viewing a political scientist's position to determine whether it is liberal, one should ask whether the author is arguing that there are specific political ills which can be cured within the present political framework of society once certain specific reforms are undertaken. If the answer to this question is "yes," then for our purpose the author may be considered a liberal.

What is socialism?

Socialists are opposed to a society based on private property as the fundamental principle of social organization with a small elite obtaining the greatest benefits. They believe that those who do the work should operate the work places, with no special class of managers to control the work of others. Socialists hold that utility should be the criterion for production of goods and services, and distribution based on the principle of need. There should be and need be no inherited wealth, since everyone has the right to sufficient material goods and social services to ensure health and well-being. Social and political structures should be organized so that each person may develop individual talents while participating in a fair share of the necessary work of society, even work no one undertakes by choice.

People often see radical change as violent and disruptive and are repelled by that prospect. Although change may be brought about through violence, fear of chaos is often used by conservatives and liberals as an argument against attempting to undertake far-reaching change. Some socialists, however, contend that radical alteration of the political system can be based on nonviolent activity. Mass movements, political parties, and the formation of new institutional structures based on socialist principles are cited by them as examples of nonviolent radical activities. These are attempts, according to socialists, to institute an alternative society based on the needs of the many and their own conceptions of those needs, rather than on the needs of the few or the perception of the few of what the many need.

The socialist approach to political institutions reformulates the issue by arguing that real change does not take place simply by convincing people to change their attitudes or by modifying existing institutions. The problem is inherent in the structures of capitalist society. Specific political problems are surface manifestations of a form of political organization which benefits the powerful few and not the great masses of people. What is required to solve this problem, say the socialists, is a revolution by peaceful or violent means which will replace capitalism and its political institutions with a qualitatively different form of human society. Until this transformation occurs, political problems will exist as inevitable features of the structural relationships of capitalist society. Thus, existing political institutions are to be questioned, and if found wanting should be changed or replaced.

Contrary to Jo Freeman, Shulamith Firestone in her analysis of sexism postulates the theory that reform is irrelevant and radical reformulation of a structure—in this case the family—is necessary if sexism is to be eradicated.

In the radical feminist view, the new feminism is not just the revival of a serious political movement for social equality. It is the second wave of the most important revolution in history. Its aim: overthrow of the oldest, most rigid class/caste system in existence, the class system based on sex. . . . All institutions that segregate the sexes . . . must be destroyed. [9]

Socialism views social and political institutions as having been constructed by people and therefore always open to the possibility of being destroyed by people and reconstructed along different lines. People are not passive objects inevitably overwhelmed by external forces. Neither are they totally free individuals able to make and carry out whatever decisions they choose. Therefore no social or political structure can continue to exist in the face of the near total resistance of people joined together to oppose it. The very nature of structures of control inherent in large-scale bureaucratic institutions begins to generate opposition from those who are subjected to conditions in which they are separated from participation with others in control over their political leaders, their work, and their lives. The alienation which results from the imposition of hierarchical structures on people is a basic weakness which they oppose in all bureaucratic systems.

Socialism views the potential for massive political transformation as an interaction between the crises that result from the basically flawed structures of capitalist society and the social movements that result from alienation. The task of a socialist political scientist, then, is twofold: (1) to provide a clear analysis of the oppressive structures of capitalist society; and (2) to engage with others of like mind in doing both the theory and practice of constructing institutional structures based on socialist principles.

The basic stances of our three political traditions toward political institutions may then be set forth as follows:

Conservative: Conditions defined as problems by liberals and socialists do not really exist as such. The liberal and socialist definition of a problem usually stems from rising expectations. If correctly analyzed, things are better than they seem; furthermore, actions taken by liberals and radicals to resolve what they deem to be problems can often result in worse situations than if left well alone. Therefore, it is usually best to retain the current *modus operandi* and, if possible, to redefine the situation. In this way the problems can be contained by those few of the elite who are in the best position to comprehend and control them.

Liberal: Conditions exist as problems when a number of people define them as problematic. Solutions are to be obtained by the application of knowledge through existing political and institutional structures. Social science plays a large role in bringing this knowledge to the attention of policy makers in technically evaluated format so that action may be taken.

Socialist: Political problems are really manifestations of political conflicts between those people who hold economic and political power in our society and those who do not. A basic transformation of American society is called for so that every person may acquire the necessities of life by right. Power must be taken from the haves by the have-nots in order to accomplish meaningful changes in their poor conditions of life. Lesser remedies that accept the current distribution of power and resources in American society do little to relieve oppressive conditions.

In essence, conservatives stand firmly for a status quo that preserves their privileged position in society. Only those changes that serve to buttress their position of power in American society are considered acceptable. Liberals identify and decry abuses against the people that are perpetrated by all political institutions. They propose changes and work for reforms but seldom make structural recommendations sufficient to deal with the problems. Liberals are often fearful of too greatly disturbing the functioning of existing institutions. In trying to maintain a balanced view of the good and evil features of political institutions liberals incline to accept ambiguity. Socialists see all political institutions as pawns of America's corporate elite. The elite uses these institutions to control dissatisfaction with the unequal distribution of power. Socialists propose new institutions to distribute power and resources equally.

Both conservatives and liberals use the theory of pluralism. Conservatives use the theory that the existence of a variety of competing groups must be supported to defend an elite that is under attack. This elite is viewed by them as being just one of a number of relatively equal groups. This approach to pluralism is the conservative style. Liberals believe that the concept of pluralism is a basic element in American democracy. A variety of groups—unions, corporations, voluntary associations, and so on—each have the power to veto the desires of the other groups. Political decisions are a result of accommodation and compromise between these groups. This is the liberal approach to pluralism. Socialists believe that pluralism of either variety is a myth. Conservative pluralism is a justification of elite rule. Liberal pluralism is an ideology of well-intentioned people who fool themselves into thinking that they hold power when they do not. Socialists believe that if redistribution of power is to be brought about in America, the people must decide who actually does and who does not have power.

Question 4.   How can the political position of an analysis of a political institution be discerned when it is not openly stated? In other words how are students to read what academic authors write?

Sometimes the political values of an analysis are not readily discernable because they are only implicit in the content of an essay. Political language is often deliberately unclear because authors intend it to be so. Many political authors attempt to influence people who disagree with their politics. They cannot openly say they are conservative, liberal, or socialist because readers might be turned off. Conservatives may imply they are liberals, while liberals often broaden their terms so everyone will agree to them. Therefore, it is often difficult to decide the political position of an author. In Chapter 11, an essay we have identified as conservative, "Political Parties: Contributions to Democracy," may be seen by some to be liberal. In Chapter 14, an essay we have identified as liberal, "How Banks Destroy the Economy," may be seen by some as conservative.

In ordering the selections used in this book into three categories we have made *our* judgment as to which are conservative, liberal, or socialist. Even though each article is headed by the word conservative, liberal, or socialist, we encourage students to make their own judgment. You are free either to agree or disagree with us. Our purpose is not only to get you to concur with our analysis; it is also to help you to make your own.

In drawing your own conclusions be aware that the use of words and data, footnotes, and quotes from authorities are all devices used by writers to gain the sympathy of readers. For example, a conservative may refer to the Central Intelligence Agency (CIA) as "vital to America's national security." A socialist, on the other hand, might term the CIA "an illegitimate, undemocratic force." Students must look at the connotations of words and phrases in order to tell the political perspective of an author.

The political position of a writer can seldom be taken for granted. Historical circumstances may change, and what is considered conservative today may be considered liberal tomorrow. For example, from 1949 to 1972 the People's Republic of China was seen by conservatives to be an enemy of the United States. Today, many of those same conservatives see China as tolerable. Political figures, such as former President Richard Nixon, who once always referred to China as "Red China," since 1972, when Nixon visited China, have made a point of calling it the People's Republic of China. Politics involves shifting definitions of reality. The use of words is a means of reinforcing political power, or delegitimating it—getting people to believe or disbelieve.

Conservatives, liberals, and socialists have different goals for the future of American society. Politics is the use of any means necessary to attain political goals. Political writing is one of those means.

NOTES

1. This idea was originally suggested by Marvin Surkin and Alan Wolfe, eds. in *An End to Political Science* (New York: Basic Books, 1970), p. 7.

2. There is a problem about which rubric to use for the Left position on the political spectrum. The possibilities considered were radical, Marxist, critical, and socialist. Each has its problem as a generic term. *Radical* has been used to refer to the extreme Right, as well as the Left. The term *Marxist* implies a specific theory of large-scale social change, giving priority of influence to the means of production and to the economic area of society rather than to other material factors or to issues of consciousness.

The term *critical* denotes a revised Marxist theory in which a higher priority of influence is imputed to the level of ideas and consciousness. A broader term, *socialism,* also has its difficulties. On the one hand, "socialism" has been associated for many with the particular programs of a number of socialist political parties in the United States and elsewhere. On the other hand, some theories of socialism combine Marxist goals with liberal means. Yet, socialism is perhaps the broadest, yet most specific term for what we wish to connote. It seems to represent the Left position on the political spectrum in a more accurate sense than radical, Marxist, and critical. These latter, however, are more precise and will be used for specific instances.

The conservative, liberal, and socialist definitions utilized have in their general frame been adapted from Henry Etzkowitz, ed. *Is America Possible?* (St. Paul: West Pub., Co., 1974).

3. Surkin, Wolfe. p. 18. See also, James Petras, "Ideology and United States Political Scientists," *Science and Society* (Vol. xxix, No. 2, 1965).

4. Max Weber. "Science as a Vocation," in *From Max Weber*, Gerth and Mills, eds. (New York: Oxford Univ. Press, 1958), pp. 129–156.

5. See, Robert A. Dahl. *Modern Political Analysis.* (Englewood Cliffs: Prentice-Hall, Inc., 1963), p. 100.

6. Michael Parenti. "The Possibilities for Political Change," *Politics and Society* (Vol. 1, No. 1, Nov. 1970), pp. 79–80.

7. Daniel Bell. "The Revolution of Rising Entitlements," *Fortune* (April 1975), p. 182.

8. Jo Freeman. *The Politics of Women's Liberation.* (New York: David McKay Co., Inc., 1975), p. 6; p. 244.

9. Shulamith Firestone. *The Dialectic of Sex.* (New York: Bantam Books, 1972), p. 15; p. 208.

*

Part one

Where do
I stand?

In this part of *Is America Necessary?* we will show how conservatives, liberals, and socialists each view the American political system from different premises. Partisans of these groups have conflicting assumptions about how American political institutions should operate and what their goal's should be; in fact there is even disagreement on the fundamental question of which institutions in America are political. Uncovering these often hidden premises and assumptions is the task of the student.

We will not analyze in full the position of conservatives, liberals, and socialists towards political institutions in this part of the book. We will, however, describe the over-all framework used by each in their analysis of the political system. Students must proceed from that point to develop a more complete understanding of how different ideologies, (people's ideas of how society works based on their self or class interest) view American political institutions. The next task of students is to relate their own political ideas to the positions of conservatives, liberals, and socialists. The purpose here is not to develop a definitive and final statement of political principles but to clarify and bring forth one's own political premises and assumptions for self-examination. The authors hope that this process will enable students to be more aware, effective, and active in developing and translating into action their own political concerns.

Conservatives maintain that government must tend to its own concerns and that industry must be left alone to concentrate on making money. Since corporations are fundamental to American society, it is in the interest of every member of society to see that they are productive, profitable, and stable. The role of government is mainly to protect Americans from foreign and domestic threats, not to ensure that the social and economic needs of Americans are met. Individuals, through voluntary group organizations, must do what they can to solve their own problems—government is not a problem solver. According to conservatives, political problems in the 1970s exist because government has tried to do too much for too many people with the result that most Americans have become pleasure seekers who have lost their moral and individualistic underpinnings. Such Americans believe the world owes them a living. If these people would only return to the frontier spirit of rolling up their sleeves and working for what they want, rather than waiting for government to give it to them, the American political system would be relatively problem-free.

In contrast, liberals believe that government exists to insure political rights and to maintain a decent standard of living for American citizens. They hold to the philosophies of Presidents Theodore Roosevelt, Woodrow Wilson, and Franklin D. Roosevelt[1], that a strong government must protect the people from abuses that corporations will engage in if left alone. Liberals separate the political system from the economic order in their analyses of American political institutions. The essence of liberal thought is that that government is best which acts to protect people from abuses. Government is the American citizen's best friend: it gives people rights and liberties; it maintains these liberties; it protects people from foreign enemies, and it protects them from overwhelming natural, economic, and political forces. Flawed as it is, government is the only instrument available to allocate values, goods, and services in such a way that the public is served.[2]

Socialists maintain that the American political system is run and dominated by a ruling class made up of economic magnates, political leaders, and military elites. Some refer to this constellation of forces as "the power elite." Socialists hold that these elite groups operate the American political system to further their own interests. If the public is at all served by this system it is purely accidental, or a by-product of the catering to elites. Americans are generally unaware of their domination by elites, and this lack of awareness is a major prop of elite power. The solution to elite control of the political process as perceived by socialists is twofold: (1) Americans must recognize that conservative and liberal solutions to political problems are not in their interest. (2) The American corporate political system must be destroyed and replaced by socialism. When the nation moves on socialist gears, the people will be served rather than exploited. Through elected councils in every sector of society people will be participants in decision-making instead of its objects. In other words, the people themselves will decide what is best, rather than having the few make their decisions. In essence, socialists maintain that the American political process as it now exists, does not serve the needs and interests of the American people. The replacement of this oligarchic system—rule by the few—is the only solution to this dilemma.

Some socialists hold that this transformation can be achieved through structural reform by means currently available. Electoral campaigns, formation of parties, the creation of additional institutions socialist in nature, the publicizing of socialist ideas, are some examples of working within the system to restructure it. Others maintain that transformation of the political order can only take place through (1) a general economic collapse, or (2) a revolution by force of arms. Socialists who believe in far-reaching change are therefore forced to face up to this issue. They are confronted with deciding whether they are willing to take up arms against the government to overthrow it, or to engage in a long-term process of political organization. In other nations both these strategies, or combinations of them, have been tried and have succeeded or failed. American socialists have a distinct requirement to draw up and carry out a strategy for change that relates to the particular conditions and historical circumstances of American society, rather than applying a model from abroad, or the past, which may not fit in the United States. Though lessons may be drawn from other struggles in working out their strategy, American socialists must decide for themselves through their own theorizing and practical political activity how to make their own kind of American socialist revolution.

The authors are socialists committed to the restructuring of American society along humane and egolitarian lines. We are troubled by contemporary political, social, and economic affairs in the United States and believe change is essential. Our perspective is set forth in the passages we have written. Though we are personally committed to socialist change, we have endeavored to select conservative, liberal, and socialist writings which fairly represent these respective political perspectives.

NOTES

1. Theodore Roosevelt, President from 1901–1909, attempted to limit the size of big business, maintaining he was interested in supporting a "Square Deal" for Americans. Woodrow Wilson, President from 1913–1920, continued the Theodore Roosevelt policy of reform. Franklin D. Roosevelt, President from 1933–1945, under the rubric of a "New Deal" for Americans, engaged in developing a fantastic number of government agencies which would aid Americans in combatting the Depression of the 1930s. For further liberal analyses of these men see: Richard Hofstadter, "Theodore Roosevelt, the Conservative as Progressive," in his *The American Political Tradition*, New York: Vintage Books, 1959. John Morton Blum, *Woodrow Wilson and the Politics of Morality*, Boston: Little, Brown and Co., 1956. William E. Leuchtenburg, *Franklin D. Roosevelt and The New Deal*, New York: Harper Torchbooks, 1963.

2. See Robert A. Dahl, ed., *Modern Political Analysis*, Englewood Cliffs: Prentice-Hall Co., 1963. Although Dahl is a conservative political scientist, portions of his analysis are used by liberals. Students will see throughout *Is America Necessary?* that liberal and conservative analyses often intersect.

※

Conservative

Daniel Bell. The revolution of rising entitlements.

The great historian is one who, looking back at the long sweep of a nation's history—say, two hundred years—can identify the salient and enduring factors, the axial principles, that account for its distinctiveness and the course the polity has taken. Even greater, and rarer, are those who, at the onset of a distinctive phase in a nation's history, at the time when the first tracks are being cut through the virgin forest, can identify those that will remain and become the roads for future generations.

What makes Alexis de Tocqueville so relevant today is that, one hundred and forty years ago, he saw one of the roads clearly. The opening lines of his introduction to *Democracy in America*, written in 1835, set the motif:

"No novelty in the United States struck me more vividly during my stay there than the equality of conditions. . .

"I soon realized that the influence of this fact extends far beyond political mores and law, exercising dominion over civil society as much as over the government; it creates opinions, gives birth to feelings, suggests customs, and modifies whatever it does not create.

"So the more I studied American society, the more clearly I saw equality of conditions as the creative elements from which each particular fact derived, and all my observations constantly returned to this modal point."

No single person or social movement shaped this idea of equality. A theme that is so protean has many diverse sources. It is, in a direct way, a fruit of the Reformation, of Martin Luther's idea of the priesthood of all believers, in which individual conscience and not institutional authority is the source of judgment. In the U.S., the idea of equality flourished because there was no tradition of hierarchical feudal institutions. And, of course, the idea was helped along by the expanding frontier, in which no man could "lord it" over others.

American society was also set apart from others by its belief in material progress. The industrial revolution and the capitalist order were combined powerfully in the U.S. and were soon creating a rising standard of living and holding out a tangible promise of plenty for all.

Yet the System has been transformed in recent years, and those original impulses are today being caricatured in ways that threaten the stability of American society. The promise of plenty has been transformed into a revolution of rising expectations. This need not in itself have been a problem; rising expectations for themselves might, in principle, lead people to feel more responsible for the health of their society. But the expectations in America have become hedonistic, concerned with consumption and pleasure, and lack any moral underpinning.

Meanwhile, the promise of equality has been transformed into a revolution of rising "entitlements"—claims on government to implement an array of newly defined and vastly expanded social rights. Here again, this need not have been a problem; there is nothing inherently wrong with turning to government to secure one's rights. But the process has been unfolding in a peculiarly destructive way in the U.S. Just about *all* grievances now get dumped into the lap of government, while the voluntary associations that once furthered the claims of different groups are withering.

Both revolutions have a lot of momentum behind them, but there is no doubt that the entitlements have more. The increasing tendency of Americans to turn to the government to solve their problems is reflected dramatically in some figures on spending by government at all levels. In 1950, spending by government to buy goods and services, and to effect transfer payments, represented 18 percent of gross national product. By 1974 the figure was 32 percent. There is every sign that the proportion will increase steadily, and that major economic decisions in the society will turn, necessarily, on the decisions of government.

Where the battles will be fought

All this portends the emergence of a new kind of political economy. The major conflicts, increasingly, are not between management and labor within the framework of the economic enterprise but between organized interest groups claiming their shares of government largess. The political cockpit in which these battles are fought is the government budget. These battles have become the "class struggles" of the present and the future.

One large question that the American System now confronts is whether it can find a way to resolve these conflicts. Lacking rules to mediate rival claims, the System will be under severe strains.

The equality that Tocqueville wrote about was generally considered to be equality of opportunity. It implied conditions that allowed each man, whatever his origins (although color was then a question apart), to make his way on the basis of ability. In recent years the demand for equality has broadened considerably, and the term now refers to a wide range of political, economic, and social demands. The demands, furthermore, are now defined as rights.

Clearly, the demand for equality now goes far beyond equal opportunity, or protection against unfair hazards. Too many Americans who got that protection still came out losers. What is now being demanded is equality of result—an equal *outcome* for all.

New tasks for the government

It has always been a function of government to provide goods and services that individuals cannot purchase for themselves—military defense, roads, railways, etc. In the last forty years, however, government has been transformed by its acceptance of three new responsibilities.

The first, which originated in the 1930's, was for the health of the economy. Government spending aims to control the level of economic activity; tax and monetary policy powerfully influence the timing of investment; transfer payments effect a continuing redistribution of incomes through Social Security, revenue sharing, etc.

The second responsibility, which emerged in the 1950's, was for science and technology. Much of the new effort was at first linked to defense, but the decisive role played by science in a modern society has drawn the government into supporting it on a broader front. It has been estimated that about one-half of all those working in science these days are directly or indirectly dependent on government funding. Decisions about who should be educated in the sciences, and how far they should go, and what fields they should work in, are today less matters of individual choice than of government policy.

The third task of government was a commitment that first took shape in the 1960's. It involved social policy; and what it came down to was an expanding effort to remedy the inequalities and injustices of our society. The efforts covered civil rights, housing, environmental policy, health care, and income support (the more genteel term, these days, for welfare policy—though the implications are much broader than merely helping the indigent).

Much of this came pell-mell and piecemeal, and much of it is still taking shape. Nevertheless, the direction of events is clear: the government has made a commitment, not only to create a substantial welfare state, *but to redress all economic and social inequalities as well.* And the commitment is largely irreversible.

Public satisfaction for private "wants"

The acceptance of these tasks has created new and sharp dilemmas for American society. In the past, the claims of different groups could be dealt with by "the market," which meant that the responsibility for any outcome was dispersed. But when the government is the arbiter of claims, the conflicts become explicit and focused. Moreover, the government budget becomes the arena for the fulfillment, not only of public needs, but of private "wants"—previously the province of the market economy.

And when the basic allocative power is political rather than economic, there arises a question about restraints. The economic constraint on private wants is the amount of money that a man has, or the credit he is able to establish. But what are the constraints on political demands?

"One of the great puzzles of twentieth-century history," Professor Charles Lindblom of Yale once observed, "is that masses of voters in essentially free democratic societies do not use their votes to achieve a significantly more equal distribution of income and wealth, as well as many of the other values to which men aspire . . . What needs explaining is why they do not try."

My argument is that such an effort is now being made.

Let a thousand programs bloom

Since 1950, federal spending for social-welfare purposes has risen from $10.5 billion to almost $170 billion—from less than one-fourth of the federal budget to about half. If we include comparable expenditures by state and local government, it appears that we are spending about $250 billion for social programs. Outlays for those programs, which were 4 percent of national income in 1950, are about 15 percent today.

It is true that the bulk of this spending is concentrated in a few programs: about 70 percent is accounted for by Social Security payments, Medicaid and Medicare, and welfare payments to the poor. The increase in the number and variety of social-welfare programs is nevertheless extraordinary. In the early years of the Kennedy Administration, there were about 200 programs; today there are over 1,100, bearing upon almost every aspect of social life. And as one of the oldest and surest laws of bureaucracy puts the case, once a program is started, it can

never be disbanded, and its budgets inch up incrementally each year.

A vast array of Americans are now employed in administering those programs. About 3.7 million are working in the health field, about 3.3 million in education. An article in *Science* a while back reported on a one-day census of persons under institutional care in California in 1969. Out of 19.8 million people in the state, around eight million were in social care on any one day—i.e., in schools, hospitals, prisons, old-age homes, day-care centers, and the like. That number was equivalent to the state's entire civilian labor force (and, indeed, some 8 percent of the labor force was engaged in looking after the seven million).

All of which raises the question of how the revolution of rising entitlements is to be paid for. During the 1960's, Congress voted for many of these programs on the ground that their costs would be financed by budgetary surpluses based on steady economic growth. In fact, one of the lovely "problems" posed by the Council of Economic Advisers in the mid-1960's was the prospect of a continuing surplus that we must find ways to spend if the economy was to continue growing. That rosy view has been replaced by the specter of a slowdown of economic growth and large and continuing budget deficits.

When the solvent disappears

Economic growth has become a "political solvent." It provides the means to finance rising government expenditures without redistributing income (always a politically difficult matter) or burdening the poor (almost equally difficult). In a trillion-dollar economy, a 1 percent increase in the growth rate implies a net addition of $100 billion over a decade. The Johnson Administration found that Congress infinitely preferred to finance the social-welfare costs of the Great Society out of economic growth than out of higher tax rates.

And yet, paradoxically, economic growth may be the source of a distinctive "contradiction'' of capitalism—a contradiction that may prove to be its undoing. For growth has become inextricably linked with inflation, and it seems unlikely that any democratic society can abolish inflation without disastrous political consequences.

It is not as though Americans look upon inflation without concern; every survey taken in the last few years shows that inflation is an object of profound fear. Inflation is especially devastating to the middle class, which, as Aristotle observed, is the foundation of democracy. And yet every imaginable anti-inflationary policy impinges on the welfare of some major interest group. The simple fact is that no one wants to pay the price of ending inflation, and modern democratic governments find it politically difficult to make any sizable group pay the bill.

The mismatch between goals and resources

The dilemma associated with economic growth and inflation is only one of many that now beset American society. We confront such "incompatibilities" in many different ways. We want increased automobile-engine efficiency to cut down on consumption of gasoline; yet we also want to cut down on pollution, and most of the proposals for doing so reduce engine efficiency. We want to have independent sources of energy; yet we are reluctant to strip-mine coal in the western lands, where we would end up with large tracts of scarred acreage.

A somewhat larger incompatibility is reflected in the striking mismatch between the national goals we have set ourselves and the resources available for implementing them. In 1974 the National Planning Association made an effort to cost out some of the nation's human-welfare goals (those cited by the Eisenhower Commission in 1959). According to the N.P.A., the cost of attaining all the goals, as they were conceived, would entail spending $265 billion more in 1980 than in 1969.

In part because of these incompatibilities, it has become increasingly clear in recent years that the revolution of rising entitle-ments may become unmanageable. Because of this prospect, we suffer increasingly from a crisis of belief. If this process is not reversed, it will work to undermine the legitimacy of our society.

The crisis of belief has several manifestations. One is a loss of nerve on the part of the Establishment; in fact, it often seems as though the chief characteristic of the Establishment is an eagerness to repudiate its own existence. There is also a widespread questioning of the legitimacy of institutions, especially on the part of the educated young, who would normally be preparing to move into elite positions in these institutions. In the population at large, there is a feeling of being let down by leaders.

The major consequence of this crisis is the loss of *civitas*—that spontaneous willingness to obey the law, to respect the rights of others, to forgo the temptations of private enrichment at the expense of the public weal. Instead, each man goes his own way, pursuing his private vices, while the public weal is forgotten.

The weakened political parties

The foundation of any liberal society is the willingness of all groups to compromise private ends in order to protect the public interest. But when *civitas* begins to erode, interests may become polarized and passions so inflamed that terrorism and group fighting ensue. Or the loss may mean that every public exchange becomes a cynical deal, in which the most powerful segments benefit at the expense of the weak.

One consequence can be a considerable increase in political instability. As loyalty to some conception of the public interest is replaced by loyalty to the "interest group," we may see the breakup of the party systems as we have known them. There seems to be, especially among the middle classes, a revulsion against "politics," a mood that, in the past, has led to the weakening of strong party rule and the fragmentation of legislative bodies. It is a striking fact that in 1975 no single party holds a majority in the legislatures of Norway, Sweden, Denmark,

France, Germany, Holland, Belgium, and Italy.

In the U.S., the political party is in a state of decay. Most party machines are weak in finances, personnel, and resources. Party identification has weakened; one-third of the electorate now designates itself as "independent." True, party systems are deeply embedded in the institutional life of Western societies. They are often legally reinforced, as is the two-party system by most U.S. state voting laws; they still have patronage and cadres. But it is also likely that one will see more "invasions" of the parties by more extreme factions, like the McGovern new left in the Democratic party, and the Young Socialists in the German S.P.D.

In all this, there is a large danger. Politics always involves some mixture of material interests and symbolic expressions of belief. One may set aside the interests, yet still retain the beliefs; or one may lose the beliefs, yet retain an interest in the well-being of the society. But where trust in a society and its institutions is battered, the possibilities are explosive.

The neo-neo-Marxists are waiting

For more than a century, Marxists have been predicting the demise of capitalism. The theory originally underlying the predictions held that the demise would follow from the unplanned and anarchic nature of the market. This would lead to an excessive concentration of industry, resulting in declining profit margins as unemployment rose and demand fell off.

The theory had to be amended in the 1930's, after extensive intervention by the state worked to prop up demand. The new Marxist argument was that capitalists and legislators would support the system by voting money for armaments and defense, but would not vote for social expenditures. Capitalism, therefore, would be entirely dependent on a war economy and would ultimately destroy itself in war.

Now there is a third version—neo-neo-Marxism, it might be called—which notes the new emphasis on social expenditures, argues that they are necessary to the maintenance of capitalism, but insists that the state will ultimately be unable to pay the bill. The difficulty, it is said, is that the commitment to social expenditures represents a "drag" on the System, which will be increasingly unable to accumulate the capital it needs, and therefore unable to grow and raise revenues. James O'Connor, a young, contemporary Marxist economist, has put the case this way: "The fiscal crisis of the capitalist state is the inevitable consequence of the structural gap between state expenditures and revenues."

O'Connor may be right. But if the reason for capitalism's demise is the expansion of social expenditures, the "victory" for Marxist theory will be a conceit. For socialism too confronts all the difficulties presented by the need to accumulate capital while meeting overwhelming social demands.

But there is no doubt that the revolution of rising entitlements presents some peculiar difficulties to any society in which the level of taxes, and of public expenditures, is always an issue on the agenda—a society that Joseph Schumpeter called the "tax state." Schumpeter, one of the most farsighted economists who has lived in this century, made this chilling analysis fifty-five years ago: "The fiscal capacity of the state has its limits...If the will of the people demands higher and higher public expenditures, if more and more means are used for purposes for which private individuals have not produced them, if more and more power stands behind this will, and if finally all parts of the people are gripped by entirely new ideas about private property and the forms of life—then the tax state will have run its course and society will have to depend on other motive forces for its economy than self-interest. This limit, and with it the crisis which the tax state could not survive, can certainly be reached. Without doubt, the tax state *can* collapse."

The ultimate problem presented by the revolution of rising entitlements is not that it will cost a lot of money—although it will certainly do that. What is potentially more dangerous is the threat that the revolution presents to our political system. It threatens to overload the system, to confront it with far more grievances than legislators and judges know how to cope with. What makes this threat especially devastating is the absence, thus far, of any agreed-upon rules for settling the differences between all the contending interest groups.

Balancing appetite and responsibility

At some point, a society needs to take stock of itself, to seek to reaffirm in a self-conscious way the values to which it is committed and to redesign its institutions to match the current realities.

The United States was founded, in part, on a belief in a radical individualism. Jeremy Bentham, who created utilitarian philosophy and profoundly influenced much of American political thought, went so far as to deny that there was any such entity as a community. It was, he said, a fictitious body: "The interest of the community then is, what?— the sum of the several members who compose it." But it is quite clear that the "sum total of individual decisions" frequently has antisocial results: everyone wants to be free to drive on an open highway, but when everyone gets on it the highway becomes a nightmare of congestion. So the problem of balancing private appetite and public responsibility is a real one. How is it to be solved?

In the future, far greater weight will doubtless be given to the values represented by public responsibility. Yet there is also no doubt that, in the United States, the government's efforts to balance social and individual rights will please no one. Corporations resent government regulation, for the degree of interference with managerial authority is real. Liberals are increasingly suspicious of government and planning, even though their first reaction to any issue is still to call for more "government action," as if that abstraction were coterminous with the public good. And the state management that will emerge will be a cumbersome, bureaucratic monstrosity, wrenched in all

directions by the clamor for subsidies and entitlements, yet gorging itself on the increased appropriations to become a Leviathan in its own right.

To help us strike a balance between social and individual rights, there must be a recognition of the public character of needs. But there must also be some agreed-upon principles that can enable us to differentiate between needs and "wants." Finally, we must learn more about the relationship of means to ends in public-policy formation.

For example, we have a lot to learn about the possibilities of the market mechanism as a means to achieve social ends. In many public-policy discussions, it is assumed that our choices are either administrative regulation to achieve those ends—or abandoning the ends. But the market can often be used to achieve them efficiently. The market provides for self-adjustment and self-regulation, within a framework of rules. Thus, in dealing with pollution, a system of effluent charges, with the cost element becoming the lever of compliance, would be preferable to a system of administrative regulation.

Rediscovering old virtues

What some liberals and some new leftists have rediscovered are the virtues of decentralization and competition. Without competition, one is left at the mercy of the indifferent private monopoly or the slovenly bureaucratic agency. Yet, without public mechanisms for the transfer of payments and the setting of standards, one cannot have effective power for the achievement of social ends.

There is a need to strengthen local government and make it a good deal more flexible and responsive. Here again, Tocqueville was remarkably prescient. In many ways, he was wary of equality. Its natural effect, he thought, was to make men individualistic and selfish. But he was hopeful that these tendencies would be restrained in America and he thought that our society had a special stability built into it. What set it apart was the considerable degree of local autonomy given to towns and counties, i.e., in taking care of such matters as roads, relief for the poor, and schools—in contrast to the central bureaucracy in France.

It is the nature of decentralized institutions to tie individual self-interest to public-spiritedness. A man who wanted a road or a canal could seek to get it through local government, but he would have to show that it would benefit other interests as well. Thus local government united initiative, self-interest, and public need.

But what the U.S. has today is a vast, lopsided growth of federal power matched by total disarray in local government. Professor Samuel Huntington, the Harvard political scientist, has remarked that while the U.S. has had the most dynamic economy in the world, it has had a Tudor political system—with many institutions going back to the seventeenth century. We have municipalities, townships, counties, and states whose boundaries follow no rational economic, social, or cultural divisions. The boundaries of Midwest counties are still laid out to the limits of how far a man could drive in a single day by horse and buggy, to reach a county seat.

It is important to restore the vitality of local institutions. For local government provides those basic services—security and efficient law enforcement, the collection of garbage and the sweeping of streets, the wise spending of school moneys and the like—that give people a sense that government is effective and responsive. And we need far better definitions than we now have to help us determine what is appropriate for a neighborhood to decide on, what for a town, a regional unit, and the like.

An agreement on the common good

But means are viable only within the framework of ends, i.e., the conceptions of social justice that a society seeks to embody. A definition of ends would appear to be critical in a period when the satisfaction of private wants and the redress of perceived inequities are pursued, not individually through the market, but politically by the interest group. We need a way to define the common good; without the definitions, we have no way to adjudicate the conflicting claims about rights.

I cannot make any claim to having a satisfactory definition of the ends we need. But I believe that any serious effort to agree on ends would lead most thoughtful Americans to certain conclusions. They would feel obliged to reject the hedonistic emphasis on the satisfaction of private appetites, which is involved in so much of the pursuit of goods. They would want to retain political liberalism, with its concern for individual differences and liberty.

"The public philosophy," wrote Walter Lippmann, "is addressed to the government of our appetites and passions by the reasons of a second, civilized, and therefore acquired nature. Therefore the public philosophy cannot be popular. For it aims to resist and to regulate those very desires and opinions which are most popular."

In the classical view, a public philosophy could be implemented only in a republic of small size, since as Montesquieu said, "In a small republic, the public good is more strongly felt, better known, and closer to each citizen." Yet, among the Founding Fathers, where the issue was debated, Madison wrote a sophisticated rebuttal to the classical view. He believed that strongly felt views presented a special problem to a free society. The danger in any democracy, he argued, is the possibility that "a passionate majority" might "sacrifice to its ruling passion or interest both the public good and private rights. . ."

The solution to the problem, Madison believed, lay in size and diversity. Whereas a small direct democracy along classical lines "can admit of no cure for the mischiefs of faction, a representative republic opens a different prospect and promises the cure for which we are seeking." The greater the size, the greater the "variety of parties and interests," and hence the smaller the probability "that a majority of the whole will have a common motive to invade the rights of other citizens . . . ''

There were—and are—two special requirements for equity in a "representative republic.'' First, that all interests must be represented; and second, that all issues must be viewed as negotiable.

The mechanisms of compromise still exist. The question today is whether there is a will to use them. Here, too, there is a prior condition for their use—the need for some transcendent tie to bind individuals sufficiently for them to make the occasional necessary sacrifices of self-interest.

Historically, what has united a people has been a ruler, a doctrine, or a destiny—sometimes, in the great periods of a people, a fusion of the three. In the U.S., what gave purpose to the republic at its founding was a sense of destiny—the idea, expressed by Jefferson, that on this virgin continent God's design would be unfolded. On a virgin continent, men could be free, prodigally free, to pursue their individual ends and celebrate their achievements. The doctrine was shaped by a Protestantism that emphasized sobriety and work, which resisted the temptations of the flesh. By and large, the belief in the "great man'' was more muted in the U.S. than in other societies.

Over the years, this quiet sense of destiny and harsh creed of personal conduct were often replaced by a virulent "Americanism,'' a manifest destiny that took us overseas, and a materialist hedonism that provided the incentives to work. Today that manifest destiny is shattered, the Americanism has worn thin, and only the hedonism remains. It is a poor recipe for national unity and purpose.

Recognizing the limits of power

Yet in this time of trial and defeat, it is possible to see the outlines of a new purpose: one based on a self-conscious maturity that dispenses with ideologies, charismatic leaders, and manifest destinies, and that seeks to redefine the self and the liberal society on the only basis on which they can survive. The redefinition would be based on a recognition of the limits of our power, individual and social, to deal with unlimited appetites and wants.

Any such purpose would be the basis of a new social compact—but of a compact that does not ignore the past. It was the hubris of classical liberalism, and of socialist utopianism as well, that in each new generation men could start afresh and discard the past. It is true that, within limits, men can remake themselves and society. But the knowledge of power must coexist with the knowledge of its limits. This is, after all, the oldest and most enduring truth about the human condition—if it is to be human.

Liberal

Mark V. Nadel. The hidden dimension of public policy: Private governments and the policy-making process.

Public policy, like obscenity, is usually defined in practice by Justice Potter Stewart's maxim: "I don't know how to define it, but I know it when I see it.'' On a superficial level, most definitions are in basic agreement and differences are primarily semantic. Overcoming the diversity of more specific definitions, the new Policy Studies Organization defines policy as "actual and potential government programs and actions designed to cope with various social problems.''[1] More specifically, Robert Salisbury's definition states: "Public policy consists in authoritative or sanctioned decisions by governmental actors. It refers to the 'substance' of what government does and is to be distinguished from the processes by which decisions are made. Policy here means the outcomes or outputs of governmental processes.''[2]

Common to these and most other definitions of public policy is the broad notion that public policy is what government does.

What differences there are in definitions involve policy—the question of defining that "what" in what government does. It is widely assumed that by definition public policy is *government* policy. The present analysis is intended to examine and challenge that assumption.

Defining policy

When we go beyond the brief definitions of policy, we do find important substantive differences in the way that that concept is operationalized for purposes of research. It is not our purpose here to analyze all such conceptual differences, but an overview of several important defining characteristics reveals the confines of the current discussion of public policy among political scientists.

First, David Easton distinguishes between "outputs" and "outcomes." Outputs are the formally announced decisions and intended consequences of government action. Outcomes are the second order effects of policies and the over-all real world effects of policies.[3]

A second, although related, distinction involves the problem of empirically conceptualizing policy outputs. Frequently, outputs are conceptualized in terms of quantitative measurement. For example, Herbert Jacob and Michael Lipsky categorized current measurements primarily by level of expenditure, program quality (teacher/pupil ratios, doctor/patient ratios, and so forth), and policy impact by outcomes (such as dropout rates, literacy rates, and so forth).[4] Probably because of its ease of measurement, the most commonly used of these is "expenditure level." The question of measurement involves not only how *much* but also the more fundamental *what* the policy is. For example, do we discuss a state's educational policy in terms of how much is spent per pupil or in terms of reading achievement levels or by some other less precise measurement? While the Eastonian distinction between outputs and outcomes is generally acknowledged, as yet no consensus on the parameters of a public policy has been reached.

A third definitional problem was noted by Theodore J. Lowi, who urged that policy be distinguished from decisions.[5] Lowi faults those who equate decision-making with policy-making and who treat all decisions as policies. Although he does not state explicitly how the two concepts should be differentiated, his argument is basically that decisions are merely components (micro) of larger entities (macro) that should properly be labeled as policies.

Finally, an important definitional issue is the question of symbolic policy introduced by Murray Edelman.[6] In an analysis that is analogous to the distinction between policy output and outcome, Edelman argued that there was frequently a great difference between policy as formally pronounced and as actually implemented. A formal pronouncement (progressive tax system, careful and rigid inspection of food and drugs) could become symbolic policy that masked the realities of the policy as actually implemented. Although Edelman does not directly confront the issue, the question arises of how we define the policy. Is it to be defined in terms of the objectives of the original legislation or executive action, subsequent amendments, administrative implementation, or public belief? This problem extends beyond any particular policy and applies to the general concept of public policy.

Although the conceptual difficulties summarized above illustrate the diversity of possible conceptions of public policy, a common strand runs through them: the differences all hinge on the definition and conceptualization of the term "policy" rather than the qualifier "public." The disagreement concerns the content and scope of governmental actions that can be called "policy," but fundamentally they agree that public policy is something that *government* does. Thus the *Encyclopedia of Social Sciences* article on "public policy" uses that term synonymously with "the policies of government." Going back to Salisbury's definition, public policy "consists in authoritative or sanctioned decisions by *governmental* actors [emphasis supplied]." Few political scientists would disagree with Austin Ranney: "A *public* policy is one special case [of policy], albeit of central importance for political scientists. Its special character consists in the fact that it is adopted and implemented by what David Easton calls 'the authorities' in a political system."[7]

But what about the actions of private organizations—labor unions, corporations, associations, and so forth? Can these organizations be said to have policies? It is generally acknowledged that some aggregate of the decisions of all organizations can be labeled "policies." Thus in a review article, Lowi summarizes the definitions of several scholars: "Policy is simply any output of any decision maker, whether it be an individual or a collectivity, a small collectivity or a large one, a government or a nongovernment."[8] Again, it is assumed that the policies of government are, by definition, public policies while the policies of private organizations are not. The latter policies may be studied by economists, business administration scholars, organizational sociologists, but not normally by political scientists.

The boundary between public and private

The equation of public policy with government policy would be on firmer ground if there were a clear distinction between governmental (public) organizations and nongovernmental (private) organizations. Although the line between public and private policies is sharply drawn, the line between public and private organizations has not been so exact. Indeed, that organizational boundary line has long been questioned by a number of scholars.[9] This question is both paradoxical and indicative of the need to expand the meaning of "public" in the concept "public policy."

In an early discussion of the subject, for example, Charles Merriam pointed out that the "lines between 'public' and 'private' are not absolutes, but . . . there are zones of cooperation and cohesion in the common cause and on a common basis in many fields of human action."[10] Merriam, however, argued that a line between public and private existed although he did not posit firm criteria for public functions other than some consideration of the common good.

Attempting a major formulation of the problem, Robert A. Dahl and Charles E. Lindblom go farther than Merriam and dismiss the sharp public-private distinction as being foolishly rigid, unrealistic, and unnecessarily limiting of the real choices at hand. They demonstrate that the situation is more accurately conceived as a continuum on which organizations display varying degrees of public and private function. On this continuum, which shows some of the choices available between government ownership and private enterprise, the possibilities run from "an enterprise operated as an ordinary government department such as the post office" to "a hypothetical small proprietorship subject only to common law" on the private end. Various types of enterprise in the middle of the Dahl and Lindblom continuum, like subsidized corporations, the TVA, and government contracts, point out the fuzziness of the public-private boundary (and, they argue, its lack of utility.)[11]

Probably because they are the largest and most pervasive entities that are popularly regarded as "private," much discussion of the private-public boundary question concerns corporations. Increasingly, the public character of the large corporation is acknowledged. For example, Dahl argues that large corporations are political entities and asserts that "it is a delusion to consider [the great corporation] a *private* enterprise. General Motors is as much a public enterprise as the U.S. Post Office."[12] But surely there are some differences—particularly in law and public conception. The question is whether there are inherent and substantial differences in function. Gordon Tullock addresses this very question:

What then, is the difference between a government and a corporation? The answer to this question is simply that we have grown accustomed to calling one particular type of collective organization a government. Characteristically, there is one collective apparatus in society that is more powerful than any other and that can, if it comes to a battle, win over others. This apparatus we call the government. It should be emphasized, however, that the difference between this organization and a general contract is less than one might suppose.[13]

Thus, scholars in a variety of fields have come to regard the distinction between public and private, between governmental and nongovernmental as rather tenuous and artificial—particularly with regard to the management of large-scale economic enterprise. This blurring of boundaries between public and private organizations and functions has several aspects. First, the extensive co-operation between governmental and nongovernmental bodies makes it difficult to know where one ends and the other begins. The defense procurement policies instituted by Secretary of Defense Robert S. McNamara are an extreme but good example. Weapons systems were developed through the coequal co-operation of the Pentagon and "private" industry.[14] The provision of government-sponsored job training programs by private industry through the old Job Corps is another example. Morton Grodzins has shown that the interconnectedness of public and private may be even greater at the local than at the national level. In many small localities private businesses and associations perform a variety of planning and service functions in co-operation with or instead of local government agencies.[15] Also, new forms of enterprise have evolved which themselves straddle whatever distinctions may exist between governmental and nongovernmental. Comsat and Amtrak are two prominent examples.

A second feature of boundary blurring is the impact and nature of actions taken by private entities on their own. Thus, Dahl argues that large corporations are political systems:

By its decisions, the large corporation may:

Cause death, injury, disease, and severe physical pain, e.g., by decisions resulting in pollution, poor design, inadequate quality control, plant safety, working conditions, etc.;

Impose severe deprivations of income, well being, and effective personal freedom, e.g., by decisions on hiring and firing, employment practices, plant location, etc.;

Exercise influence, power, control, and even coercion over employees, customers, suppliers, and others by manipulating expectations of rewards and deprivations, e.g., by advertising, propaganda, promotions, and demotions, not to mention possible illegal practices.[16]

A third aspect of the boundary problem was extensively analyzed in studies by Grant McConnell[17] and Theodore J. Lowi.[18] Both studies are critical of the direct policy-making role played by private interests. This policy-making role is based on the delegation of governmental functions by the government to private groups—groups that are essentially unaccountable to many of those affected by the policy decisions they make. In the present context the essential point about these critiques is that the phenomenon they attack is not so much a usurpation of a policy-making role by private interests as a voluntary delegation of that function by the government. While this aspect of the boundary problem is closely related to the other two aspects, it is distinct in that it emphasizes the utilization of private organizations to perform explicitly governmental functions.

Although Lowi and McConnell explicitly deal with the co-optation of governmental functions by private entities, the ultimate conception of *public* in public policy is substantially unchanged. The co-optation is both a process and a policy. It is a process in that it is an ongoing method of creating policy outputs, one in which the official governmental input is consistently intertwined with the private input. More important, the co-optation itself is a result of explicit government policies ceding to private entities certain functions that had been or reasonably could be performed by the government. It is this initial governmental policy of voluntary co-optation which is the problem. The resultant outputs are considered public policy because of that initial series of decisions and because of the ongoing policy process. Thus the thrust of their analyses questions the legitimacy of that process. But in both cases public policy is still defined ultimately as the policies of government—even when government has allowed itself to be usurped.

A final aspect of the blurring of the public-private boundary is more fundamental and more controversial than the others: the alleged dominance of private elites in public life. Since a good many articles and books have been devoted both to positing and criticizing this proposition, it would be redundant and beyond our present purpose to re-hash that debate.[19] Suffice it to say that the power elite model holds that effective power in communities is actually held by a ruling class rather than by elected officials responsible to a widely dispersed plurality of interests. The elite is neither conspiratorial or completely cohesive but does have a nexus of interests to which the formal government normally responds. The actual positive policy outputs thus emanate from the government although the decisions behind those policies are reached by the elite acting with and through the government. The power elite model, then, is also part of the orthodoxy in defining public policy. Power elite theorists part company with the pluralists in the analysis of the policy-making *process;* the argument is over the degree of concentration of influence on government as policy-maker—but they both see the government as the only source of formal public policy outputs.

It can be seen that we are left with a major paradox. On the one hand, it is readily acknowledged that in many instances no clear distinction can be drawn between governmental and nongovernmental organizations. But on the other hand, public policy is viewed as emanating exclusively from the government. But how can the latter definition be useful when, in many instances, it is not clear what is a government? The answer must be that the prevalent definitional equation of public policy with government policy is therefore limited and unrealistic. An alternative and preferable strategy would be to analyze the nature of public policy and to determine who makes it. One potential utilization of such a strategy can be seen if we consider the expanded and innovative analysis of the role of private elites that was posited by Peter Bachrach and Morton S. Baratz.[20] According to their conception, the power of elites to influence policy should not be measured solely by their positive ac-

tions toward their objectives, which lead to victory in a controversy, but also by their ability to keep that controversy from surfacing in the first place. Achieving a "nondecision" in an area where Participant X has an interest in maintaining the status quo is as much a demonstration of influence as if Mr. X had fought in a public controversy and won.

This line of argument is far from being without critics. The most comprehensive critique of the utility of the nondecision concept was presented by Raymond Wolfinger, who argues that it is inherently impossible to determine empirically the existence of a nondecision.[21] Wolfinger's discussion of the matter is, of course, more comprehensive and complex, but for our purposes it is enough to note as the thrust of his argument the fact that we can not know what should have happened and therefore we can not study what did not happen without engaging in hopeless metaphysics.[22]

There is, however, a basic utility to looking at nondecisions—a utility masked by the current framework of discussion about the nondecision concept. A major reason for the present difficulty in utilizing the nondecision concept is that Bachrach and Baratz as well as their critics all ultimately view the matter from the perspective of formal governmental institutions. That is, Bachrach and Baratz view nondecisions as issues on which the political structure of the community begs off because of anticipated reactions from the nongovernmental power structure. So the result is a nondecision by government.[23] This conception leaves the analyst with the task of trying to study a non-event—something which can be an exercise in metaphysics, as Wolfinger implies. But the conceptual trouble arises only insofar as one attempts to study the influence of powerful private interests on the formal government, and such a study leaves aside the crucial consideration that the nondecision is only a nondecision by the government (whether or not it is a conscious suppression of an issue). Decisions on the issue (or non-issue if you please) may still be made by nongovernmental bodies. Thus there are decisions and cumulatively there is a policy—policy which I will argue may be

Figure 1   Range of nongovernmental group involvement in public policy-making

	Type of group					
Noninvolvement in public policy-making	Nonpolitical groups (social fraternal, etc.)	Interest groups	Large scale government contractors	Delegated power recipients (Farm Bureau, medical and bar associations)	Local elites and some corporations	Monopoly of public policy-making
	Neutrality	Influence	Intervention	Co-optation	Nondecision and direct policy-making	

Type of involvement

public policy in many instances. For example, air pollution may be a nonissue in a community. When no governmental regulation exists, the decisions as to air quality are left to the polluter. In a large city with many polluters, no one in fact makes the decision. The resultant policy about pollution is established by the "tyranny of small decisions." But in a single industry town, or region, real and visible decisions about pollution levels are in fact being made unilaterally.[24]

Let us recap the analysis of the role of private organizations in policy-making. We have proceeded from the participation of private organizations in governmental policy-making to the co-optation or delegation of policy-making functions to private organization and finally to a monopoly of policy-making functions by private organizations in the face of governmental noninvolvement (via nondecision) in a policy area. The subject is shown graphically in Figure 1.

It is readily acknowledged that policy outputs on the left end of the continuum constitute "public policy" regardless of the participation of private groups and regardless of the blurred lines between public and private organizations. Indeed this understanding is inherent in the conceptual orientation and in the actual role of government. As noted before, even in the case of co-optation it is ultimately the government that makes the positive decision to allow co-optation and it is the government that defines the permissible range of alternatives to its (private) delegated decision-makers.

As we get to the right end of the continuum, however, the situation becomes more debatable. Who is making policy and what is the nature of that policy (if any)? Fundamental to the discussion of the nondecision question is whether government officials make an identifiable decision to stay out of an issue-area. That question can readily be bypassed and can be transformed into an inquiry about who does make the decisions relating to the policy area. The nature of such decisions is fundamentally different from those reached through all the other mixtures of public and private policy-making participation. Even in the case of co-optation, authority ultimately is traceable to the government and a specifiable boundary of decisions is discernible. Where the government is completely uninvolved, no such delegation of authority is present and no boundaries are set. The question then becomes: "Is the resultant set of decisions 'public policy?'" The answer often must be in the affirmative if we view public policy more comprehensively than has hitherto been the case. The distinction is demonstrated in Figures 2 and 3. In highly simplified form, Figure 2 represents the prevalent model of the policy-making process. The in-

Figure 2

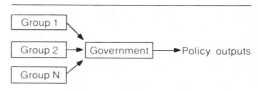

WHERE DO I STAND?   33

fluence of various groups is filtered through the government. Most scholarly debate concerns the relative weight of influence of the various groups and elites and the process by which their influence is transmitted through the government. The present argument, however, is that the realities of policy-making by some nongovernmental groups necessitate a broader view of the policy process, represented by Figure 3. In this conception most interests contribute to public policy through government, but some interests are able to make public policy directly. To establish the validity of that rather unorthodox assertion it is first necessary to explore the essential components of public policy.

Figure 3

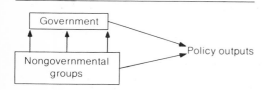

The components of public policy

Since so many definitions of public policy are based on David Easton's work—or at least have his framework implicit in them—it is appropriate to examine his definition of public policy and its conceptual relationship to government. Easton writes that a policy "consists of a web of decisions and actions that allocates values."[25] Since political science, however, is concerned with the authoritative allocation of values for a society, not all policies are within the purview of the discipline.[26] The scope is limited to policies that are authoritative allocations of values. Thus a public policy is implicitly defined as an authoritative value allocation for society. Or, in another formulation, public policy is seen as the outputs of the political system—outputs that are produced by the authorities in the political system.[27] Furthermore, inherent in the nature of authoritative outputs is that members of the system "consider or are compelled to accept [them] as binding."[28]

We can readily accept the Eastonian components of public policy: authority, bindingness, and allocation of values for society. To these we would add another requirement—intent. Like bindingness, intent is actually implicit in any definition that equates public policy with government policy. There is no question that the authorities formulate policy outputs (although not necessarily *outcomes*) with deliberate intent. To establish the validity of the concept of nongovernmental public policymakers, it is necessary to make explicit the intent of such policy. Without fulfilling the criterion of intent, private group actions with public consequences would simply be nothing more than transactions that incidentally affect society. Of course, unintentional policies may also have a significant impact on society, but we are concerned here with public policy rather than with all public effects. In this way we are adhering to a more conservative and rigorous concept of public policy than one that would include all significant social effects.

To sum up, a public policy is a allocation of values that is authoritative, binding, and intentional. The question is whether these criteria must be limited to the outputs of the formal government.

Allocation of values

Allocation of values is a relatively simple concept. Gabriel Almond and G. Bingham Powell define allocations in the political system as the distribution of "goods, services, honors, statuses and opportunities."[29] Although they distinguish between allocations and extractions, for our purposes it is more convenient to consider extractions simply as the allocations of costs. With this comprehensive view, subsidies, taxes, a military draft, public offices (both substantive and honorary), welfare, medical care, education, and many other values may all be policy outputs—values that are allocated by the political system.

Easton cautions that the proper scope of political science (and, implicitly, public policy) includes not all allocations, since this would be hopelessly universal, but only those that are authoritative and that are society-wide.[30] He notes the variety of organizations and institutions whose members accede to their authority—churches, employers, and so on. Yet the policies of such organizations are not public policies because they are not authoritative for the whole of society. While Easton acknowledges that many government policies apply only to some people or regions within a society, he argues that this differential effect is distinct from the similarly limited effect of private group policies because government policies are considered to be authoritative by all members of society.[31] We will deal with the question of authority below. At this stage, the important point is that a public policy must be an allocation of values but that allocation need not apply equally to the whole society. Indeed, it may even have a very narrow scope of application as long as it is authoritative.

Authority and bindingness

In Easton's formal system the authorities are, by definition, the government, and he is very clear and explicit on the role of the government in making public policy (rendering outputs). It is a completely exclusive role by definition: "Fundamental to the present conceptualization of outputs is the idea that they consist of a stream of activities flowing from the authorities in a system. It is the fact that they are produced by the authorities that distinguishes them as outputs."[32] As for the political role and power of non-authorities, he acknowledges that they may engage in activities that "may flow into the environment" such as large scale political strikes, and they may even dominate the formal authorities. Nonetheless, Easton asserts that "the politico-economic elite making the decisions involved in this behavior are not to be considered as producing political outputs in my sense of the term." Such an expansion of the conception of outputs, he asserts, would make the study of outputs "equivalent to the examination of all political behavior."[33] It is precisely this formulation that is contrary to the present

analysis. While it is no doubt useful in Easton's model of the political system, it is, nonetheless, needlessly limiting in selectively examining the formation and content of public policy per se. Indeed, when we move from the identity of the authorities to what the authorities do, we see that the case is less clear for equating public policy with government policy.

The function of authorities in a political system is to produce outputs—to make public policy. As we have seen, Easton argues that the authorities are the exclusive producers of outputs. The source, however, is not the only characteristic of outputs. Inherent in the character of authoritative outputs is that they are binding. Citizens must conform their behavior as specified by the particular output—pay taxes, pay the minimum wage, and the like. Easton distinguishes between "authoritative" and "associated" outputs on the basis of the binding character of the former. Associated outputs may also emanate from the authorities in a political system, but they are not binding. What consequences they have result only from their being associated with authoritative outputs. Such associated outputs include legislation introduced but not enacted, various policy proposals and the informal and/or sub-rosa granting of favors. But because they are not binding and formal they are not authoritative outputs. Easton concedes that such outputs may border on being binding but maintains that there is a discernible boundary line although he is not specific on what it is.[34] It is also not quite clear whether associated outputs constitute public policy, but if they do it must be because they are linked to *binding* authoritative outputs.

Nearly all definitions of public policy include its binding nature. Like the definition of public, however, that binding nature is usually conceived of as stemming from the government—from the *binder*. Thus public policy is binding because it stems from the government. We are told by Easton and others, however, that a distinguishing characteristic of government is that it makes binding policy. We are left with the circular conclusion that outputs are binding only because they are governmental, and they are governmental because they are binding. If, however, we view the "bindingness" of policy from the perspective of the affected citizens—the "bindees"—we can start constructing a more comprehensive and realistic view of policy. From this perspective a policy is authoritative for society if it is binding—regardless of the source of the policy.

The essence of binding policy is the absence of effective choice by the affected party. A's policy is binding on B if B must conform his behavior to the dictates of A's policy regardless of B's own preferences in the matter. A policy may be binding through two situations. First it may be enforced by sanctions after the fact. For example, I file an income tax return and pay taxes even though I do not want to because the policymaker (in this case the federal government) will punish me if I do not. In this case we have physical freedom but legal compulsion. I can act in a way contrary to the binding policy, but it is irrational for me to do so because I would then be punished. We can call this type "sanction bindingness." In the second type of situation, I do not even have the option of resisting the binding policy. Once I am sentenced to jail, my freedom is eliminated, and by physical coercion the state does with me what it will, in accord with its binding policy. Physical coercion and violence are not the only implements of this kind of binding policy. All that is required is removing from the bindee all options of resistance. For example, I do not have the option of not paying income taxes which have already been withheld from my paycheck. The government, acting through my employer, has removed that option. This kind of bindingness we can call "situational bindingness" because the total situation is controlled.

The question now is whether nongovernmental entities can employ either or both of these kinds of binding policies. The answer is clearly "yes." For example, the New York Stock Exchange may punish individual violators of Exchange regulations by prohibiting member firms from employing them for a specified period of time. Just as in government, a corporation may thus cause an indi-

vidual to act against his own preferences or face the more unpleasant alternative of a severe deprivation of material and status values—a sanction little different in effect from a judicially imposed fine. Of course the sanctions of a corporation are unlikely to be physical, but the economic sanctions represent a coercive force as powerful as a judicially imposed fine or an attachment of wages or assets by a governmental unit.

The second kind of binding policy, situational bindingness, is even more pervasive as an element of nongovernmental policymaking. This bindingness largely includes many externalities of corporations. Environmental degradation is probably the most obvious and pervasive example of situational bindingness. For example, the citizens of Gary, Indiana, suffer a binding deprivation of health and aesthetic values due to the air pollution emanating from the plants of United States Steel. Now, they may consider this a worthwhile trade-off for employment and prosperity, but they are nonetheless bound by the policy outputs (pollution) of the industry. Similarly, all citizens of large urban areas suffer the binding policy outputs of automobile pollution. The point to be emphasized is that pollution, to continue the example, does not simply occur as a spontaneous act of God. It is, rather, the result of identifiable decisions made by corporate officials in the first instance. It is, in short, a policy made by those officials.

In one sense, this formulation of bindingness as authoritative outputs is congruent with Easton's own conception of authority since he notes that society has a variety of authority relationships. Easton, however, differentiates between nongovernmental authority figures and those that he calls the authorities. As we have seen, this distinction leads to an automatic equation of public policy with government policy. The problem is that such a scheme arbitrarily excludes authority figures who are functionally equivalent to "the authorities." Furthermore, it is not always clear just who are "the authorities" in a political system. When we say that a member of the school board in Sheboygan, Wisconsin, is part of "the authorities" but the president of General Motors is not, we cannot go very far in understanding political behavior or public policy.

It can be readily conceded that nongovernmental public policy, while authoritative, need not be legitimate. That is a different question. Easton and most other scholars regard legitimacy as an adjunct to government and an important element of governmental power. The belief in the "rightness" of the authorities' role as policy-makers enables the authorities to rule with a minimum of coercion. Privately made public policies may prevail even though citizens do not regard them as legitimately made. Citizens may be unable or unwilling to change those policies or upset the position of the policy-makers. Thus, one useful distinction between government public policy and nongovernment private policy may be that of legitimacy.

It should not be assumed, however, that legitimacy offers an automatic or mutually exclusive distinction between government and nongovernment policy. The relationship between the government and groups which have authority over their members may be such that those groups' legitimacy is positively accepted by the government. For example, when a state government delegates professional licensing power to local bar or medical associations the authority of those groups over their members is, in effect, no different from the authority and legitimacy of the state in comparable circumstances. Similarly, when federal legislation provides for a union shop, then the union is also an authoritative and legitimate allocator of values—particularly in industries like construction where hiring is done through union officials. As with governmental laws that apply differentially by region and person, such private uses of authority also are considered to be legal and binding for all who fit into whatever categories are prescribed.

Intent

In assessing the question of intent, we can start with the situational binding policy of pollution. We need not go as far as Ralph Nader, who labels environmental degradation as "chemical warfare," to appreciate pollution as a binding public policy. It may be objected that corporations do not produce pollution as a primary goal and that such externalities are certainly not intended—at least not as a goal. Cigarette companies do not market their product in order to produce lung cancer, and steel manufacturers do not produce steel in order to produce pollution. However, while some binding externalities do not constitute policy, others do. These externalities constitute binding policy when the social risk of the externality becomes known to the decision-makers. Once the danger of the transaction or production process becomes known, someone must decide on how much danger to allow and how to assess the costs of preventing the danger. When an explicit government policy exists on the subject (for example, the National Environmental Policy Act) the government is the effective policy-maker. In the absence of government public policy, however, corporate officials themselves decide on the cost they find acceptable to prevent negative consequences. They decide on the allocation of negative values to the total number of affected citizens. In doing so, they make public policy. Even if they do not intend negative externalities as their goal, they do intend them as an allowable cost to be assessed on society. In the intended allowance of risk, the corporation policy-makers are acting in the same fashion and with the same consequences as government policy-makers who also allow for a certain level of risk in regulatory measures. The results are all public policy; the only difference is in who makes the public policy.

A good example is the automobile industry. Prior to the National Traffic and Motor Vehicle Safety Act of 1966, the question of automobile safety was largely left to the unilateral discretion of the automobile manufacturers. Their policy was that only minimal expenditures would go to automobile safety and that even such low-cost devices as effective restraint systems and collapsible steering columns would not be provided. Such policies were made even in the face of abundant evidence that these devices would save a significant proportion of the 50,000 lives lost annually in crashes.[35] As a result of new government policy, such devices were eventually mandated. It is an empty exercise in formality to say that the corporate decisions about automobile safety were not public policy while the government's decisions were public policy. In both cases, the decisions had binding consequences for most citizens. Returning to the question of intent, in deciding on vehicle-safety requirements and other regulations, government officials do not intend that a certain number of people should die or be injured but that a certain risk is acceptable. Nonetheless, it is universally conceded that the policy is intentional. In the same sense, the cost calculations of auto makers and other corporate officials who make these decisions also constitute intentional public policy.

Nongovernmental public policy

To say that private entities may make public policy is not enough. As a proposition it goes no further than simply arguing the inadequacy of prevailing definitions of public policy. Just as with governmental public policy it is necessary to differentiate among different types of policy.[36] Therefore, a typology of privately made public policy is formulated here for three reasons: first, it further demonstrates the character of such policies as public policies; second, it differentiates between different types of such policies; finally, it allows comparisons between policy-makers and political systems.

Given the great number of existing policy categorizations, it might be objected that the last thing needed is yet another one. The problem with simply utilizing existing paradigms, however, is that they are all predicated on the implicit assumption that public policy must be limited to government policy. To get past this limitation requires a modification of some existing typologies and also requires that such a modification allow for comparison among private makers of public

policy and between them and government policy-makers. Such a comparison makes necessary functional categories with a high degree of abstraction. The typology is loosely based on the well-known categories posited by Theodore Lowi[37] as well as the more functional categories of Almond and Powell.[38] Lowi's original three categories are regulative, distributive, and redistributive. In a later exposition he has added constituent policy, which includes reapportionment, voting rights, and the like.[39] Almond and Powell posit four categories: extractions, allocations, regulations, and symbols. Like other abstract categories, both of these classifications present problems. For example, it is not clear why subsidies, which Lowi lists as distributive policies, can not be seen as redistribution— from the poor to the rich in agriculture subsidies or from the rich to the poor in low-income housing subsidies. Similarly, with Almond and Powell a tax policy can be viewed as an allocation (hidden subsidies via tax policy) or as they conceived it, an extraction from citizens.[40] Although such abstract categories can probably never be completely mutually exclusive, a large part of these problems can be alleviated by collapsing the various categories of the distribution of values (that is, Lowi's distributive and redistributive and Almond and Powell's allocations and extractions) into a single category. This category is labeled "resource transfer," and it includes all binding allocations of costs and benefits. In this way the fuzziness between allocations that are distributive and those that are redistributive is avoided, and all allocations are recognized as actually transfers carrying with them extractions to pay for those allocations. The second category is "regulatory" with much the same meaning as is utilized in that category elsewhere. Regulation involves control over personal conduct. The third category, constituent policy, is adapted from Lowi's formulation, and it includes policies that affect the procedures by which societal decisions are made. While this category may appear to be a policy process rather than a substantive policy output, its conception hinges on a time dimension. At the time a constituent policy (for example, reappointment) is formulated, it is a policy output. Once in force it clearly becomes a part of the policy-making process. Furthermore, such constituent policy outputs are conceived here as the political equivalent of resource transfers. Rather than material resources, constituent policy involves transfers of political power resources. Just as with material resources, they are valued not only for their own sake but for what they can be converted into.

A series of brief examples can make the nature of privately made public policy and its categorization clearer. Because of their predominant position as nongovernmental makers of public policy, the examples focus on large corporations.

Resource transfer

In terms of the impact on citizens, the most pervasive form of corporation-made public policy involves resource transfer—the extraction and allocation of material values. By the same token, this category is predominant in government policy. This fact can be seen by simply looking at the extent of government taxation—an activity that directly affects more citizens than any other. Indeed, taxation by private industry is the major mode of private resource transfer. The concept of taxation by private organization is not a novel one. Thurmond Arnold noted that "taxation by industrial organizations is a pleasanter way of paying tribute than taxation by government."[41] Arnold argued sarcastically that the distinction was a convenient myth.

No one observed the obvious fact that in terms of total income of an individual it made no difference whether his money went for prices or taxes. Men believed there was a difference because prices were automatically regulated by the laws of supply and demand. If any great corporate organization charged too much, in the long run it would be forced out of business by other corporations which did not charge so much. This might not be true if the corporation had a monopoly but our antitrust laws protected us from anything like that. . . .

Arnold viewed the entire pricing and investment structure of industry as "taxation."

We need not go as far as that to appreciate some industry practices as a form of taxation. The very purpose of corporations is to effect resource transfers by procuring, producing, and distributing goods and services. Yet only a small proportion of these transactions (and their externalities) constitutes public policy. The distinction lies in the degree of control that a particular corporation exercises over its transactions and can be most readily seen in the form of taxation by administered prices.

Administered pricing is a major form of corporate resource transfer policy. Rather than setting prices as a reaction to competitive pressures expressed through the "law" of supply and demand, some corporations in highly concentrated industries are able to exercise considerable (although not unlimited) discretion in setting their own prices. This kind of situation, which results from a market wherein a few competing producers predominate, was described by Gardiner Means:

(1) Prices tend to be administered, and not sensitive to short-run changes in demand and supply. (2) Competing producers tend to set the same prices or maintain the same price differentials over considerable periods of time. (3) There is apt to be one producer who is looked to as the leader in making price changes. (4) Prices tend to be set in terms of long-run considerations and not in terms of the short-run variations in demand and supply factors which dominate prices set by competition.[42]

A Senate antitrust subcommittee concluded that administered pricing was the general situation in the steel industry. Despite wide fluctuations of demand over time, steel prices rose steadily through the 1950s. The situation contrasts sharply with the price of scrap metal where the selling market is composed of many small firms.[43] In the steel industry, United States Steel is the price leader, and the other companies have historically matched its price rises to the penny.[44] As Gardiner Means points out, the setting of administered prices is not an unlimited power. United States Steel cannot set prices at *any* level it chooses. There are vaguely defined lower and upper limits. But, as Means says, "the price leader in steel operates within an area of pricing discretion such that within a significant range it can set one price rather than another."[45] In this situation, the price leader is engaging in the same kind of pricing power as that exercised by a governmental agency in a regulated industry. There, too, the power is not unlimited but rather is utilized within reasonable lower and upper limits. In both cases a binding resource transfer is effected by a public policy-maker. The public policy role of the administered price leader was implied in the statement of United States Steel Chariman Roger Blough before the Senate Antitrust Subcommittee when he stated, "I commend to the thoughtful consideration of this committee the question of whether or not our price action was responsible and in the public interest."[46] While there is considerable disagreement as to whether administered prices lead to excessive or exorbitant profits, the point remains that such a system consists of unilateral price setting in a regulated price structure. Just as the CAB makes public policy when it sets airline fares, so too does United States Steel when it sets steel prices.

Given the impact of steel prices on automobiles, artificially high steel price hikes represent a nationwide regressive tax (particularly when coupled with a "voluntary" steel import agreement reached with Japan in 1972).

Another major type of resource transfer is in the form of investment. While most investment decisions are conditioned by considerations of risk and potential return, there is considerable latitude for discretion within those broad parameters. It is within the bounds of that discretion that public policy-making occurs. The major forms of investment as policy-making involve the financing of major projects by banks and insurance companies through the extension of credit, the placement and removal of major corporate installations, and large-scale property development. These decisions have had a particularly significant effect in major cities whose viability has been damaged as major corporations pull out, locate in the suburbs, and channel their investments away from central-city areas.[47] Nor is this impact confined to urban ghettos. Unilateral decisions by large private land-development corporations have a profound impact on community life in suburban and rural areas.[48]

It should not be thought that the effects of corporation-made public policy are necessarily malevolent. Corporate "charity," which is a frequent mode of resource transfer policy, includes support of the arts, grants to educational institutes, programs for ameliorating inner-city conditions, and a variety of other such subsidies. They are all essentially public policy in that the individual corporation (or group of corporations acting jointly) unilaterally decides on allocation of societal resources for public purposes. Whether the federal government or Gulf Oil formulates and pays for a minority training program, the process still involves public policy. This was certainly true during the Johnson administration when private corporations received government contracts to run Job Corps centers, and it is no less true when corporations perform the same function unilaterally.

Regulatory policy

A widespread type of private regulatory policy is the regulatory framework established by manufacturers or parent corporations in their relationships with retail distributors or franchise holders. This practice is particularly pervasive in the automobile industry. Until the passage of the Automobile Dealers Day in Court Act (1956), auto manufacturers had complete control over their dealers and could terminate their franchises at will. Exhibiting one of the classically posited requirements of a state, the manufacturers even had their own judicial system for adjudicating disputes between dealers and manufacturers. Naturally, the manufacturers usually prevailed in those disputes—a problem which led to the passage of the 1956 legislation. Nonetheless the auto manufacturers still have control over their dealers, and according to the representative of one large dealers association the 1956 legislation has done little to affect the regulatory power of the manufacturers.[49] Indeed, the distributive system of automobiles is still in the form of a controlled regulatory framework. The heart of the system is the manufacturers' ability to control dealer entry through the granting of nonexclusive franchises. In controlling entry into the retail end of the business, the auto manufacturers function like such entry controlling regulatory commissions as the FCC and the ICC. Similarly, the manufacturers place a series of continuing requirements on franchised dealers once entry is granted. These include requirements that only certain replacement parts supplied by the manufacturer be used, minimum sales quotas, and the providing of highly detailed financial information. Furthermore, as is the case with some industries regulated by government, franchises can not sell their franchise except to an approved buyer. If the manufacturer has any financial interest in the dealership (an increasing trend), the manufacturer gets voting control of the dealer.[50] This situation is unique among sellers of high volume "big ticket" items such as major appliances. If we make the reasonable assumption that the retail selling of cars is a business distinct from their manufacture, the automobile manufacturers are thus in the position of controlling entry and otherwise regulating another entire industry. This practice is normally, and correctly, thought of as a public policy formulated by government. In this case, however, the "government" is an automobile manufacturer.

Private regulation also extends beyond situations that are analogous to government economic regulation. It is a process of social control that includes sanctions to affect individual behavior and can be similar to the highly coercive use of police power by the state. For instance, the early struggle to unionize the coal mines and other basic industries saw the utilization of private police and even private armies to control workers.[51]

Private regulative policy also involves all those activities that promote or adversely affect individual welfare—binding alloca-

tions or deprivations of such values as life, health, and pleasure. They include food and drug regulation, occupational safety, pollution control, and so forth.

Let us take the case of pollution control. It is clearly public policy when a government requires installation of various pollution abatement devices either in industry or automobiles. It is also public regulatory policy when an industry unilaterally decides to install or not to install such devices—precisely what happened in the automobile industry. There was not even the problem of a "nondecision"; The Big Three plus American Motors formulated a public policy of not developing and installing pollution abatement devices. In 1955, the four auto manufacturers agreed to a cross-licensing arrangement on antipollution devices. As later adduced by a federal grand jury, the arrangement consisted of agreements not to publicize competitively any solution to the problem of automobile emissions; to adopt a uniform date for the announcement of the discovery of any control device; and to install such devices only on an agreed date.[52] The industry enjoyed a virtual monopoly of policy-making until 1964 when California approved four emission control devices and, in accord with a previous California law, required the installation of qualifying devices on all 1966 cars sold in the state. Although the Automobile Manufacturers Association in February 1964 had stated that the devices would be ready for the 1967 model year, the grand jury found that the auto companies in fact already had developed devices at the time the AMA resolution was issued. In any event, the automobile manufacturers managed to comply with the California requirement in 1966, all their previous protestations notwithstanding. Nonetheless, their conspiracy resulted in the lack of any voluntary development and installation of antipollution devices between 1954 and 1967. As the Antitrust Division noted in its summary of the grand jury investigation, the evidence proved:

the existence of an industry wide agreement and conspiracy among the auto manufacturers, through AMA, not to compete in the research, development, manufacture and installation of motor vehicle air pollution control devices for the purposes of achieving interminable delays, or at least delays as long as possible. The cross-licensing agreement was used as a cover and focal point of the conspiracy.[53]

The case was eventually settled by a consent decree.[54]

Just as the Clean Air Act of 1970 was a public policy placing maximum limits on polluting automobile emissions, the 1955 agreement among the automobile manufacturers was a public policy in the opposite direction. The only difference is that the former was a policy of the federal government, while the latter was a policy of private governments. They both, however, were public regulatory policies.

Constituent policy

Constituent policy is more procedurally oriented than the other two policy types. It involves the setting of the structure and procedures of formal governance in a society. For example, the United States Constitution is our basic constituent policy and the Federal Election Campaign Act of 1971 is a more recent example. It might, therefore, be thought that this kind of policy can only be associated with public governments. Such a supposition, however, is more of a normative wish than an analytical statement. Private governments (in the present case, corporations) also formulate constituent policy in two broad ways.

First, corporations have their own internal structures of government.[55] The charter of the corporation sets forth the purposes of the corporation, the responsibilities of the directors, the rights of stockholders, and so forth.[56] Additionally, the usual rules and regulations divide resonsibility in any large organization. For corporations that are public policy-making entities in their own right, the charter and other procedural policies are also constituent policy for the society as a whole.

But this internal structure is only the most routine and universal form of corporate constituent policy. Less frequent, but more important, are those instances in which corporations are constituent policy-makers not for themselves but directly for governmental bodies. The most blatant example is the old style company town, which still exists, although in declining numbers, particularly in the South. We need not re-enter the hoary community power debate to note that the local political life of some small communities is *totally* dominated by a single industry. There is, for example, the case of St. Mary's, Georgia, chillingly documented by Peter Schuck and Harrison Wellford.[57] The town is a fiefdom of the Gilman Paper Company, which employs nearly all the town's workers. The town's attorney is also the mill's attorney and was the state representative for the district. The town mayor is a mill employee and is also president of his union local which is, de facto, a company union. The political machine of the town is run directly within the company's plant. In 1970 a local doctor, Carl Drury, narrowly managed to unseat the mill's incumbent candidate for state representative (he lost in St. Mary's but carried the surrounding area of the legislative district). Subsequently, he was framed on a rape charge allegedly orchestrated by the company/town attorney (and former incumbent). Although the case fell apart when brought to the grand jury, Drury later paid a price for his independence when he was badly beaten up. In spite of the several eye witnesses, the assailant was acquitted by a jury dominated by mill employees or their relatives. Additionally, during Drury's campaign, the mill spied on employees to ferret out any who might be supporting Drury. Several were fired, businessmen in the surrounding county who supported Drury or were merely suspected of supporting him suffered economic retaliation.

Of course, a major reason for the extraordinary efforts at total domination is the resulting economic advantage. By running the town the paper company, in effect, can set its own local taxes—with a very advantageous result for itself. But given the economic dependence of the town on the company, such advantages would probably accrue anyway. Schuck and Wellford suggest that domination is craved also for its own sake. They note that "there is a traditional view among southern mill owners, captured by W.J. Cash in his *Mind of the South*, that it's no one else's damn business how they run their town."[58] In short, the paper company runs the show in St. Mary's. Furthermore, the traditional pluralist safeguards are absent. The local press is not independent (the only local paper is controlled by mill interests and gave no coverage to the election), and no countervailing interest groups exist.

The system of campaign financing is the most pervasive form of constituent policy. Unlike the other corporate public policies, this form is directly traceable to the decisions (or lack thereof) of governmental bodies and the needs of politicians in the electoral system as it is presently constituted. Campaigns cost a lot of money. In the absence of provisions for public financing of campaigns or of effective limits on spending, corporations have the ability to deliver the requisite funds (usually by various subterfuges), and they have the incentive to use their economic resources to invest in politicians they deem favorable to their own interests.[59] If public financing of campaigns in the future would be a public policy, corporate financing is currently a public policy with the specific allocations of resources being determined by each corporation.

Conclusion

Our thesis all along has been that it is extremely shortsighted to limit our conception and analysis of public policy to only those policies emanating from governments. We have argued that private governments, particularly giant corporations, are significant public policy-makers. It is equally important, however, not to go overboard in utilizing this broader conception of public policy—there are still limits to what can be considered privately made public policy. Specifically we issue three caveats.

Caveats

First, not all the effects of corporate enterprise upon citizens can be considered to be public policies. Probably most of the impact of corporations on society is due to the social and economic consequences of modern technology, a pervasive capitalist ideology, and large-scale industrial organization. One must distinguish these generalized conditions from specific instances of corporate public policy-making—which requires intentional policies that are specifically identifiable. The line between specific policy and social environment may sometimes be vague, but it should be kept in mind. Even with specifiable policies, the line between those that are purely private and those that are public is not precise. In this respect the situation is analogous to the fuzzy line between public and private organizations. Further research and analysis must precede an attempt to establish more exact criteria of "publicness" for both organizations and policies.

Second, the thesis being advanced is not a conspiracy or a "power elite" theory. We make no claim that hidden powerful interests are pulling the strings of government or that government is nothing more than a reflection of powerful economic interests. What we are asserting, rather, is that a significant amount of *public* policy is made by corporations and other private governments without having to go through formal government authority. Furthermore, there is no claim here that all or even most public policy originates in this manner. But a significant number of public policies do so originate— enough to warrant increased public and academic concern.

Finally, it is not contended that all the effects of corporate policy-making are evil. While we need not accept the conservative view that the only valid criteria for assessing business performance are economic, it should still be emphasized that large corporations provide such benefits as goods, services, and employment. Most of this activity, however, does not constitute public policy-making. Corporate participation in the Urban Coalition and other such enterprises indicates that corporate policy-making may be beneficent and may coincide with the interests of other groups in society. Furthermore, the corporate policy-makers have some economic limits on their power and they may exercise self-restraint in using their political power.

Implications

There are two sets of implications of this conception of public policy: one relates to the study of politics, and one relates to democratic values. One major implication for political studies has been stated earlier with reference to the problem of nondecisions. Public policy research can be organized around the analysis of what constitutes a particular policy and the determination of who makes the policy. Indeed such a strategy is essential if we accept the validity of the concept of nongovernmental public policy. A second implication concerns the study and importance of policy impact. Impact studies have traditionally related only to the outputs of governments and have assumed that such outputs were the totality of public policy in a given area. The present broader conception of policy, however, alters this focus in two ways. First, the impact of a policy must include the outputs of all the relevant policy-makers—including the nongovernmental policy-makers. Otherwise we will deal only with partial impacts in such areas as health care, transportation, occupational safety, and other fields with a heavy nongovernmental policy component. Second, impact is not a separable sphere of inquiry but rather is a defining characteristic of what constitutes a *public* policy. Again, although the lines are still blurred, a public policy is any policy whose fundamental impact is a binding allocation of values for a significant segment of society. The final implication relates to the "relevance" of political science. As noted above, David Easton among others argues that extending the concept of public policy beyond the formal government would hopelessly broaden and dilute political science. Yet I would argue that another risk is even more pressing.

Limiting the concept of public policy to government policy tends to trivialize political science in that such a narrow concept misses some of the most significant allocations of values for citizens. Furthermore, these nongovernmental allocations are increasingly intertwined with the activities of formal government.[60] To factor out only governmental outputs for research thus tends to make policy studies a heuristic exercise divorced from the real world of policy-making and policy impacts. Such a limited concept is analogous to prebehavioral political science, in which the focus was on the legal and formal institutions of government to the exclusion of much of the world of political behavior. Similarly, the challenge now is to analyze public policy—whatever its source.

The second set of implications concerns political accountability and democratic theory. Nongovernmental policy-makers may be benevolent and restrained in their exercise of power. But, as noted by Morton Baratz, "this is hardly a satisfactory arrangement for a society which places a high value on a decentralized power structure."[61] Baratz approvingly cites Peter Drucker who writes, "the important fact about 'enlightened despotism'—also the one fact 'enlightened despots' always forget—is that while it appears as enlightenment to those in power it is despotism pure and simple to those under it."[62]

This last point is at the heart of the problem. We would not countenance a totally nonelected self-perpetuating oligarchy in government merely because many of the policies of that oligarchy were beneficent. Corporations also make public policy. When they do so, however, there is not even the formal accountability to the public that we have in government. The task for scholars and the public alike is to assess the amount of public policy that is privately made and to formulate ways of limiting such policy-making power—or at least of making it more accountable.

NOTES

1. *Policy Studies Journal,* 1 (Autumn 1972), 2.

2. "The Analysis of Public Policy: A Search for Theories and Roles," in *Political Science and Public Policy*, ed. Austin Ranney (Chicago: Markham Publishing Co., 1968), 152.

3. *A Systems Analysis of Political Life* (New York: John Wiley & Sons, Inc., 1965), 351–352.

4. "Outputs, Structure, and Power: An Assessment of Changes in the Study of State and Local Politics," *Journal of Politics*, 30 (May 1968), 515.

5. "Decision Making vs. Policy Making: Toward an Antidote for Technocracy," *Public Administration Review*, 30 (May/June 1970), 314–325.

6. *The Symbolic Uses of Politics* (Urbana: University of Illinois Press, 1964).

7. "The Study of Policy Content: A Framework for Choice," in *Political Science and Public Policy*, ed. Ranney, 7.

8. "Decision Making," 317.

9. See Sanford A. Lakoff, ed., *Private Government* (Glenview, Ill.: Scott, Foresman & Co., 1973) for a relevant anthology.

10. *Public and Private Government* (New Haven, Conn.: Yale University Press, 1944), 16.

11. *Politics, Economics, and Welfare* (New York: Harper & Brothers, 1953), 9–16.

12. Robert A. Dahl, *After the Revolution?* (New Haven, Conn.: Yale University Press, 1970), 120.

13. *Private Wants, Public Means* (New York: Basic Books, 1970), 53.

14. See, for example, William W. Kaufman, *The McNamara Strategy* (New York: Harper & Brothers, 1964), 168–203.

15. "Local Strength in the American Federal System: The Mobilization of Public-Private Influence," in *Continuing Crisis in American Politics*, ed. Marian D. Irish (Englewood Cliffs, N.J.: Prentice-Hall, 1963).

16. "A Prelude to Corporate Reform," *Business and Society Review*, 1 (Spring 1972), 18.

17. *Private Power and American Democracy* (New York: Alfred A. Knopf, 1966).

18. *The End of Liberalism* (New York: W. W. Norton & Company, 1966).

19. The classic formulation asserting the dominance of an elite is C. Wright Mills, *The Power Elite* (New York: Oxford University Press, 1956). See also Floyd Hunter, *Community Power Structure* (Chapel Hill: University of North Carolina Press, 1953); Jack L. Walker, "A Critique of the Elitist Theory of Government," *American Political Science Review*, 60 (June 1966), 285–295. The leading affirmation of pluralist theory in the community power debate is still Robert Dahl, *Who Governs?* (New Haven, Conn.: Yale University Press, 1961). See also Nelson W. Polsby, *Community Power and Political Theory* (New Haven, Conn.: Yale University Press, 1963) for a concise summary of the leading community power studies and a lucid analysis of the issues.

20. "Two Faces of Power," *American Political Science Review*, 56 (December 1962), 947–952; "Decisions and Non-Decisions: An Analytical Framework," *American Political Science Review*, 57 (September 1963), 632–634.

21. "Nondecisions and the Study of Local Politics," *American Political Science Review*, 65 (December 1971), 1,063–1,080. Also see Frederick Frey, "Comment: On Issues and Non-issues in the Study of Power," *American Political Science Review*, 65 (December 1971), 1,081–1,101; and Richard M. Merelman, "On the Neo-Elitist Critique of Community Power," *American Political Science Review*, 62 (June 1968), 451–460.

22. In his comment on Wolfinger's article, Frey is more optimstic about the utility of the nondecision concept. He asserts that it is possible to identify situations where one would expect influence to be attempted by aggrieved or disadvantaged parties but where such an attempt does not occur. Frey, "Issues and Nonissues," 1,094–1,099.

23. They also urge attention to the "mobilization of bias" within a community, "the dominant values, the myths, and the established political procedures." This analysis, however, precedes the central inquiry which is "the extent to which and the manner in which the status quo oriented persons and groups influence those community values and those political institutions…which tend to limit the scope of actual decision-making to 'safe' issues." "Two Faces of Power," 952.

24. Cf. Matthew Crenson, *The Un-Politics of Air Pollution* (Baltimore, Md.: The Johns Hopkins University Press, 1970).

25. *The Political System* (2d ed.; New York: Alfred A. Knopf, 1971), 130.

26. *Ibid.*, 129.

27. Easton, *Systems Analysis*, 349.

28. *Ibid.*, 352.

29. *Comparative Politics: A Developmental Approach* (Boston: Little, Brown & Co., 1966), 198.

30. *Political System*, 131–134.

31. *Ibid.*

32. *Systems Analysis*, 205–206.

33. *Ibid.*, 349–350.

34. *Ibid.*, 352–362.

35. Ralph Nader, *Unsafe at Any Speed* (New York: Grossman Publishers, Inc., 1965), chaps. 2, 3, *passim*.

36. On the utility of policy differentiation, see Theodore J. Lowi, "American Business, Public Policy, Case Studies, and Political Theory," *World Politics*, 16 (July 1964), 677–715; also

Lewis A. Froman, Jr., "The Categorization of Policy Contents," in *Political Science and Public Policy*, ed. Ranney, 41–52.

37. "American Business," 686–715.

38. *Comparative Politics*, 195–201.

39. "Four Systems of Policy, Politics, and Choice," *Public Administration Review*, 32 (July/August 1972), 298–310.

40. Cf. Larry L. Wade, *The Elements of Public Policy* (Columbus, Ohio: Charles E. Merrill, 1972), 6.

41. *The Folklore of Capitalism* (New Haven, Conn.: Yale University Press, 1937), 263.

42. *Pricing Power and the Public Interest: A Study Based on Steel* (New York: Harper & Brothers, 1962), 20.

43. U. S., Congress, Senate, *Administered Prices, Steel,* Report of the Committee on the Judiciary, Subcommittee on Antitrust and Monopoly, 85th Cong., 1st sess., 1958 (Washington, D.C.: Government Printing Office, 1958), 8, 18–22.

44. *Ibid.*, 14–15.

45. *Pricing Power*, 43.

46. U. S., Congress, Senate, Committee on the Judiciary, *Administered Prices, Hearings* before the Subcommittee on Antitrust and Monopoly, 85th Cong., 1st sess., 1957, 214.

47. See, for example, Karen Orren, *Corporate Power and Social Change: The Politics of the Life Insurance Industry* (Baltimore, Md.: The Johns Hopkins University Press, 1973), for an analysis of housing investment.

48. Robert Fellmeth, *The Politics of Land* (New York: Grossman Publishers, Inc., 1973).

49. Statement of Raphael Cohen, Metropolitan Independent Dodge Chrysler Dealers Association, *Hearings* before U.S., Congress, Senate, Committee on Small Business, a Senate Select Committee on Small Business on the role of giant corporations, 92nd Cong., 1st sess., 1971, pt. 1, 45–67.

50. *Ibid.*

51. See, for example, W. G. Broehl, Jr., *The Molley McGuires* (Cambridge, Mass.: Harvard University Press, 1965).

52. Department of Justice Antitrust Division memorandum on grand jury proceeding, cited by, Mark J. Green et al., *The Closed Enterprise System* (New York: Bantam Books, 1972), 255.

53. *Ibid.*, 257.

54. Although three of the four Justice Department attorneys on the case recommended both civil and criminal actions, Antitrust Division Chief Donald Turner declined to ask for indictments. The grand jury wanted to issue indictments, but did not do so because they did not realize that they could have done so even in the absence of a Justice Department request. A Justice Department civil suit was filed on January 10, 1969. In spite of protests from many congressmen and the State of California, the Justice Department under the leadership of Attorney General John Mitchell did not go to court but signed a consent decree with the automobile industry. The auto industry agreed not to further conspire to inhibit the development of antipollution devices without admitting that they had done so in the first place.

55. See, for example, Richard Ells, *The Government of Corporations* (New York: The Free Press, 1962.

56. In theory the charter is supposed to be a manifestation of public control of the corporation which is exercised in exchange for a variety of privileges. In reality, the charter has lost this original function and is currently the loosest kind of document allowing maximum freedom to corporate management. The new charter results from competition among the states to offer the most advantageous requirements to corporations. Currently Delaware is the champion, with one-third of all New York Stock Exchange listed corporations. See James Phelan and Robert Pozen, *The Company State* (New York: Grossman Publishers, Inc., 1973), 163–171.

57. "Democracy and the Good Life in a Company Town," *Harper's Magazine,* May 1972, 56–66.

58. Schuck and Wellford, "Company Town," 64.

59. See, for example, "Convention Financing: Corporate America's Role," *Congressional Quarterly Weekly Report*, 30 (July 8, 1972), 1,656–1,660.

60. Cf. Charles A. Reich, "The New Property," 73 *Yale Law Journal* 733 (1964).

61. "Corporate Giants and the Power Structure," *Western Political Quarterly*, 9 (June 1956), 415.

62. *The Concept of the Corporation* (New York: John Day Co., Inc., 1946), 72.

Socialist

William Domhoff. State and ruling class in corporate America.

On top of the gradually-merging social layers of blue and white collar workers in the United States, there is, a very small social upper class which comprises at most 1% of the population and has a very different life style from the rest of us. Members of this privileged class, according to sociological studies, live in secluded neighborhoods and well-guarded apartment complexes, send their children to private schools, announce their teenage daughters to the world by means of debutante teas and debutante balls, collect expensive art and antiques, play backgammon and dominoes at their exclusive clubs, and travel all around the world on their numerous vacations and junkets.

There is also in America, an extremely distorted distribution of wealth and income. Throughout the twentieth century, the top 1% or so of wealth-holders have owned 25–30% of all wealth and 55–65% of the wealth that really counts, corporate stock in major businesses and banks. But even that is not the whole story, for a mere .1% have at least 19% of all the wealth in the country—190 times as much as they would have if everyone had an equal share. As for income, well, the maldistribution is not quite as bad. But one recent study argues that if income from capital gains is included, the top 1.5% of wealthholders receive 24% of yearly national income. And, as all studies on matters of wealth and income are quick to point out, these estimates are conservative.

It is not hard for most of us to imagine that the social upper class uncovered in sociological research is made up of the top wealthholders revealed in wealth and income studies. However, it is not necessary to rely on our imaginations, for it is possible to do empirical studies linking the one group to the other. The first systematic studies along this line were reported by sociologist E. Digby Baltzell, but there have been others since.

In most countries, and in most times past in our own country, it would be taken for granted that an upper class with a highly disproportionate amount of wealth and income is a ruling class with domination over the government. How else, it would have been argued, could a tiny group possess so much if it didn't have its hooks into govern-

ment? But not so in the United States of today. This nation is different, we are assured. It has no social classes, at least not in the traditional European sense, and anyhow there is social mobility—new millionaires are created daily. Besides, many different groups, including organized labor, organized farmers, consumers, and experts, have a hand in political decisions—at least since the New Deal. There is no such thing as a ruling class in America.[1]

In this paper I am going to suggest that in fact a ruling class does dominate this country, a suggestion which not only flies in the face of prevailing academic wisdom, but raises problems for political activists as well. To support this suggestion, I will describe four processes through which the wealthy few who are the ruling class dominate government. Let me begin by defining two terms, "ruling class" and "power elite." By a ruling class, I mean a clearly demarcated social upper class which

a. has a disproportionate amount of wealth and income;

b. generally fares better than other social groups on a variety of well-being statistics ranging from infant mortality rates to educational attainments to feelings of happiness to health and longevity;

c. controls the major economic institutions of the country; and

d. dominates the governmental processes of the country.

By a power elite I mean the "operating arm" or "leadership group" or "establishment" of the ruling class. This power elite is made up of active, working members of the upper class and high-level employees in institutions controlled by members of the upper class.

Both of these concepts, I contend, are important in a careful conceptualization of how America is ruled. The distinction between ruling class and power elite allows us to deal with the everyday observation, which is also the first objection raised by critics of ruling-class theory, that some members of the ruling class are not involved in ruling, and that some rulers are not members of the upper class. Which is no problem at all, in reality. There always have been many members of ruling classes who spent most of their time playing polo, riding to hounds, or leading a world-wide social life. And there always have been carefully groomed and carefully selected employees, such as Dean Rusk of the Rockefeller Foundation, Robert McNamara of Ford Motor Company, Henry Kissinger of the Council on Foreign Relations, and Herb Stein of the Committee for Economic Development, who have been placed in positions of importance in government.

Now, many other criticisms have been raised about ruling-class theory, and many different kinds of evidence have been put forth to deal with these criticisms. One typical criticism is that the ruling class is never specified in a way that it can be studied empirically. But this argument can be met by reputational, positional, and statistical studies which show that certain social registers, blue books, prep schools, and exclusive clubs are good indicators of upper-class standing.

Another usual comment is that there is no reason to believe the alleged ruling class is "cohesive" or "class conscious," a criticism which can be countered by pointing to systematic evidence on interregional private school attendance, overlapping club memberships, interlocking corporate directorships, and nationwide attendance at annual upper-class retreats like the Bohemian Grove and the Ranchero Visitadores.

Then there is the assertion that members of the upper class have lost control of corporations and banks to middle-class managers and technocrats, which flies in the face of facts on corporate ownership, on the social backgrounds of corporate directors, and on the motives and goals of corporate managers.

Perhaps the most important criticism, however, is that championed by political scientists, who say proponents of ruling class theory do not spell out the mechanisms by which the ruling class supposedly dominates government. Not content to infer power from such indicators as wealth and well-being statistics, they want the case for governmental domination by a ruling class demonstrated in its own right, without appeal to statistics on wealth, income, health, and happiness.

My first attempt to satisfy the political science fraternity on this score was to show that members of the power elite hold important governmental positions, especially in the executive branch of the federal government, which I assume everyone now agrees is the most important part of American government.[2] But critics were not satisfied by a sociology-of-leadership approach, which infers "power" to be present when a disproportionate number of people from a given class, ethnic, racial, or religious group appear in positions of responsibility in a given institution. Although no one questions the findings of this method when it is used to show anti-ethnic or anti-racial discrimination on the part of banks, corporations, and universities, weaknesses are discovered in it when it is used to study the powerful instead of the powerless. Now the critics want to see the position holders in action, to see the various means by which they supposedly rule in the interests of themselves and their class.

Such critics often argue, as sociologist Arnold Rose did in his earlier-cited book on *The Power Structure*, that members of the power elite may not act in the interests of the ruling class while in governmental positions. Instead, they may act in the "national interest," a claim that probably strikes many people as a little empty when they contemplate oil industry tax favors, subsidies to corporations and rich farmers, defense contract overruns, loans to failing corporations, and the general social science finding that most human beings rarely if ever transcend their class, religious and/or ethnic background in viewing the world.

In my second effort to satisfy the concerns of those who wonder about the precise relationship between the state and the ruling class in corporate America, I turned to the problem of policy formation, developing information which suggests that non-partisan, seemingly objective dis-cussion groups like the Council on Foreign Relations and the Committee for Economic Development are in fact exclusive policy-planning organizations wherein members of the power elite join together with their hired experts to develop plans which are then brought to the government through blue ribbon commissions, position papers, friendly politicians, and not least, govern-mental appointees who are members or em-ployees of these groups.[3] But this was not quite good enough either, mostly because it did not deal with the role of political parties and elections. Despite the generally nega-tive response I have received from political scientists, I would like to take another stab at satisfying their major criticism of ruling-class theory. Perhaps it is masochism that motivates this near-hopeless task, but I have a new way of thinking about the prob-lem of ruling class and government that may put things in a new light. Simply put, I think there are four general processes through which economicially and politically active members of the ruling class, operating as the leaders of the power elite, involve them-selves in government at all levels. I call these four processes:

1) the special-interest process, which has to do with the various means utilized by wealthy individuals, specific corporations, and specific sectors of the economy to satisfy their narrow, short-run needs;

2) the policy-planning process, which has to do with the development and imple-mentation of general policies that are im-portant to the interests of the ruling class as a whole;

3) the candidate-selection process, which has to do with the ways in which members of the ruling class insure that they have "access" to the politicians who are elected to office; and

4.) the ideology process, which has to do with the formation, dissemination, and en-forcement of attitudes and assumptions which permit the continued existence of policies and politicians favorable to the wealth, income, status, and privileges of members of the ruling class.

Let me now turn to each of these processes to show their role in ruling class domination of the government. Although my focus will be on the federal government in Washington, I believe the general schema can be applied, with slight modifications, to state and local governments.

The special-interest process, as noted, comprises the several means by which specific individuals, corporations, or busi-ness sectors get the tax breaks, favors, subsidies, and procedural rulings which are beneficial to their short-run interests. This is the world of lobbyists, Washington super-lawyers, trade associations, and advisory committees to governmental departments and agencies. This is the process most often described by journalists and social scientists in their exposés and case studies concern-ing Congressional committees, regulatory agencies, and governmental departments. This process also has been the target of the excellent investigations by Ralph Nader and his colleagues.

I do not think I need spend any time giving examples of how this process works. In-deed, each reader will have his or her favor-ite studies for demonstration purposes. For myself, I am partial to what Richard Harris, in *The Real Voice*, and Morton Mintz, in *By Prescription Only*, have revealed about the machinations of the drug industry, and to the superb study of *The Politics of Oil* by Robert Engler. My favorites among the Nader studies, by a small margin, are Robert Fellmeth's *The Interstate Commerce Omission* and James Turner's *The Chemical Feast*. For a panoramic view, I prefer rela-tively recent books like Joseph Goulden's *The Super-Lawyers,* Drew Pearson and Jack Anderson's *The Case Against Congress*, Morton Mintz and Jerry Cohen's *America, Inc.*, and Robert Sherrill's *Why They Call It Politics*. But I stress that there are many other fine studies of this process, and that more are appearing all the time.

The information in these studies might seem on its face to be impressive evidence for ruling-class theory. After all, it shows that members of the ruling class are able to realize their will on innumerable issues of concern to them. They can gain tax breaks, receive subsidies, subvert safety laws, and dominate regulatory agencies, among other things. However, in the eyes of most political scientists this is not adequate evidence, for it does not show that the various "interests" are "coordinated" in their efforts. Moreover, it does not show directly that they dominate policy on "big issues," or that they control either of the political parties. This typical view is even expressed by Grant McConnell, the political scientist most sensitive to the many ways in which various private interests have taken over the piece of government of greatest concern to them. After concluding that "a substantial part of government in the United States has come under the influence or control of narrowly based and largely autonomous elites," he then asserts there is no need to talk of a power elite because

> These elites do not act cohesively with each other on many issues. They do not rule in the sense of commanding the entire nation. Quite the contrary, they tend to pursue a policy of noninvolvement in the large issues of statesmanship, save where such issues touch their own particular concerns. [4]

Moreover, the big interests do not dominate the government as a whole. The political parties and the Presidency seem to be beyond their reach:

> Fortunately, not all of American politics is based upon this array of small constituencies. The party system, the Presidency and the national government as a whole represent opposing tendencies. To a very great degree, policies serving the values of liberty and equality are the achievements of these institutions. Public values generally must depend upon the creation of a national constituency. [5]

In order to deal with the kind of argument presented by McConnell, it is necessary to consider next the policy-formation process, the process by which policy on "large issues" is formulated, for it is in the policy process that the various special interests join together to forge general policies which will benefit them as a whole. The central units in the policy network are such organizations as the Council on Foreign Relations, the Committee for Economic Development, the Business Council, the American Assembly, and the National Municipal League,

which are best categorized as policy-planning and consensus-seeking organizations of the power elite. I will not repeat here the information on the financing and leadership of these organizations which shows beyond a doubt that they are underwritten and directed by the same upper-class men who control the major corporations, banks, foundations, and law firms.[6] More important for our purpose is what goes on in the off-the-record meetings of these organizations.

The policy-planning organizations bring together, in groups large and small, members of the power elite from all over the country to discuss general problems—e.g., overseas aid, the use of nuclear weapons, tax problems, or the population question. They provide a setting in which differences on various issues can be thrashed out and the opinions of various experts can be heard. In addition to the group settings, these organizations also encourage general dialogue within the power elite by means of luncheon and dinner speeches, special written reports, and position statements in journals and books.

It was in groups such as these that the framework for a capital-labor detente was worked out at the turn of the century, that the bill for a Federal Trade Commission was drafted, that the plans for social security were created, that the ideas behind the Marshall Plan were developed, that national goals for the 1960's were projected, and the "population problem" was invented.[7] I do not have the space in this paper to spin out any of the case examples that are available in the works I just cited. Let me be content to summarize the policy-planning network by means of the diagram on the next page, and to list some of the most important functions of this process:

1. They provide a setting wherein members of the power elite can familiarize themselves with general issues.

2. They provide a setting where conflicts within the power elite can be discussed and compromised.

3. They provide a setting wherein members of the power elite can hear the ideas and findings of their hired experts.

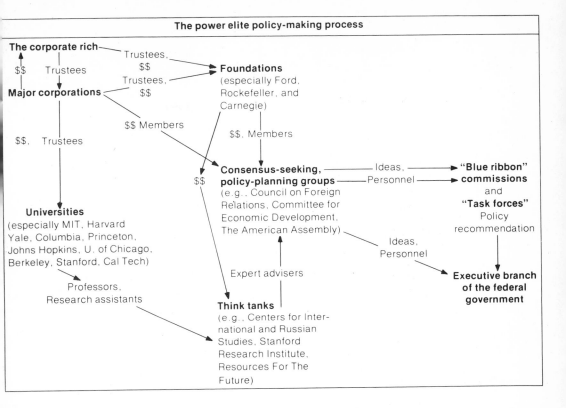

The power elite policy-making process

The corporate rich

$$ Trustees

Trustees, $$

Trustees, $$

Major corporations

$$ Members

Foundations
(especially Ford,
Rockefeller, and
Carnegie)

$$, Members

$$, Trustees

$$

**Consensus-seeking,
policy-planning groups**
(e.g., Council on Foreign
Relations, Committee for
Economic Development,
The American Assembly)

Ideas, —— **"Blue ribbon"**

Personnel —— **commissions**
and
"Task forces"
Policy
recommendation

Ideas,
Personnel

Universities
(especially MIT, Harvard
Yale, Columbia, Princeton,
Johns Hopkins, U. of Chicago,
Berkeley, Stanford, Cal Tech)

Professors,
Research assistants

Expert advisers

**Executive branch
of the federal
government**

Think tanks
(e.g., Centers for Inter-
national and Russian
Studies, Stanford
Research Institute,
Resources For The
Future)

4. They provide a "training ground" for new leadership within the ruling class. It is in these organizations that big businessmen can determine which of their peers are best suited for service in the government.

5. They provide a framework for commissioned studies by experts on important issues.

6. Through such avenues as books, journals, policy statements, press releases and speakers, they can greatly influence the "climate of opinion" both in Washington and the country at large.

There are several points for political scientists and other critics of ruling-class theory to consider in contemplating the policy-planning network. First, it provides evidence that businessmen, bankers, and lawyers concern themselves with more than their specific business interests. Second, it shows that leaders from various sectors of the economy do get together to discuss the problems of the system as a whole. Third, it

suggests that members of the power elite who are appointed to government are equipped with a general issue-orientation gained from power-elite organizations that are explicitly policy oriented. Fourth, it reveals that the upper-middle-class experts thought by some to be our real rulers are in fact busily dispensing their advice to those who hire them.

In short, if political scientists were to take the idea of a policy-planning process seriously, they would not be able to agree with Grant McConnell when he downgrades the importance of the Business Council by saying "the really effective participants in business politics are those [organizations] which direct their energies almost wholly to hard, specific matters of immediate economic concern to business firms."[8] Instead, they would say that trade associations are among the most important influences in the special-interest process and that the Business Council is one of the Archimedean points of the policy process.

Etzkowitz & Schwab—Is America Necessary—5

If I am right that members of the ruling class gain their narrow interests through the well-known devices of the special-interest process and their general interests through the little-studied policy-planning process, then the question immediately arises: how is all this possible when we have a government elected by the people? Shouldn't we expect elected officials to have policy views of their own that generally reflect the wishes of the voters who sent them to office? There is certainly one group of political scientists who believe this to be the case—they have developed a detailed argument to suggest that the deep-seated political ambitions of individuals and parties lead them to take the policy stands which will get them a majority of the vote, thereby insuring that the policy views of politicians will reflect more or less the views of the people.

To answer questions about our elected officials, we must examine the political parties and the candidates they nominate. When it comes to the parties, political scientists have suggested that a fully developed political party fulfills four functions: (1) integrating conflicting regional, ethnic, and class identifications; (2) selecting candidates to fill offices; (3) political education; and (4) policy making. In the United States, however, the parties have little or nothing to do with political education or policy making: "Particularly in our own century," writes political scientist Walter Dean Burnham, "American political parties have been largely restricted in functional scope to the realm of the constituent [integrative function] and to the tasks of filling political offices."[9] Another observer, the executive director of the National Committee for an Effective Congress, puts the matter even more strongly:

For all intents and purposes, the Democratic and Repulican parties don't exist. There are only individuals [candidates] and professionals [consultants, pollsters, media advisers].[10]

It is because American politics is restricted largely to office-filling functions that I prefer to talk about the candidate-selection process rather than the political process. The term political process gives the impression that more is going on in our electoral system than is really the case. And it is precisely because the candidate-selection process is so individualistic and issueless that it can be in good part dominated by means of campaign contributions from members of the ruling class. In the guise of fat cats, the same men who direct corporations and take part in the policy groups play a central role in the careers of most politicians who advance beyond the local or state legislature level in states of any size and consequence. To quote again from Walter Dean Burnham: "Recruitment of elective elites remains closely associated, especially for the more important offices and in the larger states, with the candidates' wealth or access to large campaign contributions."[11] Moreover, the role of the wealthy middlemen seems to be especially crucial in the nomination phase of the process. At least this was the conclusion of one of the most thorough studies ever done of campaign finance, by political scientist Alexander Heard:

The necessity for obtaining essential election funds has its most profound importance in the choosing of candidates. The monies can usually be assured, and often can be withheld, by the relatively small corps of political specialists whose job it is to raise money.... As a consequence, money probably has its greatest impact on the choice of public officials in the shadow land of our politics where it is decided who will be a candidate for a party's nomination and who will not. There are many things that make an effective candidate, but here is a *choke point* [my italics] in our politics where vital fiscal encouragement can be extended or withheld.[12]

The fat cats, of course, are by and large hard to distinguish in their socioeconomic outlook whatever their political party. Indeed, most corporations, banks, and law firms try to have personnel who are important donors to both parties. Then too, many of the fattest cats of the opposing parties join together as leaders of such policy-planning groups as the Council on Foreign Relations and Committee for Economic Development. For example, in 1968 there were 144 members of the Council on Foreign Relations who gave $500 or more to the Republicans, 56 who contributed $500 or more to the Demoncrats. One hundred twenty-six members of the National Council of the Foreign Policy Association donated sums of $500 or more to Republicans, 71 gave to Democrats. At the Committee for Economic Development, there were 95 Republican donors and 16 Democratic donors. Although well-connected in both parties, we can see a power elite preference for the Republican Party, at least in 1968. There is one other difference among fat cats worth noting— Southern and Jewish members of the upper class are more likely to be Democrats than are their WASPY counterparts.[13]

What kind of politicians emerge from this individualistically-oriented electoral politics that has to curry favor with large contributors? The answer is available from several studies. Politicians are first of all people from the higher levels of the social ladder: "The wealthiest one-fifth of the American families contribute about nine of every ten of the elite of the political economy."[14] They are secondly, at least among those who wish to go beyond local and state politics, quite ambitious men who are constantly striving for bigger and better things. They are thirdly people who are by and large without strong ideological inclinations; the exceptions to this statement are well known precisely because they are so unusual. Finally, with the exception of the local level, where businessmen are most likely to sit on city councils, they are in good part lawyers, an occupational grouping that by training and career needs produces ideal go-betweens and compromisers. The result of the candidate selection process, in short, is (1) men who know how to go along to get along, and (2) men who have few strong policy positions of their own, and are thus open to the suggestions put forth to them by the fat cats and experts who have been legitimated as serious leaders within the framework of the policy-planning network.

When we consider the interaction between the policy process and the political process, it is not surprising that there is a considerable continuity of policy between Republican and Democratic administrations. As columnist Joseph Kraft wrote

about the Council on Foreign Relations, "The Council plays a special part in helping to bridge the gap between the two parties, affording unofficially a measure of continuity when the guard changes in Washington."[15] Nor is it surprising that Hubert Humphrey would reveal in early 1973 that he had asked Henry Kissinger before the election in 1968 to serve as *his* foreign policy adviser should he win the Presidency. But David Halberstam's *the Best and The Brightest* best reveals the degree to which politicians defer to representatives of the policy process. After winning an election based upon "new frontiers" and non-existent missile gaps, President-elect John F. Kennedy called in Republican Robert Lovett, a Wall Street financier who hadn't even voted for him, and asked him for his advice as to whom should be appointed to important government positions. Kennedy did this because he only knew mere politicians, not the kind of "serious men" who were expert enough to run a government:

He had spent the last five years, he said ruefully, running for office, and he did not know any real public officials, people to run a government, serious men. The only ones he knew, he admitted, were politicians, and if this seemed a denigration of his own kind, it was not altogether displeasing to the older man. Politicians did need men to serve, to run the government.[16]

Among Lovett's suggestions were Dean Rusk of the Rockefeller Foundation, Robert McNamara of Ford Motor Company, and Douglas Dillon of Dillon, Read, who, as we all know, ended up as Kennedy's choices to head the state, defense, and treasury departments.

So politics in America has little to do with issues and public policy. It is an exercise in image-building, name-calling, and rumor mongering, a kind of carnival or psychological safety valve. Thus, a Richard M. Nixon can unctuously claim he is dealing with the issues in the 1972 campaign, when in fact even the *Wall Street Journal* has to admit that all he does is wave the flag and accuse people who disagree with him of being traitors.[17] And at about the same time he is pretending to discuss the issues, he can quietly tell his campaign strategists not to worry about what the platform says because "Who the hell ever read a platform?"[18] Then, after the election, the President's press secretary can calmly admit that the issue of spending cuts in domestic programs was purposely hidden during the campaign. It would have been "naive" to raise this issue explained Herb Klein when he was asked why the President did not mention his plans to cut back domestic programs during the campaign. "You don't raise unnecessary issues in the middle of a Presidential campaign," Klein explained.[19]

I conclude that the notion of public policy being influenced to any great extent by the will of the people due to the competition between the two political parties is misguided. "Politics" is for selecting ambitious, relatively issueless middle- and upper-middle-class lawyers who know how to advance themselves by finding the rhetoric and the rationalizations to implement both the narrow and general policies of the bi-partisan power elite.

At this point I can hear the reader protesting that there is more to American politics than this. And so there is. I admit there are serious-minded liberals who fight the good fight on many issues, ecologically oriented politicians who remain true to their cause, and honest people of every political stripe who are not beholden to any wealthy people. But there are not enough of them, for there is also a seniority system dominated by ruling class-oriented politicians who have a way of keeping the insurgents off the important committees and out of the centers of power. There is in addition a Southern Democratic delegation which retains its stranglehold on Congress despite all the claims of the mid-Sixties that its star was about to fade. Then there are the machine Democrats who aid the Southerners in crucial ways even while they maintain a liberal voting record. And finally, there are the myriad lobbyists and lawyers who are constantly pressuring those who would resist the blandishments of the power elite. As former Congressman Abner Mikva once said, the system has a way of grinding you down:

The biggest single disappointment to a new man is the intransigence of the system. You talk to people and they say, "You're absolutely right, something ought to be done about this." And yet, somehow, we go right on ducking the hard issues. We slide off the necessary confrontations. This place has a way of grinding you down.[20]

In short, even though there is more to American politics than fat cats and their political friends, the "more" cannot win other than headlines, delays, and an occasional battle. The candidate-selection process produces too many politicians who are friendly to the wealthy few.

Contemplation of the ways in which the special-interest, policy-planning, and candidate-selection processes operate brings us to the $64 question: why do we, the general public, acquiesce in this state of affairs? Why is it, as Marx warned, that the ruling ideas of any age are the ideas of the ruling class? Why does the ruling class have what the Italian Marxist Antonio Gramsci called "ideological hegemony," by which he meant that "the system's real strength does not lie in the violence of the ruling class or the coercive power of its state apparatus, but in the acceptance by the ruled of a "conception of the world" which belongs to the rulers?"[21] Unfortunately, no one has given an adequate answer to these interrelated questions. Such an answer would involve insights from a variety of disciplines including history, anthropology, and psychology as well as political science and sociology, and would quickly lead to age-old problems concerning the origins of the state and the general nature of the relationship between leaders and led.

However, at the sociological level which concerns me in this paper, we certainly can see that members of the ruling class work very hard at helping us to accept their view of the world. Indeed, we can be sure from past experience that they will stop at nothing—despite their protestations of "democracy" and "liberalism"—to get their views across.[22] Through the ideology process, they create, disseminate, and enforce a set of attitudes and "values" that tells us this is, for all its defects, the best of

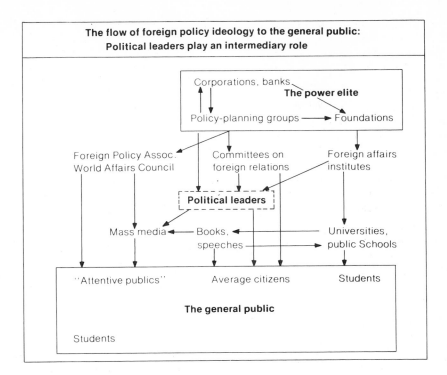

**The flow of foreign policy ideology to the general public:
Political leaders play an intermediary role**

Corporations, banks
The power elite
Policy-planning groups ⟶ Foundations

Foreign Policy Assoc.
World Affairs Council

Committees on
foreign relations

Foreign affairs
institutes

Political leaders

Mass media ⟵ Books,
speeches

Universities,
public Schools

"Attentive publics"   Average citizens   Students

The general public

Students

all possible worlds. At the fount of this process are the same foundations and policy-planning groups which operate in the policy process. For in addition to providing policy suggestions to government, these policy-planning organizations also provide the new rationales which make the policies acceptable to the general public. Thus, in the case of the ideology process we must link these organizations not to the government, as in the policy process, but to a dissemination network which includes middle-class discussion groups, public relations firms, corporate-financed advertising councils, special university and foundation programs, books, speeches, and various efforts through the mass media.

The dissemination apparatus is most readily apparent in the all-important area of foreign policy. Perhaps most critical here is the Foreign Policy Association and its affiliate, the World Affairs Council. Tightly interlocked with the Council on Foreign Relations, the Foreign Policy Association provides literature and discussion groups for the "attentive public" of upper-middle-class

professionals, academics, and students. For local elites, the Council on Foreign Relations sponsors Committees on Foreign Relations in over 30 cities around the country. These committees meet about once a month during the nonsummer months to hear speakers provided by the Council on Foreign Relations or the government. The aim of this program is to provide local elites with information and legitimacy so they may function as "opinion leaders" on foreign policy issues. In addition to the Foreign Policy Association and the Committees on Foreign Relations, there are numerous foreign affairs institutes at major universities which provide students and the general public with the perspectives of the power elite on foreign policy. Then too, political leaders often play an intermediary role in carrying foreign policy positions to the general public.

The enforcement of the ideological consensus is carried out in a multitude of ways that include pressure, intimidation and violence as well as the more gentle methods of persuasion and monetary inducement.

Those who are outspoken in their challenge to one or another of the main tenets of the American ideology may be passed over for promotions, left out of junkets, or fired from their jobs. They may be excluded from groups or criticized in the mass media. If they get too far outside the consensus, they are enmeshed in the governmental law enforcement apparatus which is shaped in the policy-formation process with a special assist from the ruling-class dominated American Bar Association and its affiliated institutes and committees.[23] But I do not think we need spend much time considering the bitter details of ideology enforcement, for they are all too fresh in our minds after years of struggle over civil liberties and the war in Southeast Asia.

NOTES

1. For typical expressions of this view, consult sociologist Arnold Rose, *The Power Structure* (Oxford University Press, 1967), political scientist Robert Dahl, *Pluralist Democracy in the United States* (Rand McNally, 1967), or political scientist Grant McConnell, *Private Power and American Democracy* (Alfred A. Knopf, 1966).

2. G. William Domhoff, *Who Rules America?* (Prentice-Hall, 1967).

3. G. William Domhoff, *The Higher Circles* (Random House, 1970).

4. McConnell, *op. cit.*, p. 339.

5. *Ibid.*, p. 8.

6. Domhoff, *The Higher Circles, op. cit.*

7. On the capital-labor detente and the Federal Trade Commission, see James Weinstein, *The Corporate Ideal in the Liberal State* (Beacon Press, 1968). On Social Security, see Domhoff, *The Higher Circles, op. cit.* On the ideas behind the Marshall Plan, see David Eakins, "Business Planners and America's Postwar Expansion," in *Corporations and The Cold War,* David Horowitz, ed. (Monthly Review Press, 1969). On national goals see G. William Domhoff, "How The Power Elite Set National Goals," in *The Triple Revolution Emerging,* Robert Perrucci and Marc Pilisuk, eds. (Little Brown and Co., 1971). On the "population problem" see Steve Weissman, "Why the Population Bomb is a Rockefeller Baby," *Ramparts*, May, 1970, and William

Barclay, Joseph Enright, and Reid T. Reynolds, "Population Control in the Third World," *NACCLA Newsletter,* December, 1970.

8. McConnell, *op. cit.*, pp. 292–293.

9. Walter Dean Burnham, "Party Systems and the Political Process," p. 279. In *The American Party Systems*, William Chambers and Walter Dean Burnham, eds. (Oxford University Press, 1967).

10. John S. Saloma III and Frederick H. Sontag, *Parties* (Alfred A. Knopf, 1972), p. 295.

11. Burnham, *op. cit.*, p. 277.

12. Alexander Heard, *The Costs of Democracy* (Doubleday, 1962), p. 34.

13. G. William Domhoff, *Fat Cats and Democrats,* (Prentice-Hall, 1972), for the information in this paragraph.

14. Kenneth Prewitt and Alan Stone, *The Ruling Elites* (Harper & Row, 1973), p. 137.

15. Joseph Kraft, "School for Statesmen," *Harper's Magazine,* July, 1958, p. 68.

16. David Halberstam, *The Best and The Brightest* (Random House, 1972), p. 4.

17. James P. Gannon, "Is GOP Campaign Rhetoric Too Hot?," *Wall Street Journal,* Sept. 8, 1972, p. 8.

18. "Republicans: Cloth-Coat Convention," *Newsweek,* August 7, 1972, p. 23.

19. "Post-Election Candor," *Newsweek,* March 26, 1973, p. 15.

20. Robert Sherrill, "92nd Congress: Eulogy and Evasion," *The Nation,* February 15, 1971.

21. Giuseppe Fiori, *Antonio Gramsci: Life of a Revolutionary* (NLB, London, 1970), p. 238.

22. G. William Domhoff, "The Power Elite, the CIA, and the Struggle for Minds," *The Higher Circles* (Random House, 1970), for an account of how moderates and liberals within the power elite subverted various American institutions in their efforts to "save" an "open" society.

23. The bottom level of the enforcement apparatus, the police, didn't do their job quite right in the late Sixties. While injecting the required amount of fear into many citizens, they also created many new dissenters among students, Blacks, and Chicanos by their heavy-handed tactics. So the Ford Foundation spun off a $30 million Police Foundation to fund the university programs, special institutes, consultants, and books which are being used to teach the police to be more sophisticated in the containment of dissent in the future.

Part two

The typical American Government textbook describes the operation of the political system in terms of checks and balances of the three major organs of government—executive, legislative, judicial—and attempts to analyze how they function. Individual leaders and their actions are paid great attention while the operation of underlying institutional and historical forces are neglected. The traditional approach to the study of American government is an analysis of powerful leaders and official institutions.

Very recently alternative analyses to the traditional approach have appeared.[1] Although they offer a broad overview of unofficial, as well as the official institutions which comprise the American political process, they seldom incorporate a detailed accounting of the institutions and their inner workings.

The following chapters of this part of the book offer contrasting analyses of the three institutions that we believe are the most important, powerful, and presently most visible in the American political system. In 1956, C. Wright Mills published *The Power Elite*[2] in which he argued that three institutional structures, in coordination, determined the goals of American society. They were the military (the Joint Chiefs of Staff), the polity (the Office of the Presidency), and the economy (heads of major corporations). We feel that in the succeeding years other institutions have emerged as major visible power centers in American society. The Central Intelligence Agency (CIA) and the Federal Bureau of Investigation (FBI), often thought of as adjuncts to the exercise of American power, have now shown themselves to be capable of setting the direction for American and foreign societies. The uncovering of their operation permits us to include them as full-fledged members of the political elite. This is not to say that other institutions that Mills identified, such as the corporations, are less powerful. They may, in fact, be more so. We only feel them to be currently less visible.

The structure of this book does not set forth in order the more powerful and then the less powerful political institutions. Rather, it operates from the principle of moving from the more obvious to the less obvious political institutions, at least insofar as we view these institutions. We recommend that students keep this in mind. We recommend further that students keep the purposes of this framework in mind as they read the following articles. We hope that students reach their own conclusions as to which individuals or institutions are the most important in running

The visible power elite

America. They should also try to come to grips with the question of whether these institutions are useful or necessary in achieving what they want American society to be.

NOTES

1. See for example, Karl A. Lamb, *The People, Maybe: Seeking Democracy in America*. Belmont, California: Wadsworth Pub. Co., 1971. Michael Parenti, *Democracy for the Few*. New York: St. Martin's Press, 1974. Milton C. Cummings, Jr., David Wise, *Democracy Under Pressure: An Introduction to the American Political System*. New York: Harcourt Brace Jovanovich, Inc., 1971. Robert A. Isaak, Ralph P. Hummel, *Politics for Human Beings*. North Scituate, Mass: Duxbury Press, 1975. Robert Sherrill, *Why They Call It Politics*. New York: Harcourt Brace Jovanovich, Inc., 1972. Alfred de Grazia, *Politics for Better or Worse*, Glenview, Illinois: Scott, Foresman & Co., 1973.

2. C. Wright Mills. *The Power Elite*. New York: Oxford University Press, 1956.

*

2 The Presidency

The basic questions this chapter will address are:

(1) How powerful or powerless is the President?

(2) Which interests does the President serve?

(3) What are the sources of information the President receives and how valid is this information?

(4) How powerful should the President be in setting the direction of our society?

These questions represent the major issues which the authors in this chapter argue from explicit and implicit conservative, liberal, and socialist principles.

The conservative position holds that the Presidency should be the basic goal-setting institution of our society. It accepts the Presidency as the most important institution in our society and argues that it is in everyone's interest to keep it so. The liberal position argues that the Presidency is the most important institution but that it has some structural deficiencies which lead to its not always acting in the best interests of the people. Liberals want to reorder some of the goals of society and believe this can be done by filling the Presidential office with the right individual. The right individual, such as a Franklin Roosevelt or a John Kennedy, is held by his leadership to be able to reorder priorities by changing how the office works. The socialist position does not see the problem in terms of how the office works. The very existence of the Presidency as the preeminently powerful institution in our society is a basic problem. This is so because the enormous power accumulated in this institution is used to serve a small class of people who control society through their control of the economy. The power is used in the interest of this small elite rather than for the great masses of people. The solution therefore is not seen in a restructuring of the Presidential office but in changing fundamentally the economic/political system of the United States.

In the articles you will read in this chapter, the office of the Presidency is analyzed, and the above questions and following issues are dealt with.

Amos Perlmutter, in his article "The Presidential Political Center and Foreign Policy," says that the Presidency is and ought to be the center of decision-making in foreign policy. The presidential political center consists of people chosen on the basis of merit and expertise. These people know what they are doing and know what is best for the country. They have the right to act.

The President is the decision-maker in foreign policy because he has been granted power by the Constitution, Congress, and the Supreme Court, and he has taken advantage of that power. In addition to this delegation of power, Presidents have taken the initiative in defining new areas of power under their control. This initiative has been formulated from John Locke's theory of *Prerogative,* which allows that for the good of society many things should be left to the discretion of the executive.[1] Formulated in the seventeenth century in *Of Civil Government*, this theory was taken by American Presidents and turned into the inherent power theory. Harry Truman put into words what has long been part of American political tradition: "The President must use whatever power the Constitution does not expressly deny him."[2] This means that Presidential actions are based not only on statutory authority, that is, laws passed by Congress and powers explicitly granted to the President in the Constitution, but on inherent authority, that is what the President thinks he wants to do. This doctrine of inherent powers has been approved by the Supreme Court in a number of cases. For example, in the best known of these cases, *U.S. v Curtiss Wright*, the Court said that "if embarrassment [in foreign affairs] is to be avoided and success for our aims achieved, congressional legislation . . . must often accord to the President a degree of discretion and freedom from statutory restriction . . . . "[3]

Delegated and inherent powers exist in the Presidency in very large part, according to Perlmutter, because Congress, which is also constitutionally delegated power in foreign affairs, is too disorganized and disunited to act. Perlmutter maintains that one man, even the President, cannot make decisions alone. He needs at his side competent and expert advisors. From this framework it follows that the President would want to find the most expert people available, chosen on the basis of demonstrated ability and wisdom. With the help of these experts the President acts. Together they make rational decisions. The Presidency is presently organized so that the best people the country has to offer are in power and make decisions that are in the best interests of the nation.

According to this analysis little criticism is called for, since the optimum decision-making structure has been achieved. Perlmutter criticizes detractors of this analysis who claim that decisions are made on a criteria other than pure merit—such as class position.

The underlying presupposition of Perlmutter's analysis is that the President is, and ought to be, the center of decision-making, particularly in the area of foreign affairs. A small, tightly organized and efficient structure is necessary to conduct foreign policy so that United States power can be maintained and strengthened. This thesis is based on the further assumption that the United States by right ought to be the most powerful nation in the world, setting the basic framework within which other countries make their decisions. This is an expression of the doctrine of Manifest Destiny—that the United States has a right to expand to its fullest limits, on its own continent and internationally. Any challenge to American authority must be met by the Presidential office because any loss of power to this office is detrimental to the country.

Any slight to the nation is taken very seriously by the President and his advisors, who have the power to focus world-wide attention to the actions they will take. The capture of a ship in a dispute over international boundaries, such as North Korea capturing the *Pueblo,* and Cambodia the *Mayaguez,* is taken as a personal affront and "What will the Presi-

dent do?'' becomes the question everybody asks.
captures a British trawler in a dispute over fishing
portant to the concerned parties and few people in
it.

Because of the attention given the Presidency, mind
with as major mishaps and the question of what the ⎜
becomes of vital interest in Moscow, Peking, Bonn, ⎜   ⎣⎯ ⎯ the
capitals of smaller states.

This perspective of Presidential power sees the Presidency as symbolic
of the country. The President stands for the United States and all it represents in the same way as ''The Star-Spangled Banner'' and the flag.
As it is wrong to tear up the flag or make fun of the national anthem, so it
is wrong to criticize the Presidential office. Like the flag, the Presidential
office has become inviolable.

This philosophy of the Presidency can be traced back to Plato's *Republic*, in which he argued that only the best must rule, those who are
wisest, virtuous, and most reasonable. Everyone has their place in
society: workers must work, those talented in soldiering must soldier,
and those with reason must rule.

The city-state was for Plato what the nation is for those who hold to the
conservative perspective of the Presidency: office should be held by
those few who have reason and intelligence. By accepting this theory of
how society should work, one must accept a converse theory that those
who presently hold power are reasonable and wise. Most of the press
and the public reinforce this theory. This is where the concept ''the office
makes the man'' comes from—the Presidency lends wisdom and reason
to those who hold it. Harry Truman, who, as Vice-President projected an
image of an intellectual lightweight, was as President, seen to possess a
new level of decision-making capability. In either case, a system of rule
is legitimated by which the few have the right to rule the many. If wise
people are in power, fine; if not their office will lend them wisdom. Both
sides of this concept form a complete system of thought which can be
used to justify any status quo.

George Reedy, in his article ''The American Monarchy,'' represents the
liberal position on the Presidency. He accepts the premise that the major
decisions in American society ought to be made by the White House. In
the past few decades, as a result of Congressional delegation of power
and public acquiescence to that power, the American President has
become a super-powerful figure.

This power has also been increased by modern technology. Computers,
jet planes, taping systems, push-button telephones are all available to
give the President instant information and control over its use. According
to Reedy these instruments of technology have actually isolated the
President in his oval office rather than expanded his awareness. There is
however, the appearance that all this technology provides the President
with more knowledge than you or I could ever have access to.

This technology produces such a wealth of information that no one person could select and review it himself. An entire staff is necessary to separate the important from the unimportant. The President must be supplied with summaries of information selected by the intelligence services, cabinet officers, personal advisors, and newspapers. For example, one Presidential advisor chooses articles and editorials from a selection of newspapers for the President to read each morning. Rarely do Presidents read newspaper articles other than those selected for him. According to Reedy, you and I often have more information at our disposal through a complete reading of *The New York Times* than does the President. After leaving office in 1969 Vice-President Hubert Humphrey claimed that he knew very little about the intensity and number of Vietnam dissenters because the newspaper articles selected for him to read deemphasized such information.

Reedy maintains that the use of this massive gathering and editing of information makes the President dependent on a few people. These advisors have become so infatuated with the power and authority of their positions that they will do anything to keep their jobs and remain in the President's favor. They give the President only the information they believe he would like to hear, which will put them in a good light in his eyes.

In conclusion, Reedy states that in reality the President often has very little valid information at his disposal with which to make adequate decisions. For Reedy, the problem is not the structure of the Presidency itself but the atmosphere of the White House. The President is not as busy as he would like us to think he is. If he made a greater effort to obtain information from a wider variety of sources and at the same time deemphasized the monarchial trappings of the White House, he would become more in touch with reality and be better able to do his job.

Essentially the liberal perspective of the Presidency is that the office is powerful and ought to be so. The President should look after the interests of Americans at home and abroad. His office is the central institution in the American political system. Liberals however, believe that this institution is not flawless. If it were corrected by placing better individuals in the office who would correct abuses of power, the Presidency would function in the interests of all the people better than any other governmental institution. In the *Federalist Papers* debates over ratification of the Constitution, John Jay argued for a strong Presidency. It is, he said, the sole institution capable of speaking with one voice, listening with one set of ears. Congress, particularly in foreign affairs, was too disorganized to function with one voice in the name of all the people.[4] Thus, the liberal approach to a strong Presidency has its underpinnings in the very origins of the American Republic. Alexander Hamilton, James Madison, and John Jay, all of whom wrote the *Federalist Papers* assumed that a reasonable and wise man would fill the Presidential role; there was no reason to believe, therefore, that he would abuse his powers. Liberals generally feel that abuse of Presidential power is an abberation which can be corrected by electing a wise and good person as President.

Whereas Perlmutter and Reedy accept the structure of the Presidential office as acting in the best interests of the nation as a whole, Gabriel Kolko in "The Men of Power" sets forth the thesis that the Presidential office acts in the interest of only a small number of Americans.

Most of the people who serve in high levels of the Presidential office come from business, corporate law, banking, and industry. They act on behalf of the sources of power from which they come. While Perlmutter and Reedy argue that those who serve the President are the best qualified for their jobs, Kolko disagrees. It is his belief that lawyers, bankers, and industrialists are not necessarily the most intelligent but are merely well-fixed and both represent and serve powerful economic interests.

The solution does not lie in restructuring the Presidency but in altering the economic underpinnings of our society. As things stand, a few control most of the resources and therefore have the ability to control the Presidency and use it to maintain and advance their specific interests.

Elements of the socialist critique of the Presidency can be seen in Thomas Jefferson's fears of a strong central government. It was his belief that by establishing alternate sources of power in the states the growth of the central government could be prevented. The rights and liberties of the people could best be protected by preventing accumulations of power in a central government which, like Great Britain over the American colonies, could become very oppressive. Since any government structure tends to accumulate power it should be dismantled periodically and rebuilt. As Jefferson said, "The tree of liberty must be watered every twenty years."[5]

Socialists feel that the Presidency serves the interests of a few economic giants. In order to deal with this situation the economic structures themselves would have to be dismantled. The Presidency is more a spokesman for these interests, and thus merely altering its structure does not do anything to change its fundamental values. The socialist alternative is to eliminate the Presidential office, replacing it with a series of coordinating bodies, responsible to the people, who could make decisions in their interest. One man or a small number of men would not make these decisions. Foreign policy and other decisions, would be made by these coordinating bodies, or conventions, whose fealty would be to the people rather than to economic interests. These bodies would be representative of the population because they would come from the population. The socialist ideal of the withering away of the state does not mean that there would be no political coordinating mechanism, but that everyone will participate in political decisions.

NOTES

1. John Locke. *Of Civil Government: Second Treatise.* Chicago: Henry Regnery Co., 1964. p. 135.

2. Harry S. Truman. *Years of Trial and Hope: 1946–1952.* New York: Signet Pub., 1956. p. 535.

3. *United States v. Curtiss-Wright.* 299 U.S. 304 (1936).

4. See, *The Federalist Papers,* Number 64.

5. See, Richard Hofstadter. ''Thomas Jefferson: The Aristocrat as Democrat'' in *The American Political Tradition.* New York: Vintage Books, 1959. p. 24. See also, Charles M. Wiltse. *The Jeffersonian Tradition in American Democracy.* New York: Hill & Wang, 1960.

Conservative

Amos Perlmutter. The Presidential political center and foreign policy: A critique of the revisionist and bureaucratic-political orientations.[*]

The foreign policy elite and its challengers

Political philosophers, social theorists, and moralists have been examining the nature of power since time immemorial. This search for a definition, which still goes on, has exhibited certain characteristics. First, the most intensive quests for what constitutes power have been initiated in times of political and moral crises or during periods of revolution and profound social change. Next, because the most conspicuous aspect of power is personal power—institutional power being more complex and less apparent—analysts have tended to focus on rulers and their corollary, the ruled. Finally, in examining this dichotomy between the rulers and the ruled, analysts have sought to discover the sources of crises, revolution, and change.

Devising a theory of the power elite became an honorable professional occupation for theorists at the time of the French Revolution: its antagonists were heavily engaged in historical, social, and methodological controversies. Some time later, Karl Marx emerged as the first, most astute analyst of power of the modern age, although his political analysis was marred by a preoccupation with economics and historical materialism. To Marx, the ruler was a single power construct: the few owners of the means of production. The real producers, the proletariat, were the ruled. Rationally conscious of their permanent need to protect their power, the owners used instruments of coercion and violence—the police, the military, and the state—to uphold their economic power and status. Thus, they were the oppressors of the real producers— the actual workers whom they exploited. In this battle between exploiters and producers, according to Marx, lay the heart of the class struggle, which could be resolved only by violence and revolution.

Outraged by Marx and Marxism, conservative political theorists rose to challenge him in the late nineteenth and early twentieth centuries, notably the Italians Gaetano Mosca and Vilfredo Pareto, and Roberto Michels, a German professor teaching in Italy.[1] Arguing that Marx's class theory was not social-scientific but ideological, they elevated his analysis of the elite into a science and an ideology.[2] Whereas Marx's science afforded an ideology for the proletariat, this group assured the middle classes that socialism would become "bourgeoisified," and that the "iron law of oligarchy" would not discriminate between the left and the right. In this sense, socialism would develop as a class movement with a conservative orientation.[3]

With the rise of a complex and affluent industrial society in the twentieth century, the "classical" ruling-class theory reappeared under a new guise—that of the power elite. Its most renowned spokesman was the sociologist C. Wright Mills.[4]

According to Mills, power in modern times is institutional. Corporate linkage produces the cohesiveness of the "power elite." Domination, then, "will be in large part determined by the closeness of the links between the institutional hierarchies." The political directorate (the conglomerate of political, industrial, and military corporate hierarchical elites) takes advantage of the interchange and complementarity of institutional proximity.[5] Above all, the conspiracy of the power elite is hatched by the hierarchy—a cabal of the industrial, military, and university institutions.

Mills identifies the power elite with the political elite around the surrogate political center, the office of the President. It consists of corporate business executives, military professionals, armchair strategists, university professors, scientists, and technocrats. Their social status and background may provide access to the presidential political center, but it does not guarantee political power. Corporate, intellectual, and technocratic elites are by nature more co-

[*]From World Politics XXVII, no. 1 (October 1974), pp. 87–106. Reprinted by permission of Princeton University Press.

hesive than the political, elective, and representative elites. Clustered around the office of the Presidency, they become ever more cohesive, conscious, and conspiratorial. Class backgrounds and loyalties are subordinated to the power of the center.

In this article I will challenge the concept of "power" that is derived from cohesiveness—the conspiratorial theory. I will suggest instead that the division over ideology and class within each elite cluster is greater than any division between the elite and the masses. The implications, of course, cut at the heart of Mills' monolithic theory. Further, I will attempt to demonstrate that foreign policy—ideologically, institutionally, and behaviorally—has been and probably will remain the area of "competence" of the few whose cohesion (i.e., political power) is derived from their proximity to the presidential political center, rather than (according to Mills), from class, social, and institutional proximity.

The "conspiracy theory" of the power elite, and therefore its influence on foreign policy and national security, stems from an analytical failure to identify the dynamics of power. Power is obtained through the dynamics of politics, and not merely from being a member of a cohesive corporate group that, naturally and by design, converts institutional proximity to power. The gap between power and powerlessness cannot be seen as a simple dichotomy between "rulers" and "ruled," or "government" and "the people." It is not a simple struggle between elites and non-elites, or between the "elite" and the "masses." Basically, it is between the politics of the politically elected and the appointed experts—a rivalry between the regime's institutions and the competition between and within their respective elites. The gap between power and powerlessness must be explained by the fact that supremacy over defense and security policy making is an end in itself which transcends any psychological make-up of the "elite," its organizational abilities, and its control over economic resources and the distribution of offices.[6] In other words, the political struggle between "in" and "out" elites is over the dom-ination of the political center and the center of the center—the Presidency and its most coveted power: the power over foreign affairs and defense.

Consensus is a central elitist concept and a major weapon of the foreign policy elites. Consensus, according to power-elite theorists, is the instrument of mass manipulation by the power elite. Foreign policy consensus is that instrument which buttresses *a small, well-integrated elite* (*or coalition of elites*) *clustered at the political center.*

When we speak of the school of social-political scientists (or the bureaucratic-politics group), we are speaking of analysts of political and organizational power who have identified the strategic elites as the bureaucratic-politicians.[7] When members of this group analyze the politics of these "bureaucrats," they are actually analyzing the politics of the strategic elites.[8]

The "bureaucratic-politics school," although less ideologically oriented than the power-elite theorists, also fails to offer any viable alternative to the presidential political center. Its "value-free" analysis of the politics of security and diplomacy is dominated by modern organizational theories which are used to explain the mechanisms and complexity of political-bureaucratic decision making at the highest levels of foreign policy formulation and execution. These analysts do not attempt to alter the political power structure of the United States. They correctly identify the focus of foreign policy as being the presidential political center, but their analysis breaks down when they invest members of the court with disproportionate power, failing to discern the court's master—the President—as the real source.

The dichotomy of bureaucratic versus monarchical politics stems from the *unequal* relationship between the President and the members of his court. Most of the bureaucratic-politics analysts, like the power elitists, fail to see that the political struggle over foreign policy in the United States is neither a function of bureaucratic politics nor a struggle between elected politicians and experts, but a central institutional-constitutional political struggle.

The power-elite theorists and the foreign policy center

The new power-elite theorists are original in singling out the processes of American foreign policy making as proof par excellence of the persistence of the power-elite theory in the United States. On their own grounds, I wish to challenge their argument.

For the present purpose, I shall lump the revisionist-historians with the anti-cold war moralists. Their arguments are as follows:

1. American foreign policy is dominated by the few who make key decisions: the foreign policy directorate (i.e., the presidential court and the elites of the cold-war consensus).

2. The political directorate, the military, and the industrial elites are linked by virtue of their institutional proximity.

3. The power of the military-industrial complex stems from the "institutional mechanism" (or, as Richard Barnet calls it, the bureaucratic revolution) of the modern corporation and complex organizations.

4. The link between the political directorate and corporate power stems also from their common educational background (Ivy League schools) and their common war experiences (World War II, Korea, the cold war, Vietnam).

5. The consciousness of the foreign policy directorate is, in a Marxist sense, that of monopoly capitalism.

6. Above all, these decision-makers form a conspiratorial group, one that expresses a common will for action.

7. Their consensus ideology is the pursuit of militant anti-communism, American globalism, and the maintenance of the cold war. Psychologically, they are identified by their organizational commitments (corporate-technocratic) and by their association with complex organizations.

It should be mentioned here that although revisionists and moralists agree on the directorate's cohesiveness and consciousness, they differ on what constitutes the conspiracy of the directorate. Revisionists argue that surrogate economic monopoly capitalism is the root of the directorate's power and conspiratorial inclinations, whereas the moralists regard the power as stemming from social class, skills, or both, and the conspiracy as incidental.

Where the power-elite theorists fail is in their lack of any social, scientific, and historical-comparative analyses of the behavior of the directorate in the context of American Political power. (It would behoove the power elitists to modify their anti-power elite ideology, but that would probably be morally abhorrent to them.) Kolko and Chomsky tend to attack the directorate on Marxian grounds, i.e., social and economic elitism;[9] Barnet, Stone, and others tend to challenge it on Michelian organizational grounds.[10] Like Marx, however, the moralist-revisionists do not address themselves either to political and institutional sources or to the purposes of political power and political elites and the ensuing political behavior. One finds no reference in their works to Weber, the great analyst of political institutions, authority, and status. Neo-Marxists, like the old master, consider politics epiphenomenal. They fail to heed the counsel of Bendix and Lipset "that the facts of politics must be studied in their own right and *not just inferred from the politicians' social background.*"[11] In other words, this group either fails to perceive the critical relevance of the political center or ignores it. For instance, as issues of national security and foreign policy become more complex, they are accompanied by rivalry between and within the military-industrial complex. The division is not between civilians and the military, but between conflicting orientations, based on their perceptions of the enemy.

The power elitists propagandize, too, for an alternative system of values and beliefs, for a new consensus, a counter-elite. The moralists are not "value-free" social scientists. Kolko and Chomsky would have us believe that the chief malady of American political life lies in the high immorality of the foreign policy elite; that foreign policy directorates and multiversity corporate intellectuals are the equivalent of Marx's "oppressors." Economic corporations and monopoly capitalism have been linked to atavistic political realism, all conspiring at the top. Imperialism no longer becomes a Hobbesian-Leninist "last stage of capitalism," but the raison d'être of the American foreign policy directorate.

The above is, of course, a simplistic interpretation of the power and purpose of the foreign policy elites and of the political behavior of the President. Despite their expertise, the strategic elites are in no sense a political directorate. How powerful is a group which can be dismissed at the President's whim? After all, Robert McNamara, the arch-technocrat of them all, the "super imperialist," after seven years at the helm of a "political directorate"—the Defense Department—was relieved by a President suspicious of his failing loyalties, i.e., his growing doubts about Vietnam.

William A. Williams envisions an American empire set on an inexorable path toward economic imperialism since 1890, when capitalistic farmers discovered foreign markets.[12] The Open Door policy, for instance, is perceived as a policy of economic imperialism. Again, a single factor analysis of this sort simply is insufficient as an explanation for the behavior of American policy in the 1960's and 1970's. Kolko's and Williams' theory of "imperialists as economic exploiters"—that power relations within a society are derived from the power of the bank, that in the absence of the sword, power follows property (a view shared by the philosopher James Harrington)—simply does not explain motivations behind the war in Vietnam. And yet, as Charles Maier, a critic of the revisionists, has written, "They are unwilling to accept any description that tends to stress the decentralized nature of decision-making, or that envisages the possibility of expansionist policy taking shape by imperceptible commitments and bureaucratic momentum."[13]

Foreign policy and bureaucratic politics

Not unlike the concept of elite, that of bureaucracy has become all-encompassing and multi-purpose. Among other things, it now connotes management, administration, rational organization, and a type of authority legitimation. Even Max Weber, the most profound social theorist and analyst of bureaucracies in modern times, did not resolve the question of the conceptual and actual dividing lines between government, authority, and administration, or between types of domination and bureaucratic staffs.[14] Nor has the issue of the dividing lines between administrators, civil servants, bureaucrats, and politicians been resolved.

Inherent in the analysis of the bureaucratic-politics group (although not alluded to in their theories), is the pluralistic concept of power in society: that power in modern society is diffuse, that advanced societies are characterized by complex and highly differentiated organizations, and that power is dispensed in response to the diversification of interests. This pluralist orientation, combined with social scientific (and game theory) analyses, is the intellectual and methodological foundation of the bureaucratic-politics group.[15]

In contradistinction to the power-elite group, this group analyzes the elements of foreign policy in the proper context—politics. For that purpose, it uses the highly sophisticated concepts and methods of modern organizational analysis and game theory. There is no more analytically comprehensive approach to the study of the elements and the behavioral output available today.[16]

But that analysis contains a serious conceptual flaw. However sophisticated the approach of the bureaucratic-politics group, it is prey to the same pitfalls as that of the power-elite theorists. Although they correctly identify the locus and the pyramid of foreign policy decision making, they fail to identify where political power really rests. They make no clear distinction (even if it is inferred) between the President and the strategic elite, and they offer no theory concerning the dynamics of the relationship between the President and his court. The bureaucratic-politics group dodges any analysis of the politics of integrating the strategic elite (the bureaucratic politicians) into the office of the President. These theorists demonstrate no understanding of the dynamics of bureaucratic politicians—their power and influence. They also fail to see that relationships alter significantly over time, depending upon the changing nature of problems and the differing styles of succeeding administrations.

In the relationship between the President and his court, there are, after all, serious gaps of politics, power, and status. The bureaucratic-politics model of decision making along rational and organizational lines should lead serious theorists to infer the existence of inherent and actual disproportions of power between the President and his advisors. Unfortunately, the emphasis of the bureaucratic-politics authors is upon the conflict among members of the strategic elite within the court. They therefore give recognition and priority to position papers, options, stratagems (so well elaborated in the *Pentagon Papers*), and organizational-bureaucratic behavior; they do not even allude to the process by which the bureaucratic politicians—the court—gradually surrender to the monarch. And yet, the case studies of Cuba and Vietnam do not demonstrate the action or organization of an independent, autonomous, and authoritative political elite. On the contrary, they demonstrate the *subservience* of the court to the monarch—how bureaucratic politicians responded *after* the President had decided upon the priorities of the situation. The outcome (less so in the case of Cuba) demonstrates either that the bureaucratic politicians were as wrong as the President, or that in a foreign policy crunch only the President can act.

The study of bureaucratic politics is the study of the politics of conformity. The strategic elite maneuver exclusively against each other. They cannot challenge the President in office. They are his scribes; there is no alternative political center. Senate committees have been unsuccessful in their attempts to challenge the President; the universities and foundations are outside the presidential center and therefore powerless. The power of political authority in the United States is derived from the set institutional framework of the American political system. Only in the absence of the presidential political center (or when the President is weak), do strategic elites seem politically important and significant.

The study of bureaucratic politics ought to explain the degree of bureaucratic-political influence on the outcome of specific challenges. For example, could the court have helped persuade the President to postpone or cancel his decision concerning the first bombing of North Vietnam? Could the court, or its influential members, have persuaded the President to keep the Russians informed during the early stages of the Cuban missile escalation, thus possibly preventing the Cuban missile crisis? Can the court mobilize its collective effort to persuade a President, or is it so divided by cliques, groups, and opinions (i.e., is it so non-integrated) that it is a check on its own influence? How is influence distributed in the court—a very complex organization of differentiated statuses, roles and persons? When does this influence come into play—before, during, or after the President has made a decision on crucial issues?

The bureaucratic-politics school cannot provide answers to these questions, for its members have ignored the relationship between power and the political foundations of power. Power is inadequately defined in terms of organizational behavior, which subordinates political to bureaucratic-organizational explanations. Thus the "politics" of the court (not unlike the "politics" of the corporation) is used to explain the behavior and politics of American national security. The politics of national security is autonomous, and not connected with the inner politics of the court. Therefore the degree of the elites' political autonomy should be the central conceptual factor in differentiating bureaucratic politicians from elective politicians. Because the former (i.e., Mills' political directorate) possess no independent power, they are at the mercy of their monarch.

The extraordinary power accumulated by a non-elected expert such as Henry Kissinger (who, like other academic colleagues, was originally part of the Kennedy-Johnson court), cannot be explained by the bureaucratic-politics approach. In Kissinger's case, power does not stem from his role as a presidential court bureaucrat, nor from successful confrontations with lesser rivals. The source of Kissinger's present power is political. Direct negotiations with the leaders of the U.S.S.R. and China have established for him an autonomous credibility with the most prominent international figures. His friendly relations with members of Congress and with the press, and the esteem in which he is held by the American electorate, have established an independent constituency for him. These are raw sources of political power which have nothing to do with the restricted bureaucratic influence of the presidential court. Kissinger, however, is not totally invulnerable. Depending upon his own actions and choices, Kissinger is at all times potentially a member of the presidential court. Not unlike the others, he could therefore become dispensable.

Because the bureaucratic-politics school incorrectly identifies the "governmental process" with politics, its members offer no cogent analysis of the dynamics of security and diplomacy within the context of the American political system. There is no explanation, for instance, from Graham Allison as to *why* Kennedy opted for a blockade and not for invasion during the Cuban missile crisis, although there is a careful delineation of the President's management of the situation: the "governmental process." When Allison refers to the "behavior" of the government and the narrowly defined "unitary rational decision-maker"—centrally controlled, completely informed, and value-maximizing—what he is actually explaining is the political behavior of the bureaucratic politicians.[17] The politics of the latter is the politics of the court; the court is the instrument of the dominating monarch, whose politics in turn can be explained only within the context of the American political and constitutional systems. "For those who stress history as bureaucratic process, all questions of historical responsibility can appear ambiguous and even irrelevant. Foreign policy emerges as the result of a competition for fiefs within governmental empires. Bureau-

cratic emphases can produce a neo-Rankean acquiescence in the use of power that is no less deterministic than the revisionist tendency to make all policies exploitative in a liberal capitalist order."[18] What distinguishes the bureaucratic-political analysts from the power-elitist group is that the latter allege that foreign policy is dominated by a super-conglomerate imbued with Machiavellian or Hobbesian immorality, while the former convey a Kafkaesque caricature of the so-called "political directorate."

Both, however, exaggerate the role of the "political directorate." The bureaucratic-politics analysts have failed to identify the locus and the dynamics of real political power in foreign and security affairs. They have confused action on the part of the strategic elites with politics, and processes of integration in the presidential court with influence over foreign policy. Political wisdom (or non-wisdom), political power, and political influence (or lack of it) cannot be explained in terms of a theory of action in a complex organization—in this case, the presidential court. The vicissitudes of action—i.e., bureaucratic short circuits, loss of direction, routine, lack of imagination, plain ambition, and so forth—explain only the dynamics of action of the few, in specific organizational and bureaucratic contexts. A theory of bureaucratic action explains the nature of the staff and its behavior: it does not explain the direction and purpose of the political system.

The Presidential political center and foreign policy

Fundamental to modern politics is the fact that the politics of national security and foreign diplomacy are central to society. Historically, foreign and security politics have been main priorities of the political center, conducted primarily on that level. Political theorists from Aristotle to Hobbes have identified the *raison d'être* of political centers as the direction of security affairs. In recent times (since 1945 in the United States), these political centers have gained predominance because administrative staffs in the Weberian sense—persons, structures, institutions, and machines—which handle functions of security and diplomacy are exclusively administered by the presidential political center.[19] In the absence of well-integrated political elites, a highly centralized political party or parties, and a powerful and permanent bureaucracy and civil service (especially administrative staff at the highest level), this presidential political center has become pivotal, with almost exclusive control over foreign affairs and national security—a function not shared equally by any other source of authority in U.S. society. In fact, both classical and modern political and social theorists define a ruling organization as political insofar as it is charged with the safeguarding of the territorial area.

Through most of the history of the United States, there has been no geographical center of values, beliefs, and symbols. Although Washington is not the country's economic, social, or intellectual center, the geographic and political focus of government—the executive, the legislative, and the judiciary—is located there. The governmental system in Washington is not the only source of authority (political power being diffuse), but it is the highest and final system of authority. In this sense, the federal bureaucracy becomes the agent of the political center. Its authority being derivative, it is also revocable. In other words, precisely because there has been no single center of values and symbols, the federal system has developed into the central authority system. Parsons maintains that American society is characterized by the "nonpolitical stress in American social structure." He argues convincingly that, for historical reasons, the American political system (i.e., the government) lagged behind that of the economy. According to Parsons, this is a function of "the economic emphasis inherent in our system of values, and the relative lack of urgency of certain political problems because of our especially protected and favored national position."[20]

Every four years the presidential political center (in particular the Departments of State and of Defense), is "occupied" by a newly elected President and his bureau-cratic, appointed entourage—his court—composed of experts, counselors, advisors, and cronies. This process, after all, is the constitutional prerogative (as well as political practice) of the office of the Presidency. Drawing upon major reservoirs of values, symbols, and beliefs, the presidential center recruits its members from a variety of elites throughout the country.

The presidential political center, therefore, is dominated by elective party politicians, bureaucrats (civil service, military, scientists), and intellectuals. Neither the American political parties nor the governmental bureaucracy, however, are in a position to dominate the central functions (i.e., foreign policy and national security affairs) of the presidential political center exclusively.

The presidential political center has been and remains dominated by a small group most often referred to by derogatory titles such as "the elite," "the establishment," "the power elite," "the political directorate," "the rulers," "the power structure," "the military-industrial complex," and "bureaucratic politicians." Of course, each title has a different connotation. "The power elite" refers only to the "military-industrial complex"; "the bureaucratic politicians" bear little relationship to Mosca's "rulers"; the "power structure" implies a broad coalition of social, economic, intellectual, and political power; and "the political directorate" signifies a coalition of the "real" rulers (i.e., the corporate, political, and military-industrial elites). Nonetheless, in general, use of the term "the power elite," be it by Mosca, Pareto, Michels, or C. Wright Mills, refers to the elite that dominates the presidential political center. Precisely because in recent times the focus of the presidential political center has been on foreign policy, "power elites" in general have erroneously become identified with foreign policy and national security.

Talcott Parsons shrewdly observed that "American society has not developed a well-integrated political-governmental elite, in the sense that it has developed a relatively well-integrated business-executive group."[21] This picture has now been completely reversed. The federal system has finally become the "political center," primarily due to *economic* and external challenges. The great depression called for a revolution of priorities and of values. This meant government expansion and intervention. The wild growth of corporate industrial powers also called for the development of what Parsons called the political system, by which he meant the federal government.[22] The American involvement in the second World War and the cold war promoted the growth of the federal system in size, level of influence, and scope to an extent American society had never known before. Before 1914 one could still distinguish the political center from the federal government. After 1945 the two converged, in the minds of many, into a single monolith. Between 1933 and 1941 the federal system—the government—wrested more and more influence away from the diffuse economic centers. After 1941, national security and foreign affairs became the major indicators of the federal government's growing scope of political influence (if not actual size). The defense budget is now unquestionably the highest spending item of the federal government and a considerable portion of the GNP. The defense budget and military spending have become dominant items on the agenda of the political center, thus reinforcing the presidential political center.

The dynamics of the presidential political center

My analysis of the dynamics of the presidential political center will examine: (1) the constitutional, institutional arrangements of the political center in its foreign affairs and national security functions; (2) the type of elites attracted and recruited to the presidential center; and (3) the structure of their internal contradictions.

There is little doubt that the Constitution (as interpreted since Lincoln's Presidency) arrogated to the federal executive as commander-in-chief an awesome political power: defense of territory, the maintenance of peace, and, above all, command of the armed forces. "Despite their strong fear of standing armies, the authors of *The Federalist* tried to convince their readers of the necessity for such an army."[23] The Federalists delegated to the chief executive the central political power: the security system of the United States. The necessity for political domination of standing (i.e., professional) armies was one of the strongest reasons behind Federalist support of the Union, "for they maintained that peace among the several states depended upon *having a central government which alone had the authority to maintain a professional army.* Indeed, without this provision a federal state would dissolve into component elements, each finding it necessary to support a standing army. A continuous condition of military rivalry would make it impossible to sustain republican governments."[24]

Since 1941 this power has reached staggering proportions. Because of the concentration of political power at the center, especially in the office of the Chief Executive, and because of the nature of modern warfare and diplomacy, the office of the President has become the single dominant power in national security and foreign affairs. Some argue that executive-legislative coalitions and the so-called bipartisan foreign policy enhanced the political power of the President in foreign affairs. It may well have buttressed the political center's consensus over foreign policy. In my view, however, the power of the President over foreign affairs was intensified by (a) the constitutional interpretation of his *inherent* power, and (b) the predominance of foreign policy. The President's towering power over the Senate in foreign affairs—constitutional, institutional, and behavioral—is not a simple matter of elite domination and bureaucratic politics. Constitutionally and institutionally, Congress is both the President's chief partner and his rival in the central functions of the political center, but Congress has not met the challenge inherent in this relationship.

Had the above powers simply been "given" to the President with the stipulation that they be used with "the advice and consent of the Senate," the diffusion of power still would keep the Senate from exercising a controlling power in the realm of foreign affairs. Again, this is due primarily to the absence of power in the hands of political parties at the center. The Senate has been and is an important element of the political center—a fact often overlooked by analysts who refer to it in terms that imply it is outside the center of government. It has indeed been less influential than the President in deliberations of foreign affairs, not so much because of the separation of powers within the federal system, but because of the development of the American political system wherein the Senate had only derivative constitutional powers—advice and consent—rather than the inherent power that is in the hands of the President.

The Senate's political impotence has institutional as well as constitutional origins. Despite the fact that its members are elective officers—many are brilliant politicans—the Senate's political elite suffers in a behavioral sense from its lack of integration. Precisely because it lacks cohesion, particularly in confrontation situations with the President, the Senate cannot take advantage of the diffuse political center. Moreover, the Senate's attempts to challenge the President's court by recruiting its own bureaucratic strategic elite to staff key Senate committees dealing with security and diplomacy (Armed Services and Appropriations) have been dismal failures. The President, on the other hand, can take full advantage of his "inherent" constitutional and institutional powers, which give his office supremacy in the realm of security and diplomacy. Because the President exercises almost complete freedom in the choice of his advisors and appointees, his court is a potential base for a well-integrated elite. Despite the lack of challenge from elective officers, the effectiveness of the Presidential court depends upon what James Meisel refers to as the three C's—cohesion, continuity, and conspiracy ("common will to action").[25]

The dynamics of national security and foreign affairs must be explained not only in terms of executive-legislative competition

and rivalry, or in terms of rivalries within the well-integrated strategic elite of the President's office, but in terms of (a) the President's handling of the security-diplomacy consensus; (b) the President's manipulation of the strategic elites; and (c) the still untested congressional restraints on the President's powers as Commander-in-Chief. (The Cambodian Resolution may be an extraordinary exception of congressional restraints.)

Thus, the Senate's constitutional lack of powers equal to those of the executive, and the Supreme Court's interpretation of the President's role as Commander-in-Chief have considerably reduced the power of the Congress over foreign affairs. Further, the absence of a cohesive national political party has restricted the power of the Senate and left its most prominent members isolated. The Senate's key structures for domination over national security and foreign affairs, the Committees on Foreign Relations, Armed Services, and Appropriations are also diffuse. The chairmen of these committees are not only elected politicians, but independent, powerful Senators with different backgrounds and orientations, who often checkmate one another. The power they possess is equal. The same applies to the members of the committees in which power is diffuse, autonomous, and equal.

By contrast, the President—as chief administrator—is the singular and authoritative officer. Elected by all Americans, the President is Commander-in-Chief, in charge of all national security and foreign affairs. His partners in fulfilling these functions are not elective equals, but bureaucratic subordinates who are in no position to seriously challenge their supreme commander. The office of the President may be likened to those of the Monarchs, Emperors, and Caliphs of the historical bureaucratic empires.[26] Unlike the rulers of the historical centralized empires, however, the President is not a patrician or a usurper, but a democratically elected official. As the master of his house, he is rarely challenged by the other members of the political center. (Very seldom does the Senate fail to confirm a cabinet member or an ambassador. Nor can it challenge his appointments of private advisors.) In a Weberian sense, the office of the President is a ruling organization where members are subjected to rational domination by virtue of the established and legitimate rational political order.[27] And, like the rulers of the historical centralized bureaucratic states, he has almost unlimited autonomy in security and diplomacy functions. Since 1941 he has been free to develop autonomous political and national security goals.

A. The presidential court

The elite recruited for the presidential court can be described as a non-elective, private set of bureaucrats, advisors, counsellors, public relations men, scribes, intellectuals, and cronies. (Functionally, this group resembles the court of the historical centralized empires.) Despite their differences in social status, educational background, and achievement, these dignitaries, ex-politicians, learned men, super-managers, technicians, and Nobel Prize-winning scientists are all equal in being subject to the whims of the President. As members of the court, they live under the shadow of his total power.[28]

To summarize, the President's court has emerged in the absence of a cohesive political center, a central political party, and a centralized and continuous bureaucracy. Another element has been the perpetuation of the bureaucratic malpractices of modern complex organizations in the State and Defense Departments; Henry Kissinger has characterized these departments as rigid and non-innovative bodies, where the "machine becomes a more absorbing occupation than defining its purpose," and where "studying the problem can turn into an escape from coming to grips with it."[29] The President's court has thus been organized to bypass the professional military and diplomatic corps and the systems of merit and tenure. In addition, it serves to shield the President from Congress and the press.

What are the characteristics of the court? The President's recruiting policy depends greatly upon his personal style, experience, and *Weltanschauung*. During Eisenhower's administration there was a preponderance of conservative businessmen, bond lawyers, military officers, and small-town bankers. Kennedy's court was composed of technicians, foreign policy and national security professionals, scribes, intellectuals, belle-lettrists, and non-conservative military professionals. The Johnson court was full of Texans and what Eric Goldman has called "pragmatic liberals." Nixon's court, with the exception of Kissinger and Schlesinger, and formerly Shultz and Moynihan, was packed with public relations and advertising executives and assorted lawyers, generals, and politicians.[30]

The most significant aspect of the President's recruitment strategy is the fact that the criteria by which the elite is chosen have to do with what conservative and liberal Presidents alike take to be the most advanced representatives of the values, symbols, and beliefs of American society. The members of the court are not chosen— as power theorists would have us believe— because of their class or status, their power in American society, or their institutional proximity to power (i.e., the military-industrial and multiversity complexes). The court is selected in the knowledge that the President will dominate and manipulate it and use it to create a consensus for his decisions. The members are his creatures, whose course of action he dictates. Their reputations and credibility are at his mercy.

The above further buttresses my theory concerning the political center in the United States: constitutionally, it is divided. The disparate, pluralistic centers of values, symbols, and beliefs are the reservoirs from which it recruits its elite. Drawing upon the same reservoirs, the presidential political center itself becomes a temporary focus of symbols, values, and beliefs. *But it is only in the realm of national security and foreign affairs that the court represents an American consensus—a spectrum of the opinions and ideas of the United States* (minus the extreme poles of radical left and right). Again, this can only be explained behaviorally within the context of the American political system.

The President's function is to represent the progressive ideas of the nation. (These need not include the most up-to-date ideas and practices, nor the extreme poles or those filled with moral indignation.) Take, for instance, the intellectual-educational foreign policy elite and the armchair strategists: a list of members of the Executive Committee of the Harvard Center for International Affairs is testimony to the court's being recruited from the "center of the intellectual universe."[31] The same holds for recruitment from the business, industrial, and technocratic universes. Class, status, social and educational background of the courts' strategic elite may be relevant factors, but they fail to distinguish one administration's recruitment policy from another's. Nor do they underline a specificity of recruitment among carefully selected elites.

The elite may emanate from widely differing places. Nonetheless, it should represent society's centers of values, symbols, and beliefs. Although some Presidents (as was mentioned earlier) are not really interested in recruiting persons who are most representative of contemporary American values, the latter still gain entrance to the court.

B. The structure of consensus and the court

A valid argument can be made that there are considerable differences of ideological orientation, emphasis of values, and manipulation of symbols between one court and another or within a single court. In fact, since 1965 we have witnessed a marked change in ideologies and placement of values, and a shift in priorities between and within the political center. To those who are morally indignant, or those who believe in a total revolution, this may well seem irrelevant. To those, however, who believe in reform and incremental but cumulative change, it is most relevant. Thus, when we speak of consensus we speak of several factors.

First, consensus is the broadest and most generalized acceptance of specific but universal orientations, beliefs, practices,

and procedures. Consensus is a basis for actions and a pillar for successful policy-making. Consensus is not a program or policy; it is a collective perception and identification of friends and foes, and of issues. In foreign affairs, consensus is also an aspect of community support for regimes and authorities.[32] It is, however, an analytical and non-empirical concept. For this reason, there is no adequate definition of consensus or even an acceptable procedure for its measurement. We do know that consensus is a property of the political community that is articulated (if not invented) on the whole by elites outside the political center. This consensus becomes the support of any policy executed by the President and his court.

When we speak of consensus as policy, however, we refer to those who identify consensus with a specific political orientation or action. At that point, it ceases to be a property of voters and consumers, and becomes a property of authority. When the foreign-affairs elites speak of consensus, there is little doubt that they refer to the seldom-challenged property of the elites of the presidential political center. In this respect, consensus is a most influential variable, dominating the integration of the court's elite. Consensus is the security and diplomatic ideology (Pareto's derivative) of the presidential court. The elites outside the presidential political center who are not oriented toward the ideology of the consensus will not join the court. They become the counter-elites, conspiring against the center and aspiring to enter the court on their own condition: that their dissent should become the court's new consensus. In Mannheim's sense, the ideology of the elite becomes the utopia of the counter-elite. Consensus, therefore, is not only a criterion for elite recruitment, but an instrument by which the elite is politically integrated once it has reached the presidential political center. The function of the court, then, is to inculate the consensus into the political community. The maintenance of consensus and its support is crucial to the presidential function in national-security policy.

The court's elite becomes the guardian of the consensus-perpetuated ideas of "cold war," "peaceful coexistence," "polycentrism," "the balance of terror," or "detente." Broad and diffuse, consensus becomes the structure of a system of support for policies as diverse as lifting the Berlin blockade, helping the Greek regime in 1947, supporting anti-Communists praetorian "progressives" in Asia and Africa, maintaining the balance of terror, and so on. The cold war had the assent of the relevant community—the foreign policy elite. Paradigmatically in Thomas Kuhn's sense, the cold war was the "normal science" of the 1950's (when theory and fact were in close agreement and were affirmative).[3]

Revolution, according to Kuhn, has nothing to do with nature; it is a state of mind. Consensus, then, in his sense, is a response to a crisis, to an anomaly. A change in perception or in vision is tantamount to a new paradigm, a new consensus. It follows, then, that the character of the new paradigm—that the cold war only exists in the minds of the power elite at the center, and that the new consensus is not a change in the state of nature but in man's mind—also denies the basis for the old consensus. Yet the function of the court is to insist on "normal science," the accepted paradigm, and to refine, extend, and articulate it. One should not expect authority to perceive and act against its accepted cognitions. In the absence of serious antagonists in the realm of security and diplomacy elsewhere in the political center, the presidential court will continue to function in this manner.

Any attempt to analyze American foreign policy or to identify who really dominates it must begin with an analysis of the locus and degree of power within the American political-behavioral and constitutional context.

NOTES

1. See analysis in T. B. Bottomore, *Elites and Society* (New York 1964), 31–41; Geraint Parry, *Political Elites* (London 1969), 27–29.

2. *Ibid.*, 20–27.

3. On the writings and critique of the power elite, see Parry's analysis (fn. I); also Dankwart Rustow, "The Study of Elites: Who's Who, When, and How," *World Politics*, XVIII (July 1966), 690--717.

4. C. Wright Mills, *The Power Elite* (Oxford 1956). Mills was promptly challenged by a very specific group of social and political theorists, the pluralists. These were mainly professional political scientists and sociologists (inaccurately known as the "end-of-ideology" school). The pluralists, in turn, were challenged by the morality contingent, including professionals (political scientists and sociologists), but also by linguists, belle-lettrists, and journalists indignant about the slow process of social justice and an allegedly immoral war. Mills' disciples moved to restate the power-elite theory and applied it to the analyses of security and diplomacy.

5. *Ibid.*, 3–7.

6. See Parry (fn. 1), 30–63.

7. Suzanne Keller, *Beyond the Ruling Class* (New York 1957), distinguishes between a ruling elite (the elective or political elite) and the strategic elite primarily concerned with administration and technocracy—the elite of merit.

8. Although the field of bureaucratic politics is as old as the seminal studies of Weber and Michels, the political science profession in the United States has its origins with students of public administration and government—Woodrow Wilson, Frank Goodnow, and Bernard Moses, to mention only a few. The new school of bureaucratic politics in political science mainly focuses on the politics and management of foreign affairs. Among the early political scientists and writers were Richard E. Neustadt (*Presidential Power: The Politics of Leadership*, New York 1950) and Samuel P. Huntington (*The Common Defense*, New York 1961). The field of arms control is dominated by political scientists influenced by modern theories of organization and economic management, such as Thomas Schelling, *Arms and Influence* (New Haven 1966).

9. Gabriel Kolko *The Politics of War* (New York 1968); Noam Chomsky, *American Power and the New Mandarins* (New York 1960).

10. Richard J. Barnet, *Roots of War* (New York 1972); I. F. Stone, *The Hidden History of the Korean War* (New York 1952).

11. Rustow (fn. 3), 703; emphasis added.

12. William A. Williams, *The Roots of the Modern American Empire* (New York 1969).

13. Charles S. Maier, "Revisionism and the Interpretation of Cold War Origins," *Perspectives in American History*, IV (1970), 339.

14. See Alfred Diamant, "The Bureaucratic Model: Max Weber Rejected, Rediscovered, Reformed," *Comparative Public Administration* (1959), 59–96.

15. The group includes the professional political scientists Graham Allison and Morton Halperin, who are considered to be the "high priests" of bureaucratic politics. Leslie Gelb should also be

mentioned. Interestingly, the moralists I. F. Stone and Richard Barnet have made considerable use of the concept of bureaucratic politics. See Allsion *The Essence of Decision* (Boston 1971); Allison and Halperin, "Bureaucratic Politics," *World Politics*, XXIV (Supplement 1972); Halperin, *Bureaucratic Politics and Foreign Policy* (Brookings, April 1972); and Barnet (fn. 10). In fact, John Newhouse, in *Cold Dawn* (New York 1973), identifies bureaucratic politics with the different schools' positions and doctrines on arms control. (Halperin's and Gelb's writings certainly have been influenced by the politics of arms control.)

16. I shall here deal only with key conceptual assumptions.

17. Allison (fn. 15), 63.

18. Maier (fn. 13), 344.

19. See Max Weber, *Economy and Society*, ed. C. Wittich and G. Roth (Bedminster 1968), I, 212–15.

20. Talcott Parsons, *Structure and Process of Modern Societies* (New York 1960) 216, 213.

21. *Ibid.*, 216.

22. Parsons' is a narrow definition of the political system, i.e., "government," which certainly does not include the American political system.

23. I am in debt here to David Rapoport's perceptive analysis of the Federalists on executive power in its civil military context, "Praetorianism: Government without Consensus," unpub. Ph.D. diss. (University of California, Berkeley 1958), 174.

24. *Ibid.*, 175; emphasis added.

25. See James Meisel, *The Myth of the Ruling Class* (Ann Arbor 1965); also Parry (fn.)

26. See S. N. Eisenstadt, *The Political Systems of Empires* (New York 1963).

27. Weber (fn. 19), I, 212–54.

28. See George Reedy, *The Twilight of the Presidency* (New York 1970); Harry McPherson, *A Political Education* (Boston 1972); Eric Goldman, *The Tragedy of Lyndon Johnson* (New York 1969).

29. Kissinger, "Domestic Structure and Foreign Policy," *Daedalus*, vc (April 1966), 344. See also Kissinger, *The Necessity for Choice* (New York 1969), 340–58.

30. See Barnet (fn. 10) for an adequate but opinionated review of the types of court recruitees. Here *The Power Elite* could be cited as a major source of inspiration.

31. Robert Bowie was a high official in the Eisenhower administration. Samuel Huntington was a Humphrey advisor (1968). Both were members of the Policy Planning Staff of the State Department. Henry Kissinger was President Nixon's National Security Advisor and Secretary of State, and was an advisor to Presidents Kennedy and Johnson. Edward S. Mason was a close advisor to Secretary McNamara. Thomas C. Schelling was also an advisor to Secretary McNamara.

32. On the conceptual and analytical aspects of support, see David Easton, *A Systems Analysis of Political Life* (New York 1965), 170–89. While I do not accept the conceptual usefulness of this functional analysis, I know of no other author who has posed the problem analytically.

33. Thomas S. Kuhn, "The Structure of Scientific Revolution," *International Encyclopedia of Unified Science*, 2nd ed., II, No. 2 (Chicago 1970).

Liberal

George E. Reedy. The American monarchy.

A president cannot have problems which are personal to him alone. His troubles are the troubles of the nation and if they become disastrous, the nation is in peril. It is vital, consequently, to identify those aspects of his position which are most likely to bring him to grief. And the most important, and least examined, problem of the presidency is that of maintaining contact with reality. Unless a president starts giving thought to this question—and on the available evidence, very few do—immediately following the fine flush of his election victory celebration, he is headed inevitably for trouble.

There are very few warnings to the president-elect that this problem will be encountered. No one has placed over the White House door the admonition *"facile decensus Averni."* No one comes rushing to him with somber warnings and Dutch-uncle talk. The state of euphoria induced by political success is upon him at the very moment that caution, introspection, and humility are most needed. The process of erosion by which reality gradually fades begins the moment someone says, "Congratulations, Mr. President."

There is built into the presidency a series of devices that tend to remove the occupant of the Oval Room from all of the forces which require most men to rub up against the hard facts of life on a daily basis. The life of the White House is the life of a court. It is a structure designed for one purpose and one purpose only—to serve the material needs and the desires of a single man. It is felt that this man is grappling with problems of such tremendous consequence that every effort must be made to relieve him of the irritations that vex the average citizen. His mind, it is held, must be absolutely free of petty annoyances so that he can concentrate his faculties upon the "great issues" of the day.

To achieve this end, every conceivable facility is made available, from the very latest and most luxurious jet aircraft to a masseur constantly in attendance to soothe raw presidential nerves. Even more important, however, he is treated with all of the reverence due a monarch. No one interrupts presidential contemplation for anything less than a major catastrophe somewhere on the globe. No one speaks to him unless spoken to first. No one ever invites him to "go soak your head" when his demands become petulant and unreasonable.

In theory, privilege is accorded to, and accepted by, a man in accordance with his responsibilities. It is a supposed compensation for heavier burdens than those carried by lesser mortals. In practice, privilege is a status that feeds upon itself—with every new perquisite automatically becoming a normal condition of life. Any president upon entering office is startled—and a little abashed—at the privileges that are available to him. But it is only a matter of months until they become part of an environment which he necessarily regards as his just and due entitlement—not because of the office but because of his mere existence.

It is doubtful whether even Harry S. Truman—the most democractic of contemporary presidents—wore the same size hat when he left the White House as he did the day he entered.

This status was built into the American government by the Constitution itself. The founding fathers had rejected the concept of the divine right of monarchy. But when they sat down to write a constitution that would assure freedom, they were incapable of thinking of government in any terms other than monarchy. Someone, they reasoned, must reign and rule. Someone must give orders that could not be questioned. Someone must have ultimate and final authority. Therefore, their conclusion, although not stated in these terms, was a solution which placed in office a monarch but limited the scope of the monarch's activities.

In the context of the late eighteenth century, the solution was an excellent one. First, the founding fathers analyzed the functions of the government and divided them into three basic categories—the determination of policy, the execution of policy, and the adjudication of disputes arising out of the determination and the execution. The determination of policy was granted to Congress and the adjudication of disputes to the judiciary. The execution of policy they lodged in the hands of the president and within that area they gave him, for all practical purposes, total authority, not so much by affirmation but by failing to set many boundaries on what he could do. They felt that by dividing functions they had created competing power centers within the government and that the competition would prevent any one center from assuming a complete monopoly of power. As an additional safeguard, they limited the term of the president to four years (with an option for renewal if mutually agreeable between the president and the electorate) and gave Congress the authority to remove the president from office, although only on the basis of cumbersome machinery.

The accent was on stability and the firebrands of the Revolution—Tom Paine, Patrick Henry, James Otis—were given short shrift, the traditional fate of revolutionaries when men meet to put the pieces together after the crockery has been smashed. But the founding fathers were neither reactionary nor timorous. They provided—whether consciously, intuitively, or by sheer luck—ample room for the constitutional institutions to react in new ways to new circumstances, as long as the institutions themselves did not change in any fundamental respect. Generally, this objective was achieved by indirection.

The president, for example, was forbidden to legislate or adjudicate, but there was remarkably little definition of his executive powers. As a result, the size of the president in office at any given time determined the extent of what he regarded as his mandate. It was inevitable that strong men such as Jackson, Lincoln, and the two Roosevelts would interpret the absence of specific prohibitions as the presence of specific authority and act accordingly. Harry S. Truman even invoked the doctrine of "inherent" presidential powers to seize the nation's steel mills despite the lack of any legislative authorization—an effort that did not succeed because his popular following at the time was far short of his own supply of willpower.

Of equal importance was the failure to provide a method of determining whether acts of Congress transgressed the permissible boundaries of the Constitution. It was inevitable that such questions would arise and would be regarded differently by men whose function was to represent the popular will and men whose function was to administer a theoretically impersonal body of law. Had the doctrine of judicial review of legislative acts not been established by John Marshall, it is virtually certain that one of his successors would have done so. This particular gap was so huge that it had to be plugged somehow. But it is only a matter of time until a body which has succeeded in acquiring the power to forbid (which is essentially the power of the Supreme Court over Congress and the executive) also takes over the power to direct. This is the process that has made the judiciary a major agency for social change in the past two decades.

The framers of the Constitution had no way of foreseeing the effects of their most important decision—to give the presidency the functions of both chief of state and chief of government. It is doubtful whether they were aware at the time that the functions could exist separately. They knew that there had to be someone who spoke for all the

government. They also knew that there had to be someone to manage the affairs of the country. The concept that these functions could be separated was alien to their experience, even though the origins of separation were already apparent in the relationship between the king of England and the English prime minister.

They lived in a universe dominated by the concept of ownership and in which management independent of ownership was unknown. The parallel to government seemed obvious in their minds. Furthermore, they were confronted with an immediate and apparent problem which far overshadowed what could then only be abstract ideas of the distinction between reigning and ruling. They had a nation which was being pulled apart by the centrifugal forces of state pride. Their task was to devise some method by which thirteen quite independent political units could be merged into a collective whole. Their problem was to find some counterweight that would balance forces of disunity and induce Americans to think of themselves as citizens of the United States rather than as citizens of Connecticut, New York, Virginia, or Georgia.

The most practical method of unifying people is to give them a symbol with which all can identify. If the symbol is human, its efficacy is enhanced enormously. The obvious symbol was the president—the man who held the role of commander-in-chief of the armed forces; the man to whom all could pay respects as the first citizen. In short, the founding fathers established the presidency as a position of reverence and, as they were truly wise and sophisticated men, their efforts were as effective as human wisdom could make them.

The consequences of this decision were ultimately inescapable although not immediately discernible. In the simple society of the eighteenth-century United States, it was not easy to conceive of the Federal government in terms of grandeur. An Abigail Adams could hang her washing in the East Room; a Dolly Madison could act as a porter, running to safety with important works of art in advance of British occupation; an Andrew Jackson could invite all his frontier friends into the White House for a rollicking party where they could trample the official furniture with muddy boots and pass out dead drunk on the plush carpets of the Oval Room. But even in a nation as close to the realities of the frontier as the United States, a position established to inspire awe and reverence would inevitably pick up the trappings of reverence. And the trappings could not fail to have an effect upon the man whom they served as a buffer against the rest of the world.

Among the fundamental characteristics of monarchy is untouchability. Contact with the king is forbidden except to an extremely few people or as a rare privilege to be exercised on great occasions. The king's body is sanctified and not subject to violation by lesser mortals unless he himself so wishes. He is not to be jostled in crowds; he is not to be clapped on the back; he is not to be placed in danger of life or limb or even put to the annoyance of petty physical discomfort. Nor can he be compelled to account for his actions upon demand.

By the twentieth century, the presidency had taken on all the regalia of monarchy except robes, a scepter, and a crown. The president was not to be jostled by a crowd— unless he elected to subject himself to do so during those moments when he shed his role as chief of state and mounted the hustings as a candidate for reelection. The ritual of shaking hands with the president took on more and more the coloration of the medieval "king's touch" as a specific scrofula. The president was not to be called to account by any other body (after the doctrine of executive privilege was established). In time, another kingly habit began to appear and presidents referred to themselves more and more as "we"—the ultimate hallmark of imperial majesty.

These are the conditions under which a president-elect enters office in the modern era. In fact, the aura of majesty begins to envelop him the moment it becomes apparent that the electorate has decided upon its next president. Trusted assistants who have been calling him by his first name for many years switch immediately to the deferential "Mr. President." The Secret Service agents who have been protecting him during the campaign are suddenly joined by their chiefs who, up to that point, have stayed away from him and the other candidates in order to emphasize their neutrality. Members of the Army Signal Corps almost silently appear with communications equipment such as he has never seen before. All these developments take place as he bathes in the universal congratulations that always come to the successful candidate, even from his bitterest opponents. The agents that corrupt the democratic soul creep into his life in the guise of enthusiastic supporters, tactful policemen, self-effacing telephone linemen, and well-trained house servants. Even the members of the press, for a few months at least, regard him with some awe. The apotheosis has begun.

During the early days of a president's incumbency, the atmosphere of reverence which surrounds him acquires validity in his own eyes because of the ease with which he can get results. Congress is eager to approve his nominees and pass his bills. Business is anxious to provide him with "friends" and assistants. Labor is ready to oblige him with a climate of industrial peace. Foreign ambassadors scurry to locate suitable approaches.

It is a wonderful and heady feeling to be a president—at least for the first few months.

The environment of deference, approaching sycophancy, helps to foster another insidious factor. It is a belief that the president and a few of his most trusted advisers are possessed of a special knowledge which must be closely held within a small group lest the plans and the designs of the United States be anticipated and frustrated by enemies. It is a knowledge which is thought to be endangered in geometrical proportion to the number of other men to whom it is passed. Therefore, the most vital national projects can be worked out only within a select coterie, or there will be a "leak" which will disadvantage the country's security.

Obviously, there *is* information which a nation must keep to itself if it is to survive in the present world climate. This means that the number of minds which can be brought to bear on any given problem is often in inverse proportion to the importance of the problem.

The steps that led to the bombing of North Vietnam were all discussed by a small group of men. They were intelligent men—men of keen perception and finely honed judgment. It is doubtful whether any higher degree of intelligence could have been brought to bear on the problem. But no matter how fine the intelligence or how thoroughgoing the information available, the fact remained that none of these men was put to the test of defending his position in public debate. And it is amazing what even the best of minds will discover when forced to answer critical questions. Unfortunately, in this as in many other instances, the need to comment publicly came after, and not before, irreversible committment.

Of course, within these councils there was always at least one "devil's advocate." But an official dissenter always starts with half his battle lost. It is assumed that he is bringing up arguments solely because arguing is his official role. It is well understood that he is not going to press this points harshly or stridently. Therefore, his objections and cautions are discounted before they are delivered. They are actually welcomed because they prove for the record that decision was preceded by controversy.

As a general rule, the quality of judgment usually varies directly with the number of minds that are brought to bear upon an issue. No man is so wise as to play his own "devil's advocate," and workable wisdom is the distillation of many different viewpoints which have clashed heatedly and directly in an exchange of opinion. To maintain the necessary balance between assurances of security and assurances that enough factors have been taken into consideration is perhaps the most pressing problem of statecraft. The atmosphere of the White House, in which the president is treated constantly as an infallible and reverential object, is not the best in which to resolve this problem.

In retrospect, it seems little short of amazing that President Kennedy would ever have embarked upon the ill-fated Bay of Pigs venture. It was poorly conceived, poorly planned, poorly executed, and undertaken with grossly inadequate knowledge. But anyone who has ever sat in on a White House council can easily deduce what happened without knowing any facts other than those which appeared in the public press. White House councils are not debating matches in which ideas emerge from the heated exchanges of participants. The council centers around the president himself, to whom everyone addresses his observations.

The first strong observations to attract the favor of the president become subconsciously the thoughts of everyone in the room. The focus of attention shifts from a testing of all concepts to a groping for means of overcoming the difficulties. A thesis which could not survive an undergraduate seminar in a liberal-arts college becomes accepted doctrine, and the only question is not *whether* it should be done but *how* it should be done. A forceful public airing of the Bay of Pigs plan would have endangered the whole project, of course. But it might have prevented disaster.

On a different level can be cited the far less serious setback suffered by President Lyndon B. Johnson when he attempted to merge the Commerce and the Labor departments into one agency. Out of a desire for a "surprise" headline, this proposal was held in the utmost secrecy between the president and his speech writers until a few moments before his State of the Union message was scheduled for delivery. Quick calls were made to the secretaries of labor and commerce, who were pressed for a quick response and who reacted as any government official reacts to such a call from the White House. They said, "Yes."

In a matter of days, it was apparent that the project had as much chance of getting off the ground as a kiwi. To organized labor, still headed by men with long memories, the Labor Department was a sacrosanct institution for which they had fought and bled in their youth. They had no intention of acquiescing to the removal from the cabinet of what they regarded as "our spokesman."

Business, while far less emotional, made it quite clear that industrialists did not relish the prospect of "our agency" being merged with what they regarded as the opposition. The president quietly buried the whole idea.

The truly baffling question, however, is how a man with the political sensitivity of Lyndon B. Johnson would ever embark on such a futile enterprise. The basis of his success as the Senate Democratic leader had been his insistence upon touching every base before launching a project. He was famous throughout the political community for "taking the temperature" of every affected group in advance and laying careful plans to meet any objections they might have before the objections were even raised. And yet here was an instance where even a perfunctory conversation with a few of his friends would have made clear that humiliation was the only conceivable outcome of his proposal.

The only conclusion that an observer can draw is that the atmosphere of the White House—the combination of sycophancy and a belief in the efficacy of closely held knowledge—had done its work. The man regarded as the outstanding politician of the mid-twentieth century had stepped into a buzzsaw which could have been foreseen by a wardheeler in any major city of America.

A reader of history will find innumerable and startling examples of political bloopers committed by men with a record of political sagacity. How is one to explain President Truman's inept handling of the Communist spy scare of the late 1940s—a mistake which opened up the era of Joe McCarthy? How is one to explain Franklin D. Roosevelt's futile effort to "pack" the Supreme Court? How is one to explain Woodrow Wilson's clumsy treatment of the Senate, which led directly to its refusal to permit United States participation in the League of Nations? None of these men had shown themselves politically inept on such a grand scale at any previous moment of their lives. It is only an inference but an inescapable one that the White House is an institution which dulls the sensitivity of political men and ultimately reduces them to bungling amateurs in their basic craft—the art of politics.

The real question every president must ask himself is what he can do to resist the temptations of a process compounded of idolatry and lofty patriotic respect for a national symbol. By all the standards of past performance, he should be well equipped to face it. As a general rule, he has fought his way up through the political ranks. He has flattered and been flattered—and the mere fact that he has survived to the threshold of the White House should indicate a psychological capacity to keep flattery in perspective. He has dealt with rich people, poor people, wise men, fools, patriots, knaves, scoundrels, and wardheelers. Had he not maintained his perspective on human beings generally, it is doubtful that he would ever have received his party's nomination.

But the atmosphere of the White House is a heady one. It is designed to bring to its occupant privileges that are commensurate in scope with the responsibilities that he must bear. A privilege is, by definition, a boon not accorded to other people. And to the extent that a man exercises his privileges, he removes himself from the company of lesser breeds who must stand in line and wait their turn on a share-and-share alike basis for the comforts of life. To a president, all other humans are "lesser breeds."

Furthermore, a president would have to be a dull clod indeed to regard himself without a feeling of awe. The atmosphere of the White House is calculated to instill in any man a sense of destiny. He literally walks in the footsteps of hallowed figures—of Jefferson, of Jackson, of Lincoln. The almost sanctified relics of a distant, semimythical past surround him as ordinary household objects to be used by his family. From the moment he enters the halls he is made aware that he has become enshrined in a pantheon of semidivine mortals who have shaken the world, and that he has taken from their hands the heritage of American dreams and aspirations.

Unfortunately for him, divinity is a better basis for inspiration than it is for government. The world can be shaken from Mount Olympus but the gods were notoriously inefficient when it came to directing the affairs of mankind. The Greeks were wise about such matters. In their remarkable body of lore, human tragedy usually originated with divine intervention and their invocations to the deities were usually prayers of propitiation—by all that is holy, leave us alone!

A semidivinity is also a personification of a people, and presidents cannot escape the process. The trouble with personification is that it depends upon abstraction and, in the course of the exercise, individual living people somehow get lost. The president becomes the nation and when he is insulted, the nation is insulted; when he has a dream, the nation has a dream; when he has an antagonist, the nation has an antagonist.

The purpose of this book is to examine the effects of this environment upon the president of the United States. This has become a matter of great urgency. It is increasingly evident that the tasks of the presidency are more and more demanding. It is also increasingly evident that presidents spend more of their time swimming in boiling political waters. There is even a respectable body of thought which holds that the problems are out of control and that, in the present context, the nation must look forward to a series of one-term persidents, incapable of holding the office for more than four years.

As a general rule, efforts to remedy the deficiencies of the presidency center on proposals to bring a greater administrative efficiency to the White House itself. It is held that the problems would become manageable if the president had better tools at his command. In my mind there is a strong suspicion that the problems are no more unmanageable today than they have been in the past. They are, of course, bigger in terms of consequence. But they are still decision rather than management problems. Perhaps a more fruitful path lies in an exploration of the extent to which the atmosphere of the White House degrades a man's political instincts and abilities. Our

thoughts should be centered not on electronic brains but on the forces that would foster the oldest, the noblest, and the most vital of all human arts—the art of politics.

Socialist

Gabriel Kolko. The men of power.

To comprehend the nature and function of power in America is to uncover a critical analytic tool for assessing the character of the American historical experience and the role of the United States in the modern world. The failure of most of an entire generation of American intellectuals and scholars to make the phenomenon of power a central concern has permitted a fog of obscuritanism and irrelevance to descend upon the study of American life in the twentieth century.

Stated simply, the question is: What are the political and economic dimensions of power in American society, how does power function, and who benefits from it? The correlations of these structural aspects of power are either curious or critical, incidental, and perhaps colorful, or of decisive importance. The structure of power may be described empirically, but power may also reflect a more elusive configuration of social attitudes and forces that makes it possible for one class to prevail in American history—or it may involve aspects of both the tangible and the intangible.

For the most part, the handful of students of American power have concentrated on the investigation of the social status and origins of men of power, an exercise that has meaning only if one can show distinctive political behavior on the part of men of power with lower social status. Indeed, one must assess the psychology of decision-makers, the genesis of their power, and the source of their conduct in the context of the structure and function of American power at home and in the world, a critical evaluation that permits one to determine whether a "military-industrial complex," a unique bureaucratic mentality, or something more substantial is the root of American policy nationally and internationally. It forces us to determine whether, for example, the presence of a Harriman-family lawyer in one key post is, in itself, crucial to understanding the goals and motives of his behavior and American policies, or whether powerful men freely use one decision-making mechanism or another in a situation in which the results are largely the same because more fundamental interests and goals define the range of action and objectives of all decision-makers. The permanence and continuity in American national and international policy for the better part of this century, scaled to the existence and possibilities of growing national strength, suggests that the study of power in America must also define the nature and function of American interests at the same time.

If, in the last analysis, the structure of power can only be understood in the context in which it functions and the goals American power seeks to attain, the fact that the magnitude of such a vast description requires a full history of twentieth century America should not deter social analysts from highlighting the larger contours of the growth of modern American bureaucracies, if only to make the crucial point that these bureaucratic structures are less the source of power than the means by which others direct power in America for predetermined purposes. That society is one in which bureaucrats do not represent their own tangible interests, save if they wear other and more important hats, but those of what one must tentatively call that of the "power system," and when their own aspirations become dysfunctional leaders remove them on behalf of more pliable men. For behind the bureaucrats exist levels of economic and political power, whether latent or exercised, the objectives and maintenance of which no one can abandon without far-reaching, indeed revolutionary, alterations in policy and the very nature of American society itself. It is this ultimate power that defines the limits of bureaucratic conduct and the functions of the state.

Politicians create bureaucracies for specific purposes, and that these structures develop their own administrative codes and techniques, or complex mystifying rationales, is less consequential than their objective and functions. Congress created such bureaucratic power in the United States first during the era 1887–1917 as a result of class-oriented elements seeking to rationalize via political systems the unpredictable elements of economic life in a modern technology. To study *how* rather than *why* political power operates in a class society, a formalism that Max Weber contributed to conservative descriptive social analysis, is to avoid the central issue of the class nature and function of the modern state. After the turn of the century the political parties cultivated bureaucracy purely as an instrumentality serving and reflecting class interests—bureaucracy with no independent power base and nowhere to find one within the American power structure. Given the decisive role of the businessmen in the creation of modern American bureaucracy and the "positive state," it should be neither surprising nor impractical that they staff the higher levels of the bureaucratic mechanisms of American power with men from business.

Policy, in brief, preceded bureaucratic rationalism, with Congress serving as a lobby for, and objective of, various business interests. Given the consensual nature of social and political priorities in America, and the essentially repressive manner in which the authorities handle nonconformity to consensus when it becomes a potential threat, political power in American society is an aspect of economic power—economic power often sharply in conflict by region or size or interest, but always operative within certain larger assumptions about the purposes of victory for one side or the other. Often this disunity among competing economic interests is so great as to mean mutual neutralization and ineffectuality, and frequently the divergent factions couch their goals in rhetorical terms—"anti-monopoly" being the most overworked—which has made "liberal" phraseology the useful ideology of corporate capitalism.

This diversity and conflict within the ranks of business and politicians, usually described as a pluralist manifestation, has attracted more attention than it deserves and leads to amoebic descriptions of the phenomenon of interbusiness rivalry in a manner that obscures the much more significant dimensions of common functions and objectives. The critical question for the study of what passes as conflict in American society must be: What are the major positions, and who wins and why? The motives of the losers in the game of politics, or of those who created pressures others redirected for their own ends, is less critical than the actual distribution of power in society. It is in this context of the nature of power and its function that the scholar should study bureaucracies, with less concern for social mobility than the concept of purpose and goals the bureaucracy serves. Only in this manner can we understand the interest and actions that are functional and irrevocable as part of the logic of American power and not the result of mishap, personalities, or chance. If powerful economic groups are geographically diffuse and often in competition for particular favors from the state, superficially appearing as interest groups rather than as a unified class, what is critical is not who wins or loses but what kind of socioeconomic framework they *all* wish to compete within, and the relationship between themselves and the rest of society in a manner that defines their vital function as a class. It is this class that controls the major policy options and the manner in which the state applies its power. That they disagree on the options is less consequential than that they circumscribe the political universe.[1]

Despite the increasingly technical character of modern political and economic policy, and the need to draw on individuals with appropriate backgrounds for the administration of policy—especially businessmen—it is the structural limits and basic economic objectives of policy that define the thrust of American power nationally and internationally. The source of leadership is important, and has been since the turn of the century, but it may not be decisive. What is ultimately of greatest significance is that whether leadership comes from Exeter-Harvard or Kansas, the results have been the same, and an outcome of the nature of power in America and the role of the United States in the world.

The limits of consensus

American politics in the twentieth century has been a process of change and shifting rewards within predictable boundaries and commitments that are ultimately conservative and controlled as to the limited social and economic consequences it may achieve. No decisive or shattering social and economic goals have cracked the basic structure and distribution of power in all its forms, and if some have used democratic and liberal rhetoric to explain motion within these boundaries it is less consequential than the functional material contours of the system itself. Indeed, it is the illusion of the possibility of significant change—of true freedom in society—that helps make possible its practical suppression via liberal politics and gradualism which, as historical fact, never exceed predetermined orbits and assumptions.

One must never infer that such illusions are the sole source of conservative order—as witnessed by the response of those with power during rare periods when genuine opposition shatters the mythologies. For though freedom is a posture decision-makers tolerate among the politically impotent, those in power act to make certain that all others remain ineffectual. When their own policies are subject to severe trials, or appear to be failing, they cannot afford the luxury of organized opposition and functional freedoms which can shatter their hegemony over the normal, usually passive social apathy. The history of civil liberties in the United States is testimony to the fact that when freedom moves from rhetoric to social challenge it is suppressed insofar as is necessary. Functional freedom is the ability to relate to power or forces with the potential for achieving authority, that is, the decision-making establishment or those who seek to transform or replace it. So long as intellectuals or the people exercise this right "responsibly," which is to say to endorse and serve the consensus their rulers define, abstract freedoms flourish in public pronouncements and slogans because they lead nowhere. Hence the dissenter has the freedom to become a victim in the social process and history, and a battery of sedition, espionage, criminal anarchy, or labor laws exist in readiness for the appropriate moment of social tension and the breakdown in the social and ideological consensus which exists during periods of peace and stability. The celebrants of American freedom rarely confront the concepts of order that underlie the large body of law for suppression that always exists in reserve.

A theory of consensus is indispensable for comprehending the nature of decision-making and power in American society, but a social analyst must always consider that theory from the viewpoint of its role when some socially critical and potentially dynamic groups and classes cease to endorse or sanction the consensus, because then consensus is based on discipline and becomes, for practical purposes, authoritarian on matters of measurable power. For only challenges to a political and social system and crises reveal its true character—when established power threatens to break down and formal democracy is nearly transformed into functional, true freedom.

The essential, primary fact of the American social system is that it is a capitalist society based on a grossly inequitable distribution of wealth and income that has not been altered in any essential manner in this century. Even if there has not been *decisive* class conflict within that structure, but merely conflict limited to smaller issues that were not crucial to the existing order, one can accurately describe American society as a static class structure serving class ends. A sufficiently monolithic consensus might voluntarily exist on the fundamental questions indispensable to the continuation of the existing political and economic elites, and the masses might respect or tolerate the primary interest of a

ruling class in the last analysis. The prevailing conception of interest, the critical values of the society, did not have to be essentially classless, as Louis Hartz and recent theorists of consensus have argued, but merely accepted by those segments of society without an objective stake in the constituted order. This dominant class, above all else, determines the nature and objectives of power in America. And for this reason no one can regard business as just another interest group in American life, but as the keystone of power which defines the essential preconditions and functions of the larger American social order, with its security and continuity as an institution being the political order's central goal in the post-Civil War historical experience.

On the national level, reform and legislation have led to class ends and the satisfaction of class needs, and that the purposes of decision-makers in 1968 should be any different than in 1888 makes sense only if one can posit and prove a drastic alteration in the distribution of economic power.

One may base such an analysis on a functional view of American reform, on the consequences of legislation rather than the motives of all reformers, motives that are ultimately paramount among those who are to be regulated and who have power. Social theory, muckrakers, and intellectuals did not and do not influence important businessmen, who have never aspired to have reforming crusaders regulate and direct their affairs. Businessmen have always preferred that their own lawyers and direct representatives play that role in matters of the most intimate relevance to their economic fortunes, though not necessarily in lesser affairs, and it is a fact that the government has ultimately drawn most critical political decision-makers from, or into, the higher reaches of economic life. In this setting, we should see American reform primarily as a question of technical and efficiency engineering—of social rationalization—to advance the welfare and interests of specific business interests first and society generally, but always within critical ideological boundaries and assumptions. With only occasional differences on tangential points, political authorities have shared, or conformed to, the practical applications of this conservative consolidation usually called "progressivism" or "liberalism."

Yet the critical question arises as to why, in such an economic context of inequality, poverty, and many years of unemployment, there has never been a class opposition to constituted politics and power. In brief, quite apart from the efficacy of the alternatives, why has no anti-capitalist mass movement emerged, as in Western Europe, to create that essential political option which is the indispensable precondition for true pluralism and freedom in America? For the United States is a class society, with measurable oppression, but also without decisive class conflict as of this time. It is also a society serving class ends with the consensual support or apathetic toleration of the dispossessed classes. This consensus, which serves the interest of a single class rather than all of society, exists in an altogether different situation than what theorists of consensus have described, but the social and historic outcome is the same.

The phenomenon of consensus and its causes are simply too complex to describe in light of existing evidence. But it is necessary to pose certain critical questions in order to comprehend whether consent alone is important in explaining the nature and durability of American power and the decision-making structure. What happens when the consensus is shattered and ceases to receive traditional adherence or toleration? Does the fact that all of society may at times share an ideology legitimate it? Or is it more consequential that the economically critical and powerful class endorses the ideology that serves it best—a fact that makes the ideology operate during those rare periods when consensus breaks down? And can core commitments of the public be evaluated by any measurable techniques that permit valid social generalization?

If the history of Left politics in the United States is cooption for some, it is also repression for many others: grandfather clauses, poll taxes, and other means for applying the stick when the carrot was insufficient or deemed inappropriate. The history of the militant labor movement, black struggles, southern populism, socialism, and even the current anti-war and civil rights movements all bear testimony to the fact that when politics and social movements do not legitimize the existing order consensus becomes mandatory conformity and suppression. Authority and power exist quite beyond general social sanctions and rest on specific interest and the ability to impose restraints, and the ruling class has never permitted decision-makers in the governmental apparatus who do not advance and conform to the interests of the state—for psychological reasons or whatever—to introduce dysfunctional elements or policies into governmental affairs. This enforced consensus from above and social cohesion due to the relatively rare exercise of ever latent authority and repression has been the truly revealing aspect of the nature and purpose of American power and capitalist interests. Yet whether voluntaristic or otherwise, these shared values make the origins of decision-makers, or the identity of their special governmental agencies, less consequential than the binding and permanent commitments of ruling groups and their social and economic system.

For this reason, mass consent in a society based on a relatively small elite predominance is less significant, and the operative causal agents in society are the interest and goals of men of power—and their will and ability to retain their mastery—rather than masses who also endorse those objectives. It is the commitments of those able to implement their beliefs and goals, rather than of the powerless, that creates racism in the employment practices of corporations; and it is elite authoritarianism, which remains constant in the historical process, rather than working class biases—which vary with circumstances and interest and often disappear functionally—that leads to authoritarian institutions.

Yet even if the social and power weight of specific opinion and class interests, as opposed to its existence among all sectors of society, is primary, it is still vital to comprehend the elusive character of what is now called "public opinion" or "consensus." What is more significant than opinion is the ultimate implications of apathy and ignorance of elite sanctioned policies, a condition that reveals the limits of the integrative possibilities of elite-controlled "mass culture" from above. For the most part, in matters of foreign affairs, workers are no more or less belligerent or pacifistic than executives and professionals—when they are forced to register an opinion. The theory of public attitudes as the fount of the decision-making process reinforces a democratic theory of legitimacy, which, for reasons of sentimental tradition at home and ideological warfare abroad, is a useful social myth. But the close and serious student of modern American foreign relations will rarely, if ever, find an instance of an important decision made with any reference to the alleged general public desires or opinions. What is more significant is the fact of ignorance and lack of interest among the vast majority of the population during a period of crisis as to the nature of essential issues and facts, a condition that neutralizes their role in the decision-making process even more and cultivates an elitist contempt for the inchoate role of "the people" as nothing more than the instrument or objective, rather than the source, of policy.[2] The persistent fluctuations in such mass attitudes alone assure that for practical guidance the decision-makers must refer to their own tangible and constant values and priorities. Yet what no one has ever shown is the extent to which this mass apathy reflects the manipulative and moronizing impact of modern communications, or a superior intelligence based on the individual's awareness that he has no power or influence after all, and that he has a very different identity and interest in the social process than the managers and rulers of society.

The versatile rulers

If the manipulated values and consensual ideology coincide with the objective and material interests of the decision-makers, the fact is important but not necessarily the sole causal factor of their conduct, for even where personal interests do not exist the policies are the same. The function of bureaucracy is to serve constituted power, not itself. While it often can be relevant that an individual in government is directly connected with a business interest, even one in a field deeply concerned with the topic over which he has jurisdiction, we can determine the ultimate significance of this connection only if more disinterested men adopt different policies. Historically, by and large, they have not. In our own era the reasons for this continuity in policy and action are critical, and they reveal the institutional and interest basis of American power in the world, a power that transcends factions and men.

American diplomacy has traditionally been the prerogative of the rich and well placed. Even if they had a lifetime career in government, the intrinsic nature of the structure until 1924 required professional diplomats to be men of independent means, and that tradition persisted until today in various forms. In 1924 the Diplomatic Corps, which paid salaries so low that only the sons of the well-to-do and rich could advance very far in it, was merged with the Consular Corps into the Foreign Service to establish a merit system. In 1924, 63 percent of the diplomatic officers were Harvard-Princeton-Yale graduates, as opposed to 27 percent of the ambassadors for the years 1948, 1958, and 1963. Of the 1,032 key federal executive appointees between March 4, 1933, and April 30, 1965, 19 percent had attended these three elite schools, ranging from 16 percent under Roosevelt to 25 percent during the Johnson Administration. Somewhat lower on the scale of rank, in 1959 the three universities produced 14 percent of all Foreign Service executives, while nearly two-thirds of those in the Service were the sons of business executives and owners or professionals. At the level of all civilian federal executives above GS-18 ranking, or the very highest group, 58 percent were the sons of this upper income and status occupational category.[3]

Sociologists such as C. Wright Mills, and often journalists as well, have made too much of these social origins, for while interesting and important there is no proof such connections are decisive. Twenty-six percent of the highest federal executives come from working class and farmer origins, and an increasingly larger percentage from the non-Ivy League schools, and there is no evidence whatsoever to prove that social and educational origins determine policies of state. That elite origins and connections accelerated personal advancement is now sufficiently self-evident not to warrant excessive attention, much less to make these standards the key criterion for explaining the sources and purposes of American power. In brief, the basic objectives, function, and exercise of American power, and not simply its formal structure and identity, are paramount in defining its final social role and significance. Without denigrating the important contribution of Mills, which was brilliant but inconsistent, such an approach fails to come to grips with the dynamics of American power in its historical setting.

A class structure and predatory rule can exist within the context of high social mobility and democratic criteria for rulership, perhaps all the better so because it co-opts the elites and experts of the potential opposition and totally integrates talent into the existing society. The major value in essentially static structural studies of key decision-makers is to illustrate the larger power context in which administrators made decisions, but not to root the nature of those decisions in the backgrounds or individual personalities of an elite. In brief, correlation may not be causation in the power structure, and should high status, rich men ever seek to make decisions dysfunctional to the more permanent interest of dominant power interests, even more powerful leaders would immediately purge them from decision-making roles. The point is that while such men are unlikely to make socially dysfunctional decisions so is anyone else who rises to the top of a structure with predetermined rules and functions. To measure power that is latent as well as active, it is often easier to study the decision-makers themselves. The other approach, and by far the more difficult, is to define objective and impersonal interests and roles for the larger classes and sectors of American society, their relationship to each other and to the world, and the manner in which they have exercised their relative power.

The analyst must utilize both approaches, and should consider everything useful, including the investigation of status, celebrities, core elites, military elites—the important and trivial, as Mills discovered—and he should discount the trivial and establish the correlations in the hope of revealing causes. If Mills made it clear that there were levels of power among those who shared it, and an inner power core that transcended local society and celebrities, he slighted the economic basis of American politics and exaggerated the causal and independent importance of the military.[4] To him, the social and educational origins of the elite were too critical, thereby excluding the possibility of a power elite "democratized" within its own ranks or selection process but still in the traditional dominant relationship to the remainder of society. Offhand, I assume that in this process it is worth striking a final balance and integration and rejecting certain factors. Social origins and education, and the possibility of the existence of an Establishment based on common heritage and interests, are of lesser concern than the currently operative ties of decision-makers, for the father's words or the impressions of old school days wear off, and the responsibilities of men are measurable in the present rather than in the past.

A more select group reveals far more than a collection as large as W. Lloyd Warner's 12,929 federal executives, and on this assumption I investigated the career cycles and origins of the key American foreign policy decision-makers from 1944 through 1960, excluding the Presidents. My major premise was that even if I could show that such men neither began nor ended in business, there were still many other and more valid ways of gauging the nature of foreign policy. We examined the State, Defense or War, Treasury and Commerce Departments, plus certain relevant executive level agencies indicated in the "Note on Methods" on page 140, and considered only those with the highest ranks.[5] The study included 234 individuals with all their positions in government during 1944–60, comprising the lesser posts if an individual attained the highest executive level. As a total, these key leaders held 678 posts and nearly all of them were high level and policy-making in nature.

The net result of this study, however imperfect, revealed that foreign policy decision-makers are in reality a highly mobile sector of the American corporate structure, a group of men who frequently assume and define high level policy tasks in government, rather than routinely administer it, and then return to business. Their firms and connections are large enough to afford them the time to straighten out or formulate government policy while maintaining their vital ties with giant corporate law, banking, or industry. The conclusion is that a small number of men fill the large majority of key foreign policy posts. Their many diverse posts make this group a kind of committee government entrusted to handle numerous and varied national security and international functions at the policy level. Even if not initially connected with the corporate sector, career government officials relate in some tangible manner with the private worlds predominantly of big law, big finance, and big business.

Of the 234 officials examined, 35.8 percent, or eighty-four individuals, held 63.4 percent of the posts (Table I). Thirty men from law, banking, and investment firms accounted for 22 percent of all the posts which we studied, and another fifty-seven from this background held an additional 14.1 percent—or a total of 36.1 percent of the key posts. Certain key firms predominated among this group: members of Sullivan & Cromwell, or Carter, Ledyard & Milburn, and Coudert Brothers, in that order among law firms, held twenty-nine posts, with other giant corporate-oriented law firms accounting for most of the remainder. Dillon, Read & Co., with four men, and the Detroit Bank, with only Joseph M. Dodge, accounted for eighteen and ten posts, respectively, and two men from Brown Brothers, Harriman held twelve posts—or forty posts for three firms. It was in the nature of their diverse functions as lawyers and financiers for many corporate industrial and investment firms, as Mills correctly perceived, that these men preeminently represented the less parochial interests of all giant corporations, and were best able to wear many hats and play numerous roles frequently and interchangeably as each corporate or government problem—or both—required. Nothing reveals this dual function more convincingly than their career cycles. Despite the fact that Sullivan & Cromwell and Dillon, Read men tended to go into the State Department, or lawyers from Cahill, Gordon, Zachry & Reindel to the Navy Department, general patterns of distribution by economic interests—save for bankers in the governmental banking structure—are not discernible. And with one possible exception, all the men from banking, investment, and law who held four or more posts were connected with the very largest and most powerful firms in these fields.

In the aggregate, men who came from big business, investment, and law held 59.6 percent of the posts, with only forty-five of them filling 32.4 percent of all posts[6] (Tables I and II). The very top foreign policy decision-makers were therefore intimately connected with dominant business circles and their law firms. And whether exercised or not, scarcely concealed levels of economic power exist beneath or behind the government, and indeed high mobility in various key posts reinforces such interlockings. This continuous reality has not altered with successive administrations, as the state has called upon Fair Dealers and modern Republicans alike to serve as experts in running a going operation which they are asked to administer efficiently within certain common definitions of its objectives. Whether Democrats, such as James Forrestal of Dillon, Read, or Republicans, such as John Foster Dulles of Sullivan & Cromwell, the continuous contact and advice they have received from their colleagues in the world of finance, law, and business have always colored their focus. The operative assumption of such men, as Forrestal once put it, is that "What I have been trying to preach down here is that in this whole world picture the Government alone can't do the job; it's got to work through business. . . . that means that we'll need to, for specific jobs, be able to tap cer-

Table 1 Occupational origin of individuals with four or more posts in government and those with less than four posts, 1944–60

Occupational origin	Individuals with four or more posts				Individuals with less than four posts			
	No. of indi-viduals	% of all indi-viduals	No. of posts held	% of all posts studied	No. of indi-viduals	% of all indi-viduals	No. of posts held	% of all posts studied
Law firms	12	5.1	55	8.1	33	14.1	72	10.6
Banking and investment firms	18	7.7	94	13.9	24	10.3	24	3.5
Industrial corporations	8	3.4	39	5.8	31	13.2	49	7.2
Public utilities and transportation companies	0	.0	0	.0	4	1.7	4	.6
Miscellaneous business and commercial firms	7	3.0	32	4.7	17	7.3	35	5.2
Nonprofit corporations, public service, universities, etc.	7	3.0	37	5.5	7	3.0	12	1.8
Career government officials—no subsequent nongovernment post	15	6.4	85	12.5		4.7	19	2.8
Career government officials—subsequent nongovernment post	8	3.4	38	5.6	12	5.1	13	1.9
Career government officials—subsequent nongovernment post and return to government post	8	3.4	45	6.6	6	2.6	15	2.2
Unidentified	1	.4	5	.7	5	2.1	5	.7
TOTALS	84	35.8	430	63.4	150	64.1	248	36.5

Table 2 Number of key positions in government, 1944–60, held by individuals designated by nongovernment career origin and by a government career origin

Nongovernment and career government category	No. of individuals	% of individuals	State Dept.	Defense Dept.	War Dept.	Treasury Dept.	Commerce Dept.	Navy Dept.	Army Dept.	Air Force Dept.	White House staff	International Bank for Reconstruction and Development	Export-Import Bank	E.C.A.—M.S.A.—I.C.A.	Budget Bureau	C.I.A.	Japan and German military governments	Miscellaneous government departments	No. of positions	% of positions
1 Key law firms	45	19.2	16	12	12	7	1	15	8	8	2	1		4	2	5	3	31	127	18.7
2 Banking and investment firms	42	17.9	19	7	3	8	7	8	4	1	4	7	4	8	3	1	4	30	118	17.4
3 Industrial corporations	39	16.7	9	5	1	2	12	1	4	9	3	1		9		1		31	88	13.0
4 Public utilities and transportation corporations	4	1.7						1		1			1		1				4	.6
5 Miscellaneous business and commercial corporations	24	10.3	8	5		3	1	8	2	2	5			12	6			15	67	9.9
TOTAL: 1-5	154	65.8	52	29	16	20	21	33	18	21	14	9	5	33	12	7	7	107	404	59.6
6 Nonprofit, public service, and universities	14	6.0	4		1	1	1		2	1	3			10	4	3	3	16	49	7.2
TOTAL: 1-6	168	71.8	56	29	17	21	22	33	20	22	17	9	5	43	16	10	10	123	453	66.8
7 Career officials—no subsequent nongovernment position	26	11.1	26	1	1	4	2	4	2	1	2	1	1	10	4	1	1	43	104	15.5
8 Career officials—subsequent nongovernment position	20	8.5	7	4	1	2	2	2	2	1	1	4	5	4	4	1	1	10	51	7.5
9 Career officials—subsequent nongovernment position and return to government	14	6.0	12	5	1	1	1	1	1		1	3	2	9	2		2	19	60	8.8
TOTAL: 7-9	60	25.6	45	10	3	7	5	7	5	2	4	8	8	23	10	2	4	72	215	31.8
UNIDENTIFIED	6	2.6	1			1						1	2	1	1	1	1	1	10	1.5
COMBINED TOTAL	234	99.9	102	39	20	29	27	40	25	24	21	18	15	67	27	13	15	196	678	100.1

tain people . . . ."[7] It is this process of "tapping" for high level policy tasks that has accounted for high mobility and the concentration of posts in few hands.

Perhaps of even greater interest is the special nature of the government career officials and their relationship to business during their extended professional lives. These sixty men, 25.6 percent of the total, held 31.7 percent of the posts considered, in part because, being full-timers, they were available for a greater number of tasks. But for many of these men government became a stepping stone toward business careers, and we can only speculate on how this possible aspiration influenced their functional policies on economic and other questions while they were in government. "The lure of industry was such that I couldn't pass it up," a former career officer and head of the C.I.A. for fourteen months, Admiral William F. Raborn, Jr., confessed in discussing why he had taken his government post in the first place. "I went there with the thought I could go when I wanted to."[8] Over half these men, perhaps enticed in the same manner, later took up nongovernmental posts, though a significant fraction returned to government for special tasks. Conversely, however, any government employee thwarting the interests of American businesses, as expressed in foreign and national security affairs, risks losing possible future posts, even if he goes to foundations or university administrations. Most of these new private positions were in law firms and industry. But certain of those key career officials who never left for business or new careers the State Department had selected under its pre-1924 or conventional rules, where independent wealth and social connections were always helpful. The fact that John M. Cabot, Assistant Secretary of State and a Boston Cabot, also held the largest number of posts among the twenty-six full-time career officials we examined is not inconsequential. It is within this career group that the conventional elite social background predominates.

For the most part, the technical and policy nature of foreign policy and military security issues has necessitated the selection of men with requisite business backgrounds. The choice of William L. Clayton, rags-to-riches head of the largest world cotton export firm, to deal with United States foreign economic policy between 1944–47 was rational and both a cause and reflection of policy.[9] What is most instructive was that Woodrow Wilson and Cordell Hull, President and Secretary of State (1933–44), a professor and small town politician, formulated the essential foreign economic policy, and it is here that we must see the larger ideological and consensual definition of foreign policy as ultimately transcending the decision-maker recruitment process.

Business as the fount

The organizational rungs of governmental power take many other businessmen into the lower hierarchies of administration in much the same manner as their seniors function at the very highest levels. These lower tiers of operation are too extensive to measure in their entirety here, but it is sufficient to point to several readily documented expressions. Such lines of contact are perfectly logical, given the objectives of American policy abroad, and given the fact that Washington generally assigns the management of the Government's relationship to various problems to the businessmen or their representatives with business connections or backgrounds in the various areas. And it is both convenient and more than logical that key federal executives recruit former associates for critical problem-solving posts for which they have responsibility. There is no conflict of interest because the welfare of government and business is, in the largest sense, identical.

This will mean that key law firm executives with major corporate connections will draw on former clients, whom they may again soon represent at the termination of their governmental service; it will simplify the task of the business representatives in Washington—about two-thirds of the top two hundred manufacturing firms maintain them on a full-time basis—who may wish assistance with marketing, legislative, or legal matters. The Government will invariably choose advisers to international raw materials and commodity meetings from the consuming industries, and will select key government executives concerned with specific issues—such as oil—from the interested industry. The existence of businessmen and their lawyers in government, in short, gives the lobbyists and those not in government something to do—successfully—insofar as it is to their interest. These men interact in different roles and at various times, for today's assistant secretary may be tomorrow's senior partner or corporate president. However much such men may have competing specific economic objectives, conflicts that may indeed at times neutralize their mutual goals, what is essentially common among such elites, whether or not they are cooperative, makes them a class with joint functions and assumptions and larger economic objectives that carry with it the power to rule. This is not to say such well placed officials with industry backgrounds are the only source of government policy, but that they exist and, more important, given the larger aims of government it is entirely rational to select personnel in this fashion. From this viewpoint the nature of the bureaucracy is essentially an outcome rather than a cause of policy.

Examples of interlocking government-business leadership are numerous even below the highest decision-making echelons. In the Department of the Interior, to cite one instance, the large majority of key personnel in the Office of Oil and Gas or the Petroleum Administration for Defense in the decade after 1946 came from the industry, often just on loan for fixed periods of time. These bodies, which are largely a continuation of wartime boards, have permitted the regulation of the petroleum industry via governmental agencies, free from the threat of antitrust prosecution and for the welfare of the industry. Pleased with the arrangement, the industry has supplied many of the key administrators and consultants the government needs on a no-compensation basis.[10]

No less typical is the Business and Defense Services Administration of the Department of Commerce (BDSA), created in the fall of 1953. Composed of 184 industry groups during the period 1953–55, the BDSA committees dealt with a vast number of goods and the problems of their industry, recommending action to the government that was the basis of profitable action and regulation of various economic sectors. These ranged from the division of government purchases among industry members to the review of proposed Export-Import Bank and World Bank loans for the construction of competing industries abroad. In effect, BDSA committees have served themselves via the government in a classic fashion, the precedents for which range back to the early nineteenth century.[11] In this regard they are no different in genesis and function from the federal regulatory movement initiated in 1887.

At every level of the administration of the American state, domestically and internationally, business serves as the fount of critical assumptions or goals and strategically placed personnel. But that this leadership in foreign and military affairs, as integrated in the unified hands of men who are both political and economic leaders, comes from the most powerful class interests is a reflection as well as the cause of the nature and objectives of American power at home and abroad. It is the expression of the universality of the ideology *and* the interests and material power of the physical resources of the ruling class of American capitalism, the latter being sufficient should consensus break down. The pervasiveness of this ideological power in American society and its measurable influence on mass culture, public values, and political opinions is the most visible reality of modern American life to the contemporary social analyst. It means that one can only assess the other institutional structures, the military in particular, in relation to the predominance of the economic ruling class which is the final arbiter and beneficiary of the existing structure of American society and politics at home and of United States power in the world.

NOTES

1. I have attempted to trace the origins of modern federal bureaucracy and power in my book, *The Triumph of Conservatism* (Chicago,

1967 [paperback ed.]); I have outlined the economic context of power in my *Wealth and Power in America* (New York, 1962).

2. Paul A. Smith, "Opinions, Publics, and World Affairs in the United States," *Western Political Quarterly*, XIV (September 1961), 698–714; Martin Kriesberg, "Dark Areas of Ignorance," in *Public Opinion and Foreign Relations*, Lester Markel, ed. (New York, 1949), 49–64; Gabriel A. Almond, *The American People and Foreign Policy* (New York, 1950), 85 ff.

3. Martin B. Hickman and Neil Hollander, "Undergraduate Origin as a Factor in Elite Recruitment and Mobility: The Foreign Service—A Case Study," *Western Political Quarterly*, XIX (June 1966), 337–42; W. Lloyd Warner *et al.*, *The American Federal Executive* (New Haven, 1963), 14–129, 163; David T. Stanley, Dean E. Mann, and Jameson W. Doig, *Men Who Govern: A Biographical Profile of Federal Political Executives* (Washington, 1967), 126.

4. C. Wright Mills, *The Power Elite* (New York, 1956), 28–29, 288–96, and *passim; United States News*, May 23, 1947, 20–21; "Who Really Runs the State Department. . . ," *U.S. News and World Report*, May 5, 1950, 32–33; Warner, *et al.*, *American Federal Executive*, 163; G. William Domhoff, *Who Rules America?* (Englewood Cliffs, N.J., 1967); Paul M. Sweezy, "Power Elite or Ruling Class?" in *C. Wright Mills and the Power Elite*, G. William Domhoff and Hoyt B. Ballard, eds. (Boston, 1968), 115–32, for the best critique of Mills.

5. Note on Methods. We examined four Cabinet-level Departments for the period 1944–60: the State, War and Defense, Treasury, and Commerce Departments, their Secretaries, Under and Assistant Secretaries, and Special Assistants to the Secretaries. We included this last-named post because these officials are traditionally the links between the Cabinet members and major problems. In addition, we examined positions designated "Deputy" or "Special" Secretary, Under or Assistant Secretary.

Also surveyed were the Army, Air Force, and Navy Departments, which have similar organizational structures. The other agencies, however, are organized along different lines, and it was possible only to estimate the equivalents of Cabinet posts. Only a random selection of the highest officers is included in the case of the White House staff, the military governments of Germany and Japan, and the E.C.A.-M.S.A.-I.C.A. foreign aid organizations, while the aid organizations incorporate a number of lower level officials. Moreover, the category of "Miscellaneous Government Departments" includes *all* the key individuals' Government posts—in the agencies indicated or others—that do not otherwise qualify for study. The net effect of this technique is to minimize slightly the percentage of posts individuals with law or business backgrounds held. In brief, these data are conservative estimates of the extent of private control of public office.

The data on career backgrounds and history may be found in various issues of *Moody's Industrials, Moody's Manual of Investments, Poor's Register of Directors and Executives, Who's Who, Who Was Who, Martindale-Hubble Legal Directory, Congressional Directory*, and the *New York Times*.

6. My preceding data were collected in 1966, and in September 1967 the Brookings Institution published *Men Who Govern*, by David T. Stanley, Dean E. Mann, and Jameson W. Doig. The Brookings volume is far superior to any hitherto published study and is unmarred by debilitating ideological biases masked as methodology. It covers 1,041 individuals who held 1,567 key executive appointments from March 1933 to April 1965. These included persons who attained posts—nearly one-third the total—too low to be included in my sample, another one-quarter were Kennedy-Johnson appointees, and somewhat less than this figure served prior to 1944. The authors included all Cabinet-level positions, while I included only four Cabinet agencies. My sample, therefore, covers a more select group of leaders over a shorter time span.

The authors of the Brookings study show that 39 percent of their 1,041 leaders received a private preparatory education, with 60 percent, 46 percent, and 44 percent for the State, Treasury, and Defense Departments, respectively. Nineteen percent attended Yale, Harvard, or Princeton. Twenty-four percent of *all* appointees were principally businessmen before appointment, this figure reaching 40 percent for the Cabinet Secretaries, 56 percent for Military Secretaries, and 42 percent for Under Secretaries. Twenty-six percent of all appointees were lawyers, though the Brookings study does not explore the size or nature of their firms. Sixty-three percent of all Cabinet Secretaries, 86 percent of the Military Secretaries, 66 percent of all Under Secretaries, and 50 percent of all Assistant Secretaries were either businessmen or lawyers prior to political appointment, generally corroborating my findings for a more selective sample.

Including ranks lower than those I considered, the Brookings study revealed that 16 percent of their State Department sample, 1933–65, were principally businessmen before their appointments, and this figure grew to 39 percent in Defense, 57 percent in Commerce, and 60 percent in the Navy Department. While businessmen and lawyers accounted for 60 percent of the Eisenhower appointees, the Johnson Administration had the lowest, at 40 percent. President Johnson also appointed more men with master's and doctoral degrees than any of his predecessors, which only tends to prove my contention that the origins of individuals are less responsible for the continuity of the policies of the nation than most critics have cared to admit.

Manufacturing provided 44 percent of the persons designated as businessmen, finance 23 percent, and other forms of capital the remainder. Defense contractors provided 12 percent of the executives considered in the defense-related agencies, reaching a peak of one-fifth under Kennedy. If one removes retirements, deaths, and other statistical imbalances, nearly half the State Department executives had subsequent business and private professional careers, mainly in law, this percentage reaching over three-quarters for most of the other agencies included in my sample.

7. Telephone conversation between James F. Forrestal and Reese H. Taylor, March 25, 1947, in James F. Forrestal Papers, Princeton University Library, box 73. See also Forrestal memo to Dean Acheson, May 17, 1947, Forrestal Papers, box 70, for an example of how this was done.

8. *New York Times,* June 26, 1966.

9. *Business Week*, April 14, 1945, 18–19.

10. U.S. House, Committee on the Judiciary, *Hearings, WOC's and Government Advisory Groups.* 84:1–2 (Washington, 1955–56), 1570 ff., 2267–2580. See Paul W. Cherington and Ralph L. Gillen, *The Business Representative in Washington* (Washington, 1962), *passim*; Robert Engler, *The Politics of Oil* (New York, 1961), 310--17.

11. U.S. House, Committee on the Judiciary, *Interim Report of the Anti-trust Subcommittee . . . on WOC's and Government Advisory Groups.* 84:2. April 24, 1956. (Washington, 1956), 8–16, 29, 56–62, 90, 143, 150, 161–62; Committee on the Judiciary, *WOC's and Government Advisory Groups,* 282–83, 521 ff., 1878–2146; for an excellent summary, see Michael D. Reagan, "The Business and Defense Services Administration, 1953–57," *Western Political Quarterly*, XIV (June 1961), 569–86.

3 The Pentagon

The basic questions this chapter will address are:

(1) Who is the military? Is it the army, navy, air force, and marines? Or does the military incorporate a larger complex of individuals and institutions including major industries and other branches of government?

(2) What is the role of the military in American life, and which interests does it represent?

(3) What role does the population have, if any, in influencing the formation of military strategy?

(4) What should the role of the military be in the republic of the United States?

These questions represent the major issues which the authors in this chapter argue from explicit and implicit conservative, liberal, and socialist principles.

Conservatives hold that the military consists of the bureaucrats of the Pentagon and the branches of the armed services. They believe that the existence of the United States fundamentally depends on the strength of our military, for the military is the only instrument that the United States has to call on when our national security is in danger. No other institution exists which can effectively defend the territory of the United States. Any criticism of the military is seen as wrong because it weakens American military might and thus threatens the existence of our nation. Conservatives think that most problems can be solved by force. For example, in Vietnam no real and honest attempt was ever made by the United States government to negotiate the differences that existed between the parties. Negotiations were used only as a delaying tactic until a further application of force could be initiated. The use of armed force was seen as the only effective way of solving the Vietnamese war.[1] In the domestic sphere, armed force is seen as the ultimate way of solving intractable social problems. When, in 1967, Detroit ghettos erupted into violence because the social and economic needs of the ghetto were not met, federal troops were sent in to control the situation. Conservatives were unwilling to meet the demands of the people who desired a better way of life, and thus force rather than arbitration had to be the answer.

Conservatives do not see the American public as important in setting military strategy because ordinary people are seen to be ignorant of military affairs. These are held to be highly complicated issues only to be dealt with by technical experts. The overall perspective of conservatives is that the military is the fundamental political institution upon which the very existence of our nation rests and it should be accorded due respect as the guarantor of our sovereignty.

According to liberals, the military consists of the Pentagon and the armed services. But, because of the enormous power the Pentagon wields in contracting for goods and services, it has the ability to misuse its authority. An example of this misuse is cost overruns in producing military equipment. Liberals believe that the Pentagon and armed ser- ✝

+ vices keep many military matters secret in order to increase their power. During Lyndon Johnson's presidential administration, Laos, in Southeast Asia, was bombed on orders of the President and the Pentagon without Congress and the American public being informed. It was believed that if Congress and the public were asked to support such a policy they might not do so. Consent, therefore was never requested for the bombing.[2]

Liberals believe that military abuses can be corrected if the people, through their Congressional representatives, demand the cessation of secrecy and military abuse of power. Liberals accept the basic structure of the military. They believe its efficiency could be increased and waste eliminated. Funds that are saved could be used to meet pressing domestic needs.

Socialists hold that the military is interconnected with the political and economic system that exists in the United States. According to this perspective the Pentagon acts on behalf of corporate elites to further their interest and power. Many military expenditures are utilized primarily for the interests of these elites. It has been argued by many socialist authorities that the United States sent marines into the Dominican Republic in 1965 to support a regime that would allow American corporate interests to operate and control the sugar industry of that country.[3]

Socialists further believe that liberal and conservative arguments for the necessity of a strong military to defend the territory of the United States are merely an excuse to further the power of elites and to legitimate the military in the eyes of the American people.

The essential argument of socialists regarding the military is that the military is a prop for an economic and political system controlled by a small elite. The idea that the United States is always threatened by attack is used by the military and its supporters to argue for the necessity of a strong defense establishment. Military provocations are engaged in so as to bring forth a response from the opposing side in order to justify that a real threat exists. Socialists say that a constant state of military tension between major nations is a means of calling forth support for the American status quo. Therefore this threat should be seen as contrived so that the existence of the armed forces as an institution is unnecessary to the well-being of the population. They believe in general disarmament and unilateral initiatives by individual countries to bring it about.

In the articles you will read in this chapter the military establishment is analyzed, and the above questions and following issues are dealt with.

Henry Kissinger, Secretary of State under Presidents Richard Nixon and Gerald Ford was, at the time he wrote the article "Force and Diplomacy in the Nuclear Age," Professor of Government at Harvard University. Kissinger argues that the United States must create respect for itself if it is to be potent in international affairs. To do this it must be militarily prepared to fight all wars at all times, whether they be traditional, insurgent, or nuclear. Our major adversary is the Soviet Union, and has been since the end of World War II. Although there may be respites in the tension between the USSR and the USA, a cold war—political, economic, psychological, sometimes military—continues as a contest over which nation will be the preeminent world power.

Kissinger's argument is twofold. The United States should build up a super arsenal of weapons, traditional and nuclear, and make it clear to the Soviet Union that it has a strategy in which these weapons will be used if circumstances warrant. Thus, preparedness and a constant development of new weapons systems is a major element of his strategy. This in turn will create inhibitions on the part of Soviet leaders. They will be unwilling to challenge or threaten the United States, and if they do so we will have the policy and weaponry which will force them to back down. The Cuban missile crisis of 1962, in which President Kennedy threatened eventually to use the full weight of American military weapons against the Soviet Union if they did not remove the missiles they had placed in Cuba was an example of the use of this policy.

A major part of Kissinger's strategy is that nuclear weapons are seen as part and parcel of American military strategy. They are not seen as weapons too terrible to use. In essence, the strategy is that the United States will progressively escalate, or threaten to escalate military force, and include the threat and use of nuclear weapons as one step on the scale of escalation. Through this policy the Soviet Union will see that we mean business in a confrontation between our two countries. They will know that they cannot depend on us not to use nuclear force. The element of doubt created in their minds as to the possibility that we will use nuclear weapons is an essential threat that the United States must retain and use in its dealing with other nations.

This is a rejection of the doctrine of massive retaliation put forth by President Dwight Eisenhower and his Secretary of State John Foster Dulles in the 1950s. This doctrine held that nuclear weapons were the primary element of our nuclear strategy and would be used to retaliate massively against any form of Russian aggression. Accordingly, we would destroy Russia over a minor incident provoked by the Soviets in any part of the world. This was seen as so terrible a prospect that the Soviet Union would back off. Kissinger however knew, and rightfully so, that we would not use nuclear weapons over a minor issue. He understood that the Russians also realized this and that our nuclear striking power would not deter them from aggressive behavior. Thus the need for an overall military strategy which incorporated all weapons to obtain the maximum effect of American power.

The assumption of Kissinger and conservative military policy in general is that the United States must have the greatest possible military strength. We must be able to defeat an opponent in war and, if possible, to forestall through threat of arms the use of military, political, and economic force by any adversary. The overall effect of this strategy is that all powers must see us as more ready to use force than they are. And to Kissinger this is true in particular of the Soviet Union which is the only other state that comes close to matching American weaponry.

Milton Mankoff and Linda Majka, in their article "Economic Sources of American Militarism," argue that a key reason for the heavy military expenditures of the last three decades has been to protect and expand United States overseas investments. They maintain that our overseas investments in the developed and developing nations are so extensive and so important to our own economy that political systems in these countries must be kept under our control. The ultimate assurance for this is the exercise of American military power. Thus, a massive military program is required for the maintenance of American political and economic power.

Mankoff and Majka link the military with United States foreign economic expansion; the profit motive is the key to our military buildup. Further, the United States pushes its military expansion so that new markets abroad are opened for capital investment. Some authorities state that the United States maintains its military presence in South Korea so as to support a government that allows American business to operate factories with low-cost labor, no strikes, and maximum repatriation of profits. Mankoff and Majka essentially maintain that corporate interests dictate our military policy. They do not challenge the basic structure of the United States military. But they do call for a public to arouse itself and press the Congress to restrain the Pentagon and the President from engaging in foreign military adventures.

Their overall analysis questions the ill effects of the application of military force; it wants restraints placed on the military. The article is muckraking in that it publicizes specific abuses of the military and calls upon the people to correct those abuses. Liberals seldom come to the conclusion that the very existence of the military, as it is now in American society, must be questioned and fundamentally altered to achieve their goals.

Seymour Melman, in "The State-Management," maintains that the Kissinger proposals for an aggressive military posture were implemented by President Kennedy and his Secretary of Defense Robert McNamara in the early 1960s. In order to multiply their military options Kennedy and McNamara increased America's force level.

In a matter of three years the defense budget grew to fifty-six billion dollars (an increase of some 40 percent) with fifteen billions being spent on nuclear weapons. The number of nuclear weapons available to the United States was increased by 100 percent. There was a 45 percent increase in the number of combat ready army divisions (with 400,000 men being stationed in Western Europe alone), an increase of 175 percent in our procurement of airlift aircraft, and an increase of some 500 percent in counter-insurgency forces. The number of Polaris submarines and Minuteman missiles was doubled, and the number of manned bombers standing ready on fifteen-minute alert increased by 50 percent. The num-

ber of ICBM's was more than tripled from a beginning point inherited from Eisenhower of 200, while the Nike-Zeus anti-missile missile program was initiated along with the Nike-X surface to air missile.[4]

Kennedy and McNamara created a military government in which they were able to control the activities of civilian producers of goods and services.

According to Melman the Pentagon is no longer merely a civilian-controlled military bureaucracy, but is in fact the largest business establishment in the United States. The Kissinger/Kennedy/McNamara program created a new industrial-manager class. Because of the huge amount of subcontracting engaged in by the Pentagon and the direct managerial controls instituted over these contractors they in effect became subsidiaries of the Pentagon. Much as Frigidaire and Chevrolet are subunits of the General Motors organization, McDonnell-Douglas and Grumman Aircraft are subsidiaries of the Pentagon. Rather than being units that deal independently with one another, they are part of one integrated bureaucratic system of control.[5]

In the past, proponents of the power elite thesis argued that there was a constant interchange between business, political, and military leaders. Melman argues that since 1961 there has been no need for interchange. They are now part of an integrated network. The political/military/industrial complex referred to in the past was in actuality a series of structures bound together by individuals moving from one structure to the other. The state-management thesis holds that these are no longer separate and related structures but are all part of one single unit.

Melman and other socialist analysts of the military argue that the Pentagon is now a part of the larger economic system of power which is used to extend itself. It is a motor in the engine of capitalism. Despite the fact that military programs are justified in the name of defense, their existence has become an integral part of the growth of American capitalism.

A socialist would maintain that the first step in altering the military structure is to understand the real purposes that it serves. The next step is refusal to serve in the armed forces, refusal to pay taxes to support it. A further step is to organize political groups to disrupt and dismantle the American military machine. The War Resisters League and the Vietnam Veterans Against the War are examples of such groups. The military in large measure depends on the people's believing that it is acting in their interests. Once it is recognized as acting against their interests and they refuse to participate in it and support it financially, the military will begin to collapse.

Although it may appear that antimilitary activity has little effect on such a powerful force military leaders have privately acknowledged the effects such activities, as antiwar newspapers, antiwar coffee houses, war resisters and deserters, have on maintaining control over soldiers. The fundamental basis of any armed forces is the unquestioning acceptance and following by soldiers of orders from their commanders. This is the weakest link in the military structure. Just imagine if on a certain day in 1967 all United States servicemen in Vietnam went on strike? This is not so outlandish a possiblity given the fact that often soldiers and entire units refused to participate in military actions in Vietnam.

The socialist ideal would be a world society in which military forces did not exist. Threats of force and wars would play no part in the interaction among peoples. Each society would conduct its own affairs without fearing the threat or exercise of force against it.

NOTES

1. See *The Pentagon Papers*. New York: Bantam Books, 1971.

2. Fred Branfman. "Presidential War in Laos, 1964–1970." In, *Laos: War and Revolution*, ed. by Nina S. Adams and Alfred W. McCoy. New York: Harper & Row, Pub., 1970.

3. For a detailed analysis of this issue see, James Petras, "Patterns of Intervention: U.S. Foreign Policy and Business in Latin America," in Marvin Surkin, Alan Wolfe, eds. *An End to Political Science: the Caucus Papers*. New York: Basic Books, 1970.

4. Peter Schwab, J. Lee Shneidman. *John F. Kennedy.* New York: Twayne Publishers, Inc., 1974. p. 106.

5. For a discussion of this issue and its relationship to the Persian Gulf see Michael T. Klare, "The Political Economy of Arms Sales: United States—Saudi Arabia," *Society* (Vol. 11, No. 6, Sept./Oct. 1974), pp. 41–49.

Conservative

Henry A. Kissinger. Force and diplomacy in the nuclear age.

In his whimsical essay "Perpetual Peace" written in 1795, the German philosopher Kant predicted that world peace could be attained in one of two ways: by a moral consensus which he identified with a republican form of government, or by a cycle of wars of ever-increasing violence which would reduce the major Powers to impotence.

There is no evidence that Kant's essay was taken seriously in his lifetime, or indeed for a century and a half afterwards. But much of current thought about the impact of the new weapons of today carries a premonition of Kant's second proposition. We respond to every Soviet advance in the nuclear field by what can best be described as a flight into technology, by devising ever more fearful weapons. The more powerful the weapons, however, the greater becomes the reluctance to use them. At a period of unparalleled military strength, the President has best summed up the dilemma posed by the new weapons technology in the phrase "there is no alternative to peace."

It is only natural, of course, that an age which has known two world wars and an uneasy armistice since should have as its central problem the attainment of peace. It is paradoxical, however, that so much hope should concentrate on man's most destructive capabilities. We are told that the growth of thermonuclear stockpiles has created a "nuclear stalemate" which makes war, if not too risky, at least unprofitable. The Geneva "summit" conference has been interpreted as a nonaggression treaty: a recognition by the U.S. and the U.S.S.R. that war is no longer a conceivable instrument of policy and that for this reason international disputes can be settled only by means of diplomacy. Mr. Stassen has maintained that the peaceful application of nuclear energy has made irrelevant many of the traditional reasons for wars of

aggression because each major Power can now bring about a tremendous increase in its productive capacity without annexing either foreign territory or foreign labor. And many of the critics of Mr. Dulles' interview in *Life* were concerned less with the wisdom of the specific threats than with the fact that a threat of war was made at all.

These assertions have passed almost without challenge. They fit in well with a national psychology which considers peace as the "normal" pattern of relations among states and which has few doubts that reasonable men can settle all differences by honest compromise. So much depends, however, on the correctness of such propositions that they must be subjected to close scrutiny. For the impact of the new weapons—as every revolution—has not only a technical but a conceptual side. Until power is used, it is, as Colonel Lincoln from West Point has wisely said, what people think it is. But except for the two explosions of now obsolete bombs over Hiroshima and Nagasaki, no nuclear weapons have ever been set off in wartime; there exists, therefore, no previous experience on which to draw. To a considerable extent the impact of the new weapons on strategy, on policy, indeed on survival, depends on our interpretation of their significance.

It therefore becomes of crucial importance that the United States not paralyze itself by developing a calculus of risks according to which all dangers would seem to be on our side. But this is precisely what has happened to us recently. The slogan "there is no alternative to peace" is the reverse side of the doctrine of "massive retaliation." And both deprive us of flexibility—"massive retaliation" because it poses risks for us out of proportion to the objectives to be achieved, and "there is no alternative to peace" because it relieves the Soviets of a large measure of the risk of aggressive moves. This is true despite Soviet reiteration of the horrors of a hydrogen war. For apart from the fact that these statements are usually addressed to foreigners and may therefore, be designed to increase the inhibitions of others, it makes all the difference which side has to initiate thermonuclear war. And as long as the Soviets retain a sufficiently flexible weapons system, they can confront us with contingencies from which we can extricate ourselves only by initiating such a war. To be sure, the President has said explicitly (December 17, 1954), "Let no man think that we want peace at any price." But the price of peace cannot be determined in the abstract. The growth of the Soviet nuclear stockpile is certain to increase our reluctance to run the risks of an all-out war; the line between what is considered "vital" and what is "peripheral" will shift if we must weigh all objectives against the destruction of New York or Washington or Chicago.[1]

It may be argued that the emphasis on the rôle of force mistakes the main thrust of the current Soviet threat, which presents more ambiguous and subtle challenges than overt aggression. To be sure, the present period of revolutionary change will not be managed by a military doctrine alone; imaginative diplomacy and a consistent program are necessary if our aims are to be identified with the aspirations of humanity. But we always seem in danger of focussing so much attention on the current Soviet threat that we are taken unawares by the Soviet Union's frequent changes of tactics. During the period of Soviet militancy we were so preoccupied with building defensive barriers that we neglected the supporting psychological and political framework. And now, with the Soviet emphasis on more indirect methods of penetration, we stand in danger of forgetting that economic development must be accompanied by a modicum of security against foreign invasion. Moreover, it is one of the most difficult tasks of statesmanship to relate what a Power says it will do to what it is able to do. If the international order possessed the sanctions that prevail in domestic arrangements—courts and enforcement machinery, for example—relations could be conducted largely on the basis of what states assert their intentions to be. But in an international order composed of sovereign states, the principal sanction is the possession of superior force; any adverse change in power relationships involves the possibility that the gain in strength will be used with hostile intent. This

is the real meaning of "atomic blackmail." As the Soviet nuclear stockpile grows, overt threats have become unnecessary; every calculation of risks will have to include the Soviet stockpile of atomic weapons and ballistic missiles.

If the phrase "there is no alternative to peace" were to become accepted doctrine, it could lead only to a paralysis of policy. It would be tantamount to renouncing power and staking everything on the professions of another sovereign state. This would have been difficult at any period; it becomes an invitation to disaster when we are confronted with a revolutionary Power which prides itself on its superior understanding of "objective" forces, and to which policies unrelated to a plausible possiblity of employing force will seem either hypocrisy or stupidity. Force and diplomacy are not discrete realms; on the contrary, the ultimate pressure during negotiations has always been the possibility that recourse might be had to force. To the extent that the slogan "there is no alternative to peace" is taken seriously by the Soviets as a statement of American intentions, it will remove a powerful brake on Soviet probing actions and any incentive for the Soviet Union to make concessions. At best the doctrine "there is no alternative to peace" can achieve only an indefinite continuation of the status quo. In this context, our frequent pronouncements that we refuse to accept the satellite orbit will seem hollow or will even backfire: they will give impetus to Soviet peace offensives without generating a meaningful pressure on the Soviet sphere.

The discussion about war being "inconceivable" has, however, performed this useful purpose: it has drawn attention to the paradox that we are preparing for a war which we did not fight even when we possessed an atomic monopoly and that we have not yet found a rationale for such a war when weapons have become incomparably more destructive. On the contrary, far from giving us freedom of action, the very power of modern weapons seems to inhibit it. In short, our weapons technology and the objectives for employing them have become incommensurable. No more urgent task confronts the United States than to bring them into harmony.

II

But perhaps this incommensurability is inherent in the new weapons and not in the military doctrine? Perhaps we are moving into a new era of international relations in which the Powers will have to adjust themselves to the fact that force can no longer be used? What about "nuclear stalemate?"

Of course, "stalemates" have occurred before in the history of war, particularly in the relation of offense to defense. The distinguishing feature of the current use of the term is that it refers not to a balance on the battlefield, but to a calculus of risks: with each side possessing the capability to inflict catastrophic blows on the other, war is said to be no longer a rational course of action. It is important, however, to be precise about the deterrent effect of the "nuclear stalemate:" it deters not only aggression, but resistance to it; and it deters not war as such, but all-out war. The side which can present its challenges in less than all-out form may, therefore, be able to use the "nuclear stalemate" to its advantage.

Moreover, even if a nuclear stalemate does exist, it does not make for stability in the present volatile state of technology— much less for a sense of harmony. The spectre of a technological breakthrough by the other side would always loom large; it would lend an apocalyptic quality to all current international relations.

For the purpose of national policy, however, the significance of the term "stalemate" resides not in the technical but in the psychological aspect. For the "stalemate" is not anything new. Actually it has existed ever since the explosions over Hiroshima and Nagasaki. To be sure, it was not a physical stalemate; for nearly a decade the United States was relatively immune from Soviet retaliation. But it was a stalemate nonetheless in the sense that we never succeeded in translating our military superiority into a political advantage. This was due to many factors: a theory of war

based on the necessity of total victory, the memory of the wartime alliance with the Soviets, humanitarian impulses, lack of clarity about the process in which we found ourselves involved. But whatever the reason, our atomic monopoly had at best a deterrent effect. While it may have prevented a further expansion of the Soviet sphere, it did not enable us to achieve a strategic transformation in our favor. Indeed, even its importance as a deterrent is questionable. Assuming that there had never been an atomic bomb, would we really have acquiesced in the Soviet Union's taking over Europe? Would the U.S.S.R. have risked a general war so soon after having its territory devastated by the Germans and having lost, by the most conservative estimates 10,000,000 dead? Not even a dictatorship can do everything simultaneously.

But apart from the questionable assumption that all-out war was prevented by our atomic monopoly, the decade witnessed the consolidation of a satellite orbit in Eastern Europe, the triumph of Communism in China and, most fundamental of all, the growth of the Soviet atomic stockpile. Those who expect great things from technological breakthroughs would do well to study American actions after Hiroshima and Nagasaki. No foreseeable technological breakthrough is likely to be more fundamental than the discovery of the A-bomb. Yet possession of it did not enable us to prevent another Power which never hid its hostile intent from expanding its orbit and developing a capacity to inflict a mortal blow on the United States.

How did this come about? Primarily because we added the A-bomb to our military arsenal without integrating its implications into our thinking; because we saw it merely as another tool in a theory of warfare which had showed a poverty—indeed almost an absence—of political conception during the two world wars, and which became completely inapplicable after the explosions over Hiroshima and Nagasaki.

For over a century before the outbreak of World War I, wars were an extension of policy. Because they were fought for specific political objectives there existed a rough commensurability between the force employed and the goal sought. But with the outbreak of World War I, war suddenly seemed to become an end in itself. After the first few months, none of the protagonists would have been able to name an objective other than the total defeat of the enemy or, at least, they would have named objectives, such as the German demand for the annexation of Belgium, which amounted to unconditional surrender. There had occurred a hiatus between military and political planning which has never subsequently been bridged. The military staffs had developed plans for total victory, because it is in such plans that all factors are under the control of the military. But political leadership proved incapable of giving this conception a concrete expression in terms of peace aims. The result was four years of war of ever increasing violence which carried its hatreds into a peace treaty that considered more the redressing of sacrifices than the stability of the international order.

The notion that war and peace, military and political goals, were separate had become so commonplace by the end of World War II that the most powerful nation in the world found itself paralyzed by the enormity of its own weapons technology. In every concrete instance, even in the matter of the regulation of the atom which affected our very survival, we found ourselves stalemated by our own preconceptions. The consequences of military actions which we might take always seemed to outbalance the gains to be achieved. Thus our policy became entirely defensive. We possessed a doctrine to repel overt aggression, but we could not translate it into a positive goal. And even in the one instance where we resisted aggression we did not use the weapon around which our whole military planning had been built. The hiatus between military and national policy was complete. Our power was not commensurate with the objectives of our national policy and our military doctrine could not find any intermediary application for the new weapons. The growth of the Soviet atomic stockpile has merely brought the physical equation into line with the psychological one; it has increased the reluctance to engage in a general war even more. But it has not changed the fundamental question of how the political and military doctrines can be harmonized, how our power can give impetus to our policy rather than paralyzing it.

One way of avoiding this problem is to deny that it exists. It is possible to argue that the term "stalemate" is illusory, that in an all-out war one side is almost certain to be able to "win" in the sense of being able to impose its will on its antagonist. This is technically correct. But it does not affect the calculus by which the decision to enter the war is taken: in its crudest form, whether it is "worth" fighting the war in the first place. Obviously no Power will start a war it thinks it is going to lose. But it will also be reluctant to start a war if the price of victory may be its national substance. The capacity to inflict greater losses on the enemy than one suffers is the condition of policy; it cannot be its objective.

The transformation imposed by the "nuclear stalemate" is not that victory in an all-out war has become technically impossible but that it can no longer be imposed at an acceptable cost. Nor is this conclusion avoided by an appeal to military rationality. For example, in Paul Nitze's hypothetical general war confined to airfields and S.A.C. installations, the bombing of cities would be unwise in the early stages of the war and unnecessary in the later ones after air superiority has been achieved.[2] But this assumes that victory is the only rational objective in war. It overlooks the fact that war is not only the instrument for imposing one's will on the defeated but is also a tool for frustrating this intent by making the effort too costly. An air battle would be a rational strategy for the side which has a strategic advantage either in terms of base structure or in weapons potential, for it would put the enemy at its mercy at a minimum cost. But for the side which stands to lose the air battle and which seeks to exact a maximum price for its own defeat, the most rational strategy may well be to inflict maximum destruction. Such a Power may at least attempt to equalize the *threat* of nuclear destruction by inflicting its *actuality* on the enemy and thereby deprive him of the fruits of his victory, or at least make it too risky for him to seek total victory. Unconditional surrender—or depriving the enemy of his nuclear capability, which amounts to the same thing—cannot be achieved by subterfuge.

III

But does the stalemate, defined as the impossibility of achieving total victory at an acceptable cost, apply to lesser conflicts? In other words, is limited war a conceivable instrument of policy in the nuclear period? Here we must analyze precisely what is meant by limited war.

One can think of many models: a war confined to a geographic area, a war that does not utilize the whole weapons system, a war which utilizes the whole weapons systems but limits its employment to specific targets. But none of these military definitions seems adequate, since a war may be confined geographically or in terms of targets and yet be total in the sense of exhausting the national substance, as happened to France in World War I. The fact that the whole weapons system is not employed, or that the destructive capability of the existing weapons system is small, is not of itself a factor of limitation. In the Thirty Years' War the number of men in each army was small by present-day standards, the power of the weapons was negligible compared to modern armaments, and yet it is estimated that at least 30 percent of the population of Germany died during the course of it.

A distinction based on the difference between nuclear weapons and "conventional armaments" is no more fruitful. Apart from the fact that the distinction becomes increasingly nebulous as we develop nuclear weapons of very low yield, it will be impossible to reverse present trends. The very existence of nuclear armaments on both sides seems to insure that any future war will be nuclear. At a minimum, forces will have to deploy *as if* nuclear weapons might be used, because the side which concentrates its forces might thereby give its opponent the precise incentive he needs to use nuclear weapons. But if forces are dispersed, they will not be able to hold a line or achieve a breakthrough with conventional weapons, because the destructive power of conventional weapons is so much smaller. Finally, nuclear weapons, particularly of the low-yield type, seem to offer the best opportunity to compensate for our inferiority in manpower and to use our superiority in technology to best advantage.

It is not for nothing that Soviet propaganda has played on two related themes: 1, there is no such thing as a "limited" nuclear war, and 2, "ban the bomb." For both emphasize the corollary "there is no alternative to peace" and both deprive our policy of flexibility and sap our resistance to the preferred forms of Soviet strategy: peripheral wars, subversion and atomic blackmail.

Our discussion up to this point thus leads to these conclusions: Any war is likely to be a nuclear war. Nuclear war should be fought as something less than an all-out war. There exists no way to define a limited war in purely military terms. On the contrary, wars can be limited only by political decisions, by defining objectives which do not threaten the survival of the enemy. Thus an all-out war is a war to render the enemy defenseless. A limited war is one for a specific objective which by its very existence will establish a certain commensurability between the force employed and the goal to be attained.

Limited war, therefore, presents the military with particular difficulties. An all-out war is relatively simple to plan for, because its limits are set by military considerations and even by military capacity. The characteristic of limited wars, on the other hand, is that there are ground rules which define the relationship of military to political objectives. Planning here becomes much more conjectural, much more subtle and much more indeterminate, as we found when considering intervention in Indo-China. The political leadership must therefore assume the responsibility for defining the framework within which the military are to develop plans and capabilities. The prerequisite for a policy of limited war is the re-introduction of the political element into our concept of warfare and the surrender of the notion that policy ends when war begins or that war has goals different from those of national policy.

IV

This raises the question to what extent the nuclear age permits a policy of intermediary objectives. Do any of the factors apply today which formerly led to a diplomacy of limited objectives and a military policy of limited wars?

In the great periods of European cabinet diplomacy between the Treaty of Westphalia and the French Revolution and between the Congress of Vienna and the outbreak of the First World War, wars were limited because there existed a political framework which induced the major Powers to conduct a diplomacy of limited objectives. This political framework was due to several factors. There was, to begin with, a conscious decision that the upheavals of the Thirty Years' War and of the Napoleonic Wars should not occur again. More important was the fact that the international order did not contain a revolutionary Power. No state was so dissatisfied with the peace settlement that it sought to gain its ends by overthrowing it and no Power considered that its domestic notion of justice was incompatible with that of other states. Again, the domestic structure of most governments set a limit to the proportion of the national resources which could be devoted to war. Not even the most absolute ruler by the grace of God could think of conscripting his subjects or confiscating their property. Finally, in an era of stable weapons technology, both the strength of the Powers and their assessments of those strengths were relatively fixed and as a result the risks of surprise attack and of unforeseen technological developments were relatively small.

If we inquire which of these factors—fear of war, legitimacy, limits on the domestic exercise of power and a stable power relationship—is present today, little cause

for optimism remains. Under conditions of nuclear plenty, no major Power will be forced to adopt a policy of limited objectives because of insufficient resources. Moreover, for over a generation the U.S.S.R. has proclaimed the incompatibility of its domestic notion of justice with that of other states and has built an internal control system on the theory of a permanently hostile outside world. Peaceful coexistence, too, is justified by the Soviets on the basis that it will enable them to subvert the existing structure by means other than all-out war.

Nor is the nature of power relationships more reassuring. Even with a less volatile technology, a two-Power world would have an element of inherent instability because an increase in strength of one side cannot be made up by superior political dexterity but is tantamount to an absolute weakening of the other side. Actually, the weapons technology is far from stable. Almost up to the outbreak of World War II a weapons system would be good for a generation at least, while today it may be outdated when it has barely passed the blueprint stage. In this technological race, moreover, the side which has adopted a policy of letting its opponent strike the first blow is at a distinct disadvantage; it cannot afford to fall behind even for an instant. It must phase its planning and procurement over an indefinite period while its opponent, if he is determined on a showdown, can plan for a target date.

But if neither an agreed legitimacy nor a stable power relationship exists today, they may be outweighed by the third factor in the equation: the fear of thermonuclear war. Never before have the consequences of all-out war been so unambiguous, never have the gains seemed so incommensurable with the sacrifices. What statesman who declared war in 1914 would not have recoiled had he known the shape of the world in 1918? Today every weapons test augurs much worse horrors. There exists, therefore, a limiting condition to every diplomatic move. The distinction between tactical and strategic nuclear weapons may be nebulous in military terms, but every state has a powerful incentive to make some distinction, however tenuous its logic. The fear that an all-out thermonuclear war might lead to the disintegration of the social structure should be utilized to guarantee the "limits" of war and diplomacy.

The key problem of our present-day strategy is therefore to devise alternative capabilities to confront our opponent with contingencies from which he can extricate himself only by thermonuclear war, but to deter him from this step by our retaliatory capacity. All Soviet moves in the postwar period have had this character; they have faced us with problems which by themselves did not seem "worth" an all-out war[3] but which we were unable to deal with by an alternative strategy. We refused to defeat the Chinese in Korea because we were unwilling to risk an all-out conflict; we saw no solution to the Indo-Chinese crisis without dangers we were reluctant to confront. A doctrine for the graduated employment of force might reverse or at least arrest this trend. Graduated deterrence is thus not an alternative to massive retaliation but its complement, for it is the capability for "massive retaliation" which provides the sanction against expanding war.

V

A doctrine for the graduated employment of force would enable us to escape the vicious circle in which we find ourselves paralyzed by the implications of our own weapons technology. The idea that the most effective strategy is the thermonuclear bombardment of cities is a legacy of World War II, when we could attack production centers without fear of retaliation. Because the destructive power of individual weapons was then relatively small, a decisive victory on the battlefield could be achieved only by using quantities too large to stockpile; munitions and weapons had to be supplied out of current production. Under these circumstances it made sense to attempt to win through attrition, by bombing production facilities. The destructiveness of modern weapons, however, makes attrition the most wasteful

strategy. Under conditions of nuclear plenty, existing stockpiles will probably suffice to achieve a decision; nuclear weapons may therefore be more decisively employed on the battlefield or against military installations such as airfields than against production centers.[4]

Moreover, while the growth of the Soviet strategic air force and atomic stockpile should cause us to revise our concepts regarding air warfare, the introduction of nuclear weapons on the battlefield will shake the very basis of Soviet tactical doctrine. No longer will the Soviets be able to rely on massed manpower and artillery as in World War II. On a nuclear battlefield, dispersion is the key to survival and mobility the prerequisite of success. A great deal depends on leadership of a high order, personal initiative and mechanical aptitude, all qualities in which our military organization probably excels that of the U.S.S.R. To be sure, there are many types of aggression to which nuclear weapons offer no solution, either for political or military reasons—civil war and guerrilla actions, for example—and we must retain a conventional capability to deal with them. The fact remains that the most fruitful area for current strategic thought is the conduct and efficacy of limited nuclear war, the "war gaming" of situations in which nuclear weapons are used by *both* sides, and a consideration of what would constitute victory in such a war.

The graduated employment of force, however, presupposes a capability which is really "graduated." If we build our whole strategy around "absolute" weapons of megaton size, professions of limited objectives will be meaningless and any use of nuclear weapons is likely to touch off an all-out war. The possibility of keeping a limited nuclear war limited depends on our ability to extend the range of low-yield weapons of a kiloton and below, and to devise tactics for their utilization on the battlefield.

At the same time, a doctrine for the graduated employment of force and the renunciation of unconditional surrender should not be confused with the acceptance of a stalemate. The flexibility of our diplomacy will increase as our military alternatives multiply. And militarily, the notion that there is no alternative between total victory and the *status quo ante* is much too mechanical. If the military position of an enemy became untenable and if he were offered choices other than unconditional surrender, he might accept local withdrawals without resorting to all-out war. If S.A.C. retains its retaliatory capacity, the other side may decide that amputation is preferable to suicide. In these terms the calculus of risks by which a limited nuclear war is expanded into an all-out thermonuclear exchange is almost the same as that by which a limited conventional war is expanded into an all-out war. Whether we can obtain local adjustments will thus depend on: 1, the ability to generate pressures other than the threat of thermonuclear war; 2, the ability to create a climate of opinion in which national survival is not thought to be at stake in every issue; 3, the ability to keep control of public opinion should a disagreement arise over whether national survival is at stake.

But is it possible to bring about a climate in which national survival is thought not to be at stake? Pressures severe enough to cause withdrawal may, after all, be severe enough to be thought to threaten survival, especially in a régime like that in Soviet Russia. On the other hand, the problem is not how to reassure the Soviets, which is probably a well-nigh impossible effort, but how to give effect to the one interest we presumably have in common: that we both wish to avoid all-out thermonuclear war. Given this attitude, total war is likely in only two contingencies: if the Soviets see an opportunity to achieve hegemony in Eurasia by peripheral actions which we are not able to deal with by a graduated employment of force; or if the U.S.S.R. should misunderstand our intentions and treat our every military move as if it were the prelude to an all-out war.

It therefore becomes the task of our diplomacy to convey to the Soviet bloc that we are capable of courses other than all-out war or inaction, and that we intend to use this capability. Fortunately, the imbalance in our national strategy has been caused less by our diplomacy than by our military policy. Indeed, our difficulty has been precisely the fact that our moderate pronouncements have seemed incongruous in the face of an all-or-nothing military policy and that our diplomacy has been deprived of flexibility because "massive retaliation" has had as its logical corollary the slogan "there is no alternative to peace." A modification of our military doctrine would, therefore, go a long way towards creating a framework of limited objectives; the next step would be to convey this change to the outside world. Others have suggested details of such a diplomatic program.[5] Possible measures might include proposals for conventions regarding open cities, greater publicity for tests of low-yield nuclear weapons, and a high-level pronouncement which defines as precisely as possible what is meant by the "graduated" employment of force.

Such a program should be distinguished sharply from the Soviet "ban the bomb" propaganda, however. We cannot afford even the implication that nuclear weapons are in a special category, apart from modern weapons in general, for this undermines the psychological basis of the most effective United States strategy. If nuclear weapons were outlawed, Soviet superiority in manpower would again become a factor and its stockpile of conventional weapons would place Eurasia at the mercy of the Soviets, at least in an intermediary period while we adjusted our procurement, training and organization. "Ban the bomb" proposals, moreover, distract from the real security problem which is Soviet aggression, a fact that American diplomacy should not permit the world to forget. The diplomatic and psychological framework for the graduated employment of force is created not by "ban the bomb" proposals but by defining the conditions of its use. To be sure, a diplomatic program for the graduated employment of force will not inevitably prevent an all-out war; if the Soviets feel strong enough to knock us out by a surprise attack, they will presumably do so. But it may prevent an all-out war caused by our failure to develop alternatives or by

Soviet miscalculation or misunderstanding of our intentions.

Moreover, while the Marxist philosophy has heretofore imparted great flexibility to Soviet policy we may be able to use it as well to give effect to a policy of graduated deterrence. The belief in inevitable triumph is after all as consistent with tactical withdrawal as with an effort to fill every power vacuum. All of Soviet history testifies to the fact that this is not a régime for last stands if other alternatives present themselves. One need only study the abject efforts of the Politburo in the months before the German invasion to come to a settlement with Hitler to realize that if confronted with superior power the Soviets do not hesitate to apply Lenin's dictum, "One step backward, two steps forward." And this tendency is supported by all of Russian history. Russia has always been less able to apply force subtly than massively; she has always been more vulnerable to wars outside her territories than within, and to limited rather than all-out war.

The strategic problem for the United States, then, can be summed up in these propositions:

1. Thermonuclear war must be avoided, except as a last resort.

2. No power possessing thermonuclear weapons is likely to accept unconditional surrender without employing them and no nation is likely to risk thermonuclear destruction except to the extent that it believes its survival to be at stake.

3. It is the task of our diplomacy, therefore, to make clear that we do not aim for unconditional surrender, to create a framework in which the question of national survival is not involved in every issue. But equally we should leave no doubt about our determination to achieve intermediary objectives and to resist by force any Soviet military move.

4. Since diplomacy which is not related to a plausible employment of force is sterile, it must be the task of our military policy to develop a doctrine and a capability for the graduated employment of force.

VI

The discussion up to this point has been primarily concerned with the impact of our diplomacy and of our military policy on the Soviet bloc. Its impact on our allies and the uncommitted nations is no less important. The truism that the contemporary crisis cannot be solved solely by the exercise of power should not be confused with the notion that power plays no role in contemporary affairs. Peace has never been maintained except by making aggression too costly; the benefits of diversity which the free world still enjoys are due to the shield afforded by American military strength. For this reason alone, the quest for an adequate American military doctrine concerns not only us but also the rest of the world.

There can be little doubt that our system of alliances is undergoing a crisis. Many reasons for this exist: the Soviet peace offensive, the domestic problems of France, the economic stagnation of Britain, Canada's increasing sense of vulnerability. But surely one fundamental cause is the absence of a unifying military doctrine. The argument most frequently advanced for our coalition policy is that we require overseas bases. But whatever sense this policy makes to us, it is not persuasive to countries who want above all to avoid another round of bombings and occupation. Our allies realize, moreover, that in an all-out thermonuclear war the ground strength of our NATO partners will be almost irrelevant; in terms of the doctrine of massive retaliation our allies see little military significance in their own contribution. The growth of the Soviet atomic stockpile compounds these difficulties. Heretofore, a nation threatened with attack would generally resist because the potential destruction was insignificant compared to the consequences of surrender. But now, when most of our NATO partners consider the outbreak of a war as leading inevitably to national catastrophe, our system of alliances is in dire jeopardy. It can be restored, if at all, only by two measures: one, by a military doctrine and capability which makes clear that not every war is necessarily an all-out thermonuclear war, even in Europe; two, by measures such as the air defense of NATO, which reduce the sense of impotence felt by our allies in the face of the threat of thermonuclear war.

The problem with respect to the uncommitted nations, particularly those newly independent, is more complicated. Where our NATO partners suffer from a perhaps excessive awareness of the reality of power, the former colonial states seem hardly conscious of its existence and nature. This is understandable. The leaders of the newly independent states achieved their positions by distinguishing themselves in the struggle with the former colonial Powers. But the independence movements almost without exception provided a poor preparation for an understanding of modern power relationships. Based on the dogmas of late nineteenth century liberalism, especially its pacifism, the independence movements relied more on ideological agreement than on an evaluation of power factors. Indeed, the claim to superior spirituality remains the battle cry of Asian nationalism. Moreover, the bad conscience of the colonial Powers and their preoccupation with European problems gave the struggle for independence more the character of a domestic debate than of a power dispute. To be sure, many of the leaders of the newly independent Powers spent years in jail and suffered heroically for their cause. It is not to deny the measure of their dedication to assert that the results achieved were out of proportion to their suffering. Empires which had held vast dominions for hundreds of years disappeared without a battle being fought.

And if it is difficult for the leaders to retain a sense of proportion, it is next to impossible for the mass of the people. On the whole they were involved in the struggle for independence only with their sympathies; to them the disappearance of the colonial Powers must seem nothing short of miraculous. Moreover, most of the people of the newly independent states live in pre-industrial societies. It would be difficult enough for them to grasp the full impact of industrialism; it is too much to expect them

to understand the meaning of nuclear technology. It is therefore understandable that in most former colonial areas there is an overestimation of what can be achieved by the power of words alone. Nor is this tendency diminished by the rewards that fall to the uncommitted in the contest for their allegiance waged by the two big power centers. There must be an almost overwhelming temptation to defer the solution of difficult internal problems by entering the international arena, to solidify a complicated domestic position by triumphs in the field of foreign policy.

But however understandable, it is a dangerous trend. If this were a tranquil period, nothing would be involved but minor irritations. But in the present crisis, the dogmatism of these newly independent states makes them susceptible to Soviet "peace offensives," and their lack of appreciation of power relationships may cause them to overestimate the protection afforded by moral precepts.

The power chiefly visible to the newly independent states is that of Soviet or Chinese armies on their borders. The United States must counter with a twentieth century equivalent of "showing the flag," with measures which will permit us to make our power felt quickly and decisively, not only to deter Soviet aggression but to impress the uncommitted with our capacity for action. This does not mean "rattling the atom bomb." What it does require is greater mobility and a weapons system that can deal with the tensions most likely to arise in the uncommitted areas—tensions which do not lend themselves to the massive employment of thermonuclear weapons: civil war, peripheral attacks or a war among the uncommitted.

To be sure, this is an ungrateful and indeed an unpopular course. But we will not be able to avoid unpopularity. In the short run, all we can hope for is respect. Moreover, condescending as it may seem, we have an important educational task to perform in the newly independent countries on the subject of power in the nuclear age. Within a generation, and probably in less time than that, most of these states will possess nuclear power plants and therefore the wherewithal to manufacture nuclear weapons. And even if this should not prove the case, the Soviets may find it advantageous to increase international tensions by making available nuclear weapons, on the model of their arms deal with Egypt. But nuclear weapons in the hands of weak, irresponsible or merely ignorant governments present grave dangers. Unless the United States has successfully established ground rules for their graduated employment, many areas of the world will begin to play the traditional role of the Balkans in European politics: the fuse which will set off a holocaust.

VII

One of the difficulties in the nuclear period has been our tendency to treat its problems primarily as technical. But power is meaningless in the absence of a doctrine for employing it. The debate provoked by Mr. Dulles' interview in *Life* has again emphasized this dilemma: the enormity of modern weapons makes the thought of war repugnant, but a refusal to run any risk would amount to giving the Soviets a blank check. Our dilemma has been defined as the alternative of Armageddon or defeat without war. We can overcome the paralysis induced by such a prospect only by creating other alternatives both in our diplomacy and in our military policy. Such measures require strong nerves. We can make the graduated employment of force stick only if we leave no doubt about our readiness to face a final showdown; its effectiveness will depend on our willingness to face up to the risks of Armageddon.

NOTES

1. For a more detailed discussion of the doctrine of "massive retaliation" see the author's "Military Policy and the Defense of the Grey Areas," *Foreign Affairs*, April 1955.

2. Paul Nitze, "Atoms, Strategy and Policy," *Foreign Affairs*, January 1956.

3. See, for example, Thomas K. Finletter's letter to the *New York Herald Tribune*, December 22, 1955.

4. For application of these ideas to the conduct of a military campaign, see Richard C. Leghorn, "No Need to Bomb Cities to Win Wars," *U.S. News & World Report*, January 28, 1955.

5. For example, Rear Admiral Sir Anthony W. Buzzard, *Manchester Guardian*, November 3, 1955.

Liberal

Milton Mankoff and Linda Majka.   Economic sources of American militarism.

Since the end of World War II, the American government has expended over $1 trillion on military preparedness and activity. The belief that war profiteers are largely responsible for the enormous military expenditures of the federal government, and are also principal architects of military activity around the world, has long preoccupied social critics. The famous Special Committee on Investigation of the Munitions Industry, chaired by Senator Gerald Nye, conducted a lengthy investigation in the 1930s to uncover the extent and effect of war profiteering in the United States during World War I. It rejected the notion that arms manufacturers caused war. Nevertheless, by having a vested interest in military production and by stimulating an arms race through indiscriminate sale of the instruments of war to governments throughout the world, producers of weapons were held by congressional analysts to have contributed to a war psychology.

The current concern with war profiteering, while similar in many respects to that which motivated Senator Nye and his colleagues, assumes greater significance insofar as a military sector of the economy has taken on characteristics of permanence since the end of World War II. Whereas previously the nation mobilized for war and then rapidly demobilized afterward, the postwar military budget has remained quite high as a proportion of federal expenditures compared to previous postwar outlays. This suggests that the drive toward militarism may be rooted in the industrial sector to a greater extent than ever before.

The fact that the top 100 defense suppliers in 1970 received almost 70 percent of the total contracts of $10,000 or more, and that 68 of the 100 biggest contractors were among the 500 largest industrial corporations in the United States also implies that military manufacturers are not simply a dispersed and marginal component of American capitalism, but are among its most concentrated and economically potent representatives. As of 1969, all but four of the twenty-five largest industrial corporations in the United States were among the 100 largest Pentagon contractors.

Although the evidence suggests that a military-oriented industry of considerable economic power and concentration exists in the United States, this has not persuaded most scholars that the needs of the industry determine the development of American militarism. While the top industrial corporations are also among the largest defense contractors and many of the top defense contractors are among the top industrials, only a small proportion of the major corporations and contractors are dependent upon military production. For example, a company such as General Motors, the largest industrial corporation and the tenth largest defense contractor in 1968, had a ratio of military contract dollar value to the dollar value of total sales of only .031. There are a few giant firms such as McDonnell-Douglas which have huge total sales and owe them largely to military production, but this is not generally the case.

Economic reconversion

Other research indicates that reconversion of the economy to peacetime needs would not cripple American industry. For example, Wassily Leontief has argued that a 20 per-

cent decrease in military spending would "mean a reduction in total output and employment in only ten of the nation's fifty-six industrial sectors," principally those involved in aircraft, ordinance, research and development, electronics equipment and nonferrous metals. Robert G. Kokat has stated that a 50 percent cut in military expenditures would "have an expansionary impact on the majority of industries."

Most economic analysts treat military production as if it were no different from any other kind. They contend that nonmilitary government expenditures could be substituted for military contracts without damaging the corporate economy or the preeminent positions of most of the largest industrial corporations. However, there are several reasons why assumptions of equivalence in military and nonmilitary spending may not be tenable. As a number of analysts have argued, government military expenditures are particularly attractive to large, oligopolistic capitalist firms because (a) they promote relatively low risk and infinitely expandable production, and (b) they facilitate the protection and extension of overseas investments.

Commercial production aimed at the private consumer involves enormous risks in promoting new commodities and/or retaining consumer loyalty to old ones. Government social production (e.g., roads, schools) is low risk, but does not permit an infinitely expandable volume of output since social spending in many areas can become exhausted (roads and schools last for decades and do not require rapid replacement). By contrast, military production is no riskier than any other prepaid, government-oriented production. Moreover, continued replacement of self-destructing arms, as well as the "need" to improve existing weapons, assures a steady flow of business as long as war or the threat of it are ever-present.

The development and reinforcement of a sense of insecurity regarding national defense sustains a continual publicly accepted rationale for endless and wasteful military outlays that would be difficult to justify for social welfare spending, where need and performance are more easily calculated. The uncertainties of measuring national security in the face of relatively unknown or rapidly changing military capabilities of actual or potential adversaries, and the fact that many highly sophisticated weapons systems will never be tested in warfare, stands in sharp contrast to the ways in which ordinary citizens can assess their need for social services and the satisfaction of those needs. It is simpler for most people to determine whether there are enough medical or educational facilities in their community and whether they work adequately than to estimate if an intercontinental ballistic missile is required to maintain military security. Given these advantages, the producers of military goods and services will naturally be reluctant to dispense with such production in order to pursue more elusive or self-limiting business in the private sphere or public welfare sectors of the economy.

Drawbacks and incentives

Military production does have some drawbacks which might cause firms to be wary of making a heavy commitment to obtaining defense contracts to the exclusion of other forms of economic activity. For example, there is a certain degree of competition within the defense industries. Large contracts are bid for by a number of firms; thus there are always more losers than winners for any given contract. At the same time, because military expenditures are subject to political decisions, there might be a general reduction of outlays, which would severely hurt companies that are too dependent upon defense production.

Yet, despite these possible disadvantages, firms that have received significant shares of the defense dollar have generally managed to maintain high profits and keep their relative dominance in the defense industries throughout the postwar years. Moreover, there does not appear to be any significant movement toward reconversion among defense industries, even those most heavily dependent on military production.

A number of analysts have argued that a primary function of militarism has been to protect and expand American overseas investments and export markets. In evaluating the importance of foreign markets for American corporations, it is important to consider not only the significance of foreign trade and investment for the economy as a whole or even for those corporations with overseas operations, but for the largest and most powerful firms as well. Thus, it is conceivable that the vast majority of corporations have little to gain from foreign markets, and that the small number having a major interest in them are of marginal importance to the American system. The fate of the largest corporations, however, is intimately tied to the overall prosperity of the economy. In 1969, for example, the twenty-five largest (by sales) industrial corporations accounted for 22 percent of the sales and 34.7 percent of the after tax profits of all industrial corporations in the United States. Our examination of annual company reports and other sources indicated that by 1970 after tax profits from foreign economic activity represented an average of 32 percent of total after tax profits for the largest thirty industrials.

One can argue that corporate investment overseas is not entirely (or even largely) dependent upon America's military might. A relatively small and diminishing proportion of American foreign investment is currently located in the underdeveloped world. The bulk of overseas investment is in Western Europe and Canada, rather than in Latin America, Southeast Asia or Africa. Given the minimal Soviet military threat to Western Europe and Canada and the relative political stability in the developed countries, on the surface it seems implausible that American military preparedness is necessary to keep foreign markets open to corporate penetration.

However, a closer look reveals a different picture. Although the value of direct foreign investment in the underdeveloped countries in 1969 represented 28 percent of the total direct foreign investment, the much higher profit rates available on investment in the underdeveloped countries (18.7 percent to

8.3 percent) meant that the share of earnings from these areas accounted for 47 percent of all foreign earnings. This evidence refutes the contention that investment in underdeveloped, politically unstable societies is less valued by American businessmen than investment in advanced industrial societies. The fact that some Western European societies (e.g., France, Italy) continue to face substantial political threats from powerful mass anti-capitalist movements also lends credibility to the view that America's military presence in Europe might have an imperialist basis even now.

Coordination of production and expansion

If militarism and foreign economic expansion are linked with each other, what are the modes by which expansion and military production can be coordinated? Given the growth of multipurpose corporations, which produce a wide variety of commodities and services, as well as the emergence of giant conglomerates, in which firms primarily associated with a single commodity or service have been controlled by corporations with different orientations, it is possible that corporations with a large stake in foreign markets might be tied to companies preoccupied with military-related economic activity.

Most of the top thirty industrials have a significant stake either in overseas operations or military-oriented production. Of these corporations only Boeing had at least 20 percent of its profits rooted in both military production and foreign economic activity in 1970. Thus, coordination of both military production and economic expansion abroad appears not to be focused primarily within individual firms.

Although giant industrial corporations do not seem to be significantly involved in both overseas investment and sales as well as military production, firms that specialize in one function might have structural ties with those oriented towards other functions. In examining structural linkages between corporations, analysts have typically investigated boards of directors to learn whether the members of one firm's board are also found on that of another firm. If this occurs, the two firms are said to have interlocking directorates.

There is a great deal of controversy as to whether boards of directors in modern corporations exercise genuine control over important company operations or largely serve in an advisory capacity. In either case, interlocking directorates minimally provide corporations with a greater understanding of the needs and desires of other corporations. The extent of interlocks among corporations in the United States is considerable. Our analysis of data on interlocking directorates demonstrated that 44 percent of the top twenty-five defense contractors have a total of twenty interlocks with the largest thirty industrials. Among those defense contractors having interlocks with the top industrials, 61 percent of the eighteen interlocks with corporations classifiable in regard to type of production were with foreign-oriented corporations (those with at least 20 percent of after tax profits coming from overseas markets), 33 percent were with domestic nonmilitary producers and 6 percent were with military producers. Moreover, 82 percent of the interlocks with foreign-oriented industrials involved military producers which clearly did not recieve 20 percent or more of their total profits from military production, despite being among the largest defense contractors.

While direct ties between military producers and overseas operators are not always present, it is possible that indirect linkages exist through common interlocks with financial institutions. A number of scholars have pointed to the importance of financial institutions in the corporate world, but there is considerable disagreement as to the degree of control, if any, financial institutions have over nonfinancial corporations. Since banks and insurance companies seem to be at the core of several interest groups involving sets of interlocking corporations, these institutions might better be able to coordinate the interdependent interest of military and foreign-oriented corporations.

What stake do financial institutions have in militarism and foreign economic expansion? Victor Perlo, in *Militarism and Industry: Arms Profiteering in the Missile Age*, made the following observations:

Unquestionably a large volume of business flows to the banks and other financial institutions by virtue of the military budget. This includes loans to munitions makers, stock flotations for the numerous companies coming into existence or expanding on account of military business and the massive operations in the Federal debt, amounting to tens of billions yearly for refunding alone.

At the same time, financial institutions benefit greatly from corporate activity abroad through loans to firms expanding operations in foreign countries and investment in foreign-oriented corporations. In addition, financial institutions seek to expand overseas through, for example, the creation of banking facilities abroad. The continued use of the dollar as the primary currency in the captialist world is enormously profitable for financial capitalists. Thus, financial institutions have a significant stake in both militarism and foreign economic expansion.

Our research on interlocks between the largest eight banks and five insurance companies (by assets), on the one hand, and the top thirty industrials and twenty-five largest defense contractors on the other, showed that all the foreign-oriented companies and big military producers had interlocks with one or more of the largest financial institutions. Moreover, all the major financial institutions had interlocks with one or more leading military producer or company heavily involved in overseas economic operations. This data suggests that financial institutions, many of whose top executives have served on foreign policymaking bodies in government and in key advisory groups such as the Council on Foreign Relations, may be strategically located to coordinate overseas economic expansion and the military preparedness which serves to buttress it.

Militarism and history

Recent historiography indicates that key American government and business officials in the years during and following World War II were extremely concerned about the possibility of a recurring Great Depression in the absence of expanded foreign markets. Although initial antimilitarist sentiments were expressed in business and government circles, and there was a desire to return to peacetime production (except for a small number of arms manufacturers who feared rapid conversion), many businessmen and public officials recognized that military spending was the most potent method of combating the massive unemployment of the recent past. They counseled against a return to prewar levels of military outlays.

Evidence that these leaders perceived the link between militarism and economic expansion abroad is somewhat harder to obtain, if one must rely solely on written or oral documents in an age when public figures are increasingly sensitive to the judgment of future historians. Yet some material, such as *The Pentagon Papers,* supports the view that foreign policymakers were aware of the utility of militarism in maintaining an "open door" for capital investment and exports.

The great concern over foreign markets is consistent with the diminishing orientation toward "radical" social reform by 1940. Business opposition to the New Deal led to a growing reliance upon foreign expansion and military spending to stabilize the social order. Postwar elite antipathy to great social welfare outlays has generally been far more vehement than concern over large military expenditures.

With complete data far from being available, it is impossible to make definitive statements about the motives of government decision makers in the past generation. It is especially difficult to draw conclusions about the reference groups of Presidents, who have ultimate authority in many facets of military and foreign policy. This might be ascertained only by examining memoranda, reports and diaries not meant for public exposure. However, the evidence on reference groups that does exist is inconclusive. Some public officials over the years have clearly advocated and engaged in conscious deception of the citizenry, whereas others have been victimized by faulty intelligence from subordinates.

Do officials in the former category lack a sense of obligation to the public interest or do they believe that "noble lies" best serve it? The famous remark of former Secretary of Defense Charles Wilson ("What's good for General Motors is good for the country") may well answer that question, given the extensive social and occupational ties of most of those involved in national security management with the world of corporate capitalism. Most foreign policymakers believe they are serving the entire citizenry, but since they draw their conception of national interest from those in their social milieu, their decisions function primarily in the interests of that unrepresentative group. Whether awareness of possible flaws in their conceptual world would change their behavior is not clear; however, persons acting outside of government who have a vested interest in militarism can put great pressure upon political leaders who might radically alter their world views.

Counterproductive functions

Inflation, the channeling of brainpower away from projects which might improve industrial productivity of civilian goods and a concomitant adverse effect upon the balance of trade are some of the counterproductive functions of militarism which have eroded American capital's preeminence within the world economy. In addition, the human and material costs of militarism, along with the inequitable distribution of benefits, raises doubts about the quality and purpose of government. Warfare, even more than economic depression, has tended to polarize political life. In the twentieth century, mass left-wing movements grew in Europe—and to a lesser extent in the United States—during and immediately after wars. In the underdeveloped world, revolution was not an infrequent outcome of wartime

burdens placed upon fragile and anachronistic social systems. In many ways, military victory has been pyrrhic and defeat has been catastrophic for those identified in the public view with war making.

The future relationship between militarism and economic expansion may be less pronounced than at the present time. Whereas foreign policymakers may have felt that world military and political hegemony was a precondition for economic penetration in the period immediately after World War II, the emergence of a revitalized and economically expansive Western Europe and Japan, without the aid of militarism, has strengthened those political and economic elites who have begun to look more critically at American militarism.

Even if one concedes that militarism is most helpful, if not essential, for the maintenance of American capital's access to world markets, overseas expansion does not necessarily have to continue for the well-being of American capitalism. Although expansion abroad may be the most advantageous strategy, under adverse circumstances it may be modified or even abandoned without destroying the capitalist mode of production. A post-imperialist capitalism would undoubtedly require enormous tranformations of the social structure, a vast increase in government social spending and a weakening of capitalist class domination. This has happened in England to a great extent and that country— with its greater initial stake in foreign markets and the need for them—was far less favorable to demilitarization than the United States. English leaders, economically and militarily weakened after World War II, reluctantly followed a largely post-imperial path.

The growing awareness of the costs of militarism, and even of overseas economic expansion, to business and government elites as well as ordinary citizens might lay the groundwork for a reorientation of the American political economy. However, if the citizenry continues to play as passive a role in formulating and pressing for alternatives to militarism in the present as they have previously, economic and political elites will be able to pursue strategies that are least likely to meet the needs of the vast majority of Americans. Only an aroused and articulate public can insure a demilitarized future with social justice.

Socialist

Seymour Melman. The state-management.

In the name of defense, and without announcement or debate, a basic alteration has been effected in the governing institutions of the United States. An industrial management has been installed in the federal government, under the Secretary of Defense, to control the nation's largest network of industrial enterprises. With the characteristic managerial propensity for extending its power, limited only by its allocated share of the national product, the new state-management combines peak economic, political, and military decision-making. Hitherto, this combination of powers in the same hands has been a feature of statist societies—communist, fascist, and others—where individual rights cannot constrain central rule.

This new institution of state-managerial control has been the result of actions undertaken for the declared purposes of adding to military power and economic efficiency and of reinforcing civilian, rather than professional, military rule. Its main characteristics are institutionally specific and therefore substantially independent of its chief of the moment. The effects of its operations are independent of the intention of its architects, and may even have been unforeseen by them.

The creation of the state-management marked the transformation of President Dwight Eisenhower's "military-industrial complex," a loose collaboration, mainly through market relations, of senior military officers, industrial managers, and legislators. Robert McNamara, under the direction of President John Kennedy, organized a formal central-management office to administer the military-industrial empire. The market was replaced by a management. In place of the complex, there is now a defined administrative control center that regulates tens of thousands of subordinate managers. In 1968, they directed the production of $44 billion of goods and services for military use. By the measure of the scope and scale of its decision-power, the new state-management is by far the largest and most important single management in the United States. There are about 15,000 men who arrange work assignments to subordinate managers (contract negotiation), and 40,000 who oversee compliance of submanagers of subdivisions with the top management's rules. This is the largest industrial central administrative office in the United States—perhaps in the world.

The state-management has also become the most powerful decision-making unit in the United States government. Thereby, the federal government does not "serve" business or "regulate" business. For the new management is the largest of them all. Government *is* business. That is state capitalism.

The normal operation, including expansion, of the new state-management has been based upon preemption of a lion's share of federal tax revenue and of the nation's finite supply of technical manpower. This use of capital and skill has produced parasitic economic growth—military products which are not part of the level of living and which cannot be used for further production. All this, while the ability to defend the United States, to shield it from external attack, has diminished.

From 1946 to 1969, the United States government spent over $1,000 billion on the military, more than half of this under the Kennedy and Johnson administrations—the period during which the state-management was established as a formal institution. This sum of staggering size (try to visualize a billion of something) does not express the cost of the military establishment to the nation as a whole. The true cost is measured by what has been foregone, by the accumulated deterioration in many facets of life, by the inability to alleviate human wretchedness of long duration.

Here is part of the human inventory of depletion:

1. By 1968, there were 6 million grossly substandard dwellings, mainly in the cities.

2. 10 million Americans suffered from hunger in 1968–1969.

3. The United States ranked 18th at last report (1966) among nations in infant mortality rate (23.7 infant deaths in first year per 1,000 live births). In Sweden (1966) the rate was 12.6.

4. In 1967, 40.7 percent of the young men examined were disqualified for military service (28.5 percent for medical reasons).

5. In 1950, there were 109 physicians in the United States per 100,000 population. By 1966 there were 98.

6. About 30 million Americans are an economically underdeveloped sector of the society.

The human cost of military priority is paralleled by the industrial-technological depletion caused by the concentration of technical manpower and capital on military technology and in military industry. For example:

1. By 1968, United States industry operated the world's oldest stock of metal-working machinery; 64 percent was 10 years old and over.

2. No United States railroad has anything in motion that compares with the Japanese and French fast trains.

3. The United States merchant fleet ranks 23rd in age of vessels. In 1966, world average-age of vessels was 17 years, United States 21, Japan 9.

4. While the United States uses the largest number of research scientists and engineers in the world, key United States industries, such as steel and machine tools, are in trouble in domestic markets: in 1967, for the first time, the United States imported more machine tools than it exported.

As civilian industrial technology deteriorates or fails to advance, productive employment opportunity for Americans diminishes.

All of this only begins to reckon the true cost to America of operating the state military machine. (The cost of the Vietnam war to the Vietnamese people has no reckoning.) Clearly, no mere ideology or desire for individual power can account for the colossal costs of the military machine. A lust for power has been at work here, but it is not explicable in terms of an individual's power drive. Rather, the state-management represents an institutionalized power-lust. A normal thirst for more managerial power within the largest management in the United States gives the new state-management an unprecedented ability and opportunity for building a military-industry empire at home and for using this as an instrument for building an empire abroad. This is the new imperialism.

The magnitude of the decision-power of the Pentagon management has reached that of a state. After all, the fiscal 1970 budget plan of the Department of Defense—*$83 billion*—exceeds the gross national product (GNP) of entire nations: in billions of dollars for 1966—Belgium, $18.1; Italy $61.4; Sweden $21.3. The state-management has become a para-state, a state within a state.

In its beginning, the government of the United States was a political entity. The managing of economic and industrial activity was to be the province of private persons. This division of function was the grand design for American government and society, within which personal and political freedom could flourish alongside of rapid economic growth and technological progess. After 1960, this design was transformed. In the name of ensuring civilian control over the Department of Defense and of obtaining efficiencies of modern management, Secretary of Defense Robert McNamara redesigned the organization of his Department to include, within the office of the Secretary, a central administrative office. This was designed to control operations in thousands of subsidiary industrial enterprises undertaken on behalf of the Department of Defense. Modeled after the central administrative offices of multi-division industrial firms—such as the Ford Motor Company, the General Motors Corporation, and the General Electric Company—the new top management in the Department of Defense was designed to control the activities of subsidiary managements of firms producing, 1968, $44 billion of goods and services for the Department of Defense.

By the measure of industrial activity governed from one central office, this new management in the Department of Defense is beyond compare the largest industrial management in the United States, perhaps in the world. Never before in American experience has there been such a combination of economic and political decision-power in the same hands. The senior officers of the new state-management are also senior political officers of the government of the United States. Thus, one consequence of the establishment of the new state-management has been the installation, within American society, of an institutional feature of a totalitarian system.

The original design of the American government was oriented toward safeguarding individual political freedom and economic liberties. These safeguards were abridged by the establishment of the new state-management in the Department of Defense. In order to perceive the abridgement of traditional liberties by the operation of the new managerial institution, one must focus on its functional performance. For the official titles of its units sound like just another government bureaucracy: Office of the Secretary of Defense, Defense Supply Agency, etc.

The new industrial management has been created in the name of defending America from its external enemies and preserving a way of life of a free society. It has long been understood, however, that one of the safeguards of individual liberty is the separation

of roles of a citizen and of an employee. When an individual relates to the same person both as a citizen and as an employee, then the effect is such—regardless of intention—that the employer-government official has an unprecedented combination of decision-making power over the individual citizen-employee.

In the Soviet Union, the combination of top economic and political decision-power is a formal part of the organization and ideology of that society. In the United States, in contrast, the joining of the economic-managerial and top political power has been done in an unannounced and, in effect, covert fashion. In addition to the significance of the new state-management with respect to individual liberty in American society, the new organization is significant for its effects in preempting resources and committing the nation to the military operations that the new organization is designed to serve. Finally, the new power center is important because of the self-powered drive toward expansion that is built into the normal operation of an industrial management.

The preemption of resources takes place because of the sheer size of the funds that are wielded by the Department of Defense. Its budget, amounting to over $80 billion in 1969, gives this organization and its industrial-management arm unequalled decision-power over manpower, materials, and industrial production capacity in the United States and abroad. It is, therefore, predictable that this organization will be able to get the people and other resources that it needs whenever it needs them, even if this requires outbidding other industries and other organizations—including other agencies of the federal and other governments.

Regardless of the individual avowals and commitments of the principal officers of the new industrial machine, it is necessarily the case that the increased competence of this organization contributes to the competence of the parent body—the Department of Defense. This competence is a war-making capability. Hence, the very efficiency and success of the new industrial-management, unavoidably and regardless of intention, enhances the war-making capability of the government of the United States. As the war-making department accumulates diverse resources and planning capability, it is able to offer the President blueprint-stage options for responding to all manner of problem situations—while other government agencies look (and are) unready, understaffed, and underequipped. This increases the likelihood of recourse to "solutions" based upon military power.

Finally, the new government management, insofar as it shares the usual characteristics of industrial management, has a built-in propensity for expanding the scope and intensity of its operations—for this expansion is the hallmark of success in management. The chiefs of the new state-management, in order to be successful in their own eyes, strive to maintain and extend their decision-power—by enlarging their activities, the number of their employees, the size of the capital investments which they control, and by gaining control over more and more subsidiary managements. By 1967–1968, the scope of the state-management's control over production had established it as the dominant decision-maker in U.S. industry. The industrial output of $44 billion of goods and services under state-management control in 1968 exceeded by far the reported net sales of American industry's leading firms (in billions of dollars for 1968): A.T.&T., $14.1; Du Pont, $3.4; General Electric, $8.4; General Motors, $22.8; U.S. Steel, $4.6. The giants of United States industry have become small- and medium-sized firms, compared with the new state-management—with its conglomerate industrial base.

The appearance of the new state-managerial machine marks a transformation in the character of the American government and requires us to re-examine our understanding of its behavior. Various classic theories of industrial capitalist society have described government as an essentially political entity, ideally impartial. Other theories depict government as justifiably favoring, or even identifying with,

business management, while the theories in the Marxist tradition have depicted government as an arm of business. These theories require revision.

Theories of government —business power

The classic theory of imperialism explained the behavior of government, in part, as the result of the influence of private industrial managers and chiefs of financial organizations. In this view, a ruling class, located in private enterprise, used the political instruments of government in the service of private gain. Thereby, the central government's political, legal, and military powers were utilized at home and abroad to maintain and extend the decision-power of this ruling class, through sponsoring and protecting private property rights, foreign trade, and foreign investment.

These classic theories of imperialism do not help us understand one of the most important of recent United States government policies—participation in the war in Vietnam and preparation for a series of such wars. At the time of this writing, the United States government had expended not less than $100 billion in military and related activities in connection with the Vietnam war. This excludes the economic impacts of an indirect sort within the United States caused by this war.

No one has demonstrated any past, present, or foreseeable volume of trade or investment in Vietnam and/or adjacent areas that would justify an outlay of $100 billion. The accompanying data on location and size of United States foreign investments speak for themselves. Indeed, there is substantial evidence to indicate that an important segment of the industrial corporations of the United States are not beneficiaries of participation by the American industrial system in military and allied production. (Thus, a Marxist political economist, Victor Perlo, has judged that about one-half of the major American industrial firms would gain materially from a cessation of military production.) Moreover,

U.S. private direct long-term investments abroad, 1966* (In billions of dollars)

Total	$54.2
Canada	$16.8
Western Europe	16.2
Latin American republics	9.8
Other Western hemisphere	1.6
Africa	2.0
Middle East	1.6
Far East	2.2
Oceania	2.0
Miscellaneous international	2.0

*Source: *Statistical Abstract of the United States, 1968,* U.S. Department of Commerce, 1968, p. 792.

criticism of the Vietnam war by important institutions of the American establishment, such as *The Wall Street Journal* and *The New York Times,* is not consistent with the ideas that the war has been conducted to suit the requirements of private finance and industry.

However, the operation of Vietnam war policies by the federal government is quite consistent with the maintenance and extension of decision-power by the new industrial management centered in the Department of Defense—for the management of the Vietnam war has been the occasion of major enlargement of budgets, facilities, manpower, capital investment and control over an additional million Americans in the labor force and more than one-half million additional Americans in the armed forces.

In his notable volume *The Power Elite,* C. Wright Mills, writing in 1956, perceived a three-part system of elites in the United States: economic, military, and political. At different times in American history, Mills wrote, this elite has been variously composed. That is, one or another of these three principals exercised primary decision-power. Mills concluded:

The shape and the meaning of the power elite today can be understood only when these three sets of structural trends are seen at their point of coincidence: the military capitalism of private corporations exists in a weakened and formal democratic system containing a military order already quite political in outlook and demeanor.

Mills stated further:

Today all three are involved in virtually all ramifying decisions. Which of the three types seems to lead depends upon the tasks of the period as they, the elite, define them. Just now, these tasks center upon defense and international affairs. Accordingly, as we have seen, the military are ascendent in two senses: as personnel and as justifying ideology. That is why, just now, we can most easily specify the unity and the shape of the power elite in terms of the military ascendency.

In a similar vein, Robert L. Heilbroner, writing of *The Limits of American Capitalism,* supports the Mills analysis that a system of elites wields primary decision-power in American society: the military, professionals—including technical experts—and government administrators. "There is little doubt," Heilbroner wrote,

...that a military-industrial-political interpenetration of interests exists to the benefit of all three. Yet in this alliance I have seen no suggestion that the industrial element is the dominant one. It is the military or the political branch that commands, and business that obeys: ...the role of business in the entire defense effort is essentially one of jockeying for favor rather than initiating policy.

The analysis by C. Wright Mills was a reasonable one for his time. It was appropriate to a period of transition, whose closing was marked by the famous farewell address of President Dwight Eisenhower.

In his final address as President, Eisenhower gave his countrymen a grave message. "In the councils of government we must guard against the acquisition of unwarranted influence, whether sought or unsought, by the military-industrial complex. The potential for the disastrous rise of misplaced power exists and will persist." Here and in subsequent addresses, Eisenhower did not offer a precise definition of what he meant by military-industrial complex. It is reasonable, however, to see the meaning of this category in the context in which it was stated. Military-industrial complex means a loose, informally defined collection of firms producing military products, senior military officers, and members of the executive and legislative branches of the federal government—all of them limited by the market relations of the military products network and having a common ideology as to the importance of maintaining or enlarging the armed forces of the United States and their role in American politics.

The military-industrial complex has as its central point an informality of relationships, as befits the market form which underpins its alliances. The understanding, therefore, is that the main interest groups concerned tend to move together, each of them motivated by its own special concerns, but with enough common ground to produce a mutually reinforcing effect. It is noteworthy that neither Eisenhower nor anyone else has suggested that there was a formal organization, or directorate, or executive committee of the military-industrial complex. The new industrial management in the federal government is, by contrast, clearly structured and formally organized, with all the paraphernalia of a formal, centrally managed organization, whose budget draws upon 10 percent of the Gross National Product of the richest nation in the world.

The formal organization and powers of the new state-management also bear on the meaning of the various elite theories. It is true that various groups in society obviously have greater power over the course of events than ordinary citizens. But the elites are not equal. Some are "more equal than others." Primacy in decision-power among major elites is determined by the extent of control over production and by the ability to implement policies whose consequences are favorable to some elites, even while being hurtful to the others. By these tests the new state-management dominates the field. It manages more production than any other elite. Its policies of military priority, military build-ups, and the Vietnam wars program have been damaging to the decision-power of other elites. (This will be shown in the following chapters of this book.) In sum, an understanding of the normal operation of the new state-management and its consequences is essential for a meaningful theory of contemporary American economy, government, and society.

During recent years, many writers have been intrigued by the panoply of technological power displayed by the immense and complicated stockpile of weapons fashioned for the Department of Defense. There has been a tendency in some quarters to focus on control over weaponry rather than on decision-power over people. In December, 1967, Arthur I. Waskow told the American Historical Association, "The first major trend event of the last generation in America has been the emergence of what could almost be seen as a new class, defined more by its relation to the means of total destruction than by a relation to means of production."

In a somewhat similar vein, Ralph E. Lapp, in his recent volume *The Weapons Culture,* concluded: "It is no exaggeration to say that the United States has spawned a weapons culture which has fastened an insidious grip on the entire nation." While I admire the excellence of Lapp's analyses of military organization and weaponry and the consequences of their use, it seems to me that to emphasize the idea of a weapons culture, implying a kind of weapons-technological Frankenstein, is less than helpful for appreciating the sources of recent changes in the American government and its policy.

Lapp declared: "The United States has institutionalized its arms-making to the point that there is grave doubt that it can control this far-flung apparatus." He may be correct in his judgment that the whole affair has gone beyond the point of being halted or reversed. But in order to make this judgment, it seems altogether critical to define exactly what it is that has been institutionalized. Where is the location of critical decision-power over "the weapons culture," with several million Americans involved directly or indirectly in military organization and in its support? Should we understand that one person, or one part, of this network is as important as any other?

In my estimate, it is important to identify the crucial decision-makers of the largest military organization (including its industrial base) in the world. Apart from these considerations, I am uneasy about theories viewing man as the captive of his weapons. This is a self-defeating mode of understanding, rather different from identifying the top decision-makers and their mode of control. Men may be captives, but only of other men. The concept of man in the grip of a Frankenstein weapons system has a severely limiting effect on our ability to do anything about it, if that is desired.

Recently, two writers have developed theories of convergence between military industry and government. Better-known are the ideas of John Kenneth Galbraith, as formulated in his volume *The New Industrial State*. Galbraith states: "Increasingly, it will be recognized that the mature corporation, as it develops, becomes part of the larger administrative complex associated with the state. In time the line between the two will disappear." In this perspective, the major military-industrial firms, as part of the larger family of major enterprises, merges with governmental organization. But this theory does not specify which of the managerial groups involved becomes more important than the other. Indeed, one of the theoretical contributions of *The New Industrial State* is the idea of a "technostructure," a community of technically trained managers operating on behalf of enterprises, public and private, with their movements among these enterprises serving as a bond between public and private institutions. But the technostructure idea homogenizes the men of the managerial-industrial occupations on the basis of their skills and work tasks. This bypasses the fact that an accountant, for example, in the state-management participates in a power-wielding institution of incomparably greater scope than the management of any private firm. Being in the state-management amplifies the significance of his work tasks, which may be qualitatively undifferentiable from those in a private firm.

In a similar vein, a former economist for Boeing, Murray L. Weidenbaum (now Professor of Economics at Washington University), presented another convergence hypothesis before the American Economic Association in December, 1967. In Weidenbaum's view.

The close, continuing relationships between the military establishment and the major companies serving the military establishment is changing the nature of both the public sector of the American economy and a large branch of American industry. To a substantial degree, the government is taking on the traditional role of the private entrepreneur while the companies are becoming less like other corporations and acquiring much of the characteristics of a government agency or arsenal. In a sense, the close, continuing relationship between the Department of Defense and its major suppliers is resulting in a convergence between the two, which is blurring and reducing much of the distinction between public and private activities in an important branch of the American economy.

The Weidenbaum thesis is close to the analyses which I am presenting in this book. My purpose here, however, is to underscore not convergence but the managerial primacy of the new managerial control institution in the Department of Defense, and the consequences for the character of American economy and society that flow from this.

When the Kennedy-Johnson administration took office in 1961, the President's aides were impressed with the problem of ensuring civilian White House control over the armed forces. From this vantage point, one of the main accomplishments of Robert S. McNamara was to reorganize the Department of Defense so as to give top decision-power to the newly enlarged and elaborated office of the Secretary of Defense—clearly a civilian control office superior to and separate from the Joint Chiefs of Staff. McNamara obviously drew upon his experience as a top manager of the Ford Company central office to design a similar organization under the Office of the Secretary of Defense. There is a similarity between these two central offices, but the difference in decision-power is very great. The Pentagon's management is by far the more powerful in the industrial sphere, and is tied to top decision-power in the military and political spheres as well.

It is true that the top echelons of the Department of Defense were reorganized in a manner consistent with the goal of establishing firmer civilian control. This result, however, was achieved by methods that also established an industrial management of unprecedented size and decision-power within the federal government. One result is that it is no longer meaningful to speak of the elites of industrial management, the elites of finance, and the elites of government and how they relate to each other. The elites have been merged in the new state-management.

This development requires a review of many of our understandings of the role of the federal government in relation to individual freedom in our society. For example, antitrust laws, and their enforcement by the executive branch of the government, have been designed to preserve individual freedom by limiting combinations and preventing conspiracies in the econo-

mic realm. The laws have been enforced with varying intensity, but have pressed in particular on the largest firms by restraining them in their growth relative to smaller firms in the same industry.

These laws exempted government because government, in particular its executive branch, was seen as acting for the nation as a whole: With the new development of the state-management, the government-management is now acting for the extension of its own managerial power.

It is worth recalling that Eisenhower warned against the acquisition of unwarranted influence by the military-industrial complex, *"whether sought or unsought."* One of the controlling features of the new industrial management is that, like other managements, it may be expected to act for the acquisition of additional influence; such behavior is normal for all managements.

✳

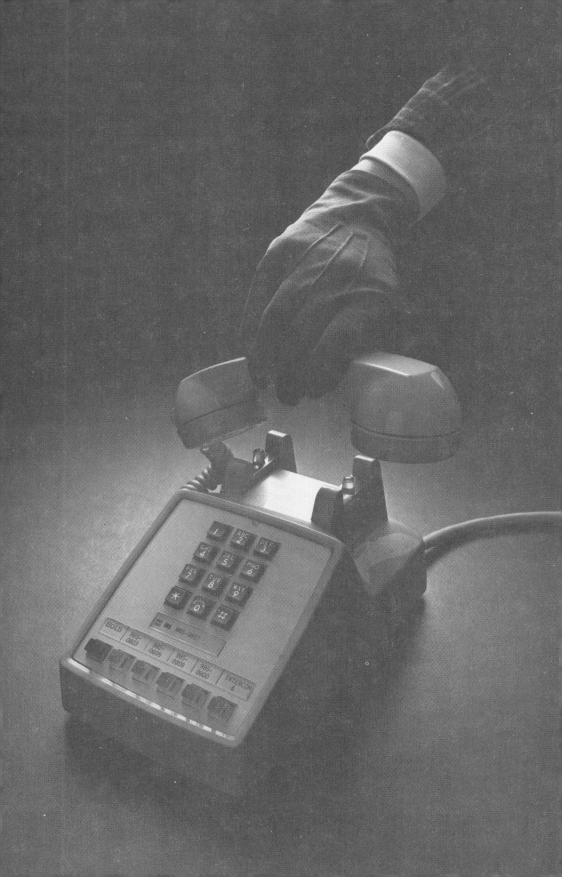

4 The secret police

The basic questions this chapter will address are:

(1) Does the United States have a secret police?

(2) Who are they?

(3) What are the functions of the American secret police?

(4) Is the secret police under the control of any force in American society? Or does it act independently?

(5) Is it necessary for the well-being of the United States as a democratic republic to have a secret police establishment?

These questions represent the major issues which the authors in this chapter argue from explicit and implicit conservative, liberal, and socialist principles.

Conservatives hold that there should be a secret police establishment but they prefer to call it the Central Intelligence Agency and the Federal Bureau of Investigation. These are the only agencies that they would include under their definition of "secret police." According to conservatives, a secret police is necessary if the United States is to be protected from its enemies abroad who are using against us secret police tactics that must be countered with similar and better strategies. Further, the CIA should operate within the territory of the United States insofar as it is necessary to carry out successfully its foreign missions. Foreign agents in the United States and Americans in contact with them must be followed closely and neutralized.

The CIA and FBI must be allowed to act in secrecy. Any attempt by the public or other government agencies to publicize FBI/CIA activities is harmful to the security of the United States. If this secrecy is violated the very completion of their mission becomes impossible. The breaching of secrecy and the raising of too many questions will impair the operation of these agencies. Conservatives hold that the FBI and CIA must be given the power to police their own operations. If other agencies attempt to correct abuses there is the danger that there will be further losses in secrecy. Too much of a loss in secrecy could, in their view, make both the CIA and FBI unviable. In a dangerous and violent world the CIA and FBI are seen as integral and positive institutions necessary for the maintenance of American security. The successful functioning of the American political system is dependent upon a respected, smooth-running, powerful, and publically supported secret police establishment.

Liberals believe that a secret police should exist but should be maintained in a far more restricted format. They hold that the CIA should be only an information gathering agency, and that the FBI should be merely an investigatory agency. Clandestine operations, engaged in by both agencies, should be prohibited. Liberals believe in the use of espionage to obtain information but not in undertaking actions which shape or eliminate foreign governments.

The CIA and FBI are viewed by liberals as evils necessary for the protection of the United States. These agencies are not instruments for carrying out foreign policy but are secondary and supportive institutions to its conduct.

Abuses of power by the FBI and CIA must be made known to the public, but secret information-gathering activities should remain known only to the President and Congressional leaders. Supervision of these agencies should be a Congressional responsibility. Congressional committees should receive ongoing information, which can be accomplished by Congressional hearings. These hearings will lead to legislation that will limit abuses by the CIA and FBI. The passing of legislation is regarded as an effective means of controlling secret activities.

Liberals are often confused over their attitude towards the CIA and FBI. They are not sure whether they can live with or without them, nor how much of what these agencies do should be private or public. This is the essence of the liberal dilemma vis à vis the secret police.

Liberals sometimes believe in the secret police and sometimes reject its necessity. Congressional hearings, they feel, are necessary, but too much information might come out in the hearings. They want strong protections against abuses of the FBI and CIA but at the same time are fearful of hamstringing these agencies. Liberals find it difficult to set a clear standard for judging how much authority should be allowed to these agencies, and how much control should be exercised over them.

The basic reason for the existence of the FBI and CIA, according to socialists, is to repress political dissenters at home and to influence the makeup of political regimes abroad. Socialists accept the analysis that the secret police includes not only the FBI and CIA but also intelligence networks that exist in other government agencies, such as the following: the Internal Revenue Service, Federal Bureau of Narcotics, Immigration and Naturalization Service, Postal Service. Accordingly, these networks together form one of the most powerful forces in setting the direction of American politics. Sometimes these agencies act independently of the President, their official controller, and other times they act at his behest. There are times also when these agencies act on behalf of elites directly rather than through the office of the Presidency. For example, some individuals who have investigated the events surrounding the 1963 assassination of President John Kennedy hold to the belief that the CIA was, in one way or another, involved in the assassination. In 1974/75 Daniel Schorr, a CBS television correspondent, publicized these allegations with the result that the Rockefeller Commission was forced to include this question in their investigation of the CIA. At the time of this writing the pressure on government has not been sufficient to force the release of the conclusions of this assassination investigation. It has also been hypothesized by investigative reporters researching the events surrounding Watergate that the CIA was involved in instigating, organizing, or furthering disclosures of the Watergate activities and the coverup.[1]

Socialists hold that although the major official mission of the CIA is to counter supposed Soviet threats, the CIA is relatively ineffective in this area due to the strength and effectiveness of the KGB, the Soviet secret police. The CIA's greatest area of effectiveness is in the weak and underdeveloped countries where it can develop and control the secret police, government, and military forces of these countries.[2] Socialists further believe that the CIA encourages and publicizes dissent, and its own activities in combatting this dissent, in order to justify its existence. The FBI operates in the same manner. In 1969/1970 seven prominent antiwar advocates, Jerry Rubin, Dave Dellinger, Tom Hayden, Rennie Davis, Bobby Seale, Abbie Hoffman, and John Froines, were tried for conspiring against the United States by collectively discussing means by which they could together force the Vietnamese war to a conclusion, and crossing state lines with intent to incite a riot. The United States government, in its attempt to prosecute the Chicago Seven, brought forth to the witness stand a number of FBI informants. Though they had very little information regarding the alleged conspiracy, their presence at the trial allowed the FBI to publicize its own activities. This had the effect of showing the American public that they were vigilant and on guard.

Socialists believe the CIA and FBI and other secret police agencies must be eliminated. Their real purpose is not in furthering the security of individual Americans, but rather in extending their control over Americans by undemocratic means. Realization that control of the American people is the real purpose of the secret police is the first step toward weakening their power over us. Exposure of agents, stealing their documents, making their activities publicly known, and openly conducting activities of dissent is one strategy to counter their repression. The surest defense against control of dissent by the secret police is to organize open protest movements with large numbers of participants and leaders. If policy formation is conducted openly no small number of agent provocateurs can work their way into positions of power and influence in these movements for long—they will soon be recognized. The surest way to fall under the prey of the secret police is to follow their model of organizing secret groups. Secret groups are of necessity small and easily manipulated by a few persons.

Elimination of these secret police agencies by itself is not enough, for they are merely one instrument of the corporate elites who control the entire American political process. Eradication of the capitalist corporate economy is the prime goal for socialists. The secret police is only one part of this visible power elite. Any analysis of its organization, purposes, and activities, and any strategy for eliminating it must include an analysis and strategy for dealing with the overall power elite.

In the articles you will read in this chapter the secret police establishment is analyzed, and the above questions and following issues are dealt with.

The "Report to the President by the (Rockefeller) Commission on CIA Activities Within the United States," the summary of which follows, examined alleged abuses of the CIA. These included opening of mail, establishment of a special operations group to investigate dissident organizations, and drug dealing.

The CIA, established under the National Security Act of 1947, was, according to its statutory authority, only to engage in the gathering and collation of information received from abroad. It was not given any legal authority to gather domestic intelligence nor to engage in political or military activities at home or abroad.

The Rockefeller report found that the CIA did engage in domestic activities contrary to its charter. It found, for example, that from 1953 to 1973 more than 2.5 million pieces of mail sent to or from the USSR were either opened or photographed. This was done in collusion with the Postal Service. The Commission also found that the CIA, in 1967, established a special operations group known as Operation CHAOS. The purpose of this group was to collect information about, and to evaluate the extent to which foreign powers influenced domestic dissidents. CHAOS accumulated a huge amount of material on domestic dissidents who had no relation to any foreign power. During the period of its known operation, Operation CHAOS compiled files on more than 7000 American citizens and used its computers to index more than 300,000 persons and their organizations considered by the CIA to be politically questionable. The Commission also found that the CIA tested the influence of LSD on people unaware that they were being experimented on. One person died as a result of these tests and others were permanently mentally impaired.[3] The Commission concluded that although these activities were illegal the correction of the abuses should be left to the CIA and the President, in other words, that all evils should be self-corrected. Congress should play merely a secondary role: to create legislation making acts such as the above illegal. The CIA, according to these proposals, was to ensure that these illegal activities would not take place again.

The underlying assumption of the Rockefeller Commission report is that the CIA must necessarily exist. Fundamentally, the CIA is a key instrument in conducting foreign affairs and protecting the United States from its enemies abroad. Nowhere was the CIA strongly criticized. No important CIA official was publically condemned. The CIA's basic purpose as an institution was upheld. The Commission's report was an expression of the conservative perspective on the secret police; it is vital to the United States, and the Commission did everything it could to protect the CIA and to limit criticism of it. The Commission Report's underlying thesis is that the public must understand the necessity for such a secret agency, and like the Commission itself must limit its criticism.

Richard J. Barnet, in his article "Dirty Tricks and the Intelligence Underworld," maintains that the CIA actually engages in the formation and conduct of U.S. foreign policy, almost always acting illegally. Not only does the CIA gather intelligence information, it even takes political and military actions. The CIA acts primarily in the Third World—Africa, Asia, Latin America, the Middle East—in an attempt to influence the construction and operation of governments there. According to Barnet, the CIA should exist as an information-gathering agency to defend the United States from terrorist acts, and to uncover information regarding other countries. The underlying assumption of this statement is that the United

States needs some sort of intelligence agency to defend its sovereignty. Barnet is against the dirty tricks utilized by the CIA but he is not opposed to the CIA's acting in accordance with its charter. It is his belief that the illegal actions of the CIA have detracted from the liberties of American citizens and have not increased their security. He calls for gathering intelligence openly while opposing covert operations.

This position seems typical of the liberal predicament. Two opposing principles, mutually contradictory, are set up and agreed with. Actions in specific circumstances are to be decided upon in the light of these two principles. Sometimes one will be upheld, other times its opposite will be followed. Still other times both will be attempted to be followed at one and the same time. Liberals are often caught between these opposing concepts and are rarely certain which one to select. This is why liberals who hold good credentials can come down on opposite sides of a question and still be seen to be upholding liberal principles.

Alan Wolfe, in his article "Repression Through Political Intelligence" maintains that all intelligence agencies have two purposes: (1) To repress political dissidents; and (2) to influence and control foreign governments. He believes that private intelligence operations, such as the Pinkerton Detective Agency, and public agencies, such as the FBI and CIA, act in the interest of the power elite. They act for management, against labor; for government, against its constituents; for foreign policy decision-makers, against foreign governments. Wolfe also holds that these agencies often publicize their illegal achievements so that people will be frightened of them. People will fear that they are being watched and followed and, it is to be hoped, will not act as dissidents. The spreading of this fear of the omnipotence and omnipresence of secret police agencies allows them to extend their control beyond what their actual resources will allow.

Socialists believe that the secret police of both official government and corporate enterprise often coordinate their activities and goals. They claim that one notable example of this joint operation was the overthrow of President Salvador Allende of Chile in 1973. Together, the CIA, International Telephone and Telegraph (ITT)—Chile, and Anaconda Copper Co., successfully worked to eliminate the government of President Allende. This was accomplished, they say, by destroying the economy through pushing down copper prices, withdrawing bank credits, and reducing all but military aid. The objective of these actions was to activate potential antisocialist forces in Chile against Allende, particularly the military and the middle class. As much as possible the CIA and American corporations wanted to cover up their own direct involvement in the overthrow of the Chilean government. They made it appear that the overthrow was a result of a popular uprising against the policies of Allende.[4]

Socialists believe that the solution to the abuses of the secret police lies in the elimination of these secret police agencies. Since they rule in the name of corporations and national elites, and their power in large measure derives from these elites, a strategy of dismantlement of these agencies must include an attack on the ruling elites themselves. The attack must be general because the secret police is only one expression of the hegemony of the ruling class.[5]

NOTES

1. See the articles of Seymour M. Hersh in *The New York Times*, 1973 through 1975. *Washington Post* reporters Carl Bernstein and Bob Woodward, who investigated Watergate and its cover-up, wrote about the CIA's role in the events surrounding Watergate in *All the President's Men*, New York: Simon & Schuster, 1974.

2. On this issue see in particular Philip Agee, *Inside the Company: CIA Diary*. New York: Stonehill Press, 1975. He deals in great detail with CIA involvement in Mexico, Ecuador, and Uruguay. See also, Victor Marchetti, John D. Marks, *The CIA and the Cult of Intelligence*. New York: Alfred Knopf Pub., 1974; and David Wise, Thomas B. Ross, *The Invisible Government*. New York: Random House, 1964.

3. An excellent analysis of the CIA's involvement in drug running can be found in Alfred W. McCoy, with Cathleen B. Read, and L.P. Adams II, *The Politics of Heroin in South East Asia*. New York: Harper & Row, 1972.

4. See, James F. Petras, Robert LaPorte, Jr., "Chile: No," *Foreign Policy* (Summer, 1972), pp. 132–158.

5. For an analysis of the FBI see Fred J. Cook, *The FBI Nobody Knows*. New York: The Macmillan Co., 1964. See also Max Lowenthal, *The Federal Bureau of Investigation*. New York: Harcourt Brace, Jovanovich, 1972.

Conservative

From: Summary of: report to the president by the (Rockefeller) commission on C.I.A. activities within the United States.

D. Significant areas of investigation

Introduction. Domestic activities of the CIA raising substantial questions of compliance with the law have been closely examined by the Commission to determine the context in which they were performed, the pressures of the times, the relationship of the activity to the Agency's foreign intelligence assignment and to other CIA activities, the procedures used to authorize and conduct the activity, and the extent and effect of the activity.

In describing and assessing each such activity, it has been necessary to consider both that activity's relationship to the legitimate national security needs of the nation and the threat such activities might pose to individual rights of Americans and to a society founded on the need for government, as well as private citizens, to obey the law.

1. The CIA's mail intercepts (Chapter 9)

Findings. At the time the CIA came into being, one of the highest national intelligence priorities was to gain an understanding of the Soviet Union and its worldwide activities affecting our national security.

In this context, the CIA began in 1952 a program of surveying mail between the United States and the Soviet Union as it passed through a New York postal facility. In 1953 it began opening some of this mail. The program was expanded over the following two decades and ultimately involved the opening of many letters and the analysis of envelopes, or "covers," of a great many more letters.

The New York mail intercept was designed to attempt to identify persons within the United States who were cooperating with the Soviet Union and its intelligence forces to harm the United States. It was also intended to determine technical communications procedures and mail censorship techniques used by the Soviets.

The Director of the Central Intelligence Agency approved commencement of the New York mail intercept in 1952. During the ensuing years, so far as the record shows, Postmasters General Summerfield, Day, and Blount were informed of the program in varying degrees, as was Attorney General Mitchell. Since 1958, the FBI was aware of this program and received 57,000 items from it.

A 1962 CIA memorandum indicates the Agency was aware that the mail openings would be viewed as violating federal criminal laws prohibiting obstruction or delay of the mails.

In the last year before the termination of this program, out of 4,350,000 items of mail sent to and from the Soviet Union, the New York intercept examined the outside of 2,300,000 of these items, photographed 33,000 envelopes, and opened 8,700.

The mail intercept was terminated in 1973 when the Chief Postal Inspector refused to allow its continuation without an up-to-date high-level approval.

The CIA also ran much smaller mail intercepts for brief periods in San Francisco between 1969 and 1971 and in the territory of Hawaii during 1954 and 1955. For a short period in 1957, mail in transit between foreign countries was intercepted in New Orleans.

Conclusions. While in operation, the CIA's domestic mail opening programs were unlawful. United States statutes specifically forbid opening the mail.

The mail openings also raise Constitutional questions under the Fourth Amendment guarantees against unreasonable search, and the scope of the New York project poses possible difficulties with the First Amendment rights of speech and press.

Mail cover operations (examining and copying of envelopes only) are legal when carried out in compliance with postal regulations on a limited and selective basis involving matters of national security. The New York mail intercept did not meet these criteria.

The nature and degree of assistance given by the CIA to the FBI in the New York mail project indicate that the CIA's primary purpose eventually became participation with the FBI in internal security functions. Accordingly, the CIA's participation was prohibited under the National Security Act.

RECOMMENDATION (13). a) The President should instruct the Director of Central Intelligence that the CIA is not to engage again in domestic *mail openings* except with express statutory authority in time of war. b) The President should instruct the Director of Central Intelligence that *mail cover* examinations are to be in compliance with postal regulations; they are to be undertaken only in furtherance of the CIA's legitimate activities and then only on a limited and selected basis clearly involving matters of national security.

2. Intelligence community coordination (Chapter 10)

Findings. As a result of growing domestic disorder, the Department of Justice, starting in 1967 at the direction of Attorney General Ramsey Clark, coordinated a series of secret units and interagency groups in an effort to collate and evaluate intelligence relating to these events. These efforts continued until 1973.

The interagency committees were designed for analytic and not operational purposes. They were created as a result of White House pressure which began in 1967, because the FBI performed only limited evaluation and analysis of the information it collected on these events. The stated purpose of CIA's participation was to supply relevant foreign intelligence and to furnish advice on evaluation techniques.

The CIA was reluctant to become unduly involved in these committees, which had problems of domestic unrest as their princi-

pal focus. It repeatedly refused to assign full-time personnel to any of them.

The most active of the committees was the Intelligence Evaluation Staff, which met from January 1971 to May 1973. A CIA liaison officer attended over 100 weekly meetings of the Staff,[1] some of which concerned drafts of reports which had no foreign aspects. With the exception of one instance, there is no evidence that he acted in any capacity other than as an adviser on foreign intelligence, and, to some degree, as an editor.

On one occasion the CIA liaison officer appears to have caused a CIA agent to gather domestic information which was reported to the Intelligence Evaluation Staff.

The Commission found no evidence of other activities by the CIA that were conducted on behalf of the Department of Justice groups except for the supplying of appropriate foreign intelligence and advice on evaluation techniques.

Conclusions. The statutory prohibition on internal security functions does not preclude the CIA from providing foreign intelligence or advice on evaluation techniques to interdepartmental intelligence evaluation organizations having some domestic aspects. The statute was intended to promote coordination, not compartmentation of intelligence between governmental departments.

The attendance of the CIA liaison officer at over 100 meetings of the Intelligence Evaluation Staff, some of them concerned wholly with domestic matters, nevertheless created at least the appearance of impropriety. The Director of Central Intelligence was well advised to approach such participation reluctantly.

The liaison officer acted improperly in the one instance in which he directed an agent to gather domestic information within the United States which was reported to the Intelligence Evaluation Staff.

Much of the problem stemmed from the absence in government of any organization capable of adequately analyzing intelligence collected by the FBI on matters outside the purview of CIA.

RECOMMENDATION (14). a) A capability should be developed within the FBI, or elsewhere in the Department of Justice, to evaluate, analyze, and coordinate intelligence and counterintelligence collected by the FBI concerning espionage, terrorism, and other related matters of internal security. b) The CIA should restrict its participation in any joint intelligence committees to foreign intelligence matters. c) The FBI should be encouraged to continue to look to the CIA for such foreign intelligence and counter-intelligence as is relevant to FBI needs.

3. Special Operations Group—"Operation CHAOS" (Chapter 11)

Findings. The late 1960's and early 1970's were marked by widespread violence and civil disorders. Demonstrations, marches and protest assemblies were frequent in a number of cities. Many universities and college campuses became places of disruption and unrest. Government facilities were picketed and sometimes invaded. Threats of bombing and bombing incidents occurred frequently. In Washington and other major cities, special security measures had to be instituted to control the access to public buildings.

Responding to Presidential requests made in the face of growing domestic disorder, the Director of Central Intelligence in August 1967 established a Special Operations Group within the CIA to collect, coordinate, evaluate and report on the extent of foreign influence on domestic dissidence.

The Group's activities, which later came to be known as Operation CHAOS, led the CIA to collect information on dissident Americans from CIA field stations overseas and from the FBI.

Although the stated purpose of the Operation was to determine whether there were any foreign contacts with American dissident groups, it resulted in the accumulation of considerable material on domestic dissidents and their activities.

During six years, the Operation compiled some 13,000 different files, including files on 7,200 American citizens. The documents in these files and related materials included the names of more than 300,000 persons and organizations, which were entered into a computerized index.

This information was kept closely guarded within the CIA. Using this information, personnel of the Group prepared 3,500 memoranda for internal use; 3,000 memoranda for dissemination to the FBI; and 37 memoranda for distribution to White House and other top level officials in the government.

The staff assigned to the Operation was steadily enlarged in response to repeated Presidential requests for additional information, ultimately reaching a maximum of 52 in 1971. Because of excessive isolation, the Operation was substantially insulated from meaningful review within the Agency, including review by the Counterintelligence Staff—of which the Operation was technically a part.

Commencing in late 1969, Operation CHAOS used a number of agents to collect intelligence abroad on any foreign connections with American dissident groups. In order to have sufficient "cover" for these agents, the Operation recruited persons from domestic dissident groups or recruited others and instructed them to associate with such groups in this country.

Most of the Operation's recruits were not directed to collect information domestically on American dissidents. On a number of occasions, however, such information was reported by the recruits while they were developing dissident credentials in the United States, and the information was retained in the files of the Operation. On three occasions, an agent of the Operation was specifically directed to collect domestic intelligence.

No evidence was found that any Operation CHAOS agent used or was directed by the Agency to use electronic surveillance, wiretaps or break-ins in the United States against any dissident individual or group.

Activity of the Operation decreased substantially by mid-1972. The Operation was formally terminated in March 1974.

Conclusions. Some domestic activities of Operation CHAOS unlawfully exceeded the CIA's statutory authority, even though the declared mission of gathering intelligence abroad as to foreign influence on domestic dissident activities was proper.

Most significantly, the Operation became a repository for large quantities of information on the domestic activities of American citizens. This information was derived principally from FBI reports or from overt sources and not from clandestine collection by the CIA, and much of it was not directly related to the question of the existence of foreign connections.

It was probably necessary for the CIA to accumulate an information base on domestic dissident activities in order to assess fairly whether the activities had foreign connections. The FBI would collect information but would not evaluate it. But the accumulation of domestic data in the Operation exceeded what was reasonably required to make such an assessment and was thus improper.

The use of agents of the Operation on three occasions to gather information within the United States on strictly domestic matters was beyond the CIA's authority. In addition the intelligence disseminations and those portions of a major study prepared by the Agency which dealt with purely domestic matters were improper.

The isolation of Operation CHAOS within the CIA and its independence from supervision by the regular chain of command within the clandestine service made it possible for the activities of the Operation to stray over the bounds of the Agency's authority without the knowledge of senior officials. The absence of any regular review of these activities prevented timely correction of such missteps as did occur.

RECOMMENDATION (15). a) Presidents should refrain from directing the CIA to perform what are essentially internal security tasks. b) The CIA should resist any efforts, whatever their origin, to involve it again in such improper activities. c) The Agency should guard against allowing any component (like the Special Operations Group) to become so self-contained and isolated from top leadership that regular supervision and review are lost. d) The files of the CHAOS project which have no foreign intelligence value should be destroyed by the Agency at the conclusion of the current congressional investigations, or as soon thereafter as permitted by law.

4. Protection of the agency against threats of violence—Office of Security (Chapter 12)

Findings. The CIA was not immune from the threats of violence and disruption during the period of domestic unrest between 1967 and 1972. The Office of Security was charged throughout this period with the responsibility of ensuring the continued functioning of the CIA.

The Office therefore, from 1967 to 1970, had its field officers collect information from published materials, law enforcement authorities, other agencies and college officials before recruiters were sent to some campuses. Monitoring and communications support was provided to recruiters when trouble was expected.

The Office was also responsible, with the approval of the Director of Central Intelligence, for a program from February 1967 to December 1968, which at first monitored, but later infiltrated, dissident organizations in the Washington, D.C., area to determine if the groups planned any activities against CIA or other government installations.

At no time were more than 12 persons performing these tasks, and they performed them on a part-time basis. The project was terminated when the Washington Metropolitan Police Department developed its own intelligence capability.

In December, 1967, the Office began a continuing study of dissident activity in the United States, using information from published and other voluntary knowledgeable sources. The Office produced weekly Situation Information Reports analyzing dissident activities and providing calendars of future events. Calendars were given to the Secret

Service, but the CIA made no other disseminations outside the Agency. About 500 to 800 files were maintained on dissenting organizations and individuals. Thousands of names in the files were indexed. Report publication was ended in late 1972, and the entire project was ended in 1973.

Conclusions. The program under which the Office of Security rendered assistance to Agency recruiters on college campuses was justified as an exercise of the Agency's responsibility to protect its own personnel and operations. Such support activities were not undertaken for the purpose of protecting the facilities or operations of other governmental agencies, or to maintain public order or enforce laws.

The Agency should not infiltrate a dissident group for security purposes unless there is a clear danger to Agency installations, operations or personnel, and investigative coverage of the threat by the FBI and local law enforcement authorities is inadequate. The Agency's infiltration of dissident groups in the Washington area went far beyond steps necessary to protect the Agency's own facilities, personnel and operations, and therefore exceeded the CIA's statutory authority.

In addition, the Agency undertook to protect other government departments and agencies—a police function prohibited to it by statute.

Intelligence activity directed toward learning from what sources a domestic dissident group receives its financial support within the United States, and how much income it has, is no part of the authorized security operations of the Agency. Neither is it the function of the Agency to compile records on who attends peaceful meetings of such dissident groups, or what each speaker has to say (unless it relates to disruptive or violent activity which may be directed against the Agency).

The Agency's actions in contributing funds, photographing people, activities and cars, and following people home were unreasonable under the circumstances and therefore exceeded the CIA's authority.

With certain exceptions, the program under which the Office of Security (without infiltration) gathered, organized and analyzed information about dissident groups for purposes of security was within the CIA's authority.

The accumulation of reference files of dissident organizations and their leaders was appropriate both to evaluate the risks posed to the Agency and to develop an understanding of dissident groups and their differences for security clearance purposes. But the accumulation of information on domestic activities went beyond what was required by the Agency's legitimate security needs and therefore exceeded the CIA's authority.

RECOMMENDATION (16). The CIA should not infiltrate dissident groups or other organizations of Americans in the absence of a written determination by the Director of Central Intelligence that such action is necessary to meet a clear danger to Agency facilities, operations, or personnel and that adequate coverage by law enforcement agencies is unavailable.

RECOMMENDATION (17). All files on individuals accumulated by the Office of Security in the program relating to dissidents should be identified, and, except where necessary for a legitimate foreign intelligence activity, be destroyed at the conclusion of the current congressional investigations, or as soon thereafter as permitted by law.

5. Other investigations by the Office of Security (Chapter 13)

A. Security clearance investigations of prospective employees and operatives

Findings and conclusions. The Office of Security routinely conducts standard security investigations of persons seeking affiliation with the Agency. In doing so, the Office is performing the necessary function of screening persons to whom it will make available classified information. Such investigations are necessary, and no improprieties were found in connection with them.

B. Investigations of possible breaches of security

1. PERSONS INVESTIGATED

Findings. The Office of Security has been called upon on a number of occasions to investigate specific allegations that intelligence sources and methods were threatened by unauthorized disclosures. The Commission's inquiry concentrated on those investigations which used investigative means intruding on the privacy of the subjects, including physical and electronic surveillance, unauthorized entry, mail covers and intercepts, and reviews of individual federal tax returns.

The large majority of these investigations were directed at persons affiliated with the Agency—such as employees, former employees, and defectors and other foreign nationals used by the Agency as intelligence sources.

A few investigations involving intrusions on personal privacy were directed at subjects with no relationship to the Agency. The Commission has found no evidence that any such investigations were directed against any congressman, judge, or other public official. Five were directed against newsmen, in an effort to determine their sources of leaked classified information, and nine were directed against other United States citizens.

The CIA's investigations of newsmen to determine their sources of classified information stemmed from pressures from the White House and were partly a result of the FBI's unwillingness to undertake such investigations. The FBI refused to proceed without an advance opinion that the Justice Department would prosecute if a case were developed.

Conclusions. Investigations of allegations against Agency employees and operatives are a reasonable exercise of the Director's statutory duty to protect intelligence sources and methods from unauthorized disclosure if the investigations are lawfully conducted. Such investigations also assist the Director in the exercise of his unreviewable authority to terminate the employment of any Agency employee. They are proper unless their principal purpose becomes law-enforcement or the maintenance of internal security.

The Director's responsibility to protect intelligence sources and methods is not so broad as to permit investigations of persons having no relationship whatever with the Agency. The CIA has no authority to investigate newsmen simply because they have published leaked classified information. Investigations by the CIA should be limited to persons presently or formerly affiliated with the Agency, directly or indirectly.

RECOMMENDATION (18). a) The Director of Central Intelligence should issue clear guidelines setting forth the situations in which the CIA is justified in conducting its own investigation of individuals presently or formerly affiliated with it. b) The guidelines should permit the CIA to conduct investigations of such persons only when the Director of Central Intelligence first determines that the investigation is necessary to protect intelligence sources and methods the disclosure of which might endanger the national security. c) Such investigations must be coordinated with the FBI whenever substantial evidence suggesting espionage or violation of a federal criminal statute is discovered.

RECOMMENDATION (19). a) In cases involving serious or continuing security violations, as determined by the Security Committee of the United States Intelligence Board, the Committee should be authorized to recommend in writing to the Director of Central Intelligence (with a copy to the National Security Council) that the case be referred to the FBI for futher investigation, under procedures to be developed by the Attorney General. b) These procedures should include a requirement that the FBI accept such referrals without regard to whether a favorable prosecutive opinion is issued by the Justice Department. The CIA should not engage in such further investigations.

RECOMMENDATION (20). The CIA and other components and agencies of the intelligence community should conduct periodic reviews of all classified material originating within those departments or agencies, with a view to declassifying as much of that material as possible. The purpose of such review would be to assure the public that it has access to all information that should properly be disclosed.

RECOMMENDATION (21). The Commission endorses legislation, drafted with appropriate safeguards of the constitutional rights of all affected individuals, which would make it a criminal offense for employees or former employees of the CIA wilfully to divulge to any unauthorized person classified information pertaining to foreign intelligence or the collection thereof obtained during the course of their employment.

2. INVESTIGATIVE TECHNIQUES

Findings. Even an investigation within the CIA's authority must be conducted by lawful means. Some of the past investigations by the Office of Security within the United States were conducted by means which were invalid at the time. Others might have been lawful when conducted, but would be impermissible today.

Some investigations involved physical surveillance of the individuals concerned, possibly in conjunction with other methods of investigation. The last instance of physical surveillance by the Agency within the United States occurred in 1973.

The investigation disclosed the domestic use of 32 wiretaps, the last in 1965; 32 instances of bugging, the last in 1968; and 12 break-ins, the last in 1971. None of these activities was conducted under a judicial warrant, and only one with the written approval of the Attorney General.

Information from the income tax records of 16 persons was obtained from the Internal Revenue Service by the CIA in order to help determine whether the taxpayer was a security risk with possible connections to foreign groups. The CIA did not employ the existing statutory and regulatory procedures for obtaining such records from the IRS.

In 91 instances, mail covers (the photographing of the front and back of an envelope) were employed, and in 12 instances letters were intercepted and opened.

The state of the CIA records on these activities is such that it is often difficult to determine why the investigation occurred in the first place, who authorized the special coverage, and what the results were. Although there was testimony that these activities were frequently known to the Director of Central Intelligence and sometimes to the Attorney General, the files often are insufficient to confirm such information.

Conclusions. The use of physical surveillance is not unlawful unless it reaches the point of harassment. The unauthorized entries described were illegal when conducted and would be illegal if conducted today. Likewise, the review of individuals' federal tax returns and the interception and opening of mail violated specific statutes and regulations prohibiting such conduct.

Since the constitutional and statutory constraints applicable to the use of electronic eavesdropping (bugs and wiretaps) have been evolving over the years, the Commission deems it impractical to apply those changing standards on a case-by-case basis. The Commission does believe that while some of the instances of electronic eavesdropping were proper when conducted, many were not. To be lawful today, such activities would require at least the written approval of the Attorney General on the basis of a finding that the national security is involved and that the case has significant foreign connections.

RECOMMENDATION (22). The CIA should not undertake physical surveillance (defined as systematic observation) of Agency employees, contractors or related personnel within the United States without first obtaining written approval of the Director of Central Intelligence.

RECOMMENDATION (23). In the United States and its possessions, the CIA should not intercept wire or oral communications[2] or otherwise engage in activities that would require a warrant if conducted by a law enforcement agency. Responsibility for such activities belongs with the FBI.

RECOMMENDATION (24). The CIA should strictly adhere to established legal procedures governing access to federal income tax information.

RECOMMENDATION (25). CIA investigation records should show that each investigation was duly authorized, and by whom, and should clearly set forth the factual basis for undertaking the investigation and the results of the investigation.

C. Handling of defectors

Findings. The Office of Security is charged with providing security for persons who have defected to the United States. Generally a defector can be processed and placed into society in a few months, but one defector was involuntarily confined at a CIA installation for three years. He was held in solitary confinement under spartan living conditions. The CIA maintained the long confinement because of doubts about the bona fides of the defector. This confinement was approved by the Director of Central Intelligence; and the FBI, Attorney General, United States Intelligence Board and selected members of Congress were aware to some extent of the confinement. In one other case a defector was physically abused; the Director of Central Intelligence discharged the employee involved.

Conclusions. Such treatment of individuals by an agency of the United States is unlawful. The Director of Central Intelligence and the Inspector General must be alert to prevent repetitions.

6. Involvement of the CIA in improper activities for the White House (Chapter 14)

Findings. During 1971, at the request of various members of the White House staff, the CIA provided alias documents and disguise material, a tape recorder, camera, film and film processing to E. Howard Hunt. It also prepared a psychological profile of Dr. Daniel Ellsberg.

Some of this equipment was later used without the knowledge of the CIA in connection with various improper activities, including the entry into the office of Dr. Lewis Fielding, Ellsberg's psychiatrist.

Some members of the CIA's medical staff who participated in the preparation of the Ellsberg profile knew that one of its purposes was to support a public attack on Ellsberg. Except for this fact, the investigation has disclosed no evidence that the CIA knew or had reason to know that the assistance it gave would be used for improper purposes.

President Nixon and his staff also insisted in this period that the CIA turn over to the President highly classified files relating to the Lebanon landings, the Bay of Pigs, the Cuban missile crisis, and the Vietnam War. The request was made on the ground that these files were needed by the President in the performance of his duties, but the record shows the purpose, undisclosed to the CIA, was to serve the President's personal political ends.

The Commission has also investigated the response of the CIA to the investigations following the Watergate arrests. Beginning in June 1972, the CIA received various requests for information and assistance in connection with these investigations. In a number of instances, its responses were either incomplete or delayed and some materials that may or may not have contained relevant information were destroyed. The Commission feels that this conduct reflects poor judgment on the part of the CIA, but it has found no evidence that the CIA participated in the Watergate break-in or in the post-Watergate cover-up by the White House.

Conclusions. Providing the assistance requested by the White House, including the alias and disguise materials, the camera and the psychological profile on Ellsberg, was not related to the performance by the Agency of its authorized intelligence functions and was therefore improper.

No evidence has been disclosed, however, except as noted in connection with the Ellsberg profile, that the CIA knew or had reason to know that its assistance would be used in connection with improper activities. Nor has any evidence been disclosed indicating that the CIA participated in the planning or carrying out of either the

Fielding or Watergate break-ins. The CIA apparently was unaware of the break-ins until they were reported in the media.

The record does show, however, that individuals in the Agency failed to comply with the normal control procedures in providing assistance to E. Howard Hunt. It also shows that the Agency's failure to cooperate fully with ongoing investigations following Watergate was inconsistent with its obligations.

Finally, the Commission concludes that the requests for assistance by the White House reflect a pattern for actual and attempted misuse of the CIA by the Nixon administration.

RECOMMENDATION (26). a) A single and exclusive high-level channel should be established for transmission of all White House staff requests to the CIA. This channel should run between an officer of the National Security Council staff designated by the President and the office of the Director or his Deputy. b) All Agency officers and employees should be instructed that any direction or request reaching them directly and out of regularly established channels should be immediately reported to the Director of Central Intelligence.

7. Domestic Activities of the Directorate of Operations (Chapter 15)

Findings and Conclusions. In support of its responsibility for the collection of foreign intelligence and conduct of covert operations overseas, the CIA's Directorate of Operations engages in a variety of activities within the United States.

A. Overt collection of foreign intelligence within the United States

One division of the Directorate of Operations collects foreign intelligence within the United States from residents, business firms, and other organizations willing to assist the Agency. This activity is conducted openly by officers who identify themselves as CIA employees. Such sources of information are not compensated.

In connection with these collection activities, the CIA maintains approximately 50,000 active files which include details of the CIA's relationships with these voluntary sources and the results of a federal agency name check.

The division's collection efforts have been almost exclusively confined to foreign economic, political, military, and operational topics.

Commencing in 1969, however, some activities of the division resulted in the collection of limited information with respect to American dissidents and dissident groups. Although the focus was on foreign contacts of these groups, background information on domestic dissidents was also collected. Between 1969 and 1974, when this activity was formally terminated, 400 reports were made to Operation CHAOS.

In 1972 and 1973, the division obtained and transmitted, to other parts of the CIA, information about telephone calls between the Western Hemisphere (including the United States) and two other countries. The information was limited to names, telephone numbers, and locations of callers and recipients. It did not include the content of the conversations.

This division also occasionally receives reports concerning criminal activity within the United States. Pursuant to written regulations, the source or a report of the information received is referred to the appropriate law enforcement agency.

The CIA's efforts to collect foreign intelligence from residents of the United States willing to assist the CIA are a valid and necessary element of its responsibility. Not only do these persons provide a large reservoir of foreign intelligence; they are by far the most accessible source of such information.

The division's files on American citizens and firms representing actual or potential sources of information constitute a necessary part of its legitimate intelligence activities. They do not appear to be vehicles for the collection or communication of derogatory, embarrassing, or sensitive information about American citizens.

The division's efforts, with few exceptions, have been confined to legitimate topics.

The collection of information with respect to American dissident groups exceeded legitimate foreign intelligence collection and was beyond the proper scope of CIA activity. This impropriety was recognized in some of the division's own memoranda.

The Commission was unable to discover any specific purpose for the collection of telephone toll call information or any use of that information by the Agency. In the absence of a valid purpose, such collection is improper.

B. Provision and control of cover for CIA personnel

CIA personnel engaged in clandestine foreign intelligence activities cannot travel, live or perform their duties openly as Agency employees. Accordingly, virtually all CIA personnel serving abroad and many in the United States assume a "cover" as employees of another government agency or of a commercial enterprise. CIA involvement in certain activities, such as research and development projects, are also sometimes conducted under cover.

CIA's cover arrangements are essential to the CIA's performance of its foreign intelligence mission. The investigation has disclosed no instances in which domestic aspects of the CIA's cover arrangements involved any violations of law.

By definition, however, cover necessitates an element of deception which must be practiced within the United States as well as within foreign countries. This creates a risk of conflict with various regulatory statutes and other legal requirements. The Agency recognizes this risk. It has installed controls under which cover arrangements are closely supervised to attempt to ensure compliance with applicable laws.

C. Operating proprietary companies

The CIA uses proprietary companies to provide cover and perform administrative tasks without attribution to the Agency. Most of the large operating proprietaries—primarily airlines—have been liquidated, and the remainder engage in activities offering little or no competition to private enterprise.

The only remaining large proprietary activity is a complex of financial companies, with assets of approximately $20 million, that enable the Agency to administer certain sensitive trusts, annuities, escrows, insurance arrangements, and other benefits and payments provided to officers or contract employees without attribution to CIA. The remaining small operating proprietaries, generally having fewer than ten employees each, make nonattributable purchases of equipment and supplies.

Except as discussed in connection with the Office of Security (see Chapters 12 and 13), the Commission has found no evidence that any proprietaries have been used for operations against American citizens or investigation of their activities. All of them appear to be subject to close supervision and multiple financial controls within the Agency.

D. Development of contacts with foreign nationals

In connection with the CIA's foreign intelligence responsibilities, it seeks to develop contacts with foreign nationals within the United States. American citizens voluntarily assist in developing these contacts. As far as the Commission can find, these activities have not involved coercive methods.

These activities appear to be directed entirely to the production of foreign intelligence and to be within the authority of the CIA. We found no evidence that any of these activities have been directed against American citizens.

E. Assistance in narcotics control

The Directorate of Operations provides foreign intelligence support to the government's efforts to control the flow of narcotics and other dangerous drugs into this country. The CIA coordinates clandestine intelligence collection overseas and provides other government agencies with foreign intelligence on drug traffic.

From the beginning of such efforts in 1969, the CIA Director and other officials have instructed employees to make no attempt to gather information on Americans allegedly trafficking in drugs. If such information is obtained incidentally, it is transmitted to law enforcement agencies.

Concerns that the CIA's narcotics-related intelligence activities may involve the Agency in law enforcement or other actions directed against American citizens thus appear unwarranted.

Beginning in the fall of 1973, the Directorate monitored conversations between the United States and Latin America in an effort to identify narcotics traffickers. Three months after the program began, the General Counsel of the CIA was consulted. He issued an opinion that the program was illegal, and it was immediately terminated.

This monitoring, although a source of valuable information for enforcement officials, was a violation of a statute of the United States. Continuation of the operation for over three months without the knowledge of the Office of the General Counsel demonstrates the need for improved internal consultation. (See Recommendation 10.)

8. Domestic activities of the Directorate of Science and Technology (Chapter 16)

Findings and Conclusions. The CIA's Directorate of Science and Technology performs a variety of research and development and operational support functions for the Agency's foreign intelligence mission.

Many of these activities are performed in the United States and involve cooperation with private companies. A few of these activities were improper or questionable.

As part of a program to test the influence of drugs on humans, research included the administration of LSD to persons who were unaware that they were being tested. This was clearly illegal. One person died in 1953, apparently as a result. In 1963, following the Inspector General's discovery of these events, new stringent criteria were issued prohibiting drug testing by the CIA on unknowing persons. All drug testing programs were ended in 1967.

In the process of testing monitoring equipment for use overseas, the CIA has overheard conversations between Americans. The names of the speakers were not identified; the contents of the conversations were not disseminated. All recordings were destroyed when testing was concluded. Such testing should not be directed against unsuspecting persons in the United States. Most of the testing undertaken by the Agency could easily have been performed using only Agency personnel and with the full knowledge of those whose conversations were being recorded. This is the present Agency practice.

Other activities of this Directorate include the manufacture of alias credentials for use by CIA employees and agents. Alias credentials are necessary to facilitate CIA clandestine operations, but the strictest controls and accountability must be maintained over the use of such documents. Recent guidelines established by the Deputy Director for Operations to control the use of alias documentation appear adequate to prevent abuse in the future.

As part of another program, photographs taken by CIA aerial photography equipment are provided to civilian agencies of the government. Such photographs are used to assess natural disasters, conduct route surveys and forest inventories, and detect crop blight. Permitting civilian use of aerial photography systems is proper. The economy of operating but one aerial photography program dictates the use of these photographs for appropriate civilian purposes.

RECOMMENDATION (27). In accordance with its present guidelines, the CIA should not again engage in the testing of drugs on unsuspecting persons.

RECOMMENDATION (28). Testing of equipment for monitoring conversations should not involve unsuspecting persons living within the United States.

RECOMMENDATION (29). A civilian agency committee should be reestablished to oversee the civilian uses of aerial intelligence photography in order to avoid any concerns over the improper domestic use of a CIA-developed system.

9. CIA relationships with other federal, state, and local agencies (Chapter 17)

CIA operations touch the interest of many other agencies. The CIA, like other agencies of the government, frequently has occasion to give or receive assistance from other agencies. This investigation has concentrated on those relationships which raise substantial questions under the CIA's legislative mandate.

A. Federal Bureau of Investigation

Findings and Conclusions. The FBI counterintelligence operations often have positive intelligence ramifications. Likewise, legitimate domestic CIA activities occasionally cross the path of FBI investigations. Daily liaison is therefore necessary between the two agencies.

Much routine information is passed back and forth. Occasionally joint operations are conducted. The relationship between the agencies has, however, not been uniformly satisfactory over the years. Formal liaison was cut off from February 1970 to November 1972, but relationships have improved in recent years.

The relationship between the CIA and the FBI needs to be clarified and outlined in detail in order to ensure that the needs of national security are met without creating conflicts or gaps of jursidiction.

RECOMMENDATION (30). The Director of Central Intelligence and the Director of the FBI should prepare and submit for approval by the National Security Council a detailed agreement setting forth the jurisdiction of each agency and providing for effective liaison with respect to all matters of mutual concern. This agreement should be consistent with the provisions of law and with other applicable recommendations of this Report.

B. Narcotics Law Enforcement Agencies

Findings and Conclusions. Beginning in late 1970, the CIA assisted the Bureau of Narcotics and Dangerous Drugs (BNDD) to uncover possible corruption within that organization. The CIA used one of its proprietary companies to recruit agents for BNDD and gave them short instructional courses. Over two and one-half years, the CIA recruited 19 agents for the BNDD. The project was terminated in 1973.

The Director was correct in his written directive terminating the project. The CIA's participation in law enforcement activities in the course of these activities was forbidden by its statute. The Director and the Inspector General should be alert to prevent involvement of the Agency in similar enterprises in the future.

C. The Department of State

Findings and Conclusions. For more than 20 years, the CIA through a proprietary conducted a training school for foreign police and security officers in the United States under the auspices of the Agency for International Development of the Department of State. The proprietary also sold small amounts of licensed firearms and police equipment to the foreign officers and their departments.

The CIA's activities in providing educational programs for foreign police were not improper under the Agency's statute. Although the school was conducted within the United States through a CIA proprietary, it had no other significant domestic impact.

Engaging in the firearms business was a questionable activity for a government intelligence agency. It should not be repeated.

D. Funding requests from other federal agencies

In the spring of 1970, at the request of the White House, the CIA contributed $33,655.68 for payment of stationery and other costs for replies to persons who wrote the President after the invasion of Cambodia.

This use of CIA funds for a purpose unrelated to intelligence is improper. Steps should be taken to ensure against any repetition of such an incident.

E. State and local police

The CIA handles a variety of routine security matters through liaison with local police departments. In addition, it offered training courses from 1966 to 1973 to United States police officers on a variety of law enforcement techniques, and has frequently supplied equipment to state and local police.

In general, the coordination and cooperation between state and local law enforcement agencies and the CIA has been exemplary, based upon a desire to facilitate their respective legitimate aims and goals.

Most of the assistance rendered to state and local law enforcement agencies by the CIA has been no more than an effort to share with law enforcement authorities the benefits of new methods, techniques, and equipment developed or used by the Agency.

On a few occasions, however, the Agency has improperly become involved in actual police operations. Thus, despite a general rule against providing manpower to local police forces, the CIA has lent men, along with radio-equipped vehicles, to the Washington Metropolitan Police Department to help monitor anti-war demonstrations. It helped the same Department surveil a police informer. It also provided an interpreter to the Fairfax Country (Virginia) Police Department to aid in a criminal investigation.

In compliance with the spirit of a recent Act of Congress, the CIA terminated all but routine assistance to state and local law enforcement agencies in 1973. Such assistance is now being provided state and local agencies by the FBI. There is no impropriety in the CIA's furnishing the FBI with information on new technical developments which may be useful to local law enforcement.

For several years the CIA has given gratuities to local police officers who had been helpful to the Agency. Any such practice should be terminated.

The CIA has also received assistance from local police forces. Aside from routine matters, officers from such forces have occasionally assisted the Office of Security in the conduct of investigations. The CIA has occasionally obtained police badges and other identification for use as cover for its agents.

Except for one occasion when some local police assisted the CIA in an unauthorized entry, the assistance received by the CIA from state and local law enforcement authorities was proper. The use of police identification as a means of providing cover, while not strictly speaking a violation of the Agency's statutory authority as long as no police function is performed, is a practice subject to misunderstanding and should be avoided.

10. Indices and files on American citizens (Chapter 18)

Findings. Biographical information is a major resource of an intelligence agency. The CIA maintains a number of files and indices that include biographical information on Americans.

As a part of its normal process of indexing names and information of foreign intelligence interest, the Directorate of Operations has indexed some 7,000,000 names of all nationalities. An estimated 115,000 of these are believed to be American citizens.

Where a person is believed to be of possibly continuing intelligence interest, files to collect information as received are opened. An estimated 57,000 out of a total of 750,000 such files concern American citizens. For the most part, the names of Americans appear in indices and files as actual or potential sources of information or assistance to the CIA. In addition to these files, files on some 7,200 American citizens, relating primarily to their domestic activities, were, as already stated, compiled within the Directorate of Operations as part of Operation CHAOS.

The Directorate of Administration maintains a number of files on persons who have been associated with the CIA. These files are maintained for security, personnel, training, medical and payroll purposes. Very few are maintained on persons unaware that they have a relationship with the CIA. However, the Office of Security maintained files on American citizens associated with dissident groups who were never affiliated with the Agency because they were considered a threat to the physical security of Agency facilities and employees. These files were also maintained, in part, for use in future security clearance determinations. Dissemination of security files is restricted to persons with an operational need for them.

The Office of Legislative Counsel maintains files concerning its relationships with congressmen.

Conclusions. Although maintenance of most of the indices, files, and records of the Agency has been necessary and proper, the standards applied by the Agency at some points during its history have permitted the accumulation and indexing of materials not needed for legitimate intelligence or security purposes. Included in this category are many of the files related to Operation CHAOS and the activities of the Office of Security concerning dissident groups.

Constant vigilance by the Agency is essential to prevent the collection of information on United States citizens which is not needed for proper intelligence activities. The Executive Order recommended by the Commission (Recommendation 2) will ensure purging of non-essential or improper materials from Agency files.

NOTES

1. The liaison officer was Chief of the CIA's Special Operations Group which ran Operation CHAOS, discussed in Chapter 11 of this Report.

2. As defined in the Omnibus Crime Control and Safe Streets Act, 18 U.S.C. Secs. 2510–20.

Liberal

Richard J. Barnet.   Dirty tricks and the intelligence underworld.

After Watergate it is not difficult to make a strong case against secret intelligence operations. The costs and risks of maintaining an intelligence underworld sealed from public scrutiny and free from legislative accountability have become obvious. The "misuse" of the Central Intelligence Agency (CIA), one of the counts in the Article of Impeachment adopted by the Judiciary Committee, can occur whenever an insecure President feels tempted to use this classic instrument of dictatorial rule against some domestic "enemy." Although the CIA in the Watergate Affair demonstrated some resistance to improper involvement, there are no institutional safeguards to prevent wigs and burglary tools from being supplied to "the wrong people" again.

Former Attorney General Nicholas Katsenbach and others have persuasively argued that maintaining extensive clandestine operations endangers American democracy and should be ended. The danger is no less when the CIA and other intelligence agencies act "properly," i.e., when they perform the missions they are supposed to perform. CIA clandestine services represent a special sort of secret army. The very existence of such an army undermines American democracy because the people's elected representatives are supposed to decide when and where to go to war. The maintenance of a large bureaucracy whose purpose is deception breeds suspicion and cynicism about government in general.

Systematic lying to the public, an institutionalized habit in such bureaucracies, has eroded confidence in government to an unprecedented extent. Ironically, the widespread use of the political lie in the name of national security has helped undermine a crucial foundation stone of national security—public confidence. In the last days of the Nixon Administration, only about 25 percent of the American people had confidence in either the President or Congress.

The stock in trade of the intelligence underworld is deceit. Its purpose is to create contrived realities, to make things appear different from what they are, for the purpose of manipulation and subversion. More than 200 agents, according to a recent *New York Times* article, pose as businessmen abroad. The CIA has admitted that more than thirty journalists have been on its payroll since World War II. "Proprietary" corporations—Air America and other Agency fronts, fake foundations, student organizations and church organizations—are all part of the false-bottom world that has confused the American people as much as it has confounded foreign governments.

We have pretended to ourselves that we can support murder, arson, larceny and deceit abroad and still continue to enjoy democracy at home. Indeed, the official myth has been that unless the United States prosecutes the ''backalley war'' with all the brutality of which we are capable, we will lose democracy in America. The Watergate Effect suggests that the United States is not immune from social processes which have corrupted past empires. What the state does abroad has an impact on domestic society eventually. It is not possible to maintain a bureaucracy of hired killers, thieves and con men for use against foreigners who get in our way without soon feeling the effects at home. No system of law and order can survive in a schizophrenic environment in which government is invited to subsidize assassination and crop contamination abroad and at the same time is expected to turn square corners with its own citizens. That contradiction can perhaps be maintained for short periods of warfare (although we have seen how each war the United States has fought has taken its toll on civil liberties), but it cannot be maintained under a state of permanent warfare. In the backalley war there are no truces and no peace treaties.

The secrecy shrouding covert operations distorts the foreign policymaking process in a number of specific ways. First, covert operations are typically discussed by a small group with special clearances. (As a general rule, those able to get the clearances already have a vested interest in the operation.) Second, covert operations encourage adventurism because they create the impression, often falsely, that they can be disavowed if they fail. Third, covert operations often close options rather than open them. One of the reasons President Kennedy decided to go ahead with the Bay of Pigs operation was Allen Dulles' warning that the Cuban refugees recruited for it would expose it if they did not get the chance to carry their flag to Havana. Similarly, to protect the existence of secret bases in such places as Pakistan and Ethiopia, the United States has had to make special concessions to those countries it would not otherwise have made. Fourth, the lack of control over covert operations leads to minor diplomatic disasters, such as the recent incident in Thailand when a CIA agent faked a letter from a guerilla leader to the Bangkok government for the purpose of discrediting his movement. (The Thai government was not amused and the CIA station chief was recalled.)

In the name of national security

As Morton Halperin and Jeremy Stone have pointed out, the secrecy necessary to maintain an intelligence underworld distorts our constitutional processes in a number of ways. Congress loses its ability to monitor foreign policy when important operations such as the raids on North Vietnam in 1964 are concealed from it, and it is asked to make crucial decisions, such as the fateful Gulf of Tonkin resolution, on the basis of a highly misleading picture of reality. Similarly, it loses the power of control over the Treasury when concealed and unaccounted funds can be used at the discretion of the executive. Protecting foreign statesmen from embarrassment about their involvement with the Agency or concealing some of the Agency's own indiscretions become grounds for misleading or muzzling the press. National security is the holy oil that converts felonious acts into patriotic exploits.

The fundamental reason why the secret war bureaucracy threatens the rule of law is that by all democratic norms, it is inherently a criminal enterprise. Perjury, subornation, torture, property destruction, assassination, fraud, impersonation and a variety of other acts for which ordinary citizens go to jail become the dictates of duty. The activities of the intelligence underground are shrouded in secrecy because they violate some accepted principle of constitutional or international law. If there were no international consensus against staging coups, contaminating crops, assassinating leaders, bribing parliaments and suborning politicians, there would be no need for the elaborate shield of deception behind which these activities take place. Governments resort to clandestine operations precisely because they wish to act in contravention of established legal principles and specific promises they have made to the outside world and to their own people.

The dangers which a large extra-legal enterprise pose for the establishment of an international legal order or for domestic constitutional order in the United States are obvious. Even the highest officials of the intelligence community will admit publicly that there are risks. It is conventional to call for strict controls and better accountability, but there is a fundamental contradiction between the perceived need for a freewheeling, highly secret worldwide intelligence apparatus and effective political control. The handful of senators and congressmen who are permitted even a peek into the secret life of the United States government are, by some mysterious process of selection, wholly sympathetic with what Victor Marchetti and John Marks, coauthors of *The CIA and the Cult of Intelligence*, call the "clandestine mentality" and the peculiar code of the intelligence underworld. To read the account of the closed hearings on the nomination of ex-CIA Director Richard Helms to be ambassador to Iran (subsequently published because of Watergate) is to realize that congressional watchdogs are blind and toothless.

Dismantling covert intelligence

The inescapable fact is that effective control over an apparatus of the size and character of the United States intelligence community is impossible. The choice is between trusting that those in charge are honorable men, as Helms urged in 1971, or dismantling the covert intelligence arm of the United States. The necessity for the second choice is overwhelming.

An inherent problem of the intelligence underworld is that it is to a great extent uncontrollable. A criminal enterprise, such as the "dirty tricks" department, does not respond to ordinary political controls be-

cause it is made up of people who have been trained to respect no law but the command of the superior. E. Howard Hunt characterized the break-in of Daniel Ellsberg's psychiatrist's office as "an entry operation conducted under the auspices of competent authority." The habit of mind prevailing in the intelligence underworld includes what Richard Bissell, former deputy director of the CIA in charge of clandestine services, calls the "higher loyalty," a definition of national security developed and communicated in secret by higher ranking bureaucrats hermetically sealed from public scrutiny.

But despite the code of obedience, agents in the field have both the power and the motivation to trap their superiors by giving them a distorted picture of reality, wittingly or unwittingly. The spectacular intelligence failures—Bay of Pigs, Pueblo— are examples of this phenomenon. The law that operates in more benign bureaucracies also operates here: bureaucrats tend to keep doing what they have been doing, on an expanding scale, if possible. Thus, extraordinary efforts from the top are necessary to turn off operations once they are begun. The deeper the cover, the more impervious to political control.

But the most covert intelligence activities are carried out in direct support of clearly defined United States foreign policy objectives. Indeed, some of those objectives require the maintenance of an intelligence underworld of the character that has emerged. With all of its spectacular failures and the pretentious banality of the world of spies, buggers, code-snatchers, crop contaminators, covert philanthropists and secret political manipulators, the intelligence underworld is a necessary institution for managing a modern empire. If we cannot find security in the world without trying to run it, then the dirty tricks department must remain a fixture of our national life.

Managing political and social change around the world and opposing national revolutions, such as the recently exposed "destabilization" campaign in Chile, requires covert action. As long as the United States maintains its extravagant policy of trying to make the world safe for established political and economic power, there will always be men ready to lie, steal and kill in that higher cause. The CIA now seems a more important political instrument than ever because of improved techniques for "low profile" interventions, the growing desire to control resource-producing Third World countries and the increasing difficulties in mounting conventional military operations abroad. If state legitimization of criminal activity at home and abroad is undesirable, then the United States must stop trying to set conditions for the internal development of other nations.

It is important to distinguish covert action from covert intelligence gathering. Covert action is secret warfare. Clandestine intelligence collection, by contrast, is not designed to influence political affairs in other countries, but it does have that effect. Both covert action and covert intelligence collection are primarily directed against those societies least able to hurt the United States because they are least able to protect themselves from penetration.

The underdeveloped world "presents greater opportunities for covert intelligence collection," as Bissell explained to a Council on Foreign Relations study group in January, 1968, because their governments "are much less highly oriented; there is less security consciousness; and there is apt to be more actual or potential diffusion of power among parties, localities, organizations, and individuals outside the central governments." Thus, the same internal suspicions, rivalries and bribery that keep poor nations from effectively organizing themselves to overcome mass poverty make them attractive targets of the intelligence underworld. Real and exaggerated fears of being infiltrated help to keep such societies in a continual state of political disorganization. As Bissell points out, the less totalitarian the society, the easier it is to find out and to influence what goes on there. Salvador Allende's tolerance of forces opposing him made it easy for the CIA and other intelligence agencies to work with them to hasten his downfall. The CIA destabilization campaign (which, according to recent revelations of CIA Director William Colby's secret

testimony, was strongly pushed by Henry Kissinger) would not have worked had the regime been more repressive. That lesson is one of the uglier legacies of the dirty tricks department.

Disorientation of underdeveloped societies

The deliberate disorientation of societies by means of bribery, assassination, black propaganda, subornation and other methods helps keep them poor and dependent. When they are manipulated for United States foreign policy purposes rather than their own development purposes, their capacity even to begin to deal with the overwhelming problems of mass poverty is undermined. Unfortunately, United States foreign policy purposes in most areas of the Third World have been defined in such a way as to conflict directly with local development needs. The crushing problems of Asia, Africa and Latin America—mass poverty, unemployment and growing inequality—require structural changes in those societies, polite terminology for overthrowing local elites that run them as personal holding companies or throwing out foreign business interests that are often equally exploitative. Consistently, the CIA's continuing secret war has been in support of local and foreign interests threatened by structural change, the maintenance of a repressive "stability" that stifles hope for the majority of the population. The capability of the United States to support reactionary regimes, and its clear intent to do so wherever possible, has been a powerful political factor in preserving a highly inequitable and ultimately explosive status quo.

For the most part, CIA intervention has not been successful against countries with the capacity to destroy the United States. (Some exceptions include the cultivation of famous defector Colonel Penkovsky, who did provide important military information on Soviet missile strength when it could not be obtained by observation satellites; some propaganda victories in the fight for the "hearts and minds" of European intellectuals in the early postwar period; limitation of Soviet influence in the international labor movement; and collection of Kremlin gossip by bugging Party limousines.) But in the weak countries of the Third World, the CIA can make a crucial difference in setting political direction and it often has. If the secret warfare that makes the United States government the enemy of political change around the world is to be abandoned, the United States must stop attempting to influence the direction of internal politics in other countries in order to serve its military and corporate interests.

CIA revision

In the aftermath of Watergate, the CIA has been revising the official rationale for its extensive clandestine operations. According to Miles Copeland, a former CIA official, the Agency is now explaining its mission for the mid-1970s in congressional briefings as follows:

1. Meticulous monitoring of the detente. 2. Collection of data on international terrorist groups. 3. Protection of access to strategic materials. 4. Cooperation with multinational corporations.

Certainly the detente must be "meticulously monitored," if that phrase means keeping track of what the Soviet Union is doing. The most important information about the Soviet Union relevant to detente is the character and state of readiness of the armed forces. Satellite observation and the collection of order of battle intelligence by conventional means is the best way to monitor this information. Spies in the Kremlin, if indeed there are any, and document snatchers are unlikely to provide reliable information in a society that invests as much as the Soviet Union does to avoid penetration. The effort itself jeopardizes detente. "Testing" the Soviet air defenses by penetrating their air space is a provocation which serves no legitimate military purpose.

The best way to obtain information about Soviet attitudes toward detente is to press them hard for real measures of disarmament. The problem is not one of finding some piece of esoteric information that will provide the key to Soviet behavior, but rather of developing an analysis comprehensive and dynamic enough to utilize the vast amount of information already available.

Terrorism will be an increasing problem in a world where avenues of peaceful change appear blocked. There is no way to monitor real or imagined terrorist groups without violating the civil liberties of thousands of people. There is no evidence to suggest that a worldwide surveillance network could prevent random acts of terror typically the work of individuals or small splinter groups. Even if the prospects for preempting terrorist attacks through surveillance were more probable, the political damage caused by widespread surveillance in other countries outweighs any possible benefits.

Using covert action to protect United States access to strategic materials and energy sources is nothing new. Many CIA operations in the Mediterranean and Latin America have been precisely for this purpose. If there is no way to maintain the United States economy other than spreading intimidation, confusion and murder in the Third World, then the intelligence underworld will always have a place in American foreign policy.

To say that clandestine services must be available to aid United States-based multinational corporations is to make a virtue of the classic imperialist relationship in which the power of the state is used to bail out private interests abroad. The United States traditionally equates the "national interest" with the interests of International Telephone & Telegraph or Kennecott or some other corporation in conflict with the local government. But such a policy risks involvement in military interventions, frustrates possibilities of development and confirms the charge that the United States is interested only in a structure of peace that preserves its power to dominate weak economies.

United States corporations should be required to stand on their own in their dealings with other countries. If they are prepared to do business in a way that will benefit the host country, they do not need espionage or dirty tricks supplied at the taxpayers' expense. Similarly, access to raw materials is a problem of bargaining skill and technological innovation. Unless the United States is prepared to make war on the producing nations of the Third World in order to obtain access to resources on its terms, the CIA has no role in this drama.

It is frequently asserted that the United States must make extensive use of espionage and other secret means of collecting information about other nations in order to protect national security. The crucial issue concerns basic choice in foreign policy. Certain kinds of policies require certain kinds of information. If the foreign policy of the United States dictates a large-scale destabilization program for Chile, the information needed to conduct it can be obtained only by secret means. Data such as the names of Chilean subversives prepared to conspire with a foreign government against their own constitutional system, and the amount it will take to bribe or equip them become vital national security information. Since every government takes some pains to keep such information out of hostile hands, it can only be collected through an undercover operation. Had the decision been made to permit the survival of a freely elected government in Chile, such information would not have been required.

If the United States were genuinely prepared to live in a world of diversity, as it sometimes claims, political information would still be needed, but not through illegal and subversive means. Indeed, if the United States actually engaged in building a structure of peace evolving toward global equity instead of seeking to freeze a highly unjust and unstable status quo, then most information could be obtained from open sources and direct inquiry.

The principles of espionage were developed for war, and the more closely diplomacy resembles war, the more it must rely on espionage. Undercover operations against other countries are no more nor less justifiable than war itself, but they have a way of surviving the wars they are supposed to support. The *Pueblo* was captured off North Korea in 1967 while engaged in eavesdropping operations that might have been defensible during the war that concluded fourteen years earlier, but served no plausible purpose in 1967. Similarly, much of the covert intelligence apparatus was developed for a backalley war with the Soviet Union that has been overtaken by events.

The clandestine mentality

There is an information and analysis gap, but the information the United States needs most is not under the control of any foreign nation and cannot be wrested from it. The necessary analysis cannot be done by professional spies. The clandestine mentality fostered by intelligence bureaucracies is a form of trained inability to see the importance of information that does not have to be stolen. Witness the profound crisis in the economic underpinnings of the postwar world. The behavior of the world political economy is confounding experts, who, only a few months ago, professed to understand the "laws" under which the worldwide flow of goods and services was supposedly operating. Today, it is commonplace to read public admissions from such experts that they do not understand what is going on—why we have inflation and recession at the same time, and why the old economic remedies, such as the manipulation of interest rates, do not work. There is a crisis of understanding about what is happening to our institutions, and it has assumed the status of a national security crisis (as well as an international security crisis).

The greatest cost to the United States in maintaining an anachronistic secret warfare department, besides its damage to the reputation of the nation and the corrosion of American institutions, is that it distorts the country's perspectives. The United States spends billions a year acquiring knowledge useless for solving the most urgent problems.

On June 27, 1970, at a meeting of the 40 Committee, Henry Kissinger declared: "I don't see why we need to stand by and watch a country go Communist due to the irresponsibility of its own people." The problem, as Kissinger conceived it, was how to overturn a popular election in a foreign country (Chile) that produced a result the United States government did not like. Once defined in this way, the problem became simple. The United States could employ some of the same methods used in Guyana against Cheddi Jagan, in Guatemala against Arbenz, in Brazil against Goulart. The information needed to carry out such a policy was easy to identify and to obtain.

But the problem of Chile remains. Because the United States made it clear from the outset to Allende's opposition that they need not compromise with the Unidad Popular because they were backed by the United States, the internal politics of the country became polarized. The Junta has not merely repealed the reforms of Allende's abortive peaceful revolution, but has turned the clock back two generations, and, in a burst of gunfire, has obliterated reforms won under conservative and Christian Democratic presidents. The economic situation, bad under Allende, is now desperate. Inflation is worse than ever. Large parts of the middle class are considerably worse off than under the regime they were so happy to be rid of. The incompetence of the Junta has brought tens of thousands in the bottom strata of the population to the brink of starvation. (The price of food has risen precipitously, real wages have fallen and, incredibly, crops are being exported to earn foreign exchange to buy manufactured goods from abroad.) It is hard to see how the "success" in Chile has advanced the interests of the American people. (That it has advanced the interests of a few United States firms that had been or were about to be nationalized is clear.) Adding another "sick man" to the international economy is not going to solve the problems that now challenge our basic institutions.

The intelligence gathered with respect to Chile aggravated the economic problems of Chile, but did not solve them. That operation also had the effect of complicating United States relations elsewhere in the hemisphere. In his State of the Union Speech, Mexico's President Luis Echevarria made it clear that the lessons of the Chile "success" have not gone unnoticed:

[Terrorist groups are] easily manipulated by covert political interests, whether national or international, that use them as irresponsible instruments [for] acts of provocation against our institutions.

This manipulation and control from outside is conducted with great dexterity, and at times one might think that. . . . it is the work of extreme leftist groups; but when one realized the ideological unpreparedness of these groups and that their object is really to provoke repression, what one may call a "witch hunt," one is immediately led to think that it could very well be that they are using covert methods to provoke repression with the effect of halting the function of our institutions, as had occurred in other countries, and to cause the curtailing of our liberties when we have only just begun to follow a policy of economic nationalism in our country. In several Latin American countries, coups d'etat have been preceded by rumor campaigns that have their origin in certain irresponsible groups of businessmen and have also been encouraged by these acts of terrorism which attempt to sow confusion.

If in or outside of Mexico there are interests that try to divide the Mexicans, to create discord, let us remember that in 1848 we lost half of the territory we inherited from our indigenous and Spanish fathers, after an unjust war with the United States, in which internal division played a fundamental role. . . . If these groups that try to divide us wish some day to provoke the intervention in any form by any of the powerful nations, let them know that we have full historic awareness of what has happened in Mexico. . . .

This is an extraordinary statement from the chief of a state as thoroughly dependent upon the United States as Mexico. That the President of Mexico would make such a thinly veiled accusation against the United States is evidence not only of the depth of distrust that dirty tricks brought about, but it is also an indication of the erosion of American power. Ironically, the United States spy network is creating a political backlash in Thailand, Greece and Mexico as well, with the result that these traditional clients are seeking a more independent course. How much better it would have been for United States-Greek relations if the CIA apparatus had been withdrawn before it was expelled.

Cooperation and exchange of information

Thus, the sort of knowledge developed by clandestine collection services creates problems in the present world situation. The knowledge needed to solve the overwhelming institutional crises cannot be obtained by adversary means. Cooperation and exchange of information—about the workings of national economies, the structural changes in world economy, the successes and failures of social experiments and the impact of domestic policies of one country upon another—are absolutely essential if any country is to develop a comprehensive understanding of the world political economy in order to devise practical policies and solutions. The development of a much higher level of international trust is necessary to combat the real threat facing the American people—inflation, unemployment, loss of liberty and in the background, nuclear war. The intelligence underworld is a serious obstacle to the building of that new relationship between the United States and the world now necessary for survival.

From time to time, CIA officials reassure the public that the tax dollars with which they support the intelligence underworld (amount undisclosed) are well spent. The classic argument in support of a large secret warfare department is that other nations have them too. The clandestine mentality pervades the Soviet Union and the record of the KGB (Soviet Committee of State Security) for murder, theft, torture and forgery is probably unmatched. But do criminal activities of other countries require us to maintain our own? Certainly, some counterintelligence effort against penetration and manipulation of our government and theft of military secrets is necessary. That is a job principally for the Federal Bureau of Investigation to carry out within the framework of United States constitutional safeguards. As the Watergate experience demonstrates, there is a point rapidly reached at which the costs of ferreting out "enemies" and preventing leaks far outweigh the benefits.

If the United States were out of the covert action business, its counterespionage requirements would be drastically reduced. Much effort is now devoted to preventing the penetration of our intelligence underworld by the Soviet intelligence underworld. If we did not have one, we would create an unemployment problem for the KGB. Similarly, if habitual lying in the "national interest" were no longer a dictate of duty, then the government would not have to spend so much money concealing things from other governments and from the American people. But counterespionage, which within limits is a legitimate defensive activity, is one thing, and secret warfare against other nations is another. (There is, to be sure, the risk that one can be disguised as the other.)

The dirty tricks gap, if indeed there is one, is no more justification for the United States to corrupt its own society and to distort foreign relations than the missile gap or the bomb shelter gap or all the other arms races. There is nothing to suggest that adding a spy to the payroll will cause the Soviets to retire one or that "winning" the dirty tricks race is a significant victory. Indeed, most United States clandestine operations in the Third World do not appear to be effectively countered by the Soviet Union at all. The backalley war, which Allen Dulles said required fighting fire with fire, was a reasonable description of the Cold War confrontation over Europe. It does not describe what is happening in the Third World where the war is not between United States and Soviet intelligence agents, but between United States agents and weak indigenous political forces which, as in Chile, have received little help from the Communist powers.

United States covert action and clandestine intelligence collection (excepting satellites) could be abandoned unilaterally with a net gain in security for the American people. This is so not only for the reasons already discussed, but because most of the information so expensively and dangerously procured by secret agents is politically worthless. The work product of the spy is inherently suspect because specialists in espionage are in the business of producing disinformation as well as information. Indeed, the more esoteric and elaborate the deception required to produce data, the less likely the spy's political superiors are to believe it. Thus, some of the great intelligence coups of history, such as the advance warning to Stalin of the impending German attack, have gone unheeded. Only a short time ago advance warning of the Defense Information Agency that the Egyptians and Syrians were about to attack Israel was ignored by policymakers who questioned its reliability.

For the protection of our own society, the dirty tricks department must be recognized for what it is, a criminal enterprise. Dismantling it and preventing its reappearance in newer and slicker disguises would be one of the first acts of a new administration genuinely concerned about preserving constitutional liberty and stopping the wreckage dirty tricks have caused around the world.

Socialist

Alan Wolfe.   Repression through political intelligence.

A second form of violent repression in liberal society is political intelligence and espionage. Here it is of no concern whether the state's activities are formally defined as "legal," that is, whether they are supported by legislative statute. Much of domestic political espionage is legal in that sense; much of it is also illegal or extralegal. It makes little difference. This form of repression is characterized by the use of covert means by the state to control political dissidents. Since, by definition, this form is covert, information on it is less available when compared to other forms of repression. Nonetheless, every now and then the state is willing to reveal how extensive its infiltrative mechanisms are, for if it did not, who would be intimidated by them? From these acts of revelation, enough information can be assembled to place the use of political intelligence by the democratic state into a meaningful perspective.

Obtaining political information covertly is an old human custom. In the Bible, Delilah would appear to be the first agent, working for the Philistines against Israel.[1] The use of spies and informers for domestic political purposes has been traced back at least as far as medieval England.[2] Since Americans think of themselves as both religious and shaped by English law, it is not surprising that Delilah's techniques were quickly adopted. What is interesting is that political intelligence was first used by private groups and only later by the government.

The Pinkerton Detective Agency—which flourished at the end of the nineteenth century—was instrumental in developing tactics of repression through political intelligence. Of the many colorful individuals who rose to prominence in this profession, the career of the most well known is illustrative of a whole pattern. James McParland—subject of a Hollywood movie in 1970—caught the eye of Allen Pinkerton when he successfully infiltrated the semisecret labor organization known as the "Molly Maguires" in the Pennsylvania coalfields.[3] Eventually becoming a key leader of the organization, he often acted as a *provocateur*, pushing the group into an illegal action and then informing the authorities so that the group could be suppressed. McParland was highly successful, and his testimony against the group in court ensured its demise. This led to a promotion for the young intelligence officer, and he went farther west to continue roughly the same sort of work.

In 1906, McParland and the Pinkertons reemerged to work actively in repressing the IWW. Arrested and charged with the murder of former governor Frank Steunenberg of Idaho were three key leaders of the IWW—William Haywood, George A. Pettibone, and Charles H. Moyer. The arrests were illegal; the men were kidnaped across state lines so that Idaho could ignore extradition proceedings. Since little evidence was presented linking the men to the crime, McParland, instinctively understanding the tortured mind of a self-confessed murderer, obtained a confession that implicated the three officials, and a political trial was begun. In this case, Clarence Darrow broke through the confession, and the men were found not guilty. Nonetheless, the expense and harassment associated with the trial hurt the IWW and was a sign of its future treatment.

What is the role of the state in this tale? At one level the state (of Idaho) cooperated with McParland and the Pinkertons in their work. But more important is something revealed by McParland himself in a letter to his boss, written during these events:

This is one of the most important operations ever undertaken in the Portland District, and if through our offices we are successful, it will mean a great deal to the Spokane office so far as the mine operators are concerned, in fact all mine operators in the whole district.[4]

It did mean a good deal to the mine owners. In situations of this sort, the Pinkerton Agency was explicitly working for those who constituted the ruling class at that time. One could infer that repression by the state was contracted out to a private organization with all the advantages (fewer scruples) that such a move entails. Intelligence of this sort, though conducted privately, is clearly an affair of state and should be considered as such.

Private intelligence intensified after this period. The use of industrial spies led to strikes and resulted in violence in Kentucky in 1933 and 1934.[5] In fact, the amount of industrial espionage leaped in the 1920s and 1930s. Fortunately one aspect of the American government investigated the actions of another, resulting in the hearings before the Subcommittee of the Senate Education and Labor Committee, often called the La Follette Civil Liberties Committee.[6] These 1936 hearings, the most comprehensive collection of information about industrial espionage ever gathered, reveal a vast system of private intelligence, working for the powerful, designed to repress labor organizations of all varieties, including the least revolutionary. The hearings uncovered the existence of at least 225 private detective agencies engaged in the business of spying on labor unions.[7] Spy reports, filed by agents, cover in meticulous detail every event at meeting after meeting of a labor union. Employers knew union affairs more thoroughly than union leaders themselves. Also informative from these hearings were

lists of contributions made by various corporations to "employer's associations," money that went immediately into espionage.[8] The La Follette hearings show an extensive network of intelligence operative working for corporations—with the expressed sympathy of the state—whose sole function is the violent repression of those groups whose interests run counter to the interests of the rulers of the democratic state.

One should not get the impression that because private groups were engaged in repression for the state that the state itself was idle. In 1917, the Bureau of Investigation of the Department of Justice gave its blessing to a group called the American Protective League, a private organization that would ferret out "subversives" and others endangering the war effort.[9] So zealous were these patriots that vigilantism mushroomed throughout the country. The violence became so intense that the bureau realized it must itself take on the job of political repression, in a more covert and "professional" manner. Repression, it discovered, is a tricky business best left to the experts. Shortly thereafter, in June 1917, an assistant to the attorney general was hired to coordinate "war work," and he in turn hired an assistant named J. Edgar Hoover. In September, the first raids by the bureau against the IWW were taken. In those few months, the foundations of the modern FBI were laid, and national government increasingly became involved in repression through political intelligence.

The proudest moment in this period occurred in 1922. In 1920, while the Soviet Union was being undermined by the presence of American troops aiding the White Army, Francis Morrow was hired by the Department of Justice to spy on radical organizations, eventually including the American Communist party, which was formed in 1921. Morrow became a party official in Camden, New Jersey, and he periodically sent reports to Washington. It was Morrow who relayed enough information to make possible a raid on the party's Bridgman (Michigan) Convention, an affair held after the most elaborate precautions were taken to ensure that the government would be unable to find the then "underground" organizations. Many leaders were arrested, documents were seized, and the importance of a professional intelligence system for purposes of political repression was demonstrated to all who remained skeptical.[10] What soon became the Federal Bureau of Investigation had a major part of its mission defined.

What is the current status of repression through political intelligence? The general use of intelligence techniques in law enforcement seems certain to have risen. At least twelve federal agencies keep extensive intelligence records: FBI, Federal Bureau of Narcotics, Bureau of Customs, Alcohol Tax Unit, Immigration and Naturalization Service, Internal Revenue Service (Intelligence Division), Civil Aeronautics Administration, U.S. Maritime Commission, Post Office Department, Interstate Commerce Commission, Department of Agriculture, and Department of Labor.[11] States and municipalities also keep such information; California, for example, has five state agencies that perform key intelligence operations.[12] The importance of effective intelligence for police work in general has been summarized in a police textbook on the problem:

Police operational intelligence has probably made more advances in the last twenty years than it did in the previous century. Though an embryo service, *the future appears exceptionally bright, full of vast unexplored areas for research and development not yet unveiled. Police agencies throughout the country are experimenting in one degree or another with the application of intelligence techniques.* The product of this experiment coupled with *current research in the fields of psychology, criminology, sociology,* and data processing techniques should bring forth a highly effective tool for future police administrators.[13]

One would expect, given the increasing reliance on intelligence for general law enforcement, that the use of such techniques for political repression is bound to increase as well. This is especially true when we consider that to those who enforce the law, political dissidents themselves are just a special sort of criminal. The standard police textbook on intelligence discusses communism in the same chapter with crime,

right after Al Capone and Salvatore Luciana. The authors' reason for making this linkage is to emphasize the "true nature" of the Communist *conspiracy:* "Any idiot or pseudo-intellectual that thinks Communism has any relationship to the Latin root is grossly ill informed." They must realize instead that "Communism is a pseudoscientific, atheistic philosophy perpetuated by a criminal conspiracy of power hungry dictators."[14] (This is in a textbook designed for professional use.) If political dissidents are indeed so dangerous, they are criminals and all law enforcement tactics can be used, including intelligence.

In a 1955 speech to the International Association of Chiefs of Police, J. Edgar Hoover told those responsible for law enforcement this:

It is through the efforts of confidential informants that we have been able to expose the Communist conspiracy in the past and *through which we must stake much of the future security of the United States.* That is why such a vicious attack has been made against former Communists who have firsthand knowledge of the secret diabolical purpose of the Communist Party.[15]

If Hoover is considered a biased spokesman, the speech at the same meeting by Assistant U.S. Attorney General William Tomkins is even more interesting, because it illustrates the legitimacy that liberal intellectuals like Learned Hand have, in their desire to ensure balance, given to the more nefarious aspects of political repression:

With reference to the propriety of using informants, very little need be said. Judge Learned Hand, in affirming the conviction in the celebrated Dennis case, tried before Judge Medina in New York City, announced this contention simply and succinctly by stating that "courts have countenanced the use of informers from time immemorial." *What our critics fail to, or will not recognize, is that those who are engaged in a criminal enterprise have no right to be free from such surveillance*. . . .[16]

The function of repression through intelligence is more than merely to render a group ineffective. One reason for keeping tabs on political dissidents is to strengthen other forms of political repression, especially of the legal variety. The information gathered through the intelligence network is dramatically "revealed" to the public in a highly visible political trial. A close examination of the evidence at *all* recent political trials indicates that the only "evidence" presented by the state is the word of informers. In the Dennis trial, the government's case consisted of four converts (those who joined the party sincerely and were "sickened") and seven informers (those who joined the FBI and then joined the party).[17] In the Chicago conspiracy trial of 1969, one of the defendants noted that "as for concrete evidence of lawbreaking activity, the government puzzled us further by introducing almost nothing."[18] All the government did was to parade its undercover agents on the stand, and their number alone seems to have convinced the jury that the defendants were indeed dangerous and, therefore, guilty.

In addition, repression through intelligence provides to the repressors of the democratic state continued reason for their own existence. There are now many liberals within the United States who would like to deemphasize this form of repression, but those who control it have entrenched themselves within the bureaucracy and with the public and are unmovable. J. Edgar Hoover's death, it has been suggested, will bring a liberal to head the FBI, to win back confidence in its mission. (Acting Director Gray has already taken steps in this direction.) But intelligence is now more than one man. It is an apparatus, and what keeps an apparatus operating is its work. Parkinson's law is accurate for intelligence work: the information uncovered will expand to match the number of people doing the uncovering.

At the present time, this problem has become most serious. Sophisticated technological improvements have been combined with traditional espionage techniques to create a repressive apparatus that is truly startling. Electronic surveillance is widely used,[19] which creates a dilemma. In reviewing the conviction of a labor leader convicted on the basis of a wiretap of his phone, the Supreme Court recently noted

that "...the use of secret informers is not *per se* unconstitutional."[20] There is the rub. Since liberal theory does not want to render the state powerless, it admits in principle the legitimacy of the new devices. But once admitted, these devices have a way of multiplying to their technological limits. (It is, after all, a capitalist economy that makes and sells the new equipment.) Thus, one has reason to believe that the new techniques are seen as highly relevant to the control of political dissidents. Nobody knows how much wiretapping takes place; the very secrecy of it leads to wild rumors. The feeling that one's phone is tapped is effective in shaping political conduct, whether the phone actually is or not.

This discussion would suggest that repression through intelligence cannot be explained in totally rational terms. Further evidence of this comes from the heavy emphasis on converts in this sort of work. In the speech quoted earlier, J. Edgar Hoover indicated the importance of apostates to political work. Indeed, the Bridgman raid, the first successful federal repression of the Communist party, was directed by a Russian who sympathized with the Russian Revolution.[21] The presence of so many converts adds a psychological dimension to the problem. Is it possible that the democratic state finds itself controlling so many groups because the state needs to manufacture its own opposition? The possibility must at least be admitted. If order is an end of the democratic state, what could be more ordered than controlling one's own antithesis? *There is evidence, in short, that the function of repression through intelligence is not to destroy such groups but to keep them functioning.* Their existence is needed, sometimes desperately. In 1964, when the Communist party of the United States was weak, divided, and a threat to nobody or nothing, by any objective standard, the director of the FBI said:

The Communist Party, USA, stepped up its programs on all domestic fronts during the 1964 fiscal year.... The Party worked unremittingly to increase its influence in the racial struggle; gain new members through an intensive youth recruitment campaign; and promote the false impression that it is a legitimate political party.[22]

Many people manufacture their own devils. What made this man's devils so interesting was not that he was just another person, but that he was in charge of repression through intelligence in the democratic state. He could have reached such a position only with the support of the whole system.

One should not, however, conclude that such repression is totally irrational. Kirchheimer has noted that "Informing will be a somewhat smaller threat to larger movements, which neither need nor want to consider violence a necessary or exclusive means of undermining the foundations of an existing regime, but are intent and able to concentrate their efforts on a broader front. Due to the wider nature of their appeal, they are more immune to turncoats and traitors."[23] It follows that this form of repression is most used against small groups. If they are not engaged in violence, and hence no threat to public order, infiltration is little justified, though heavily used. If they are a threat by their emphasis on violence, it must be remembered that the group might not have decided on a violent course were it not for the agent in their midst urging violence upon them. (Consider the "plot" to kidnap Henry Kissinger, strongly advocated by a police agent.) In short, the function of repression through intelligence is not to allow the group to have a choice. The democratic state can no longer draw the line between groups that threaten order and those that do not. Control is the basis of the democratic state, and repression through intelligence is still an effective and highly rational form of control.

Such repression bothers some people. Writing in 1863, the British historian Sir Thomas Erskine May expressed the problem eloquently:

Men may be without restraints upon their liberty; they may pass to and fro at pleasure; but if their steps are tracked by spies and informers, their words noted down for crimination, their associates watched as conspirators—who shall say they are free? [Espionage] haunts men like an evil genius, chills their gaiety, restrains their wit, casts a shadow over their friendships, and blights their domestic health. The freedom of a country may be measured by its immunity from this baleful agency.[24]

If that immunity is to be the measure, it is unfortunate for the government of the United States. For it is not only clear that the government will fail the test, but every indication is that it will continue to fail it, perhaps with even lower scores.

NOTES

1. Judges 16: 9–24.

2. Richard C. Donnelly, "Judicial Control of Informants, Spies, Stool Pigeons, and Agent Provocateurs," *Yale Law Journal* 60 (November 1951): 1091.

3. This section is based on James D. Horan, *The Pinkertons* (New York: Crown, 1967), pp. 445–79.

4. Quoted in ibid., p. 461.

5. Taft and Ross, "American Labor Violence," p. 321, 332–34.

6. U.S. Senate, *Hearings Before a Subcommittee of the Committee on Education and Labor*, 75th Cong., 3rd sess.

7. See the list included in a book summarizing the hearings: Leo Huberman, *The Labor Spy Racket* (New York: Modern Age Books, 1937), pp. 165–69. Also dealing with the findings of the LaFollette Committee is Clinch Calkins, *Spy Overhead: The Story of Industrial Espionage* (New York: Harcourt Brace, 1937). An engrossing "inside" picture of the problem, which contains much material linking the state to industrial espionage, is GT-99, *Labor Spy* (Indianapolis: Bobbs Merrill, 1937).

8. Huberman, *Labor Spy Racket*, pp. 178–79.

9. This paragraph is based upon the Bureau's own "official" history. See Don Whitehead, *The FBI Story* (New York: Random House, 1956), pp. 34–39.

10. See the full story in Theodore Draper, *The Roots of American Communism* (New York: Viking, 1957), pp. 366–75.

11. Donald O. Schultz and Loran A. Norton, *Police Operational Intelligence* (Springfield, Ill.: Charles C. Thomas, 1968), p. 77.

12. Ibid., p. 78.

13. Ibid., p. 26. Emphasis added.

14. Ibid., p. 91.

15. J. Edgar Hoover, in the *Law Enforcement Bulletin* (June 1955). Quoted in Malachi L. Harney and John C. Cross, *The Informer In Law Enforcement* (Springfield, Ill.: Charles C. Thomas, 1968), p. 19. Emphasis added.

16. William F. Tompkins, in the *Law Enforcement Bulletin* (June 1955). Quoted in ibid., p. 70. Emphasis in original.

17. Donnelly, "Judicial Control of Informants," pp. 1124–25.

18. Tom Hayden, "The Trial," *Ramparts* 9 (July 1970): 19.

19. See Alan F. Westin, *Privacy and Freedom* (New York: Atheneum, 1967). Also informative is Samuel Dash, *The Eavesdroppers* (New Brunswick, N.J.: Rutgers University Press, 1959).

20. Hoffa v. U.S., 385 U.S. 311 (1966).

21. Draper, *Roots of American Communism*, p. 368.

22. *Annual Report of the Attorney General*, 1964, p. 373. Mr. Hoover's annual remarks on Communist party repression are contained in the section entitled "Protecting Democracy."

23. Kirchheimer, *Political Justice*, p. 237.

24. Thomas Erskine May, *Constitutional History of England*, vol. 2 (London: Longmans, Green, 1863), p. 275. Quoted in Donnelly, "Judicial Control of Informants," p. 1131.

꙼

Part three

Some institutions are readily perceived as political institutions. The people who act within them are known as politicians, legislators, or judges. They identify themselves as politically or legally motivated and everyone thinks of them as acting from political or legal motives.

Other institutions are not clearly political. Although they exert power in directing and controlling American society, people who act within them maintain they are acting strictly to make money. These economic institutions, whether they be multinational corporations or criminal families, are also political institutions for they structure and influence the operation of the overtly political institutions. Elite clubs and associations operate within the same framework to influence the official political institutions.

The exercise of power, whether it be invisible and hidden or visible and public, must be studied if an understanding of the American political process is to be achieved. It is often very difficult to obtain valid and documented information on the workings of the invisible power structures. This does not make it less important to analyze them, but only more difficult to learn about them. Still, this task of ferreting out data on multinational corporations, organized crime, elite clubs and associations, and other relatively invisible political entities must be undertaken if their true range of effects on us is to be understood and acted upon.[1]

NOTES

1. One of the many groups engaged in this process is The American Committee on Africa. Formed in 1965 by returned Peace Corps Volunteers, it publishes a monthly journal, *Southern Africa*. The Committee attempts to uncover the political manipulations of multinational banks, such as the Bank of America, and Chemical Bank of New York, in the Republic of South Africa. The committee has also investigated Gulf Oil Corporation's relationship with the colonial policy of Portugal in Mozambique. Under the colonial Portugese regime, Gulf benefitted from oil investments in Mozambique. In return Gulf supported financially Portugal's attempt to prevent revolutionary movements in Mozambique from being successful. Although Mozambique became independent in 1975 as a result of a revolution in Portugal itself, the policy that Gulf followed allowed it to profit heavily from its investments in Mozambique while it interfered in the politics of that country. Much of this information would not have become known had it not been for the research conducted, and published, by The American Committee on Africa.

The invisible power elite

The basic questions this chapter will address are:

(1) How are these groups formed?

(2) Who gets to be a member?

(3) How do these elite clubs and associations work?

(4) Do these groups formulate the priorities that the formal political institutions of American society carry out?

(5) If they do formulate priorities should they continue to be permitted to make public policy?

Elite clubs and associations include groups such as the Foreign Policy Association—a voluntary association representing business, law, and banking interests whose purpose is to formulate and influence foreign policy decisions; Bohemian Grove—a group of extraordinarily wealthy businessmen and politicians who meet at a California resort to renew ties and form new ones. One of the purposes of this overtly social group and other similar ones is to influence and make public policy. An elite club or association can be a highly organized group or a loosely structured social unit. In either case its defining characteristic is that it brings together wielders of great economic and political power.

The conservative position on elite clubs and associations is that they are purely social organizations of like-minded people. These groups exert no disproportionate influence in comparison to any other sector of society. Although their members are often extraordinarily wealthy these individuals do not use their wealth to promote private ends. You and I have as much influence on decision-making in the United States as any member of these elite clubs and associations.

Elite clubs and associations, according to conservatives, generate political influence upon government in the same manner as other organizations. Registered lobbyists represent the interests of their organizations by calling upon congressional representatives and government bureaucrats. Congress members respond to this pressure according to the merits of a lobbyist's argument. Rarely do legislators take bribes or act in the expectation of receiving campaign contributions from wealthy and powerful groups. They act only in the best interest of the nation. Essentially, conservatives see no conflict of interest whatsoever and they feel that critics of elite clubs and associations are raising a false specter in the minds of the public when these critics claim that there are super powerful and secret groups controlling the formation of public policy.

Liberals accept the theory that there are differences in power among groups in American society. They believe that economic elites, if permitted, can exert undue influence on government. This influence can be limited by government legislation. Some of the means liberals advocate to curtail abuses of power are: registration of lobbyists; economic groups submission to Congress of their financial records; and legislation prohibiting gifts, bribes, and favors. Liberals hold that countervailing groups—a number of relatively equal groups each exerting power in opposite directions—neutralize any excesses of power exercised in one direction or another. Since they accept the pluralist thesis, liberals believe that voluntary associations, financially secure and well organized, can influence government in much the same way as any elite group.

Ralph Nader is an example of someone who has organized from the premises of this theory. It is Nader's belief that through research, conducted by both volunteers and professionals, abuses of power can be discovered. In publicizing these abuses, and bringing them to the attention of the American people, pressure groups can be formed to influence Congress to correct these abuses.

In general, liberals hold that undue elite influence can be thwarted by citizen participation in the political process. They refuse to recognize the control economic magnates have over the political system. They focus on how elite clubs and associations operate rather than on the concentration of wealth and power that these groups represent. That some groups in American society wield more inordinate power than others does not fit into their pluralistic framework.

In this chapter we have chosen "How the Power Elite make Foreign Policy" as the liberal perspective because the article deals with a group that has established its own public identity. The article is also representative of the intersection of liberal and socialist perspectives on elite clubs and associations. Both liberals and socialists acknowledge their existence as wielders of power in American society. Liberals tend to look at these associations in a narrower context than do socialists. G. William Domhoff, in this article, straddles the liberal and socialist positions.

The socialist position is that elite clubs and associations are a key institution in formulating goals for American society. Its membership is made up of society's wealthiest and most powerful people. Some have been known for generations, such as the Mellon's, Carnegie's, and Rockefeller's; others, such as Robert Abplanalp and Felix Rohatyn,[1] emerge publicly only when it becomes necessary to handle a delicate situation, while a third group never becomes known. Members of this latter group often do not even register with elite directories such as Who's Who. This makes it extraordinarily difficult to do thorough research on individuals who control the American power structure. These elites believe that their power is best exercised in private. When their names become public they attempt, through public relations and favorable publicity, to convince the American people that they are acting in their best interests.

Socialists believe otherwise. They hold that these individuals act only to further their own welfare and their class interests. These elites run the biggest banks, corporations, and industrial enterprises, and coordinate their affairs and conciliate their differences through the meetings of elite clubs and associations. Socialists maintain that although these elites publicize their actions as being for the national good, it is their class interest that is served. They take their class interest to be for the national good.

These elites wield extraordinary power. To deal with this, the public must be made to see what they are up to. The political, rather than purely social nature of their dealings must be displayed. For example, the official purpose of the Council on Foreign Relations is to educate the people and increase public awareness of foreign affairs, and to establish links between foreign and domestic elites. In reality, a major function of the Council on Foreign Relations is to develop experts on foreign policy and to have them placed in key government positions. In this way the Council, whose membership represents corporate interests, ensures that American foreign policy will represent its own interests. John Foster Dulles, Secretary of State under President Eisenhower, Dean Rusk, Secretary of State under Presidents Kennedy and Johnson, and Henry Kissinger, Secretary of State under Presidents Nixon and Ford were all members of the Council on Foreign Relations. The Council operates as *the* institution which represents elite interests in the conduct of American foreign policy.

Socialists hold that in addition to groups such as the Council on Foreign Relations, which has a public identity, there are other formal and informal elite groups that operate in private. They consist of people who attend similar schools, intermarry, and work together.[2] Socialists believe that the question of elite clubs and associations is part of a larger complex of power in American society. This complex is not only represented by organizations, but by extended families and social networks that on other levels of society serve mainly as kinship and friendship ties. For the elite, these relationships of family and friends serve as a means to perpetuate self-interest and class rule.

NOTES

1. *Robert Abplanalp* was the inventor of the aerosol can. As a result of being involved in the Watergate scandal through financial dealings with President Richard Nixon, he was forced to defend his actions publicly. It was alleged that he had benefited financially, and illegally, by loaning Nixon money to purchase a house in San Clemente, California. Taxes were not paid, and, in fact, Nixon deducted the cost of the house on his tax return by claiming that after his presidency the house would be given to the federal government. *Felix Rohatyn,* a partner in the investment banking house of Lazard Frères & Co., surfaced publicly in 1974 because of the economic crisis. He set forth conservative proposals for the maintenance of the capitalistic system. Up to that time he had not even registered in *Who's Who in Finance and Industry.*

2. An analysis of such a group is found in G. William Domhoff, *Bohemian Grove*, New York: Harper Colophon books, 1975.

*

Conservative

Lewis Anthony Dexter.
Influence. . . information
. . . intelligence.

According to the Washington representatives quoted at the beginning of the last chapter, they can provide their clients with "guidance. . . information. . . influence." The phrasing is neat. But it is an oversimplification.

For, in fact, it is only on rare occasions that Washington representatives can really "provide," or "offer," that is to say, sell or rent influence. The notion, however, that this can frequently be done is common; it confuses clients, employers, potential clients, journalists, and a good many observers of government.

The best way to show the irrelevance of the notion to most Washington representation is to start out with a discussion of some typical occasions when influence is actually supposed to have been sold or rented. This provides a contrast with the more characteristic and realistic ways in which Washington representatives can help clients exert influence: *by discovering for the clients facts and techniques which permit the focusing and orienting of previously unexercised sources of influence.*

Reflections about the discovery of such facts and techniques lead directly into consideration of the kinds of information which a Washington representative can usefully provide his client or employer. In summary, the Washington representative must select, process, and handle information so that it becomes "intelligence," in the sense in which that word is used in military planning. For, in one way or another, clients and employers are concerned with actions or contemplated actions; and information is only useful to them if it affects plans for action.

I

Influence can be most effectively sold or rented—from the client's standpoint, pur-

chased—when the issue is that of awarding a specific favor. A contract is given to a corporation. A pardon is granted so-and-so. A tax decision benefits such-and-such a company. Broad issues of policy do not ordinarily arise on such matters. People who are, *chiefly,* concerned with them are not (in the sense in which the terms are used in this book) as such engaged in "Washington representation" or "government relations."

Nevertheless, of course, a good many Washington representatives spend part of their time on issues of policy and the rest on contracts, favors, special awards. Does it pay a client to try to hire somebody who has special influence, if part of the work in Washington is to get special favors?

Obviously, the answer to any such general question may vary with specific cases. But, ordinarily, it is of dubious value to the client.

First: There is rarely any way of telling whether influence or "pull" really did make the difference. The requirements of bureaucracy and the insistence upon honesty in government operate so that there is no clarity on the matter. Even if a decision is made on the basis of pull, the client cannot be sure at all that this is so—the decision-making official will not furnish any proof to that effect.

Second: We hear a good deal about ways in which special interests mislead public servants. There is also the reverse situation. Public servants may mislead—and do mislead—special interests in the following way.

They indicate to an organization that they will pay unusual attention to such-and-such a former employee or political supporter or relative. So, the organization hires the person. But, in fact, its claims are handled on their merits, just as they would have been anyway. With perhaps one additional handicap: some subordinates in the executive agencies, dealing with the organization are careful to lean over backward, because they foresee that if the political climate changes, some allegation of scandal may occur. So the organization, if anything, loses on the deal.

This is, as a matter of fact, one of the best ways in which politicians can provide for friends and allies and supporters.

There is a story told about Speaker Rayburn, and probably also about other distinguished politicians, which illustrates the point. Some time after he had become majority leader, a man came to him, who had done substantial favors for him years before in Texas. "What," said the Congressman, "can I do for you?"

"Just this—let me be seen with you! Let me walk with you from your office to the floor or over to dinner. That's all."

"That's all?" commented the Congressman. "You ask a lot less than most!"

"Yes," replied the man, "if I am seen enough with you, people will think I am somebody."

Probably, the somebodies who really counted in this story were interests engaged in hiring a Washington representative. And the man could have made a good thing, financially, out of the situation. Would his clients have got their money's worth? Only if the administrative agencies were as naive as they, and assumed because the man was seen in the Congressman's company in public, that he had real influence.

Yet, what less expensive way for the Congressman to repay past favors? And all things considered what great public disadvantage was involved?

Third: Influence is, in the nature of the case, usually a wasting asset. Mr. A may have helped Senator Y in a close election. Or Mr. C may have been prominent in the professional deliberations which took place before a new commissioner or bureau chief was chosen. And Mr. C may have played the decisive role in getting the professional group to support Commissioner X's candidacy.

It may be that Senator Y and Commissioner X are men who feel strongly that favors should be repaid, and would make a real effort to do so. Messrs. A or C might be able to get unusual favors from them—once or twice or possibly a third time. But then, two things would happen: first, the Senator

and the Commissioner would feel that the account now balanced. And, second, due to the lapse of time, they would discount the favor; the Senator, for instance, would be more concerned about the next election than about a previous one.

On a one-shot basis, considerable favors can be obtained, no doubt, from some office-holders, because of gratitude or some other claim to special, personal attention. But a professional Washington representative will be extremely careful as to what claims he makes to be sure that he gets the best possible return on his earlier investment in the man's career, and, above all, he will be eager not to ask for too much. For a frequent source of ill will in politics (as in other human relations) is the demand by one man that he get better treatment than the other thinks he is entitled to.

We have supposed here that Senator Y and Commissioner X are men who acknowledge favors readily and gladly repay them. There are, of course, such men in politics. But there are others, like the late Mayor LaGuardia, who at the celebration, the evening of his first election, started his victory speech to his supporters: "I have one qualification for mayor. That is my capacity for monumental personal ingratitude."

More common, perhaps than either those who are grateful or who are purposefully ungrateful, are those who esteem the favor as demanding only limited gratitude; they have enough self-confidence, and they are personally sure they would have made it anyhow, so the man who helped them was after all investing in a sure thing.

Fourth: Also, almost anyone who has achieved a prominent position has *many* obligations, and ties, and considerations. A close associate of the late Governor Paul Devor of Massachusetts—one of those unfortunate men, temperamentally speaking, who did not forget obligations, who felt strongly he ought to try to repay them—said of the Governor:

"Poor Paul! He just could not get away from the people who had helped him over the years. He would walk out of the office and there in the waiting room would be half-a-dozen guys who had helped him in the great victory of 1948—who wanted something. And then on the other side of the office would be some fellows who had clung to him in the dreary, discouraging 1946 campaign for Lieutenant-Governor. And, if he went into the hall, he would probably see several fellows he had worked with in the Navy. Then, there would be a bunch who helped him in the 1940 Governorship race which looked like a close one. And, when he got downstairs there would be fellows who worked for him in the Attorney-General's office—where he did some pretty big things—and others who worked for him in the three A.G. fights—and don't forget that recount! that took a lot out of people. And, I am certain, when he got back home to Cambridge, there would be fellows who helped him in his campaigns for State Rep and others who started him out in politics. He could not shake them off!"

But the result was—and is—that no one man, no matter how much he may have done for a public figure, has as big a claim as he thinks he has—because there are a lot of others with big claims on the man.

II

More or less the same sort of analysis might be made of other kinds of pull. A senator or a bureau chief may have a close personal friend, one who goes out of his way to entertain him and whose company he genuinely likes—and may do one or two or three favors for such a person. But in Washington, nowadays, after all, there are "as good fish in the sea as ever came out of it," and few important officials will risk serious jeopardy to their reputations by repeated acts of favor to some personal friend. Friends are easier to replace in Washington in 1968 than reputation and position.

It is, no doubt, possible to think of extreme and exceptional cases—blackmail or extraordinary sexual attraction—where the limitations here spoken of do not apply. But they are so exceptional as not to be important in any general discussion.

III

I should also, perhaps, emphasize that I am speaking only of Washington in the period since 1933. I do not know enough about other capitals or about Washington before that date to say much about them. My suspicion is that in some state capitals, and in the capitals of some underdeveloped countries, pull is much more significant than in Washington today. It may have been more significant in Washington before the development of the present system of specialized communications. Nowadays, many people in a particular industry or profession throughout the country hear through all sorts of channels what is going on of interest to them in Washington. They well hear very quickly about, and some of them will resent, any allegations of favoritism. Before the development of newsletters, before the frequency of personal visits by professional and industry leaders to Washington, it may have been easy to get away with favoritism. It is more difficult now.

IV

On this matter of "pull"—a clarification is in order. Influence is certainly desirable, and where one has influence or can easily acquire it, it is likely to be helpful. But the difference between "pull" and "influence" lies precisely in the notion that "pull" is illegitimate, influence legitimate. Trying hard to get pull is likely to have the difficulties referred to above and below. A Washington representative can very rarely—if ever—legitimize an organization or demand or movement which is not already regarded as legitimate. Of course, as we point out below, through the use of information and intelligence, a skillful Washington representative can channel or mobilize influence which would otherwise not be effectively employed.

V

It is unquestionably easier to get specific favors through pull than to get general rules or regulations or policies established or changed through favor.

If a particular favor is worth enough to a given favor-seeker, it may be rational from his standpoint to exercise a good deal of pull in trying to get the favor. But it is rarely rational to exert a great deal of pull in order to get a general rule or regulation or policy established or changed; because one of two things is likely to be the case:

a. either competing interests are not very powerful or shrewd, so that the rule or regulation or policy could be established without pull; or

b. competing interests are powerful and shrewd enough so that if they discover that pull has been used, they will set to work to discover their own sources of pull. And, since public officials are under obligations to so many people, this can nearly always be done.

So, it is really not worthwhile—except under rather exceptional circumstances—to *try* to use pull to get a *general* policy established or changed. Opponents will offset such pull; the net result will merely be to increase the cost of doing business in Washington.

There are, apparently, state and city governments where middlemen exist who expect rake-offs on pull. But, in Washington, this is not the custom, and there is no advantage to most interests in acting so as to change that situation.

VI

The preceding discussion does not mention one kind of influence which may be especially attractive to some clients or would-be clients. There are a number of persons who are advisors, money-raisers, confidants of political and administrative figures, and who themselves make a good deal of money out of being Washington representatives. Their relationship with the prominent is continuing. They will raise money in the next campaign as well as having done so in previous ones. They will be consulted on various difficulties. Their influence rests as

much on future expectations as on past services.

But how much can and do they do for their clients?

This is one of the real mysteries of Washington. Certainly any client hiring them should know that normal notions about "conflict of interest" do not apply. They feel a greater loyalty to their political friends than to the clients who pay them. So, they will not push anything which would embarrass these political friends, even if such action would be helpful to the client.

Similarly—so far as their own time is concerned—if the political friends call on them, they will respond, often at the expense of effort which is committed to paying-clients. Consequently, in Presidential years, for instance, advisors of this sort are not particularly good representatives. They are too busy with other things.

Of course, some such people in fact only go through the motions themselves personally. They are the glamour boys of their firms; but they hire competent associates who do much the same sort of job any other Washington representative would do. The advantage for the firm may be that it can charge higher fees, because of the glamour boy's reputation. And, no doubt, the glamour boy does get quicker access, and more detailed information in some agencies—bureaucrats hope he will remember them the next time he talks to the President or to the Secretary of Defense. Whether this access outweighs the disadvantages of paying higher fees for what is not otherwise a different level of performance is a matter for the individual client to assess. Of course, many clients cheerfully pay for the privilege of hobnobbing with the famous and for the hope that they themselves will be introduced to the President or have a chance to breakfast with distinguished political leaders. If this is an expectation, it will often lead to disappointment; as a hope, how much is it worth?

There is one other disadvantage attaching to the employment of Washington representatives who are well known as advisors to the famous. Those in Congress to whom they are *not* advisors or potential advisors—usually the overwhelming majority—and a good many bureaucrats are suspicious of them. So, although, on the one hand, they may have more "influence" in some places because of their close associations, they may have less in others for the same reason. Anyone eager to do a neat study of balances of influence might well try to calculate the balance in regard to several such figures.

VII

However, there are two kinds of influence which some Washington representatives can to an extent rent out. A man who is respected for his integrity and judgment in a given field or by a given senator can confer credibility, to a degree, upon a few clients. If he takes a client, it will be assumed that the latter is respectable—if nothing or little was known about the client before, or if the previous feeling was mixed. But, obviously, a man who has earned this sort of respect has to be careful to keep it by taking only respectable clients! He cannot practice according to the lawyer's notion: "Everybody is entitled to a defense." Or, if he does take a client whose case is weak, he has to be perfectly open about it with his Washington associates. This sometimes happens: a respectable Washington representative will say: "Look, this client wants this. (For example, this foreign government). There's a lot of exaggeration and a lot of shoddiness in the situation; but on the whole, this part of what they want seems to me, after looking at it, justifiable, despite and disregarding all these weaknesses. Will you look at it from that point of view?" But, obviously, not very many Washington representatives can do this often; and it probably is a rare approach.

The other kind of what looks like "influence" that a good many competent Washington representatives can sell is "access," the opportunity to be heard. Many clients present their own cases too badly or too emotionally to be heeded. And, in any case, a man who has been around Washington for awhile has established contacts with people

so that they will listen to him. But, although access is useful, *access is by no means the same as influence. It is simply a route towards influence—and in many cases, the route is blocked.*

A senior committee clerk or a committee chairman, a bureau chief or a White House aide, a commissioner in a regulatory agency, may listen a little sooner and a little longer to someone whom they already know. There are times when this can make the margin of difference. It probably is particularly important when the issue is new and the Washington representative has the rhetorical skill to define the issues in a memorable way, favorable to his client. (But, of course, many people who have access enough do not possess this skill).

But, in fact, a well-put case on any issue of importance will usually be heard by committee chairmen, White House aides, and commissioners anyway—regardless of who puts it. The occasions when access really "helps" *in the short run* are usually precisely those occasions when *in the long run* the case is doomed to failure. A person who has access, who is a friend or former coworker, who is respected or politically prominent, can and will get a rehearing for an issue already decided; he can get consideration given to an extremely weak case, but he cannot get a favorable verdict. Access, that is, can drag out and delay a decision—which may at times be important—but it rarely influences the final verdict unless during the period of delay some change happens in the factual situation.

VIII

Now we come to a restatement of a central emphasis of the entire book. *The kind of influence which a Washington representative can best provide is that arising from professional competence.*

A way of showing what this sort of professional competence consists in is by stressing why it is that most presentations to congressmen or bureaucrats—requests for changes in law or policy—coming spontaneously from those desiring the changes are not effective. They are ineffective because most people, making such presentations, do not take account of the history and complexity of the issue nor do they pay attention to the organizationally derived point of view of members of Congress or of the bureaucracy.

That is to say, issues—with the rarest exceptions—do not come before Congress or a bureau with a clean slate. On the contrary, in one form or another, executives, bureaucrats, legislative aides, and congressmen have dealt with closely related matters before. They know (or think they know) that any action to accomplish the particular purpose which interest A desires will be criticized by interests B, C, and D. They believe, on the basis of experience which is (or is thought to be) relevant, that if they actually do what an organization in terms of official policy presses for, sooner or later it may happen that some in that very organization protest the results of the change. As a parallel, it is well known that "good government" organizations at the local level which succeed in persuading or coercing public officials to enforce ordinances or taxing provisions "without fear or favor" sometimes discover that some of their own most prominent members protest the new dispensation quite vigorously. Similar problems happen in regard to numerous Federal decisions, although reasons of space forbid my citing those that come most quickly to mind.

An example wherein granting a request might create dissatisfaction somewhere else is provided by the case already discussed several times in this book. Suppose Senator Personal Service had taken the stand desired by the industry in his state; and some measure of action against foreign imports had been undertaken in consequence. In that same state there is a big port city, which probably has as high a proportion of business leaders opposed in principle to import restriction as any city in the country. They might conceivably have protested the action the Senator's other constituents desired. Or suppose that one of the biggest industries in the very town from which the protest came found, as is possible, that such an action made it more diffi-

cult to sell its products in the country which would be most hurt by the requested import restriction—perhaps the Senator a couple of years later would be trying some action to take care of a protest arising out of this situation.

Such aspects of the situation could have created problems for the Senator. Yet, to explain them briefly to Mr. Industrialist would have been dangerous; many people react to such an explanation by labelling the explainer as a "mere opportunistic politician." And to explain them at length would have taken more time than it would have been reasonable to expect from a senatorial office on what was after all a relatively minor issue from the Senator's standpoint.

But a competent Washington representative would have been aware of these aspects of the matter and of others like them.

A qualified Washington representative would be able to look at the situation, not only from the standpoint of the client, but from the standpoint of the Senator and his colleagues. With such an approach, he would be able to try to think of ways of asking for action which would lessen the risks to the Senator or he would have prepared himself to convince the Senator's staff that the threat of bother to the Senator was not really very great.

Similarly, since after all the real decisions would be made by administrative agencies, the Washington representative would be able to present the case to the latter in a way which minimized the risk of trouble to them, if it could be minimized, or, if it could not be, showed awareness of agency problems. From the standpoint of the agencies which might have done something to protect the industry, the significant question would almost certainly be: Why treat this industry differently? For, clearly, other industries might claim whatever protection was given this industry.

In fact, it is unlikely that a strong case could have been made for protection for the industry, in terms of the then prevailing viewpoints in Congress and the executive branch. But it is probable—if the industry's statements about barriers against selling its product in Canada were true—that on that matter there was a basis for special aid to the industry which would have been admitted both in Congress and in the State Department. And, so, the *"influence"* of the Washington representative would have consisted in his finding out to whom in government an acceptable and helpful case could be presented.

Likewise, if the industry could have accomplished something for itself in regard to materials allocation at the end of the Korean War, the "influence" of the Washington representative would have lain, precisely, in his ability to determine where and how presentations on this matter could best be made.

Now, a competent Washington representative is not, of course, concerned only with the arguments for or against a case, logically interpreted. He will recognize that in any governmental organization there are traditional ways of doing things, traditional hostilities, etc., which determine what is regarded as natural and proper. He knows that in any agency an issue is assessed partly in terms of that agency's own position in relationship to other agencies and the public, and partly in terms of the notions of propriety common in the agency. And he will be able to judge, in consequence, what agencies are the most likely to respond favorably to particular demands of a client at a given time. So, he will try to see what basis exists for presenting the case to the most favorably disposed agencies. And, vice versa, of course, if agencies to whom the case might most logically be presented are likely to be unsympathetic, he will inquire vigorously into alternative possibilities.

IX

This kind of "influence" is secured by information about the internal workings of government. But a capable Washington representative should often spend effort in focusing *outside* influence upon governmental officials. For this purpose, he needs to know who outside government will actually have influence with those inside it who

may pass on his case. He also needs to know how influential outsiders can be encouraged or persuaded to support it.

The most familiar example here is the Washington representative who stage-manages a presentation, brings in well-known experts to testify, and then gets constituents to see individual congressmen. The congressmen want to feel that important people favor the proposed bill; and they want also to feel that people in their own constituencies are paying attention to the matter and will appreciate what they do about it. Yet, in most cases, the experts would not have testified and the constituents would not have pushed the matter, unless the Washington representative had done the planning and coordinating.

Such presentations are often arranged by coalitions of groups and interests—the civil rights coalition consisted of well over 100 different organizations in 1964-1965. And, of course, a great deal of the exchange of information between representatives of different groups in such a case as this is about how to influence whom. One organization will feel it has a lead to a given congressman because of a religious tie; another will report that its representative talked with another congressman's executive assistant who seemed to be worried about a peripheral aspect of the proposal; a third will recollect that its national officers happen to be active in state politics in the home state of still another congressman and might be willing to call on him the next time he goes home. And someone else will suggest that, in fact, the newspaper coverage in certain states and cities from which key congressmen come has been poor—can anything be done about that?

Such coalitions exist on issues much more limited than civil rights. The lumber-paper company representatives in Washington meet together; the pharmaceutical company representatives also in practice meet together, in regard to such issues as the cost of Medicare items and how to handle drug regulations. In such coalitions there is a tendency to divide up responsibility, so that the representative of the company which has the most influence with a given committee chairman or the representative of the company which is the most involved in a specific issue becomes the "action agent" for that issue. He keeps the other representatives alerted; and then, on the next issue, some other company representative will become "action agent."

Coalitions have been developed more systematically in regard to legislation than in regard to relationships with administrative agencies. But this represents, more than anything else, the fact that all political reactions are a little behind the times. There probably have been coalitions, which I have not encountered, designed to influence some administrative agency. If there have not yet been full-fledged administratively oriented coalitions, there surely will be. Geography would count for less in coalitions of this sort, and professional alignment for more. A group, trying to influence the Public Health Service or the National Institutes of Health on some matter, might well divide officials up according to professional background—so that some members of the coalition would attempt to influence hospital administrators; others, surgeons; others, psychiatrists; and still others, professional civil servants.

Or consider an effort to get support for an Institute of Inter-American Studies, affiliated with the University of Puerto Rico, similar to the East-West Institute in Hawaii. Although congressional support would be useful and welcome in nurturing the idea, congressmen would not be of preeminent importance in the early period of its development. A member of the House Foreign Affairs Committee could, for instance, exert less influence than a section chief in A.I.D. in the early stages, unless he made it a real priority issue.

The advocates of such an institute would have to try to get support both inside and outside the government—from people with some weight in the educational-philanthropic community or in the field of Latin-American affairs.

The advocates of any proposal of this sort have to make at least nine separate kinds of calculations:

1. First, they have to determine who could kill the proposal by open hostility—in the particular case, the Governor of Puerto Rico almost certainly could, and the congressional delegate from Puerto Rico probably could. It is possible that real objection by various Pan-American or Inter-American secretariats would be lethal, also. And, at the University of Puerto Rico, substantial opposition from leading faculty members might well take place and could hurt a good deal.

It would not be necessary to secure the support of all or any of the above (though it would be helpful), but it would be wasteful to go ahead if they were seriously opposed.

2. What agencies in the Latin-American or Caribbean affairs field or in the educational-philanthropic community (or locally in Puerto Rico) might be in a position to provide necessary financial support. These agencies might be either private or public— foundation or business as well as governmental.

3. What the formal channels of getting such support would be.

4. What the informal ways of communicating with those who later might be formally approached are.

5. What kind of support from outside the government or outside a foundation or business firm might help to make government agencies or foundations or business firms feel the idea worthwhile. In such a case as this, professional support would probably count for much more than public or constituency backing. To be sure, a senator from New York State might respond favorably to a request from Puerto Rican constituents that he endorse the proposal, but it would be highly unlikely that any significant number of Puerto Ricans in New York would vote differently in the next election or even provide more or less in the way of campaign funds because of whatever he did on such an issue. It is not likely to have enough priority. Whereas officials in Health, Education, and Welfare, Foreign Aid administrators, and foundation executives will be continuously concerned with the judgments of university associations, professional

groups in social science and the humanities, etc. It might turn out that library facilities would be a key factor with such groups and associations—and that the best way to get their support, or at any rate avoid their opposition, would be to improve libraries at the University of Puerto Rico. Similarly, Foreign Aid administrators, the State Department, and the like will respond partly in terms of their guess as to the way in which Caribbean nations regard Puerto Rico—and it may be the case that the university can do something to affect such guesses. It might show that Puerto Rico is more popular with and admired by Caribbean and Latin American *intellectuals* than it is with Caribbean and Latin American *governments* (some of which have not been enthusiastic about the Popular party social-democratic regime in Puerto Rico). On the other hand, there may be nothing that the University of Puerto Rico can do to affect such guesses, for they may be dependent upon historic, demographic, and cultural factors, quite beyond control.

6. Among those whose favorable support is important after calculations (2) through (5), which are the most likely to be *sympathetic* and therefore provide good starting points and

7. Among those whose favorable support is important after calculations (2) through (5), which are the most *accessible*.

8. Among those whose favorable support is important after calculations (2) through (5), which ones are the most *able to provide really effective support.*

9. Then there is a final calculation—weighing possible sympathy, accessibility, and power against each other, where should the start be made? The temptation is of course to start with the most accessible; but this is often wasteful; they may only be mildly predisposed to sympathy and/or not powerful.

It is worth reporting that, although I spent some weeks in 1961 trying to develop plans for such an institute in Puerto Rico, neither I, nor any of those with whom I worked, as far as I recollect, got beyond mere formal arguments and approaches. Yet, we, because of a background in politics, were

more predisposed than most academics to be aware of the need for analyzing influence.

Calculations of the sort just listed help to locate and focus influence; they can help to make latent influence active; *but they can rarely create influence.* This is not to say that it is impossible to create influence. But the creation of influence is more a matter of "public relations" or propaganda than of government relations; it will not be discussed in this book, although there are government relations specialists and Washington representatives who also spend a good deal of time on public relations, propaganda, and political campaigning. But the techniques are different. They have been discussed so frequently elsewhere that there is no occasion to deal with them here.

X

What has just been said is really this: *The effective Washington representative provides influence for his client by acquiring and translating relevant information.* In this sense, of course, he does "provide influence and information..." but this is probably not the sense in which inexperienced clients expect to buy or rent influence. And, in fact, clients often have to be taught that this is what they can in fact get and use.

It is desirable to underline the point that the Washington representative deals with two kinds of information. The first kind is apparent enough—information about the factual and legal aspects of the issues with which his clients are concerned. Second, he supplies relevant information about influence relationships or influence potentialities in a given situation. If, for instance, it is known that a given congressman is in debt because of campaign expenses, it is more likely that he will be particularly responsive to an invitation to address a trade association meeting for a fee. Or, if the most active commissioner of a given regulatory agency is supporting a particular presidential aspirant, to whom victory in a particular state primary is important, representations by lawyers, active in the politics of that particular state, may be especially helpful. Or if a medical or educational officer in the Department of Health, Education, and Welfare, whose support is desired for a certain ruling, is a candidate for the presidency of a given university, a trustee of that university may have better access to and more influence with him than most people.

However, there is a danger which may affect some Washington representatives and clients. Information about these influence relationships can be helpful; in most instances, however, their effect is marginal. Some people are in a sense unduly Machiavellian in viewpoint—they exaggerate the role of power and pull in U.S. governmental decisions, or simply have a passion for the "inside dope," the "real reason." They can and do waste a good deal of time in focusing on influence relationships rather than on the merits of the case—or in trying to cultivate influence of their own through contacts, rather than dealing with the issues. The latter type is dismissed by some sophisticated Washington hands with a phrase about "those guys who think government relations is playing golf out at Burning Tree . . ." (Prominent people supposedly relax at Burning Tree; and are then more susceptible, supposedly, to blandishments from representatives of business firms and other organizations).

On the whole, in Washington, my *impression*—without any hard evidence to support it—is that more Washington representatives pay too *little* explicit attention to the influence factor than pay too *much* attention to it. My *impression*, also is that the situation is just the reverse in some state capitals.

There is one other approach to information which must be included in a sophisticated government relations program. That is the *intelligence* approach, the approach designed to take account of contingencies which could develop. The careful Washington representative will, for instance, keep track of bills and resolutions which are filed—to see if any of them *might* affect the interests of his organization. Of course, the overwhelming majority of bills and resolutions have nothing to do with his particular organization—but, sometimes, there are unexpected consequences from proposals which do not, at first glance, appear connected. For instance, should representatives of a university or of associations of college professors or students take any stand on a proposal for penalizing travel to Europe in order to protect the balance of payments? Or could the National Parking Association benefit from some proposal to finance training of school dropouts?

Certainly, too, the great majority of bills and resolutions are not going anywhere. They will be filed and that will be the end of them. But, as a measure of protection, it may be desirable to see if there is a sleeper among seemingly hopeless proposals.

Similarly, of course, a sophisticated government relations staff monitors, *within the limits of available time and personnel,* committee reports and hearings which may be relevant.

And, even more important, a sophisticated program involves keeping track of regulations and proposals for regulations which may be relevant to the client's interests.

Of course, no one person can possibly follow, comprehendingly, most of the numerous proposals for bills, investigations, and regulations. There are too many—their implications are too broad. It is for this reason that experience is vital in much Washington representation. For, it is experience, aided by study and imagination, which can enable a person to guess that such-and-such a form of words may well mean that a proposed bill or regulation or investigation might affect his organization's interests. At any rate, the perception of such possible contingent connections is a specific kind of skill, which some persons who know a great deal about government lack. ·

Of course, in a government relations program of any size, it is not necessary that everyone possess this skill. But it is highly useful in such a program to have someone in its employ who does possess it.

XI

In any presentation of the sort made in this chapter, it is difficult to steer a straight course between Scylla and Charybdis. On the one hand, there is a tendency to write so as to confirm familiar impressions (in this case that would mean to support the notions which many have derived from newspaper stories about corruption and pull in government). On the other, there is a temptation, in challenging the familiar and conventional impressions, to overstate one's case (or at least to write so that one appears to do so).

Were we starting this discussion with a naive faith in rational democracy, ignorant of the existence of interests and organizations, and of their role in politics and government, no doubt much emphasis would have to be placed upon the role of deals, special access, etcetera, in government and governmental decision-making. But we are not starting out on any such basis; in fact, the literature of lobbying and pressure politics, ever since the days of Mark Hanna and the Populists, has emphasized the role of wheeler-dealers in legislation and administration. Anyone who has, for instance, read Drew Pearson's columns over the years will have learned that deals do happen, influence is exerted, people are paid off, and so forth.

Accordingly, it is not at all necessary to stress these matters. However, in calling attention to the far greater importance of other forms of exerting influence I have probably failed to take enough account of three respects in which pull, very crude deals, and so forth, may work:

a. The "one-shot" operator probably can on occasion help himself a good deal by buying pull—and if he has enough resources, he may be able to pay a high enough price genuinely to buy it. But, in fact, there are not very many one-shot operators. *And in any case this book is written from the standpoint of the organization that is likely to have a continuing relationship with government.* Few one-shot operators would read it or be guided by it. (By a "one-shot" operator, I mean a man who has one very important favor or ruling to get from government and will not need any subsequent concessions of any great importance. An example might be a firm dependent for survival upon a particular land concession, but, which, if granted the land rights, might not need to go again to Washington for ten years.)

b. I have emphasized that what I say applies only to Washington—and not necessarily to states or cities, and still less to certain foreign governments. But there is a great difference in the organizational ethics and climate of different departments and regulatory agencies; I do not pretend to know all of the bureaus in Washington. It is possible, perhaps even probable, that there is some bureau or regulatory commission which practices politics and government in the fashion of some of the states, rather than like other Washington agencies. I am speaking, in other words, about what is characteristic of Washington, not what is necessarily true of every agency, bureau, and section.

I would be speaking out of unsupported suspicions if I were to name current examples as illustrating such exceptions; but it does seem to have been the case that the Alien Property administration just after World War II was more vulnerable to pull and rather crude deals than most agencies. It also seems definitely to have been the case that just prior to World War II the consular service was similarly susceptible; although in this case it might be regarded as more of a "one-shot operation" where persons desiring special favors could and did make very high payments to underpaid officials.

c. It is important to stress that the general freedom of the Washington bureaucracy from susceptibility to illegitimate pull or crude deals is *in part* due to support from the highest executive and congressional officials. (Vice versa, of course, politicians coming to Washington are often more honest and objective than they were in earlier careers in state politics, because the cumulative impact of the Washington bureaucracy, the national press, and the Washington tradition pushes them toward a greater degree of honesty and integrity). During the Harding administration, notably, there were some occasions when top executives connived at or benefited from crudely dishonest deals. There have been a few such instances since; and no doubt any given organization or Washington representative might be dealing with men who similarly violate the Washinton tradition in the future. But in dealing with such executives or congressmen, the warnings given in this whole chapter apply. And, in particular (and this is very different from the situation in many state governments) an organization which engages in bribery and corruption of a Washington official of any prominence may well be handicapping itself for years to come; for, in the Washington situation, such bribes and corruption may well be exposed, and, if they are, all those who deal with the bribing organization in the future may well lean over backwards to avoid any suspicion of favoritism towards it.

Of course, in principle, it is possible that the national government as a whole might become genuinely corrupt and come to resemble highway departments, for instance, in such states as Oklahoma, West Virginia, and Indiana, not long ago. The odds against such a development appear to me, however, to be very great; the whole thrust of our times towards bureaucratic accountability and efficiency and professionalism seems to be moving us, as a nation, in the opposite direction. Indeed, a change in this direction in our national government would be as much of a revolution as the New Deal in its time or the Jacksonian introduction of the spoils system in the earlier days of the republic. Not only this book, but much of what is now written about government in Washington, would become outdated should this direction alter.

Liberal

G. William Domhoff.   How the power elite make foreign policy.[1]

This essay will attempt to show that American foreign policy is initiated, planned, and carried out by members and organizations of a power elite that is rooted in and serves the interests of an upper class of rich businessmen and their descendants. It will be claimed that none of the factors often of importance in domestic issues—Congress, labor, public opinion—has anything but an occasional and minor effect on foreign policy. If there is one issue-area truly and solely the domain of the power elite, it is foreign policy. Given the great importance of foreign policy in determining the framework within which all types of policy-making take place, power elite dominance of this single issue-area gives them a great influence on all aspects of the political process.

The making of foreign policy takes place within an environment or setting: the international community of nations, American public opinion, mass media, political interest groups, agencies of the executive branch and committees of Congress. However, it is possible to suggest that public opinion is rarely felt and that Congress is usually by-passed. Moreover, it is possible to be much more concrete in spelling out the specific mechanisms within which the decision-makers function. In general, the most important institutions in foreign policy decision-making are large corporations and banks, closely intertwined charitable foundations, two or three discussion and research associations financed by these corporations and foundations, and the National Security Council, State Department, Defense Department, and specially appointed committees of the federal government. Admittedly, this is only the most important core, for there are several other private and university-affiliated research and opinion-molding organizations, as well as several other agencies of the federal government.

The Council on Foreign Relations

To give empirical flesh to these generalizations, there is no better starting point than the Council on Foreign Relations (CFR). It is the key middle term, so to speak, between the large corporations on the one hand and the federal government on the other. By studying its connections in both directions, it is possible to establish the first link we are looking for in showing the specific mechanisms by which the power elite formulate and transfer their wishes into government policy. While it would be hard to underestimate the importance of this organization in understanding the overall framework for American foreign policy, I do not want to overemphasize it, and we will see that there are other links between big business and big government.

The Council on Foreign Relations is a nonpartisan research and discussion group dedicated to informing citizens about world affairs and creating an interest in international relations. Despite its reputed prominence and the fact that it was founded in 1921, most information on it comes from its own publications: a fifteen-year history, a twenty-five-year history and annual reports. One of the few who has written on it, Washington journalist Joseph Kraft, noted in 1958 that it was mentioned only five times in *Time* magazine in the period 1953–1958.[2] We can go one step further and say that there never has been any research paper on it in any scholarly journal indexed in the *Social Science and Humanities Index*. While this may suggest it is not very important, there are several ways to establish its crucial role, including testimony by journalists and scholars, the acknowledged preeminence of its journal (*Foreign Affairs*), the nature of its financial backing, the composition of its leadership and membership, and the presence of its members in federal government positions.

To begin with expert testimony, CFR was called by Kraft a "school for statesmen [which] comes close to being an organ of what C. Wright Mills has called the Power Elite—a group of men, similar in interest and outlook, shaping events from invulnerable positions behind the scenes."[3] Douglass Cater, a journalist from Exeter and Harvard who served on the staff of President Lyndon B. Johnson, has noted that "a diligent scholar would do well to delve into the role of the purely unofficial Council on Foreign Relations in the care and breeding of an incipient American Establishment."[4] *The New York Times* calls it "a testing ground for new ideas, with enough political and financial power to bring the ideas to the attention of the policy makers in Washington."[5] Political scientist Lester Milbrath notes that "The Council on Foreign Relations, while not financed by government, works so closely with it that it is difficult to distinguish Council actions stimulated by government from autonomous actions."[6]

Empirically speaking, such reputational testimony is the least important of our evidence. Far more important is CFR's financing and leadership. Aside from membership dues, dividends from invested gifts and bequests, and profits from the sale of *Foreign Affairs*, the most important sources of income are leading corporations and major foundations. In 1957–58, for example, Chase Manhattan, Continental Can, Ford Motor, Bankers Trust, Cities Service, Gulf, Otis Elevator, General Motors Overseas Operations, Brown Brothers, Harriman, and International General Electric were paying from $1,000 to $10,000 per year for the corporation service, depending upon the size of the company and its interest in international affairs. (The benefits of subscribing to this corporation service are as follows: free consultation with all members of the CFR staff, subscriptions to *Foreign Affairs* for leading officers of the corporation, the use of the Council's excellent library which is second to none in its field, and the right to nominate one "promising young executive" to participate in seminars which the Council conducts each fall and spring for the benefit of the corporations.)[7] More generally, in 1960–61, eighty-four large corporations and financial institutions contributed 12% ($112,200) of CFR's total income. As to the foundations, the major contributors over the years have been the

Rockefeller Foundation and the Carnegie Corporation, with the Ford Foundation joining in with a large grant in the 1950's. According to Kraft, a $2.5 million grant in the early 1950's from the Ford, Rockefeller, and Carnegie foundations made the Council "the most important single private agency conducting research in foreign affairs."[8] In 1960–61, the foundation money accounted for 25% of CFR income.

The foundations which support the CFR are in turn directed by men from Bechtel Construction, Chase Manhattan, Cummins Engine, Corning Glass, Kimberly-Clark, Monsanto Chemical, and dozens of other corporations. Further, to complete the circle, most foundation directors are members of CFR. In the early 1960's, Dan Smoot found that twelve of twenty Rockefeller Foundation trustees, ten of fifteen Ford Foundation trustees, and ten of fourteen Carnegie Corporation trustees were members of CFR[9]. Nor is this interlock of recent origin. In 1922, for example, former Secretary of State Elihu Root, a corporation lawyer, was honorary CFR president as well as president of the Carnegie Corporation, while John W. Davis, the corporation lawyer who ran for President on the Democratic ticket in 1924, was a trustee of both the Carnegie Corporation and CFR.

A consideration of the leadership and membership of CFR is equally conclusive in establishing its relationship to the power elite. Its founders included two lawyers and two bankers from Wall Street. The single permanent official of CFR at its outset, Hamilton Fish Armstrong, and the first editor of *Foreign Affairs*, Archibald Coolidge, were both from well-known, upper-class families. Indeed, Hamiltons, Fishes and Armstrongs have been involved in American foreign policy since the beginnings of the Republic. Nor has anything changed since the early 1920's, with fourteen of the twenty-two recent or current directors as of the early 1960's being listed in the Social Register. Among the most prominent of the recent directors highly visible in the corporate elite are Frank Altschul, Elliott V. Bell, Thomas K. Finletter (one-time Secretary of the Air Force),

Devereaux C. Josephs, John J. McCloy, David Rockefeller and Adlai E. Stevenson.

The CFR limits itself to 700 New York area residents and 700 non-New York residents (no women or foreigners are allowed to join). As of the mid-sixties, 46% of the resident members and 49% of the non-resident members, most of whom are big businessmen and lawyers, were listed in the Social Register.[10] The Council's only other formal associates are the Committees on Foreign Relations that have been formed in about thirty cities across the country. These committees come together at dinners and other occasions to hear speakers (mostly supplied by CFR) and exchange ideas. This committee program has been financed since 1938 by the Carnegie Corporation.[11] We were able to locate information on 509 committee members from twenty-nine cities ranging in size and importance from Philadelphia, Detroit and Atlanta to Albuquerque, Boise and Little Rock. A significant minority of those studied (41%) were corporate executives and bankers. Twenty-one percent were lawyers, almost half of whom (44%) were also corporate directors. Thus, a small majority (51%) were directly involved in business enterprises. Another significant group consisted of educators (22%), most of whom were college presidents, political scientists, economists, and deans. Seven percent of those studied were editors or publishers, with the remainder being small numbers of government officials, politicians, church leaders, physicians, accountants and museum directors.

Turning to the all-important question of government involvement, the presence of CFR members in government has been attested to by Kraft, Cater, Smoot, CFR histories and *The New York Times*, but the point is made most authoritatively by John J. McCloy, Wall Street lawyer, former chairman of Chase Manhattan, trustee of the Ford Foundation, director of CFR and a government appointee in a variety of roles since the early 1940's: "Whenever we needed a man," said McCloy in explaining the presence of CFR members in the modern defense establishment that fought World War II, "we thumbed through the roll of council members and put through a call to New York."[12] According to Kraft, "When John McCloy went to Bonn as US High Commissioner, he took with him a staff composed almost exclusively of men who had interested themselves in German affairs at the Council."[13] CFR members also were prominent in the US delegation to the founding of the United Nations, and several dozen have held high posts in postwar administrations. One *Annual Report* spoke as follows in an obituary notice:

[John Foster] Dulles was a member of the Council almost from the start. He wrote an article on "The Allied Debts" for the first issue of *Foreign Affairs* and six more articles thereafter, including two while Secretary of State. He participated in numerous study and discussion groups over the years and spoke often at Council afternoon meetings and dinners, twice as Secretary of State.[14]

Theodore White, in recounting how Lyndon Johnson won the Presidency in 1964, wrote as follows about the relationship of the Council to government:

Its roster of members has for a generation, under Republican and Democratic administrations alike, been the chief recruiting ground for Cabinet-level officials in Washington. Among the first eighty-two names on a list prepared for John F. Kennedy for staffing his State Department, at least sixty-three were members of the Council, Republicans and Democrats alike. When, finally, he made his appointments, both his Secretary of State (Rusk, Democrat) and Treasury (Dillon, Republican) were chosen from Council members; so were seven assistant and undersecretaries of State, four senior members of Defense, ... as well as two members of the White House staff (Schlesinger, Democrat; Bundy, Republican).[15]

Now that we have located the CFR in sociological space as an institution controlled by members of the upper class, we are in a position to see what it does and how effective it is in shaping foreign policy. As to what the CFR does, in addition to serving as a talent pool and training ground for government service, it is a tax-exempt, nonpartisan organization which sponsors education, discussion and research on all aspects of foreign affairs. As part of its educational effort, it brings before its exclusive membership leading scholars and government officials from all nations to make off-the-record speeches and to answer questions from the members. And, as Kraft notes, this not only educates the members, it gives them a chance to size up important leaders with whom they will have to deal.[16] Also under the heading of education, CFR publishes *Foreign Affairs*, by far the most important journal in its field, and three annual surveys: *Political Handbook of the World, The United States in World Affairs,* and *Documents on American Foreign Relations.*

Despite the importance of speeches and publications, I think the most important aspects of the CFR program are its special discussion groups and study groups. These small groups of about twenty-five bring together businessmen, government officials, military men and scholars for detailed discussions of specific topics in the area of foreign affairs. Discussion groups explore problems in a general way, trying to define issues and alternatives. Such groups often lead to a study group as the next stage. Study groups revolve around the work of a Council research fellow (financed by Carnegie, Ford and Rockefeller) or a staff member. This group leader usually presents monthly papers, which are discussed and criticized by the rest of the group. The goal of such study groups is a detailed statement of the problem by the scholar leading the discussion. In 1957–58, for example, the Council published six books which grew out of study groups. Perhaps the most famous of these was written by Henry Kissinger, a bright young McGeorge Bundy protégé at Harvard who was asked by the CFR to head a study group. His *Nuclear Weapons and Foreign Policy* was "a best seller which has been closely read in the highest Administration circles and foreign offices abroad."[17] As to his study group, it included "two former chairmen of the Atomic Energy Commission, a Nobel Prize winner in physics, two former civilian secretaries in the Defense Department and representatives just below the highest level from the State Department, the Central Intelligence

Agency and the three armed services."[18] When economists Percy Bidwell of the CFR staff led a discussion on foreign tariff, an issue that will be discussed later, the study group included ten corporate representatives, ten economists, two communications experts from MIT's Center for International Studies, a minor Defense Department official and a foreign service officer.[19]

It is within these discussion groups and study groups, where privacy is the rule to encourage members to speak freely, that members of the power elite study and plan as to how best to attain American objectives in world affairs. It is here that they discuss alternatives and hash out differences, far from the limelight of official government and mass media. As *The New York Times* says of these unpublicized luncheons and closed seminars: "Except for its annual public Elihu Root Lectures, the Council's talks and seminars are strictly off the record. An indiscretion can be grounds for termination or suspension of membership…"[20] Such discussions also help to reduce the effect of political changes. In Kraft's language: "…the Council plays a special part in helping to bridge the gap between the two parties, affording unofficially a measure of continuity when the guard changes in Washington."[21]

Given its privacy as to discussions (it is quite open about everything else), can we know the relationship between CFR and government policy? Can we go beyond the fact that CFR conducts research and discussions and that its members hold responsible positions in the federal government? It is not only secrecy which makes this question hard to answer; there is also the problem that CFR as an organization does not take a partisan stand. To even begin to answer such a question completely would require a large number of studies of various decisions and their outcomes. In lieu of such studies, the most important and easy of which would be on the origins of the bipartisan foreign policy of postwar years, several suggestive examples will have to suffice, along with the general testimony of Kraft ("It has been the seat of some basic government decisions, has set the context

for many more") and *The New York Times* ("Discussion groups, scholarly papers and studies sponsored by the Council laid the groundwork for the Marshall Plan for European recovery, set American policy guidelines for the North Atlantic Treaty Organization, and currently are evolving a long-range analysis of American attitudes toward China").[22] More concretely, Kraft claims that CFR action was responsible for putting Greenland out of bounds for the Nazis, for shaping the United Nations charter, and for softening the American position on German postwar reparations, among others. One of the most impressive evidences is that four CFR planning groups, set up in 1939 with aid from the Rockefeller Foundation, were taken (along with most of the personnel) into the State Department in 1942 "as the nub of its Advisory Committee on Postwar Planning Problems."[23] And it was supposedly a special CFR briefing session in early 1947 that convinced Undersecretary of State Robert Lovett of Brown Brothers, Harriman that "it would be our principal task at State to awaken the nation to the dangers of Communist aggression."[24]

Despite the fact that the CFR is an organization most Americans have never heard of, I think we have clearly established by a variety of means that it is a key connection between the federal government and the owners and managers of the country's largest financial institutions and corporations. It is an organization of the power elite. If it is not all-embracing in its importance, it is certainly a considerable understatement to speak of CFR members and members of similar power elite associations, as one scholar does, as "external bureaucrats" who supply the government with information, perspectives, and manpower.[25] In my view, what knowledge we have of CFR suggests that through it the power elite formulate general guidelines for American foreign policy and provide the personnel to carry out this policy. But I also know that the evidence I have presented is not enough for those scholars who prefer to analyze actual decisions. Then, too, skeptics can point out that CFR has no policy (other than the all-important policy of international involvement, as opposed to isolationism, for which it is called "Communist" and "Un-American" by older-fashioned, nationalistic critics). Furthermore, skeptics can say that CFR's members have other institutional and associational affiliations that may be more important in determining their outlook. For all of these reasons, I will let the case for CFR rest at this point, noting the presence of its directors and members only in passing, and instead emphasizing the direct corporate connections of important decision-makers. In closing this discussion of the CFR as an organization of the power elite, it should be noted that Kraft is among the skeptics. Despite all the comments we have quoted from him on the importance of CFR, he concludes that "even that cock will not fight" as far as the CFR being part of any power elite. This is because CFR has assumed "semi-official duties only in emergencies," because it "has never accepted government financial support" and because its recommendations "have subsequently all stood test at the polls or in Congress." Furthermore, there are "divergent views" within the Council, and such an organization is necessary because issues are too complicated for the ordinary citizen, who is all wrapped up in his private life. Kraft's concluding sentence seems to be a challenge to those who might criticize—he quotes Voltaire, asking, "What have you got that's better?"[26]

Other policy-planning groups

The Council on Foreign Relations is by no means the only power elite link between the corporations and the federal government in the issue-area of foreign policy. There are many others, perhaps the most important of which are the Committee for Economic Development, the RAND Corporation and a handful of research institutes affiliated with elite universities. Turning to the first of these, the Committee for Economic Development (CED) is a tax-exempt research organization which is in many ways the counterpart on economic policy of the Council on Foreign Relations. While its concentration on monetary and economic problems makes it more prominent on

issues involving the Department of Treasury and Commerce, it has on several occasions played a major role in shaping foreign policy.[27] Organized in the early 1940's to prepare for postwar reconversion to a civilian economy, the leaders in its formation were financier Jesse Jones, then Secretary of Commerce, and millionaires Paul Hoffman and William Benton. These three men brought together corporation executives and bankers with outstanding economists for weekend study sessions which were intensified versions of the CFR study groups. Out of these sessions came the guidelines for American economic policy in the postwar era, including some of the provisions of the Employment Act of 1946, the stabilized budget concept, long-range fiscal and monetary policy, and certain aspects of the Marshall Plan. Perhaps the most impressive evidence of CED prominence in foreign policy is that its corporate elite members and hired economists were the men who moved into the government to administer the Marshall Plan. That CED head Paul Hoffman of Studebaker and the Ford Foundation became administrator of the Marshall Plan is only the surface of the iceberg.

The relationship of the CED to the corporations really does not need to be established, for membership is limited to big businessmen and a handful of university presidents. Among its original and most active members have been Ralph Flanders, the Vermont toolmaker and Boston banker; Thomas B. McCabe, head of Scott Paper Company; Clarence Francis of General Foods; Marion B. Folsom of Eastman Kodak; William L. Clayton of Clayton, Anderson; William L. Batt of SKF Industries; Charles E. Wilson of General Electric; Eric A. Johnston of the Brown-Johnston Company; Chester C. Davis of the Federal Reserve Bank of St. Louis; and S. Bayard Colgate of Colgate-Palmolive-Peet. As with the CFR, many CED members become officials of the federal government: thirty-eight of the trustees during the first fifteen years of CED held elective or appointive positions.[28] Flanders and Benton became senators, McCabe became head of the Federal Reserve Bank under President Truman, and

Folsom, Clayton, William C. Foster, and Wayne C. Taylor held important posts in major departments. As of the early 1960's, forty-eight of 190 CED trustees were at the same time members of CFR.

Perhaps the best known of the power elite's large research organizations is the RAND Corporation, a name which is an acronym for "research and development." It has been credited with many technical innovations and operational suggestions. Started after the war with government research contracts and Ford Foundation money to "think" for the Air Force, it has since expanded its staff and facilities to provide this service for the entire federal government. Its 500-man professional staff is well-paid and well-educated (150 have Ph.-D.'s) due to the fact that RAND was purposely set up as a non-governmental agency so that civil service rules and salary scales could be avoided in order to attract the finest talent money could buy. It is governed by a board of trustees which is made up of members of the power elite. In 1963, when RAND published a report on its first 15 years, the board included executives from CBS, Hewlett-Packard, Owens-Corning Fiberglas International, Monsanto Chemical and New England Electric System, as well as the president of one of the Carnegie foundations, a leading official in the Council on Foreign Relations, the former vice president of the Carnegie Corporation (then president of Cornell) and the presidents of MIT and Rice University.[29] Seven of the seventeen trustees were members of the CFR. Of fifteen former trustees, seven were leading figures in the corporate world. The rest were university administrators or physicists. The most important of these former trustees was H. Rowan Gaither, a West Coast attorney, banker, and Ford Foundation trustee who was one of the key organizers of RAND. His legacy is seen in two of the 1963 trustees not with one of the companies listed above: Frederick Anderson is a partner in the investment firm of Draper, Gaither, and Anderson; Edwin E. Huddleson, Jr., is a partner in the law firm of Cooley, Crowley, Gaither, Godward, Castro, and Huddleson.

In addition to CFR, CED, and RAND there are many other associations and research organizations controlled by members of the power elite. About 300 study centers consult for the Defense Department alone.[30] Rather than trying to outline any more of these specific links, I want to turn instead to a more general, less direct link between the power elite and the federal government: the world of academic scholarship. As we have seen in the case of CFR, CED and RAND, members of the power elite are not averse to seeking advice from professional researchers, a fact which has led some to claim that "experts" control the country. Without emphasizing the direct power of these scholars, for they are often ignored and seldom have decision-making roles, it can be added that the power elite pay for their training and encourage them by monetary inducements to study certain questions rather than others. This is accomplished, first, by the general framework created at major universities through financing and through service on boards of trustees. Second, it is accomplished by foundation grants which encourage research on specific questions. Thus, Rockefeller, Carnegie, and Ford money are responsible in one way or another for almost all American research in non-Western areas.[31] While many of these grants are to universities to provide scholarships and to individuals to undertake specific research projects, the foundations also provide money for institutes affiliated with universities. For example, Ford and Carnegie money finance a Russian Research Center at Harvard, Rockefeller money finances a Russian Research Center at Columbia. Scholars from these institutes are frequent consultants to the Council on Foreign Relations.

The interrelationship of corporate-controlled foundations, think factories, and university research institutes can be demonstrated by studying the prefaces to leading books in the field of foreign affairs. For example, Gabriel A. Almond, of the very prominent Princeton Center of International Studies (publisher of *World Affairs*, which is second only to CFR's *Foreign Affairs* in this field), offers thanks to the Carnegie Corporation for the funds which made possible his study of *The Appeals of Communism.* Carnegie also supplied the funds for *The Civic Culture: Political Attitudes and Democracy in Five Nations,* coauthored by Almond and Sidney Verba. Thomas C. Schelling of the Center for International Affairs at Harvard wrote *The Strategy of Conflict* during a year-long stay at the RAND Corporation, and Herman Kahn did most of the research for *On Thermonuclear War,* published by the Princeton Center, while at the RAND Corporation. Lucian Pye's *Aspects of Political Development* was written while at the MIT Center for International Studies, with the help of Carnegie money. Walt W. Rostow of the MIT Center, a leading adviser to Democratic presidents during the 1960's, wrote his "non-communist manifesto," *Stages of Economic Growth,* during a "reflective year" grant provided by the Carnegie Corporation. Harry Eckstein edited *Internal War* for the Princeton Center with the help of Carnegie funds; an earlier version of Eckstein's own contribution, "On the Etiology of Internal Wars," was published in *Social Science and National Security,* a book which had government circulation only. Apparently, such secret books are not unusual. According to one source, it is "standard procedure at MIT and elsewhere" to publish two versions, "one classified for circulation within the intelligence community, the other 'sanitized' for public consumption."[32] While I do not believe for a minute that the power elite dictate to these scholars as to what to say, it should be clear that members of the power elite see no reason to discontinue their support of such efforts. The relationship has been explained by political scientist David Easton:

...a deeper social reason for the failure of political science to transcend its limitations ...lies in the proximity of political research to social forces that determine social policy. ...Entrenched power groups in society, those who have a firm hold on a particular pattern of distribution of social goods, material and spiritual, have a special reason to look askance at this probing into the nature and source of their social positions and activities. They are prone to stimulate research of a kind that does not inquire into the fundamentals of the existing arrangement of things.[33]

NOTES

1. I wish to thank undergraduate research assistant Mark Goldowitz for his help in gathering and organizing material for this essay, an earlier version of which appeared in *Corporations and the Cold War,* David Horowitz, ed. (New York: Monthly Review Press, 1969). This new version benefited from the comments of Douglas Fox, David Horowitz and Richard Hamilton.

2. Joseph Kraft, "School for Statesmen" (*Harper's Magazine,* July, 1958), p. 64.

3. *Ibid.,* pp. 64, 68.

4. Douglass Cater, *Power in Washingon* (New York: Random House, 1964), p. 247.

5. "Experts on Policy Looking to Youth" (*The New York Times,* May 15, 1966), p. 34.

6. Lester Milbrath, "Interest Groups and Foreign Policy" in James N. Rosenau, ed., *Domestic Sources of Foreign Policy* (New York: Free Press, 1967), p. 247.

7. *Annual Report of the Council on Foreign Relations,* 1957–58.

8. Kraft, *op. cit.,* p. 68.

9. Dan Smoot, *The Invisible Government* (Dallas: The Dan Smoot Report, 1962), pp. 168–71.

10. John F. Whitney, Jr., "The Council on Foreign Relations, Inc." (Unpublished research paper, Texas A and I University, January, 1968).

11. Smoot, *op. cit.,* p. 21.

12. Kraft, *op. cit.,* p. 67.

13. *Ibid.,* p. 68.

14. *Annual Report of the Council on Foreign Relations,* 1958–59, p. 4.

15. Theodore H. White, *The Making of the President 1964* (New York: Atheneum Publishers, 1965), pp. 67–8.

16. Kraft, *op. cit.,* p. 66. A perusal of any annual report of the CFR will show that a foreign official visiting in New York who is anyone at all will be speaking or meeting with members of the Council.

17. *Ibid.*

18. *Ibid.*

19. Percy W. Bidwell, *What the Tariff Means to American Industries* (published for the Council on Foreign Relations by Harper & Row, New York, 1956).

20. "Experts on Foreign Policy Look to Youth," *op cit.,* p. 34.

21. Kraft, *op cit.,* p. 68.

22. *Ibid.,* p. 64; "Experts on Foreign Policy Look to Youth," *op. cit.,* p. 34.

23. Kraft, *op. cit.,* p. 67. Much of Kraft's information on CFR involvement in specific issues seems to be drawn from CFR's self-published 25-

year history. It contains further details and information on other issues as well. See *The Council on Foreign Relations, A Record of Twenty-five Years,* New York, 1947.

24. Quoted in Kraft, *op. cit.,* p. 68.

25. Chadwick F. Alger, "The External Bureaucracy in United States Foreign Affairs (*Administration Science Quarterly*, June, 1962).

26. Kraft, *op. cit.,* p. 68.

27. Karl Schriftgiesser, *Business Comes of Age* (New York: Harper & Row, 1960).

28. *Ibid.,* pp. 25, 62, 162.

29. RAND Corporation, *The First Fifteen Years* (Santa Monica, California: The Rand Corporation, 1963).

30. Arthur Herzog, *The War-Peace Establishment* (New York: Harper & Row, 1965), p. 54.

31. George M. Beckmann, "The Role of Foundations" (*The Annals of the American Academy of Political and Social Science,* November, 1964).

32. David Wise and Thomas D. Ross, *The Invisible Government* (New York: Random House, 1964), p. 243.

33. David Easton, *The Political System* (New York: Alfred A. Knopf, Inc., 1966), pp. 50–1.

Socialist

C. Wright Mills.
Metropolitan 400.

The little cities look to the big cities, but where do the big cities look? America is a nation with no truly national city, no Paris, no Rome, no London, no city which is at once the social center, the political capital, and the financial hub. Local societies of small town and large city have had no historic court which, once and for all and officially, could certify the elect. The political capital of the country is not the status capital, nor even in any real sense an important segment of Society; the political career does not parallel the social climb. New York, not Washington, has become the financial capital. What a difference it might have made if from the beginning Boston and Washington and New York had been combined into one great social, political, and financial capital of the nation! Then, Mrs. John Jay's set ("Dinner and Supper List for 1787 and 1788"), in which men of high family, great wealth, and decisive power mingled, might, as part of the national census, have been kept intact and up-to-date.[1]

And yet despite the lack of official and metropolitan unity, today—seventeen decades later—there does flourish in the big cities of America a recognizable upper social class, which seems in many ways to be quite compact. In Boston and in New York, in Philadelphia and in Baltimore and in San Francisco, there exists a solid core of older, wealthy families surrounded by looser circles of newer, wealthy families. This older core, which in New York was once said—by Mrs. Astor's Ward McAllister—to number Four Hundred, has made several bids to The Society of America, and perhaps, once upon a time, it almost succeeded. Today, in so far as it tries to base itself on pride of family descent, its chances to be truly national are subject to great risks. There is little doubt, however, that among the metropolitan 400's, as well as among their small-town counterparts, there is an accumulation of advantages in which objective opportunity and psychological readiness interact to create and to maintain for each generation the world of the upper social classes. These classes, in each of the big cities, look first of all to one another.

1

Before the Civil War the big-city upper classes were compact and stable. At least social chroniclers, looking back, say that they were. "Society," Mrs. John King Van Rensselaer wrote, grew "from within rather than from without...The foreign elements absorbed were negligible. The social circle widened, generation by generation, through the abundant contributions made by each family to posterity...There was a boundary as solid and as difficult to ignore as the Chinese Wall." Family lineage ran back to the formation of the colonies and the only divisions among upper-class groups "were those of the church; Presbyterians, Dutch Reformed and Episcopalians formed fairly definite sections of a compact organization."[2]

In each locality and region, nineteenth-century wealth created its own industrial hierarchy of local families. Up the Hudson, there were patroons, proud of their origins, and in Virginia, the planters. In every New England town, there were Puritan ship-owners and early industrialists, and in St. Louis, fashionable descendants of French Creoles living off real estate. In Denver, Colorado, there were wealthy gold and silver miners. And in New York City, as Dixon Wecter has put it, there was "a class made up of coupon-clippers, sportsmen living off their fathers'' accumulation, and a stratum like the Astors and Vanderbilts trying to renounce their commercial origins as quickly as possible.[3]

The richest people could be regarded as a distinct caste, their fortunes as permanent, their families as honorably old. As long as they kept their wealth and no newer and bigger wealth threatened it, there was no reason to distinguish status by family lineage and status by wealth.[4] The stability of the older upper classes rested rather securely upon the coincidence of old family and great wealth. For the push, the wealth, the power of new upper classes was contained by the old, who, while remaining distinct and unthreatened, could occasionally admit new members.

In the decades following the Civil War, the old upper classes of the older cities were overwhelmed by the new wealth. "All at once," Mrs. Van Rensselaer thought, Society "was assailed from every side by persons who sought to climb boldly over the walls of social exclusiveness." Moreover, from overseas the immigrants came, like southerners, and later westerners, to make their fortunes in the city. "Others who had made theirs elsewhere, journeyed to New York to spend them on pleasure and social recognition."[5]

From the eighteen-seventies until the nineteen-twenties, the struggle of old family with new money occurred on a grandiose national scale. Those families that were old because they had become wealthy prior to the Civil War attempted to close up their ranks against the post-Civil War rich. They failed primarily because the new wealth was so enormous compared with the old that it simply could not be resisted. Moreover, the newly wealthy could not be contained in any locality. Like the broadening national territory, new wealth and power—in family and now in corporate form as well—grew to national size and scope. The city, the county, the state could not contain this socially powerful wealth. Everywhere, its possessors invaded the fine old families of metropolitan society.

All families would seem to be rather "old," but not all of them have possessed wealth for at least two but preferably three or four generations. The formula for "old families" in America is money plus inclination plus time. After all, there have only been some six or seven generations in the whole of United States history. For every old family there must have been a time when someone was of that family but it was not "old." Accordingly, in America, it is almost as great a thing to be an ancestor as to have an ancestor.

It must not be supposed that the pedigreed families do not and have not admitted unregistered families to their social circles, especially after the unregistered have captured their banking firms. It is only that those whose ancestors bought their way into slightly older families only two or three generations ago now push hard to keep out those who would follow suit. This game of the old rich and the parvenu began with the beginning of the national history, and continues today in the small town as in the metropolitan center. The one firm rule of the game is that, given persistent inclination, any family can win out on whatever level its money permits. Money—sheer, naked, vulgar money—has with few exceptions won its possessors entrance anywhere and everywhere into American society.

From the point of view of status, which always tries to base itself on family descent, this means that the walls are always crumbling; from the more general standpoint of an upper social class of more than local recognition, it means that top level is always being renovated. It also means that, no matter what its pretensions, the American upper class is merely an enriched bourgeoisie, and that, no matter how powerful its members may be, they cannot invent an aristocratic past where one did not exist. One careful genealogist has asserted that at the beginning of this century, there were "not ten families occupying conspicuous social positions" in either the moneyed set or the old-family set of New York "whose progenitors' names appeared on Mrs. John Jay's dinner list."[6]

In America, the prideful attempt to gain status by virtue of family descent has been an uneasy practice never touching more than a very small fraction of the population. With their real and invented ancestors, the "well-born" and the "high-born" have attempted to elaborate pedigrees and, on the basis of their consciousness of these pedigrees, to keep their distance from the "low-born." But they have attempted this with an underlying population which, in an utterly vulgar way, seemed to glory in being low-born, and which was too ready with too many jokes about the breeding of horses to make such pretensions easy or widespread.

There has been too much movement—of family residence and between occupations, in the lifetime of an individual and between the generations—for feeling of family line to take root. Even when such feeling does strengthen the claims of the upper classes, it is without avail unless it is honored by the underlying strata. Americans are not very conscious of family lines; they are not the sort of underlying population which would readily cash in claims for prestige on the basis of family descent. It is only when a social structure does not essentially change in the course of generations, only when occupation and wealth and station tend to become hereditary, that such pride and prejudice, and with them, such servility and sense of inferiority, can become stable bases of a prestige system.

The establishment of a pedigreed society, based on the prestige of family line, was possible, for a brief period, despite the absence of a feudal past and the presence of mobility, because of the *immigrant* situa-

tion. It was precisely during the decades when the flow of the new immigration into the big cities was largest that metropolitan Society was at its American peak. In such Yankee ghettoes, claims for status by descent were most successful, not so much among the population at large as among those who claimed some descent and wanted more. Such claims were and are involved in the status hierarchy of nationality groups.

But there came a time when the lowly immigrant no longer served this purpose: the flow of immigration was stopped, and in a little while everyone in North America became—or soon would become—a native-born American of native-born parents.

Even while the supply of immigrants was huge and their number in the big cities outnumbered those of native parentage, liberal sentiments of nationalism were becoming too strong to be shaped by the barriers of strict descent. "The Americanization of the Immigrant"—as an organized movement, as an ideology, and as a fact—made loyalties to one ideological version of the nation more important than Anglo-Saxon descent. The view of the nation as a glorious melting pot of races and nations—carried by middle classes and intelligentsia—came to prevail over the Anglo-Saxon views of those concerned with "racial" descent and with the pedigreed, registered society. Besides, each of these national groups—from the Irish to the Puerto Rican—has slowly won local political power.

The attempt to create a pedigreed society has gone on among an upper class whose component localities competed: the eastern seaboard was settled first; so those who remained there have been local families longer than the families of more recently populated regions. Yet there are locally eminent families who have been locally eminent in many small New England towns for as long as any Boston family; there are small-town southern families whose claims for continuity of cousinhood could not be outdone by the most fanatic Boston Brahmin; and there are early California families who, within their own strongly felt framework of time, feel older and better established than any New York family might be. The localities competed economically as well. The mining families and the railroad families and the real-estate families—in each industry, in each locality and region, as we have said, big wealth created its own hierarchy of local families.

The pedigree is a firm and stable basis of prestige when the class structure is firm and stable. Only then can all sorts of conventions and patterns of etiquette take root and flower in firm economic ground. When economic change is swift and mobility decisive, then the moneyed class as such will surely assert itself; status pretensions will collapse and time-honored prejudices will be swept away. From the standpoint of class, a dollar is a dollar, but from the standpoint of a pedigreed society, two identical sums of money—the one received from four generations of inherited trusts, the other from a real kill on the market last week—are very different sums. And yet, what is one to do when the new money becomes simply enormous? What is Mrs. Astor (the pedigreed lady of Knickerbocker origin married to old, real-estate wealth) going to do about Mrs. Vanderbilt (of the vulgar railroad money and the more vulgar grandfather-in-law) in 1870? Mrs. Astor is going to lose: in 1883 she leaves her calling card at Mrs. Vanderbilt's door, and accepts an invitation to Mrs. Vanderbilt's fancy-dress ball.[7] With that sort of thing happening, you cannot run a real pedigreed status show. Always in America, as perhaps elsewhere, society based on descent has been either by-passed or bought-out by the new and vulgar rich.*

* But not only the fast-moving mechanics of class upset the show. Almost anything fast moving does. For the conventions of a style of life are important to the prestige of local society, and only where class and status relations are stable can conventions be stabilized. If conventions are truly rigid, then dress becomes "costume," and conventions become "traditions." High prestige of ancestors, of old age, of old wealth, of antiques, of "seniority" of residence, and membership and of old ways of doing anything and everything—they go together and together make up the status conventions of a fixed circle in a stable society.

When social change is swift, prestige tends to go to the young and the beautiful, even if they are the damned; to the merely different and to the

Here, in the social context of the self-made man, the parvenu claimed status. He claimed it *as* a self-made man rather than despite it. In each generation some family-made men and women have looked down upon him as an intruder, a *nouveau riche*, as an outsider in every way. But in each following generation—or the one following that—he has been admitted to the upper social classes of the duly pedigreed families.

2

The status struggle in America is not something that occurred at a given time and was then done with. The attempt of the old rich to remain exclusively prominent by virtue of family pedigree has been a continual attempt, which always fails and always succeeds. It fails because in each generation new additions are made; it succeeds because at all times an upper social class is making the fight. A stable upper class with a really fixed membership does not exist; but an upper social class does exist. Change in the membership of a class, no matter how rapid, does not destroy the class. Not the identical individual or families, but the same type prevails within it.

There have been numerous attempts to fix this type by drawing the line in a more or less formal way. Even before the Civil War, when new wealth was not as pushing as it later became, some social arbiter seemed to be needed by worried hostesses con-

"novel," even if they are the vulgar. Costumes then become "old-fashioned," and what matters, above all, is to be "fashionable." The appearance value of one's house, and even of one's manners and one's self, become subject to fashion. There is, in short, an appreciation of the new for its own sake: that which is new is prestigeful. In such a situation, money more easily decides who can keep up with such a dynamic and steeply graded pattern of consumption differences in dresses, cars, houses, sports, hobbies, clubs. It is, of course, to such a situation as this, and not to a stabilized leisure class, that Veblen directed his phrases: "ostentatious consumption" and "conspicuous waste." For America, and for the second generation of the period of which he wrote, he was generally correct.

fronted with social decisions. For two generations before 1850, New York Society depended upon the services of one Isaac Brown, sexton of Grace Church, who, we are told by Dixon Wecter, had a "faultless memory for names, pedigrees, and gossip." He was quite ready to tell hostesses about to issue invitations who was in mourning, who had gone bankrupt, who had friends visiting them, who were the new arrivals in town and in Society. He would preside at the doorstep at parties, and some observers claimed that he "possessed a list of 'dancing young men' for the benefit of newly arrived party-givers."[8]

The extravagant wealth of the post-Civil War period called for a more articulate means of determining the elect, and Ward McAllister, for a time, established himself as selector. In order that "society might be given that solidity needed to resist invasion of the flashiest profiteers," McAllister wished to undertake the needed mixture of old families with position but without fashion, and the "swells" who had to entertain and be smart in order to win their way." He is said to have taken his task very seriously, giving over "his days and nights to study of heraldry, books of court etiquette, genealogy, and cookery. . ." In the winter of 1872–3, he organized the Patriarchs, "a committee of twenty-five men 'who had the right to create and lead Society' by inviting to each ball four ladies and five gentlemen on their individual responsibility, which McAllister stressed as a sacred trust." The original patriarchs were old-family New Yorkers of at least four generations, which, in McAllister's American generosity, he thought "make as good and true a gentleman as forty."[9]

During the 'eighties, McAllister had been dropping comments to newspaper men that there were really "only about 400 people in fashionable New York Society. If you go outside that number you strike people who are either not at ease in a ballroom or else make other people not at ease."[10] In 1892, when both the exclusiveness of the Patriarchs and the popularity of Ward McAllister were beginning seriously to decline, he published his list of "400," which in fact contained about 300 names. It was simply the rollcall of the Patriarch Balls, the inner circle of pre-Civil War New York families, embellished by unattached daughters and sons who liked to dance, and a select few of the new rich whom McAllister deemed fit for admittance. Only nine out of a list of the ninety richest men of the day[11] appear on his list.

The attention given McAllister's list of the "400," and his subsequent retirement from high society, reflect the precarious situation of the old upper classes he tried to consolidate. Not only in New York, but in other cities as well, all sorts of attempts have been made to preserve the "old-guard" from the social entrée of new wealth. McAllister's demise symbolizes the failure of all these attempts. The only sensible thing that could be done was to admit the new wealth, or at least selected members of it. This, the most successful attempt, *The Social Register*, has done.

In the gilded age of the 1880's, a New York bachelor who had inherited "a small life-income and a sound though inconspicuous social standing," decided to publish "a list of the Best People from which advertising was wisely excluded but which merchants might buy."[12] *The Social Register* presented a judicious combination of the old with the new, and, with the hearty support of friends among such New York clubs as Calumet and Union, became an immediate success. The first *Social Register* of New York contained some 881 families; in due course, lists were published for other cities, and the business of compiling and publishing such lists became incorporated as The Social Register Association. During the 'twenties, social registers were being issued for twenty-one cities, but nine of these were later dropped "for lack of interest." By 1928, twelve volumes were being printed in the autumn of each year, and ever since there have been Social Registers for New York and Boston (since 1890), Philadelphia (1890), Baltimore (1892), Chicago (1893), Washington (1900), St. Louis (1903), Buffalo (1903), Pittsburgh (1904), San Francisco (1906), Cleveland (1910), and Cincinnati (1910).[13]

The Registers list the "socially elect" together with addresses, children, schools, telephone numbers, and clubs. Supplements appear in December and January, and a summer edition is published each June. The Association advises the reader to purchase an index containing all the names in all the Registers, this being useful in so far as there are many intermarriages among families from the various cities and changes of addresses from one city to another.

The Social Register describes the people eligible for its listing as "those families who by descent or by social standing or from other qualifications are naturally included in the best society of any particular city or cities." The exact criteria for admission, however, are hard to discern perhaps because, as Wecter has asserted, "an efficient impersonality, detachment, and air of secret inquisition surround The Social Register. A certain anonymity is essential to its continued success and prestige."[14] Today, the Social Register Association, with headquarters in New York, seems to be run by a Miss Bertha Eastmond, secretary of the Association's founder from the early days. She judges all the names, some to be added, some to be rejected as unworthy, some to be considered in the future. In this work, she may call upon the counsel of certain social advisers, and each city for which there is a Register has a personal representative who keeps track of current names, addresses, and telephone numbers.

Who are included in the some 38,000 conjugal family units now listed,[15] and why are they included? Anyone residing in any of the twelve chosen cities may apply for inclusion, although the recommendations of several listed families must be obtained as well as a list of club memberships. But money alone, or family alone, or even both together do not seem to guarantee immediate admittance or final retention. In a rather arbitrary manner, people of old-family are sometimes dropped; second generations of new wealth which try to get in are often not successful. To say, however, that birth and wealth are not sufficient is not to say that they, along with proper conduct, are not necessary.

Moderately successful corporation executives, once they set their minds to it, have been known to get into the Register, but the point should not be overstressed. In particular, it ought to be made historically specific: the thirty-year span 1890–1920 was the major period for entrance into the registered circle. Since the first decade of the twentieth century, in fact, the rate of admission of new families into the Social Register—at least in one major city, Philadelphia—has steadily declined: during the first decade of this century, there was a 68 per cent increase, by the decade of the 'thirties, the rate of increase was down to 6 per cent.[16]

Those who are dropped from The Social Register are often so well known that much is made of their being dropped; the "arbitrary" character of the Register is then used to ridicule its social meaning. Actually, Dixon Wecter has concluded, "unfavorable publicity seems as near as one can come to the reason for banishment, but this again is applied with more intuition than logic . . . It is safe to say that anyone who keeps out of [the newspaper's] columns—whatever his private life may be, or clandestine rumors may report—will not fall foul of The Social Register."[17]

With all the seemingly arbitrary selection and rejection, and with all the snobbery and anguish that surrounds and even characterizes it, The Social Register is a serious listing that does mean something. It is an attempt, under quite trying circumstances, to close out of the truly proper circles the merely nouveau riche and those with mere notoriety, to certify and consolidate these proper circles of wealth, and to keep the chosen circles proper and thus presumably worthy of being chosen. After all, it is the only list of registered families that Americans have, and it is the nearest thing to an official status center that this country, with no aristocratic past, no court society, no truly capital city, possesses. In any individual case, admission may be unpredictable or even arbitrary, but as a group, the people in The Social Register have been chosen for their money, their family, and their style of life. Accordingly, the names contained in these twelve magic volumes do stand for a certain type of person.

3

In each of the chosen metropolitan areas of the nation, there is an upper social class whose members were born into families which have been registered since the *Social Register* began. This registered social class, as well as newly registered and unregistered classes in other big cities, is composed of groups of ancient families who for two or three or four generations have been prominent and wealthy. They are set apart from the rest of the community by their manner of origin, appearance, and conduct.

They live in one or more exclusive and expensive residential areas in fine old houses in which many of them were born, or in elaborately simple modern ones which they have constructed. In these houses, old or new, there are the correct furnishings and the cherished equipage. Their clothing, even when it is apparently casual and undoubtedly old, is somehow different in cut and hang from the clothes of other men and women. The things they buy are quietly expensive and they use them in an inconspicuous way. They belong to clubs and organizations to which only others like themselves are admitted, and they take quite seriously their appearances in these associations.

They have relatives and friends in common, but more than that, they have in common experiences of a carefully selected and family-controlled sort. They have attended the same or similar private and exclusive schools, preferably one of the Episcopal boarding schools of New England. Their men have been to Harvard, Yale, Princeton, or if local pride could not be overcome, to a locally esteemed college to which their families have contributed. And now they frequent the clubs of these schools, as well as leading clubs in their own city, and as often as not, also a club or two in other metropolitan centers.

Their names are not in the chattering, gossiping columns or even the society columns of their local newspapers; many of them, proper Bostonians and proper San Franciscans that they are, would be genuinely embarrassed among their own kind were their names so taken in vain—cheap publicity and cafe-society scandal are for newer families of more strident and gaudy style, not for the old social classes. For those established at the top are "proud"; those not yet established are merely conceited. The proud really do not care what others below them think of them; the conceited depend on flattery and are easily cheated by it, for they are not aware of the dependence of their ideas of self upon others.*

---

* A word about Thorstein Veblen's *The Theory of the Leisure Class* (1899) which—fortunately— is still read, not because his criticism of the American upper class is still adequate, but because his style makes it plausible, even when the criticism is not taken seriously. What he wrote remains strong with the truth, even though his facts do not cover the scenes and the characters that have emerged in our own time. It remains strong because we could not see the newer features of our own time had he not written what and as he did. Which is one meaning of the fact that his biases are the most fruitful that have appeared in the literature of American social protest. But all critics are mortal; and Veblen's theory is in general no longer an adequate account of the American system of prestige.

The Theory of the Leisure Class, is not *the* theory of *the* leisure class. It is a theory of a particular element of the upper classes in one period of the history of one nation. It is an account of the status struggle between new and old wealth and, in particular, it is an examination of the *nouveau riche*, so much in evidence in Veblen's formative time, the America of the latter half of the nineteenth century, of the Vanderbilts, Goulds, and Harrimans, of Saratoga Springs and Newport, of the glitter and the gold.

It is an analysis of an upper class which is climbing socially by translating its money into symbols of status, but doing so in a status situation in which the symbols are ambiguous. Moreover, the audience for the Veblenian drama is not traditional, nor the actors firmly set in an inherited social structure, as in feudalism. Accordingly, consumption patterns are the only means of competing for status honor. Veblen does not analyze societies with an old nobility or a court society where the courtier was a successful style of life.

In depicting the higher style of American life, Veblen—like the actors of whom he writes—seems to confuse aristocratic and bourgeois traits. At one or two points, he does so explicitly: "The aristocratic and the bourgeois virtues—that is to say the destructive and pecuniary traits—should be found chiefly among the upper classes...."[18] One has only to examine the taste

Within and between the various cliques which they form, members of these proud families form close friendships and strong loyalties. They are served at one another's dinners and attend one another's balls. They take the quietly elegant weddings, the somber funerals, the gay coming-out parties with seriousness and restraint. The social appearances they seem to like best are often informal, although among them codes of dress and manner, the sensibility of what is correct and what is not done, govern the informal and the natural as well as the formal.

Their sense of civic service does not seem to take direct political form, but causes them gladly to lead the charitable, educational, and cultural institutions of their city. Their wealth is such—probably several millions on the average—that they do not usually have to use the principal; if they do not wish to work, they probably do not have to. Yet their men—especially the more substantial older men—generally do work and sometimes quite diligently. They make up the business aristocracy of their city, especially the financial and legal aristocracy. The true gentleman—in the eastern cities, and increasingly across the nation—is usually a banker or a lawyer, which is convenient, for those who possess a fortune

are in need of trusted, wise, and sober men to preserve its integrity. They are the directors and the presidents of the major banks, and they are the senior partners and investment counselors of the leading law firms of their cities.

Almost everywhere in America, the metropolitan upper classes have in common, more or less, race, religion, and nativity. Even if they are not of long family descent, they are uniformly of longer American origin than the underlying population. There are, of course, exceptions, some of them important exceptions. In various cities, Italian and Jewish and Irish Catholic families—having become wealthy and powerful—have risen high in status. But however important, these are still exceptions: the model of the upper *social* classes is still "pure" by race, by ethnic group, by national extraction. In each city, they tend to be Protestant; moreover Protestants of class-church denominations, Episcopalian mainly, or Unitarian, or Presbyterian.

In many cities—New York for example—there are several rather than one metropolitan 400. This fact, however, does not mean that the big-city upper classes do not exist, but rather that in such cities the status structure is more elaborate than in those with more unified societies. That there are

of the small businessmen to know that this is certainly not true.

"Conspicuous consumption," as Veblen knew, is not confined to the upper classes. But today I should say that it prevails *especially* among one element of the new upper classes—the *nouveau riche* of the new corporate privileges—the men on expense accounts, and those enjoying other corporate prerogatives—and with even more grievous effects on the standard and style of life of the professional celebrities of stage and screen, radio and TV. And, of course, among recent crops of more old-fashioned *nouveau riche* dramatized by the "Texas millionaires."

In the middle of the twentieth century, as at the end of the nineteenth which Veblen observed, there *are* fantastic goings-on: "Tenor Mario Lanza now owns an outsize, custom-built white Cadillac with a gold-plated dashboard...Restaurateur Mike Romanoff ships his silk and pongee shirts air express to Sulka's in Manhattan for proper laundering...Construction Tycoon Hal Hayes...has a built-in bar in his Cadillac plus faucets for Scotch, bourbon, champagne and

beer in his home...."[19] But in established local society, the men and women of the fourth and fifth generation are quietly expensive and expensively quiet; they are, in fact, often deliberately inconspicuous in their consumption: with unpretentious farm houses and summer retreats, they often live quite simply, and certainly without any ostentatious display of vulgar opulence.

The terms of Veblen's theory are not adequate to describe the established upper classes of today. Moreover...Veblen's work, as a theory of the American status sytem, does not take into adequate account the rise of the instituted elite or of the world of the celebrity. He could not, of course, have been expected in the eighteen-nineties to see the meaning for a truly national status system of "the professional celebrities," who have arisen as part of the national media of mass communication and entertainment, or anticipate the development of national glamour, whereby the debutante is replaced by the movie star, and the local society lady by the military and political and economic managers—"the power elite"—whom many now celebrate as their proper chieftains.

social feuds between competing status centers does not destroy the status hierarchy.

The family of higher status may belong to an exclusive country club where sporting activities and social events occur, but this pattern is not of decisive importance to the upper levels, for "country clubs" have spread downward into the middle and even into the lower-middle classes. In smaller cities, membership in the best country club is often the significant organizational mark of the upper groups; but this is not so in the metropolitan status market. It is the gentlemen's club, an exclusive male organization, that is socially most important.

Gentlemen belong to the metropolitan man's club, and the men of the upper-class stature usually belong to such clubs in more than one city; clubs for both sexes, such as country clubs, are usually local. Among the out-of-town clubs to which the old upper-class man belongs are those of Harvard and Princeton and Yale, but the world of the urban clubs extends well beyond those anchored in the better schools. It is not unusual for gentlemen to belong to three or four or even more. These clubs of the various cities are truly exclusive in the sense that they are not widely known to the middle and lower classes in general. They are above those better-known arenas where upper-class status is more widely recognized. They are of and by and for the upper circles, and no other. But they are known and visited by the upper circles of more than one city.*

To the outsider, the club to which the upper class man or woman belongs is a badge of certification of his status; to the insider, the club provides a more intimate or clan-like set of exclusive groupings which places and characterizes a man. Their core of membership is usually families which successfully claim status by descent. From intimate association with such men, newer members borrow status, and in turn, the accomplishments of the newer entrants help

* Even in 1933, some fifty New Yorkers maintained their full-rate dues in Boston's Somerset Club. [20]

shore up the status of the club as a going concern.

Membership in the right clubs assumes great social importance when the merely rich push and shove at the boundaries of society, for then the line tends to become vague, and club membership clearly defines exclusiveness. And yet the metropolitan clubs are important rungs in the social ladder for would-be members of the top status levels: they are status elevators for the new into the old upper classes; for men, and their sons, can be gradually advanced from one club to the next, and so, if successful, into the inner citadel of the most exclusive. They are also important in the business life within and between the metropolitan circles: to many men of these circles, it seems convenient and somehow fitting to come to important decisions within the exclusive club. "The private club," one national magazine for executives recently put it, is becoming "the businessman's castle." [21]

The metropolitan upper classes, as wealthy classes having control of each locality's key financial and legal institutions, thereby have business and legal relations with one another. For the economy of the city, especially of a metropolitan area, is not confined to the city. To the extent that the economy is national and big-city centered, and to the extent that the upper classes control its key places of big-city decision—the upper classes of each city are related to those of other cities. In the rich if gloomy quiet of a Boston club and also in the rich and brisk chrome of a Houston club—to belong is to be accepted. It is also to be in easy, informal touch with those who are socially acceptable, and so to be in a better position to make a deal over a luncheon table. The gentlemen's club is at once an important center of the financial and business network of decision and an essential center for certifying the socially fit. In it all the traits that make up the old upper classes seem to coincide: the old family and the proper marriage and the correct residence and the right church and the right schools—and the power of the key decision. The "leading men" in each city belong to such clubs, and when the leading men of other cities visit them, they are very likely to be seen at lunch in Boston's Somerset or Union, Philadelphia's Racquet or Philadelphia Club, San Francisco's Pacific Union, or New York's Knickerbocker, Links, Brook, or Racquet and Tennis.[22]

4

The upper-class style of life is pretty much the same—although there are regional variations—in each of the big cities of the nation. The houses and clothing, the types of social occasions the metropolitan 400 care about, tend to be homogeneous. The Brooks Brothers suit-and-shirt is not extensively advertised nationally and the store has only four branches outside New York City, but it is well-known in every major city of the nation, and in no key city do the "representatives" of Brooks Brothers feel themselves to be strangers.[23] There are other such externals that are specific and common to the proper upper-class style, yet, after all, anyone with the money and the inclination can learn to be uncomfortable in anything but a Brooks Brothers suit. The style of life of the old upper social classes across the nation goes deeper than such things.

The one deep experience that distinguishes the social rich from the merely rich and those below is their schooling, and with it, all the associations, the sense and sensibility, to which this educational routine leads throughout their lives.

The daughter of an old upper-class New York family, for example, is usually under the care of nurse and mother until she is four years of age, after which she is under the daily care of a governess who often speaks French as well as English. When she is six or seven, she goes to a private day school, perhaps Miss Chapin's or Brearley. She is often driven to and from school by the family chauffeur and in the afternoons, after school, she is in the general care of the governess, who now spends most of her time with the younger children. When she is about fourteen she goes to boarding school, perhaps to St. Timothy's in Maryland or Miss

Porter's or Westover in Connecticut. Then she may attend Finch Junior College of New York City and thus be "finished," or if she is to attend college proper, she will be enrolled, along with many plain middle-class girls, in Bryn Mawr or Vassar or Wellesley or Smith or Bennington. She will marry soon after finishing school or college, and presumably begin to guide her own children through the same educational sequence.*

The boy of this family, while under seven years of age, will follow a similar pattern. Then he too will go to day school, and, at a rather earlier age than the girls, to boarding school, although for boys it will be called prep school: St. Mark's or St. Paul's, Choate or Groton, Andover or Lawrenceville, Phillips Exeter or Hotchkiss.[25] Then he will go to Princeton or Harvard, Yale or Dartmouth. As likely as not, he will finish with a law school attached to one of these colleges.

Each stage of this education is important to the formation of the upper-class man or woman; it is an educational sequence that is common to the upper classes in all the leading cities of the nation. There is, in fact, a strong tendency for children from all these cities to attend one of the more fashionable boarding or prep schools in New England, in which students from two dozen or so states, as well as from foreign countries, may be readily found. As claims for status based on family descent become increasingly difficult to realize, the proper school transcends the family pedigree in social importance. Accordingly, if one had to choose one clue to the national unity of the upper social classes in America today, it would best be the really exclusive boarding school for girls and prep school for boys.

* "The daughter of the industrial leader, of the great professional man must thrive in a complex civilization which places little premium upon its women's homelier virtues: meekness and modesty, earnestness and Godliness. Yet such a man must, according to the *mores* of his kind, send his daughter to one of a handful of institutions whose codes rest upon these foundations...Of the 1,200-odd private schools for girls in this country, curiously enough only a score or more really matter...so ephemeral are the things which make one school and mar another that intangible indeed are the distinctions."[24]

Many educators of the private school world feel that economic shifts bring to the top people whose children have had no proper family background and tone, and that the private school is a prime institution in preparing them to live at the top of the nation in a manner befitting upper-class men and women. And whether the head-masters know it or not, it seems to be a fact that like the hierarchy of clubs for the fathers—but in more important and deeper ways—the private schools do perform the task of selecting and training newer members of a national upper stratum, as well as upholding the higher standards among the children of families who have long been at the top. It is in "the next generation," in the private school, that the tensions between new and old upper classes are relaxed and even resolved. And it is by means of these schools more than by any other single agency that the older and the newer families—when their time is due—become members of a self-conscious upper class.

As a selection and training place of the upper classes, both old and new, the private school is a unifying influence, a force for the nationalization of the upper classes. The less important the pedigreed family becomes in the careful transmission of moral and cultural traits, the more important the private school. The school—rather than the upper-class family—is the most important agency for transmitting the traditions of the upper social classes, and regulating the admission of new wealth and talent. It is the characterizing point in the upper-class experience. In the top fifteen or twenty such schools, if anywhere, one finds a prime organizing center of the national upper social classes. For in these private schools for adolescents, the religious and family and educational tasks of the upper social classes are fused, and in them the major tasks of upholding such standards as prevail in these classes are centered.*

These schools are self-supporting and autonomous in policy, and the most proper of them are non-profit institutions. They are not "church schools" in that they are not governed by religious bodies, but they do require students to attend religious services, and although not sectarian, they are permeated by religiously inspired principles. The statement of the founders of Groton, still used today, includes this fundamental aim: "Every endeavor will be made to cultivate manly, Christian character, having regard to moral and physical as well as intellectual development. The Headmaster of the School will be a clergyman of the Protestant Episcopal Church."[27]

"The vitals of a prep-school are not located in the curriculum. They are located in a dozen other places, some of them queer places indeed: in the relations between boys and faculty; in who the boys are and where they come from; in a Gothic chapel or a shiny new gymnasium; in the type of building the boys live in and the sort of thing they do after supper; and, above all in the headmaster."[28] There is a kind of implicit ideal for the school to be an organized extension of the family, but a large family in which the proper children from Boston and Philadelphia and New York together learn the proper style of conduct. This family ideal is strengthened by the common religious practices of the school, which tend to be Episcopalian; by the tendency for given upper-class families to send all their sons to the same schools that the father, or even grandfather, attended; and by the donations as well as the social and sentimental activities of the alumni associations. The underlying purpose of the Choate School, for example, is to prove that family and school may

* "These schools for boys," the editors of *Fortune* have written, "are conspicuous far out of proportion to the numbers enrolled in them. More than seven million boys and girls in the U.S. now (1944) receive secondary education, 460,000 of whom are in private schools. Of this number more than 360,000 were in Catholic schools (1941 figures, latest available) and more than

10,000 in military schools, whose special purposes are obvious. Of the remainder, girls' schools, whose job is also relatively well defined, accounted for almost 30,000 more. Forty thousand odd were in co-educational schools, largely day schools. Some 20,000 were in the schools for boys, the group that particularly desires self-justification."[26]

be effectively combined, so that a boy while gaining the benefits that school provides—in particular "spiritual leadership" and "association with boys of purpose"—will retain the intimate influences that ought to characterize a proper home.

Daily life in the exclusive schools is usually quite simple, even Spartan; within its atmosphere of snobbish simplicity, there is a democracy of status. Everyone follows more or less the same routine, and there are no opportunities for officially approved inclinations for ostentatious display or snobbery.[29]

These schools are not usually oriented to any obvious practical end. It is true that the boys' schools are invariably preparatory for college; while those for girls offer one curriculum for college preparation, and one terminal course for girls contemplating earlier marriage. But the middle-class ethos of competitiveness is generally lacking. One should, the school seems to say, compare one's work and activity not with the boy or girl next to you, but with what you and your teacher believe is your own best. Besides, if you are too interested, you become conspicuous.

Certainly competition for status among students is held to a minimum: where allowances are permitted, they are usually fixed at modest levels, and the tendency is for boys to have no spending money at all; the wearing of school blazers by boys, or a uniform jumper or blouse, skirt and sweater by girls, is not, as it is usually interpreted by outsiders, so much upper-class swash as it is an attempt to defeat displays of haberdashery within the exclusive group. And girls, however rich, are not usually allowed to own their own horses.

The elders of the school community are those older children in the higher Forms, and they become the models aspired to by the younger children. For young boys, up to eight and nine, there are carefully chosen Housemothers; between twelve and thirteen, they are weaned from women and have exclusively male teachers, although the wives of instructors often live with their husbands in apartments within the boys'

dormitories and continue a virtual kinship role with them. Care is taken that the self-image of the child not be slapped down, as it might by an insecure parent, and that manners at table as elsewhere be imbibed from the general atmosphere rather than from authoritarian and forbidding figures.

Then one will always know what to do, even if one is sometimes puzzled. One will react appropriately upon meeting the man who is too carefully groomed and above all, the man who tries too hard to please, for one knows that that is not necessary if one is "the right sort of person." There will be the manner of simplicity and the easy dignity that can arise only out of an inner certainty that one's being is a definitely established fact of one's world, from which one cannot be excluded, ignored, snubbed, or paid off. And, in due course, as a young broker, banker, executive, one will *feel* smooth and handsome, with the easy bonhomie, the look of superior amusement, and all the useful friendships; one will have just the proper touch of deference toward the older men, even if they *are* members of your own club, and just the right degree of intelligence and enthusiasms—but not too much of either, for one's style is, after all, a realization of the motto of one's schooling: nothing in excess.[30]

Harvard or Yale or Princeton is not enough. It is the really exclusive prep school that counts, for that determines which of the "two Harvards" one attends. The clubs and cliques of college are usually composed of carry-overs of association and name made in the lower levels at the proper schools; one's friends at Harvard are friends made at prep school. That is why in the upper social classes, it does not by itself mean much merely to have a degree from an Ivy League college. That is assumed: the point is not Harvard, but which Harvard? By Harvard, one means Porcellian, Fly, or A.D.: by Yale, one means Zeta Psi or Fence or Delta Kappa Epsilon; by Princeton, Cottage, Tiger, Cap and Gown, or Ivy.[31] It is the prestige of a properly certified secondary education followed by a proper club in a proper Ivy League college that is the standard admission ticket to the world of urban clubs and parties in any major city of the nation. To the prestige of the voice and manner, constructed in such schools, local loyalties bow, for that experience is a major clue to the nation-wide upper class that is homogeneous and self-conscious.

Among those who are being educated in similar ways, the school naturally leads to marriage. The prep schools for boys are usually within a convenient range of boarding schools for girls of similar age, and several times a year the students from each are thrown together for chaperoned occasions. There are, in addition, the sisters of the other boys and the brothers of the other girls. And for those attending the more exclusive boys' and girls' colleges, there are formally arranged visits and parties—in short, dating patterns—established between them. On the college level, the exclusive schools become components of a broadened marriage market, which brings into dating relation the children of the upper social classes of the nation.

5

The rich who became rich before the Civil War also became the founders of most old American families, and those who have become rich since then have joined them. The metropolitan upper class which they have formed has not been and is not now a pedigreed society with a fixed membership, but for all of that, it has become a nationally recognized upper social class with many homogeneous features and a strong sense of unity. If new families are added to it, they are always wealthy families, and new or old, their sons and daughters attend the same types of exclusive schools and tend to marry one another. They belong to the same associations at the same set of Ivy League colleges, and they remain in social and business touch by means of the big-city network of metropolitan clubs. In each of the nation's leading cities, they recognize one another, if not strictly as peers, as people with much in common. In one another's biographies they recognize the experiences they have had in common; in their financial positions of brokerage firm, bank, and cor-

poration, they recognize the interests they would all serve. To the extent that business becomes truly national, the economic roles of the upper classes become similar and even interchangeable; to the extent that politics becomes truly national, the political opinion and activity of the upper classes become consolidated. All those forces that transform a confederation of localities and a scatter of companies into a corporate nation, also make for the coinciding interests and functions and unity of the metropolitan 400.

The upper social classes have come to include a variety of members concerned with power in its several contexts, and these concerns are shared among the members of the clubs, the cousinhoods, the firms, the law offices. They are topics of conversation around the dinner table, where family members and club associates experience the range of great issues in a quite informal context. Having grown up together, trusting one another implicitly, their personal intimacy comes to include a respect for the specialized concerns of each member as a top man, a policy-maker in his own particular area of power and decision.

They spread into various commanding circles of the institutions of power. One promising son enters upon a high governmental career—perhaps the State Department; his first cousin is in due course elevated to a high executive place in the headquarters of a corporation; his uncle has already ascended to naval command; and a brother of the first cousin is about to become the president of a leading college. And, of course, there is the family law firm, whose partners keep in close touch with outlying members and with the problems they face.

Accordingly, in the inner circles of the upper classes, the most impersonal problems of the largest and most important institutions are fused with the sentiments and worries of small, closed, intimate groups. This is one very important meaning of the upper-class family and of the upper-class school: "background" is one way in which, on the basis of intimate association, the activities of an upper class may be tacitly coordinated. It is also important because in such circles, adolescent boys and girls are exposed to the table conversations of decision-makers, and thus have bred into them the informal skills and pretensions of decision-makers; in short, they imbibe what is called "judgment." Without conscious effort, they absorb the aspiration to be—if not the conviction that they are—The Ones Who Decide.

Within and between the upper-class families as well as their firms and offices, there are the schoolboy friendships and the prep schools and the college clubs, and later the key social and political clubs. And, in all these houses and organizations, there are the men who will later—or at the time of meeting—operate in the diverse higher circles of modern society.

The exclusive schools and clubs and resorts of the upper social classes are not exclusive merely because their members are snobs. Such locales and associations have a real part in building the upper-class character, and more than that, the connections to which they naturally lead help to link one higher circle with another.

So the distinguished law student, after prep school and Harvard, is "clerk" to a Supreme Court judge, then a corporation lawyer, then in the diplomatic service, then in the law firm again. In each of these spheres, he meets and knows men of his own kind, and, as a kind of continuum, there are the old family friends and the schoolboy chums, the dinners at the club, and each year of his life the summer resorts. In each of these circles in which he moves, he acquires and exercises a confidence in his own ability to judge, to decide, and in this confidence he is supported by his ready access to the experience and sensibility of those who are his social peers and who act with decision in each of the important institutions and areas of public life. One does not turn one's back on a man whose presence is accepted in such circles, even under most trying circumstances. All over the top of the nation, he is "in," his appearance, a certificate of social position; his voice and manner, a badge of proper training; his associates, proof at once of their acceptance and of his stereotyped discernment.

NOTES

1. Cf. Dixon Wecter, *The Saga of American Society* (New York: Scribner's 1937), pp. 199ff., which is the standard work on the history of American "Society." The best examinations of the "societies" of particular big cities are Cleveland Amory, *The Proper Bostonians* (New York: E. P. Dutton, 1947); and Edward Digby Baltzell Jr., *The Elite and the Upper Class in Metropolitan America: A Study of Stratification in Philadelphia*, (Ph.D. thesis, Columbia University, 1953), both of which I have used.

2. Mrs. John King Van Rensselaer, *The Social Ladder* (New York: Henry Holt, 1924), pp. 30–32.

3. Dixon Wecter, op. cit. pp. 294–5.

4. Cf. J. L. Ford, "New York of the Seventies," *Scribner's Magazine*, June 1923, p. 744.

5. Mrs. John King Van Rensselaer, op. cit. pp. 53–4.

6. W. J. Mills, "New York Society," *Delineator*, November 1904. Cf. Also Ralph Pulitzer, "New York Society at Work," *Harper's Bazaar*, December 1909.

7. Cf. Harvey O'Connor, *The Astors* (New York: Knopf, 1941), p. 197.

8. Wecter, op. cit. pp. 209–10.

9. Ibid. pp. 212, 214.

10. Cited in ibid. p. 215.

11. See FIVE: The Very Rich, and notes to that chapter.

12. Wecter, op. cit. pp. 232–3.

13. See Mona Gardner, "Social Register Blues," *Collier's*, 14 December 1946 and G. Holland, "Social Register," *American Mercury*, June 1932. On the volumes of *The Social Register* published up to 1925, see Wecter, op. cit. p. 233.

14. Wecter, op. cit. p. 234.

15. As of 1940. Cf. Baltzell Jr., op. cit. Table 2.

16. See ibid. Table 14, pp. 89 ff.

17. Wecter, op. cit. pp. 235, 234.

18. Thorstein Veblen, *The Theory of the Leisure Class*, 1899 (New York: New American Library, Mentor Edition, 1953), p. 162. Cf. also my Introduction to that edition for a fuller criticism of Veblen's theory.

19. *Time,* 26 October 1953.

20. See "Boston," *Fortune,* February 1933, p. 27.

21. *Business Week*, 5 June 1954, pp. 92–3.

22. From private estimations. Cf. Baltzell Jr., op. cit. p. 178.

23. Cf. ibid. footnote 5, p. 172.

24. "Miss Chapin's, Miss Walker's, Foxcroft, Farmington," *Fortune,* August 1931, p. 38.

25. See Porter Sargent, *A Handbook of Private Schools*, 25th ed. (Boston: Porter Sargent,

1941); "Schools for Boys," *Fortune*, May 1944, pp. 165 ff.; "St. Paul's, St. Mark's, Groton, Andover, *et. al.*," *Fortune*, September 1931, pp. 76 ff. Cf. also George S. Counts, "Girls' Schools," *Fortune*, August 1931 and "Twelve of the Best American Schools," *Fortune*, January 1936, pp. 48 ff.

26. "Schools for Boys," op. cit. p. 165. Cf. also "Boys' Prep School," *Life*, 1 March 1954, which deals with Hotchkiss. Compare Eleanor Roosevelt's feelings upon sending her youngest son, John, to Groton, as reported by her in *This I Remember* (New York: Harper, 1949), p. 43.

27. Cf. Frank D. Ashburn, *Peabody of Groton* (New York: Coward McCann, 1944), pp. 30, 67-8.

28. "St. Paul's, St. Mark's, Groton, Andover, *et al.*," op. cit. p. 76.

29. Cf. Allan Heely, *Why the Private School?* (New York: Harper, 1951).

30. Cf. John P. Marquand, *H. M. Pulham Esquire* (New York: Bantam Edition, 1950), pp. 76, 60; and W. M. Spackman, *Heyday* (New York: Ballantine Edition, 1953), p. 12.

31. Cf. Baltzell Jr., op. cit. pp. 218-20.

6 Multinational corporations

The basic questions this chapter will address are:

(1) Are multinational corporations solely economic institutions? Or are they essentially political institutions that also conduct business?

(2) What are the effects of multinational corporations on the United States?

(3) What effects do multinational corporations have on countries other than the United States?

(4) Can multinational corporations be controlled by any other political institution?

Multinational corporations operate in a number of countries and have the ability to shift personnel and resources from one country to another, effectively removing themselves from domination by any national government.

Conservatives believe that multinational corporations are economic organizations that play a positive role in the development of poor countries and in the economic expansion of rich countries. Because multinationals are effectively organized, well-financed, and well-run, they are eminently suited to coordinate world economic development. Conservatives hold that multinational corporations are, at present, the only organizations that have a world perspective and the capacity to engage in effective economic development. Such corporations must be left alone to conduct their own business. National governments should not be permitted to hamper their activities. Both developed and developing countries should recognize and support the role that multinational corporations play in agrarian, industrial, and technological development.

Liberals maintain that multinational corporations, left to their own devices, will abuse the power their financial and economic resources give them. They believe that the economies of poor countries are stunted by the monopolization of economic enterprise by multinationals. The economies of the Western world can also be hurt if there is no control over them. An example of this type of activity is the arrangement that international oil companies made with producing nations, in 1973–74, to increase sharply the price of oil.[1]

Multinationals are accepted by liberals as an economic fixture in the world. They hold that if permitted, multinational corporations will exert political power over national governments. For liberals, government legislation is the answer to the abuses of power that multinationals engage in if given the chance. Countervailing forces exist which can limit the undue influence exerted by multinational corporations. These are labor unions, small business, and government. The first two are discounted as viable forces because they have little means of exerting authority across national boundaries. The ability to transcend national boundaries is the key element that gives multinational corporations their extensive power. The power of unions and small business has been vitiated by this very ability of the multinationals to operate in more than one country. Small business cannot compete effectively with multinational corporations, and labor unions lose their membership and clout when multinational corporations move their operations from one country to another. Government is the only force left that can place controls on multinational corporations. Liberals believe that governments are not able to deal with the economic and political power of multinational corporations through existing means for these giant industries can conceal their operations through transferring resources from one national subsidiary to another.

Government legislation established in the late nineteenth and early twentieth centuries to limit large business combinations is not adequate, according to liberals, to deal with international corporations.[2] New legislation is necessary if the political power of multinationals is to be controlled. However, liberals feel that government does not recognize the necessity of new legislation. Government elites, on the other hand, do not hold to the thesis that multinational corporations abuse their power unduly. Some of these national leaders believe that the interests of the multinationals and of the nation-state converge. Liberals prescribe two strategies to deal with this problem: (1) government must be made aware of the fact that multinational corporations may abuse their power; and (2) legislation must be passed to limit their power.

The socialist perspective is that multinational corporations are a primary component of the power elite. Such international corporations, together with Western industrial states, successfully inhibit economic development in the Third World. Because these giant businesses monopolize world industry, creating world-wide economic needs (which serve them), and because they control investment capital, poor countries that accept the capitalist framework don't stand a chance of developing economically. Firestone Rubber in Liberia, Anaconda Copper in Chile, and United Fruit in Latin America are examples of multinational corporations that control the economic and political systems of these areas. Socialists believe that Western governments do not want to limit the power of multinational corporations. The people who run these corporations also influence the operation of Western governments, so the interests of Western governments and multinational corporations coincide.

The answer to the situation does not lie in reform of multinational corporations. It lies in the destruction of these corporations and the power elite which they are part of. This can be accomplished by consumers refusing to buy the products of multinational corporations, or by limiting their consumption as much as possible. Since the multinational corporations' very existence is based on the acceptance of their products by a world public, counter-advertising that exposes the repressive political actions of multinationals could be used to curtail their business. Another part of the socialist strategy is publicizing the availability of other competing goods and services from little-known sources such as cooperatives and small businesses. For instance, one must question whether products such as Pepsi Cola or Coca Cola are refreshing or helpful, or whether we have been trained to like them better than homemade lemonade. This strategy also entails the setting up of alternative economic institutions.[3] One reason for developing these institutions is that multinational corporations refuse to market products that may be beneficial to people but harmful to themselves. For example, international rubber companies, such as Firestone, Goodyear, B.F. Goodrich, have for years had the knowledge to produce an automobile tire that would virtually not wear out. They refused to market this product because it would severely cut into their future profits.

Socialists seldom consider going beyond a critique of capitalism to engage in the theory and practice of constructing social organizations according to socialist principles. One example of an attempt to establish a new technology which relates to socialist principles is the development of solar power. Prohibited for years because it would interfere with existing energy monopolies over coal, oil, and electricity, the controlled development of solar power is now of interest to energy cartels since it has become a public issue. The strategy of multinationals is that if they cannot prevent the development of a new technology that interferes with their control of existing technologies, then they themselves must gain control of this new technology and destroy any potential competitors.[4]

The formation of new economic institutions by socialists must become a prime factor in any socialist strategy to deal with the existing economic arrangements of capitalist societies. Socialist forms of work and economic organization must be presented to people as a living reality even if the examples seem small and short-lived. If people are to destroy the institutional arrangements of capitalism they must see that other ways of organizing society are possible.

NOTES

1. The classic study on the relationship between international oil companies, oil producing states, and Western nations is Robert Engler, *The Politics of Oil: Private Power and Democratic Directions.* Chicago: The Univ. of Chicago Press, 1969.

2. The primary legislation utilized is the Sherman Antitrust Act of 1890, and the Clayton Antitrust Act, passed during the administration of Woodrow Wilson.

3. Henry Etzkowitz and Gerald Schaflander, in *Ghetto Crisis*, Boston: Little Brown and Co., 1969, describe an attempt to organize an alternative economic organization which marketed goods and services and used its profits to support community services.

4. The Consumers' Solar Electric Power Corporation, organized by Gerald Schaflander, is an example of an alternate economic institution which is attempting to develop a new technology and keep it out of the control of multinational corporations. His organization, and the attempts of multinationals to disrupt its success, is described in, Alexander Cockburn, and James Ridgeway, "The Merchant of Sunlight, or the Saga of Schaflander and the Sunshine Boys," *The Village Voice*, April 7, 1975, pp. 12–15, 19.

*

Conservative

John Diebold. Why be scared of them?

Let me begin with three assumptions: During the next two decades there will be a large transfer of manufacturing industry from the three rich industrial areas of the world (North America, northwest Europe, Japan) to the poorer areas to the south. This transfer will include manufactures of both finished goods and components for export back to the richer countries. Between now and 1993, the rich third of the world will increasingly find both economic and social reasons to move into the post-manufacturing age; to shift manufacturing to the less-developed countries (LDC's).

The multinational corporation (MNC) will be the mechanism initially most favored for this southward transfer of manufacturing. Often this will mean a wholly-owned American (or European or Japanese) subsidiary. There are some advantages as well as disadvantages for LDC's in this. The best strategy for a developing country should be to put itself into a position where it can choose. My guess for the next two decades is that if a developing country has a thriving domestic business sector, then it is likely that the multinational corporations will seek it out. It will then be up to the developing country to choose the terms to allow them. The development policy that will *not* succeed will be one that stops the growth of a domestic business ethos, and that then erects barriers against the participation of foreign firms that, as a result of these factors, will not want to come in anyway.

In some cases host governments will inhibit economic development, either by mistake or because they do not want it. In many developing countries, the class struggle today is really between the "new men of government" and the "new men of business" (both domestic and foreign). These "new men of government" may win the struggle in some countries, either because they have the military on their side, or because the masses can be won to support them by a mixture of economic apathy and emotional romanticism (fostered by nationalism, anti-colonialism, anti-Americanism, anti-capitalism, etc.). But while this scenario is convincing as a sketch of what will happen in many of today's poorer countries some of the time, it is not convincing as a sketch of what will happen in all of them all of the time. At least some of today's poorer countries are likely to climb eagerly onto the development bandwagon, and there will then be an incentive to follow them. Those leading the climb will be the "new men of business" in the developing countries. Sometimes (as in Mexico and Japan) the policy they carry through will be one that restricts the import of technology through the particular medium of MNC's; sometimes (as in Brazil and Singapore) they will be self-confidently liberal in importing technology through the MNC's. My belief is that both policies will sometimes work.

Gathering pace

Business generated by multinational enterprises outside their home countries already amounts to about $350 billion worth of goods and services a year (three-fifths of it by U.S. companies). This is one-eighth of the gross product of the non-Communist world. The proportion is increasing rapidly, because the production of MNC's seems to be expanding at about 10 percent a year. On a crude extrapolation of recent trends, one could expect MNC's to be responsible for one-fourth of the production of the non-Communist world by the early 1980's.

If the host countries continue to receive multinationals, there is a strong probability that this last figure will prove to be an underestimate. Trends suggest that the growth of multinational business activity is likely to be even faster in the near future than in the immediate past, partly because (a) American companies have mastered the techniques of multinationalism; but largely because (b) Western Europe and Japan are very likely in the period 1973–93 to follow America's 1950–70 trend, and start "exporting companies and know-how, much more than goods, to the outside world."

The essence of the first argument is that there is a certain technique in "going multinational": namely, acquiring a degree of expertise in foreign tax laws, employment customs, written or unwritten business regulations, and social and political habits. That technique was pioneered in the 1950's and 1960's by the giants, and is to some extent now almost available in packaged form (especially for U.S. companies) as well as being made easier by the presence abroad of U.S. chambers of commerce, U.S. banks, and the like. Smaller U.S. firms may now take advantage of this development in countries where U.S. multinational corporations are already well established.

The key statistic for the second argument is that, at present, overseas production by European and Japanese companies is less than the annual value of their exports. This was true of America until the 1950's, but now production by U.S. companies abroad *exceeds* U.S. exports by five to one. The U.S. multinationals' production abroad has therefore become, quite suddenly, the most important form of American involvement in the world economy. During the next 20 years, it is likely that the same will become true of the EEC countries and Japan, and that their investment and export of knowhow—like that of the United States—will go especially to the LDC's.

Until the last few years, Japan's industry has been based on high-wage big firms, and on low-wage small firms from which the big firms have bought their components. The "lifetime employment" system in Japan meant that the small firms held on to their cheap labor. The big Japanese firms thus broke down their production processes into systems where component work could be subcontracted to small firms, which made these components in ways that were efficient but did not require the use of much highly skilled or well educated craft labor. Now, however, young Japanese will not go into low-wage small firms, and wages are leveling up. The Japanese, who unlike the Northern Europeans certainly do not intend

to allow mass immigration of unskilled foreign workers, intend to set up these "small firm" industries in some profusion in other parts of Asia with cheaper labor. They have already begun to do so. North American and West European industrialists might do well to study (and imitate) some of the ways in which the Japanese thereby subdivide their production.

Developing countries should also study Japanese experience. Big Japanese firms are used to dealing with large numbers of small Japanese subcontractors, which regard themselves as independent firms. Some relationships between big Japanese firms and small Japanese subcontractors are not in the subcontractors' interests (e.g., credit terms, monopoly dealing, etc.), but others provide an excellent framework within which small independent firms can grow. Governments of developing countires would be well-advised to study the terms under which they would like locally-owned firms in their own countries to develop along this potentially profitable road, as subcontractors to big Japanese companies. These governments should suggest the sorts of subcontract arrangements into which local firms should and should not enter. And they should then encourage maximum competition to get the contracts which seem desirable. This effort might sometimes be aided by changes in local law (including the law of bankruptcy and debt collection), local credit facilities, local import and export regulations, etc.

Should they want multinationals?

The recommendations above assume that developing countries should want multinational corporations in their lands. There are strong arguments to the contrary.

The arguments of the critics need to be taken as seriously as the arguments of the proponents. But it will be convenient to discuss the latter first, concentrating on those in italics in Table I. The arguments in italics are those that I take most seriously on either side.

Table 1   The debate over the multinational corporation (MNC)

Its proponents say	Its critics say
1. By focusing on *economic rationality*, the MNC represents the interests of all against the parochial interests of separate nations. It is the most effective available counter to rampant nationalism. Its only political weapon is that it can remove its benefits from developing countries that are politically unreliable or confiscatorily anti-business; and this is an incentive towards responsibility that is in the poor countries' own interests.	1. The MNC removes a significant part of the national economy from responsible political control, without escaping improper political influence, including influence from the governments of the MNC's home countries. The MNC is an invasion of sovereignty and frustrates national economic policies. It fragments industries, causing proliferation without hope of consolidation.
2. The MNC is the best available mechanism for training people in countries for modern managerial skills.	2. *It does not train people in entrepreneurial skills*, which is what a developing country most needs.
3. No more effective instrument has been found for the diffusion of technology.	3. The transfer of technology is often minimized because (a) R & D is generally carried out by the parent company; (b) the training of nationals of the host country for R & D posts is often neglected; (c) the technology itself is often closely held.
4. The MNC is the most promising instrument for the transfer of capital to the developing world and its role will be crucial in overcoming the income gap.	4. The cost of the capital brought by the MNC is far higher than the host government would be charged as a direct borrower in capital markets. The MNC invests relatively little of its own capital, and buys up foreign enterprises with local capital. The profits of the MNC are exhorbitantly high, and too low a proportion of them are reinvested.
5. The MNC's integrated and rationalized operations in many lands make it *incomparably efficient*. It has proven to be the only really effective instrument for economic development.	5. The rationalization of production is sometimes a *tax dodge*. The MNC distorts development programs by channeling its reported profits to countries where taxation is lowest, by manipulating charges for services and transactions to disguise real earnings.
6. The MNC enhances competition and breaks local monopolies. To the consumer, it provides a better product at a lower cost. To the host country it can provide a *new export industry for tomorrow*.	6. Its sheer size and scope represents unfair competition to local enterprises. It tends to preempt the fast-growing, advanced-technology industries where profits are highest, ignoring older, more competitive fields.
7. Management of the MNC is becoming increasingly flexible, sensitive to local customs, and genuinely international in fact and in spirit.	7. The interest of the parent company must remain dominant and the MNC cannot ever become genuinely international. Often, the MNC has resisted genuine internationalization by declining (a) to put foreigners into management and (b) to make shares of its affiliates available to nationals of the host country.
8. The MNC is an agent of change which is altering value systems, social attitudes, and behavior patterns in ways which will ultimately reduce barriers to communications between peoples and establish the basis for a stable world order.	8. Far from breaking down barriers between peoples, the MNC aggravates tensions and stimulates nationalism. Moreover, there is every indication that *these tendencies will intensify in years ahead*.

The main advantages of multinational companies to developing countries are said to be economic rationality, efficiency, and the growing importance of the companies as exporters. I believe that this last point is going to become the crucial one for Latin America. Experience has shown that it is wise to try from the beginning to direct industrial development in Latin America in ways whereby the new industries have incentives to keep down inflation. Export-oriented industries have such incentives, because cost increases prevent the selling of more exports. By contrast, development on the basis of attempted import-substitution is much more likely to breed inflation.

Unfortunately, attempted import-substitution was the mainspring behind most development programs in LDC's during the 1950's and 1960's, and it helped foster inflation rates of 50 percent a year and more. The switch to inflation-countering, export-oriented production came largely with multinationals. To quote Raymond Vernon's study, *Sovereignty at Bay:*

The capacity to use the less-developed countries as areas of production for export appears to have been intimately related to the multinational character of the exporters. Without multinational links, the subsidiaries probably would not have increased their exports on anything like the same scale. Illustrative of that tie is the fact that although U.S.-controlled manufacturing subsidiaries accounted for 41 percent of Latin America's manufactured goods exports in 1966, they were responsible for less than 10 percent of Latin America's gross manufacturing value added in that year. Even more to the point was the type of goods being exported. These were the products of industries in which barriers to entry were relatively high and in which successful marketing required a relatively advanced degree of sophistication and control. As a result, the marketing process itself generally required the services of affiliates as well as the supervision of the parent.

Critics will point out that often the subsidiary does not export to its country of origin, in order to avoid competing with the parent company and causing trouble with the labor force at home. But my guess is that this will be progressively mitigated by three factors: (a) consumer tastes are becoming more and more international; (b) the tremendous growth of new products; (c) the educational and training revolution which will make the training of labor in the LDC's a much quicker, more scientific process.

On the second point, the biggest expansion in developing countries' manufacturing for export during the period 1972–92 may well take place in new products.

The reason why new products are especially successful exports for LDC's is partly that the know-how for producing them tends to be codified in a form easily transmitted to inexperienced labor forces. But it is chiefly because they developed so quickly that production begins abroad almost before U.S. labor unions and business lobbies back home are sufficiently organized to realize that such industries existed!

A greatly expanding proportion of world manufacturing production during the period 1972–92 will consist of entirely new products. When the products are not entirely new, manufacturers will pretend that they are.

My third point above is that we are on the edge of a breakthrough in the whole concept of our learning and information processes. Business will probably adapt well to the new educational technology—better indeed than many schools and universities—because its focus is more on results than on defending institutional methods.

The training and information revolution is likely to include a huge expansion in computer-based education. In step with this codification of the learning process, multinational computerized data banks will become available that will aid decision-makers in choosing where to locate production facilities all around the world, with an eye on the trainability of labor as well as on other advantages. Thus the head offices of MNC's will use computers to handle logistic functions (such as purchasing raw materials, services, tools, components, and equipment); to plan and control the marketability of different countries' products in third countries; to handle all credit transactions (by the 1980's most foreign exchange transactions will be carried out by multinational computer systems which link together, on-line, both large and small international banks); and to codify worldwide research.

We are also moving into a world in which the price of telecommunications will no longer depend on distance. Once enough satellites are put into space, and equipment installed, the marginal cost of making a picture telephone call to China should be no more than the cost of telephoning the office next door.

Norman Macrae, of *The Economist,* has suggested where these trends might lead for business organization by the beginning of the twenty-first century, when three-fifths of today's population should still be alive:

As a prototype for the most successful sorts of firm in 30 or 40 years time, it may be most sensible to visualize small groups of organizers or systems designers, all living in their own comfortable homes in pleasant parts of the world and communicating with others in the group (and with the systems designers) by picture-phone: arranging for the telecommunication of the latest best computerised learning programme on how to make a better mousetrap (or, more probably, how to make the next-successor-but-five to integrated circuits) rooftop to rooftop to about 2,000 quickly trainable, even if only newly literate, workers assembled before their two-way-teaching-in-computer terminals by some just tolerably efficient organising subcontractor (also taught by long-distance telecommunicated computer lessons) in West Africa or Pakistan.

The logical and eventual development of this possibility would be the end of nationality and national governments as we know them. Less and less would people live out their lives where they were born; more and more would they live where they choose. Those people working in systems-designing and knowledge-producing jobs would merely have to live "hooked into" what would become easily transportable two-way terminals to the big computer networks. Those people working in goods-producing and goods-transporting jobs would have to take on-site jobs for their working years; but probably the working year for these people would become much shorter.

However, this is looking fairly far forward towards what some people will not regard as a world Utopia.

Objections to multinationals

I suggest that the three most valid objections to MNC's in developing countries, as underlined in Table I, are (a) they do not encourage local inhabitants in entrepreneurial (as distinct from operative and executive) skills; (b) they often fail to carry as large a tax burden as they might; and (c) MNC's can aggravate tensions and stimulate nationalism, with every indication that these tendencies will intensify in years ahead.

On the first point, I suspect that there is an easy rule of thumb. If a country can tap real entrepreneurial abilities among its own people, as in Japan and Mexico, then there probably will be a sufficient inflow of licensing agreements, proposals of joint ventures, etc., to bring about the transfer of technology on terms acceptable to local people, without letting the MNC's dictate their own terms. But I suspect that the remaining LDC's will, by the end of this century, include a sad number which have kept out MNC's on the grounds that they think that they have sufficient local entrepreneurial talent, but which have found no support in the world market for their view.

On the second point, I suspect that many of even the biggest MNC's may soon run into a conflict. Intra-company transfers are used to make it appear that profits do not arise in high-tax countries, but rather mainly in low-tax ones. It is not sensible to say that poor countries should respond to this situation by giving generous tax concessions to MNC's, because this would be a beggar-my-neighbor policy; and some are very poor beggars already. I would be in favor of poor countries banding together to give competing tax concessions to MNC's (although they should be sensible and not make the standard tax rates exorbitant either); and employing some commission or international referee to report when intracompany transfers to dodge taxes have been made.

It is the last point—the aggravation of tensions and nationalism—that is the most difficult. In confronting it we do not handle easy and computable things like market research reports and tax assessments but rather difficult things like emotions.

Probably the best idea for tactful operation by multinationals has come from Professor Howard Perlmutter, who classified them as ethnocentric, polycentric, or geocentric. But he sees these terms not as being permanently descriptive of particular companies, but rather quite often as phases through which a single company may pass. He points out that to be genuinely international is a state of mind, and that many MNC's are extremely ethnocentric. He tabulates the characteristics of his three types of MNC's as shown in Table 2.

Clearly, it seems desirable to move towards the right in this spectrum. The trouble is that this diluted solution always sounds easy to advocate, but will generally be very difficult to carry out.

Nationalism and the future

C. P. Kindleberger has argued that "the nation state is just about through as an economic unit." This view is naturally not welcome in Africa and Asia, at just the moment when countries there have emerged from the colonial link and become independent nation states for the first time. The leading men in those countries have reached the top by sometimes dangerous political endeavor, and they understandably do not like to be told that the eminence they have attained is pretty pointless anyway. This is one of the reasons for an angry socialist ideology in some of these countries, and in some parts of Latin America. It is one reason why the governments of some developing countries, after deciding that the "time is ripe" to set up some domestic industry (often on very unscientific evidence), then try to raise capital and other resources domestically and set up an indigenous plant—perhaps resorting to some "buying-in" of technology and management ideas from abroad on a contract basis. The

danger is that they may then purchase the wrong type of production know-how and management from abroad, getting second-class inputs.

Nevertheless, this feeling of nationalism has to be lived with. My conclusions and recommendations therefore begin with some suggestions for developing countries and conclude with those for MNC's.

The two most important determinants of events in this field will be:

1. What governments of the LDC's try to do; and

2. How businessmen react.

I believe that LDC governments can improve their position—to get more out of the MNC's, if you will—in a way with which businessmen can come to terms. That at least is the promise. It is to that end that I have tried to formulate my recommendations.

Recommendations for developing countries

We are left finally with recommendations for the governments of developing Latin-American countries. Many American businessmen will disagree with these, but I think that they are realistic.

1. Gear policy to the assumption that much export-oriented manufacturing production will be switched in the period 1973–93 to the LDC's, especially to countries where the domestic tone of goverment is not anti-business (with the attitude to local business often being more important even than that to MNC's).

2. Examine and spur the increasing possibilities for small independent firms to become subcontractors to big foreign manufacturers (with a special eye on the great opportunities and particular problems involved in being subcontractors to big Japanese industry). Test whether this "subcontracting revolution" can be aided by changes in local import/export regulations,

Table 2 Three types of headquarters orientation toward subsidiaries in an international enterprise

Organization design	Ethnocentric	Polycentric	Geocentric
Complexity of organization	Complex in home country, simple in subsidiaries	Varied and independent	Increasingly complex and interdependent
Authority; decision-making	High in headquarters	Relatively low in headquarters	Aim for collaborative approach between headquarters and subsidiaries
Evaluation and control	Home standards applied for persons and performance	Determined locally	Find standards which are universal and local
Rewards and punishments; incentives	High in headquarters, low in subsidiaries	Wide variation: can be high or low, rewards for subsidiary performance	International and local executives rewarded for reaching local and worldwide objectives
Communication; information flow	High volume to subsidiaries; orders, commands, advice	Little to and from headquarters; little between subsidiaries	Both ways and between subsidiaries; heads of subsidiaries part of management team
Identification	Nationality of owner	Nationality of host country	Truly international company but identifying with national interests
Perpetuation (recruiting, staffing, development)	Recruit and develop people of home country for key positions everywhere in the world	Develop people of local nationality for key positions in their own country	Develop best men everywhere in the world for key position everywhere in the world

Source: Columbia Journal of World Business (*January–February, 1969), p. 12.*

credit arrangements, business law, and government handling of foreign contracts.

Recognize, though, that simply to require local procurement runs the great risk of encouraging high-cost production among subcontractors. Ways should be found to insure that local procurement requirements do not become a burden on the whole enterprise in its ability to export competitively.

3. Do everything possible to import education and training by telecommunicated, computer-assisted, visual-aid-assisted means. It may be worth buying these programs competitively from multi-national service corporations; giving performance contracts to profit-making as well as to non-profit-making bodies that will provide pioneer educational experiments in particular areas; certainly buying course broadcasting via satellites from the great universities of the world. I also believe that nutrition is a field in which it ought to be possible to hire the services of a multi-national service corporation of a new type. The MNC ought to be a specially useful instrument in the struggle to overcome malnutrition because it combines almost all the elements needed in the search for solutions: a capacity for large-scale research and development (R & D); access to the most advanced technologies; experience in, and knowledge of, other countries and cultures; and production and marketing know-how. To improve nutrition means primarily finding ways either to raise the protein content of food that is grown or to add to it in processing. Both entail dealing with age-old tastes and preferences. It may involve developing tastes for a vegetable having a texture with which the individual is unfamiliar. Or it may involve persuading a woman to alter her cooking habits and the eating habits of her family. All this requires local partners for the MNC of exceptional awareness and imagination. The developed countries, especially the United States, have not provided incentives for doing socially useful things. I believe that one of the great challenges before the developing world is to succeed in this field where the developed world has largely failed.

4. Recognize that investment and production decisions will increasingly be taken on the basis of information retrieved from giant multinational and computerized data banks. Take advantage of this, and gear your policies in a way that will not unnecessarily make all these data banks list you as a bad risk country to invest in.

5. Recognize that multinational operations, rather than joint ventures, may be better initially for export-oriented industries (including some extractive industries), and large-scale advanced technology industries. But these MNC's should be required to put out more and more of their subsidiary functions for competitive local tender.

6. Recognize that joint ventures can be a very good way of important technological know-how if the developing country has a large enough local business infrastructure to have several competing joint ventures in the industry concerned. But if your developing country cannot thus set up competing joint ventures, then it may sometimes be better to allow an ordinary foreign MNC to enter on generous but non-monopolistic terms (because another foreign MNC might then come and compete with it), or else try to import foreign technology on competitive (i.e., open to tender) fee-paying, or contractual terms.

7. Do not allow protection for the home market of more than say 30 percent of domestic value added.

8. Try to ensure that as many local industries as possible (especially those with multinational participation) become capable of exporting competitively. Even industries whose main purpose is to substitute for imports should not receive very high protection once they are established.

9. Do not force—or even encourage—MNC's to pay wages above the local average, because this will cost you your main international competitive advantage. Try to impose proper taxes on the MNC instead, while allowing it the advantage of cheap local labor. Also, use the taxes to improve the non-wage standard of living of your people, as through the development of infrastructure.

10. Set up a joint arbitrating mechanism to decide whether taxes are being dodged

through the manipulation of charges for services and transactions by the head office of the MNC back in America or Europe on behalf of its local subsidiary. An arbitrating mechanism will shame the MNC out of trying the most obvious dodges that do exist, while rigorous unilateral searching by your country's own tax inspectors will sometimes be unfair, and often be expected to be.

Recommendations for American and European MNC's

Pending the development of clear and relatively stable policies toward MNC's by Latin-American governments, American and European MNC's would be well-advised not to overplay their hands. While these policies may or may not parallel the recommendations outlined above, they will eventually delineate—either formally or informally—the constraints and incentives under which the MNC's will be expected to operate.

American and European MNC's currently have no effective means of speaking with one voice, even if broad consensus were to be achieved. Therefore it is incumbent upon MNC's to operate under a set of informal ground rules such that the constraints that the governments eventually do impose, and the concessions they grant, will be most favorable.

The ground rules I suggest are far fewer in number than my recommendations for the Latin-American governments, and fall under the broad *caveat* of avoiding the impression that the host country is being exploited, particularly economically.

More specifically, the American and European MNC operating in Latin America should hire out as much work as possible to local subcontractors, repair shops, service contractors, and the like, and acknowledge an obligation to give local nationals a sense of participation by training and employing nationals in top management, as well as conducting some R & D locally.

The second of these informal ground rules involves neither seeking nor accepting special concessions unavailable to local businessmen, nor attempting to achieve domination by buying out local companies in traditional fields long favored by local investors.

And finally, in recognition of the fact that the host country benefits more from taxes that help infrastructure development than wage inflation for favored labor forces, the MNC must refrain from avoiding taxes by manipulating charges for services and transactions on behalf of a particular affiliate, so as to disguise real earnings. Thus the higher productivity of the MNC can be of benefit both to the corporation and to the host government.

Liberal

Richard Barnet and Ronald Miller. The Latin–Americanization of the United States.

1

At a particularly tense moment in the Watergate crisis, the veteran White House correspondent of *Time* magazine archly referred to the United States as a banana republic. Indeed, the constitutional crises provoked when the President is investigated to determine whether he is committing high crimes in office or the Vice-President is forced to resign for pettier crimes committed in a lesser office are more reminiscent of Latin-America than what has generally been thought to be the world's most stable political system. Such parallels can be overdone. The hysterical political metaphor is not a substitute for analysis. The United States is not "becoming" another Brazil any more than it is "becoming" another Nazi Germany or Soviet Union, despite dire predictions from the left and the right. Nevertheless, it is now possible to discern certain structural changes in the United States which are causing the world's richest nation to take on some of the aspects of an underdeveloped country. Some of these changes are directly related to the rise of the global corporation.

To understand the impact of the global corporation on the majority of the people of the United States, which is the subject of the remainder of this book, we need to recall the principal elements of the global transformation we have been describing thus far. In the first place, the rise of the global corporation represents the globalization of oligopoly capitalism. In perhaps simpler terms, the new corporate structure is the culmination of a process of concentration and internationalization that has put the world economy under the substantial control of a few hundred business enterprises which do not compete with one another according to the traditional rules of the classic market.

Second, the interest of these enterprises is *global* profit maximization, which may, as we have seen in our study of under-developed countries, require profit *minimization* in certain countries under certain circumstances. This is but one example of how the interests of global corporations and countries in which they conduct their operations may conflict. As we shall see in the chapters that follow, conflicts also exist between U.S.-based global corporations and their home country.

Third, the poor nations of Asia, Latin America, and, soon, Africa, long the hewers of wood and drawers of water for the international economy, are increasingly becoming the principal sites of new production. This dramatic shift from north to south, which could not have been predicted even ten years ago, is changing employment patterns and living standards in the United States.

Finally, this global economic process is producing a new concentration of political power in what are, in legal and political terms, private hands. In short, the managers of the global corporations are neither elected by the people nor subject to popular scrutiny or even popular pressure,

despite the fact that in the course of their daily business they make decisions with more impact on the lives of ordinary people than most generals and politicians. The principal source of their power is their control of knowledge of three specific kinds: the technology of production and organization—i.e., how to make, package, and transport; the technology of obtaining and managing finance capital—i.e., how to create their own private global economy insulated from the vicissitudes of national economies by means of shifting profits and avoiding taxes; the technology of marketing—i.e., how to create and satisfy a demand for their goods by diffusing a consumption ideology through the control of advertising, mass media, and popular culture.

In this chapter and those that follow we shall be looking specifically at the effects on the United States of the reorganization of the world economy into a Global Shopping Center and a Global Factory. We shall be looking particularly at three sorts of changes in American society which we believe are intimately associated with the new role of the global corporation in the U.S. economy. These changes have the effect of changing the pattern of production, the distribution of income, and the balance of power within American society to increase its resemblance to an underdeveloped country.

As we shall explore in the next chapter, the gap between rich and poor in the United States, as in underdeveloped countries, is widening. Dramatic changes in personal economic circumstances are occurring. Our large prosperous middle class, long considered the foundation of American stability, is increasingly squeezed by shrinking employment opportunities, high taxes, and inflationary prices. The members of many a $15,000-a-year family are merely honorary members of the middle class. The unemployed or absurdly underemployed university graduate, a familiar figure in India and Mexico, is no longer a rarity in the United States. While increasing numbers have pushed their way into the middle class during the last decade, membership involves a much more precarious existence than the purveyors of the American Dream promised.

The decline in jobs and the rise in prices have hit those below the middle class much harder. The welfare population largely comprises unskilled workers for whom jobs do not exist. In the center of every large city hundreds of thousands of Americans are living without decent food, light, plumbing—and without dignity or hope. As in Brazil, the first to feel the squeeze of a tightening economy are minority groups. In the United States the unemployment rate among blacks is two to three times the rate among whites. But even the moderately well-to-do face reductions in key aspects of their standard of living. There are meatless days even in Winnetka. The price and scarcity of gasoline have begun to restrict the use of the automobile as entertainment. The shortage of heating fuel and electric power means colder houses in winter and hotter houses in summer than many Americans are used to. Compared with what most of the world endures, these indicators of a decline in the standard of living are perhaps barely worth talking about. But in the context of American expectations of something bigger and better every year, they are significant indeed.

What do these changes have to do with the rise of the global corporation? As we shall show in succeeding chapters, a great deal. The argument can be summarized briefly. In the interest of maximum global profits, the managers of the world corporation are creating, often unconsciously, a global system in which the long-term role assigned to the United States is completely changing what it produces and consequently what its people do. Production of the traditional industrial goods that have been the mainstay of the U.S. economy is being transferred from $4-an-hour factories in New England to 30-cents-an-hour factories in the "export platforms" of Hong Kong and Taiwan. Increasingly, as the cars, TVs, computers, cameras, clothes, and furniture are being produced abroad, the United States is becoming a service economy and a producer of plans, programs, and ideas for others to execute. The effect is to eliminate traditional jobs on the assembly line and thereby to reduce the blue collar work force and to replace these jobs with others (probably a smaller number) requiring quite

different skills. Because people are not fungible, the man who assembles radios cannot easily become a computer programmer or a packaged-food salesman, to name two recent growth occupations. Unemployment and reduced income result.

As in underdeveloped countries, such as Brazil, for example, the effects of unemployment are not equally distributed over the entire population. They are concentrated in certain regions. The counterpart to Brazil's Northeast, a crisis region of a developing economy, is Appalachia, an area that the energy industry has exploited but not developed. Certain formerly industrial communities of New England, the Midwest, and the Pacific Coast now face the same fate.

The change in employment patterns—the decline in labor-intensive production and the corresponding rise of skilled service jobs—has led to a redistribution of wealth and income which, once again, is more in the tradition of the underdeveloped world than in that of the Affluent Society. A careful look at income statistics reveals that the average employee, as opposed to top executives, is earning a *decreasing* share of the national income. John Kenneth Galbraith has called our attention to the commonplace but still curious phenomenon that pleasant work is generally much better paid than unpleasant work. But the global corporation is eliminating unpleasant jobs on American soil either by automating them or by exporting them. All of this means that, contrary to the American Dream, there is a trend in the United States toward greater inequality. The patterns of distribution of income and wealth are nowhere near so stark as in underdeveloped countries, but some of the same processes we have just examined with respect to Latin America are at work here.

The United States trading pattern is beginning to resemble that of underdeveloped countries as the number one nation becomes increasingly dependent on the export of agricultural products and timber to maintain its balance of payments and increasingly dependent on imports of finished goods to maintain its standard of living. To earn the foreign exchange to buy the energy and certain raw materials on which Americans are increasingly dependent, and the TVs, cameras, and other basic consumer goods which, more and more, are produced abroad, the United States must export increasing amounts of grain, lumber, and other agricultural products. (Unlike poor countries, however, the U.S. also exports "software"—i.e., technical knowledge.) In recent years this trading pattern has resulted in food shortages and skyrocketing food prices at home, a phenomenon long familiar in poor countries but a new one in the United States.

2

This chapter begins our inquiry into the connections between corporate growth and the adverse social changes in the United States to which we have just alluded. We shall be focusing on the role of global corporations and banks in this process. Although all but a few of the top 500 industrial firms in the U.S. and almost all the top banks qualify as centrally planned global enterprises, important segments of the economy are still in the hands of primarily national firms. Although small business is not global in either outlook or operation, much of it is dependent on global firms for survival. Certain giant firms which concentrate on domestic services, such as constructing office buildings and operating the telephone system, do not plan or act like global corporations. Government too is an important actor in the economy. We will not be concerned with the activity of these primarily national sectors of the U.S. economy, because it is the global corporation which is the most rapidly growing sector and the most dynamic agent of change.

Probably the most dramatic illustration of the planning power of global corporations and what it can mean for ordinary American citizens is provided by the energy industry. The international petroleum giants have been the pioneer global corporations. They were the first to develop global planning, to locate a high percentage of their assets abroad, and to perfect the art of transfer pricing and the science of tax avoidance.

About 6 percent of the world's population lives in the United States, but these 200 million people consume over 30 percent of the world's energy output. (During much of the last generation before the Japanese and Europeans began to be big oil consumers, the percentage was higher.) Until recently, Americans burned fuel at a bargain rate. But between 1970 and 1973, even before the Arab boycott and the official proclamation of the Energy Crisis, the price for crude rose 72 percent. In some cases the price of natural gas has risen 200 percent since 1970. James E. Akins, formerly the State Department's chief petroleum expert, predicts that "world consumption within the next twelve years is now expected to exceed total world consumption of oil throughout history up to the present time."

Although consumption in the United States has been cut back by government programs, blackouts, brownouts, service-station shutdowns, winter school closings, and rationing, demand, both U.S. and worldwide, far outpaces the *available* supply. This situation is a direct consequence of some of the structural changes in the world economy to which we have alluded. The decisions about production, pricing, research and development, and distribution in the energy field have been substantially in the hands of the global energy companies, the "seven sisters"— British Petroleum, Gulf, Mobil, Shell, Texaco, Exxon, and Chevron (Standard Oil of California). (Purely domestic energy companies account for approximately one-third of annual U.S. energy consumption.) For many years Exxon and other global energy companies have been earning substantially higher profits abroad than in the United States. Because 300 billion barrels of the proved 500-billion-barrel world oil reserves are in the Arab countries of the Middle East, the companies have been concentrating their development activities there. Because of their oligopolistic control over the world energy market, they have held the commanding power to decide how much oil is produced, where it shall go, the price to be charged, and where, through transfer pricing techniques, to declare their profits.

The power of the global energy companies in the U.S. economy is based on a combination of special privileges: uniquely favorable oil concessions in foreign countries backed by the power of the U.S. Government in the name of "national security" (in 1948 Aramco's concession area in the Middle East was larger than the combined areas of Texas and California); special tax advantages unavailable to any other industry (a 22-percent—until recently, 27.5-percent—depletion allowance plus a secret "national security" tax concession making royalty payments to foreign governments eligible as a credit against U.S. taxes); near-monopoly control of oil reserves, transportation, refining and marketing facilities. In 1949, according to the Federal Trade Commission, the "seven sisters" controlled 65 percent of the estimated crude reserves in the world, 88 percent of crude production outside the United States and the U.S.S.R., 77 percent of the refining capacity outside the United States and the U.S.S.R., two-thirds of the tanker fleet, and all major pipelines outside the United States and the U.S.S.R. (It need hardly be added that the same companies dominated production, refining, marketing, and distribution within the United States.) Despite recent nationalizations and the rise of a few European and Japanese companies, 8 global companies, 5 of them U.S.-based, still control 48 percent of world production and a degree of vertical integration and market sharing permitted no other industry. Immunity from antitrust prosecution has been justified on "national security" grounds. (One documented piece of evidence of conspiracy in the industry is found in a Swedish parliamentary committee report that the local subsidiaries of Shell, Texaco, Gulf, and Jersey Standard arranged weekly meetings to "fix uniform rebates, commissions, bonuses, discounts, and other selling terms.")

Because the petroleum companies have had near-monopoly power over production and distribution, they have, for much of the last generation, been able to set world market prices at will. This explains, in part, their extraordinary profits. Oil companies such as Exxon like to advertise that their profit rates are lower than those in many other industries. This is true if one looks at the consolidated balance sheet of the energy companies in which oil, coal, uranium, and other less immediately profitable energy operations are lumped together. But if one looks just at the oil business, the return has been immense. Between 1948 and 1960, the net income of the oil companies derived from the Middle East alone was over $14 billion. While profit rates have been declining in the U.S. and Venezuelan operations, the annual rate of return on fixed assets invested in the Middle East rose from 61 percent in the 1948–1949 period to 72 percent a decade later. This is due to the fact that costs are much lower in the Middle East. (A Chase Manhattan Bank study of the early 1960's computed the cost of producing a barrel of Middle East oil at 16 cents, as compared with $1.73 a barrel for U.S. oil.) The companies have been able to use their enormous profits from foreign operations to finance their expansion into the energy fields which they hope to dominate in the next generation—shale, coal gasification, nuclear power, etc. When Standard Oil (New Jersey) changed its name to Exxon at a cost of some $100 million, it announced thereby not only that it had outgrown New Jersey but that it had transcended the oil industry itself.

Global oligopolies develop ever greater and more concentrated power through various forms of "cross-subsidization." John Blair, former counsel to the Senate Anti-Trust Committee, defines this term as "the actual use by a conglomerate of monopoly profits earned in another industry to subsidize sales at a loss or at an abnormally low profit." Throughout the American economy the giants are using their dominant position in one sector of the economy to acquire a commanding position in another. For example, a successful seller of soft drinks can use its oligopoly profits to subsidize a foray into related industries like the potato-chip business or unrelated industries like the trucking business. Because it can afford to outadvertise smaller established companies, it ends up with a large share of their market. Nowhere is this process of cross-subsidization clearer than in the world of oil and related products. The big companies can use their enormous Middle East profits to consolidate their hold on the distribution system in the United States or to forestall competitors from exploiting alternative energy sources. Thus the same people, essentially the managers and directors of the "seven sisters," end up controlling the pace of exploitation, distribution, and price of petroleum and future energy sources to replace it such as coal, natural gas, and uranium.

Because the energy industry pioneered the globalization of American business, it is one of the best and most instructive examples of the planning power of global corporations—and how this power can be misused. The oil companies are largely responsible for what the former State Department petroleum expert James Akins calls "spectacularly wrong" projections about supply and demand. These estimates of their own domestic well capacity were accepted uncritically by government petroleum planners and they were "almost always exaggerated." (Domestic oil production is down about 8 percent since 1970, and this trend is likely to continue. The addition of approximately 2 million barrels a day by 1980 from Alaska's North Slope is likely to be more than offset by the rapid dwindling of the Texas and Oklahoma oil fields.) At the same time, the decline in natural-gas production and its effect on the demand for oil were largely ignored in the government. In 1970, President Nixon's Task Force on Oil Imports, dominated by representatives of the industry, predicted no significant rise in the price of crude and projected a demand in the United States in 1980 of 18.5 million barrels a day, of which no more than 5 million would need to be imported. By 1973 the United States was already importing well over 6 million barrels, and some revised projections for 1980 are as high as 24 million barrels a day. (Akins estimates that about 35 percent of projected U.S. consumption in 1980 must come from the Eastern Hemisphere.)

Because the information about oil reserves, real costs of drilling and distribution, and their own long-range strategies is in the exclusive hands of the companies, it is impossible to know the extent to which the celebrated Energy Crisis that began in 1973 is real or manipulated. There is considerable evidence, as committees of Congress began to discover in 1974, that available supplies are far more ample than the long lines at gas stations and "crisis messages" from the White House would suggest. Indeed, fuel stocks in the U.S. were at an all-time high in 1974. The critical issues have concerned pricing and timing. It has been in the interest of the companies to orchestrate the worldwide flow of oil in such a way as to maximize profits. In times and places of surplus, it has been company strategy to keep petroleum products off the market. Moreover, during the 1974 energy crisis, when the U.S. domestic price of crude was controlled below that of Europe and Japan, oil companies maximized global profits by maintaining their previous level of imports and increasing the supply to Europe and Japan. This, in part, explains why Japanese and European consumers did not experience the same serious shortages as did motorists and homeowners in the United States. (Company advertisements that appeared in major newspapers in 1974 claiming that the tankers lining up off the American coast could not unload their cargo for technical reasons understated industry resources and resourcefulness.)

An "energy crisis" which pushes up the price of oil, drives smaller, independent producers out of business, and ensures historic industry profits is something less than a disaster from the companies' viewpoint, however much it may disrupt, inconvenience, or impoverish other citizens. (If it can be presented to the public as a natural disaster compounded by "Arab greed" rather than a massive planning error—real or deliberate—the companies can qualify for relief in the form of additional government subsidies or immunity from environmental controls.) Some knowledgeable students of the petroleum industry such as former Occidental executive Christopher Rand and MIT professor Morris Adelman offer impressive evidence that there is no shortage of fossil fuels in the ground and that indeed, in Rand's words, "the inventories of the world's available fuel have been increasing rather than diminishing, even when measured against the annual rise in the rate of the world's consumption." The suddenness with which lines at gas stations appeared and disappeared, the puzzling display of sudden anger and sudden friendship from the Arab boycotters, and the quick jump in gas prices and oil-company profits all within a few short winter months in 1974 aroused widespread public suspicion that the Energy Crisis was stage-managed. Certainly the profit statements of the "seven sisters" suggest that this was a marketable crisis. When it miraculously lifted, the public was grateful for the opportunity to buy 60-cent gasoline, and a number of troublesome independent operators in the petroleum industry had been eliminated. The extent to which the crisis was the result of conspiracy may not be known until historians are given access to the oil companies' equivalent of the Pentagon Papers.

There is little doubt that the oil companies made serious planning errors. When oil-company executives are subjected to the sort of scathing public questioning by Senate committees that once was reserved for suspected subversive screenwriters, and whispers of nationalization are heard in the corridors of Congress, it is evident that management has been careless with the company image. But up to now the energy giants have been able to profit from their planning errors by pushing their results onto the public.

In the late 1950's, the oil companies finally went too far in taking advantage of their superior bargaining power with the producing countries. Accustomed to renting pliable sheiks along with their oil reserves, they assumed that they could continue indefinitely the cheap and easy access to Arab oil supplies that had financed their mammoth growth. In 1958 and 1959, the major companies reduced their posted prices and tax payments to oil-producing nations and thereby stimulated the creation of OPEC—at first a weak protective society, but now grown into an effective sellers' cartel to offset the cartel power of the companies. (According to conservative estimates, between 1973 and 1985 Kuwait, Saudi Arabia, and the smaller sheikdoms of the Persian Gulf are in a position to earn $227 billion in oil revenues.)

The worldwide energy crisis is not a problem of absolute shortages of energy sources. It is a political crisis over who shall control these resources; who shall decide where, when, and how they are to be distributed; and who shall share in the enormous revenues. The United States is rich in coal and shale. Solar energy, nuclear fusion, wind, and even the recycling of wastes are all possible alternative sources of energy to run the world industrial machine. There may not be an energy crisis in fifteen or twenty years. Rand attributes the lack of refinery capacity in the United States to the fact that "the major American oil companies have neglected to build refineries in the past few years because there has not been as yet enough profit in the enterprise." But, for the present, the problem remains: how are the factories, houses, offices, and cars of the world, with their ever-increasing demand, to be fueled during these transition years until such alternatives are developed? Energy sources that can be exploited only with nonexistent technology or at prohibitive cost, no matter how abundant they may be, are irrelevant to this transitional crisis. Having absorbed well their lessons at the Harvard Business School and the London School of Economics, the new oil technocrats of the Middle East have elected to limit the exploitation of their reserves to delay their exhaustion and to maximize their profits. Their optimum schedule for producing oil is not the same as the schedule of consumption in the industrialized world. It is correct to argue, as Professor Adelman and other petroleum experts do, that there is no worldwide shortage of recoverable oil in the ground, but it is an academic point if those who control the reserves will not permit them to be exploited fast enough to meet rising demand.

While the U.S.-based oil companies now issue standard warnings about the Energy Crisis, they are engaged, in the words of David Freeman, head of the Energy Policy

Study, in a "massive exercise in picking the pocket of the American consumer to the tune of billions a year." Not only do energy companies pass on the cost increases of crude to the consumer, but, as Professor Adelman has calculated, they "increase their margins and return on investment" as a result of price increases. In Britain, for example, a recent tax increase of 28 cents a barrel was matched by a price rise of 42 cents a barrel. Because the energy giants are classic oligopolies (in 1969, 8 companies controlled 81.8 percent of all production in OPEC countries), they need not worry about price competition and hence can afford to take a relaxed view of price increases. As long as they can pass such increases on to American motorists and homeowners, they have no great incentive to drive a hard bargain with the Arab countries—particularly when the Arabs are in a position to restrict the supply. Thus Professor Adelman charges the global oil companies with being mere tax collectors for the sheiks, and Senator Henry Jackson calls for government intervention in the negotiating process because the companies "cannot be credible bargainers with OPEC." Confidential papers of the Arabian-American Oil Company subpoenaed by the Senate Subcommittee on Multinational Corporations show that the company welcomed price increases because "their profits increased in proportion to the price rise."

Given world petroleum needs and the distribution of supply, the bargaining power of the Arab states can only increase. The Shell Oil Company now estimates that by 1985 total U.S. import requirements will rise to 15 million barrels a day, of which 78 percent will have to come from Arab countries. At the same time, the company predicts that world consumption will double. Since other industrial countries such as Japan are even more dependent on Middle East oil supplies than the United States and since the Arab countries wish to exhaust their reserves at a slower rate than the companies would like, oil shortages and skyrocketing prices which are then likely to be charged will by that year cost the United States an estimated $70 billion a year in the loss of foreign-exchange reserves. To try to keep the U.S. balance of payments in equilibrium, the United States must export increasing amounts of agricultural products. As the 1972 Soviet wheat deal made clear to customers at the supermarket, huge shipments of grain exported abroad reduce the short-run supply in the United States and drive up the price of bread and meat. Thus while the energy companies are able to adjust to the new realities of international oil politics by translating scarcity into profits, the U.S. consumer (and his counterpart in other countries as well) is paying the price in many ways.

As the bargaining power of those in control of energy resources increases, the United States will be faced with a series of uncomfortable choices. One would be a sharp decline in the use of energy in the United States. Homes at 65 degrees, auto-less Sundays, and a ban on nonessential electric appliances might be just the beginning. Furthermore, emergency power to ration and allocate scarce resources would further strengthen and centralize the power of the Executive in Washington. (More optimistically, it could also lead to some basic rethinking about the wisdom of maintaining economic growth on ever-increasing consumption and waste of finite natural resources, but as yet there is no sign of this.)

By 1980, Chase Manhattan Bank experts project, the foreign-exchange reserves of Arab countries from their oil revenues will be in excess of $400 billion. (In 1970 their foreign-exchange reserves were about $5 billion; four years later they had jumped tenfold.) These huge dollar reserves pose a serious problem for the world monetary system. A dollar represents a claim on goods and services. The world is fast approaching the point at which the claims outstanding may well exceed the goods, services, and investment opportunities of interst to the oil-producing nations. Additional dollars will then become as unappealing a medium of exchange for their precious oil as Indian rupees. The Arab sheiks can spend only a fraction of their bulging dollar reserves on Cadillacs and Mediterranean cruises, and their sparsely populated countries even under the most ambitious development schemes could not absorb more than a small fraction. The Arab states are attempting to buy into retail, refining, and marketing operations in the U.S. petroleum industry through joint ventures with U.S.-based companies. Saudi Arabia is becoming a major holder of real estate on the West Coast and by early 1974 had already acquired two California banks. But none of these acquisitions makes much of a dent in the dollar stockpiles of the Middle East. The unanswered question now plaguing the world's bankers is whether the international monetary system can find any way to recycle the extraordinary foreign-exchange holdings of the oil-producing states. In the the next few years they will continue to be absorbed in Eurodollar deposits and U.S. Treasury bills, but, as a senior Chase Manhattan Bank executive predicts, within a few years "there will be severe difficulties" unless there are "structural changes" in institutional markets. Thus the glut of dollars no less than the scarcity of oil threatens the stability of the international structures for the creation and maintenance of wealth.

The Energy Crisis is perhaps the most dramatic illustration of these growing vulnerabilities that make the United States look more like an underdeveloped country, but it is only a part of a larger problem. Increasingly, poor countries of the underdeveloped world are coming to understand that their very survival depends upon their taking control over their natural resources and using their increased bargaining power to end what has amounted to a subsidization of the rich nations. (To the argument that the favorable oil concessions of two and three generations ago merely represented what the traffic could bear, their reply is that the traffic pattern is now beginning to change and that, increasingly, they will resist being drained on other people's terms.) This shift in viewpoint, as we saw in the last chapter, is present in the manufacturing industries as well. As the leading U.S. producers of drugs, electronics, packaged food, chemicals, automobiles, and engines become more dependent upon "export platforms" in poor countries, the politicians and generals in charge of those countries may be expected to exact a large share of the profits of global corporations to pre-serve their own political position. If the governments of underdeveloped countries can succeed in keeping more finance capital in the country, thereby restricting its use for financing of worldwide expansion, they will profoundly affect the way global corporations do business.

Some indication of how important the extraordinary profits available to global corporations in weak and underdeveloped societies have been for their worldwide operation was given us by a top manager of a large U.S.-based manufacturing corporation operating in Latin America. He told us that it was standard practice for his firm, and he believed for many others, to finance expansion in the United States and Western Europe from the excess earnings generated in Latin America. When the "profit faucet," as he termed it, is turned off because local politicians have learned how to police transfer pricing and technology transfers, the expansion programs are threatened, especially when outside capital is scarce and expensive. We have noted . . . how extensive the practice of transfer pricing is and what huge disguised profits this practice can generate.

Their greatest achievement, the global corporations claim, has been to sustain an unprecedented standard of living in the major industrial countries in which their headquarters are based. That is the great source of their power and the basis for their extraordinary claims on the future. But how important to the maintenance of that standard of living has been the power to exact extraordinarily favorable terms and conditions from poor countries? What will happen to the industrial societies when those terms and conditions change? We have no idea how much our prosperity depends upon the cheap and easy access to raw materials and labor in weak and dependent societies. We do know that our dependence on imported raw materials and foreign labor will increase significantly in the next few years and that changes in bargaining power will force the affluent society to reexamine patterns of consumption that have come to be accepted as laws of nature. It is then that the three-way conflict between the global corporation, American consumers, and poor countries is likely to become more acute. How it is to be resolved will determine how much peace or justice we can expect in the twenty-first century.

3

We must now ask ourselves a troublesome question. If we are right in the assessment that the policy decisions of U.S.-based global corporations in many areas, such as in the energy field, are causing the United States to begin to resemble underdeveloped societies in important respects, how is it that these decisions are allowed to be made? How is it that global corporations continue to exercise the key planning function in American society—in energy policy, transportation policy, and employment policy, to give three examples—when those decisions are producing plainly irrational results for the majority of Americans?

The answer in the United States, as in poor countries . . . can be found only by examination of the distribution of power in American society. An understanding of the process by which the power to make crucial economic decisions for a society becomes concentrated in a few hands and the cumulative effects of that concentration is the intellectual key to understanding how and why such decisions are made. Major social analysts such as Max Weber, Thorstein Veblen, and Joseph Schumpeter have amplified and explained the obvious relationship between economic power and political decisions and in particular why concentrated power produces decisions to the advantage of the few and to the disadvantage of the many. So undebatable is the relationship between concentrated economic power and narrow self-serving political decisions that it represents a meeting ground for Karl Marx and Adam Smith. The prophet of socialism believed that the state under capitalism was the executive committee of an exploitative ruling class. But Adam Smith, the prophet of capitalism, also worried about the social effects of concentrated economic power. Capitalists are forever trying "to widen the

market and narrow the competition," and the latter is always against the public interest. "By raising their profits above what they naturally would be [capitalists] levy for their own benefit an absurd tax upon the rest of their fellow citizens."

In the remainder of this chapter we shall be examining why the process of globalization itself has been accompanied by a steep rise in the rate of concentration. In short, there are intrinsic requirements of global oligopoly capitalism that lead to ever-increasing concentration of power and wealth. The problem is not that certain individuals who have risen to preeminent ownership or managerial positions in global corporations are greedy or lacking in public concern. After all, greed is the oil of capitalism. Greed, or to put it in less Biblical terms, acquisitiveness, is supposedly the motivation that makes the system work. The drive for ever-greater accumulation is integral to that system and does not depend upon personal idiosyncrasies. Under traditional capitalist theory, private greed was supposed to lead to public good because of the character of the market. Competition would restrain the selfishness of each to the benefit of all.

However, certain structural changes in world capitalism that we have considered and others that we are about to consider now make it increasingly difficult to reconcile entrepreneurial acquisitiveness with the public interest—if we define public interest to include the health, safety, welfare, and comfort of at least 60 percent of the population. The global corporation, essentially because it does most of its trading with itself, has delivered the coup de grâce to the market. True, the power accumulated by giant oligopolies by the late 1950's to control supplies, set prices, and create demand had made an anachronism of the classic concept of the market even before Big Business became global. But globalization completed the process. At the minimum, almost half of the transactions involving U.S.-based global firms are those in which the buyer and the seller are essentially the same—i.e., intracorporate sales, loans, and other transfers. In such situations the notion of a fair market price is lost. When parties to a transaction are not dealing at arm's length, there are no external criteria for judging the public consequences. The negation of the market means that global profit maximization becomes the guiding star in every transaction and that corporate managers have far more freedom than classic entrepreneurs to arrange profit-maximizing strategies at the expense of the public interest.

Thus by ushering in a postmarket economy and transforming the nature of competition, the rise of globally oriented companies has removed constraints that formerly restricted the size, power, and audacity of the firm. The concentration of power necessarily involves the decline of countervailing power. When a firm buys its former competitors, it is removing checks on its power. Similarly, as we shall show, when a corporation develops the mobility to move its plants out of the United States, it has already gone far to defang its less mobile union adversaries. The rise of the global corporation over the U.S. economy has thus occurred simultaneously with the accelerating concentration of power in the hands of the 500 biggest U.S. corporations. Virtually all of these corporations are global—in the location of their assets, the source of their profits, and their production and marketing outlook. Each is dependent to a significant degree on its foreign operations.

Just as they did in the underdeveloped world, during the course of the last generation the top 500 corporations have dramatically increased their position of dominance in the American economy. In 1955, 44.5 percent of all Americans working in manufacturing and mining worked for the top 500 corporations; by 1970, the figure had risen to 72 percent. In the same period, the top 500 increased their share of all manufacturing and mining assets in the country from 40 to 70 percent. There is an accelerando to the concentration process as one nears the pinnacle. In 1970, the top 9 corporations in the industrial and mining sectors accounted for some 15 percent of total assets and sales in the country. Furthermore, during 1955–1959 the largest 200 industrial corporations increased their share of total industrial assets each year by an average of 1 percent. Ten years later, this average rate of concentration had doubled: they were taking over an additional 2 percent of total assets each year.

The rhythm of accelerated concentration is sustained by the perpetual process of merger. Between 1953 and 1968, there were over 14,000 mergers of manufacturing corporations in the United States, in which the acquiring corporations obtained $66 billion in new assets. The top 100 corporations accounted for only 333 of these mergers, but in the process they acquired $23 billion in new assets, or roughly 35 percent of all merged assets acquired during the period. In the late 1960's, the merger of industrial giants accelerated at an exponential rate. Almost 60 percent of the $23 billion of new assets were acquired in the four most recent years studied (1965–1968). (In 1965, for example, 1,496 domestic firms disappeared through merger, the highest number in the history of the United States up to that time.) Although comprehensive data for the following years are not available, many indications point to a continuation of the same trend of accelerating concentration. Despite antitrust laws written with a ferocity to intimidate the uninitiated, prosecutions are few and courts are lenient. (Of all the mergers between 1950 and 1967, only 199 were challenged. Almost half of these, it might be added, were small firms of less than $100 million in sales. The government won 90 of these challenges, and in only 48 out of 14,000 mergers during the period were the companies required to divest themselves of anything.)

If we turn to the service sector, the pattern of cumulative increases in concentration is equally striking. The term "service sector" includes lawyers, dishwashers, travel agents, and masseurs, but when we are focusing on the services that earn most of the money in the United States (as opposed to those that employ the most people) we mean banks, insurance companies, other financial institutions, and the communications and transport industries—in short, the social infrastructure of the country.

In looking at poor countries, . . . we noted that the control of ideology by global corporations through the mass media was as important a source of their power as their control of finance and technology. It was the interaction of the three that enabled powerful corporate interests, mostly foreign-based, to make major planning decisions which adversely affected the problems of mass poverty, unemployment, and inequality. The same mutually supporting use of these three elements of corporate power can be seen in the United States, and with some of the same effects.

Any discussion of the power of the mass media in the United States must of course begin with television and radio. The typical American spends three and a half hours a day watching TV and two and one-half hours listening to the radio. The industry estimates that about 87 percent of the population is exposed to television each week and 90 percent to radio. Because the network's franchises, its most valuable property, cost next to nothing (a few million dollars in legal fees to obtain or protect its right to broadcast over the fifteen stations it is allowed to own and the 200-odd affiliate stations), profits are enormous. The networks have used these profits to finance their expansion into many unrelated areas. CBS owns Steinway Piano; Holt, Rinehart and Winston publishers; and, formerly, the New York Yankees. RCA, NBC's parent, owns Random House, Hertz car rentals, and Cushman & Wakefield real estate. While the electronic media are not the sole source of information beyond the village, as in countries with large illiterate populations, they are, as the editors of *Look* and *Life* discovered, increasingly replacing magazines, as well as books and newspapers, as the primary source of news and entertainment. About 96 percent of the entertainment to which 87 percent of the population is exposed each week is produced by the three networks. About 75 percent of the country looks to the three networks as its primary source of news.

The principal purpose of this mass diffusion of news and entertainment is to sell products. Each year, it is estimated, the average viewer sees 40,000 commercials. In 1968, advertisers spent over $3 billion on television. (Total advertising revenues in all media have jumped since 1945 from $3 billion to $20 billion. About 30 percent of the advertising business is handled by the ten largest agencies, which nearly doubled in size during the 1960's.)

Advertising is also the mainstay of the newspaper business. (The average newspaper devotes 60 percent of its space to ads.) The marketing function of newspapers is more important to those who finance them than the communication function. For this reason, size of the market rather than quality of the content is the crucial determinant of whether a newspaper shall live or die. The bigger a newspaper's readership, the more advertising revenue it can command. In rational economic terms most cities cannot "support" more than one newspaper. Thus, less than 15 percent of the 1,500-odd cities in the United States with a daily newspaper have more than one and at least half the nation's daily papers are owned by newspaper chains. Seventy-five percent of all newspaper news is supplied by the two major wire services, Associated Press and United Press International.

The same groups (the banks and financial institutions) that are the major sources of noncorporate finance capital also have significant interests in the communications media. The process by which large corporations use their predominant power to gain increasing control within one sector of the economy and then to use that power to gain control over other sectors—i.e., cross-subsidization—goes far to explain the rapidity with which the global corporations accumulate ever-increasing power and undermine sources of countervailing power.

4

No one understands this process better than bankers. Nine of the top ten companies in the United States in terms of assets are global banks. Of 13,000 banks in the United States, the top 4—the Bank of America, Chase Manhattan, the First National City

Bank, and Manufacturers Hanover Trust—had in 1970 over 16 percent of all bank assets. The top 50 had 48 percent. More important, the top 4 had increased their rate of concentration dramatically. From 1965 to 1970 they were increasing their share of total bank assets at roughly twice their expansion rate during the previous ten years. As in the control of technology and mass media, the concentration of power has proceeded in the finance sector at an exponential rate.

That the rich get richer is well established as folk wisdom ("Nothing succeeds like success") and Biblical truth ("To him who hath shall it be given"). There is nothing especially mysterious about why large banks grow faster than small banks. What is striking about the growth of banks is not so much that a few financial giants have come to dominate the money industry as that they also dominate other sectors of the economy as well. The largest banks exercise significant influence in a number of the country's leading manufacturing and mining companies, the transportation industry, the media, and public utilities.

Banks have certain advantages over other corporations in their ability to use cross-subsidization. The most mobile of business enterprises, they can change the focus of their activities from country to country as financial conditions change. Thus the top U.S. banks which invaded London during the Eurodollar boom of the 1960's are now retrenching somewhat in the City and expanding their activities elsewhere. Similarly, they are more flexible in dealing with regimes of all political hues. As the world economy becomes more integrated, even the most militant Communists, who also need hard currency, cannot afford to offend the international bankers.

The process by which banks have expanded their control of the nonbanking sectors of the U.S. economy has involved three major strategies. The first is the use of their enormous holdings of industrial stocks which they either own or manage for customers in trust accounts. In 1971 banks owned $577 billion in corporate securities in their own portfolios and had control of an additional $336 billion in trust funds. Together these assets in the hands of banks amount to almost $1 trillion. Trust funds are portfolios of securities given to banks to manage, usually for widows, children, estates, pension funds, or charitable institutions. In 1971, in addition to the banks' own holdings, bank trust departments held 22 percent of all the outstanding voting shares of all publicly held U.S. corporations. For more than 80 percent of these shares the bank had "sole investment responsibility"—which meant that it could buy and sell the shares at will and vote the stock at shareholder meetings.

Thanks to the continuing investigative work of Congressman Wright Patman's Subcommittee on Banking and Currency and Senator Lee Metcalf's Subcommittee on Budgeting, Management and Expenditures, we know a good deal about how banks have translated that trillion dollars into what one subcommittee calls "enormous potential power for good or evil." Economists generally agree, and managements are acutely aware, that a shareholder in control of 5 percent of a publicly held corporation cannot be safely ignored. According to the Patman Subcommittee, there is "considerable evidence" that corporations seek to establish "close contact" with such shareholders, who are almost invariably large institutional investors. Corporate management regularly consults them on "any major corporate decision, such as a proposed merger, a new stock issue proposal or any pending decision which may seriously affect the company's operations." Corporate managers listen to the bankers' answers, since they have the power to sell off large blocks of stock and cause a decline in its value, thereby hurting the reputation of management and, perhaps more importantly, the value of its stock options. Moreover, when a bank or insurance company controls 5 percent of a company's stock, it can exert crucial voting power in the event of a proxy battle. (It is much easier to enlist the support of a 5-percent shareholder than to recruit 5,000 small investors.) Institutional investors dominate annual shareholders' meetings on the relatively rare occasions when fundamental issues of corporate policy are put up for a vote.

The top 49 banks have a 5-percent or greater share in 147 of the top 500 industrials. They have a 5-percent or greater interest in 17 of the top 50 transportation companies, 29 of the top 50 life insurance companies and 5 of the top public utilities. Some specific examples provide a more vivid picture of the power of America's largest global banks.

By examining interlocking directorates and stock ownership of the leading U.S. banks, the economist Peter Dooley has identified fifteen major financial groups in the United States. A group is a collection of nominally separate corporations which pool their resources to enhance their combined power. By far the most powerful is the Rockefeller-Morgan group, the coordinated financial operations of the descendants, beneficiaries, and employees of John D. Rockefeller and J. P. Morgan. As early as 1904, John Moody, the founder of *Moody's Industrials*, still the leading directory to the labyrinth of high finance, concluded that it was impossible to talk of the Rockefellers and Morgans as separate economic actors, so intertwined were their various activities.

Taking another look at the Rockefeller-Morgan empire in the mid-1960's, Peter Dooley concludes that ''it is not possible to separate these groups.'' The power base of the Rockefeller-Morgan group is the control of six of the country's largest banks: the Chase Manhattan Bank, the Rockefeller family depository, of which David Rockefeller is chairman; the First National City Bank; Manufacturers Hanover Trust; the Chemical Bank of New York; the Morgan Guaranty Trust; and Bankers Trust. In the mid-1960's, according to Patman Subcommittee research, these banks dramatically increased their holdings of one another's stock and consolidated the interlocks among their boards. Together four large interlocking New York banks, according to a 1973 Senate Government Operations Committee report, hold 21.9 percent of United Airlines, 24.7 percent of American Airlines, and 13.8 percent of Western Air-

lines. The Chase Manhattan Bank alone holds substantially more than 5 percent of United, American, Northwestern, and Western. Chase (with two other Rockefeller-Morgan banks) has voting rights to 23.1 percent of the stock of CBS, to 24.6 percent of ABC, and to 6.7 percent of NBC. In addition to the principal airlines and the three major networks, the Rockefeller-Morgan group has effective control of key sectors of the mining industry. (It is scarcely necessary to mention the Exxon Corporation, until recently Standard Oil, the largest energy corporation in the world and the source and constant nourisher of the Rockefeller family fortune.) In 1967, Chase had a 5.5-percent interest in Reynolds, and Morgan had a 17.5-percent interest in Kennecott (which in turn owns Peabody Coal, the world's largest coal company) and a 15.5-percent interest in American Smelting and Refining.

No committee of Congress or anyone else has been able to show exactly how large banks use their power in the communications and transportation industries and how their huge holdings may affect the public interest. We have some ideas on this, which we shall take up in the next section. Whether banks have too much power over other parts of the economy is controversial. Whether Congress should have the information to determine whether this is so is not. Public authorities do not have the regular access to the information on the interaction of crucial institutions necessary to understand the present U.S. economy and how it works.

Banks have reinforced their concentration of ownership and control by means of a second strategy, the liberal use of the interlocking directorate. The Patman Subcommittee found that the top 49 commercial banks had 5 percent or more stock control *plus* interlocking directorates with 5,270 companies. Dooley's 1966 study ''The Interlocking Directorate'' in the *American Economic Review* concludes that ''most of the larger corporations have been interlocked with other large corporations for many decades.'' What are interlocking directorates and why are they important? An interlock occurs when a corporation elects an executive or director of another corporation to be on its board of directors. There are many possible motives behind the practice. Sometimes it is to get expert business advice from a proved success in another field; sometimes to embellish an annual report with an eminent name. Still another possibility is to suppress competition by inviting representatives of competing firms to share in coordinated planning for the industry. (This practice is prohibited by the Clayton Act of 1914, but Dooley's study shows that "nearly one in every eight interlocks involves companies which are competitors.") There are special reasons why corporations like to invite bankers to sit on their boards and why bankers like to accept. "By electing a banker to the board of directors," Dooley notes, "a company may expect to have more ready access to bank funds while the banker can watch over the operation of the company and reduce the risk of lending to a distressed borrower." On the other hand, banks like to elect company officers to their boards to "attract large deposits" and "reliable customers" for large loans. Adolph Berle, perhaps the most influential analyst of the American corporation, describes how interlocking directorates enhance the power of banks:

As trustees, these banks are large stockholders. As suppliers of credit, they have the influence of lenders. With interlocking directorates, they potentially can influence the decision-making function of the operating corporate managers.

In 1914, Louis Brandeis branded the practice of interlocking directorates "the root of many evils" because of the "fundamental law that no man can serve two masters." In the early years of the century populist sentiment was running high, and even Woodrow Wilson was condemning the bankers for their "monopoly" of money. Running for office against banks in Texas a generation ago was the equivalent of running against King George in the Irish wards of Chicago. Today most populist attacks against bigness, banks, and interlocking directorates have a faintly quixotic air since the U.S. economy has been hurtling for so many years in the opposite direction.

The third and most important strategy of banks for extending their influence over the nonbanking sectors of the economy has been the use of cross-subsidization. Just as oil companies could use their economic power to enter the coal business or the nuclear-energy field or a newspaper chain could use its oligopoly profits to buy TV stations, so the largest banks have in the last ten years systematically used their power over the banking sector to enter, and eventually to dominate, unrelated fields such as insurance and equipment leasing. It had been an article of faith in the New Deal days that the speculation of banks in the stock market was a prime cause of the Great Crash. Accordingly, until the mid-1960's banks were effectively prohibited by law not only from dabbling in the stock market but from venturing into virtually all other new financial pastures. Essentially, they were supposed to confine their business to gathering in deposits and lending out money.

The Bank Holding Act of 1956 was designed to reaffirm control of banks, but it contained a rather obvious loophole that permitted nonbanking corporations to own both banks and nonrelated industries. Though ostensibly intended for the small-town rural banker who might want to own the local hardware store along with the family bank, the one-bank holding company has been used to establish the banking conglomerate in which a single corporation controls travel services, insurance, commercial paper, consumer credit, credit cards, leasing of industrial equipment, data processing, and certain types of mutual funds. No single lawyer's invention has contributed more to the concentration of wealth in America; banks can use cross-subsidization to drive independent entrepreneurs out of all these businesses.

The First National City Bank, which took the lead in creating a one-bank holding company, Citicorp, and the other banking giants that followed expanded their activities in this direction—not only because of their own passion for growth but also because their foreign competitors were thinking and acting the same way. In the mid-60's similar developments in the banking industry were taking place in France, Britain, and Germany, where legislation was already more permissive than in the United States. Thus, as in the industrial field, the intensification of worldwide oligopolistic competition forced further concentration in the U.S. economy.

The one-bank holding company permits banks to transcend legal and financial restrictions that pertain to banks and to cross geographical borders otherwise barred to them. The size of the banking giants permits them to achieve certain economies of scale which in effect pay for their expansion. Thus, for example, banks went into the data-processing business with virtually no initial investment because they had unused time in their own computers. In 1969 new legislation was passed—supposedly to close the loopholes that had permitted banks to escape much intended regulation; but as it finally emerged from the Congress, the new law almost perfectly suited the interests of the large commercial banks. While it helped to prevent the takeover of banks by nonbanking conglomerates, it ratified the right of banks to expand into other ''closely related'' financial activities. Thus, Americans hold over 56 million BankAmericards, owned by Bank of America, or Master Charge cards, owned by Inter-Bank, a consortium of the Rockefeller-Morgan-controlled New York banks. For the banks the card is a way of selling 18-percent loans without taking up a bank officer's time. Leasing arrangements are now responsible for what is probably the most rapid and significant growth in the power of banks over nonbanking activities. Banks are consolidating their hold over the aviation industry by financing both the seller and the buyer of the same equipment, the aircraft manufacturers and the airlines. Between 1971 and 1974 about $15 billion in sales have been financed through such arrangements. The leasing of equipment is thus one more device for accelerating the diversified growth of banks. ''Tomorrow Citicorp will be bigger and in more places,'' the company promises.

That the same institutions which have become global banks have also extended their power into almost every strategic sector of the U.S. economy is clear. What that extension of power means is a matter of debate. Indeed, the proper role of bankers in our society has been a matter of controversy even before Andrew Jackson's clash with Nicholas Biddle over the chartering of the National Bank shook the foundations of the young republic. Despite the advertising campaign to convince anyone with a steady income that ''you have a friend at Chase,'' most people do not think so. The popular image of the banker—a rather stuffy man who arrives at the office late and from time to time forecloses on mortgages—was established in turn-of-the-century melodramas and, despite millions spent in institutional advertising, is not yet wholly refurbished. Commercial banks, Wright Patman notes, having ''crept into every crevice of the American economy,'' are in a position to make too many crucial decisions affecting the rest of us. Some Marxist critics are strongly impelled to show that banks dominate the industrial economy because this thesis represents the fulfillment of Hilferding's and Lenin's prophecies about the evolution of capitalism. The conflict of interest between industrialists and bankers is seen as part of a ''fatal contradiction'' which will lead to the collapse of capitalism.

Our view is different. Banks play two different roles—one in the regulated and another in the nonregulated sector of the economy—with different public consequences. In the nonregulated, dynamic sectors such as the drug, computer, and communications industries and the fast-growing industrial conglomerates like ITT and Gulf & Western, banks played a crucial role in supporting company management by facilitating its acquisition campaign. This is Wright Patman's summary of what happened:

One of the favorite pastimes of concentrated financial power is promoting concentration in nonfinancial industries. There is substantial evidence that the major commercial banks have been actively fueling the corporate merger movement. A 1971 congressional report, for example, found that major banks financed acquisitions, furnished key financial personnel to conglomerates, and were even willing to clean out stock from their trust departments to aid in takeover bids. Thus Gulf and Western, one of the most aggressive conglomerates of the 1950's and 1960's (92 acquisitions involving almost a billion dollars in eleven years), expanded hand in glove with Chase Manhattan. Friendly representatives of Chase made funds available and provided advice and services that assisted Gulf and Western in its acquisitions. In return, in addition to the customary business charges for Gulf and Western's accounts and loans, Chase secured banking business generated by the newly developing conglomerate that formerly had gone to other banks, and was recipient of advance inside information on proposed future acquisition.

Indeed, the accelerating increase in the power of banks is a direct result of the feverish pace of global corporate expansion. Banks have grown in large measure in the last ten years because the dynamic industries have high cash-flow requirements. Following their clients overseas, the largest banks have formed consortia to cap their control over the Eurodollar market. Although large industrial firms such as IBM and GM have traditionally financed most of their expansion from internal capital, they are increasingly resorting to outside financing, particularly for their foreign operations (over 30 percent of their capital requirements in the United States and 50 percent of their capital requirements overseas are met through outside financing). But despite the fact that banks hold large blocks of the stock of such corporations and have representatives on their boards, there is no evidence that the banks have "taken over" these dynamic corporations. (It must be said at the outset, of course, that there is little evidence of anything concerning the internal relationships of banks and corporations because not only are the deliberations secret but much of the financial data to prove or disprove the thesis that banks dominate industry is also beyond the examination of the Executive, Congress, or the public.) That role of outside financing for

U.S.-based global corporations, however, has now become most crucial as the need for additional capital to keep pace with Japanese and European competitors becomes more acute. German and Japanese banks directly control major industries in their countries. Oligopolistic competition may well encourage similar developments in the United States.

Thus in the nonregulated growth industries, principally the global giants we have been considering up to now, the question whether banks use their financial power and stockholdings to dictate to the management of such firms scarcely arises because their interests are the same. The bank is as interested as the corporation's own management in promoting corporate policies that will produce growth so that its holdings will appreciate and its loans will be repaid. Edward S. Herman, professor of finance at the Wharton School, puts it this way:

What impresses me most in examining intercorporate relationships is not centralized control, banker or otherwise, but the network of personal and business affiliations and contacts and the mutually supportive character of so much of the business system . . . . One can deduce that activities carried out by substantial business firms, no matter how odious, will not be subject to open criticism by important businessmen who are part of the corporate-banking network. If [Dow, GE, Honeywell, North American Rockwell and other major Vietnam war suppliers] were to produce gas chambers under contract with the Pentagon, their decisions would be accepted in silence by the community of leading business firms.

The issue, it seems to us, is not whether the interests of bankers and the interests of corporate management are in conflict but whether bankers are in a position to use their concentrated financial power against the public interest.

When we turn to the regulated sector of the U.S. economy, however, a different picture emerges. It is in the regulated industries that the banks' "enormous potential power for good or evil" is crucial. These industries—power companies, airlines, radio and television, railroads, telephone companies—represent essential services of the society, the social infrastructure on which all other economic growth depends. The one characteristic of these companies is that they are all heavily subsidized by government. Though all are technically private firms, and are privately owned, the government will not allow any of them to stop performing its essential services. They cannot be permitted to go out of business however great their financial losses.

The power of banks over the transportation sector and how that power is used has recently been illustrated by the Penn Central debacle. The Patman Subcommittee notes that "a number of financial institutions played a major and perhaps dominant role in the management of the Penn Central and its predecessors." The chairman of the world's largest privately owned railroad at the time it went into bankruptcy was Stuart T. Saunders, a director of the Chase Manhattan Bank and of the large Philadelphia commercial bank First Pennsylvania Banking and Trust Company. Chase and its closely interlocked ally Morgan Guaranty were major creditors of the railroad. The chief financial officer of the railroad was David C. Bevan, president of a large Philadelphia bank. Beginning in 1963 at the behest of these and other bankers who dominated the railroad's board, Penn Central began a major diversification program, principally into real estate, with the heavy use of commercial bank loans. At a time when service was declining and rolling stock needed replacement, the Patman Subcommittee notes, the real estate operations "were competing with the Railroad for the same limited sources of credit at a time when the Railroad was having trouble obtaining needed financing." In short, Penn Central's finance capital was used to cross-subsidize the real estate expansion. The "disastrous expansion program," according to the Subcommittee, produced a net cash drain of $175 million. The same bankers in charge of Penn Central had also pushed heavily for a merger with the New York Central two years before the final collapse. "Thus, we see," the Subcommittee report notes, "that those most anxious to see the merger consummated were people in the financial aspects of the transaction, and who knew or cared little or nothing about running a railroad. Ultimately, the financial experts' judgment proved to be disastrous."

It is characteristic of regulated industries that they incur much greater debt than other firms dare incur. The reason they are such good customers for banks is that they are stable. Their growth rates are steady and predictable, their stocks have high yields, and they cannot be permitted to go out of business. It is the near-certain prospect of government rescue that makes no-risk social-infrastructure investment attractive for banks. Unlike the situation in the private sector, where fairly large corporations can disappear, even bankruptcy does not mean the end of a railroad, airline, or major military contractor or a default on its loans. If necessary, the Federal Government will keep it in operation and eventually satisfy its creditors.

This arrangement, which would make Adam Smith wince, might be termed bankers' socialism. A good illustration of how it works is seen in the case of the 1971 Lockheed loan. In 1969, Lockheed, then the number one defense contractor, borrowed $400 million from a consortium of 24 banks. In 1970, while working on the L-1011 Airbus, the company ran into such serious financial difficulty that bankruptcy seemed imminent. Six representatives of the major banks that had lent the $400 million met in March of that year with Deputy Secretary of Defense David Packard to negotiate their rescue. The result was a $250-million loan guarantee, which the Nixon Administration proposed and the Congress narrowly passed in August 1971, by which the U.S. taxpayer relieved the rescuing banks of all risk. The case illustrates the hold that huge corporations—particularly those in transportation, utilities, and the defense industry—have on the rest of the society. Despite its inefficiency and mismanagement, Lockheed was subsidized by the U.S. taxpayer because of its very size. Too much was at stake to permit Lockheed to fail—24,000 jobs, $2.5 billion in outstanding contracts, $240 million advanced by airlines. (The collapse of Lockheed, the banks argued in support of the rescue operation, would lead to the collapse of TWA.) A number of the same banks that had lent so much money to

Lockheed (Chase, Morgan Guaranty, Bank of America, Wells Fargo, Bankers Trust) had also lent money to the major airlines threatened by a Lockheed bankruptcy.

If we turn our attention to the public utilities, we see the same combination of huge external debt owed to banks and the heavy representation of bankers on the board of directors that we saw in the Penn Central case. Consolidated Edison of New York, the power company that services the New York City area, operates under a board of directors made up of individuals who are also directors of some of the country's largest banks and insurance companies: Manufacturers Hanover, Metropolitan Life, First National City, Chemical Bank. Indeed, not only is Con Ed dominated by men with important bank connections, but the great majority of such connections are with institutions included within the Rockefeller-Morgan network. Six of the ten largest shareholders are commercial banks. (Indeed, according to Senator Lee Metcalf's investigations, Chase Manhattan is among the top ten holders of 42 utilities, Morgan Guaranty Trust is among the top ten of 41 utilities, Manufacturers Hanover Trust is among the top ten of 31 utilities.)

Utilities are exceedingly good customers for banks. More than 50 percent of the total capitalization of Con Ed of New York is in long-term debt financing. Because it is a regulated monopoly, it need fear no competition. Its customers have nowhere else to turn to run their electric kitchens or their office-building elevators and air conditioners. Bronx Borough President Robert Abrams calls this enviable position "a cost-plus relationship with society." Utilities, he charges, need not cut costs to maintain profits. They need merely raise prices to the customers. Between 1964 and 1969, Con Ed reduced the amount spent on plant additions nearly 10 percent at a time when expansion of service was clearly needed, but increased its payments to the holders of its long-term debt by about 9 percent a year. (By 1969 the power company was paying 93 percent of its annual income to banks and other holders of its stocks and bonds.) No one can prove a direct relationship between this sort of financial management and the

persistent power failures that plague the city of New York but the New York State Public Service Commission blames Con Ed's faulty equipment for the massive 1973 power failure in Queens. There is strong evidence here, as in the Penn Central case, that putting bankers in charge of public utilities is no way to run either a power company or a railroad.

A whirlwind tour of who owns America, such as we have just completed, is essential to an understanding of the preeminent power of the global corporations over American society. Moreover, as we noted in our discussion of Latin America, one cannot understand global corporations without comprehending their interconnections with global banks. There is also an intimate and necessary connection between growth and concentration. In a world dominated by oligopolistic competition, the quest for the one leads inevitably to the other. The result is that managerial control of the technology, the finance capital, and the instruments for developing and disseminating ideology vest in a few hundred individuals. The principal decision makers in the 200 top industrial corporations and the 20 largest banks, which control such a huge proportion of the nation's wealth and its capacity to produce wealth, number fewer than a thousand persons. These individuals are the planners for our society.

Since the days of Thorstein Veblen analysts of the American corporation have theorized about what it means that salaried executives have taken over the day-to-day management of the great business enterprises from the owners. Veblen dreamed of the socially minded engineer who, free of the temptation to accumulate a personal fortune, would run the corporation in accordance with the public interest. Berle and Mean's classic analysis of the separation of ownership and management laid the foundation for Galbraith's concept of the technostructure—essentially propertyless sellers of skill whose vision of the corporation was broader than the traditional entrepreneurial vision. If in fact the interests of the technostructure and the interests of owners were different, such diversity in outlook between them would, it was argued, provide a crude system of checks and balances. It did not really matter that the Rockefeller family owned the largest energy company, the largest banks, the largest insurance companies, etc., because the managers of these enterprises were not necessarily responsive to their will. Thus the answer to the Wright Patmans was that it was hard to translate huge holdings into political power because the owners did not make the crucial decisions.

Although the theory is somewhat more elegant than our simplification suggests, it has never been supported by much empirical evidence. The simple fact that managers are easier to get rid of than owners should cause a certain skepticism about the vaunted managerial takeover. Recent studies confirm our skepticism about the supposed conflict in interest and outlook between the very rich and the aspiring rich. In brief, the distinction between owners and managers is disappearing as top management in the major corporations acquires substantial blocks of stock through options, bonuses, and special opportunities. Professor Wilber Lewellen's study for the National Bureau of Economic Research *The Ownership Income of Management* indicates that in recent years top managers are steadily earning substantially more of their income from ownership of their own corporations than from salary. By the early 1960's the leading members of the technostructure were earning more than 50 percent of their total income from their stockholdings in their own corporations. Our own studies updating these findings, discussed in the next chapter, confirm the trend through 1972.

It is now common for corporate managers of major corporations to have holdings of several million dollars. The gulf between these respectable fortunes and the super-fortunes of the major stockholders is great, to be sure, but the manager who depends on his shares in his own corporation for the major share of his own income has precisely the same personal interest in maximizing

corporate growth as the $100-million shareholder.

6

Ever-greater concentration of economic power through a process of cross-subsidization across industrial sectors and geographical frontiers is now a crucial dynamic of the world political economy. The acceleration of this process by which a small number of large economic units employ their advantages to acquire ever-greater market shares appears inescapable as long as corporate executives and government managers continue to think as they now do. One reason why concentration is proceeding at an exponential rate is the rapid erosion of sources of national power that might have been expected to restrain this expansionary process.

We must now ask the same crucial political question about the United States we posed in connection with Latin America: why is there so little countervailing power to resist the corporate takeover? If our analysis is correct that global banks are increasingly coming to dominate the vital social services of the society—transport, utilities, etc.— and are using their enormous influence to promote good financial return often at the expense of good public service, why has this been allowed to happen? If global corporations, having assumed the principal planning power in our society, are unable to deal satisfactorily with our major social problems— inflation, unemployment, the energy crisis, pollution—why do they continue to exercise such power?

The answer is structural weakness in major institutions of our national life, which might have been expected to balance off the power of the global corporations. As a result, the United States is looking more and more like an underdeveloped country. As in Latin America, the obvious candidates to oppose the power of the corporations— labor unions, small businessmen, and, especially, the government—are completely inadequate. Why should this be so?

Of these three candidates, we shall have little to say here about the first two. The decline of the power of labor in the face of the globalization of business is so important a matter that it deserves a separate chapter. The decline of small business and regional business is a vital part of the structural transformation in the American economy, but it is a relatively simple matter to explain. During the nineteenth century and the early years of the twentieth century, interests of Southern farmers, New England mill-owners, and New York bankers often conflicted, and these regional and sectional differences served to fractionate and hence to check the power of business as a whole. By the mid-twentieth century, however, the United States had been fully integrated into a national market and these historic conflicts among entrepreneurs had largely disappeared. The same techniques now being used to develop the global market—modern transportation, accounting, marketing, etc.—were successfully employed to create the integrated U.S. market, and in the process local pockets of resistance to the march of the great corporations were eliminated. The decline of competition and the disappearance of thousands of small firms with competing interests have consolidated the political power of business.

But why does government lack the power to control global corporations? In Latin America, as we saw, government bureaucracy is weak, corrupt, and inefficient, but the Nixon scandals notwithstanding, that is hardly a fair description of the U.S. Government. Inefficiency abounds and corruption exists, but the government is not weak. Indeed, over the past generation, the Federal state apparatus has claimed and exercised ever-greater power. The centralization of authority over the economy in the Executive Branch and, finally, in the President's office has made this the era of Big Government. Yet Big Government is unable to control Big Business.

The easy explanation is that politicians who achieve high office and the public ad-ministrators they appoint have little desire to control the expansion and exercise of corporate power. The dominant ideology in mid-century America is the celebration of growth and bigness. No government dedicated to steady, spectacular economic growth as the prime tool for maintaining social peace can afford to take a tough line with big corporations. For those who have come to power in America in the last thirty years, the notion that there were any fundamental conflicts between corporate interests and the public interest simply did not arise. The power of the United States rested so clearly on the power of the great corporations.

Therefore, it has seemed quite reasonable to the last five administrations to staff those parts of the Federal Government that regulate the economy with men on loan from the great corporations and banks. The Federal Government is in a position to exercise little countervailing power against big corporations in large measure because of government–business interlocks in the most strategic areas of the economy. The interlocking process begins with the campaign contribution. The stark truth is that no one can be elected President of the United States under our present system without massive financial contributions from big business. This has been a fact for almost one hundred years, but its true significance was dramatized in the Nixon Administration. So anxious were the managers of such corporations as Gulf Oil, Braniff Airways, Phillips Petroleum, Ashland Oil, American Airlines, Minnesota Mining and Manufacturing, Goodyear Tire and Rubber, and Carnation to contribute to the President's already overflowing campaign chest that they broke the law (for which they received suspended jail sentences and small fines). It is clear from the behavior of ITT, milk producers, and banks that corporations regard campaign contributions as investments, not charity. They are buying shares in an Administration which they have reason to expect will be responsive to their interests. Here is a list of some of the major corporate contributors to the Nixon 1972 campaign:

Robert Allen	Gulf Resources & Chemical Corp.	$ 100,000
	American Airlines	75,000
Elmer Bobst	Warner-Lambert Pharmaceutical Co.	100,000
Nathan Cummings	Consolidated Foods Corp.; board chairman, Assoc. Products Inc. (manufacturing and wholesale food)	44,356
Frederick L. Ehrman	Lehman Corp. (investment banking)	63,578
Harvey, Leonard & Raymond Firestone	Firestone Tire & Rubber Co.	212,153
Max M. Fisher	Chairman, Fisher-New Center Co., co-chairman Finance Committee	125,000
Henry Ford II & Family	Ford Motor Company	99,775
J. Paul Getty	Getty Oil	75,000
Howard Hughes		150,000
	National Airlines	50,000
	Standard Oil Co. of California	50,000
	Phillips Petroleum Co.	100,000
Roger Milliken	Deering Milliken Inc. (textiles)	84,000
John A. Mulcahy	President, Quickley Co. (steel subsidiary of Pfizer, Inc., pharmaceuticals)	573,559
W. Clement Stone	Combined Insurance Co. of America	2,000,000
Arthur K. Watson	Former board chairman, IBM World Trade	300,000
Claude C. Wild	Gulf Oil Crop.	100,000

(Some of Mr. Nixon's ambassadorial appointees from large corporations apparently felt a touching sense of obligation to the man who made it possible for them to be addressed for life as "your Excellency." The ambassadors to Ireland, France, Britain, Jamaica, Switzerland, Trinidad, and the Netherlands together invested slightly over $1 million in the 1972 campaign.)

From the start, regulatory agencies have been dominated by the industries they were supposed to regulate. When the first regulatory agency, the Interstate Commerce Commission, was being debated in 1884, Charles Adams, director and later president of the Union Pacific Railroad, characterized with refreshing candor what is still the predominant attitude of industry toward Federal regulation. Writing to a Massachusetts Congressman who had asked his help in defeating a "radical" regulatory measure, he observed:

What is desired, if I understand it . . . is something having a good sound, which will impress the popular mind with the idea that a great deal is being done, when, in reality, very little is intended to be done.

As the historian Gabriel Kolko has shown, the railroads were proponents of moderate regulatory legislation as an alternative to the tougher measures the antirailroad forces in the country were pushing. The ICC was staffed from the beginning with a high proportion of railroad lawyers and others sympathetic to the industry. The ICC is still dominated by proindustry commissioners. Whether one accepts Kolko's view that regulatory agencies have always been captives of the industries they are supposed to regulate or the more conventional view that they begin as crusaders and gradually ossify, the effect is the same. In the words of former Federal Communications Commissioner Nicholas Johnson, the regulatory agency is now "a leaning tower of Jell-o."

An impressive qualification for becoming an FCC commissioner is to own a television station, just as it is helpful to have worked for the gas industry if you want to serve on the Federal Power Commission. The plausible argument for taking businessmen on loan to be regulators of their own industry is that they are the ones with the experience to do the job. But the theory that it takes one to catch one is contradicted by consistent practice. The business journal *Forbes* notes that "it is hard to see how the troubled natural gas industry could have a regulator more to its tastes than the new chairman of the Federal Power Commission" (John N. Nassikas, a Manchester, New Hampshire, utilities lawyer). Other recent FPC commissioners include Rush Moody, Jr., a Texas lawyer representing Pennzoil, an oil conglomerate; and Carl E. Bagge, a Boise lawyer who also represented Pennzoil. In 1972 the Federal Power Commission granted the natural-gas industry huge price increases and, in the words of former FPC Chairman Lee White, "abandoned the consumer."

Bankers are even better represented in government than utilities lawyers. Peter Flanigan, Special Assistant to President Nixon for International Economic Affairs, was vice-president of Dillon Read, the investment house, before his public service, as was C. Douglas Dillon before serving as Under Secretary of State and Secretary of the Treasury in the Eisenhower, Kennedy, and Johnson Administrations. David Kennedy, Nixon's first Secretary of the Treasury, was (and is once more) chairman of Continental Illinois National Bank. Charles E. Walker, who resigned as Under Secretary of the Treasury in 1972, had been chief lobbyist for the American Bankers Association. Chase Manhattan, the Rockefeller family bank, has been particularly generous in lending its officers for service in strategic government posts, particularly in international economic regulation. Some of the more prominent Chase alumni include Paul A. Volcker, Under Secretary of the Treasury for Monetary Affairs; John R. Letty, Assistant Secretary of the Treasury (international affairs); and Charles Fiero, Director of the Office of Foreign Direct Investments in the Commerce Department. Members of

the board of directors of Chase Manhattan have been equally public-minded. John McCloy (longtime chairman and counsel) and Eugene Black ran the World Bank from 1947 to 1962 before passing it on to George Woods of the First Boston Corporation. (Other Chase directors include John Connor, Secretary of Commerce in the Johnson Administration; William Hewlett of Hewlett-Packard, member of various Presidential advisory boards and a partner of David Packard, Nixon's first Deputy Secretary of Defense; and Gilbert Fitzhugh, Chairman, President's Blue Ribbon Defense Panel.)

"The value of your stock will rise," Wright Patman pointed out to David Kennedy during the Secretary of the Treasury's testimony in favor of the one-bank holding company. (Kennedy still had major stockholdings in Continental Illinois National Bank and Trust Company, of which he had been chairman and to which he would soon return.) Bankers in government have been protective of their own interests, as have businessmen on loan from utilities and defense contractors. To a greater or lesser degree this has always been true since the United States became an industrial nation. The government—business interlock goes a long way to explain why the world's most powerful government is ineffective in checking the expanding power of business. To a significant degree, Big Business and Big Government represent identical interests.

Although the blurring of private and public interests is an old story, a new dimension must now be added. Even if the U.S. Government were run by a thousand Wright Patmans it would still lack the power to control effectively the activities of global corporations. Any government, however strong its motivation to keep the power of business in check, lacks the tools to manage a national economy in such a way as to balance off competing interests and hence ensure long-term stability as long as global corporations are so powerful. The reason for this, as we shall explain more fully in the next chapter, is that our public legal and political institutions have not kept pace with the extraordinary changes in the private productive system. We still have a tax system, a monetary policy, an employment policy, and a trade policy that are barely adequate for controlling national firms at a time when big business has gone global. There has thus developed a structural lag between the public and private sectors of our social system. The very machinery of government, whoever operates it, is currently inadequate to cope with the globalization of Big Business. As we shall see, the government planners do not have enough knowledge about the activities of global corporations to make the crucial planning decisions for the society. Thus the managers of the corporations have become the principal planners for the society by default.

It has been a persistent theme of this book that knowledge is the critical component of power. In Latin America, as we saw, global companies are able to build their power and, at an accelerating rate, to neutralize government control because their near monopoly of the technologies of production, finance, and marketing permits them to elude government's relatively feeble efforts to regulate them. The same power that enables corporations in Latin America to conceal their ownership, plans, and intra-corporate dealings and hence frustrate government control over them operates also in the United States. It is one key structural reason, in our view, why the world's richest society is looking more and more like an underdeveloped country.

Existing disclosure requirements are hopelessly inadequate to permit government to exercise power over global corporations. In March 1972, to give one example, Senator Lee Metcalf attempted to obtain from the Securities and Exchange Commission a list of the largest shareholders of what are probably the two most strategic companies in the American economy, GM and Exxon, and was told that the Commission did not have that information. When the Senator wrote the companies directly, he was told that the information was "privileged and confidential." The U.S. Government now has no way of knowing how and by whom the largest corporations in the country are controlled.

But the business-government interlock has been so strong that controlling the misuse of corporate power has been something less than an obsession. The dominant role of Big Business in both political parties, the financial holdings of certain key members of Congress, the ownership of the mass media, the industry-government shuttle in the regulatory agencies, and, most important, the ideology prevailing throughout the society of salvation through profits and growth all help to explain why the government of the world's mightiest nation musters so little power to protect the interests of its people.

Socialist

James O'Connor. International corporations and economic underdevelopment.

I

United States, European, and Japanese international corporations presently own or directly control between 20 and 30 per cent of the monetized resources in the underdeveloped countries (including Canada). Indirect control of local capital in Asia, Latin America, and Africa is equally pervasive: the mobilization of local capital,[1] control of subcontractors and other suppliers, "management contracts" which afford foreign capital day-to-day control of joint ventures,[2] and licensing agreements which restrict the use of technology by prohibiting "fundamental investigation and research"[3] extend the sway of foreign capital still further, and multiply the quantitative impact of the international corporations on the misutilization of resources abroad.

The general reasons for the expansion of foreign capital during the 1950s and 1960s, especially capital organized by the giant United States international corporations, are well known: In the first place, the United States economy tends to generate more economic surplus than large-scale business can profitably absorb at home. Foreign investments absorb some of the surplus in the short run, but generate even greater amounts of surplus in the long run. The large corporations are thus compelled to become even more expansion-minded and seek fresh investment opportunities.[4] As shown below, branch plant investments of U.S. corporations absorb surplus generated in the United States by providing major export markets for parent corporations.

In the second place, modern technology requires special raw materials, mainly metals, many of which are found only in underdeveloped countries. In addition, short supplies of raw materials in the North American continent have compelled U.S. corporations to exploit new sources in the underdeveloped world. More, U.S. corporations are under constant pressure to develop fresh raw material sources, as a hedge against competitors and as a way to reduce business risk by diversifying supplies.[5]

It is also well known that U.S. corporations have been operating in an especially favorable economic and political environment since the end of World War II. There have been few important political barriers preventing American capital from insinuating itself into the defeated empires of Germany and overseas Japan, and the decayed empires of Britain, France, and Holland in Asia and Africa. In Latin America, the failure of national-oriented import-substitution industrialization policies to promote ongoing economic development has accelerated the conquest of Latin American capital by U.S. corporations.

Another familiar story concerns the general political-economic effects of U.S. control of an increasing part of the capitalist world's economic resources. Canada's independent economic foreign policies are confined to the agricultural sphere, still under the control of Canadian capital. India's domestic economic policies are influenced at every turn by the United States, due to her dependence on U.S.

"aid," U.S. government control of a large share of India's money supply, and the growing penetration of U.S. private capital. Fiscal and monetary policies in Brazil, Argentina, and many smaller countries are often dictated by the U.S.-dominated International Monetary Fund. Everywhere in the underdeveloped world the World Bank influences or controls development plans, due to the Bank's monopoly position in the international market for long-term capital funds. Only Cuba has escaped the bondage of U.S. imperialism, although in Guatemala, Colombia, Bolivia, Angola, and elsewhere revolutionary forces are fighting to free these countries as well.

Less familiar is the story of how U.S. corporations actually cause economic underdevelopment, or prevent on-going development in the underdeveloped countries. Thanks to the work of Andre Gundar Frank, Clifford Geertz, Gunnar Myrdal, and others, but above all due to Paul Baran's path-breaking book, *The Political Economy of Growth*, the general historic mechanisms of the process of development-underdevelopment are understood. Almost invariably, when pre-capitalist societies were integrated or re-integrated into the world capitalist system the result was underdevelopment in the economically more backward poles and development in the advanced poles. Economic development and underdevelopment did not merely go hand in hand historically; the one *caused* the other. Only in a handful of regions, such as West Africa, where the existence of unused land and underemployed labor opened the possibility of expanding subsistence and export production simultaneously, did specialization in raw material production for export fail to undermine subsistence agriculture, small-scale local manufacturing, and, in general, any local base for autonomous development. Although not the typical case, Britain's relations with her economic and political colonies highlight the development-underdevelopment process. Britain developed a balanced industrial economy which was able to "capture" economies of large-scale production and external economies of scale *because* most of her colonies (including her Latin American economic colonies in the last half of the nineteenth century) were *underdeveloped*—that is, because they became unbalanced, nonindustrial economies specializing in the production of raw materials for export.

We do not have a comparable comprehensive account of how the development of international corporations, based mainly in the United States, prevent the development of Asia, Latin America, and Africa, or cause the underdevelopment of these regions. It goes without saying that this is a question worth studying. Fortunately, there are enough partial studies now available to attempt a beginning, general analysis of the subject. This is in fact the purpose of the present article.

II

As a beginning, it is well to list the main types of U.S. foreign investments, in rough order of their historic priority. First, of course, are investments in raw materials production, including the necessary infrastructure investments (e.g. Anaconda's copper mines in Chile and Reynolds' bauxite mines in Jamaica and Guyana). Second are investments in raw material processing, such as the nickel-processing facilities in pre-Revolutionary Cuba. Third are investments in manufacturing facilities, chiefly final assembly operations taking the form of branch plants of parent U.S. corporations. These are the so-called "tariff hopping" investments, which import many raw materials, intermediate goods, parts, and sometimes, even fuel from the parent corporation or elsewhere in the developed countries, and sell final products in the local market. Branch-plant investments have become increasingly popular since World War II, and, in fact, constitute the only way that many underdeveloped countries are able to acquire foreign private capital. A good example are the many automobile assembly plants in Latin America. Fourth, there are the true "multi-national" investments, plants that purchase inputs from one branch of a corporation located in the same or a different country and sell outputs to another branch of the same corporation located elsewhere—that is, investments characterized by "product-by-plant" specialization. Multi-national investments are mainly confined to petrochemicals and computers, although electronic and other assembly plants in cheap labor havens such as northern Mexico, Puerto Rico, Formosa, and South Korea often produce for re-export to the parent company.

Most international corporations confine their foreign investments to only one or two of the above types, although a handful— International Telephone and Telegraph and Standard Oil of New Jersey are two examples—are represented in all four categories. For expository purposes, and because each type of investment works somewhat different effects in the underdeveloped regions, our analysis will focus on the specific effects of the various forms foreign investment takes.

Next, what is required is a general description of the world capitalist system from the standpoint of the international corporations. These companies provide the institutional framework—or the accounting framework for resource utilization—for many underdeveloped countries, especially the smaller, more vulnerable economies. Integrating more and more resources into their own structures, the international corporations are able to mobilize, transform, and dispose of capital on a regional, or even world-wide scale—in effect, constituting themselves as extra-territorial bodies.

Production goals and techniques, investment policies, labor relations, prices, profit allocation, purchasing, distribution, and marketing policies are all decided from the standpoint of the profit goals of the international corporation *whether or not these goals are consistent with local economic development*. The corporations are the channels for the diffusion of technology and consumption patterns; again, profits come first, local needs second. Even big business ideologists are coming close to admitting what has long been a truism for Marxists; one of them concedes the possibility that the "utilization of resources to maximize profits" may not be "compatible" with the interests of the "host country."[6]

In what specific ways are the goals and policies of the international companies detrimental to local economic development? We will consider in turn the effects of corporate *investment, production,* and *purchasing and sales policies* on the local economy, subsequently discussing the effects of the international corporations on *technological change*, and the *balance of payments* in the underdeveloped countries.

The effects of foreign investments in raw material production and processing are too well known to require more than brief mention.[7] In a nutshell, raw material investments tend to make underdeveloped countries mere appendages of developed countries, depriving them of any opportunity for autonomous, on-going economic development, and thwarting the development of industry and an industrial bourgeoisie.

Foreign investments in manufacturing in the form of branch plants and wholly or partially owned subsidiaries have less familiar effects. The basic purpose of these investments is to control markets by affording the large corporation the opportunity to retain and expand export markets in the face of high tariffs, that is, to control the market for parts, components, and raw materials. In India, for example, Pavlov has shown that Indian tariff policy largely determines the industrial and sectoral composition of joint ventures and wholly-owned subsidiaries of foreign corporations.[8] Surveying the key international corporations, the National Industrial Conference Board concluded that "marketing strategy was clearly the dominant element in investment decisions." A study made by the U.S. Department of Commerce in 1963 disclosed that over one-third of the corporations sampled invested abroad mainly to expand exports. More evidence is provided by data on U.S. exports to Latin America: in 1964, of total U.S. exports to manufacturing affiliates of U.S. firms in Latin America, 57 per cent consisted of parent exports of capital equipment and materials for processing and assembly to affiliates.[9] Profit figures provide more evidence of the importance of export markets for foreign investments; some parent corporations make most of their money abroad by exporting materials and equipment to their branch plants; next in importance are revenues from royalties and fees; dividend revenue for these corporations is marginal.[10]

Put briefly, the significance of this for the underdeveloped countries is that investment decisions are not made on the basis of local priorities, or the ranking of alternative yields, but rather on the basis of promoting exports. Thus in an economy receiving private foreign capital in the form of branch plants there is a tendency toward overinvestment, high costs, and excess capacity—that is to say, there are too many production units, all of them too small for efficient operations. Cy Gonick describes the global results of this process in Canada in the following words:

. . .Canada has an economy which in some sectors is made up of a large number of small productive units, more than a country of our size would warrant. What other comparable country has as many automobile-producing units, or companies producing refrigerators and other appliances? Now the Americans can afford to enter every field of economic endeavor and set up three or more corporations in oligopolistic competition. But this is an absurdity for a country the size of Canada. The only way that a country our size can survive economically is to specialize and achieve pre-eminence in a limited series of lines, as successful small European countries have done. We have only managed to set up this crazy patchwork quilt because of the economics of the international corporation which makes a high-cost additional outlet an interesting proposition.[11]

In addition, in the branch plant economies there is a tendency for existing local industry to be eroded away as a result of the effects of over-crowding on the rate of profit, particularly since local industry, unlike the affiliates, cannot charge losses back to a parent corporation. Foreign capital, in the words of David Felix, outcompetes local capital partly due to its ability "to self-insure against risk and to inflate the capital base of subsidiaries by transferring to them already depreciated equipment and designs from their more advanced home plants." Local capital thus tends to be either co-opted by foreign capital, or confined to especially risky undertakings. Further, branch-plant industrialization fragments the local capital market; branch-plant savings are not ordinarily available to other sectors of the local economy, being reinvested, used to purchase facilities from local capital, or repatriated. All in all, branch-plant investments promote the misutilization of capital, and generate severe immobilities in the local capital market.

The third type of foreign undertakings are the pure "multi-national" investments. Again, investments are not made on the basis of local priorities, or with an eye to the local resource base and local needs. Rather the motive is to minimize costs of production to the corporation. Thus, once a sizable market for a standardized commodity has been established in the advanced countries, the corporations are free to make long-term commitments to build production facilities in the underdeveloped countries where labor costs are low.[12] The facility imports the bulk of its inputs, exports nearly all of its output, and hence remains totally unintegrated into the local economy.

III

Next we will consider the impact of corporate production policy on the development of underdeveloped countries. So far as raw materials are concerned, Baran has shown that production is optimum only from the standpoint of the corporation's total profit picture, or from the standpoint of the needs of the developed countries. In Chile, for example, the two international corporations which monopolize copper production have acquired more profits by expanding output in competing areas, which also enables the monopolies to pressure the Chilean government for more favorable treatment locally. Examples could be multiplied no end; two more are drawn from the Caribbean: in recent years, rivalries between metropolitan-based international corporations which dominate Caribbean banana production have helped to ruin small-scale peasant producers by promoting an unlimited expansion of production. Again in recent years,

Bookers Sugar Estates Ltd. and the Demerara Co., which control nearly all of Guyana's sugar production, have established sugar plantations in Nigeria from profits made in, and in competition with Guyana.[13]

The effects of corporate production policy in the industrial sphere present somewhat different problems. Three key features stand out. First, it is clear that the international corporations have every motive to defend their export markets, and hence order their branch plants to discriminate against local supplies in favor of imports from the parent company. There is no evidence that the governments of the smaller underdeveloped countries have been able to compel the corporations to produce with local supplies, although some of the larger countries, such as Brazil, have partially succeeded in doing this.

Second, it is also clear that the international corporations—excepting the true multi-national companies—have little or no interest in producing for *export*, especially when export production competes with other branches of the same corporation in the international market. The significance of this is that an economy which is undergoing "branch-plant industrialization" is developing little or no export capacity, a process which was crucial to the growth of the developed countries of Europe, as well as Japan and the United States.

Third, in the underdeveloped countries the demand for commodities is increasingly based on the diffusion of "tastes" from the developed countries, together with the prevailing social structure and distribution of income. As Levitt has pointed out, the international companies seek to homogenize world demand in order to spread fixed costs and capture economies of scale in research, product design, and technology. ". . . . The profitability of the parent corporation," she writes, "is assisted by every influence which eliminates cultural resistance to the consumption patterns of the metropolis. The corporation thus has a vested interest in the destruction of cultural differences and homogenization of the

[U.S.] way of life, the world over." In addition, as Stavenhagen points out, "the diffusion of manufactured articles is directly related to the overall level of technology as well as to effective demand [in the underdeveloped country]."[14] We must return to the basic Marxist theory of consumption to assess the significance of this for economic development. Marx demonstrated not only that production creates the objects that satisfy economic needs, but also the economic needs satisfied by the objects; in short, production determines consumption. Today consumption in the underdeveloped countries tends to be determined by production in the developed countries, and hence economic needs in the former are satisfied poorly or imperfectly. In specific, branch-plant production of a wide variety of heavily advertised differentiated products is very wasteful in poor countries with small markets.[15]

IV

Let us turn next to the effect of corporate purchasing and sales policies on economic development. As expected, these policies reinforce the negative effects of corporate investment and production decisions. Borrowing from the work of John Kenneth Galbraith, who argues that the large corporation subjects decisions previously made in the market to administrative control, Girvan and Jefferson have developed a framework for an analysis of this problem.[16] In this model, the international corporation seeks the fullest possible utilization of capacity in all its vertically and horizontally integrated activities. The basic motive is to spread overhead costs and avoid paying profits to other corporations. Thus the international company places a large "premium on intra-company product and factor flows" which creates "rigidity in the product and factor flows between companies producing similar sets of commodities, whether these companies are producing in the same region or in the same country, or not." The result is regional economic fragmentation; for example, some of Reynolds' Guyana bauxite production

reaches the aluminum smelting industry of Venezuela via Reynolds alumina plants in the United States. Another result is national economic fragmentation; according to Girvan and Jefferson, "Reynolds bauxite output in Guyana and Jamaica has not so far been available to the existing processing capacity in both countries because the capacity is owned by a different company."[17] Still another result is that intra-corporation purchases tend to be insensitive to changes in foreign exchange rates; for example, the 1962 Canadian devaluation was accompanied by a 17 percent *increase* in imports.

Economic fragmentation means that many of the "resources of [the Caribbean and Latin America] reach the other in a more finished form via processing plants in the U.S." On the one side, the bulk of U.S. imports of raw materials take the form of imports from subsidiaries and branches to the U.S.-based parent corporation; leading examples are Caribbean bauxite; Mexican iron ore, manaterese, flourspar, lead, zinc, and asbestos; Chilean copper, lead, and zinc; and Brazilian manganese. On the other side, in the Caribbean alone, over one-third of the imports of *metal* manufactures, machinery, and transportation equipment by the four largest Commonwealth territories is supplied by the United States.

From this line of analysis, Girvan and Jefferson rightly conclude that the existing *competitiveness* of underdeveloped countries is a poor guide to potential economic *complementarity*. Moreover, the present built-in bias toward importation of supplies from parent corporations inhibits import-substitute industrialization programs. The Caribbean offers the extreme case—local governments have actively promoted industrialization for years; one result has been a growth of per capita income, but there has been no simultaneous change in the structure of imports. At best, import-substitute industrialization under the auspices of the international corporation merely changes the composition of imports, leaving the dynamic of expansion with the traditional export sector.

A general understanding of the impact of purchasing and sales policies on underdeveloped countries requires a brief review of corporate price policies. In general, the international corporation is an effective instrument for maximizing the appropriation of surplus from satellite economies by metropolitan economies. On the one hand, the parent corporation charges its branch plants (both in the raw materials and manufacturing sectors) the highest price possible, in order to maximize profits on exports, as well as a hedge against local government restrictions on profit remittances. (The exception are corporations that intend to reinvest abroad and thus desire to maximize foreign profits and minimize profits reported at home, in order to escape U.S. taxes.) Meanwhile, the parent corporation's interests are best served by keeping final product prices in the underdeveloped country as high as possible, consistent with the role of the branch plant as the parent's export market.

On the other hand, the parent buys raw materials from its branches and subsidiaries at the lowest possible price. Bauxite, iron ore, and copper—among other minerals— all tend to be undervalued.[18] The reasons are plain: first, the large corporations seek to purchase the outputs of small independent producers at depressed prices; second, low prices discourage the development of new independent producers, and hence potential competition; third, depressed prices reduce foreign exchange risks when local governments attempt to reduce profit remittances; and, last, low buying prices mean that the corporations pay fewer taxes and lower royalties and wages.

V

We have finally to discuss the impact of the international corporation on technological change in underdeveloped countries, as well as on the satellite economies' balance of payments. As we have seen, the international corporations seek to keep control over technology themselves. In Alavi's words,

"typically, strict control is sought over the use to which the techniques imported are put. . . . The supplier of the new technique is often fully protected from imparting a complete technology by clauses which specially exclude 'fundamental investigation and development' . . . the Indian concern is often effectively prevented from adapting products or processes to local conditions and materials, or from encouraging local ancillary industries and so becomes even more dependent on imported supplies."[19] In effect, control of technology (foreign capital tends to be more technologically integrated than local capital, and foreign production more specialized) means control of markets.

Besides licensing agreements restricting local control of technology, the international corporations often discourage their branches from applying technological resources to *local* technological bottlenecks. Thus U.S.-owned sugar firms in pre-Revolutionary Cuba conducted little research into the problems of raising cane yields, increasing the sucrose content of cane, or mechanizing the harvest. Again, U.S. aluminum companies in Jamaica spend nothing on iron separation techniques, even though Jamaican bauxite has a high iron content; on the other side, the same companies finance intensive research into the problem of recovering aluminum from high-alumina clays in the United States.

In the underdeveloped countries undergoing some degree of branch-plant industrialization, the impact of the international corporations is equally negative. Assembly plants and other facilities oriented to higher stages of manufacturing are relatively small-scale, fail to capture economies of large-scale production, and frequently embody out-of-date techniques. Saddled with small-scale production units and obsolete equipment, the branch-plant economies are characterized by "perpetual and certain backwardness in research and technology."[20]

The international diffusion of technology is thus under the control of the international corporations. Perhaps the most significant consequence for the underdeveloped countries is that the large corporations make technological decisions with an eye to the resource base (or "relative factor supplies") of the United States or world capitalism as a whole, and not to the resource supplies of the underdeveloped country or region. In Felix's words, "Despite their involvement in activities in which sustained profits are supposed to depend on a continual replenishment of technological advantages, neither domestic nor foreign-owned firms [in Latin America] have tried to modify imported technology or products through local research and development." This has led to the use of techniques which generate little additional employment of labor in the underdeveloped world. Branch-plant industrialization thus not only assures technological backwardness and prevents the development of production processes and products more suitable to local conditions, but also inhibits the growth of manufacturing employment. In Latin America as a whole, for example, industrial production compared with total production rose by 16.5 per cent from 1950 to 1960; meanwhile, industrial employment in relation to total employment *fell* by 10 per cent.[21]

At this point, we can turn our attention to the impact of the international corporations on the balance of payments of the underdeveloped countries. Taken together, the specific effects of the corporations discussed above cause a heavy and increasing burden on the local balance of payments. For one thing, the lack of integration of foreign investments into the local economy, especially branch plants which exist only to provide a market for the parent corporation, places heavy pressures on foreign exchange reserves. As Furtado has shown, the shift away from traditional raw material exports to import-substitute industries producing final commodities compels the underdeveloped countries to accelerate imports of capital goods, and hence suffer severe balance of payments problems.[22] Second, repatriated profits, whether in an open or disguised form, place a greater drain on scarce foreign exchange and constitute a kind of permanent debt service. So do technological monopolies, which mean costly royalties, management fees, and salaries of foreign technicians. In addition, local consumption patterns based more on demand in the developed countries than on local needs lead to needless imports of both consumer and capital goods. And, finally, the lack of *regional* integration prevents trade and investment between the underdeveloped countries and unnecessarily uses up even more scarce hard currencies. Although there seems to be no simple way to estimate the quantitative impact of these factors on the balance of payments of the underdeveloped world, the burden is bound to be very great indeed. Taking the case of Latin America during the period 1961–1963, profit remittances, debt service, royalties, and other invisible financial services alone accounted for nearly 40 percent of the region's foreign exchange earnings.

VI

Although the critical study of the role of international corporations in underdeveloped countries (especially in manufacturing industries) remains in its infancy, it may not be premature to offer some general observations about the relationship between economic development and underdevelopment in the present era. The evidence at our disposal strongly suggests that the development of the large international corporation at home and abroad, and hence the development of the advanced capitalist countries, *causes* the underdevelopment of the economically backward countries and regions. The relationship between the developed and underdeveloped poles in the world capitalist system thus has not been fundamentally changed, even though many of the forms of exploitation have been altered.

Certainly this conclusion can be applied to the small underdeveloped countries, as it has been by Lloyd Best in his summary description of the Caribbean economy. The international companies, Best writes:

. . .form parts of wider international systems of resource allocation. This is true of the mining corporations, the sugar companies, the hotel chains, the banking, hire purchase and insurance houses, the advertising companies, the newspapers and the television and radio stations . . . .Insofar as there is harmonization among these concerns, it is for the most part achieved within the context of the metropolitan economies where they are based, and not in the peripheral economies of the countries where the companies actually operate. Moreover, the policies of the corporations are determined by their parent companies operating somewhere in the northern hemisphere and not by local need to integrate industries and to increase interdependence between different sectors of the economy. The economy is therefore hardly more than a locus of production made up of a number of fragments held tenuously together by Government controls—themselves often borrowed from elsewhere. In other words. . .it seems to be inherent in the structure of the international corporations which operate in the region that the Caribbean economies remain fragmented and unintegrated. . . .[23]

The political significant of economic "balkanization" should be obvious. In the case of Bolivia, after the nationalization of the tin mines, the U.S. government enjoyed a great deal of leverage in its maneuvers to push the Bolivian government to the right, partly because the country "remained beholden to the same big companies for processing and sale."[24] In Canada, Levitt describes the process of the "balkanization of the political structure whereby the growing economic powers of the corporations and the provincial governments threaten to destroy the [Canadian] nation state."[25] And of course Cuba has maintained her political independence from the United States only at a very high economic cost. Economic and political fragmentation thus lie at the very heart of the nature of neocolonialism, as indicated by the report of the Third All-African People's Conference, held in Cairo in 1961. Among the "manifestations of Neo-Colonialism in Africa" were "regrouping of states, before or after independence, by an imperial power in federations or communities linked to that imperial power. . . .Balkanization as a deliberate political fragmentation of states by creation of artificial entities, such as, for example,

the case of Katanga, Mauritania, Buganda, etc. . . .The economic entrenchment of the colonial power before independence and the continuity of economic dependence after formal recognition of national sovereignty. . . .Integration into colonial economic blocs which maintain the underdeveloped character of African economy."[26] In the extreme cases—some Caribbean countries, South Korea, and Thailand are examples—the international corporations are in a position to play off one against another, just as domestically they play off one State against another in an attempt to obtain low business taxes, cheap unskilled labor, a reserve of skilled, technical labor, and other concessions.

This line of analysis leads into the question of economic reform and, in particular, the efficacy of economic integration within the underdeveloped regions and countries. The general subject of economic reform is large and complex, and we cannot even begin to give it adequate treatment here, except insofar as it relates to economic integration.

Certainly in Brazil, Mexico, and India, governments have had a certain degree of success in "legislating" *national* economic integration by compelling the international corporations to purchase more and more of their supplies locally. Meanwhile, however, foreign capital, especially in Brazil, has taken over a larger share of the local economy. Further, even though from a strictly economic standpoint there is considerable scope in these countries for the development of a great number of capital goods industries, every country in the underdeveloped world remains largely dependent on imported machinery and other capital equipment. The truth is that nowhere has there been, nor can there be save by socialist revolution, the structural changes in agriculture, state policy (especially tax policy), wealth and income distribution, and so on necessary for on-going, self-generated development. Only Mexico has had a significant "agrarian reform"—that is, the displacement of the *ejido* sector by the capitalist sector dominated by large corporate farming. But income distribution in

Mexico is far too unequal to sustain a domestic market for any length of time, and, as a consequence, Mexico is looking hungrily at Central America, long dominated by the United States. Tax reform in most of the underdeveloped world is a joke; the Chilean government, for example, has not used taxes and royalties to integrate the copper mining industry into the local economy (nor did Chile use nitrate royalties to this end in the nineteenth century), but rather to increase imports of consumer goods and to finance the government payroll. And of all the underdeveloped countries, only Cuba has promoted a deep-going redistribution of wealth and income.

Proposals for *regional* economic integration in the form of free trade areas and common markets—especially in the Caribbean, Central America, Latin America, and Africa—should also be viewed skeptically given the prevailing pattern of integration imposed by the international corporations. As of 1966, the Central American Common Market's Economic Integration Program (EIP) has developed only two "integrated industries"—one in tire and tube, another in caustic soda and insecticide production. The Program has not gotten off the ground because the international corporations do not want Central America to develop its own basic capital goods industries, and because there are few business interests in Central America which are willing and able to develop local markets for themselves. The corporations do not want to be controlled by EIP, which insists on regulating prices to prevent monopoly abuses, determining the pattern of industrial location, and sharing in other basic economic decisions. Thus the large corporations have confined their investments to indivdual Central American countries, where development is not guided by EIP and where there is little or no resistance to more branch plants and subsidiaries producing and assembling consumer goods.

In Latin America, the most significant development in economic integration has been the Latin America Free Trade Area (LAFTA). Largely the brain-child of the Economic Commission for Latin America (ECLA), and for a long time opposed by the United States government, economic integration is now seen in reform circles as the "solution" to Latin American development. Needless to say, much of Latin America is *already* integrated by the international corporations. Reductions of tariffs, elimination of import quotas, and removal of controls over foreign exchange can only strengthen the position of the corporations.[27] As *Fortune* magazine puts it, "for U.S. private enterprise, the common market spells enticing new opportunity.... U.S. businessmen are beginning to see in the Latin American the advantages that they seized upon in the European Common Market: the chance to move to the broader, more competitive, and potentially more profitable task of supplying a market big enough to be economic on its own terms. ...In many a boardroom, the common market is becoming a serious element in planning for the future."[28]

Certainly here we have the reason why the U.S. government now favors economic integration, and why, finally, there has developed a "harmony of interests" between the U.S. and the ECLA reformers. Apart from revolutionary forces in the underdeveloped world, there are few if any remaining economic and political interests which cannot be contained within or reconciled with the international corporations. Such is the nature of modern imperialism, a worldwide system of social production in which the giant, conglomerate international corporation stands as the highest (and final) form of social integration consistent with private ownership of the means of production.

NOTES

1. As of 1964, 95 per cent of U.S. investments in Canada were raised from Canadian sources, 17 per cent from Canadian financial institutions, and 78 per cent in the form of retained earnings (Kari Levitt, "Canada: Economic Dependence and Political Disintegration," *New World Quarterly*, IV, 2, 1968, p. 74). As of 1957, 74 per cent of U.S. investments in Brazil were raised in Brazil, 36 per cent from Brazilian financial institutions and other sources, and 38 per cent from depreciation and retained earnings (Claude McMillan, *International Enterprises in a Deve-*

oping Economy: A Study of United States Business in Brazil [East Lansing, 1964], p. 205).

2. "Management Contracts Abroad," monograph published by Business International, 1963.

3. Hamza Alavi, "Indian Capitalism and Foreign Imperialism," New Left Review, 37, May–June, 1967, p. 83.

4. Paul A. Baran and Paul M. Sweezy, Monopoly Capital (New York, 1966), pp. 104–108. A more detailed analysis of the process of surplus absorption and creation abroad is provided in James O'Connor, The Meaning of Economic Imperialism (Radical Education Project, Ann Arbor, 1968), pp. 12–21.

5. Far and away the best account of the importance of raw materials for modern capitalism is in Harry Magdoff, The Age of Imperialism (New York, 1969).

6. Gibert Clee, "Guidelines for Global Business," Columbia Journal of World Business, 1, 1, Winter, 1966.

7. Baran, op. cit.; Andre Gundar Frank, Capitalism and Underdevelopment in Latin America: Historical Studies of Chile and Brazil (New York, 1967); C. Rollins, "Mineral Development and Economic Growth," Social Research, Autumn, 1956; Alvin Wolfe, "The African Mineral Industry," Social Problems, Fall, 1963; Dudley Seers, "Big Companies in Small Countries," Kyklos, XVI, 4, 1963; James O'Connor, The Origins of Socialism in Cuba (Ithaca, 1970).

8. V.I. Pavlov, India: Economic Freedom Versus Imperialism (New Delhi, 1963), p. 92, footnote.

9. Norman Girvan and Owen Jefferson, "Corporate vs. Caribbean Integration," New World Quarterly, op. cit., p. 53.

10. This analysis tends to confirm the thesis that within the giant corporation "production literally 'takes care of itself' " and that financing is no longer a problem, thus that "the corporate decision-maker may be left with one main function—merchandising" (James O'Connor, "Finance Capital or Corporate Capital?" Monthly Review, December, 1968, pp. 34–35). In general, however, branch profits and dividends far exceed royalties, licenses, and rentals, probably because of the heavy concentration of manufacturing investments in advanced capitalist economies.

11. Besides being unable to seize advantages from economies of large-scale production, branch-plant industry fails to benefit from locational specialization and from complementaries of inputs in the use of natural and technical resources (W. Demas, The Economics of Development in Small Countries with Special Reference to the Caribbean [Montreal, 1965], pp. 8–10).

12. See the model developed in Raymond Vernon, "International Investment and International Trade in the Product Cycle," Quarterly Journal of Economics, May, 1966.

13. George Beckford, "Issues in the Windward-Jamaica Banana War," New World Quarterly, II, 1, 1965; Horace B. Davis, "The Decolonization of Sugar in Guyana," Caribbean Studies, 7, 3, 1967, p. 37.

14. Rodolfo Stavenhagen, "Seven Fallacies About Latin America," in James Petras and Maurice Zeitlin (eds.), Latin America: Reform or Revolution? (New York, 1968), p. 25.

15. Mention of the "production" of bank credit by branches of metropolitan banks is in order. In the smaller underdeveloped countries which are still dominated by foreign banks, branch banks tend to be more responsive to liquidity conditions in the metropolitan countries than in the local economy. In the Caribbean, for example, branch banks have contracted credit during export booms—that is, when the local economy has relatively high foreign exchange reserves and thus a real base for expanding credit locally.

16. John Kenneth Galbraith, The New Industrial State (Boston, 1967); Norman Girvan and Owen Jefferson, "Corporate vs. Caribbean Integration," New World Quarterly, op. cit., pp. 52–54.

17. A recent study concludes that national or regional integration in aluminum is highly unlikely because the prospects for the development of smelters and processing capacity in the underdeveloped countries are small (Sterling Brubaker, Trends in the World Aluminum Industry [Baltimore, 1967]). It should be noted that in the oil industry there is a widespread practice of exchanging crudes and oil products between companies.

18. Girvan and Jefferson, op. cit.; Seers, op. cit.; Frank, op. cit.

19. Alavi, op. cit.

20. Levitt, op. cit., p. 81.

21. The "industrialization" of Trinidad and Tobago offers the extreme example of the negative effects of branch-plant investments on employment (Edwin Carrington, "Industrialization by Invitation in Trinidad and Tobago since 1950," New World Quarterly, op. cit.). As Baran has shown, imported technology creates little employment even in the traditional raw materials sectors. In Chile, the copper industry employs only 5 per cent of the labor force; in Venezuela, petroleum production provides jobs for only 3 per cent of the labor force.

22. Celso Furtado, Development and Underdevelopment (Berkeley, 1967), Chapter Five. In this article, we have confined our analysis to the impact of private international corporations, and have ignored the role of the U.S. government and the international lending agencies. Needless to say, public policies tend to reinforce the existing pattern of resource misutilization. For example, Furtado exposes the reactionary role of the International Monetary Fund, which continues to push "monetary" solutions to structural

economic problems which generate monetary symptoms.

23. Lloyd Best, "Size and Survival," *New World Quarterly,* Guyana Independence Issue, 1966, p. 61.

24. Allen Young, "Bolivia," *New Left Review,* 39, September/October, 1966, p. 66.

25. Levitt, *op.cit.,* p. 81.

26. "Neo-Colonialism," *Voice of Africa,* I, 4, April, 1961, p. 4.

27. Miguel Teubal, "The Failure of Latin America's Economic Integration," in Petras and Zeitlin, *op. cit.*

28. Quoted by Edie Black, "Whose Common Market Is It?" *NACLA Newsletter,* August 1967.

✼

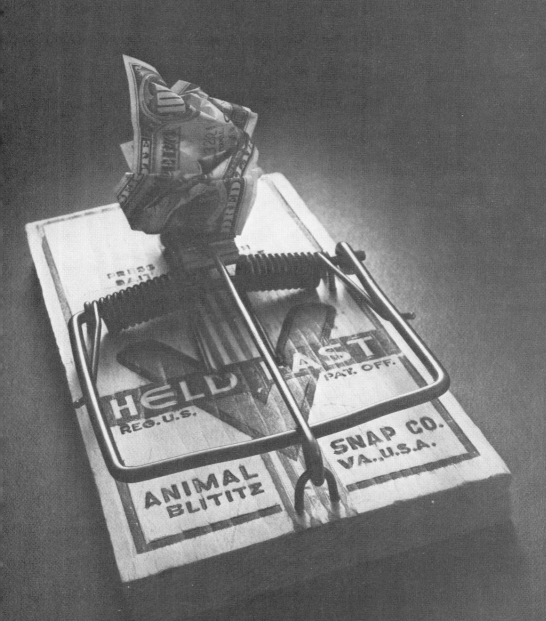

7 Organized crime

The basic questions this chapter will address are:

(1) Is crime organized into large-scale organizations much as business and government are?

(2) What is the role of organized crime in American society?

(3) How is its influence exerted?

(4) Why is organized crime usually seen as criminal activity, while similar activities carried on by other institutions are not so defined?

Conservatives maintain that criminal activities exist in the United States but that they are not structured and organized along bureaucratic lines. They define criminal activities as being clearly illegal acts, such as burglary, assault and battery, and murder. People who argue that there is a well-structured, highly organized criminal confederation in the United States are posing a false issue. The depiction of crime as conducted by large-scale organizations is a myth. The existence of organized crime is not supported by available evidence, only by vague assertions and unproved allegations. Conservatives hold that popular images, such as that of "The Godfather",[1] are accepted because Americans are fascinated by conspiracy theories. Essentially, conservatives do not believe in the existence of organized crime. They hold that it is a Hollywood fiction that has been swallowed whole by the American people.[2]

Liberals view crime differently. They believe that organized crime exists, particularly in the form of the Mafia.[3] It is their contention that such groups are well-structured. These organizations corrupt individual legislators, policemen, and judges. Liberals also hold that poorer sections of American cities are often at the mercy of these criminal organizations. Gambling, which is seen to be controlled by the Italian and Black Mafias, syphons off the meager resources of the poor.[4]

It is the contention of liberals that organized crime continues to exist in the United States because government law enforcement agencies are not vigilant enough. The power of organized crime can be limited by legislation and vigorous law enforcement officers. Liberals clearly separate the conduct of organized crime from the operation of the Federal political process. Organized crime can be eradicated only if the political system is mobilized by an aroused public to enforce the laws.

Socialists maintain that organized crime is as much a part of the American political process as are multinational corporations. It is their thesis that organized crime is an institution fundamentally based on the same economic principles as other capitalist institutions. Organized crime works in cooperation and coordination with other political institutions. For example, it has been alleged that the Mafia, together with the Central Intelligence Agency (CIA), under the direction of the

President, planned various assassination attempts on Cuban Premier Fidel Castro.[5] These events allegedly took place during the administrations of Presidents John Kennedy, Lyndon Johnson, and Richard Nixon. At the time of this writing the United States Senate is investigating this issue.

Socialists contend that the solution to the problem of organized crime does not lie in ferreting out and capturing particular individuals such as Al Capone, Frank Costello, or Meyer Lanksy. Once again, the solution lies in understanding the network of institutions, both legal and illegal, through which the political system operates. The head of a Mafia family is, to a socialist, as much a criminal and business leader as the head of General Motors or the Ford Corporation.

Why do most people consider syndicated crime leaders to be violating the law, and the President of General Motors or the Ford Corporation to be in accord with the law? The answer, as socialists see it, is that individuals have been socialized—trained—to identify only violators of explicitly defined laws as criminals. It seems apparent that factory owners, who produce goods on assembly lines which are unsafe and whose machines kill and maim people,[6] are as much murderers or felons as anyone who takes a "contract" out on someone's life. Manufacturers who produce pajamas for children that go up in fire upon the slightest contact with direct heat or flame are murderers even though they never pull a trigger or order an execution.[7] Mafia heads, and the institutions they direct, must be seen to be essentially no different than corporations and their presidents. Socialists assert that this must be understood by the American people if any effective strategy to alter the political system is to be developed.

NOTES

1. Thought to be a legitimate term used among Mafia families, "Godfather" has been popularized by Mario Puzo, *The Godfather*, New York: G.P.Putnam's Sons Co., 1969.

2. A foremost expositer of this thesis is Daniel Bell. See his *The End of Ideology*, New York: The Free Press, 1960, particularly the chapter, "Crime as an American Way of Life," pp. 127–150.

3. See, in particular, Donald Cressey, *Theft of a Nation*, New York: Harper & Row Pub., 1969. See also the *Report of the President's Commission on Law Enforcement and Administration of Justice*, Washington, D.C., U.S. Government Printing Office, February, 1967. In particular note the section "The Challenge of Crime in a Free Society," pp. 187–200.

4. Francis A.J. Ianni. *Black Mafia, Ethnic Succession in Organized Crime*, New York: Simon and Schuster, 1974. Interesting also is James A. Inciardi, *Careers in Crime,* New York: Rand McNally/College Pub. Co., 1975.

5. The *Report to the President by the (Rockefeller) Commission on CIA Activities Within the United States* dealt with this subject. The Commission however, has not, at this writing, released its findings. During the period May–July 1975 *The New York Times* published a number of articles dealing with this matter.

6. A full treatment of this subject is found in Dan Georgakas, Marvin Surkin, *Detroit: I Do Mind Dying,* New York: St. Martin's Press, 1975.

7. John Galloway, in *Consumer Reports,* wrote a number of articles on flammable clothing. See in particular, "Childrens Flammable Sleepwear," February 1972, p. 106.

Conservative

Gordon Hawkins. God and the Mafia.

A perplexing and elusive problem confronts the student seeking information about organized crime. It concerns the concept "organized crime" itself. For a curious feature characterizes almost all the literature on the subject, up to and including the Task Force Report on this topic published in 1967 by the President's Commission on Law Enforcement and Administration of Justice. This is that a large proportion of what has been written seems not to be dealing with an empirical matter at all. It is almost as though what is referred to as organized crime belonged to the realm of metaphysics or theology.

Indeed the analogy with theology is quite striking. Nor is it merely a matter of occasional similarities or likenesses, but rather of a systematic resemblance recurring in a wide variety of different sources. The parallelism is so pervasive that it is difficult to dismiss it as altogether fortuitous. But before considering its significance it may be well to illustrate it.

Take first the question of the existence of organized crime, a matter about which, like the existence of God, doubts have been expressed. On this subject Estes Kefauver, in his *Crime in America,* which is based on testimony taken at the hearings before, and upon reports of, the Senate Crime Committee between 1950 and 1951, writes as follows:

A nationwide crime syndicate does exist in the United States of America, despite the protestations of a strangely assorted company of criminals, self-serving politicians, plain blind fools, and others who may be honestly misguided, that there is no such combine. . . . The national crime syndicate as it exists today is an elusive and furtive but nonetheless tangible thing. Its organization and machinations are not always easy to pinpoint. . . . However, by patient digging and by putting together little pieces of a huge and widely scattered puzzle, the picture emerges. . . . Behind the local mobs which make up the national crime syndicate is a shadowy, international criminal organization known as the Mafia, so fantastic that most Americans find it hard to believe it really exists.

Now, apart from the bizarre nature of its content, one of the most remarkable facts about this quite categorical statement, which occurs in the first chapter of Kefauver's book, is that the evidence necessary to substantiate it is never produced. Indeed Daniel Bell in his *The End of Ideology* comments as follows:

Unfortunately for a good story—and the existence of the Mafia would be a whale of a story—neither the Senate Crime Committee in its testimony, nor Kefauver in his book, presented any real evidence that the Mafia exists as a functioning organization. One finds public officials asserting before the Kefauver committee their *belief* in the Mafia; the Narcotic Bureau *thinks* that a world-wide dope ring allegedly run by Luciano is part of the Mafia: but the only other "evidence" presented—aside from the incredulous responses both of Senator Kefauver and Rudolph Halley when nearly all the Italian gangsters asserted that they didn't know about the Mafia—is that certain crimes bear "the earmarks of the Mafia." (Author's italics.)

Others have been equally skeptical. Thus, Burton B. Turkus, in *Murder Incorporated*, writing at the time when the Senate Crime Investigating Committee was publishing its findings, said:

If one such unit had all crime in this country under its power, is it not reasonable to assume that somewhere along the line, some law agency—federal, state, county or municipal—would have tripped it up long before this? No single man or group ever was so clever, so completely genius, as to foil all of them forever. . . . In fact, as a factor of power in national crime, Mafia has been virtually extinct for two decades.

Gus Tyler, editor of *Organized Crime in America,* prefaces the section devoted to the Mafia with an essay in which he says that the Mafia "whose existence is assumed by some government agencies" is "a still unproven fact." He adds, however, that "while the existence of the Mafia is still legally conjectural, theories of its existence cannot be ignored."

But the "theories of its existence" prove on examination to consist of little more than a series of dogmatic assertions. Thus, the Final Report of the California Special Crime Study Commission on Organized Crime (1953) speaks of The Mafia, which it says is "now known as L'Unione Siciliana," as "the most sinister and powerful criminal organization in the world (with) headquarters on at least two continents." But after giving a somewhat desultory account of a variety of "illegal enterprises," and making further reference to "a criminal organization extending all over the world," the report falls back on the argument that "The study of these crimes over the years shows a definite pattern, the repetition of which in case after case cannot be laid to coincidence." This incidentally bears an extraordinary resemblance to one of the best known arguments for the existence of God: that is "the argument from design" in the form in which it was used by the eighteenth- and nineteenth-century rationalist theologians. But it is neither probative nor particularly persuasive.

Divine attributes

Another respect in which assertions about the existence of organized crime in general, and a Mafia in particular, resemble statements about the existence of God is that in neither case is it clear what would be regarded as constituting significant counterevidence. Thus, in the Third Interim Report of the Special Committee to Investigate Organized Crime in Interstate Commerce (i.e., the Senate Crime Committee, or the Kefauver Committee), it is said that "Almost all the witnesses who appeared before the committee and who were suspected of Mafia membership, either denied that they had ever heard of the Mafia, which is patently absurd, or denied membership in the Mafia."

The only exception to this which stood up under cross examination was a witness who said "that the Mafia was freely discussed in his home when he was a child." It is not at all clear what the significance of this childhood reminiscence is supposed to be. What is perfectly clear however is that whatever witnesses had said would have been construed as evidence for the existence of Mafia. Acknowledgment of membership in, or awareness of the existence of a Mafia would have been accepted at face value. Denials, on the other hand, merely demonstrate that the Mafia "is a rare 'secret' society whose existence is truly secret"; secrecy being enforced by "Mafia killings" that themselves "are surrounded with the secrecy that has proved to be most difficult to penetrate."

But even when organized crime is not identified with a Mafia it is still referred to in terms that imply divine attributes, such as invisibility, immateriality, eternity, omnipresence, and omnipotence. Thus, in the President's Commission Task Force Report on Organizied Crime, it is said that "organized crime affects the lives of millions of Americans, but . . . preserves its invisibility." Again, organized crime is said to have its own discipline, but "the laws and regulations they obey, the procedures they use, are private and secret ones that they devise themselves, change when they see fit, and administer summarily and invisibly." Moreover, "Agents and employees . . . cannot implicate the highest level figures, since frequently they have neither spoken to nor even seen them." Another Task Force Report, "Assessment of Crime," states that "Organized crime thrives on invisibility. . . . No one knows whether it is getting bigger or smaller. . . ." And F. J. Cook, in The Secret Rulers, speaks of "a secret organization, an invisible government of crime." (My italics.)

As for immateriality, we are also told by the President's Commision:

But to discuss the impact of organized crime in terms of whatever direct, personal, everyday effect it has on individuals is to miss most of the point. Most individuals are not affected in this sense, very much. . . . Sometimes organized crime's activities do not directly affect individuals at all.

And one writer, "the former attorney for an illicit New York organization," is quoted as speaking in mystical terms of "a mysterious, all pervasive reality."

The Task Force Report also emphasizes the perpetually enduring nature of organized crime. "[O]rganized crime maintains a coherent, efficient organization with a *permanency of form that survives changes* in working and leadership personnel." And Gus Tyler, in an article on "The Roots of Organized Crime," speaks of ". . .its *eternal life* . . . an institutional longevity extending far beyond the natural life span of its more mortal leadership." (My italics in both cases.)

With regard to omnipresence and omnipotence, Robert F. Kennedy said that "The insidious influence of organized crime can reach into almost every facet of our life, corrupting and undermining our society." The Task Force Report goes further and states that "Organized criminal groups are known to operate in all sections of the Nation." Professor D. R. Cressey writing of "the American confederation of criminals," in his paper on "The Functions and Structure of Criminal Syndicates," which is printed as an appendix to the Task Force Report, says that "while organized criminals do not yet have control of all the legitimate economic and political activities in any metropolitan or other geographic area of America," they have started "to undermine basic economic and political traditions."

As with the Deity, moreover, direct knowledge of this phenomenon is apparently not vouchsafed to us. "While law-enforcement officials now have detailed information about the criminal activities of individual men," Professor Cressey writes, "knowledge of the structure of their confederation remains fragmentary and impressionistic." He goes on to say that "Our knowledge of the structure that makes 'organized crime' organized is somewhat comparable to the knowledge of Standard Oil that could be gleaned from interviews with gasoline station attendants." But there is nothing tentative about his explicit statement that "in the United States, criminals have managed to organize a nationwide illicit cartel and confederation." And in a lengthy chapter beginning, "The structure of the nationwide cartel and confederation which today operates the principal illicit businesses in America, and which is now striking at the foundations of legitimate business and government as well came into being in 1931," sufficient baroque detail is provided to suggest that interviews with gasoline station attendants may not be totally uninformative for those with ears to hear.

The code of the underworld

Yet, as Professor Cressey acknowledges, "some officials, and some plain citizens, remain unconvinced." And, although he regards skepticism as "misplaced," he does not, like Senator Kefauver, define unbelievers as criminals, self-servers, blind fools, and so on. This is, in the circumstances, prudent. For when only "fragmentary and impressionistic" data about an "elusive and furtive" phenomenon are available for judgment, it is unwise to assume that doubt must be disingenuous or perverse.

Thus, as an instance of the sort of thing that might occasion doubt on the part of a plain citizen, consider the tenets of the code that Professor Cressey says "form the foundation of the legal order of the confederation." He states frankly that he was "unable to locate even a summary statement of the code" and that his statement of it is based only on "the snippets of information we have been able to obtain." Yet, on this presumably exiguous basis, he constructs a code that, in regard to form and content, compares favorably with more easily accessible examples of such systems of general rules regarding conduct.

The sinister underworld code that "gives the leaders exploitative authoritarian power over everyone in the organization," reads like the product of collaboration between Rudyard Kipling and Emily Post. Most of it would not appear incongruous if embroidered on a sampler. Organized criminals are enjoined to "be loyal members of the organization," to "be a member of the team," to "be independent," and yet not to "rock the boat." At the same time, they are told to "be a man of honor" and to "respect womanhood and your elders."

The organized criminal "is to be cool and calm at all times"; "is not to use narcotics...not to be drunk on duty...not to get into fights...." "He does not whine or complain in the face of adversity." "The world seen by organized criminals is a world of graft, fraud, and corruption, and they are concerned with their own honesty and manliness as compared with the hypocrisy of corrupt policemen and corrupt political figures."

In a world of corrupt police and politicians, it must be difficult to preserve these standards. But Professor Cressey explains that, by a "process of recruitment and indoctrination," the leaders of organized crime "have some degree of success" in inculcating "a sense of decency and morality—a sense of honor—so deep that there will be absolute obedience." It is no surprise when we are told that Mr. Vito Genovese, who is said to have been, in 1957, leader of the "All-American 'Commission'" which is "the highest ruling body in the confederation," was "invested with charismatic qualities by his followers. He was almost revered, while at the same time being feared, like an Old Testament divine. Even his name had a somewhat sacred quality...."

The truth is that this sounds very much like what Gus Tyler calls "the fantasy of the Mafia," and Daniel Bell refers to as the "myth of an omnipotent Mafia" all over again. Indeed, Professor Bell, in a subsequent article entitled, "The Myth of Cosa Nostra" (*The New Leader,* 1963), seems to have been one of the few persons to have remained unpersuaded by the later evidence that we shall examine critically in some detail. For others, however, the same sparsity of data supports an equally grandiose inferential superstructure. "Since we know so little," Professor Cressey says, "it is easy to make the assumption that there is nothing to know anything about." But the scarcity of "hard facts" does not appear to constrict him unduly. And although some of what he says sounds plausible in a nonderogatory sense, when it comes to the question of the *existence* of "the American confederation of criminals" he uses a form of argument that comes close to what one might call logical legerdemain.

The argument is worth examining briefly. Under the heading, "The Structural Skeleton," Professor Cressey provides an outline of the "authority structure" or " 'organizational chart' of the American confederation." Twenty-four criminal "families," each with its "boss," are said to operate under the "commission" that "serves as a combination board of business directors, legislature, supreme court and arbitration board." After giving some details of "the formal structure of the organization," Professor Cressey deals briefly with street-level operations and more informal functions. He then concludes briskly:

[T] he skeleton has more bones than those we have described, as our discussion of informal positions and roles indicates. *The structure outlined is sufficient to demonstrate, however, that a confederation of "families" exists.* (My italics.)

It scarcely seems necessary to point out that if "to demonstrate" here means "to prove by reasoning" or "to establish as true," the existence of the confederation cannot be said to have been demonstrated.

It may be said here, parenthetically, that the details of criminal hierarchies given by Professor Cressey and others in the literature on organized crime are curiously reminiscent of the details of celestial hierarchies to be found in the literature of angelology. Both the "Lord of Hosts" and the "Boss of all Bosses" stand at the apex of a pyramidal structure. Just as the "Lord of Hosts" is attended by superior orders of angelic being like Archangels and Seraphim, so the "Boss of all Bosses" has his attendant Counsellor (or Consigliere) and Underbosses (or Sottocapi). The Cherubim and ordinary angels are paralleled by the Lieutenants (Caporegime) and Soldiers, lower-echelon personnel who, like the lower orders of angels, may have particular missions as agents, messengers, guards, and enforcers. Possibly in the light of this analogy, Professor Cressey's description of Vito Genovese, sometime "Boss of all Bosses," as "like an Old Testament divine" may not seem altogether incongruous.

But we come now to what must in this context and in the present state of knowledge be crucial questions. The first of these concerns what may be called the mythopeic factors that operate in this field. For it is important to recognize that, quite apart from the evidence available, the notion that behind the diverse phenomena of crime there exists a single mysterious omnipotent organization that is responsible for much of it, is one that has long exerted a powerful influence on the minds not only of journalists, but also of law enforcement agents and serious students of crime. The second question which we have to ask is, leaving aside nonevidential and irrational considerations, what kinds of evidence may be regarded as providing a means of ascertaining the truth in this matter; and further what sorts of argument may be adduced as, if not being fully probative, at least having a significant bearing on the question at issue.

Folklore and myth

With regard to the first question, it is evident that there is a considerable *folklore* relating to organized crime. Much of the literature on the subject consists of myths and folktales. The point is made in Earl Johnson's article, "Organized Crime: Challenge to the American Legal System" that:

America has a new folklore. This folklore has grown up around—organized crime. Next to Westerns, war and sex, it is probably the chief source of material for TV plots, books—both fiction and non-fiction—and newspaper exposés. The names of "Scarface" Al Capone, Frank "The Enforcer" Nitti, Tony Accardo, Frank Costello, and "Lucky" Luciano have become as familiar to most present-day Americans as Pocohantas, Jesse James, "Wild" Bill Hickock, Paul Bunyan, or Nathan Hale.

The significance of this development has nowhere been fully analyzed, but in the light of the functionalist interpretation of myth made by anthropologists, it would be unwise to dismiss it as of little account. Bronislaw Malinowski, for example, holds that "Myth fulfills in primitive culture an indispensable function: it expresses, enhances and codi-

fies belief; it safeguards and enforces morality; . . ." Nor, is this something confined to primitive cultures, although the character of the myths will obviously be different in different cultures. In regard to our own society, Ruth Benedict has pointed out that

the fundamental opposition of good and evil is a trait of occidental folklore that is expressed equally in Grimms' fairy tales and in the *Arabian Nights* . . . . It determines some of the most deeply seated world views of western religions and western civilizations. The opposition of God and the devil, of Christ and Antichrist, of heaven and hell, is part of the fundamental intellectual equipment of those who participate in these civilizations.

It is probable that a large part of the appeal of such television series as "The Untouchables," "Target: The Corrupters," and "The F.B.I.," to mention only three, is that they dramatize the struggle against organized crime in terms of this fundamental myth. In this, too, it seems likely lies some of the appeal of televised and reported congressional investigations, newspaper accounts of "crusades" against organized crime, and a vast literature dealing with law enforcement efforts against it.

Another function of mythology, however, is that it provides an *explanation*, in that it helps to introduce some intelligible order into the bewildering diversity of phenomena surrounding us. Thus, Ruth Benedict says that "Man in all his mythologies has expressed his discomfort at a mechanistic universe and his pleasure in substituting a world that is humanly motivated and directed." But all myths are not of a cosmic character, and discomfort can be induced just as much by an apparently formless and unstructured field of experience as by the theory that all natural processes are mechanically determined. Whenever alarm and uneasiness are induced by an apparently chaotic upsurge of crime and lawlessness, or whenever explanation in terms of anonymous and intangible "social forces" is found unsatisfying, it is likely that the attribution of responsibility to a group of identifiable human agents for a large proportion of the disturbing happenings could be both intellectually and emotionally reassuring.

Yet, something more than a demand for simplicity and order is involved. In this connection, the way in which anger and distress lead to a demand for the identification of a responsible individual or group, which is brought out by Professor Allport in his discussion of the psychological process of "scapegoating," is directly relevant to our discussion. "The common use of the orphaned pronoun 'they,'" says Allport, "teaches us that people often want and need to designate out-groups—usually for the purpose of venting hostility. . . ." And Daniel Bell attributes part of the attractiveness of the

theory of a Mafia and national crime syndicate to the fact that there is in the American temper, a feeling that "somewhere," "somebody" is pulling all the complicated strings to which this jumbled world dances. In politics the labor image is "Wall Street" or "Big Business"; while the business stereotype was the "New Dealers."

In the field of crime, the national crime syndicate provides a specific focus or target for fear and discontent.

There is, of course, nothing exclusively or peculiarly American about this process. The popularity of "conspiracy" theories throughout history reflects a general human tendency. The objectification and institutionalization of fear reactions is not a native American development. Yet, as Richard Hofstadter demonstrates in his brilliant essay on "The Paranoid Style in American Politics," American history is singularly rich in examples of "conspiratorial fantasy." It is true that Hofstadter says, "the paranoid style is an international phenomenon." But he also admits that "it can be argued . . . that certain features of our history have given the paranoid style more scope and force among us than it has had in many other countries of the Western world." It is relevant to note here that, in describing "the basic elements in the paranoid style," Hofstadter says that "the central image is that of a vast and sinister conspiracy, a gigantic and yet subtle machinery of influence set in motion to undermine and destroy a way of life."

Yet, so much having been said about irrational factors that may be regarded as conducive to the acceptance of the notion of an all-powerful syndicate that dominates American crime, it remains true that the validity of an idea and the reasons for its popularity may be quite independent of one another.

Liberal

Daniel P. Moynihan. The private government of crime.

One of the largest and surely one of the most profitable industries in the United States is that unusual complex of skills and services known as organized crime. There is nothing secret about this modern big business. Tens of millions of Americans regularly come in contact with crime when they patronize a numbers runner, a bookmaker, or an after-hours drinking club, as well as when they become more than casually involved in any of the fifty-odd areas of racket infiltration, ranging alphabetically from advertising to transportation, that the Kefauver Committee uncovered.

Organized crime obviously has something to sell that many people want to buy. Yet always behind the pleasures of vice lie the ugliness of degradation and the terror of violence. It is pleasant to think of winning a lot of money, not so pleasant for an Irish tenement kid to stare at what is left of his father's face after the smiling bookies' psychotic "enforcers" have collected the hard way. We can all sympathize with the shame of parents who learn that their son in college has been paid off to shave the score of a basketball game, but most of us find it difficult even to imagine the feelings of Puerto Rican parents the first time their daughter comes down from the roof "high" on heroin.

But even thousands of personal tragedies like these may not be the worst by-products of organized crime in the United States. If any moderately determined amateur gambler can find a place to put down a bet nearly anywhere in this country, why can't the police find the same places? The question itself suggests to many people that law enforcement in this country is really phony, that the laws don't really mean what they say, and above all that government at many levels is controlled by massive and sinister commercial interests that the individual dare not defy.

The head of the Department of Justice's Special Group on Organized Crime declared about a year ago: "The underworld gets about $9 billion of the estimated $47 billion spent annually on illegal gambling . . . Fully half of the syndicates' income from gambling is earmarked for protection money paid to police and politicians." Since the total salaries of the municipal police forces in the United States probably do not come to $1 billion a year, these figures would indicate that the American police receive more money from criminals than from taxpayers. Probably that is an exaggeration, but there is no question about the validity of the conclusion to which the figures point: corruption by organized crime is a normal condition of American local government and politics.

It is hardly surprising therefore that for the last quarter century organized crime has been a major political issue in the United States. It is, however, an issue that the voters by and large have recognized and responded to on their own rather than having it thrust upon them by the political parties, journalists, and academics who usually attempt to set the agenda for American politics. Those political leaders who have put themselves forward as challengers of the criminal hegemony have almost invariably found themselves the spokesmen for one of the most deeply rooted concerns of the American people.

The issue first appeared as a national rather than a purely local one about the time it became evident that organized crime had not gone away with the ending of Prohibition. Thomas E. Dewey became an aspirant for the Republican Presidential nomination in 1940 at the age of thirty-eight purely and simply on the basis of his record as a prosecutor of racketeering in New York City, a record that was highlighted by the conviction of Lucky Luciano and Jimmy Hines, the twin symbols of Italian mobster and Irish politician. In 1952 Estes Kefauver came to the Democratic convention with a vast national following and almost a majority of the delegates largely because of his Senate investigation of organized crime. More recently, John F. Kennedy made his first widespread impression on the American public through the hearings of the McClellan Committee, of which his brother Robert was chief counsel.

The fallacy of the new broom

As with many important popular undercurrents in American history, the reaction against organized crime has suffered both from a lack of effective leadership and from the too easy acceptance of simple solutions. The way most people think about crime has not advanced very far beyond the stage reached at the turn of the century, when Lincoln Steffens discovered that the Tammany chief of police ran crime in New York City—a matter of common knowledge to all of the police reporters. This revelation led to the notion that the major problem lay in the selection of police chiefs, and thence to the "throw-the-rascals-out" approach that has plagued most Good Government efforts ever since. It has been taken for granted that the installation of energetic and incorruptible public officials *of itself* would put an end to organized criminal activities carried on with official connivance. This has left reform leaders and their supporters woefully unprepared for the discovery that organized crime is a far more complex and persistent problem than they had imagined—that in effect organized crime constitutes a kind of private government whose power rivals and often supplants that of elected public government.

The quintessential experience in this regard is that of Thomas E. Dewey. Elected governor of New York in 1942 as a crime buster, Dewey promptly dropped the subject. During his first eight years in office his annual messages to the legislature were devoid of any reference to crime except for an occasional mention of juvenile delinquency or parole procedure.

When the Kefauver Committee began exposing organized criminal activities in New York City, Dewey was jubilant. In October, 1950, he told a campaign audience: "I have said before and I say again, that this could not happen were there not a definite link between the big-time gambling racketeer and those in high office. What we see revealed in New York City is what happens when crooked political bosses take control of a party and hand-pick their stooges.... The scandals in New York City could not happen if there were an aggressive, honest administration, owing nothing to the big party bosses. Tammany and 'Paving Block' Ed Flynn and their gang are responsible...."

Kefauver then moved his investigation to upstate New York—and found pretty much the same conditions he had found in the city. The "big-time gambling racketeer" was operating wide open in Saratoga, with liquor licenses provided by the state; all this was going on with the full knowledge of the state police—not to mention nearly everyone else in Albany. Kefauver then began asking why Dewey, who had put Lucky Luciano in jail in 1936, had seen fit to let him out of jail in 1946, ostensibly for helping in the war effort. Dewey did not answer. He went abroad.

It next developed that the Republican majority leader of the state senate had been visiting the racketeer Joey Fay in Sing Sing. Then it turned out that the Republican hierarchy (with the Democrats cut in) had been making fabulous profits out of harness-track franchises—involving just the same underworld characters Kefauver has turned up in New York City.

Dewey's last four years in office were devoted largely to the subject of crime commissions and harness-track czars, in a nearly frantic effort to clean up the mess that had suddenly been uncovered. But it was too late. In 1954 the Democratic gubernatorial candidate, Averell Harriman, made crime his principal campaign issue. "The story of the harness tracks," he declared, "has punctured for all time the myth about the integrity of the present-day leadership of the Republican Party of New York. For the first time, we see scandal reaching the Governor's closest and most intimate associates."

Harriman won, whereupon *his* administration promptly dropped the subject of crime. The issue was not mentioned in any of his first three annual messages. There was a flutter when it developed that the boys had tried to fix a parole-violation charge for one of Frank Costello's associates, "Socks" Lanza, but things were generally quiet until 1957, when the McClellan Committee began hearings on labor racketeering in New York connecting the Teamsters with the underworld. That summer, Albert Anastasia was executed in a New York barbershop, and on November 14 the state police arrested fifty-eight men at what was prompty labeled a "crime convention" near the upstate hamlet of Apalachin. At this point all hell broke loose, and Nelson Rockefeller did not fail to make the most of it in the 1958 state election.

The experience of the New York governors is not uncommon. Again and again across the country it has been demonstrated that electing a crime buster is not the same thing as busting crime. A fundamental reason is that while criminal jurisdiction has remained limited and local, crime has grown into a nation-wide operation.

A managerial revolution

Rackets—a Hell's Kitchen term for big parties, to which local tradesmen were often "asked" to buy tickets—existed in a number of industries at the turn of the century, and there were loose associations of criminals at that time. But crime first got organized along modern business lines during Prohibition. This development has been clearly documented, although the reasons for it have been somewhat confused.

As an illicit industry, bootlegging tended

to attract persons from marginal social groups, including a large number of Sicilian immigrants. This led to the notion—still the official theory of the U.S. Treasury Department—that the Sicilians brought organization over with them, in the form of the Mafia. But this is much too simple. Obviously the Southern Italians had qualities that made for successful organization men in this field: nerve, first of all, but also the peasant habit of group loyalty and a relative imperviousness to alcohol and narcotic addiction. Nor were they disheartened by the occasional necessity to settle disputes with violence. But the process by which crime became organized was essentially no different from that by which a score of small, fragmented industries have been gradually consolidated into ever larger units, tending always toward the commercial ideal of monopoly.

When Prohibition was abandoned, the new criminal groups turned to similar businesses, mainly gambling and, on a smaller scale, narcotics. The general corruption of local government that took place under Prohibition continued, making possible a great expansion of racketeering, in which threats of violence were used for commercial purposes. With law-enforcement agencies corrupted, the persons or corporations threatened had little recourse save to submit to the fiat of the private government that had usurped the publicly elected government's monopoly on the use of force. During the 1930's a good deal of hot money seems also to have gone into real estate, in which political connections are always useful.

These enterprises flourished, especially gambling. In the words of an American Bar Association report on organized crime, the operators of the illegal gambling industry in America "acquired control of an enterprise of fantastic proportions, with all the power that flows from the control of great wealth. The result has been a new type of criminal, living in luxury, flanked by expensive attorneys and advisors, able to cut deeper into our social structure by corrupting weak officials than he ever did by open defiance and violence."

Where Steffens stopped

For all its obvious importance, the subject of organized crime has rarely engaged the serious attention of American political scientists. In the decade of the 1950's, which began with the Kefauver hearings and ended with those of the McClellan Committee, not a single item on crime appeared in the *American Political Science Review.* There are, of course, formidable difficulties in collecting data on the subject. But the most likely explanation for the gap is simply ignorance.

In general, the academic view of crime remains that formulated by the muckrakers. Crime has been regarded as a governmental pathology that would not normally occur in a wholesome municipal atmosphere. Hence a half century of reform movements, which may have improved city government somewhat but have not bothered crime much at all.

The press has done no better, confining itself to periodic disapproval but rarely seeking adequate understanding. As a result, to the extent there is a consensus on what to do about organized crime, it consists of three very general, very old ideas: we must clean up the slums, which breed crime; we must break up the political machines, which tolerate crime; and we must keep a critical eye on the trade unions, which are generally associated with the dangerous assertion of raw power.

This ingenuous approach fails to take account of the changed meaning of the term "crime." At the turn of the century, protected crime generally involved only small, local operations: prostitution and some gambling as well as the traditional felonies such as burglary, which are estimated currently to account for only two per cent of the total "cost" of crime. There were few laws against drinking or narcotics ("Honey, have a whiff on me!"), and communications did not facilitate nation-wide betting. It was only with new prohibitions and new technology that a mass market was created for illicit goods and services. The executives who run these businesses are a different breed from the solitary pickpocket who relieved Steffens of his pay envelope under the benign surveillance of precinct detectives.

Thus it is probably too late to get at crime by cleaning up the slums: organized crime has moved to the suburbs and the underworld has become café society. The sociologist Lloyd E. Ohlin has suggested that this development may even account for the increase in juvenile violence. Traditionally, organized crime has offered one of the most attractive career opportunities open to the youth of the slums. This prospect, Ohlin notes, taught them "to curb overly aggressive and violent conduct. In the world of semiprofessional and organized crime there is no place for the impulsive, explosive, and undisciplined individual." Ohlin goes on to point out that "changes in criminal organization may be expected to have important consequences for delinquent youngsters in slum areas who aspire to an adult criminal career. Changing patterns of recruitment, in which skills such as accounting, public relations, legal and organizational ability are highly valued, may well lessen the appropriateness of delinquency as a training ground. . . . The encroachment of organized crime on legitimate business, such as trucking and the garment trades, appears likely to place recruitment of new personnel on a functional rather than a geographical basis." The delinquents will indeed be rebels without a cause when crime itself is closed to them.

As to the second part of the reformers' assumptions about the ways to wipe out crime, the effort to break up the political machines that tolerated and profited from crime has been largely successful. But far from having solved the problem of commercial crime, the elimination of the machines seems to have eliminated the one social force that was able to contain it. The decline of Tammany Hall since Steffens's time is a case in point. Over the years the New York police department has become steadily freer of politics, notably so during the Wagner administration. But this freedom has hardly been followed by an end of organized crime. The situation in policy offers an excellent example.

A major industry in Harlem

Policy (from the Italian *pòlizza*, lottery ticket) is the most popular form of illegal gambling in New York City. It appears that some 1,500,000 New Yorkers—almost a third of the adult population—buy something to look forward to for a few hours by placing a small bet on the last three digits of parimutuel totals or the U.S. Treasury balance each day. It is a poor man's game and a sucker's game—the "split" is 60-40—but it flourishes, despite official disapproval. It is pre-eminently the type of crime that the Tammany of Lincoln Steffens's day would have controlled to the last nickel.

In 1958, when Congressman Adam Clayton Powell led a revolt against the Tammany leaders in Harlem, it was commonly agreed that much of his popular support came from the Negro numbers runners who were tired of working for white men who ran policy from outside Harlem. At the time, an N.A.A.C.P. official remarked that Carmine De Sapio's overstuffed officialdom didn't have a chance in competition with the runners turned poll workers, who, after all, called on the housewives of Harlem almost every day of the week. Just so. The regulars were clobbered and Powell's team took over. But two years later, Negroes still did not control policy.

Powell took to his pulpit to say that while he certainly did not approve of the numbers racket, he was "going to fight for the Negro having the same chance as an Italian." He also read into the *Congressional Record* a list of the names and addresses of the white gamblers who, he charged, were "pauperizing" Harlem. "Here we find a community lower in income than any other in the city and yet we spend $50,000,000 a year to support Italian and Jewish policy bankers."

In order to correct this situation, Powell called on the then Police Commissioner Stephen P. Kennedy to appoint a Negro deputy police chief. Kennedy was precisely the type of police chief Steffens dreamed of: he fought crime with a furious, consuming energy. Kennedy replied that Congressman Powell had only recently become a Tammany district leader and was perhaps on that account not fully aware that district leaders no longer made appointments to the New York City police force. A stirring retort. But was it not also a clear indication that no open and public institution, neither the police nor the party, could really claim to have any control over crime? The police commissioner was incorruptible, but the rackets flourished still—answerable only to themselves. Or, perhaps, they were answerable only to police officers further down the line.

The shame of our cities

Perhaps the single most important development in local government since Steffens' time has been the fragmentation of the political power formerly held by party machines, where they existed, into the complex of groups and individuals who influence events in the vast metropolises of today. Both the growth of the urban areas and the diminution of political power have lessened the ability of society to control a phenomenon such as organized crime. The criminal thrives. Here and there, from time to time, he actually dominates.

Take Kansas City. It appears that in Tom Pendergast's heyday ten per cent of the city police force had criminal records, and parts of the town were, of course, wide open. There was never any question about who was boss in Kansas City. But when the machine was broken and its leader sent to prison for income-tax evasion, the underworld, led by Charles Binaggio, moved in to fill the vacuum. Appropriately, Binaggio was shot down in his First Ward Democratic headquarters. Just recently a grand jury charged that a syndicate connected with the Mafia has for seven or eight years been operating a "criminal playground" in Kansas City under a pact with the police that has given organized crime free reign in its particular field in return for a pledge to refrain from major burglaries and similar crimes against property.

Take Schenectady, a city of enlightened capitalism and nonrevolutionary socialism, which has even had Walter Lippmann in its municipal employ. Some time after Assembly Speaker Oswald Heck, its leading citizen, denounced Harriman on the subject of crime, a pair of gamblers called on the Republican city manager and informed him that they wanted the chief of police dismissed from his post immediately. The chief did not wait to find out whether he would be fired. He resigned, fled, and has been in hiding ever since.

In neighboring Albany, where the O'Connell clan runs one of the last thriving urban Democratic machines in the nation, there is no shortage of bookmakers. But the mind boggles at the thought of what would happen to one such who tried to intimidate the chief of police!

In the past, crime tended to be associated first and foremost with the big Democratic cities. This may even then have been an exaggeration, but it is certainly true no longer. The rackets also flourish in Republican suburbs, and are well established in Republican cities and states. The New York State Commission of Investigation recently identified the Republican stronghold of Syracuse as the center of a vast bookmaking and policy network, a number of whose operatives were distinguished by the variety of police courtesy cards they carried. Despite Earl Warren's administration, Kefauver in 1951 found "Crime, vice, and corruption in California had a special flavor—exotic, overripe, and a little sickening." John Gunther reported of Missouri: "Kansas City is the heart of Democratic power...St. Louis the heart of Republican." Kefauver's chapters on these cities are entitled "Kansas City: Law of the Jungle," and "The St. Louis Area: Where Gambling Is Big Business." Thus the change of party which normally accompanies the election of a reform administration is rarely as much a blow to the criminal interests as it first appears—and as the reformers often innocently assume.

The fate of John Acropolis

The third widely endorsed nostrum for controlling crime, that of keeping a sharp eye on the trade unions, might have had some effect had it taken the form of vigilant public support for legitimate trade-union leaders threatened by criminal incursion, but this has not generally been the case. The record of major industries actually employing criminals as labor-relations advisers is well known. Few industrialists can have felt much personal alarm to learn that a Jewish labor organizer had been stabbed to death in the garment district of New York or that a cargo net had been dropped on some Polish stevedore over in Jersey City. The alarm has normally only come later when the criminals have begun to make their new operation pay.

As Robert Kennedy made dramatically clear in the McClellan hearings, the activities of criminals in the labor movement are quite different from the *condottiere* operations of the 1930's, when racketeers offered their goon services to labor and management alike with fine impartiality. A typical example of the present situation is the garbage-removal business in the suburbs of New York. Robert Kennedy has written: "When there is a monopoly control, the refusal to remove garbage or waste can put a company out of business.... Because it is comparatively easy to gain and maintain control, gangsters and racketeers have been attracted to the multimillion-dollar industry. Important in their organization is a friendly labor union which can act as an enforcing arm." When John Acropolis, the Teamster official concerned with garbage in Westchester, defied the mob, he was simply murdered. The business was turned over to a local run by two hoodlums, Joe Parisi and Bernard Adelstein, and in short order the $50-million business was being run at the direction of James Squillante, the *soi-disant* godson of Albert Anastasia. It is important to note that this is a new industry, created by the new shopping centers and new shifts in population, that Squillante is a new man— he was not sixteen years old when Prohibition came to an end.

Money talks

In some part at least, the persistence of criminal power can be accounted for by the general shift of attention, particularly of the special interests, away from local government. Crime remains as one of the few big commercial, cash-in-hand interests on the local scene. This is already obvious in the relatively small but significant area of campaign contributions. Alexander Heard, in his book on campaign finances, estimates that organized crime currently pays for fifteen per cent of campaign expenditures at state and local levels. In 1952 that would have been some $16 million—ten times the national contribution of organized labor. Heard quotes the remark of one mob official: "Show me a punk who wants to run for office, and I'll show you a man who can be had."

Judges, of course, are particularly important to organized crime. For a long time there have been indications that municipal benches and higher have been reached by criminals. As for most other types of public office, all the underworld requires of the incumbent in return for financial support is that he keep out of the way where crime is concerned. This is the point at which the problem extends beyond the existence of crime, bad as that may be. There was a wisecrack going around a few years ago that if a New York City official returned from lunch to find he'd had calls from the governor, the mayor, and Frank Costello— he would call Costello back first. For such officials, the problem[s] of crime get priority, and other problems wait. As for what sort of officials the Costellos are likely to choose in the expectation that their calls will be returned first, the answer will be obvious to anyone with experience in American local government: stupid.

Crime has not only corrupted American government for its own purposes; it has also tended to immobilize government for many other purposes. The problems of the American city, to speak only of that level, are not going to be solved by the dimwits whose campaigns are financed by the syndicate. And is there any reason to suppose that the leaders of organized crime are incapable of perceiving that they will be better off if American municipal government remains fragmented, unco-ordinated, and in the hands, as much as possible, of incompetents? In some ways there are no more vigorous guardians of local government than these criminal states' righters.

What about the FBI?

The most common reaction to the seeming insolubility of the crime problem at the local level is to try to solve it at the state or Federal level. According to this argument, local governments are too small to resist corruption, they do not retain the services of capable officials long enough to accomplish anything, and since crime has become national in scale anyway, it must be fought by large units of government. It also is pointed out, quite correctly, that while corruption is practically the normal condition of American municipal police forces, the FBI and most state police organizations have maintained the highest standards of integrity.

This approach will be recognized as a variant of the original "get a new police chief" thesis. It is not to be discarded on that ground, but it must be pointed out that it involves the danger that in raising the level on which the fight against organized crime is waged, we may at the same time raise the level at which the corruption of organized crime takes place.

For whatever motives, it is quite clear that those law-enforcement organizations which have kept themselves free of corruption and infiltration by organized crime have done so by avoiding jurisdiction over the problem. The state troopers are what they are because they confine their attentions to traffic safety and crimes of passion. In the same pattern, the FBI has not hesitated to take on the toughest problems of national security but has successfully stayed away from organized crime.

Perhaps unintentionally, much of this success has stemmed from the presumption on the part of the public that the FBI is already fighting organized crime. The hundreds of thousands of men, women, and children who take the FBI tour at the Department of Justice each year are shown through a fantastic gallery of submachine guns, death masks, and ransom notes depicting an unceasing pursuit of the criminal all across the nation. One of the most popular features is the gallery of pictures of the Ten Most Wanted Fugitives of the moment. The free booklet *The Story of the Federal Bureau of Investigation* tells how crime met its match in 1934 when the FBI was given general jurisdiction over Federal crimes. John Dillinger, Pretty Boy Floyd, and Baby Face Nelson were dispatched, one-two-three. "The underworld finally realized that never again could it openly and brazenly flaunt justice and order." An accompanying pamphlet reassures law-abiding householders that the FBI has in its possession the fingerprints of 34,027,049 "Criminals and Suspects," illustrated by a sinister figure in a trench coat with smoking revolver and cigarette.

All this is quite overwhelming, but a closer look will make it clear that none of the criminals, or the offenses so dramatically illustrated on the tour, have any real connection with organized crime. Their post-office faces look out at you: the bewildered Middle Westerners who— once—tried bank robbing in the depression when farming failed, the idiot rapist, the sullen Negro auto thief, the rather seedy swindler by mail, the youth who blew up his Mom in an airplane. These are not the men of the syndicates who appoint judges, make police chiefs wealthy, or contribute $16 million a year to political campaigns.

"Crime is essentially a local matter," Hoover has written, and for thirty-seven years he has sought to avoid any assignment that would involve the FBI directly with problems that have often appeared to be insoluble. And he gets his way. The one significant bit of legislation that came out of the Kefauver period, the requirement that gamblers register with the Federal government and pay a fee, is enforced not by the FBI but by the Internal Revenue Service. In fact, the Treasury Department gets most dirty work of this kind. . . .

Legalized gambling?

Far from putting a stop to crime, some laws actually seem to promote its growth. When a government attempts to forbid certain activities that large numbers of citizens do not really disapprove of, it runs the risk of expanding rather than reducing the areas in which criminals find inviting opportunities to operate. It may be that a central difficulty with many of this nation's traditional notions about how to control crime is that they have often reflected the tastes as well as the morality of upper-middle-class persons who have not generally been attracted to the forms of entertainment—or vice, as you will—that criminals have found it profitable to purvey. At least not since Prohibition. Gambling, like the consumption of alcohol, is and always has been a universal phenomenon. As the sociologist Herbert A. Bloch observes, the volume of gambling has remained at a relatively high level so far this century, and no efforts to control it have succeeded.

Gambling provides the base on which other and far more ugly forms of organized crime can rise. This point was made just two years ago by a Brooklyn grand jury which declared: "Gambling is the very heartbeat of organized crime both on a local and national scale. Strangely enough, this vital finding, which should be apparent to everyone concerned with the problem of law enforcement, is recognized in theory but virtually ignored in practice.... Actually, if you scratch the professional operator of gambling ventures you find the narcotics peddler, the loan shark, the dice game operator, the white slaver and the murderer."

An increasing number of public officials faced with the impossible task of enforcing the betting laws have been coming forth with proposals for legal off-track betting, government lotteries, and so on. Such proposals, of course, inevitably run into strong, deeply felt opposition from the Protestant churches and their congregations. Protestant opinion does not appear to be solid on this subject, but a united front is maintained in deference to those groups for which gambling is an issue of urgent moral concern. There are certainly moral questions involved here. And one of them is whether it is better to leave gambling in the hands of the underworld or to bring it out into the open under public control.

The next step?

Past experience has certainly shown that no single solution can solve a problem as deep and complex as that of organized crime in America. What we have to reckon with is not only the existence of crime but also of a large, wealthy, and firmly entrenched criminal class. The end of Prohibition did not destroy this class, and it is not likely that the end of certain gambling restrictions would do so. So long as there are rules against something a lot of people really want, there are profits to be made in getting around them, and criminals will take advantage of that opportunity. The report of the American Bar Association on organized crime, which appeared during the Korean War, noted that gambling was by far the richest source of criminal revenue at that time, but that it could be expected that black-market revenues would soon exceed even those of gambling. Thus new strongholds are constantly being created for the barons of crime.

It is common enough to call for more light on any social problem, but organized crime is one that cries out both for understanding and for action. In the aftermath of the Apalachin meeting, of which so much has been said but so little proved, Edwin J. Lukas of the Society for the Prevention of Crime asked, without result, for "a thorough canvas of all the existing and known significant rackets that currently victimize the American community" and "an effort, in depth, to identify clearly the factors in our society which serve to cause and perpetuate rackets." More information is needed on this subject, and needed urgently.

The time of naïve faith in simple solutions is past. The private government of organized crime must be recognized as a national rather than a purely local problem. This does not mean that the no man's land in which city and state governments have shown they cannot wage war effectively must be occupied by the Federal government alone. The attack must be co-ordinated among all the various law-enforcement agencies. Only through this sort of cooperation can we avoid the dangers that may lie in the extension—and possible corruption—of Federal power, without leaving the job of fighting crime in the hands of the ill-sorted combination of various groups that prefer for both idealistic and practical reasons to maintain the present cozy relationship between outlaws and the law. But most important of all, we must realize that an enterprise that has become many-sided and national in scope can only be controlled by a many-sided and national effort.

This is a moment of rare opportunity. A vigorous Attorney General has pledged the full support of the national government to bring organized crime under control. The gambling fever of the postwar period, in which full employment coincided with a shortage of goods on which to spend the pay checks, seems to have abated somewhat, and there are no great commodity shortages to feed the black market. Crime, for the moment, is more vulnerable than it has been for some time.

The opportunity must be seized. In the words of the Attorney General, "If we do not on a national scale attack organized criminals with weapons and techniques as effective as their own, they will destroy us."

Socialist

Nicholas Gage.   Meyer Lansky —underworld genius.

When Maier Suchowjansky arrived on Ellis Island from Grodno, Russia, in 1911, his mother, in all the confusion, could not remember the day or even the month in which he had been born nine years earlier.

So the immigration officials gave him July 4 as a birth date, hoping, perhaps to instill in the boy a sense of patriotism and high aspirations.

In many ways Maier Suchowjansky, who Americanized his name to "Meyer Lansky," lived up to those hopes. He became so patriotic that he moved heaven and earth to get his oldest son into West Point. He is as ardent a supporter of United States involvement in Vietnam as any man in America. As for material success, he set his aspirations high and has achieved the directorship of a network of enterprises as big as General Motors. His personal fortune is estimated to be somewhere between $100 million and $300 million.

The thing that sets Meyer Lansky apart from most men who have achieved the American Dream is his line of business. He chose to pursue his ambitions not in steel or oil, not in automobiles or banking, but in crime. In that field he is as much of a visionary and innovator as Andrew Carnegie, Henry Ford, and John D. Rockefeller were in theirs. Lansky is the main architect of the giant conglomerate that is organized crime in the United States. Forty years ago he helped pull together a group of rival gangs, including the Mafia, into a national network and then proceeded to shape it into a silent, streamlined colossus that is now, in his own words, "bigger than U.S. Steel."

As a director of the organized crime syndicate, of which the Mafia is the biggest branch, Lansky is so powerful that he controls legitimate corporations, runs a gambling network that stretches from Las Vegas to the Middle East, and "buys" whole governments with bribes. Even the United States Navy once had to plead for his help.

He has convinced the syndicate that it should deemphasize such high-risk enterprises as narcotics, prostitution, and murder-by-contract and enter new fields such as banking, investments, manufacturing, and real estate by using thousands of fronts, some so sophisticated they may never be penetrated. In addition, he has developed new ways to promote the underworld's most lucrative traditional source of income—

gambling—in the Caribbean, England, Europe, and the Middle East.

Lansky the man is a fascinating series of contradictions. His personal style is radically different from that of the cigar-smoking professional mobster portrayed by Edward G. Robinson in *Little Caesar* or by Rod Steiger in *Al Capone*. At sixty-nine, Lansky is gray-haired, thin, even ascetic in appearance. In many ways he is indistinguishable from a successful Scarsdale investment broker on a two-week Miami Beach vacation. His suits are conservatively cut, and his home, until 1969, was a modest three-bedroom ranch-style house in Hallandale, Florida, a suburb of Miami. He drives rented Chevrolets, walks the family dog, and goes home every night to his wife. He brags about the grandchildren, takes his wife with him on annual vacations, and carefully shields her from contacts with his underworld friends. On the few occasions when he has been pushed into the public spotlight, Lansky has shown occasional flashes of dry humor and a quiet, relaxed demeanor.

Early in 1969 Lansky sold the house in Hallandale and moved to a beachfront apartment building with tight security at 5001 Collins Avenue in Miami Beach, a short walk from the Fontainebleau and Eden Rock hotels. He reportedly made the move because he feared that the suburban home exposed him to the danger of being kidnapped for ransom by the "young Turks" in the underworld, a fate that had befallen certain New York gang leaders late in 1968.

In the summer of 1970 Lansky moved to Israel and settled down in a suite in the Dan Hotel in Tel Aviv. At about the same time federal agents were investigating the skimming of millions of dollars worth of gambling profits from the Flamingo Hotel in Las Vegas from 1960 to 1967.

In March, 1971, Lansky was indicted by a federal grand jury in Miami of conspiring to engage in illegal gambling activity and to conceal proceeds from the Flamingto Hotel. Lansky, of course, declined to return to the United States to face the charges.

When he was still in the country and the law began to crowd him, Lansky resorted to a favorite ploy: he pretended to be deathly ill. Whenever the heat was on—an investigation made public, a grand jury inquiry, a new task force of federal crime fighters on his trail—the story circulated that Lansky was dying of cancer or some other terminal illness. A report in the files of the New York State police, dating from the 1920's, states that there is no need to worry about Meyer Lansky's criminal activities because he will not live for more than a year. The police report, to say the least, was greatly exaggerated. Lansky today is in the pink of health and looks ten years younger than his age. "He'll probably live to be one hundred," says an old friend and former racketeer.

Acting like any good businessman with a social conscience, Lansky makes occasional contributions to reputable charities. But the contributions are always small— between $2,500 and $5,000—in keeping with Lansky's image. Lansky has made at least two small contributions to Brandeis University at the behest of his friend Joseph Linsey, a Boston businessman with underworld links who is a large contributor to the university. Lansky treasures a 1962 letter from Abram Sachar, former president of Brandeis, thanking him for a contribution arranged by Linsey.

Even Lansky's tax returns, it is said, portray a retired investor living in moderate comfort off the returns from a few prudent holdings. Lansky can justify every penny of every expenditure; indeed he often does not even take the deductions to which he is entitled.

His holdings include $90,000 worth of oil and gas leases, which he bought in 1960 from Sam Garfield, a Michigan businessman who, over the years, has been associated in a number of deals with Lansky. To justify the sudden possession of such a large amount of cash, Lansky made it known first that he had received a loan from a friend for $90,000, and then he started making payments to Garfield for the leases. He is still drawing dividends from this investment, which is quite legal and helps him justify some of his modest expenditures.

Another ploy he used to justify an increase in his income came to light in November, 1969. The Toronto *Telegram* told the story of a bemused Toronto stockbroker who, not knowing who Lansky was, arranged to purchase $250 worth of mining claims in Canada for him. Four months later, Lanksy had the broker handle the sale of the same mining claims to two New York brothers for $40,000. Lansky subsequently claimed the $38,750 "profit" on the deal as a capital gain and paid tax on it, much to the dismay of the Internal Revenue Service. The IRS believes that Lansky himself gave the brothers the $40,000 to buy the claims and thereby legitimatize, or "dry-clean," nearly $40,000 of mob profits. Because the deal had taken place in Canada, the IRS had no legal recourse.

In spite of being rich and powerful, Lansky maintains his modest life style down to the last detail, and with good reason. He has only to remember the fate of his more flamboyant colleagues to realize what happens to gangsters who flaunt their wealth. He started out in the rackets with such men as Joe Adonis, Frank Costello, Vito Genovese, Louis Lepke, Lucky Luciano, Dutch Schultz, and Bugsy Siegel. All loved to let their money show, and all wound up executed, assassinated, deported, imprisoned, or deposed.

So Lansky hides his wealth and courts anonymity with a passion worthy of Howard Hughes. He does not even bother to answer requests for interviews, and when he takes a walk, he never ventures more than a two-minute trot from his doorway. When he was still living in Miami Beach, I drove by his apartment building while he was taking a stroll, but as soon as he saw my car slow to a stop, he ran back into the building. He seldom went out then, and when he did it was only to restaurants and clubs operated by old friends in the rackets. Word went out early that "Joe Meyer" (Lansky's favorite code name) would be visiting that evening. A quiet table in a dark corner would then be reserved for him.

He likes plain food and one, at most two, bourbons before dinner. He has never been a heavy drinker or a ladies' man. He smokes cigars after meals and cigarettes in between. He is greatly concerned about the health dangers associated with cigarettes, but he has not managed to quit. He does not like the taste of filtered cigarettes, so he uses a three-inch cigarette holder, which he believes helps keep out tar and nicotine.

Lansky's main pleasures are simple. He likes to travel, to go for walks, and to lie in the sun. Often he can be seen stretched out on a reclining chair by the swimming pool of his hotel, soaking up the sun. He is only 5 feet 4 inches tall, and in swimming trunks he loses his otherwise rather imposing presence. He likes to walk so much that he sometimes interrupts his business conferences to go for a stroll on the beach.

Like many other self-made millionaires, Lansky is distinctly right-wing politically. On Vietnam, for example, "he thinks we should go in there and blow Hanoi to pieces," according to an acquaintance. "He's really disgusted with all these demonstrations against the war."

Lansky's fervent conservatism and anti-Communism may have something to do with the end that Fidel Castro put to his flourishing gambling setup in Cuba in 1959. But at least one federal agent believes that a right-wing outlook is concomitant with underworld success. "A lot of your mob chiefs are fierce conservatives," he says. "They're guys who came to this country with nothing and who did very well here, who found this a land of plenty. So, in the right-wing sense of the word, they're quite the ardent patriots."

Lansky is so patriotic, in fact, that in 1949 he used all the political influence at his command to win an appointment to West Point for his oldest son, Paul. The appointment was made by the late New York State Supreme Court Justice Arthur G. Klein, who was then a congressman. Paul Lansky did fairly well at the academy and rose to the rank of captain in the Air Force before resigning in 1963 to begin an engineering career on the West Coast. He now lives in Tacoma, Washington, with his wife and children and is a respected member of his community. To keep Paul's life from being affected by the Lansky name, Meyer has spread the rumor that his son broke with him several years ago and that they have not spoken to each other in a long time. This is not true, however. Lansky talks frequently with Paul on the telephone, and speaks proudly to his friends of the kind of life Paul has made for himself.

Lansky has two other children, a son named Bernard and a daughter, Sandra. Bernard, who is known as Buddy, lives in a comfortable house near his father's old home in Hallandale, Florida, and is often seen in supervisory positions in hotels and motels in which Meyer is said to have an interest. Lansky is very close to Bernard, who has been physically handicapped since childhood, and spends a lot of time with him.

Lansky's daughter, Sandra, has been married twice and had a reputation as a swinger when she was young. During that period she got into scrapes that gave her father more than a few sleepless nights. One of the scrapes would have gotten Lansky into trouble with his Mafia colleagues if he had not been so highly thought of in the underworld.

Most Italians in the underworld share the opinion of Angelo "Gyp" De Carlo, who, in a phone conversation taped by the FBI in New Jersey, referred to Lansky as the most respected non-Italian in the underworld. "There's only two Jews recognized in the whole country today," he said. "That's Meyer and . . . Moe Dalitz, but he [Dalitz] ain't got much recognition." (Dalitz is one of the founders of the uniquely successful "Cleveland Syndicate" and one of the men responsible for supervising the underworld's investments in Las Vegas.)

Lansky is easily the most heeded leader in the underworld, and for several good reasons. First, he has survived longer than anyone else in the underworld. In his fifty years in crime he has spent only three months in jail. Second, anyone who has

associated himself with Lansky has made big money. Third, and most important, Lansky has the best brain in the underworld.

While he was still living in the United States, Lansky made annual trips to Europe with his wife and managed to combine business with pleasure. In his hotel rooms, where he spent most of his time, the syndicate's overseas representatives came to report to the chairman. Mrs. Lansky was never introduced to any of these men, and the meetings were never held in her presence.

These and other signs indicate that Lansky keeps his wife, an attractive sometime blonde twenty years his junior, at least partially in the dark about his real wealth and position. On the rare occasions when they go out together, he is careful to tip much less than when he is with friends or dining alone. When a reporter knocked at the Lansky home a few years ago, Mrs. Lansky informed him through the screen door that her husband was "misunderstood by the press and the FBI."

It was Lansky who developed the worldwide network of couriers, middlemen, bankers, and front men that allows the underworld to take profits from illegal enterprises, send them halfway around the world, and then have the money come back laundered clean to be invested in legitimate businesses.

The way this works is beautifully simple. Lansky's couriers take the Mafia's "black money"—profits from illegal activities—to secret bank accounts in Switzerland, where the money is "washed clean in the snow of the Alps," as the joke goes. Middlemen in Europe send the money from the Swiss accounts back to the United States as mortgages and loans, and on other legal pretexts. This "clean money" is then used for legitimate investments. There is no way to find out the ultimate source of the money because it can be traced back only to the Swiss banks, which will not divilge the names of depositors.

Occasionally, however, one can glimpse the faces of the men behind the underworld's money-laundering operations, and law enforcement officials are not surprised to find that many of those faces are easily recognizable as close friends and associates of Meyer Lansky.

Early in 1967, for example, a group of gangsters tried to defraud the Chase Manhattan Bank of almost $2 million, using the Exchange Bank of Geneva, Switzerland, as a cover. The scheme was uncovered before the money was transferred to the Geneva bank. An investigation ultimately resulted in an indictment of the Exchange Bank as a co-conspirator in the caper. It was revealed that the Swiss bank had served as a "laundry shop" for Mafia money for years. It was also discovered that the bank was owned by a group of Americans. The two principal owners were businessmen with clean records. But other owners included Edward Levinson, the Las Vegas casino operator who fronts for the Lansky syndicate, and Benjamin Siegelbaum, another Lansky associate.

In Europe Lansky's chief watchdog and head of operations is John Pullman, a former bootlegger who started out in the rackets with Lansky in the 1920's. Pullman was born in Rumania, naturalized an American citizen, and then denaturalized in 1954. He became a Canadian citizen, and finally moved to Switzerland as Lansky's chief overseas representative. He lives in Lausanne, but is always shuttling to Geneva, Rome, Paris, London,, and Toronto for meetings with Lansky's representatives.

Meyer Lansky got an early start in crime. He was first picked up by the police when he was sixteen. By the time he was twenty-seven he had been arrested five times on charges ranging from disorderly conduct to suspicion of homicide. But not once were the police able to make the charges stick. An incident in 1926 explains why. A man named John Barrett was found near death from bullet wounds in a New York alley and rushed to a hospital. When he recovered consciousness, he told the police he had been shot and then pushed from a car by Lansky because of an argument over the loot from a warehouse robbery. Barrett agreed to testify against Lansky and was placed under heavy guard. When he discovered that his hospital food had been laced with arsenic, however, he decided that he could not rely on police protection and he bought his life by refusing to sign a complaint against his assailant.

By this time Lansky had become a close friend and partner of Benjamin "Bugsy" Siegel's. The short and hawk-faced Lanksy so admired the tall, boyishly handsome Siegel that he borrowed his idol's nickname, and for a while called himself Bugs Meyer. They first hired themselves out as gunmen to Legs Diamond and then started their own gang. The Bugs and Meyer Mob, as it was called, did a thriving business protecting liquor shipments from hijackers for the various gangs then operating in New York and New Jersey.

When various East Coast gangs formed an alliance to coordinate rumrunning on the Eastern seaboard, Siegel and Lansky were made members of the governing board. Lansky was appointed controller of the merged group, which came to be known as the Eastern Syndicate.

Early in the 1930's, . . . the Eastern Syndicate began to link up with the Cleveland and Reinfeld syndicates—groups that specialized in smuggling bootleg booze from Canada—and other regional mobs to form a national syndicate. The tie-in with the Cleveland Syndicate provided important lessons in Lansky's education as a gangster. The four leaders of this group— Moe Dalitz, Morris Kleinman, Sam Tucker, and the late Louis Rothkopf—were more subtle, and often more effective, than crime leaders in the East. They relied more on the bribe than the bullet, led inconspicuous personal lives, and hid behind numerous and effective fronts. Lansky was to study their methods, refine them, and use them to lead organized crime in the United States into a new era.

But all that took time. In the 1930's Lansky and his underworld associates were still toiling in the usual vineyards— narcotics, prostitution, hijacking, extortion, gambling. For a time Lansky, Bugsy Siegel, Louis Lepke, and Lucky Luciano ran a factory in the Bronx section of New York to extract morphine from an opium base for the illicit drug market. Each man had other things going and none took it too hard when this project failed to fulfill its early promise. Lepke, for one, teamed up with Gurrah Shapiro to recruit a group of vicious contract killers such as Albert Anastasia and Abe Reles into the infamous Murder Inc. That organization served as the enforcement arm of the new Eastern Syndicate, which had succeeded the Bugs and Meyer Mob. But Lepke, an inventive man, broadened the base of Murder Inc. and offered murder as a marketable service to all comers.

Murder Inc. ended the lives of an estimated eight hundred persons before prosecutors Burton Turkus and the late Thomas E. Dewey moved forcefully against the New York mobs some thirty-five years ago. Their racket-busting almost shattered the Eastern Syndicate altogether, and several of its leaders stayed as far as possible from New York while the investigations were in progress.

Bugsy Siegel went to Hollywood, California, where he socialized with the movie stars he had always envied. (He shook down a number of them, but was so popular anyhow that Jean Harlow became godmother to two of his children.) Lansky went to Hollywood, Florida, although he returned often to New York, where he kept an apartment until 1953.

Lucky Luciano, the top man at the time, refused to leave the center of his operations at all. He was ultimately convicted by Dewey on so many counts of white slavery that he was sentenced to fifty years in prison.

Dewey thus eliminated some of the syndicate's most powerful members, but indirectly he did the organization a favor. Under the pressure of his investigation many of the remaining leaders, who had become rather parochial, left New York, spread their operations, and made the syndicate truly national.

Lansky, for one, built a whole new empire in southern Florida and the Caribbean by imitating the Cleveland group, particulary in the use of bribes to secure the cooperation of police officials and politicians.

The efficiency of the bribes was dramatized in the Kefauver Committee hearings in 1953. Walter Clark, sheriff of Broward County, Florida, from 1933 to 1952, admitted, for example, that he not only provided "special policing" for Lansky's illegal gambling establishments but also deputized the men who drove armored cars carrying cash from casinos to the bank.

In 1937 Lansky explored the possibility of expanding his operations to Cuba. He found a willing listener in Fulgencio Batista, the former army sergeant then in power, and the two made plans for turning Havana into a playground for the rich. World War II, however, put an end to this initial effort. "There weren't any boats on the seas," Lansky later told the Kefauver Committee. "You can't live from the Cuban people themselves."

During the war Lansky played a key role in one of the strangest deals in which the United States government has ever been involved. The full story has never been told; but as it was outlined during the Kefauver hearings, naval intelligence decided that it needed the help of the Mafia to protect East Coast shipping from sabotage. Lucky Luciano was the only man who could arouse the Mafia to such a service, but he was still in prison—and not likely to be feeling patriotic.

The Navy turned to Luciano's attorney, Moses Polakoff, who promised to talk to his client. But he said that he had to take along someone whom Luciano would trust— Meyer Lansky. For several months Polakoff and Lansky visited Luciano regularly and ultimately, as Polakoff recalled in 1970, Luciano "agreed to be of whatever service he could. He passed the word along." (Luciano owed Lansky a big favor. When Luciano was trying to rise to the top of the Mafia, Lansky made room for him by having some of his men kill the then head of the group, Salvatore Maranzano.)

How much Luciano's cooperation contributed to the nation's welfare is still a military secret, but it certainly contributed to Luciano's welfare. He was paroled at the war's end and allowed to return to his native Italy, on condition that he never again set foot in the United States.

From exile Luciano continued to influence the syndicate, but active leadership passed to Joe Adonis, Frank Costello, and Meyer Lansky. Right after World War II, however, Lansky ran into a series of problems that kept him from enjoying his new prestige. First, his ally, Fulgencio Batista, failed to win the presidency in Cuba, and Lansky once more had to postpone his plans for developing Havana.

Second, his personal life became quite complicated. Right after the war, Lansky met Thelma Schwartz, a manicurist at a New York hotel, and decided to marry her. But first he had to persuade his wife, the former Anna Citron, to give him a divorce while allowing him the companionship of their two sons and one daughter.

Finally, Lansky's old friend Bugsy Siegel was causing trouble for the syndicate. He was spending too much of its money to build the Flamingo Hotel in Las Vegas. And he was ignoring advice and getting involved in a factional struggle within the underworld for control of the wire service that supplied bookies with racetrack information. In short, he was showing the kind of growing independence and recklessness that threatened the subtle organization that men like Lansky were building. So, early in 1947, syndicate leaders met in a Havana hotel suite with Lucky Luciano to decide what to do about Bugsy. Luciano had sneaked back from Italy hoping to re-enter the United States. What occurred is not known, but it is certain that Lansky, a man who would not hesitate to put the organization above loyalty to an old friend, went along with the decision reached at the meeting.

On June 20, 1947, Siegel was sitting in the Beverly Hills home of his mistress, Virginia Hill, when two steel-jacketed slugs from an Army carbine tore through the window and into his face. One bullet smashed the bridge of his nose and drove into his left eye. The other entered his right cheek, passed through the back of his neck and shattered a vertebra. His right eye was later discovered on the dining-room floor fifteen feet away.

The Flamingo Hotel, which had gotten Siegel into trouble, started paying dividends the very day Bugsy was shot. Lansky, one of the original twenty-one investors, got back many times over the $62,500 he had put up. So did other syndicate leaders. They went on to build bigger and better hotels and casinos and to make even more money, thanks to a large degree to the ill-fated Bugsy. For it was Siegel who had awakened them to the gold in Las Vegas years before, when all they could see there was sand. However, it did not help Bugsy at all in the end.

(The Flamingo later changed hands several times, but Lansky continued to follow the fortunes of the old place with keen interest, as his recent indictment demonstrates. In 1960, when the Parvin-Dohrmann Company of Los Angeles, which owned the Flamingo at the time, was trying to sell it, Lansky turned up once again. Parvin-Dohrmann, a distributor of hotel supplies and equipment, paid Lansky $200,000 as a finder's fee for helping in the sale of the hotel. "Flamingo recognizes and acknowledges that it has been solely through the information and advice supplied by Lansky that the sale may be made . . ." said a contract signed by Lansky and Albert Parvin, then head of the company, on May 12, 1960.)

Lansky worked feverishly to take advantage of the post-war boom by launching hundreds of new operations all over the country. He started real-estate companies in several states; set up jukebox-distribution outlets in Baltimore, Philadelphia, and New York; opened a string of new casinos that stretched from Miami, Florida, to Saratoga, New York; and bought into several television manufacturing and servicing companies. The money from all these ventures rolled in with such speed that even Lansky had difficulty counting it. Records show that two of his illegal casinos in Florida—Greenacres and La Boheme—brought in $1.6 million during one four-month period in 1949 alone.

Then in 1950 the Kefauver Committee turned the spotlight on Lansky, and America caught a glimpse of his power for the first time. The heat of the investigation forced officials in Florida and New York to shut down Lansky's casinos and to make noises about sending him to prison. He was indicted for gambling violations in both states and an effort was started to have him deported. But in the end he served only a three-month sentence in New York—the first and last time Lansky ever went to jail.

When he got out, he headed for Cuba to revive his old dream of turning havana into a gambling paradise. His old friend Batista, who had won back the presidency in 1952 with syndicate financing, gave him free rein.

Lansky made Cuba a gambling monopoly for himself and selected syndicate friends. He had a law passed that allowed gambling only in hotels worth $1 million or more, and proceeded to build the only hotels that would qualify. To safeguard his employees, he had Cuban immigration regulations adjusted so that his dealers, pit bosses, and stick men would be classified as "valuable technicians."

During this period the triumvirate that ruled the syndicate began to break up. First, Joe Adonis was deported to Italy; then Frank Costello was persuaded to retire, not because of old age or poor health but because of overexposure. He was too well known and too well identified with crime to remain the leader of the kind of organization the syndicate was becoming. (Shortly afterward Costello was replaced as head of his Mafia family as well. He did not protest either demotion and was allowed to go on living.)

As soon as he became a primary force in the underworld, Lansky began instituting a number of changes that enabled the syndicate to penetrate deep into the economic life of America. He curtailed the practice of buying up small companies through friends and relatives. Such men always turned out to be more loyal than competent, and the

businesses never got very far. Instead, he started sending syndicate money to secret accounts in Europe, from which authorized middlemen would lend it to American executives in urgent need of capital. "Some of the biggest mergers and acquisitions in recent years have been financed with syndicate money from Europe," says a Securities and Exchange Commission official.

To represent the syndicate in the sophisticated businesses it was financing, Lansky began recruiting bright young men with no links to the underworld. He trains them in the art of being invisible, which he has perfected. These men will be the inheritors of power in organized crime, making the job of law enforcement officials in the future even more difficult than it is now. "At least the old bunch had records and we knew them," says one police official. "It will take us years just to identify this new button-down breed. And some we'll probably never know."

The admiration Lansky won for his innovations was slightly tarnished in 1959 when he lost Cuba to Fidel Castro. Lansky flew out of Havana on the same day that Batista did, but he left his brother Jake behind to see if he could arrange a deal with Castro's men. Not only did the Cuban revolutionaries refuse to play ball, but they kept Jake hostage for twenty-five days before letting him return to Florida.

Lansky was so angry that he called a meeting of the syndicate's board and persuaded it to put a $1 million price on Castro's head. It was partly this bounty that worried United States officials when Castro later visited New York for a United Nations session and refused to abide by security restrictions. But the concern was unnecessary. By that time Lansky had withdrawn the bounty. Never a man to live in the past, he had become resigned to losing Cuba and was already focusing on the Bahamas.

In 1963 a plush new hotel, the Lucayan Beach, was built in Freeport on Grand Bahama Island by a group of companies under the control of Wallace Groves, an ex-convict who had settled on the island twenty years previously. Just before the Lucayan Beach was finished, Groves got permission from the Bahamian government to operate a casino in the hotel.

Soon after it opened, the casino was running with an efficiency worthy of the best gambling parlors controlled by Lansky in Las Vegas. And with good reason. The men in charge turned out to be three long-time Lansky associates—Max Courtney, Frank Ritter, and Charles Brudner. Another key operative was Dan "Dusty" Peters, a Lansky courier of long and loyal service, who was observed making frequent trips to Miami Beach for meetings with Lansky.

Then in 1966 it was revealed that some of the highest officials in the United Bahamian party had received secret payments from several companies controlled by Groves. Sir Stafford Sands, then minister of finance and tourism, later acknowledged to a Commission of Inquiry that Lansky had offered him $2 million in 1960 to permit gambling on Grand Bahama. Sands said he had turned the gangster down. He insisted that the $1.8 million he had received from Groves's companies was for "consultant and legal fees."

These revelations toppled the United Bahamian party from power. Sands left the Bahamas for a castle he owns in Spain, and Lansky's men were expelled from the islands. Fear of Lansky's continued influence in the Bahamas has remained strong, however. When one of the new managers of the Lucayan Beach casino, Hyman Lazar, was observed fraternizing with Lansky in Miami Beach, the present operators of the casino quickly dismissed him.

With the heat on in the Bahamas, Lansky turned his attention to the growing number of casinos that were opening in England, Europe, and the Middle East. In England, for example, hundreds of small casinos and several large ones opened after Parliament in 1960 passed a law permitting gaming under certain conditions. It was hardly surprising that Lansky's man Dino Cellini should show up as manager of the Colony Club, a posh casino in London's Berkeley Square, after being kicked out of the Bahamas.

Cellini was followed by another of Lansky's old friends—George Raft. The actor's associations with underworld figures go back to his premovie days, when he worked as a beer runner for Owney "The Killer" Madden. His trip to Hollywood was financed by the mob, and it was he who introduced Bugsy Siegel to Hollywood society in the late 1930's. Over the years Raft has been a front for a travel agency in California and a supermarket in Arizona. He worked for Lansky at the El Casino de Capri in Havana, ostensibly as an entertainment director, until Castro closed the place.

Both Cellini and Raft were expelled by British authorities, and the Colony Club was closed, but their departure in no way ended Lansky's interest in English casinos. He merely turned to less identifiable fronts recruited locally. At present Lansky is known to control at least five major casinos in England, mainland Europe, and the Middle East—and to be shopping around for others. His self-exile to Israel to avoid prosecution in the United States has not meant that he is slowing down, as the string of syndicate emissaries who come to Tel Aviv every month clearly demonstrates.

At an age when several of his old partners in crime are selling their interests in the syndicate, setting up trusts for their children, and retiring, grateful for the chance to die of natural causes, Lansky is still scanning the world for new outlets for syndicate activities. He has more money than he can use, and at present he has very little opportunity to enjoy it. He has reached the top of the ladder unscathed, while the closest friends of his youth have been jailed, deported, or executed in gangland killings. Why doesn't he cash in his chips and retire?

The only answer that seems to make sense is that he thrives on the challenges that go with being in the vanguard of organized crime. Just as his former idol Bugsy Siegel always had a secret yen to be a movie star, Lansky has always wanted to be a powerful business executive. In a thoroughly unorthodox manner he has achieved his goal. He sees the syndicate as a huge corporation whose growth and profits depend on his efforts. The new generation of syndicate members with Brooks Brothers suits and degrees in accounting looks to him for guidance. Henry Ford and Andrew Carnegie could not give up the risks and challenges of a lifetime at sixty-five, and neither can Lansky.

He has spent most of his life trying to reach a position where he could play the big executive: developing plans for vast new enterprises around the world, making decisions that involve millions. He has extorted, robbed, and murdered to get where he is, and now he cannot give it all up even though it means he can never enjoy his great wealth as long as he goes on. Meyer Lansky, a victimizer of men and laws for half a century, is himself a victim of his own dream.

Part four

Congress, the courts, regulatory agencies, political parties, and academia are examples of institutions or groups which support the operation of both the visible and invisible elements of the power elite. They are not in and of themselves the core of the American political process. They are subsidiary institutions that aid in the exercise of power. Although most people view congress and the judiciary as part of the core of the political system, it is our belief that they are not.

Students should consider the possibility that the very public nature of these institutions serves a purpose. Socialists contend that when these groups receive publicity attention is distracted from the central economic and political forces that direct our society. People who serve in these institutions are also in the public eye. Students look to professors as role models. The black robes of judges give the impression of wisdom and propriety. Many members of congress are celebrities. An implicit deduction can be that publicity is an indication that people who receive it are really important. But only some power is based on the ability to gain the attention of the media. Other sources of power are more effective still because they exercise their power outside the glare of publicity.

In reading the following chapters students should attempt to make their own judgments as to whether this supporting cast of institutions is more or less powerful than the editors state. We have offered our own outline of how the American political system works. It is up to students to come to their own conclusions.

※

The supporting cast

8 Congress

The basic questions this chapter will address are:

(1) What is the actual role that Congress plays in the American political system?

(2) Is Congress a legislative body whose role is to obscure the real wielders of power in America?

(3) What groups in American society have the ability to get the legislation they want passed?

(4) Do the American people have any role to play in making Congress an effective national political institution representing their interests?

Conservatives and liberals believe that both houses of Congress—the Senate, the House of Representatives—play a primary role in policy-making. In this role, the Senate holds hearings, conducts investigations, and debates issues. This organ has the ability to take a long perspective and to develop issues which take extended periods of time to incubate. Also, the Senate develops public opinion on these issues through hearings, debates, and investigations. As far as conservatives and liberals are concerned, the Senate is a public forum and publicity machine.

The House of Representatives is viewed as a more specialized body than the Senate.[1] Because it has more members[2] it can divide itself into more committees and pay detailed attention to special areas. The House is often seen as reacting to the publicity generated by the Senate in its "Great Debates." Conservatives see Congress as playing as important a role in the formulation and passing of legislation as the Office of the President.

Although the President often initiates legislation, he just as often responds to the initiatives of Congress, particularly in domestic affairs.[3] The weaknesses of Congress as perceived by liberals are seen by conservatives to be strengths. For example, the seniority system—where length of time served in Congress is the determining factor to being assigned to head a committee—viewed as anti-democratic by liberals, is seen by conservatives to be an asset because it allows Congressmembers to mature in office before attaining great power. This system also acts as an incentive to encourage good performance. Conservatives believe in the importance of Congress and maintain that it functions as a primary instrument of policy formation. The legislative structure in the United States is well suited to perform its task of policy formation, and, according to conservatives, it really accomplishes this.

Liberals accept the legislative structure that exists in the United States. They believe that this structure has the ability to initiate, formulate, and enforce legislation. Its weaknesses are threefold: (1) Structural defects; (2) the right person is not always elected to Congress; and (3) the public does not always arouse itself to pressure Congress in the same manner as do special interests.

Liberals have developed political strategies to remedy these problems. They have proposed structural reform of Congress so that it will be more responsive to public needs. For example, liberal Democrats have organized a congressional caucus to further liberal goals. One tactic has been to eliminate the seniority system which has served to perpetuate conservative control of legislation. The liberal caucus has attempted to replace the seniority system with direct congressional election of committee chairpersons. It is believed that direct election will allow more liberals to gain positions of power.

In order to get more liberals elected to Congress, liberal groups have organized to obtain nation-wide support for liberal candidates in congressional elections. For example, in the early 1960s physicist Leo Szilard organized a campaign to fund and support candidates opposed to the testing of nuclear weapons.

Liberals believe that in order for Congress to act, the public must be aroused. An example of successful public pressure on Congress was the fight to halt funding of the Super Sonic Transport plane (SST). In 1969–1970 a coalition of environmental organizations, peace groups, and public-interest organizations organized sufficient public pressure on Congress to obtain a majority vote against federal funding of the SST. In this instance a broad liberal coalition was able to defeat elements of big business, that is, aircraft companies and their political allies.

The public however does not always arouse itself to pressure Congress in the same manner as do special interests. For example, despite the fact that more than 80 percent of the American people want strong gun control legislation, gun lobbyists together with corporate interests have made such legislation impossible to achieve. Another flaw in the legislative process is the amount of money needed by congressional candidates to run for office. Because it is so expensive to conduct a campaign, congressional candidates are at the mercy of special interests since they need them to obtain campaign funds.

The strategy that liberals use to deal with these problems is threefold: (1) Citizen participation in well organized groups must be increased so that these groups can effectively counter and overcome special interest pressure. (2) Congressional campaigns must be publicly funded so that Congressmembers are not at the mercy of corporate campaign contributors. (3) The right people must be elected to office.

Socialists maintain that members of Congress are either corporate figures themselves, such as former Senator and oil magnate Robert Kerr of Oklahoma, or are representatives acting on their behalf. They therefore believe that Congress is one segment of the corporate elite. Socialists do not believe that Congress can reform itself by eliminating its relationship to corporations. They do not believe that the "right people" by themselves will make much difference because the pressures of the existing political system are so strong that new people will be co-opted by it. A socialist strategy holds that: (1) The public must become aware

of what the real position of Congress in our corporate society is. (2)
Using their awareness, the people must either refuse to vote for candidates representing corporate interests, and should instead vote for socialist candidates in primaries of the major parties, or should vote for candidates of a mass socialist party. The Democratic Socialist Organizing Committee,[4] led by socialist author and theorist Michael Harrington, is an example of the former. The National Interim Committee for a Mass Party of the People,[5] led by Arthur Kinoy, is an example of the latter.

Even though this socialist electoral strategy promises no early or easy success, it is one means of raising socialist consciousness. Electoral platforms give socialists an opportunity to present their kind of ideas and political alternatives to the public. These opportunities to make socialism a public issue are not ignored by committed socialists. Yet, too often many socialists refuse to use means within the existing political system because they feel they will be inevitably co-opted by the structure. Whether or not this is a hazard, socialists must recognize that they are forced to risk open and direct political activities if they are to advance their cause. Otherwise socialist groups remain simply educational societies, social and cultural groups, or minor parties.

NOTES

1. An informative book detailing the inner workings of the House of Representatives and its members is Charles L. Clapp, *The Congressman: His Work as He Sees It.* Garden City: Anchor Books, 1964.

2. The Senate has 100 members; two Senators for each state. The House of Representatives has 435 members. A state's representation is determined by its population. The larger states, in terms of population, have more Representatives.

3. John S. Saloma III, *Congress and the New Politics,* Boston: Little, Brown and Co., 1969, represents this viewpoint.

4. See their pamphlet, Michael Harrington et al., *We are Socialists of the Democratic Left.* New York: Democratic Socialist Organizing Committee, 1973. They can be reached at, 853 Broadway, Rm. 617, New York, New York, 10003.

5. Arthur Kinoy. "A Party of the People," *Liberation* (December, 1973). The National Interim Committee for a Mass Party of the People can be reached at 156 Fifth Ave., Rm. 812, New York, New York, 10010.

*

Conservative

Nelson W. Polsby. Policy analysis and Congress,

One of the functions of the United States Congress is to act as a machine for making decisions about public policy. In what sense does Congress engage in analytic activity in the process of decision-making? How can Congressional decision-making be made more receptive to the kinds of policy analysis that are carried on elsewhere, both within the government and outside it?

The fact that Congress is organized differently from conventional bureaucracies leads many observers to assert overhastily that Congressional decision-making is inefficient, cumbersome, and in need of instant reform. Consider, for example, the fact that Cabinet officers are asked to justify certain aspects of their programs in much the same language before authorization and appropriation committees in both houses, adding up to four presentations in all— clearly an inefficient use of a busy executive's time, according to the busy executive and his friends.[1] Yet this same busy executive insists as a matter of course that programs coming up the line to his office be justified repeatedly to program review committees, bureau chiefs, department level staff, and departmental budget officers, and he would think nothing of justifying the program again to other interested executive branch departments, the President and the budget bureau. Cabinet-level officers quite commonly make presentations, formal and informal, justifying their programs to the general public, to interest groups, to newspapermen. Why, then does alleged inconvenience to an executive officer of the government provide an excuse for the recommendation that Congress change its structure if the same reasoning does not lead (for example) to an outcry to consolidate those three well-known extra-constitutional entities, "Face the Nation," "Meet the Press," and "Issues and Answers"?

This is one of the little mysteries of Washington politics, wrapped inside the bigger enigma that the organizational structure of Congress presents to most of the outside world. As an outsider myself I cannot pretend to know all the ins and outs of Congressional decision-making, but I believe nevertheless that some attempt has to be made to comprehend the unique qualities of the two houses in order to capture a sense of why they interact as they do with one another, with the executive branch, and with the rest of their environment.

The structure of an organization, after all, maps the topography of its economizing devices. So in viewing the structures of the House of Representatives and the Senate whole and from a distance, it may be easier to see how rational calculation enters into the wiring diagram of Congressional decision-making, how Congress does research, how "politics" aids and deters rational calculation, and how increased professionalization in policy analysis can improve the political position of generalist politicians.

I

As institutions, the House and the Senate differ markedly in their essential character. The House is a highly specialized instrument for processing legislation. Its great strength lies in its firmly structured division of labor. This division of labor provides the House with a toehold in the policy-making process by virtue of its capacity to farm out and hence, in some collective sense, to master technical details. House members are frequently better prepared than senators in conferences,[2] and usually have the better grasp of the peculiarities of the executive agencies they supervise. This is an artifact of the strong division of labor that the House maintains: Members are generally assigned to one or two committees only; and floor debate is generally limited to participation by committee members. There is an expectation that members will concentrate their energies, rather than range widely over the full spectrum of public policy. Patterns of news coverage encourage specialization; general pronouncements by House members are normally not widely reported. Senators, because they are fewer, more socially prominent, and serve longer terms (hence are around long enough for newsmen to cultivate), and allegedly serve "larger" districts, can draw attention to themselves by well-timed press releases almost regardless of their content.

The coordination of an organism like the House is difficult because it cannot entail excessive centralization of power. Decentralization is necessary for the House to maintain its capacity to cope with the outside world (that is, through its complex and specialized division of labor). And this in turn produces the House's major career incentive, namely the opportunity accorded a tenth to a fifth of its members to possess the substance of power in the form of a committee or subcommittee chairmanship or membership on a key committee. At present seniority acts as a bulwark of this incentive system, by guaranteeing a form of job security at least within the division of labor of the organization.[3]

Thus, as I once observed in another connection:[4]

To that large fraction of members for whom the House is a career and a vocation, the longevity of members above them in the many hierarchies of the House—not the entirely predictable congressional election returns in their home districts—is the key to the political future.

The essence of the Senate is that it is a great forum, an echo chamber, a publicity machine.[5] Thus "passing bills," which is central to the life of the House, is peripheral to the Senate. In the Senate the three central activities are (1) the cultivation of national constituencies (that is, beyond state lines) by political leaders; (2) the formulation of questions for debate and discussion on a national scale (especially in opposition to the President); and (3) the incubation of new policy proposals that may at some future time find their way into legislation.

This conception of the Senate is, in some respects, novel, since it focuses on an aspect of Senate life that is much deplored by aficionados of the "inner club" conception of the institution, who often defend the curious thesis that the persons anointed by the mysterious chemistry of Senate popularity are the very elite that keeps this nation from the mob scene in *The Day of the Locust.*

I think, however, that there is considerable use in a democratic republic for an organization that encourages—as the Senate currently does—the generation of publicity on issues of public importance. One must grant there have been abuses in the pursuit of publicity by senators; but Senate "great debates," investigations, and hearings have also performed considerable public service.

Where the House of Representatives is a large, impersonal, and highly specialized machine for processing bills and overseeing the executive branch, the Senate is, in a way, a theater where dramas—comedies and tragedies, soap operas and horse operas—are staged to enhance the careers of its members and to influence public policy by means of debate and public investigation.

In both the House and the Senate the first commandment to newcomers is "Specialize." But this means vastly different things in the two house[s].[6] "Specialize" to a representative means "tend to your knitting": Work hard on the committee to which you are assigned, pursue the interests of your state and region. In the Senate everyone has several committee assignments. Boundaries between committees are not strictly observed: Occasionally a senator who is not a committee member will sit in on a hearing if a subject interests him. On the floor, quite unlike the House, virtually any senator may speak for any length of time about anything. Thus the institution itself gives few cues and no compulsions to new senators wondering what they should specialize in. For the Senate, specialization seems to mean finding a subject matter and a nation-wide constituency interested in the subject that have not already been preempted by some more senior senator.

It is a cliché of academic political science that in legislative matters, it is the President who initiates policy, and Congress which responds, amplifying and modifying and rearranging elements which are essentially originated in the executive branch. Not much work has been done, however, on following this river of bills-becoming-and-not-becoming-laws back to its sources. Where do innovations in policy come from *before* the President "initiates" them?

Old Washington hands know the answer. There is very little new under the sun. A great many newly enacted policies have "been around," "in the air" for quite a while. In the heat of a presidential campaign or when a newly inaugurated president wants a "new" program, desk drawers fly open all over Washington. Pet schemes are fished out, dusted off, and tried out on the new political leaders.

There is often a hiatus of years—sometimes decades—between the first proposal of a policy innovation and its appearance as a presidential "initiative"—much less as a law. Commentators have greatly underestimated the role of the Senate in gestating these ideas, by providing a forum for speeches, hearings, and the introduction of bills going nowhere for the moment. This process of gestation accomplishes a number of things. It maintains a sense of community among far-flung interest groups that favor the innovation, by giving them occasional opportunities to come in and testify. It provides an incentive for persons favoring the innvoation to keep up to date information on its prospective benefits and technical feasibility. And it accustoms the uncommitted to a new idea.

Thus the Senate is in some respects at a crucial nerve-end of the polity. It articulates, formulates, shapes, and publicizes demands, and can serve as a hothouse for significant policy innovation.

Hence proposals to increase the structuredness of the Senate, to force germaneness in debate, to tighten committee assignment procedures, and to reduce the number of assignments per senator misunderstand the nature of the Senate and the contribution it can uniquely make to the political system. What is needed in the Senate is as little structure as possible; its organizational flexibility enables it to in-cubate policy innovations, to advocate, to respond, to launch its great debates, in short to pursue the continuous renovation of American public policy through the hidden hand of the self-promotion of its members.

II

What has this to do with analysis in policy-making? It suggests that the analytic roles that Congress plays in the process are somewhat more varied than the customary "President proposes, Congress disposes" overview would suggest. Let us decompose the policy-making process into stages.[7]

1. *Initiation.* How are policies initiated in the American political system? The process is by no means uniform, or clear. It is certainly not generally true that policy innovation begins with a presidential message to Congress. For behind each presidential message lurk months of man-hours of work and sometimes years of advocacy and controversy. The two great fountainheads of policy seem to be: (1) sudden demands upon government that spur bureaucrats to ad-hoc problem solving that ultimately has to be codified or rationalized as "policy"; and (2) a longer range build-up in the society of some demand upon the government where the formulation of a "solution" may first be made by a professor, or by technical support personnel attached to an interest group, or by a government "expert." On rare occasions, experts attached to a Congressional committee will initiate a policy. More often, I think, Congress is in on the beginning of a policy innovation because it provides the first sympathetic ear for an innovation concocted by outside experts.

2. *Incubation.* Many of our most important policy innovations take years from initiation to enactment. Surely the idea of medicare, to take an obvious example, was not "initiated" by the Johnson administration in the 89th Congress when proposals incorporating its main features had been part of the landscape since the early Truman administration. Medicare, like other great policy innovations, required *incubation*—a process in which men of Congress often

play very significant roles. Incubation entails keeping a proposal alive while it picks up support, or waits for a better climate, or while the problem to which it is addressed grows. Senators and (to a lesser extent) representatives contribute to incubation by proposing bills that they know will not pass, making speeches, making demands for data and for support and from interest groups favoring the proposal. Sometimes a sympathetic committee chairman can be persuaded to allow hearings on such a proposal. Hearings focus public attention, mobilize interest groups for and against, and provide an occasion for the airing of a proposal's technical justifications.

3. *Formulation.* When, finally, a proposal moves toward enactment it is usually the executive branch that focuses the energy sufficient to overcome inertia. A presidential priority is a tremendous advantage in clearing away obstacles, but the President's support is usually purchased at a price: The proposal becomes his. This is not merely a matter of credit, although who gets credit is no trivial matter. The executive branch begins the process of bargaining by including some features of the proposal and dropping others, adding bait here and padding there. In some cases (e.g., foreign aid, civil rights) executive branch control over bargaining is tight and continues right through the legislative mill. In others (e.g., surtax, medicare) influential members of Congress establish which provisions will survive and which will be sacrificed. Sometimes (e.g., the HUD bill in the Kennedy administration) the most significant battle is precisely over who will control the bill.

4. *Modification.* The legislative gauntlet is too well known to require discussion here. The analytical questions at the focus of attention during this part of the policy-making process are: Who wants the proposal? Who wants it to fail? How resourceful and well mobilized are they? By what means (invocation of party loyalty, promises of future help, log-rolling, the sacrificing of certain provisions, etc.) are coalitions for and against the proposal built? In addition, committee staffs generally assemble competent justifications on the merits for legis-

lation. Often these reports reflect work done by the downtown bureaucracies. Hearings provide additional evidence on the merits as do interest group representatives on a more informal basis.

5. *Appraisal.* After a bill is enacted it goes into effect. Presumably this has an impact upon members of the general public, who in turn communicate with their congressmen about this and myriad other topics. By monitoring the tides of complaint and appeals for assistance from constituents, Congress keeps track of the activity of the entire federal government. Congressmen learn quickly enough which agencies are throwing off benefits to their constituents, which cause the people back home grief, which preoccupy them, which they ignore.

This appraisal process operates day and night on a piecemeal basis, and separately from the more formally organized oversight activities of the Congress: investigative hearings, budgetary hearings, confirmation hearings, on-site inspections of physical plant, informal briefings, conferences, and so on.

III

In short, Congress in the normal course of events gathers great amounts of information, processes this information according to reasonably well-known criteria, and matches what it learns against goals. That is, it conducts a tremendous amount of policy analysis. This simple fact is generally somewhat obscured by two important conditions under which policy analysis takes place on Capitol Hill. Much Congressional policy analysis takes place under adversary circumstances. Thus Congressional decision-makers ordinarily cannot enjoy the luxury of examining alternative means to stipulated ends. In an adversary process ends are not stipulated but contested. Agreement on means is often sought as a substitute for agreement on ends. Ends are often scaled down, pulled out of shape, or otherwise transformed. In short, from the standpoint of an outside observer whose focus is as often as not on some pressing problem in society, the Congressional process of policy analysis looks chaotic at best, perversely insensitive at worst.

Insensitivity in Congressional policy analysis is not altogether curable. It can come about because the strength of a demand in society as it is felt by an observer has no counterpart equally strong within the Congressional process itself. Sometimes Congress does not reflect "needs" as defined in the society at large because Congress itself is malapportioned, or because the "wrong" sorts of people dominate the relevant committee. Thus a wave of short-run, intense demands may break futilely across the superstructure of any institution. Given the stately metabolism decreed for it by the founding fathers, Congress could hardly be expected to operate efficiently with respect to short-run demands in the best of circumstances.

The second basic condition under which Congress conducts policy analysis is inexplicitness and fragmentation. All knowledge on a particular topic is rarely collected in a single spot or systematically marshalled. Nevertheless, the executive branch does impose some order, principally because the Congressional division of labor is organized according to executive agencies so as to provide oversight. Thus jurisdictional anomalies in the executive are echoed in the legislature. Fragmentation can be spatial— as when a bill's best friends and worst enemies are not members of the relevant committee—or temporal, when excellent analytic work is done in the incubation process but is not picked up in the formulation or enactment stages. There are often structural as well as coincidental reasons for this phenomenon when it occurs— jurisdictional jealousies between committees may prevent efficient communication, for example.

All this suggests that the analytic activity undertaken by Congress, while formidable in amount, is inexplicit with respect to some matters regarded as crucial outside and systematically skewed toward the reduction of the sorts of uncertainty about which most members of society are indifferent. Yet Congressmen, as elected officials, *must* ask who will get the credit—or the blame. They must know who is for what and how strongly, because these matters affect not only their own future efficacy but also their present chances of assembling a coalition "on the merits."

Is there a practical alternative to policy analysis in which alternative policies are put to such tests? The alternative, for a legislature, is total passivity. Legislative arenas, as contrasted with legislative institutions having transformative effects (and therefore "insensitivities"), can faithfully reflect the balance of forces as they are generally arrayed in society, and they can if they like commission policy analysis. But they are powerless to incorporate such analysis into their deliberations because legislative arenas do not deliberate, they merely transmit. The sponsorship of research by parliamentary bodies that are principally "electoral colleges" is at best a means of lobbying the cabinet or the prime minister.

IV

Under the circumstances, is there any use in considering the improvement of explicit policy analysis by Congress? I believe the answer is yes, principally because most substantive policy that Congress is concerned with affords nearly complete freedom from constituent knowledge, much less pressure. The adversary process may be muted or perfunctory, or capable of drastic modification by the infusion of detailed technical knowledge. Thus explicit policy analysis, although it comprises only a fraction of the policy analysis actually going on at any one time in Congress, is well worth improving.

Where does Congress get technical knowledge? Principally from committee staff personnel, who virtually monopolize the activity of explicit policy analysis in most subject matter areas. But while the executive branch has systematically been engaged in professionalizing its search for technical detail over the past decade or more, Congress on the whole has not done so. It is romantic for Congressmen to think of themselves as not in need of expert and detailed explicit analysis because they are "generalists." Generalism is too often a genteel name for ignorance. Like all other modern institutions, Congress can only preserve its autonomy and effectiveness by reducing ignorance.

Are there means by which Congress can do so? Two such come readily to mind. Both seek to apply to Congressional committee staffs lessons from the executive branch, where the professionalization of economic forecasting and defense procurement led to tremendous increases in the power of political decision-makers to identify options and choose among them. This is precisely the battle many Congressmen feel they are losing. Yet if they choose to do so, they can professionalize their own committee staffs, thereby increasing the efficiency of their explicit analytical activities and enhancing their own knowledge and power.

To "professionalize" implies continuous contact with a community outside the world of Capitol Hill. Professional economists, operations researchers, psychologists, and so on, maintain standards of performance by participating in professional communities through meetings, scholarly journals, and similar specialized communications media. Typically, nowadays, the top economists of the executive branch—the men who formulate fiscal policy, antitrust policy, international trade policy, and so forth—are first and foremost professional economists. The primacy of loyalty to professional craft standards on the part of executive technical personnel vastly increases the probability that the options presented to political executives will be feasible and technically sound.

Typically, Congressional committees are staffed by an older, less effective process of patronage.[8] This produces loyal service, and by the standards of an earlier day, highly competent service. But unswerving loyalty to the chairman is seldom enough to produce technically advanced criticism of executive proposals, sophisticated insight into alternatives, or sensitive awareness of emerging problems in the world. Yet these are what Congress needs. Hence, here are two modest proposals, both of which have already been tried out in small ways on Capitol Hill. Committees should be encouraged to constitute outside advisory groups to advise the chairman on the technical competence of the work they are receiving from their staffs.[9] Secondly, exchanges for one-year or two-year hitches of service should be instituted between Congressional committee staffs and staff persons in the executive branch, private business, labor unions, social service organizations, and universities.[10]

The purpose of these proposals is to bring to bear upon explicit policy analysis on Capital Hill some of the standards—and the considerations—that are commonly employed in policy analysis within the executive branch and elsewhere in society. It is not contemplated that steps such as these will necessarily bring Congress into harmony with the executive branch in areas where they now disagree, since there is no reason to suppose that a large number of disagreements over national policy are *based* upon ignorance—although some may be. These disagreements should be resolved. Other disagreements may rear their heads, if Congress chooses to equip itself with more professional analytic personnel, since not all executive branch proposals are free from controversy even when they are grounded in thorough professional knowledge. Thus more professionalism in explicit analysis can assist Congress in finding disagreements and weak spots in executive branch recommendations and can increase the probability that Congress itself can initiate policy. These proposals, therefore, genuinely attempt to strengthen Congress rather than the opposite—as is the case with so many proposals for Congressional reform.

Many of these proposals, in my opinion, make a fundamental mistake: They attempt to force Congress into an organizational format that mimics the hierarchical arrangement of the executive branch. For example, PPBS (Planning—Programming—Budgeting

System), where it has been used successfully in the executive branch, is in part a political device for forcing decisions upward in the hierarchy. There is a point, however, beyond which this technique cannot go. PPBS is a technique for comparing alternative and substitutable methods of achieving specific goals. But it is not and cannot be a device for selecting desirable goals. In rare cases, where costs differ greatly, PPBS can help decision-makers identify goals as more or less achievable given limited resources, but in the end political and not technical decisions are the outcome of PPBS analyses.

Thus Congress is at present satisfactorily organized to assess the results of PPBS analysis in each of the sectors to which it can be or has been applied. The Armed Services Committees have for some time received the benefit of detailed discussion of cost-benefit analysis by Pentagon planners. There is no reason to assume that the same sort of information would not be forthcoming from other agencies that succeed in using PPB techniques, and presented to the appropriate committees of Congress.

Some observers may assume that because on the executive side an aggregation process takes place in the Bureau of the Budget and the executive Office of the President that establishes priorities in the funding of programs, some similar explicitly synoptic act of aggregation ought to be instituted on the legislative side. This is a mistake. It assumes that the act of establishing priorities is a technical, not a political, matter in the Executive Office Building, when in fact judgments are being made about items that are incommensurable and nonsubstitutable by technical criteria. Secondly, it ignores the fact that just as the executive branch employs a method of aggregation suitable to its organizational design, so too does Congress. Decomposition of budgetary and program proposals by subject-matter specialties and the assembling of successive majorities around specific proposals is a process of setting priorities and aggregating preferences no more political than the analogous activities in the top of the

executive branch. It merely entails politics appropriately responsive to the relatively decentralized character of a complex legislative institution.

Unlike the Supreme Court, the legitimacy of Congress does not rest even in small measure upon the intellectual excellence of its work. Congress legitimizes policy because it embodies the will of the people by giving voice to the collective judgment of their duly elected representatives. Technical competence and intellectual excellence in one phase of policy analysis are therefore not strictly necessary for Congress to be important in the American system of government. But sound and sophisticated explicit policy analysis can increase the capacity of Congress to contribute to the solution of the problems besetting America. Since Congressmen must choose among solutions, they may as well equip themselves as best they can for the task. This aim does not require the revamping of Congress itself, but rather greater attention to unused resources currently well within the power of Congress to command.

NOTES

1. A recent summary of this sort of complaining is contained in John P. Leacacos, *Fires in the In-Basket* (Cleveland and New York: World Publishing Co., 1968), pp. 180 ff.

2. Although the question has not been studied systematically or in great detail, this conclusion seems to be fair on the basis of a number of case studies. See, for instance, Richard F. Fenno, Jr., *The Power of the Purse* (Boston: Little, Brown, 1966), pp. 616 ff.; Gilbert Y. Steiner, *The Congressional Conference Committee* (Urbana: University of Illinois Press, 1951); James M. Landis, "The Legislative History of the Securities Act of 1933," *George Washington Law Review*, XXVIII (1959–60), pp. 29–49; or the following recent comment by Senator Lee Metcalf (formerly a member of the House Ways and Means Committee): "No matter what the Finance Committee does or the Senate does, when we come back from conference with the House we have given in to Wilbur Mills. He runs both committees" (*Washington Post*, January 14, 1969).

3. Nelson W. Polsby, Miriam Gallaher, and Barry Spencer Rundquist, "The Growth of the Seniority System in the U.S. House of Representatives," *American Political Science Review* (in press; to appear in September 1969), goes into

the history of seniority more fully. See also Michael Abram and Joseph Cooper, "The Rise of Seniority in the House of Representatives," *Polity*, I (Fall 1968), pp. 52–85.

4. Nelson W. Polsby, "Two Strategies of Influence: Choosing a Majority Leader, 1962," in R. L. Peabody and N. W. Polsby, eds., *New Perspectives on the House of Representatives* (Chicago: Rand McNally, 1963), p. 244.

5. Different points of view on the nature of the Senate are expressed by William S. White, *The Citadel* (New York: Harper, 1956); Donald Matthews, *U.S. Senators and Their World* (Chapel Hill: University of North Carolina Press, 1960); Joseph S. Clark, *et al.*, *The Senate Establishment* (New York: Hill and Wang, 1963); and Ralph K. Huitt and Robert L. Peabody, *Congress: Two Decades of Analysis* (New York: Harper and Row, 1969), especially pp. 159–208.

6. A more familiar view of Senate specialization may be found in Matthews, *op. cit.*, pp. 95–97.

7. These stages are inspired by Harold D. Lasswell's "The Decision Process: Seven Categories of Functional Analysis," reprinted in N. W. Polsby, R. A. Dentler, and V. Smith, eds., *Politics and Social Life* (Boston: Houghton Mifflin, 1963), pp. 93–105.

8. The only scholar who seems to have devoted close attention in recent years to the professional capabilities of committee staff is John F. Manley, who has looked with some care into tax policy. See his "Congressional Staff and Public Policy-Making: The Joint Committee on Internal Revenue Taxation," *Journal of Politics*, XXX (November, 1968), pp. 1046–1067. Manley gives very high marks to the staff of the Committee on Internal Revenue Taxation, in particular for its even-handedness under the present staff director, Lawrence Woodworth, in dealing with members of the Committee alike who are defenders and critics of current tax policy. This was far less true, Manley reports, under Woodworth's predecessor, the legendary Colin F. Stam. Under both the Stam and the Woodworth regimes the Committee staff has enjoyed a high reputation for technical accuracy in forecasting.

9. The Select Committee on Government Research of the U.S. House of Representatives (1963–64) under the chairmanship of Representative Carl Elliott used this device. I know of no published evaluation of the efficacy of the Committee's General Advisory Committee, but I have the impression from talking with members of the Committee, advisors, and staff that the net effect of the advisory committee was to help. No doubt other committees have experimented from time to time with similar bodies.

10. I am aware that a small number of programs like this are currently operating. I think it would be useful to see an evaluation of their effects. This recommendation reflects my judgment that such an evaluation would be strongly favorable.

Liberal

Michael J. Harrington. The politics of gun control.

In April 1971, a special assistant to the Secretary of the Treasury named G. Gordon Liddy represented the Administration in a panel at the annual meeting of the National Rifle Association. Liddy, described by the NRA's magazine the *American Rifleman* as an "attorney, conservationist, and pistol shooter," told his audience that the Administration opposed gun registration and had established an "open, clear dialogue" between the White House and the firearms field. "High ranking members of the White House staff," he pointed out, "have already held two mutually helpful conferences at the White House with representatives of firearms organizations, manufacturers, and gun publications."

The NRA and its allies are doing well in their battle to frustrate advocates of gun control in this country. Yet it seems to me that the so-called gun lobby remains an enigma to its opponents, who feel on much firmer ground in analyzing the oil lobby, the dairy lobby, the highway lobby and the AMA. Most lobbies represent readily definable business interests, and that makes them easy to understand and criticize. General knowledge of the gun lobby is more limited: its sources of funds, the nature of its political tactics, the base of its members—even its motives—are difficult to pin down.

The lobby's shadowy image is perhaps one major reason that the issue of gun control itself is so perplexing. Environmentalists have won some modest victories over the oil companies in the 1970s, and consumer advocates have forced some setbacks on the car manufacturers, but citizen activists have made little headway on gun control. To understand why, it is necessary to consider not only the lobby but the qualities of pro-control advocates, the attitudes of the American public, and the nature of Congressional response to organized and disorganized group interests.

Founded in 1871 by some officers of the New York National Guard—who had been distressed by the ineptitude of Northern riflemen during the Civil War—the National Rifle Association today numbers more than a million dues-paying members. That makes it larger than all but three of the country's labor unions (the Teamsters, the Steelworkers and the UAW) and more than three times as big as Common Cause. The association operates out of its own modern 8-story structure in Scott Circle in Washington, where it employs a full-time staff of 250, maintains communications with 11,500 affiliated clubs, works on programs in marksmanship and firearms safety, plans and sponsors thousands of annual shooting tournaments, and publishes the *American Rifleman*. As the governing body of competitive rifle and pistol shooting in the United States, the NRA sponsors the big annual tournament for gunmen, the National Matches. Because of its semi-official status, the association also selects the rifle and pistol teams who represent the United States in the World Olympics and the Pan-American games. Its impressive range of activities is backed by assets of $19 million and an annual budget of almost $8 million.

The association is not the sum of the gun lobby armada, however, but rather its highly visible and imposing flagship. Central to the lobby's unapparent economic power are the country's gun manufacturers (Remington Arms, Winchester, Browning Arms, Colt Industries, Smith and Wesson, Savage Arms, Sturn-Ruger, Daisy) and gun dealers (New York's dignified Abercombie & Fitch, Interarmco in Virginia), which do an estimated annual business of $1.5 billion. The gun industry's financial support is essential to the NRA, since 22 per cent of the NRA's annual income flows from manufacturer and dealer advertising in *American Rifleman*.

The industry's money also goes directly into the treasuries of sympathetic politicians. When Common Cause successfully sued the Committee to Re-Elect the President last September to force identification of secret campaign donors, a total of $345,000

was recorded from dominant shareholders of a single gun manufacturing interest—the Olin Mathieson Corp., whose Winchester-Western Division is one of the country's two largest gun makers. This dollar figure made Olin the fourth largest known source of contributions to the committee during the period before April 7, 1972, at which time new disclosure requirements went into effect.

Also charter members of the gun lobby are an astonishing number of national hunting and sporting publications (*Field & Stream*, with an annual circulation of 1.5 million; *Guns and Ammo*, with 200,000; *Shooting Times*, *Sports Afield*, *Trap and Field*, *Shooting Industry*, *Argosy*, *Guns and Hunting*, *Gunsport*, *Gun World*, *Guns*), all of them pipe lines to the 21 million Americans who participate in hunting, and all of them recipients of advertising revenue from the firearms industry.

Surprisingly, the lobby includes conservation and wildlife preservation groups like the National Wildlife Federation, the Wildlife Management Institute, the Isaac Walton League, and numerous state wildlife and conservation departments. The key to this improbable environmental link is also economic—firearms hunters spend about $72 million a year on hunting licenses and $27 milion a year in federal excise taxes on guns and ammunition, most of which is committed by state laws to conservation and wildlife programs.

Finally, the membership of the NRA includes hundreds of state and local political leaders, more than twenty-five Congressmen, and the President of the United States, who became a "life member" in 1957 and who remains officially on the rolls, though the Administration claims he resigned after the 1968 election.

Despite these varied and impressive trappings of power, the most formidable source of the gun lobby's clout lies in its grass-roots following—those million NRA members, 21 million hunters and an estimated 60 million American households which have guns. For the most part, these people are decent and law-abiding, and the importance they attach to firearms defies the arguments of gun-control proponents in Congress and elsewhere.

The views of those who oppose gun control are easy to describe: people have the right to bear arms for pleasure and self-protection without interference from big government; criminals will get guns despite gun-control laws; all gun-control proposals—whether they advocate registration, licensing, record keeping, or anything else—are undesirable because they will lead inevitably to other more restrictive measures.

Gun-control opponents promote these beliefs through several methods.

They make use of political contacts in the executive branch and Congress, as the Gordon Liddy incident illustrates.

They use campaign contributions from sources like the Olin Corp.

They put the pressure on opposing groups. This past June, *American Rifleman*, in an editorial entitled, "Say Goodbye to the Y?," reported that the YWCA "had thrown its full feminine weight" behind gun control at its annual assembly. The group's decision "may turn out to be a self-inflicted financial problem," the *Rifleman* observed. "The Sportsmen's Alliance of Michigan, a highly active and vocal organization of gun owners, has already expressed the view that its members should refrain from contributing to community drives whose proceeds go in part to supporting the YWCA. Others may follow suit." They may indeed, but they probably wouldn't have if the magazine hadn't given the ploy national circulation.

They use their extensive media connections to misstate the details of proposed bills, and to play to fears about race, government domination and subversion by radicals. In July 1965, when the modest proposals to regulate mail-order sales were first proposed in the Senate, *Guns and Ammo* ran an article called "The Real Facts Behind S.1592" which began, "If you, as a collector, hunter, target shooter, gun dealer, gunsmith, or small manufacturer,

wish to lose your rights to own guns, to go hunting, target shooting, or deal in firearms, read no further. This bill will ultimately confiscate your guns, and make it impossible for you to hunt or stay in business."

In fact, the 1965 proposal, which was not enacted into law until three years later, was a thoroughly mild reform. All persons selling firearms are now required to obtain a federal license, the interstate sale of firearms through the mails is prohibited, and the possession of firearms by certain people—including convicted criminals, aliens residing illegally in the United States, and mental incompetents—is forbidden. The law poses no threat whatsoever to respectable collectors, hunters, target shooters, gun dealers, gunsmiths or small manufacturers.

Later that year, after the Watts rioting, *Guns and Ammo* editorialized, "In the final analysis, rampaging hoodlumism such as experienced in Los Angeles, Chicago and other major cities may yet be a blessing in disguise which will do a great deal to preserve our precious right to keep and bear arms."

But most of all, the lobby stirs an avalanche of grassroots sentiment, usually in the form of letters. Ultimately, as I suggested earlier, it is the lobby's outside following, rather than its inside connections, that most effectively discourages Congressional action. The lobby's ability to elicit letters from its constituency is phenomenal.

During the 1965 controversy, for example, the NRA sent a bulletin to all its members, urging them to write the President and Congress about the mail-order bill. "Write now," urged the NRA, "or it may be too late." Included with the letter was a list of instructions, entitled, "How to Write Your Letter," The bulletin featured exhortations like, "Do not doubt for one second the effectiveness of your one voice," and "If the battle is lost, it will be your loss and that of all who follow you."

Guns and Ammo chimed in, saying in its August issue, "Nothing impresses an elected lawmaker as much as a massive amount of mail from people who vote in his district. It is the one proven way to persuade a legislator to act."

Journalist Richard Harris describes in *The New Yorker* the results the association's bulletin produced:

During the month preceding the campaign set off by the NRA, the White House received fifty letters on S. 1592 [the Senate bill], divided just about equally pro and con. During the following month, it received 12,000 letters, all but a few opposing the bill. Within two weeks after Orth [an official of the NRA] alerted his followers, the Subcommittee to Investigate Juvenile Delinquency [which was handling S. 1592] got 1,400 letters, forty-seven of them favoring the bill, and the Commerce Committee [also considering the legislation] got over 2,000, four of them favoring it.

The reaction was predictable. Sen. Jacob Javits was quoted as saying, "I have received an enormous amount of mail, really enormous, almost unbelievable, expressing opposition to this bill." Sen. Gale McGee of Wyoming said, "I can recall no issue, either international or domestic, in my tenure in the Senate that has aroused the people of Wyoming as this one."

Three years later, the deaths of Robert Kennedy and Martin Luther King triggered a temporary counter reaction in favor of gun control, but even then the lobby was so strong that the bill which finally passed was a much amended ghost of its former self. The lobby, however, still declared war on supporters of the 1968 measure, and chose its targets for political retribution accordingly. "Every Congressman who lost his seat in 1970 is convinced he lost because he voted for the gun-control bill," said Rep. Abner Mikva, a leading control advocate, who lost his own seat two years later. *American Rifleman*, in an article reviewing plusses and minuses of the 1970 elections, began the column by quoting Maryland's Joseph Tydings, another spokesman for control who had just lost his re-election fight in the Senate, as saying, "I suppose this will discourage others from taking on the gun lobby."

At this point in a discussion of gun control and Congress' failure to support it, control advocates can be expected to point out that, as early as April 1938, the Gallup poll showed 84 per cent of the American public in favor of requiring firearms registration. In eight polls conducted by the Gallup organization between 1959 and 1972, posing the question, "Do you favor or oppose a law requiring a police permit to buy guns?," those in favor have never dropped below 68 per cent.

Given these polls, supporters of control say, the politician should realize that he has little to fear from the gun lobby, that the lobby simply looks bigger than it is by generating an intense reaction from its hard-core membership, and that, in fact, the case for gun control is almost universally conceded.

However, a special interest does not necessarily have to convince a politician that its positions reflect the feelings of the majority of voters in his district or state. In elections, politicians worry not only about the views of the majority but about the possible sources of the *margin* of victory or defeat. They believe that most of their constituents make up their minds according to their general perceptions of a variety of issues, and that supporting a concept like gun control is not likely, by itself, to win many additional votes. On the other hand, elected officials may sense that the anti-control voters mobilized by the gun lobby are apt to engage in a kind of bullet voting, and decide their voting preferences on the basis of the gun question alone. This view of gun-control opponents and other special interest voters, which is not calculated but intuitive, leads the politician to treat particular groupings in his area—union people, peace activists, members of a particular profession—with great care, especially if they have a high degree of internal ogranization. Politicians want very much to avoid controversy, and will go a long way to placate people who harass them.

In that case, it may be asked, why haven't gun-control supporters organized to provide the margin of victory or defeat in the other direction? The answer, I think, is the same that explains why there is no well-organized group to oppose the oil interests on the depletion allowance or the medical-health establishment on national health insurance: "special interests" can focus resources and efforts, while the "general interest" is by definition broad, unfocused and difficult to defend.

The pro-gun control forces in this country tend to be governmental agencies and officials concerned with the entire area of crime prevention, religious and civic organizations whose primary activities lie elsewhere, "public interest" and "citizen action" groups designed to represent the public against the special interests but spread thin across the entire spectrum of political issues, and public figures who lend their names and time to the cause. Thus, in 1972 the Americans for Democratic Action assembled a coalition which included Detroit Mayor Roman Gribbs, the American Baptist Convention, Common Cause, the ACLU, the AFL-CIO, the UAW and the American Jewish Committee. In 1968, after the shock of the assassinations, former astronaut John Glenn chaired an "Emergency Committee for Gun Control" composed of people like Warren Beatty, Truman Capote, Joe DiMaggio, Vince Lombardi and Archibald Cox.

Both coalitions were modestly funded, loosely organized, and designed to self-destruct at the conclusion of the particular legislative fight then being waged. The National Rifle Association, meanwhile, was going full steam before they started and after they disbanded.

Currently, consumer groups, tax reform groups, political reform groups and women's groups all see gun control as a desirable goal, but the issue falls in the chinks between each organization's specific program planks. "We're an organization of somewhat limited resources," an official of the National Women's Political Caucus said recently, "and we've had to devote those resources to matters directly affecting women's ability to participate in the political process. As far as gun control is concerned, I can't think of a time when the issue has even come up."

The only group which now exists solely to promote gun control and organize for its adoption is the National Council for a Responsible Firearms Policy, headed by David Steinberg. Steinberg is the most informed and thoughtful proponent of gun control in the country, but because the council is small and unable to attract substantial funds, he must serve as its only staff member in a part-time capacity. He circulates on Capitol Hill, consulting with committees and interested Congressmen, providing solitary counterbalance to the NRA's 250 employees on the other side of the issue.

Thus, members of Congress confront a situation in which a special interest is organized to threaten them with the margin of defeat, while the "public interest" is represented with tenacity and dedication, but without adequate backing. Under such circumstances, it might still be reasonable to expect our elected political leaders to *lead*, to take the dangerous but responsible policy position, and to find ways to educate and mobilize those substantial majorities who, according to the Gallup poll, agree with gun control.

In fact, quite often a politician may feel that he could defeat the economic, political and media strength of a given special interest—if he devoted a major part of his political capital to the effort. But very likely he will have a variety of such interests to cope with, and rather than take on all of them, he is apt to fall back to one of the first precepts of play-it-safe politics: people often don't give you credit for agreeing with them, but they never forget when you disagree. The politician, particularly the incumbent, is likely to settle for the *status quo* and keep his boats from rocking.

In my opinion, this outlook characterizes much of the behavior of Congress, which ordinarily takes so much time to see which way the wind is blowing that the storm is over before it ever acts—whether in response to the war in Vietnam, Presidential vetoes of social programs, or the gun situation.

Moreover, the Congressional inclination toward caution becomes more pronounced in the absence of Presidential pressure to act. The 1968 laws regulating mail-order sales passed only after President Johnson, acting through people like Atty. Gen. Ramsey Clark, made the matter a legislative priority. Attitudes changed greatly in the White House after 1968, as I attempted to illustrate at the beginning of this article.

These points about interest group tactics and the reactions they draw from politicians are probably true for many controversies. But it seems to me that there are attributes of the gun question which make it distinct from, say, the oil lobby problem and the pharmaceutical lobby problem. While the gun lobby has many of the marks of a conventional special interest which sets out to frustrate a widely acknowledged "public interest," quite a few members of Congress are disturbed by the grass-roots element of the lobby, and the nagging apprehension, if not the outright conviction, that the voters in their areas are not telling Dr. Gallup everything he ought to know.

In weighing these apprehensions, it is important that intellectuals, journalists, reformers and politicians from the Northeast understand the regional dimensions of the gun issue. Almost everywhere else in the country—the South, the Midwest, the Far West, wherever rural influences are more pronounced—firearms are basic to the environment. According to Carl Bakal, a long-time writer on the gun question, an amazing 59 per cent of individuals in the South own a gun, compared to 34 per cent in the East. An aide to South Dakota Sen. James Abourezk told the *Chicago Tribune,* "Our constituency is very emotional about guns. Guns are a way of life and their attitude is, if you take away my guns, you'll take away my wife next." *The Wall Street Journal* wrote, in an editorial, "Behind Gun-Control Furor: A Clash of Cultures," "The real pressure for gun control comes from cosmopolitan America, which sees it as the plainest common sense. The real resistance comes from the redoubts of bedrock America, which sees gun control as another

symptom of encroachment by a new culture."

The rural area representatives who dominate the Congressional committee structure through the seniority system may very well feel they have ample reason to interpret those thousands of letters from gun-control opponents as being fairly representative of their constituents' convictions. To their minds, a "yes" or "no" question in a national poll about the specific idea of "police permits to buy guns" does not mirror the complicated feelings of the voters back home.

Similar conclusions have apparently been reached in the White House, where the Administration's ardent courtship of the National Rifle Association fits nicely into its "Southern strategy" and its appeals to "Middle America." To many politicians, as well as to many other observers, there appear to be a number of social and cultural factors in American life today which make broad unambivalent public support of gun control unlikely.

One can begin by reciting the historical factors, unique to the United States—our nostalgia for the American frontier, reverence for self-reliance and individual strength, and insistence on a tough kind of masculinity in our country's males. In a quite pessimistic essay, *America as a Gun Culture*, historian Richard Hofstadter writes that "for millions of American boys, learning to shoot and above all graduating from toy guns and receiving the first real rifle of their own were milestones of life, veritable rites of passage that certified arrival at manhood."

These traditional inclinations have assumed a fresh tone of immediacy with the stunning growth of the nation's crime rate. Millions of citizens genuinely fear their neighborhood streets after dark, and the notion of defending oneself and one's family, of "fighting back," rather than relying solely on the police, has apparently gained great appeal, despite the proven impracticality and ineffectuality of such efforts. Women enroll in self-defense courses, *New York* magazine chronicles the growth of citizen vigilante groups, Sen. William Proxmire evokes a national reaction when he stands up to two muggers who accost him during his jogging. "I wouldn't want to see a lot of gun-control laws," a young volunteer for a major women's rights organization remarks, "if it would deprive women of a means of defending themselves."

An additional current of feeling reinforces public reservations about gun control, a current which, if anything, is apt to grow stronger in light of Richard Nixon's disturbing use of Presidential power. "Another belief of American gun enthusiasts enjoys a wide currency in the United States, extending to a good many liberals, civil libertarians, and even radicals," historian Hofstadter remarks, "It is the idea that popular access to arms is an important counterpoise to tyranny."

A dozen years ago, invocation of this fear of centarlized government as a reason for resisting gun control would have been dismissed as near paranoia. Now, while Professor Hofstadter rightly describes belief in the value of "popular access to arms" as both naive and dangerous, the suspicions behind the belief perhaps cannot be so easily argued away. Recent evidence has emerged of the government's illegally wire-tapping newspapermen and its own officials, misusing data-bank information, burglarizing private offices, and spying on dissident groups. It isn't altogether surprising that many people might hesitate to accept assurances that the federal government would never abuse its regulatory powers over firearms.

The Christian Science Monitor, a consistent advocate of gun control, recently featured an article with the headline, "Many Gun Owners Distrust Government." When considerable numbers of citizens come to distrust the individuals they have democratically elected to office, that seems to me one of the greatest tragedies which can befall a democracy.

I have been most concerned with describing the nature of the gun lobby.

Though I have not discussed them here, the arguments for gun control—the statistics on the number of firearms homicides, the correlation in particular states between strict control laws and low firearms murder rates, and the history of effective gun control in England and other countries—are quite well known. A question remains: what can be done to advance the cause of gun control in the face of the forces I have been discussing?

A wholly satisfactory answer would require an additional article, but I can suggest some ways to begin. First, gun-control supporters should proceed with an awareness of the issue's complexities, and especially with respect and empathy for the concerns which motivate the grass-roots opposition.

Second, gun control should be made part of a tough, effective anti-crime program for the nation. Conventional liberal analyses of national issues have not been cohesive and convincing in the area of crime prevention; yet many Americans will hesitate at the most modest regulation of their firearms as long as they feel threatened by criminals.

Third, gun-control advocates should work to elect a President who will curb the federal government's increasing incursions into individual civil rights and liberties, as well as institute an anti-crime program which includes gun control. Given the imperfections of Congress and the regional strength of the gun lobby, strong national leadership on the issue must come from the Chief Executive.

The activist core of the gun lobby—the NRA, the manufacturers and dealers and the hunting and gun publications—will persist in fighting effective gun control. But the grass-roots element, essential to the lobby's continued strength, could, in my opinion, be persuaded of the merits of the pro-control position. These people have been grief-stricken by the assassinations of the last decade, believe in the responsible use of firearms, wish to be free of the fear of crime, and want to trust their government. In the past, liberal reformers have had trouble talking persuasively to "bedrock America" about gun control—or, for that matter, about the welfare problem, civil rights, dissent, the cities, the 1972 Presidential election and change in general. However, these are the people who have to be convinced; then progress in gun control could very likely follow.

Socialist

Mark Green, James M. Fallows, and David R. Zwick. Who owns Congress?

The influence of big money on government has been a theme of critics ever since the founding of the Republic. Were it not for the sordid tales of bribery and payoffs regularly floating out from behind the Capitol Curtain, scandal columnists would long ago have gone on unemployment compensation. But for all their titillating impact, the crudest forms of bribery are vastly overshadowed as a corrupting influence by a much more sophisticated and widespread practice. Instead of going into the congressman's pockets, the money is instead put in the campaign coffers for the next (or sometimes the previous) election.

Of course, when a big campaign contribution is given in return for an assurance of receiving special treatment, it doesn't matter what the transaction is called. It's still nothing more than good old-fashioned graft in a very thin disguise. But who needs to extract a promise from a politician if spending enough money at election time can put a "reliable" man into office? Or better yet, if spending enough money at primary election and nominating time can ensure that *all* the surviving candidates by the time the general election rolls around are "reliable." Whether campaign contributions buy an entire election or favored treatment or simply special access to politicians, they are the main reason why the rich men who make them get richer while the average citizen gets what little is left over.

Expensive merchandise

Part of the problem is inflation. Like meat, congressmen have risen in price. As the cost of U.S.-Prime political influence has soared, casual buyers have fled the market and left it to the truly rich or the corporate purchasers. Expenses weren't always so high. In the election campaign of 1846, friends of Abraham Lincoln collected a fund for his first try for Congress. The $200 they scraped together would barely cover one week's phone bills for a modern candidate. But at the end of the campaign, Lincoln returned $199.25 of it. The rest had gone for his one campaign expense, a barrel of cider for local farm hands.

Honest Abe might have spent the rest of his life chopping rails if he'd tried the same thing much later. The turning point for campaign expenses came with the Civil War. As the newly powerful corporate empires began to buy political favors—and as the politicians of the time showed themselves willing to be bought—competition pushed the prices up. The mounting expense, however, did not curb demand, since the companies saw the hard business advantage of friendly politicians. In 1903, a Standard Oil agent (who was himself a member of Congress), screening a "loan request" from a senator, wrote to the company's vice-president John Archbold, "Do you want to make the investment?"

The return on investments like this was a Congress increasingly populated with men like Senator Boies Penrose. Penrose was a Pennsylvanian, a Republican, and a devoted glutton.[1] But his deepest allegiance was to the welfare of Corporate America. He explained his philosophy of economy and life to a group of his business beneficiaries: "I believe in a division of labor. You send us to Congress; we pass laws under . . . which you make money; . . . and out of your profits you further contribute to our campaign funds to send us back again to pass more laws to enable you to make more money." A good operating guideline, he once confided to an associate, was to work on "legislation that meant something to men with real money and let them foot the bill" (as when Archbold of Standard Oil gave him $25,000 on one proven occasion).

Today's politicians can afford neither Penrose's candor nor his appetite, but his mottoes live on. Where does the money go? Before the coming of television as a political tool, most of it went to the old-fashioned paraphernalia of an election—billboard ads and two-cent stamps, campaign workers and envelope lickers, whistle-stop tours and barbecue rallies. Occasionally, of course, it went to buy votes outright. Oklahoma's Senator Fred Harris has fondly recalled his baptism in this old style of campaign spending, in the 1954 Oklahoma election, which found one oil millionaire (Robert Kerr) who held a Senate seat facing another oil millionaire (Roy Turner) who wanted it. Harris, who worked for Turner, says:

Some [people] wanted to be county or town campaign managers for whichever candidate would pay the most. An unprincipled preacher offered to bargain away supposed influence with his unsuspecting congregation. An Avon saleswoman was willing to consider—for a price—adding a pitch for a candidate to her usual sales promotion to regular-route customers. And there were the ubiquitous importunings of hundreds of poll haulers and hangers-on. They wanted everything from $25,000 to carry a county to a half-pint of whiskey to make the day. From fifty dollars for "gas and expenses" to get to the district church conference, to a thousand dollars to pay back taxes to keep a weekly newspaper publishing . . . .

One young man in the Turner headquarters had as his principal duty running to the Federal Reserve Bank every day as soon as it opened to bring back a thousand or so dollars in cash to be doled out to those who came in declaring that victory in their counties required a little money "to put on a barbecue" or "to hire some woman to pick up old folks on election day."

But Darwin rules in politics as in nature, and the richest survive. Turner ran out of money midway through the campaign and had to quit. Kerr kept his seat.

If Turner were running his campaign in 1972, the daily money deliveries would have to be closer to ten thousand than to one. As election techniques have risen from barbecues and preacher-bribing to the higher

technologies of media advertising, costs have soared. One of the new, and costly, techniques is air travel. Congressmen who languish in Washington learn the truth of out-of-sight, out-of-mind. In election years, congressmen and their staffs spend much of their time in the air between Washington and the home-state voters. One Senate staffer told Haynes Johnson of the *Washington Post* that to mend political fences he averaged twenty-two trips per year, at an annual cost of $10,500. Trips for government affairs can be deducted as business expense, but not campaign junkets. The results? "I can't describe to you what a constant worry that is or how I would go out of my way through this maze or that, trying to cover these bills. The only way to do it was through campaign contributions."

The real thrust behind skyrocketing costs, however, is television advertising. When saturation campaigns of one-minute spots or half-hour specials took over from more primitive, and cheaper, forms of publicity, election funding became a truly big business. As recently as 1952, when Eisenhower first ran for the presidency, the total spent in national election campaigns was "only" $140 million (according to the Citizens Research Foundation). Over the next twelve years, the total rose slowly; in 1964, it was an estimated $200 million. But only four years later, in the 1968 campaigns, the figure had risen by 50 percent, to $300 million. More than any other factor, television was the cause.

The most extreme example of television's effect on campaigns is the 1970 senatorial elections. Of the fifteen major candidates in the seven largest states, eleven were millionaires. The four who were not lost. One of the nonmillionaires was Charles Goodell, the liberal Republican who was trying to hold his seat in New York. Goodell spent $1.3 million in the campaign—more than half of it for television. Goodell raised the money through an executive finance committee. This was a group of fifteen wealthy men who called other wealthy men and asked them to donate between $1,000 and $10,000 apiece. But Goodell still ended up outspent by the opposition and $400,000 in debt. "We were always on the verge of a [TV] blackout because of lack of money," he told reporter Johnson. A TV blackout, as Goodell knew, would mean political death, given the voters' residual ignorance about him, and given his opponents' free-spending ways. The eventual winner, Conservative James Buckley, reported spending $2 million, while Democrat Richard Ottinger invested $4 million in his losing effort.

If the apparent lesson is that money won't necessarily buy victory, it is worth remembering that Ottinger, who had not been widely known in the state, won the Democratic primary almost solely through an overwhelming, expensive television campaign.

As costs have risen to the point where even the millionaires must borrow, so too rises the certainty that politicians must turn to rich special interests for help. President Eisenhower, in an era of what now looks like small-change campaigns, was appalled by the "outrageous costs of getting elected to public office." Later, Robert Kennedy agreed that "we are in danger of creating a situation in which our candidates must be chosen from among the rich [like the Kennedys] . . . or those willing to be beholden to others."

Who "owns" the politicians? A look at campaign fund sources shows two main stockholders, one holding so many shares that it is content to be silent, the other feisty but much weaker. The small shareholder is the organized labor movement. A relative newcomer to big money politics, unions became an important force in the 1950s. A key starting point was the AFL-CIO's decision to set up a political action arm, the Committee on Political Education (COPE). Federal law bars unions from using their own funds in political campaigns, so committees like COPE serve as a handy and legal conduit for members' contributions. Aside from COPE, the committee list now includes the teamsters' DRIVE, the United Auto Workers' Good Government Fund, and many others. Together, according to Americans for Constitutional Action, they contributed more than $4 million to candidates in the 1970 elections.

While union contributions might potentially be a necessary counterweight to big-business spending, the tactics some unions use to collect their funds give the working class a bad name. One of the more notorious examples is the Seafarers International Union (SIU). The SIU has long been a big giver; in 1968, its 80,000 members came up with more than three times as much campaign money as the 1.4 million United Auto Workers. The money has been put to effective use, too. Much of the more than $600,000 collected that year was spread among friends of the maritime industry in Congress, where it oiled the way for a series of lush subsidies to the U.S. merchant fleet. So far, so good for the SIU. But along the way, there had been technical troubles. In 1970, eight of the union's officers were indicted for making illegal contributions of $40,000. This was allegedly part of a conspiracy involving donations of $750,000 over many years. The source of these huge funds is supposed to be "voluntary" contributions from union members, but grumblers claim that the word is used in a sense no one outside the SIU would recognize. As an aid to voluntarism, some SIU members have said, "goon squads" show up at collection time (a charge denied by union spokesmen). According to Jerry Landauer of the *Wall Street Journal*, the SIU collects from all crewmen on a U.S. ship— including foreigners, whose interest in American politics is presumably slight.

Campaign collectors in the business community are delighted when exploits like the SIU's come to light. Together with the well-publicized contributions from COPE and DRIVE, the union horror stories are just the thing to spur businessmen to greater spending sacrifices for *their* favorite candidates. It is a tribute to the determination of the fundraisers, and to the businessmen's refusal to be complacent, that the money still rolls out in response to the union threat. For, as all the available evidence shows, the business world has nothing to worry about.

It is difficult to total up the business contributions as exactly as those from labor. Unlike the unions, who typically trumpet each dollar they collect from the members and pass on to the candidate, business interests prefer to keep their work largely invisible. A few have COPE-type committees—such as the American Medical Association's AMPAC (a reported $693,000 in 1970) or the National Association of Manufacturers' BIPAC ($539,000)—but most shun even that degree of publicity.

Some rough estimates are available. From extensive research into Democratic party contributions, reported in his *Fats Cats and Democrats*, Professor William Domhoff estimates that roughly half the party's money comes from corporate moneymen (55 percent). The rest comes from labor (20–25 percent), racketeers and gangsters (10–15 percent in some metropolitan areas), and Apple Pie Middle-class Americans (roughly 15 percent). Domhoff says that the Republicans' contributors (who typically outspend their Democratic counterparts by 6 to 4 or 7 to 3) are much more heavily weighted toward industrialists, bankers, and other moguls.[2] A final estimate comes from Senator Russell Long, who speaks from long experience on the receiving end. In a speech on the Senate floor in 1967, Long said, "Most campaign money comes from businessmen. Labor contributions have been greatly exaggerated. It would be my guess that about 95 percent of campaign funds at the congressional level are derived from businessmen. At least 80 percent of this comes from men who could sign a net worth statement exceeding a quarter of a million dollars." In a crucial last sentence, Long added, "Businessmen contribute because the Federal Corrupt Practices Act prohibits businesses from contributing." Like the unions, corporations find troublesome regulations standing between them and the politicians they want to buy. Dodging the rules takes two steps—getting "voluntary" contributions from employees through tactics reminiscent of the SIU, and finding ways to send the money to the right candidate.

Where seafaring men might use a goon squad, Texaco uses an interoffice memorandum. "We must as individual citizens support those candidates who understand and appreciate the validity of our position," intones a letter from Texaco's vice-president for public relations and personnel. It closes with a request that employees contribute $5 per month, or $60 for the entire year. Sterling Drug Inc., applying a means test, asks its 525 executives who earn more than $15,000 per year to give at least one-half of one percent of salary, up to ceiling of $200. "Specifically, we're asking for a *voluntary* contribution from you," the letter says, "for a political fund to be allocated to those legislators … whose… election is *important* to our industry and to *Sterling Drug Inc.*" (emphasis in original) The volunteer donor—eager to help his industry's patrons, and curious about the use of his money—might ask the company who the important legislators are. Upholding the best professional traditions of confidentiality, Sterling refuses to tell.

Other corporations, more considerate of their workers, may add "bonuses" to executive paychecks with the understanding that the money will be passed on to a candidate. Still others—like the Union Oil Company and the Cleveland-based defense firm Thompson-Ramos-Woolridge (TRW)—avoid the middleman by simply deducting an arranged amount for "campaign contributions" from the paychecks of cooperating employees. The Public Affairs Council, whose members include two hundred corporate titans, is so struck by the plan that it is working for the day when the nation's thousand biggest companies will all have automatic campaign funding.

A possible flaw in the project is a new federal campaign finance law, which went into effect on April 7, 1972. One of its clauses forbids government contractors to participate "directly or indirectly" in campaigns. The citizen organization Common Cause went to court against TRW, claiming that its deduction plan violates the law, since the company, not the employees, decides where the money will go.[3] It is not yet clear whether this is an "indirect" participation in campaigns—or how strictly "contractor" will be defined (since nearly all the biggest corporations have some government contracts). But for the moment the law is holding up wider use of automatic funding plans. Once the Justice Department clears the doubt with a legal ruling, the way may be open for the biggest round of political inflation yet.

Clever as these ploys may be, they do not begin to cover the range of deceptions available to the determined business contributor. Another effective ruse is to use a company lawyer as a broker: the company pays him "legal fees," which he then passes on to a grateful politician. More directly, a group can support its candidate by paying him an appropriate honorarium for a good speech (as can any other interest group, for that matter). In 1971, seventy-six senators reported speaking fees totaling $787,433. How much more was paid and received is unknown, since listing the amounts is voluntary. If the businessmen don't want to put up with a speech, their corporation may simply buy large blocs of tickets for $100- or $1,000-per-plate fundraising dinners, which no one but a few lobbyists need even attend.

Payments also come "in kind." Some companies keep men on the payroll to loan as campaign workers to deserving candidates. Others give special discounts on, or offer free, products ranging from air travel to hotel rooms to printing presses. Companies can donate computer time to a candidate, or take expensive surveys and give away the results. Boeing, recognizing a politician who had earned its support, did just that for Scoop Jackson during his doomed run for the presidency. A traditional means of hidden contributions to the national party occurs every four years, when companies buy ads at ludicrously inflated rates in the parties' convention programs.

The effect of these twisting and hidden paths is, as might be expected, to thoroughly deter attempts to find who's sending money to whom. Journalist Walter Pincus (now heading the Nader Congress Project's campaign finance investigations) discovered how tangled the threads could be when, in 1970, he tried to survey campaign reports from eight states and the District of Columbia. At the end of his labors, he had turned up undercover spending programs run by General Electric, U.S. Steel, Procter and Gamble, Union Carbide, and other corporations, totaling more than $1 million. But piecing together the evidence required a detective effort that would do credit to Scotland Yard. To track down one small item—a secret Union Carbide fund of at least $20,000—six researchers had to spend ten weeks looking through reports filed by individual candidates and cross-checking names of hundreds of contributors with lists of corporate executives. Small wonder that few members of the public know what industries are supporting which politicians.

The campaign disclosure laws have not been much help. The scripture of modern politics, the Federal Corrupt Practices Act of 1925, had deficiencies so obvious that Lyndon Johnson called it "more loophole than law." For a start, the law did not even apply to primaries—where so much of the spending goes on, particularly in one-party states. For everything after the primaries, Senate candidates were required to file spending reports with the secretary of the Senate, and House candidates with the clerk of the House. Just how seriously the law was taken is indicated by a few of the filed reports. In his 1968 reelection campaign in South Dakota, George McGovern's total expenditures were "none." The explanation is that the candidates must only report funds used with their "knowledge and consent." McGovern's executive assistant George Cunningham kept McGovern in blissful ignorance by being "very careful to make sure that Senator McGovern never sees the campaign receipts."

Another clause making for hilarity at the public's expense is the provision that all donors of $100 or more must list their names and addresses. Witty contributors get around this by making as many $99.99 donations as they want to various campaign committees working for the same candidate. The most important loophole in the 1925 law, however, was its provision that campaign committees would have to report their contributors only if the committee operated in two or more states. There was ample office space in the District of Columbia for thousands of campaign committees, and none of them had to report their activities. Along with the cherry trees, another rite of election-year springs in Washington has been the flowering of campaign committees for candidates all over the country. To choose two illustrations among the many offered in 1970: Congressman Thomas O'Neill of Massachusetts, august chairman of the House Special Subcommittee to Investigate Campaign Expenditures, demonstrated the need for such an investigation by setting up a dummy committee in the District of Columbia. Similarly, James Buckley took in $400,000 toward his New York Senate seat through a series of false-front D.C. committees. More receptive to the spirit of the law than many deadpan candidates, Buckley's staff invented names like "Committee to Keep a Cop on the Beat," "Neighbors for Neighborhood Schools," and "Town Meeting Preservation Society" for their groups. "We made a game of it," staffer David Jones said.

Figuring that even a good joke may get stale after forty-seven years, the public pressured Congress to enact a new law in February, 1972. The Federal Election Campaign Act will take much of the fun and suspense out of old-style campaigning. It extends coverage to financing of primaries, runoff and special elections, party caucuses, and nominating conventions. A candidate can no longer feign ignorance of funds spent by others on his behalf.

But Congress, determined to have the last laugh, relented at the last minute and left in a few amusing provisions. The least subtle of these was the "grace period"—the two-month delay between the bill's passage in February and the date when candidates would first have to report contributions. With a joyous, free-for-all spirit not seen since the Oklahoma Land Rush, candidates from all parties scrambled to pack their campaign chests before the April 7 deadline. Led by the president—whose chief fundraiser, Maurice Stans, openly exhorted businessmen to get their money in on time—many congressmen lost all inhibitions in their eagerness to make the most of the remaining time. The only barrier was fatigue: one lobbyist, hand presumably sore from reaching for his wallet, complained to Arizona Congressman Sam Steiger that he had to attend 162 fundraising parties between February 23 and April 7.

With such freewheeling times behind them, private interests still have to rely in the future on the bill's more restrained loopholes. One, a minor revision of the $99.99 clause, now says that only contributions of "more than" $100 must be reported. Another, which will probably turn out to be the secret contributor's bread and butter, is the evasion known as "earmarking." This means that a contributor sends money to a campaign committee, with instructions that an equal amount of money be passed on to his candidate. Since one committee, such as the Democratic Senatorial Committee, handles contributions for dozens of candidates at one time, the trails become blurred as the money passes through the committee. By making the contribution in two steps—donor to committee, committee to candidate—there is no way of knowing, from the outside, which of the funds coming in are linked to those going out.

The Public Affairs Council's director, Richard Armstrong, has prepared a brief lesson on earmarking for his corporate pupils. In a memo to officials of Humble Oil, GM, IBM, R. J. Reynolds, and others, he told of "another possible dodge.":

For years many corporate committees have contributed political funds through four campaign committees (Republican senatorial, Republican congressional, Democratic senatorial, and Democratic congressional). To some extent this has been a "smoke screen." Customarily, they will "trade checks" with you. (I.e., you want to give $500 to Congressman X's campaign. But you do not want to report it and do not want him to report it. Therefore, you make a contribution to the Congressional Campaign Committee of $500. The Campaign Committee makes out a check to Congressman X. They may even let you deliver it.) So, it may be possible for a political fund to file a report simply saying that it gave equal amounts to each of these four committees. On the surface, it would appear that the fund just wanted to help everyone. Actually, *every nickel could be directed to specific candidates.* [emphasis in original]

Like crooks lugging baskets of dirty money to be washed through legitimate business fronts, the corporations may cleanse their contributions in the purifying waters of the campaign committee. The overseers of this cleansing operation—the committee directors—have indicated that the role does not upset them. "If it isn't illegal, and it isn't," John t. Calkins, director of the Republican National Congressional Committee, told reporter James Polk, "I don't see how we can refuse to do it—swap checks with them."

As if such a sign were needed, Congress has given one further indication that it did not intend this new law to veer into the realm of seriousness. To enforce the tough new provisions, Congress avoided calling in any outside supervisors or creating a scrupulous watchdog agency. The guardians of the new law will instead be the same old crew that chuckled through the old law: the House clerk, the Senate secretary, and the Justice Department. The clerk and the secretary are both paid employees of Congress; over the years they have surprised absolutely no one by their reluctance to crack down on their masters. If, for unknown reasons, one of them begins to take his job too seriously, Congress can quickly right matters by removing all his staff. Ohio's Wayne Hays, chairman of the House Administration Committee, has already given House clerk W. Pat Jennings a taste of what to expect if he gets too nosy: Jennings asked for thirty-eight staff officials to administer the new law, but Hays gave him nineteen. (Hays took away the clerk's computerized equipment, and he forced a rise in the price the public must pay for copies of the politicians' reports, from ten cents per page to one dollar. Common Cause went to court and got an order reversing the price rise.) Neither Hays nor anyone else has figured out what to do about the clause allowing the public to look at the reports, but they take some comfort in knowing that the public is in a race with the clock. The reports are kept on file and publicly available for only one

election term—two years in the House—before they vanish.

There is, of course, a final member of the trio of enforcers: the U.S. Department of Justice. Those who have watched this crack organization at work against ITT and other corporate suspects will not be surprised by its performance in regulating campaign finance. For years, the law was openly and massively violated, yet Justice never acted. Then in 1968, newly elected house clerk W. Pat Jennings surprised everyone by sending over to Attorney General Ramsey Clark a list of violations from the 1968 campaign. Before the list got any further, Clark was out of office, replaced by President Nixon's new attorney general, John Mitchell. Mitchell, fresh from firsthand experience with campaign contributors during his year as Nixon's campaign manager, was fascinated by Jenning's list; he and his colleagues at Justice kept it so close that it seemed to have disappeared. Jennings, slow to get the message, sent other lists in 1969 and 1971—each time with the same result. One of the violators himself then tried to help out. A defeated candidate from Vermont's 1970 House election, Dennis Morrisseau, wrote to Mitchell that he was deliberately violating the law and asked to be prosecuted. The merciful Justice Department turned the other cheek.

The new 1972 law has received roughly similar treatment. One day after President Nixon signed it, Ralph Nader and his action group, Public Citizen, tried to sting Justice into action by filing a lawsuit demanding strict enforcement. Their complaint was accompanied by a ninety-two-page list of hundreds of unprosecuted campaign finance violations (for example, candidates who had waited to file until after the election, "thus defeating the purpose of pre-election disclosures," or who had failed to file reports at all).

The suit is still not decided, but the Justice approach appears to be. In June, 1972, Common Cause asked the clerk of the House to investigate ninety-one candidates from Alabama, Indiana, Ohio, Pennsylvania, and the District of Columbia who had ignored the reporting requirements of the new law. Shortly afterwards, Common Cause charged that more than two-thirds of California's 1972 congressional candidates had failed to file correct disclosures before the May primary. As of September, 1972, the Justice Department has never prosecuted a single candidate for breaking the campaign finance laws.

Wise shoppers

The special interest investors, who would not dream of pouring their money into dud stocks, are equally careful when it comes to choosing their legislative portfolio. A freshman legislator with a seat on a dull committee won't cost much, but won't yield much return, either. The logical result is the money goes to the men who rule Congress—the members of the key committees, the party leaders of each of the houses, and those aging powers who have stored up seniority, the committee chairmen. Following this guideline, the political arm of General Foods—the "North Street Good Government Group"—did not squander its money on Armed Services committee members. Instead, it aimed at three men whose influence on questions dear to General Foods equaled that of a hundred other congressmen combined: three powerful members of the House Agriculture Committee. The bankers' group, BankPAC, similarly excludes anyone not on committees which affect the industry.

For congressmen who happen to be in the key positions, this arrangement can ease many of life's problems. Congressman Wayne Aspinall, for example, must theoretically rely on his Colorado constituents to vote him into office again and again. But the money Aspinall uses for his campaigns comes mainly from private interests in other parts of the country. In 1970, for example, 79 percent of the $50,000 Aspinall reported that he spent came from outside his district. The reason is that Aspinall is chairman of the House Interior Committee, and, as such, one of the men who does most to

determine the profit rates in the mining, timber, and oil industries. Aware of this, Kennecott Copper sent Aspinall nine separate checks in 1970; Humble Oil mailed seven checks from Texas; and Shell Oil, Martin Marietta, and American Metal Climax and Oil Shale Corporation also chipped in. From Washington, D.C., help came from lobbyists and executives of Union Oil, Atlantic Richfield, Dow Chemical, Burlington Northern Railroad, and the Southern tobacco industry. The hewers of logs, whose hewing depends on regulations Aspinall passes, joined in as well: the Southwest Forest Industries of Phoenix and the Western Wood Products Association of Portland, Oregon, sent funds.

Given the shape of the corporate economy, the importance of government regulations in making rich men richer, and the vulnerability of politicians to financial persuasion, it takes little imagination to see how campaign contributions can influence the activity of Congress.

It used to be that corporations helped their candidates in return for an even larger slice of the government's pie; nowadays many big businessmen find they already have as much as they can decorously eat. Their main concern is to guarantee against shrinkage, and they view their campaign contributions as a kind of insurance policy. As a member of the Senate Finance Committee explained to the Atlantic's Elizabeth Drew, "By and large, the big contributions come from the privileged. They're not asking for any new privileges. Therefore, a man can say, 'Sure, I got a lot of money from the oil companies, but they never asked me for a thing.' That's because what they want is protection of the status quo. . . . By and large, Wall Street gives you money because you're against the war, or for health, but you think long and hard before being against capital gains or depreciation on real estate."

This benign approach may rapidly change if the businessmen see signs of impending danger. In 1955, for example, the Texas oil industry noted that congressional proposals to change the industry's tax subsidies had not been killed as quickly as usual. Anxious to set things right, the president of the Texas oil trade association told his fellows that "it seems only fair to tie a few strings to the contributions we make to political organizations and candidates." When, in 1958, the oil depletion tax loophole was up for its biennial round of criticism in Congress, a staff member of the Democratic senatorial campaign committee went to see some candidates from the Western states. "I was informed that if I could get some of these fellas out West to express their fealty to the golden principle of 27.5 percent [depletion allowance], there might be a pretty good piece of campaign change involved," he later told Ronnie Dugger of the *Texas Observer.*

In each case, the contributions would obviously have a purpose—to get those sympathetic to the oil lobby into Congress and to convince those already there to open their hearts to oil. But the bargain need not be stated that baldly. "Don't kid yourself about the 'no-strings attached' to a contribution," one congressional staffer with long experience in the wilderness of fund-raising has said. "There's always a string attached. It may not be a black string, but it's a string, and some day it's going to get pulled."

These invisible links may swell to chain-like dimensions when the contributions pull a candidate out of a predicament like the one Congressman Edward A. Garmatz of Maryland nearly succumbed to in 1966. As primary election time approached, polls showed him doing badly. Then, the Seafarers International Union appeared to rescue him. The $17,000 in publicly reported contributions from the SIU for Garmatz was the largest amount of money any lawmaker got from any reported source. Garmatz sailed through and then returned the favor. He was able to do so through his position as chairman of the Merchant Marine and Fisheries Committee, which doles out the subsidies to the shipping companies that hire the SIU. In 1968, 90 percent of Garmatz's funding came from shipping interests. In 1970, the industry raised a reported $37,000 for him, even though he was unopposed for reelection.

Men in Garmatz's position often point to the old chicken/egg questions: Do they do what they do because of the campaign contributions they received? Or do they receive the contributions because they do what they do? As one House staff aide noted, "There are some guys around here who honestly *believe* that industry is getting screwed by the consumers." When contributions make the difference between a career in Congress and another twenty years tending the small-town car dealership or law firm, the answer is that the distinction doesn't really matter. In 1970, six of the many candidates struggling for victory in the congressional primaries of North Carolina, Texas, and Pennsylvania found themselves blessed with contributions from the National Association of Manufacturers (through its political committee, BIPAC). All six went on to win. BIPAC relies on campaign gifts rather than direct lobbying, because, as its newsletter editor Edward Maher has put it, "if you get the right group down there, you don't have to lobby."

Even when their contributions are not likely to be decisive, contributors often spread money for good will with whoever ends up in office. The more cautious contributors go further and hedge their bets by sprinkling a little good will among all likely near-or-distant winners—provided, of course, that they are "reasonable on the issues" (in the words of one Union Carbide operative). Thus if Tweedledee and Tweedledum are running a close race, a little butter may be applied to both. Even though a congressman is not dominated by any one special interest, his donors expect that he will remember gratefully those who helped him along. After his brief campaign for the presidency had foundered, Ways and Means Committee Chairman Wilbur Mills was $91,000 in debt. In June, 1972, the heads of ten breweries sent contributions of $6,000. This could hardly "buy" Mills, but as Robert A. Schmidt, president of the Olympia Brewing Company, explained, "Being in the brewing industry, you have to play both sides of the street. If they don't know that you contribute, the next thing you know, you might get an extra tax you don't like."

If those good-will contributions succeed in buying nothing else, they inevitably buy that vague but crucial commodity, *access* to an elected official. "We're not trying to buy votes," says a money handler for the oil industry. "We're trying to buy an entrée to talk about our problems." The purchase is usually successful. Politicians make way on their appointment schedules for potential or past contributors. As one congressional aide explained, "I'd always tell the Old Man, 'You don't want to know where it [the money] comes from, but if I tell you to see a guy, you'd better damn well see him.'"

More than dramatic payoffs and scandals, it is this entrée that twists the direction of government policy. Reporter James Polk has described the "fraternal" atmosphere that springs from these cordial talks; politicians naturally begin to "understand" their patrons' problems better than they otherwise might. Few congressmen would admit that they can be "bought," but their protest is like that of a free-living woman who decides she might as well take money for what she enjoys, but insists she is not a prostitute. With their more sympathetic view, they can open up the range of government favors to private interests: subsidies, lucrative contracts, tax exemptions, toothless regulatory laws, restraints on overeager regulating agencies, protective tariffs, foreign policies to protect private investment, domestic policy that stimulates demand. Those who suffer when the favors are passed out—the taxpayers, the purchasers of overpriced goods—never get a chance to sit down with the politicians in the same chummy atmosphere.

The next time you buy a quart of milk, you might reflect on how the alliance of politicians and private interests can affect you. Early in 1971, the dairy industry was demanding that the government raise the guaranteed price it paid farmers for "manufactured milk"—raw milk used to make many dairy products. The increase they wanted would raise retail food prices by hundreds of millions of dollars, at a time when inflation was already rampant. It

would also, U.S. Department of Agriculture officials predicted, lead to serious milk surpluses piling up in government warehouses—an extra burden on an already strained federal budget.

Weighing these disadvantages, Secretary of Agriculture Clifford Hardin announced on March 12, 1972, that the price would not go up. Concern for the food budgets of hard-pressed families had apparently persuaded the administration to resist.

But not for long. Dairy representatives swung into action, and by March 25—less than two weeks later—the administration had caved in. Citing "new evidence," Secretary Hardin announced a 6 percent price boost, just what the milkmen had asked for. The cost of the decision to the American eater, who spends one out of every seven food dollars on dairy products, will be an estimated $500 million per year (one cent extra per quart, plus large increases in other dairy prices).

What did the milkmen have going for them that the housewife didn't? They've got a lot of pure homogenized Grade A cash, milked from the housewife in inflated prices. Like the shrewd John Archbold of Standard Oil, they invest their money wisely; by putting it into politics, they earn the legal right to bilk the housewife of more money, a small portion of which they can again invest in politics. The dairymen hit on the tactic several years earlier, when—as William A. Powell, president of Mid-America Dairymen, explained in a letter to one of his organization's members—they learned "that the sincere and soft voice of the dairy farmer is no match for the jingle of hard currencies put in the campaign funds of the politicians by the vegetable fat interests, labor, oil, steel, airlines, and others.

The obvious remedy was to make sure the farmers could match the other jingles with an ample jingle of their own. In their first two years of political fundraising, they put together a war chest of $1 million. More than $500,000 of this they sunk in the congressional elections of 1970. So, in their time of trouble one year later, they could turn to those they had helped. The list was formidable: starting with Speaker Carl Albert and working down through Congressmen W. R. Poage (chairman of the House Agriculture Committee) and Page Belcher (ranking Republican on the committee), key House members could look back on dairy donations. Even though Poage had no opposition for reelection, the dairymen spent $11,500 on a dinner for him and gave $500 apiece to him and Belcher. In the Senate, the dairy groups concentrated on Edmund Muskie, then a front-runner for the presidency, and Hubert Humphrey (member of the Agriculture Committee), Gale McGee (chairman of the Agricultural Appropriations subcommittee), and William Proxmire (the senator from lacteal Wisconsin, and a member of McGee's subcommittee).

The investment paid off. Within a week of Hardin's first announcement, the industry had drafted a bill that would have taken the price decision out of the Agriculture Department's hands by making an increase mandatory. In the House, 116 members—50 of whom had received dairy contributions—jumped on the milk wagon as cosponsors. There were 29 sponsors in the Senate, including consumer advocate Gaylord Nelson. Twelve of these senators had run in 1970—8 of them with dairy contributions.

But another dairy beneficiary, the Nixon administration, beat Congress in making the move. The clincher was the $255,000 the farmers sent to Nixon's election fund to help him make up his mind. Of this, $35,000 was a down payment, funneled into Republican campaign committees only days before Hardin announced the price rise. The rest was paid out in installments, stretching several months past "delivery." The first of these, a $45,000 installment, was paid on April 5, just four days after the new price went into effect.

What happened just before Hardin's turnabout announcement is revealing. The first big contribution was on March 22. It got quick results. The next day, President Nixon invited sixteen dairy and farm representatives to the White House. Their audience with the president—the ultimate in purchased political access—lasted nearly an hour, twice as long as scheduled. The meeting with the president was later described by William Powell, president of the Mid-America Dairymen, in a letter to one of his members:

We dairymen as a body can be a dominant group. On March 23, 1971, along with nine other dairy farmers, I sat in the Cabinet room of the White House, across the table from the President of the United States, and heard him compliment the dairymen on their marvelous work in consolidating and unifying our industry and our involvement in politics. He said, "You people are my friends and I appreciate it."

Two days later an order came from the U.S. Department of Agriculture increasing the support price of milk . . . which added from $500 million to $700 million to dairy farmers' milk checks. We dairymen cannot afford to overlook this kind of economic benefit. Whether we like it or not, this is the way the system works.

The only thing unusual about the dairy campaign was the publicity it received. Fresh off the farm, the dairymen at first made the mistake of filing a candid set of financial reports. An amazed Democratic campaign hand told Frank Wright of the *Minneapolis Tribune*, "My God, we've been doing that sort of thing for years, and we've never, never had it reported so publicly." The milkmen's efforts at concealment may have been a bit rough around the edges, but they had learned their basic lesson well: they paid their money and patiently waited for the dividends. The rest of us should think about changing the whole political marketplace.

NOTES

1. He weighed 350 pounds and kept in condition with meals like the following: one dozen oysters, pots of chicken gumbo, a terrapin stew, two ducks, six kinds of vegetables, a quart of coffee, and several cognacs.

2. A few candidates in each party also receive contributions from citizens', environmental, and peace groups. The amount of such contributions is small, however, and they are generally earned by those who have offended the large corporate givers by taking strong environmental stands, or are given to the opponents of incumbents with blatantly insensitive records on these issues.

3. In response, TRW dropped its plan temporarily and Common Cause dropped the suit. Another TRW fund, in which the employees get to designate where the money goes, was not challenged by Common Cause.

9 The courts

The basic questions this chapter will address are:

(1) What interests does the legal system serve?
(2) Can justice be obtained through the courts?
(3) Can justice be obtained by other means?
(4) Should there be a legal system?

Conservatives believe that the judicial system in America is both a legal structure and a political institution. The legal system is exemplified by the Supreme Court which decides cases and controversies arising between individuals, states, and the federal government, and also has the power to set national goals.[1] The Supreme Court, as conservatives view it, rules substantially in accord with the will of the majority, and only occasionally defends minority rights. This is the Court's correct role because democracy means majority rule.[2] The role of the Supreme Court is not to correct social abuses; these questions should be decided by individuals and local communities.

In general, conservatives maintain that the judicial system should confine itself to the business of deciding legal controversies. The Supreme Court should not attempt to correct all social inequities. It should act strictly in accord with the Constitution. Conservatives believe that the Supreme Court presently acts in accord with the President and Congress and that the basic purpose of the Court is to legitimate presidential decisions and Congressional legislation.

Liberals maintain that there are two problems in the legal system of the United States: (1) The system is set up to serve the rich and not the poor. Since judges are either selected by political parties or the President, or owe their position to the people in power, too often they act in the interest of these "sponsors." Most skilled lawyers work for the very wealthy. Even though a system now provides lawyers for people who cannot afford the going legal rates, these Legal Aid lawyers are overburdened and can seldom give the same attention and expertise to a case as can a lawyer in private practice. (2) The wrong people often become judges or lawyers.[3] Many individuals who are just interested in making money and have little social conscience enter the legal profession. They are seldom concerned with the ideals of the law, but rather use the law to serve their own financial interests.

The liberal solution to the defects of the judicial system is quite simple. Judges should be elected by the people rather than selected by politicians. Law schools should include social science and humanities courses in their curricula to enhance the social awareness of law students. Liberals accept the legal structure that exists in the United States. The defects which exist in the legal system can be easily corrected.

Socialists hold that the entire legal system works together with the rich and powerful to maintain the political system. The courts act for whites and against minority groups; for the rich against the poor; for management against workers. Socialists believe that law is used against the people. Belief in the law keeps people in line. Handling disputes within the judicial system prevents people from organizing into mass movements.

Socialists believe that minorities, women, workers, and the poor seldom receive justice through the court system.[4] People should not regard the court system as the only mechanism for redressing their grievances. Neither should the judicial system be ignored. Socialists want people to act both within and outside of the rules of the court structure to obtain justice. Within the structure legal tactics and strategems should be used to their fullest. Socialists have shown ingenuity in defending themselves by making the system work for rather than against them. Radical lawyers have developed successful and effective techniques to get their clients off conspiracy charges. Lawyers such as Leonard Boudin, Charles Garry, William Kunstler, Gerald Lefcourt, and Leonard Weinglass have caused major eruptions within the courtroom in order to make clear to juries that government prosecution of their clients is based on often spurious and exaggerated charges[5] and that their clients are victims of political repression. Juries are seen as the most potentially radical element in the judicial system; their selection has become a key process. Sociologist Jay Schulman, using techniques of survey research, gathers together a group of researchers in the community where the trial takes place. Together, they develop sociological patterns of the community to predict how people from different backgrounds will act in a courtroom. Through this research they aid lawyers in selecting juries that will be fair to their clients.[6] Public demonstrations, and seemingly flamboyant political actions should also be undertaken to make the courtroom an arena for raising larger issues. The actions of Bobby Seale and Abbie Hoffman during the Chicago Seven trial are examples of this strategy.[7]

Overall, socialists believe that the legal system is part of the corporate structure of American society. Working within the system, the structure, they feel, should be democratized. Juries should be made up of true peers. If a woman is on trial, the jury should be made up of women; if an ex-convict is on trial, the jury should be made up of ex-convicts.[8] The second part of socialist strategy is the destruction of the legal system as it presently exists. Legal knowledge must be simplified so that all people can comprehend the workings of the law. This way, anyone should have the opportunity to become a judge, a lawyer, or a public defender. If this is made possible, socialists contend that the creation of power for the few, by legalisms, will be demystified. The power can then be transferred to, and possibly exercised by, the people themselves in a manner that is truly democratic.

NOTES

1. The Supreme Court's decision in Brown v. Board of Education, 347 U.S. 483 (1954) is an example of a case where national goals were established. In deciding that schools

must be integrated in South Carolina, Virginia, Delaware, Kansas, and the District of Columbia, the Court declared that the Constitution, under the equal protection clause of the 14th Amendment, guaranteed equal protection for all students in the United States. Thus, a new national goal was established by the Supreme Court. "We have now announced," the Court said, "that [school] segregation is a denial of the equal protection of the laws."

2. This belief is based on the arguments put forward by James Madison in *Federalist Papers,* No. 10. His argument was that a Republican form of government, with its Representatives chosen by a majority of the population, could best preserve democracy. The Representatives would protect democratic rights and liberties because their "wisdom may best discern the true interest of their country, and whose patriotism and love of justice will be least likely to sacrifice it to temporary or partial considerations."

3. Liberals believe that the best example of a "good" judge is former Associate Supreme Court Justice Oliver Wendell Holmes who served on the Court from 1902–1932. He interpreted the Constitution in the interests of the nation, and reached decisions based on his deep social commitment. See, in particular, Felix Frankfurter (himself a former Associate Justice of the Supreme Court), *Mr. Justice Holmes and the Supreme Court.* Cambridge: Harvard Univ. Press, 1938. See also, Paul A. Freund, *The Supreme Court of the United States.* Cleveland: Meridian Books, 1965.

4. Students should be sure to read George Jackson, *Soledad Brother.* New York: Coward McCann Pub., 1970.

5. The *National Lawyers' Guild* is an organization of lawyers that encourages lawyers to be more radical in their approach to their profession. They are presently in the process of organizing a law school, that will aid them in effecting their ideas. They can be reached at 23 Cornelia Street, New York, New York. See also, Jonathan Black, ed., *Radical Lawyers: Their Role in the Movement and in the Courts.* New York: Avon Books, 1971.

6. At this writing Schulman's organization is aiding the lawyers defending inmates of Attica Correctional Facility in Attica, New York. These present, or former inmates, are accused by the government of murder for the role they played in the uprising there between Sept. 9–13, 1971. Schulman's organization can be reached at 70 West 95th St., New York, N.Y., 10024. For information on Attica see, "The Official Report of the New York State Special Commission on Attica," *Attica,* New York: Bantam Books, 1972.

7. Jason Epstein, *Great Conspiracy Trial.* New York: Random House, 1970.

8. See Nick DiSpoldo. "How To Be A Jailhouse Lawyer," *Win Magazine* (July 10, 1975), pp. 14–16.

*

Conservative

Robert A. Dahl. Decision-making in a democracy: the Supreme Court as a national policy-maker.

To consider the Supreme Court of the United States strictly as a legal institution is to underestimate its significance in the American political system. For it is also a political institution, an institution, that is to say, for arriving at decisions on controversial questions of national policy. As a political institution, the Court is highly unusual, not least because Americans are not quite willing to accept the fact that it *is* a political institution and not quite capable of denying it; so that frequently we take both positions at once. This is confusing to foreigners, amusing to logicians, and rewarding to ordinary Americans who thus manage to retain the best of both worlds.

I

A policy decision might be defined as an effective choice among alternatives about which there is, at least initially, some uncertainty. This uncertainty may arise because of inadequate information as to (a) the alternatives that are thought to be "open"; (b) the consequences that will probably ensue from choosing a given alternative; (c) the level of probability that these consequences will actually ensue; and (d) the relative value of the different alternatives, that is, an ordering of the alternatives from most preferable to least preferable, given the expected consequences and the expected probability of the consequences actually occurring. An *effective* choice is a selection of the most preferable alternative accompanied by measures to insure that the alternative selected will be acted upon.

No one, I imagine, will quarrel with the proposition that the Supreme Court, or indeed any court, must make and does make policy decisions in this sense. But such a proposition is not really useful to the question before us. What is critical is the extent to which a court can and does make policy decisions by going outside established "legal" criteria found in precedent, statute, and constitution. Now in this respect the Supreme Court occupies a most peculiar position, for it is an essential characteristic of the institution that from time to time its members decide cases where legal criteria are not in any realistic sense adequate to the task. A distinguished associate justice of the present Court has recently described the business of the Supreme Court in these words:

It is essentially accurate to say that the Court's preoccupation today is with the application of rather fundamental aspirations and what Judge Learned Hand calls "moods," embodied in provisions like the due process clauses, which were designed not to be precise and positive directions for rules of action. The judicial process in applying them involves a judgment. . . . that is, on the views of the direct representatives of the people in meeting the needs of society, on the views of Presidents and Governors, and by the construction of the will of legislatures the Court breathes life, feeble or strong, into the inert pages of the Constitution and the statute books.[1]

Very often, then, the cases before the Court involve alternatives about which there is severe disagreement in the society, as in the case of segregation or economic regulation; that is, the setting of the case is "political." Moreover, they are usually cases where competent students of constitutional law, including the learned justices of the Supreme Court themselves, disagree; where the words of the Constitution are general, vague, ambiguous, or not clearly applicable; where precedent may be found on both sides; and where experts differ in predicting the consequences of the various alternatives or the degree of probability that the possible consequences will actually ensue. Typically, in other words, although there may be considerable agreement as to the alternatives thought to be open [(a)], there is very serious disagreement as to questions of fact bearing on consequences and probabilities [(b) and (c)], and as to questions of value, or the way in which different alternatives are to be ordered according to criteria establishing relative preferability [(d)].

If the Court were assumed to be a "political" institution, no particular problems would arise, for it would be taken for granted that the members of the Court would resolve questions of fact and value by introducing assumptions derived from their own predispositions or those of influential clienteles and constituents. But, since much of the legitimacy of the Court's decisions rests upon the fiction that it is not a political institution but exclusively a legal one, to accept the Court as a political institution would solve one set of problems at the price of creating another. Nonetheless, if it is true that the nature of the cases arriving before the Court is sometimes of the kind I have described, then the Court cannot act strictly as a legal institution. It must, that is to say, choose among controversial alternatives of public policy by appealing to at least some criteria of acceptability on questions of fact and value that cannot be found in or deduced from precedent, statute, and Constitution. It is in this sense that the Court is a national policy-maker, and it is this role that gives rise to the problem of the Court's existence in a political system ordinarily held to be democratic.

Now I take it that except for differences in emphasis and presentation, what I have said so far is today widely accepted by almost all American political scientists and by most lawyers. To anyone who believes that the Court is not, in at least some of its activities, a policy-making institution, the discussion that follows may seem irrelevant. But to anyone who holds that at least one role of the Court is as a policy-making institution in cases where strictly legal criteria are inadequate, then a serious and much debated question arises, to wit: Who gets what and why? Or in less elegant language: What groups are benefited or handicapped by the Court and how does the allocation by the Court of these rewards and penalties fit into our presumably democratic political system?

II

In determining and appraising the role of the Court, two different and conflicting criteria are sometimes employed. These are the majority criterion and the criterion of Right or Justice.

Every policy dispute can be tested, at least in principle, by the majority criterion, because (again: in principle) the dispute can be analyzed according to the numbers of people for and against the various alternatives at issue, and therefore according to the proportions of the citizens or eligible members who are for and against the alternatives. Logically speaking, except for a trivial case, every conflict within a given society must be a dispute between a majority of those eligible to participate and a minority or minorities; or else it must be a dispute between or among minorities only.[2] Within certain limits, both possibilities are independent of the number of policy alternatives at issue, and since the argument is not significantly affected by the number of alternatives, it is convenient to assume that each policy dispute represents only two alternatives.[3]

If everyone prefers one of two alternatives, then no significant problem arises. But a case will hardly come before the Supreme Court unless at least one person prefers an alternative that is opposed by another person. Strictly speaking, then, no matter how the Court acts in determining the legality or constitutionality of one alternative or the other, the outcome of the Court's decision must either (1) accord with the preferences of a minority of citizens and run counter to the preferences of a majority; (2) accord with the preferences of a majority and run counter to the preferences of a minority; or (3) accord with the preferences of one minority and run counter to the preferences of another minority, the rest being indifferent.

In a democratic system with a more or less representative legislature, it is unnecessary to maintain a special court to secure the second class of outcomes. A case might be made out that the Court protects the rights of national majorities against local interests in federal questions, but so far as I am aware, the role of the Court as a policy-maker is not usually defended in this fashion; in what follows, therefore, I propose to pass over the ticklish question of federalism and deal only with "national" majorities and minorities. The third kind of outcome, although relevant according to other criteria, is hardly relevant to the majority criterion, and may also be passed over for the moment.

One influential view of the Court, however, is that it stands in some special way as a protection of minorities against tyranny by majorities. In the course of its 167 years, in seventy-eight cases, the Court has struck down eighty-six different provisions of federal law as unconstitutional,[4] and by interpretation it has modified a good many more. It might be argued, then, that in all or in a very large number of these cases the Court was, in fact, defending the rights of some minority against a "tyrannical" majority. There are, however, some exceedingly serious difficulties with this interpretation of the Court's activities.

III

One problem, which is essentially ideological in character, is the difficulty of reconciling such an interpretation with the existence of a democratic polity, for it is not at all difficult to show by appeals to authorities as various and imposing as Aristotle, Locke, Rousseau, Jefferson, and Lincoln that the term democracy means, among other things, that the power to rule resides in popular majorities and their representatives. Moreover, from entirely reasonable and traditional definitions of popular sovereignty and political equality, the principle of majority rule can be shown to follow by logical necessity.[5] Thus to affirm that the Court supports minority preferences against majorities is to deny that popular sovereignty and political equality, at least in the traditional sense, exist in the United States; and to affirm that the Court ought to act in this way is to deny that popular sovereignty and

political equality *ought* to prevail in this country. In a country that glories in its democratic tradition, this is not a happy state of affairs for the Court's defenders; and it is no wonder that a great deal of effort has gone into the enterprise of proving that, even if the Court consistently defends minorities against majorities, nonetheless it is a thoroughly "democratic" institution. But no amount of tampering with democratic theory can conceal the fact that a system in which the policy preferences of minorities prevail over majorities is at odds with the traditional criteria for distinguishing a democracy from other political systems.[6]

Fortunately, however, we do not need to traverse this well-worn ground; for the view of the Court as a protector of the liberties of minorities against the tyranny of majorities is beset with other difficulties that are not so much ideological as matters of fact and logic. If one wishes to be at all rigorous about the question, it is probably impossible to demonstrate that any particular Court decisions have or have not been at odds with the preferences of a "national majority." It is clear that unless one makes *some* assumptions as to the kind of evidence one will require for the existence of a set of minority and majority preferences in the general population, the view under consideration is incapable of being proved at all. In any strict sense, no adequate evidence exists, for scientific opinion polls are of relatively recent origin, and national elections are little more than an indication of the first preferences of a number of citizens—in the United States the number ranges between about forty and sixty per cent of the adult population—for certain candidates for public office. I do not mean to say that there is no relation between preferences among candidates and preferences among alternative public policies, but the connection is a highly tenuous one, and on the basis of an election it is almost never possible to adduce whether a majority does or does not support one of two or more policy alternatives about which members of the political elite are divided. For the greater part of the Court's history, then, there is simply no way of establishing with any high degree of confidence whether a given alternative was or was not supported by a majority or a minority of adults or even of voters.

In the absence of relatively direct information, we are thrown back on indirect tests. The eighty-six provisions of federal law that have been declared unconstitutional were, of course, initially passed by majorities of those voting in the Senate and in the House. They also had the president's formal approval. We could, therefore, speak of a majority of those voting in the House and Senate, together with the president, as a "lawmaking majority." It is not easy to determine whether any such constellation of forces within the political elites actually coincides with the preferences of a majority of American adults or even with the preferences of a majority of that half of the adult population which, on the average, votes in congressional elections. Such evidence as we have from opinion polls suggests that Congress is not markedly out of line with public opinion, or at any rate with such public opinion as there is after one discards the answers of people who fall into the category, often large, labelled "no response" or "don't know." If we may, on these somewhat uncertain grounds, take a "lawmaking majority" as equivalent to a "national majority," then it is possible to test the hypothesis that the Supreme Court is shield and buckler for minorities against national majorities.

Under any reasonable assumptions about the nature of the political process, it would appear to be somewhat naive to assume that the Supreme Court either would or could play the role of Galahad. Over the whole history of the Court, on the average one new justice has been appointed every twenty-two months. Thus a president can expect to appoint about two new justices during one term of office; and if this were not enough to tip the balance on a normally divided Court, he is almost certain to succeed in two terms. Thus, Hoover had three appointments; Roosevelt, nine; Truman, four; and Eisenhower, so far, has had four. Presidents are not famous for appointing justices hostile to their own views

on public policy nor could they expect to secure confirmation of a man whose stance on key questions was flagrantly at odds with that of the dominant majority in the Senate. Justices are typically men who, prior to appointment, have engaged in public life and have committed themselves publicly on the great questions of the day. As Mr. Justice Frankfurter has recently reminded us, a surprisingly large proportion of the justices, particularly of the great justices who have left their stamp upon the decisions of the Court, have had little or no prior judicial experience.[7] Nor have the justices—certainly not the great justices—been timid men with a passion for anonymity. Indeed, it is not too much to say that if justices were appointed primarily for their "judicial" qualities without regard to their basic attitudes on fundamental questions of public policy, the Court could not play the influential role in the American political system that it does in reality play.

The fact is, then, that the policy views dominant on the Court are never for long out of line with the policy views dominant among the lawmaking majorities of the United States. Consequently it would be most unrealistic to suppose that the Court would, for more than a few years at most, stand against any major alternatives sought by a lawmaking majority. The judicial agonies of the New Deal will, of course, quickly come to mind; but Mr. Roosevelt's difficulties with the Court were truly exceptional. Generalizing over the whole history of the Court, the chances are about one out of five that a President will make one appointment to the Court in less than a year, better than one out of two that he will make one within two years, and three out of four that he will make one within three years. Mr. Roosevelt had unusually bad luck: he had to wait four years for his first appointment; the odds against this long an interval are four to one. With average luck, the battle with the Court would never have occurred; even as it was, although the "court-packing" proposal did formally fail, by the end of his second term Mr. Roosevelt had appointed five new justices and by 1941 Mr. Justice Roberts was the only remaining holdover from the Hoover era.

Table 1 The interval between appointments to the Supreme Court

Interval in years	Per cent of total appointments	Cumulative per cent
Less than 1	21	21
1	34	55
2	18	73
3	9	82
4	8	90
5	7	97
6	2	99
—	—	—
12	1	100
Total	100	100

Note: The table excludes the six appointments made in 1789. Except for the four most recent appointments, it is based on data in the Encyclopedia of American History 461–62 (Morris ed., 1953). It may be slightly inaccurate because the source shows only the year of appointment, not the month. The twelve-year interval was from 1811 to 1823.

It is to be expected, then, that the Court is least likely to be successful in blocking a determined and persistent lawmaking majority on a major policy and most likely to succeed against a "weak" majority; e.g., a dead one, a transient one, a fragile one, or one weakly united upon a policy of subordinate importance.

IV

An examination of the cases in which the Court has held federal legislation unconstitutional confirms, on the whole, our expectations. Over the whole history of the Court, about half the decisions have been rendered more than four years after the legislation was passed.

Of the twenty-four laws held unconstitutional within two years, eleven were measures enacted in the early years of the New Deal. Indeed, New Deal measures comprise nearly a third of all the legislation that has ever been declared unconstitutional within four years after enactment.

It is illuminating to examine the cases where the Court has acted on legislation within four years after enactment—where the presumption is, that is to say, that the lawmaking majority is not necessarily a dead one. Of the twelve New Deal cases, two were, from a policy point of view, trivial; and two, although perhaps not trivial, were of minor importance to the New Deal program.[8] A fifth[9] involved the NRA, which was to expire within three weeks of the decision. Insofar as the unconstitutional provisions allowed "codes of fair competition" to be established by industrial groups, it is fair to say that President Roosevelt and his advisers were relieved by the Court's decision of a policy they had come to find increasingly embarrassing. In view of the tenacity with which Mr. Roosevelt held to his major program, there can hardly be any doubt that had he wanted to pursue the major policy objective involved in the NRA codes, as he did, for example, with the labor provisions, he would not have been stopped by the Court's special theory of the Constitution. As to the seven other cases,[10] it is entirely correct to say, I think, that whatever some of the eminent justices might have thought during their fleeting moments of glory, they did not succeed in interposing a barrier to the achievement of the objectives of the legislation; and in a few years most of

Table 2 Percentage of cases held unconstitutional arranged by time intervals between legislation and decision

	New Deal legislation	Other	All legislation
Number of years	%	%	%
2 or less	92	19	30
3– 4	8	19	18
5– 8	0	28	24
9–12	0	13	11
13–16	0	8	6
17–20	0	1	1
21 or more	0	12	10
Total	100	100	100

Table 3   Cases holding legislation unconstitutional within four years after enactment

Interval in years	New Deal No.	%	Other No.	%	Total No.	%
2 or less	11	29	13	34	24	63
3 to 4	1	3	13	34	14	37
Total	12	32	26	68	38	100

the constitutional interpretation on which the decisions rested had been unceremoniously swept under the rug.

The remainder of the thirty-eight cases where the Court has declared legislation unconstitutional within four years of enactment tend to fall into two rather distinct groups: those involving legislation that could reasonably be regarded as important *from the point of view of the lawmaking majority* and those involving minor legislation. Although the one category merges into the other, so that some legislation must be classified rather arbitrarily, probably there will be little disagreement with classifying the specific legislative provisions involved in eleven cases as essentially minor from the point of view of the lawmaking majority (however important they may have been as constitutional interpretations).[11] The specific legislative provisions involved in the remaining fifteen cases are by no means of uniform importance, but with one or two possible exceptions it seems reasonable to classify them as major policy issues from the point of view of the lawmaking majority.[12] We would expect that cases involving major legislative policy would be propelled to the Court much more rapidly than cases involving minor policy, and, as the table below shows, this is in fact what happens.

Table 4   Number of cases involving legislative policy other than those arising under New Deal legislation holding legislation unconstitutional within four years after enactment

Interval in years	Major policy	Minor policy	Total
2 or less	11	2	13
3 to 4	4	9	13
Total	15	11	26

Thus a lawmaking majority with major policy objectives in mind usually has an opportunity to seek for ways of overcoming the Court's veto. It is an interesting and highly significant fact that Congress and the president do generally succeed in overcoming a hostile Court on major policy issues.

Table 5   Type of Congressional action following Supreme Court decisions holding legislation unconstitutional within four years after enactment (other than New Deal legislation)

Congressional action	Major policy	Minor policy	Total
Reverses Court's policy	10[a]	2[d]	12
Changes own policy	2[b]	0	2
None	0	8[e]	8
Unclear	3[c]	1[f]	4
Total	15	11	26

Note: For the cases in each category, see footnote 13.

It is particularly instructive to examine the cases involving major policy. In two cases involving punitive legislation enacted by Radical Republican Congresses against supporters of the Confederacy during the Civil War, the Court faced a rapidly crumbling majority whose death knell as an effective national force was sounded with the election of 1876.[14] Three cases are difficult to classify and I have labelled them "unclear." Of these, two were decisions made in 1921 involving a 1919 amendment to the Lever Act to control prices.[15] The legislation was important, and the provision in question was clearly struck down, but the Lever Act terminated three days after the decision and Congress did not return to the subject of price control until World War II, when it experienced no constitutional difficulties arising from these cases (which were primarily concerned with the lack of an ascertainable standard of guilt). The third case in this category successfully eliminated stock dividends from the scope of the Sixteenth Amendment, although a year later Congress enacted legislation taxing the actual income from such stock.[16]

The remaining ten cases were ultimately followed by a reversal of the actual policy results of the Court's action, although not necessarily of the specific constitutional interpretation. In four cases,[17] the policy consequences of the Court's decision were overcome in less than a year. The other six required a long struggle. Workmen's compensation for longshoremen and harbor workers was invalidated by the Court in 1920;[18] in 1922 Congress passed a new law which was, in its turn, knocked down by the Court in 1924;[19] in 1927 Congress passed a third law, which was finally upheld in 1932.[20] The notorious income tax cases[21] of 1895 were first somewhat narrowed by the Court itself,[22] the Sixteenth Amendment was recommended by President Taft in 1909 and was ratified in 1913, some eighteen years after the Court's decisions. The two child labor cases represent the most effective battle ever waged by the Court against legislative policy-makers. The original legislation outlawing child labor, based on the commerce clause, was passed in 1916 as a part of Wilson's New Freedom. Like Roosevelt later, Wilson was somewhat unlucky in his Supreme Court appointments; he made only three appointments during his eight years, and one of these was wasted, from a policy point of view, on McReynolds. Had McReynolds voted "right," the subsequent struggle over the problem of child labor need not have occurred, for the decision in 1918 was by a Court divided five to four, McReynolds voting with the majority.[23] Congress moved at once to circumvent the decision by means of the tax power, but in 1922 the Court blocked that approach.[24] In 1924 Congress returned to the engagement with a constitutional amendment that was rapidly endorsed by a number of state legislatures before it began to meet so much resistance in the states remaining that the enterprise miscarried. In 1938, under a second reformist president, new legislation was passed, twenty-two years after the first; this a chastened Court

accepted in 1941,[25] and thereby brought to an end a battle that had lasted a full quarter-century.

The entire record of the duel between the Court and the lawmaking majority, in cases where the Court has held legislation unconstitutional within four years after enactment, is summarized in Table 6.

Table 6 Type of Congressional action after Supreme Court decisions holding legislation unconstitutional within four years after enactment (including New Deal legislation)

Congressional action	Major policy	Minor policy	Total
Reverses Court's policy	17	2	19
None	0	12	12
Other	6*	1	7
Total	23	15	38

*In addition to the actions in Table 5 under "Changes Own Policy" and "Unclear," this figure includes the NRA legislation affected by the *Schechter Poultry* case.

Thus the application of the majority criterion seems to show the following: First, if the Court did in fact uphold minorities against national majorities, as both its supporters and critics often seem to believe, it would be an extremely anomalous institution from a democratic point of view. Second, the elaborate "democratic" rationalizations of the Court's defenders and the hostitility of its "democratic" critics are largely irrelevant, for lawmaking majorities generally have had their way. Third, although the Court seems never to have succeeded in holding out indefinitely, in a very small number of important cases it has delayed the application of policy up to as much as twenty-five years.

V

How can we appraise decisions of the third kind just mentioned? Earlier I referred to the criterion of Right or Justice as a norm sometimes invoked to describe the role of the Court. In accordance with this norm, it might be argued that the most important policy function of the Court is to protect rights that are in some sense basic or fundamental. Thus (the argument might run) in a country where basic rights are, on the whole, respected, one should not expect more than a small number of cases where the Court has had to plant itself firmly against a lawmaking majority. But majorities may, on rare occasions, become "tyrannical"; and when they do, the Court intervenes; and although the constitutional issue may, strictly speaking, be technically open, the Constitution assumes an underlying fundamental body of rights and liberties which the Court guarantees by its decisions.

Here again, however, even without examining the actual cases, it would appear, on political grounds, somewhat unrealistic to suppose that a Court whose members are recruited in the fashion of Supreme Court justices would long hold to norms of Right or Justice substantially at odds with the rest of the political elite. Moreover, in an earlier day it was perhaps easier to believe that certain rights are so natural and self-evident that their fundamental validity is as much a matter of definite knowledge, at least to all reasonable creatures, as the color of a ripe apple. To say that this view is unlikely to find many articulate defenders today is, of course, not to disprove it; it is rather to suggest that we do not need to elaborate the case against it in this essay.

In any event the best rebuttal to the view of the Court suggested above will be found in the record of the Court's decisions. Surely the six cases referred to a moment ago, where the policy consequences of the Court's decisions were overcome only after long battles, will not appeal to many contemporary minds as evidence for the proposition under examination. A natural right to employ child labor in mills and mines? To be free of income taxes by the federal government? To employ longshoremen and harbor workers without the protection of workmen's compensation? The Court itself did not rely upon such arguments in these cases, and it would be no credit to their opinions to reconstruct them along such lines.

So far, however, our evidence has been drawn from cases in which the Court has held legislation unconstitutional within four years after enactment. What of the other forty cases? Do we have evidence in these that the Court has protected fundamental or natural rights and liberties against the dead hand of some past tyranny by the lawmakers? The evidence is not impressive. In the entire history of the Court there is not one case arising under the First Amendment in which the Court has held federal legislation unconstitutional. If we turn from these fundamental liberties of religion, speech, press and assembly, we do find a handful of cases—something less than ten—arising under Amendments Four to Seven in which the Court has declared acts unconstitutional that might properly be regarded as involving rather basic liberties.[26] An inspection of these cases leaves the impression that, in all of them, the lawmakers and the Court were not very far apart; moreover, it is doubtful that the fundamental conditions of liberty in this country have been altered by more than a hair's breadth as a result of these decisions. However, let us give the Court its due; it is little enough.

Over against these decisions we must put the fifteen or so cases in which the Court used the protections of the Fifth, Thirteenth, Fourteenth and Fifteenth Admendments to preserve the rights and liberties of a relatively privileged group at the expense of the rights and liberties of a submerged group: chiefly slaveholders at the expense of slaves,[27] white people at the expense of colored people,[28] and property holders at the expense of wage earners and other groups.[29] These cases, unlike the relatively innocuous ones of the preceding set, all involved liberties of genuinely fundamental importance, where an opposite policy would have meant thoroughly basic shifts in the distribution of rights, liberties, and opportunities in the United States—where, moreover, the policies sustained by the Court's action have since been repudiated in every civilized nation of the Western world, including our own. Yet, if our earlier argument is correct, it is futile—precisely because the basic distribution of privilege *was* at issue— to suppose that the Court could have possibly acted much differently in these areas of policy from the way in which it did in fact act.

VI

Thus the role of the Court as a policy-making institution is not simple; and it is an error to suppose that its functions can be either described or appraised by means of simple concepts drawn from democratic or moral theory. It is possible, nonetheless, to derive a few general conclusions about the Court's role as a policy-making institution.

National politics in the United States, as in other stable democracies, is dominated by relatively cohesive alliances that endure for long periods of time. One recalls the Jeffersonian alliance, the Jacksonian, the extraordinarily long-lived Republican dominance of the post-Civil War years, and the New Deal alliance shaped by Franklin Roosevelt. Each is marked by a break with past policies, a period of intense struggle, followed by consolidation, and finally decay and disintegration of the alliance.

Except for short-lived transitional periods when the old alliance is disintegrating and the new one is struggling to take control of political institutions, the Supreme Court is inevitably a part of the dominant national alliance. As an element in the political leadership of the dominant alliance, the Court of course supports the major policies of the alliance. By itself, the Court is almost powerless to affect the course of national policy. In the absence of substantial agreement within the alliance, an attempt by the Court to make national policy is likely to lead to disaster, as the Dred Scott decision and the early New Deal cases demonstrate. Conceivably, the cases of the last three decades involving the freedom of Negroes, culminating in the now famous decision on school integration, are exceptions to this generalization; I shall have more to say about them in a moment.

The Supreme Court is not, however, simply an agent of the alliance. It is an essential part of the political leadership and possesses some bases of power of its own,

the most important of which is the unique legitimacy attributed to its interpretations of the Constitution. This legitimacy the Court jeopardizes if it flagrantly opposes the major policies of the dominant alliance; such a course of action, as we have seen, is one in which the Court will not normally be tempted to engage.

It follows that within the somewhat narrow limits set by the basic policy goals of the dominant alliance, the Court can make national policy. Its discretion, then, is not unlike that of a powerful committee chairman in Congress who cannot, generally speaking, nullify the basic policies substantially agreed on by the rest of the dominant leadership, but who can, within these limits, often determine important questions of timing, effectiveness, and subordinate policy. Thus the Court is least effective against a current lawmaking majority—and evidently least inclined to act. It is most effective when it sets the bounds of policy for officials, agencies, state governments or even regions, a task that has come to occupy a very large part of the Court's business.[30]

Few of the Court's policy decisions can be interpreted sensibly in terms of a "majority" versus a "minority." In this respect the Court is no different from the rest of the political leadership. Generally speaking, policy at the national level is the outcome of conflict, bargaining, and agreement among minorities; the process is neither minority rule nor majority rule but what might better be called minorities rule, where one aggregation of minorities achieves policies opposed by another aggregation.

The main objective of presidential leadership is to build a stable and dominant aggregation of minorities with a high probability of winning the presidency and one or both houses of Congress. The main task of the Court is to confer legitimacy on the fundamental policies of the successful coalition. There are times when the coalition is unstable with respect to certain key policies; at very great risk to its legitimacy powers, the Court can intervene in such cases and may even succeed in establishing policy.

Probably in such cases it can succeed only if its action conforms to and reinforces a widespread set of explicit or implicit norms held by the political leadership; norms which are not strong enough or are not distributed in such a way as to insure the existence of an effective lawmaking majority but are, nonetheless, sufficiently powerful to prevent any successful attack on the legitimacy powers of the Court. This is probably the explanation for the relatively successful work of the Court in enlarging the freedom of Negroes to vote during the past three decades and in its famous school integration decisions.[31]

Yet the Court is more than this. Considered as a political system, democracy is a set of basic procedures for arriving at decisions. The operation of these procedures presupposes the existence of certain rights, obligations, liberties and restraints; in short, certain patterns of behavior. The existence of these patterns of behavior in turn presupposes widespread agreement (particularly among the politically active and influential segments of the population) on the validity and propriety of the behavior. Although its record is by no means lacking in serious blemishes, at its best the Court operates to confer legitimacy, not simply on the particular and parochial policies of the dominant political alliance, but upon the basic patterns of behavior required for the operation of a democracy.

NOTES

1. Frankfurter, The Supreme Court in the Mirror of Justices, 105 U. of Pa. L. Rev. 781, 793 (1957).

2. Provided that the total membership of the society is an even number, it is technically possible for a dispute to occur that divides the membership into two equal parts, neither of which can be said to be either a majority or minority of the total membership. But even in the instances where the number of members is even (which should occur on the average only half the time), the probability of an exactly even split, in any group of more than a few thousand people, is so small that it may be ignored.

3. Suppose the number of citizens, or members eligible to participate in collective decisions, is n. Let each member indicate his "most preferred alternative." Then it is obvious that the maximum number of most preferred alternatives is n. It is equally obvious that if the number of most preferred alternatives is more than or equal to $n/2$, then no majority is possible. But for all practical purposes those formal limitations can be ignored, for we are dealing with a large society where the number of alternatives at issue before the Supreme Court is invariably quite small. If the number of alternatives is greater than two, it is theoretically possible for preferences to be distributed so that no outcome is consistent with the majority criterion, even where all members can rank all the alternatives and where there is perfect information as to their preferences; but this difficulty does not bear on the subsequent discussion, and it is disregarded. For an examination of this problem, consult Arrow, Social Choice and Individual Values (1951).

4. Actually, the matter is somewhat ambiguous. There appear to have been seventy-eight cases in which the Court has held provisions of federal law unconstitutional. Sixty-four different acts in the technical sense have been construed, and eighty-six different provisions in law have been in some respects invalidated. I rely here on the figures and the table given in Library of Congress, Legislative Reference Service, Provisions of Federal Law Held Unconstitutional by the Supreme Court of the United States 95, 141–47 (1936), to which I have added United States v. Lovett, 328 U.S. 303 (1946), and United States ex rel. Toth v. Quarles, 350 U.S. 11 (1955). There are some minor discrepancies in totals (not attributable to the differences in publication dates) between this volume and Acts of Congress Held Unconstitutional in Whole or in Part by the Supreme Court of the United States, in Library of Congress, Legislative Reference Service, The Constitution of the United States of America, Analysis and Interpretation (Corwin ed., 1953). The difference is a result of classification. The latter document lists seventy-three acts held unconstitutional (to which Toth v. Quarles, supra, should be added) but different sections of the same act are sometimes counted separately.

5. Dahl, A Preface to Democratic Theory, c. 2 (1956).

6. Compare Commager, Majority Rule and Minority Rights (1943).

7. Frankfurter, op. cit. supra note 1, at 782–84.

8. Booth v. United States, 291 U.S. 339 (1934), involved a reduction in the pay of retired judges. Lynch v. United States, 292 U.S. 571 (1934), repealed laws granting to veterans rights to yearly renewable term insurance; there were only twenty-nine policies outstanding in 1932. Hopkins Federal Savings & Loan Ass'n v. Cleary, 296 U.S. 315 (1935), granted permission to state building and loan associations to convert to federal ones on a vote of fifty-one per cent or more of votes cast at a legal meeting. Ashton v. Cameron County Water Improvement District,

298 U.S. 513 (1936), permitting municipalities to petition federal courts for bankruptcy proceedings.

9. Schechter Poultry Corp. v. United States, 295 U.S. 495 (1935).

10. United States v. Butler, 297 U.S. 1 (1936); Perry v. United States, 294 U.S. 330 (1935); Panama Refining Co. v. Ryan, 293 U.S. 388 (1935); Railroad Retirement Board v. Alton R. Co., 295 U.S. 330 (1935); Louisville Joint Stock Land Bank v. Radford, 295 U.S. 555 (1935); Rickert Rice Mills v. Fontenot, 297 U.S. 110 (1936); Carter v. Carter Coal Co., 298 U.S. 238 (1936).

11. United States v. Dewitt, 9 Wall. (U.S.) 41 (1870); Gordon v. United States, 2 Wall. (U.S.) 561 (1865); Monongahela Navigation Co. v. United States, 148 U.S. 312 (1893); Wong Wing v. United States, 163 U.S. 228 (1896); Fairbank v. United States, 181 U.S. 283 (1901); Rassmussen v. United States, 197 U.S. 516 (1905); Muskrat v. United States, 219 U.S. 346 (1911); Choate v. Trapp, 224 U.S. 665 (1912); Evans v. Gore, 253 U.S. 245 (1920); Untermyer v. Anderson, 276 U.S. 440 (1928); United States v. Lovett, 328 U.S. 303 (1946). Note that although the specific legislative provisions held unconstitutional may have been minor, the basic legislation may have been of major policy importance.

12. Ex parte Garland, 4 Wall. (U.S.) 333 (1867); United States v. Klein, 13 Wall. (U.S.) 128 (1872); Pollock v. Farmers' Loan & Trust Co., 157 U.S. 429 (1895), rehearing granted 158 U.S. 601 (1895); Employers' Liability Cases, 207 U.S. 463 (1908); Keller v. United States, 213 U.S. 138 (1909); Hammer v. Dagenhart, 247 U.S. 251 (1918); Eisner v. Macomber, 252 U.S. 189 (1920); Knickerbocker Ice Co. v. Stewart, 253 U.S. 149 (1920); United States v. Cohen Grocery Co., 255 U.S. 81 (1921); Weeds, Inc. V. United States, 255 U.S. 109 (1921); Bailey v. Drexel Furniture Co., 259 U.S. 20 (1922); Hill v. Wallace, 259 U.S. 44 (1922); Washington v. Dawson & Co., 264 U.S. 219 (1924); Trusler v. Crooks, 269 U.S. 475 (1926).

13a. Pollock v. Farmers' Loan & Trust Co., 157 U.S.429 (1895); Employers' Liability Cases, 207 U.S. 463 (1908); Keller v. United States, 213 U.S. 138 (1909); Hammer v. Dagenhart, 247 U.S. 251 (1918); Bailey v. Drexel Furniture Co., 259 U.S. 20 (1922); Trusler v. Crooks, 269 U.S. 475 (1926); Hill v. Wallace, 259 U.S. 44 (1922); Knickerbocker Ice Co. v. Stewart, 253 U.S. 149 (1920); Washington v. Dawson & Co., 264 U.S. 219 (1924).

b. Ex parte Garland, 4 Wall. (U.S.) 333 (1867); United States v. Klein, 13 Wall. (U.S.) 128 (1872).

c. United States v. Cohen Grocery Co., 255 U.S. 81 (1921); Weeds, Inc. v. United States, 255 U.S. 109 (1921); Eisner v. Macomber, 252 U.S. 189 (1920).

d. Gordon v. United States, 2 Wall. (U.S.) 561 (1865); Evans v. Gore, 253 U.S. 245 (1920).

e. United States v. Dewitt, 9 Wall. (U.S.) 41 (1870); Monongahela Navigation Co. v. United States, 148 U.S. 312 (1893); Wong Wing v. United States, 163 U.S. 228 (1896); Fairbank v. United States, 181 U.S. 283 (1901); Rassmussen v. United States, 197 U.S. 516 (1905); Muskrat v. United States, 219 U.S. 346 (1911); Choate v. Trapp, 224 U.S. 665 (1912); United States v. Lovett, 328 U.S. 303 (1946).

f. Untermyer v. Anderson, 276 U.S. 440 (1928).

14. Ex parte Garland, 4 Wall. (U.S.) 333 (1867); United States v. Klein, 13 Wall. (U.S.) 128 (1872).

15. United States v. Cohen Grocery Co., 255 U.S. 81 (1921); Weeds, Inc. v. United States, 255 U.S. 109 (1921).

16. Eisner v. Macomber, 252 U.S. 189 (1920).

17. Employers' Liability Cases, 207 U.S. 463 (1908); Keller v. United States, 213 U.S. 138 (1909); Trusler v. Crooks, 269 U.S. 475 (1926); Hill v. Wallace, 259 U.S. 44 (1922).

18. Knickerbocker Ice Co. v. Stewart, 253 U.S. 149 (1920).

19. Washington v. Dawson & Co., 264 U.S. 219 (1924).

20. Crowell v. Benson, 285 U.S. 22 (1932).

21. Pollock v. Farmers' Loan & Trust Co., 157 U.S. 429 (1895).

22. Nicol v. Ames, 173 U.S. 509 (1899); Knowlton v. Moore, 178 U.S. 41 (1900); Patton v. Brady, 184 U.S. 608 (1902); Flint v. Stone Tracy Co., 220 U.S. 107 (1911).

23. Hammer v. Dagenhart, 247 U.S. 251 (1918).

24. Bailey v. Drexel Furniture Co., 259 U.S. 20 (1922).

25. United States v. Darby, 312 U.S. 100 (1941).

26. The candidates for this category would appear to be Boyd v. United States, 116 U.S. 616 (1886); Rassmussen v. United States, 197 U.S. 516 (1905); Wong Wing v. United States, 163 U.S. 228 (1896); United States v. Moreland, 258 U.S. 433 (1922); Kirby v. United States, 174 U.S. 47 (1899); United States v. Cohen Grocery Co., 255 U.S. 81 (1921); Weeds, Inc. v. United States, 255 U.S. 109 (1921); Justices of the Supreme Court v. United States ex rel. Murray, 9 Wall. (U.S.) 274 (1870); United States ex rel. Toth v. Quarles, 350 U.S. 11 (1955).

27. Dred Scott v. Sandford, 19 How. (U.S.) 393 (1857).

28. United States V. Reese, 92 U.S. 214 (1876); United States v. Harris, 106 U.S. 629 (1883); United States v. Stanley (Civil Rights Cases), 109 U.S. 3 (1883); Baldwin v. Franks, 120 U.S. 678

(1887); James v. Bowman, 190 U.S. 127 (1903); Hodges v. United States, 203 U.S. 1 (1906); Butts v. Merchants & Miners Transportation Co., 230 U.S. 126 (1913).

29. Monongahela Navigation Co. v. United States, 148 U.S. 312 (1893); Adair v. United States, 208 U.S. 161 (1908); Adkins v. Children's Hospital, 261 U.S. 525 (1923); Nichols v. Coolidge, 274 U.S. 531 (1927); Untermyer v. Anderson, 276 U.S. 440 (1928); Heiner v. Donnan, 285 U.S. 312 (1932); Louisville Joint Stock Land Bank v. Radford, 295 U.S. 555 (1935).

30. "Constitutional law and cases with constitutional undertones are of course still very important, with almost one-fourth of the cases in which written opinions were filed [in the two most recent terms] involving such questions. Review of administrative action . . . constitutes the largest category of the Court's work, comprising one-third of the total cases decided on the merits. The remaining . . . categories of litigation . . . all involve largely public law questions." Frankfurter, op. cit. supra note 1, at 793.

31. Rice v. Elmore, 165 F.2d 387 (C.A. 4th, 1947), cert. denied 333 U.S. 875 (1948); United States v. Classic, 313 U.S. 299 (1941); Smith v. Allwright, 321 U.S. 649 (1944); Grovey v. Townsend, 295 U.S. 45 (1935); Brown v. Board of Education, 347 U.S. 483 (1954); Bolling v. Sharpe, 347 U.S. 497 (1954).

Liberal

Richard Tench. Whose side are the lawyers on?

The Holmes legacy

What ever happened to Oliver Wendell Holmes, Jr.? Literally he is dead, of course. He was dead in that sense before I first knew that he still lived on in his cultural contributions, those creative acts that make a man everlasting in a practical way, not in the way we pray for immortality in our churches. For him, practical immortality took the form of pieces he added to the mosaic that we recognize as man's organized common sense, and that we call constitutional law. His literal dying was but an event, perhaps no more than an occasion for other men to renew their faith in the part of him that lives beyond death.

If you happen to have forgotten Holmes's cultural contributions, you are at least in good company. Constitutional lawyers have too, men specifically charged with remembering them. However, what is worse for those lawyers is that they have forcibly displaced those concepts of law that Holmes once erected as a foundation for a constantly growing civility. So that today, when American law is so thoroughly represented by our own native versions of what the Russians call "Apparatchiks" and the Germans "Gauleiters," an active exercise of will is needed to jog the memory about Holmes's life and contributions.

Holmes, then, was a United States Supreme Court Justice. He was appointed to that Court by Theodore Roosevelt, who later came to wish that he had never heard of Holmes, since, like all Roosevelts, Theodore had a very personal view of the presidency, and Holmes had a most catholic attitude towards the law. Even when Holmes was appointed, there were old senators who complained, with no apparent sense of irony, that he was too old for the job, the same old senators who subsequently opposed Justice Brandeis because he was too Jewish. Hypocrisy masquerades; the higher the setting, the more outlandish the costumes. Actually, those old senators knew that Brandeis, like Holmes, would interpret the Constitution too "liberally." They were right. He did. They were right too that Holmes when appointed had almost reached the retirement age set by corporations, universities, and virtually every segment of society except the United States Congress.

Yet Holmes sat on the Supreme Court for more than thirty years, with such intellectual virility that along with Brandeis and Pound he fathered the sociological view of constitutional law. Their brainchild was not named "sociological" until much later, and is still not recognized publicly for what it is by Supreme Court justices, bar associations that recommend them, presidents who appoint them, senators who confirm them, and most teachers of constitutional law, not excepting those at Holmes's alma mater, Harvard, where he once lectured on the common law. Today such worthies still often talk like old senators, dividing Court justices into two categories: those who interpret the Constitution "strictly," and those who interpret it "liberally." Yet a smart school boy reviewing the record knows that "strict constructionists" have always been guardians of what is, veritable hydras of the status quo, whereas "liberal constructionists" in varying degrees have always been "sociological," determining what is currently constitutional by Holmes's own test: the felt necessities of our times.

The Court itself has been most often on the side of the smart school boy when it has discussed constitutionality, however much it may act differently on its cases. Justices at various times have admitted that precedents established by earlier cases—or *stare decisis* for those who insist on Latin—have no part in consitutional law other than in the area of broad basic principles, which is where continuity of the law comes in (and is the only place where it should). Previous court decisions, which are everything in civil and criminal law, are so much fluff so far as the Constitution is concerned. The whole matter was boiled down by Chief Justice Hughes, who, in effect, declared: "The Constitution says what the Supreme Court says it says when it says it."

Law for the black man

Law regarding the education of the black child in America tells the Court's sociological story well. When state school segregation was presented as a *fait accompli* to the Supreme Court, the majority, over the dissent of Justice Harlan, adopted the theory of the aptly christened Slaughter House Cases to conclude that states could segregate their schools on color lines so long as black and white schools were equal, which they never were and still are not. Eighty years later, without a pertinent word of the Constitution changing, the Warren Court concluded that segregating school children by race is inhuman. Then, as though ignorant of the innumerable methods by which constitutional decisions are ignored without punishment for con-

tempt of court, Warren's decision gave states an indefinite period in which to desegregate schools.

Words in the Constitution need not change for the Court to change its mind. Justices, as someone said, read the newspapers too. In fact, it was the pressure of politics that induced the *volte-face* in the Supreme Court. Now, many years later, increasing political pressure is forcing states to obey the Court's latest decision rather than its first one. Two questions then arise: why does political pressure work on the Supreme Court, a nonelected autocracy, and not on an elected Congress? And why do people still refer to these divergent judicial opinions, one humane, the other inhumane, as simply different interpretations of a written document, blithely content with their nonsociological, nonpolitical view of the Supreme Court?

Holmes was an acceptable hero in my day at the Law School of the University of Florida, though that institution was racist to its bell tower and parochial beyond belief. I was not aware of that then. Racism was not for us at issue. Ours was a legal generation never taught that racial injustices existed, and we were so immersed in the conveniences of injustices that we never noticed them. Our teaching impressed upon us that it was better to hang a man whose lawyer had improperly pled the common law rules than to bend the rules to save his life, for to do so would destroy the continuity of the law exactly where, I see now, it required scrutiny, and it should have been destroyed.

Holmes was acceptable at the University of Florida because he was what we call today "an establishmentarian liberal." He believed that American democracy was more human and workable than any other type of government, and that its faults could be corrected by the diligent efforts of good men and good education. But looking back through the waters of aging eyes and the prisms time cuts for reflection, I see now that in the mid-thirties in all of Gainesville, Florida, including the university, the only man I knew comparable to Holmes was the mailman, Lonnie Brown. We called him "colored" then, and it was he who taught me that there was a racial problem, as Holmes might have done. As a result I committed two daring acts. First I embarrassed him by shaking his hand in front of my fellow students rocking on the front porch of our boarding house, all of whom fancied themselves Johnny Rebs. And then later, at his invitation, I stole into the Quarters for Sunday night dinner at his house. We spoke of his children then attending Florida's colored university, the Agricultural and Mechanical College, in connection with the racial problem I had just discovered. By the time we had lit our pipes we decided that good black and white people like us (I am not sure we didn't say "good black and white men") would one day break the color bar. Without knowing it, we were part of the Holmes legacy.

As Justice Holmes would be thought "establishmentarian" today, so Lonnie Brown would be an "Uncle Tom." But such expressions are too easy, too self-serving, too unwitting. Holmes could turn the establishment on its head at times. What lawyer putting Holmes down with such a label would have said as he did, that he did not think the Union would end if power for reviewing congressional legislation were withdrawn from the Supreme Court, but that it might end if the Court could not review legislation by the states?

The prime virtue of a written constitution is that it delineates the limits of a government's power over its people. In the American Constitution the Fourteenth Amendment was added to set limits on state power as they were hammered out by Lee and Grant at Appomattox. Any layman priding himself on his ability to understand the written word in the context of history should read the first section of the Fourteenth Amendment to determine for himself whether or not it says that no state may discriminate against a citizen of the United States. Even a cursory reading of history reveals that that at least is what the Civil War was all about, and that a whole people would have had to be insane to endure such terrible trials of blood and agony only to ratify a constitutional amendment meant to leave the positions of citizens and states just where they were before. But that is exactly

what a bare majority of the Supreme Court said the American people people did. In the Slaughter House Cases five years after that amendment was ratified, the Court simply said there is no such thing as a citizen of the United States except in exclusively federal instances—that is, when he is abroad, being drafted, flying over state lines, or when Congress wants to punish, rather than help him.

The Slaughter House Cases established states' rights so firmly that former black slaves were turned into freed zombies. Corporations, furthermore, were made into legal persons, so free of federal restraints that they could buy whole states simply by buying a few legislators. And, finally, the cases laid the groundwork for the Confederacy to take over Congress. Using Southern fried courtesy where rebellion had failed, Southern congressmen contrived a set of internal Senate and House rules with no more constitutional standing than the rule against spitting in congressional corridors. (There are spittoons, by the way, on chamber floors.) Legislation was bound up in a Gordian congressional committee system, and that system was tied tightly to the continued reelection of white supremacists, which guaranteed Southern committee chairmen who were selected by seniority.

In view of such shenanigans, it is little wonder that hardly anybody has ever heard of the second section of the Fourteenth Amendment, which provides that whenever a state disenfranchises any of its population, Congress may reduce that state's seats in the House of Representatives proportionately. Through decades in which blacks were denied a vote, this constitutional provision was never mentioned by liberal or conservative Congresses alike. "Congress," as the eminent Constitutionalist Professor Corwin put it, "has never taken the second section of the Fourteenth seriously."

Law, politics, sociology

Congressional antics such as these were long considered "political" by the Supreme Court, and thus outside its province, freed from judicial attacks by anyone. Gerrymandering, for example, the process by which political power groups can draw voting lines in a state in order to concentrate power in areas they control, was also at one time declared beyond the Court's jurisdiction. Ultimately the Court changed its mind, and states were ordered to redistrict so that the vote of each citizen has approximately equal weight.

For the Supreme Court may even alter its course about the limits of its own power. This is quite logical, as a matter of fact, since by a simple five-to-four vote the Court could decide for itself that it never had the power of judicial review to start with. After all, there is nothing in the Constitution about judicial review; the Court's power in this respect derives largely from a linguistic interpretation made long ago by Chief Justice Marshall. Limits of the Court are set only by judicial restraint. It is a bit surprising, therefore, that we have not heard more than we have in the past that our Supreme Court is indeed acting unconstitutionally whenever it decides for the nation the constitutionality of lower courts' decisions.

One of the Court's self-imposed restraints that has turned into a veritable bonanza for those who buy legislators is its refusal to examine the motives of legislators to ascertain what they mean by the legislation they vote. Courts in general do not hesitate to look into a man's motives to determine his intent to commit murder or to knock down contracts fraudulently. Motives, one might think, are the key to what a man does, and his words often no more than a façade. But with this kind of peddler's world, or Freudian world, where hidden motives lie behind language, the Supreme Court has nothing to do; its region is the pure one of words themselves. Too often it refuses to move into the language of laws beyond the committee room discussions that led up to them, when the motivational words that really count are actually bandied about by legislators in the cloakroom.

If, therefore, you are a legislator and you want to keep the poor from drinking whiskey for whatever reason, the procedure is clear.

You don't pass a bill with words forthrightly saying that the poor cannot drink while the rich can, since that would violate the Supreme Court's ruling about equal protection of the laws. What you do instead is to pass legislation taxing whiskey beyond the reach of the poor, declaring meanwhile to everyone who has ears, including the Court, that the whiskey tax is for revenue. Or, if you are a bureaucrat and don't like someone, you harass him with picayune violations of fire and zoning codes, indiscriminate arrests, expensive administrative law suits that you know you will win. In either example, whether one enacts laws or executes them, the letter, not the motive, is what will count as judicial decisions are made.

If, then, the Supreme Court is to be kept in the business of constitutional law under Holmes's kind of sociological definition, why not appoint sociologists to the Court instead of lawyers? Probably the best answer is: for the same reason that we should never have appointed lawyers. Nothing in present law prohibits the appointment of sociologists, any more than cannon law requires that Popes be priests, though, paradoxically, most states demand that lowly justices of the peace be lawyers. No, the better reason is probably that sociologists, like lawyers, are themselves too compartmentalized by their discipline to comprehend the broadest, most humane, nay even sociological implications of the law.

Experts of all sorts are more often than not captives of their own expertise, which is why they perform best as advisors or practitioners, to be trusted until they fail. Historically, experts have been notoriously fatal as policy makers, as was Jean Jacques Rousseau, as were the "Crisis Managers" of President Kennedy. So, while it might perhaps be useful to have expert judges on evidence, expert county agents on agricultural questions, expert sociologists on the matter of segregating black and white children in our schools, and so on, the law, as Holmes knew, needs more than narrowness.

Lawyers, unfortunately, are educated in the techniques of the law, not its majesty.

Majesty is reserved for the few like Holmes, Brandeis, and Pound, who spent existential lives plumbing what was once known as "the natural law," or what Holmes himself referred to as "the study of man's experience." The result of such plumbing is a product of wisdom, not of law schools or sociology departments. Certainly sociologists are not precluded necessarily from wisdom, nor from bringing to their specialized field their own personal flair. Nor are today's lawyers. Merely because I know of no such lawyers in several states does not mean that there are not one or two in each. I know for sure, however, that to put any legal technician on the Supreme Court is to send a mechanic to do the job of an architect, or a clinical psychologist where the need is for a political philosopher.

A lawyer's milieu, the Nuremburg example

What really puts the cat amongst the pigeons is that the lawyer's education, including his apprenticeship, is more "mal" than "ill" because it trains him away from constitutionalism. Were that not so, lawyers in the last few decades would have been able to incorporate the decisions of the Nuremburg trials into man's organized common sense, as Justice Jackson would have had them do. He was then on leave from the Supreme Court as America's jurist representative at Nuremberg.

Taken at face value, the Nuremburg decisions switched the parties of international law from nation states to individual persons, contiguously declaring the institutional person "unconstitutional." Nuremburg replaced a man's state or institutional domination with his personal experience; he was judged by the expression of his subjective, individual conscience within the realm of the objective conscience of mankind. It was this latter effect that makes it jejune to compare the conscience of a conscientious objector with that of Tojo.

When the Nuremburg trials were first mooted, Senator Taft (with me agreeing from a graduate school level) argued that they were revenge posturing as justice. Taft stressed the *ex post facto* nature of the trials; crimes were defined in 1946 for acts committed before then. He added that, in any event, by international law no man can be held responsible for acting under orders from his state, which could legally execute him if he disobeyed. But the Nuremburg court interpreted the law differently. It said that each defendant German general had committed crimes against nature, of which his conscience made him aware and for which his personal responsibility could not be institutionalized away.

Yet inside America when the Nuremburg decisions have been raised as bases of defense for young men refusing compulsory military service, such bases have always been brushed aside by federal judges who maintained that Nuremburg has no bearing on purely internal law, and no standing against subsequent U.S. Statutes or variegated treaties. Which is exactly the bearing that the Nuremburg court said they did have.

May we absolve the lawyer for not seeing the broad sunlit uplands of Nuremburg inasmuch as he does not see the fallow fields of injustice at home? Or is the query pertinent? The lawyer himself may be but a servant of oracular law. Law may, therefore, be the complete amoral profession. When he has passed the bar, the lawyer takes an oath that makes him an officer of the court, tying him singly (and collectively through his bar association) to the nation's court hierarchy. Yet his court association may raise the question of his obligations without providing any full answer. Like the German general, the lawyer's profitable and privileged position in society and his daily practice of his profession make it impossible for him to be unaware of injustices under the law. Here, anyway, the dogma that ignorance of the law is no defense makes sense; while everybody else must sometimes plead ignorance of the law because of sheer human limitations, the lawyer cannot honestly do so. His trade is law. Manipulating people is his life and his humor. It seems utterly unlikely that those who sup so well at the Law's table should say that the origin of the feast is beyond their ken.

A lawyer's knowledge, in fact, spreads widely. He knows, for example, that over the years commerce and competition have removed the need for lawyers in vast areas—the law of wills, property transfers, divorce, industrial death and injury compensation, debt collecting (including garnishment), and so on. Yet legislation demands that lawyers continue to preempt such fields at preposterous fees. Indeed, were it not for lawyers, a good deal of the law of property could be moved from courts to public and private agencies, with more justice more speedily rendered at less cost. With one fell swoop the problem of overcrowded courtrooms could be solved. Lawyers' motives in fighting such changes stand out like braille when one looks at their opposition to no-fault insurance, which in such states as Massachusetts has emptied the courts of those contests between perjurers called damage suits, and has reduced insurance costs as much as twenty-seven percent. No-fault insurance simply provides that in automobile accidents each insuror pay the damages of his own insured, thus stopping court haggling over who is at fault. The funniest lawyer's argument against no-fault insurance is that it ignores the first law of nature—that people will drive more recklessly if they are not held to fault for accidents that cost their insurance companies money. Besides being funny, this is also a prime instance of a lawyer's principled stance: for him, much too often, a typical legal argument is one that is above all self-serving.

The rest of us may blame our mal-education upon educational bureaucrats over whom we have no control and with whom we have no personal contact. Lawyers have only themselves to blame. Legislatures have given them almost complete autonomy over both their own education and practice in the law. Bar associations accredit new schools, set the bias of teaching in them, decide which of their graduates get to practice. Arguments that bar examinations decide impartially falter on two points: first, the basic illogicality of such examinations as a requirement for law practice; and, second, the statistics on black admissions to the bar, which echo much too accurately statistics on abysmally low black memberships in construction and other tight unions. However much the conscience of the law practitioner may rankle, bar associations still require membership as a prerequisite to practice. The practice sets its own ethics, and what is more says which lawyers will be prosecuted for violations of its ethical code and which will not. Presidents and governors accept the association as a chief advisor in selections of appointments to the judiciary. Hardly mute testimony as to the association's impact on presidential court selections may be read in the deadly list of racist federal judges and attorneys general appointed even by President Kennedy.

Equality under the law

In Lincoln's time the Supreme Court held that when the courts are closed the Federal government may reopen them by means of martial law. For all the effect that decision has had, the Court might just as well have been speaking about the ease with which court room doors swing on their hinges. For a court to be opened effectively there must exist inside a climate of justice in which each person entering is possessed of the same tools as everyone else. The most essential tool, of course, is an adequate lawyer, for no matter what the Constitution says about equal protection of the laws, in practice the law is equal only for all men with socially equal, equally competent lawyers. That puts the burden of who is entitled to a lawyer upon the individual conscience of the lawyers, which is where it does not belong. A proper lawyer at the proper time is one of those procedural rights without which the substance of freedom is as empty as a Fourth of July speech. The Warren Court at last stated this specifically in its later cases involving police interrogation. In courts, procedures often stand as large as the constitutional law with which they are concerned, and since both means and ends are inextricable, so in the law both must be promulgated to the fullest measure.

This anomaly between theoretical and actual rights persists in the very linchpin of freedom, freedom of speech and press. In practice this has worked out so that the corporations own the presses, the transmitters, the statellites, the education and training of audiences. The individual citizen, meanwhile, owns a megaphone. In theory both citizens and corporations have freedom of speech and press, the citizen as if shouting through his megaphone to an empty field, they transmitting to every attentive eye and ear in the land. Legally all the citizens can do is shout louder and louder.

Where we are

I am not suggesting that lawyers are more wicked than anyone else. Competition in wickedness these days is too stiff. It is simply that knowledge of the law carries with it the burden and the knack of bending law without breaking it. And lawyers seldom make their bends in the right direction. Granting that with the same knowledge and conditioning other people would do likewise, one nevertheless wishes that the profession would stop visualizing itself in the mantle of Holmes, whose wisdom and plain human decency make laymen of most of today's lawyers. Natural intelligence does not even distinguish our lawyers today, if Dean Prosser of California's law school at Berkeley was correct when he told a Western Conference of Law Schools a few years back: ''We don't get the brains any more.''

Law schools today might get the brains if they recognized that the carrot of incentive for many prospective law students is not money, or that the law has possibilities of new horizons, new interpretations within the walls of legal academia. The current word today is ''relevancy.'' The law is only relevant at the justice-of-the-peace level, say the small, new breed of young lawyers intent on propounding the philosophy that the ideal is also the practical. It always was, although in my law school days and those thereafter lawyers have been told that ideals did not buy hamburgers, or memberships in the

best country clubs for that matter, and were in fact deviant ghosts to be buried with other pubescent fantasies. What we learned at the University of Florida in the thirties, and what continued to be the bias of all law schools well into the sixties, is that the law is only relevant at the corporate level. What is clear to many of the best young minds now looking at the profession is that corporate law is utterly irrelevant to them and to our society.

Yet, where we see encouraging signs in one direction, discouragement lies in another. It is, of course, amusing to read of a poll indicating that some huge percentage of our populace, upon hearing transcripts of the First and Fifth Amendments to the Constitution, believe that what they hear is Communist propaganda. Why this is amusing is something to ponder, since our schools are principally responsible. Can the schools be taking the Constitution seriously when from Clearwater, Florida, to Siletz, Oregon, we see schools compelling children to recite school prayers and flag salutes that the Supreme Court has declared unconstitutional? Such ''edcuation'' must be one of the better ways to undermine the legal structure of our culture, but it does instruct us in the pragmatic truth that custom is often more powerful than law, whether for or against organized common sense.

Coming back to an adult level, we see that the great mass of lawyers never seems to allow their pronouncements about the Constitution on the Fourth of July to seep unduly into what they do the other 364 days of the year. Bench and bar in every state will be found lined up solidly behind John C. Calhoun's doctrine of interposition, the theory Calhoun invented to interpose the sovereignty of the state between its people and the sovereign power of the Union. Legally, Calhoun's doctrine was never more than a rebel yell, but spiritually it lives in the hearts and actions of lawyers and the people they serve. It is a double-standard, two-tiered law—that for them and that for us, them being the privileged and us being the underprivileged.

Some cracks in the cloisters of the privileged may last and may even widen.

The Jehovah's Witnesses began the cracking with constitutional actions in the courts against the public's repression of an irregular and despised religion. Their work led to cases brought by the National Association for the Advancement of Colored People to permit an unpopular race the use of public schools and public places. Now these organizational actions have expanded into class actions for amorphous groups like consumers, and those with common political causes that are *démarché* from the rigor of party politics. In these we see beginnings of direct cooperation of the people in situations that somehow must be determined by themselves. The indivdual, meanwhile, is finding a personal candor essential, so that he lives more existentially the life style he preaches, as opposed to the conflicting say-do style of his parents.

Private and communal activities, sometimes rescuing participatory government from its mere rhetoric, are finding it more and more necessary to excuse lawyers of my generation from the further conduct of their affairs. Still, we old-timers may go happy and well fed to the grave, humming: "Oh, what a tangled web we weave, When first we practice to deceive!" The new breed, being lawyers, should always be viewed with caution. We can only hope that they practice law with the same idealism and relevance that they brought with them into their legal studies, and that their help increases in the search Holmes began for a growing civility.

Socialist

Robert Lefcourt. Law against the people.

To the person who waits all day to pay a traffic fine, the young man who spends a few months in jail for possessing marijuana, the woman who finds no remedy in court for an exorbitant rent hike, the Black who still cries for implementation of "civil rights" legislation, and the student who resists serving in an illegal war, the judicial process appears to worsen pressing problems rather than solve them.

It is not only that the legal apparatus is time-consuming and expensive; that unjust laws remain unchanged; that the Supreme Court has long refused to consider such "political" questions as the continuing wars in Southeast Asia and the exclusion of non-whites, young and poor people from most juries; and that the legal system has failed to meet the expectations of certain segments of society. The legal system is bankrupt, and cannot resolve the contradictions which, like air pollution, have grown visibly more threatening to society but whose resolution still is not given high priority.[1]

This bankruptcy is clearest in the priorities of law enforcement and in the criminal courts. Criminal courts protect existing economic, political, and social relations. Historically this role has created a pattern of selective law enforcement practices of which the white upper and middle classes are the beneficiaries. Bail requirements and plea bargaining victimize propertyless defendants who are, in effect, prejudged. The roles of the judge, the prosecuting attorney, and even the defense lawyer for the poor and near-poor reinforce the bias, because they are geared only to the efficient administration of overcrowded, understaffed, and dehumanized court bureaucracies. The proposed solutions of many court officials concentrate on material rather than human problems—automating court procedures, expanding facilities, allocating more funds. But the crisis in the legal system is more fundamental and cannot be cured by technical reform: it lies in the class-based and racist character of social relationships and in the court structures which maintain these relationships.

Who does the law protect?

"Jail the Real Criminals"
—A poster seen at various demonstrations in the 1960s

The myth of "equality under law" would have us believe that everyone is subject to society's laws and those who violate the laws are subject to prosecution. Yet in criminal courts across the country it can be easily observed that law enforcement affects almost exclusively the working-man and the poor, and, in recent years, the political activist. In the big cities nonwhites predominate in regular court appearances. The other criminals, the extremely wealthy, the corporations, the landlords, and the middle class white-collar workers are rarely prosecuted and almost never suffer the criminal court process as defendants.

It is impossible to enforce all laws against all lawbreakers. One survey by the President's Crime Commission reports that ninety-one percent of all Americans have violated laws that could subject them to a term in prison.[2] Choices are made as to which laws will be enforced against which people, and law enforcement officials necessarily use guidelines to make these choices.

One of the most important guiding principles behind law enforcement decisions can be inferred from the Crime Commission report. On the one hand it is stated that

Each single crime is a response to a specific situation by a person with an infinitely complicated psychological makeup who is subject to infinitely complicated external pressures. Crime as a whole is millions of such responses.[3]

Accordingly, a corporate executive who arranges to fix prices for the sale of his company's milk product is just as much a "criminal" as a man who steals food from a vegetable market. On the other hand, it is argued that the individual perpetrator of a crime must be seen in the context of his or her environment.

...crime flourishes, and has always flourished, in city slums; those neighborhoods where overcrowding, economic deprivation, social disruption, and racial discrimination are endemic.[4]

.... so long as the social conditions that produce poverty remain, no reforms in the criminal process will eliminate the imbalance.... The poor are arrested more often, convicted more frequently, sentenced more harshly, rehabilitated less successfully than the rest of society.[5]

Despite the fact that "individual responsibility" is the stated basis of our criminal law enforcement, just as "social conditions" explain the why of selected law enforcement, it is still the individual's economic and social class and the color of his skin that determine his relationship to the legal system.

Just as power in a capitalist society is not concentrated in the capitalist as an individual, the law's protection of the middle and upper classes is not exercised directly by individuals. The enforcement of criminal sanctions is dictated by the necessities of the economic and political system in which the profit motive is central. For example, it is not surprising that no law prevents industrial managers from laying off thousands of workers, or from moving plants to new locations in order to maximize profits. The people whose lives and communities may be shattered have no recourse in the legal system. No law requires institutions which control and profit from the materials and means of production to share their wealth equally among the people who produce it and need it. Despite the lip service, it is not a priority of any elected official to urge a district attorney's office to arrest the property owners and corporate managers who violate air and water pollution laws, antitrust laws, housing codes, and the health and safety laws of the drug and auto industries. The pollution, sickness, and death resulting from such illegalities have had little effect on law enforcement agencies; in fact, the corporate class exercises such control over Congress and law enforcement agencies that there are few statistics documenting abuses. The public continues to drink polluted water, breathe poisoned air, and ride unsafe automobiles.

The protection of lesser economic interests, such as those of the middle class, serves to camouflage the abuses of those higher up the ladder. The broker who sells phony stocks, the builder who deliberately uses defective materials, the dairy company executive who fixes prices, the embezzler and the tax evader are the white collar criminals. As the Crime Commission report states, ''These criminals are only rarely dealt with through the full force of criminal sanctions.''[6] Through a multitude of regulatory statutes, the law regulates the food and drug and other industries; but the law is not enforced. ''The crucial fact is that these laws are violated on a vast scale, sometimes in deliberate disregard of the law, sometimes because businessmen, in their effort to come as close to the line between legality and illegality as possible, overstep it.''[7]

Avoiding taxes is the common practice for many middle class business people. Of the more than forty billion dollars collected on personal income each year, eighty-six percent comes from people in the lower brackets. These figures reflect not only the vast scale of tax evasion, but the fact that the tax law rewards a capitalist's skillful shuffling of paper. Inheritance stipends and stock dividends are subject in practice to fewer taxes than the $10,000 or less in salary earned by carpenters or secretaries.[8]

Middle class ''interest groups'' also are favored in law enforcement practice. White New York City high school teachers are employed in a school system that is mostly nonwhite. Teachers who closed down schools in January 1969 were not arrested, although they clearly broke the law against strikes by public employees; but a headline the next month announced a legal crackdown on students who protested the conditions in those same schools. While the anti-strike law is aimed at crushing worker demands, it will not be used against white, or for Black, interests. In the teachers' strike, the law defended a white middle class constituency against Blacks who were making inroads in the white-controlled school system.

White racism is rarely prosecuted, especially when property interests are involved. For example, real estate interests continue to profit from the age-old practice of ''blockbusting'' (although the courts may soon be forced to face the problem). This is a tactic used by speculators involving the sale of one or two homes in a white neighborhood to Blacks to persuade the remaining white home owners to leave the neighborhood, selling at low prices. The realtors then resell the homes to middle class Blacks at high prices. In spite of Supreme Court rulings upholding the civil rights of Blacks, the law has not been enforced against Southern politicians and landowners who discriminate in schools, public facilities, housing, and jobs. In 1970 a public park in one Southern town was returned by the Supreme Court to its original white owners. A will had turned the park over to the city with the restriction that only whites could enjoy the facilities, and the Court, rather than ordering the integration of the public park, chose to respect the interest of the dead property owner by returning the land to his estate.

Legal oppression of the innocent

''Much better hang wrong feller than hang no feller.''
Charles Dickens, Bleak House

No matter how willingly or unwillingly a criminal defendant cooperates with the rules of the legal game, he is forced to submit to his own undesirability, and in effect, his prejudged guilt under the law. The prejudgment is finalized by two traditional court practices: the requirements of monetary bail and the pressure to ''cop a plea,'' whereby a defendant pleads guilty instead of going to trial. Less blatant than these techniques is the cooperation among officials—the judge, the prosecuting attorney, and the poor person's defense lawyer—who use the legal techniques to isolate the prejudged defendants. Common class and racial bonds unite court officials and set apart the defendant, more or less according to the particular crime he or she is alleged to have committed. In one study of arrests in Washington, D.C., ninety percent of the people taken into custody had incomes of less than $5,000; Blacks have a significantly higher rate of arrests nationally than whites in almost every offense category; nearly forty-five percent of all arrests are for crimes

Etzkowitz & Schwab—Is America Necessary—23

without victims, such as drunkenness, gambling, vagrancy, and prostitution.[9]

The poor and nonwhite, arrested at a proprotionally higher rate than the rest of the population, are more likely to be jailed after arrest because of the court practice of imposing monetary bail. If the defendant cannot post the amount set by a judge or give a bail bondsman security to post it for him, he remains in jail. One study of New York bail practices indicates the extent to which the courts tend to incarcerate the innocent prior to trial: twenty-five percent of all defendants in this study failed to make bail at $500, forty-five per cent failed at $1,500, and sixty-three percent at $2,500.[10]

The Eighth Amendment guarantees against excessive bail and the Supreme Court has ruled that the only function of bail is to help guarantee the appearance of the defendant in court. But bail is most often used against a defendent to "teach him a lesson" or to "protect the community."[11] A poor or nonwhite defendant languishes in jail weeks, months, and even years before trial. Nor does this preventive detention count toward whatever sentence may be imposed if the defendant is convicted; thus more pressure is placed on the accused to plead guilty quickly.

It may surprise most people that there are almost no criminal trials in the United States; but since seventy percent (over ninety percent in many states) of all defendants plead guilty, the need for most trials is eliminated.[12] In 1966, there were 9,895 felonies recorded in New York City; 9,501 of these ended in convictions by a plea of guilty. The pressures on lower class, poor, or nonwhite defendants to plead guilty has received little attention, perhaps because those who are arrested and detained illegally are generally thought to be guilty anyway.

This huge number of guilty pleas is produced by the practice known as plea copping, in which the accused pleads guilty to an offense lesser than the one originally charged, or in exchange for a promise of leniency from the judge. Frequently, the accused will be charged with more crimes than actually took place in order to persuade him to plead guilty to lesser charges. A man may be charged with armed robbery on five counts: robbery first degree, assault second degree, assault third degree, carrying a dangerous weapon, and petit larceny. If the defendant goes to trial and is convicted on every count he faces many years in prison. Instead, if he has no previous record, he is offered a lesser charge—simple assault or petit larceny—to which he can plead guilty on the spot. Regardless of whether he committed the crimes, he will plead guilty to the misdemeanor because the risk of conviction at trial, especially for a Black man or woman, is great. Meanwhile the court saves the time and expense of a trial. In many states defendants in capital cases can avoid convictions carrying a mandatory death sentence only by pleading guilty. In such cases defendants who wish to exercise their right to trial by jury risk death.

In the practice of plea copping more than in any other court ritual the common class interest of all the participants in the "adversary system" of law is apparent. It is generally thought that the defense lawyer and prosecuting attorney are opponents whose struggle will bring out the true guilt or innocence of the accused. In reality, it is through the cooperation of the judge and the prosecuting and defense attorneys that bail requirements are established or a guilty plea obtained. Because there is no conflict in the class interest of judge, defense, and prosecuting attorneys, there is no reality to their apparent opposition in court. Their task is the disposition of cases, not the trial of people. Their function is to keep the guilty guilty.

The aim of the prosecutor is to "get" people. Obtaining the guilty plea is as necessary to his personal image as it is to the smooth functioning of the system. Election campaigns play up his conviction rate like a batting average. Whether a district attorney is elected or appointed, he must have the support—financial and otherwise—of the Democratic or Republican Party, and many prosecutors use their offices as political stepping stones or to build future careers in the business world. The prosecutor must therefore avoid disrupting the traditional court practices. His stake in the status quo leads him to view defendants as criminals who should be punished if they are even slightly implicated. The prosecutor's influence is great, as he determines whom the police arrest, the volume of cases in the courts, and whether convicted offenders are imprisioned.

The judge exerts a powerful influence on all stages of the criminal process. His enforcement of class distinctions in rulings, sentencing practices, and in the speed with which he disposes of cases determines many decisions by police, prosecutors, and defense counsel. Like the prosecutors, the judges have a stake in the status quo. They are chosen by professional politicians, after nomination by the Democratic and/or Republican Parties, or appointed according to the patronage of local, state, or federal executives. It is therefore not unusual for judges to work hand in hand with prosecutors. A rebel Black judge from Michigan, George W. Crockett, Jr., states the relationship clearly: "I personally think that it's unfortunate that, for the most part, our judges are made up of members of the former ranks of the prosecutors' offices, or the U. S. District Attorney's office. I think they come to the bench conditioned to believe everything the policeman says and everything the prosecutor says."[13] Because a defendant can expect little from a court controlled by an Establishment judge, he is the more influenced to plead guilty.

Although the judge only acts as a rubber stamp in this process, his powers of setting bail and of sentencing, and the psychological effect of the aura of power that surrounds him, all serve to force the guilty plea. The great symbol of justice in the criminal courts, he in fact uses the prestige of traditional courtroom respect to cloak the procedure that takes place behind closed doors or before the bench itself. All must rise when the judge enters. U.S. District Court Judge Marvin E. Frankel writes, "Sitting on raised platforms, all draped in black, judges (even of lower courts) sometimes have ludicrously inflated images of themselves and of the supposed Olympian qualities of their decisions."[14] Because his role is the least questioned and the most respected of all the participants, the judge's decisions seem to confirm the guilt of the undesirables who plead guilty.

In a recent experiment in one Western county the prosecutor exchanged places in the courtroom with the defense attorney, supposedly so that each could learn the difficulties of the other's position. That the experiment could take place at all demonstrates the overt cooperation between supposedly opposing forces. The defense lawyer's role is that of a friend who leads the unsuspecting to the slaughterhouse. Of course the defense attorney is supposed to try to prove the innocence or defend the interests of his client; this is what he does when hired by a wealthy influential client. It is also true when a Movement attorney volunteers to defend a political activist. But a defense attorney for the poor or workingman, whether the state or a private agency reimburses him or whether the client pays directly, does not identify above all with the interests of the client. He is more interested in seeing the court process function smoothly—which means that his client should plead guilty.

Each year about sixty percent of all defendants in federal and state courts are financially unable to afford counsel. Most states provide lawyers by one or both of two methods. In the assigned counsel system, which covers about two-thirds of all indigent defendants, the county clerk uses a list of available lawyers to appoint an attorney for the indigent on a case-by-case basis. In large cities the "defender" system is in greater use. Here lawyers are mostly full-time salaried government employees. Since the 1963 *Gideon* decision, in which the U. S. Supreme Court decided that any person alleged to have committed a felony must have access to an attorney, the defender system has grown enormously.

Recent studies comparing both the defender and assigned counsel to the traditional private lawyer have shown that lawyers for the poor advise their clients to plead guilty somewhat more often than privately retained attorneys.[15] However, the experts do not begin to explain the relationship between the guilty plea and its class and race basis. The private "lawyer regulars," as one criminal lawyer calls them, use their professional role as attorneys to exploit moderate income and working class clients. These lawyers are

highly visible in the major urban centers of the nation; their offices—at times shared with bondsmen—line the back streets near courthouses. They are also visible politically, with clubhouse ties reaching into judicial chambers and the prosecutor's office. The regulars make no effort to conceal their dependence upon police, bondsmen, jail personnel, as well as bailiffs, stenographers, prosecutors, and judges.[16]

The private "lawyer regular" is not concerned with guilt or innocence—nine out of ten times he will lose in court—so he collects his fee in advance, then convinces his client that pleading guilty will be best because the charges or the sentence will be lessened. The trusting client agrees, forgetting that in so doing he is forfeiting his right to a trial by jury and, as in many states, getting a presentence hearing before a judge over facts that might mitigate the offense.

"As members of a bureaucratic system, defense attorneys become committed to rational, impersonal goals based on saving time, labor, and expense and on attaining maximum output for the system."[17] The assigned counsel or public defender has a close working relationship with the "impartial" judge and the "enemy" prosecutor. They appear again and again in the same courtroom, whereas clients come and go. One who has observed the casual offstage and onstage relations among the defense and prosecuting lawyers and the judge understands that the ties among these individuals override the interests of a particular defendant. This is not corruption in the traditional sense, although that also exists; this is the normal way that guilt is determined for the undesirables in our society. As a judge who sits on a higher court described the reality of the lower courts,

Despite the presumption of innocence, the defendant in these police and magistrate courts is, prima facie, guilty. He is almost always uncounseled and sometimes he is not even informed of the charges against him until after the so-called trial. Often no records are kept of the proceedings, and in the overwhelming majority of cases, these courts are, in practice, courts of last resort.[18]

Law and power in a "pluralistic" society

Karl Marx noted that "judicial relations, like state forms, can be explained neither as things in themselves, nor by the progress of the human mind; they are rooted in the material conditions of life." As the economic organization of our society is grounded in property relations, so the law serves the most powerful property interests. The masses of people who have little or no connection to the centers of economic power are governed by rules intended to maintain existing power relationships. Criminal law enforcement controls the activities of those who are powerless because of their material conditions. While the lower classes and nonwhites dominate the court calendars, the court officers represent the interests of the power structure. The class and racist practices inherent in the bail system and plea bargaining contradict democratic principles at the same time as they uphold the economic relationships of a capitalist society. The legal superstructure is not designed to dispense justice to a whole community nor to allow changes in property relations. It legitimizes the power of the few and punishes those who have been defeated by or who challenge this power.

American social scientists use the term "pluralism" to describe American "representative democracy." They depict a society in which widely varied groups compete with each other, in which decision-making rests on give-and-take among various groups. Groups compromise, make deals, and pressure each other; public officials and lawmakers respond to these various group pressures so that no one political, economic, social, religious, regional, or racial group will dominate. This creates the "natural" system of checks and balances which maintains a democracy. People become part of the decision-making process as soon as they organize: as big labor checks big business, Catholics check Protestants, farmers check urbanites, students check school administrators.

The plausibility of this description is such that today many people are claiming that the answer to poverty is community control and that racism can be ended by supporting Black power as a check on white power. Yet the poor cannot check the rich and Blacks will never balance whites; pluralism masks the fact that some groups and individuals hold power in capitalist society while certain classes and races are excluded. It cannot be denied that important changes occur when pressures are exerted. High-level interest groups struggle for control in the top brackets of industry; the passage of civil rights legislation in 1964 and after came as a result of the nonviolent demands of the early 1960s. What can be denied is that property relations can be changed by the pluralist process. Economic guidelines and laws give the major corporations in this free enterprise system ownership of the means of production, while the populations underlying the upper class are divided (into income, religious, ethnic, and racial groups) so that they are prevented from determining the material conditions of their lives or the policies of their government. It is now a well-established (though not so well-known) fact that economic inequality within the United States has remained generally constant throughout this century,[19] showing that the "potential for unity"[20] of the upper class is much greater than that of the middle and lower classes. Sociologists have shown that a cohesive white upper class, consisting of approximately one-half of one percent of the people in this country, controls every major bank and corporation and personally owns over one-quarter of the country's wealth, while eighty percent of all stock value is owned by less than two percent of all families.[21]

The wealthy exercise their power through corporations.

. . . great corporations are the important units of wealth, to which individuals of property are variously attached. The corporation is the source of the basis of continued power and privilege. All the men and the families of great wealth are identified with large corporations in which their property is seated.[22]

John Kenneth Galbraith and other apologists for monopoly capitalism argue that the increased need for technical knowledge and management expertise has come between large industrial enterprises and their owners and has democratized the corporations. Yet the profits of the top fifty corporations represent about forty percent of all industrial earnings, and the corporations are now struggling for still greater control of the economy by means of a new phenomenon, the conglomerate. It is estimated that by 1975 three hundred corporations will own two-thirds of the industrial assets of the world.[23]

Occasionally laws are passed which challenge ruling class interests, e.g., New Deal legislation resulting from workers' struggles strengthened unions and, to some extent, redistributed income. These changes, however, did not substantially diminish corporate wealth and control. The workers were diverted from the struggle to gain control over economic forces by the creation of a legal administrative bargaining structure in which the perpetuation of the power structure was assumed. Other examples of laws which challenge corporate control are consumer safety regulations concerning food and drugs and, recently, air and water pollution. The laws restrict those capitalists whose activities are so obviously harmful that public anger at them is a potential threat to corporate power. They have clearly been forced to respond in some measure to popular outcries; but the corporate elite, through its influence over law enforcement, insures that these new laws are not used to impair basic operations.

"Legality" depends not only on who is powerful but also on the intensity of the struggle by the people, which can transform legal relationships. A labor union in the early nineteenth century was defined as an illegal conspiracy to interfere with employees' freedom of contact. Courts enjoined organizing activity and jailed organizers. Company thugs were praised as protectors of law and order—that is, company property—while workers out on strike were criminals. By the late 1930s union organizing and the right to strike were protected (except among weak groups like agricultural workers and public employees) and bosses were required to bargain. Union contracts became enforceable in court. What had been criminal became legal and previously legal activity was not illegal. The changing law reflected the new power of the movement, but it also coopted it. Property relations had been slightly modified by the struggles of the people; nevertheless, the right of ownership was safe.

Because the legal superstructure is largely powerless against the pervasive abuses of the corporate world and its oppression of the large segment of the population, it opens the way for popular attacks directed at its most valued assumption, its impartiality. Resistance to the legal oppression of the lower classes and non-white peoples has in recent years resulted in the arrests, jailing, and even murders of many who are aware that the system will not change itself. This resistance, especially among the Black population—supported by a growing number of white youth—has focused attention on the role the courts play in maintaining an illegitimate order. Those who are captured in the criminal court process experience its oppressiveness concretely and are radicalized by their experience; this process leads radicals to argue that all "criminals," as defined by the Establishment, are political prisoners.

For the majority, however, the legal superstructure does not seem to impose on daily life. The separation of the law from the people obscures the true class and racist nature of the entire economic and political system. People are now focusing their resistance on the institutions which directly affect them—at their schools, on their jobs, in their neighborhoods. But as the Establishment uses its law to cut off resistance, people will begin to see legal relationships

as they actually are, coexisting with the economic and political system. Law will be demystified. People will no longer tolerate a system in which large corporations, wealthy individuals, and property owners receive the greatest benefits. They will no longer accept the pluralist mask behind which the law pretends to be an impartial voice among conflicting groups or individuals. The people themselves will then assume authority and become their own lawmakers.

NOTES

1. See *The New York Times*, April 3, 1970, p. 48. "The Ford Foundation has appropriated $1,000,000-plus for grants to study what it feels is a growing lack of faith in this country's judicial process."

2. *The Challenge of Crime in a Free Society*, A Report by the President's Commission on Law Enforcement and the Administration of Justice. New York: Avon Books, 1968. Hereafter, the *Crime Commission Report*.

3. Ibid., p. 87.

4. Ibid., p. 88.

5. Patricia Wald, "Poverty and Criminal Justice," in the *Crime Commission Report*, p. 151.

6. The *Crime Commission Report*, p. 156.

7. Ibid., p. 157.

8. Gabriel Kolko, *Wealth and Power in America*. New York: Frederick A. Praeger, 1962, pp. 30–45.

9. The *Crime Commission Report*, pp. 149–50, 195.

10. Caleb Foote, "A Study of the Administration of Bail in New York City," *University of Pennsylvania Law Review*, Vol. 106 (1958), p. 633.

11. Ibid.

12. The percentage of trials in all states varies from none (South Dakota) to forty-five percent (Texas). The median is twelve percent. Lee Silverstein, *Defense of the Poor: The National Report*. Chicago: American Bar Foundation, 1965, Vol. I.

13. George W. Crockett, "Racism in American Law," *The National Lawyers Guild Practitioner*, Fall 1968, p. 178.

14. Marvin E. Frankel, "Remarks on Law and Revolution," *Bar Bulletin*; New York County Lawyers' Association, Vol. 26, No. 2, 1968-1969, p. 51.

15. See Silverstein, *Defense of the Poor*, for a comparison of legal aid systems.

16. Abraham S. Blumberg, "Lawyers With Convictions," *Transaction*, July 1967, p. 18.

17. Ibid.

18. J. Skelly Wright, ''The Courts Have Failed the Poor,'' *New York Times Magazine,* March 9, 1969, p.26.

19. Kolko, pp. 13–14.

20. William Domhoff, *Who Rules America?* Englewood Cliffs, New Jersey: Prentice-Hall, 1967, pp. 151–52.

21. Ibid., p. 11.

22. C. Wright Mills, *The Power Elite.* New York: Oxford University Press, 1957, Chapter 7.

23. See *Fortune,* May 15, 1969, for the Establishment's listing of the top corporations in the U.S., and some crude justifications for the growth of conglomerates.

*

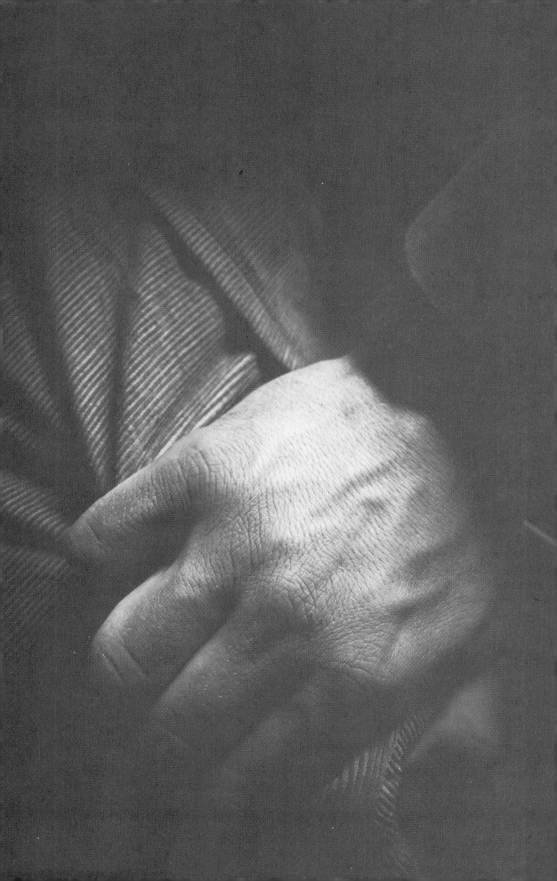

The basic questions this chapter will address are:

(1) Do regulatory agencies serve the interests of the American people?

(2) Do regulatory agencies regulate corporations, or do corporations direct the regulatory agencies?

(3) Can regulatory agencies be reformed, or must they be eliminated?

A regulatory agency is a formal independent institution established by, and under the nominal control of Congress. Its purpose is to oversee industries whose goods and/or services need control to best serve the public. Regulatory agencies are known as the fourth arm of government. The Federal Trade Commission, established by the Pure Food and Drug Act, sees that food products meet health standards and drugs are safe for human consumption. The Interstate Commerce Commission sets rates for industries whose enterprises cross state boundaries.

The public position of conservatives on regulatory agencies is simple: they interfere with the development of free enterprise, therefore they should not exist. Regulatory agencies are an inefficient overlay of bureaucratic regulation that increases the retail cost of products. Regulation of business should be done by business itself through organizations such as the Better Business Bureau. Conservatives maintain that government regulation opens the door to a "communist welfare state," in their eyes, the devil. In the line of conservative thinking, there should be no government regulation whatsoever.

Given the existence of regulatory agencies conservatives believe that they should be controlled by people who will act on behalf of industry. Their public position on this issue is that regulatory agencies should be staffed by experts. And industry produces the relevant experts. The real position of conservatives is that regulatory agencies can be made into useful devices to protect industry from public pressure. Conservative success in controlling regulatory agencies is due to the fact that many liberals believe that industry's viewpoint should be given considerable weight and that regulatory agencies should not act solely on behalf of the public.

Liberals believe in government regulation of private enterprise. Without regulation major corporations will rob the public blind. Government regulation keeps small businesses from being eliminated by the few large companies who corner the market. According to liberals, government regulation ensures economic competition and defends the public from corporate abuses of power. For example, fair rates must be set for companies such as Bell Telephone which has no competitors. The issuance of licenses for corporations that use public facilities such as the air waves must be granted to those who will serve the public interest. In another aspect of regulation, constant testing of consumer goods must be carried on so that product safety is insured.

Liberals feel that regulatory agencies can be improved by making them stronger and by filling their managerial posts with individuals who have not had prior connections to the companies they are supposed to regulate. With the right people holding office, with administrative enforcement, and with stronger legal powers to enforce controls for the public good, regulatory agencies could serve the function for which they were intended.[1]

Socialists maintain that regulatory agencies both represent the corporations they are supposed to control and are part of the corporate establishment. Most individuals in the upper echelons of these agencies originally came from industry. They hold a corporate perspective, are often still on the corporate payroll, and expect to receive future corporate advancement if they treat the corporation favorably. Typically, regulatory agency personnel return to industry when they complete their terms of office. For example, William D. Ruckelshaus, Director of the Environmental Protection Agency from 1970–1973, is now a lobbyist for the Polyvinyl Chloride industry. His job is to influence the people who formerly worked for him in the Environmental Protection Agency. Ruckelshaus is no exceptional case; this is the way regulatory agencies operate.

Socialists argue that regulatory agencies do not protect the public. They are a useless sham intended to make the public believe it is being protected, while in reality they serve only corporate interests. To socialists, regulatory agencies are part of the overall problem of capitalism. Some socialists argue that these agencies can never be improved by reforming their operations. Instead, the American capitalistic system must be replaced with a socialist economy. Other socialists maintain by gaining control of key congressional committees that oversee regulatory agencies radical changes could be effected in the way these agencies function. Laws to control corporations, which presently exist, are seldom enforced. If they were enforced, capitalism could be significantly altered, and a step towards socialism effected.

NOTES

1. This approach is represented in Harmon Zeigler, *Interest Groups in American Society*. Englewood Cliffs: Prentice-Hall, Inc., 1964.

Conservative

James Q. Wilson. The dead hand of regulation.

After decades of public and journalistic neglect, the government agencies that set prices, control entry, and regulate conduct in many of our most important industries have suddenly found themselves in the limelight. Owing to the efforts of Ralph Nader and other advocates of "consumerism," a considerable segment of attentive opinion has become convinced that the prosaic, often arcane decisions of these little understood commissions are not always in the public interest. Such a view is correct, and for dramatizing the fact we owe Nader and the others a debt of gratitude.

But dramatic confrontations between "raiders" and "bureaucrats," however useful in creating an issue, are not so useful in understanding the issue. Persons easily convinced that the government is not acting rightly tend to assume that it is because the government is not righteous; if industries are being regulated wrongly, then (in this view) it must be because bad people are doing the regulating. It would be unfortunate if the resolution of the regulatory issue were framed in terms of the moralistic premises that first gave rise to it.

It would be all the more unfortunate considering that a number of scholars, chiefly economists, have developed over the last ten years a substantial set of analytical tools and empirical findings which, taken together, constitute an impressive contribution to our knowledge of what happens when the government tries to intervene in the economy. Yet compared to the enormous influence of those economists who have developed ways of managing our tax, fiscal, and monetary policies, the influence exercised by the regulatory economists has been negligible. About the only serious effort to move in the direction suggested by their analyses was President Kennedy's 1962 transportation message calling for the abandonment of minimum-rate regulation in the shipment of bulk commodities on trucks, trains, and barges. The plan was buried in Congress, opposed by the truckers, the barge operators, and the rate setters (in this case, the Interstate Commerce Commission).

If the economists' success in getting their aggregate strategies accepted reaffirmed what the invisible hand of the market could do under proper guidance, their failure in getting government to accept their critique of non-aggregate strategies testified to the enduring strength of the dead hand of regulation. Paul W. MacAvoy of MIT in *The Crisis of the Regulatory Commissions* (New York: Norton, 1970) summarizes the most important analyses of regulatory economics as an "accumulation of substantial quantitative findings" leading to the general conclusion that "regulation has imposed considerable costs on public utility company operations without providing compensating benefits."

The problems of regulatory agencies go beyond price setting, however, and involve issues ranging from allocation (e.g., deciding who will get a television broadcast license) through the approval of business practices (e.g., deciding which firms may merge and which may not) to the control of what may or may not be broadcast (e.g., deciding whether radio stations will be allowed to editorialize or whether television stations show too much violence or too many commercials). In evaluating these and other kinds of government regulations, there are two standards one may employ— efficiency and equity. By "efficiency" I mean that a given regulatory policy achieves a desirable objective at minimal cost; by "equity" I mean that the regulatory policy, whether efficient or not, treats those subject to it fairly—that is, treats like cases alike on the basis of rules known in advance and applicable to all.

Until the end of the 1950s, the many criticisms of regulatory commissions were generally based on rather narrow or truncated versions of these two criteria. Those concerned with efficiency tended to emphasize the problem of who would determine what the desirable social objective should be and thus to whom regulatory agencies would be accountable. This in general was the concern of the Hoover Commission and of the political scientists who complained that the commissions were a "headless fourth branch" of government and were being "captured" by the very industries they were supposed to regulate. Typical of the reform proposals of such commentators, most of whom accepted without much question the desirability of regulation, were suggestions that the commissions have "stronger leadership," "clearer mandates," "popular support," and "effective management." Rarely did any of these authors say to what concrete ends that leadership and popular support should be directed or what should be contained in the clear mandate. And as for industry influence over commissions, the best answer came from Louis Jaffe of the Harvard Law School: Whether a commission does or does not serve the ends of industry is much less important than whether it serves the correct ends, and these may or may not be what industry wants.

Critics concerned with equity, who on the whole were less favorably disposed to the idea of administrative regulation at all, concentrated their fire on the administrative procedures of the commissions, and sought by various legal and judicial remedies to insure that parties appearing before the commissions would receive ample notice, a fair hearing, an opportunity for review, and the other elements of due process as then conceived. The culmination of this movement was the passage of the Administrative Procedures Act of 1946. Though its proponents, mostly lawyers, hailed it as marking a new era in administrative law, the new era did not arrive. In the opinion of most observers, the influence of the act was marginal, and such effect as it did have was generally in the direction of making regulation slower and more costly rather than fairer.

Indeed, insofar as it sought to treat affected parties more justly, the act was doomed from the start, for it was based on a fundamental misconception of much of the regulatory process. Adjudication, as it occurs in a court of law, is (in the words of Lon Fuller) an "institutionally protected opportunity to present proofs and arguments" to support a claim of right deriving from some previously agreed to standard. This is what we do, for example, when we sue a person for failure to pay a debt. But most regulatory commissions do not have such standards, nor do most of their clients have a "right" to (for example) a vacant television license, an airline route, or a particular price for long-distance telephone calls. In deciding who shall receive the license or fly the route or what the price shall be, the agency has no single solution to which the affected parties can direct their arguments. Equity or justice in cases of this sort does not consist so much in providing the opportunities for court-like speeches as in enunciating and adhering to a reasonable standard, applicable to all, that will permit the affected parties to conduct themselves free of the fear of capricious governmental action.

The effects of regulation

The economists have cut through much (though as we shall see, not all) of the fuzzy rhetoric and empty reforms addressed to these issues and have asked instead the simple questions, "What effect does a regulatory policy have and, given certain goals, how can that effect be improved?" The first thing to decide was whether regulatory policies, especially in the rate-fixing area, *had any effect at all*. Everyone, of course, assumed that they had. Why else would businessmen complain so much about these rates and an aroused public demand even lower ones? The landmark study on this issue has been the effort of George J. Stigler and Claire Friedland to determine whether or not state control over the prices that electric utilities could charge had any effect on what prices they did charge. They compared the rates charged by utilities in states with regulation to those charged in states without it during the period (before 1937) when there was a significant number of unregulated states. They did not compare the rates directly—for obviously many factors other than regulation will affect prices—but compared the "residual rates" after controlling for the effects of urbanization, the price of fuel and the incomes of consumers.[1] In calculations for various years from 1912 to 1937, the existence of regulation had no significant effect. Nor was there in unregulated as opposed to regulated states any evidence of greater price discrimination (between, for example, domestic and industrial consumers) or of differences in utility profit levels as measured by stockholder experience. Stigler and Friedland explain their findings by the absence of long-run monopoly power in the hands of electric companies (they face competition from other energy sources) and the inability of a regulatory body to determine what rates ought to be relative to costs, or even to learn what the costs are.

That the incompetence of the agency as much as the nature of the industry may make price regulation so chancy a phenomenon will suggest to some readers what it has suggested to several generations of reformers: the need to have "better" commissions, perhaps ones staffed with economists as able as Professor Stigler. After all, what is required is simply to set prices so as to provide a "reasonable return on investment." And there are some firms that are so nearly in the position of a natural monopoly that regulation is the only means short of public ownership to prevent them from charging monopoly prices. It remains only to determine what the investment or the production costs are, and then to set the price. But as Felix Frankfurter and Henry Hart pointed out over 35 years ago, a fair and defensible determination of the rate base is maddeningly hard to make. Initial capital investment obviously will not do, as the value of the plant has no doubt appreciated since it was built. Replacement cost seems a better alternative, until one realizes that estimating it for an electric light or telephone company requires a kind of economic science fiction almost impossible to justify. What is the cost of "replacing" a utility that grew with the surrounding community's growth from village to metropolis and now exists in such close inter-

connection with the people it serves that to "replace" it would require virtually replacing the community itself? And in any case, assessing the value of a company can take (and has taken) years, hardly an arrangement conducive to regular and flexible adjustments in rates to meet changing economic conditions. And as for using the costs of production as the basis for price fixing, what a firm chooses to term a cost (as opposed to an investment), how it chooses to allocate costs between the regulated and unregulated aspects of its business, and what service levels it is willing to provide to its customers under various cost conditions are all matters that, if knowable at all, are known only to an array of accountants prepared to conceal as much as they reveal. Furthermore, taking even knowable costs as the basis for price setting by a commission may eliminate much of the firm's incentive to reduce costs or adopt more efficient technological innovations. The intention of government price setting may be to protect the helpless consumer, but its effect may be to protect the incompetent producer.

Just because it is hard to fix rates does not mean that rates are not fixed. They are, and often with quite significant results to the consumer. This is perhaps best illustrated in the field of transportation. Anyone who buys an airplane ticket or ships his furniture to another city is paying a price that is affected by, and sometimes uniquely determined by, a government agency. Merton J. Peck of Yale has studied the results of this process for shippers and Richard E. Caves has studied it with respect to airlines. Both conclude that prices would be lower to the consumer if they were not regulated. Peck estimates that abolishing government-set minimum rates for rail, truck, and barge shipments of bulk and agricultural commodities would save the consumer in excess of $400 million annually *and* at the same time increase the profitability of the railroads. Caves offers no dollar estimates, but concludes that the airline industry is sufficiently competitive to insure good service without government control over either prices or the right of a new firm to enter the industry. (Maintaining safety standards would, of course, be required, but that can be done by inspecting and certifying aircraft and air crews and does not require economic regulation.)

Efficiency

The inefficient use of economic resources in fields such as transportation does not result from the fact that stupid or corrupt men regulate these industries, but from the fact that well-meaning and reasonably intelligent men do. The Interstate Commerce Commission sought to prevent railroads from gouging farmers during the period when trains afforded almost the only way of shipping many farm products to market. I do not know how successfully the ICC protected the farmer when railroads had oligopoly positions, but today, when they do not, the ICC protects him very well. According to John Meyer, Merton Peck, John Stenason, and Charles Zwick,[2] rail revenues during the period 1939 to 1959 represented between 120 and 140 per cent of costs for agricultural products, while revenues for manufactured products have averaged between 165 and 203 per cent of costs. Nor do prices discriminate only among kinds of things shipped. Short-haul rail prices are a lower fraction of costs than long-haul prices, and many places are grouped for the purpose of calculating rates. Thus, the price to ship some things from California to Maine has been the same as from Idaho to Pennsylvania, even though the distances vary by as much as a thousand miles.

These and other anomalies result from the fact that the ICC has felt it necessary to set rates on an item-by-item, point-to-point basis, partly because it sought originally to protect the farmer (at the expense of the manufacturer) and partly because the railroads themselves practiced this form of price discrimination in the days before they had much competition. The ICC decided to strike a compromise between the interests of farmers and those of the railroaders by tinkering with existing prices rather than by starting all over. What began as tinkering wound up as a set of 75,000 separate rate schedules and an administrative procedure for handling (in 1962) over 173,000 proposed tariffs submitted by truck and barge as well as rail firms. Among the rates the ICC now "sets" are ones which distinguish, as Phillip Locklin has noted, between horses for slaughter and horses for draught, between sand used to make glass and sand used to make cement, and between lime used in industry and lime used in agriculture. Of course, no agency could "set" all these rates every year; the best it can do is look at a few, change any flagrant ones, and hope for the best.

The chief cumulative cost to society of ICC rate setting is not its administrative confusion or intellectual untidiness, but the distortions it causes in the effort to create a balanced and efficient transportation system. When trucks came onto the scene, they did not seek out those routes for which they were the most efficient carriers (e.g., short-haul carriage of agricultural products) but, as Peck points out, those where they could make the most money even though they might be the least efficient (that is, long-haul carriage of manufacturing products for which the rates were kept artificially high in part by government action). The ICC responded, not by deregulating railroads so they could compete, but by regulating trucks so they could not. It did not quite succeed, however. The best it could do was to set truck and rail prices at the same level, but then the competition turned on quality of service (at which trucks had the advantage because they could go anywhere a road was to be found), and the railroads suffered anyway.

The Civil Aeronautics Board has been a better friend to the airlines than the ICC has been to the railroads. Prices on the high-density, big-city air routes are higher than they would be if competitively set. It costs less per mile, for example, to fly from Los Angeles to San Francisco (an intrastate route not subject to CAB regulation) than from New York to Washington, D.C. (an interstate route that is CAB-regulated). The CAB justifies this in part by requiring the airlines serving the high-density, over-priced routes also to serve low-density, unprofitable routes in order to insure that the nation has a complete airline system. Even assuming that it is in the national interest to guarantee that virtually any city can be reached by air, and that to do it a subsidy is required, it is not clear why the cost of that subsidy should be borne by passengers on the high-density routes rather than by the nation as a whole, or why the subsidy should be conferred covertly (by internal fare regulation) rather than openly (by cash payments). Or rather it *is* clear—it is politically easier to subsidize if it is done inconspicuously and in ways that do not appear to be a charge on the tax rate.

Nor are the economic inefficiencies limited to the transportation field. By a combination of policies administered by various agencies, we insure that the nation produces too much crude oil and too little natural gas. Restrictions ("quotas") on the importation of foreign oil guarantee that the price of oil in the United States will be higher than it need be (i.e., than the world price) and that there will be more drilling in scarce domestic oil reserves than is justified. At the same time, the Federal Power Commission until recently has set the field price of natural gas below the rate necessary to clear the market, and thus below the rate many think is necessary to encourage vigorous exploration for new sources of supply. This means that while present-day consumers of gas may have been benefited because prices have been kept low, future consumers may well have been harmed because of the shortages they will encounter (and to some extent, already are encountering).[3]

Who has captured whom

Scholars as diverse as the radical historian Gabriel Kolko and the conservative economist George Stigler offer a simple explanation for the behavior of these and other regulatory agencies: They have been captured by, or were created to serve the interests of, the industries they are supposed to regulate. To Kolko, business regulation, like all other "reform" efforts in American government, has had the intended effect of making secure the control over wealth exercised by the dominant economic class. To Stigler, any industry with sufficient political influence will use the coercive power of the state to limit entry into the industry and thus to restrict competition; failing that, it will take the second-best strategy of obtaining cash subsidies from the government to help defray the cost of competition. ("Second best," because a cash subsidy, without entry control, would have to be shared with all new entrants into the industry, and the bigger the subsidy the more numerous the entrants.)

There are examples of regulation that seem to have no other explanations than those. The benefits given to the petroleum industry by import quotas and tax-depletion allowances represent an enormous subsidy (perhaps as much as $5 billion a year). The CAB has not allowed the formation of a new trunk airline since it was created in 1938. At one time the butter producers virtually suppressed the use of margarine by obtaining laws that forbade coloring margarine to look like butter. Plenty of other instances could no doubt be added.

But just as striking are the cases contrary to the theory of industry capture. The Federal Power Commission can hardly be called the tool of the natural gas producer interests; until recently it has set well-head prices below what the producers would like and indeed what the public interest probably requires. If the ICC was once dominated by the railroads, it is not today: So generous has that agency been to the chief rivals of the railroads, the truckers and barge lines, that today the rail industry favors deregulation altogether. Television broadcasters (such as WHDH in Boston) that have lost their license to a rival claimant because of the action of the Federal Communications Commission, or newspaper owners who face the possibility of having to divest themselves of television station ownership, or television networks that have had the amount of programming they could supply in prime viewing time reduced by a half-hour each day are not likely to think of themselves as playing the role of captor with respect to the FCC.

Indeed, there may well be as many industries that have been "captured" by their regulatory agency as agencies captured by the industry. But the term "capture" reflects a simplistic view of the politics of regulation. Though there have been very few good studies of agency politics, what probably happens is this: An agency is established, sometimes with industry support and sometimes over industry objections, and then gradually creates a regulatory climate that acquires a life of its own. Certain firms will be helped by some of the specific regulatory decisions making up this climate, others will be hurt. But the industry as a whole will adjust to the climate and decide that the costs of shifting from the known hazards of regulation to the unknown ones of competition are too great; it thus will come to defend the system. The agencies themselves will become preoccupied with the details of regulation and the minutiae of cases in whatever form they first inherit them, trying by the slow manipulation of details to achieve various particular effects that happen to commend themselves from time to time to various agency members. In a burst of academic masochism, Paul MacAvoy recently read all 1,041 pages in Volume 42 of the *Federal Power Commission Reports*, and concluded that it is hard to find any consistent policy preference concealed in their bureaucratic and ponderous language; hints appear here and there in the few important cases, but it would be hard to call them a "policy." The net effects of the FPC's actions often are clear, but whether they are intended, and if so on what grounds, is not clear.

Louis Jaffe has probably stated the political situation more accurately—the agencies are not so much industry-oriented or consumer-oriented as *regulation-oriented*. They are in the regulation business, and regulate they will, with or without a rationale. If the agencies have been "captured" by anybody, it is probably by their staffs who have mastered the arcane details of rate setting and license granting. Take the Anti-Trust Division of the Justice Department: No one supposes that this division is animated by any clear, consistent, and economically defensible theory of the impact of firm size on market performance,

and indeed it is not. Some may suppose that in the absence of such a theory it will be guided instead by political pressures or White House inclinations; but despite the efforts of Nader's Raiders to find evidence of such influences, there is little to support this supposition. As far as anyone can tell, the Anti-Trust lawyers are guided chiefly by their trained habits to find a case that with available evidence and under prevailing court opinions can be made to stick. Any case.

In any event, most regulatory agencies have been doing pretty much what Congress has asked of them. Congress never intended that competition should govern in transportation, and the ICC has seen to it that it hasn't. The ICC was supposed to "coordinate" our transportation system, and though one may question (and I certainly question) whether co-ordination can be achieved by detailed regulation, the fact is that the ICC, supposedly "owned" by the railroads, has in the name of co-ordination been quite generous to the trucking and barge industries—so much so that now the railroads are in favor of deregulation. Indeed, if any agency has been "captured" by its clients, it has been, under certain presidents, the National Labor Relations Board; but again, this is exactly what Congress intended in the Wagner Act. (Curiously, academic criticism of business domination of regulatory agencies rarely extends to organized labor influence in the NLRB.) The Securities and Exchange Commission has had a running feud with much of Wall Street, just as Congress hoped it would. Indeed, if any single political force benefits from economic regulation, it is Congress—or more accurately, those key Congressional committee and subcommittee chairmen with a substantive interest in, or appropriations responsibilities over, the regulatory agencies. The FCC has been reluctant to make any change in its controls over cable communication without checking with key Senators, and the NLRB regularly hears from members of the House Education and Labor Committee about matters pending before it.

But even Congressional intervention, like industry control, is not in itself a problem;

everything depends on the ends toward which such intervention or control is directed. The problem of efficiency, in short, is not wholly a problem of clientelism, political meddling, or agency incompetence; in substantial part it is a problem of the nature of the tasks which we have given the agencies. These tasks probably could not be performed well even in theory, and amid the practical realities of confused ends and ambiguous standards they are, through the fault of no one in particular, performed abominably.

Equity

The economic analyses thus far described have rather little to say explicitly about the problem of equity, though their criticism of piecemeal rate making has clear implications about the fairness with which (for example) shippers of similar products over similar distances are treated. The general question of equity is not raised by economists, and those who do raise it—chiefly business firms that feel unjustly treated—are often ignored on grounds, quite plausible in many cases, that they are engaged in special pleading.

But the issue remains, even if it is difficult to get people to take it seriously. Not that people are generally indifferent to considerations of justice and fair play; far from it. But they tend to limit their concern to victimized individuals and groups with whom they have sympathy. Those who publish books and articles rarely, if ever, argue that a person should be subject to arbitrary arrest, or that *ex post facto* laws should be tolerated, or that demonstrations should be allowed or forbidden at the pleasure of an administrator. Or do they? Consider the following statement, written by a man who was later to become a Justice of the United States Supreme Court:

Unless the police officer has effective bargaining power, little can be expected. He must have sanctions or desired favors which he can trade for changes in behavior . . . . He may be asked to exercise his discretion, for example, to allow a certain demonstration to take place. Then, if the need of the demonstrators is sufficiently urgent,

a trade may be consummated. In return for the favor of the police officer, the demonstrators may change their speeches and leaflets in accordance with the police officer's conception of equity and justice.

I venture that most readers would find this statement shocking and odious. The idea that the right to demonstrate should be subject to arbitrary powers and the content of the demonstration modified by the capacity of a policeman to bargain with the demonstrators seems the height of unfairness. .

Now, I must confess that the Justice-to-be (Abe Fortas, as it turns out) did not exactly say this. Instead, Fortas was writing, in 1937, about how the staff of the SEC should behave. His exact words were as follows:

Unless the administrator has effective bargaining power, little can be expected. He must have sanctions or desired favors which he can trade for changes in practices . . . . He may be asked to exercise his discretion, for example, to accelerate the effective date of registration [of a new security]. Then, if the need of the registrant is sufficiently urgent, a trade may be consummated. In return for the favor of the administrator, the registrant may amend his practices in accordance with the administrator's conception of equity and justice.

Most people, other than securities registrants, would find this statement at worst to be a candid but scarcely shocking glimpse into the real-life behavior of bureaucrats. Political scientists would probably cite this approvingly as an example of how the informal use of "necessary" administrative discretion can lead to the more "effective management" of the economy. I am perfectly aware, of course, that there are differences, perhaps decisive ones, between free speech and securities registration; but I think it behooves all who unhesitatingly condemn the first quotation and approve the second to think through rather carefully just what these differences may be and why speech should have near-absolute protection and commerce near-zero protection.

Whether or not we place the interests of the firm on the same plane as the interests of the writer or speaker, it seems clear (again, hardly anyone has examined the problem) that a person or corporation subject to regulation cannot in many cases know in advance where he stands, nor expect to be treated tomorrow by the same rule that governed his actions today. The theory of regulation advanced in the earlier part of this paper—that it tends to be an ad hoc, particularistic process, affected, but not determined, by a policy habit or inclination—suggests not only that agencies will not operate on the basis of general rules, but that they will go to some pains to avoid developing such rules.

There are two reasons for this. One is that the greater the codification of substantive policy, the less the power the agency can wield over any client in the particular case. As Michel Crozier has argued with respect to bureaucracy generally, power depends in part on uncertainty—I have power over you to the extent you cannot be sure in advance what my reactions to your behavior will be. If the agency could only apply known rules to corporate behavior, it would still constrain that behavior, but far less than if it improvised its action in each case. In a baseball game the umpire has power because he can call me out after three strikes; but his power over me would be much greater if every time I came to the plate he told me that how many strikes I would be allowed depended on how well I swung the bat, or maybe on how clean my uniform was.

The second reason for avoiding codification is related to the first: The agency and its staff wish to be able to achieve particular goals in particular cases. Though the goals may be ambiguous and the cases all different, the general desire to realize a particular state of affairs is more important to the agency than the desire simply to insure that the rules are followed. To continue the analogy, it is as if the baseball umpire desired not just to see that the game was played fairly, but also that a certain number of runs were scored (so the fans would be happy), a certain number of pitches thrown (so the pitcher would get a good workout), and a certain price charged by the owners (so they would be either happy or unhappy, depending on his intentions).[4]

Regulating the broadcasters

Television and radio renewals display many of the attributes of a form of regulation deliberately without policy or rules. Each license must be renewed every three years, and the vast majority are in fact renewed almost automatically, or with only perfunctory review. But the power not to renew, and the actual shifting of licenses in some cases (technically, WHDH in Boston only had a "temporary" permit, not a regular three-year one) and the threatened shift in other cases, give to the FCC vast potential influence over the owners of stations and their conduct. To some extent that power is used to serve desirable objectives, such as that represented by the diversification rules. These are intended to encourage competition and specify that no applicant for a license may own more than one outlet in any one market area or more than seven outlets nationwide.

But increasingly, that power is used (or more accurately, its use is hinted at) to achieve a wide range of not very clear, not very consistent, and in many cases not very desirable social policies. Though the diversification rules are presumably intended to insure competition, the local ownership rules seem designed to prevent it. A radio or television station is supposed to be locally owned by people who have past broadcast experience, a record of participation in civic affairs, a willingness to engage in "public service" (i.e., unsponsored but "worthwhile") broadcasting, a capacity to find out (by opinion surveys and other means) what their audience wants, and so on. In short, they are supposed to be "good guys," somehow defined, even if they run to a certain bland sameness.

Furthermore, the owners are supposed to be fair. They have, in the Commission's words, "an affirmative duty generally to encourage and implement the broadcast of all sides of controversial public issues over their facilities" and to "play a conscious and positive role to bring about the balanced presentation of opposing viewponts." The fairness doctrine as interpreted by the FCC means that a station broadcasting a program in favor of fair employment practices must also broadcast a program opposed to it, that a station indicating opposition to the nuclear test ban treaty must find and put on the air a spokesman who favors it, and that a station discussing the nutritive value of vitamin pills and white bread must seek out persons with different views. These are actual cases; there are others.

In principle, no one is opposed to fairness and in practice many of us may welcome, as a last resort, the existence of the fairness doctrine as a weapon with which to challenge the most egregious examples of one-sided broadcasting by stations with monopoly positions in their communities. But by now we should have learned that the existence of a federal power stimulates a demand for its use, and thus what begins as an ultimate weapon for extreme cases becomes a ready weapon for everyday cases. The United States Court of Appeals in Washington, D.C. has recently held that a station which shows a commercial for a high-powered automobile or leaded gasoline can be compelled to show programs, free of charge, about the dangers of air pollution. It is obvious that pollution is a problem and that cars contribute to it (many of us, we should recall, learned those facts from television!); but the implication of this decision is that showing anything (even a paid advertisement) about a controversial public issue creates an obligation to show something on the other side—free if necessary, and even if the other side has already expressed its views on other stations or in other media. If the purpose of the decision was to insure vigorous public debate, its effect, if it stands, is likely to be the opposite. Vigorous debate arises from boldness, while the decision is likely to inspire timidity.

Consider the necessary implications of the agency's position in this matter: Part of the government is empowered, on the basis of an inevitably vague standard, to control access to, and to influence (though not determine) the content of, an important medium of communication. No government agency has that power over newspapers, books, or magazines, and very few of us, I imagine, would want such an agency to exist.

Radio and television, of course, are supposed to be different from other media, but whether they really are is not clear. It surely is not because of their monopoly power—there are far more broadcast stations than newspapers serving most (perhaps all) American cities. And it cannot be because the public "owns" the airwaves; for the need to control their use (other than to prevent interference) does not follow from the fact of "ownership." But it is hard to see in what sense the airwaves are "owned" at all or, if they are somehow in the public domain, why they are any more so than the forests out of which newsprint is made or the public streets on which newspapers are sold. It may be that radio and television have a greater, perhaps even hypnotic effect on their audience, which thus must be protected. No one has shown this empirically to be the case[5], and in any event, no one suggested a Federal Motion Picture Commission when the movies were supposed to be the dominant (perhaps hypnotic) form of entertainment and persuasion. Perhaps it is because radio and TV are more directly available to children that we give them special treatment; but so are comic books, and the influence of either medium on young people is hard to assess.

I think that in fact we accept government regulation of broadcasting because we have it, we are used to it, and we all know of things we would like to see improved in radio and TV. If the First Amendment had never been added to the Constitution, and if it therefore had been possible to have a Federal Newspaper Commission, we probably would have one in some form and expect it to "improve" our daily reading matter, eliminate objectionable advertisements, reduce the violence portrayed on the printed page, and allow only "balanced" editorial viewpoints (which is to say, no editorial viewpoints at all other than trivial ones). We would especially accept this form of control if those who would make use of it were people with views similar to our own.

Is the FCC to blame?

The FCC is no more solely responsible for the bland sameness of TV than the ICC is for our unbalanced and excessively costly transportation system. The central facts about the broadcast medium, especially television, are: (1) It must attempt to secure the largest possible number of viewers; (2) there is a shortage of creative talent with which to satisfy all of those viewers all of the time and some of those viewers any of the time; (3) until the general advent of cable television or other technologies there will be a lack of channels with national linkages to serve specialized audiences.

But the FCC has helped in its own way to make matters worse. The local ownership rule eliminated the possibility of regional stations; the initial decision to favor VHF over UHF broadcasting kept down the number of available channels; the local and public service programming rules have helped insure that there will be some programs on the air that almost nobody wants to watch; the anti-network decisions have reduced the contribution of almost the only group with the capacity to attract the most expensive (and usually the most gifted) talent; the fairness doctrine has helped inhibit (though it has not prevented) the growth of editorializing and the showing of controversial programs; and the ban on the cable importation of distant signals into the largest markets has impeded the growth of cable television and thereby conferred a hidden subsidy to over-the-air broadcasting.

Perhaps more importantly, FCC discretionary power over licenses has been increasingly encouraging to anybody who wishes to "improve" radio and television and increasingly worrisome to those who run stations. Community groups, often aided by "public interest" law firms, can and will object to license renewals for any station that has offended them and may succeed in time in switching licenses to owners whom they are willing to approve. The attacks of Vice-President Spiro Agnew on newsmen are bound to have more of a chilling effect on an industry (such as TV) that knows its very existence depends on government approval than on one (such as newspapers) entirely independent of such authority. It is doubtful that the FCC will become the agent of Agnew's views, but nothing is more natural than for broadcasters to suspect it may have become so and to act accordingly. (If Agnew really wishes to change broadcasting, he might have his supporters hire a law firm of their own and challenge some offending stations at renewal time.)

The extent to which citizens' groups will be able to use renewal hearings as a means of controlling broadcasting is not yet clear, but the momentum is growing. In Des Moines a radio station is being challenged because it intends to stop playing "progressive rock," while a Syracuse station is being challenged because it has stopped playing classical music. In Los Angeles, a Mexican-American group has charged NBC-TV with portraying Mexicans in a demeaning manner on a long list of network programs and has demanded that NBC sign an agreement allowing the citizen organization to monitor all scripts and to veto any programs it considers "racist." Italian-American groups made sure long ago that most persons portrayed on television as gangsters will not have Italian names.

We can always hope, of course, that the FCC will reject any challenges that seem to inhibit free political communication, as they often have in the past. When a California FM radio station was challenged on the grounds that its programming was subversive and indecent, the FCC eventually cleared the station after an investigation. But why should there have been even the possibility that the station could thus have been put out of business? (If it had violated any proper law by its actions, there were civil and criminal remedies available to the regular law-enforcement agencies.)

One rejoinder to this criticism of the FCC is that we already have radio and television censorship, but it is practiced by network executives and station owners who are accountable to nobody. And to a considerable extent, this is true. While the degree of conscious control over television news by network executives is less than one might expect (their overriding concern is to find ways of creating visual entertainment and audience appeal out of roughly the same news stories everybody else is covering), it does exist: There seem to be cases of controversial documentaries being dropped or modified, of certain continuing stories (such as Vietnam) being covered from a particular perspective, and of views offensive to listeners or advertisers being tempered or quashed. But given the nature of the medium, that is almost inevitable. It is a *mass* medium supported by advertiser revenue, and TV executives would properly be judged incompetent if they aided their competitors by deliberately narrowing their appeal or reducing their revenues.

Those on the FCC who have attempted to create more diversity in television have acted as if they did not understand this and thus have adopted methods likely to make the problem worse. There is no way the FCC can regulate talent, diversity, or controversy *into* television; the best (or worst) it can do is to regulate *out* things it or someone else finds objectionable, and to otherwise keep the station owners on tenterhooks. The only way to free broadcast executives from the constraints under which they now operate is either to restructure the medium so that all or part of it is free from the need to advertise (as with pay television), or to create so many channels, nationally linked, that minority audiences with special tastes can be reached in sufficient numbers to warrant advertiser investment (as may perhaps be possible with cable television). No regulation can ever be successful if it is based on an effort to thwart powerful motives of self-interest; regulation works when it harnesses self-interest to public purposes.

The FCC has issued rule after rule apparently intended to require broadcasters to be better people with higher motives; but when faced with requests for pay television, it has either refused them or allowed only small experiments under conditions seemingly designed to insure failure. And, for all practical purposes, cable has been kept out of the one hundred largest markets, in which over 80 per cent of all television receivers are to be found. (This limitation will probably be partially lifted in the near future).

It is beyond the scope of this article to dwell on ways in which the necessary allocation of broadcast frequencies can be made without asking an agency to assess the character of the would-be owners or to monitor the content of their broadcasting. Ten years ago Ronald H. Coase suggested in the *Journal of Law and Economics* that the simplest means would be to auction off broadcast licenses, thereby both insuring a non-political allocation process and recovering for the public treasury some of the considerable value of the license. The advent of cable television offers opportunities for so increasing the number of TV channels available and so lowering the cost of origination that hardly anyone need be excluded from access on economic grounds; it also may make possible a feasible pay-TV system using one or more channels on a national scale. And there are other possibilities.

I doubt that anyone in the broadcast industry would favor either the auction or the cable, or that many would support any fundamental changes in the FCC's regulatory powers. On almost any decisive issue the broadcasters will support the Commission as it now operates, not because business has "captured" it (many broadcasters are deeply suspicious of the Commission and view its actions as wrong or capricious), but because the regulatory climate created by the Commission is what the industry knows and has more or less learned to live with. Besides, however offended any individual broadcaster may be by an FCC decision, the broadcasters' trade association is hardly likely to curry FCC ill-will by a frontal attack.

The unlikelihood of change

Neither industry nor the agencies have much need to fear major reforms, or at least reforms that reduce the item-by-item discretionary regulation that now exists. Quite the contrary. The reform impulse, except among economists who specialize in the problems of better use of regulated resources, is now of an entirely different sort—increased regulation, increased discretion, more numerous challenges to existing corporate practices. Commissioner Nicholas Johnson of the FCC has even published a book, *How To Talk Back To Your*

Television Set, that is a manual of ways to challenge broadcasters; if its lessons were followed by a large number of citizen groups, the already considerable tendencies of broadcasters to provide programs that offend absolutely no one would be given a powerful impetus. What the pursuit of audience ratings has started, the law suits and renewal hearings would consummate. (In fairness it should be noted that Commissioner Johnson has also been an advocate of cable television and the greater diversity it promises.)

With respect to rate-fixing agencies, a move toward greater reliance on market forces in industries where competition is adequate is also unlikely. Not only would the agencies oppose it, but some groups will lose in the short run from any deregulated rate: Consumers might have to pay more for natural gas, oil companies might earn less from crude oil, and some shippers would pay more in rail and truck rates. Everyone who stands to pay more will naturally oppose deregulation, and those who will pay less (consumers, future generations, some firms) are typically not organized to seek such benefits—if, indeed, they are even aware of them.

But most importantly, the most articulate segment of public opinion has recently become aroused by the issue of "consumerism," and this almost surely will lead to demands for increasing the power and aggressiveness of the regulatory agencies. There is, of course, necessary contradiction between a desire to protect the consumer and the desire to use scarce resources more efficiently; the efforts of the Federal Trade Commission or the Food and Drug Administration to insure that false and misleading claims are not made for products and that harmful substances are not sold to unwitting buyers are in principle unobjectionable. Indeed, one of the ironies of economic regulation is that it has generally existed with respect to those tasks it can do only poorly (such as setting rates and prices and controlling market entry) and has not existed, or has been indifferently managed, with respect to those tasks it could do well (such as controlling the effects of business

activity on third parties or on the environment). Reducing the emission of noxious fumes or preventing the sale of a harmful drug is conceptually and perhaps administratively easier than deciding what allocation of television licenses will be in "the public interest" or what price levels are "reasonable"; yet until recently Congress has encouraged the agencies to do the latter but not the former. In so far as the contemporary concern for ecology and public health redresses this balance, it is all to the good.

But it is unlikely that the desire to improve and perfect human affairs will stop there. An effort will be made to "protect" the consumer by setting the price he can pay or forbidding him to buy certain products of whose dangers he is fully aware. Moreover, enhancing the powers or stimulating the activity of regulatory agencies for whatever reasons will lead the agencies themselves to enlarge their mandate and extend their influence. Consumer advocates, including as they do many of those most skeptical on other grounds of the manageability of large government organizations, should be the last to suppose that bigger consumer-protection agencies will work as intended; but of course, they are among the first to suppose it.

NOTES

1. For the technically-minded reader, regulation-nonregulation was a dummy variable in a regression equation in which the dependent variable was the log of the average revenue per kilowatt hour and the predictor variables were the log values of the population in cities over 25,000, the cost of coal per BTU, the per capita income, and the proportion of power from hydroelectric sources.

2. *The Economics of Competition in The Transportation Industries* (Cambridge: Harvard University Press, 1964).

3. The extent to which there is or may be a shortage depends in part on estimates of the size of the natural gas reserves, and this is a hotly disputed issue; it may also be ultimately unanswerable. Whatever the size of the reserves, the issue remains as to whether wellhead rates are high enough to encourage exploration for new fields and whether there is enough competition to insure that market prices will not be monopoly prices. Studies by Paul

MacAvoy suggest that field prices are (or without regulation, would be) competitive.

4. Some agencies have codified their policies; the NLRB is one. As Roger G. Noll has pointed out, the NLRB is almost unique in dealing with two influential, well-organized, and competitive interests—labor and management. It is, therefore, under steady pressure to define its policies, and its decisions are appealed to the courts much more frequently than those of any other agency.

5. For a discussion of one such effort to prove it, see my article, "Violence, Pornography, and Social Science," in *The Public Interest,* Winter, 1971, pp. 45–61.

Liberal

Norton E. Long.   Power and administration.

There is no more forlorn spectacle in the administrative world than an agency and a program possessed of statutory life, armed with executive orders, sustained in the courts, yet stricken with paralysis and deprived of power. An object of contempt to its enemies and of despair to its friends.

The lifeblood of administration is power. Its attainment, maintenance, increase, dissipation, and loss are subjects the practitioner and student can ill afford to neglect. Loss of realism and failure are almost certain consequences. This is not to deny that important parts of public administration are so deeply entrenched in the habits of the community, so firmly supported by the public, or so clearly necessary as to be able to take their power base for granted and concentrate on the purely professional side of their problems. But even these islands of the blessed are not immune from the plague of politics, as witness the fate of the hapless Bureau of Labor Statistics and the perennial menace of the blind 5 per cent across-the-board budget cut. Perhaps Carlyle's aphorism holds here, "The healthy know not of their health but only the sick." To stay healthy one needs to recognize that health is

a fruit, not a birthright. Power is only one of the considerations that must be weighed in administration, but of all it is the most overlooked in theory and the most dangerous to overlook in practice.

The power resources of an administrator or an agency are not disclosed by a legal search of titles and court decisions or by examining appropriations or budgetary allotments. Legal authority and a treasury balance are necessary but politically insufficient bases of administration. Administrative rationality requires a critical evaluation of the whole range of complex and shifting forces on whose support, acquiescence, or temporary impotence the power to act depends.

Analysis of the sources from which power is derived and the limitations they impose is as much a dictate of prudent administration as sound budgetary procedure. The bankruptcy that comes from an unbalanced power budget has consequences far more disastrous than the necessity of seeking a deficiency appropriation. The budgeting of power is a basic subject matter of a realistic science of administration.

It may be urged that for all but the top hierarchy of the administrative structure the question of power is irrelevant. Legislative authority and administrative orders suffice. Power adequate to the function to be performed flows down the chain of command. Neither statute nor executive order, however, confers more than legal authority to act. Whether Congress or President can impart the substance of power as well as the form depends upon the line-up of forces in the particular case. A price control law wrung from a reluctant Congress by an amorphous and unstable combination of consumer and labor groups is formally the same as a law enacting a support price program for agriculture backed by the disciplined organizations of farmers and their Congressmen. The differences for the scope and effectiveness of administration are obvious. The presidency, like Congress, responds to and translates the pressures that play upon it. The real mandate contained in an Executive order varies with the political strength of the group demand embodied in it, and in the context of other group demands.

Both Congress and President do focus the general political energies of the community and are so considerably more than mere means for transmitting organized pressures. Yet power is not concentrated by the structure of government or politics into the hands of a leadership with a capacity to budget it among a diverse set of administrative activities. A picture of the presidency as a reservoir of authority from which the lower echelons of administration draw life and vigor is an idealized distortion of reality.

A similar criticism applies to any like claim for an agency head in his agency. Only in varying degrees can the powers of subordinate officials be explained as resulting from the chain of command. Rarely is such an explanation a satisfactory account of the sources of power.

To deny that power is derived exclusively from superiors in the hierarchy is to assert that subordinates stand in a feudal relation in which to a degree they fend for themselves and acquire support peculiarly their own. A structure of interests friendly or hostile, vague and general or compact and well-defined, encloses each significant center of administrative discretion. This structure is an important determinant of the scope of possible action. As a source of power and authority it is a competitor of the formal hierarchy.

Not only does political power flow in from the sides of an organization, as it were; it also flows up the organization to the center from the constituent parts. When the staff of the Office of War Mobilization and Reconversion advised a hard-pressed agency to go out and get itself some popular support so that the President could afford to support it, their action reflected the realities of power rather than political cynicism.

It is clear that the American system of politics does not generate enough power at any focal point of leadership to provide the conditions for an even partially successful divorce of politics from administration. Subordinates cannot depend on the formal chain of command to deliver enough political power to permit them to do their jobs. Accordingly they must supplement the resources available through the hierarchy with those they can muster on their own, or accept the consequences in frustration—a course itself not without danger. Administrative rationality demands that objectives be determined and sights set in conformity with a realistic appraisal of power position and potential.

The theory of administration has neglected the problem of the sources and adequacy of power, in all probability because of a distaste for the disorderliness of American political life and a belief that this disorderliness is transitory. An idealized picture of the British parliamentary system as a Platonic form to be realized or approximated has exerted a baneful fascination in the field. The majority party with a mandate at the polls and a firmly seated leadership in the Cabinet seems to solve adequately the problem of the supply of power necessary to permit administration to concentrate on the fulfillment of accepted objectives. It is a commonplace that the American party system provides neither a mandate for a platform nor a mandate for a leadership.

Accordingly, the election over, its political meaning must be explored by the diverse leaders in the executive and legislative branches. Since the parties have failed to discuss issues, mobilize majorities in their terms, and create a working political consensus on measures to be carried out, the task is left for others—most prominently the agencies concerned. Legislation passed and power granted are frequently politically premature. Thus the Council of Economic Advisers was given legislative birth before political acceptance of its functions existed. The agencies to which tasks are assigned must devote themselves to the creation of an adequate consensus to permit administration. The mandate that the parties do not supply must be attained through public relations and the mobilization of group support. Pendleton Herring and others have shown just how vital this support is for agency action.

The theory that agencies should confine themselves to communicating policy suggestions to executive and legislature, and refrain from appealing to their clientele and the public, neglects the failure of the parties to provide either a clear-cut decision as to what they should do or an adequately mobilized political support for a course of action. The bureaucracy under the American political system has a large share of responsibility for the public promotion of policy and even more in organizing the political basis for its survival and growth. It is generally recognized that the agencies have a special competence in the technical aspects of their fields which of necessity gives them a rightful policy initiative. In addition, they have or develop a shrewd understanding of the politically feasible in the group structure within which they work. Above all, in the eyes of their supporters and their enemies they represent the institutionalized embodiment of policy, an enduring organization actually or potentially capable of mobilizing power behind policy. The survival interests and creative drives of administrative organizations combine with clientele pressures to compel such mobilization. The party system provides no pressures to compel such mobilization. The party system provides no enduring institutional representation for group interest at all comparable to that of the bureaus of the Department of Agriculture. Even the subject matter committees of Congress function in the shadow of agency permanency.

The bureaucracy is recognized by all interested groups as a major channel of representation to such an extent that Congress rightly feels the competition of a rival. The weakness in party structure both permits and makes necessary the present dimensions of the political activities of the administrative branch—permits because it fails to protect administration from pressures and fails to provide adequate direction and support, makes necessary because it fails to develop a consensus on a leadership and a program that makes possible administration on the basis of accepted decisional premises.

Agencies and bureaus more or less perforce are in the business of building, maintaining, and increasing their political support. They lead and in large part are led by the diverse groups whose influence sustains them. Frequently they lead and are themselves led in conflicting directions. This is not due to a dull-witted incapacity to see the contradictions in their behavior but is an almost inevitable result of the contradictory nature of their support.

Herbert Simon has shown that administrative rationality depends on the establishment of uniform value premises in the decisional centers of organization. Unfortunately, the value premises of those forming vital elements of political support are often far from uniform. These elements are in Barnard's and Simon's sense "customers" of the organization and therefore parts of the organization whose wishes are clothed with a very real authority. A major and most time-consuming aspect of administration consists of the wide range of activities designed to secure enough "customer" acceptance to survive and, if fortunate, develop a consensus adequate to program formulation and execution.

To varying degrees, dependent on the breadth of acceptance of their programs, officials at every level of significant discretion must make their estimates of the situation, take stock of their resources, and plan accordingly. A keen appreciation of the real components of their organization is the beginning of wisdom. These components will be found to stretch far beyond the government payroll. Within the government they will encompass Congress, Congressmen, committees, courts, other agencies, presidential advisers, and the President. The Aristotelian analysis of constitutions is equally applicable and equally necessary to an understanding of administrative organization.

The broad alliance of conflicting groups that makes up presidential majorities scarcely coheres about any definite pattern of objectives, nor has it by the alchemy of the party system had its collective power concentrated in an accepted leadership with a personal mandate. The conciliation and maintenance of this support is a necessary condition of the attainment and retention of office involving, as Madison so well saw, "the spirit of party and faction in the necessary and ordinary operations of government." The President must in large part be, if not all things to all men, at least many things to many men. As a consequence, the contradictions in his power base invade administration. The often criticized apparent cross-purposes of the Roosevelt regime cannot be put down to inept administration until the political facts are weighed. Were these apparently self-defeating measures reasonably related to the general maintenance of the composite majority of the Administration? The first objective—ultimate patriotism apart—of the administrator is the attainment and retention of the power on which his tenure of office depends. This is the necessary pre-condition for the accomplishment of all other objectives.

The same ambiguities that arouse the scorn of the naive in the electoral campaigns of the parties are equally inevitable in administration and for the same reasons. Victory at the polls does not yield either a clear-cut grant of power or a unified majority support for a coherent program. The task of the presidency lies in feeling out the alternatives of policy which are consistent with the retention and increase of the group support on which the administration rests. The lack of a budgetary theory (so frequently deplored) is not due to any incapacity to apply rational analysis to the comparative contribution of the various activities of government to a determinate hierarcy of purposes. It more probably stems from a fastidious distaste for the frank recognition of the budget as a politically expedient allocation of resources. Appraisal in terms of their political contribution to the administration provides almost a sole common denominator between the Forest Service and the Bureau of Engraving.

Integration of the administrative structure through an overall purpose in terms of which tasks and priorities can be established is an emergency phenomenon. Its realization, only partial at best, has been limited to war and the extremity of depression. Even in wartime the Farm Bureau Federation, the American Federation of Labor, the Congress of Industrial Organizations, the National Association of Manufacturers, the Chamber of Commerce, and a host of lesser interests resisted coordination of themselves and the agencies concerned with their interests. A presidency temporarily empowered by intense mass popular support acting in behalf of a generally accepted and simplified purpose can, with great difficulty, bribe, cajole, and coerce a real measure of joint action. The long-drawn-out battle for conversion and the debacle of orderly reconversion underline the difficulty of attaining, and the transitory nature of, popularly based emergency power. Only in crises are the powers of the Executive nearly adequate to impose a common plan of action on the executive branch, let alone the economy.

In ordinary times the manifold pressures of our pluralistic society work themselves out in accordance with the balance of forces prevailing in Congress and the agencies. Only to a limited degree is the process subject to responsible direction or review by President or party leadership.

The program of the President cannot be a Gosplan for the government precisely because the nature of his institutional and group support gives him insufficient power. The personal unity of the presidency cannot perform the function of Hobbes' sovereign since his office lacks the authority of Hobbes' contract. Single-headedness in the Executive gives no assurance of singleness of purpose. It only insures that the significant pressures in a society will be brought to bear on one office. Monarchy solves the problem of giving one plan to a multitude only when the plentitude of its authority approaches dictatorship. Impatient social theorists in all ages have turned to the philosopher king as a substitute for consensus. Whatever else he may become, it is difficult to conceive of the American President ruling as a philosopher king, even with the advice of the Executive Office. The monarchical solution to the administrative problems posed by the lack of a disciplined party system capable of giving firm leadership and a program to the legislature is a modern variant of the dreams of the eighteenth century savants and well nigh equally divorced from a realistic appraisal of social realities.

Much of administrative thought, when it does not assume the value of coordination for coordination's sake, operates on the assumption that there must be something akin to Rousseau's *volonté générale* in administration to which the errant *volonté de tous* of the bureaus can and should be made to conform. This will-o'-the-wisp was made the object of an illuminating search by Pendleton Herring in his *Public Administration and the Public Interest*. The answer for Rousseau was enlightened dictatorship or counting the votes. The administrative equivalent to the latter is the resultant of the relevant pressures, as Herring shows. The first alternative seems to require at least the potency of the British Labour party and elsewhere has needed the disciplined organization of a fascist, nazi, or communist party to provide the power and consensus necessary to coordinate the manifold activities of government to a common plan.

Dictatorship, as Sigmund Neumann has observed, is a substitute for institutions which is required to fill the vacuum when traditional institutions break down. Force supplies the compulsion and guide to action in place of the normal routines of unconscious habit. Administrative organizations, however much they may appear the creations of art, are institutions produced in history and woven in the web of social relationships that gives them life and being. They present the same refractory material to the hand of the political artist as the rest of society of which they form a part.

Just as the economists have attempted to escape the complexities of institutional reality by taking refuge in the frictionless realm of theory, so some students of administration, following their lead, have seen in the application of the doctrine of opportunity costs a clue to a science of administration. Valuable as this may be in a restricted way, Marx has more light to throw on the study of institutions. It is in the dynamics and interrelations of institutions that we have most hope of describing and therefore learning to control administrative behavior.

The difficulty of coordinating government agencies lies not only in the fact that bureaucratic organizations are institutions having survival interests which may conflict with their rational adaptation to overall purpose, but even more in their having roots in society. Coordination of the varied activities of a modern government almost of necessity involves a substantial degree of coordination of the economy. Coordination of government agencies involves far more than changing the behavior and offices of officials in Washington and the field. It involves the publics that are implicated in their normal functioning. To coordinate fiscal policy, agricultural policy, labor policy, foreign policy, and military policy, to name a few major areas, moves beyond the range of government charts and the habitat of the bureaucrats to the market place and to where the people live and work. This suggests that the reason why government reorganization is so difficult is that far more than government in the formal sense is involved in reorganization. One could overlook this in the limited government of the nineteenth century but the multi-billion dollar government of the mid-twentieth permits no facile dichotomy between government and economy. Economy and efficiency are the two objectives a *laissez-faire* society can prescribe in peacetime as overall government objectives. Their inadequacy either as motivation or standards has long been obvious. A planned economy clearly requires a planned government. But, if one can afford an unplanned economy, apart from gross extravagance, there seems no compelling and therefore, perhaps, no sufficiently powerful reason for a planned government.

Basic to the problems of administrative rationality is that of organizational identification and point of view. To whom is one loyal—unit, section, branch, division, bureau, department, administration, government, country, people, world history, or what? Administrative analysis frequently assumes that organizational identification should occur in such a way as to merge primary organization loyalty in a larger synthesis. The good of the part is to give way to the reasoned good of the whole. This is most frequently illustrated in the rationalizations used to counter self-centered demands of primary groups for funds and personnel. Actually the competition between governmental power centers, rather than the rationalizations, is the effective instrument of coordination.

Where there is a clear common product on whose successful production the subgroups depend for the attainment of their own satisfaction, it is possible to demonstrate to almost all participants the desirability of cooperation. The shoe factory produces shoes, or else, for all concerned. But the government as a whole and many of its component parts have no such identifiable common product on which all depend. Like the proverbial Heinz, there are fifty-seven or more varieties unified, if at all, by a common political profit and loss account.

Administration is faced by somewhat the same dilemma as economics. There are propositions about the behavior patterns conducive to full employment—welfare economics. On the other hand, there are propositions about the economics of the individual firm—the counsel of the business schools. It is possible to show with considerable persuasiveness that sound considerations for the individual firm may lead to a depression if generally adopted, a result desired by none of the participants. However, no single firm can afford by itself to adopt the course of collective wisdom; in the absence of a common power capable of enforcing decisions premised on the supremacy of the collective interest, *sauve qui peut* is common sense.

The position of administrative organizations is not unlike the position of particular firms. Just as the decisions of the firms could be coordinated by the imposition of a planned economy so could those of the component parts of the government. But just as it is possible to operate a formally unplanned economy by the loose coordination of the market, in the same fashion it is possible to operate a government by the loose coordination of the play of political forces through its institutions.

The unseen hand of Adam Smith may be little in evidence in either case. One need not believe in a doctrine of social or administrative harmony to believe that formal centralized planning—while perhaps desirable and in some cases necessary—is not a must. The complicated logistics of supplying the city of New York runs smoothly down the grooves of millions of well adapted habits projected from a distant past. It seems naive on the one hand to believe in the possibility of a vast, intricate, and delicate economy operating with a minimum of formal overall direction, and on the other to doubt that a relatively simple mechanism such as the government can be controlled largely by the same play of forces.

Doubtless the real reasons for seeking coordination in the government are the same that prompt a desire for economic planning. In fact, apart from waging war with its demand for rapid change, economic planning would seem to be the only objective sufficiently compelling and extensive to require a drastic change in our system of political *laissez-faire*. Harold Smith, testifying before the Senate Banking and Currency Committee on the Employment Act of 1946, showed how extensive a range of hitherto unrelated activities could be brought to bear on a common purpose—the maintenance of maximum employment and purchasing power. In the flush of the war experience and with prophecies of reconversion unemployment, a reluctant Congress passed a pious declaration of policy. Senator Flanders has recorded the meager showing to date.

Nevertheless, war and depression apart, the Employment Act of 1946 for the first time provides an inclusive common purpose in terms of which administrative activities can be evaluated and integrated. While still deficient in depth and content, it provides at least a partial basis for the rational budgeting of government activities. The older concept of economy and efficiency as autonomous standards still lingers in Congress, but elsewhere their validity as ends in themselves is treated with skepticism.

If the advent of Keynesian economics and the erosion of *laissez-faire* have created the intellectual conditions requisite for the formulation of overall government policy, they do not by any means guarantee the political conditions necessary for its implementation. We can see quite clearly that the development of an integrated administration requires an integrating purpose. The ideals of Locke, Smith, Spencer, and their American disciples deny the need for such a purpose save for economy and efficiency's sake. Marx, Keynes, and their followers by denying the validity of the self-regulating economy have endowed the state with an overarching responsibility in terms of which broad coordination of activities is not only intellectually possible but theoretically, at least, necessary. Intellectual perception of the need for this coordination, however, has run well ahead of the public's perception of it and of the development of a political channeling of power adequate to its administrative implementation.

Most students of administration are planners of some sort. Most Congressmen would fly the label like the plague. Most bureaucrats, whatever their private faith, live under two jealous gods, their particular clientele and the loyalty check. Such a condition might, if it exists as described, cast doubt on whether even the intellectual conditions for rational administrative coordination exist. Be that as it may, the transition from a government organized in clientele departments and bureaus, each responding to the massive feudal power of organized business, organized agriculture, and organized labor, to a government integrated about a paramount national purpose will require a political power at least as great as that which tamed the earlier feudalism. It takes a sharp eye or a tinted glass to see such an organized power on the American scene. Without it, administrative organization for overall coordination has the academic air of South American constitution making. One is reminded of the remark attributed to the Austrian economist Mises; on being told that the facts did not agree with his theory, he replied "*desto schlechter für die Tatsache.*"

It is highly appropriate to consider how administrators should behave to meet the test of efficiency in a planned polity; but in the absence of such a polity and while, if we like, struggling to get it, a realistic science of administration will teach administrative behavior appropriate to the existing political system.

A close examination of the presidential system may well bring one to conclude that administrative rationality in it is a different matter from that applicable to the British ideal. The American presidency is an office that has significant monarchical characteristics despite its limited term and elective nature. The literature on court and palace has many an insight applicable to the White House. Access to the President, reigning favorites, even the court jester, are topics that show the continuity of institutions. The maxims of LaRochefoucald and the memoirs of the Duc de Saint Simon have a refreshing realism for the operator on the Potomac.

The problem of rival factions in the President's family is as old as the famous struggle between Jefferson and Hamilton, as fresh and modern as the latest cabal against . . . [a Cabinet officer]. Experience seems to show that this personal and factional struggle for the President's favor is a vital part of the process of representation. The vanity, personal ambition, or patriotism of the contestants soon clothes itself in the generalities of principle and the clique aligns itself with groups beyond the capital. Subordinate rivalry is tolerated if not encouraged by so many able executives that it can scarcely be attributed to administrative ineptitude. The wrangling tests opinion, uncovers information that would otherwise never rise to the top, and provides effective opportunity for decision rather than mere ratification of prearranged plans. Like most judges, the Executive needs to hear argument for his own instruction. The alternatives presented by subordinates in large part determine the freedom and the creative opportunity of their superiors. The danger of becoming a Merovingian is a powerful incentive to the maintenance of fluidity in the structure of power.

The fixed character of presidential tenure makes it necessary that subordinates be politcally expendable. The President's men must be willing to accept the blame for failures not their own. Machiavelli's teaching on how princes must keep the faith bears re-reading. Collective responsibility is incompatible with a fixed term of office. As it tests the currents of public opinion, the situation on the Hill, and the varying strength of the organized pressures, the White House alters and adapts the complexion of the administration. Loyalties to programs or to groups and personal pride and interest frequently conflict with whole-souled devotion to the presidency. In fact, since such devotion is not made mandatory by custom, institutions, or the facts of power, the problem is perpetually perplexing to those who must choose.

The balance of power between executive and legislature is constantly subject to the shifts of public and group support. The latent tendency of the American Congress is to follow the age-old parliamentary precedents and to try to reduce the President to the role of constitutional monarch. Against this threat and to secure his own initiative, the President's resources are primarily demagogic, with the weaknesses and strengths that dependence on mass popular appeal implies. The unanswered question of American government—"who is boss?"—constantly plagues administration. The disruption of unity of command is not just the problem of Taylor's functional foreman, but goes to the stability and uniformity of basic decisional premises essential to consequent administration.

It is interesting to speculate on the consequences for administration of the full development of congressional or presidential government. A leadership in Congress that could control the timetable of the House and Senate would scarcely content itself short of reducing the President's Cabinet to what in all probability it was first intended to be, a modified version of the present Swiss executive. Such leadership could scarcely arise without centrally organized, disciplined, national parties far different from our present shambling alliances of state and local machines.

A presidency backed by a disciplined party controlling a majority in Congress would probably assimilate itself to a premiership by association of legislative leadership in the formulation of policy and administration. In either line of development the crucial matter is party organization. For the spirit of the party system determines the character of the government.

That the American party system will develop toward the British ideal is by no means a foregone conclusion. The present oscillation between a strong demagogic presidency and a defensively powerful congressional oligarchy may well prove a continuing pattern of American politics, as it was of Roman. In the absence of a party system providing an institutionalized centripetal force in our affairs, it is natural to look to the presidency as Goldsmith's weary traveler looked to the throne.

The presidency of the United States, however, is no such throne as the pre-World War I *Kaiserreich* that provided the moral and political basis for the Prussian bureaucracy. Lacking neutrality and mystique, it does not even perform the function of the British monarchy in providing a psychological foundation for the permanent civil service. A leaderless and irresponsible Congress frequently makes it appear the strong point of the republic. The Bonapartist experience in France, the Weimar Republic, and South American examples nearer home, despite important social differences, are relevant to any thoughtful consideration of building a solution to legislative anarchy on the unity of the executive.

The present course of American party development gives little ground for optimism that a responsible two-party system capable of uniting Congress and Executive in a coherent program will emerge. The increasingly critical importance of the federal budget for the national economy and the inevitable impact of world power status on the conduct of foreign affairs makes inescapable the problem of stable leadership in the American system. Unfortunately they by no means insure a happy or indeed any solution.

Attempts to solve administrative problems in isolation from the structure of power and purpose in the polity are bound to prove illusory. The reorganization of Congress to create responsibility in advance of the development of party responsibility was an act of piety to principle, of educational value; but as a practical matter it raised a structure without foundation. In the same way, reorganization of the executive branch to centralize administrative power in the presidency while political power remains dispersed and divided may effect improvement, but in a large sense it must fail. The basic prerequisite to the administration of the textbooks is a responsible two-party system. The means to its attainment are a number one problem for students of administration. What Schattschneider calls the struggle for party government may sometime yield us the responsible parliamentary two-party system needed to underpin our present administrative theory. Until that happy time, exploration of the needs and necessities of our present system is a high priority task of responsible scholarship.

Socialist

Gerald M. Schaflander. The "balanced" liberal ideology at the Federal Trade Commission: A due process radical alternative.

Pluralists maintain that there is a series of built-in checks and balances within the administrative and legislative branches of Government that blocks big business corporations from monopolizing the economy and controlling the political process. Many radicals maintain that large corporations have completely taken over the economy and totally and irreversibly dominate the polity. Some liberals proclaim a "balanced view" by saying that there are two relatively equal sides to the political and economic battles in our society. By doing so they legitimate the perpetuation of corporate control over much of American society. I will argue in this analysis that although oli-

gopolistic[1] companies and industries have effectively penetrated the polity, many of the democratic values inherent in the culture and in the constitution still survive.

The fight for democracy and the protection of consumers from unfair, deceptive, and manipulative business practices depend, in large part, upon exposing "balanced-view liberals." They must be removed from decision-making posts within the polity in order to stop the destruction of a free economic and political marketplace. The Federal Trade Commission (FTC) is one of the key battlegrounds on which radicals and liberals contest their conflicting values and goals.

A careful and critical analysis of the FTC, its bureaucratic, pro-business practices, and the need for structural reforms at and by the Senate Commerce Committee and at the FTC itself, must be creatively and carefully considered. A radical alternative using due process strategies must be attempted before a political verdict for the future is drawn. To accept a monolithic analysis of the polity without engaging in a democratic fight to alter the FTC would make this analysis into a self-fulfilling prophecy.

Deception and manipulation are practiced daily upon the American consumer by corporations. Strategies and tactics have to be developed in order to stop big business from overwhelming consumers and wiping out their capacity to protect themselves from being manipulated. Only after the fight to implement new institutional reforms has been made can radicals and their supporters consider further action. Through institutional conflict (such as restructuring the FTC and Senate Commerce Committee), large numbers of people can be involved—across the political spectrum—to determine the success or failure of various strategies and tactics. In this way, one can build a constituency for social and political change that responds to consumer issues and actions rather than to abstract rhetoric.

To say that there is no use in fighting oligopoly under the present system and to offer only the hope of a future utopian dream, of a nonspecific, nonblueprinted vague form of socialism, inevitably checks the support of large numbers of potential allies.[2] And how do we know we will fail to institute basic, structural reforms if we don't try, now? Will people respect us if we don't even try? If we say dogmatically that there is no hope under this system? Building mutual hope, trust, and respect is the first step in building a constituency for political and social change. Offering strategy and tactics that might build a broad constituency to reform the FTC is a first step necessary to effect institutional change.

Millions of Americans are seriously disturbed by the blackmail price-rise tactics of the oil, food, and utility oligopolies. People will listen to programs to combat these noncompetitive industries. They will respond to proposals on their merits, if they are talked to with respect and in the accepted terms of American democracy. With this perspective, we can analyze the recent activities of the Federal Trade Commission, the one institution empowered to stop unfair, manipulative, and deceptive business practices perpetrated on the American people. This vital regulatory agency, by law, can be one key to reversing the escalating growth of oligopoly, by protecting American consumers from being "ripped-off."

At its creation in 1914, the Federal Trade Commission was empowered to deal with antitrust problems. The FTC Act and the Clayton Act, along with the Sherman Antitrust Act, were an indication by Congress that it intended the FTC to carry out a variety of functions to combat monopolies.

The FTC Act prescribed procedural forms for establishing violations, halting them through the issuance of Cease and Desist orders, and enforcing such orders by civil penalties.[3] The Wheeler-Lea Act of 1938 specified that the FTC was to be involved directly in consumer-protection, and it gave the FTC a critical enforcement role in that regard. Because of widespread consumer deception that accelerated during the depression of the 1930s, Congress mandated the FTC to deal with consumer protection. The specific provisions added to the FTC Act in 1938 not only outlawed "deceptive acts and practices" but also gave the FTC enforcement powers over particularly dangerous deception areas. The FTC was thus authorized to *seek both criminal penalties* and *temporary injunctions to prevent deceptive advertising of foods, drugs,* and *cosmetics* (FTC Act, Sections 12, 14, and 15). But Cease and Desist orders became institutionalized as an endless process that did not stop deception by a rapidly expanding advertising industry. The injunction process—to stop food, drug and cosmetic deceptions immediately—has never been used on behalf of consumers, as a weapon against deceptive advertisers. Cease and Desist orders became a bureaucratic nightmare to exponents of rapid and effective deterrents against deceptive advertisers.

The struggle for consumer protection by the FTC started in 1938, but the full powers of the FTC to immediately halt advertising deception by the food, drug, and cosmetic industries have never been used. The injunction powers in Section 13(C), of the FTC Act, have not been invoked.

The Federal Trade Commission procedure

The FTC is the key regulatory agency insofar as effective regulation of antitrust and consumer protection activities are concerned.[4] Here, briefly, is how the FTC is supposed to work from the initial complaint to final decision in protecting the consumer from unfair, deceptive, and manipulative business practices:

An application for complaint is filed with the FTC by either a consumer, businessman, member of Congress, or anyone from a local, state, or federal government agency.

Each application is reviewed to determine if it falls under the jurisdiction of the FTC statute.

If so, an investigation is begun.

Based on the information obtained in the investigation, a decision is made either 1) to close the case for failure to find that a violation has occurred or 2) to issue a formal complaint, along with a Cease and Desist Order. If the latter takes place, the case can be settled by a "consent order" wherein the charged party certifies that the challenged practices will be corrected or discontinued.

If the charged party disagrees with the proposed order, the complaint is issued and public hearings before an FTC examiner are held.

The examiner hears the arguments and decides either to issue the Cease and Desist Order or to dismiss some or all charges.

If the hearing examiner's initial decision is not appealed, it may be adopted by the Commission, requiring the businessman or company to comply.

The Federal Trade Commission in practice

The FTC was established to serve the public by attacking unfair and deceptive acts or practices in commerce. Ralph Nader's study group on the FTC charged that it is pro-business, pro-monopoly, and pro-large advertisers.[5] Further, Nader's Raiders charged that,

When viewed after a cursory examination of FTC public relations, the failures of the FTC reveal an outstanding feature of its operation—its continual and consistent violation of its own statutes with regard to deceptive practices. . . . It has avoided congressional (oversight) or other investigation or review for a decade by consistently responding to the vector theory of power—feeding and serving those who would or do not threaten it.

(Substantially, this means serving and feeding big business and subservient Congressional interests).[6] The Raiders went on:

We will show how the FTC has failed to do its job in four specific regards. Unless it addresses itself to correcting these failures, the FTC will never work with any effectiveness.

1. The FTC has failed to detect violations systematically.

2. The FTC has failed to establish efficient priorities for its enforcement energy.

3. The FTC has failed to enforce the powers it has with energy and speed.

4. The FTC has failed to seek sufficient statutory authority to make its work effective.[7]

The FTC staff at the Washington office is divided into administrative offices and operating bureaus. The major operating bureaus are those of Consumer Protection, Economics, Competition, Field Offices, Industry Guidance, Textiles and Furs. The major administrative offices are those of the Secretary, Program Review Officer, General Counsel, Hearing Examiners, and Executive Director. The FTC Commission itself is composed of five members (commissioners) appointed by the President, with the advice and consent of the Senate, for staggered seven-year terms. The Chairman, appointed by the President, has extensive powers and responsibility in the management of the FTC. He is its top administrative officer and is responsible for hiring and promoting persons on the staff and at the Bureau level.

The American Bar Association, under the antitrust committee leadership of Miles Kirkpatrick—prominent Philadelphia lawyer—substantially confirmed the Nader report charge of FTC ineffectuality on behalf of the consumer and the free, competitive marketplace. As a result of this Kirkpatrick-ABA report, President Nixon appointed Kirkpatrick chairman of the FTC in 1970. Kirkpatrick then appointed Robert Pitofsky, formerly counsel of the ABA antitrust committee and New York University law professor, as director of the key FTC Bureau of Consumer Protection.

After the advent of the Kirkpatrick regime at the FTC, and after Pitofsky started his job, accelerated activities (mostly public relations and a cool style) were publicly noticed at the FTC, which began to *seemingly* test its authority in a wide-ranging number of cases and programs. Its basic assignment and responsibility, however—to protect consumers and small businesses against unfair, deceptive, and anticompetitive advertising and business practices—did not become evident. The accuracy of this perception is quite critical since the FTC is the sole legal institution (the heart of the "pluralist" check and balance myth of democracy) specifically authorized to protect the consumer and guarantee perpetuation of a free, competitive marketplace.

Michael Pertschuk, Chief Counsel to the Senate Commerce Committee (under the chairmanship of Senator Warren Magnuson), is a long-time liberal, with a consumer advocate reputation. He works very closely with Nader, the FTC commissioners and staff, while also maintaining solid industry and trade association contacts. He noted in a statement to the author:

Kirkpatrick is doing some very tough things. The whole tone, spirit, and commitment to consumer protection is vigorous and much progress has been made, especially under Robert Pitofsky's Bureau of Consumer Protection. The knowledge that key members of the Senate Consumer Subcommittee (under Magnuson and Moss) and the Senate Commerce Committee favor these changes has had a supportive effect.

Pitofsky, three years later, became counsel to an anti-FTC, big business, super law firm, Covington & Burling. Kirkpatrick is back practicing law in Philadelphia, along with Pitofsky, also representing clients against the FTC. Not one iota of evidence exists to document or support Pertschuk's thesis that consumers were or are being "*vigorously protected*." Pitofsky's influence is still *deeply felt* at the FTC. His successors and colleagues, namely Jodi Bernstein, Jim Cohen, Gerald Thain, and E. Roush (current head of the Bureau of Consumer Protection under Republican Chairman, Lewis Engman) have a deep bureaucratic and career investment in the Pitofsky practices that were initiated under the Kirkpatrick regime. And they are all still operating under the Bureau of Consumer Protection umbrella at the FTC—though many job title and hierarchial shifts have taken place.

From 1970 to 1973, the FTC appeared as if it were starting to move beyond its old role of merely issuing Cease and Desist orders against deceptive advertising and offending advertisers. There was a proposal that advertisers must substantiate all advertising claims. This new ad substantiation program promised action by threatening the removal of commercials if the product and ad limitations were not made fully known to the public. Some examples of deceptive advertising follow.

Over the counter drugs: The multibillion dollar overdose

Here's how to turn that mood around: Just take two *Bayer Aspirin* for your headache, sit down for a few minutes, and relax. [8]

You can trust *Anacin* to relieve headache pain in minutes. Then its nervous tension and painful pressure on nerves go, too. *Anacin* lets you do a better job. Lets you function better. [9]

When you take two *Exedrin* you're able to cope with your problems a lot better. [10]

In 1970 the American public spent over $500 million for nonprescription analgesic drugs. This figure includes the sale and consumption of approximately 17,500 tons of aspirin (the principle analgesic ingredient), a yearly average of 225 tablets for each American. In 1970 the drug companies that manufacture and sell these analgesic products spent over $100 million in advertising and sales promotion. The major proportion of this expenditure went into television advertising campaigns.

For example, "To relieve a headache fast Bayer Aspirin's got the best help there is." Ad agency Dancer-Fitzgerald-Sample claimed for Cope, a product of Sterling Drug: "Important studies made at the world's leading headache clinic show that for relief of severe nervous tension headaches, a combination of a pain reliever and a sedative provides greater relief than either medication alone."

Again, Sterling Drug, through the Benton & Bowles advertising agency, claimed, "When you get a headache we think you should take Vanquish." And last, but not surprisingly, the same Sterling Drug, via the Thompson-Koch advertising agency, claimed that Midol has "medically approved ingredients that relieve headache."

The competition, not to be outdone, struck back. Bristol-Myers, through its agency Ted Bates, claimed, ". . . Bufferin speeds its pain-reliever to your headache twice as fast as simple aspirin." Through the Young & Rubicam ad agency Bristol-Myers claimed, "For Excedrin headaches you want the Excedrin formula, with four ingredients, to relieve pain and its tension." And once again, Young & Rubicam for Bristol-Myers deceivingly maintained, "Excedrin PM is the extra-strength nighttime pain reliever." At a minimum, Bristol-Myers has distorted facts and manipulated the consumer on two out of three products.

Finally, the third in our line of pain-reliever companies, American Home Products, through the John F. Murray Advertising Agency, claimed, "Anacin gives you 100% more of the strong pain-reliever doctors recommend most for headaches than the other leading extra-strength tablet."

Can they all be correct? Obviously not. Someone is lying! Perhaps they are all lying?

Let us see what medical and pharmacological experts have to say about these ($88 million worth of) claims.

The following are excerpted segments of the testimony of Drs. Beaver and Simmons given before Senator Gaylord Nelson's Select Small Business Subcommittee:

Staff Director, Mr. Gordon: Which products are these?

Dr. Simmons:[11] These are *Anacin* and *Excedrin* . . .

In sum, the OTC analgesics represent a class of drugs manufactured in an endless variety of dosages, but containing basically three analgesic agents. They are promoted with techniques that bombard consumers with terminology which confuses, rather than enlightens and informs.

None of these preparations are known to be any better for pain than aspirin and some in fact are inferior.

Senator Nelson: Looking at the ingredients of Vanquish, does the caffeine or acetaminophen or aluminum hydroxide or the various milligram dosages listed there have any analgesic effect that you are aware of?

Dr. Beaver: . . . the caffeine, as far as we know, does not really do anything.

Senator Nelson: Does a milligram of acetaminophen have about the same effect as a milligram of aspirin?

Dr. Beaver: In those conditions where studies have been done, it seems to be about equi-analgesic [equal] on a milligram basis.

Dr. Simmons: In the main, nothing in the OTC drug market has yet been shown to surpass aspirin as an analgesic, antipyretic, anti-inflammatory agent.

Dr. Beaver: Very few of the OTC analgesics have ever been tested extensively for headaches, surprisingly enough.

Dr. Simmons: In comparability ad claims, much promotion is based on statements such as "stronger than aspirin," "extra-strength pain-relief," "fast" or "faster" pain-relief, "more prolonged relief," or "gentler" or "less irritating." The consumer is not told that the two leading competitive products featuring "stronger than aspirin" claims simply provide more aspirin per tablet and are combined with other ingredients that contribute little or nothing to the product.

Mr. Gordon: Here is an advertisement for Anacin, of which I am handing you a copy. It mentions tension headaches and it says: "Clinical tests by doctors on over 500 patients who complained of tension headaches prove Anacin relieves nervous tension headaches just as effectively as the expensive leading prescription." Is there any evidence that Anacin is less irritating, faster acting, and relieves tension?

Dr. Simmons: No. We have no evidence to support either of those last three claims. The particular quote this article talks about, that Anacin has been shown in studies to relieve nervous tension headaches just as effectively as the leading prescription, unfortunately doesn't go on to point out that both the leading prescription product and Anacin are not known to be any more effective than aspirin alone. [12]

Toothpaste

The "brightening toothpastes" are highly abrasive. Their greatest danger is to those over thirty-five, the age when many adults (approximately 25 percent) begin to suffer a general gum recedence. This exposes part of the root or cemetum above the gum. The highly abrasive material common to the "whitening toothpastes," while possibly dangerous to enamel itself, is more likely to be dangerous to cementum. On January 1, 1969, the American Dental Association issued a warning about the product. How many Americans know of the warning? Probably no more than a few thousand. Yet the makers of Plus-White, Ultra-Brite, Ipana, Macleans, and others seem to feel no compunction about withholding this information. Indeed, they feel no compunction about continuing to advertise the sex appeal and general virtue of abrasive toothpastes.[13]

Cigarettes

Sports, music, travel, vacations, jewelry, cosmetics, and clothing are the principal areas of interest chosen for cigarette premium promotions. These leisure, fun, and hedonistic appeals to the potential or "hooked" cigarette smokers go a long way to re-establish a health-fun-love brand-image for smoking and to overcome the death and disease threats inherent in the legal warnings which are required to be displayed on all cigarette advertising. In fact, if you look at the miniscule size of the small end-of-the-pack picture, the minute type, and the obscure words of the health warning, chances are that.

WARNING: THE SURGEON GENERAL HAS DETERMINED THAT CIGARETTE SMOKING IS DANGEROUS TO YOUR HEALTH

will be lost in a pictorial sea of blue water or green grass, inhabited by handsome men and women, clothed in exquisite sports or swim ensembles, glamorously adorned with jewelry—vitality personified. What a way to die!

The cigarette advertising in the pages of *Esquire, Time, Newsweek, Sports Illustrated,* and so on, are guilty of the exact same technique of utilizing nature-health pictorial and other beneficial imagery to drown out or obscure the somber and dangerous health warning required by law. Advertising manipulation of this "heart disease and cancer causing" industry is highlighted by tobacco companies like R. J. Reynolds, American Brands, Inc., Lorillard (a division of Loews), Philip Morris, Liggett-Myers, and Brown & Williamson, selling both filter-tip and nonfilter cigarette brands, competing against each other as separate brands while being manufactured and marketed surreptitiously by the same company.[14] It is perfectly acceptable in the manipulative-deceptive advertising departments of the major cigarette companies and their advertising agencies, to perpetuate this shrewd reverse charade on a frightened, smoking public.

Recent cigarette advertising is obscenely bizarre. *Newsweek* (September 22, 1975, p. 79)

"ALIVE WITH PLEASURE - NEWPORT . . ."

(Smoking Newport could just as well leave you *dead* with heart disease and cancer.)

Sports Illustrated (September 23, 1975) . . .

"L & M - THE PROUD SMOKE"

(*Proud* to die of emphysema?)

"THERE'S A LITTLE EVE IN EVERY WOMAN . . . TRY TODAY'S EVE: FLOWERS ON THE OUTSIDE"

(And flowers on the grave too—because of cancer and heart disease on the smoker's *insides*?)

And quite hidden, way off in the wild blue yonder, those immortal words—obscured in each of the above advertisements:

WARNING: THE SURGEON GENERAL HAS DETERMINED THAT CIGARETTE SMOKING IS DANGEROUS TO YOUR HEALTH

FTC responses

The headlines in *Ad Age*, the bible of the ad industry, revealed industry concern, anger, and even threats of legal action against the FTC and the Commission, or even outright withdrawal of all advertising from media that supported corrective advertising policies. As time went by, the ad industry was content to let the FTC and the public think that corrective advertising was a serious deterrent to deceptive advertising and that the ad industry was concerned and frightened by this vigorous new protection tool purportedly advanced by the FTC on behalf of the consumer. In 1975, the FTC is still spending endless days and hours negotiating for corrective advertising penalties with huge expenditures of money, manpower, and publicity supporting this massive effort. But, in fact, the corrective advertising program has been a *total and colossal failure* insofar as deterring deceptive advertising. And though publicity still generates attention, it is becoming more obvious daily that corrective advertising is ineffectual and only protects bureaucratic jobs for Bureau of Consumer Protection (BCP)-FTC Personnel. Yet, while serious deception and unfair advertising and marketing practices rage on unchecked by the FTC, the public relations battle over corrective advertising also rages loudly and furiously!

There obviously is no doubt as to the FTC's right to force corrective ads; misrepresentation, deception, or unfair manipulation is within their legal purview. There is, however, considerable question about whether the FTC can or will push the Federal Communications Commission (FCC) hard enough to implement the FTC suggestion that "counteradvertising" rebuttals from consumer advocates might be put into five-minute blocks of prime broadcasting time as a public service.[15] Another FTC recommendation was "open availability," meaning that anyone who wants to rebut an advertiser can do so by paying for the rebuttal, just as any commercial advertiser does (as part of the "fairness doctrine").[16] The Federal Communications Commission never responded. The Pitofsky ploy for counteradvertising fell on "expected" deaf ears at the FCC. Nevertheless, the pseudovigorous Bureau of Consumer Protection plowed ahead with its "new" programs.

Corrective advertising became the keystone of the Pitofsky thrust. As interpreted by the FTC, corrective advertising must be run by an advertiser who has previously had his claims declared unfair and deceptive by the FTC and so must now publicize that deception.

An example of the use of corrective advertising is the case of Profile bread (ITT Continental Baking Company). Gerald Thain (Pitofsky appointee), Director of National Advertising, stated:

Profile runs the corrective commercials more than 25% of the time. One of the interesting reasons for their going along with Corrective Ads is that some of the general public response to the corrective ads, is: "What candor, what honesty."[17]

It is clear that Profile would not be running the corrective advertising if it hurt the product of corporate image. In this case, Profile's corrective advertising helped the product image. Corrective advertising actually aids and encourages Profile and other advertisers to go ahead with their regular deceptive advertising. If the FTC catches them, they negotiate a corrective advertising settlement that inserts changes in their commercials to build consumer confidence in the product's candor and honesty. Deception is thus rewarded—not punished. No basic corrective repudiation would be tolerated for one minute by a powerful national advertiser.

Robert Pitofsky promised that there would be several other agreements negotiated before the fall of 1972 so that corrective advertising, as an ongoing policy, would be functioning in cases "other than ITT-Profile." None has been seen on television or in print as of September 1975.

Ford, Chrysler, and General Motors, the three oligopolistic giants of the automobile industry, have been caught in manipulative and deceptive advertising practices through the FTC initiation of the ad substantiation program. But no specific actions or basic alterations in automobile advertising by the Big 3 have resulted from any FTC actions brought against them...at least up until September 25, 1975. On that day, a Reuters news story appeared in the The *Los Angeles Times*[18]—three years after the ad substantiation FTC program originated:

CHRYSLER MILEAGE ADS FALSE, FTC JUDGE RULES

Washington—Chrysler Corporation has run false advertisements of gasoline mileage of its small cars, a Federal Trade Commission administrative judge has ruled.

The ruling...may be appealed to the commission within 30 days, but if upheld would force Chrysler to end such claims for its Plymouth Valiants and Dodge Darts.

Judge Miles Brown found that Chrysler falsely advertised that *Popular Science* magazine had reported that all Chrysler's small cars were superior in gasoline mileage to all Chevrolet Nova cars.

In reality, he said, the magazine reported that Valiants and Darts equipped with six-cylinder engines obtained better mileage than Novas, but when equipped with eight-cylinder engines were inferior in mileage to Novas.

The advertisement in newspapers and magazines in 1973 and 1974 was also misleading...because it did not say that *Popular Science* reported both Nova sixes and eights were superior in mileage to Valiant and Dart eights.

Who regulates the regulators?

The principal antibusiness enforcement weapon still used by the FTC to police the vast majority of consumer frauds and deceits has been the Cease and Desist Order. In 1938, a minority of the House Committee reporting the Wheeler-Lea Act recognized and described the inadequacy of such a limited enforcement power.

Unless the disseminator of a false advertisement knows at the time of the dissemination that he may at some time in the future be held account-

able by a criminal or civil penalty action for the unlawful dissemination, he will NOT be deterred from such dissemination. It is just this deterring effect that is lacking when dependence is placed upon Cease and Desist Orders for enforcement.[19]

The Committee's fears proved well founded. Each subsequent decade has brought forth indictments of the FTC's incapacity to enforce Section 5 (a) (1) of the Federal Trade Commission Act.

The FTC's caution in withholding endorsement of the Moss-McGovern Truth in Advertising Bill, 1972, differs sharply in motivation from the self-serving attacks made by the Association of National Advertisers (ANA). In effect, however, they both served the same purpose. They both thwarted attempts to establish new law on behalf of beleagured consumers.

(1) In order for consumers to be protected, Congress must be pressed to pass the FTC Improvement Act to strengthen the FTC and give it the preliminary injunction powers to go into federal court and to stop unfair, deceptive advertising at inception. The FTC, however, hasn't used the power it already has to halt unfair food, drug, or cosmetic advertising through present injunctive powers.

(2) Through a Truth in Advertising bill, the consumer must be given the right to ask the advertiser directly for ad substantiation documentation. The consumer would then get the right to seek financial redress, up to $10,000 dollars, if he or she could prove unfairness and deception in court. This bill, which would give teeth to the consumer advocacy movement, could also serve notice to advertisers that if found guilty they can and will be punished severely from both a marketing and financial standpoint. They will not have the present, cozy option of stalling through the FTC internal bureaucratic procedures and through long, enervating FTC and/or court action, while continuing their suspect advertising campaigns.

As Warren Braren, of Consumers Union, pointed out in 1971, the ad substantiation program has been too slow and way behind yearly model changes. No significant action has yet been taken against Ford, Chrysler, GM, Norelco, and others.

The (FTC) Commission's request for and release of the documentation is certainly commendable [reference to advertising substantiation of claims program initiated by FTC]. But it is a Johnny-come-lately action! Most of this advertising [Ford, Chevy, Chrysler, and Norelco] ran for months before the Commission requested the documentation and then it took several more months before the Commission released it. The time delay—releasing old information on last year's models—is not in the consumers' best interest.

Why does the FTC delay and not deliver in the consumer's best interest?

Anyone working at the FTC, at the National Advertising division, or at the Bureau of Consumer Protection, knows that the ad substantiation program (and corrective and counter ad programs) are ineffective. Public relations efforts have neither focus, substance, nor structure behind them. What the FTC actually has is the form, not the substance of consumer protection programs. And this is either because of bureaucratic ponderousness, or advertising-industry political pressure.

Stylized, public relations activities are clever, but meaningless, as the utter failure of the corrective advertising and ad substantiation programs proves. But these stylized, pseudocreative and highly publicized programs have lulled many consumer advocates and groups into accepting the FTC and Congressional committees as a force for consumer protection and substantive action. The ineffectual and spiritless results of FTC work have been harmful because many liberals and consumer advocates have been sympathetic and "understanding" of the negligible or slow progress of FTC programs. The pluralist thesis of check-and-balance democratic regulation—an effective FTC check on big business—simply does not exist.

In the same manner as some liberals legitimated and made the Vietnam War acceptable (Bundy, Rostow, McNamara, Kissinger, Schlesinger); and as some liberals such as Lee White, Dave Freeman,

Stuart Udall, and John Carver have fronted for the seven sisters—the oil-energy corporations—in their oil-gas-coal-uranium price gouging; so too have the major big-business oligopolists had "their" liberals fronting for them on regulatory commissions and Congressional committees.

Leading the way has been Senator Warren Magnuson; Senate Commerce Committee Staff Director Mike Pertschuk; former Commissioner Mary Jones; FTC Consumer Protection officers, Bob Pitofsky, Gerry Thain, Jodi Bernstein, Chris White, and Jim Cohen—all "balanced" and fair-minded liberals—all looking at all sides of the difficult struggle confronting consumers. These liberal forces have put up phoney, irrelevant battles; that is, ad substantiation, corrective and counter ad programs, fighting the wrong forces with the weakest of weapons; all the while legitimating the status quo. Is there evidence to support this serious charge? Just read your papers and magazines, and watch television nightly. Look at the deceptive, unfair advertisers selling consumers merchandise they don't really need at gouging prices.

Advertising is admittedly only one key part of the entire process. Other aspects are: unfair discounting of network rates; barring entry of competitors by means of distribution and shelf space dominance because of massive pre-sold advertising to consumers; informal joint price fixing; coordinated lobbying to restrict consumer protection bills. All are part of the whole anticompetitive process which the FTC is supposed to prevent.

Louis M. Kohlmeier, Jr., formerly Washington correspondent of the *Wall Street Journal*, points out in his book, *The Regulators:*

Congress...conferred on the commission unusually large powers to look into the books and records of private corporations. It said in the Federal Trade Commission Act, the Commission's enabling law, that the FTC was empowered to investigate any corporation. The FTC's inquisitorial powers today are broader in their reach than those of any other agency of government that oversees business conduct. And Congress in 1914, established clear lines of communication between the Commission, on the one hand, and Congress and the President, on the other. The FTC Act said the Commission was to report to the legislative and executive branches whenever it concluded from its investigations that additional anti-trust or other economic legislation was necessary. The FTC was to use its power of investigation and its public hearing procedures to explore and air issues of industrial concentration, in particular industries, or in the economy at large. It could probe corporate records and require the presidents of the nation's largest corporations to appear before it, to testify on matters relating to an industry at large or to a single corporation.[20]

The potential power of the FTC, then, is considerable. Why does the FTC, now that it has established clear-cut guidelines and definitive criteria for unfair and deceptive advertising practices, still plod along on a case-by-case basis, allowing so much automobile, gasoline, cereal, drug, food, cosmetic, household bleach and detergent, toy, soft drink, and other manipulative advertising to continue uninterruptedly? Many of these industries, through their ads and sales promotion practices use the identical phrases, half-truths, partial disclosures, incomplete statements, exaggerated manipulations, and faulty comparisons that companies receiving Cease and Desist orders were guilty of. The FTC must obtain quicker results and broader protection of consumers—under the FTC Act. All ads of course would not have to be checked. Priorities must be established at the FTC, priorities that deal with the major deceptive advertisers. These can be easily determined each year by analyzing both *Advertising Age* and *National Advertising Investments*, which yearly publish lists of the leading, top 100 advertisers. These publications not only list the top advertisers by their gross, yearly ad expenditures, but they also encompass at least the first and second companies (in spending) of each of the leading advertising industries, which, coincidentally, 1) are the most oligopolistic and concentrated, 2) advertise most intensively for the most product-differentiated brands, and 3) have been caught or charged the most times for deceptive, manipulative, and unfair business practices by the ineffectual FTC.

The list covers: food, household products, autos, OTC drugs, cigarettes, cereal, soft drinks, candy, and snack industries.

The table on the following page, using *Ad Age*'s August 18, 1975, list for 1974 and *National Advertising Investments*' 1973 list, ranks these priority companies in order of total gross and ad expenditures.

An aggressive FTC, honoring its Congressional mandate to vigorously pursue antitrust suits and deceptive advertising, might some day be a key factor in protecting the American consumer from anticompetitive, unfair, and deceptive business practices. Isn't it time for Nader to take a long, overdue second look at the FTC? Furthermore, the Congress of the United States bears the responsibility for overseeing laws to protect the American consumer.

Proposed solutions; new laws

The late Senator Estes Kefauver's brilliant work in the Senate led to the passage of the Celler-Kefauver Act, strengthening the hand of anti-monopoly forces in America. His painstaking and indefatigable exposure of the weaknesses in the FDA and the drug laws led to the Kefauver-Harris bill, with the consequent increase in protection of the consumer-citizen from the hazards of newly introduced drugs. As Chairman of the Judiciary Committee's Subcommittee on Anti-Trust, the hearings helped break up Westinghouse and General Electric price-fixing practices. Kefauver had the kind of integrity and character that is rarely found in the U. S. Senate. His analysis of businessmen who didn't really believe in free, honest, and open competition in the marketplace is deserving of special attention. It is particularly relevant now, as corporate self-regulation, social purpose, and responsibility are debated within many corporation board meetings. Particularly noteworthy is his statement as to what to expect and understand about most business executives:

Under a system of free enterprise, it is basically illogical to expect businessmen to subdue the acquisitive urge to social ends. Profit-seeking is the accepted purpose of their undertakings; self-interest is the motivating force that drives them. Does it make sense to admonish business leaders to pursue courses of conduct that may endanger the security of their own corporate domains? Can we really expect executives, steeped in the tradition of protecting the interests of their stockholders, voluntarily to relinquish opportunities for profit in order to serve the public welfare? [21]

Officers and executives of the leading oligopolistic corporations and their counterparts in the largest advertising agencies

cannot be expected to act against their own best interests. That is why the charade and myth of self-regulation must be exposed once and for all. It won't happen!

Consumer advocates and critics of current advertising practices include Ex-FCC Commissioner Nicholas Johnson; the Consumer Federation of America (CFA); attorney Ralph Nader; consumer-advocate Robert Choate; Associate Director of Consumers Union, Warren Braren; and many others, such as Drs. Berger, Grow, Latham, Condry, and Blake; economists Blair,

Advertisers ranked in order of total gross ad expenditures

Leading national advertisers (1974). Compiled by Ad Age, 8/18/74, p. 1			National advertising investments (1973). Compiled & published by leading National Advertisers, Inc., Vol. 25, No. 2 (from: PIB, BAR, LNA Services)	
(in thousands of dollars)				
Proctor & Gamble	①	$325,000.0	(1) Proctor & Gamble	$231,220.3
General Motors	①	247,000.0	(2) General Foods	126,359.0
Sears			(3) Amer. Home Products	115,178.3
General Foods	②	189,000.0	(4) Bristol-Myers	109,003.3
Warner Lambert	①	156,000.0	(5) General Motors	103,078.2
Bristol-Myers	②	150,000.0	(6) Ford Motor	93,047.1
Amer. Home Products	③	135,000.0	(7) Colgate Palmolive	91,465.9
Ford Motor	②	132,000.0	(8) Sterling Drug	86,998.8
Colgate-Palmolive	①	118,000.0	(9) Sears	
U.S. Government		110,800.0	(10) Lever Brothers	69,320.1
R.J. Reynolds	①	102,000.0	(11) General Mills	62,923.0
AT&T			(12) Gillette	
Heublein Inc.	②	95,600.0	(13) Philip Morris	56,728.5
IT&T			(14) R.J. Reynolds	55,829.1
Chrysler	③	86,200.0	(15) Warner Lambert	52,170.5
Lever Brothers	③	85,000.0	(16) Chrysler	52,122.7
Sterling Drug	④	85,000.0	(17) Kraftco	
RCA Corporation			(18) Nabisco	46,361.6
Richardson-Merrell	⑤	83,500.0	(19) AT&T	
Philip Morris	②	81,000.0	(20) S.C. Johnson & Son	45,059.9
			(21) Heublein	43,753.6
			(22)	
			(23) Coca-Cola	40,980.9
			(24) Schering-Plough	38,587.8
Coca-Cola	①	74,400.0	(25) Miles Lab	38,215.9
			(26)	
			(27)	
General Mills	①	72,700.0	(28) Nestle Company	36,818.4
			(29) Pepsico Inc.	36,040.1
American Brands	③	70,000.0	(30) Kellogg	34,324.5
Brown & Willamson	④	69,400.0	(31)	
			(32) Ralston-Purina	32,989.7
Nabisco	②	68,100.0	(33)	
Ralston-Purina	③	66,000.0	(34)	

Numbers circled indicate rank of corp. in their industry of markets.

Scherer, Mueller, and Bain; Judith Sarson and Peggy Charren of Action for Children's Television (ACT).

Many of these concerned citizens have, in addition to their fact finding and critiques, put forward various recommendations for action. These advocates, and psychological and health experts, have made a series of proposals and requests for regulatory and legislative action. They want to protect children and adults alike from unfair, deceptive, and manipulative acts and practices in media programming and advertising; to stop program (cartoon) violence; to prevent promotion of non-nutritional candy, food, and drug products to children; to halt promotion of a pill or drug for every new problem or mood; to eliminate cigarettes, which kill; and to prohibit polluting or other unsafe products from all media advertising.

Some of their recommendations, and most of mine, include:

(1) A tax on all advertising.

(2) Large fines to be levied against advertisers, advertising agencies, and media for unfair, deceptive, or manipulative advertising. Fines would extend to one-half of the time, space, and production expenditures spent on advertising by the offending advertiser for one year.

(3) Elimination of all television commercials during P.M., and during weekend children's programming.

(4) Regulation and/or restriction of all children's television programs by a broad committee representing doctors, educators, child development psychologists, humanitarian organizations, parents, consumer advocates, ACT officers, and advertising and media representatives.

(5) The banning of all unsafe automobile, truck, gas and oil, OTC drug, non-nutritional sugared-food and drink advertising on television and other media.[22]

(6) Banning from all media any advertising from an advertiser or agency which produces or delivers unfair, deceptive, or manipulative advertising after being "caught" by the FTC or FCC a second time.

(7) Government funding of a Citizens Public Communications Company, which would prepare commercials, and special programs, for consumer groups to "counter" advertising that is unfair, deceptive, or presents only one side of a controversial issue. Time would be provided by advertisers and networks, on a weekly, half-hour program basis, on all three major networks.

(8) The government should strengthen the Public Broadcasting System network already underway. This can be done by taxes (on sales of all TV sets, TV tubes, public lotteries, percent of media-sales receipts, etc.). An independent, national public network free of commercials and commercial TV patronage or influence should be established similar to those found in Canada and Great Britain.

(9) The banning of all emotional or psychosocial (unconscious) advertising, with only informational or factual statements allowed in all advertising.

(10) The total elimination of the discriminatory media discount structure in advertising.

(11) All advertising to be checked and precleared by the Federal Trade Commission before it is allowed into print or broadcast.

(12) All new products and/or "questionable products" advertising to be pretested and precleared by FDA, Bureau of Standards, National Institute of Health (NIH), or by a newly created Consumer Protection Agency before the product can be advertised or sold to the American consumer.

(13) Prevent oligopical consumer-goods advertisers from making any acquisitions or mergers for five years—by a new law, or by establishment of new antitrust rules at the FTC and Justice Department.

(14) Every company with $250,000,000 or more in yearly gross sales to be divested of ownership or control of holdings, divisions, subsidiary companies or products, until its sales are reduced to the more competitive level of no more than $250,000,000 in gross sales yearly.

I further propose that we join more specifically in support of practical, legislative and regulatory action as follows:

Response to deceptive advertising

(1) Rules and mandatory guidelines must be instituted at the FTC to support and extend the Advertising Substantiation of Claims campaign. Full publicity, as well as quick, effective injunctions, Orders and Complaints, should follow in all cases where unfair and deceptive advertising claims are not completely satisfactorily substantiated. This should be done while the ads are first running in media—not one year or three years later, as is now the case.

(2) Passage of a Federal Trade Commission Improvement Act Amendment, providing the Commission with the power to seek preliminary injunctions, to initiate actions in U.S. Federal District Court seeking specific cash-fine redress for consumers injured by unfair or deceptive acts or practices, and to secure criminal penalties for knowing violations of the FTC Act.

(3) Full support must be mobilized to pass the old Moss-McGovern Bill. This Truth in Advertising Act will require the furnishing of documentation of advertiser claims first concerning safety, performance, efficacy, characteristics, and comparative prices of advertised products and services to consumers (upon request from them) made directly to advertisers. A class action $10,000 award—fine on offenders to consumers—is imperative.

(4) The initiation and institution of effective product testing by the government, developing standards to help the consumer make rational decisions. The Bureau of Standards could well develop such a program along the lines of the successful Consumers Union program.

(5) The restriction of the televising of commercials (by either regulatory rules, or by new law) to no more than four minutes of commercial matter in any clock hour, bunched in no more than two periods for each clock hour, on the hour and half hour.

Oligopoly break-up

(1) The FTC must apply the principles of the Robinson-Patman Act to disallow all media discount rates as discriminatory to small and medium regional and national advertisers. Advertisers who in effect spend .50¢ dollars (because of total aggregate discount media rates), competing with smaller companies who spend .80¢ dollars, bar entry to a free, competitive marketplace and encourage anticompetitive behavior and acquisitions.

(2) De-concentration of the oligopical, high-intensity advertisers in the consumer goods industries is an essential step for the FTC and Anti-Trust Division of the Justice Department to undertake. The FTC Order and Complaint against the cereal industry is a prime example of what should happen to the concentrated automobile, OTC drug, package goods, cigarette, tire, and oil industries—all of which have companies, four or less, controlling between 50 and 70 percent of each of these industries or sales markets.

(3) The FTC should require that all OTC Drug advertising must include the same warnings and counterindications now legally required for all OTC packages and labels.

(4) Finally, we should extend to law or regulatory rule a program that all "chronic violator" advertisers (those charged by the FTC for unfair and deceptive and/or manipulative advertising)—in areas of past abuse—must have their ad substantiation claims pre-checked and pre-cleared by the FTC, EPA, and FDA, prior to the running of print and broadcast advertising in the media. If they break the law, $25,000 personal fines and mandatory two-year prison sentences should be imposed on the president, vice president, marketing vice president, sales, and ad managers of the guilty advertising companies. This also applies to the president, vice president, account supervisor, account executive, and copy chief at the ad agency.

(5) The rapid turnover of lawyers shuttling from the FTC to superlawyer Washington corporations has a terrible effect within the FTC. The "advertiser" ex-

FTC lawyers have an intimate knowledge of just how bureaucratic and unwieldly many of the FTC administrative procedures are. They practice (for their clients and against consumers) a brilliant, minutiae kind of delaying tactic on behalf of deceptive advertisers. They know how to "work" the FTC and know how to tie up potential action—no matter how ineffectual—in endless conferences and bureaucratic letter writing. This leads to endless postponements and continuing manipulative advertising by their clients, while the complaints are stalled.

FTC lawyers should be barred from practicing for private law firms and their clients, against the FTC for at least five years after they leave the FTC. Five-year contracts upon being hired by the FTC at starting salaries of over $15,000 should be mandatory, to provide continuity and experience.

Strategies and tactics

The absence of critical, tough, and constant oversight hearings by the Senate Commerce Committee (Magnuson & Pertschuk) is a serious factor in the ineffectiveness of FTC personnel. Pertschuk is a buddy of most of the commissioners and Bureau personnel. He helped many of them get their jobs, and has a deep, bureaucratic investment in their careers (and his), in seeing that they agree with him in doing what has to be done. Regular televised hearings are an absolute must, and Nader's lobbyists and the Consumer Federation of America's lobbyists must have full opportunities to ask questions and raise criticisms—out in the open glare of national publicity—if consumer protection is ever to become a reality. The implications of the national scandal inherent in neglecting the injunctive powers of the FTC over deceptive food, drug, and cosmetic advertising, in itself, would enrage millions of Americans. Small, unpublicized hearings of the Sub-Committee on Consumers, with no follow-up questions ever asked by gentle, nice, Senator Frank Moss, are no substitute for full Committee hearings with Nader's Raiders invited to follow up on their famous report and see what, if anything, has changed at the FTC.

If Oversight Hearings are not called by Pertschuk, Public Interest Lawyers have a deep obligation to the consumer movement to file Class Action law suits against the FTC Commissioners, Senator Warren Magnuson, and Michael Pertschuk for malfeasance in office or law-breaking at the highest levels of government. The FTC Act is not being carried out by the Commerce Committee, or the FTC. Congresspersons Dellums, Rosenthal, Corman, Abzug, Kastenmaier, Burke, and others, could demand joint hearings along with Congressman Moss's House Interstate Commerce Committee, and should take appropriate action if such hearings aren't undertaken.

The willful and deceptively bureaucratic FTC fight against establishing priorities for deceptive advertisers and advertising—heretofore mostly ignored by the FTC—must be completely exposed. Working on piecemeal, insignificant deceptions by ineffectual, small advertisers plays into the hands of the concentrated, oligopolistic advertisers who constantly "rip-off" the consumer in both advertising, business practices, and anticompetitive behavior. Key criteria must be institutionalized around the concept of confining deceptive and manipulative charges only to those key advertisers who rule the print and electronic media and who deceive in their ads. The current haphazard FTC monitoring system is a joke. The FTC has no plan for setting priorities.

More than any specific lies or deceptions, however cruel they may be, what is most disturbing is the way that the "advertising ideology" has been able to distort and change our central value system. For decades we have been ruthlessly sold false images and expectations. Now we have begun to accept them. Worse, we have begun to accept them knowing that they are false. We have been taught to purchase, made to buy. We have seen the institutionalization of a central value system of drivenness and repetitive consumption with FTC silent approval.

The price we pay for this acceptance is fixed. We are permitting ourselves to become more callous and more tolerant of untruth. We are becoming increasingly less honorable and so is our government. We are, as a society, becoming more apathetic and more alienated and estranged from one another. We have in fact, begun to lose that one quality on which every workable society finally depends: trust, the ability to believe in others.

Drivenness, deception, manipulation, exploitation, dishonesty, and concentrated power in advertising, business, education, government, and in every part of our public and personal lives, has to be fought and fought hard. The opposing economic and political forces are exceedingly powerful, but they are not as powerful as an aroused citizenry.

The message then is not simply that our central value sytem is on trial but that we, as a free people, with the potential of influencing decisions that vitally affect our lives, are on trial also. We must start to fight back! And that fight should start with a counterattack against the FTC and the Senate Commerce Committee.

NOTES

1. Two to four companies dominating more than 50 percent of sales within a market or industry.

2. Arnold Kaufman, *The Radical Liberal* (New York: Simon and Schuster, 1968), p. 52. "They [radicals] subject the system they repudiate to an abusive hammer attack that inspires the converted and alienates everyone else. Hence, like those liberals they so bitterly criticize, members of the Movement create a gap between their own rhetoric and their social reality. To the extent that this is so, they are at least as insincere as those they condemn. Worse—they are ineffectual."

3. "The Commission is empowered and directed to prevent persons . . . or corporations . . . from using unfair methods of competition in commerce and unfair and deceptive acts or practices in commerce." Section 5 (A), (6).

4. "Unfair methods of competition in commerce, and unfair or deceptive acts or practices in commerce, are declared unlawful."

5. Edward Cox, Robert Fellmeth, and John Schulz, *"The Nader Report" on the FTC.* (Grossman, New York: 1969) p. 39.

6. Ibid., pp. 38, 39.

7. Ibid., p. 39.

8. CBS, NBC TV; 9/22, 9/23, 9/24.

9. Ibid.

10. Ibid.

11. Director, Bureau of Drugs and Medication, Food and Drug Administration, Public Health Services Dept., DHEW.

12. Hearings, Subcommittee on Monopoly, Select Committee; Small Business, U.S. Senate, 92nd Congress, 1st Session, of Proprietary Medicine, Part 1, p. 261.

13. Cox, Fellmeth, and Schulz, pp. 25–26.

14. Camels, Winston-Salem are also R. J. Reynolds products.

15. Counter advertising is allowing equal, unpaid time for consumer advocates to oppose an advertiser's advertising (commercial) claims.

16. Both clever "Pitofsky" public relations ploys—that temporarily appeased consumer advocates—but were never seriously considered by the FCC.

17. *Minneapolis Tribune,* Minneapolis, Minnesota, April 3, 1972.

18. The *Los Angeles Times.*

19. Report on the Senate Committee on Commerce, on S. 986, 92nd Congress, Report No. 92–269, Calendar No. 263, U. S. Government Printing Office, Washington, 1971 (64–665), pp. 1, —6.

20. Louis M. Kohlmeier, Jr., *The Regulators* (Watchdog agencies and the public interest) (Harper & Row, New York, 1969), p. 253.

21. Estes Kefauver, *In A Few Hands: Monopoly Power in America* (Penguin Books, Baltimore, Maryland, 1965), p. 207.

22. Cigarette Print Advertising, which includes premium promotions, horse races, tennis tours should be banned as a public health menace.

*

11 Political parties

The basic questions this chapter will address are:

(1) Why are there only two major parties in the United States?

(2) What is the role of parties in the American political process?

(3) Which groups in American society do the Democratic and Republican parties represent?

(4) What alternatives to the two-party system are there?

Conservatives believe that a large number of parties can lead to chaos and confusion so the two-party system best represents the varied interests of the American people. A party's primary role is to bring together into a coherent whole the many needs of Americans. In this way a small number of demands can be posed to the decision-makers and then be met by the government.

Political parties are not democratically run, nor, in fact, should they be. Though they are, according to conservatives, autocratic in structure, they nevertheless uphold democratic principles. Parties are responsive institutions—they meet the needs of Americans. If they were not responsive they would not have lasted: the Republican Party has been in existence since the mid-nineteenth century; the Democratic Party traces its origins to Thomas Jefferson and the Republicans of the late eighteenth century.[1] Any alternatives to America's two-party system might result in disorder, and even the end of the American political system as we know it.[2]

Liberals also believe in the two-party system. If parties are not responsive to the needs of the people, it is because the people have not pressed the parties to select the right candidates for office. Liberals hold that the "right" candidate is not a radical of the Right or Left. The "correct" person is one who represents the center position in American politics. This candidate wants change so that more people can benefit from the political process. At the same time this person accepts the premises upon which the political system is based: capitalism, representative government, democracy, the two-party system, and a President, strong but not all-powerful. A candidate with this vision of government helps the American party system to function smoothly and fulfill its ideals. Compromise with political opponents becomes easy since these leaders are rational. Liberals also feel that if more people voted than presently do, political parties could be strengthened since candidates would be forced to meet the peoples' demands. Increased citizen participation can put the right people in office, and can make our party system work well.[3]

Socialists believe that neither of the two major parties represents the will of the American people. They reject the liberal thesis that the Democratic Party represents labor, minorities, and the poor, and that the Republican Party represents business. Both parties represent a corporate/political/military elite. Essentially, socialists hold that the creation of socialist mass parties, and nominating socialist candidates under the two-party rubric are means of combatting elite control over the party process.[4]

NOTES

1. See, Joseph Charles, *The Origins of the American Party System*. New York: Harper Torchbooks, 1961. Note also, Vincent P. De Santis, "The Republican Party Revisited, 1877–1897," in H. Wayne Morgan, ed., *The Guilded Age, A Reappraisal*. Syracuse: Syracuse Univ. Press, 1963. This gives a good description of the Republican Party's program and ideology.

2. Conservative analyses of the party system in America can be found in: Clinton Rossiter, *Parties and Politics in America,* Ithaca: Cornell Univ. Press, 1960; Gabriel A. Almond and G. Bingham Powell, Jr., *Comparative Politics: A Developmental Approach,* Boston: Little Brown and Co., 1966, see in particular their chapter, "Interest Aggregation and Political Parties;" Frank J. Sorauf, *Political Parties in the American System.* Boston: Little Brown and Co., 1964.

3. An interesting selection of "good," "correct" individuals and an analysis of why they are so defined is found in Saul K. Padover, *The Genius of America.* New York: McGraw-Hill Book Co., 1960. An interesting thesis which claims the two-party system is really a four-party system is James MacGregor Burns, *The Deadlock of Democracy.* Englewood Cliffs: Prentice-Hall, Inc., 1964.

4. For a fuller discussion of this thesis see chapter 8, "Congress." See also G. William Domhoff, *Fat Cats and Democrats.* Englewood Cliffs: Prentice-Hall, Co., 1972.

Conservative

Robert A. Dahl.   Political parties: contributions to democracy.

In the light of long experience, not only in the United States but in all other democracies, there is no longer any substantial ground for doubting that political parties make substantial contributions to the operation of a democracy—at any rate to a large democracy. To most democrats who reflect on the problem, the positive contributions of parties far outweigh their negative aspects. But in many democracies, not least the United States, the negative aspects stimulate a lively interest in the possibility of reforming the parties or the party system.

The principal contributions of parties, it might be suggested, are three:

They facilitate popular control over elected officials.

They help voters to make more rational choices.

They help in the peaceful management of conflicts.

Yet each of these propositions must be qualified. To explore adequately the contributions and defects of parties, even American parties, would require a volume in itself. The essays, monographs, and full-scale books that appraise political parties and advance or criticize proposals for reform would form a sizeable library.

A brief discussion can nonetheless open up some of the major questions.

Parties and popular control

One of the strongest claims made for political parties is that they assist the electorate in gaining some degree of control over elected officials and, thus, over the decisions of government.

For one thing, they carry on much of the organizing that makes a large-scale system of elections, representation, and legislation workable. The ambitions that induce party politicians to carry on these organizing tasks may repel democratic purists who would prefer motives closer to those invoked in the noble rhetoric with which men good and bad usually cloak their deepest purposes. Yet, whatever one may think of the motives of party politicians, these men (and women) perform some functions that are essential if democracy is not to dwindle into flatulent ineffectuality: Nominations, for example. In the absence of concerted effort, an election in which a candidate satisfactory to a majority *might* have emerged victorious may be won instead by a candidate who is satisfactory only to a minority. Surely, it is no virtue if a majority of like-minded voters are presented with three satisfactory candidates to run against a fourth candidate they agree is worse; for if they distribute their votes over the three they like, the fourth may win even though he be the most objectionable. Once like-minded voters see that it is worthwhile to organize themselves around a single candidate they have already acquiesced in the beginnings of a party.

The organization furnished by party is particularly necessary if an opposition is to exist. The dominant forces have somewhat less need of party organization; a President might, for example, operate with a sort of non-party coalition. This is no doubt why party machinery fell into decay when opposition temporarily became merely an exercise in futility during the long death-agonies of the Federalists and before the re-appearance of new cleavages around which an opposition could form. When there was no opposition, there were no effective parties. One could also put it the other way around. When there is no party, there is not likely to be an effective opposition. To displace the incumbents, who have the resources of government at hand, an opposition needs to organize, focus its forces, keep up the pressure, draw in every possible ally—all of which spells party. It is, thus, no accident that in Europe it was usually the Labour or Socialist opposition parties that first developed modern party organization—during the lengthy period they dwelt in opposition before assuming office.

Then, too, the sheer efficiency of party organization for winning political victories means that a single party, unchecked by another, would be a danger in a republic. One party needs to be counterbalanced by another. Let there either be no parties, or at least two parties, but never only one party, the citizens of a republic might well resolve. For if there is only one party, those among us who disagree with it will surely be outweighed, even though we be more numerous than our opponents. Since we cannot prevent at least one party from forming, lest by doing so we destroy our republican liberties, let there always be two parties or more. In this way, we shall insure another kind of separation of powers and create additional checks and balances to sustain our liberties.

A fourth way in which parties assist popular control is to enable the many to pool their resources to offset the advantages of the few. This is doubtless one reason why Federalists looked upon parties with less enthusiasm than did Republicans. The chief resources of the many are their numbers and their votes; unorganized and leaderless they are no match for smaller numbers with wealth, skills, information, and informal organizational networks. Even when parties are internally oligarchical, as they generally are, a party competing for the votes of the otherwise unorganized many gives them more power than they would have if there were no parties at all.

Despite these contributions, parties have been subjected to a barrage of criticism on the ground that they are internally undemocratic and are ruled by oligarchies.[1] The charge is in considerable measure true. That the nominations and policies of political parties tend to be controlled by leaders, rather than the rank and file of members or registered supporters, seems undeniable. There is, as we saw, more decentralization and diffusion of control in the two American parties than in many European parties; even so, both the Democratic and Republican parties would be more accurately described as coalitions of oligarchies than as democratic organizations.

Given the democratic ideology prevailing among Americans, it was to be expected that efforts would be made to "democratize" control over nominations in American parties; these efforts have diffused power, but they have not by any means turned the parties into democratic systems. As we saw, presidential candidates were first nominated by the Federalist and Republican caucuses in Congress. While the caucus continued to be used for several decades for presidential and vice presidential nominations, an alternative system began to develop for nominating candidates to other offices, national, state, and local. This was the nominating convenion, which, being a representative system, seemed more appropriate than the caucus to the spirit of democracy. The caucus fell into even worse repute because it sometimes dramatized for all to see the fact that nominations were made by unrepresentative cliques. One such episode, in 1824, killed the congressional caucus as a device for nominating presidential candidates. Of two hundred sixteen Republicans in Congress who were invited to attend the nominating caucus that year, only sixty-six attended. This small minority proceeded to nominate for President of the United States a minor league politician, W. H. Crawford. In the election Crawford ran well behind Andrew Jackson, who led the other candidates in popular and electoral votes, and also behind John Quincy Adams, who trailed Jackson but ultimately won the Presidency when the House of Representatives had to decide the election. The convention made its first appearance for a presidential nomination in September, 1831, when the brief-lived Anti-Masonic party nominated candidates for President and Vice President at a convention in Baltimore. Henry Clay's National Republicans (soon to become the Whigs) followed suit in December, also in Baltimore. Jackson's followers, the Democratic Republicans, met in the same city in May, 1832, to nominate Jackson and Van Buren.[2] Ever since then, the national convention has been used for nominating presidential and vice presidential candidates.

Although national nominating conventions are representative in form, probably no one who knows how they work would argue that they are in any genuine sense democratic. At most, the convention is a contest among oalitions of state and local oligarchs. Because representative democracy seemed to have failed, advocates of democratic control over nominations turned to direct democracy: party members or supporters would themselves choose the candidate of their party. This was the direct primary.

Toward the end of the last century the convention began to be displaced by the direct primary, which is now almost universally employed for party nominations to executive offices other than the Presidency and the Vice Presidency. Yet even the direct primary has not democratized the parties—in part, of course, simply because most people do not participate in crucial day-to-day decisions or, for that matter, even in the primaries. In examining fifteen non-Southern states over the period 1932–1952, the late V. O. Key discovered that "in three out of four primaries...the total Democratic primary

vote plus the total Republican primary vote did not exceed 35% of the number of citizens 21 years of age or over...At the extreme of high participation in only one out of twelve primaries did more than 50% of the potential vote turn up at the polls"[3] (Table 1).

Running a party, like operating any other complex institution, is a full-time business; and as in other institutions, power tends to accrue to those who make it a full-time business. Consequently, neither American political parties nor those of any other country are likely to be very democratic in their internal operations. But how much does internal party democracy really matter? Political parties are sometimes likened to business firms competing for customers—the customers being in this case the voters. And just as business firms are driven by competition to satisfy consumers, even if they are *internally* not

Table 1 Gubernational primaries in selected states according to percentage of potential electorate voting in Republican or Democratic primary, 1926–1952[a]

Participation percentage	Number of primaries[b]	Percentage of primaries	Percentage of general elections
10–14	9	5.1	0.0
15–19	22	12.5	0.0
20–24	23	13.1	0.0
25–29	37	21.0	1.1
30–34	39	22.2	2.8
35–39	15	8.5	5.7
40–44	5	2.8	4.5
45–49	10	5.7	9.7
50–54	9	5.1	13.1
55–59	4	2.3	8.0
60–64	2	1.1	13.6
65–69	1	0.6	14.2
70 and over	0	0.0	27.3
	176	100.0	100.0

[a]The states included in this tabulation are Vermont, North Dakota, Maine, Wisconsin, Michigan, New Hampshire, Pennsylvania, Kansas, Massachusetts, Illinois, Wyoming, Ohio, Colorado, West Virginia, and Missouri. The selection of states for inclusion in this table was dictated chiefly by the availability for the period covered of the types of data needed for the analyses made in [V. O. Key] Table 16 and Figure 14.
[b]In the enumerations of this column one primary equals a pair of simultaneous primaries, Republican and Democratic. Thus in nine primaries, so defined, between 10 and 15 per cent of the potential electorate voted for either Democratic or Republican aspirants for the gubernatorial nomination.

Source: V. O. Key, Jr. *American State Politics*, New York, A. A. Knopf, 1956, p. 135.

governed by consumers in the way that a consumers' cooperative is, so, it is sometimes argued, competitive parties will fulfill all of the essential functions of democratic control . . . even though each party is internally controlled by its leaders.[4]

Seen from this perspective, the most important question is not who runs the parties but to whom are the parties responsive? To the leaders themselves, to the rank-and-file registered party member, or to the voters? If the main function of competing parties is to insure that the views of voters are translated into government policies then it is less important that parties be internally democratic than that they be responsive to the views of the voters.

In actual practice, American parties seem to respond to all three forces: to the party leaders, to the rank-and-file, and to the voters. What happens if a party responds more to its leaders than to the voters? The answer seems obvious: It will probably be defeated in elections—if the other party is closer to the views of the electorate.

There is some interesting evidence bearing on this point. In 1957–1958, three social scientists surveyed about half the delegates and alternates to preceding presidential nominating conventions and compared the views of these party "leaders" with a national survey of voters. The results revealed that on five major categories of issues—public ownership of resources, government regulation of the economy, equality and welfare, taxes and foreign policy—the differences in views were as follows:

The greatest difference in views was between Democratic and Republican leaders.

Almost equally great was the difference between Republican leaders and Democratic followers.

Democratic followers and Republican followers showed the slightest—and indeed often negligible—differences in their views.

There were relatively small differences in views between Democratic leaders and Democratic followers.

But—the most startling finding—the differences between Republican leaders and Republican followers were almost as great as the difference between Republican leaders and Democratic followers.

And there was actually a greater difference between Republican leaders and Republican followers than between Democratic leaders and Republican followers![5]

What these findings strongly suggest, then, is that by the late 1950s the Republican leaders big and small around the country, the activists who exercise dominant influence over nominations and policy no longer represented their Republican followers, nor—and this is even more important—did they represent the great bulk of the voters, Republicans or Democrats.

During this period . . . voters continued their steady shift in allegiance toward the Democratic Party. Then, in 1964, the most ideologically conservative activists in the Republican Party, whose views probably represented only a minority among Republican voters and an even smaller minority in the electorate as a whole, seized control of the nominating convention from the Republican "establishment," nominated Senator Goldwater, and suffered one of the three or four worst defeats in the entire history of the party.[6]

The lesson seems fairly clear: When the policies of party leaders get too far out of line with those desired by the voters, support for the party will erode, and the party is likely to get beaten in elections.

In sum: The main contributions that parties make to democracy are not to be found in their internal operations but in their external effects—in competing for votes, organizing elections and legislatures, strengthening the opposition, providing offsetting checks to one another, and helping the many to overcome the otherwise superior resources of the few.

Parties and rationality

Of what value is popular control, however, if voters are simply duped by party leaders or mindlessly vote for their parties without weighing the candidates and the issues? It might be argued that even if parties do help the electorate to gain some degree of control over elected officials, the control of the voters is in large measure spurious because it is irrational. Do parties reduce the irrationality of politics—or do they actually increase it?

It would be absurd to attribute to political parties all the forms of irrational and non-rational behavior that have ever been commonplace in human affairs and that exist in political systems of all sorts. The relevant question is whether parties change the amount and kinds of "irrational" behavior from what would exist in the absence of parties.

Unhappily, the question is all but unanswerable. "Levels" or "amounts" of irrationality are terms that at best have only metaphorical meaning. No one has been able to measure changes in "the amount of rationality" in political systems. The most extreme cases of collective irrationality in modern times have occurred in dictatorships, I believe, where whole populations have fallen under the absolute domination of paranoid leaders like Stalin and Hitler. By comparison, the stable democracies appear to be models of rational action. The question is, then, whether democracies would be more—or less—rational without competing parties.

One could theorize endlessly in response to this question without arriving at a conclusive answer. Let me therefore confine my conjecturing—for this it must be—to two aspects that everyone would agree do characterize political parties: (1) Parties present to voters a very small number of alternatives out of the total number theoretically available. This effect is particularly strong in a two-party system with single-member districts; for at elections the voter is usually confronted with only two rival candidates. (2) Each party develops a core of followers whose loyalty is fortified by non-rational factors like sentiment, pride, jealousy, combativeness, gamesmanship, and habit.

Reducing alternatives

Consider the first point. A voter presented with two rival candidates, might prefer neither of them so much as a third possible candidate who failed to win a nomination by either party. Similarly, on some matter of policy a voter may like the policy proposed by both parties less than some other alternative neither party is willing to advance. Reasoning along these lines, one might conclude that multi-party systems would offer voters a more rational choice than two-party systems. Yet, if four parties are better than two, are eight parties better than four? And sixteen parties better than eight? Or, for that matter, why not a separate candidate for every point of view held by any citizen in the country? But suppose the voter were confronted with a choice among twenty parties and twenty candidates. Might he not then reason as follows: These are too many alternatives; I cannot possibly appraise them all. Anyway, what do I gain if the man I vote for wins? If there are twenty parties in the parliament, my representative and all the others will have to make many compromises by the time they reach the final decision. How do I know what compromises they will make? Would it not be much better if most of the compromises had been made already, so that I could then choose between two possible coalitions, knowing roughly the direction in which each would go if it won a majority of seats . . .?

Evidence does, in fact, suggest that the need to choose among a large number of parties is, for all except a small minority of voters, highly confusing and may lead, as in France, to seriously discrediting the whole party system.[7]

Such reasoning might cause a voter to oscillate between two poles. At one pole, accepting the need for eliminating alternatives in order to arrive at a decision, he would enjoy the advantage of being confronted at elections by only two major alternatives. At the other pole, accepting the need to have his favorite alternative presented to him in order to have full freedom of choice, he would enjoy the advantage of being confronted at elections by a wide array of alternatives. Carried to an extreme, the first would result in a plebiscite, like those under the French Fifth Republic, where the only choices were to vote yes or no to a simple proposition. In this case, the voter might feel badly cheated and powerless because the choices were too narrow. The second solution, carried to the other extreme, would result in an array of choices so great that no voter could possibly estimate the effect of his vote on the ultimate outcome of the election and parliamentary bargaining. In this case, he might feel badly cheated and powerless because the choices were far too many.

The fact remains, then, that whenever a diversity of viewpoints and desired alternatives exists among the citizens of a democracy, the citizens must, sooner or later, by one process or another, reject all but one alternative (even if the final choice is, in effect, the null alternative of inaction). There is no escaping this process; it is the essence of "rationality;" the only question is where and how it takes place. Much of the process of winnowing out alternatives could take place *before* an election, or *in* the election itself, or in negotiations *after* the election. All party systems do some winnowing *before* an election, making the *election* itself more decisive by reducing the alternatives, thus leaving less winnowing to be done *after* the election by bargaining and negotiation among members of different parties. The contrast is most marked between the British two-party system and a multi-party system like that of Italy, or France under the Third and Fourth Republics. The American party system, like the multi-party systems of the Scandinavian countries or the Netherlands, stands somewhere in between.

The notion, then, that parties increase irrationality in making choices by reducing the alternatives is based upon too simple a

picture of the processes by which collective political decisions can be made, for all such processes necessarily involve a drastic reduction in the alternatives. Although the question is obviously exceedingly complex, it seems much more reasonable to conclude (as most students of the party do) that on the whole the parties play a beneficial role in this process.

Consequences of party loyalty

Consider now the second aspect of parties, the fact that they develop a core of followers loyal to the point of blind, nonrational support. The more the parties succeed in their efforts, it might be said, the more the weight of reason in politics is bound to decline. Parties may be the backbone of democracy; but all bone and no brain makes for a dull system. Does party loyalty insure the rationality of voters?

There are four markedly divergent answers.

The first and oldest, traceable to Rousseau, was the dominant theme of one of the earliest systematic analyses of British and American parties, that by M. Ostrogorski in 1902.[8] "Ostrogorski's conception of democracy," a modern critic has said, "was essentially atomistic. He thought of a democratic society as one in which isolated individuals engage in the rational discussion of public affairs, freely combining with other individuals on the basis of identity of views on particular issues."[9] To Ostrogorski all permanent parties are bad. Party loyalty turns into a kind of religious dogma:

. . . To prevent the great mass of adherents on whom rests the power of the party from escaping it, their minds and their wills must be inveigled by every kind of device, . . . [Ostrogorski wrote] They unite their contingents in superstitious respect for pure forms, in a fetish-like worship of the "party," inculcate a loyalty to its name and style, and thus establish a moral mortmain over men's minds . . . They stereotype opinion in creeds which enforce on it a rigid discipline, they conceal the divergences of views that arise by composite programmes in which the most varied problems are jumbled together, which promise everything to everybody.[10]

Ostrogorski's solution was simple. It consisted

in discarding the use of *permanent* parties . . . and reserving to party its essential character of a combination of citizens *formed specially for a particular political issue* . . . Party holding its members, once they have joined it, in a viselike grasp would give place to combinations forming and reforming spontaneously, according to the changing problems of life and the play of opinions brought about thereby. Citizens who part company on one question would join forces in another. [11]

Although in the United States, as we shall see, the parties approximate the condition described in the last sentence more closely than Ostrogorski could have known, in this country as in every other democracy his specific solution has been decisively rejected in favor of permanent parties. A second view, seemingly more in keeping with reality, became much more widely accepted than Ostrogorski's. This is the view that while the great bulk of the voters are party loyalists who act not so much in pursuit of rational aims as from nonrational loyalties, a considerable body of independents stands outside the two parties. It is the votes of these independents, the argument runs, that essentially determine elections. And independents, it is said, are relatively rational and reflective: It is they who give genuine consideration to the candidates and programs of the two parties and then make their choices. Consequently, so long as the number of these thoughtful independents is sufficiently large and the number of loyalists on each side is less than a majority, the independents determine the outcome. Hence party competition places the decisive voice in elections exactly where it belongs, with the more thoughtful, judicious, and reflective citizens committed to neither party. Unlike Ostrogorski's appraisal, this view is on the whole favorable to the role of parties: They are useful, at any rate, as long as they do not gain so many partisans that they no longer need to contest for the votes of the independents.

Alas for this optimistic view, it was based almost exclusively on data available within easy reach of the armchair. Beginning with the presidential election of 1940, social scientists used the new techniques of opinion surveys in a series of studies that have revolutionized our knowledge about American voters.[12] From these studies, based upon lengthy and carefully analyzed interviews with a scientifically selected sample of the electorate, a new picture emerged—based for the first time, it seemed, on hard fact. In this new group portrait, the face of the rational voter is all but invisible. For social scientists have learned what was plausible enough all along: People who are most interested and most informed about politics are also likely to be the most partisan, and the least partisan voters are likely to be uninterested and uninformed about issues, personalities, and other aspects of a campaign. Unfortunately for the older portrayal of the independent as the ideal voter, it now became clear that the less partisan or more 'independent' of party loyalties a voter is, the less likely he is to be interested in politics, to be informed about candidates and issues, to go to the polls, or, if he does, to make up his mind judiciously after carefully reflecting on the alternatives. The portrait of the voter painted by these studies is, then, rather gloomy. On the one hand, it appears, most voters are party loyalists who vote less out of an intelligent concern for policy than from sheer loyalty, habit, and inertia. On the other hand, the reflective independent, once honored for his contribution, scarcely exists in real life. A voter who is not interested enough in politics to be partisan is unlikely to be interested enough to have an intelligent judgment on the election.

In the light of the evidence from these recent studies, campaigns and elections began to seem rather meaningless. The overwhelming number of interested voters, these surveys revealed, make up their minds even before the campaign starts. In fact, the more interested a voter is the more likely he is to make up his mind even before the candidates are nominated! To be sure, some voters are open-minded. Those who have "open" minds during the campaign and do not decide how they will vote until the

Table 2 Percentages of those who voted in preceding Presidential election shifting in preference and in reported vote from one major party to the other

Period of shift	In pre-election preference	N*	In post-election report of vote	N*
1936–40	17%	(12,031)	16%	(4319)
1940–44	14	(12,086)	11	(1673)
1944–48	18	(5,223)	13	(1795)
1948–52	17	(6,120)	20	(1795)
1952–56	13	(2,789)	(not given)	
1956–60	21	(4,295)	22	(1857)

*N is the total number of persons in the sample or in the *combined* samples from several surveys.

Source: V. O. Key, *The Responsible Electorate,* Cambridge, Harvard University Press, 1966, Table 22, p. 19.

polling day draws near are very likely to have minds so open, it seems, as to be downright vacant. An election, looked at in the bleakest light shed by the data, seemed to be little more than sound and fury, signifying nothing . . . a tale told by an idiot.

Combined with a measure of healthy iconoclasm endemic among social scientists, the hard facts of election studies helped to give wide credence to this perspective among social scientists engaged in studying elections. Yet there is some reason for thinking that, as is often the case, a plausible view had been pushed too far. In a book which he was unable to complete before his death, the late and highly distinguished political scientist V. O. Key

had moved to a counterattack with an impressive array of evidence drawn from opinion surveys covering every presidential election from 1936 to 1960.[13] According to Key's evidence, even if not many voters change their minds as a result of a campaign, many more decide from one presidential election to the next to shift their vote from the presidential candidate of one party to that of the other party. The proportion of voters who shift between one presidential election and the next probably fluctuates somewhere in the neighborhood of 15–20 per cent. (Table 2). If we add to these "shifters" the new voters (i.e., who have not voted in a previous election), then the rest, the "standpatters" who do not change from one election to the next are in the

Table 3 Percentages of new voters, shifters, and standpatters in Presidential elections, 1940–1960

	Election	New voters	Shifters	Standpatters	
1940					
	Pre-election preference	16%	14%	70%	100%
	Post-election report	16	13	71	100
1944					
	Pre-election preference	15	13	72	100
	Post-election report	13	10	77	100
1948					
	Pre-election preference	23	14	63	100
	Post-election report	16	11	73	100
1952					
	Pre-election preference	30	12	58	100
	Post-election report	20	16	64	100
1956					
	Pre-election preference	27	10	63	100
	Post-election report				
1960					
	Pre-election preference	27	15	58	100
	Post-election report	14	19	67	100

Source: Key, *The Responsible Electorate,* Table 23, p. 20.

neighborhood of 60–70 per cent of the electorate (Table 3). More important, Key also found a moderately close connection between one's views on policy and one's chances of shifting or standing pat. Far from being will-less partisans, the standpatters tend to be voters whose views are closer to those of the party they support than to the other party. The shifters tend to be people who, by shifting, give support to the party that is closer to their views than the party they had supported in the preceding elections, the portrait that emerges from Key's analysis is, on the whole, a benign one: ". . . voters are not fools. To be sure, many individual voters act in odd ways indeed; yet in the large the electorate behaves about as rationally and responsibly as we should expect, given the clarity of the alternatives presented to it and the character of the information available to it."[14]

Whatever the experts may have thought, on Key's showing the American voter appears to cast his vote with a reasonably intelligent judgment as to which party is the more likely to pursue the kinds of policies he prefers.

NOTES

1. Among the most famous and most influential criticisms of this kind were those of M. Ostrogorski, *Democracy and the Organization of Political Parties* (1902), recently edited and abridged by S. M. Lipset, 2 vols., Garden City New York, Anchor Books, 1964; and Robert Michels, *Political Parties* (1915), New York, Collier Books, 1962. For an appraisal of Ostrogorski, see Austin Ranney, *The Doctrine of Responsible Party Government,* Urbana, University of Illinois Press, 1962. For a critique of Michels, see John D. May, "Democracy, Organization, Michels," *American Political Science Review* (June, 1965), pp. 417–429.

2. These events are described in Ostrogorski, *op. cit.,* Vol. II, *The United States, pp. 17–39.*

3. Key, *American State Politics,* p. 134.

4. An interesting and important theoretical analysis bearing on this subject will be found in Anthony Downs, *An Economic Theory of Democracy,* New York, Harper & Brothers, 1957.

5. Herbert McClosky, Paul J. Hoffman, and Rosemary O'Hara, "Issue Conflict and Consensus among Party Leaders and Followers," *American Political Science Review,* Vol. 54, (June, 1960) 406–427, Table 1, p. 410, and *passim.*

6. For an analysis, see P. E. Converse, A. R. Clausen, and W. E. Miller, "Electoral Myth and Reality: The 1964 Election," *American Political Science Review,* Vol. 59 (June, 1965) 321–336. The percentages of the total popular vote received by the Republican presidential candidate in their four great defeats were:
 1964, Senator Goldwater, 38.5%
 1936, Alfred M. Landon, 36.5
 1912, William H. Taft, 23.2*
 1856, John C. Fremont, 33.1
 *In 1912 Theodore Roosevelt, the Progressive candidate, received 34.9 per cent of the votes, many of them from Republicans; Woodrow Wilson, the Democratic candidate, received only 41.9 per cent of the votes.

7. Philip Converse and Georges Dupeux, "Politicization of the Electorate in France and the United States," in *Elections and the Political Order, op. cit.,* Ch. 14, esp. pp. 277–278.

8. M. Ostrogorski, *Democracy and the Organization of Political Parties* (1902), edited and abridged by S. M. Lipset, 2 vols., Garden City, New York, Anchor Books, 1964.

9. Ranney, *op. cit.,* p. 115.

10. Ostrogorski, *op. cit.,* Vol. II, p. 354.

11. *Ibid.,* p. 356 (emphasis added).

12. The principal studies for the following elections are:
1940: Paul F. Lazarsfeld, Bernard Berelson, and Hazel Gaudet, *The People's Choice,* 2nd. ed., New York, Columbia University Press, 1948.
1944: Sheldon J. Korchin, "Psychological Variables in the Behavior of Voters," Doctoral dissertation, Harvard University, 1946.
1948: Bernard R. Berelson, Paul F. Lazarsfeld, and William N. McPhee, *Voting,* Chicago, University of Chicago Press, 1954.
1952: Angus Campbell, Gerald Gurin, and Warren E. Miller, with the assistance of Sylvia Eberhart and Robert O. McWilliams, *The Voter Decides,* Chicago, Row-Peterson, 1954.
1954: Angus Campbell and Homer C. Cooper, *Group Differences in Attitudes and Votes, A Study of the 1954 Congressional Elections,* Ann Arbor, University of Michigan, 1956.
1956: Angus Campbell, Philip E. Converse, Warren E. Miller, Donald E. Stokes, *The American Voter,* New York, John Wiley & Sons, 1960.
1960: Angus Campbell, Philip E. Converse, Warren E. Miller, Donald E. Stokes, *Elections and The Political Order,* New York, John Wiley and Sons, 1966; Ithiel de Sola Pool, Robert P. Abelson, and Samuel P. Popkin, *Candidates, Issues and Strategies, A Computer Simulation of the 1960 Presidential Election,* Cambridge, M. I. T. Press, 1964.

13. V. O. Key, Jr., with the assistance of Milton C. Cummings, Jr., *The Responsible Electorate, Rationality in Presidential Voting 1936–1940,* Cambridge, Mass., Harvard University Press, 1966.

14. *Ibid.,* p. 7.

Liberal

Theodore J. Lowi. A "critical" election misfires.

The 1972 elections leave us once again with a profound political question: Why do we have so many problems and so few issues?

Most of America's dilemmas seemed to come to a head in the late 1960s. By 1968 rioting was widespread among lower-income groups, and disaffection was so rampant among the middle groups that an incumbent President was not even welcome at a convention of his own party. Yet the 1968 campaign was empty of everything except a moderate suspense as to the outcome, and even the question of winning was interesting only because politics has become good box office, another entertainment in TV's Wide World of Sports.

The midterm elections of 1970 also occurred amid widespread confrontations. Cambodia and Kent State brought many things into focus. Congress' sigh of *mea culpa* on the war made debate possible and dissent respectable. There were signs of maturity in the approaches to America's race problems. Yet the cumulative effect of the 1970 elections was utter boredom and irrelevance. All the war talk sounded moderately dovish, and all the domestic talk sounded moderately law-and-orderish, washed as they were into obscurity by a detergent called the "social issue." There were no issues at all. Everyone seemed to see society's problems in about the same way, and the candidates appeared mere mouthpieces for a consensus that had existed before the election—that seemed always to have existed.

So too with 1972. Before the political year began we were apparently overrun with problems. We were still suffering from what Meg Greenfield of *The Washington Post* had in the early 1960s called the "problem problem." Cities were less safe, yet more expensive; peace was closer but war had never been so vicious; governments had never tried so hard, taxed so much, or been so close to bankruptcy.

Yet for the duration of the campaign there were no issues. Not once did Mr. Nixon have to take off the Presidential cloak; no threat ever made that necessary. America's problems were simply not translated into points of political relevance. The best we came up with was the question of George McGovern's character. That being the case, something has gone wrong with American political institutions.

Most of our elections, including national elections, are routine affairs. Mandates are rarely more than the idle bluster of the winner. Elections are important because they give a few people license to rule for a limited period of time; and that is important, whether an issue was settled or not. But every generation or so we have expected more from an election, and we have gotten it. Every thirty to forty years conditions seem to be ripe for a "critical election." It is a situation in which political parties suddenly spring apart on important issues, candidates honestly and consistently differ, and the citizenry turn out to vote in unusually high proportion, exhilarated by the prospect of a real choice.

Critical elections usually occur during or after a serious domestic crisis. They usually follow a period in which one of the major parties has gone through a serious defeat and regeneration, because it is usually in such a period that a party is weak enough to be permeated by new leaders intensely committed to a specific solution for a defined social problem. The 1932 and 1936 elections were the last occasions when we witnessed a party coming out of reconstruction with a clear electoral orientation, a program and a commitment to change. The results of decisions and electoral realignments made at that time still affect us today.

Similar conditions prevailed in 1972. In fact many of the most astute political historians have been expecting a critical election since 1964, because they felt that conditions were by then comparable to 1932. Reasonable observers can of course disagree on when conditions are sufficient, but one datum alone suggests that by 1972 we were surely ready. That single fact is that more than 80 per cent of the delegates at the Democratic National Convention were in attendance for the first time.

George McGovern's nomination is still another indication of the presence of sufficient conditions for a critical election. He was an outsider who seized his party's nomination as the leader of a movement of outsiders. The movement was clearly the culmination of concerns over the war, to which several domestic preoccupations attached themselves. This movement took over the convention by a surprisingly effective combination of unconventional direct-action politics (learned in the 1960s) and respectable, conventional party politics (learned in the aftermath of the failure of 1960s direct-action politics). No better example of critical election politics has been seen since the nomination of William Jennings Bryan led the Democratic Party into the critical election of 1896.

Now that the election is over it is patent to almost everyone that George McGovern could not have won. But in a critical election winning is surprisingly irrelevant. What matters is how the campaign is fought and whether it realigns the electorate into voting components roughly relevant to the real problems of the day. That is precisely how, in a mass democracy, problems are translated into issues. It is not done simply by candidates wishing it or voters demanding it. It happens only when the whole thrust of party politics is directed toward one or two intensely felt and clearly stated problems.

George McGovern came in on a peace movement, but as matters turned out, especially Nixon's skillful manipulation of international news, it was impossible for Democrats to win with peace as the issue. Nevertheless, peace was the basis of the McGovern movement, and it could have won in the way most movements win, by establishing the fact that peace and America's place in the world are issues over which the American people have a right to

exercise some long-range control. This was the "new politics." It was a "new politics" in the same way that we have had new politics several times before in our history. This movement made George McGovern a one-issue candidate. He tried to be a multi-issue candidate. He became a non-issue candidate.

At the personal level, George McGovern's conduct let down the movement that got him the nomination. But the personal side is irrelevant. It is only indicative of a more general failure of party politics to solve problems for American democracy. Somehow the vital energies of this movement were snuffed out by party structures. The consequences of this turn of events are so important that they will be the subject of analysis and explanation for many years to come. Here I want to take note of the most salient apparent consequences and then turn to a first effort at explanation.

The outstanding feature of 1972 is the extent to which the election itself was out of joint with the other political developments of that year. This already begins to suggest that the election suppressed the natural tendencies already at work, the strongest indication being that most of the politically significant changes of 1972 took place before the election. For example, thirteen members of the House lost their seats in the spring and summer primaries. Ten of these were Democrats, and their departure represented a loss to Congress and to the Democratic Party of 202 years of seniority (computed by counting the number of years served beyond the first term). Three of the Democratic losers were chairmen of important committees. An additional thirty members of the House retired altogether from politics (two by death); thirteen of these were Democrats, two of them committee chairmen; a large percentage, one may assume, were moved to retire by a depressing assessment of their chances for re-election. These retirees represent a seniority loss of 186 years to Democrats and to the Congress.

In contrast, a total of only thirteen incumbents lost in the election, and a mere eight of these were Democrats—several of whom lost because of redistricting rather than campaigning. These losses deprived Democrats in Congress of no committee chairmen and only 106 years of seniority.

All told, counting also those who retired voluntarily to seek higher office, the House of Representatives will in 1973 be almost 1,000 years younger than it was in 1972, but only a tiny proportion of this rejuvenation is attributable to the $500 million spent on the campaign. In fact, more than 80 per cent of all the incumbents running for re-election were successful. What a moment of frustration it is to ponder the contrast between the 80 per cent of new delegates at the Democratic convention and the 80 per cent of old incumbents returned to Congress by the election!

Or consider the following as a further example of how the election was out of joint with all of the other results of 1972. Despite the defeat of the liberal McGovern, only seven of all departing Congressmen had compiled ADA or "liberal" support records better than 70 per cent. The large majority of departing members actually had liberal support records of less than 50 per cent, and nearly a third of these were actual conservatives, with liberal scores below 14 per cent. Contrast this to 1964, when the Republican Presidential candidate took an equivalent shellacking. Forty Republicans were defeated in the general elections alone, causing the GOP to lose 244 years of Republican seniority in the House, along with several ranking members of such important committees as Rules, Ways and Means, and Appropriations (seven of the twenty Republicans on Appropriations were defeated and an eighth retired). All but four of the Republicans who went down with Goldwater had liberal support scores below 25 per cent, and thirty-one of these supported liberal legislation less than 14 per cent of the time. In 1964, that is, defeat was consistent; in 1972, defeat was almost completely meaningless. The terms of discourse and the lines of conflict will be irrelevant to electorates for at least another four years.

When the complete theory of the 1972 election is written, a large part of the failure of American politics will probably be seen to stem from the stress put on electoral victory as the only test of political virility. In our political system nothing is quite so ignominious as defeat. That is largely because we tend to define politics as a game. Winning and losing are the only dimensions that seem to concern us, and usually this comes down to the very narrow question of *who* won. There is little concern for *what* won, or how. And as long as winning remains the test of virility, party politics will continue to suppress issues because, even though the need to face problems may be compelling, the risks of losing are too great when problems are raised to the pro or con clarity of issues.

Defining politics as a game is natural to a politician like Richard Nixon, who has a game plan for damned near everything. But it seems evident that politics-as-a-game had almost everything to do with the McGovern strategy as well. In the end this seems to be what led him to forsake his movement. McGovern, or his staff, killed a historic opportunity by redefining it in conventional party terms. This definition provided them with a guide to their responsibilities, which boiled down to a single imperative: use all resources rationally to win the game.

If victory is all that counts, even when you are doomed to lose, the main thing is to decide what you think the voters think. The key to the whole silly effort is to gain rapport in order to attract votes. And the main job, then, is to study the polls.

The trouble is that this sort of thing can be done, and in this case was done, irrationally. The polls were accurate this year, but accurate only in reporting gross voter inclination between the two major candidates. Almost nothing else about polling, this year or any other year, is a matter of accurate forecasting. It is all a matter of interpretation, and the urge to win led the McGovern people to serious errors of interpretation and therefore of judgment.

Organizations like Gallup or Roper design questionnaires to solicit the opinions of respondents on a variety of substantive concerns. These are "issues" in one sense, because each question is framed as an issue, in order to get a distribution of opinions on "both sides." One good example would be something like, "Some people feel that all children should attend integrated schools, even if public transportation is required. Would you strongly agree, agree, be neutral, disagree, or strongly disagree with their position?" Simple as such questions may seem—and there is indeed a science to making questions simple—they, like hypnotism, produce serious distortions when put in the wrong hands. The first distortion is the impression polls give to the uninitiated that there is an issue corresponding to the question. The poll defines bussing as an issue by posing a question for the ayes and the nays and the don't knows. But the entire extent to which bussing has been employed, and the existing law and practice on bussing, are left out of the background of the question. The complex matter of school quality is left out. The complex history of abuse of bussing by white suburbs is left out. What is it that a person is saying aye or nay to?

As it turns out, the most serious and knowledgeable respondents would actually be obliged to respond "don't know" to almost any opinion question, unless each question were prefaced by a monograph of explanation. It is in this respect that the poll can give a false sense of the existence of an issue.

A second serious type of distortion arises from the cumulative impression made by all the opinion questions on a given questionnaire. If you ask twenty opinion questions you will tend to get a distribution of yesses, no's and don't knows on all twenty. Moreover, the don't knows will normally be less than 10 per cent of the total, because people usually do not know enough, or lack the courage to say they do not know enough, about an important problem. But if an "issue" is by definition a public problem on which a significant number of people disagree, then each of the twenty questions *is* an issue. The rest is easy to picture. George McGovern's staff studied these responses, interpreted each result as an

"issue," and then decided that a rationally conducted campaign should include position papers on each of these issues, with the candidate expressing his views on each of these issues in a significant section of the country. In this manner, George McGovern was killed by the extreme rationality of his staff and by his own sense of responsibility to take courageous positions on all the things that seemed to preoccupy the voters. By taking a stand on every so-called issue, Mr. McGovern pulled the fuse from his own movement, and at the same time heaped upon himself all of the hostilities that an electorate invariably feels when something it does not understand seems to be happening.

A third type of distortion, which I wrote about at length after the 1970 campaign ("Politics of Dead Center: The Artificial Majority," *The Nation*, December 7, 1970) is the Illusion of Central Tendency that the polls unintentionally produce. That is, along with the illusion that voters are neatly arranged on two sides of a well-defined issue, the polls produce the illusion that the preponderance of voters are located at the center of each issue, mildly for versus mildly against. Often this is true, but often it is not: on some questions the voters are really far apart—or polarized. Yet when a pollster asks a question in an area where the issue is poorly defined—as, for example, "Do you favor or oppose bussing?"—the typical voter, who may be faintly aware of all the conflicting possibilities, must respond "maybe" or "moderately," even though he may feel very strongly negative on some aspects of the issue and very strongly the other way on other aspects. For example, if the question dealt strictly and exclusively with the prospect of bussing blacks from the center city out to suburban and upperwhite city schools, the distribution of responses would almost certainly be quite different from the results if the question were one of bussing in both directions. When all such elements are masked in one basket question about "bussing," the attempt to respond becomes a neurotic situation for the person answering. He must engage himself in an inner dialogue, take the various implicit components of the question into balance, and then "on net," report a moderate yes or a moderate no or a don't know and go away feeling that the poll was kind of silly. And he would be right.

George McGovern's sincere effort to be an issue candidate was ultimately undermined by the equally sincere urge of his staff and the Democratic National Committee to be rational. That is what turned "new politics" into old politics, and it happened without anybody noticing. The preconvention momentum was lost and the campaign doomed—not to defeat, because that seemed foreordained—but to meaningless defeat.

But should the rest of us take it lightly that the party system quashed our once-in-a-lifetime opportunity to have a plebiscite on peace? The militants of the 1960s should be most indignant, because all that promise about the effectiveness of conventional politics proved to be nothing but the right to embrace the existing leadership—to embrace not the American system of democracy but an increasingly outmoded system of party politics. But the non-militants of Left and Right should also be indignant, because the party system is so irrelevant even when the opportunity for relevance is so close at hand. How else can one interpret the fact that a spectacularly bona-fide mass movement of early 1972 was, by late 1972, nothing but a passive audience for some of the silliest political promises ever made? It was the polls, not the conscience, that made cowards of them all.

This most recent national campaign proves only that the primary function of elections and of political parties in America is conquest. More effectively than the military and the FBI, "democratic participation" brought most of the disaffected of the 1960s back into the system. But conventional politics no longer means the right to use the franchise to bring about nonviolent change; it means only the opportunity to be a member of a status quo. The earlier militancy had proven that obstructive tactics and trashing were almost instantly counterproductive. Now after 1972, it is proven that a militant commitment to conventional

politics is also useless. This may turn out to be counter-productive for the system itself i it demoralizes thousands of young people by giving the impression that there are no routes at all to political change.

In fact, there seems to be only one other route to political change that is as yet untried, and it may be attractive because it is as unconventional as militancy, but as nonviolent as conventional participation. This route is *abstentionism*.

Abstentionism has no special political meaning in English. The Oxford Dictionary defines it only in terms of holding back, whether from drinking whiskey or signing a manifesto. But the French and many other Europeans look at it somewhat differently. They see it as a political act, an act questioning the ligitimacy of what is going on. The Argentines were apparently threatening to engage in this kind of abstentionism until the military rulers agreed to bring Perón from exile.

America teaches that good citizenship involves giving support to the system. It means showing respect for the symbols and objects of power, and that often extends to showing respect even for individual power holders and their interest groups. It implies voting, but tends to define voting as an act of giving consent. Citizenship has come, therefore, to be defined rather narrowly, as in "vote for the candidate of your choice." This is comparable to our narrow and stilted definition of religion as "worship at the church of your choice." It seems that citizenship was never supposed—in the United States—to mean *withholding* consent.

Consequently, participation has become a *pro forma* matter of voting yes or no to a referendum, or yes or yes[no] to one of two major candidates. The only alternative, even as defined in the scientific study of political behavior, is "non-voting," or "non-participation," which amounts to virtual non-citizenship. In the election just held, scarcely more than half the electorate voted, and this is widely taken as a sign that the democratic process is seriously sick. And so it is, if the voters stay home from apathy or because they find both the candidates distasteful; and particularly it is so if they nurse their dissatisfactions in privacy, being both absent and not counted. The alternative to this in the past has been obstructionism, which is illegal.

But there is a third way—voting by abstention: actual participation by refusing, on publicly expressed principle, to participate. In brief, it is sometimes an exercise of citizenship to refuse to give consent to be governed. That does not imply an obligation of civil disobedience. It means only that, for a certain period, you will obey only because those who govern hold power over you and can punish you severely for not obeying. It means that in your opinion the exercise of power is illegitimate because it was gained illegitimately and that you will obey the illegitimate power only because you have no choice.

Abstentionism is almost the only counterweapon citizens have when arbitrariness, or corruption, or surveillance, or suppression is widespread. It should be engaged in when, as in 1972, there is too much concern for winning. Mort Sahl put it all together in 1960 when he suggested that we "vote no for President." The rest of his line was ". . . and leave the White House empty for another four years." The White House is going to be occupied no matter what we do, but a national "vote no for President" movement, led by a few thousand people who command public respect and can voice public indignation, might well give that occupant of the White House, whoever he is, a strong sense that he had better so conduct himself as to earn the legitimacy that he does not yet enjoy.

Something drastic must be done to bring the politician back to a proper political role, and abstentionism may be just the thing, because it may be the only effective way to vote against the political system without indicating an intention to destroy it. Abstentionism may be a way to hold a political system to its own pretensions, which you cannot do by merely voting against the incumbent. That is what Southern Blacks used to try when both candidates were racists. But true abstentionism was not available to Southern Blacks, because they participated only on sufferance, and their consent was neither needed nor desired.

Seen in this way, abstentionism is a kind of third party. True, it will elect no candidates, but in this country the function of third parties, when they are in any measure effective, is not to win elections but to raise issues. Voters who declare themselves abstentionists gain a power hitherto unsuspected. They can deprive politicians of consent, which is something politicians desperately need. Their only recourse would be to try to regain that consent, and it seems clear that their response would have to involve some effort to change their own ways. And what would our conditions be? Quit lying, quit hiding the truth, quit misrepresenting. Quit being all things to all people. Try, for a change to be *some* things to *some* people. The election of 1972 makes the notion of abstentionism a good deal more attractive and plausible than it ever was before.

Such a stand might very well end up producing a multiparty system. This is always a tendency when politicians set their goals at something short of a majority. But we have really operated under a multi-party system for many years! There have consistently been three parties on the national scene, the Republicans, the Democrats and the Southern Democrats. Mr. Nixon's "opening to the Left" may well reveal still a fourth party. These separate third and fourth parties have been masked over by the requirements of the electoral college and the committee system in Congress. But it has been clear at least since 1968 that the electoral college is a dangerous as well as a silly instrument for electing Presidents, and the talk about abolishing it subsided only because George Wallace did not become a third-party candidate for President in 1972. Abolition of the electoral college might all by itself relieve politicians of the obsession to gain rapport with every single voter, and that would make national campaigns for President a good deal more honest.

Meanwhile, the behavior of politicians must be changed, and there must be a means to express our dissatisfaction with the behavior of politicians. Abstentionism could be that means.

Socialist

Michael P. Lerner. How to put socialism on the agenda.

The recent surge of articles and proposals concerning the formation of a new socialist party is a welcome sign of political maturation for the American left. But the debate around the specific details of such a party could very easily take the place of building it. The questions that must concern us now are those that are likely to arise during the next decade. It makes more sense to assess what can be accomplished within that period and build an instrument appropriate to these tasks than to try now to develop forms that will be appropriate to every possible contingency between the present moment and the revolution. And if we approach the construction of a party with that kind of tentativeness, we will feel less traumatized if the new tasks of a future period require important changes in the organization of the party.

The party must be built to confront and transform the present realities. A key obstacle: the unrealistic assessment of possibilities that has so often prevented the left from developing sensible expectations and programs. We went from the millenarian and utopian expectations of the late sixties ("Revolution Now!") to a period of extreme defeatism in which serious struggles for power, particularly on the national level, have been rejected as premature and unrealistic. Neither extreme makes sense: utopian expectations yielded disillusionment and pessimism, and the present over-intoxication with an empirical account of our present weakness is self-fulfilling and forgets how quickly the political realities of the early 1960s were transformed by the

intervention and activism of what was initially a small band of militants.

It is unrealistic to expect that a socialist revolution can be made in America in the next eight years. What can be accomplished is the following: we can place socialism on the agenda. We can make socialism the central political issue of the late 1970s and early 1980s, shaping the political debate and redirecting all political activity, much as we made the issue of immediate and unconditional withdrawal the central issue of the late 1960s and early 1970s. To put it on the agenda is not the same as to win it: nevertheless, we can achieve a monumental goal by making the desirability and possibility of a socialist society the major political concern, and one which will have to be addressed by anyone seeking a political base within the American working class. That is a goal far short of taking and holding state power, and far greater than any implicit in the existing practice of the left.

Toward a mass party

It is this strategic goal that provides a framework within which we can develop appropriate weapons for the struggle. We are immediately confronted with the need for a mass political party. The recognition of that need grows out of the actual experiences of those who have worked on local projects and have tried to raise the issue of socialism. They have invariably found the following response: "Oh, your idea of socialism sounds very nice. But where is the force that can institute this socialism idea? Until there is one, it is impractical for me to side with you, or back demands that have socialism as their logical extension, because I'll just be an individual (or we'll just be this one local union local, or one local city council, or local health care clinic, etc.) isolated, alone, vulnerable, and somewhat powerless. So for the time being, I'll stick with realistic demands that can actually be won on the local level, or within the context of political forces that I can clearly see exist (e.g., the liberal wing of the Democratic Party)." Faced with this response, many old new leftists have either given up on politics themselves, changed their politics, or temporarily shelved their wider vision and agreed to a narrowing of focus that would seem concrete, practical, realistic, etc. The point is that demands for society-wide transformation will never be taken seriously until there is the prospect of a society-wide force which at least potentially would be the agent for such change.[1]

Originally, the New American Movement was conceived in such a way, but a counter-tendency to make it a sectarian political organization rather than a protoparty formation won out. The differences are critical: a sect group may often see itself as the leader of the masses, but not as the organization that the masses join. A party, on the other hand, must be the organization for the masses of working people: it must provide a form and style that encourages mass participation. The mass party must take itself seriously as the correct political vehicle for this period: its goal is to be the representative and expression of the movement for socialism. It talks in its own name, boldly and self-confidently, as the voice of those who seek basic social transformation.

NAM [The New American Movement] never did this. It barred the media from its founding convention and has largely avoided seeking public attention on a national level. It has refused to call in its own name for national demonstrations around energy, inflation, or any other political issue. And its argument is: "Who are we, so small, so weak, so unknown, to call anything or to speak in the name of the oppressed?" The answer: You will remain unknown and small and weak as long as you do nothing to call yourself to the attention of the American people, as long as you conceive of yourself as weak and powerless. It is only when a political organization begins to take itself seriously as the vehicle through which people can act to change things that anyone not already in it gets attracted to it. NAM's typical response: "But we had to define our politics better." Answer: None of the refinements introduced since June of 1972 are refinements likely to make NAM more attractive to the American working class. It is not as if all these people are just waiting for

NAM to get its politics more clearly articulated before they join. NAM's problems were never that it needed better self-definition than it achieved in its founding document pre-Davenport 1971: rather that it needed to change that self-definition into a reality by beginning to act in the political world of public politics.

NAM developed some important work in the theory of socialist-feminism; imagine the difference, however, if it had developed a program for public political action that brought such an analysis to the attention of the American public. We are past the days when action is counterposed to theory, but in practice NAM has failed to become more on a national level than a political debating club in which different local groups get to exchange information and debate their politics. Imagine, to give a local example, the impact NAM would have had if it had taken its analysis of socialist-feminism and set up continued demonstrations and disruptions at San Francisco North Beach nightclubs that exploit women's bodies. Imagine that it demanded that newspapers give equal space to feminist reviewers of movies and that it demanded from owners of movie theaters showing sexist flicks that they allow five minutes before or after the show for a feminist to explain how people were being indoctrinated in sexist attitudes. You can invent your own examples for your own scene, and you may dislike some of my specific examples, but the point still stands: working women will be attracted to a political movement that is actively confronting sexism, and the early NAM analyses of feminist-socialism were adequate for attracting those women had they been put into public political practice. The internal political life and education of a party is critical, but it risks becoming sectarian unless that internal life is continually related to an external political practice that aims at speaking to the largest constituencies that will presently listen. The party we need to build must avoid this kind of sectarianism: it must start from a solid political foundation with a clearcut commitment to socialism and a sound analysis of racism, sexism, and imperialism and their roots in capitalism, and a well-thought-out analysis of work, leisure, and the problems of everyday life— but it must immediately move its primary energy outward to the world rather than inward to refining its politics.

Because it takes itself seriously, the party aims to be the major expression of those who seek basic change. As such, it is competitive with the Democratic Party on the one hand and the left sects on the other: it is not open to people who wish to win adherents to these alternative forms. At the same time, it does not impose an exclusivity on its members: they are encouraged to work in other organizations and struggles, e.g., the trade union movement, the independent women's movement. But wherever it works, it does so not to take over secretly other alternatives, but to proclaim publicly and openly the necessity for a socialist perspective, and it urges other political groups that agree to affiliate with the party itself, which is the coordinator and voice of the socialist movement.

The mass party is not an organization of organizers: it is a structure that will have organizers and full-time political activists, honored and paid for their commitment, but it is primarily built around people who are not going to give the bulk of their time to political activity. While it must counter the passivity generated by the Democratic and Republican parties, where membership consists solely of voting in primaries and elections, it must also avoid the image of an organization for people who never get bored and whose sole concern is politics. A plausible goal here is the following: monthly meetings of local party chapters, structured to focus on the primary political issues facing the chapter on the national and local levels, together with a biweekly internal bulletin that publicizes debate on important issues, and a bimonthly meeting to settle organizational issues exclusively. Questions like this may seem trivial, but it is precisely at this level that organizations get structured in ways that make mass participation impossible, either by allowing no avenues of participation (as the capitalist parties operate) or by demanding such a high degree of involvement that only a few feel comfortable enough to venture forth.

Of course, a party must have organizers and paid staff (at an income high enough to be competitive with a good factory job so that the staff isn't composed simply of people in their twenties doing a stint before getting to their real-life occupation, and at a level low enough so that anyone on staff feels the same economic problems as the majority of Americans we hope to organize). But paid staff members have as their primary responsibility the development of organizational forms and political activities that allow for the greatest participation of the rank and file. It should be possible for a factory worker, an office clerk, or a housewife to play a leadership role, to be a spokesperson for the organization around a particular struggle or issue, without having to become a full-time activist and leave job and family. So the functions of the staff are primarily internal: to structure meetings, provide political forms, develop internal political education, that have as their openly stated goal the direct involvement of membership in all external activities aimed at changing the society and recruiting more people to the party. To ensure that the staff doesn't develop interests of its own, its primary positions must be elected by the general membership, and it must be held accountable to the membership in its decision-making. Supervising the staff and coordinating political activities must be an elected political leadership, at local, regional, and national levels. In order to ensure accountability, leadership must make frequent attempts to submit central political issues to a referendum of the membership, and the right to immediate recall of leadership must be institutionalized within the party. At the same time, because working people will be reluctant to take leadership positions and relinquish their steady jobs, real care must be taken to ensure that leaders can afford to live, that defeated leadership is helped to find alternative employment, and that working people who become involved in party activity be financially assisted whenever necessary.

The party must care about the needs of its members as human beings and as political people. We understand the importance of this when it comes to building non-sexist practices, fighting internal racism, and engaging in political education. But we also need to worry about a host of other problems: employment, housing, child care, health, psychological well-being, etc. Of course, short of societal transformations we cannot adequately deal with these problems, but neither can we leave it at that—dismissing such concerns with some sharp analyses of how we need to change the system. We may not handle them adequately, but a party that makes some effort in this direction can make a profound impression on its members that far transcends particular political disagreements within the party. A working-class party, of course, will have to develop working-class forms, which means that the cultural chauvinism of the new left must be overcome. Our party will have lectures, but bowling leagues as well, and it will speak in a language that respects the intelligence, decency, and humanity of the American working class.

Extending our social base

Given our present situation, any party that is formed now would have a disproportionate number of people who are not part of the industrial work force. So the immediate problem is to transform the social base of the party, to the extent that it becomes more representative of the working class as a whole, rather than of just one sector of it. NAM provides us with a perfect example of how *not* to do this: by spending time in further refining political strategy, debating internal structure, and shying away from publicity and national attention. The party will only be taken seriously by working people when they hear about it, and hear about it from some other source than the party's own leaflets and newspaper. The party must, from the start, be in the public arena, seeking publicity for its programs, and its programs must clearly address the basic issues facing working people. Had such a party been in existence in the past several years, for instance, it would have focused on inflation and energy, and would have raised the demand for socialism within that context. It would have clearly and loudly explained why only a full-scale socialization of the economy could possibly deal with the problems being raised.[2] It would have sponsored national demonstrations, marches, sit-ins, disruptions, electoral initiatives, and electoral campaigns around that theme.

But isn't it premature to raise the demand for socialism? Wouldn't we be dooming ourselves to irrelevance? No.[3] Here our central task is not merely to accept the established dynamic in the political order, but to transform it. The scenario could be similar to that of the sixties: when we demanded ''immediate withdrawal'' from Vietnam in 1965 many condemned us as being utopian and politically unrealistic. However, because our demand was the only one that made real sense and because we were willing to engage in confrontations to bring it to the attention of the American people, it eventually was seen as the most logical position and gained the support of the majority in the society. Certainly the demand for socialization will be resisted more strenuously by the press and by ''responsible political leaders.'' Nevertheless, it is the only demand that can make sense in the period ahead, and if put forth intelligently and vigorously it could spread rapidly, creating a new reality which the rulers will have to confront (one likely direction for them: the emergence of a ''pro-socialist'' sector of the Democratic Party, whose ''socialism'' will be some variant of state control, with the state remaining in the hands of the ruling class).

Of course, it would be foolish to suggest that a party need only announce its existence and everyone will come rushing towards it. Bourgeois ideology has a tremendous grip, and a party must be intelligent and imaginative in the ways in which it confronts that ideology. Yet the Vietnam war and Watergate have ripped tremendous holes into the picture of the world that the rulers would like to paint. And the increasing crisis in the economy, certain to deepen and intensify in the next several years, will widen the crisis of confidence in the present system and open up to sectors of the working class alternative explanations of their reality. Those alternatives will almost certainly come from the far right, and the right will have the advantage of playing on prejudices and aspects of bourgeois indoctrination to support their side. But this same situation presents tremendous opportunities for the left, because people will be increasingly open to interpretations different from those being fed them through the media and established political leaders. And while the left has to break through a heavy conditioning to get its message heard, it has a significant advantage: it speaks the truth about the world, and most people are capable of responding to the truth in the not-too-long run. Hence the tremendous growth of popularity for the left in the sixties; only we could explain the war, and only we had a solution that made sense. Obviously, not everybody came flocking around the moment we articulated it, but because we stayed around, became increasingly visible, and reminded people of our analysis year after year—while patiently and yet dramatically working, on every level from the electoral to mass demonstrations—a large number of people eventually recognized the validity of our message.

Although it is true that the demand for socialism will face even more obstacles than the call for America to give up the war, it is also probable that the economic crisis will be more pressing on the consciousness of most Americans than the war, so that the left will be less pressed to raise the issue, since it stares people in the face every time they buy food, pay rent, and purchase commodities. Further, the increasing pressure on resources—human and material—raises directly and concretely questions about the rationality of production in capitalist society with an immediacy that is potentially revolutionary. The key is to see the potentialities: the crisis is real and is happening right now, but how people interpret that crisis— whether they see it as a crisis for capitalism or merely as a personal problem that they need to deal with in their own lives—depends on the existence of a serious and imaginative left.

Combining the social and the political

In an otherwise instructive article in *Socialist Revolution* 18, John Judis suggests that the primary focus for a party must be the taking of state power, and not merely the focus on what he calls the "social struggle" that takes place "in every institution of capitalist society—in the home, in the schools, in the factories and offices, churches and union halls—wherever the social relations of capitalist society are reproduced." He cites approvingly a NAM caucus statement that "the object of the struggle remains as always the production-property system; the pivot of the struggle is the society-wide political-ideological contest for state power and social hegemony." The problem with this dichotomy between object and pivot is that it leaves intact the very division that we want to break down. Our goal is the politicization and democratization of all the institutions of the society, and most centrally the democratization of the productive apparatus of the society. It is therefore mistaken to focus on the political apparatus and the struggle for power within it; doing that only strengthens a pattern of thought and a conceptualization of the political world that we oppose.

What I am suggesting is that we fight *now* for what we want eventually: a full democratic transformation. Our struggle for power must mean and appear to be something dramatically different from the struggle of the Democrats versus the Republicans. We are not for the replacement of the present ruling elite by a better, more moral, or even more "socialistic" elite. We are for total democratization of the society. Then our strategy must be that: to extend the realm of the political precisely where it was considered inappropriate before.

Part of making that struggle will involve elections and campaigns for public office. These are critical because (a) they are the traditional avenue through which Americans express their political preferences, and it would be contradictory to propose democracy but be unwilling to put up our candidates for scrutiny by the electorate; (b) elections allow one some limited access to the media not otherwise available; and (c) winning some electoral offices gives the party a platform for putting forward its program. An electoral presence is critical for national elections, because any program for basic economic change would have to be coordinated nationally, and failure to have some national agent for change will make local operations seem isolated and essentially futile. However, there are serious reasons why electing candidates has great limitations: (a) a poor showing may be interpreted as lack of support for left programs, when in fact it represents a popular feeling that the programs are good but are unlikely to command enough support now, so that it would be a mistake to throw a vote away when it could go to some liberal who has the power to make some minimal changes now; (b) competing for votes in an arena largely controlled by the capitalist media can set in motion very negative dynamics within the party (e.g., the desire to moderate programs, to choose leaders on the basis of their being "responsible," appealing to the bourgeois media); (c) focus on candidates and voting tends to increase the passivity of party membership, whereas we want an organization that increases self-activity and sense of creativity among participants.

The solution is not to avoid running candidates, a move which guarantees a high degree of political impotence. We do not want a repeat of the collapse of the anti-war movement, where our demand, finally legitimized, was taken up by established parties and, with its radical thrust diluted and undermined, was then used to strengthen the credibility of the capitalist system as a whole. An impossible scenario if our demand is socialism? No. Look at the political scene in Western Europe and see how, when necessary, the parties that do not want to challenge capitalist rule (e.g., Britain's Labour Party) can accommodate themselves to the demand for socialism, and even nationalize (though not socialize) sectors of the economy which might otherwise be failing. A similar strategy for America has been proposed by John Kenneth Galbraith, and would be an extremely likely move if our party starts to generate mass support. We absolutely must have an electoral wing that is the expression of the movement that created the demand for socialism.

Nevertheless, our use of the electoral arena would be different from that of the Democratic and Republican parties, whose political activity consists in running candidates and little else. Our candidates must be so overshadowed by the content of our program that they are seen as incidental to it, as one of several ways to get that program better known. We must see the running of candidates as a less important way to use electoral politics than the device now available in a majority of the states: the electoral initiative. The initiative provides a party with the unique opportunity of placing its main proposals on the ballot in a language that it chooses. Using this avenue is critical: by putting proposals directly before the people we are doing now what we want in a transformed society. It is critical that we pose the issues sharply and dramatically: I envision that by 1980 we could have ten or fifteen states voting on an initiative proposal that calls for workers' control of factories, or for a democratically elected council to plan what new industries will be allowed, or a confiscatory tax scheme on the rich. Done on a local level the old arguments about industry and capital moving out of a state become central; but done as part of a nationally coordinated effort, and in the climate of a society that has been faced by a growing popular movement for socialism, these efforts take on a credibility and impact that would be very dramatic and far-reaching. Only a national party that has built up an electoral presence can successfully coordinate such an effort.

Needless to say, the mass work of a party goes far beyond electoral activity. An important way to grow is through demonstrations that give political expression to popular frustrations. In the years ahead, the party should be involved in visible confrontations with the capitalists and the state. It should sponsor mass demonstrations that capture national publicity. It should lead consumer boycotts and eventually society-wide moratoriums and strikes. And it should do so always with its politics up-front and central. Its goal should be mass demonstrations for socialism itself by the late 1970s.[4]

A primary focus of the party's work should be in the arenas described by Judis as the "social struggle." And the aim of that work should be to convert the "social" into the political realm. For instance, an important party activity at the workplace is directed at popularizing the notion of workers' control of their own work situation and of the economy as a whole. Within the unions the party pushes for these kinds of demands as integral to any strike or struggle. At first, the idea seems utopian: "What does this have to do with my immediate needs?" Our answer: "Everything." And we explain why and how. Next likely counter: "OK, I can see how things would be better that way, but it's so far off that it doesn't make sense to talk about that now." Here, the only counter will be our success, *outside the factory*, in having popularized the demand and given it such wide public attention (e.g., through demonstrations, initiatives, public statements by party members) that industrial workers will see that it is not just this local party member who is discussing a particular proposal, but that it is a real society-wide issue. At this point our next approach makes sense: "By fighting for workers' control here, we will be part of a much larger movement, which will tend to be more successful if we do something here." Work inside the trade union movement should have the same focus: to make the central demand that of socialism. The party must reject the strategy of various sectarian groups that seek to build rank-and-file caucuses around the issue of providing a more militant leadership in the unions. We want militancy, but not around the same old demands: we want a new orientation for the demands, and the way to get that is to start *now* (and not in some mysterious later time that never comes) to demand workers' control as a central part of a union program. Again, isolated from a national movement that commands publicity and attention, such a program will sound absurdly sectarian and silly: hence, the experience of current workplace organizers leads them into more localized demands and into narrow struggles for liberal, less corrupt leadership of the unions. In the absence of a national party, this seems to flow from and be required by the present reality. The socialist party transforms that reality by creating a climate in which agitation for socialism becomes as normal and pervasive a phenomenon throughout the society as agitation against the war was in the late sixties.

Politicizing everyday life

The same model applies throughout each area of the society: everywhere we must struggle to politicize and democratize basic concerns. Whether around schools or health care, transportation or housing, we agitate now for a socialist program, which has as its first step the right of the people to decide for themselves how to deal with these issues. We challenge authoritarianism in social relations, sexism, racism, not simply by agitation on a one-to-one basis or through small groups, but by developing programs that bring it into the public realm. For instance, it has recently been suggested that women should be paid for housework. This demand is not adequate for several reasons: most importantly, because it would confirm women in this position rather than liberate them from a sex-stereotyped occupation. Nevertheless, an initiative (sic) campaign around that kind of demand, which takes an area of everyday life typically thought to be immune from politics and politicizes it, is one way to raise issues around women's liberation that might potentially unify the struggle of women isolated as individuals or in small groups. A better example might be an initiative that guarantees to workers certain rights on the job (e.g., the right to supervise their own production within a shop, to elect and recall foremen, and to secure job tenure). Since the demand for socialism *is* the demand for democratization, it is this very process that legitimates and makes plausible the basic demand for socialism. We need not fear that such demands will be granted and co-opted: even should such referenda pass, the courts will attempt to strike them down and the legislatures will rush to limit the rights of initiative-style legislation. At that point, the movement that has fought for the substance must move directly to the fight for the process: and that struggle for the people's democratic sovereignty is the battle for socialism.

One reason that an explicitly socialist politics has been eschewed in the past is that the left itself has little vision of what socialism would look like concretely, and hence hasn't been able to devise programs for the socialization of particular sectors. Making the demand for socialism concrete is the precondition for putting socialism on the agenda. The party seeks to involve a majority of people in the running of the society: but to do so, that majority must know concretely how it will run the society, and what specifically it will do. Needless to say, many of these questions cannot be settled a priori, and we don't need more utopian fantasies. What we do need are concrete programs for specific institutions and issues that provide a way of fighting for larger and larger areas of democratic control. But such plans will never develop in the abstract. Only when we have a party that can utilize those plans to advance political debate will people put serious energy into developing them. It is false to argue that we don't have a sufficiently developed strategy to have a party yet. The strategy only emerges when there is a social force looking to implement a strategy. We have enough of a direction right now, in terms of realizable goals for the next decade, to warrant the immediate creation of a party.

The development of detailed strategies also provides a critical way for the party to begin to implement a process that a socialist revolution would finally complete: the direct involvement of people in structuring their own lives. One central task for the party in this period is to build workers' discussion groups and councils that seek to develop plans about how particular factories, offices, and other workplaces could be reorganized in a more democratic, creative, and humanly satisfying way. Who would be better at developing those plans than the workers themselves? And what better way to involve people in the struggle for a new society than for them to see that such a society could be one that they themselves constructed? That very process will be resisted at first by many workers who see themselves as incapable of that kind of thinking, and who regard such thinking as utopian speculation not worth spending time on. But as the demand for socialism becomes louder and clearer, involvement could spread very quickly and the very participation in that kind of activity would have a great liberating effect on many workers, convincing them that they are much more competent and intelligent than the society has led them to believe, and hence much more able to trust themselves and their fellow workers with the task of running a society without an authoritarian structure from on top. The creation of workers' discussion groups, along with democratic participation in party meetings, would go a long way towards convincing people that a socialist revolution could really be democratic.

The workers' discussion groups and councils, besides strengthening the workers' self-conceptions and self-confidence in their ability to run a new society, could be an important force in shifting the trade unions leftward and encouraging them to align with a mass socialist party. The existence of an organizational form that is separate from the trade union bureaucracy will be seen at first as a tremendous threat, but in their efforts to co-opt such a development the union leadership will be forced to provide more space for genuine political discussion and debate. Workers who have begun to feel their strength in these small discussion groups will be encouraged by the party to participate more actively inside the trade union movement, pushing for an explicit socialist politics. Struggles for a new progressive leadership will be supported only to the extent that such a leadership has a clear anti-capitalist orientation. Organized independently of the unions, the councils and discussion groups will still focus some of their attention on how the trade union movement has been co-opted and on how it could be transformed. At first, these discussions might seem utopian, but as a mass socialist party becomes increasingly visible in the media, people will increasingly feel themselves to be part of something larger and hence capable of winning something real inside the trade union movement.

Conclusion

The ideas, the strategy, the politics for a new socialist party exist. The potentiality for mass response, the objective economic conditions, and the disillusionment with the American political apparatus have set the stage for tremendous possibilities. What is absent is a left that is willing to move and provide leadership. Every national and nearly every local institution of the left is dominated by people who see themselves as powerless and defeated. When new people come into contact with the left they are overwhelmed by this sense of futility and cynicism. Those who think something can and must be done are quickly driven away. Those who remain become socialized into the spirit of despair, vicariously reliving the defeats of the sixties through those who experienced them. My own conclusion is that no matter what the world's objective possibilities, nothing can be accomplished until this subjective sense of powerlessness has been overcome. For that reason, I have begun to work in psychology, studying Reich, Gramsci, and others who would give us some clues as to how to deal with mass psychological disorders, and I have begun working as a therapist with people who are daily living their powerlessness. Whatever objective factors may be contributing to people's sense of powerlessness, there seems to be a clearly irrational element holding people back and which is holding back the left at this historical moment. A high immediate priority is to develop a psychology and a therapy that can deal with the collective neurosis of the American left.

I used to believe that winning concrete victories would be sufficient for overcoming people's sense of powerlessness. But the way the left continually interpreted its successes as defeats in the past decade has convinced me that political achievement is only a necessary condition, not a sufficient one. And this points toward another major activity that a party must see as its immediate concern: the struggle against powerlessness is not restricted to the left, but is central for the entire working class, and must be fought not just on the political level,

but also through the development of a socialist approach to mass psychology, culture, organizational life, and the family. Important contributions have been made already by the women's movement, but the struggles in these arenas are only beginning, and a party would have to view this as something integral to the task of putting socialism on the agenda. The historical split between the personal and the political must be challenged within the party, and to do this we must take very seriously the personal problems of our members, and of our potential members. When people do not feel good about themselves, they easily lapse into political defeatism and irrational behavior that can destroy any political movement. While personal struggle cannot ultimately occur independent of the political struggle, neither can a party that seeks socialist revolution fail to develop, within itself, forms for nurturing support and development of the individual's self-realization. At the same time, the party must create forms for dealing with these problems that are outwardly generalizable, so that its very concern with the psychological well-being of its members becomes a further reason why people outside it, from all sectors of the working class, are attracted to it.

NOTES

1. This is a dialectical process: it can't be big until it first exists, and starts addressing questions in a way that could reach millions of Americans. It must start small, given the present realities of who would initially hear about and be attracted to such a party. But it must be "mass" in conception: allowing for tremendous growth through its program and structure.

2. Socialization equals nationalization plus workers' control. This demand should include putting directly to the people the question of national politics in particular industries, or the election by the people of the board of directors of a socialized industry. Workers' control must ensure that the industry being socialized begins to provide a model for what work would look like in a worker-controlled society.

The demand for workers' control is a central part of the demand for socialism—but only a constituent part, because socialism will include a national and later an international plan for the allocation of resources and human time. A further discussion of how to balance the needs of local control with the needs for rational planning can be found in the chapter on socialism in my book, *The New Socialist Revolution* (New York, 1973).

3. It is this kind of thinking that has kept the Socialist Workers Party from playing an important role. It has always shied away from raising its inner politics in a public way, putting forward instead programs around single-issue demands that could become immediately popular. In effect, this has retarded the development of mass political consciousness, because SWP's dogged determination to keep its front organizations single-issue has conflicted with the logic of political development—to show the interrelationship of all the issues within the common problem source, capitalism itself.

The SWP's failures, however, go beyond its approach to program. How could anyone believe that such an organization would, if followed, lead the working class to power when it is so undemocratic and stingy about power within its own framework? No party can grow into a mass organization with millions of adherents if it is hierarchically structured. Internal opposition within the SWP is frequently squelched and expelled. Members' initiative is limited to implementing policies, rarely questioning their basic assumptions and directions. Hence, the kind of person likely to survive in such an organization will be a cheery young bureaucrat, willing to leave politics to the experienced people on top. This attitude can never generate the kind of approach that would lead to a mass party—an approach that politicizes by raising basic questions in ways in which they have not been raised before, that goes to the root of institutions and challenges their hidden political assumptions. Indeed, it was the rebellion against this old left conception of politics that helped to fuel the

energy of the sixties and will also probably inspire a movement in the period ahead. Our problem is that the reaction against the old left was so severe that we allowed no room for the legitimacy of national and even regional or local leadership, no room for taking seriously the experience of those who had led previous battles, no room for national vision.

The new party must embody the internal democracy and anti-authoritarianism of the new left while simultaneously leaving room for a genuine leadership to emerge, a leadership that is committed to internal democracy, but a leadership that is willing to lead and not just respond. We want to encourage neither anarchy and leaderlessness (e.g., a national leadership that thinks it can do nothing but coordinate local activity and exchange information about what is happening at the local level) nor the kind of runaway, unaccountable, hierarchical leadership that so stifled old left organizations. Now that we have a clearer picture of what we want to avoid in terms of the excesses of both the old left and the new left, it may be possible to develop a style of leadership that synthesizes the best in both. But such leadership isn't "born"—it develops—and a high priority is to create a climate in which imaginative, bold, but still accountable leadership can emerge while being both appreciated and given real space to innovate and experiment.

4. These demonstrations, of course, are not demands that the ruling class give us socialism, but rather mass demonstrations of strength and determination to fight for socialism. They are important because they liberate the closet socialists, and make it possible for those who have been afraid even to look at the left's analysis realize that if they get turned on by socialism they will not be alone. Mass demonstrations can also be confrontational when that is appropriate.

*

12 Academia

The basic questions this chapter will address are:

(1) What is academia?

(2) What is the role of faculty and students in the university?

(3) Are universities run according to democratic principles or are they autocratic institutions?

(4) Can the university be transformed so that it serves the community in which it exists?

Conservatives believe that universities do not exist in a vacuum. They are part of American life. Professors have a predilection to see themselves as intellectual elites while both college faculty and students tend to look down on other less educated people. Conservatives maintain that this elite stance of the university population is not right, but at the same time education does make some people more knowledgeable than others.

Conservatives see the university and industry working together to better American life. The underlying assumption is that academic experts must aid industry in developing new techniques and products. According to this analysis, there is or ought to be a close relationship between the university and the world outside the university. For example, science faculties should work together with government to develop space technology or new weapons systems. Political scientists, anthropologists, sociologists, and economists should work together with the military in developing counter-insurgency techniques for the conduct of any future wars. Psychologists should work with prison authorities in helping the latter rehabilitate and control inmates. If academics do not work with and support the government, then it is questionable whether universities should be supported by government funds. For conservatives, the university should accept its role as maintainer of the status quo and be proud of it. They do not understand why some professors and students are unwilling to accept their defined place in American society as they see it.[1]

Some liberals think that academics must engage in "objective" research in their laboratories and libraries and that the university campus should be an independent center of thought, beholden to no outsiders. While research should be engaged in for its own sake, researchers should not be held responsible for the uses others may make of their findings. Publication of scientific results must be freely and openly available to all. Academicians have the responsibility to publish whatever they have learned.

Other liberals believe that faculty should be socially and politically aware and should translate that awareness to their students. Teachers have great power over shaping the minds of their students; therefore it is their responsibility to make students conscious of issues such as racism, sexism, and discrimination against the aged. Professors should not confine their lectures to facts and theories from a textbook; they should encourage their students to participate in the real world. For instance, to understand prison life students should visit prisons; to understand courts students should attend night court; to understand how young children are socialized, students should work in a day-care center during the summer.

Liberals hold diverse opinions about political participation by academics within and outside of the university system. Some want direct involvement, others hold that academics should maintain a distance from the political arena. Some believe that faculty should maintain neutrality in the classroom, while others hold that teachers should take a political stand. It is often difficult in academia to distinguish between a liberal and a conservative for many adhere to various combinations of liberal and conservative positions.

Socialists believe that academics serve the interests of capitalism and capitalists.[2] It can be no other way. From a socialist standpoint this is evidenced by universities which either refuse to hire radicals as faculty members, or fire them whenever possible. They also cite the example of professional journals which generally exclude radical articles that are submitted for publication. Faculty promotion and tenure committees seldom give credit to publications which appear in radical journals. Professional associations are usually led by individuals having close links with the government. They are the professors who receive federal funding for their research and whose research findings are used by the government for its own purposes. In the discipline of political science, pluralism does not exist. Socialists point out that the major journal, the *American Political Science Review*, is controlled by conservatives. Departments in almost all universities are controlled by liberals or conservatives. Book publishers, with few notable exceptions, do not publish socialist literature.

Socialists see the solution to the problem of conservative/liberal control of academia in several ways. They believe in establishing alternative universities by and for radicals. For example, the Free Association, in New York City, offers courses seldom found in college catalogues.[3] Socialists also hold that the Ph.D. degree is a mechanism for excluding people from teaching and scholarship and hence should be demystified as a qualification for scholarship and eliminated as a qualification for teaching. Faculty should not allow themselves to be co-opted by government or industry; further, scholarly work, which could be used by elites against the people, should not be published. It is best that grants and scholarships from government and industry be declined, or possibly taken and turned against them. To further the growth of socialism, courses with a radical perspective should be offered. Faculty members should encourage their students to take jobs that have a social and political import.

Socialist academics should be politically active in building an American socialist movement. Their task is not only providing scholarly research for this movement, but to engage in the practical tasks of building political organizations. In the university, socialist academics work to separate the university, as much as possible, from the status quo. They attempt to radicalize their students so that they can see the underlying contradictions of the American political system and encourage them to act to change it.[4]

NOTES

1. Among the foremost expositors of this school of thought are Professors Sidney Hook and Ithiel de Sola Pool. See Sidney Hook, "Barbarism, virtue, and the university," *The Public Interest* (No. 15, Spring 1969), pp. 23–39; Ithiel de Sola Pool, "The Necessity for Social Scientists Doing Research for Governments," *Background* (No. 10, August 1966).

2. For an excellent analysis of this thesis see Marvin Surkin, "Sense and Non-Sense in Politics," in Marvin Surkin, Alan Wolfe, *An End to Political Science.* New York: Basic Books, Inc., 1970. pp. 13–33.

3. The *Free Association* is located at 5 W. 20th St., New York City. Among the courses the College offers are: Socialism and Feminism; Marx and Freud; Modern Music under Capitalism; Political Economy; History of the Family. Some liberals have also established colleges which can surely be considered novel. *The School of New Resources,* set up by Joe McDermott, is an example of such a college. In an attempt to attract people back to school, The School of New Resources gives Life Experience credits to students. To obtain this credit they must write up their life and social history. Courses are also offered. Included among them are Legal Rights, Field Work in Ghetto Communities, Socialism. Although the school presently has three campuses, at Co-op City in the Bronx, at Union DC37 in Manhattan, and at the College of New Rochelle, in New Rochelle, New York, the school can be reached at its main office at the College of New Rochelle.

4. For those students interested in finding out more about socialism in political science or socialist institutions we offer the following list of professors of political science and where they can be reached. This is only a handful of the many socialists who are presently teaching or writing and the list is meant as an aid rather than as a listing. Bertell Ollman—New York Univ., New York City; Ira Katznelson—Univ. of Chicago, Chicago, Illinois; David Nasaw—The Free Association, New York City; Lourdes Beneria—Livingston College, Rutgers University, New Brunswick, New Jersey; Alan Wolfe—Richmond College, Staten Island, New York City; Marvin Surkin—Brooklyn College, New York City; Mary Edwards—State Univ. of New York, Purchase, New York; James O'Connor (Political Economy)—San Jose State University, San Jose, Calif.; Peter Schwab and Henry Etzkowitz can be reached at State Univ. of New York, Purchase, New York.

Conservative

W. Henry Lambright and Laurin L. Henry. Using universities: the NASA experience.

One of the most significant results of government's modern relationship to science and technology is the blurring of lines between public and private sectors. Government raises and distributes a great deal of research and development money, but industry and the universities perform most of the actual work. As the problems of Lockheed with the C5A and Boeing with the SST attest, the government-industry partnership can be highly uncertain for both parties. Even more problematic, however, are the relationships between government and the universities.

There is a considerable congruence of sponsor and performer interest where the government and industrial laboratories are involved. Government specifies what it wants as precisely as it can, and the performer delivers—usually through a research group which has service to government and other external clients as its primary mission. The performer's underlying concern with making a profit is usually not incompatible with other aspects of the transaction, despite occasional problems of scheduling and price overrun.

But when government sponsors research at universities, the "interface" situation is more complex. The university's mission is broader than research; it is primarily an institution of higher education. Thus the university prefers to do research of a fundamental or basic character which it chooses itself, and seeks arrangements in which its research and teaching functions strengthen one another. The university feels its essential character to be threatened when government attempts too firmly to direct it along any given path. The freedom that is the educator's traditional prerogative, the pursuit of truth for its own sake that is the highest value of the basic researcher, and the pluralistic character of the university combine to make the university an extremely independent member of the research partnership.

The federal government's relationship to higher education today presents many difficult issues. The financial plight of the colleges and universities is great, but the government shrinks from the cost and both sides dislike the control implications of large-scale direct general subsidy. Congress and the administration continue to grope for limited arrangements involving aid to students instead of their institutions, or aid to institutions in special circumstances, or aid and compensation to universities for activities, such as research, which are needed and justified for other governmental purposes. Federal support for university research has been a major activity since World War II, but this relationship now is being re-examined and criticized from several viewpoints. Many in government are increasingly skeptical of the value of the social return from government-sponsored university research. Many friends of the university, like Robert Nisbet, call upon it to repent its entanglements and return to the purer life of yesteryear.[1] They contend that the university has tried to do too much for too many "customers," losing its own sense of distinct mission in the process. But there are others, like Franklin Long, who worry about present trends that would push government and universities further apart and argue that the university has not done enough for the public weal. Long admonishes:

Pressure the universities if you will; castigate their occasionally overly narrow behavior; insist on changed structures and reward mechanisms. But for earth's sake, don't count them out. Without their active involvement, the future will be a good deal dimmer than it might otherwise appear.[2]

The National Science Foundation, an agency traditionally sympathetic to the universities, certainly has not counted them out of its new "Research Applied to National Needs" (RANN) program. This effort, which typifies the new federal mood stressing applied research, faces an uncertain future, however, in part because of uncertainty as to the universities' capacity to produce policy-relevant results. *Science* comments: "The RANN program could mark the beginning of a change in federal support for science in the universities. Or it could wind up as a fiasco in NSF management—one on the order of the Mohole Project."[3]

Regardless of the NSF program, there remains uncertainty about the role of universities in the R & D programs of the so-called "mission" agencies. The mission agencies are those that support research in the pursuit of more specific social goals than science per se. Since all agencies except NSF fall into this category, the question of mission agency-university relationships is of paramount importance. Historically, most university support has funneled through mission agencies, but two agencies that have been particularly prominent in the past, the Defense Department and the National Aeronautics and Space Administration, are now reducing their roles. It is not at all clear whether new relationships can and will be forged between the mission agencies of growing priority, such as Housing and Urban Development, Transportation, and the Environmental Protection Administration. What is certain is that many of the dilemmas that emerged under older arrangements will be even more perplexing in any new mission agency dealings.

Clark Kerr said in 1963 that the university had become, through the research partnership, "a prime instrument of national purpose."[4] Because of its resources for basic research and training, as well as its immense need for external financial support, the university's engagement in national endeavors was inevitable. But who determines "national purpose"? And who articulates the role of the university therein? Rhetoric is as unlikely to determine the role of universities in future R & D programs as it has been in the past. The process by which agencies and universities determine their mutual interests and roles is inherently a political one, subject to bargaining and power considerations. Some of the uncertainties were illustrated in an attempt in the 1960s by NASA to develop a program that would enable universities to become more effective instruments of national purposes. Though no longer "alive," this innovative effort—known as the Sustaining University Program (SUP)—is worthy of close examination today for its relevance to the future.[5]

The NASA Sustaining University Program

Extending from 1962 to 1970, this program attempted to *help* universities, to *use* universities, and, most importantly, to *change* universities. That NASA rather than some presumably more "appropriate" agency should serve as the government's principal innovator in government-university relations in the 1960s is incidentally illustrative of the role that chance, accident, and administrative entrepreneurship play in federal policy-making. For SUP sppears to have been uniquely the invention of an unusual individual who happened to be at an ideal place at the right time. This was James E. Webb, NASA Administrator from 1961 to 1968.

A former Director of the Bureau of the Budget and Under Secretary of State, Webb was chosen by President Kennedy to head NASA in 1961 because of his combination of political and administrative qualifications. Webb's forte was large-scale management in a public setting. He knew little of science and technology as such, although he appreciated their role in economic growth and sensed their relevance to broad social problems. A man accustomed to manipulating organizations, he found the government-industry-university superorganization of NASA a challenge. And the institution that intrigued him most was the one that he had personally never managed—the university.

Webb, the son of a North Carolina school superintendent, won a Phi Beta Kappa key at Chapel Hill. He later studied and practiced law, but for most of his career alternated between business and executive positions in Washington. However, he liked to think of himself as an educator as well as a professional manager. Recent political science tends to play down the role of individual personality in the policy process. To do so in the case of SUP would be to belie the reality, for without Webb there probably would not have been a NASA Sustaining University Program.

Launching SUP, 1961–63

SUP was planned in the aftermath of Kennedy's decision to shoot for the moon—a setting that encouraged thinking big and moving fast. As defined within NASA, SUP was to have three basic elements:

1. A training grants (fellowship) program to increase the number of Ph.D.'s in space science and related disciplines. NASA would award funds for blocks of fellowships to various universities, which in turn would choose the students to receive them. (This contrasted with NSF's national fellowship competition among individual applicants, after which recipients could take their grants to whatever universities they chose.)

2. A program of rather large, three-year, step-funded grants to universities for interdisciplinary research in broadly identified areas.

3. A facilities grants program to provide new laboratory buildings to universities expected to play particularly large roles in the space program.

There was nothing in the Space Act of 1958 calling for such an ambitious program of grants to universities. Prior to 1961, NASA had increased its spending through universities above that of its predecessor agency, the National Advisory Committee for Aeronautics. But the connecting link was almost exclusively the project contract or grant—an award emanating from a particular program officer of NASA who wanted a particular professor to do a particular piece of research for a particular purpose. This was the primary mechanism used by almost all agencies, although there were some limited precedents for more broadly based awards by the National Institutes of Health, the National Science Foundation, and the Advanced Research Projects Agency of the Department of Defense.

Project grants were frequently criticized by university leaders, and by some government officials. Closely tied to mission needs of agencies, they were subject to unanticipated starts and stops, tight schedules, and fluctuating budgets. Awarded almost entirely on the basis of scientific "excellence" or specialized competence, project grants tended to concentrate at a select handful of institutions. Even within the favored institutions, grants produced imbalances between have and have-not departments, and enabled federally-funded individual academic stars to disregard department chairmen and university administrators. Certain universities, fields of science, and scientists did quite well, while universities and faculties as institutions lost coherence. By 1961, most federal agencies knew the effects of project grants but still found it difficult to contemplate significant reforms in existing relationships. Behind the banner of excellence lay vested interests in government and academe.

When Webb came on the scene he soon perceived an opportunity simultaneously to advance the interests of the universities, NASA, and society at large. It was clear that the Apollo decision meant a substantial increase in contracts and grants to universities for specialized projects; NASA needed manpower and research that only the universities could supply. Webb conceived SUP to complement the project grants, give the universities some things *they* wanted, provide insulation from the disadvantages of the project system, and help the universities help NASA. The fellowship program would help many universities attract more good students instead of having an elite gravitate to a handful of prestige institutions. The multi-year broad research grants would give faculties more freedom to choose their projects while simultaneously encouraging the interdisciplinary combinations needed to advance the space effort and science in general. The facilities grants would provide totally-financed buildings for university expansion. Because NASA needed more scientists and research than existing heavily funded institutions could provide, SUP grants would go to many respectable but underfinanced universities in various parts of the country; Webb made geographical dispersion of grants an overt policy. This would enlarge the nation's scientific resources, give many universities a stake in space, and enlarge the base of support that would be needed to sustain the Apollo program for a decade. Thus SUP could serve goals that were at once academic, idealistic, and political.

In the way of such a program were a series of institutional roadblocks. First, there were competing claimants inside NASA for the money projected for SUP. Second, there was the President, or, more precisely, his watchdog on untoward agency initiatives, the Bureau of the Budget. Third, there was Congress. And fourth, there were the universities themselves, who had to understand that there was a *quid* for SUP's *quo*.

The first hurdle was overcome fairly easily. Webb was the boss and he wanted the program. In a period of rapid financial build-up there seemed money enough for all!

The Bureau of the Budget was more of a problem. SUP was listed in the FY 1963 NASA budget materials that BoB reviewed in the fall of 1961. At first BoB questioned the appropriateness of NASA's entering the higher education scene in this broad way. It took a forceful presentation by Webb, a former BoB Director, before the then incumbent, David Bell, to remove Budget objection to the program. One consequence of the meeting, however, was Webb's decision, to which BoB acquiesced, to "bury" the funds for SUP in the agency's big-money hardware programs rather than include a line item in the budget that went to Congress. By "reprogramming" for SUP from already appropriated funds, NASA could avoid premature Congressional debate and let SUP "surface" when politically ripe.

The problem with Congress was the one to which BoB had been sensitive—a great many legislators were simply opposed to federal aid to education. Kennedy had been trying to get money for education at all levels substantially increased, but Congress was balking. Could NASA be a politically more acceptable route than, say, the Office of Education? Without any mention of SUP,

the FY 1963 NASA budget sailed through Congress. A few key Democratic legislators were informed of SUP—how it was important to getting to the moon, how it might help them in their districts and states—but most Congressmen were unaware.

Early in 1962, before Congress even had cleared the FY 1963 budget, Webb was launching the program—making the first grants to universities for fellowships, research, and facilities. Money was reprogrammed from funds already allotted in FY 1962. The same procedure was followed in 1963. This involved sizeable amounts—$4.6 million the first year, $31.9 the second.

In 1963, when the FY 1964 budget did show Congress a line item for SUP, some legislators criticized Webb's tactics. Colorado Senator Gordon Allott, ranking Republican on NASA's appropriations subcommittee, complained: "We suddenly found that we were confronted with a project which, essentially, is a federal aid-to-education measure.... [NASA] says that every dollar in its budget is 'tight'; yet we suddenly find that it is projecting $20 to $28 million...into a [fellowship] program that no one ever heard of before." To quell the unrest, Senator Clinton Anderson, head of the Space Committee, promised a full investigation of the new program. This was carried out quickly with no unfriendly witnesses. NASA's budget went through and SUP received $36.6 million and the legitimation represented by a line item.

The Webb strategy of "reverse budgeting"—acting first, justifying later—had presented Congressional critics with the more difficult problem of killing a program in being rather than preventing one from starting. After two years of grant-giving, SUP had by this time acquired a clientele. Moreover, by this time, the President, his science advisory apparatus, and a number of major legislators had become strong proponents of the program. Helping to solidify this support was a study by the President's Science Advisory Committee, released in late 1962, that cited a severe shortage in engineering, mathematical, and physical sciences manpower. Calling for immediate acceleration in the production of scientific manpower, the study commended NASA for its positive action.

Implementation, 1963–1967

The Sustaining University Program ran from 1962 to 1970, accounting for about one-third of the money NASA spent in universities in that era. (See Table 1.) However, 1963–67 was the period of full flowering. This was also a period of intense interaction among Webb, elements of his staff, and the universities over implementation.

With SUP, NASA was expanding the nation's resources in space-related sciences, which was the mission-related justification for the program. Webb also was aware that the money was being spent in ways much desired by the universities. Consequently he felt justified in seeking from the universities a special response beyond the immediate terms of the grants themselves—"something extra" that would serve both public and NASA's long-range interests.

Webb discussed his goals and sought understandings with the leaders of universities receiving major SUP grants. From presidents of institutions receiving NASA's most handsome benefits—grants for new buildings without any requirement of matching funds—Webb required their personal signature of a Memorandum of Understanding expressing the university's commitment to certain broad goals. The 34 memoranda[6] signed between 1962 and 1967 varied in detail to suit individual cases, but they all emphasized a few broad points:

Table 1   NASA SUP budget

FY	$ Million
1962	4.6
1963	31.9
1964	36.6
1965	45.1
1966	45.7
1967	31.0
1968	10.9
1969	9.3
1970	7.0
1971	0

First, the university would make availab its total competence for space-relate research. This included not just the physic and life sciences and engineering, but soci science, business administration, law, an all the rest.

Second, the university would seek, in a "energetic and organized fashion," to pro mote multidisciplinary research on problem in space research or having to do with th organization and implications of the spac effort.

Third, the university would seek ways c diffusing the results of space-related re search and putting those findings to work i advancing development and solving tech nological, economic, and social problems— particularly in the universities' own region but to some extent the nation as a whole.

What did Webb really want? Althoug goals were stated in the memoranda and re stated many times in his speeches, letters t universities, and notes to his staff, th specifics remained elusive. But clearl Webb was asking universities for change both internally and in relation to their en vironments. By providing institutional grant and dealing directly with the universit presidents, Webb sought to avoid furthe splinterings of the universities and pu resources, and therefore leverage fo change, in the hands of the top leadership By pressing for multidisciplinary research h tried to break down internal barriers achieve genuine intellectual exchange in th university as a whole, stimulate the de velopment of new knowledge that could onl come from such cross-fertilization, and en able the university to tackle problems tha required interdisciplinary solutions.

Webb also wanted to bring the universi ties into the direct and effective service o society in practical and visible ways. He encouraged university researchers to assis in utilization of research by the industries o their regions, promoting new industry and economic growth, and applying knowledge derived from NASA experience to govern mental and social problems, including the growing urban crisis. Finally, in promoting intellectual and organizational unity in the universities, and strengthening their leaders, he hoped for emergence of *institutional* capability and feelings of responsibility for meeting new challenges and responding to social need—including solving complex policy problems that might be referred to them by government administrators.

Webb did not cite specific models or precedents, but apparently he had been impressed by such developments as Route 128, the North Carolina Research Triangle, and the Southern California aerospace complex. One can discern background elements of the land grant college at the high noon of agriculture, the Wisconsin Idea, traces of the University of North Carolina's long-standing concern with regionalism—and perhaps also foreshadows of the "relevant" university that began to be demanded by reformers shortly after Webb left office.

If they could be stimulated, the NASA Administrator thought these developments would be to everyone's good. If universities could become more effective in economic development and otherwise meeting the needs of their respective areas, then the leaders who controlled the resources of those areas would come forth with generous support to the universities. Such developments, fostered by NASA and spreading the fruits of space research, would close the loop, demonstrate the value of the nation's investment in space, and assure NASA of political support. Webb the idealist and Webb the practical bureaucratic politician were not easily separable.

Whatever the ambiguities in Webb's mind when he signed the memoranda, a more interesting question may be what was in the university presidents' minds. Perhaps they saw the memos as just one more piece of bureaucratic red tape required to obtain needed funds. Perhaps they sincerely intended to have their institutions fulfill the obligations undertaken. Perhaps.

The principal NASA office for administering SUP was the Office of Grants and Research Contracts. Also involved to a much lesser degree was an Office of Technology Utilization. For a brief period Webb had a personal aide oversee the university and technology utilization efforts—an attempt to bring together university and industry-related activities toward a common purpose of technology diffusion and regional development. This administrative apparatus included some very able and dedicated individuals, but most of them had learned research grant administration in other agencies, and inevitably they were burdened with processing applications and monitoring grants from the traditional kinds of criteria that had to be observed regardless of Webb's unconventional ambitions. Neither their place within NASA nor their contacts at the universities provided the kind of leverage needed to move the universities very far along the line Webb desired.

By conventional science program standards, the universities made good use of the NASA money. The fellowship program was generally highly regarded by the academic community; the NASA stipend-level became a model for other agencies. The facilities grants provided badly needed buildings, although on most campuses construction was still under way or barely finished when SUP began to fade. The research money was put to work in ways that could be described as interdisciplinary as compared to traditional research groupings, although in most cases this involved fairly comfortable accommodations between scientific disciplines. There were not many unconventional combinations, and effective marriages of physical and social science—which was what Webb seemed most interested in—were rare indeed.

Webb's greatest disappointment, however, was the university response to the obligation in the Memorandum of Understanding to seek new and more effective ways of making research results available to external clienteles. At some institutions with strong traditions of basic research, the scientists were indifferent or hostile to such notions. Other institutions reported things like industrial advisory committees, conferences on applications of new findings, outside consulting relationships of individual faculty members, and so on. But most of this seemed trivial to Webb. He was seeking a more profound response, basic attitude changes, major restructuring on the campus, and new external relationships for university personnel at all levels. Although he bombarded them with letters and badgered them with visits, the university leaders, with one or two exceptions, never quite caught or accepted Webb's vision. Or, if they did believe in it, they could see no way to make it manifest except over very long periods of time. The built-in rigidities of the university were too great and the resources at their disposal too small, even with Webb's SUP money. Their replies to his queries became increasingly evasive and noncommittal.

Webb harangued his staff and eventually reorganized and changed the leadership of the Office of Grants and Research Contracts, but with little effect. A task force he appointed to study NASA-university relationships suggested that the problems of SUP were not necessarily internal to NASA. In its 1968 report, the task force said:

The failure of the universities to respond to the explicit agreements of the memorandums—technology transfer and multidisciplinary research—suggests that the SUP goals, which they contained implicitly, were not achieved. Thus, the SUP facilities program cannot claim to have developed concern for societal problems, capability for institutional response, awareness of a service role, or strengthened ties with industry and the local and regional community.

The major criticism that must be made of the universities' response to the Memorandums of Understanding is that they did not try. They clearly committed themselves to make an "energetic and organized" effort to implement the memorandums, and then did not make it.[7]

The task force did not seek to say exactly why the universities did not try to make the "energetic and organized" effort. In the conclusion to this paper we will attempt an explanation. But first, let us bring the story of SUP to its close.

Survival struggle and death, 1967–70

The year 1967 was a turning point in SUP's history. From $31 million in FY 1967, the budget plummeted to $10.9 in FY 1968. The whole program was revamped in acco with the limited resources; the faciliti grants were phased out. The decline funding mirrored to some extent Webb disappointment with the universities' re sponse to the broader goals he had se More responsible for SUP's downfall wa the changing environment of NASA and R D generally.

The Apollo program had reached its pea and all other programs in NASA felt th pinch as extra money to realize the manne lunar landing goal had to be squeezed fro other parts of the agency. The Apollo fir that took the lives of three astronauts i 1967 brought NASA's management capa bility under scrutiny and criticism for vi tually the first time. The administration ha begun to press NASA for economies a demand rose for funding of Vietnam an domestic programs. As the environment ha been permissive at the time of SUP' launching, now it was growing restrictive They key decision against SUP, however came from President Johnson.

President Johnson was given to poring over agency budgets in great detail.[8] B 1967, he was looking for savings every where and was increasingly irritated b criticism of his policies emanating from the campuses. Responding to a cue from the Budget Bureau that SUP was dispensable he told Webb to kill the program. Webb promised him a drastic curtailment but go permission for a short delay to fulfill out standing commitments and carry out a few low-cost projects he had in mind before closing up altogether. These late initiatives included research in administration and management, engineering systems design, and aid to black colleges. These were important, but it was downhill for SUP from 1967 to 1970. Webb himself left in 1968. The FY 1971 NASA budget submitted by President Nixon contained no funds for SUP despite energetic appeals by Webb's successor, Dr. Thomas Paine.

Congress did not come to the rescue. This was due in part to the fact that after several years of reduced funding, SUP had lost most of its clout on the Hill. More imrtantly, Congress reflected a general ublic impatience with universities. Vietnam opposition, student riots, and apparent loss control by presidents and faculties led any in Congress to be unsympathetic to ny notion of "sustaining" universities. At e same time, congressional strikes gainst military involvements on campus, as eflected in the Mansfield Amendment estricting Pentagon-financed research on ampus to the strictly mission-related,[9] ere influencing legislative thinking with espect to all the mission agencies.

SUP in retrospect

n its lifetime, SUP obligated more than 200 million for research, training, and acilities, to complement and facilitate IASA's much larger project research effort. Over 2000 graduate students at over 100 niversities were financed in space-related isciplines; about 1400 faculty members articipated in research and design projects t NASA centers during the summers; 37 esearch laboratories were built on iniversity campuses; and over 3000 space-elated endeavors were carried out under he research portion of SUP.

SUP was a successful program by the standards that were customary in the 1960s. t increased the supply of trained man-power; it enhanced university involvement in aeronautics and space; it broadened the base of competence for project-oriented research; it consolidated closely related activities into "space centers" on many campuses; it established precedents for nstitutional grants and geographic disper-sion as federal support policies.

Webb, however, had broader goals for SUP. He hoped to see more innovation and change in universities—broader capabilities for multidisciplinary research, university concern with the technology transfer process, increased involvement with in-dustry and community and regional prob-lems, developing capability for institutional response to societal need. These hopes were largely disappointed. By the late 1960s there was evidence on some campuses of

movement in the directions Webb sought, but just as these were appearing SUP ended.

The reasons for SUP's limited achieve-ment lay in part with NASA. Below Webb there were jurisdictional uncertainties among those supposed to follow up on the Memos of Understanding. Operating offi-cials were kept busy with the routines of managing a large university-grants program that had sprouted almost overnight, and did not find ways to press their university clients toward goals that seemed visionary, vague, and distant. NASA funds, although large, were never really big enough to have a massive impact in moving the universities toward reform. Moreover, the 1960s were the "golden years" of university support, and there were other agencies toward which universities could turn for funds if NASA pushed too hard.

In one sense, perhaps, Webb's goals were unrealistic, stemming from insufficient understanding of the nature of universities. He did not fully perceive the rigidity of departmental structures, the strength of forces that keep scholars working within disciplinary lines, and the disdain for practi-cal outcomes, particularly in the commer-cial sphere, held by many of the most distinguished research scientists. He probably did not fully perceive the differ-ences in character and potential respon-siveness to his efforts among such varied institutions as MIT, Chicago, Berkeley, Pittsburgh, and Rensselaer Polytechnic. He did not seem to realize how unusual were his efforts to deal with universities as wholes through their hierarchical leaders; he seemed to assume that university presidents exercised the kind of authority he had in his agency and business leaders had in their corporations. He did not understand the lack of mechanisms within the university by which change and innovation, as implied in the Memos of Understanding, could be induced by central administrators.

Webb may not have fully understood these characteristics of the university, but certainly he did understand them in part— indeed, they were some of the features he was trying to change. But the university leaders did not do the things he thought they had agreed to do. Not only Webb but several outside consultants and NASA review teams came to the same conclusion: Few university presidents were energetic and innovative in pursuing their obligations under the Memoranda of Understanding. Some of them did not really try, despite the resources and potential leverage Webb was trying to put in their hands. One can speculate that many university presidents, despite occasional verbalizing about lack of power, have internalized the prevailing faculty view that administrators should be weak; therefore they wait for faculty initiatives and fail to recognize or shrink from exercising power resources even when they are available.

Relevance to the future

Webb's frustration may have been because of prematurity. In the 1960s, universities were not ready for interdisciplinary, problem-oriented research; in the 1970s they are moving in that direction, pushed by both internal and external forces. In their various ways, students, faculty members, and external clienteles demand "relevance," a sharper focus on widely perceived societal problems. The universities have fewer options in research support, and a shrinking market for their graduates to teach in the academic disciplines. Thus policy studies are coming into vogue, and the universities are groping for ways to apply what is known and direct new research toward pressing national problems. Numerous authorities, including the President's Science Adviser, confirm that in the coming decade federal relationships with science will be substantially reoriented with less attention to disciplines, more attention to goals defined by society; and these goals will expand beyond defense, space, and health to include a wide range of social, urban, and environmental problems.[10] NSF's RANN is one thrust of this orientation, and plans are developing in other domestic agencies with more specific and probably more urgent missions.

It is already clear that there will b substantial university response to these nev emphases. Universities have some sensi tivity to the requirements of the times, an they urgently need support for faculty re search and graduate students. As federa money for problem-oriented work become available, proposals will emanate from universities.

The probable character of the universit response is not so clear. Undoubtedly a great deal of useful problem-oriented research and training will occur. But the NASA experience suggests that federa policymakers should not expect too much Universities are adept at converting problem-oriented money into discipline-oriented activity. Establishment of, for example, an institute of transportation studies does no necessarily mean that all of the university's resources potentially related to transportation problems will become involved University administrators, as in the past, will hesitate to set priorities about what problems their institutions will research, to change structures and incentive systems to free and encourage faculty members of all disciplines to participate, or—least of all— to press their faculties to develop coordinated answers to the problems of policymakers.[11]

Whether the universities "pull themselves together," either organizationally or conceptually, depends in part on what the government does. Webb exhorted the universities to unify themselves to become more effective in dealing with him and meeting the nation's requirements for research and service. But the response was limited by the simultaneous efforts of the universities to respond to the initiatives of other agencies as well as NASA. Could there be a coordinated university response to an uncoordinated government? What exists is not a simple government-university research partnership but a host of legitimate and uncoordinated scientific enterprises that pair off across the government-university line. This fragmentation limits the impact on the university of either any single agency or the government as a whole and diminishes the university's ability to address cietal problem at the highest levels of complexity.

If government and universities are to work together to society's benefit in this decade, there probably will have to be a more ordered set of federal priorities and a more coherent response from universities than characterized the 1960s. But how far should these changes go? The compartmentalization and inwardness of universities are frustrating both to those who deal with them from outside and to many within who are sensitive to the needs of society beyond the ivy. However, it does no one any good if the universities are pushed to overrespond. Universities should not be expected to turn themselves inside out establishing interdisciplinary, problem-oriented institutes and programs for every new priority arising on the federal agenda. Neither is it desirable to attempt to reduce government-university research connections to a single set of relationships. The government might not choose its priorities well, or have difficulty in adjusting them to changing needs. Faculty members who have other priorities could become indifferent, either nonparticipating or pressed into reluctant service as the price of academic survival and advancement. In a certain amount of pluralism there is long-run protection for both government and universities. Striking the right balance between centralized and decentralized approaches is a never-ending process of mutual adjustment to changing needs and problems.

What such disparate critics of the multiversity as Webb and Nisbet have pointed up are the consequences of the rampant pluralism that characterized the 1960s. While money was plentiful, the implications of this pluralism were glossed over or ignored by most decision-makers in governments and the university. Now that the old sources of funds, such as NASA, are drying up, while at the same time pressures build on universities to respond to new imperatives, the necessity for considering a restructured government-university relationship must be faced.

The dilemma is two-fold: First, how to preserve the independence of universities in a period of potentially increasing and essential interaction with government; and second, how to enable universities to play a more useful role in collaboration with government in addressing complex social problems. The SUP suggests certain concepts that may be helpful in forging a new relationship that is more adequate from the point of view of both partners. For example, government as a whole should recognize, as NASA did, that universities cannot be truly useful if they are tottering on the brink of bankruptcy. They must have institutional support, however the formula for supplying that support is worked out. Such support should come openly and unambiguously in the name of higher education, not, as in the 1960s, primarily through the back door of space. This may require a new National Foundation for Higher Education, or a much larger, broader National Science Foundation, or their administrative equivalent. The point is that the agency should be independent of categorical, mission-oriented research and development responsibilities. It should be able to view the university as an entirety rather than in its specialized segments. Such a government institution would serve to protect the universities against shifting and possibly inappropriate demands from mission agencies. It would allow them to retain their vigor, and thus be able to establish their own sense of priority in addressing specific agency needs.

As SUP suggests lessons for government, it also provides ideas for universities. Webb believed universities could be strong only if society came to regard their support as an investment policy rather than charity. He wanted universities to find mechanisms for responding to social needs and pressures in ways that would preserve their distinctive strengths yet permit evolution with changing times. He felt university administrators should lead their institutions rather than be led by fragmented faculties and government administrators. The Memoranda of Understanding pointed directions, leaving it to university presidents to decide whether, how, and when to move. In this case there was little motion, at least in the short run, in the directions Webb hoped the universities would go.

Nevertheless, there is merit to the idea that university central management must be bolstered if the institution is expected to make a coordinated response to government. If university leaders cannot lead, the sub-parts will splinter and establish whatever external relationships may be expedient and lucrative at a given moment. The resulting fragmentation damages the university in two ways: By trying to perform piecemeal for a multitude of sponsors the university tends to perform poorly, from the government's perspective, and increases government suspicion that it is incapable of keeping a bargain or effectively performing interdisciplinary policy-oriented research. By haphazard attempts to be "relevant" to external needs it finds itself accused of neglecting its teaching and basic research responsibilities—of failing, in Nisbet's words, to "mind its own business."

It is the fragmentation and lack of leadership that endangers the university's traditional function, not the interdisplinary activity *per se*. If integration and synthesis of knowledge are the essence of the university's function, then interdisciplinary, problem-oriented research is justified for educational reasons, not governmental needs. Long, for example, argues:

College students must learn a genuinely interdisciplinary approach; this can only happen when their professors have personal knowledge of and commitment to interdisciplinary research and when there are programs wherein students can learn by doing—in short, when an interdisciplinary approach permeates the universities.[12]

But how to strike the right balance? The university must respond to social needs but it must also protect its institutional integrity, identity, and reputation. Stronger, more innovative central leadership may help in this regard, but may not be sufficient. A variety of administrative techniques and structures will have to be tried; what "works" at one university may not at another.

Harvey Brooks has suggested one possible strategy of general applicability: the creation of "buffer" institutions. Just as a federal agency devoted solely to "sus-

taining" institutional capabilities could buffer universities against the vagaries and misuses of universities by mission agencies, so also might university-based buffer institutions better permit universities to mobilize and focus their resources and adapt to mission-oriented user demands without endangering educational functions.

As Brooks explains it, these would be organizations

. . . with both operational and research responsibilities which translate knowledge into application, especially in areas of public responsibility and in relation to local and state problems. These buffer institutions should be closely connected to universities but independently organized and managed. They should be placed where students and faculty could participate in real world problem-solving but they should have their own permanent career staff, with a separate career line and reward structure.[13]

The buffer institution concept gives greater potential for coherence and initiative in university dealings with government. It has forerunners in the existing defense laboratories and agricultural experiment stations. The known weaknesses and limitations of these existing institutions, such as their tendency to be not only physically but intellectually remote from the campus, should stimulate thinking on ways to make the newer buffer institutions more helpful to the university proper as well as to governmental clients. If universities do not consider their organization for the future, others will do their thinking for them.

There is little chance that the university will return to the ivory tower of former days. "Involvement" in social crises of the day is an inevitable by-product of the knowledge requirements of postindustrial society. The questions are primarily how, on whose terms, with what consequences, and through what mechanisms that involvement will take place.

Government and the university must recognize and respect the fact that they have overlapping but distinct interests. The differences in mission are bound to cause tensions and frustrations on both sides. But the two partners must find imaginative ways to cooperate as the old arrangements and the old programs (such as SUP) give way to the new. A continuation of the research partnership is in the interest of government and the university. The futures of both are at stake.

NOTES

1. Robert A. Nisbet, "The University Had Better Mind Its Own Business," *Psychology Today*, IV (March 1971), 22.

2. F.A. Long, "Interdisciplinary Problem-Oriented Research in the University," *Science*, CLXXI (March 12, 1971), 961.

3. "The RANN program could mark the beginning of a change in federal support for science in the universities. Or it could wind up as a fiasco in NSF management—one on the order of the Mohole Project." "NSF: Is Applied Research at the Take Off Point?" *Science*, CLXXII (June 25, 1971), 1315.

4. Clark Kerr, *The Uses of the University* (Cambridge: Harvard University Press, 1963), p. 87.

5. Readers interested in a much more detailed account of the evolution of SUP to 1967 should consult *Launching NASA's Sustaining University Program*, by W. H. Lambright, with the assistance of E. A. Bock; and *The NASA Memorandum of Understanding*, by Laurin Henry. Both case studies were prepared under a NASA grant and published in limited editions in 1969 by the Inter-University Case Program, Inc.

6. The universities that received facilities grants and signed memoranda of understanding included Stanford, Chicago, Iowa, California (Berkeley), Minnesota, MIT, Colorado, California (Los Angeles), Rennselaer Polytech, Wisconsin, Michigan, Pittsburgh, Denver, Texas A&M, Maryland, Rice, Cornell, Purdue, NYU, Washington (St. Louis), Georgia Tech, Arizona, Illinois, and Brooklyn Tech.

7. Homer Morgan, *et al.*, *A Study of NASA University Programs* (Washington, D.C.: NASA, 1968), p. 58.

8. "Science Policy: An Insider's View of LBJ, DuBridge, and the Budget," *Science*, CLXXI (March 5, 1971), 874, 875.

9. Public Law 91–121, Title II, Sec. 203 (Nov. 19, 1969).

10. Edward E. David, Jr. "The Integrity of Purpose," an address delivered November 2, 1971; reprinted in *Science Policy Reviews*, IV (No. 4, 1971), 13–20.

11. Gabor Strasser has argued that although the universities produced a great amount of useful defense and space research in the 1950s and 1960s, they lagged in developing the concepts of systems engineering needed to integrate knowledge for the solution of complex new problems—that sort of thinking was done by the non-profits and sophisticated consulting firms. Accordingly, says Strasser, we may again have to look to the "think-tanks" to produce the "orchestrators" of research needed to handle the social and environmental problems of the 1970s. "What Is In Store for our Scientific Technological Establishment?", *Science Policy Reviews*, IV (No. 4, 1971), 3–12.

12. Long, *op. cit.*

13. U.S. House of Representatives, Committee on Science and Astronautics, Subcommittee on Science, Research, and Development, *Hearings, National Science Policy* (Washington, D.C.: Government Printing Office, 1970), pp. 141, 142.

Liberal

Robert B. Denhardt.*
Exploring political alternatives.

Unlike acts of power, which are usually observable if not even highly visible, the definitions of power in a society lie beneath the political surface, emerging fully only in times of crisis. However, only where a particular version of societal power—including its content, its acquisition, and its limits—is maintained, can a governmental system be said to exist. For this reason governments employ many devices to ensure the continued acceptance of certain basic assumptions. In this way, civic education—the process of acquiring political orientations through encounters with political reality— becomes crucial to the distribution of social power.

In *The Eclipse of Citizenship*. Pranger suggests a distinction between two forms of civic education. The first, "political socialization," is "that political truth which is mediated by groups and their members" (Pranger, 1968: 43); the second, "political education," on the other hand, emphasizes "the free man armed with enough political sophistication to participate in politics as a

* "Exploring Political Alternatives," by Robert B. Denhardt is reprinted from *Teaching Political Science* Vol. 2 (Jan. 1975), pp. 212–226 by permission of the publisher, Sage Publications, Inc.

person with the capacity for independent judgment." "Political education emphasizes above all the artificiality of political order and the citizen as a creative actor within this order" (Pranger, 1968:44). Though found in mixed proportions, political socialization is usually associated with a politics of power, and political education with a politics of participation. We will argue here that political socialization has come to dominate both our thinking and our practice in the area of civic education, nearly to the exclusion of political education. We will suggest some reasons why this is true, then examine some ways in which political education might be promoted.

I

Social scientists typically describe the process of socialization in rather bland (value-free?) terminology, but always emphasize the group mediation of values. Langton in 1969, for example, writes, "we shall view political socialization as the process, mediated through various agencies of society, by which an individual learns politically relevant attitudinal dispositions and behavior patterns." This recent definition varies only slightly from that presented over a decade ago by Hyman, who described the socialization of the individual as "his learning of social patterns corresponding to his societal positions as mediated by various agencies of society" (Hyman, 1959: 18). Those patterns or dispositions which comprise the content of socialization are, of course, not randomly distributed; rather, what is "politically relevant" is that which is selected as such by the dominant political culture. This is simply another way of saying, as many researchers have, that political socialization serves to generate political support. Almond notes that "all political systems tend to perpetuate their cultures and structures through time...mainly by means of the socializing influences" (Almond, 1956: 391-409).

Partially because our vision has been blurred by the persuasiveness of socialization studies, our comprehension of political

education—those experiences which tend toward the development of individual judgment about what is politically acceptable—has been restricted. Basically, political education seeks authentic political expression through personal commitment to civic virtue. It suggests that the citizen be fully and creatively involved in structuring and restructuring the political order. Where political socialization restricts the role possibilities of the citizen, political education extends the scope and range of political activities for the individual. Where political socialization moderates the search for alternatives, political education encourages the exploration of political potentialities.

II

Since the most obvious attempts by government to develop personal values consistent with existing norms are those found in the schools, we will concentrate here on the role of the school in civic education. While our comments are drawn from experiences at the high school level, they should be equally applicable to the highly symbolic political experiences of students in early grades as well as the more complex content of college courses in government. We will ask whether such efforts, obviously attempts to socialize, might also generate experiences contributing to political education.

Courses devoted to civic education have been subject to extensive critiques recently. The schools have been generally indicted for their failure to make civic education meaningful to life situations, a failure stemming from the schools' lack of relevance, their misinterpretation of political reality, their discrimination against minorities, and their implicit bias toward existing systems. Space does not permit a detailed analysis of the shortcomings of civic education in the schools; however, a few brief points of special relevance to the difference between political socialization and political education should be elaborated. These may be stated as follows:

(1) Current programs of civic education, by presenting statements of value masked as fact, orient the student toward an acceptance of the existing political system. Rather than presenting a range of alternative political possibilities from which the individual may choose, the schools concentrate on an elaboration of traditional structures.

(2) Such programs, moreover, in their presentation of operative values demand conformity rather than creativity. Students are instructed to accept attitudes and behavioral standards consistent with dominant norms.

(3) Finally, such programs restrict the range of political activities in which the individual may engage to those which are not disruptive to the political order. The role possibilities for the individual citizen are limited to acts such as voting, keeping informed, or paying taxes. Creative questioning or demands for political change on the part of the citizen are excluded.

A word needs to be said about each of these criticisms and their contribution to the political socialization of young people, for when viewed in this light the criticisms extend beyond their usual context. To say, for example, that social studies efforts present a view of politics firmly geared to the maintenance of the current system is simply to reiterate a fairly standard contention. What is often overlooked, however, is the restrictive nature of such value inculcation. In order to emphasize established structures, other political possibilities are selected out with the effect that civic education programs not only emphasize system-sustaining expressions of value, but also limit students who might wish to explore other systems. Alternative political possibilities, either existing in the real world or in the mind of student or teacher, are rarely considered and even where consideration is given, the alternatives are quickly dismissed (often on rather questionable grounds). Students are rarely encouraged to explore creatively the potential of various political orders; rewards are given for conformity rather than imagination.

A similar situation obtains with respect to the operative political values a student en-counters as part of his civic education. Certain values, such as obedience and civic duty, are assumed to be consistent with the requirements of the existing order and are therefore emphasized by the educational system. The effect of this procedure, however, is to depress the political potential of possible challengers to the system by bringing their views in line with those of the majority. Langton and Jennings in a well-known study comment on this possible outcome, though in somewhat different language (Langton and Jennings, 1968: 863-864). They suggest that while civics courses have little effect on white middle-class students, they may alter the belief patterns of blacks. Langton and Jennings suggest that the reason for this is that the blacks are receiving new information in civics courses, where the values whites encounter here simply reinforce those already developed in the home and peer group (Langton and Jennings, 1968: 863-864). This interpretation is on the surface probably sound, yet it fails to point out that blacks like whites have received political data prior to entering school. Their perceptions of politics as developed in the home and peer group are much more likely to be antagonistic to the structure of social power currently in existence. What the civics course ultimately attempts is a replacement of antagonistic values or alternative values with those acceptable to the system.

Finally, we should note that typical civic education programs also present a limited range of possibilities for individual civic action. From all the possible forms of political involvement, relatively harmless efforts are given emphasis. In a particular junior-high-school textbook, for example, we find that the good citizen is to "pay taxes cheerfully, support the public schools, and keep informed." Not only is this statement misleading through its lack of discrimination (should we support racially segregated public schools?), but it is also extremely limiting in its definition of the range of citizen activities. The citizen is taught to see his role as a very minor one in the whole of the political order. It is a system, he is told, in which all participate. . .but not too much. Real political systems require more in order for change to take place than the acts listed here. Students should be introduced to the full range of political activities which persons find effective, including even conflict and violence. To present less both distorts political reality and denies the individual a part of his role as a citizen.

III

An explanation of the role of political socialization in securing acceptable definitions of power in a society is incomplete without attention to the various social forces which support this role. As pointed out earlier, it is the demand for appropriate expressions of power which stimulates concern for political socialization. But the particular forms of political socialization found in schools today are more than simply the results of political manipulation; they are in fact broadly supported by other manifestations of the dominant culture. Two of these will be considered here: the first relates to what is being taught (objective knowledge); the second is concerned with the circumstances under which education occurs (the bureaucratic imperative). In either case, we will argue that an illusion is provided which conceals the fact that "educational" activities reflect and reinforce the unequal distribution of social power.

Objective knowledge. The positive science view of knowledge plays an important part in structuring our perception of what goes on around us. We have come to depend so much on this version of truth that we find it difficult to visualize alternative modes of thought. In line with what we have been taught, we consider the "scientific" version of reality beyond question; we have a special reverence for the scientist who pursues "facts" through a careful and restrictive methodology. "Objectivity" in this view becomes the supreme technique and "fact" the ultimate product. We even make the philosophic assumption that all our problems derive simply from our lack of objective knowledge. If we had all the facts, we could easily solve all our problems.

The positive science model described here has had a tremendous, though subtle impact on the way in which knowledge is distributed in society. One of the things the positive science model tells us is that students need only be told the facts; that any judgments they might make about the facts are up to them. For this reason teachers of civics and other social studies are very careful that their statements are not construed as "value judgments." The job of the teacher is to explain the facts and let the students draw their own conclusions. As Levinson has noted, given this perception of the teacher's role, the modern educator supposedly dispenses facts, having mastered the relevant data in his field (Levinson 1969: 600).

But of course what is factual is itself a matter of some controversy. As an example let us examine the factual statement "America is an oppressive society." Obviously if we were to include this statement of fact (and its many implications) in our program of civic education, we might certainly create great changes in consciousness and activity. But in spite of the compelling evidence and experience which might attract us to this fact, there are several aspects of the positive science view of objective knowledge which we can use to justify not incorporating this statement of fact into our classroom presentations.

As teachers considering the possible use of this fact, we might first say that the statement is really a value judgment and that we can only be concerned with empirical reality. This rationalization, however, requires that we assume that oppressiveness is inevitably a term laden with value, that it can never exist in fact. Since we know this is untrue, we may turn to another aspect of positive science: scientific explanation requires the agreement of many persons—it demands "intersubjective validity." Under this guise we may retreat further from our statement of fact by arguing that consensus does not exist. But even if we became convinced some agreement were present, we might then challenge the statement as an unanswerable hypothesis. Our view of social science implies that fact can only be produced by testing hypotheses, and given the current limits of science, this particular hypothesis would be considered untestable. Moreover, we might suggest that the statement is after all unduly generalized, and that even though we might be fascinated with such demographic data as the number of people who go to bed hungry each night we cannot jump so easily to the broad implications of these facts. Finally, as teachers considering a classroom topic we realize that our view of objective knowledge, the positive science view, deals ultimately with the regular not the unusual, with stability not change. The statement of fact we are considering obviously does not contribute to the regularity of the political system. Therefore, we reason, it should not be used.

In truth, however, our selection of those values which are to be called facts depends on our own perception of the distribution of social power. While the hesitancy of teachers to address controversial issues in the classroom is often rationalized through reference to the positive science distinction between fact and value, in reality teachers make judgments according to "how much the traffic will bear." If they feel their commentary will arouse little concern, they are likely to be quite open about their values; if they expect a bitter reaction by outside powers, they will remain silent. A teacher in a racist community has little hesitance condemning advocates of black power; a teacher who might be fired for defending such persons might not bring the subject up. In either case, a judgment—a political judgment—is made. Those values which are ultimately selected are usually those consistent with the particular structure of power in a community or nation. Those values which have the support of power achieve the status of facts. The result is a view of the political system which is not only supportive of that system but which excludes consideration of alternative possibilities. And though this view is derived from the structure of social power, it is justified in terms of the positive science view.

The bureaucratic imperative. The positive science view has been complemented by the increasing bureaucratization of American society. Not only have bureaucracies come to dominate the social landscape, they have also provided models for human association. The pattern of thought and action demanded by large and complex organizations has been transmitted through society. We will not argue here that such a frame of reference is useless; in terms of productive capabilities it has proven quite useful. However, as this bureaucratic orientation extends beyond the boundaries of the organization of production, especially into the realm of politics, its influence is questionable. As bureaucratic standards become pervasive forces in society, they contribute to a pattern of political socialization and detract from political education.

A number of bureaucratic qualities such as hierarchy, impersonality, and coercion impinge directly on the educational process. Because students find themselves located in a bureaucratically organized school system and because they are being prepared for bureaucratic positions in later life, they are instructed in ways consistent with the maintenance of bureaucracies.

Students are likely to see the teacher as a role model after which they will pattern their own behavior. They observe and respond to the total personality of the instructor. If we ask what lessons are learned by students as they observe their teachers, we are struck immediately by the fact that many of these lessons are structured by the bureaucratic milieu in which students and teachers interact. In a school situation very definite lines of authority and hierarchy are drawn and recognized by all members of the educational community. Not only do these include the relations of student and teacher but also those of teacher and principal.

In the classroom, for example, the teacher is seen to exercise authority in petty and arbitrary ways, yet demand unquestioning obedience. On the other hand, the teacher is seen by the students as submitting meekly to the authority of the principal. (Obviously, teachers often disagree vigorously with their principals, yet there is an unwritten rule that disagreements are to be voiced away from student audiences. Before the students, the teacher is quite obedient.) In the situation described here, there is much to suggest that the American school system has become an extremely effective instrument for the inculcation of authoritarian values. Much the same pattern appears if we look at other bureaucratic norms, such as impersonality and hierarchy, as they affect the shaping of students personalities. The important point, however, is that through experiences such as these, experiences growing out of the bureaucratic nature of society generally and the school system in particular, children are being taught values which may be antithetical to norms of political change. Such a conclusion is of course not surprising. The orientations provided by an organizational society contribute ultimately to the political socialization of students. Rather than adopting norms of inquiry, students are taught acceptance. Rather than patterns of creativity, students are taught deference. The supposed "necessity" of bureaucracy contributes to an enforcement of existing structures of power.

In the final analysis the dual norms of positive science and bureaucratic rule are highly supportive of the political socialization of students. Moreover, they interact with one another in a pattern of reinforcement. That is, bureaucratic structures are most often themselves rationalized in terms of a positive science interpretation of administrative life which suggests that it is possible to distinguish between the ends (values) and the means (facts) of organizational life. In turn, bureaucracies, being equipped to accept inputs of facts rather than values (which might be challenging), aid in establishing the social norm of objectivity. In any case, political socialization benefits from the interaction of positive science and bureaucratization in that both tend to stress "objectivity" and "deference" to established techniques. As Pranger writes, "Education in the context of hierarchical power deals with knowledge—analytical, logical, objective: Education in participatory situations emphasizes understanding—empathetic wisdom, personal commitment, subjectivity" (Pranger, 1968: 48).

IV

If we are serious about stimulating political education, we should explore the avenues through which persons might gain creative outlooks and individual orientations toward politics. As Pranger correctly points out, political education may be submerged during some periods but rarely dies out completely. Even under the most authoritarian regimes there are opportunities for political education; surely we should expect such possibilities in a more open society. One way to approach this problem is to explore those spaces in which political education now occurs. By analyzing the emergence of alternative views of political order, we can specify ways in which political education might be emphasized.

Obviously in this country recently, the chief sources of alternative viewpoints about politics have been the poor, the black, and the young. That the poor and the black have developed extraordinary political ideas can be explained through their confrontation with the political realities of economic exploitation and racism. In response to the oppressiveness of the dominant society, these persons have been forced to develop new political alternatives. Being presented with a social condition which emphasized terminal values such as efficacy, power, status, and wealth, but does not provide the instrumental values necessary to achieve these ends, these persons are forced to make certain accommodations. Jackson notes in *Soledad Brother,* "Whenever a man builds an image of himself and of his surroundings that he cannot live up to and does not conform to the *de facto* situation, the end result must be confusion and emotional breakdown" (Jackson, 1970: 93). Out of such an understanding, there may also grow political education.

The development of alternative political viewpoints among affluent, upper- and middle-class white youths is less clear. These persons have not found it necessary to respond to direct oppression. They have, however, been forced to deal with incongruities between learned values and social realities with important consequences for

heir political education (Denhardt and
Allen, 1971). The confrontation of humanist
outh with the positive science view forms
n important theme in the youth culture. In
he Making of A Counter Culture, Roszak
rgues that the "myth of objective con-
ciousness" subordinates the visionary
xperience (which we might associate with
olitical education). "Science, under the
echnocracy, has become a total culture
empting the lives of millions . . ." (Roszak,
969: 216). Roszak sees the youth counter-
ulture as rejecting this notion and in such a
ejection arriving at a truly embracing
ppositional culture.

The youth counter-culture has also
ejected the bureaucratic imperative. In-
leed, some analysts have suggested that
anti-bureaucratic feelings lie at the heart of
student rebellion. Flacks argues that the
iumanistic youth of the middle class find it
lifficult to reconcile learned values with the
cold efficiency and manipulation of massive
organizations (Flacks, 1970: 340–357).
Berger notes, "Modern childhood is marked
by values and by a consciousness that are
emphatically personalistic. Modern bureaucracy, by contrast, has an ethos of impersonality. Put simply, an individual shaped by
modern childhood is most likely to feel
oppressed by modern bureaucracy" (Berger
and Newhaus, 1970: 37). Such a background hardly prepares youth to be content
with either the nature or the content of
efforts at political socialization. Indeed their
raining leads them to directly confront the
wo cultural themes specified earlier as
underlying efforts at political socialization.

The rejection of the positive science view
and the bureaucratic imperative by
iumanist youth in the sixties does not in
tself demonstrate that political education
prevailed for this group. Rather we must
examine the responses of these persons, as
we must examine the responses of the poor
and the black, to determine whether their
confrontation with social and political
realities led to a creative questioning of
existing political structures and a search for
new alternative modes of politics.

While many oppressed blacks and many
disillusioned youth have turned away from
politics, many others have tried diligently to
examine and to understand the possibilities
of other political viewpoints. Some they
sought through experience, as in travels to
Africa or to Cuba. Others they sought
through more intellectual, less experimental
channels. That contemporary leftist politics
presents such a congeries of political
ideologies is less a criticism of the left than
an indication of the broad interests of its
members. At least in terms of civic education, this diversity of viewpoints should be
seen as a strength rather than a weakness.

This is not to argue that the civic education of the left is necessarily superior to that
of the right in American politics. Rather the
point here is simply that political education,
seen as the creative questioning of the
political order and the postulation and
examination of alternative political systems,
exists today among a significant portion of
our population. If we are really interested in
developing civic experiences for all persons
which would encompass not only political
socialization but also political education, we
should view these situations quite carefully.
We should attempt to see whether the
process of radical education bears lessons
for political education generally.

V

These remarks are suggestive of several
areas in which current civic education
practices, including those in formal
education settings, could benefit. First, the
experience of radical education has once
again pointed up the importance of conflict
in the educational process. A number of
education theorists have explored the
creative impact of conflict, and most classroom teachers have themselves experienced the impact of group conflict in
generating new ideas and in sharpening
those already held. Such conflict however is
too often accidental. Educators have not
fully explored the creative uses of classroom
conflict. Teachers might well investigate
further the possibilities of generating
constructive conflict through the use of

debate, role-playing, simulation, and other techniques.

A second lesson growing from the experience of radical education regards the importance of comparison. Students need to confront alternative political systems and to analyze and to evaluate them in comparison with the existing political order. In part, such comparisons can be developed through the cross-national study of government structure; in part they can be developed from cross-cultural and subcultural comparisons of political behavior. For example, the political experience of the emerging African Nations or of postrevolutionary Cuba has proven quite valuable in stimulating discussions of alternative forms of political activity in this country. Students, however, should not be limited simply to an examination of existing systems but should be encouraged to design and operate political structures of their own making.

A third lesson from the radical experience is drawn from the realization that civic education does not stop where the classroom stops. As Illich has noted, the school itself provides "hidden curricula" in that certain lessons are learned in the process of "certification" efforts (Illich, 1971: 7). Others have used the same phrase to refer to political lessons learned as persons engage in day-to-day political activities ranging from street gangs to environmental action. Those in the schools interested in improving the political education of their students should recognize and emphasize a continuity between what the student learns and does in the classroom and his activities outside the school. Even formal efforts at civic education can be integrated into the political world outside through activities emphasizing community involvement. Teachers must reject the notion that what children learn "in the streets" is antithetical to the achievement of a liberal education. To the contrary, it may be essential.

Efforts at political education then must finally emphasize the elusive element of political creativity. By involving students subjectively in political exercises of various types, teachers may aid in achieving elements of commitment and engagement which efforts at political socialization fail to produce. Today's students will live in a rapidly changing world. To the extent that political change requires involvement rather than observation, political education rather than political socialization is required.

REFERENCES

Almond, G. (1956) "Comparative political systems." J. of Politics 19: 391–409.

Berger, P. and R. Newhaus (1970) Movement and Revolution. Garden City, N.Y.: Doubleday.

Denhardt, R. B. and H. D. Allen (1971) "Youth responses to cultural incongruities." Youth and Society 3: 237–255.

Flacks, R. (1970) "Social and cultural meanings of student revolt." Social Problems 17: 340–357.

Hyman, H. (1959) Political Socialization. New York: Free Press.

Illich, I. (1971) "After deschooling, what?" Social Policy 2: 7.

Jackson, G. (1970) Soledad Brother: The Prison Letters of George Jackson. New York: Bantam.

Langton, K. and K. Jennings (1968) "Political socialization and the high school civics curriculum in the United States." Amer. Pol. Sci. Rev. 63: 863–864.

Levinson, S. (1969) "On 'teaching' political science," in P. Green and S. Levinson (eds.) Power and Community. New York: Bantam.

Pranger, R. J. (1968) The Eclipse of Citizenship. New York: Holt, Rinehart & Winston.

Roszak, T. (1969) The Making of a Counter Culture. Garden City, N.Y.: Doubleday.

Socialist

Alan Wolfe. The professional mystique.

The Caucus for a New Political Science has been interested not only in changing the nature of the reality which political scientists study, but also in changing the way in which they study it. This concluding essay is designed to represent that interest. It summarizes the criticisms made by a number of younger scholars of the profession it-self, and then it suggests some difficulties and alternatives which grow out of those criticisms. What some of us have discovered is that if there is a bias in the methods and means by which reality is sought, it is hardly likely that the one found will be neutral. In this sense, a concern for a proper definition of professionalism is an integral part of the search for a new political reality. The intellectual and the organizational aspects of the caucus' activities are not distinct. Without some change in the rigidity with which academic professionals study politics, all other reforms will be meaningless. Any examination of this proposition must begin with the very word "professional" itself.

There is something powerful about professionalism. In an essay describing his experience teaching a seminar on the professions, Everett C. Hughes relates how, even though the course is one in sociology, people from fields as diverse as insurance, nursing, probation, and public health eagerly register. "As often as not, they want to write a paper to prove that some occupation—their own—has become or is on the verge of becoming a true profession."[1] The reasons are not hard to find. Hughes' comments on the insurance salesmen apply with few changes to any other similar group striving toward professionalism:

The insurance salesmen try to free themselves of the business label; they are not selling, they are giving people expert and objective diagnoses of their risks and advising them as to the best manner of protecting themselves. They are distressed that the heads of families do not confide in them more fully. [2]

Desires are often turned into realities. Title VIII, Articles 131–151 of the New York State Educational Law has given legal sanction as professions in recent years to such occupations as nursing, pharmacy, accounting, surveying, and shorthand reporting.[3] Two books dealing with institutions in urban areas have concluded that a drive toward professionalism on the part of school teachers and policemen is necessary for an understanding of their collective behavior in recent years.[4] In the face of this tendency to professionalize everyone, one can respond, as did Harold Wilensky, by being

critical of the absurdity of the whole movement.[5] But I find it hard to criticize people for wishing to have more status attributed to the way they spend forty or more hours each week. The demand of groups such as these for professional status occurs at the same time as the economies of advanced, industrial societies offer fewer and fewer personal satisfactions on the job. As computers take the guess-work out of estimating, as programmed materials are presented to the teacher, as pharmacists have a ready-made pill for any prescription presented, one can summon up little indignation, but only pathos, at those who claim prestige for work which can be quite humiliating. Do we really care when the bail-bondsman tells his Long Island neighbors that he is "in insurance"?

Indignation may more justifiably be present when professionalism is claimed without the need for status being present, which is the case when we move beyond the occupations already mentioned to scholarship. In those "professional associations" like the Modern Language Association, the American Physical Society, and the American Psychological Association, a desire for status in the eyes of the rest of the population is rarely an important motive. Scholars and teachers know that they can achieve all the status they want by manipulating their classes into a submissive acceptance of their own authoritarian role. With a choice of being either "doctor" or "professor," with a captive audience that increases year by year, with the right to wear imposing and expensive academic paraphernalia at each graduation, with special parking lots, with the privilege of not paying library fines, with waitress service in the eating-place—college professors have much to buttress their claim to special status.[6] Any understanding of the professional activities they engage in must look elsewhere, then, to explain the attraction of professionalism.

Looking elsewhere, an alternative explanation for the importance of professionalism for academics might be found in the motives of groups traditionally labeled as professional. There is something positive about the word professional, especially when compared to one of its opposites, the word amateur. At one time, professionals were considered to be a group of people whose expertise, fairness, and devotion were so unquestioned that decisions about who was to be admitted to the group could be made by the group itself, privately, under special sanction from the state. So doctors, lawyers, and clergymen, to name the three most prominent traditional professions, developed apprentice systems and qualification tests for membership in the profession. The service to society performed by these groups was so demanding and important that only they should have the right to determine entry, they claimed. Much of the argument was valid. One has only to compare the strides made by modern medicine with the charlatanism of a not too distant past to realize the service which professionalism has performed in certain areas of life. The same comparison, however, also reveals the great danger always inherent in professionalism, that the chartering practice will lead to an exclusivist clique based, not on external expertise or fairness, but on internal conformity to certain values of the dominant professionals. Since most groups traditionally called professionals have both these external and internal functions associated with them, any evaluation of their performance should seek to find which was dominant in the minds of the ruling professionals at any one time.

From this point of view, there is much to be said that the purpose of academic professionalism, and of its organizational counterpart, academic professional associations, is more conformity within the profession than external service to society. This is especially true of many of the social sciences, including political science, for reasons of the ideology governing the field. If we are to listen to its practitioners, we would come away believing that political science is a neutral, "pure," science, not a body of expert and immediately applicable knowledge, like law or medicine. Therefore, service to any clientele, an important part of the traditional professions, is not a salient characteristic of the social sciences, except for certain fields like social work and educational psychology. Of course, we know that the ideology is false, that social science is

very active in supporting a particular societal clientele.[7] But it is nonetheless interesting that the formal ideology of a field like political science, by implication, denies the external rationale for professionalism. If this interpretation is correct, here is a clue that those who maintain the value-free ideology *and at the same time* call for professionalism are doing so because the internal functions are uppermost in their minds. Why have professional political scientists? There would seem to be no reason as far as society is concerned. But there are many reasons as far as the professionals themselves are concerned. Having rejected the desire for status and external service as these reasons, let us now look at what are to me more convincing reasons, particularly those dealing with internal conformity.

A valid explanation of the contemporary attraction among academics for professionalism must take into account some of the changes taking place within academia at this time. For many years, it was just assumed that academics were professionals and were expected to act as such. After all, most universities had clauses somewhere in their by-laws or procedures to the effect that faculty members were not expected to engage in "unprofessional" conduct. Left intentionally vague, such clauses implied that there was such a thing as *professional* conduct which all college professors could fairly easily determine. Judging by the way such clauses were implemented, it would seem to be true that so long as a faculty member did not engage in illicit sexual relations with his students, his conduct was professional. Such clauses were not codes of ethics; they had nothing to say about a faculty member like J. Sterling Livingston, who turned a position at the Harvard Business School into a personal fortune; a university like the University of Pennsylvania which conducted secret research into biological and chemical warfare; or about the various institutes which helped fight wars overseas and have been recently recruited to help fight wars in American cities.[8]

In the last few years, academics have become more and more concerned that a proper definition of a professional role be developed. In part this is due to the various questionable activities which have taken place within universities, but even more it is due to the undertakings of the critics of these activities. For these critics have raised embarrassing questions about the proper role of the professoriate. Can one proclaim value-neutrality and still do counterinsurgency research? Can one remain silent in the face of an immoral war and counter that he is not being political? Does academic freedom give a faculty member the right to teach a course in riot-control? Is it the proper role of younger faculty to accept all the rules of careerism determined for them by tenured faculty? Is the demand for publication really a demand for political conformity? All of these are difficult questions. In many cases, young and radical faculty members and graduate students found that, when they raised them, no answers were forthcoming. Instead, the questioners themselves were attacked. A "responsible" and "professional" scholar does not take public positions on controversies where he does not have expertise. Nor does he appeal to the masses (i.e., students) in emotional terms when issues are dividing a campus, for such conduct is demagogic. Nor does the responsible academic question strenuously the rules of scholarly promotion, for then he will soon find himself no longer an academic. One convenient rubric which could be used for all of these charges was that the dissenter was acting "unprofessionally."

In this way, conservatives within universities made a distinction between acting politically and acting professionally. In the former capacity, the professor is equal to anyone else who acts similarly. So long as he publicly takes political positions outside his area of expertise, he has the same civil liberty as the barber or welder who does likewise. When the professor acts professionally, on the other hand, different criteria arise. It is then that he can use the umbrella of academic freedom, presumably because now he will never need it.[9] It is then that he is presumed to speak with authority. It is also then that his application for promotion will be considered more seriously. In other words, this attempt to define professional

conduct is a political act, among other reasons because it is really an attempt to define political conduct. To those who make this distinction, what is political is unprofessional and vice versa. The concept of professionalism now beginning to emerge in many academic disciplines, then, stems from a motive which fears politics, challenge, and dissent. Advocating professionalism becomes a way by which academic conservatives can latch on to a respectable-sounding phrase to justify their adherence to the status quo. To paraphrase the famous character from Molière, they have only recently discovered that they have been acting professionally all their lives.

The attempt to operationalize this dichotomy between political and professional conduct can be seen throughout academia at this time. Take the changes going on within academic professional associations, for example. There, insurgent groups in a variety of fields have organized for different ends. Sometimes they have asked professional associations to go on record as condemning the war in Vietnam; this was countered, until it recently became more popular to take such positions, by the argument that to take political positions as an institution is an unprofessional way of acting. In addition, other groups, like the Caucus for a New Political Science, have decided to run candidates for office within the professional association as a way of demonstrating alternative approaches to the discipline. When the caucus announced that it was going to run a list of candidates for the elected positions within the American Political Science Association, marking the first contested election among political scientists in the twentieth century, the idea was expectedly denounced as unprofessional, even by groups running their own slate of candidates (presumably only as a last-gap measure to bring the profession back to its senses). One political scientist, Donald Herzberg, with the support of some of the most well-known scholars in the field, devoted nearly full-time to fulminating about the election. First, he formed a group called the Ad Hoc Committee for a Mail Ballot, designed (successfully) to insure that the election be taken out of the hands of any face-to-face group and be placed in the hands of an impersonal mail ballot. Herzberg had read the book by a former president of the association, David Truman, which showed how resorts to the mail are frequently used by the leaders of groups to keep themselves in power when dissenters begin to emerge.[10] Then, Herzberg formed another group called the Ad Hoc Committee for a Representative Slate. Under its name, he circulated a letter to all the members of the association (cost: $780) which made this statement:

This election will determine whether the Association is to be a *professional organization based on shared interests and expertise in scholarship, research, and teaching or whether it is to be a political action group.*

The Ad Hoc Committee for a Representative Slate wants to maintain the Association as a *professional organization* devoted to shared *professional purposes.*

For this reason we ask you to vote for the Ad Hoc Slate, all of whose members were chosen for *professional, rather than political reasons.* [Emphasis added]

The superficiality of this distinction is so apparent that the only thing more remarkable than the fact that an allegedly neutral and politically sensitive scholar made it is the fact that allegedly similar scholars will adhere to it.[11] A letter which claims to be nonpolitical but which urges people to vote for a particular slate is an interesting enough phenomenon. But this one goes beyond that. One of the two people supposedly picked for professional rather than political reasons is much more well known in his political capacity. He was one of the most outspoken critics of President Perkins at Cornell during the racial soul-searching there, and one of the first to announce his resignation. Since then, he has become a prominent speaker on the anarchy caused by white and black student unrest and the need for firm discipline to remedy it. But people are being asked to believe that his name is put forward at this time because of his (very good, as it happens) scholarship on the two-party system. At least Herzberg has made the paradoxes clear; we can see from this letter that, for many, acting "professionally" is a way of acting politically by denying the fact. Acting "professionally" does not allow one to escape from politics; it only appears to let him do so.

This same distinction between political conduct and professional conduct is used in academic departments with much more serious consequences. Because the removal of a member of a department for reasons of his politics is a direct violation of the conventional wisdom of academic freedom (and because it may also lead to censure from the AAUP), the rubric of unprofessional conduct has found a whole new outlet for its use. Surely a person who acts unprofessionally has no recourse to academic freedom, for that is a protection for professionals only. Therefore, firing such an individual, while certainly distasteful, is still defensible. Consider the grounds for such action against a person dismissed from his position as a teacher of international relations. While teaching at San Francisco State College, John Gerassi helped students break into a building during a demonstration and, in a public speech, urged them to close down the college. Both a departmental committee and a faculty ad hoc committee agreed that Gerassi was guilty of "unprofessional conduct" (made punishable by the state's education code), and he was fired. Here politics is blatantly associated with professionalism. But in defending this action, one of the faculty members instrumental in firing him also said this:

. . .he declined to exercise the normal responsibility of academic authority. For example, he gave all his student's "A's." In style, dress, associations, and deportment, he made it clear that he regarded the students, and not the faculty, as his peer group.[12]

The indictment, if it is meant to be one, is devastating. If you cannot get someone on his politics, get him on his deportment. If it is true that there is a direct correlation between informal dress and left-wing politics, one or the other would do. The possibilities are endless.

Another example is more interesting

because it grows out of the "good side" in an academic freedom case. In 1969, Angela Davis was fired from the UCLA philosophy department by the California Regents because she was a member of the Communist party, although that action will most likely be reversed by the courts. Unlike the 1950's, when such an action would have been met with partial silence, the whole university has jumped to her defense. On the surface this would appear to be a positive development, for it indicates that people really believe in academic freedom. But a further look leads to a different conclusion, for defenders of Miss Davis may inadvertently be laying the groundwork for more political repressions. In a statement issued on September 23, 1969, David Kaplan, Associate Professor of Philosophy and Vice-Chairman of the Philosophy Department at UCLA, took a strong stand in support of Miss Davis. After giving the conventional reasons for academic freedom, he goes on to note: "Academic freedom is not a license for irresponsible behavior. Indeed the academic profession has its own code of professional ethics, and one which many would find quite demanding." Kaplan then goes on to list these responsibilities, which include the intellectual honesty, avoidance of indoctrination, and respect for the opinion of others.[13] Angela Davis has all these qualities, so she should be defended. But the real question would concern those who allegedly did not meet these "responsibilities." I, for one, do not meet them, for there are others whose opinions I do not respect (at all) and whom I am quite intolerant of. Among them are outspoken racists, militarists, and neofascists. Does that mean that my conduct is irresponsible and hence not deserving of academic freedom? One could see how the case could be made. Were I to be fired, not, of course, for my politics but because of this "irresponsibility," where would those who defend Angela Davis on the quoted grounds stand? One would hope that they would have the sense to see how, even in defending someone, they are stating the opposite case from the one they intended. One would hope they would also have the sense to see how "responsible" and "professional" modes of behavior can be used as ways of insuring acceptable modes of political conduct.

At this point the argument I am making can be summarized. Recent talk of the importance of academic professionalism in many disciplines has not grown out of the external relationships between the discipline and society but out of internal pressures for political conformity. Hence the demand for professional conduct is a demand for a conservative politics. To evaluate such a thing as "the profession of political science," then, is to talk about politics. I have found that those who defend many of the present practices of political scientists do so under the name of professionalism. Among these practices are the following: accepting the emergence of an elite within the field which sets standards with little review or question; excluding points of view other than the prevailing ones; affiliating with client groups which are supportive of the status quo; and developing a model of proper scholarship which is exclusionary in effect. These practices are familiar enough to anyone who knows the discipline of political science, and repeating them here will add little information and much boredom. But there are still some who are unfamiliar with them, and more importantly, the connection between these practices and how professionalism is used to rationalize their existence has yet to be made.

1. Professionalism is used to justify the formation of an unrepresentative elite which has determined the character of the discipline. In another paper I have shown how a small, unrepresentative sample of the membership of the American Political Science Association has dominated the important positions within that body.[14] No contested elections were ever held, until last year. No outlets were provided for the general membership to express its opinions. The affairs of the association, and to an extent the profession, were carried out by the APSA's Executive Director, Evron Kirkpatrick, a man trained in the arts of anti-communism to the extent of affiliating himself with more than one CIA front-group. No procedures were available for independently investigating his behavior. The constitution of the association mitigated against the emergence of democracy or representative government within it. Most of the member-

ship felt unable to protest, but did denounce, in the only survey taken, the "establishment" which had developed. In short, political scientists—who always tell others how to govern themselves—did not do a very good job when it came to their own house.

The more interesting question is the relationship between the oligarchic character of the APSA and professionalism. Within the APSA, a kind of gentlemanly club atmosphere prevailed in which decisions were made by a small group of notables. In the strange logic which imbues these things, supporting this unrepresentative oligarchy and desiring little voice in the association which made decisions affecting your life was considered responsible and professional, while trying to change it through means considered highly proper in the larger political system (voting, persuasion, organization) was considered demagogic, unprofessional, and generally beneath contempt. This seems to be one of those cases, which political scientists should know about, where elites, in order to insure their position of power, define standards to which everyone in the political system is expected to adhere. Most people do, because they have not thought of other standards and because they aspire to or identify with those already existing elites. Whether the standards are good or bad is beside the point; it's who makes them up which matters. Professionalism, seen as such a standard, easily becomes translated into political quiescence, even by the quiescent.

2. Professionalism has been used to justify the exclusion of points of view from the discipline which run contrary to the established ones. The way this works has been summarized in the Gerassi and Davis cases discussed above. Few people dispute the idea that departments use the rhetoric of professionalsim to gain total adherence within a department to one point of view.[15] In departments of political science, this refers not only to political viewpoints but methodological ones as well. There are departments which will not hire someone, no matter what his qualifications, if he is not trained in mathematics. There are others

which will dismiss as unqualified anyone with extensive mathematical training. Both types of departments are suspicious of anyone who claims that the knowledge uncovered by a political science must be used by insurgent groups who are challenging those who now have power in America. People affiliated with the Caucus for a New Political Science, for example, have already found themselves blacklisted from many political science departments. One person, whose teaching and scholarly credentials were astounding in their excellence, was denied jobs at three different universities on the basis of his connections with the caucus. Many others have had similar experiences.

The secrecy and confidentiality which surrounds faculty-hiring procedures permits such informal blacklisting to take place. There are some senior professors who, when they hear of a caucus person being considered for a job in another department where they have a friend, dash off an immediate letter to him dropping the crucial code word, "unprofessional conduct." That is the end of the applicant's chances for a job, for what self-respecting department will hire an unprofessional when they can have a professional? The applicant does not know what happened because he can never see the letter which blackballed him, and in some cases, he may never know that a letter was written. The whole process of confidential letters, which is usually cited as the "professional" way of making new appointments, can easily be turned into a procedure which has no due process, no chance to reply to charges, and no redress.

In spite of the rubric of secrecy, there has been one study of the hiring process, and, even though it was done in an allied field, sociology, its findings are relevant to political science as well.[16] By studying 185 letters of recommendation written by 167 sociologists, Lionel Lewis strongly questioned the validity of this statement by Caplow and McGee: "The data leaves us with a strong impression . . . that although the scholar's judgment of his colleagues is often blind and biased, and occasionally crazy, it *is* professional."[17] On the contrary, says

Lewis, interpersonal considerations dominate the letters written by sociologists. Portions of his analysis are indicative of his findings.:

It is manifest, then, that departments are not interested in recruiting men who will disrupt social relationships and upset the *status quo* within a department. The distinguishing personality traits a prospective department member should have to ensure that he will not be an irritant are friendliness (amiable, warm, personable, pleasant) . . . gentleness (patient, modest, quiet, easy-going, relaxed), and soundness of mind (stable, well-adjusted, balanced, even-tempered). Possessing, or seeming to possess such traits is deemed of greatest importance in defining a suitable colleague.[18]

Lewis feels that his analysis supports neither the traditionalists who argue that universities do operate rationally or critics who argue that it should. But it certainly is supportive of those who argue that it doesn't. What I find most interesting about it is that although professional conduct does not operate as a significant variable in letters of recommendation, unprofessional conduct does. An assertion of the candidate's friendliness, gentleness, and soundness of mind is an assertion that he can be trusted not to turn into a political radical, who would, of course, be bitter, distrustful, and intellectually insufficient.

3. Professionalism has been used to justify an affiliation with client-groups which are supportive of existing American policies, national and international. In spite of its ideology of neutrality, there is little doubt that most political scientists are working hard to support the contemporary American status quo. The ideology of pluralism is only the most blatant example. Many political scientists work directly for the State and Defense Departments at research institutes at universities like Columbia, Stanford, and Harvard. In addition, political scientists, despite an early promise to the contrary,[19] find themselves collecting all sorts of information on nonelites, while totally ignoring research on elites, to the extent, according to Karl Deutsch, of spending about one hundred times the effort on the former compared to the latter.[20] Finally, as the in-

troduction to this volume has pointed out, in their adherence to a value-free, limited-objective, "scientific" state of mind, political scientists have assured themselves that they would be incapable of dealing with the power of privileged groups in this country even if they accidentally stumbled across them.

The connections between this overwhelming proximity to power and the drive toward professionalism are intertwined with all of the things discussed so far. Power in America, insofar as it touches political scientists, does so through the foundations. Part of being a professional political scientist is doing research which has foundation support. Yet, it does not require much insight to conclude that foundations are going to be receptive to certain ideas—the ones defined by the discipline as compatible with professionalism—and hostile to others, those the profession has put outside the pale. Foundations, says Robert Dahl, "because of their enormous financial contributions to scholarly research, and the inevitable selection among competing proposals that these entail, exert a considerable effect on the scholarly community."[21] That effect, despite Dahl's denial of the point, is to reinforce notions acceptable to the foundations and to the national power-elite which funds them. Not only are left-wing scholars, particularly those who study the power-elite, cut off from foundation support, but even partially critical institutes, the moment they become critical of the direction of American policies, find themselves without funds.[22] Note the word "direction." To criticize the war in Vietnam is acceptable to the foundations; to even mention American imperialism is not. Once again, a situation exists in which support for existing power relationships is not considered "political" activity, while nonsupport for the same relationships is considered political. The urge to become professional, in other words, becomes so compelling that political scientists cannot even develop a sufficient definition of their own subject matter. But few seem to mind, for adherence to an incomplete definition of politics, which only views the action of insurgents as politics, is also a professional thing to do, while attempts to promote a more comprehensive definition of politics is not.

4. Professionalism has been used to justify a model of research which has been quite exclusionary in effect. Political scientists know that there are two kinds of journals, acceptable ones and non-acceptable ones. The former are those which, by some arbitrary criteria, are considered authentic publications in the constant search for new jobs. The latter group, demeaned as "popular" or "journalistic" are to be avoided and ignored, although they are (perhaps in secret) read more avidly than those in the first group. Acceptable journals are also considered professional journals; when one writes for them, one is writing for a group of similarly trained professionals. The others are considered "lay"; when one does write for them, he talks down to the audience, for they do not understand the details contained in the more sophisticated periodicals.

Since only "professional" journals count in one's career, most political scientists think only of publishing there. But what is acceptable for publication in such a journal must meet further standards justified under the name of professionalism. These standards cannot be dismissed as simply scientific criteria which apply equally to all. A study by Diana Crane of allied journals concluded that "the evaluation of scientific articles is affected to some degree by non-scientific factors."[23] That this proposition carries over to the *American Political Science Review* is scarcely debatable. Whether or not those nonscientific standards include political bias is the more interesting question. From everything I have been able to conclude, they do, but never explicitly so. Rather than reject articles for the critical stance of their politics and accept others because of their status quo politics, the Review determines the former to be unprofessional, while the latter, it is decided, meet the standards of the profession.

Since I have not been able to obtain (professional secrecy once again) any systematic information on which articles are accepted and rejected for the *American Political Science Review*, I can only use secondary evidence. David Kettler, who worked as an assistant to the editor of the *Review* for a few years, does not doubt that political factors play a role in the selection of articles.[24] His point is confirmed by an analysis of the actual articles published. In the last few years, articles in the *Review* can be broken down into the following categories: those with a political bias which is conservative; those with a political bias which is centrist; those with radical political biases; those which have no political bias because they are solely methodological or mathematical; those which had no political bias because of other reasons; those which formally had no political bias but which concluded by justifying the existence of current political institutions; and those which had no formal political bias but which concluded by justifying existing American policies. Since the categories are subjective ones, I did not rigidly break down all articles from one period to another into each category, but instead read through some recent issues to see, in my own mind, which categories predominated. I found that articles with explicit *left or right* biases were rare.[25] Nearly half the articles were scientific and "professional," while most of the remaining half, by implication, had implicit political biases which were supportive of existing institutions (nearly all the articles on the House of Representatives fit here) or policies (most articles on Latin America or foreign policy fit there). Thus, there is a bias against articles which are explicit in their politics but not those that are implicit. The norms of professionalism, then, discriminate against committed political scientists whose politics run in either direction. The only way to take a political position is to sneak it by the everwatchful editors under the guise of "science" and "responsible scholarship." Since those who tend to have these implicit politics are supportive of the status quo, professionalism once again is used to justify the exclusion of divergent points of view.

To the extent that traditional professionalism supports and justifies these practices, critics of academia will find themselves becoming more and more distrustful of the use of the term "professionalism." Any merits which may have been present in the idea—insight, intelligence, critical stance—will become lost as the term more and more becomes synonymous with the politics of quiescence. Pseudoprofessionals will guarantee that no room is left for true professionalism. While this is happening, those dissatisfied with what professionalism has come to mean will attempt to develop for themselves some guidelines for their own action. In an important sense, the formation of groups like the Caucus for a New Political Science is the first step in this process of redefinition. As one involved in redefining, I think it might be helpful to conclude this essay with some observations about what this process involved.

The profession of political science, as presently constituted, is not receptive to extended criticism. Certainly it should be, but merely to say so does not help very much. Everyone will agree *in abstracto* with the proposition that an academic discipline should welcome to it people of all points of view, in other words, that it should be guided by the principle of pluralistic liberalism. The trouble with such assertions, however, is that pluralism rarely works. It was under a permissive liberalism that the present situation came about. All were allowed to do their own thing, and all wound up doing the same thing. Is there a causal relationship between the two clauses of that sentence? I think there probably is. In the American political system, within the universities, and, as I have been trying to show in this essay within the academic professional associations, a rhetoric of liberalism has long been present. Yet the reality of the situation in all three cases has been to deny the development of any true pluralism, underrepresenting dissenting points of view in all three. In my view, this is not a coincidence. The ideology of liberalism becomes a two-edged sword. It guarantees diversity within the tenants of liberalism itself (where it is not needed), but it is incapable of extending those benefits outside of itself (where it is). To simply assert the need for many points of view, then, is not enough. Something must be developed which will actually bring that about.

Whatever that something is, it will probably run counter to the central principles of liberalism.

Two activities have been the principal vocation of radicals within the academic disciplines until this point. Both are initially essential; both have now reached the point where at least in political science they are counterproductive. The first activity was to "muckrake" within one's profession. Proving the existence of political bias, showing how oligarchies control professional associations, confronting the limitations of the received wisdom of academic freedom—all of these activities, which I have been doing now for about two years, are fun. All of them, in addition, have become tiring. There is only so much rationality within the universities and the academic professions. Some will be convinced of the justice of your cause, but more will ingeniously develop rationalizations to avoid the points you are making. Thus, there reaches a point in the development of insurgent groups within academic disciplines where they have to stop being internally critical of the practices and content of their profession and turn their attention to more important things. I personally find, therefore, that this will be the last essay I write on the state of the political science profession, all my points having been made. And I similarly urge organizations like the caucus to turn their attention away from the discipline and its problems to more productive enterprises.

A second type of activity is organizing within the academic professions for radical ends. This grew out of a movement which was recently popular on the left called "radicals in the professions."[26] Recognizing that radicals would constitute a minority in whatever profession they happened to enter, this movement discussed organizing techniques for expanding the radical constituency. When it turned out that some professions, particularly secondary school teaching and welfare work, were attracting a high proportion of left-leaning college graduates, there was some possibility of creating relatively permanent organizations. Teachers for a Democratic Society, organized in New York City, is one such organization. Its success (measured by its continued existence, no small accomplishment these days) is proof of the basic lesson learned from all these activities: that radical organizing cannot take place in professions where there are few radicals.

I mention this experience because it is directly relevant to the problem of what radicals in the profession of political science can do. Political science is one of those professions in which radical organizing does not make sense. Something seems to happen to people when they become political scientists, or maybe people who become political scientists were strange to begin with. But whatever the causal relationship, this profession is one of the least movable there is. (Economics may be worse). Allied disciplines such as sociology and history have recognizable subgroups of scholars whose dissents from the prevailing orthodoxies were well-known to incipient radicals.[27] This means that these professions may be more likely to see radical organizing succeed. But in political science, the only criticims of pluralism, the dominant ideology, came from people who were excellent scholars, but who could hardly be considered political radicals.[28] With a dearth of radical thought at the left end of the discipline, it is no wonder that political science is so conservative at the center and on the right. What other discipline has seen the development of a right-wing Conference—not Donald Herzberg's group but a group of actual *National Review*-type political scientists—to counter the "New Left" tendencies of the Caucus for a New Political Science? This is especially remarkable in the face of the caucus' own tendency to deny its radicalism by adopting a liberal rhetoric and welcoming to its ranks anyone interested in making political science "relevant."

Radicals, in a few words, do not really exist in the discipline of political science. At the September 1969 convention of the American Political Science Association, while the leaders of the association and *The New York Times* all waited for the young militants to disrupt the meetings, as was happening at the same time with sociologists in San Francisco and the psychologists in Washington, those of us who knew about these things were laughing. We knew that there might be somewhere between five and ten political scientists in the United States willing to challenge the basic notions of pluralistic liberalism, and only four or five of them were at the convention. This lack of radicalism within the profession does not contradict the point that radicals have been discriminated against in the profession. Rather, the two propositions feed each other. The rules of professional conduct discussed in this essay—the hostility of the professional journals, the difficulty of getting a job teaching, the lack of funds, the exclusion from the professional association—have left their toll. The reason radicals were not in New York at the APSA convention was that they were either in San Francisco with the sociologists or at home with themselves. The study of power and governance, it seems clear, has been left to those who deny the importance of power and governance.

With both internal criticism and radical organizing becoming less productive within the profession of political science, the question becomes one of defining certain positive steps which those branded as "unprofessional" can take. One of these would be to turn to places where there would be some support. The caucus is currently (and rightly, I feel) exploring the possibility of joining with insurgents in other disciplines around a journal and other activities for similar ends. The problem is that insurgents in other fields have more to do within their disciplines, but there is nothing in that problem to stop their also working with groups outside their own. This would make political science the weak sister in any such coalition, but it is better than being an only child.[29] In addition, dissenting political scientists can also obtain support by joining with people from other fields within their own university. This has the disadvantage of bringing together people who speak different languages, but at least it gives them a chance to speak. Both of these alternatives, however, are not the end of the problem; they are simply suggestions to avoid the problem of the radical political scientist going stir-crazy.

Ultimately, the "unprofessional" political scientist could, if he does somehow obtain job security somewhere, realize the virtues of a true academic professionalism, not because he hopes to convince anyone of his purity, but because it could be a very satisfying thing to do. In discussing the caucus and similar groups, David Kettler has noted that:

these groups will dissipate their energies and get caught in the senseless escalation of expectations to the point of cynical passivity if they do not recognize that their political activities within these associations and professions must first and foremost serve the theoretical goal of making the disciplines places where we can do our work, including, of course, work between teachers and students.[30]

This "work" is called by Kettler, in the title of his paper, "The Vocation of Radical Intellectuals." If we have been denied by others the title of professional, the answer is to claim for ourselves the title of vocational. In our process of redefinition, we could conclude that the true academic professional is one who never uses the word professional, because of its suggestion of internal conformity. Furthermore, true professionals would, in all likelihood, know that they were professionals and not have to repeat it every time they take an action which they feel might be unpopular. The true professional, on the contrary, has a vocation, and that vocation is the promotion of his own radical truth. It may be, because the university is what it is, that he will be unable to pursue that vocation within it. But that should not stop him, for neither Marx nor Voltaire pursued his vocation within a university. So long as our true professional does not allow the pseudoprofessionalism of academia to convince him that he is crazy and they are sane, he, more than anyone else, can follow his questions where they lead him. So long as he maintains his real interest in questions of power and governance, it is he, and not those who currently misuse the title, who will be active in the profession of political science.

NOTES

1. Everett C. Hughes, "Professions," in Kenneth S. Lynn, ed., *The Professions in America* (Boston: Beacon Press, 1965), p. 4.

2. *Ibid.*, p. 5.

3. As cited by Arthur Niederhoffer, *Behind the Shield* (Garden City: Doubleday Anchor, 1969), p. 20.

4. *Ibid.*; and David Rodgers, *110 Livingston Street* (New York: Random House, 1968).

5. Harold L. Wilensky, "The Professionalization of Everyone?" *American Journal of Sociology*, 66 (January 1961): 325–334.

6. Jerry Farber has made all of these points in an essay entitled *Student as Nigger* (Ann Arbor: Radical Education Project, n.d.). Farber's experience had been at one school, California State College at Los Angeles, and since I teach at an experimental college which was highly informal and brand new, I tended to discount his essay as exaggerated. However, I recently taught a summer quarter at Cal State, L.A., and halfway through the summer I remembered that it was Farber's school. I then kept my eyes open to see whether he was overdoing it. He wasn't.

7. See the essay by Marvin Surkin in this volume for more on this proposition.

8. Livingston and Penn are discussed in James Ridgeway, *The Closed Corporation* (New York: Random House, 1968), pp. 70–74, 126. For a good overview of the research institutes, see David Horowitz, "Sinews of Empire," *Ramparts*, 8 (October 1969): 32.

9. This point is relevant to an understanding of the proposition that academic freedom has been achieved. Walter P. Metzger, in *Academic Freedom in the Age of the University* (New York: Columbia Paperback, 1955), seems to feel that academic freedom is much more of a reality now than it ever was. The only way he can maintain this position, it seems to me, in the face of the University's demands for near-total conformity, is to focus on the narrow issue of overt political conduct. From that point of view, there will never be an academic freedom case at any major university because all the scholars there have been turned into professionals. Once again, those who would need the protection of academic freedom are excluded from the university before they could ever use it, and those who are in the university and able to use it will never allow themselves to do so.

10. "A device that must be classified with internal propaganda in most instances, although it superficially would not appear so, is the referendum. This is a widely employed instrument in chambers of commerce, trade associations, labor unions, and *professional associations*. By this device a question of public policy on which the association is to take a stand is sent to the members or constituent societies, frequently together with arguments on both sides of the issue. The recipients are to indicate their choice

of policies on a ballot. The practice has been particularly used by the Chamber of Commerce of the United States. It is classed along with propaganda because judgments of it almost universally are that *it serves primarily to emphasize unity, to give sanction to previously determined decision, and, by the appearance of wide rank-and-file participation in policy making, to strengthen the group internally* and make it more effective externally." (Emphasis added.) David B. Truman, *The Governmental Process* (New York: Knopf, 1962), pp. 197–198.

11. Not all scholars. Herzberg's letter so incensed James Prothro of the University of North Carolina, one of the foremost scholars in the field of American Government, that he circulated to political science departments a defense of the men attacked in Herzberg's letter. This shows some humanity in the field, but does not deny the point. Prothro's approach was to show that the men under attack were indeed professionals, and not to question the whole notion of what professionalism is.

12. Marshall Windmiller, "Trouble at San Francisco State," *New York Review of Books*, 10 (April 11, 1968), pp. 41–42. That Windmiller is a member of the executive committee of the Caucus for a New Political Science only indicates to me how far the doctrine of professionalism has been allowed to go.

13. Press statement of David Kaplan, September 23, 1969.

14. Alan Wolfe, "Practising the Pluralism We Preach," *Antioch Review*, 29 (Fall 1969): 353–373.

15. When I wrote an essay devoted to making this point ("The Myth of The Free Scholar," *Center Magazine*, July 1969), few people disputed that it happened. Seymour Martin Lipset, certainly one prone to find nothing but goodness in existing institutions, argued that it would be "futile" to deny the point. He instead noted that ". . . as compared with other institutions and professions the university is the most critical one we have." (See *Center Magazine*, September 1969, pp. 93–94). Now I would agree that all institutions and professions have degrees of unfreedom. One of the activists in the Berkeley Free Speech Movement, for example, has been denied admission to the California Bar despite his excellent credentials. This exclusion was done, not for his left-wing views, but because of his having spent some time in jail (unprofessional) for offenses which grew out of his political views. Admittedly, the distinction is a difficult one for nonlawyers to grasp. Whether the university is less likely to engage in exclusionary tactics like this one is an interesting empirical proposition. It is not resolved by concluding, as Lipset did, that "scholars who are competent are as free as they choose to be." In face of all the unfreedom in the university, an unfreedom which Lipset has admitted is present, the only way for such a statement to make sense is through a narrow definition of competence. This would equate competence with "responsible" and "professional" behavior. Then the statement would read that scholars who accepted the rules of professional conformity are as free as they choose to be. That is exactly the point.

16. Lionel S. Lewis, "The Puritan Ethic in Universities and Some Worldly Concerns of Sociologists," *American Sociologist*, 4 (August 1969): 235–241.

17. Theodore Caplow and Reece J. McGee, *The Academic Marketplace* (New York: Basic Books, 1958), p. 93.

18. Lewis, *op. cit.*, p. 238.

19. That promise can be seen in the early works by behavioral political scientists which did deal rather comprehensively with elites. See Harold Lasswell, *Politics: Who Gets What, Where, How* (New York: Meredian Books, 1958); and E. E. Schattschneider, *Politics, Pressures and the Tariff* (New York: Prentice Hall, 1935) as representative examples.

20. As quoted in David Horowitz, "Billion Dollar Brains," *Ramparts*, 7 (May 1969): 42.

21. *Ibid.*

22. The story of how the Ford Foundation, Standard Oil, and powerful individuals in Washington and California brought about the end of the Institute of Hispanic American and Luso-Brazilian Studies at Stanford University, which had been critical of American policy, and replaced it with a heavily financed and more controllable institute is fully told in Horowitz, "Sinews of Empire," pp. 39–40. Few can read that story and come away with idealistic thoughts about contemporary American universities.

23. Diana Crane, "The Gatekeepers of Science: Some Factors Affecting the Selection of Articles for Scientific Journals," *American Sociologist*, 2 (November 1967): 200.

24. In a letter to *P.S.*, newsletter of the APSA.

25. I considered an article by Wilmore Kendall and George Carey to have an explicit right bias, one by Lewis Lipsitz or Peter Bachrach to have a left political bias, one by Nelson Polsby to have implicit support of existing institutions, and any article on a socialist country to be implicitly supportive of American policies.

26. See the *Radicals in the Professions Newsletter* for insights into this movement's philosophy and tactics.

27. Historians with dissenting views were attracted to the University of Wisconsin, particularly by William Appleman Williams and Harvey Goldberg, but also for William R. Taylor and George Mosse. After obtaining their degrees, they went to other institutions where they carried on the tradition. Sociologists were attracted by the works of Robert Lynd and C. Wright Mills, although they could attend

Columbia only with difficulty because of Paul Lazarsfeld and Robert Merton. What they tended to do was to go someplace else, but to read the dissenting books on the side. The result is that there are some radical sociologists in little groups throughout the country and in Canada.

28. Particularly Henry Kariel and Theodore Lowi. See the essay by Michael Parenti in this volume for references.

29. There are two already existing umbrella groups of radicals within universities, the New University Conference and the Socialist Scholars Conference. Neither has very many political scientists associated with it.

30. David Kettler, "The Vocation of Radical Intellectuals," in Godfried van den Bergh and David Kettler, eds. *Reason Against Power* (Amsterdam: Vangenner, forthcoming).

*

Part five

We see the media, banks, and unions as political institutions. Although they are not formally organized as political decision-making institutions in the way that the three branches of government are, they nevertheless exercise significant political power by other means: financial, ideological, and through the workings of organized labor. The exercise of their power, or the withholding of their resources can have as great a political effect as an act of Congress or the functioning of the secret police. As such, these institutions must be included in any examination of decision-making in the United States.

This has not always been seen to be so. Until Vice-President Spiro Agnew began attacking the press in 1969,[1] only a few radicals raised questions about the political importance of the media. Banks were not considered as potent political forces by the general public until the mid-1970s when they openly began to dictate policy to city officials who had requested financial support.[2] Union struggles for recognition and legitimacy in the nineteenth and twentieth century have long given them a political presence.[3]

Is America Necessary? is one of the few books on American Government which includes banks and the media among the primary political forces in America. There are other institutions which we have not included, among them, insurance companies and investment houses. We hope students will pay as serious attention to these unofficial political institutions as they do to the three branches of government—the Presidency, Congress, the Supreme Court. We also hope they will incorporate the analysis of these institutions into their overall judgments about American politics.

NOTES

1. Robert W. Peterson, "Agnew and the Media" in Robert W. Peterson, ed., *Agnew: The Coining of a Household Word,* New York: Facts on File Pub., 1972.

2. Robert J. Samuelson, "Bankrupt New York," *The New Republic* (May 10, 1975), pp. 17–19. See also, John D. Hicks, *The Populist Revolt.* Lincoln: Univ. of Nebraska Press, 1961.

3. David Greenstone, *Labor in American Politics.* New York: Alfred A. Knopf, Pub., 1969.

The alternative governments:
Do they really rule?

*

13 The media

The basic questions this chapter will address are:

(1) What are the mass media?

(2) Are the mass media independent? Or are they part of the corporate establishment?

(3) How do the media decide what to include in the news and what to leave out?

(4) Should government control the media? Or are the media already in accord with government thought?

Conservatives maintain that newspaper journalists must be objective, in other words, that they should not take a stand. Reporters should present fact, not opinion. Their task is to report press releases from government agencies and authoritative figures, and to report on public events ranging from society weddings to presidential activities. News that is potentially injurious to the national security should not be printed. This position was accepted by *The New York Times* when it did not print its knowledge that the United States, in 1961, was organizing an invasion of Cuba.[1] It is the belief of conservatives that the celebrity status of television anchormen has given their statements too much weight in the public mind. Together with presidential lies[2] this has created a situation of conflict between powerful Presidents and influential newscasters.[3] It has created an advocacy press in which opinion and ideology take precedence over facts, a harmful type of journalism that creates unnecessary political divisions. If newspaper and television journalists do not return to their proper role as objective reporters, then government may have to compel them to do so by persuasion or censorship. The American political system is best served by a press that does not get politically involved with the issues it reports.

Liberals strongly believe in the Jeffersonian edict that it is better to have no government and a free press, than to have a government without a free press.[4] Freedom of speech, guaranteed in the First Amendment to the United States Constitution is the first commandment of liberals. Errors of judgment the press commits must be self-corrected. Whatever news it reports must be determined by the press itself. Government must not intrude on the workings of a free press if democracy is to survive.

Socialists hold that the mass media and newspapers are part of the American power elite. Newspapers are typically run by powerful economic interests. Television and radio stations are often owned by huge corporations. The news that is presented in the media is in large part determined by corporate interests.[5] For this reason, socialists and radicals are seldom able to obtain a fair hearing of their views. The actions of elites are fully reported in the mass media, whereas the activities and statements of nonelites receive relatively little attention. According to socialists, the media work together with government and corporations, and are linked to corporate elites by financial ties and class interests.

Etzkowitz & Schwab—Is America Necessary—30

The existence of these ties does not mean that the mass media always operates to support the power elite.[6] Many reporters are on the liberal-left side of the political spectrum, and some actively attempt to get issues exposed that would limit the power of elites. For example, two reporters on the *Washington Post* spent two years investigating the "Watergate Affair." Their stories exposed the Watergate conspiracy and led to the resignation of President Richard Nixon. Their publisher supported the continuation of this investigation despite White House pressures.

Elites in American society are not always united in their policies. When they are divided, as on Watergate and the Vietnam war, a greater opportunity arises for liberals and socialists to critically analyze American institutions and publicly expose them through the mass media.

NOTES

1. Although the *Miami Herald* had published a story in April 1961 that the United States was going to sponsor an invasion of Cuba by Cuban refugees in that month, President Kennedy felt that if the story was kept out of *The New York Times* the publicity prior to the invasion would be minimal. The President called James Reston, at the time the leading editorial writer of *The New York Times* and asked him not to print the story. Reston, who had already written his story, agreed. The story was never fully printed and the invasion took place as planned. See James Reston, *The Artillery of the Press.* New York: Harper & Row, 1967. See also Robert Cirino, *Don't Blame the People,* New York: Vintage Books, 1971, particularly his chapter, "The Importance of Censorship."

2. The presidential lies which have become most public are: President Eisenhower lied, and was caught doing so, when he maintained he knew nothing about the American U-2 spy plane that was shot down over the Soviet Union in 1960; the lies Kennedy and Johnson told the American public in their defense of American participation in the Vietnamese War; the lies Nixon told in trying to hide his direct involvement in the Watergate cover up. See, Peter Schwab, J. Lee Shneidman, *John F. Kennedy,* New York: Twayne Publishers, 1974. The staff of *The Washington Post, The Fall of a President,* New York: Dell Pub., 1974. Arthur M. Schlesinger, Jr., *The Imperial Presidency,* New York: Houghton-Mifflin, Pub., 1973.

3. The best example of conflict between a reporter and a President was that between CBS White House correspondent Dan Rather, and Richard Nixon. Between 1972 and 1974 the animosity between the two was obvious to anyone watching Nixon's televised news conferences. Rather tried to extract Watergate information from Nixon, and Nixon tried to embarrass Rather through his answers. See Dan Rather and Gerry Gates, *The Palace Guard.* New York: Harper & Row, 1974.

4. See, Saul Padover, "Thomas Jefferson, the American as Democrat" in *The Genius of America,* New York: McGraw-Hill Book Co., 1960, pp. 63–64. See also Stuart Gerry Brown, *Thomas Jefferson,* New York: Twayne Pub., 1966.

5. The Pacifica Corporation is an example of a peoples media. Kept alive by voluntary contributions Pacifica operates three important radio stations, one in San Francisco, KPFA, in New York, WBAI, and in Houston, KPFT. It presents programs with a radical perspective. Examples are a live Women's Conscious Raising Group, The Free Voice of Greece, Eritreans for Independence in Ethiopia. They also present news programs in which news kept off the major networks is presented.

6. See, Henry Etzkowitz and Roger Mack, "Media, Social Researchers and the Public: Linkages of Legitimation and Delegitimation." *American Sociologist* (May, 1975).

Conservative

Paul H. Weaver.   The new journalism and the old—thoughts after Watergate.

The "fourth estate" of the realm—that was Burke's way of summing up the role of the press in his time, and when one has discounted the medieval terminology, his phrase is no less apt today. It reminds us that the press, as the coequal of other "estates," is a political institution in its own right, intimately bound up with all the institutions of government. It affects them and is affected by them in turn, and together they determine the nature of the regime and the quality of public life. Governmental institutions have political effects through their exercise of legislative, executive, or judicial powers; the press achieves its impact through the way it influences the entry of ideas and information into the "public space" in which political life takes place. So the basic question to be asked about the press is: What is its relation to other political institutions, and how does it consequently manage the "public space"?

The aftermath of Watergate provides a suitable occasion for rethinking this question—though not because the press was in any way at fault in this episode. The Watergate scandals emerge solely from the Nixon Administration's abuse of its Presidential powers in matters ranging from campaign finance and civil liberties to national security. By covering the emerging scandals as it did, the press was acting in accord with a venerable journalistic tradition that dates back to *The New York Times'* exposé of the corrupt Tweed Ring in 1871.

Yet Watergate was more than a series of criminal and corrupt actions; it also has raised basic Constitutional questions concerning the interrelationship among all our political institutions, including of course the press. One of these issues was the freedom of the press. Many of the abuses symbolized by Watergate—the Plumbers, unjustified investigations and wiretaps, and so forth—were in fact directed at the press as part of the Administration's campaign to make the news media less critical. If these efforts had been successful, they would have reduced press freedom and altered the balance between government and the press in favor of the former. For the time being at least, that danger has been averted.

So the press emerges from Watergate as free, self-confident, and enterprising as at any other time in its history. But it also emerges a bit different from what is was before. For the press today is an institution in limbo—an institution in that distinctive kind of trouble which derives from not having a settled idea of its role and purpose. It is in limbo because it now occupies an ambiguous middle ground between its long-standing tradition of "objective" journalism and a new movement for an "adversary" journalism—no longer massively committed to the one but not yet certain, let alone unanimous, about the other. To the extent that it is committed to the new movement, it is committed to a journalistic idea that is not easily compatible with American institutions in their current form, nor easily reconciled with some of its most valuable traditions. And to the extent that the press embraces this movement, its political role will remain in flux until some new practical adaptation to adversary journalism is worked out by government, public opinion, and the press itself. Watergate did not create this problem—it has been growing for a decade now—but it did intensify it. And this is the problem which confronts American journalism after Watergate.

Two kinds of journalism

To put the matter briefly: Traditionally, American journalism has been very close to, dependent upon, and cooperative with, official sources. This has been one of its problems, but it has also been its greatest strength and virtue. For in various ways this arrangement has maximized both the openness and flexibility of American government and the amount of information available to the citizenry. Over the past ten years, however, a small but significant and still-growing segment of the journalistic community has begun to revise this relationship by assuming a posture of greater independence and less cooperativeness. They see this change as a modest reform which will render American journalism purer, better, and truer to its traditional aspirations. In fact, it represents a radical change. In the long run it could make the press "freer" but also less informative and possibly more partisan; and this in turn could make the political system more closed, less flexible, and less competent.

To appreciate the meaning of what has happened, we may begin with the simple fact that journalism is the enterprise of publishing a current account of current events.[1] As such, it cannot proceed until three prior questions have been settled. First, there is the question of how, where, and on what basis to find and validate information. Second, there is the question of the point of view from which events are to be surveyed and characterized. And third, there is the question of the audience to be addressed and the basis on which it is to be aggregated. Abstractly, one can imagine any number of possible resolutions of these issues, but in practice things work out more simply. For wherever one looks in the modern world, daily journalism seems to assume one of two general forms: the partisan and the liberal.

Partisan journalism, which prevails in many European countries, and which has traditionally been represented in the United States by the "journal of opinion" rather than the newspaper, begins with an explicitly political point of view. It is ideological journalism. It aims at assembling an audience that shares its point of view; its object is to interpret public affairs from within that point of view; and it gathers information for the purpose of illuminating and particularizing such interpretation. Such a journalism is less concerned with information as such than with the maintenance and elaboration of its point of view. To it, events are more interesting for the light they cast on its "position" than for what they are, or seem, on their face.

Liberal journalism, by contrast, which prevails in the English-speaking world, is characterized by a preoccupation with facts and events as such, and by an indifference to—indeed, a systematic effort to avoid—an explicitly ideological point of view. It aims instead at appealing to a universal audience on the basis of its non-political, "objective" point of view and its commitment to finding and reporting only "facts" as distinct from "opinion." Liberal journalism strives to be a kind of *tabula rasa* upon which unfolding events and emerging information inscribe themselves. Its principal concern is to find as many events and as much information as it can, and it does this by going to "sources"—persons and organizations directly involved in the events, upon whom it relies both for information and for the validation of this information.

Throughout the 20th century, American journalism has been solidly in the liberal camp. It has sought a universal audience rather than a factional one; its central objective has been to find and publish as much information about as many events as quickly as possible; and it has striven to do this on the basis of a non-partisan, non-political, "facts-only" point of view. Or at least these have been its ideals; the extent of their actual realization has been subject, not only to the vicissitudes of human judgment, but also to two tensions inherent in the very idea of a liberal journalism.

The first of these is the tension between access and autonomy, between the effort of the press to get as much unambiguously true information about as many events as possible—which requires a maximum of access to the actors in these events, which in turn entails a maximum of dependency on these actors—and its effort to preserve its capacity for independent judgment. The second tension arises out of the desire of liberal journalists to avoid taking a political point of view, which conflicts with the inevitability that, in the course of describing events, some sort of point of view will be assumed (observation and writing cannot proceed in the absence of one), and that no point of view will ever be totally devoid of political implications.

Access and independence

To these complex problems, the established liberal tradition of American journalism provides a suitably complex resolution. As between access and autonomy, the tradition opts massively and with a clear conscience for access. This choice is reflected not only in the way newsmen go about their work, but in almost every other feature of American journalism as well, from the form of the news story to the role of the newspaper owner. By opting for access, the American press has given priority and reality to its ideals of acting as a *tabula rasa* and maximizing the amount of raw information it provides to the electorate. This same emphasis on access also goes a long way toward settling, if only unintentionally, the problem of point of view. A *tabula rasa* that is written on primarily by persons involved in events inevitably reflects their slant on the world.

In practice, then, this emphasis on access means the following:

First, virtually all the information published by the press is derived from (and is validated by) "high-level sources," i.e., persons, officials, and organizations actively involved in the events in question.

Second, what newsmen know about the events and issues they cover, and about the general context in which these occur, they acquire almost exclusively from the persons involved rather than from external professional, academic, or ideological sources and authorities.

Third, the point of view from which newsmen write is largely determined by the views, concerns, vocabularies, and situations of those actually involved in public affairs. The viewpoint of the American press is thus a practical rather than ideological or theoretical one.

And fourth, as a result of this emphasis on access, newsmen are routinely aware of—or can easily gather—a truly immense amount of information. They are authentic ringside observers of men and events. They can never publish more than a small fraction of what they know (or have reason to believe), and what they do publish is backed up by a large, if often unarticulated, familiarity with the persons, institutions, and issues involved.

Yet if the "objective" tradition defines American journalism as a primarily derivative and dependent enterprise, it also provides the newsman with a limited but still quite important sphere of independence. Partly this independence has existed by virtue of the sheer volume of events and information which are routinely available to the working newsman. He therefore is confronted with the daily and hourly necessity of choosing, and to choose is to exercise a measure of independent power. This power is enhanced by the fragmentation and indiscipline of American government. Not only do they increase the number of points of access for the newsmen seeking a given bit of information, but they also create for him the opportunity—often exploited in practice—to follow the maxim *divide et impera*, an approach whose utility is made much greater by the almost insatiable appetite of most officials for the two political resources which the newsman possesses automatically: publicity and information. The traditional journalist, then, is not utterly at the mercy of his sources.

Just as important as the fact of the newsman's power is the independent way in which the liberal tradition of American journalism has encouraged him to use that power. To begin with, the tradition demands that the newsman maintain a strict formal independence of his sources: There are to be no financial conflicts of interest, and excessively close personal or ideological relationships are frowned upon. Second, each of the newsman's uses of his selective power is subject to a process of review by his journalistic peers and superiors; not only is the newsman supposed to be free of obligations to his sources, but also he is held answerable before the court of journalistic opinion. Third and most important, there is the traditional norm of "independent" judgment. The newsman is not to have a single, comprehensive, ideological point of view, but the liberal tradition of American journalism does encourage him to have an occasional *ad hoc* opinion and to bring such views to bear in his reporting—provided they pass muster with his journalistic colleagues and superiors, and provided also that there aren't many such opinions and that they manifest themselves only infrequently. (James Reston is an exemplar of this ethos, a man of judgment rather than a man of partisan ideology.) And as vehicles for the expression of these modest and occasional opinions, the liberal tradition sanctions, in addition to "objective" reporting, the devices of muckraking and the "crusade" against a particular instance of inequity. These latter are not often used, but they do remain in the newsman's arsenal to define alternative modes of dealing with institutions and events—and to give the newsman further room for exercising independent judgment.

The liberal tradition

In the liberal tradition, then, the relationship between newsman and source, between press and government, is one of structured interdependence and bartering within an atmosphere of amiable suspiciousness. Each side knows its role. The job of government is to give access and information—*and to do so to a far greater extent than would or could be required by law*. This last point is worth emphasizing, since in this respect American government differs markedly from European (even British) governments. All European journalists are immediately struck by this difference. The American reporter not only has access to official announcements and press releases; he also has the opportunity of becoming the confidant of the official and of enjoying limited but regular access to his personal thoughts, official secrets, internal departmental gossip, and the like.

Of course, there is a price tag on such extraordinary access. The reporter is expected to be generally sympathetic to the public official and his government and to cooperate with them as far as his sense of professionalism permits. Beyond that, the

press is expected to have no strong and comprehensive ideas about the general shape of public affairs; it is officialdom which is collectively entitled to define the topography and limits of public discussion and the news—and each individual official is to have the further opportunity of attempting to shape the content of news to suit his own preferences or purposes.

But the press also has its role and rights. Its main job is to exploit its access and, one way or another, to get as much information as it can into public circulation. It has the right to select freely among the often widely divergent ideas and information circulating within officialdom and to expose corruption and foulups. In exchange, it is expected to see to it that the impression being made on the public is not radically at odds with the reality of affairs as newsmen and officials, from their "inside" perspective, know it to be.

At the level of day-to-day individual interaction, of course, the relationship between press and government in the "objective" tradition is ill-defined and highly variable. There are a few rules of thumb that all parties are expected to observe. Officials are not supposed to lie—at least, hardly ever, and then only for some good public reason. They are also supposed to keep their efforts to deceive newsmen and the public to modest proportions. And they are not ever to use the powers of government to harrass or coerce newsmen. Newsmen, for their part, are expected not to "editorialize" in their news stories and are supposed to give persons accused or disputed in a story an opportunity to tell their own side of the matter. And newsmen are also expected not to publish certain kinds of information without permission: official secrets, information about the seamy side of officials' private lives, and "inside dope" of no particular relevance to public policy. But within these limits, more or less anything goes. There is much uncertainty and much room for maneuver, manipulation, and enterprise on both sides—and for all their mutuality and cooperation, there is also endless conflict between government and press. But in this general scramble there are limits that both of the parties respect.

The great virtue of the liberal tradition of American journalism is that it enables the press to find and print a great deal of information—much more of it, and more quickly, than partisan newspapers can. For the newsman, it has the further advantage of affording him an opportunity to become truly learned and sophisticated about public affairs through an informal process of close personal observation. And for the citizen it has the virtue that it produces news which is generally intelligible. One can know that the content of news is a more or less faithful reflection of affairs as they are understood by the persons engaged in them, or at least as officialdom as a whole sees them. What is more, the general perspective on events is a practical one. News presented in this way, is sensitive to the practitioner's questions of "What next?" and "How to?" and "Who are my friends and enemies?"— and this in turn increases the possibilities that public opinion, reacting to the news, will have significant impact on the day-to-day conduct of government.

Of course, the established tradition has its shortcomings as well, and some of them are quite severe. It is a kind of journalism that is very easily (and very often) manipulated, especially by government but also by newsmen themselves. In any particular instance, the reader can never be absolutely sure that the impression being conveyed to him is a reasonably accurate reflection of the reality of affairs. And beyond that, traditional liberal journalism is perhaps excessively controlled by the ethos and conventional wisdom prevailing among "insiders" and shared by newsmen. In short, the "objective" tradition has the vices and virtues inherent in the idea of acting as a *tabula rasa*. But the virtues are substantial ones too, and the vices, serious though they are, are to no small extent inherent in the very mission of journalism as defined by the liberal tradition: publishing a current account of current events for "the general reader," i.e., the ordinary citizen.

The origins of "adversary" journalism

What I have just described is the operational reality of the liberal tradition of American journalism. The image which that journalism has of itself is not exactly congruent with the reality. Some elements of this image, to be sure, are accurate enough. For instance, newsman correctly believe that they perform three quite different public functions: For the most part, they act as neutral finders and conveyors of information; to some extent they are the "watchdogs" of government; and on rare occasions they advocate the reform of observable inequities. But in other respects, and especially as it depicts the relationship between press and government, the image is a romantic fiction. To listen to traditional newsmen, one would think that the press is completely independent of government in its quest for news, that it routinely searches out vast amounts of hidden, jealously guarded information, that it is constantly defying persons in high office, and that it is the day-in, day-out adversary of "the Establishment" and the equally faithful defender of "the People."

Now this myth of the autonomous, investigative, adversary press does serve a useful purpose. One of the greatest problems of traditional journalism is its proneness to cooptation by its sources. To the extent that newsmen believe and act on their romantic notion of who they are and what they do, the likelihood of their becoming mere uncritical puppets in the hands of their sources is diminished. Moreover, their morale would be lower, their energy smaller, and their self-respect weaker if they subscribed to a truly realistic conception of daily journalism. The romantic image of the "adversary press," then, is a myth: "functional" for certain purposes, but wholly inaccurate as a model of what newsmen actually do or can hope to achieve.

The movement for a new, genuinely adversary journalism which has gained such ground over the past decade arises out of this romantic myth; it is to the liberal tradition of our press what, in a religious context, heresy is to orthodoxy. It is the nature of a heresy to isolate a part of a tradition or doctrine and to treat the part as if it were the whole. The current "heretical" movement in American journalism is defined by the fact that it takes the mythical part of the "orthodox" tradition—the fiction of the autonomous, investigative, adversary press—for the whole of that tradition. It presents itself as an effort to make our press live up to what it always said it was: a journalism that is autonomous instead of interdependent, original instead of derivative, and in an adversary instead of cooperative relationship with government officialdom. Like religious heresies, the movement *appears* to be a "reformation"—an effort to recover the core of a partially but not irrecoverably corrupted tradition. But such appearances are misleading. For, because heresies are simplificatory, what they profess to be "recovering" is actually something that never was and that was never intended to be. What they really advocate, therefore, is the creation of something quite new and different under a smokescreen of rhetoric about restoring what is old and familiar.

Although this movement for a newly purified journalism did not attain real strength until the late 1960's its origins lay somewhat farther in the past. Within the journalistic community, three events were critical in fomenting dissatisfaction with the existing press-government relationship: McCarthyism, the U-2 incident, and the Bay of Pigs. Each cast discredit upon the Cold War itself or the spirit in which government conducted it, and together they caused newsmen to revise their opinion of American institutions and their own relationship to them.

In a way, McCarthyism was the most important. It was a powerful, nationwide movement, and no demagogue can create such a movement without a sounding board in the press. By uncritically repeating and dramatically displaying the sensational charges made by a Senator—in keeping with the usages of objective journalism—the press provided Joe McCarthy with just such a sounding board. In the aftermath of

the McCarthy era, newsmen increasingly agreed that they had permitted themselves to be used irresponsibly. A member of government had abused the power that the objective tradition gave him over the press. The answer, it was generally agreed, was that the press should become more vigilant and critical, and should exercise much more discretion about what it printed in connection with known demagogues, even those in high public office.

Then came the U-2 incident and the Bay of Pigs. In the former case, it may be recalled, various government agencies first said that the flight was for weather research and not espionage (the plane had presumably strayed off course), then said that it was for espionage but that President Eisenhower had not known about it, whereupon Eisenhower came forward and publicly declared that he had known and approved of the program. In the latter case, President Kennedy persuaded *The New York Times*, on grounds of national security, not to print a story on preparations for the Bay of Pigs invasion. After the invasion flopped he publicly stated that the *Times* should have printed the story because he would then have been forced to cancel the invasion, sparing the United States one of the worst foreign policy fiascos in its history. It was not merely that government had lied and suppressed news, and been caught at it. Nor was it only that the press had been used, used easily and with cavalier disrespect, and used wrongly. It was rather that two *Presidents* had publicly admitted lying and suppressing news, and that one of them said the press shouldn't have listened to him. Clearly the problem which the press had identified in the aftermath of McCarthyism was not confined to an occasional demagogue in Congress; it extended to the highest and most respected officials in the land. If one couldn't trust them, evidently one couldn't trust anyone.

The experience of the 1960's

These events marked the beginning of both the "credibility gap" theme in public affairs reporting and a growing truculence among newsmen. By 1966 Clifton Daniel, then managing editor of *The New York Times*, could give a speech saying that the *Times* had been wrong not to print the Bay of Pigs story and would not make such a mistake again. The *Times* is of course our preeminent jounalistic institution; it had previously been cooperative with government about national security matters; and it does not make admissions of error lightly, if at all. The speech was a watershed in modern journalistic history, and it served notice that an important article in the informal covenant between press and government was being renegotiated, if not unilaterally repudiated.

This issue might have been resolved satisfactorily had not four further developments supervened. One of these was the steep decline, during the 1960's, in the competitiveness of the "prestige" newsmarkets, especially New York, which quietly but effectively shifted the balance of power between newsmen and sources. When *The New York Times* had been actively in competition with the *Herald-Tribune*, their newsmen felt constrained to maintain friendly relationships with sources so that their opposite numbers would not get "exclusives"—and sources, as a consequence, could "whipsaw" newsmen to keep them in line. When the *Times*, the Washington *Post*, and other leading newspapers no longer had any true local competitors, their newsmen became less beholden, and sources became relatively weaker. Since these newsmen worked for newspapers which were widely respected and emulated by lesser publications, and since in any event they produced a large portion of the national news coverage published in the country, this shift had effects out of all proportion to the number of newspapers immediately involved. (Significantly, the only truly competitive comprehensive national news services—AP and UPI—have been little affected by the emergence of the movement for an "adversary" journalism.)

A second important development was the growth in the visibility, self-consciousness,

and self-confidence of the journalistic profession, and especially of the Washington press corps. Traditionally, reporting had been a low-prestige occupation; some studies reported it to rank *between* the blue-collar and white-collar occupations. In the 1960's this began to change. President Kennedy showed a special fondness for newsmen; the inauguration in 1963 of the national half-hour television news programs gave the press a new vehicle of unprecedented power and created, overnight, a batch of jounalistic celebrities; officials became ever more attentive to the press, and their efforts to manipulate the news grew in scale and sophistication; books and articles about the press began to proliferate; and by the beginning of the 1970's scale salaries at leading newspapers approached (and, in TV, exceeded) those of Assistant Secretaries. Whatever the cause, newsmen had a growing sense of their importance and a corresponding unwillingness to accept the dependency and subordination which, as it seemed, had been characteristic of the position of the press in earlier decades.

Third, there was the extraordinary political and cultural ferment of the 1960's, involving a dramatic expansion and intensification of political conflict and the emergence of countercultural, anti-establishment, and other oppositional movements. The spirit of the age had its impact on the journalistic community, especially on its younger, newly-recruited members. The psychological distance between press and government and the frequency of stories critical of established policy grew.

More important than this direct form of cultural influence, however, was the indirect influence of the spirit of the 1960's upon jounalism. As we have noted, the traditional mode of American journalism was dependent and derivative; the press largely reflected the ideas and balance of power in official circles. As the 1960's wore on, an ever larger segment of officialdom itself became sympathetic to the oppositional fashions of the decade. Not only "the kids" and other people "out there," but also Senators, committee chairmen, Washington lawyers, and Assistant Secretaries began to articulate the spirit of "confrontation" and "alienation." Thus, as ideological movements of opinion became stronger, traditional journalism found itself having to choose from among a variety of perspectives, all of which could claim some official standing. Merely by continuing to report public affairs in the traditional way, the press gave increasing exposure to the ideas and symbols of the oppositional movements.

The White House vs. the press

This led in turn to the fourth development which fostered the current movement for a "new journalism": the intensification of opposition to the movements of the 1960's, both in public opinion at large and within specific institutions and political circles. One of the ways in which such "backlash" sentiment expressed itself was by attacking the press for giving exposure to those movements, and one of the most prominent sources of such attacks was the White House, beginning with Lyndon Johnson. For a variety of reasons—good, bad, and indifferent—both Johnson and his successor chose to resist the growing truculence of the press and the exposure it gave to the growing anti-war and other oppositional movements in the country as a whole. As in Vietnam, so on the homefront: With each escalation of the President's campaign against the press, the press seemed to counter with an added measure of defiance and a little more coverage of oppositional politics.

At first the belligerents fought their battles with the conventional weapons of legitimate political warfare. LBJ used the personal approach (flattering and punishing reporters, making telephone calls to network executives, etc.) and the traditional devices of political public relations (emphasizing good news and deemphasizing the bad, manipulating the appearance of events, wheeling out various "experts" and "authorities" to defend his positions, and the like). The Nixon Administration, in its early months, added to these devices the long-range artillery of Agnewian rhetoric and an elaborately centralized system of "public information." These tactics not only didn't work, they seemed only to confirm the press in its new determination to be independent, which in context meant critical.

As feelings on both sides grew more embittered, their tactics became more unconventional and the struggle more total: It was an omen of the Watergate era to come. The Administration—which in this escalation was clearly the aggressor—launched FBI investigations of newsmen it felt to be hostile; deprived the press of traditional forms of access, such as the press conference, the casual telephone conversation, and the cocktail party; threatened television stations with loss of their licenses; in the first case of prior censorship in American history, brought suit to enjoin the publication of the Pentagon papers; and set up the Plumbers to stop unauthorized leaks. The press countered with heavy coverage of anti-Nixon political elements, publication of secret government documents (the Pentagon and Anderson papers) which they would not have dreamed of making public ten years earlier, and a growing pattern of refusing to accept the legality of subpoenas issued by courts in the course of due legal processes. There was also a certain tendency to begin ignoring traditional journalistic standards of fairness and truth. When the Supreme Court issued its "Caldwell" decision in 1972, which at most only upheld the existing rules defining the testimonial obligations of newsmen, the press interpreted this as a *change* in Constitutional law that reduced freedom of the press. A year before, in "The Selling of the Pentagon," CBS-TV editors falsified the continuity of a filmed interview with a Pentagon official. And when the actions of any newsman were challenged or criticized, increasingly the journalistic community as a whole drew together in defense of its own, right or wrong. Jack Anderson was given the Pulitzer prize for publishing a National Security Council minute concerning the American position in a current, explosive diplomatic situation, and "The Selling of the

Pentagon,'' despite its dubious editing, was cited for excellence in the television documentary category.

The new mood

The upshot of these developments was that the liberal press particularly—and to an increasing extent other parts of the journalistic community as well—found itself ever more committed to a stance of truculent independence from government and officialdom. Increasingly it felt that its proper role was not to cooperate with government but to be independent of it, or even opposed to it. Increasingly newsmen began to say that their job was to be an autonomous, investigative adversary of government and to constitute a countervailing force against the great authority of all established institutions. And increasingly they began to see as illegitimate the few traditional formal constraints upon the press: libel law, ''fair trial'' restrictions on news coverage, testimonial obligations upon all citizens to give their evidence under subpoena, and the laws defining and protecting government secrets. These sentiments, and the actions which in modest but growing number gave concrete expression to them, define the movement for a ''new journalism'' which exists today and which poses the central question which the press will have to cope with after Watergate.

It is impossible to state with any precision or sense of certainty just how widespread and securely entrenched this movement is. Its only clearly identifiable location seems to be generational: It is young reporters, in their twenties and early thirties, who seem most to share the attitudes that define the movement. In general, though, it is more a mood than a settled, behavioral pattern; a thing more of the spirit than of the flesh; a tendency or yearning more than an established and institutional accomplishment. And yet it is a fact. If it is not so widespread or influential as current conservative critics of the media insist, it is also more substantial than defenders of the

movement admit. It exists; it really is unlike that which has prevailed in our journalism for decades; it could yet become dominant; and it makes a difference.

The Blasi findings

A recent study by Professor Vince Blasi of the Michigan Law School suggests something of the extent to which the attitudes of this movement have gained ground in the journalistic community. As a means of measuring the need for and effects of ''shield'' legislation, Blasi in 1972 asked a non-random sample of almost 1,000 newsmen to respond to the following hypothetical situation:

You have a continuing source relationship with a group of political radicals. They have given you much information in confidence and this has enabled you to write several byline stories describing and assessing in general terms the activites and moods of the group. During the course of this relationship, you are present at a closed meeting with ten of these radicals at which the group vigorously debates whether to bomb a number of targets, including the local police station. The consensus is against such bombing, but two members of the group argue very heatedly in favor of bombing and are deeply upset when the others refuse to go along. These two then threaten to act on their own. The discussion then turns to another topic. Two weeks later the local police station is in fact bombed. One officer is killed by the blast and two others are seriously injured.

The first question Blasi posed was this: ''In these circumstances, would you on your own initiative volunteer the information you learned at the meeting *right after the meeting* (i.e., before a bombing took place)?'' Of those who responded, 26.2 per cent answered ''yes,'' 55.5 per cent ''no,'' and the rest gave no answer.

Question #2: ''Would you volunteer the information on your own initiative to law enforcement authorities *after the bombing* (but before you were contacted by the police or subpoenaed by a grand jury)?'' Answer: 37.6 per cent yes, 36.0 per cent no, 26.4 per cent no answer.

Question #3: "Assume that you were subpoenaed by a grand jury investigating the bombing but that an absolute legal privilege were established so that you could not be compelled to answer questions against your will. Would you voluntarily answer if the grand jury asked you whether this group of radicals had ever discussed the possibility of bombing the police station?" Answer: 45.5 per cent yes, 36.0 per cent no, 18.5 per cent no answer.

Question #4: "If the grand jury asked you to name the members of the group who had advocated bombing?" Answer: 36.9 per cent yes, 44.1 per cent no, 19.0 per cent no answer.

Question #5: "Assume that one of the members of the group who had argued vigorously *against* the bombing was indicted for the crime and that you believed, on the basis of the meeting, that it is highly unlikely that this particular member was the bomber. Would you on your own initiative volunteer this information to the prosecutor?" Answer: 60 per cent yes, 22.2 per cent no, 17.8 per cent no answer.

Question #6: "If this member's defense lawyer subpoenaed you at the trial would you testify about the meeting you had witnessed (including giving the names of those who did advocate the bombing) even if you were protected by an absolute privilege so that you couldn't be compelled to testify?" Answer: 43.2 per cent yes, 36.4 per cent no, 20.4 per cent no answer.

In the liberal tradition of "objective" journalism, newsmen cooperated with government and especially with law enforcement officials in serious felonies like bombing and murder. One may safely assume that, at some point, a traditional reporter would have given his information to the authorities and defense lawyers—albeit with a guilty conscience over having broken his pledge of confidentiality.[2] Blasi's newsmen show the opposite inclination. Even in a case of bombing, death, and serious injury, only one fourth said they would warn authorities of the possibility of a bombing beforehand; only two fifths said they would volunteer their information after the bombing; less than half were sure they would tell a grand jury that the group had discussed the possibility of bombing; and only two fifths were willing to name the persons who had advocated the bombing. And most startling of all, *almost three fifths of this sample of 1,000 reporters were unwilling to say that they would go to court to testify in defense of persons on trial for murder even if they had information tending to show the defendants to be innocent and others to be guilty.*

Issues of confidentiality

Of course, these are only attitudes; it is quite possible—even likely—that, in the crunch, no more than a handful of newsmen would actually withhold their evidence in such circumstances. But in a way that is beside the point. What is to the point is that these attitudes are widely perceived to exist among newsmen, and that a few newsmen have begun to act on the basis of them. Together these developments have raised two large and disagreeable issues which our political and legal processes are now forced to grapple with.

One of these is the problem posed by the unauthorized publication of secret or confidential government documents, ranging from White House memoranda and secret depositions before grand juries to Jack Anderson's National Security Council minute or William Beecher's summary of the U.S. fallback position in the SALT-I negotiations. In large part, to be sure, the issue here should focus more on the persons responsible for leaking documents than on the press, which merely publishes them; surely the proper initial defendant, in a legal test of this process, is not *The New York Times* but Daniel Ellsberg, not Jack Anderson but his sources (apparently in the Pentagon). Yet it is also an issue that concerns the press itself because, until recently, the press, out of regard for national security or fear of the consequences, would not have published the Pentagon papers (though it might well have written *about* them, in a veiled and guarded way). Today, obviously, it will publish them, and the result is that we are confronted squarely with a new issue that we would be better off not having to deal with.

It is an impossible issue. However it is resolved, or even if it is not resolved, we will be worse off than we were before it was raised. It involves a conflict among three valuable traditions—press freedom, confidentiality in government, and the relatively open or amorphous quality of American government. Conflicts among these traditions have heretofore been resolved on an informal, *ad hoc* basis. To attempt to resolve them systematically and formally is to lose much and to gain little, if anything. One does need secrecy and confidentiality in government: to protect national security from enemy powers, to ensure that persons in government will feel free to write down on paper their best individual judgments on issues of fact and policy, and perhaps most of all to preserve the ability of officials (especially the President) to be flexible and to take initiatives. (Premature leaks are the tried-and-true device for forestalling Presidential initiatives in policy and administration, or for rendering them ineffective once taken.) On the other hand, one does not want Congress to make any law abridging the freedom of the press in order to preserve this confidentiality. Nor does one want to take the path of enacting an official secrets act that provides severe penalties for any civil servant who leaks information without formal approval from the highest authorities. This last measure would sharply reduce the amount and range of perfectly harmless and also useful information that would be made—is now made—available to the press, usually to the benefit of us all; it would also reduce the ability of Congress to oversee the Executive, since it would know less about what was going on. Thus, by retreating from its old cooperative notion of public responsibility, the press has created an issue which cannot be resolved without changing the American system as a whole in some fundamental—and unattractive—way.

More or less the same is true of the second issue raised by the current movement for a new journalism: the question of the testimonial obligations of newsmen. In the past several years, journalists have begun to insist with increasing frequency and vehemence that they should not be compelled by grand juries or courts to disclose information they have gathered from sources on a confidential basis. To do so, they say, will cause sources to give less information to the press, which in turn will reduce the amount of information citizens can glean from newspapers. Previously, newsmen had generally cooperated with the law enforcement establishment. Now, partly because of the increasingly adversarial stance of newsmen towards government, and partly also because more newsmen have begun to cover the activities of radical, violent, or criminal groups, this has changed. A number of newsmen have chosen to go to jail rather than reveal the identity of confidential informants or the substance of what they learned from them. And in defense of this choice they have offered the further argument that the press is now subjected to so many subpoenas—over a four-year period beginning in 1968, for instance, the Chicago *Tribune* received more than 400—that its operations are truly disrupted and its freedom, as a practical matter, is reduced.

Should we then enact shield legislation exempting newsmen from their testimonial obligations? Perhaps, but to do so is not without its costs. With certain minor and traditional exceptions, all citizens are now obligated to give their evidence before courts of law. It is hard to see why newsmen should be made a class apart in this respect; and it is likely that such an exemption would render our system of criminal justice less effective. The price of immunity for journalists would be less justice for everyone else. Here, too, we have a dilemma that is created by the newsman's increasing withdrawal of his consent from the traditional covenant of cooperative suspiciousness between the press and government. To resolve the issue is to change the American system in fundamental—and, again, unattractive—ways.

A retreat from the liberal ideal

The deeper problem with this movement for a new journalism, however, is that it represents an incipient retreat, not merely from an intelligible idea of the public interest and of the responsibility of the press to serve it, but also from the entire liberal tradition of American journalism and the system of liberal democracy which it has fostered and served. The problem of the press publishing a few government secrets or withholding the names of an occasional criminal may be serious in principle but it is usually negligible in practice. But there is a larger practical question raised by "adversary" journalism that is not at all negligible: the question of the persistence of the open, fragmented, liberal system of American democracy as we have known it and benefited from it for the past many decades.

Our instinct is to assume that this system is virtually indestructible, rooted as it is in the pragmatic temper of the American people, the Constitutional system of division of powers, and other such factors apparently beyond the influence of what we do or think. This is a reasonable assumption within limits, but it isn't entirely true. The system also depends on many institutions and attitudes which are indeed changeable, and one of the most important—if least acknowledged—of these is the kind of press we have. Its capacity to find and publish vast amounts of information about politics and government, and its success in reaching universal audiences without regard to ideology or political affiliations, have contributed in an important way to the openness and flexibility of American government and to the ability of public opinion to influence the conduct of public affairs and to attain consensus. As the press has become wealthier in recent decades, its ability to gather and print information has increased; as political party organizations have declined, the need and willingness of officials to give newsmen access have also

grown; so even while the complexity of government and the amount of "classified" information have increased, the capacity of the press to help the American system realize its ideals has at least kept pace.

The new movement abroad in the journalistic community threatens all this. For the press can make its contribution to the system only by maintaining close access—a closer access, as I have said, than can ever be provided by law. The price of such access is some degree of cooperation and sympathy for government—*not* a slavish adulation, as is sometimes said, but a decent respect for authority, a willingness to see government and persons in government given the opportunity to do their job, and at least a slight sense of responsibility for and commitment to the goals inherent in those jobs. When these are not present, access diminishes. And when newsmen begin to assert they are positively the adversaries of government, access diminishes drastically, and with it not only the contribution journalism can make but also the openness and flexibility of government itself. Politicians and officials are no more than human; they have their needs and interests; above all they intend to survive. If they feel themselves to be threatened or harmed, they will eventually take steps to insulate themselves as best they can from the danger.

The history of the Nixon Administration shows some of the ways in which this can occur. At one extreme there is Watergate itself—that is, the Plumbers, wiretaps and investigations of newsmen, harrassment of news organizations, and the like. This is an irrational and pathological response which is as unnecessary as it is intolerable, and we are not likely to see a recurrence in the discernible future. But the Nixon Administration used other methods as well, and these we can expect to see more of, regardless of who is in the White House, if the movement continues to gain ground. There is "jawboning": making speeches criticizing press coverage in hopes of reducing the press' credibility and increasing its cooperativeness. More important, there is the technique of organizing and formalizing all press-government contacts through the instrument of the Public Affairs/Public Information office and the centralized public relations operation, such as the one inaugurated by Herb Klein. And most powerful of all, there is the simple device of self-isolation, on the theory that it is better to have less of a bad press than more of a good press, especially in light of the fact that the effort to seek the latter can so easily end up earning one more of the former. Such a "low-profile" strategy—with infrequent and irregular press conferences, sharply limited informal contact between officials and reporters, even reliance on a praetorian staff lacking extensive ties outside the official family—is one of Richard Nixon's original contributions to the American political tradition. It is clearly an undesirable contribution, especially in its Nixonesque form, and yet it represents a logical adaptation to the perceived existence of an adversary press; the chances are we will see more of it insofar as the new movement gains ground. By the end of his campaign, even George McGovern seemed to be changing his mind about the desirability of having an "open" staff in constant informal contact with the press. The result, as he not unreasonably perceived it, was a bad press which emphasized the confusion and in-fighting within his official family and which thus suggested that McGovern was not a competent executive. It is hard to imagine that if he had won in 1972 he would have continued his policy of openness. The price is simply too high for any rational man to want to pay, and the benefits, if any, are too few and too small.

And as government adapts to the situation created by the current movement for a new journalism, so will the entire profession of journalism—and in ways that it does not envision. As has been pointed out, the traditional form of the news story, the news organization's pattern of recruiting and training newsmen, even the format of the modern newspaper are all geared to the liberal, orthodox mode of journalism, with its preoccupation with facts and events, its relative unconcern for the problem of point of view, and its intention of appealing to a universal audience. In order to work, such a journalism needs reporters to have access to government, and when they no longer have it the capacity of newspapers to maintain the other features of the existing form is weakened, as is the whole idea of and justification for those features. Journalism will change—and the logical direction of change is toward the partisan form of journalism, with its ideological basis, politically based relationship to the government in power, and fractionated audiences. It is possible, of course, that an adversary journalism could persist indefinitely, but this seems unlikely. A stance of "pure" opposition—opposition as an end in itself, rather than as an expression of some larger, positive political commitment—is self-contradictory in theory and likely to be short-lived in practice. The probability is that an adversary press would eventually ally itself with a policital faction and so become partisan—an ideologically divisive factor rather than a politically unifying force. The consequences could be enormous.

Two scenarios for the future

Now the partisan mode of journalism has its virtues. It does not evade the problem of "point of view" as liberal journalism does, and in this sense it has an appealing honesty. It also has the capacity to create and sustain coherent bodies of political opinion; at a time when political opinion in this country is so often contradictory and inchoate, that is a very important trait. This is why "journals of opinion," existing on the margins of American journalism, have been so important and desirable.

But if, over the long run, American journalism were ever to turn massively to the partisan mode, the consequences of this development would extend to nearly every aspect of our political system. Partisan journalism would not increase the openness of the system, it would sharply decrease it. It would not reduce the scope of political conflict, but enlarge it. It would not increase the capacity of American government to act effectively and flexibly in meeting emergent needs, but would tend to paralyze it. It would not empower public opinion as a whole, but would transform it into a congeries of rigid ideological factions eternally at war with one another and subject to the leadership of small coteries of ideologues and manipulators. Indeed, it would tend to transform the entire nature of American politics: From having been a popular government based on a flexible consensus, it would become Europeanized into a popular government based on an equilibrium of hostile parties and unchanging ideologies.

The alternative to such a "Europeanization" of journalism and politics, it should be emphasized, does not have to be a massive and uncritical reversion to the way things were during the 1950's and early 1960's. Even if this were possible—which it isn't—it would clearly be undesirable. Both officialdom and the press were then busily abusing the "objective" tradition, officialdom by treating the media as an institution to be deliberately "managed" for its own expediential purposes, and the press by encouraging and acquiescing in these efforts out of inertia and a generalized avidity to print "big news" as often and as easily as possible.

There are ways to curb these abuses while still preserving the benefits of the liberal tradition of our press which the "adversary" approach would squander. Government can increase the amount of information which is formally made available on the public record. It can scale down its "public relations" operations to the point where they cannot easily operate as instruments of press management and are content instead merely to disseminate information. As Joseph Lee Auspitz and Clifford W. Brown, Jr., have suggested, the "strategic" cast of mind giving rise to, among other things, the habit of "managing" the press for purposes of personal power can be discouraged by strengthening the political party, which embeds individual actors in an institutional context, channels and restrains their ambition, and promotes a "representative" as against a "strategic" ethos. And

the press, for its own part, can help to recover the objective tradition by abandoning its flirtation with the "oppositional" posture and by ceasing to exploit public affairs for their sensation value (since the desire to exploit public affairs in this way is the main incentive leading the press to acquiesce in the manipulations of "strategically"-minded officials). The result, I believe, will be a journalism that provides more, and more useful, information to the citizenry, and a political system that, in consequence, comes a bit closer than in the past to realizing its historic ideals.

NOTES

1. I should point out that I am using the terms "journalism" and the "press" in these pages to refer to *daily* journalism only—that is, to daily newspapers and broadcast news programs. There are other forms of journalism, of course: weekly, monthly, quarterly, general purpose, special purpose, and so on. These other forms are important and interesting, and they perform crucial functions vis-à-vis government and the daily press itself. Unfortunately, space prevents me from considering them in this essay.

2. Writing in the January 15, 1973 issue of *New York*, Richard Reeves described a classic instance of the traditional relationship. "I remember. . .my first big story with *The New York Times* in the summer of 1966. . .a homicide case against a young man named Ernest Gallashaw, accused in the shooting of a ten-year-old boy during racial rioting in the East New York section of Brooklyn. . . .In ten days or so. . .I came back with notebooks full of interviews and evidence that made it clear. . .that New York City authorities were playing fast and loose with Gallashaw's life and freedom. . . .I wrote a three-column story, but just before deadline. . .I was told that it would not be published immediately and that I was to turn over our evidence to the Brooklyn District Attorney's office.

". . .Clifton Daniel, then the managing editor. . .explained. . .that homicide investigations were government business. . . .The *Times* ran the complete story a day later, beginning on page 1 with a lead saying the District Attorney was investigating new evidence in the case."

Liberal

Martin Wenglinsky. Television news: a new slant.

For at least three years now we have heard redundant public controversy over bias in television news, every political faction contending at some point that television does not portray events "accurately." And all sides are, of course, correct: television news is biased against the views from the political right, left, and center because it pursues a reality of its own, created out of the particular kind of truth for which newsmen search regardless of their own political sentiments. At its best, and under certain circumstances, television news both makes and reports the news, offering a portrait of the world wherein the perception of the viewer is the meaning of the event.

But to see all this more concretely, we should first clear away the accumulated charges and countercharges by radicals, conservatives, and liberals.

Radicals contend that television news is ruled by the interests of big business, most especially Eastern Establishment business, and so one can predict what events news programs will, as we say, "cover" and how they will cover them, or cover them up. The suffering of the poor is underplayed, and the resistance of the downtrodden to their oppressors is portrayed by television news as criminal or else sick. Indeed, ghetto riots are no longer much *shown* at all, now that networks and local stations have reflected on their coverage of certain events in the 1960's. Today, television producers seem to see themselves as acting responsibly when they censor such coverage lest it encourage others to join a dangerous action; but were they to apply this doctrine of "responsibility" for the *results* of news broadcasting evenhandedly, they would long since have stopped reporting news briefings by Presidential spokesmen, Presidents, or other self-admitted liars.

The power of the press, so the radical argument goes, is like a telescope: magnifying the importance of those in power, diminishing the grievances—and the very presence—of those with little power. When radicals themselves appear on television, it is usually on talk shows, where they entertain (and so are not taken seriously) by shocking. Radical spokesmen used to turn up on Sunday interview programs too, on the occasional slow week. But the hostile questioning of Tom Hayden on "Face The Nation" some years ago caught perfectly the style in which they were handled: the interviewers found time to ask Hayden why he was not grateful for the democratic freedom that allowed him to appear on national television in the first place—a gratuitous attempt to put a malcontent in his place, though he was in a place he had every right to be in. By that logic, the substance of freedom is that grievances vanish because they are heard. When Hayden explained that his brief appearance hardly countervailed the general tenor of public affairs broadcasting, he was asked, reasonably, why he then bothered appearing at all. He answered that it was to keep faith with his compatriots, in preparation for the period of harassment and suppression he believed the country would soon face. Prophetic or not, his defense was lame. The radicals of the 1960's were wedded to the media because they thought it the most powerful force for social control. At the same time they found it beyond their power to influence.

Perhaps the quintessential demonstration of free expression on television was a "Merv Griffin Show" of a few years ago, which Griffin announced, with much self-congratulation, as a no-holds-barred discussion of the medium itself by several of its critics, a discussion that would show just how brave and free television was. (If it was free, one wondered, why was bravery or congratulation required?) Nicholas Johnson, then a member of the Federal Communications Commission, proceeded to offer some genuinely critical remarks—the most pointed of which were edited out before the tape was broadcast.

What is further apparent to radicals is that television commentaries range only from conservative to liberal. Why no radical spokesman to join James Kilpatrick and Nicholas Von Hoffman on "60 Minutes" or Howard K. Smith and Harry Reasoner on A.B.C.? Edward P. Morgan is much subdued of late, and Sander Vanocur left N.B.C. because of what he said were restrictions on being a network newsman. I remember one delectable on-the-air discussion among N.B.C. correspondents after the assassination of Robert F. Kennedy. Vanocur had been on the plane returning to New York from Los Angeles with the Kennedy party. He was asked for the tone of things during the trip, and he said that he wasn't supposed to say: the Kennedy people thought there might be a conspiracy to kill Kennedys. Someone quickly interjected that Vanocur's answer was, of course, not seriously meant. Vanocur did not take the hint, and said the Kennedy people were quite serious. The others were clearly embarrassed, as if by a breach of taste. On television, questions of censorship are always perceived as matters of taste.

For their part, conservatives are well aware of the plentitude of liberal newsmen. George Wallace has always gotten a harsher going-over on television than other politicians. The case for segregated schools is not made, but shots of charred school buses in Michigan and violent crowds in Boston are in ample supply. Newsmen are, of course, against bureaucracy, yet they picture every new government program as quite possibly a step in the right direction, as if attempts or beginnings meant successful results. And newsmen were always soft on the Vietnam war, overcome by misgivings about refugees even as they raised few questions about the Viet Cong's taxes, drafts, and confiscations among the Vietnamese.

To be sure, many conservative objections to newscasting can be answered by saying that there simply are not two sides to every story; that in some instances no "conservative case" can be made, because in the hands of any but a few ideologues like William F. Buckley, Jr., who are continually pressed into service to defend the minority view, conservatism in this country is not so much a governmental philosophy as a defense of privilege with little consistency of principle from one case to another. But the networks disregard the fact that liberalism too is a defense of privilege, and that a great number of liberals defend their viewpoint no better than conservatives. Network people make the substantive judgment (which I share) that in our country liberal thought can justify liberal opinion, while much of conservative opinion (and, in a way, radical opinion) cannot be turned into thought and debate because it is only a defense of prejudices and nasty sentiments. Perhaps that is why, when the networks defended themselves against Vice President Agnew's attacks on bias in the news, their answers seemed disingenuous, and, at the very least, begged the question. It was as if they had no need to consider the merits of the question, only the self-serving source. By way of defense, the networks pointed out that many commentators were in fact born in the Midwest—when the point is that they are selected because they identify with a cosmopolitan point of view. Network people further maintained that every wink and raised eyebrow could seem, to the paranoid critic, an interpretation—when selectivity of coverage is the issue. And they insisted that freedom of the press must be inviolate—when, in fact, the networks have a monopoly on national news and need to be responsible to some form of pressure other than the obtuseness of their affiliates.

Conservatives also recognize in news coverage the liberal belief that the march of progress forbids retrograde speculation. An issue, once settled, is settled: no longer subject to controversy, but part of the common wisdom. Soon after the New York State law eliminating most restriction on abortion came into effect, C.B.S. denied a request for equal time by the Catholic Archdiocese of New York to present its point of view. That is, C.B.S. had been reporting on abortion clinics and the lives they saved but refused air time to those who felt C.B.S. was not considering the prenatal lives that were being lost. The corporate explanation was that C.B.S. would in the full course of normal news coverage offer a balanced representation. In short, the producing agency would decide what was a balance, how much of each side was enough, whether there was a moral issue left over about which the public might change its mind, or whether what was left over was just the honking of the unenlightened.

Pushed to the wall, liberal (and network) opinion about news on television denies that political perspective is the issue at all: the media, it claims, are attacked for being the bearers of bad but truthful tidings, and since both Left and Right attack them, they must be doing their job properly. If reportage has its limitations, they further claim, these are due to the economic and practical problems of putting on news programs daily. Newsmen cover radical violence rather than radical press conferences because there are only so many film crews, and they need something "visual." Presenting complex events, like a gold crisis, does not, furthermore, build ratings—and anyway, there is just not enough time to present enough of the facts to make such events comprehensible. And finally, such events are boring: how many shots of bullion in vaults will people watch as a "visual" for the "voice-over"?

But the view that informs the selection and presentation of news is not to be found in news producers' appeals to the non-ideological madhouse of day-to-day operations, nor even in the discrete actions or decisions that producers make on the job. Rather, it stands out in high relief in the product actually presented on the screen. First off, the principle of selection is not that of greatest visual impact. Most news stories are in fact voice-overs with only the most general relation to the picture on the screen. Stories about food shortages or agricultural problems show fields of grain with or without reapers, barns with or without livestock. Stories on transportation or gas prices or mass-transit fares show a subway or automobiles going by. Stories on rent control show buildings. Such camera shots do not explain or even present the event and could have been made years before and used for any number of stories. (One can understand the news producers' practice of using old footage of riots or bombings as

coverage of present events: they all look alike on television.) Certainly such shots do not deliver discrete information. What they do deliver is what television news in general conveys, a compendium of buildings, subways, fields, and news conferences, a travelogue of ongoing American life, with occasional film of aircraft wreckage and flooded land. Pictures of rat-infested apartments or the faces of politicians answering questions can occasionally be illuminating. But not often, and television producers know this better than we do.

Second, the working principle of news selection is not "to show the unusual": the dog-bites-man dictum. If it were, we would be spared the repetitious statements of candidates and officials and even the fact of continually rising food prices. There is nothing new in these, even if they are important. As for arrests for corruption or murder, as for forest fires and lost children, these are not even important events, unless they are explicitly connected to matters of public policy.

Inevitably, then, we have to conclude that political and social judgment *do* guide news selection: the producer selects as being important those items which affect the people at large. Rising prices and mass transit fares do affect the people at large, but Sunday backyard barbecues do not, except when they indicate changing styles of life because of price increases. Stories about what people do on a hot summer Sunday or about lost children are described by newsmen as "human interest": not real news, but sufficiently poignant or attractive to catch the viewer's attention. They provide a respite from serious news, but newsmen who overplay them are thought unprofessional. And so it is that the Governor's announcement of something or other is covered because it is believed that what he does affects our lives more than does a sit-in at a hospital by members of the local community. Protestors are of interest when they are violent; or when they are, like Cesar Chavez, seen by the newsmen as legitimate.

But news is not selected for being *immediately* important to most of us. Weather reports, if they were supposed to be informative, would be shorter. War and crime news affect us hardly at all: few of us have been mugged today, and none of us have sons at the front at the moment. Practical news of the sort that fills country newspapers—births and deaths, promotions and local festivals—is presented on television, not as a calendar of events to be used, but as a continuing report on the life of the city and the world. In New York we know there will be a report on the San Gennaro Festival in Greenwich Village every summer on local New York stations. That tells us what season it is, and furthers the idea of community that television exists to impart. Most New Yorkers don't go to the Festival but want to know it is there, just as they praise New York for its theaters, museums, and restaurants, even if these have almost nothing to do with their reason for living in New York.

Television news is in fact a marvel of construction that allows snippets of material to give us both a daily sense of the continuing drama of Watergate or Edward Kennedy or John Lindsay or Clifford Irving, and of the continuing background of floods and famine, wars and crime, poverty and consumer fads, that make up the saga of the contemporary world. We are not so much told what is important to our daily lives as what is important to and makes up public life—which is a world defined by the newsmen's sense of it. The newsman in turn is as tightly bound by the conventions of this, his genre, as is the composer of musical comedy.

Consider, for instance, that television news rarely presents the decisions and personalities of major figures in business corporations, but minor management troubles in a city agency are covered in detail: corruption in government is thought to be news, while waste and inefficiency in corporations is not. Americans believe business is more efficient than government. Is that because high overheads for office decoration and expense accounts are not made as visible or subject to inquiry as a congressional junket or political favoritism on the public payroll? Corporation officials should be no more able to escape reporters than are public officials—but they are. Economic news is clearly as important in the making as when it finally and dramatically breaks through into the consumer's life. It is just that government, like baseball, the weather, and crime, is a traditional subject in the contemporary epic of news, while, for the most part, ongoing events in large corporations and universities and literature are not.

In short, the whole of the news constitutes a world of its own. What gives dynamism and interest to a shot of a hood being hurried through a crowd to a federal courthouse is the very real art of news coverage.

But before we conclude that television news is a sort of traveling show, with its own stock characters and cliché situations, we had better remember that this particular form of entertainment is presumed to have some share of literal truth, to represent factual reality, and so influences our sense of the world. From it we are given daily a view of continuing and contending forces in the social landscape, much as in a medieval church we would be reminded of where we stood in relation to Hell, Purgatory, and Heaven. We place ourselves within this mental landscape, and, like the medieval one, it can affect major and minor decisions in our lives: we choose, say, to move to the suburbs or away from a stranger because the news keeps telling us to beware the mugger. Our experience of TV news is vicarious and archetypal experience, as in the medieval mental landscape, an unfolding tapestry into which we place, say, our dwindling savings accounts or the price-rise at our own supermarket. With inflation the official story, our own trouble with grocery bills becomes a social rather than a personal problem, just as malicious gossip about a neighbor becomes part of the cosmic drama of salvation when the preacher convinces us there is retribution for the spiteful.

One can of course be a heretic and dispute the official version—that is, find the news media's version of the Democratic convention of 1968 unpersuasive, discordant with one's own philosophy and experience and unsanctified secondary sources. But, as with other heresies, there is a price to pay for refusing the facts from the pulpit in favor of the facts of one's own life. If it seems unjust for the poor to get all that attention and sympathy from television when you have a mortgage on your semi-detached quarter-acre to worry about, you may be able to make all the economic facts fit your theory; but you will pay the price of having an unofficial theory—feeling like an outsider even as you savor the satisfaction of believing that your theory is unofficial because it is true.

Television's continuing interpretation of life gives rise, then, to a sense of being in agreement or dissent, and so to a sense of society as being divided between an establishment and the conspirators—you and I—for or against it, depending upon who agrees or disagrees with the official television view. If we think Mayor Daley is the people's man at Chicago, and the networks and the radical politicians are in conspiracy against him, that is why he looks bad on TV. Indeed, can the networks tell the truth, even if they are in agreement with some party but in conspiracy with none? That might be called honest bias, but it is bias nonetheless. Truth is terribly difficult to sift out, a matter of motives and interests rather than a product of that ideological shibboleth "objectivity." It has always been that way, deciding whether the king's representative speaks for him or on his own, whether the church or a particular preacher is for God or against Him. The difference is that we, the television viewers, experience a sort of sermon every night, and it claims a political rather than a religious truth. The church made no claim that the world it presented looked like the everyday world a peasant inhabited, only that our world had its place in the larger one, and should emulate it. Newsmen portray themselves as showing us the world we inhabit—and this they patently do not do.

We need not accuse the TV newsmen of hypocrisy, but we should look more closely at how they decide what is the socially significant story. And again, we do better to consult what appears on the TV screen than most newsmen's reflections upon their decisions, which they make, in any case, without much time to reflect. What the screen tells us is that news is not what is unprecedented—certainly not that—but what has been previously undisclosed. News is what people want to hide, or what happened to be hidden. Graft and secret treaties and memos and bombings, these are in the first category; unforeseen floods and shortages and food prices and stock crashes are in the second. "Why did this happen?" usually means "Why didn't we know about this before?" and "getting the story" means discovering lies or circumstances people could not have known about. The climactic event came when the matter went underground, or when it emerged. When was the cover-up planned, and when did the President know about it? If we have an oil crisis, what oil companies did things, in good or bad faith, that led to the lines for gasoline we see? Those lines are the present, apparent fact which has come suddenly upon us. The newsman wants to uncover the circumstances of the surprise: how something *could* be news to us, a new fact or recognition of an old fact; that is "getting to the bottom" of the story. For there to be a story, there must be a mystery to investigate, and getting scoops is what brings a newsman highest praise. It follows that all concerned assume that every story (except natural disasters or public occasions) requires unraveling and investigation. If no arduous work is required to get the story, where is the newsman's skill?

But untangling the past means neglecting the present and the obvious. It means reporting what happened that people did not know was happening, rather than reporting what is always going on and could be known but almost never is. It means neglecting the overt actions for the inner workings, which is like looking at the mechanism of a clock to find out what the time is. Rather than scanning the records to find out about a prospective appointee's past, so as to tell where he once stood, it might be useful to question him closely on where he stands now, and on the kind of person he is. (Newsmen share—and prompt—the politician's view that facts about past private misbehavior discredit someone more than what he believes today and is prepared publicly to act on.) We see little television coverage of the Bureau of Indian Affairs, but a lot about the occupation of a reservation. Senatorial ambitions are scrutinized, but not the continuing business of the Senate. Why do so few reporters emulate the exemplary I. F. Stone, who has shown how to develop immensely informative stories that get "behind" the official facade by examining the handouts, briefings, and official data which constitute that facade? By looking at *appearances* so closely, Stone reveals them as being in fact the reality of politics and policy.

The newsman's predilection for the "inside story" most clearly abuses the public in the coverage of political campaigns. For it is the politics of the campaign itself—its organizational and personal dilemmas—that we are shown, not the issues. Television covers the making of a President, not the reasons why one or another candidate should *be* President. Television does not act as a forum to help the voter decide, but as a dope sheet for betting on the outcome. The candidates are discussed according to their standing in the polls, not drawn out on the issues in a way that could affect the polls. To newsmen, the defense of an economic policy is not news, but how the opposition will counterattack is. A candidate's depth and thoughtfulness is a taboo subject, but there is nothing scandalous about his having given no thought whatever to the issue he is making a speech about. It would seem that as a public figure he is not responsible for what he says, because he is spokesman for a constituency which itself may not have thought through the issue. It would seem that we are not to expect too much of candidates too busy representing to know what they represent; we ought to be glad they can tie their own shoelaces or, with notable exceptions, are able to walk and chew gum at the same time.

True, an extreme incident may bring such taboo considerations to public attention, but in a backhanded way. The attention paid to George Romney's "brainwashing" remark in the 1968 Republican primary campaign conveyed to the public the newsmen's judgment of him as superficial, just as the significance afforded McGovern's Eagleton problem was a way to depict McGovern as wishy-washy. Yet no one insisted on Nixon's secret plan to end the Vietnam war being a little less secret before it became newsworthy: or, before Watergate, viewed Nixon's insistence on privacy as itself newsworthy. Newsmen may have sought more news conferences, but the denial of news conferences received no large headlines.

It is not that a politician's "positions" are not reported, but rather that the fact of those positions is all that newsmen usually treat as newsworthy—not the reasons for them, their logic, their implications. It follows that all positions are equally worthy of respect, because everyone has a position. This is the Theodore H. White view of the world. There is always a serious choice among candidates because they all claim to have points of view. Jeb Stuart Magruder debates with William Sloan Coffin, or Nixon with the press, and any answer, however makeshift or contradictory, is considered an answer. It is because they present every viewpoint seriously that newsmen believe they are "fair"; which is better, I suppose, than deciding not to present some viewpoints, but not as satisfactory, I think, as querying a position until, if it will, it evaporates. Feeling suddenly belligerent after Watergate, newsmen came close to calling Nixon a liar, but they hung back—understandably, since they are both palace spokesmen for the officially sanctioned view of the world and resident critics of the King, who live off court gossip. But the point stands: newsmen are so concerned with *inferring* what is true that they neglect what is remorselessly obvious in the conduct and character of men in and out of office.

Yet there are some few occasions for reporting which by their very nature force news producers to focus on precisely the appearances of things, and in such detail as to place in proper perspective the behind-the-scenes gossip the newsman relates. The quadrennial national political conventions are just such occasions, and are, to my mind, the best thing that television does. True, the conventions are often boring, non-visual, confused, but they set forth, with a unity of time and space, an interaction of visual presences and the spoken word that satisfies the conditions of valid dramatic action and meaning. Ritually organized or ritually spontaneous, the apparent events are the real ones; they not only symbolize non-visible forces and ideas but are the dramatic confrontation that gives life to those forces and orders them: the greeting to Robert F. Kennedy at the 1964 Democratic convention, and the attempt of Johnson's men to end it; Nelson Rockefeller met by boos at the 1964 Republican convention; Senator Ribicoff's remarks from the rostrum to Mayer Daley in 1968 and Daley's response. It was the sea of white faces at the 1972 Republican convention that summed up, for me, the differences between the parties. And the high point of the 1972 campaign may well have been the official appearance of the candidates: Nixon's single appearance, accepting the nomination, and McGovern's twin appearances, summing up the ambivalence that afflicted so many of his supporters. In McGovern's first appearance—to answer questions of the young Leftists in the Doral Hotel lobby— he appeared to me to be informal, calm, humane. He understood his questioners' grievances, as well as his differences with them. He was not afraid of their views and so he could engage their points. Mc-Govern's second appearance was his mis-timed and, to me, shrill acceptance speech, full of left-over rhetoric and punctuated by his embrace of a comrade-in-arms he did not know at all. This false camaraderie in compliance with old political forms was set next to a lame apology for the unusually late hour meant to show the candidate's famous independence of old political forms. It did not work well. The appearances, in more than one sense, told it all. We saw what the candidates stood for, the meanings they wished to convey—that they could not help but convey because this was the way they did politics. The conventions do not lie, and ad men cannot obscure matters as to make

politicians dissemble their own sense of things. Each convention of each party brings together what are only slowly shifting sets of American images, whose drama of reconciliation must be ritually and newly played out each time. For this reason, the public event of the televised convention is itself an important historical event in the life of the nation, fraught with consequence; it engages all of us in creating and propagating both the fact and the sense of new historical possibilities. Full of contrivances, the convention is, nevertheless, what it is—rather than a possible clue to something else.

What is true of conventions is true, *mutatis mutandum*, of all television news. News programs are not simply the reflection of events, as their defenders so often claim, but are the responses to and makers of events—are events in themselves which play the part of the official voice of the nation as an entity, having a life of its own full of ups and downs, heroes and villains, recurrent and unique problems and issues. And so, if newscasters, at least by their selectivity, implicitly judge what they present, we should not only recognize the fact but accept it as part of their job: to reflect and mold a presumptive national consensus for the viewer to embrace or stand aloof from.

As with any other consensus, its developing slowly or quickly is not the central point. Television came in time to take a critical view of the Vietnam war, and so presented the idea of a national consensus moving away from that war. Similarly, in their sympathy and then disenchantment with black militancy in the 1960's, TV newsmen conveyed what, to them, deserved respect and attention and what did not. The nondemocratic way in which the medium determines a consensus is not exactly praiseworthy; but the function of the medium in doing it is not as reprehensible as detractors—conservative, liberal, and radical— would make it out to be. How else but by human judgment can it be decided whether we shall see the Governor tonight, or a demonstration, or the worrying of Watergate until it springs a leak, or a candidate egregiously blundering through a news conference? In each case, the immediate news "policy" is a sense that something is important enough to be summarized briefly upon the screen; that a certain *appearance* may be offered as the whole reality. Was a botched news conference an exception, or the way the candidate always works? Did a news producer present Muskie's tears in New Hampshire as significant of the candidate himself or of the affront that had been offered him? A viewer cannot know—cannot expect to know—what goes into every news decision, so as to sift out bias on the way to some supposed objective residue of fact. Rather, the viewer might as well accept the newscast as a retelling, tonight, of the drama of national life, one which must be tested against his own sense of the story up to now. The viewer must select from television's images, as he would from memoirs or historical accounts, those moments which seem to him so revealing, so symbolically right, as to be pretty clearly the facts of contemporary history. To refuse or resent this task of fact-making is to prefer an authority higher than television, or a democracy, ought to afford.

Socialist

Michael Parenti. The mass media: by the few, for the many.

It is said that a free and independent press is a necessary condition for democracy, and it is frequently assumed that the United States is endowed with such a press. While the news in "totalitarian" nations is controlled, we Americans supposedly have access to a wide range of ideas and information from competing sources. In reality, the controls exerted over the media in the United States, while more subtle and less severe than in some other countries, leave us with a press that is far from "free" by any definition of the word.

The news media are important to any study of American politics. They implant the images in our heads that help us define socio-political reality. Almost all the political life we experience is through newspapers, radio and television. How we view issues—indeed, what we even define as an "issue" or "event"—what we see and hear and what we do *not* see and hear are greatly determined by those who control the media. By enlarging our vision through technology, we have actually surrendered control over much of our own sensory experience.[1]

It is argued that the mass media are not a crucial factor in political life: one can point to the many Democratic Presidents who won elections despite the overwhelming endorsement of their Republican opponents by the press. But despite a low rate of editorial endorsement, Democratic candidates do manage to buy political advertisements and receive coverage by the mass media during their campaigns, unlike radical candidates, who receive almost no exposure and almost no votes.[2] The argument also overlooks the subtler and more persistent influences of the media in defining the scope of respectable political discourse, channeling public attention in certain directions and determining—in ways that are essentially conservative and supportive of the existing socioeconomic structure—what is political reality.[3]

He who pays the piper

The primary function of television, radio and newspapers is not to keep the public informed but to make money for their owners, a goal that frequently does not coincide with the need for a vigilant democratic press. The number of independently owned newspapers has been declining in the United States, with most of the big-circulation dailies coming under the ownership of chains like Hearst, Gannett and Copely. In the last twenty years some thirty dailies have disappeared. Today only 45 out of 1,500 American cities have competing newspapers under separate ownership. According to James Aronson, more Americans "are reading fewer papers and fewer points of view than ever before."[4] (In many cities where there is a "choice," like

Chicago with its four dailies, the newspapers are all quite conservative in editorial policy.)

But if they are declining in numbers, the papers are *not* declining as business ventures. In fact, they are doing quite well. Through mergers, packaged news service and staff cutting, the larger conglomerates have paid off handsomely. In 1969 newspapers grossed $5.4 billion in advertising revenues, or 22 percent more than the total for radio and television combined. For the businessmen who own them, "newspapers are no longer entities in themselves, with individual character, courage, and a dedication to the public service, but simply properties to be listed among holdings along with real estate, fertilizer, electronics, and aerospace rocketry."[5]

As with the newspapers, so with television: big media are big business. The three major networks, CBS, NBC and ABC, made $179 million in profits in 1968 and $226 million in 1969—an increase of 12 percent in one year. Many radio and television stations and publishing houses are owned by corporations like RCA, ITT, Westinghouse and General Electric. The networks themselves have substantial international investments, owning television stations throughout Asia, the Middle East and Latin America.[6]

The influence of big-business ownership is reflected in its political content. The media are given over to trivialized "features" and gossip items. Coverage of national, state and local affairs is usually scant, superficial and oriented toward "events" and "personalities," consisting of a few short "headline" stories and a number of mildly conservative or simply banal commentaries and editorials. As one group of scholars noted after a study of the news media: "Protection against government is now not enough to guarantee that a man who has something to say shall have a chance to say it. The owners and managers of the press determine which person, which facts, which version of the facts, and which ideas shall reach the public."[7]

The business-owned media have had little to say about the relationship between the capitalist system and such things as pollution, bad housing, poverty and inflation, the relations between political and business leaders and the role of the multinational corporations in shaping American interventionist policy abroad. Almost no positive exposure is given to the socialist alternatives emerging throughout the Third World or the socialist critique of capitalism at home. Despite some recent manifestations of liberalism on such issues as Vietnam and military spending, news media content remains fundamentally conservative. There are almost no strongly liberal or radical biases expressed in the mass media. In contrast, reactionaries, militarists and ultrarightist elements have an estimated $14-million yearly propaganda budget donated by some 113 business firms and 25 public utilities, and each week across the country they make over ten thousand television and radio broadcasts—with much of the air time freely donated by sympathetic station owners.[8] In one three-week period the ultraconservative billionaire H. Ross Perot was able to present his viewpoints "supporting President Nixon's Vietnam policy in 300 newspapers with full-page advertisements and in a half hour television program. His qualifications? He had the $1 million it required."[9]

On the infrequent occasions when liberals muster enough money to buy broadcasting time or newspaper space they still may be denied access to the media. Liberal commentators have been refused radio spots even when they had sponsors who would pay. A group of scientists, politicians and celebrities opposing the Pentagon's antiballistic missile program were denied a half hour on television by all three major networks despite the fact that they had the required $250,000 to buy time. All three networks refused to sell time to the Democratic National Committee to reply to Nixon's televised statements on the Vietnam war. And on various occasions the *New York Times* would not sell space to citizens' groups that wanted to run advertisements against the war tax or against the purchase of war bonds. A *Times* executive turned down the advertisement against war bonds because he judged it not to be in the "best interests of the country."[10]

Denied access to the mass media, the political left has attempted to get its message across through local newspapers and magazines of its own, but this "underground press" has suffered many financial difficulties and official harassments. In Cambridge, Mass., street vendors for the *Avatar* were arrested fifty-eight times within a short period on trumped-up charges, and newsstand owners, under threat of arrest, refused to carry the paper, thus causing a sharp decline in circulation. In Atlanta the radical newspaper *Great Speckled Bird* was subjected to repeated police harrassments in 1972; its offices were then attacked by unknown persons three times in three weeks and were finally destroyed by fire bombs. Police seemed unable to find a clue as to who did it.

In Montgomery County, Maryland, the editor of the *Washington Free Press* was given six months in prison for publishing an allegedly obscene cartoon of a judge. In San Diego the *Street Journal and San Diego Press* suffered bullets through its office windows, theft, destruction of equipment, fire bombings and repeated staff arrests on charges that were later thrown out of court. In Urbana, Ill., the editor of the *Walrus* was arrested in 1969 for nonpossession of his draft card and imprisoned for three years. In the same city a radical printing cooperative was burglarized and destroyed by unknown persons. And in Peoria, Ill., another printer of radical publications had his press closed by authorities under a seldom enforced zoning law.[11]

The politics of entertainment

While the entertainment sector of the media, as opposed to the news sector, supposedly has nothing to do with politics, entertainment programs in fact undergo a rigorous political censorship. In the late 1960s the "Smothers Brothers Comedy Hour," after being cut several times for introducing antiwar comments and other mildly political statements, was finally removed from the air. CBS censored appeals for world peace made by Carol Burnett and Elke Sommer in their respective appearances on the Merv Griffin show. Songs that contained references to drugs, prison

conditions, the draft and opposition to war have been cut from entertainment shows.[12] When David Susskind submitted five thousand names of people he wished to have appear on his talk show to the advertising agency that represented his sponsor, a third of the candidates were rejected because of their political viewpoints. The censorship code used by Proctor and Gamble for shows it sponsored stated in part: "Members of the armed forces must not be cast as villains. If there is any attack on American custom, it must be rebutted completely on the same show."[13]

While critical socio-political commentaries are censored out of entertainment shows, there is plenty of politics of another sort. In soap operas and situation comedies, adventure programs and detective stories, comic strips and children's cartoon shows, conventional American values are preached and practiced. Various kinds of aggressive behavior are indulged in and even glorified, although dissident elements like student demonstrators and radicals have been portrayed unfavorably as violent and irrational characters. Foreign agents are seen as menacing our land and the military as protecting it. Establishment figures like judges, executive heads, businessmen, doctors and police are fair and competent—never on the take, never corrupt, never racist or oppressive. Or, if there *are* a few bad ones, they are soon set straight by their more principled colleagues. In the media world, adversities usually are caused by ill-willed individuals rather than by the economic system in which they live, and problems are solved by individual effort within the system rather than collective effort against it. Conflicts are resolved by generous applications of violence. Nefarious violence is met with righteous violence, although it is often hard to distinguish between the two. In many films the brutal and often criminal behavior of law officers has been portrayed sympathetically, as one of those gutsy realities of life. Violence on television and in Hollywood films is almost omnipresent, often linked to sex, money, dominance, self-aggrandizement and other attributes that represent "manliness" in the male-chauvinist, capitalist American culture.

In the media, women appear primarily in supportive roles as housewives, secretaries and girl friends. They usually are incapable of initiating actions of their own; they get into difficulties from which they must be extricated by their men. When not treated as weak and scatter-brained, women are likely to be portrayed as devious, dehumanized sex objects, the ornaments of male egoism. In media advertisements women seem exclusively concerned with getting a fluffy glow shampooed into their hair, waxing "their" floors, making yummy coffee for hubby, getting Johnny's clothes snowy white, and in other ways serving as mindless, cheery household drones.

Working-class people, as mentioned earlier, have little representation in the entertainment media except as uncouth, ignorant persons, hoodlums, servants and other such minor stock characters. The tribulations of working-class people in this society—their struggle to make ends meet, the specter of unemployment, the lack of decent recreational facilities, the machinations of unscrupulous merchants and landlords, the loss of pensions and seniority, the battles for unionization and union reform, the dirty, noisy, mindless, dangerous, alienating quality of industrial work, the abuses suffered at the hands of bosses, the lives wrecked and cut short by work-connected injury and disease—these kinds of reality almost never are thought worthy of dramatic treatment in the plastic, make-believe world of the mass media. The experiences of millions of working-class people are ignored because they are not deemed suitable subjects by the upper-middle-class professionals who create the programs and because the whole question of class struggle and class exploitation is a forbidden subject in media owned by the corporate rich.

Repressing the press

On those infrequent occasions when the news media do give attention to controversial events and take a critical view of official doings, they are likely to encounter intimidating discouragements from public officials. Almost without exception, government officeholders treat any kind of news that places them in an unfavorable light as "slanted" and seek to exert pressure on reporters in order to bring them around to the "correct" and "objective" (i.e., uncritical and supportive) viewpoint. Few political leaders have been more intolerant toward the press than President Nixon, who (before Watergate, and even to a large extent thereafter) regarded all critical reporting of his administration as biased and all opposition as bordering on disloyalty. Nixon professed little confidence in the American people, once observing that "the average American is just like the child in the family. . . . [If you] pamper him and cater to him too much, you are going to make him soft, spoiled and eventually a very weak individual." Beset by such paternalistic anxieties, the Nixon administration did its best to control the kind of information the childlike American was fed. Some examples:

(1) For several years Vice-President Spiro Agnew with an occasional assist from Attorney General John Mitchell leveled a series of attacks on the press for its supposedly "liberal" biases, calling upon the media to be more "responsible" in its news reports and commentaries. (This kind of attack allows the media to appear as liberal defenders of free speech against government censorship, instead of supporters of the established order as they usually are.) The effect on the already timid news media of the Agnew-Mitchell assault was a palpable one. "I think the industry as a whole has been intimidated," complained CBS newscaster Walter Cronkite.[14] At the same time, the FBI approached various network executives concerning reporters who have done stories which displeased the President.[15] While covering a story, reporter Leslie Whitten was arrested by the FBI on a trumped-up charge. Whitten's real crime, some people speculated, was having vigorously pursued the story of collusion between ITT and the CIA to stage a coup in Chile, as well as the story of ITT's illegal contribution to the Nixon campaign fund and the dairy owners' successful attempts to buy favors from the Nixon administration.[16]

(2) In June 1971 the Nixon administration tried to get a court order preventing the

publication of the Pentagon Papers (a collection of classified government memoranda and documents on how American policy in Vietnam was secretly shaped). It was the government's most serious attempt in American history to enforce prior censorship of the press. When the Supreme Court ruled in favor of the press, the Justice Department then charged Daniel Ellsberg and Anthony J. Russo, the two former government employees who had released the Pentagon Papers, with espionage. A political scientist, Samuel Popkin, who had seen the papers before their publication and refused to implicate other scholars who had studied them, was jailed for refusing to violate professional confidences before a grand jury.

(3) For most of our history, under the First Amendment guarantee against abridgements of free speech, reporters were not required to reveal those informants who gave them information about malfeasance in high places, political scandals or any other events about which the public had a right to know. In June 1972 the Supreme Court ruled that reporters could be required to disclose their information sources to grand jury investigators. With the Nixon appointees providing the winning balance, the Court decided in a 5-4 decision that the public interest involved in bringing a criminal to justice overrode the reporter's need to protect his news source.[17] The newsman who lost this decision, Earl Caldwell of the *New York Times*, declared that the decision made it "really impossible to do serious reporting in the U.S. if the government doesn't want you to." Dozens of reporters have since been jailed or threatened with long prison terms on the basis of that decision.

(4) Nixon vetoed an appropriations bill for the Public Broadcasting System because he disliked several of the public affairs programs that have appeared under its auspices. Almost all the news analysis programs that the White House disapproved of were canceled. In April 1973 the chairman of the Corporation for Public Broadcasting, Thomas Curtis, a Republican and Nixon appointee, resigned in protest, warning that public broadcasting should not become "a

propaganda arm for the Nixon Administration or for any succeeding administration."[18]

(5) In 1973 Nixon proposed a law giving the Federal Communications Commission the power to refuse to renew the license of any radio or television station that persisted in "bias." Nixon's spokesman, Clay Whitehead, explained that stations will be required to demonstrate "responsibility" and avoid "ideological plugola." "Station managers and network officials who fail to act to correct imbalance or consistent bias in the network, *or who acquiesce by silence*, can only be considered willing participants, to be held fully accountable...at license-renewal time," he concluded.[19] The government, of course, was to determine to its own satisfaction who was and was not "biased."

(6) The Nixon administration increased second-class postal rates, thereby doubling the mailing costs of publications. The increases would be a serious and perhaps fatal burden for the small, unprofitable journals that offered the kind of opposition viewpoints seldom heard in the mass media. The government defended the increase as an economy measure while at the same time continuing the heavy postal subsidy of the more than 12 billion pieces of junk mail sent out every year by business and advertising firms.

Much of the government pressure on newspapers and networks occurs outside the public view. On repeated occasions the government has subpoenaed, and received, documents, films, tapes and other materials used by news media in the reporting of events. And the government interferes in other ways: "The telephone calls from White House assistants and the visits to network executives by presidential aides are seldom publicized."[20] Such interferences impose "a *chilling effect*" on the news media, an inclination to think twice before reporting something, a propensity—already marked in most news reports—to slide over the more troublesome and damning aspects of a story—in all, a tendency to police and censor oneself to avoid the discomforts and risks of clashing with those in power.[21]

When not trying to control public opinion, the government is busy manufacturing it. After Nixon's speech announcing the mining of Haiphong harbor in the spring of 1972, a flood of telegrams in support of his policy came pouring in. Later on, it was revealed that the bulk of the mail had been sent by the Committee to Re-elect the President and had been fabricated to look like a spontaneous public response. There are certain hazards to this kind of manipulation: in December 1969, Spiro Agnew taped a speech that was scheduled by UPI news service to be broadcast one weekend over dozens of radio stations. Because of a mix-up, not a single station aired the speech. Just the same, the following Monday the UPI office was inundated with fourteen thousand pieces of mail praising Agnew for his latest attack on liberals.[22] (Not one of the letters was critical).

Attempts to control or fabricate the news are not unique to the Nixon administration. Presidents like Johnson, Kennedy and Eisenhower and their various aides were repeatedly successful in killing unfavorable stories and planting favorable ones. Much of what is reported as "news" in all our newspapers, broadcasts and telecasts is nothing more than the reporting of official releases. In more instances than can be counted, the "independent press" transmits what the government wants transmitted to an unsuspecting public.

From what has been said so far it should be clear that one cannot talk about a "free press" apart from the economic and political realities that determine who owns and controls the media. Freedom of speech means not only the right to hear both sides of a story (Republican and Democratic) but the right to hear *all* sides. It means not only the right to *hear* but the right to *be heard*, to talk back to those in government and in the network offices and newsrooms, something few of us can do at present.

What also should be clear to anyone who understands human communication is that there is no such thing as unbiased news. All reports and analyses are selective and inferential to some inescapable degree—all the more reason to provide a wider ideologi-cal spectrum of opinions and not let one bias predominate. Some measure of ideological heterodoxy could be achieved if public law required all newspapers and broadcasting stations to allot substantial portions of space and time to a vast array of political opinion, including the most radical and revolutionary.

Ultimately the only protection against monopoly control of the media is ownership by community people themselves, with legally enforceable provisions allowing for the maximum participation of conflicting views. In Europe, some suggestive developments have taken place: the staffs of various newspapers and magazines like *Der Stern* in Germany and *Le Figaro* in France have used strikes to achieve greater editorial control of the publications they help to produce. And *Le Monde*'s management agreed to give its staff a 40 percent share in the profits and a large share in policy-making and managerial decisions, including the right to block any future sale of the paper.[23]

While interesting because they point to alternative forms of property control, these developments are themselves not likely to transform the property relations of a capitalist society and its mass media. With few exceptions, those who own the newspapers and networks, and make enormous profits on them, will not relinquish their hold over private investments and public information. Ordinary citizens will have no real access to the media until they come to exercise direct community control over the material resources that could give them such access, an achievement that would take a different kind of economic and social system than the one we have. In the meantime, Americans should have no illusions about the "freedom of speech" they are said to enjoy.

NOTES

1. Robert Cirino, *Don't Blame the People* (Los Angeles: Diversity Press, 1971), pp. 30–31. Cirino's book is a well-documented study of how the news media distort and manipulate public opinion; recently reissued by Vintage, it is highly recommended to the reader.

2. For a discussion of this point see Chapter Nine, "The Sound and the Fury: Elections and Parties."

3. See Cirino, *Don't Blame the People*, pp. 181–182.

4. James Aronson, *Packaging the News, A Critical Survey of Press, Radio, TV* (New York: International Publishers, 1971), p. 14. Monopoly ownership extends across the various media. As of 1967 there were seventy-three communities in the United States in which one company or one rich individual owned or controlled *all* newspapers and local broadcast outlets.

5. *Ibid.*, p. 15.

6. Herbert Schiller, *Mass Communications and American Empire* (New York: Augustus Kelly, 1969).

7. *A Free and Responsible Press* (Report by the Commission of Freedom of the Press, 1947), quoted in Cirino, *Don't Blame the People*, p. 47.

8. Arnold Forster and Benjamin Epstein, *Danger on the Right* (New York: Vintage, 1964), p. 273.

9. Cirino, *Don't Blame the People*, p. 299.

10. *Ibid.*, p. 90 and p. 302.

11. Most of these incidents are reported in Aronson, *Packaging the News*, pp. 67–69. See also the *Guardian*, May 17, 1972, and the *Militant*, January 21, 1972. The information on Illinois is from my own observations.

12. See Cirino, *Don't Blame the People*, pp. 305–306, for various examples.

13. Murray Schumack, *The Face on the Cutting Room Floor*, quoted in *ibid.*, pp. 303–304.

14. Quoted in Aronson, *Packaging the News*, p. 80.

15. David Wise, "The President and the Press," *Atlantic*, April 1973, pp. 55–64.

16. Stephen Torgoff, "Press Freedom in Danger," *Guardian*, February 14, 1973.

17. *United States v. Caldwell*, 33 L. Ed. 2d 626 (1972).

18. *New York Times*, April 24, 1973.

19. "Mr. Nixon and the Media" ("Playboy Forum" report), *Playboy*, April 1973, p. 61. (Italics added.)

20. Wise, "The President and the Press," pp. 63–64. For a further discussion of government's use of secrecy and deception, see Chapter Fifteen, "The Politics of Bureaucracy."

21. Staggering from the blows of the Watergate exposé, the Nixon administration temporarily took a more conciliatory tack with the press in April 1973. Agnew admitted publicly that he had been too "harsh" in his choice of words. Nixon asked that the press keep giving him "hell" when he deserved it. And his press secretary, Ron Ziegler, apologized for various disparaging remarks he previously had made to reporters. Only when they no longer feel omnipotent do aggressors act civil toward others.

22. Ian Sven, Liberation News Service release, January 1970. This incident received little publicity in the establishment press.

23. Aronson, *Packaging the News*, p. 99.

14 Banks

The basic questions this chapter will address are:

(1) Are banks solely economic institutions? Or are they political structures as well?
(2) What political powers do banks have?
(3) Is there an alternative to the American banking system?

Conservatives maintain that banks are purely financial institutions, not political entities. The role of banks is to fund corporate investments. It is the underlying assumption of conservatives, who prefer to limit competition, that there are too many banks in America. Too many banks acting independently make it difficult for the large organizations such as Bank of America, Morgan Guaranty Trust Co., Chase Manhattan, First National City, Chemical-New York, to exert sufficient influence and maintain stable financial conditions. The only thing the government has to do to help the banking industry is to place large amounts of additional capital into circulation under the control and regulation of banks. Since the banking industry is not a political institution, government interference in its workings is not wanted.

Liberals hold that banks are not fundamentally political institutions, yet they can exert political pressure. For example, in 1975 the major New York City banks refused to loan funds to the city to maintain its educational structures and municipal services.[1] Liberals maintain that problems such as this can be rectified by government loaning capital when banks refuse it. The threat of government intervention would keep banks in accord with the interests of the people.

To socialists banks are fundamentally political institutions, often the instruments through which capitalists increase their profit. They loan money that enables governments to carry on war. By first advertising and furthering an economy that exists on credit, and then withholding that credit, banks have the ability to create economic chaos for individuals. The dollar, the virtual god of Americans, is manipulated and controlled by the banking industry.

The political clout of banks is enormous. They have the power to decide if cities collapse financially, or prosper. They have the power, through international loans, to decide whether poor countries will survive. They have the power to cause a depression or create prosperity. An institution as powerful as this cannot be considered to be purely financial.

Limiting or eliminating the power of banks is a key issue for socialists. One solution is the creation of alternate banking institutions. The Woman's Bank in New York City, is one example of this strategy, the Freedom National Bank, located in Bedford Stuyvesant and Harlem, in New York City, is another example. Another way of circumventing the major banks is the transferral of funds from major banking institutions to minor ones.[2] A third strategy is a refusal to live on credit. Credit cards should not be utilized, and personal loans for luxury goods should not be

Etzkowitz & Schwab—Is America Necessary—32

taken out. Use of credit cards places the individual under the economic and legal control of the corporate establishment.[3] A final strategy, in connection with an overall socialist solution, is to place the direction of banks in the hands of the people by removing control from elites.

NOTES

1. Robert J. Samuelson, "Bankrupt New York," *The New Republic* (May 10, 1975), pp. 17–19. See also issues of *The New York Times,* June/July 1975.

2. The establishment of credit unions in places of work is one example of how this can be done. The Coalition on the Economic Crisis, led by Dave McReynolds, has proposed this tactic as part of its program of economic and political action to deal with the economic crisis of the 1970s. The Coalition on the Economic Crisis can be reached at 339 Lafayette St., New York, New York 10012.

3. See, David Caplovitz, *Consumers in Trouble: Study of Debtors in Default.* New York: The Free Press, 1974.

Conservative

The great banking retreat.

Phase I of the banking revolution, the wild-and-woolly growth phase, is over—brought to a jarring halt in 1974 by inflation, recession, and the excesses of the bankers who made the revolution.

Now, banking has moved into a new, more conservative phase—the shaking out and refining that inevitably follows the sort of frenzied growth the industry has just witnessed: loans up 170% to $547-billion in a decade, assets up 143% to $917-billion. Banks became holding companies and then financial conglomerates in that decade, stretching out across the U.S. and the world.

But super growth bred super problems, and suddenly bankers, along with customers, regulators, and legislators, are having second thoughts. And it is dead certain that for banking the next 10 years will be far tamer than the past 10, with slower growth in both loans and total assets, and with fewer borrowers welcome at the banks.

"Go-go banking has had its day as a fashion," says Paul K. Kely, vice-president of First Boston Corp., the New York investment banking house. Adds M. Brock Weir, chairman and chief executive of Clevetrust Corp., the holding company ($3.9-billion in assets) that owns Cleveland Trust Co.: "There has been a change in direction in the minds of bankers. We were guilty of excesses. We got caught up in giving analysts a thrill a minute."

The banking system's problems are serious—with an overhang of very shaky loans the most visible one. The odds are now against a tidal wave of bank failures, here or abroad. But there probably will be further casualties, and another bank or two may join the list of failed giants that already includes U.S. National Bank of San Diego, Franklin National in New York, and Security National in Long Island.

So the U.S. banking system is in retreat today, and a banking system in retreat has implications for the economy as profound as a banking system in full advance. Plainly, the banks are not lending money, at home or abroad, as they did even six months ago. Nor are bankers as quick as they used to be to fund long-term loans with such short-term money as federal funds (the excess reserves of banks).

Conservative stripe

It is not banking in the manner of the 1930s and 1940s, when bankers simply waited for customers to seek them out. But it is far more conservative banking than anyone has seen in more than a decade. And it is a change mandated not only by the depth of the recession and the relative tightness of monetary policy but also by a clear acceptance by bankers that they had reached too far, taken too many risks, and must retrench before more big institutions get into trouble.

"Last summer scared the pants off some of these bankers," says John C. Poppen of Booz, Allen & Hamilton, the management consultants. "I don't mean the 60-year-old bankers, I mean the 35-year-old tigers." Says Professor Paul Nadler of Rutgers University: "A lot of the bright young tigers are not tigers anymore."

Some of this will change when monetary policy eases and the economy shows clear signs of reviving, but the crucial fact is that some elements of this new conservatism will linger through the rest of the 1970s and probably beyond that. If the buzzword of the past 10 years was "growth," then the buzzword of the next 10 years will be "quality," and that goes not only for the banks but for those who lend to and borrow from the banks.

When the chips were down last summer, after Franklin National had started its plunge toward failure and Germany's Bankhaus I.D. Herstatt had failed, it was only the giant money market banks of New York and Chicago, along with a few institutions from Boston, Philadelphia, and the West Coast, that could still get unlimited funds at the best possible price. Other banks, including the hot-shot regionals that had been in the vanguard of the new banking, either went without or paid handsomely for what they could get. This quality preference among those who lend to banks—corporate treasurers, Arab oil lands—will moderate somewhat as it becomes clear that few if any more big banks are going bust, but it will remain a fact of life for the banking system for as far ahead as anyone can see.

The big regional banks and the thousands of smaller local banks will continue to find money locally; at times they may still be able to tap the New York money market for funds, though they will usually pay a little more for it. There will be more mergers, but the regional and local banks are not going to be swept away.

Still the U.S. banking system has been heading very clearly toward a point where a mere handful of giants will dominate the nation's financial business—operating through branches where they can, and through loan production offices, electronic banking terminals, and nonbank financial subsidiaries. Comptroller of the Currency James E. Smith has already ruled that electronic terminals—customer-bank communication terminals—are not branches and that the national banks he regulates can install them anywhere in the land without regard to local branching laws. While that ruling will be fought in the courts, it is very much a straw in the wind. For a long time it seemed as though at least some of the big regional banks might make it into the titan class. Now it seems almost certain that that handful of giants will include only the big money market banks, and mostly the big New York banks at that.

Size equals quality

It is hard to assess what this enormous concentration of resources in a few hands will mean to the U.S. economy, though it has been perfectly obvious for a generation that the U.S. does not need 14,500 banks, most of them hiding behind hopelessly archaic limits on branching. Professor Paul A. Samuelson of MIT, the Nobel laureate, takes the notion calmly enough. "If you can

keep competition among big national alternative sources—A&P and Safeway, Kroger and Stop & Shop—then the demise of some Mom-and-Pop store of regional antiquity does not mean a reduction in competition," he says. "My suspicion is that the old, beloved regional banker was under less competition when the region was a captive of him."

It is easier, but more sobering, to assess the impact of what might be called the new, new banking when it is understood that the quality preference that investors have for big, rich banks is matched by a quality preference that banks have for big, rich customers. The U.S. has just come through the wildest boom in all of its economic history, and roughly $1 of every $3 borrowed in the economy came from a bank. For a businessman borrowing short-term, the figure is more than $7 for every $10. For state and local governments it is $5 of every $10.

Banks, or such nonbanking holding company subsidiaries as finance companies, leasing companies, mortgage bankers, and real estate investment trusts literally funded everyone that needed money in the past decade. They used up their own deposits and they sold certificates of deposit and holding company commercial paper and borrowed federal funds to keep the game going—creating loan/deposit and capital/asset ratios that were simply intolerable. The lesson that everyone has learned, says A. Robert Abboud, deputy chairman of First Chicago Corp., is that "the banking system cannot go out and create an unlimited amount of commitment exposure and then expect to fund 100% of these commitments."

Beyond that, many of the risks that banks assumed simply were not worthy of being financed. "Many bankers forgot that if a class of loans yielded much more, the reason is that the risk is greater," chides Brenton C. Leavitt, director of the Federal Reserve's Supervision & Regulation Div. The risk got so great that banks in 1974 had to charge off an unprecedented $1.8-billion to cover loan losses, and there still are billions of dollars in loans that are in considerable trouble—$10-billion to $12-billion in loans to real estate investment trusts alone. Even that risk might have made a certain amount of sense if the banks had profited handsomely from those loans. But between the high cost of funds—even for the banking giants—and those hefty losses, the banks' return on assets has declined precipitously in recent years.

Some won't be welcome

Now the inevitable reaction has set in. No longer will the banks or their subsidiaries finance everyone that comes along. "There is a place for high-risk loans, but not in the banking system," says Charles J. Zwick, president of Southeast Banking Corp. in Miami. A company with less than an A-rating is going to have a hard time borrowing from a bank or from one of the non-bank subsidiaries, not only this year but next year and the year after that. And the screening process is at work overseas as well.

Indeed, Thomas R. Wilcox, president of Crocker National Corp. talks about a different sort of role for banks, at least until bank capital has been built up again. "That forces you into an intermediary role," he says. "We will become more like financial architects, only retaining a sufficient share of a credit where it seems necessary to validate our endorsement." In other words, banks would merely bring borrower and lender together for a fee.

For a substantial share of the economy, however, there are no other lenders but the banks. The commercial paper market is only for the bluest of blue-chip corporations. There are the public and private bond markets. But there, too, anyone with less than an A-rating is unwelcome today—raising the obvious question of where all the money is going to come from.

Nadler of Rutgers is afraid he has an answer. "What scares the hell out of me," he says, "is that when the banks said they wouldn't lend the money to the housing industry, the government lent it." Congress is agog these days with schemes for allocating credit to sectors of the economy,

and the Federal Reserve, though it does not like to talk about it, has been pushing banks to lend to companies that it does not want to fail. Nadler fears that, at the least, the future will produce more loans to questionable borrowers, guaranteed by the U. S. government.

Government's role

Indeed, it is as certain as anything can be that the role of government in the financial markets in general and in the banking system in particular is going to grow enormously over the next 10 years with Washington making more decisions about who gets money. Certainly the link between bank and regulator will grow closer still, especially when that regulator is the Federal Reserve, with its power to create money and to act as lender of last resort to troubled banks. The other side of a Fed-directed loan to a troubled company is an implicit promise by the Fed to help a bank if the loan goes bad.

The Fed, obviously frightened by what happened to the banks in 1974, will be obliged to protect the biggest banks in order to maintain confidence in the system. The banks, in turn, will be obliged to work closely with regulators to extend their reach beyond such artificial barriers as limits on branching, and to have a guaranteed refuge in case of trouble. The result, warns Stanford University economist George L. Bach, will be increased Fed participation in decisions on how and where banks grow. "The Fed can't escape a greater participation," he says, "not so much to protect depositors as to keep a viable way of regulating money flows."

These are dramatic changes all—a few giant banks with arms that reach across the land, wedded more tightly than ever to Washington and the Federal Reserve, and less willing to take any but the choicest risks. Yet they also appear to be inevitable changes, given the way Phase I of the banking revolution worked out. "We have had the education of another generation of bankers," says Frank Wille, chairman of the Federal Deposit Insurance Corp. The experience may not sear this generation as the

Great Depression seared an earlier generation of bankers, but it will leave its mark just the same.

The generation of bankers that rose to power in the early 1960s had never known a truly sick economy. They took their ability to survive the minor economic disturbances of the 1960s as proof that they could survive anything.

"Everyone was on a drunken kick—buy your money, diversify, liability management, high multiples," charges Rutgers' Nadler. "Banking became a high-volume, low-markup business."

It was dicey enough when it was the big money market banks that were playing the new-banking game. But then came the regional banks, led by such banks as First Pennsylvania, NCNB, Citizens & Southern in Atlanta, Industrial National in Providence. Banks that once operated in a city or a state set off to match the giant money market banks. "To some extent, people were following a fad and aping the big banks," says John F. McGillicuddy, president of Manufacturers Hanover Corp. "Everybody can't be a Citibank."

Citicorp—the parent of Citibank—could keep racing ahead because the game was being played by its rules. But few banks even come close to matching its financial or management resources.

The ice got very thin

Last year pulled things apart. Inflation turned strong demand for bank money into frenzied demand. But more lending forced the banks to borrow still more, and by mid-1974 the system was stretched dangerously thin: too much questionable lending, too much borrowed money, too little capital to support swollen assets, and monetary growth that had slowed to dead zero.

The real crisis came with trouble at Franklin and at Herstatt, which threw both the domestic and international money markets into chaos. Panicked investors and depositors suddenly rushed for shelter, equating size with safety and funneling their money only to the large money center banks, leaving the aggressive regional banks high and dry. As money fled the regional banks, so did customers. By the end of 1974, Walter B. Wriston, chairman of Citicorp, was complaining that the regional banks were sending too many of their customers to New York.

Not until the memory of 1974 has faded completely is that process likely to be reversed. The immediate result was that the New York banks prospered mightily in 1974 while earnings plunged at virtually all the hot-shot regional and local banks. Now it is a matter of banks' mulling over the lessons they learned and putting them into practice.

"The most important lesson of 1974 has been that all banks cannot rely on money markets as dependable sources of funds at all times," said Ernest C. Arbuckle, chairman of Wells Fargo & Co., in his annual report. Indeed, Wells Fargo, which had covered as much as 20% of its loans with federal funds, which are mostly borrowed overnight, has cut that to closer to 10% now.

Nadler of Rutgers makes much the same point. "Banks learned in 1974 that they do not own their deposits," he says. "When there is fear, the money moves all over the lot. Now bankers realize that the old truths apply: safety, capital adequacy, decent spreads. Banking is becoming a low-volume, high markup business."

While Wriston of Citicorp does not agree, Nadler and others think that the emphasis on liability management has faded and that the emphasis will again be on the asset side—meaning on loans and investments. Plainly, the diversification craze is over for a good, long while. Few non-banking businesses earned as much as bankers hoped they would, and most did more damage to balance sheets than regulators thought they would. Even if banks wanted to reach out more, the Fed, which supervises all holding companies, would not let them. The giant banks will stay diversified, and probably more than they are even today, but that will be to provide all the various financial services that can be offered in markets where branching laws keep the bank itself from going.

The middle-grade blues

In terms of the longer-run health of the U.S. economy, though, the most important question is who will have access to bank money, and the outlook is not good. The top tier of U.S. business will be financed without question. Banks will stick with consumer installment lending because the return is so good. But the middle-grade corporation plainly faces trouble. It simply will not be able to count on a guaranteed claim on bank money, and when it does get money, the quid pro quo may be giving the bank more of a say in company management than banks have traditionally had. Chairman John Bunting of First Pennsylvania Corp. in Philadelphia is one banker who thinks bankers will have a louder voice in corporate management in coming years.

For anyone—corporation, individual, city or state—that falls below middle grade, the outlook is bleak. In the days of the new banking, they were all staked by the banks. But the days of new banking are past, and unless monetary policy turns so aggressively easy that banks have enough to supply everyone again, · the plight of those frustrated borrowers may be the most significant economic story of the next decade.

Liberal

Martin Mayer.   How banks destroy the economy.

That strange and disturbing things have been happening to big banks both here and abroad will scarcely be news to anyone who has read so much as the front pages of the past year's newspapers. What is not so well known is that these shocks are merely the surface expression of an earthquake, a revolution in the technology and function of banking that has shaken up the entire mechanism of the American economy. The revolution took place in the 1960s; looking back on that decade of talky turbulence—

Richard Hofstadter called it "the age of rubbish"—it seems somehow appropriate that the one revolution that actually came off occurred without publicity in the apparently solid structure of what was considered our most thoroughly conservative institution.

Banks have been around so long that we forget they were started with a purpose in mind. That purpose was to gather up what would otherwise be idle monetary assets and use them as grease for the wheels of commerce and industry. The forgetting process itself now has a hundred-year history: Walter Bagehot noted in 1873 that "we have entirely lost the idea that any undertaking likely to pay, and seen to be likely, can perish for want of money; yet no idea was more familiar to our ancestors." The malaise that tainted most people's contemplation of the American banking system in 1974 derived less from the handful of rather dramatic bank failures than from a sense that the system had lost its *raison d'être*. Downtown in the big cities one could scarcely wash down the sidewalk without splashing the plate-glass window of a bank, yet all over the country undertakings likely to pay could see themselves perishing for want of money.

The interest rates, of course, were high enough to inspire fear—effectively, counting the cost of "compensating balances" (money businessmen had to pay for but couldn't use), more than 15 percent per annum. "The Bank of England used to say that 6 percent would draw money from the moon," muttered Ralph Leach, chairman of the executive committee of Morgan Guaranty, studying an analysis some months ago, of what his bank would have to pay for money it was committed to lend. "They seem to have smarter people on the moon these days."

Whatever the definition of money—and however elegant the theoretical formulations, there is no really good, or even acceptable, practical definition—in modern societies the stuff is generated primarily by and through banks. The money shortages of 1974 argued a malfunction of the banking system. Nothing worked right; nothing *felt* right. We even sensed, briefly, that our monetary troubles did not result from an act of God or a sudden onslaught from abroad but were the just deserts of our own follies. The attitudes with which the country looked at the economy in mid-1974 were those of the drunk awakening on the morning after: fear, self-disgust (not unmixed with rage at "others"), and earnest resolutions not to do it again. So we dragged ourselves up to President Ford's summit, and, like the drunks we are, we perceived a remedy: the hair of the dog. All the economists and businessmen agreed that "monetary restraint" should be eased. By the end of the year, short-term interest rates were coming down; it was all but certain that the 15 percent August rate would be 11 percent in January. Thanks to the desire of the Arabs to keep their surpluses in dollars rather than in some other currency, we were back to a fair, if somewhat depressed, simulacrum of business as usual, especially at the banks.

The business now considered "as usual" in banking, however, is a most extraordinary collection of activities and attitudes never before known to this venerable institution. Even at the end of the year the interest rate was higher than it had ever been before 1969. A Rip Van Winkle of a banker awakened today after a twenty-year snooze in his office would not even understand what some of his vice-presidents were talking about. And when he did begin to understand, he would probably feel like Van Vechten Shaffer, a magnificent old man who retired a few years ago from the presidency of the Guaranty Bank and Trust Company of Cedar Rapids, Iowa, and recently expressed his admiration for "all those young men from the Harvard Business School who are wizards, just wizards, at making loans. Not quite so good at collecting them."

Assets to liabilities

The revolution at the banks can be summarized in one insufficiently jazzy phrase: the shift from asset management to liability management. These are deceptively technical, and thus comforting, terms: nothing really important to our lives, it seems, could be so described. When I hear them I think of a friend of mine from the Rand Corporation

who once blandly compared the disaster of a possible nuclear war to the disaster of a possible six-foot rise in the level of the oceans. The change the technical terms describe is among the significant sources of today's inflation, and will long be a cause of financial instability in America and financial fear in the rest of the world.

Formerly banks would take their depositors' money, lend some of it, and invest some in notes and bonds. Loans always paid the bank a higher interest rate than good bonds. When loan demands increased, the bank sold some of its bonds to raise the money to make new loans: "asset management." Today, banks will meet an increase in loan demand by borrowing from others the money they then lend to their customers: "liability management." Interest rates are flexible: the bank in effect takes a markup over the price it must pay to borrow the money.

In the days of asset management, a bank might increase its loans without changing the totals on either side of its balance sheet: the rise in loans was matched by a drop in investments. A bank's footings (its total assets: the word itself connotes stability) changed slowly. In a time of liability management, the numbers on both sides of the balance sheet go up. Instead of standing on firm footings, a bank hangs suspended from an ever-expanding balloon, and, in effect, the money supply increases.

The economists who specialize in money and banking argue that, by its control of the quantity of money in the system, the government—in the United States, the Federal Reserve—controls the behavior of the banks. By selling notes and bonds in the open market, the government takes money out of the banking system, making it harder for the banks to fund their loans (which decreases their desire to lend) and raising the interest rates (which decreases the customers' desire to borrow). In 1959 a Committee on the Working of the Monetary System (the "Radcliffe Committee") reported to the British Parliament that the reason that this strategy worked did not in fact have much to do with "the money supply" or with the direct effects of rising interest rates. What discouraged the banks, as the Committee saw it, was the fall in the bond market that accompanied the government's sale of bonds and the rising interest rates. Finding that they could fund their loans only by selling their bonds at a loss, the banks pulled back and loaned less.

That description fits what happened in the United States in 1966, before liability management had become the banks' standard operating procedure: the banks took losses totaling nearly $400 million in order to meet loan commitments they had made before the Fed tightened the money supply—and they made no new commitments. Arthur Okun, chairman of Lyndon Johnson's Council of Economic Advisers, later wrote that in 1966 the Fed had "put on *the* virtuoso performance in the history of stabilization policy. It was the greatest tight-rope-walking and balancing act ever performed by either fiscal or monetary policy. Single-handedly the Fed curbed a boom generated by a vastly stimulative fiscal policy that was paralyzed by politics and distorted by war. And in stopping the boom, it avoided a recession."

Unfortunately, nobody in America took seriously the Radcliffe Committee's proposition that the crucial factor in achieving such results was the fall in the price of financial assets. When a vice-president of one of the Federal Reserve Banks learned that I was reading the Radcliffe Report, he said he couldn't imagine why: "It's been thoroughly discredited." Friedmanite economists demanded that the Fed concentrate solely on "the money supply"; Keynesian economists insisted that only the imbalances in the federal budget and the height of the interest rate were really important. Neither of these dominant bodies of theory accorded any great importance to the bond market: neither gave any reason to believe that a shift by the banks from asset management to liability management had made much difference in the effectiveness of the Federal Reserve.

By 1966 the revolutionary doctrines of liability management had already been well accepted in the giant banks of New York, Chicago, and California. The Fed had forced these banks to sell assets that year by maintaining ceilings on the interest rates they could pay for the money they borrowed. Most of the assets they sold were state and municipal bonds. In 1966 banks owned nearly half of all outstanding state and municipal bonds, and were the customers for about two-thirds of all new issues. When the banks began selling instead of buying, the bottom dropped out of the market: states, cities, and school districts could no longer sell their bonds at all, and they came howling to the Fed (and to the Congress) for relief. The House Committee on Banking and Currency called on the governors of the Fed to defend themselves individually. Nobody wanted to go through that again. As it apparently made no difference whether the banks funded their loans by asset management or liability management, the Fed acceded to the all-but-universal demand that it get out of the business of forcing the banks to sell assets.

The move to liability management meant that the banks no longer had to sell off part of their investment portfolio to make new loans: the market price of bonds was no longer important in their planning. Now, let us suppose that the Radcliffe Committee was right. The bond-selling and money-controlling activities of the Fed would no longer work to stop the banks from making new loans. (To the extent that the fall in the value of their investments had to be deducted from their earnings, in fact, the banks might even be encouraged to expand their loan portfolio in the hope that the profits from new loans would make up for the losses on old investments.) While the reported "money supply" might rise only slowly, the lending activities of the banks would in effect create a range of money substitutes—other exchangeable credits (charge accounts, so to speak)—that could be used to inflate the alleged values of nonfinancial assets and the price levels for the economy as a whole. But, unlike money, the substitutes could not be used by everybody—only by the most creditworthy, the most speculative, and those who already had the banks over a barrel. In short, we would have the combination of inflation and tight money that we got in 1973–74.

Instant gratification

The late Joe Palmer once wrote of the "rebel yell" that rose over the streets of Louisville through the night before the Kentucky Derby. "It was not the yell of the Confederacy," he noted. "It expressed man's eternal rebellion against going to bed." Though it may seem strange to those who remember the slogans so ardently shouted in the late 1960s, the banking revolution was indeed a suitable response to the noises of that time. For what our revolutionists were demanding was that this society must become a global gratification system for its current, temporary occupants. With the elimination of the painful need to sell assets, the banks could place themselves in the vanguard of both commercial and consumer gratification.

The Chemical Bank of New York has installed a number of Docutel machines, enabling a customer with the right credit card to punch buttons at any hour and take cash from a steel drawer. It is not necessary to have money on deposit to make these withdrawals: Chemical is happy to let its customers use the equipment as a way to borrow. The steel box with the buttons, the ads and commercials say, is a "YES machine."

This nonsense was started about a dozen years ago by Chase Manhattan and the Ted Bates advertising agency (famous for its Anacin, Carter's Little Liver Pills, and other "white-coat" commercials); it was Bates that coined the slogan about "a friend at Chase Manhattan." By definition, a friend is somebody who lends you money without asking too many questions. Subsequently, New York has learned that "First National City hates to say no," and that if two lending officers turn you down at Manufacturers Hanover, the third can still okay your loan. Every city can supply its own examples, though few are quite so extreme as New York's. Pushed along in this manner, total consumer credit outstanding went from $138 billion at the end of 1971 to $180 billion at the end of 1973.

That increase was bad enough: it meant that about a third of all the money American households saved from their income in those two years was actually spent for immediate consumption by other households. Much worse, however—much more dangerous—was the way the banks used their new loan-creating capacity as a source of generosity to business. Lending officers became money salesmen rather than applications analysts, and in the process credit was made available for a range of activities never before financed by banks.

Historically, bank loans have always been a source of "working capital," a way to finance inventory and pay wages to workers producing goods that would not be sold for a while. The typical bank loan ran ninety days. Nationally chartered banks were not permitted to write mortgage loans until well into this century, and even today correct procedure calls for the bank to make the builder's loan that pays for construction, and for an insurance company or a savings-and-loan association to "take out" the bank's short-term loan with a permanent mortgage when the building is finished. Long-term loans to business were unknown in American banking until the 1930s, and did not become properly acceptable until the 1940s, when the federal government encouraged such enterprise by banks as a way to finance the rapid expansion of war production. Even then, what made such lending legitimate was the government guarantee. By definition, loans that will be paid back only over a long period of time—and are secured by the "cash flow" of the borrower rather than by collateral—are riskier than ninety-day loans secured by inventory. And bankers are not supposed to take risks: they are lending other people's money.

Actually, many of the worries about term loans were always artificial. If there was going to be a "run on the bank"—if depositors were going to come clamoring for their money—the bank would have little more luck calling its ninety-day loans that it would have calling a term loan. A self-amortizing term loan that is paid back on regular installments is likely to be more closely watched than the ninety-day loan that is automatically renewed—"rolled over"—every three months. Today, in any event, deposit insurance has put an end to runs on the bank; it cannot be said too strongly that deposits under the insured maximum of $40,000 are *absolutely* safe in any FDIC member bank. The willingness of the Fed to serve as a "lender of last resort" means that a decently run bank (even an indecently run bank, as this year's Franklin National story proves) can always lay its hands on cash to repay a depositor without any need to call a loan.

The move to liability management seemed to place an automatic limit on the expansion of term loans. Bank loans had always been made at an interest rate fixed for the duration of the loan: borrowers had to know what their loans would cost. But a bank that counted on liability management to fund its loans could never know much in advance what *its own* money costs would be. Thus the new-style, postrevolutionary bank could find itself losing money on its term loans, paying more for its own borrowings than it had agreed to charge its customers. Contemplating this problem, the revolutionists turned more radical: they began to write their term loans with interest rates that would fluctuate according to the cost of money to the banks. By 1970 virtually all term loans of any length—one of the few exceptions was the residential mortgage loan—were written in such a way that the borrower's interest costs changed from time to time.

Now the banks were in a position to serve as gratification machines for industry as well as for consumers. Liability management permitted them to expand their loan portfolio without increasing their capital or finding new deposits; variable interest rates allowed them to write new loans without worrying about the costs they incurred when they increased their liabilities. Term lending expanded dramatically; bank loans rather than the public financial markets became the leading source of expansion capital for American industry.

Three potential disasters lie hidden in this technical maneuver.

(1) To the extent that the monetary policy of the Fed was effective because of its influence on interest rates, that effectiveness would be diminished. Prior to 1970, if a customer for a term loan was confronted with a bank's insistence on a high interest rate, he might decide to postpone borrowing until rates came down; conversely, a businessman might be tempted to borrow money and use it when the Fed was expanding the money supply and rates were low. As the first purpose of monetary policy is to slow things down in booms and speed them up in recessions, borrower attitudes to interest rates could help the government get the desired results. Since the introduction of variable rates, term borrowers have little reason to pay attention to the interest rate at any given moment. If it's high today, it will go down tomorrow; if it's low now, it will rise later. Thus bank loans grew almost 2 percent a month, every month, in the first half of 1974—at an annual rate of more than 20 percent—despite the highest interest rates in American history.

(2) Loans that were once relatively safe, because capable borrowers could confidently foresee earnings that would pay a known interest cost, became considerably more risky, because a borrower's earnings might not rise to match an unpredictable increase in his interest costs. The dirty secret in American banking today is the tens of billions of dollars of doubtful and decaying loans the banks are carrying as assets on their books. (Inside auditors, outside accountants, and bank examiners have all been remarkably indulgent in "classifying" loans; in 1974 the indulgence was reinforced by fear of what might happen if realistic standards were applied.) Many— maybe most—of the borrowers now en route to going broke are losing money simply because their interest costs are so much higher than anyone expected them to be. "Here," as the Red Queen told Alice, "it takes all the running you can do, to keep in the same place."

(3) Machinery has been created that enables the economy as a whole to invest more than its component parts have voluntarily saved. This is the root of our recent problems. Before the 1930s, one of the certainties of economics was that savings

and investment had to be equal. The interest rate was the price that cleared the market for money. If investment demand exceeded savings, interest rates rose, which discouraged investment and encouraged savings, establishing an equilibrium. If savings were greater than investment demand, interest rates fell, which discouraged savings and encouraged investment, restoring the equilibrium. The great contribution of John Maynard Keynes was the demonstration that in hard times savings could persistently exceed investments: worried businessmen would have a high "liquidity preference," meaning that they would prefer to hold cash rather than put their money to work; and they might be unwilling to borrow however low the interest rate might fall.

When Keynes wrote, in the 1930s, the notion that there might be a reverse to this coin was very remote and unlikely. The long-predicted Marxist crisis of underconsumption seemed to have arrived, and the problem was not the control of inflation (which Keynes had written about most perceptively in the 1920s) but the recovery from depression. Keynes's remedy for depression was budget deficits for government, putting back into the income stream the money withdrawn by excess savings. In an unlikely future when investment demand might exceed savings at a time when the economy was already producing near its capacity, the remedy would be government surpluses. Because budget cuts involve the elimination of programs people care about, this rather casually uttered prescription turned out to be politically impossible—indeed, governments continued to run deficits even when the economy was stretched. As long ago as 1967, Sir John Hicks warned that "the implementation of pseudo-Keynesian policies by weak and irresolute governments" would produce inflation that might create "a failure of international credit."

But apart from government deficits, which are more or less visible, Keynesian orthodoxy knew no machinery by which investment could outrun savings. Banks, of course, do create money. What the depositor leaves in his checking account is money for him; and the loan the bank makes

to employ that deposit is money to the borrower. Keynes's theory relied upon the "multiplier" effect of credit creation as an initial deposit worked its way through a number of banks, each finding itself possessed of some extra funds and lending them. But this expansion could be fairly easily controlled by the government-imposed "reserve requirement" that determines how much of a deposit a bank can lend; by government operations in the bond market to increase or decrease the money supply, and—though this was never explicitly stated—by the friction between the long-term and short-term money markets caused by the banks' reluctance to make long-term loans. The expansion of bank credit, in short, would operate to fully employ the existing productive capacity of the society, and then—in the absence of government deficits—deposit creation would stop. And so would lending.

In the 1970s, however, as a result of liability management and variable-rate term loans, our banking institutions have been reorganized to gratify the productive sector of the economy when it wishes to invest beyond the savings available for the purpose—just as they can gratify consumers who wish to spend beyond their income.

Restoring the balance

Once one leaves the abstractions of the monetary realm for the real world, a certain graceful symmetry is lost. Real resources, unlike monetary resources, can be shrunk but not expanded. In the original Keynesian dilemma, when investment fails to equal savings, the balance in the real world is achieved by a reduction in resources—production declines, people are unemployed, the economy is in depression. When investment exceeds savings, however, there comes a point beyond which additional resources cannot be quickly produced to restore the balance, and the economy must in effect force its members to save. This is accomplished by inflation. To those who want to release real resources for other uses, there is no difference between the man with a $10,000 income who spends $9,000 and saves $1,000 and the man with a $10,000 income who finds it will buy him only what used to be $9,000 worth of goods and services.

The original push toward intense inflation was supplied, no doubt, by the gigantic deficits in the federal budget—especially in the second and third years of the Nixon administration. Miscalculations associated with the Russian grain sale of summer 1972 and the dollar devaluation of February 1973 further exacerbated the situation; the effectiveness of the oil producers' cartel was an added lagniappe. Simpleminded efforts to stop the juggernaut with price controls ultimately made inflation worse, as they always do (in Britain, which has not only stiff price controls but subsidizes producers to hold down the prices of key consumer staples, the rise in the cost of living in 1974 was nearly 20 percent).

But in the United States during 1973 and 1974, government deficits were small; because of revenue sharing, the total budgets of federal, state, and local governments showed a surplus in 1973. What made our desperate inflation possible in those years was the ability of our restructured, internationalized banking system to brush aside the restraining efforts of the Federal Reserve and supply ever-increasing credit to investors, speculators, and consumers. Meanwhile, the traditional users of bank credit—the builders and merchants—were out in the cold, unable to deliver (or, more accurately, promise) sufficiently high returns to justify paying those interest rates. With credit pyramiding all around them, they feared, in Walter Bagehot's phrase, to "perish for want of money." The world was upside down.

A considerable number of technological advances and procedural innovations made possible and supported the revolution in banking—wire transfer of funds, computerized controls, lock-box collection systems, certificates of deposits, federal funds, Eurodollars, et cetera. There is no space here to describe these devices, but it must be said that in banking, as in most human endeavors, *how* is more important than *why*; and nobody should dream of proposing

reforms for the banking system without getting a firm grip on the day-to-day details of its operation. Just as no single dramatic event brought forth the revolution, no grand gesture of policy will end it. History is as irreversible for us as it was for our ancestors; to poke about hoping to rectify past mistakes would be the sort of fun that ends too fast, like throwing darts at a blown-up balloon.

With luck, the current recession will be allowed to correct some of the more drastic misvaluations (especially of both urban and agricultural land, of construction labor, and of some commodities) that have been heaved up by inflationary pressures. This cannot be done painlessly: if the public finds beef prices intolerable, as it did in summer 1973, feedlot operators will go broke and farmers will slaughter calves, as they did in 1974. The resulting punishments are of course allocated inequitably. Banks, because so many of their loans are "secured" by overvalued assets, must be among the sufferers if recession is to work its curative powers: we really need some bankruptcies, to wring out the water. The price of a suburban house can come down only when builders who have paid too much for the land are sold out by creditors hoping to salvage some of the loan with which the land was bought. The market economy works, not because it rewards success (there are lots of ways to do that), but because it aborts mistakes. The longer the monster's life is sustained, the worse the horror at its death.

We are not likely to be that lucky: the notion that the government can be omnipotent in economic affairs is now very deep-rooted, and the odds are that our economy *can* be puffed up—the misvaluations preserved, the over-priced houses sold, the monsters sustained—for one more swing around the track. As noted, the banks certainly think so: they are back to business as usual. And when one considers the cost in unemployment and anguish that would result from letting nature take its course—probably briefly, but who can be sure?—it is impossible to be too critical of the Micawberish attitude that if we can just keep the GNP growing, something will turn up.

Still, the feeling that the worst is over for the banks—which apparently permeated the annual convention of the American Bankers Association in Honolulu last October—almost certainly expresses wishful rather than careful thinking. The ecology movement has harmed the efficiency of the automobile and energy industries much more seriously than it is yet fasionable to admit, so that even if the recession is brief, unemployment will be more severe than anyone is now predicting. The impending economic and human collapse of India is probably something the banks can take with equanimity, but the American economy (and especially the banks) would be badly shocked if the existing political institutions of Italy and England prove incapable of forcing the Italians and the English to live somewhere near, if not within, their means. There is always, of course, the danger that the Arabs and Israelis will resume their killing. And the next months will see two pieces of bad domestic news that could severely damage the banking system.

One of them is the forthcoming revelation—which can scarcely be delayed beyond the first quarter of 1975—of how badly the Chase Manhattan Bank, our third largest, has been managed. This does not mean that depositors in or lenders to Chase will be in any way endangered or even inconvenienced. But after the announcement last summer that Chase's securities portfolio had been substantially overvalued in a quarterly statement, the directors appointed a committee of outsiders to investigate the bank; at least the outlines of their report will become public. Several people close to the work of the committee say that, at first look, the confusion at Chase was highly reminiscent of the conditions at Wall Street brokerage houses during the chaos of 1968–69. While things may not be as bad as initial reports indicated, neither stockholders nor regulators are likely to be pleased with what they learn.

The second is the rapid unraveling of the New York City budget, a tangled weave under both the Lindsay and Beame administrations. New York, alas, really is bust, with debts far beyond constitutional limitations. The scheme has been to take as revenues whatever real-estate taxes are assessed, and to spend the money, whether or not the taxes are collected. The city's rent-controlled residential housing and vacant industrial lofts have not in fact been paying their real-estate taxes. As of last June 30, no less than $405 million of alleged tax revenues was missing from the receipts; by the end of this fiscal year, fuel oil prices and mortgage interest rates being what they are, the total may near $1 billion. The city has been selling "tax-anticipation notes" to pay its day-to-day bills, and rolling over increasing quantities of paper every quarter. In November the total amount of such paper outstanding exceeded $2 billion. It is really the Penn Central business all over again, but with public rather than corporate officers performing the deception. The losses the banks may have to take on New York City paper and on impaired or defaulted mortgages could run into the hundreds of millions—and the effect on people's attitudes may be even more destructive. Nobody has even begun to think of what effect the bankruptcy of New York might have on its ability to continue to serve as the nation's financial center.

But the greatest danger of all is that the shocks will be absorbed, that we will continue to play the great games of let's pretend that have characterized economic and social policy for the last dozen years, that we will not voluntarily, without a terrible crash that stops capital creation, accept the discipline of making our savings match our investments and our tax revenues match our public expenditures. The abuse of credit money to serve pretenses has recurred in history since John Law invented the stuff in the early eighteenth century. We thought we had exorcised these ghosts with the legislation of the early 1930s; it turns out we hadn't. But the revolutionary techniques evolved to subvert the intent of these laws were not examples of greedy misbehavior by moneybags bankers; they were widely applauded ways to get done what the society wanted banks to do, regardless of what the authors of some old laws might have said. If we want a more solid banking structure, we had better build a more solid and less sensation-seeking society. Santayana's theorem has a corollary: those who do not make provision for the future will be condemned to repeat the past.

Socialist

Paul Sweezy and Harry Magdoff. Banks: skating on thin ice.

By means of the banking system the distribution of capital as a special business, a social function, is taken out of the hands of the private capitalists and usurers. But at the same time, banking and credit thus become the most effective means of driving capitalist production beyond its own limits and one of the most effective vehicles of crises and swindle.

—Marx, *Capital*, vol. 3

The specter haunting today's capitalist world is the possible collapse of its financial institutions and an associated world economic crisis. The miasma of fear is hardly surprising in the light of the coincidence in many capitalist countries of seemingly uncontrollable inflation, declining production, and instability in financial markets. The banking and credit community is showing increasing signs of weakness. Thus, in the span of one year the United States witnessed the two largest bank failures in its history (U.S. National Bank in San Diego and Franklin National Bank in New York). In addition, according to a report in the *Wall Street Journal* of December 18, 1974, more than a dozen European banks reported big losses or failed in 1974.

The state of mind of the ruling classes of the leading capitalist countries was well illustrated in an article in *Le Monde* (October 22, 1974), Europe's most prestigious newspaper, entitled "The Bankers of New York Begin to Feel the Wind of Panic." According to the paper's special correspondent in New York, he was told by a well-known American banker:

"It is not impossible that the monetary authorities will be led in the near future to make dramatic decisions, such for example as freezing certain long-term deposits in the banks (deposits established against the issuance of CDs, i.e., certificates of deposit for which there is a very active market in the United States). It is not even possible to exclude the possibility of a panic which would drive depositors to withdraw their funds."

These somber prognostications, made during a luncheon attended by some ten people, raised no objections from the other guests, whose analyses in other respects however were quite different from those of our interlocutor, a man with world-wide experience, not confined only to the United States.

Superficial apologists are inclined to gloss over these warning signals by dwelling solely on the special and, by implication, unique errors of the banks that collapsed, thereby ignoring the fact that these so-called errors are merely distorted reflections of more basic difficulties besetting the money markets. The more responsible financial leaders of the capitalist class tend to speak more frankly. For example, Robert V. Roosa, a partner in Brown Brothers Harriman and former Under-secretary of the Treasury, observed last August, according to a *Washington Post* disptach:

"There has been a loss of confidence in the [financial] machinery most of us took for granted. There is a fear, a kind of foreboding." It is "not too much," Roosa added, to say that these concerns are similar to the kind that prevailed in the 1930s. (Published in the *Boston Globe*, August 5, 1974).

And the chairman of the Federal Reserve Board, Arthur F. Burns, in a major address to the latest convention of the American Bankers Association (October 21, 1974) also went back to the Great Depression as a point of comparison for today's critical conditions. While he did not specifically identify the decade of the 1930s, he could not have meant anything else by his opening sentence: "This year, for the first time in decades, questions have been raised about the strength of the nation's, and indeed the world's, banking system." Rather than sweep this notion under the rug, as one might expect from a conservative government official charged with the responsibility to sustain the public confidence and faith on which banks rely to stay in business, Burns went on to spell out in considerable detail why such fears are justified, tracing the problems to the fact that the "goals of profitability and growth have been receiving more and more attention [by bank managements]." He did, of course, utter the necessary endorsement of faith in the banks, but made it clear that it does not rest on the liquidity and stability of the banks themselves. Instead, he pointed out that "for the first time since the Great Depression, the availability of liquidity from the central bank has become. . . an essential ingredient in maintaining confidence in the commercial banking system. . . . Faith in our banks. . . now rests unduly on the fact that troubled banks can turn to a governmental lender of last resort." (Full text of Burn's speech in *The American Banker*, October 23, 1974.)

Why is it that matters have been permitted to reach such a state—where banks can't stand on their own feet and must hopefully rely on the government to prevent collapse? Why, indeed, when there are long-established laws and regulatory bodies—notably, the Federal Reserve Board itself—designed to prevent precisely the dangerous developments analyzed coldly and competently by Burns in the aforementioned speech? Surely, the reason can't be ignorance. The relevant data about the operations of the large commercial banks are available to the Federal Reserve Board, and are pubicly distributed by the Board itself, from week to week. Moreover, the important changes, showing increasing sources of instability, are not new, but, as we shall show below, have been developing since the early 1960s and accelerating since the mid-1960s.

The answers to these questions are not to be found in ignorance, absence of wisdom, or lack of will power. What has to be understood is that the ruling class and government officials could hardly have prevented the present situation from developing no matter how much they may have wanted to. The overextension of debt and the overreach of the banks was exactly what was needed to protect the capitalist system and its profits; to overcome, at least temporarily, its contradictions; and to support the imperialist expansion and wars of the United States. Those who now complain and tremble over excesses are the very same people who helped bring them about, or at the least did nothing to forestall them, for fear of bringing down the whole financial network. This should become clearer as we examine some of the key facts.

Before we get into the workings of the banking system in these years of inflation and credit expansion, we should understand that there are two sides to the debt explosion: (1) capitalists borrow as much as possible not only from necessity but, more importantly, as a way to increase their individual profit rates, and (2) banks and other institutions aggressively increase their lending as a means of maximizing their own profits. The first point can easily be seen with a simple arithmetical illustration.

Investment—First Stage
Let us assume that a capitalist has invested in a manufacturing process $1,000
Profit
Assume that he makes a gross profit of 20% on this investment . . . . $ 200
Assume further that he pays 50% of profits in taxes . . . . $-100
He then makes a net profit of 10% on his investment. . . . . $ 100
Investment—Second Stage
The capitalist decides to double his capacity, but, instead of plowing back his profits, he borrows another $1,000 by issuing bonds. The capital in his business then consists of

Stock investment $1,000
Bonds $1,000

Total capital $2,000
Profit
Gross profit (20%) on total capital . $ 400
Assume bondholders are paid 6% interest on their $1,000 of bonds . . . . $ -60

The capitalist then has, after interest payments. $ 340
Deduct the 50% he pays in taxes . . $-170

The capitalist now gets a profit rate of 17% on his original $1,000 invested . . $ 170

This arithmetic of profits (in our simplified example, a potential increase in the profit rate from 10 to 17 percent) is what lies behind a good deal of the vast expansion of long-term debt shown in Table 1.

As can clearly be seen from Table 1, the rapid accumulation of corporate capital since the end of the Great Depression involved both equity investment and debt, but the growth in the use of bonds and mortgages far outpaced that of stocks. Stock investment (equity capital) increased $112 billion (from $89 in 1940 to $201 billion in 1970), while debt capital (bonds and mortgages) grew by $314 billion (from $49 in 1940 to $363 billion in 1970). This shift to much greater use of debt capital has two origins: (1) the drive to increase profit rates, as explained in the foregoing arithmetical example; and (2) the constant pressure to increase the mass of profits, even though, as in Marx's words cited at the outset, this means "driving capitalist production beyond its own limits," and means relying on debt because of the insufficiency of funds capitalists are able to generate internally or through flotation of new stock issues to finance expansion. Note that we are now discussing all corporations (financial and nonfinancial); the impulse to rely on borrowed money for investment capital extends over the entire spectrum of capitalist enterprise.

As much as this long-term debt of corporations has grown, it has nevertheless proven to be insufficient to appease the capitalist appetite for accumulation. And hence corporations, with the collaboration of the banks and other financial institutions, began to depend more and more on short-term borrowing as a means of obtaining capital both for new investment in plant and equipment and for their everyday operations. Salient facts on these changes for all nonfinancial corporations are shown in Table 2.

Especially noteworthy in the data presented in Table 2 is the marked difference between the years before and after 1960. Bank loans increased in the decade of the 1950s, but pretty much in line with the general expansion of nonfinancial corporate business: bank loans as a percent of nonfinancial corporate GNP were 12.1 in 1950 and 13.8 in 1960—a rise, but not an especially significant one. Other short-term borrowing also grew in this period, but in 1960 it was still small potatoes. Now look at the decisive change that begins with 1960. Between 1960 and 1974 bank loans grew at a much faster rate than nonfinancial business activity, the ratio of the former to the latter almost doubling: from 13.8 percent in 1960 to 25.2 percent in the first half of 1974, while at the same time other forms of short-term borrowing spurted forward.

Still more interesting is the acceleration in the dependence on bank credit. Thus, if we examine the rate of increase of this dependency (as expressed in the column of Table 2 headed "Bank loans as percent of GNP"), we find that reliance on bank credit

Table 1   Investment in all U.S. corporations

Year	Long-term debt bonds and mortgages	Direct investment by owners of the corporation: stocks	Long-term debt as a percent of stock investment
	Billions of dollars		
1940	$ 49	$ 89	55.1%
1950	66	94	70.2
1955	98	113	86.7
1960	154	140	110.0
1965	210	161	130.4
1970	363	201	180.6

Source: U.S. Bureau of the Census, *Statistical Abstract of the United States: 1973*. Washington, D.C., p. 479.

Table 2 Short-term debt of nonfinancial corporations

End of year		Bank loans	Other borrowing (a)	Gross National product originating in nonfinancial corporations	Bank loans as percent of GNP	Other borrowing as percent of GNP
		Billions of dollars				
1950		$18.3	$ 1.4	$151.7	12.1%	.9%
1955		25.6	3.0	216.3	11.8	1.4
1960		37.7	6.8	273.1	13.8	2.5
1965		60.7	8.8	377.6	16.1	2.3
1970		102.5	24.3	516.1	19.9	4.7
1974	(first half)	183.6	37.6	727.9	25.2	5.2

a. Includes commercial paper sold by corporations on the open market and loans by finance companies.

Source: Data for borrowing are from *Flow of Funds Accounts 1945–1972* (Board of Governors of the Federal Reserve System, August 1973) for 1960 and previous years; *Federal Reserve Bulletin*, October 1974, for the period after 1960. Data for gross national product originating in nonfinancial corporations are from *The Economic Report of the President* (Washington, D.C., U.S. Govt. Printing Office, 1974) for the data prior to 1974; and the *Survey of Current Business*, October 1974, for first half of 1974.

increases by 17 percent between 1960 and 1965, by 24 percent in the next five-year period, and by 27 percent in only three-and-a-half years from the end of 1970 to the end of June 1974.

While this kind of debt acceleration helps keep the economy going by "driving capitalist production beyond its limits," the dependence on debt produces limits of its own. If we assume for the sake of argument that the sale of bonds and mortgages and the granting of bank loans can keep on increasing endlessly, business borrowers can still absorb this expanding debt only as long as they can make enough profit to meet the rising interest payments. Eventually, if the debt load keeps accelerating, the interest on the debt begins to choke off profits and hence also the incentive, as well as the financial ability, to keep the underlying accumulation process going.

The capitalist answer to this dilemma up to now has been to feed the fires of inflation. As interest burdens increase—the result of larger debt as well as higher interest rates stimulated by the huge demand for money capital—capitalists raise prices to meet these obligations. And as price hikes spread throughout the economy, the need for even more borrowing follows. Thus debt obligations, interest charges, and prices chase each other in the upward spiral of inflation.

Thus far we have examined only one side of the problem: the demand for money by business, assuming in effect that there is no end to the supply of money. To a certain extent, this is a tenable assumption, but only if one also assumes that the government's money-printing presses go mad and end up producing a hyperinflation that destroys the country's currency. Short of such a runaway inflation, we are beginning to see obstacles emerging in the ability of the banks to keep on supplying credit at the accelerated rate of the past. It is true that the banks, in pursuit of ever more profits for themselves, have tried to keep up with the demand for loans. But in doing so they have stretched themselves so thin that their own liquidity is in question, and legitimate fears have been raised about the possible collapse of the financial system.

To understand this aspect of the problem we need to review a few simple fundamentals of how commercial banks operate. The traditional function of such banks has been to act as a depository (safekeeper) of money. Individuals and business firms place their money in these banks in the form of deposits in checking or savings accounts, which the banks should always be able to return on request. The banks in turn accept these deposits because they can make a profit by using the major part of them either to buy bonds or to make loans. Bankers base their operations on the assumption of a certain pattern of withdrawal of deposits by customers, i.e., that only a certain portion will be withdrawn each day. To meet these withdrawals, banks keep a reserve of cash. Since one cannot be too sure that there may not be unexpected surges of deposit withdrawals, an additional part of the deposits is invested in short-term U.S. Treasury bills and notes. The prices of these investments do not fluctuate very much and, more important, they can be sold almost instantaneously in the money market to raise cash, should deposit withdrawals suddenly increase. On top of this, banks invest another part of the deposits in longer-term bonds of the U.S. Treasury, other government bodies, and corporations. On such investments banks make more money than

on short-term debt instruments, their disadvantage being that the prices of these bonds fluctuate, which means that the banks can lose money if they are forced to sell when prices are down. Still more profitable for the banks than bonds are loans to businesses and consumers, but these cannot normally be turned into cash until they mature, so they provide little or no protection against a sudden dash by depositors to withdraw funds. Hence, for the sake of safety, banks have traditionally maintained a pattern of investment which consists of retaining a margin of ready cash and then distributing their money-making assets among a variety of notes, bonds, and loans.

Against this background look at Table 3, which shows how banking practices have been changing in recent years and why doubts have been arising about the general viability of the banking system.

The rise in the percent of loans to deposits between 1950 and 1960 is not especially noteworthy. Cash reserves in

Table 3 Loans and deposits: commercial banks

End of year	Loans	Deposits	Loans as percent of deposits
	Large commercial banks (a)		
	Billions of dollars		
1950	$ 31.6	$ 87.7	36.0%
1955	48.4	105.3	46.0
1960	71.6	127.2	56.3
1965	120.3	181.8	66.2
1970	188.8	266.8	70.8
1974	319.3	389.4	82.0
	Large New York City banks		
1950	$ 9.9	$25.1	39.4%
1955	14.2	27.9	50.9
1960	18.6	31.0	60.0
1965	31.8	45.7	69.6
1970	45.5	63.2	72.0
1974	78.9	93.5	84.4

a. Banks that had total deposits of $100 million or more on Dec. 31, 1965.

Source: Data prior to 1974 are from various issues of the *Federal Reserve Bulletin.* Data for 1974 are from *Federal Reserve Statistical Release H.4.3* for the last week in 1974.

banks (and in business firms) were still very large, reflecting the cash accumulated during the Second World War. Further, the fact that 56 percent of the deposits of the large commercial banks were loaned out still left the banks in a fairly secure position, with comfortable reserves in cash and short-term securities to meet emergencies. It is the inexorable growth of the percentage of loans to deposits since 1960 that cries out for attention. The heating up of the economy under the stimulus of the Vietnam War and the consequent kindling of the flames of inflation induced an expansion of the bank-lending activity beyond any traditional understanding of the so-called fiduciary responsibility of the banks, a process that endangers the safety of the money left for safekeeping and begins to bump against the ultimate ceiling of how much money banks can lend.

Clearly, the banks cannot lend out all of their deposits; some part must be held in reserve to pay depositors who wish to withdraw their money and to cover losses arising from defaulted loans. While there is no trustworthy guide to the "proper" ratio of loans to deposits, the persistent rise in the ratio, especially since 1970, reveals that even apart from their responsibility as safe-keepers of other people's money, the banks are fast approaching the absolute limit (100 percent) of the deposits that could be loaned out. Thus, as shown in Table 3, by the end of 1974 the large commercial banks had committed 82 percent of their deposits to loans; the same pattern is seen in the large New York City banks—at the heart of the country's main money market. To see this in perspective, it should be noted that the highest ratio of loans to deposits in U.S. banks between 1900 and 1970 was 79 percent (and that in only one year, 1921); in 1929 the ratio was 73.1 percent. (Calculated from data in U.S. Bureau of the Census, *Historical Statistics of the United States, Colonial Times to 1957*, Washington, D.C., 1960.)

How the banks were able to reach the extraordinary ratios of the 1970s will be explained below. But for the present it should be noted that a sizable part of the deposits

recorded in Table 3 are far from what would be considered "normal" deposits of banks. No less than 40 percent of the deposits of the large New York City banks consists of large certificates of deposit, money borrowed by banks to facilitate the rapid growth of loans beyond otherwise practical limits; and half the increase in these deposits between 1965 and 1974 was generated by the sale of these specially issued short-term certificates of deposit. But more on this later.

This is not yet the whole story. In their search for profits and since they are bumping against limits to their outright lending power, the banks have introduced and are expanding a new technique of lending, called "standby letters of credit." (See *Business Week*, February 16, 1974, p. 120.) For a fee, they guarantee the IOUs issued and sold on the commercial paper market by big corporations. In other words, the banks commit themselves to paying the borrowed money if the corporations default. Since it is the financially weaker corporations that need such bank guarantees in order to sell their IOUs, this type of "indirect loan" is itself of the shakier variety. These letters of credit are not reported on the balance sheets of the banks and are therefore not included in the loan figures shown in Table 3. If they were included, the 1974 percentages of loans to deposits would be even larger than those shown.

Why this mad rush by the banks to expand loans? There are two basic reasons: the lust for profit and the pressure of competition. Banks operate according to the laws of capitalism expounded by Marx. Their dominant motive is the continuous search for ways to expand profits: by accumulating capital and by increasing their rate of profit. They search in every nook and cranny of the economy, using salesmen, newspaper and television advertising, testing new devices—all geared to opening up new opportunities both for lending large amounts to business firms, real estate operators, stock market speculators, finance companies, and also for extending small loans (at even higher rates of interest) to the garden-variety of citizen. This incessant drive for business and profits goes on even as the banks' lending potential (as shown in Table 3) narrows; in this fashion, they are being true to their nature as capitalist entrepreneurs.

The second stimulus for the ballooning of loans is the competition among the banks themselves. Turning down the request for a loan to an established customer always carries with it the threat that the borrower will shift his entire banking business to a competitor. If the customer is a big corporation, there is every reason to expect that another bank will stretch itself to latch on to a new source of business, even if the loan in question does not measure up to "sound" banking practice.

Both of these pressures—the drive for profits and the need to protect one's already existing market—lead to a larger and larger share of relatively unsafe loans in the banks' portfolios. It should be noted that the very ease with which the larger corporations can get loans facilitates their carrying on their own business affairs beyond safe limits, as clearly seen in the steady decline in the ratio of liquid reserves relative to what the corporations owe. (See "The Long-run Decline in Corporate Liquidity," in *Monthly Review*, September 1970.) And the harder it becomes for the corporations to repay their bank loans (because of declining liquidity), the more the banks are obliged to grant further loans to prevent borrowers from going bust and thus defaulting on the backlog of loans. As willing or unwilling collaborators in the process by which the large corporations operate closer and closer to the edge of the precipice, the banks are themselves drawn nearer to the same edge, for they can manage to lend at such a furious rate only by impairing their own liquidity. What has been happening on this score is shown in Table 4.

The last two columns of Table 4 are measures of the liquid position of the banks. In other words, they show what percentage of deposits can be got hold of quickly by bank managements to pay back depositors' money in case of an upsurge of withdrawals. The decline in liquidity shown in the penultimate column of this table (the persistent decline from 54 percent in 1950 to under 14 percent in 1974) should come as no surprise after one has examined Table 3, for this decline has been a necessary complement to the increasing percentage of loans to deposits. (This inverse relation is not precisely complementary because of the growth of bank borrowing, as will be explained presently.) Yet even this meager liquidity ratio exaggerates the reserve position of the large commercial banks. First, in order for a bank to qualify as a depository for U.S. Treasury funds, it must keep a specified reserve of U.S. treasuries to back up

Table 4   Liquidity of large commercial banks

End of year	Cash Reserves (a)	U.S. Treasury Bonds (b)	Short-term U.S. Treasury Notes (c)	Cash + all treasuries as a percent of total deposits (d)	Cash + short-term treasuries as a percent of total deposits (d)
	Billions of dollars				
1950	$13.7	$33.7	n.a.	54.0%	n.a.
1955	14.9	30.1	n.a.	42.7	n.a.
1960	14.0	30.2	$ 8.2	34.7	17.5%
1965	16.3	24.3	8.6	22.3	13.7
1970	20.2	28.1	10.3	18.3	11.4
1974	29.5	23.4	7.9	13.6	9.6

n.a.: Not available.

a. Cash in vault plus reserves with Federal Reserve banks, as required by the Federal Reserve Board.

b. Bonds here include bills, certificates, notes, as well as bonds.

c. All treasury securities that mature in less than one year.

d. The data on deposits used as the denominator are those given in Table 3.

Source: Same as Table 3.

the government's deposits. Hence, not all of the treasuries included in this liquidity ratio would be available to meet sudden large drains on deposits. Second, the data shown in the third column represent what the banks originally paid for the bonds. (This is standard accounting practice for bank assets.) The market prices of bonds, however, go up and down: as interest rates rise the prices of bonds go down, and vice versa. For example, if a bank wanted to sell a 20-year, 3-percent Treasury bond which had been bought for $1,000 (and so recorded on the bank's books), all that could be realized on that bond in the market at the end of 1974 would have been about $550. Furthermore, if several big banks began to unload their bond holdings quickly, the market price would drop even further.

It follows that the data in the penultimate column of Table 4 overstate the degree of liquidity, sharp as the drop shown has been. A more realistic picture is given in the last column of the table, where only the short-term treasuries (those with a maturity of less than one year) are counted. And here we see the same pattern: a persistent decline in liquidity, dropping by almost half from 17.5 percent in 1960 to 9.6 percent in 1974. There is an interesting feature here that is worth noting. If you look at the first column, you can see that cash reserves have been rising since 1960, not as much as the growth in deposits but a significant increase nevertheless. The reason that the banks did this was because they were forced to in order to live up to the requirements of the Federal Reserve Board. But for the next most liquid asset—short-term treasuries—there is no such pressure from the Board. What the banks do with respect to short-term treasuries is their own business. So here the investment by the large commercial banks was actually *reduced* somewhat between 1960 and 1974 while their liabilities in the form of deposits were more than tripling during the same period.[1]

Liquidity ratios are not the only way of looking at the safety problem. Traditional theory of good banking practice points out that while loans are a source of risk, banks protect themselves by maintaining special reserves in reasonable anticipation of a certain percentage of defaults, and in the final analysis rely on the bank's equity capital (bank stockholders' original investment plus accumulated profits) to make good on unexpected loan losses (thus preventing loss of deposits). But here too the ratio of equity capital to outstanding loans has been steadily dropping, most noticeably since 1960, as pointed out by Arthur Burns in the speech quoted above:

. . . this enormous upsurge in banking assets [in other words, increase in loans] has far outstripped the growth of bank capital. At the end of 1960, equity capital plus loan and valuation reserves amounted to almost 9 percent of total bank assets. By the end of 1973, this equity capital ratio had fallen to about 6 percent. Furthermore, the equity capital banks had been leveraged in some cases at the holding company level, as parent holding companies have increased their equity investments in subsidiary banks by using funds raised in the debt markets. Thus, the capital cushion that plays a large role in maintaining confidence in banks has become thinner, particularly in some of our largest banking organizations.

For a better understanding of Burns's argument we should know something about bank holding companies. A "loophole" in the amendments to the 1956 Bank Holding Company Act has been used by most of the big banks to expand their activities into a diverse range of non-traditional financial operations. What happens is that a holding company is set up which owns a bank and at the same time may own, for example, mortgage, finance, and factoring businesses. A number of these bank holding companies have gone to the money market to borrow funds in order to carry on this variety of operations, and in the process have used some of the borrowed money to increase their equity investment in their own banks. This is what Burns is referring to: even that small ratio of equity capital to assets is overstated, since some of the equity is really only debt owed by the parent company.

And now we come to where the dog is buried. How do banks manage in practice to keep on extending loans to reach such percentages as shown in Table 3? Normally, banks get resources to meet the demand for loans by increasing their capital, attracting additional deposits, or selling off investments in bonds. As we have just seen, the increase in equity capital was insufficient to support the explosion in loans. Nor have deposits increased sufficiently. Finally, the banks did not want to take the losses that would result from selling off all or a major part of their bond holdings, assuming that they could do so without destroying the market for bonds. So beginning in the 1960s the banks themselves have become major borrowers in order to enable them to indulge in their furious rush to lend. In the process they have created a complex network of borrowing and lending throughout the business world which not only further stimulated the inflationary process, but also resulted in a kind of delicately balanced debt structure that is constantly in danger of breaking down. Now let us look at the facts as shown in Tables 5 and 6.

Before discussing the significance of the facts presented in these tables, let us first explain what some of the headings mean. The first item, money borrowed "From Federal Reserve Banks and others," is a catchall, which includes among other things a usually relatively small amount of money

that the Federal Reserve Banks lend for a short period to help banks maintain their required reserves, and money borrowed by banks on their promissory notes and other collateral.[2]

The series on "Federal funds purchased" represents, in large measure, borrowings for one business day of excess reserves from other banks willing to lend their funds. There are other borrowing devices included in this category, which as in the case of the federal funds were originally designed to cope with temporary adjustment problems of the banks. But these devices became transformed during the 1960s to meet an entirely different purpose: a tool by the biggest banks to mobilize the maximum of money resources, through going extensively into debt, in order to accelerate the pace of lending.

Still another method of borrowing developed by the big banks in the 1960s was the issuance on a large scale of negotiable certificates of deposit (CDs) in minimum amounts of $100,000. These too are short-term debts of the banks. Funds raised in this fashion are used to create new loans by the banks which, in addition to being usually of

Table 5 Short-term borrowing by large commercial banks

	Borrowed money (billions of dollars)					
End of year	From Federal Reserve Banks and others	Federal funds purchased (a)	Large negotiable certificates of deposit (b)	Eurodollars (c)	Total	Short-term borrowing as a percent of total loans outstanding (d)
1950	$0.7	—	—	—	$ 0.7	2.2%
1960	1.8	$ 1.4	—	—	3.2	4.5
1965	6.2	2.6	$16.1	—	24.9	20.7
1970	1.5	18.8	26.1	$7.7	54.1	28.7
1974	4.8	54.0	92.2	4.0	155.0	48.5

a. The data for 1960 and 1965 are from a special series designed by the Federal Reserve Board, based on the 46 most active commercial banks in the federal funds market. The data for these years are not comparable with those for later years, but are given here to indicate the trend. The data for 1970 and 1974 include, in addition to federal funds purchased, securities sold under agreements to repurchase identical or similar securities, and sales of participations in pools of securities.

b. These are short-term certificates of deposit issued in minimum amounts of $100,000.

c. These data are the reported "Gross Liabilities of Banks to Their Foreign Branches." According to the Federal Reserve Bank of New York, *Glossary: Weekly Federal Reserve Statements,* this item is often used as a proxy for Eurodollar borrowings, though these data include some other types of transactions between domestic banks and their foreign branches.

d. The data on loans used as the denominator are those given in Table 3.

Source: Same as Table 3.

Table 6 Short-term borrowing by large New York City commercial banks

Borrowed money (billions of dollars)

End of year	From Federal Reserve Banks and others	Federal funds purchased (a)	Large negotiable certificates of deposit (b)	Eurodollars (c)	Total	Short-term borrowing as a percent of total loans outstanding (d)
1950	$0.4	—	—	—	$ 0.4	4.0%
1960	1.0	$ 0.8	—	—	1.8	9.7
1965	2.5	1.4	$ 6.9	—	10.8	34.0
1970	0.2	5.5	7.9	$5.2	18.8	41.3
1974	1.7	13.6	31.7	2.8	49.8	63.1

a. Same as in Table 5, except that the earlier data are based on a series for eight New York City banks.

b. Same as in Table 5.

c. Same as Table 5, except that the figure for 1974 is estimated, based on past ratios of Eurodollar borrowing by New York City banks to all commercial banks.

d. Same as in Table 5.

Source: Same as Table 3.

longer duration than the life of the CDs, do not necessarily mature at the same time. This puts the banks under constant pressure to refinance the CDs when they become due, hopefully by issuing still more CDs.

Finally, there is the resort to Eurodollar borrowing. This in effect means the borrowing by U.S. banks from their branches abroad, and is based on the dollar deposits in these foreign branches. This method began to be used in 1966, but became especially important during the credit crunch of 1969. As can be seen from the data for this item shown in the accompanying tables, this method is used intermittently.

There are various technical aspects to these data which need not be gone into here. The important thing is to understand the speculative nature of the enormous debt expansion by the banks—both as borrowers and lenders. On the one hand, the banks are gambling that businesses will be able to repay their loans despite (a) declining corporate liquidity, and (b) the fact that many firms are borrowing to pay for investment in plant and equipment that will take longer to produce the income needed than is required by the loan repayment schedules. On the other hand, the banks are speculating on being able to support this large and growing lending by having recourse to the mercurial money markets.

How rapidly this short-term borrowing has grown and how dependent banks have become on this type of debt to expand their loan load is shown in Tables 5 and 6. From Table 5 we learn that the reliance on short-term borrowing by the large commercial banks reached a point by the end of 1974 such that it represented almost 50 percent of outstanding loans. Even more striking is the case of the large New York City commercial banks, where, as can be seen in Table 6, 63 percent of their outstanding loans is accounted for by short-term borrowing.

It is also important to understand the degree of uncertainty involved in these various forms of borrowing by the banks. They are almost all interest-sensitive, which means that the quantity of such borrowing can fluctuate very widely over relatively short periods, depending on the interest differentials for various types of borrowing. Arthur Burns in the previously quoted speech refers to the "volatile character" of these borrowings. And it is on these foundations that the equally volatile structure of loans, which keep the economy going, is based.

In short, the commercial banking structure, and the entire business world that relies on this structure, is skating on thin ice that is getting progressively thinner.

Why haven't the powers-that-be done something about this? As noted above, there is good reason to believe that all this has been well known for some time by the government agencies set up to prevent such menacing developments. From time to time, these agencies, and in particular the Federal Reserve Board, have taken steps to moderate one or more abuses, only to find that the financial community either found a loophole in the regulations or discovered another avenue to stretch out the debt load. Basically, the regulatory agencies were helpless, despite all their bold stances, because they too were committed to the same ends as the ruling financial and other business circles: to increase profits and to expand business opportunities, with all that these ends entail, including imperialist expansion and the Vietnam War. Rowing in the same boat as the business community, the regulators had to close their eyes to the dangers, trusting in lucky stars. Once the excesses began to reach a critical point it was too late to retreat, for too much disturbance of the intricate and complexly interrelated debt structure could all too easily break the thin ice.

The transformations described here also illuminate how fanciful are the myths of economists, Keynesians and non-Keynesians alike, who insist that they can produce a smoothly running capitalist economy by manipulation of such matters as fiscal policy, interest rates, and the money supply. The point is that all such devices do not get to the heart of what makes the capitalist economy go.[3] At best, they cover up for a while the contradictions of the capitalist system—contradictions that cause eruptions at one time or another—with the credit and banking arrangements being, as Marx long ago explained, at the center of capitalism's vulnerability to crisis.

The advanced thinkers of the ruling class are well aware of the inadequacy of the traditional nostrums as well as of the potential threat of a United States and world-wide depression. They are therefore searching for new and more reliable ways to keep the ship from sinking. It is possible to discern from the business press two important approaches emerging. One is to get the government's finances more actively engaged in salvaging business and banking firms that begin to flounder. This, however, has certain limits, for it entails widening the money and credit stream, and thus reinforcing the inflationary trend. (Over $1 billion, and by some estimates close to $2 billion, was lent by the Federal Reserve to Franklin National, merely the 20th largest commercial bank at one time, to keep the institution's head above water until some sort of reorganization could be effected, and to sustain public faith in the banking system, thus avoiding a possible flood of withdrawals from other banks. Imagine what would be required if one of the real giants began to gasp!)

The second, and more basic, line of thought is to create a firmer financial foundation for business, so that corporations can rely more on equity capital and less on debt. For this, a greater rate of profit would be needed by business. But that alone would not be enough. The government would have to step in more actively: first, to mobilize federal finances to fatten the equity position of industrial and financial firms; and second, to rationalize monopoly capital by weeding out the weaker firms. Within the limits of capitalism, measures of this sort can have only one meaning: to cut into the living standards (wages and welfare) of the working class, the old-age retirees, the petty bourgeoisie, and smaller businessmen. This is the only way that profit rates can be beefed up and finances procured to strengthen the equity capital position of the bigger corporations.

Here lies the challenge to the working class and whatever allies may be available to it. Above all, it is necessary to destroy prevailing illusions about the possibility of regulating capitalism in such a way as to produce prosperity for all classes. The ruling class will soon be sharply drawing the class issues with the hope of stabilizing their own affairs. Only by facing up militantly to the fundamental class nature of the impending struggle, which means challenging capitalism as such, does the working class have a chance to protect its true interests.

The credit system appears as the main lever of

overproduction and overspeculation in commerce solely because the process of reproduction, which is elastic in its nature, is here forced to its extreme limits, and is so forced for the reason that a large part of the social capital is employed by people who do not own it and who push things with far less caution than the owner, who carefully weighs the possibilities of his private capital, which he handles himself. This simply demonstrates the fact, that the production of values by capital based on the antagonistic nature of the capitalist system permits an actual, free, development only up to a certain point, so that it constitutes an immanent fetter and barrier of production, which are continually overstepped by the credit system. Hence the credit system accelerates the material development of the forces of production and the establishment of the world market. To bring these material foundations of the new mode of production to a certain degree of perfection, is the historical mission of the capitalist system of production. At the same time credit accelerates the violent eruptions of this antagonism, the crises, and thereby the development of the elements of disintegration of the old mode of production.

—Karl Marx, *Capital*, vol. 3

NOTES

1. One of the common illusions concerning this subject is the belief that even if bank liquidity is inadequate the Federal Deposit Insurance Corporation (FDIC) is at hand to protect the savings of depositors. The truth is that the FDIC is only an insurance company and can therefore rescue depositors only to the extent that it has enough assets to cover bank losses. Thus, as an insurance agency the FDIC was designed to deal with occasional breakdowns of one or more banks, and not with a major financial catastrophe. The dimensions of the problem can be seen from the following facts. According to the last annual report of the FDIC, the deposits covered by FDIC insurance amounted to $465.6 billion at the end of 1973. Against this the FDIC had $8.6 billion: $5.6 billion of assets, plus the right to borrow, according to existing law, $3 billion from the U.S. Treasury.

2. A description of these various devices, including loan participation certificates, bank-related commercial paper, as well as other items covered in Tables 5 and 6, can be found in Robert E. Knight, "An Alternative Approach to Liquidity, Parts I-IV" in the *Monthly Review* of the Federal Reserve Bank of Kansas City, December 1969 and February, April, May 1970. A shorter version of these questions can be found in Donald M. De Pamphilis, "The Short-term Commercial Bank Adjustment Process and Federal Reserve Regulation," in the *New England Economic Review* of the Federal Reserve Bank of Boston, May/June 1974. This is a summary of a more detailed treatment in one section of Federal Reserve Bank of Boston Research Report No. 55 by the same author, *A Microeconomic Econometric Analysis of the Short-term Commercial Bank Adjustment Process.*

3. In addition, hands of the policy-makers are usually tied. It is impossible to devise consistent policies that can at one and the same time handle the conflicting pressures on a capitalist economy: for example, the need to finance the military budget; to keep the money markets in shape to absorb the debts of federal, state, and local governments; to support the dollar abroad; to improve the balance of payments by attracting foreign funds and stimulating exports; to try to keep inflation from getting completely out of hand; to see that the banks have enough money to rescue tottering corporations; to keep the economy expanding at a rate sufficient to provide jobs for the labor force, etc., etc.

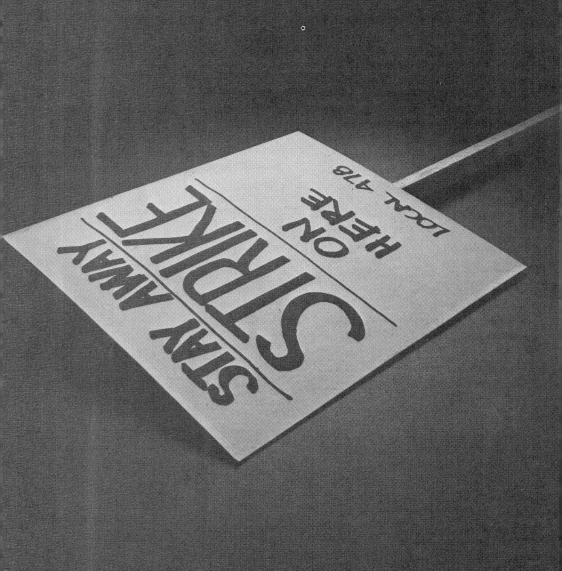

15 Unions

The basic questions this chapter will address are:

(1) Do unions serve workers or management?

(2) Is union leadership part of the corporate elite, or in opposition to it?

(3) Can unions be reformed so that they represent the interests of their constituency?

Conservatives do not believe in the existence of unions. However, since they have achieved the right to exist conservatives have to deal with them. The proper role of unions, to conservatives, is to keep their members in line and serving the interests of management. Since management is paternalistic it believes that union leadership should accept a place as a junior partner in the corporate establishment. Union leaders may maintain a facade of independence but their real interests are held to be the same as those of management.

Conservatives hold that the unruliness of workers in the 1970s[1] is due to three factors: (1) The impact of a youth society that is not oriented toward accepting decisions handed down by an authority. (2) The use of drugs. (3) The impact of the war in Vietnam. Together, these three factors have created an independent, individualistic, and undisciplined work force. The solution, as conservatives see it, is to get workers to work harder. One means to this end is the creation of sensitivity groups in industry whose purpose would be to persuade workers to accept industry goals on their own. The lack of discipline is a problem in interpersonal relationships that can be resolved through the management's use of psychotherapeutic techniques.[2]

Liberals maintain that unions are an important mechanism for the protection of workers. Obtaining and protecting jobs, increasing wages, and securing fringe benefits such as vacation time and hospitalization, are some of their major responsibilities. Unions guard workers against the abuses of industry; without them workers would be at the mercy of the corporation.

Socialists believe that most unions cooperate with management to keep workers in line. Most union leaders have accepted the ideology of the American corporate establishment and have acted to attain for themselves many of the prerequisites of corporate executives, such as high salaries, expense accounts, and elaborate offices. They have lost contact with workers and are often unaware of their needs. Workers in turn are alienated and isolated from their union leadership.[3] They often don't trust the leaders and sometimes refuse to ratify agreements negotiated by their leadership. To regain their autonomy workers conduct wildcat strikes on their own. Socialists feel that conditions of labor and false leadership need change. On this issue two strategies have been suggested by socialists: (1) The creation of alternative, representative, and responsible unions which act in the interests of their constituency.[4] (2) Formation of rank-and-file caucuses to elect new leadership for existing unions.[5] Through these two strategies socialist change can be effected.

NOTES

1. For a socialist viewpoint on the "unruliness" of workers see, Dan Georgakas, Marvin Surkin, *Detroit: I Do Mind Dying.* New York: St. Martin's Press, 1975.

2. Note, R. D. Joyce, *Transactional Analysis in Organizational Behavior.* New York: Pergamon Press, 1975.

3. G. David Garson, "Radical Issues in the History of the American Working Class." *Politics and Society* (Vol. 3, No. 1, Fall 1972), pp. 25–32.

4. Important on this issue is Stanley Aronowitz, *False Promises: The Shaping of American Working Class Consciousness.* New York: McGraw-Hill Co., 1974.

5. Dennis Bruun, professor of sociology at Bryn Mawr College, Bryn Mawr, Pennsylvania, has conducted research on this topic. For those wishing further information he may be contacted.

Conservative

Robert Schrank.   The young workers: their influence on the workplace.

This article is about the changing values of work. It is about a growing feeling that a job should be more than a place to make enough money to live on. The reason I choose to deal with changing work values, rather than the economics of employment, is that in the long run, they may be more influential in causing substantial restructuring of the workplace. The new work force, made up of the post World War II babies—all 40 million of them—is by far the best educated the workplace has ever seen. They are physically healthier and they are far more confident about what they want. They have stimulated an anti-authoritarian trend and it continues to grow. The new young worker is creating havoc with old notions about how the workplace ought to be run. Industrial organization, on the other hand, is based on an authoritarian hierarchical structure. Any challenge to that structure can mean a fundamental change of the production organization as we know it.

Who are these new young workers? They are the people who have entered the manufacturing work force in the decade of the sixties, especially the last five years. What I shall describe as the problem behavior of the new work force may refer only to a minority of the new workers. My assumption, however, is that this group represents the future, and what they are challenging represents the past. Clearly there are many new work force people who are behaving in most traditional ways. But it is the group whose behavior is new that is receiving the attention of concerned management people and behavioral scientists.

Challenging traditional ways

A major manufacturing company did a series of interviews with foremen around the country regarding the new work force. The foremen made the following comments:

"They are a hell of a lot smarter."

"They are better educated."

"I figure there are four in any ten of them with any desire to learn the job. The rest are here to do as little as possible."

"They don't give a damn. Watch 'em float around here, back and forth. I have to chase 'em to get any work done."

"They don't have a great fear of management as we had."

"Other generations didn't express themselves; this one does."

"You don't dictate to these people. Today you have to do more asking and suggesting and it sure takes time."

"The new work force presents supervision with problems they didn't know existed as little as five years ago."

"Because of low seniority many are at the bottom of the pay scale and have a tough time making ends meet."

These remarks are typical of sentiments I have frequently heard expressed. At least part of the new work force is challenging many traditional notions about taking orders, meeting production standards, showing up on time or showing up at all. How widespread is the problem? Dozens of major corporations reflect the statements I cited. While the assembly line is not typical of all production, its principles tend to dominate the workplace. It used to be the most efficient production system. Now products come off incomplete and not so well made. "Bring your Mustang back, we forgot to tighten the steering wheel." This same assembly line may have some trouble in getting itself to run because the new work force took off on Friday.

Why? A personnel director says: "Because they earned enough in the four previous days to loaf on Friday. They'll be back Monday and Tuesday when their dough runs out."

We hear about things like Chrysler giving away green stamps to get people to come to work and General Motors giving away colored glasses, just as filling stations do for customers who buy a full tank of gas. And workers are still not showing up on Monday and Friday. A training director of a major auto manufacturer said, "The Friday and Monday no show was started by the new work force. Young workers just don't care whether the cars come off the assembly line or not." This may be an example of acting out at the workplace the issue of relevancy that students on the campus have been talking about.

An international representative of the United Automobile Workers, speaking of the new work force, says: "There is a great desire for individualism as well as equality with the students on the campus." Some of the issues that students have been raising on the campus for some time are being raised in the workplace. For example, the minority rights and identity themes that have been played so loudly on the campus scene are now being heard on the job. Black militancy often gets translated into lack of interest, the questioning of instruction, and arguments—all of which slow down production. Similarly, white ethnic identity movements now appear to provide one more agenda for expression that interferes with smooth functioning of a mechanized system.

One of the underlying issues is how can the worker be relevant to the society and to himself. He asks: "What is the result of what I do? It's true I get paid, but the work I do is not contributing to a more satisfying life for me or for the consumer of my product." Indeed, the new worker sees much of the effort at the workplace increasing pollution, junk, and fatigue. As a result, he becomes concerned with the meaningless nature of his work and finds increasingly less satisfaction in his work life.

The satisfying of needs

When I was a young man going to work, there was not the slightest suggestion that working in a furniture factory or being a plumber's helper was supposed to be satisfying or meaningful. Quite the contrary. You were expected to be miserable and you

were. The workers of my generation didn't ask whether or not what they were doing was relevant. They simply wanted to know if they were going to get paid. If you got paid for working, you worked. Today, at least a part of the new work force is not accepting that premise. This young worker is becoming more aware of the impact of the workplace and the nature of his work on both himself and his community. Increasingly, he seems to feel he has a *right* to find satisfaction and pleasure in his work.

C. W. Weiss of the Bell System wrote in *Advertising Age:* "...the impact of changing youth attitudes is already being felt in the business world. There is every reason to believe that all the problems we experience today will be vastly multiplied in years ahead." This issue is generating considerable discussion in the business schools. I mention the fact because business schools are the source of future managerial talent.

A recent meeting in San Francisco brought together graduate students from the most prestigious business schools in the country. They formed an organization called The National Affiliation of Concerned Business Students. The final plank in their eight point program was: "You should feel a loyalty to both yourself and to your company. If all your efforts have been spent, which is possible (and the company does not fulfill your needs), just leave."

It would seem that many young production workers feel their efforts have been spent in trying to satisfy their needs, and so they do leave. In some companies they do it in droves. If you don't think this is much of a change consider how far a cry this is from Frederick Taylor whose philosophy of scientific management has dominated business and industry for fifty years. Taylor said:

For success, then, let me give one simple piece of advice beyond all others. Every day, year in and year out, each man should ask himself, over and over again, two questions. First, "What is the name of the man I am now working for?" and having answered this definitely, then "what does this man want me to do, right now?"

When I was growing up looking for a job in the thirties, working for the telephone company was considered having made it to the Taj Mahal. A strange contrast appears when I read management studies of the telephone company today. They talk of the crises of turnover, in some areas running as high as 200 percent. Industrial relations people in the Bell System are now coming up with extensive plans for undoing Frederick Taylor's work. Following Taylor's precepts, management advisors scaled jobs down to minimal repetitive tasks that could be performed by trained seals. Today's reformers are trying to fatten them up again and to make jobs more interesting.

Taylor's method of scientific management was designed to reduce personal friction on the job in order to maximize efficiency and raise production. The more that men could be set up to work like machines, the better the output. He urged management to relieve workers of responsibilities and to give them the simplest repetitive tasks so as to eliminate all anxieties about what they could or could not do. Today we are hearing a different tune—the work satisfaction consultants' chorus: if the worker can't control part of his activities in the workplace, he won't work.

Many years ago, I believed that the profit motive was responsible for the dehumanization of the workplace. I am now convinced that the real devil is the worship of efficiency and technology as the cure for all of man's ills. The eastern European countries share many of our problems in connection with young workers. Recent reports from the Soviet Union suggest that young workers there are similarly disrupting operations in automobile and other manufacturing plants. I suggest that these problems stem from the same source. The drive for efficiency, disregarding its effect on the workers, has the same ultimate result of creating worker alienation, no matter under what system it operates. I see the evil much more clearly now as a matter of "megatechnics" (to borrow Lewis Mumford's term), rather than hinging on who owns the means of production.

One approach to these problems has come from the human relations people. Sensitivity, T-groups, role playing, interface, etc.—mostly for supervisors—were seen as a panacea. Unfortunately, they were based on the assumption that if everyone just was nicer, understood each other better, and loved each other, everything would be fine. Actually, in most cases, the problems lay elsewhere—often in the structure of the workplace and in the task itself.

An executive of General Electric recently made this observation about the new work force: "First, we have to recognize that the needs and aspirations and motivation of our young work force are vastly different and changing everyday. If we are going to teach this source of manpower effectively, we've got a lot of work to do with getting them to understand the role of business, construction, the role of profit in providing new machines."

Another approach would be to admit that those of us in management have a lot of changing to do too. The G.E. statement is very revealing about one approach to the problems of the new work force; it says we've got to find some way to shoehorn these new workers into our system. I would suggest that, at the same time, we have to think about ways to improve life in the workplace and take advantage of opportunities for changes presented by the new work force.

Anti-authoritarianism is the common theme that runs through all these problems—as it does in other institutions, the schools, the church, and political life. It is a critical development inasmuch as authoritarian organization of power is the key to the operation of all facets of industrial societies. What is the source of increased anti-authoritarianism in the workplace and elsewhere?

The first factor, I suggest, is youth's magnitude. The percent of the population characterized as young—16 to 25 years of age—has increased from 11 percent in 1960 to 17.5 percent in 1970. By their sheer numbers, youth in the U.S. in the last 20 years have been dominant. That we are a youth-oriented culture is clear. That youth tend to be anti-authoritarian is also clear.

The second factor that has greatly influenced the workplace is the Vietnam War. The credibility gaps that came out of it have undermined authority. It seems to me that, for the first time, a substantial segment of our nation finds itself both humiliated and horrified. Increasing numbers of Americans view the war's destruction of Vietnamese land, crops, roads, and people as a grotesque abuse of authority and power. The war, like so much of what goes on in the society, relies heavily on technology. Again, Mumford's megatechnics—the kind of thinking that suggests that greater quantities are in and of themselves good and that all problems including the war have technological solutions. Many youths appear to be rejecting the megatechnic goal and are stressing the reinstatement of personal and humane social goals. Growing out of civil rights and anti-war activity, youths have been in the forefront of the attack on unresponsive authoritarian institutions to the extent of becoming almost a religious movement for a moral reawakening.

A third anti-authoritarian factor is drugs, and I am not speaking only of "grass," LSD, "red devils," and the like. The most influential drug of the past decade is "The Pill," the birth control drug which created a new freedom among our youth. This freedom quickly undermined many sexual taboos that previously operated as pregnancy preventives.

Emerging from this sexual freedom was a whole new movement of youthful sensuality. Drugs such as marijuana and LSD have been used to create a euphoria, a sense of joy, a sense of togetherness. Drug experiences have been an integral part of the lives of many of our young people, emphasizing for them the joyous, sensual side of life as against my generation's notion that hard work and sacrifice, a la Frederick Taylor, was the sure road to success. This acts as a strong counterforce to authority. Recently, there have been reports of increasing use of drugs at the workplace. This will further undermine traditional authority.

The fourth factor is that the sixties turned out to be a time of great soul searching and reappraisal for the American people. Quietly, naively, we began to review our national goals, what they should be, what we could do about poverty, inequality, discrimination, etc. The questioning of our priorities assumed that the existing institutions were not doing their job, another challenge to authority. During this time, we were led by a young president. Unlike Roosevelt, Kennedy was not faced with a depression. His was more a moral crusade against the evils of inequality, poverty, and discrimination. It was a youth crusade. It joined forces with the civil rights movement sparked by young people sitting at segregated lunch counters in the South. The Kennedy and Johnson period might be called the years of growing expectations. A better, more meaningful, more gracious life was held out as a possible reality. No group believed it more than our youth. They rallied, marched, sat in, campaigned, and fought hard. In the end, they were disappointed and unsure of what they had accomplished. They became much more anti-authoritarian.

Finally, and perhaps the strongest factor of all, is the ultimate achievement of technology—"The Bomb." It has seeded a revolt against technology and the authoritarian bureaucratic structure that operates it. While the bomb is the ultimate in pollution, technology and authority are being questioned also by people choking on polluted air. King Car is now viewed as another possible devil rather than a Merry Oldsmobile. The Great God Computer may soon be another devil. Ten years ago it was going to bring us the golden age. Today it is looked upon as a super snooper. The sixties may become known as the disillusioned enlightenment: a period of great expectations and a great deal less fulfillment. The disillusionment grew with increased awareness of technological failure.

Much of the challenge to technology comes from the youth who asked the questions about the relevancy of their education when people remained poor. The experience of the sixties (technology run rampant without making our life any richer or better) created today's atmosphere of indifference at the workplace. This indifference, I suggest, is a new form of protest, an American style of passive resistance.

Obviously, the factors I have cited do not apply to all youth; relatively few young people, I imagine, would claim to be affected by all the issues mentioned. Still, the changes I have been talking about have an indirect influence on many members of society without their taking an active role. A young assembly line worker does not necessarily have to take drugs to sense and enjoy the new freedom, pleasure seeking, and sensuality of the youth culture. The culture itself has an effect on his values.

All that I have been describing can be seen as a challenge to the organization charts which build authority like a pyramid, where power moves from the top to the bottom via the organization boxes. The behavior of the new work force is eroding authority from the bottom up; the new managers are eroding it from the middle down; and the behavioral sciences are providing the theoretical arguments for both efforts.

At the same time that managers are struggling with the new work force, the schools are experimenting with educational methods that may further undermine authority. Schools modelled on the English "open classroom," discarding traditional methods and structure, are often ungraded, noisy, confusing places that encourage students to set their own goals, determine their own schedules, plan their own work. Socializing is a significant ingredient in the learning process in these schools. Having visited some of them recently, I was left with a strong impression of a lack of authoritarian control. Teachers try to guide, not order. Children are encouraged to think independently and to raise questions. I found it very strange to see this going on in a school that is supposed to be preparing children for an industrial society. When the products of the open schools get to the workplace in significant numbers or when open schools become a generalized system of education, there will be an even greater challenge to authority. If we thought we had trouble with graduates of progessive education, wait till the "open school" kids arrive!

I had been brought up to believe that we worked to fill basic needs of food, clothing, and shelter. It is still difficult for us to act on the premise that these needs can be satisfied. Abe Maslow spoke of a hierarchy of needs and about man wanting to be self-actualized after he had fulfilled his basic needs. Despite Maslow, my generation has difficulty accepting the notion that joy and happiness and a quality of life can be issues in the real world. Yet, that is what Maslow, Goodman, Reich, Roszak, and others see in the youth culture. This is what I hear the youth work force saying to us. And we need to accept the notion that "quality of life" may be a real issue in the workplace as it is in the environment.

How do we go about improving life in the workplace? First of all, the relationship of school to work needs to be redesigned in order to permit people to alternate between school and work over their lifetimes. Work that is related to school ought to be accredited as part of the learning experience. The open school encourages students to bring the outside into the classroom. We now ought to go a step further and acknowledge that the outside *is* a good classroom. It ought to be accredited. Organizations that provide work assignments such as the Peace Corps, Vista, etc.—can be integrated into an educational program. The new work force should have opportunities to move in and out of various work and study programs. As part of their bargaining package, unions need to negotiate educational funds for their membership. These funds should be used by the union to develop new educational facilities for their members.

In the workplace itself, many changes are possible. They can be grouped into several categories:

First, laws regulating work can be re-examined with the young worker in mind. Currently, child labor laws are based on the assumption that the workplace is evil, dangerous, and corrupting. "Child labor" evokes images of tiny kids in ragged clothing, standing before the jaws of monstrous mill machines. We need to adjust these laws to permit youth to move into the work force on a work-study program. In most workplaces today, this would not be endangering their health and safety.

Once in the plant, youth need to participate more fully in the operation of equipment. In many instances, laws prevent this. In New York State, 16-year-olds cannot run power equipment on the job. While many 16-year-olds drive motorcylces, build amplifiers, run power lawn mowers or snowblowers, they must keep hands off in the plant. When we talk about high rates of unemployment among 16-21-year-olds, we have to think about laws which currently hinder their hiring.

Second, the work itself needs to be considered. Where routine, repetitive work is involved, we may need to consider offering employees two jobs, possibly in different locations. This could lighten the burden of boredom. Similarly, shifts in working hours can be tried. The nine- or ten-hour day, the four-day week, etc. are already being applied in a number of small companies. The three-day weekend apparently compensates for some part of the routine endured on the job.

Third, the structure of work tasks no longer need to be rigidly fixed. There are companies such as Texas Instruments that have permitted the work force to reorganize sections of the production process as they saw fit. Others have created worker teams that take on a series of tasks and attend to the planning, execution, and quality control. Sony in Japan went a step further. There, management took a TV assembly line, turned it over to 50 workers, and said: "You make the TVs however you want. Just give us fifty a week."

Fourth, participatory schemes are cropping up in an increasing number of companies. American unions have not been receptive to the idea in the past, seeing it as company unionism. The European experience suggests that worker participation can be useful in bringing worker representation into management policymaking

levels. While European schemes tend to be formalistic rather than substantive, they at least provide a model that we ought to consider. Recently, Volkswagen expanded its worker participation by putting two workers on its Board of Directors.

In the U.S. the new work force is organizing itself within the unions in youth caucuses, conferences, and publicity campaigns. Its members are urging the union leadership to become involved in the organization of the workplace, the nature of the task, the effect of seniority systems, the effect of the contract on flexible assignments, etc. All this goes far beyond the traditional union concepts of hours, wages and working conditions. Enlightened union leadership will seize this opportunity to revitalize their organizations with new concerns.

Unions spend a considerable amount of time telling new young members of their "valiant fights" over many years. The new worker, like the student, does not see how that relates to his problems. He is concerned with the quality of the "now," not with the past and not even much about the future. His interest in pension and insurance may be far less than it was in my generation.

Management will kick and scream that the organization of the workplace and its effects on the community are exclusively their concern. Some old line unionists will agree with them. I submit that they are both wrong. I agree with John Galbraith that corporations are no longer private institutions with the right to do as they please. They are more and more becoming public. If, in fact, tax money is used to save Lockheed, bail out Penn Central, and subsidize the airlines, then employees ought to have something to say about how these companies are run. Employees could do no worse than the present management in some companies.

These are the problems of the workplace. I am not suggesting that easy solutions exist. But I am suggesting that the new young work force will not accept current conditions simply because they are there. That kind of acceptance of tradition and authority may be past. The young worker is rightly insisting that we try to make life at the workplace more challenging, less degrading, more meaningful. That is something that all of us should subscribe to and support.

Liberal

Eileen Whalen. Working women.

More and more women are leaving the house at 8 a.m. and coming back at 6 p.m., five days a week. They're riding the buses and subways or getting a lift from a neighbor to go to the office or the plant. Though more and more hours are spent by women at their jobs away from home, there is an attitude among employers and many of us that those jobs are not their real work and need not be taken seriously.

Today's average woman has had her last child before she's thirty. So by the time she is thirty-six her children are either in school or on their own. At this age she often thinks of going back to work.

Marital status of women workers	(Approx.)
Married (husband present)	60%
Single	20%
Divorced, separated, or widowed	20%

1920: Average age: 28; usually single factory worker or clerk.
1970: Average age: 39; usually married, in variety of occupations.

If a woman with children works, her average work life will be twenty-five years. The woman who never marries works an average of forty years.

The greatest recent increase in women workers has been among young married women. This increase is probably due to the recession which brought on inflation and unsteady employment for many husbands.

About one out of three women with children under six is working, usually part-time. There also has been an increase in young wives who work full-time, putting off having children. With male teachers and engineers losing their jobs, even middle-class wives increasingly have no choice but to go to work.

Why do women work?

Are young women just passing the time waiting for a husband and children? Do married women want extra money for clothes and luxuries, or are they just bored with staying at home? These are the explanations most frequently given in the magazines. These explanations are myths which are profitable for employers. For women, they only reinforce work conditions where women have low wages and status, boring and repetitive work, with little training and promotion whether working three or thirty years.

By far the main reason women work is to keep their heads above water economically. Approximately 75 percent of the families where the wife works would have an inadequate income if she didn't work.

In two out of four families, the wife's working brings the income up to $7,000. For a family of four that means having better meat on the table and being able to buy more than one winter coat a year per family. For the third family, the wife's working brings the income up to $9,000. For that family it means having some choice in housing and going to a private doctor rather than a crowded clinic. In the fourth family, the husband's salary is adequate and the wife may work because she wants to.

Single, divorced, separated, and widowed women are supporting themselves and often their children. Ninety percent of divorced women work.

Wives working

Working wives sometimes create conflicts while easing others. Tensions and frustrations are often eased in families where the wife's salary makes the difference between being poor and getting by. Besides actual living conditions being better, and thus more relaxed, the husbands have less fear of losing their jobs and more freedom to challenge their working conditions.

For women, the psychological benefits of working are very important. Getting a pay check and having the freedom to spend money earned by herself can give a woman much strength. The socializing and friendships that working women have and often couldn't have as housewives mean a great deal to them. In low-paying jobs where the work is very boring, talking and kidding may be the only aspects of the job the women enjoy.

Many husbands resent their wives' working. In their minds a working wife indicates that the husband is a "failure." Some husbands fear their wife's job makes her less dependent upon them by giving her some economic security and some sense of equality. At the same time, the depth of men's resentment over women's "soft" work at home is probably too deep to be measured. How many housewives know the pressure the question "What have you been doing all day?" brings, and how often they have felt their answer was not accepted. This reflects a basic contradiction in our society where the work of a housewife who works an average of ninety-six hours a week is considered less valuable than the work of a man who works forty hours a week; where the housewife who cares for and maintains a worker, her husband, and future workers, her children, is not paid by society for this valuable service.

Men feel trapped in jobs they can't take pride in when the economic well-being of their families is on their shoulders. Because of this pressure and the feeling many husbands have that their wives are not as vital members of the family as themselves, they often take their frustrations out on her and the children. The unjust pressures that families are now under need close examination.

Black women

Black women workers are the most vulnerable of all working people. One-quarter of black families are headed by women. Black women have twice the rate of unemployment as white women and when they work they earn on the average 85 percent of what a white woman earns. Racism so limits the job opportunities of the black husband that a black woman's earnings are even more necessary to her family than the white woman's. The same racism limits a black woman's occupation. The largest occupation for older black women is household work. In the South the average wage is $4 to $7 a day. In the North the average wage is $15 a day with a few women ranging up to $23 a day. Nowhere are household workers guaranteed benefits such as sick days, vacation, holidays, or medical insurance, except at the discretion of their employer. The other main occupations for black women are service work, such as waitresses, restaurant workers, nurse's aides, hospital workers, hotel maids, and office cleaning women. Black women are underrepresented in clerical and sales work. Even though there are more professionals among black women than black men, these professionals are mainly elementary school teachers and nurses, the lowest-paid professionals. In the past, many black families gave their daughter an education rather than their son, knowing that a black woman could get a professional job where a black man could not. With more black men in college than black women, this is now changing. The myth that black women have prospered at the expense of the black men keeps the real causes of poverty from being seen.

Women's absences and turnover

One of the most frequently given reasons by employers for not hiring, training, or promoting women is women's absences and turnover.

Women's average absences are little more than five and one half days per year (5.8) and men's are little less than five and one half days per year (5.3). This includes days lost because of pregnancy and child-birth. Women and men have different kinds of illnesses. Women are more likely to have acute conditions such as bad colds, operations, etc., while men have chronic conditions such as heart disease, arthritis, and rheumatism. Women's acute conditions mean absences of short periods, while men's chronic conditions mean less absences but of longer periods. Because shorter absences create less disturbances on the job, studies have found that total financial loss from men's and women's absences is the same.

A statistic not favorable to women is their rate of continuous employment. Women's average rate is 2.8 years at the same job while men's is 5.2 years. While older women, married or single, have greater job stability than all men, there are several reasons why younger women, married and single have less stability.

Young married women leave jobs for childbirth and child care. Most companies have had the policy of asking women to quit their jobs some time before the baby is due. The exception to this are women workers who are protected by their union. With a vast pool of unemployed women available, companies do not hesitate to lay off a pregnant woman rather than hold her job for her. The new woman they hire will be at a lower salary since she is a beginner. A recent ruling of the law requires companies to treat maternity leave as sick leave with the same terms as any other temporary disability. Most women don't know about this ruling and employers are still taking advantage of them.

Many women want to return to their jobs but can't for lack of good, inexpensive, neighborhood child care. Most children of working women are taken care of by relatives or go to school with a neighbor keeping an eye on them. Only 2 percent of working women have children in child care facilities. Lack of child care is the most important factor keeping women from seeking work or staying on the job.

The kind of work people do has an effect on their job stability. A study of employees in a civil service agency showed that employees with lower-level jobs have more turnover and absences than employees with higher-level jobs, and women are overwhelmingly concentrated in the lower-levels. It was shown that when men and women were earning the same salary the differences were insignificant. Highly trained women occupying responsible positions were seldom absent and their turnover rate was much lower than women with fewer skills. This indicates that responsibility and skill influences the employee's morale and that in turn affects job stability.

Married women leave jobs because their husband's work demands a move to another location. When men and women begin to consider themselves equal, in any move the wife's job will be considered as important as the husband's.

Occupations and wages

Women are concentrated in a small number of occupations. There are seven major areas of work: clerical, sales in retail stores, household, teaching in elementary schools, bookkeeping, waitressing, and nursing. An important occupation for women is clerical work, with 42 percent of all clerical workers being women. Among clerical workers women do 98 percent of the typing, filing, and secretarial work, while men dominate in accounting and shipping. Men also dominate in the higher categories of clerical work in the fields of finance, insurance, real estate, and civil service. The different categories have different pay scales.

In another major occupation for women, retail sales work, women usually have salaried jobs, often at minimum wage, while the high commission sales, such as appliances and autos, are reserved for men.

In industries where women and men are separated at their work, women doing comparable work to men are paid much less than the men. In comparison, in industries where women and men work side by side doing the same job the woman earns less than the man but nothing as severe as when the sexes are separated.

In 1970 the average weekly wage for women was $95 while men's was $135.[1] *Time* magazine, in its special issue on "The American Woman," calculated that if women were paid wages equal to men, it would raise wage costs some $109 billion a year. This is money which is now industry profit.

Some of the ways employers take advantage of women

Employers hire part-time or temporary rather than full-time workers since they don't have to give them any benefits such as sick pay, vacation, insurance, etc. In part-time work, raises are infrequent and small.

Companies know they can have cheap labor when they locate close to a residential area. Many women with children can't travel far because of their home situation and lack of public transportation. At the same time that same company will pay higher wages at another branch where the employees are not at such a disadvantage.

Men are not benefiting from women's lower wages—employers are. At the same time that companies refuse women jobs in middle and higher categories, they are eager to hire women for "new" jobs. Skilled white- and blue-collar men have been "laid off" from these jobs when they were reorganized and automated to make them "new." In the field of printing and type-setting, linotype machines are being replaced by faster electronic typesetters, and women are hired as "skilled typists." Men are not usually hired for the typist position, and the salary is one-half to two-thirds of the former linotype operator's. In the electrical industry, work with heavy equipment is being broken down and automated so that women can be hired instead of men. In both instances the men were unionized and the women were not; thus they are forced to compete with each other and wages are kept low. Only 12 percent of women workers are in unions.

Marriage and work

There are other ways that industry profits from the restrictions on women's lives. One that affects all women is the way we have been brought up to expect marriage to be our "career." With the rapid increase in working married women and the large number of divorces this is far from the truth. Yet we are trained for low-skilled, low-paying jobs, no matter how many years we work. In our minds we are in conflict too, and often do not demand training, promotion, or pay to match our value. This is especially true of women who go back to work after raising children. They weren't trained before their marriage and now as older women they feel they've lost their chance and should be grateful for any job they have. Through the experience of child raising many women have become very capable people, but they are automatically shunted into jobs that use little of their ability.

A large labor force of reliable workers who hesitate to ask anything for themselves is a gold mine for industry, and since the quality of human lives is less important than profits, industry will resist any efforts by women to improve their conditions.

What can women do?

Individually a woman can apply to the Equal Employment Opportunity Commission (EEOC) for injustices such as discrimination in hiring, unequal pay for equal work, and maternity leave. But women's working conditions will not change substantially until we work together as a united force.

The way women can have the most strength is by joining a union. Some people are critical of unions. They say they are bureaucratic and only concerned with improving wages. Also the structure of unions tends to exclude women from decision-making levels, so the particular needs of women are not considered. Some union executives are corrupt at the expense of the union members and the general public.

Unions do have these serious limitations. However, joining a union is still the necessary first step if women are going to get better conditions at work. Individual solutions for working women—more women managers, more women professionals, etc.—are solutions that could only affect a tiny minority of working women. Only by working collectively, by each woman seeing her interests as identical to another woman's interests, by standing together even when our jobs are threatened can women have strength.

There are many young men workers and even more women that are challenging the *kind* of work they do. Young auto workers are rebelling against the assembly line. They want control over their jobs so that they will have respect for the work and themselves rather than being cogs in the wheel. Women are challenging the division of labor where typists have no say over what they type and filing clerks have no voice in determining the filing system. What is being challenged is not only the division between the work of men and women but also the work division between the people who have advantages such as backgrounds with money and education and the people who don't have these advantages. We must make sure that women's liberation doesn't mean an equal number of women sharing with men the professional jobs and high incomes while making sure the majority of men and women, the working class, stay in their place doing the "dumb" work.

For women's lives to begin to change we must work together to gain community-controlled child care, equal education, and democratic unions controlled by ourselves. Yet many contradictions will still exist in our lives, since we live in a society where men dominate women, and our economic system of profit forces people into competition and misuse of each other rather than cooperation and mutual aid. We have a long, hard job ahead of us making our society into one where women and men, black and white are equal.

1. These wages are based on hourly rates for a thirty-seven hour week for women and a forty hour week for men, (1970 Census Report), and do not include overtime which is a necessary ingredient of many incomes.

These wages are the average (the range of salary that most of us are in, doing the kinds of jobs most of us do), not the median, which is the figure usually published by the Labor Department. The median is often interpreted by people to be the average but it is not. It is higher, especially for men, since it is the middle mark of the total of all men's wages, including the salaries of the millionaires.

Socialist

Dan Georgakas and Marvin Surkin. Niggermation in auto: company policy and the rise of black caucuses.

I work at a small shop in Troy....Three weeks ago a woman on the day shift got her arm chopped off in a press. The week before this happened the press repeated and they said they'd fixed it and kept people working on it and then this lady got her arm chopped off. People were really freaked out; some of the people on days ended up quitting.

Denise Stevenson, in a statement to a People's Court convened by the Motor City Labor League, April 3, 1973.

One of the major concerns of the League of Revolutionary Black Workers was the deteriorating working conditions at the point of production. In 1946 some 550,000 auto workers had produced a little over three million vehicles, but in 1970 some 750,000 auto workers had produced a little over eight million vehicles. Management credited this much higher productivity per worker to its improved managerial techniques and new machinery. Workers, on the other hand, claimed the higher productivity was primarily a result of their being forced to work harder and faster under increasingly unsafe and unhealthy conditions. The companies called their methods automation; black workers in Detroit called them niggermation.

Niggermation, not automation, was clearly the watchword at Chrysler Corporation's Eldon Avenue Gear and Axle plant. Clustered alongside four other Chrysler plants—Huber Foundry, Winfield Foundry, Chrysler Forge, and Plymouth—Eldon employed a workforce of over 4000, of which 70% was black. Eldon covered over a million square feet, was surrounded by another half-million square feet of storage and siding areas, and housed 2600 machine tools of 170 types. In a report to the National Labor Relations Board on November 30, 1971, Chrysler Corporation described Eldon as "engaged primarily in machining metal parts for rear axles of most Chrysler-built automobiles, for which it is the sole source, and assembling the parts into completed axles." Workers considered this key plant the most niggermated factory in Detroit.

Even though Chrysler acknowledged how vital Eldon was to its operations, working conditions at the plant continually deteriorated. These poor conditions reached such proportions that by 1970 harassment, industrial illnesses, injuries and deaths on the job pushed Eldon workers to the breaking point. After James Johnson shot and killed two foremen and a job setter, his attorney, Ken Cockrel, said, "We'll have to put Chrysler on trial for damages to this man caused by his working conditions." The Johnson jury was taken to Eldon, the "scene of the crime," to observe for itself the conditions which Judge Philip Colista had called "abominable" and which UAW Safety Director Lloyd Utter termed "inexcusably dangerous" and evidence of "a complete neglect of stated maintenance procedures." The jury agreed and concluded that James Johnson was not responsible for his actions. That August, during the local contract negotiations, Chrysler admitted to 167 separate safety violations at Eldon; yet a

year and a half later, in January of 1971, the Michigan Department of Labor found hundreds of violations of the Michigan safety code still uncorrected. In a separate case brought against Chrysler by Johnson, he was awarded workman's compensation of $75 a week, beginning from the day of his "breakdown."

Eldon workers knew that James Johnson was not an isolated case. Serious provocations, injuries, illnesses, and deaths were the realities of their everyday work. On May 26, 1970, less than two months before Johnson fired his M-1 carbine, another death had occurred at Eldon. Gary Thompson, a black 22-year-old Vietnam veteran, had been killed when his defective jitney overturned and buried him under five tons of steel. UAW Safety Director Utter investigaged the cause of the accident. On November 12, 1970, his written conclusions were sent as an official union inter-office communication to Art Hughes, the Assistant Director of the National Chrysler Department:

I examined the equipment and found the emergency brake to be broken; as a matter of fact, it was never connected. The shifter lever to the transmission was loose and sloppy. The equipment generally was sadly in need of maintenance, having a lost steering wheel in addition to other general needs. I also visited the repair area and observed other industrial trucks in this area that were sadly in need of repair, noting: no lights, lack of brakes, horns, broken LP gas tank fasteners, loose steering wheels, leaky hydraulic equipment, etc. I was informed that there is supposed to be a regularly scheduled maintenance procedure for this equipment in this plant. I was also informed that operators are instructed to take trucks to the garage and tag them when they are in need of repairs. However, it seems to be the practice of foremen, when equipment is needed, to pull the tags off the equipment in the repair area that badly need corrective maintenance and put them back into service on the floor.... Finally, a general observation as we passed to and from the location of the fatal accident: there seemed to be little attempt to maintain proper housekeeping except on the main front aisle. Water and grease were observed all along the way, as we proceeded. Every good safety program has its basic good-housekeeping procedures. Proper steps should be taken immediately to improve conditions within this plant.

Thirteen days before Gary Thompson's death, Eldon had claimed the life of Mamie Williams, a 51-year-old black woman who had worked for Chrysler for over 26 years. Mamie Williams had been ordered by her doctors to stay home because of a dangerous blood-pressure condition. Chrysler, however, had sent her a telegram telling her to return to work or be fired and lose all the benefits she had accumulated in almost three decades of employment. An intimidated Mamie Williams had returned to her job on the first shift in Department 80. One week later, she passed out on the line and died shortly after being taken home.

A year before the deaths of Gary Thompson and Mamie Williams, Eldon had taken the life of Rose Logan, a black janitor. Rose Logan had been struck in the plant by an improperly loaded jitney whose driver's vision was blocked. Her doctor told her to stay off her feet, but Chrysler's doctors ordered her back to work. She returned to Eldon from fear of losing her job, developed thrombophlebitis in her leg, and, like Mamie Williams, ended her service at Eldon in a coffin.

Higher production at Eldon had been achieved not with advanced technology and automated assembly-line procedures, but through the old-fasioned method of speed-up. The single goal of the company was to increase profit by getting more work out of each individual worker. Eldon conditions were typical of conditions in the industry. Even when there were technological changes, usually only one segment of the assembly line was automated, so that the workers on other segments had to labor more strenuously to keep up. Often, the automation eliminated interesting jobs, leaving the more menial and monotonous tasks for people. Many of the "new" machines were not technological advances at all, but simply updated models of tools introduced as early as the 1920's and 1930's.

Health and accident data on the auto industry was difficult to obtain. Only in the early seventies did the UAW and the Department of Health, Education and Welfare begin to make studies in this area. One important report did appear in 1973. Called the HEALTH RESEARCH GROUP STUDY OF DISEASE AMONG WORKERS IN THE AUTO INDUSTRY, it was based on figures compiled by the National Institute of Occupational Safety and Health and was written by two medical doctors, Jannette Sherman and Sidney Wolfe. The report estimated 65 on-the-job deaths per day among auto workers, for a total of some 16,000 annually. Approximately half of these deaths were from heart attacks. There were also some 63,000 cases of disabling diseases and about 1,700,000 cases of lost or impaired hearing. These statistics did not include many long-term illnesses endemic to foundry workers and others exposed to poisonous chemicals and gases, nor did they include deaths and injuries by accident. Even these limited figures made it clear that more auto workers were killed and injured each year on the job than soldiers were killed and injured during any year of the war in Vietnam.

The hazardous conditions were supposedly compensated for by high wages. Auto workers were among the highest-paid workers in the United States, yet wage rates were deceptive. In the 1920's, Henry Ford made headlines by promising $5 a day to every worker in his enterprises. Ford workers soon discovered that it was not quite $5 a day for not quite everyone. Fully a third of all Ford workers never got the $5 a day. Likewise, at Eldon, the 1969 $4-an-hour average Chrysler wage proved a fiction. Before any deductions and without the cost-of-living factor, which did not cover all workers and was never more than 21¢ an hour, most job categories at Eldon paid around $3.60 an hour and none paid more than $3.94. Workers found it difficult to get figures on per-hour pay for their particular job, and they were often cheated out of increases by complex union and company clerical procedures. What the workers did know was that overtime had become compulsory and that most of them needed the time-and-a-half paid for overtime to keep pace with inflation. Census Bureau figures revealed that the value of the products shipped out of the plant, minus the cost of materials, supplies, fuel, and electricity, came to $22,500 a year per worker, as compared to an average wage of $8,000 for a worker putting in a 40-hour week. During the period 1946–1969, wages had increased by 25% while profits went up 77%, dividends 60%, personal corporate incomes 80%, and undistributed corporate profits 93%. The industry moaned about its cycle of booms and busts, but in 1970 General Motors remained the nation's (and the world's) largest manufacturing enterprise. Ford was the third largest. And Chrysler, "the weak sister," was fifth.

Niggermation at Eldon gave rise to three separate rank-and-file opposition groups. The one with the longest record in the factory was a militant trade-union group led by Jordan Sims, the black chairman of the shop stewards' committee. A radical group called Wildcat began publishing a newsletter in February 1970, and ELRUM, the local unit of the League of Revolutionary Black Workers, made its official appearance in November 1968. The three groups, separately and in various combinations, produced a steady barrage of information for the workers and succeeded in closing down the plant in several successful wildcat strikes. Chrysler was more than a little concerned about this activity. If Eldon were closed for any lengthy period, all gear and axle production would stop; and with that stoppage, all of Chrysler would stop. Chrysler remembered how, in 1937, General Motors had been forced to recognize the UAW when it occupied Fisher Body #1 in Flint and Fisher Body in Cleveland, the only plants having GM's valuable dies. Eldon had the same sort of pivotal role in Chrysler production. At this point of maximum vulnerability, Chrysler faced one of the largest concentrations of black workers in the industry. Eldon was Chrysler's Achilles' heel. Chrysler knew this, and so did the League of Revolutionary Black Workers.

ELRUM's history was similar to that of DRUM. Meetings, rallies, and newsletters built up a hard core of supporters and a much larger number of sympathizers. Leaders of ELRUM such as Fred Holsey and James Edwards found themselves under continual pressure from company, police, and union. Physical assaults were frequent, but the ELRUM leadership did not crack under the pressure. On January 22, 1969, ELRUM led over 300 workers to confront the local union leadership with a grievance list in much the way DRUM had confronted the leaders of Local 3. Five days later, ELRUM called a strike to back up its demands. ELRUM kept out 66% of the workers the first day of the strike and 50% the second. The company's retaliation was to fire some two dozen workers and to discipline 86 others.

In retrospect, the League evaluated the January 1969 strike as premature. Too many ELRUM members were knocked out of the plant, and the remaining base of support was insufficient to maintain the struggle at the same level as in the previous six months. Despite these facts, ELRUM continued to fight, and it continued to have a cadre and sympathizers in the plant. During the early part of 1970, ELRUM once more took a leading role in plant struggles, and it arrived at a working coalition with other militants.

You don't have to read about them in NEWSWEEK or see them on television. They're too dangerous. They're too dangerous to the system to have information about the kind of work being done at Eldon to be disseminated widely. This is a war we're talking about. There is literally a war going on inside the American factories. This is a violent struggle. Sometimes it is organized and guided. Most times it is unorganized and spontaneous. But in the course of this struggle more American workers have died than in all the four major wars.

John Watson, interview in QUADERNI PIACENTINI (Italy), Winter 1970.

One of the key figures in the new series of events at Eldon was a white worker named John Taylor. In August of 1972, he gave the authors a retrospective account of the events at Eldon as he had experienced them. At the time of the interview, John Taylor was a member of the Motor City Labor League. His personal testimony regarding the period from 1968 to 1970 is a textbook of what was wrong with the company and the union. It also presents a candid view of the problems within the ranks of the insurgents themselves:

"My name is John Taylor, I wasn't born in Detroit. I was born in West Virginia. My father was a coal miner who worked in the mines for 17 years. My grandfathers on both sides were coal miners. My grandfather on my mother's side was the recording secretary for the first miner's local in that part of the country back in 1916. We moved to Detroit in 1949 as part of the migration of white Appalachians northward. My father started to work at Chevrolet gear and axle plant as a production-line worker in October 1949 and he retires in 1975. My mother works at the Federals Department Store putting price tags on clothes. She's worked there since 1952 and expects to retire soon. I went to the Detroit public schools and Wayne State University. I came out with a bachelor's degree in English and a law degree. Along the way, I worked eight years for the Better Business Bureau in Detroit, a capitalist front organization, and I worked for Chrysler Corporation on the management side as a workman's compensation representative. That job took me into almost every Chrysler plant in the Detroit area. It put me into contact with literally hundreds of injured workers per week. I worked there from June 1966 to September 1968. In November of 1968, I got a job as a production-line worker at Chrysler's Eldon Avenue Gear and Axle factory, the same factory where I had worked for management.

"I was asked to resign my management job because of what they called a 'bad attitude.' The truth is that the company was fucking the workers on compensation. One of their devices was to refuse to discuss the cases with the union. They claimed workman's comp was covered by statute and

therefore not part of the contract and therefore not negotiable. My feeling was that while the substance of the decisions was not negotiable, the administration was and was therefore grievable. I thought I should discuss these cases with various shop stewards. I did what the union should have done. I gave the stewards an outline of the rights of workers—their constituents. I noticed that, during a period of nine days, about every steward in the place was in my office. I didn't find out until several years later that Jordan Sims had noticed what I was doing and had made it part of his program as Chairman of the Shop Stewards' Committee to send all of the stewards to see me. Finally, he came in himself and we had a long rap. I gave him a copy of the statutes. I used to have almost daily relations with the Labor Relations Committee. I remember on more than one day how they would say, 'Oh, we're going to have a rough afternoon coming up because Sims is coming to bargain.' That's the kind of reputation Sims had.

"After I got kicked out of Chrysler management, I went back to Wayne State; but I didn't want to be a lawyer or a teacher. I wanted to organize, and the logical place seemed to be the plant. I had the reputation in the Eldon Personnel Department of being the best comp man they had ever had. I talked them into letting me work hourly, and they put me into Department 75, first as a conveyor loader and then I worked up to being a precision grinder. That's the best job I ever had in my life. I didn't have any organizing agenda at that time. The only politics I had came out of the FIFTH ESTATE, Detroit's underground paper. I had never read Marx or Lenin. The first time I read the COMMUNIST MANIFESTO was late 1969. I thought, "This is far out. They are talking about this plant." That was an important event for me.

"One funny coincidence from that time is that I entered the plant on November 8th, 1968, and on November 10th some black workers in other departments founded ELRUM, the Eldon Avenue Revolutionary Union Movement. They had been turned on by the agitation at Dodge Main and became an affiliate of the League of Revolutionary Black Workers. I would like to relate these events in the sequence I lived them, rather than strict chronological order. I will come back later on and fill in the most important dates and events.

"Our steward in Department 75 on the third shift was a man named Frank McKinnon. I got to know him when I was in workman's comp because McKinnon was a witness in a case involving a fight. Chrysler had a policy of firing the aggressor, so the question of who started the fight was important. McKinnon gave me a statement that the worker had started the fight. I found out later he lied to me. That was the kind of steward he was. When I got to be a worker, he refused to write up my safety grievances. A number of us also had grievances relating to pay raises due us because of promotions. We were supposed to get a 5¢-an-hour raise within a week, and it took me six weeks to get mine because the foreman wouldn't do the paperwork. He was trying to save on his own budget, and McKinnon wouldn't write up the grievance about it. That's how things worked at Eldon.

"My safety grievance typifies the problems in that factory. I worked on what they call a modern grinder. We used to laugh about it because there was nothing modern about it at all. It was ancient. We had to burn off the rough edges of rangers which looked like donuts with metal teeth. This part went into the differential. There was a lot of fine dust generated by this grinding. The company put vents on the machines to hold this down, but every shift the filters would get clogged. The supervision would never give us the little time needed for someone to come and do some maintenance on them. I requested a mask. I got this thing that didn't look right and asked for the box it came in. It turned out to be for paint and gas fumes and was no help against dust. I ran all this down to McKinnon, but he refused to deal with it. So I called for a department meeting. I organized around him. The union President wouldn't schedule the meeting for more than two weeks because he said we had one word wrong in our petition. Richardson (the

President) was just pissed because he had just taken office, and now, less than two months later, there was dissatisfaction with one of his stewards. Richardson told me straight off he wanted people to cool off because he didn't want angry people in the union hall. That's another indication of the union's attitude. They do not want to deal with angry workers.

"I started seeing Sims in the cafeteria every morning. This was in early 1969, and he suggested I get on the union bylaws committee. I worked on that for a year with Sims and a guy named J. C. Thomas. We drew up some bylaws that would have made that union as honest and democratic as unions can be in this period. Needless to say, those bylaws were never presented to the membership.

"By 1970, we had gotten to a situation where Chrysler was making most of its money off small cars, the Valiant and the Dart. One reason things got so bad at Dodge Main was that is where they made those cars. Behind the need for increased production and because they wanted to harass the union, Chrysler did a lot of firing, disciplinary actions, and all sorts of bullshit. There was attempted speed-up in my department at Eldon. One foreman arbitrarily raised the quota on the grinder machine, which was totally against the contract. What we did was lower to 400 instead of the usual 700 gears, and that cooled his ass about a speed-up.

"On April 16th, 1970, things built up to what we call the Scott-Ashlock incident. There was a black worker named John Scott who was a physically small man. His foreman was a fairly large guy from Mississippi named Irwin Ashlock. They got into an argument, and Ashlock picked up a pinion gear and said he was going to smash Scott's brains out. Scott complained to his steward, and the union took it up with the company. Well, Chrysler came up with the claim that Scott had taken a knife from his pocket— you know, like all blacks carry knives. They claimed Ashlock had a right to protect himself, and rather than discipline Ashlock, they were going to fire Scott. This sparked a wildcat strike which shut the place down for the whole weekend. That was a beautifully successful strike. It had an old-fashioned unity—young and old, black and white, men and women. Everyone was militant. The skilled tradesmen went out too. At a union meeting a white worker named John Felicia, who had seen the whole thing, spoke from the stage at the hall. There were maybe a thousand people there. Felicia said there were white workers at Eldon and black workers at Eldon, but the main thing was that they were all workers and that he had seen the whole thing and that John Scott was telling the absolute truth and was totally in the right. The company needed our gears for those Valiants, so they backed down.

"Everyone thought we had won, but then, after a couple of weeks, the company started acting up. They threatened to discipline the second-shift stewards who had led the walkout. They began to have foremen follow these guys around, and then, on May 1st, they were told toward the end of the shift that they were all going to be suspended for an unauthorized work stoppage in violation of the no-strike clause of the contract. They were shown the door leading to the street. What happened was that a guy named Clarence Thornton shoved the plant guards out of the way and led everyone back into the plant. This was shift time. I remember meeting a steward, and he said, "We're shutting her down. Go home." By midnight, the factory was shut down. Chrysler went for an injunction and got it. The union lawyer from Solidarity House refused to defend Local 961 on the grounds it might bring legal action against the whole union. They sold out the strike. They advised us to go back to work without our stewards. We worked most of that summer without any stewards. Both Jordan Sims and Frank McKinnon were fired in this action.

"In response to those firings, a grouping called the Eldon Safety Committee was formed which included myself, some members of ELRUM, and the fired stewards led by Jordan Sims. Our program was to research and document the issue of safety in the plant. We got advised by lawyers Ron Glotta and Mike Adleman that we had the right to refuse to work under abnormally dangerous conditions. That would not constitute a strike, and the company could not get an injunction. We saw that we had an umbrella for closing down Eldon. We were so naive we thought words meant what they said. When you look at our leaflets of that period, you will see that we quote the law and all that stuff. We put out a few leaflets, but events overtook us. The plant was indeed abnormally dangerous. On May 26th, 1970, this was proven when a man named Gary Thompson was buried under five tons of steel when his faulty jitney tipped over. Thompson was a black Vietnam veteran about twenty-two years old. The jitney he was running was full of safety flaws.

"On May 27th, we set up picket lines. By 'we,' I mean the Eldon Safety Committee and the League of Revolutionary Black Workers. This was not as successful as the first strike, but it cost them 2174 axles over two days. We're proud of each and every one of them. The three wildcats within a month and a half cost them 2200 axles during a period when they desperately needed them for their Valiants. Chrysler immediately fired me and three members of the League: James Edwards, Alonzo Chandler, and Rob McKee.

"I need to backtrack here to tell something about ELRUM. Like I said before, they had started on November 10, 1968. My first awareness of them was when they began to put out leaflets. There was an immediate response, about 50% positive and 50% negative. The negative response came from the older black workers and of course from white workers, mainly because the ELRUM language was harsh. They called people "Toms," "Molly-Toms," "honkie dogs," "pigs," etc. No one seemed to have trouble with calling the supervision those names, but this was something different. The older people definitely had a lot of trouble with their whole tone. In early 1970, there was an election for convention delegates. That was just before the Scott-Ashlock Incident. Given their numerical superiority in that plant, black workers could have elected an all-black slate. There were like 33 separate black candidates, and ELRUM put out a leaflet calling them Molly-Toms and all that. That divided the black vote.

"ELRUM was already in bad shape by that time. In January of 1969, there was a lot of complaining about the coldness in the plant and about union discrimination against blacks. Chrysler disciplined some ELRUM people who had lost time from their jobs to do an action against the union. A wildcat followed, and after that 22 ELRUM people were fired. I think that broke the back of ELRUM right there. I think those actions were premature. There was no way to logistically support that strike. They had no outside mobilization. It was just premature. Still, everything we ever did at the plant was premature. Maybe it was vanguard activity, and they just didn't have any choice. Anyway, through 1969, the INNER CITY VOICE, the League paper, was sold at the plant. I had no personal contact until early 1970, about the time of the convention.

"At that time, I was still mainly involved in the bylaws struggle and troubles in my own department. Still, I used to see their leaflets and groups of us would discuss them, blacks and whites. I would say that we might not be able to relate to the rhetoric, but what they were saying was true. That was the position Jordan Sims took, too. A lot of his enemies said he was the secret leader of ELRUM, in an attempt to erode his base among black and white workers. Sims said their language was crude but they were telling the truth. He would defend them as aggressively as he would any militant. That was a position of principle. I should say that I wasn't all that aware of all they were doing. I can say that the young white workers didn't like them. They could relate to what I said, but they had a hard time with ELRUM.

"What really turned people off was this one leaflet they put out on the union secretaries. There was an old retiree named Butch and several white secretaries in the office. ELRUM put out a leaflet running that these white women were prostitutes for Elroy Richardson, the black President of the local. They ran all kinds of vicious stuff that people could not relate to. We knew these women and did not perceive them in that fashion. People were really put off by that issue. Another thing is that some of those young black workers who were enthusiastic about the leaflets never joined ELRUM, and some of them crossed the Safety Committee picket line. So there was this mixed response to ELRUM as we went into 1970.

"Things were very complicated by 1970. Local 961 had its first black President. This was before the Scott-Ashlock incident. ELRUM had supported the black slate in 1969, but now it had become critical and was calling Elroy a Tom, a fat-belly faggot, etc. When the wildcat came, ELRUM dropped that and supported him again. You can say that Richardson had a united plant behind him, but he was too incompetent and inept to be a leader. He had it all in his hands at the time of the wildcat following the Scott-Ashlock thing, but he blew it.

"After the wildcat, the ELRUM cadre and myself worked on the Safety Committee. I did most of the research and writing because that was an area I had expertise in. They did most of the organizing for the strike. We met at League headquarters on Cortland Street. People ask if I felt any nationalism or reverse racism, and I can say I did not. I had a lot of basic respect for what they were trying to do. When they said, "Come on over; it's all right," I did and it was. I also had a nodding acquaintance with Ken Cockrel from law school. That may have helped, but our main contact with the League was General Baker. We had a lot of contact with him and also with Chuck Wooten. They both came on the picket line with us, even though they didn't work at the plant. I would say the performance of the ELRUM people around the safety strike was exemplary.

"I need to backtrack again. By early 1970, I had come to realize that I had to get beyond Department 74 and 75. I knew you had to have an organ of some kind, a mimeoed sheet. I think that came from seeing the ELRUM example. I thought it was correct when they said whites should work with whites, which was what I was trying to do, even though I was doing it on my own from what I see now (in 1972) as correct instincts. A little earlier, a paper called WILDCAT had been given out. People in my department had picked it up and read it. Then, early in 1970, they began to put out the ELDON WILDCAT, a mimeoed plant newsletter. At that point, I was ready to leap out. I waited until they were at the gate, and I told them I worked in the factory and wanted to do some articles for them. We set up a meeting. Those people were experts at plant newsletters. I became identified with them immediately because people spotted my writing style.

"The WILDCAT people were Old Left. They were so secretive they had crossed over to paranoia. They used false names and all that stuff. They didn't want to expose their shit to open struggle. My opinion, then and now, is that that is an incorrect way to work. They strongly advised me not to distribute WILDCAT. It was their policy that outsiders distributed. My opinion was that the paper had to get into the plant. We were only covering one gate. One morning I went out and took some papers and gave them out at another gate. It soon got around the plant that I was the publisher of WILDCAT, which was a mistruth. I was only a junior member of that circle. They would edit the shit out of my articles. They would change the content and the style. Sometimes we did this together, but sometimes they said there wasn't time. I usually didn't mind, but they would put in bad stuff sometimes without consulting me, which put me into a trick as I was identified with the paper. Other workers held me responsible. I found out later that two people in the group took the position that I was only a contact and had brought my troubles upon myself by identifying with the paper in an overt way. You must remember that ELRUM was open with their thing. I thought that was correct, and I was open with mine. That made it easier to trust each other.

"What we did during that period was have ELRUM put something out one day, WILDCAT the next, and the Safety Committee the third. Then we would start the cycle going again so that there was a steady stream of information and agitation. It was like a united front. People knew I was associated with the Safety Committee, and

stewards would take me off on the side to show me violations. Management tried to keep me from going out of my department on my break. They got a guy to pick a fight with me so we both could get fired. They tried all that shit.

"ELRUM did not participate as fully as it could have in gathering information, and on that day of the strike they tried to stop distribution of the WILDCAT. My brother was giving them out, and they said this was basically a black action and he should get out. Anyway, he didn't move. I don't think that was correct, but overall ELRUM was very good. The trouble was that after Rob, Alonzo, and James were fired, they had no one else to carry on. That was after the other 22 had been fired. Their thing was just ripped. Then they made a bad mistake, which may have been unavoidable given problems within the wider context of the League. That summer and fall they only put out one leaflet. They lost their visibility. They could have had workers from other plants distribute. They could have gone to union meetings, which was something I did. They went sometimes, but they were into a program of disruption. I didn't think that was correct, and I couldn't work with them on that. I thought it was insulting to those workers who had come to the hall in good faith to take care of whatever business they thought important. I thought it was disrespectful.

"I think it would be fair to say that they were not good at dealing with people within the class who did not agree with them but who were not enemies either. I don't know what internal education the League was giving them on this. I don't know what kind of instructions they were getting. If there is not structure by which people's actions can be criticized and reviewed, you get into this kind of situation.

"ELRUM still had a few people inside, but they were essentially not doing much. Now, in 1971, union officials came up for election. ELRUM ran a candidate named Eric Edwards, a guy who I have a lot of respect for. He ran a strong third as a straight ELRUM candidate, getting 342 out of about 1000 votes. That indicated a residue of support.

The company and the union were running a heavy organized barrage against Jordan Sims, who was running against Frank McKinnon for President. Sims could have won with the solid help of older workers, but they were turned off by his association with ELRUM. Jordan and I went over to the Cortland offices and talked with Baker, Wooten, and a whole bunch of them. They had always seen Sims as a sellout and right-wing opportunist. I don't think that was correct. Anyway, he told them he didn't want their endorsement, which would be a kiss of death. The first day of the election, ELRUM did not come out in favor of Sims, and Jordan was ahead. The second day they endorsed him, and the vote turned away. I believe that was an indiciation of how negative older folks had become to ELRUM. That was one factor in his defeat. It would be interesting to know who made the decision to endorse him.

"The union ran its usual shit on us. They challenged 284 ballots because of dues default, which is strange because you have checkoffs at Chrysler so if someone is behind, it is not their fault but the union's and the company's. I analyzed those ballots, and 90% of them were in black production units, and I think they would have gone to Sims. They would have put him over as President of the local.

"The administration, the international, and the company had sold this program that we were all violent individuals. They even said I was a member of ELRUM! They said I was a violent motherfucker. We got into a situation in the hall the night we were tabulating. We were there as challengers, and they brought in armed guards with shotguns, carbines, and pistols. They were provocative as hell, trying to get us into a fight. I'm convinced they wanted to gun us down. We took our time real easy. I even took my shirt off so people couldn't claim I was strapped (carrying a gun). There was one argument which was really hot where James Edwards raised his voice, and the whole table got surrounded by those guards. These black guards were hired under the instructions of George Merrelli, the Regional Director. I got into a hot dispute with Russell Thompson, who was solid with the ad-

ministration. Some ELRUM people came over, and Thompson reached into his shirt for a piece. I saw the guards starting over, so we just split, me and the guys from ELRUM. We were not prepared to handle that shit. What is interesting is that most of the people counting the ballots were older black women, and they were physically afraid of ELRUM people. They thought ELRUM people had guns and were going to go berserk. I knew right there that there had been a tremendous failure of ELRUM. You can't have people in the plant afraid of you in that way. Also, the same women who were afraid of ELRUM were not afraid of me. Several of them went out of their way to say this.

"A similar incident occurred around the safety strike. It happened at the East Gate, which is a principal gate for the second shift coming in. The second shift is basically black and young, with little seniority. This is the 2:30–10:30 shift. James Edwards was on the gate, and at one point, James grabbed a white worker and slapped him around. Now, we had agreed there would be no violence, on advice of our attorneys, so that we could preserve the strike's legality. James violated our organizational decision. That hurt us. When people heard about that, they turned against us. They even cut a hole in the parking-lot fence so they could get in easier.

"I almost did a similar thing myself. I grabbed this one dude I had a thing on. He had caught me outside on the street one day and slugged me on my blind side. I had this plan for getting him that day, but I didn't. Maybe a policy of violence would have been better. Slapping some of those fuckers around might have made a difference. I don't know; we had decided not to, and I stuck to that decision. We sure as hell moved too fast. We hadn't organized our base correctly. We weren't ready for that strike hit. We should have agitated more around the issue of Gary Thompson and on safety in general. We could really have made it hot, but as a result we had a not totally successful strike for which we got fired. You must understand we were genuinely angry at the death of Thompson. It verified everything we had been saying. We got self-righteous. In our arrogance, we failed to note that Memorial Day was on Friday. The people were getting triple pay for working. We couldn't have picked a worse day for a strike. It's just incredible that we didn't consider that factor. We were wrong and stupid.

"These events took place in May 1970. On July 15th, James Johnson entered the factory and blew away two foremen and a job setter. He was looking for his shop steward, Clarence Thompson. That was the same guy who had led the fired stewards back into the plant by shoving the guards aside. That was exemplary because Clarence was an older dude, about 46 years old with 23 years' seniority. He was considered a good steward. Clarence was one of those sold out by the union. They left the stewards in the street for a time, and when Clarence came back he had to sign a statement that if there was any further trouble he would get permanently fired. When Johnson first approached Clarence about his grievances, Clarence told him, "I can't do much for you because I just got back myself." Clarence had been intimidated and sold out to the point where it was no longer safe for him to fight for his membership. Johnson saw his union could not function for him and decided to deal with it himself. Those connections are important. The whole preceding set of events was to break down the stewards so they wouldn't defend their people. The company refused to deal with safety and other legitimate grievances. That's why we say Chrysler pulled the trigger. Chrysler caused those deaths. Yes, indeed, James Johnson was just an instrumentality.

"It's important to note how ELRUM related to white people. The first thing is around the distribution of their leaflets. They would always refuse to give those leaflets to white workers. It wasn't until around March of 1970 that they would respect my practice enough to give them to me. Then James Edwards would go through changes about that. He would wad them up in his hand and sort of pass them to me surreptitiously, so none of the black workers would see him giving a leaflet to a white. When ELRUM had its wildcat in January 1969, there was no attempt to relate to white workers about their demands. Consequently, many white workers crossed their lines, and many black workers who had close friends in the white force took the same position. They could not relate to the strike because they perceived ELRUM as having taken a racist position. One of the interesting aspects of the safety strike was that the Eldon Safety Committee was a coalition of trade unionists, ELRUM black revolutionaries, and white revolutionaries, mainly myself.

"What happened to the Safety Committee is instructive. There was a steady process of attrition among the trade unionists, one of whom was a white named George Bauer, another of whom was Frank McKinnon. Some dropped out early. Some stuck right up to the strike. At the end, we had only Jordan Sims, J. C. Thomas, and a couple of others. During the strike, the trade unionists stayed for the first-shift picketing and then, except for Jordan Sims, were never seen again. The revolutionaries stayed with it to the bitter end because they had more than trade-union reform to fight about. That may be a clumsy formulation, but the point is they were going to fight as long as they could. George Bauer, a skilled trades steward whom I have a lot of respect for, was fired with the other second-shift stewards. He participated actively in giving us safety information, but he never took part in picketing or in various confrontations with the union. George Bauer was not and is not a racist, and he has encountered a lot of opposition with his own skilled tradesmen. They call him a nigger-lover. George had a quick temper. He used to be a professional boxer. He got into an argument outside the plant with an individual who had scabbed during the wildcat, and George decked him. This was outside the plant. Management moved to fire him, and the union wouldn't write a discharge grievance for weeks. Eventually, George got back in there, but he understood that he had better be careful.

"Our first confrontations with the union brought a reduction in the ranks of the Safety Committee. Reuther had been killed, and the international was using that as an excuse to keep the hall closed. We insisted on the right to use our own hall. We were using the conference room to get information, write leaflets, discuss strategy, etc. Elroy Richardson came in and told us to leave. We stood up and confronted him, saying he would have to throw us out. He said he'd call the police. We said, "Fine, Elroy, you want to call the police, call the police." He went away and left us alone. The next day, when we came back, the conference room was locked. Some of the unionists felt uneasy and talked about going to lunch. James Edwards and I went over to the door. I tried to pick the door with my knife, and we put our shoulders to it. Then we went outside and found a window. We got screwdrivers and got the conference-room window open. We had to actually break into our own hall. We got in and opened the conference-room door. As soon as they saw this, some of them went to lunch and never came back. We started having the meeting, and another of the stewards got more and more agitated. He got on the verge of physically attacking me because I had broken into the hall. He had a very heavy thing on how Walter Reuther had been the black man's friend and ally. He was very insulted that I, a white man, had desecrated the memory of Reuther's death. He went into this thing with me and left and never came back. That was another contradiction in our ranks.

"The reaction of the people in my own department to the strike bothered me. I was on the West Gate, where most of my department comes in. I'll never forget this. Almost unanimously, the people in my department and people I knew did not go in when they saw me picketing. They talked to me, and some of them even gave out leaflets. What a lot did, though, was go to another gate. I couldn't understand that for a long time. What it meant was that they could relate to me as a person, but not the politics of the situation. There was the additional problem of how they related to the ELRUM people who were on the gate with me. This reinforced my assessment that we moved too fast. We had to do more agitation. We cost Chrysler 2174 axles, but we could have done more. We also succeeded in exposing the Chrysler-union cooperation to the workers in the plant. That is, we produced the documentation on all the safety violations the union wouldn't deal with. This was dramaticized by the death of Gary Thompson. Even the UAW couldn't ignore that. Our strike lifted the consciousness of everybody. It used to be that workers wouldn't take the leaflets or would throw them away. Now, people at the plant almost always take the leaflet, put it in their pocket, and read it inside. That is very positive and indicates a level of consciousness, higher than in most plants and higher than it had been in their plant.

"How workers relate to material given at the gate isn't understood by most people in the movement. When WILDCAT first appeared, ELRUM tried to front them off by physical threats. The WILDCAT people came back, and ELRUM backed off. ELRUM remained extremely hostile to the WILDCAT, even after it became known I was associated with it. ELRUM had the opinion that the WILDCAT was from the Communist Party, and they had minimal respect for the CP. They thought the WILDCAT was racist and an outsider sheet.

"I would like to say something about other radical groups which made interventions from 1970 onwards. Up front, let me say that I am presently a member of the Motor City Labor League, a Marxist-Leninist revolutionary group. Now, Progressive Labor came out to the plant in the summer of 1970 and started selling their paper, CHALLENGE. I approached them at the gate one day. This was after I was fired. I looked like an ordinary worker. I was working at Budd Wheel at that time. They assumed I worked at Eldon, and I was shocked at how they related to a person whom they perceived as a typical worker. They were condescending. I ran a little bit about my involvement in the safety strike, and they were very critical of that. They said their policy was to ignore the unions. They assured me that they would be there every week and were not fly-by-night leftists. What happened was that they managed to antagonize a lot of folks, as is their fashion. This was done to the extent that one day some white workers came out and beat the shit out of them. That indicated a failure of sorts. They told me the same thing happened at Cadillac. That physical assault was the end of their presence, and they haven't been seen since.

"The reaction of the Socialist Workers Party is interesting because I'm not aware they had any reaction at all to what was going on at Eldon. They never contacted Sims, myself, or anyone in ELRUM to speak at a forum or do any internal education for them. I want to say something about their Detroit activities in the late sixties. At that time I was working for the Better Business Bureau, and I used to go to their Friday-night socialist forums at the Debs Hall. I went pretty regularly for almost a year. Not once did anyone ever approach me politically or be even minimally friendly. I was like a fixture for a year, but they just ignored me. Maybe they thought I was an agent or something, but that has always struck me as a totally ripped practice. You have to be blind or myopic to ignore what was happening at Eldon, and I have never seen them relate in any way out there. If they have worker cadre, they sure as hell aren't at Eldon, Budd Wheel, or Dodge Main.

"The only other groups to do any work are the Motor City Labor League, Revolutionary Union, and International Socialists. Revolutionary Union has mainly tried to get on with some stewards at Eldon, but they haven't distributed leaflets or done any public work. International Socialists have been extremely interested in Jordan Sims. They wanted to do a national campaign around his discharge in pretty much the way the Angela Davis thing worked for the CP. The Motor City Labor League has had a public presence in the form of leaflets, and we have been working with the various people and with Jordan Sims.

"It's a truism that struggle creates strength. It is also true that you have to find issues that affect people's lives and that you agitate and organize around those issues with the point of view of making some gains and of exposing the concrete contradictions. The aftermath of our strike was that Jordan Sims ran for President of that Local (Local 961). He maintained his membership, and was narrowly defeated by Frank McKinnon, the white steward. The election was literally stolen from Jordan. Now, there is a scandal about the embezzlement of funds by McKinnon and other officials. Very large sums have disappeared for over 10 years, and apparently George Merrelli, the Regional Director, knew about it. That would make it reach right into Solidarity House. People in the plant have gotten a pretty high consciousness about this whole set-up. We managed to get the Department of Labor into the process. We showed we were correct on the statutes and the contract. They had to expose their hand in a situation affecting the health and lives of those workers. We have developed a hard core of people at Eldon who go to union meetings. There's 60–70 people who know how to function. The company and union could just give up, but they can't do that because of the key nature of Eldon. The stakes are too high. But the company, union, and Labor Department continue to shit on people, which creates more strength for us. Eventually, they'll have to move the factory out of Detroit or let us have it."

In the stamping plant, which we know is a hazardous area anyway, I got my fingertip severed off in a press. They sewed it back on. . . . But that isn't as serious as some of the other things that have happend in the Rouge area in the past. Six men in a basic-oxygen plant were killed, and there wasn't enough left of those men to put in a decent shopping bag.

Wesley Johns, in a statement to a People's Court convened by the Motor City Labor League, April 3, 1973.

John Taylor's recounting of the struggle at Eldon points up some of the problems facing the militants who wanted to carry out the Revolutionary Union Movement (RUM) strategy. Many nationalist-minded blacks were attracted to the RUMs. Although very militant and vocal, the RUMs often held back the development of class consciousness among other workers attracted to the wider League program. This gap between secondary and primary leadership grew wider after the strike of January 1969. All the members of the League executive would have curbed some of the more counter-productive language in ELRUM leaflets, but there were occasions when Baker and Wooten sanctioned approaches some of the other League leaders would not have approved of. Excessive emphasis on the contradictions between workers not only alienated whites who might have been neutral or sympathetic, it turned away many blacks. Older workers, who had a large stake in improving working conditions, especially disliked the wholesale attacks on "honkies" and "Toms," considering them incorrect ways to get sustained and positive action. ELRUM's attitude toward individuals such as Jordan Sims and supporters of WILDCAT posed another kind of problem. ELRUM was somewhat sectarian toward them and judged that Sims, at best, was an honest reformist stuck in trade-union attitudes, and at worst could turn out to be another of those "traitors from within" the League warned about. The consequence of ELRUM's attitude was that the organization drew too rigid a line of demarcation between itself and other forces in the plant. Ken Cockrel voiced the additional criticism that the ELRUM workers fired in January had failed to build a defense committee in the plant and in the neighborhoods. He believed that the hostile ELRUM attitude toward white participation and working with non-revolutionary blacks was retarding rather than building their struggle.

ELRUM clearly failed to rally women to its ranks. Two of the workers killed at the plant during this period were women, and their deaths were an indication of the harassment and poor working conditions women faced. It was an open secret that dating foremen had its rewards, just as refusing them had its punishments. One young black woman who suffered from drowsiness caused by excessive noise got a job classification which would take her away from moving machinery, but she could not get it acted on because of union indifference and the hostility of her foremen. Several other women, in well-known incidents on the shop floor, were forced to tell off supervisors and union representatives after they became tired of fending off constant sexual advances. ELRUM bulletins spoke of the special problems facing the "sisters" in the plant, but ELRUM never developed a concrete program for dealing with such problems.

ELRUM activists generally bypassed the UAW altogether once they were out of the plant. This caused a gradual breakdown of ties with some of the more militant workers in the factory. Jordan Sims, even after being fired in 1970, went to union meetings regularly and organized his forces as he might have had he been still working inside the plant. Sims continued to contend for power in the union, and on May 23, 1973, after several highly questionable elections, he defeated Frank McKinnon 1599 to 735 and became president of Local 961. As an elected union official and still co-chairman of the United National Caucus, Sims was now able to carry on his own fight from within the UAW hierarchy. He demonstrated an honest and aggressive unionist stance during his first year in office.

Citing shortcomings in the ELRUM performance in no way diminishes the importance of the work carried out over a two-year period. A handful of revolutionary-minded production-line workers had set themselves against the company and the union, and against the timidity and weariness of many workers. Taylor, a white Appalachian, called them exemplary; and their nationalism notwithstanding, he considered them the best leadership to have emerged in the plant.

Part six

In this Part we are shifting our perspective to analyze how a current critical issue is handled by our political institutions rather than focusing on individual institutions as we have done in previous chapters.

The issue we have selected is the economic crisis of the 1970s, the greatest challenge to the political system of the United States since the Vietnamese war and the worst economic conditions this country has faced since the Great Depression of the 1930s.[1]

We are using the perspectives of conservatism, liberalism, and socialism to undertake a political, rather than a purely economic analysis of the economic crisis. A political perspective means that we are seeking to understand the arrangements of power involved in the causes, reactions, and proposed solutions to the crisis.

It is our hope that students will take the framework used here and apply it on their own to any other political issues that they consider important.

NOTES

1. See, David A. Shannon, ed., *The Great Depression*, Englewood Cliffs: Prentice-Hall Co., 1960. John K. Galbraith, *The Great Crash, 1929,* New York: Houghton-Mifflin Pub., 1972.

A critical issue

16 The economic crisis

The basic questions this chapter will address are:

(1) Is there an economic crisis?

(2) What are its causes?

(3) Who benefits and who loses from an economic crisis?

(4) Is there a solution to inflation, unemployment, recession, and depression?

Conservatives believe that there is an economic crisis but that it does not involve large numbers of unemployed persons. It has to do with the availability of capital to banks, corporations, and investors—in other words, there is a crisis of liquidity caused by too much competition among banks. In competing to loan money, banks have driven down the interest rates to too low a level to gain a reasonable return. Also the increased cost of oil due to the Arab oil producing states raising their prices has created pressure on the economy.[1] The crisis is both internally and externally caused by the flawed operation of our own financial institutions, and pressure on our economy from an outside world over which we have lost control.

To conservatives, unemployment is not a major problem. A certain amount is necessary to keep inflation under control, that is, to keep the dollar from decreasing in value. Their only concern is that too great a number of unemployed persons may lead to social unrest and government intervention in that sector of the economy not under their auspices and control. Conservatives think that a substantial rate of unemployment, between 6 per cent and 10 per cent, is economically useful to keep wages down and workers in line.

The conservative solution to the liquidity crisis is twofold: (1) A massive coordinated input of funds is transferred from the government into the corporate economy. This transfer of funds must be under the control of the corporations themselves. (2) The consolidation of banking under the control of a few major banks, such as the Bank of America, Chase Manhattan, Morgan Guaranty Trust Co., First National City, Chemical-New York. Consolidation would limit competition among banks and allow a stable control by a few superbanks over funds that circulate in the economy. Bank failures and the takeover of smaller banks by larger ones is an acceptable policy to conservatives.

Downturns in the economy are not necessarily viewed as a crisis by conservatives. Situated at the economic pinnacle, major corporations and banks increase their control over the economy in a depression. Their paper profits may seem to go down in the short term, but in the long run they benefit financially.[2] A managed recession, during which a downturn in the economy is deliberately created, is in many ways in the interest of conservatives who control the corporate economy because it allows them to increase and consolidate their power over the American economy.

Liberals maintain that the recession of the 1970s is basically a problem of too large a number of unemployed persons. They believe that unemployment has been deliberately caused by large corporations to cut costs and increase profits. Inflation and the general recession have been caused by two external factors: (1) price increases by oil-producing Arab states. (2) the $100-billion spent on the Vietnamese war by the United States. Inflation and recession are a result of the Johnson/Nixon administration's borrowing money to pay for the war rather than raising taxes to support it.

Government, according to liberals, can solve the economic crisis by undertaking two strategies: (1) Increase government regulation over corporations so that manipulation of money markets by these corporations is reduced. (2) Reallocate funds spent abroad and from the military budget to the domestic economy. For example, money spent on supporting North Atlantic Treaty Organization (NATO)/military forces in Western Europe, and on building multibillion-dollar aircraft carriers should be used in the United States to construct needed houses, better schools, mass transportation networks, and public works projects to provide jobs.[3] Liberals believe that government can cure the recession/depression if it has the will to do so. Greater public pressure on Congress and the President would force government to reallocate its priorities.[4] But public participation is necessary if government is to solve the depression of the 1970s.

Socialists maintain that the economic crisis of the 1970s must be seen in historical perspective. The present depression is part of the inevitable cyclical ups-and-downs of capitalism. Government and corporations in advanced capitalist countries work together to create economic downturns[5] in order to reduce inflation, and to limit the amount of capital available to nonelites. For example, when there is too much liquidity the Federal Reserve Bank raises interest rates to make it more difficult for borrowers to obtain money from banks. There are times however, when government and corporations lose control of the recessions they have created and depression follows. The solution as socialists see it is the overthrow of the capitalist order in the United States. Only by destroying capitalism, and the corporate economy, can new economic arrangements that are not dependent upon recession and depression be instituted. The creation of a socialist economy, well managed and organized, where goods are made to benefit the people rather than for profit or war, is the only strategy that will resolve current and future economic crises.[6]

NOTES

1. John T. Dunlop. "Inflation and Incomes Policies: The Political Economy of Recent U.S. Experience." *Public Policy* (Vol. 23, No. 2, Spring 1975), pp. 135–166.

2. American Airlines reported a $1.3 million net profit in the final quarter of 1971; Chrysler Corporation earned $3.7 million in profits in 1971, *The New York Times* (February 11, 1972). The Ford Motor Co., reported a record fourth quarter profit in 1971 of $204 million, up 35 per cent from 1970, *The New York Times* (February 15, 1972). The Caterpillar Tractor Co. earned a record net income of $109.9 million in the second quarter of 1975 at a time when unemployment was 8.2 percent according to official government

figures, *The New York Times* (July 12, 1975). International Business Machines (IBM) had a second quarter net income of $468.8 million in 1975, *The New York Times* (July 12, 1975).

3. See, Seymour Melman. *Our Depleted Society*. New York: Holt, Rinehart and Winston, 1965.

4. John W. Gardner's *Common Cause* is an example of an organization of citizens which attempts to force Congress to allocate priorities towards the needs of people. It is located at 2030 M St., N.W., Washington, D.C., 20036.

5. See Karl Marx. *Capital, A Critique of Political Economy*. New York: Modern Library, 1936 (translation). See also David Mermelstein, *The Economic Crisis Reader,* New York: Vintage Books, 1975. Bill Blum, "The Oil Connection," *Liberation* (Vol. 18, No. 6, February 1974), pp. 32–36.

6. An organization that "attempts to employ political economics in the task of changing capitalist society" is The Union for Radical Political Economics. It publishes the quarterly *Review of Radical Political Economics*. URPE can be reached at the Office of Organizational Services, Michigan Union, Ann Arbor, Mich. 48104. See in particular Frank Ackerman, Arthur MacEwan, "Inflation, Recession, and Crisis," *Review of Radical Political Economics* (Vol. 6, No. 1, 1974).

Conservative

Felix G. Rohatyn. A new R.F.C. is proposed for business.

With the country sliding rapidly into what appears to be a serious recession, suggestions are being made to revive the Reconstruction Finance Corporation as part of an overall economic program. The Democratic leadership has proposed this step and has introduced the necessary legislation.

Revival of the R.F.C. as part of a plan to get the economy on its feet is desirable without any doubt. In the Depression years of the 1930's, the R.F.C. played an important role in providing liquidity to banks and key industries, thereby preventing failures and a deepening spiral of the economic downturn. However, simply recreating the R.F.C. to provide additional credit to borrowers otherwise unable to obtain it, would be to overlook key aspects of the actual role played by the agency and to ignore basic differences between the financial structure of United States enterprise then and now. If the R.F.C. is to be recreated, let it become a vital instrument of economic growth and not just another lender of last resort.

The R.F.C. itself was a revival, in this case a revival of the War Finance Corporation of World War I. It took place in January, 1932. It was charged with providing emergency facilities for banks and other credit institutions. It was also given broad authority to make loans to agricultural, commercial and industrial enterprises. The National City Bank letter of February 1932 stated: "The enactment of the R.F.C. Act of Jan. 22 is recognition by the Government of the interest of all the people in supporting the credit granting institutions...and in bridging over the refinancing difficulties of the railways...." It went on to say, "The object of the R.F.C. is to revive industry by receiving credit."

The initial funds for the R.F.C. were to consist of $500-million of capital subscribed to by the United States Treasury and the authority to raise an additional $1.5-billion

through the sale of Government guaranteed obligations. Conceived initially as a defensive mechanism, the corporation was not perceived as a possible instrument for economic stimulation. It was only in 1933 that emergency banking legislation gave the R.F.C. the authority to purchase bank preferred stocks, thus enabling their capital base to be strengthened.

Of approximately $4-billion proposed R.F.C. expenditures for 1934, the largest portion, $1.4-billion, was earmarked for the purchase of bank preferred stocks. Eventually the R.F.C. expanded into other areas through subsidiaries such as the Commodity Credit Corporation, the Electric Home and Farm Authority, the R.F.C. Mortgage Company and the Federal National Mortgage Association. It also financed public works programs, made industrial loans and provided emergency relief.

By 1938, the R.F.C. had disbursed $10-billion, including approximately $4-billion to financial institutions, $1.5-billion to agriculture and $1-billion each to railroads and public works. The fears of many that the R.F.C. would become an instrument of creeping socialism or of state planning were unwarranted: a vast investor of public funds, the R.F.C. nevertheless was operated essentially along the lines of a private banking institution.

This brief review should be kept in mind when consideration is given to the role and the powers of a new R.F.C. in today's economic environment. Certain factors would appear to be the most obviously telling:

At every level of our economy our institutions are overburdened with debt. In the past 10 years the debt-equity ratio of individual corporations has gone from 25 per cent to 40 per cent. Inflation and the collapse of the equity markets has accelerated this trend.

The continued decline in the equity markets has resulted in 80 per cent of New York Exchange stocks presently carrying a multiple of less than 10 times earnings. A majority of such companies have market values of less than their book values. Many are unable to sell equity at any reasonable price.

The Big Board has recently estimated that the equity requirements of American industry for the foreseeable future could approximate $50-billion a year. It would appear that 1974 will produce only about $5-billion.

The United States banking system, trying to keep pace with the requirements for credit, has itself become dangerously overextended. The requirements for equity by the banking system may, in some ways, be proportionally greater than those of the industrial sector.

The dangers to the international banking system caused by the deficits of oil importing countries are too well known to require more than a mention.

This environment of fragility in both the industrial and the financial sectors exists at a time of steeply declining production, sharply increasing unemployment and continued inflationary pressures. The downward leverage, under those circumstances, would be vicious.

There exists today no public instrument for providing the only true safety net that a major corporation or bank should avail itself of when in difficulty—a major infusion of equity capital. A massive infusion of credit, such as was undertaken by the Federal Reserve System in the case of the Franklin National Bank, will provide temporary relief to cover withdrawals by depositors. It will not provide capital support to the bank in the case of a major default.

An emergency loan guarantee enabled the Lockheed Aircraft Corporation to obtain necessary short-term credits but it did not resolve the company's long-term requirements; a major restructuring of its debt and a large infusion of new equity capital will be required to do this.

At a time when loss of confidence is an almost palpable thing, accelerating the downturn of a shaky economy, a major bankruptcy either in the industrial or the financial sector is to be avoided at any

reasonable cost. The R.F.C. should be the safety net, but the cure should be permanent. From its inception, it should be an instrument empowered to make significant equity investments, in the form of either common or preferred stock, for the long-term resolution of financial problems.

There will be wide opposition to such a thesis both on ideological and practical grounds. The specter of socialism will be raised by the conservatives and the cry of "big business bail-out" will be heard from the liberals. Serious concerns with respect to the governance of such an enterprise, to its potential political power, to the possible conflicts-of-interest and corruption posed by such a mass of capital, will have to be debated and resolved. But the need for the enterprise would appear to be sufficiently great to outweigh the drawbacks.

In addition to being an investor of last resort empowered to make equity infusions into banks or industrial enterprises deemed to be "in the public interest," the R.F.C. could become a catalyst of stimulation in many areas. If a Manhattan-type project in the area of energy is ever undertaken, as is clearly required, the R.F.C. could play a major role as an investor, risk-sharer, lender and guarantor in a variety of projects. Although state-regulated concerns such as utilities should perhaps not be eligible investments, the financing of massive generating facilities, the output of which would be shared by various grids, could be considered. Construction of over $20-billion worth of generating capacity has been canceled so far this year, its effect to be felt years from now.

There can be no denying that such an organization, with the type of wide-ranging freedom described above, can be perceived as a first step toward state planning of the economy. Yet the time may have come for a public debate on this subject. Our economy is today subjected to certain traumas which have nothing to do with the result of free market interaction. The oil cartel and the prices of other basic commodities that directly affect our economy such as phosphates and alumina are the result of political rather than economic decisions, and are totally beyond our control.

At a time when the oil producing countries are levying an initial tax of $60-billion a year on the rest of the world, the United States has become capital-poor. The possible impact on this country's welfare, as well as its security, of foreign control of major enterprises has not been evaluated. The premise that, under such circumstances, the country has to husband its resources more carefully, allocate them more prudently and match its financial capabilities with its social priorities would appear to be worth considering. What many will call state planning would, to the average family, be no more than prudent budgeting.

There are many who believe that long-range economic planning, at the Federal level will become · a necessity. A plan without instruments to bring it to reality, however, is simply one more piece of paper. The R.F.C. could be one of the key instruments in this kind of approach. By injecting equity capital where none is available in quantity, it could facilitate major-restructuring for the public purpose.

For instance, if a merger of Pan American World Airways and Trans World Airlines appears to be nationally desirable, a $250-million equity investment in the merged company could accomplish much. It could cause the lenders of both corporations to convert some of their debt to equity, or reduce carrying charges or stretch out maturities. It could insure the merged company's ability to ride through the storm, achieve its savings and efficiencies and ultimately be profitable enough to provide a fair return to the investors (including the R.F.C.), a viable employer and pass some savings on in lower fares.

The R.F.C. should, thus, become a permanent part of our economic establishment, not just as a last-ditch creditor but as a vibrant instrument of both rescue as well as stimulus. It need not, and should not, be a permanent investor in any one particular enterprise. It should only remain as an investor, either as a part-owner or creditor, until such time as it can, in the public interest, divest itself of the enterprise in which it invests and this investment is eligible for normal market channels or until the markets are capable of performing their function.

The R.F.C., therefore, should, in effect, become a revolving fund—hopefully a profitable one—which steps in where no alternatives are available and which steps out when the public interest has been served and normal market forces can again operate.

An initial capitalization of $5-billion in commonstock subscribed to by the Treasury, and the authority to issue up to $10-billion in United States guaranteed obligations would provide a major safety factor to the economy in the coming times of peril, as well as simultaneously taking pressure off the banking system. These obligations could provide a logical investment for the surplus · dollars of oil-producing countries.

Financing the capital subscription should come from the private sector. It could take the form of a levy of 1 per cent of pretax profits of all enterprises earning over $1-million per annum. This would reimburse the Treasury's subscription in less than five years.

The R.F.C. should combine public purpose with prudent business practice and, with the proper leadership and oversight, should accomplish both to the ultimate benefit of the tax payers.

Liberal

Helen Ginsburg. The strategy of misery.

Gerald Ford may not agree, but unemployment is already at a disaster level. In December 1974, it shot up to 7.1 per cent. That means 6.5 million human beings are *officially* without work (unofficially, there are many more). In just three months, 1.2 million people have become jobless, and layoffs are still spreading. All kinds of workers are being cut, even the "safe" civil servants. The list grows daily, along with fear and insecurity, as the employed wonder when the pink slip will come and young people worry about the future.

Yet for all the publicity, the true nature of this unemployment crisis is scarcely recognized: it is an acute, dramatic peak rising from a continuing, long-term, quiet and usually ignored state of misery. The immediate catastrophe makes the head-lines—it is now almost certain that 1975 will bring a 7.5 or 8 per cent rate—but the chronic failure of the American economy to provide enough decent jobs for all who want to work is ignored. And the absence of a firm national commitment to full em-ployment insures the perpetuation of both situations. Short-term crises are in-creasingly frequent and stop-gap strategies to cope with them are woefully inadequate. Meanwhile, there is no long-term plan to eliminate the high unemployment that persists in so-called "good times." Even worse, permanent high rates of unemploy-ment are now widely accepted and those in power use fiscal and monetary policy to create rather than to prevent recessions.

How did the country get into this mess? Unemployment is nothing new, but the national position toward it has changed. Back in the 1940s, full employment was a major political issue. It had, after all, taken World War II to end the Great Depression and bring about full employment. There was, accordingly, a pervasive fear of a postwar depression. In labor and liberal circles it was strongly felt that unemploy-ment should never again be tolerated; that a nation capable of total mobilization for war should be able to guarantee jobs for all in peacetime and not have to rely on war to solve its unemployment problem.

In this spirit, the Full Employment Bill of 1945 was introduced in Congress. It declared that "all Americans able to work and seeking work have the right to useful, remunerative, regular and full-time employ-ment." The federal government was man-dated to "assure the existence at all times of sufficient employment opportunities." But the liberal-labor coalition was too weak to withstand the attack of big business on full employment and guaranteed jobs. Despite overwhelming Senate approval, the bill was defeated by conservatives in the House. A weaker compromise, the Employment Act of 1946, acknowledged federal responsibility to create conditions that afford "useful opportunities . . . for those willing and seeking to work." However, the changes were more than semantic. The concrete assertion of the right to a job had been replaced by the vaguer goal of "maximum employment" consistent with "other essen-tial considerations of national policy."

The Employment Act of 1946 is a legis-lative landmark, but as Prof. Bertram M. Gross of Hunter College, its chief drafts-man, recalled at a symposium last year, its actual objective was not to guarantee employment. Rather, he stated, it was to prevent the recurrence of mass depression and collapse of the American business system.

There is a feeling these days that the economy may be heading into a 1930s nose-dive, but at least until now, the Act's mission of staving off mass depression has been accomplished. And this very success has diverted attention from the long-term problem. When unemployment was a mass affliction, it could not be ignored; with less joblessness it can be. However, since the Act's passage, not only has unemployment been substantial and persistent it has also been drifting upward. From 1946 to 1973, it averaged about 4.5 per cent. But it climbed from 4.2 per cent in the first half of this era to 4.9 per cent in the last half. "Good times" have been rare. This is the sixth postwar recession. Yet who remembers that for eighty-eight months, from November 1957 to February 1956, unemployment rarely fell below 5 per cent? Or that in 1958, and again in 1961, the annual rate was nearly 7 per cent? Or that since 1948, it has never dipped below 4 per cent, except during the wars in Korea and Vietnam?

Even by comparison with other countries, the picture looks grim. True, unemployment has been rising in most industrialized capitalist nations, but it is still much higher here than in most of the others, and it has been for years. From 1960 to 1970, for example, joblessness averaged 4.7 per cent in the United States but only 0.6 per cent in Germany, 1.3 per cent in Japan, 1.5 per cent in Sweden, 2 per cent in France and 3 per cent in Great Britain. (Foreign data are adjusted to American measurement methods.) Rates considered exceedingly low here, say the 3.5 to 3.8 per cent levels attained during the war in Vietnam, would be viewed with alarm in most other countries, where there is greater worker solidarity and a stronger determination not to accept unemployment. Pressure from Socialist-oriented labor movements and political parties usually causes tension and strain at rates that would be regarded as "over full employment" in America. In Sweden, a jobless rate of about 3 per cent nearly cost the Social Democratic Party—in power for forty-one years—the 1973 election. But, as Sen. Alan Cranston noted in testimony on behalf of the ill-fated Public Service Employment Bill of 1972, "In this country the rate hovers at 6 per cent and nobody seems to care."

It's not merely that nobody cares. Big business has always preferred some unemployment because it gives more control over workers, weakens unions, and holds down wages. Contemporary economic theory now helps them justify higher and higher unemployment, all in the name fighting inflation. In the 1960s, many economists popularized the concept of the Phillips curve—the alleged trade-off between unemployment and inflation. According to this reasoning, the lower the unemployment, the more the inflation, and conversely. This implied, in the most conservative interpretation, that full employment was too inflationary and, thus, unattainable or even undesirable. (Each country was said to have its own unemployment-inflation trade-off. How else could you explain that Germany had both the lowest unemployment and inflation rates?)

In a social and political climate with little broad concern over unemployment and with practically no commitment to the concept of genuine full employment, a different meaning of "full employment" took root. At one time the concept of full employment had focused on human beings. It meant that those who wanted work could find it. But then the focus shifted from people to prices. *In many circles, full employment came to mean the unemployment rate assumed to be consistent with the degree of price stability desired by policy makers.* Over the years, the "full employment" unemployment rate was revised upward from 3 to 4 per cent, to 5 per cent and even higher. (Will it eventually mean 10 per cent unemployed?)

In this atmosphere, it is not surprising that the trade-off analysis tempted conservative American policy makers who faced inflation. Strategies deliberately designed to increase unemployment were openly pursued during Nixon's administration. In October 1968, with prices rising and unemployment at 3.6 per cent, the Business Council, an influential federal advisory group of top corporate executives, urged the next President to force unemployment up to 5.5 per cent. If that was the price for putting an end to inflation, a spokesman said, "it must be paid." (*The New York Times,* October 21, 1968.) And paid it was. Soon afterward, the Nixon regime successfully engineered a recession that drove up unemployment from 3.5 per cent in 1969 to 5.9 per cent in 1971. Not much was said about the additional 2 million jobless workers.

Despite periodic denials, the Nixon administration unofficially abandoned the 4 per cent "full employment" figure adopted by the Kennedy administration. The Council of Economic Advisers finally acknowledged a 5 per cent goal in its 1974 Annual Report:

Last year we described "maximum employment," which is the goal specified in the Employment Act, as a "condition in which persons who want work and seek it realistically on reasonable terms can find employment." We believe that condition was approximately met in 1973, even though the average unemployment rate was 4.9 per cent rather than 4.0 per cent which conventionally defines full employment.

This announcement caused hardly a political ripple, let alone any real opposition. Yet even if unemployment had been only 4 per cent in 1973, 3.6 million workers would have been officially jobless. It is absurd to call that "full employment." But the advisers made their proclamation when unemployment was nearly 5 per cent. That's 4.4 million people—seemingly small mathematical differences represent millions of lives. In a work force of 92 million people, each percentage-point rise in joblessness tosses another 920,000 onto the scrap heap. Current policies would either prevent unemployment from accidentally falling below the target or raise unemployment that is "too low." Since 1969, the game has been to keep unemployment from falling too low, not to lower unemployment—except when Nixon was up for re-election.

Nobel Laureate Paul Samuelson warned in the June 1974 *Morgan Guaranty Survey* that behind the scenes of officialdom the debate was about the desirability of countenancing and even contriving to "slow U.S. growth for two or three years, so that unemployment will remain above the 5.5 per cent level." Yet he, himself, had suggested earlier in *Newsweek* (October 15, 1973) that "to keep the average rate of unemployment below 5 per cent in the period from now to 1976, we would do well to let it rise temporarily above recent levels (repeat temporarily)." By the time of the summit conferences, the Ford Administration's target had obviously risen to at least 6 per cent. Why, then, should anyone have expected the same Administration to hurry to reduce unemployment—unless mounting political opposition forced the issue?

Inflation is a complex affair. The Phillips curve oversimplifies matters, to say the least. It spotlights attention on just two factors, *assumes* that one causes the other, and is then used as a smoke screen to obscure other roots of inflation—for example, the war in Vietnam, the growing power of monopolies, and the "peacetime" military budget.

The Johnson administration's decision in 1965 to pour troops into Vietnam set off the first round of the present inflation. Taxes could not be raised without arousing further anti-war protest, so the war was sold as a bargain. Some bargain! By 1968, direct costs had reached $30 billion a year. But the war, said the President's 1968 Economic Report, "is a burden a wealthy people can bear." In a time-honored manner, inflation financed the war. Nixon inherited that inflation and, in a desperate attempt to cool it

while maintaining the war, threw millions out of work. Yet prices kept rising until "stagflation" became a household word.

That wasn't supposed to happen, but ever since then inflation and recession have shared the same bed. This inflation cannot be attributed to wage-push. The real spendable earnings of workers have declined, while after-tax corporate profits have soared, even allowing for price changes. One reason why prices do not fall is because corporate power is growing. It's not just oil or wheat. For instance, between 1947 and 1968, the 200 largest manufacturing corporations raised their share of manufacturing assets from 47 to 60 per cent. And conglomerates now control much of our food supply. The result, as the detailed studies of John Blair, former chief economist of the Senate Antitrust Committee, show, is that when demand falls, firms in highly concentrated industries tend to raise prices, not to cut them. Witness the auto industry. The corporate hand, not the invisible hand, sets so many prices that even planned recessions that create unemployment and reduce demand don't cure inflation. In fact, they feed it. Of course, a deep and long-lasting recession would doubtless "cure" inflation.

Another factor that adds to inflation is the bloated "peacetime" military budget. As the 1974 Report of the Joint Economic Committee put it mildly, "Defense spending tends to be inflationary." Resources used by the military, the committee pointed out, can contribute to civilian shortages. Expenditures flow into the economy, but they do not produce goods and services to satisfy consumer needs. You can't eat missiles. Is that why the Council of Economic Advisers refused to conduct studies of this aspect of inflation, as requested by the committee?

Planned recessions are a neat way to take income away from the poor and middle classes and give it to the rich by eliminating jobs, charging higher prices, and increasing profits. And having created unemployment, the official attitude has been to wish it away. In the last recession, lingering unemployment was falsely attributed to the entrance of women and teen-agers into the labor force; that line is still popular. Powerless groups are simply written off as not quite legitimate members of the work force. Treasury Secretary John Connally's 1972 testimony to the Joint Economic Committee stated this quite explicitly:

It is significant that compared to the 5.9 per cent rate for total unemployment, about 17 per cent was the rate for young people and about 9 per cent was the rate for blacks. . . . If you take the unemployment rate for males, heads of families, you get down to an unemployment figure of 3 per cent. So we can't be carried away by an unemployment figure of say, 6 per cent. . . .

Apparently, only adult males matter. Preferably white.

The average unemployment rate does mask a lot, but that doesn't mean what Connally implied. It means that, while there is prosperity for one group, other groups are hit with recession and depression. At all times, most of those out of work are white. And that's important in terms of building coalitions to fight unemployment. At present, eight out of ten—5.2 million—of the jobless are white. Unemployment is not just being faced by blacks, or by the unskilled, or by the uneducated, or by any one group. A bachelor's degree no longer guarantees a job. Nor a Ph.D. But it is true that the weakest are hardest hit: minorities, the young, women, the poor and the unskilled. For two decades now, the unemployment rate of blacks has been double that of whites. In December, the figures were 12.8 per cent and 6.4 per cent. Nearly everyone except Gerald Ford admits that a 6 per cent jobless rate is a full-fledged recession. But from 1954 on, annual unemployment for blacks has never gone as low as 6 per cent and for whites has only twice reached that high. For blacks, this has meant a continuous recession interspersed with depression and frequent double-digit unemployment. And what term can describe the 37.8 per cent jobless rate of black teenagers, most of whom are out of school? Is it any wonder that inner-city crime persists? As for adult women, relatively more of them are unemployed than adult men—7.2 per cent compared to 5.1 per cent—and the gap

has been widening. Yet only the earnings of married women enable many working-class families to make ends meet. And for working women who head families, unemployment may lead to welfare.

Bad as they are, official unemployment figures are just the tip of the iceberg. They exclude, for instance, 3.4 million part-time workers who want full-time jobs but can't find them, and about 700,000 persons officially listed (1973) as too discouraged to look for work. (Unofficial estimates of discouraged workers are millions higher.) Just adding these two groups to the official roster of 6.5 million shows that, at the very least, 10.7 million people are fully or partly unemployed. Nor is even that the whole picture. Millions of fully employed Americans earn too little to live in minimal decency. All of these problems are exacerbated by the recession, but a Bureau of Labor Statistics survey has demonstrated that, even in good times, urban slums are cesspools of open and disguised unemployment and inadequate earnings. Thus, in November 1966, when national unemployment was 3.7 per cent, from 24 to 47 per cent of workers in ten large urban slums were either officially or unofficially jobless, working part time involuntarily or full time for less than the poverty level of $60 a week.

For part of the work force—especially but not exclusively minorities, women, the poor, the young and the unskilled—even good times can be bad times. And bad times are an utter disaster. Why, then, has there been so little political response? Fear of inflation? Misunderstanding of its real cause and ignorance of its extent? Unemployment insurance, which cushions the blow? (Yet in 1973, no more than two out of five of the jobless drew benefits that averaged only $59 a week.)

While each of these may explain the apathy in part, there are still other reasons. Response is weak precisely because so many of the unemployed have little status, suffer the most discrimination, have the least political power, are often outside unions or underrepresented at leadership levels within them. More of the jobless are from these groups today than in the past. Perhaps that is why ever higher unemployment has become tolerated or ignored—and not just by conservatives. Some don't know and some don't care. Increasingly, we live in differerent worlds, isolated from those unlike ourselves. And this reinforces the "I'm all right, Jack," attitude. So only when the quiet misery explodes into an acute crisis does unemployment start to generate political steam. Then, many workers who are usually fairly safe from the ravages of unemployment are threatened. They find that their immunity is only relative. When push comes to shove, more of them are sacrificed to reactionary policies.

Since 1970, poverty and income inequality have been increasing, black economic progress has halted and is even reversing. Cities have been deteriorating rapidly. Crime is more rampant than ever. Right now, in the job market it's young against old, white against black, men against women—all pitted against one another for scarce jobs. In New York, college graduates are vying with welfare mothers for a dwindling number of jobs; older civil servants may be forced into premature retirement to save younger workers' jobs. The recession has further split an already divided work force. As it deepens, divisiveness may worsen. But the situation also presents an opportunity. Can the massive assault on jobs and real earnings which now threatens so many stiffen resistance and become a unifying force?

So far, Congress has reacted weakly to the recession. Emergency unemployment benefits will be temporarily extended to many previously uncovered workers; and $2.5 billion has been authorized for public service jobs. But only $875 million has actually been appropriated for jobs. That's about 100,000 jobs—barely enough to help one out of sixty-five of the unemployed. The effect is to disguise how little is being done. The new, more liberal, Congress should be more responsive, especially as pressure builds. But even if the acute crisis eventually abates, what then? Do we go back to the quiet misery?

The goal should be guaranteed jobs for all at decent wages. But can genuine full employment actually become a potent political issue? Women are organizing—even within labor and political parties. The National Urban League has made full employment a priority issue. And the nation's mayors are calling for federal action to create jobs. Most promising is the formation last June of the National Committee for Full Employment, co-chaired by Coretta Scott King and Murray Finley, president of the Amalgamated Clothing Workers. With representation from organized labor, civil rights, black women's, religious, ethnic and other groups, the committee correctly asserts that "the guarantee of a job is a fundamental right," and that "unemployment at *any rate* is unacceptable . . . full employment means *no* involuntary unemployment." Its recent decision to engage in legislative action should give the committee greater visibility, but it is still too soon to know how it will operate. Will it remain an organization mainly of prominent though diverse leaders? Or will it blossom into a national grass-roots movement? There are other big ifs. Can the many solidarity gaps that divide people be bridged? Could a mass movement for full employment gain the momentum that the civil rights and anti-war movements once had? Can anything less make full employment a major political demand?

There's also a major new development on Capitol Hill. Reps. Augustus Hawkins and Henry Reuss and sixty-one co-sponsors have introduced the "Equal Opportunity and Full Employment Act of 1976," and Hubert Humphrey has introduced a companion bill in the Senate. The House bill would establish a national policy and create the necessary machinery to guarantee adequately paying jobs for all. It's a long-term approach, but stopgap measures don't solve long-term problems. Last March, Hawkins said that by 1976, "the platform committees of the two major parties will face a major challenge. Will they content themselves with a flatulent rhetoric of the past? Or will they commit themselves to a genuine jobs-for-all guarantee?" The question is even more pertinent today. How it is answered remains to be seen.

Socialist

Paul Sweezy and Harry Magdoff.   The economic crisis in historical perspective.

In last month's Review of the Month we argued that U.S. capitalism has once again, as in the 1930s, entered a period of persistent and prolonged stagnation. At the same time we expressed agreement with those who, while recognizing that many big banks and corporations are in very shaky condition, doubt that this time it will come to a 1933-type panic. The expectation of prompt government intervention—through some combination of debt moratoriums and emergency bail-outs—seems well founded. As *Business Week* wrote in its issue of January 27th under the heading, "When Companies Get Too Big To Fail": "The huge U.S. corporations have become such important centers of jobs and incomes that it [the government] dare not let one of them shut down or go out of business. It is compelled, therefore, to shape national policy in terms of protecting the great corporations instead of letting the economy make deflationary adjustments."

If we accept this premise, the question which we ought to try to answer is not *whether* the government will intervene to prevent a panic but what will happen *after* it is forced to intervene. What policies are being discussed in ruling-class circles? How realistic are they? What are their implications for other sectors of society, and particularly the working class? It is to questions such as these that we now turn our attention.

There is a strong tendency among capitalists and their spokesmen to see all of their troubles as stemming from an insufficiency of surplus value. Profit (one of the components of surplus value) provides the incentive to invest, and the totality of surplus value constitutes the pool from which the capital for additional investment is drawn. Since capitalist prosperity is dependent on a high rate on investment, it seems to follow that what is needed to get the system out of a slump is above all an increase in the amount of surplus value flowing into the pockets of capitalists and other recipients of income derived from surplus value. This will provide, so the argument runs, both the incentive and the wherewithal to increase the rate of investment. The policy implications of this diagnosis are of course obvious: squeeze workers and consumers generally in favor of the corporations and the wealthy. A fairly typical example of this kind of reasoning is contained in *Business Week's* special supplement on "The Debt Economy" in its issue of last October 12th:

It is inevitable that the U.S. economy will grow more slowly than it has [an implicit recognition of the new period of stagnation] . . . . Some people will obviously have to do with less . . . . Indeed, cities and states, the home mortgage market, small business, and the consumer, will all get less than they want because the basic health of the U.S. is based on the basic health of its corporations and banks: the biggest borrowers and the biggest lenders . . . .

Put simplistically, as long as corporations stay healthy, they can pay taxes and provide people with jobs . . . . But when corporations fall sick, people lose jobs and stop buying. Nobody pays taxes, governments and local authorities are not financed, and everyone—corporations, consumers, federal and local administrations alike—goes broke or gets embedded more deeply in the debt spiral . . . .

Yet it will be a hard pill for many Americans to swallow—the idea of doing with less so that big business can have more. It will be particularly hard to swallow because it is quite obvious that if big business and big banks are the most visible victims of what ails the Debt Economy, they are also in large measure the cause of it . . . .

Nothing that this nation, or any other nation, has done in modern history compares in difficulty with the selling job that must now be done to make people accept the new reality. And there are grave doubts whether the job can be done at all. Historian Arnold Toynbee, filled with years and compassion, laments that democracy will be unable to cope with approaching economic problems—and that totalitarianism will take its place.

This is remarkably reminiscent of the remedy prescribed for the German people by its ruling class in 1933. A brutal fascist regime was imposed on the country; all opposition groups, especially those of the working class, were smashed; wages were frozen; and wealth was redistributed in favor of the corporations and the rich. But there was one more essential ingredient of the Nazi success in pulling Germany out of the depression of the 1930s, and that was the enormous expenditures on war preparations which increased employment and stimulated investment both directly and indirectly.

Our analysis of the present situation, put forth in this space last month, leads to the conclusion that some comparable stimulus would be needed to push the U.S. economy onto a sustained upward course in the 1970s.[1] Without it, a policy aimed at raising the rate of surplus value might have little effect and indeed might make matters worse, since it would reduce consumption without holding out the prospect of the expanded markets which alone could justify an increase in capitalists' investment. Whether the editors of *Business Week* and those who think like them are aware that the policy they recommend (most people "doing with less so that big business can have more") requires to be supplemented by applying a powerful stimulus to the economy is not clear. Our guess would be that they lack such awareness: conservative economic analysts always have a tendency to believe that the problem of markets will take care of itself (perhaps with a little help from monetary policy) if only workers can be put in their place. Since, as the whole history of capitalism shows, this is emphatically not the case, it follows that the policy proposals of conservatives are neither very interesting nor likely to be long persisted in if actually put into practice.[2]

Less doctrinaire bourgeois analysts, while not disagreeing about the importance of expanding the flow of surplus value, recognize that the present critical, and rapidly worsening, state of the economy calls for a far more comprehensive program. In this connection attention has recently centered on a proposal, emanating from various sources, to revive the Reconstruction Finance Corporation which was created in 1932, the last year of the Hoover administration, and liquidated in 1953 under Eisenhower.[3] The RFC was itself a revival of the War Finance Corporation established during the First World War to help finance munitions plants, a function which the RFC itself also performed during the Second World War. By far the most interesting and detailed blueprint for a new RFC which has come to our attention is contained in a lead article in the financial section of the Sunday *New York Times* of December 1, 1974, by Felix G. Rohatyn ("A New RFC Is Proposed for Business"). Rohatyn is an Austrian-born partner in the international investment banking firm of Lazard Frères, a director of several large corporations (including ITT), and reportedly a very shrewd operator in the politically sensitive field of corporate mergers. Inquiries directed to sources knowledgeable in Wall Street affairs have elicited the information that he is a registered Democrat and an adviser to Senator Henry Jackson of Washington, one of the front runners for the Democratic presidential nomination in 1976. Obviously he is a man whose pronouncements on economic policy should be taken seriously.

Rohatyn makes clear at the outset that he is interested in a revived RFC not merely as a salvage operation for financially troubled corporations but as a centerpiece for a much more far-reaching economic program. "If the RFC is to be recreated," he writes, "let it become a vital instrument of economic growth and not just another lender of last resort." What this means first and foremost is that the new RFC should have the power and the financial means (to be raised through the sale of government guaranteed bonds and notes) to provide large amounts of corporate equity, i.e., to buy freshly issued stock of corporations. The purpose would be threefold: first, to halt and reverse the trend so marked in recent years for corporate debt/equity ratios to deteriorate, with a consequent impairment of credit-worthiness and decline in stock prices (Rohatyn points out that in the last decade debt/equity ratios have risen from 25 percent to 40 percent); second, through such strengthening of corporate capital structures to enable the companies themselves to raise more money through sale of stocks rather than bonds; and third, to provide corporations with the wherewithal to undertake large projects needed for the viability of the capitalist system as a whole but insufficiently profitable to attract private investors. Rohatyn does not spell all this out in any detail, but he gives enough examples to indicate not only the sort of thing he has in mind but also some of the orders of magnitude which might be involved.

"The Big Board [i.e., the New York Stock Exchange] has recently estimated," he writes, "that the equity requirements of American industry for the foreseeable future could approximate $50 billion a year. It would appear that 1974 will produce only about $5 billion." If the revived RFC is supposed, directly and indirectly, to enable U.S. corporations to sell $40 billion or more annually in new stock issues, it is indeed being conceived of as a very major new component of U.S. capitalism.

But this is not the only function to be assigned to the new RFC:

In addition to being an investor of last resort empowered to make equity infusions into banks or industrial enterprises deemed to be "in the public interest," the RFC could become a catalyst of stimulation in many areas. If a Manhattan-type project in the area of energy is ever undertaken, as is clearly required, the RFC could play a major role as an investor, risk-sharer, lender, and guarantor in a variety of projects. Although state regulated concerns such as utilities should perhaps not be eligible investments, the financing of massive generating facilities, the output of which could be shared by various grids, could be considered. Construction of over $20 billion worth of generating capacity has been canceled so far this year [1974], its effect to be felt years from now.

Furthermore, the RFC could step into messy situations which private enterprise has been incapable of straightening out—in Rohatyn's words, it "could facilitate major restructuring for the public purpose":

For instance, if a merger of Pan American World Airways and Trans World Airlines appears to be nationally desirable, a $250-million equity investment in the merged company could accomplish much. It could cause the lenders of both corporations to convert some of their debt to equity, or reduce carrying charges, or stretch out maturities. It could ensure the merged company's ability to ride through the storm, achieve its savings and efficiencies, and ultimately be profitable enough to provide a fair return to the investors (including the RFC), a viable employer, and pass some savings on in lower fares.

Whatever it may have been thought of in its earlier incarnations, Rohatyn is emphatic that this time the RFC should become an integral feature of the system:

The RFC should . . . become a permanent part of our economic establishment, not just as a last-ditch creditor but as a vibrant instrument of both rescue as well as stimulus. It need not, and should not, be a permanent investor in any one particular enterprise. It should only remain as an investor, either as a part-owner or creditor, until such time as it can, in the public interest, divest itself of the enterprise in which it invests and this investment is eligible for normal market channels or until the markets are capable of performing their function. The RFC therefore should, in effect, become a revolving fund—hopefully a profitable one—which steps in where no alternatives are available and which steps out when the public interest has been served and normal market forces can again operate.

Here again the seemingly casual mention of figures in the tens of billions of dollars for one industry and hundreds of millions for one company reveals the trend of the writer's thinking. And of course it would not be at all difficult to add to the list of projects which could use, and for the most part are not likely to be realized without, "an investor, risk-sharer, lender, and guarantor": rehabilitation of the railroads, urban mass transit, pollution control, low-cost housing, etc. Market-directed, profit-seeking private enterprise has failed miserably to meet even minimum (from the point of view of capitalism itself) social needs in these and other areas. What Felix Rohatyn is suggesting is that the capitalist class, acting through its state, should create a permanent institution capable of fulfilling the dual function of arresting the present potentially disastrous slide of the economy and subsidizing, directly or indirectly, investment in and production of goods and services which private monopolies consider too unprofitable and/or too risky to get into. If, by chance, some of these investments should turn out to be attractively profitable, they could and should be turned over to private hands: the state's job under capitalism is not to appropriate profits but to socialize losses and see that the system functions smoothly.

Rohatyn understands perfectly well that his proposals involve more than setting up a government corporation and providing it with money to invest. He brushes aside ideological objections—"socialism" from conservatives and "big business bail-outs" from the liberals—but he is quite willing to concede that the kind of RFC he has in mind can be effective only in a context of economic planning:

There can be no denying that such an organization with the type of wide-ranging freedom described above, can be perceived as a first step toward state planning of the economy. Yet the time may have come for a public debate on this subject....The premise that under [presently existing] circumstances, the country has to husband its resources more carefully, allocate them more prudently, and match its financial capabilities with its social priorities would appear to be worth considering. What many will call state planning would, to the average family, be no more than prudent budgeting.

There are many who believe that long-range economic planning, at the federal level, will become a necessity. A plan without instruments to bring it to reality, however, is simply one more piece of paper. The RFC could be one of the key instruments in this kind of approach.

Rohatyn says nothing about what other key instruments of long-range economic planning might be necessary or desirable. But others are getting into the act, and it seems certain that from now on there will be no shortage of proposals and blueprints. A story in the March 10th issue of *Business Week* clearly points in this direction:

Centralized government economic planning traditionally has been anathema to most businessmen, politicians, and economists. But with the economy in the worst slump since the 1930s, plus the added economic burden of the energy crisis, national planning is gaining new support in and out of Washington.

A group of businessmen, labor leaders, and economists, headed by Nobel Prize-winning economist Wassily W. Leontieff, wants Congress to set up an office of National Economic Planning. The proposal, which is backed by such varied people as Robert V. Roosa, senior vice president of Brown Bros. Harriman & Co. [and former Under Secretary of the Treasury for Monetary Affairs], and Leonard Woodcock, president of the United Auto Workers, would give the planning office a broad mandate including:

Authority to collect and analyze detailed economic information from all sources both in the government and the private sector.

Responsibility for developing economic plans for periods of 5 to 15 years that are to be submitted to Congress and the President.

Power to coordinate economic policy-making among such agencies as the Office of Management & Budget, the Treasury Dept., and the Council of Economic Advisers.

One other key instrument of long-range capitalist planning is likely to be some form of wage-and-price controls, often given the euphemistic name of "incomes policy," the real purpose of which is to regulate the rate of surplus value in the interests of capital. Such regulation is clearly implicit in the aim, cited above, of everyone else doing with less so that big business can have more, but its urgency is considerably less in a time of deepening depression than it was in the previous period of rampant inflation. Nevertheless, it occupies a central position in bourgeois planning literature (see, for example, J. K. Galbraith's latest book, *Economics and the Public Purpose*), and it is pretty sure to have a place in any planning scheme that may be adopted in the future.

Putting aside for the moment the question of the effectiveness of possible planning arrangements, we can say one thing with reasonable certainty: the present economic crisis and the renewed period of stagnation to which it is the prelude are bound to produce a great leap forward into state capitalism in the United States. This will take the form of extensive salvage operations which in fact are already under way in various sectors of the economy (banking, railroads, etc.). It is very likely to take the form of a massive government investment banking operation such as Rohatyn's RFC proposal. And it may involve more or less serious efforts at national economic planning. But whatever the mix, there can be no mistaking the powerful and clearly irreversible trend toward ever greater state intervention and participation in the U.S. economy.

Two brief comments are immediately in order. First, whatever conservatives and brainwashed social "scientists" may say, this has absolutely nothing to do with socialism.[4] Second, other advanced capitalist countries are much further into state capitalism than the United States, so that what is starting to happen here can be looked upon as a catching-up process.

As to whether and/or to what extent the march to state capitalism can check the present crisis and alleviate the condition of stagnation which is now in prospect, one must evidently speak with considerable caution. We have already expressed the view that the government can prevent a full-blown panic by, in effect, assuming or guaranteeing the debts of threatened banks and corporations. How much more it can accomplish is the big question mark. A careful assessment of the experience of other countries in which state capitalism is more developed than in the United States would perhaps lead to the conclusion that something can be achieved in the way of propping up investment and employment, but not very much as long as they are dependent, as most of them are, on international developments beyond their control. But it would be wrong to transfer this conclusion directly to the United States, if only because the United States is by far the biggest member of the world capitalist system and hence plays a disproportionately large part in determining the international developments which bear so heavily on the others. It might be argued that if state capitalism in the United States could

decisively improve the performance of this largest unit in the system, it would at the same time enable the others to reap the full potential benefits of state capitalism for themselves. Lacking any way to test the validity of this argument, we can only speculate on the first part of it, i.e., on how much state capitalism is likely to be able to accomplish here in this country.

And here, paradoxically (or at least so it will seem to many), the problem is much more a matter of politics than of economics. The enormous wealth and productivity of the United States confers on this country what, to use an analogy from mathematics, may be called almost unlimited degrees of economic freedom. *On paper* it should not be difficult to draw up plans which, while remaining entirely within the framework of capitalism, would eliminate some of the system's almost incredibly wasteful and absurd irrationalities and mobilize the human and material resources thus made available to tackle many of the problems which now seem hopelessly insoluble. This is not the place to spin out such plans: that can safely be left to Professor Leontieff and his associates. Suffice it to say that actual experience during the Second World War proved that, starting from an unemployment situation somewhat similar to what we have today, it was possible to increase production by roughly 100 percent while at the same time drafting millions of men and women in the most productive age groups into the armed forces. *On paper* it should be possible to do even better today, with investment being channeled (perhaps by Felix Rohatyn's RFC) into developing new energy sources, rebuilding and extending the nation's rail network, providing the cities with modernized mass transport systems, de-polluting our air and water, furnishing halfway decent housing for perhaps 25 million families, etc., etc. This would certainly not have to involve any drastic redistribution of income or any crippling (to capitalism) reduction in the rate of surplus value: easily attainable increases in production could provide more all around.

It is precisely paper dreams of this kind that dazzle our well-intentioned planners. They forget to ask where all these incredibly wasteful and absurd irrationalities came from in the first place, and they overlook the stubborn fact that each and every one of them is the fortress or hiding place of vested interests which wield enormous political power and have absolutely no intention of making the least sacrifice for the common good, even if that somewhat elusive concept is defined wholly in capitalist terms. How is the energy problem to be approached, let alone solved, with the oil giants sitting astride an ever-increasing share of the nation's profitable energy sources and firmly in control of a large delegation of senators and representatives?[5] How are the railroads and urban mass transit going to get the priority which common sense tells us they deserve in the face of the vast power of the automobile, trucking, oil, and highway interests? Who is going to sell mass low-cost housing to the real estate and mortgage-banking interests? Give us persuasive answers to these questions and maybe we'll begin to pay more attention to your paper plans. But if you have no answers, please pardon us, there are more important matters to attend to.

The working class, defined broadly to include all those who need jobs as well as those who have them, is, as always, the special victim of capitalist depression. Real wages have been declining for several years now, and unemployment is far worse than the official figure of 8.2 percent (even officially it is over 40 percent for black teenagers). Many workers are up to their ears in debt, unemployment benefits are rapidly running out, and huge numbers are being forced to go on welfare. Even those who still have jobs, knowing that their turn may come next, live in constant fear of ruin for themselves and their families. The working class in this the richest country in the world is quite literally facing a struggle for survival.

Under these circumstances, the unions, thoroughly bureaucratized, integrated into the system as a means of controlling workers rather than fighting for their interests, and in any case representing no more than about a quarter of the labor force, are not going to be magically transformed into effective instruments of working-class

struggle. Their role today will probably be similar to that of the old A.F. of L. in the early 1930s, one of impotence and obstruction. And just as then, new organizations and new forms of struggle will doubtless emerge as workers are forced to face the grim realities of capitalist breakdown.

We do not pretend to be able to predict what these new organizations and forms of struggle will be or when they will begin to take shape. Our confidence that they will indeed emerge is based on the whole history of working-class movements under capitalism: every major crisis releases dormant energies and stirs the working class to action, and there is no reason to believe it will be different this time.

In the meantime, we should be giving most careful consideration to what the role of radicals and revolutionaries should be in this new period which is now opening. As things stand in this country today, it would be foolish to imagine that they are in a position to give leadership and guidance to the coming struggles. If they are to earn the right to lead, they must first show that they understand both what is happening and the implications of what is happening. If and when they have achieved this understanding, they can begin to play a crucially important though initially modest role in the working-class movement: that of interpreter and teacher. They can make clear to increasing sectors of the working class the essentially *defensive* nature of the struggles they will be forced into. They can refuse to be drawn into, or to draw others into, the swamp of bourgeois reformism which is always ready to claim its victims. And above all they can hold high the banner of revolutionary socialism which in the final analysis holds out the only hope of a decent existence not only for American workers, but for all humanity threatened as never before with physical as well as spiritual destruction.

NOTES

1. This is of course not meant to imply that there will be no *cyclical* upturn in the visible future. As pointed out last month, the business cycle continues to operate whether the economy is buoyant or stagnant. Those who believe that the

present recession/depression will "bottom out" by the end of 1975 and give way to an up phase of the cycle may therefore be right. But the fact that, at this writing, latest reports on inventories show them to be still rising (because sales are falling faster than production) would seem to suggest that it is not very likely the present slide will come to so early an end.

2. The cases of Nixon and Ford are instructive in this connection. Both came out of the conservative wing of the Republican Party; each wanted to run his administration in accordance with the time-honored principles of Republican orthodoxy. But Nixon devalued the dollar, introduced price and wage controls, and became a "Keynesian" in matters of fiscal policy. Ford started out as a budget-balancer but soon changed his tune as the economy sank lower, and most recently has proposed a budget with the largest peace-time deficit in history. Both men became suspect to the true believers in their own party. It is of course not that either Nixon or Ford developed, or even tried to develop, an economic policy on any principles other than traditional conservatism; it is only that any attempt to practice traditional conservatism quickly results in fiasco.

3. The proposal is not new, having been put forward by the chairmen of the Senate and House Banking Committees (Senator Sparkman and Representative Patman) as long ago as 1970 in the wake of the Penn Central bankruptcy and the near-panic it touched off. More recently a number of other Democratic leaders, including Senate Majority Leader Mike Mansfield, have endorsed the idea, and it was formally included in the program adopted at the Democrats' so-called mini-convention at Kansas City in early December. Among business leaders who have backed a revived RFC, in addition to Felix Rohatyn whose contribution is analyzed below, perhaps the most prominent is Alfred Hayes, president of the Federal Reserve Bank of New York.

4. Even Marxists sometimes tend to forget that socialism is not a mode of production *sui generis* but a transitional social formation, with the process of transition centering on the modification and eventual elimination of both capital and wage labor, i.e., the abolition of the oppressive, exploitative, and essentially alienating relationship between a separate class of owners/controllers of the means of production and workers forced to sell their labor power to earn their livelihood. The bourgeois state always acts to strengthen and assure the continuation of this relationship, not to weaken or abolish it.

5. In the long run, which however may be said to have begun yesterday, the most rational solution to the energy problem is for the human race to learn to harness directly the flow of solar energy which reaches us uninterruptedly, absolutely free and in quantities which in a few days' time far exceed the total amount of energy (largely the product of past and present solar radiation) stored in the earth's crust or growing on the earth's surface. How much enthusiasm are the oil companies and their minions likely to generate for *that* solution to the energy problem?

Part seven

By this time in the readings students should be aware that conservatives, liberals, and socialists all want change, more or less. The direction of this change is dependent on the ideals that these groups stand for. In this part of *Is America Necessary?* we will discuss and analyze conservative, liberal, and socialist strategies for change. In contrast to the rest of this book we will not hold strictly to our three basic perspectives. Rather, we will also discuss movements and ideas that cross-cut our three categories or fall outside of them. We feel this is necessary in order to come to an understanding of the subtleties of political strategies, and to comprehend the sources of opposition that any single strategy will bring forth from other groups. To answer the question, What is to be done in America? a student must come to terms with the fact that there are many sides to this issue. For students to reach their own conclusions as to what solutions there are to the problems of the United States a knowledge of the strategies of various groups, and their arguments against each other is useful. We have chosen groups that represent different political positions. They are by no means a complete catalogue of those offering political alternatives. Students should feel free to seek out the political groups in their area which can offer the opportunity to learn about their efforts or participate in their activities.

Conservatives hold that there is no real necessity for major change in American institutions.[1] They believe in the maintenance of the free enterprise system as an idea, and in the strengthening of capitalism. Conservatives do not necessarily form special political groups to attain their purposes, although these groups do exist. Examples are the National Association of Manufacturers, the Business Council, the Young Americans for Freedom, and the Republican Party. The corporations, law firms, banks, and other industries are the main institutions that can deal with whatever problems do exist. For special crises, committees representing these institutions are established. For example, after the riots of the 1960s in Watts, Detroit, and Washington D.C. the Urban Coalition was formed to bring disaffected people into the corporate structure. Training programs were established, banks loaned money to businessmen at special terms, and insurance companies put up capital for the construction of housing.[2]

Essentially, conservatives believe that the American political system, as it is constituted, must be strengthened. The problem as they see it is that if corporations are weakened, society as a whole will suffer. Corporate profits are the best indicators of the health of American society for if profits are good it is felt that benefits will trickle down to the rest of soci-

What is to be done?

ety. Profit is the basic issue. When profits are high society benefits. When they are low society suffers. Therefore all Americans according to conservatives, have a personal interest in the high profit rate of corporations. This is what Charles Wilson, Secretary of Defense under President Dwight Eisenhower, and formerly president of General Motors, meant when he said "What is good for General Motors is good for America." This is the basic tenet of conservatism when it is broadened to include the other major corporations. If corporations are financially healthy they can take care of any problem.

Liberals believe something has to be done to correct economic, political, and social injustice. Working within the American political system, liberals advocate using law suits, lobbying, pressure groups, letters to Congressional representatives, and electing the right people to office. They believe in getting as many people involved in this process as possible. For example, Ralph Nader has set up a nonprofit corporation, Public Citizen Inc., to raise funds for consumer action, legal and research projects.[3] These include the Center for the Study of Responsive Law, Center for Concerned Engineering, Corporate Accountability Research Group, and the Center for Auto Safety. This last group collects information regarding automobile safety from concerned parties in the automobile industry and from consumers. This information is then collated and checked out by a staff of attorneys, engineers, researchers, and volunteers. The data derived from this process is distributed to sympathetic members of Congress who can then use their position to gain press publicity, and to initiate legislation to reform automobile industry abuses. The primary goal of the Center for Auto Safety is to get the regulatory agency for the automobile industry, the National Highway Traffic Safety Administration, to pressure the automobile industry into producing safe cars.[4] Essentially, Nader's organization attempts to organize public and Congressional pressure upon regulatory agencies so that these agencies will ameliorate the specific abuses, one by one, of capitalism.

In contrast to Nader's strategy which encourages public participation, the Center for the Study of Democratic Institutions, established in 1959 under the leadership of Robert M. Hutchins, brings together a small scholarly group of people to exchange ideas and refine liberal principles. Their major purpose is to resolve the issue of how "a free and just society [can] be maintained under the strikingly new political, economic, social, and technical conditions of the latter half of the twentieth century."[5] In addition to its own small group, the Center also invites scholars and political figures who have expertise in special areas. They meet each day for a set period of time, to exchange ideas in a free flowing dialogue. Their discussions are often published in books,[6] and in their own journal *Center Magazine*. The Center for the Study of Democratic Institutions is an elitist organization that believes that the people who have superior education and knowledge are the ones who can best solve the problems of our time. The Center does not believe that public participation in its discussions will be useful. Its goal is "the search for appropriate methods to change America's governmental institutions, in order to establish justice. For only renewed concepts of justice can bring renewed domestic tranquility."[7]

Without eliminating the basic institutions of American government, namely, corporations, universities, political parties, and so on, liberals want to make these institutions more responsive to the needs of people.[8] Liberals generally believe that people do not always know what is best for them. They must be guided to the benefits of higher education, proper housing, and good health. To bring government closer to the people, to decentralize national political institutions, to involve people in running local institutions, to participate on boards, committees, and the like are all parts of liberal strategy. The key to bringing about change is public pressure directed by the ideas of liberal elites.

Socialists believe that radical change of America's political institutions is necessary since political institutions as they are presently constructed do not serve the needs of the American people. Different strategies are proposed for effecting change. Some socialists believe in working through existing institutions. Others maintain that present-day political institutions represent the capitalist system and must be destroyed, either through violent or nonviolent tactics. Still other socialists believe that a combination of working inside and outside of the system is necessary.

The Inter-University Committee to Stop Funding War and Militarism, established by Michael T. Klare is an example of the first strategy.[9] It has as its basic aim the halting of American imperialism and militarism abroad. The organization holds that stationing American troops abroad and aiding dictatorial regimes is a mechanism by which America maintains its domination of other countries. The Inter-University Committee, through campus coordinators and steering committees, attempts to enlist faculty and student support. Through establishing a network of contacts and enlisting people to serve as coordinators on various campuses, the committee attempts to mobilize students and faculty to participate in legislative campaigns. This is accomplished by letter writing to members of Congress and by lobbying. Pressure group tactics are used to deal with the specific elements of American imperialist strategy that Congress has some leverage on. In 1975 the Inter-University Committee concentrated on three major issues: limiting United States aid to South Korea; limiting arms sales to the Third World; attempting to stop the nuclear arms race.

Another example of the first strategy, working through existing institutions, is the College for Human Services. This institution of higher education has reformulated the purposes of a traditional college program that provides theoretical knowledge to combine with practical experience in social agencies. Its goal is to bring minimum and low income people into employment at the professional level who would normally be excluded from attaining such positions because they do not have traditional educational credentials. The College for Human Services brings together the credentializing process and employment opportunities in an innovative format. Students are "selected for their . . . interest in providing humane human services . . . and inclination to human service values.''[10] Values, not grades, are taken into consideration for admission. Between 1970 and 1973 nearly 300 students completed the two-year program. The graduates, approximately half of whom were receiving public assistance at the time of enrollment, earned, in 1975, annual salaries up to $15,500. All of this is an attempt to change the educational rules of the game from inside, by gaining official accreditation for an institution that follows more radical rules than more traditional colleges.

Socialists who follow this first strategy formulate innovative ways of getting around the system. They build institutions or organizations that sound liberal but serve socialist purposes and attempt to integrate these organizations into the system without having the system co-opt them. Their aim is to get the system to serve the people and the organizations rather than have the people and organizations serving the system. They hope to provide a model for existing institutions and for the establishment of additional ones. Through this gradual process of change it is hoped that an alternate form of society, socialist in nature, will be created.

There are socialists however, who do not believe in working within the system. They believe existing institutions must be destroyed and new institutions created if a socialist society is to be brought about.

One example of a group adhering to this strategy of the building of a mass socialist organization is the New American Movement. Founded in 1971–1972, its goal as a political party is to form caucuses in factories, offices, schools, and hospitals to educate people in the need for new institutions for society. The strategy of the movement is ''to begin this task by a series of struggles in which the people begin to force changes in the economic and the political order that serve their needs and in which they exercise some power.''[11] The New American Movement does not attempt to work with the Democratic or Republican Party. Its primary goal is the establishment of a socialist movement through setting up a new, broad-based political organization whose eventual expression may be a full-fledged political party running candidates for national office. Its tactics include strikes, boycotts, mass demonstrations, and electoral activity. The New American Movement through its growth can represent working class people—blue- and white-collar—and, according to its platform, will accept nothing less than wresting power from the control of corporate elites. Structurally, it hopes to build a mass membership organization, consisting of local chapters, that carry out programs based on the priorities adopted at national conferences.[12]

The War Resisters' League also represents the second strategy. It believes in halting war, a mechanism by which, they say, corporate elites in America increase their power and profits. Through civil disobedience and other nonviolent tactics, withholding of income taxes, demonstrations, and opposition to participation in the army, the War Resisters' League hopes to destroy the American military establishment. It does not believe in reform of the military. Its goal is to eliminate it.[13]

The New American Movement and the War Resisters' League are examples of organizations that do not work within the rules of the American political system. To change the system they believe in openly and publicly breaking the rules through the use of nonviolent but constructive organizational tactics. By these means, they aim to stop the functioning of traditional institutions and bring about a system based on socialist principles. The revolutionary process is energized by putting into operation new principles to create a liberated zone within which a new order can be created. Its purpose is to form examples for the masses so that they will refuse cooperation with the existing system and join socialist mass movements.

The Weathermen is an example of a socialist political group that believes that a small core of tightly organized people can take direct and violent action to damage or destroy existing institutions. Through their example they hope to expose the corruption of American society and trigger a revolution.[14]

One of the major issues in socialist and radical movements—such as the antiwar movement—was whether the use of violent or nonviolent tactics would better achieve the goal of stopping America's imperialist wars. Proponents of nonviolence argued that larger masses of people could be drawn into the activities of the movement if peaceful tactics that involved large masses of people were the focus of the antiwar activities. Proponents of violence argued that when violence was used against the antiwar movement by police and armed forces it should have been responded to directly. This tension existed throughout the course of the antiwar movement, which was held together, often in spite of itself, by the response of the government in such acts as refusing permits for demonstrations. This set the stage for mass nonviolent civil disobedience in which large numbers of people broke the law by demonstrating. On the one hand legal forms were not adhered to, and on the other physical force was not resorted to . This compromise between legality and violence, most of the time kept the movement together on a common course of mass civil disobedience.[15]

The third strategy of simultaneously working inside and outside the system involves building new institutions to meet the needs of people. These institutions use resources from existing society but organize their institutions according to socialist principles. This strategy holds that the example of these institutions can be spread through the society by like minded people organizing similar groups.

Throughout the United States in major cities and university towns food cooperatives are being organized. A food co-op is a group of people that band together to buy food in large quantities. The members break the purchase down into small quantities and distribute it among themselves, dividing the costs. Since this is done without profit, food can be purchased far below retail prices. By dealing directly with wholesalers, the co-op avoids packaging, advertising, and supermarket costs. The prime middleman—the retailer—is effectively cut out. Sometimes these co-ops obtain their food directly from farmers, thus eliminating wholesalers. Other times, groups of co-ops are able to expand to a scale where they can eliminate wholesalers by setting up their own warehousing facilities and buying agents which deal directly with the source of food. When food co-ops or groups of co-ops deal directly with farmers who themselves are communally organized, then an entire network of socialist structure in one area of society has been created. This process of building new institutions and connecting them to each other is a strategy of institution formation. Not only are prices reduced but a political organization is created offering immediate benefits. These organizations can involve themselves in political issues relating to food as well as to other concerns. This strategy often entails organized opposition from existing institutions that the new institutions are engaged in replacing.[16]

Another area in which socialists work both in and outside the established rules of the game is in day-care centers. Cooperative day- or child-care centers have been established throughout the country to change the life of parents and to influence a change in the authoritarian manner in which children are often brought up. Parents share the everyday responsibility of bringing up children. Child-care centers remove the child and parents from isolation by sharing the raising of children. Thus, socialists claim that race, class, and sex bias can be eliminated in children; parents are free to engage in economic, social, or political activity; both parents and children together can work out new ways of formulating the activities and purposes of the child-care center. The traditional nuclear family of two parents and children, with all its authoritarian and totalitarian elements, can be broken down. Children are the responsibility of many, rather than of two people. The ideas of children about how to live their own lives are included in their up-bringing.[17]

A sector of American politics not represented in this book by their writings but very much in evidence on the American political scene are the organizations of the Radical Right, such as the National Socialist White People's Party (NAZI Party), the John Birch Society, and George Wallace's American Independent Party. Socialists perceive these groups to be clearly racist, anti-Semitic, and sexist, and that their implied objective is to eliminate elements of the population they despise and to substitute their own types of authoritarian regimes in the United States. Although at times some of these groups appear to mask their true goals to gain broader public acceptance, their real aim should not be ignored or missed. These are organizations which, and if given support, would not hesitate in implementing their dangerous policies. Many believe that when organizations such as these attain broader support they will moderate their goals and accept the terms of the American political system. On the contrary, history has shown that as movements of this kind have gained support and power they have acted to carry out and even extend their programs and goals.

There are a number of Old Left organizations, formed in the late nineteenth and early twentieth century, that believe that political power should be taken from bourgeois elites and given to workers. Among these groups are the Communist Party, the Socialist Party, the Socialist Labor Party of America, the Socialist Workers' Party. Their primary goal is the abolition of capitalism and its replacement by a socialist regime. The tightly organized group of cadres which constitute party membership devote a large amount of their time to party activities. They sometimes engage in coalitions with other groups on specific issues but they basically believe the revolution will be attained by socialists joining their party. They are usually unwilling to compromise, and this rigidity has brought about conflict within and between these parties. These conflicts lead to the breaking up of the organization into smaller splinter groups and debilitating and time-consuming fights among socialists rather than against the domination of the present elites.

Students should be aware that a multiplicity of strategies exist, sometimes in opposition to each other and at other times interrelated, that attempt to answer the question what is to be done. Conservatives and liberals accept the basic institutional structures of American society. Socialists, on the other hand, do not accept them even though some socialists may use these institutions to attain their own goals. Therefore socialists are clearly set apart from conservatives and liberals. The Radical Right is removed from all these groups by open adherence to a set of inhumane goals which would clearly lead to the eradication of large segments of the American people.

Some socialists of the New Left, who believe in working outside the rules of society, do not want to work together with those who believe otherwise. Some socialists who work within American institutions to bring about change do not always want to work together with other groups. This kind of divisiveness is of course counterproductive. If the socialist cause is to be enhanced, all socialists, whether they wish to work inside or outside the rules of the game, are obliged to find ways to coordinate their strategies and to concede respect for each other's work. If they fail in this, the New Left will undoubtedly deteriorate into a series of small sects rather than growing into a mass movement, as happened to the Old Left.

Socialists may work within the Democratic Party for social change, or build a new party. Both must be tried. If one is eminently more successful than the other then that is the time to abandon one and concentrate on the other. The same holds for educational change, or any institutional change.

If socialism is to be successful and new political institutions formed on a scale to affect a total social transformation of American society, then socialists have to learn how to work with rather than against each other. Debate and discussion among socialists over different strategies and tactics continue to be long and intense, but it should not go to the lengths of trying to destroy those socialists who follow strategies different from their own. If socialist ideas are to have effect on the future of the United States long range success is more important than the temporary or immediate success of any particular socialist group.

It is our own analysis that the problem for American socialists is to develop a broad constituency. This can be brought about through the strategy of institution formation. Institutions serving economic and social needs can have a direct political purpose. By creating social ties, isolation, cynicism, and apathy are broken down. People sharing similar political goals can use these social networks as a base from which to engage in political activity. This, we believe, is the necessary groundwork for the success of an overall socialist strategy.

This is our analysis of what is to be done. You who have read *Is America Necessary?* should, in considering these viewpoints, be better prepared to draw your own conclusions.[18]

NOTES

1. Robert A. Dahl. *After the Revolution?* New Haven: Yale University Press, 1974.

2. Jules Cohn. *The Conscience of the Corporations,* Baltimore: The Johns Hopkins Press, 1971. Karen Orren, *Corporate Power and Social Change,* Baltimore: The Johns Hopkins Press, 1973.

3. Louis G. Wark. "Consumer Report/Nader Campaigns for funds to expand activities of his consumer action complex." *National Journal* (9/18/71).

4. Ralph Nader; Ralf Hotchkiss; Lowell Dodge. *What To Do With Your Bad Car: An Action Manual for Lemon Owners.* New York: Grossman Pub., 1971.

5. This is from the Center's statement of principles. The Center for the Study of Democratic Institutions can be reached at POB 4068, Santa Barbara, California 93103.

6. Karl A. Lamb. ed., *Democracy, Liberalism, and Revolution.* Santa Barbara: Center for the Study of Democratic Institutions, 1971.

7. *Ibid.* Henry S. Ashmore, "Electoral Reform," p. 175.

8. Other liberal groups include the Federation of American Scientists, 203 C. St., N.E., Washington, D.C. 20002, and the American Civil Liberties Union, 22 East 40th St., New York, N.Y.

9. The Inter-University Committee can be reached through Professor Mark Selden, Dept. of History, Washington University, St. Louis, Mo.

10. See, "A Collaborative Program for Educating Human Service Professionals," *College for Human Services,* April 1975. The College is located at 201 Varick St., New York, New York 10014. Audrey C. Cohen or Ruth Messinger may be contacted for information.

11. From "Toward a New America," *Draft Platform of the New American Movement.* Sept./Oct. 1971.

12. The New American Movement, which also publishes a newspaper, *New American Movement,* is located at 1643 N. Milwaukee Avenue, Chicago, Illinois 60647.

13. The War Resisters' League is located at 339 Lafayette St., New York, New York 10012. See their "Manifesto for Nonviolent Revolution," by George Lakey, *WIN Magazine* (November 15, 1972).

14. See, Harold Jacobs, ed., *Weatherman.* California: Ramparts Press, 1970. See their journal *Osawatomie,* which is published periodically.

15. Dave Dellinger, *More Power Than We Know.* Garden City: Doubleday and Co., 1975.

16. For information on food co-ops write to Food Conspiracies, 165 W. Harvey St., Philadelphia, Pa. 19144. Regarding opposition to institution formation see chapter, "The Uncooperative Movement" in Henry Etzkowitz, Gerald Schaflander, *Ghetto Crisis,* Boston: Little Brown and Co., 1969. See also, Joyce Rothschild-Whitt "Conditions Facilitating Participatory Democratic Organizations." A paper given at the American Sociological Association, August 1975. The author of the paper is a graduate student at the University of California, Santa Barbara.

17. See, Henry Etzkowitz, "Sociology and Praxis: The Infant Growth Environment," *Social Theory and Practice* (Vol. 3, Spring 1971).

18. See, "Socialist Alternatives For America: A Bibliography," *Review of Radical Political Economy* (Vol. 1, Spring 1974).

*

17 Political programs

In a departure from the format followed in the preceding sections—that of selecting one essay to delineate each of the three political perspectives—the reader will have an opportunity to read a wider range of articles, and to formulate his or her own conclusions as to which of these readings presents a conservative, liberal, or socialist perspective.

This will not only be a valuable exercise in demonstrating what was learned from a careful reading and analysis of the previous chapters, but should also provide firm bases for future studies in political science. For it will be seen that categorization is a difficult task and that, in fact, in more cases than not the classification of materials or authors exemplifying one particular viewpoint will be difficult. For example, within one single essay an author may propose certain techniques easily identifiable as liberal, and at the same time promulgate theories which are much more at home within the realm of socialism. The reader will also, no doubt, when embarking on more extensive reading, find that some of these same thinkers will—on different political issues—treat one with conservative prescriptions and another with liberal remedies.

The questions brought to mind by a thorough reading of the following political strategies are endless. But it is the editors' hope that by presenting a broad choice, certain solutions will assume precedence, and the reader's ideas and options will become crystallized enough so that a clearer understanding of one's own role and thinking, and of political science as a viable tool in our society will be achieved.

Louis Banks.   The mission of our business society.

Down through history many concepts of the nature of reality have emerged, developed and disintegrated. The breakdown usually occurs when a civilization loses a positive image of its future, since the image of the future motivates actions, provides a criterion for selecting priorities, and literally forms the future for that civilization.[1]

"Disintegration" and "breakdown" are surely exaggerated descriptions of our present business and economic afflictions, but there can be little doubt that the U.S. business community lacks a positive image of its future. This lack in turn has left us with little motivation beyond individual or corporate survival, and the result, in present circumstances, may be economically counterproductive as well as morally and philosophically destructive. Also, for kindred reasons there is little sense of priority or direction in national policy other than the hope that the various combinations of restraint and expansionism will somehow get us back to "normalcy."

This sense of aimlessness is unnecessary and unjustified, and unless corrected, could indeed lead us toward a Toynbeean type of decline and fall. I believe this condition derives from a general misunderstanding of the "nature of reality" of the world that business has made, and most particularly from a failure to appreciate the developmental and even evolutionary prospects already implicit in the achievement.

We are, it is true, plagued with compound economic, political, and social problems that seem to defy analysis, let alone solutions. And legions of economists, government planners, and social scientists are at work on the specifics, as they should be. It would be preposterous to suggest that these problems can be waved away by the power of positive thinking. But there is such a thing as a power of negative thinking. And if it is true that "the image of the future motivates actions," one could argue that the work of public problem solving would be made easier with a clearer perception of our present position and some sense of potential destination.

To understand where we can go and what we can be, we must first appreciate where we are and what we are. This appreciation begins with the acceptance of a fact long shunned by academic, religious, and social thought: that the United States is a business society, or a business civilization. Thus *business,* as defined here, is something far more than one sector of national activity, and businessmen far more than a group of managers or entrepreneurs locked in conflict (as they sometimes imagine themselves) with everybody else.

Business is the United States's principal national effort. It is, as Julian Koenig has written, "the aggregator and articulator of our interests, the broker of our hopes, and the builder of our road to riches, both tangible and spiritual."[2] It would take an obtuse businessman to deny that he is the beneficiary of scholarly research, of science and technology, of education, of government policy, and even of the dominant Protestant ethic that reinforces man's inclination to express himself through work.

But this is far from saying that the diverse elements of U.S. national culture are subservient to business. Rather these elements interact continuously with business—each maintaining a sphere of independent thought and action. The business society, then, is a continuing interplay of forces whose principal expression is the production of goods and services under a profit discipline. Even if we acknowledge the widening influence of educational institutions, of nonprofit foundations, and of governmental bureaucracies, it is this productive activism that still gives purpose to the lives of most Americans and is spreading its influence to new millions in Europe and Asia.

In this article I will argue that this system bulwarks and activates the qualities that most Americans deem essential to modern life: political freedom, social achievement, humanist means, and progressive goals. Central to this argument is the notion that the business society is a *process* that enlists the major elements of national creativity, and that, while skilled at systematic problem solving, derives its regenerative force—its future—from its enterprising, somewhat serendipitous talents for opportunity exploring. Thus one can speculate, for example, that the business society possesses the sagacity, the capacity, and the flexibility to cope with impending resource limitations, to respond to ecological pressures, *and, if allowed to exercise its enterprising spirit, to circumvent conventionally defined problems by new conceptual approaches.*

The business society: a framework

Peter Drucker has observed that "the new world view...assumes process. Every single one of [our modern] concepts embodies in it the idea of growth, development, rhythm or becoming. These are all irreversible processes....All of these changes are irreversible because the process changes its own character; it is in other words self-generated change."[3]

The process that is the U.S. business society is no different. Its components are in dynamic, unbreakable relationships to each other and to the whole.

The political interaction

The continuing interaction of business and politics in American life is one that ideologists find the most difficult to accept, but it was noted nearly 150 years ago by the perceptive French lawyer and sociologist Alexis de Tocqueville. As accurately as he surveyed so many other aspects of our young nation, Tocqueville concluded that the driving force in American life was "that love of prosperity and spirit of enterprise which seem to be the distinctive characteristics of the race." And in a note that should be heartening today to dejected businessmen, he observed that even "bad laws, revolutions and anarchy [would not] be able to obliterate" these characteristics.

Tocqueville also remarked in some wonderment on the basic interrelationship between the political devotion to collective "freedom" and the individual drive for "personal welfare." "It may be supposed," he wrote, "that these passions are united and mingled in some part of [the American] character. And indeed the Americans believe their freedom to be the best instrument and surest safeguard to their welfare; they are attached to one by the other."[4]

This concept has evolved down through the decades and has kept its essential substance, if not the same form. Today's version could be this: independent corporate enterprise, operating under a profit discipline, reinforces the structure of the democratic process, and vice versa. They are indeed "attached by one to the other." On the one hand, there is a consensus that conditions of political liberty are essential to the flowering of economic opportunity in all of its risk, reward, and needs-satisfaction aspects. On the other, there is an implicit assumption that a productive economic system reinforces the individualism that is the heart and soul of political independence.

The economic promise

One fundamental result of this successful linkage of personal freedom and personal welfare is the United States's almost classless society, with its powerful promise of upward mobility, continually validated by performance. Ben Wattenberg's landmark study of twentieth-century census figures, *The Real America,* shows that the real (not inflated) family income in the United States has doubled in a generation, and that the steady upward movement of median family income has created a "massive majority middle class...something that has never happened before anywhere."[5]

The evident result of this economic progress is political stability and faith in the general long-term equity of the process. Plainly, the promise of upward mobility is principally responsible for the refusal of U.S. labor, even in the bloody organizing years, to form a political party or to consider seriously the blandishments of Marxism. As recently as the 1972 elections, the Democratic presidential candidate, Senator George McGovern, was astonished at the popular rejection of his proposal for a soak-the-rich estate tax. Pollsters showed that "the working man" did not want to foreclose the possibility that either he or his offspring might very well have the chance to build up and pass along a large estate. In short, there has been enough fulfillment of the promise of "personal welfare" for all parts of society that the democratic process has been constantly strengthened.

Being strengthened, it strengthened in return; when either the productive or the distributive process has endangered the personal welfare of any group or segment, the injured have turned to government for redress. Whether the grievance was exploitation of child labor, monopolistic oppression of small business, interference with collective bargaining, inequity of agricultural income, savings accounts at risk, racial injustice, or consumer exploitation, the polity responded with new rules for its principal activity, business.

There is no attempt here to argue in some Pollyannaish way that the accommodations have been painless (for they have been anything but), or that everything automatically turns out for the best in business's relationship with the other elements of U.S. society. Nor would I attempt to deny that a succession of governmental interventions and boons have directly benefited one aspect or another of business development in perhaps an inequitable and special interest way. Rather, my purpose here is to try to get the facts of flexibility and accommodation in perspective.

American history tends to be written in terms of politics, wars, or (more recently) social tensions. But we should acknowledge the evidence of the new business historians that business is as basic an element in U.S. history as politics.[6] We should also acknowledge that political intervention, reflecting the essence of the democratic process, has continually altered the nature of the business system so that no doctrinaire word can describe it. Our business system is indeed a political as well as an economic achievement—an economic polity or a

political economy, a business society. It is important to bear this proposition in mind as we try to decide where we are and what we are, and what forces can best help to design our future.

The social achievement

Social achievement is a moving target, and in our times there is a tendency to give it new meaning just about the time that the old meaning has been substantially realized. This is understandable and is itself a kind of search for new frontiers. But too often the fascination with new goals obscures the fact that the search itself is part of the process. By any reasonable definition, the U.S. business society has been a persistently successful vehicle for social achievement, and if one puts a premium on concomitant individual expression, it has been uniquely successful.

It is the word *vehicle* that I would emphasive in our framework of reassessment. In modern terms social achievement begins, of course, with the creation of a stream of wealth that is distributed equitably enough to provide the elementary necessities of living for an entire populace. In U.S. society achievement is propelled to higher levels by an incentive system that maintains a relationship between personal effort and living standards. Much of the social criticism of our time revolves around the equity of shares and the allocation of wealth between personal and public needs. Indeed there is urgent public business to be resolved in those debates—but not here. The relevant point in this discussion is that the business society has created sufficient wealth and distributed it successfully enough to endow richly both personal and public affairs at a whole new level of human experience.

Concurrently, as this very success has engendered new social opportunities and expectations, business itself has become society's most flexible vehicle for the diffusion of economic and social change. Some sociologists favor the theory that social change occurs as inventions come into use. In this view, the inherent flexibility of the U.S. company is socially significant, because it encourages the diffusion of innovation and makes of business "a learning system." Business, observes Donald A. Schon, has been "unsurpassed over the last 50 years in its ability to effect rapid, inventive transformations of itself without flying apart at the seams, without disappearing as a form, often without loss of identity even at the level of the individual firm."[7]

The value to society of adaptability and diffusion have been dramatically apparent in the last three or four years. Corporations have responded to political pressures embodied in a whole set of humanist laws and regulations, as well as to a new set of public expectations regarding the quality of work life. Less than a decade ago it was difficult to get business management interested in external "social responsibility" issues; today, albeit under the threat of coercion by law, regulation, or public opinion, management effort is concentrated on devising and perfecting practical mechanisms for getting women and minorities into jobs, for meeting pollution standards, for improving working conditions, and so on.

Because corporations have implemented these mechanisms, the net result is that this new set of humanist values in U.S. society now touches millions of Americans in everyday ways—and not without effect on the corporate organism itself.

"We are witnessing the development of a responsive corporation," writes Raymond A. Bauer, "which . . . should be increasingly capable of handling new issues whether they be 'business' or 'social.' It is reasonable to expect the development of a new breed of managers. They will probably have different values, as has been rather widely suggested. But, probably more importantly, they will be accustomed to and skilled at organizational change."[8]

The point to be made here is not that business is to be absolved of criticism in the important areas of social responsibility, but rather that the enormously flexible business society can, in remarkably short time spans, translate consensual social values into practice with a minimum of disruption.

This evolutionary view of the business society, with its intertwined strands of enterprise, market economics, politics, and consensual social justice, is basic to any attempt to think toward "a positive image of the future." The positive image must begin with an appreciation of the intricately balanced system that combines a central political consensus with independent-minded, opportunity-oriented, profit-disciplined centers of development, production, and service, each interacting with the other.

There seems to be prevalent in the media and in social thought an assumption that the United States must move inevitably toward government (i.e., political) domination of the economic sphere. While increasing political intervention in the economic process is undeniable—and in some cases distinctly desirable—in our business society's framework there always has been an interplay between the two forces of government and business. The delicate balance would suffer immeasurably if Americans were to accept a presumption of government over business.

Interplay between government and business

The preservation of this nondoctrinaire, pragmatically constructed, balanced system—this methodology—should be a matter of high priority. Translated into everyday action, this objective requires that all decisions involving government-business collaboration should be reviewed with a bias toward the maximum amount of nongovernmental decision making. With that said we must be prepared to accept government-business collaboration as the next logical step in opening new frontiers of development, in defining the areas ripe for economic and/or technological breakthrough, and in formulating a kind of new productionism to follow the two decades of consumerism the United States has experienced.

The new productionism

For an example of such imaginative economic action, one thinks back to the skillfull fusion of visionary planning (governmental, academic, and corporate) and business methodology that produced the Economic Cooperation Administration (Marshall Plan). Cooperation resulted in the investment of a seemingly enormous $15 billion in rebuilding Europe and Asia ("giveaways," their opponents called them) on a productive basis after World War II. This investment not only headed off the postwar depression that was then the standard economic forecast but also laid the foundation for a global surge of growth and development that has not yet run its course. Perhaps a similar hidden opportunity lies today in the strained relationships between the less-developed raw-material resource nations and the industrial democracies.

In the arena of technology there is also a historic model. Atomic power was developed by government (as an adjunct to the atomic weapons program) in contracts with educational institutions and industry. Some people saw governmental development of atomic energy as an entering wedge for ultimate governmental control over power production. But the body politic (Congress and the Eisenhower administration) ruled otherwise, and the whole apparatus of reactor production, uranium fuel processing, and power distribution was turned over to decentralized corporate enterprise— albeit under appropriate regulation.

For this discussion, perhaps the National Aeronautics and Space Administration is the most relevant technological prototype of collaboration. In executing the peaceful satellite programs and the moonshots, NASA literally created a new industry. While NASA worked out the objectives, recruited key scientists, and formulated the time-tables, there was continuous creative feedback to the planners from the highly independent and responsible corporate contractors. The government was, of course, the space program's only customer, but the contributions to a new productionism in terms of concepts, new materials, reliability factors, and general atmosphere of innovation have provided great competitive edge for high-technology U.S. industry. The longer-range potential extends almost to infinity.

Opportunity exploration

When dealing with clearly defined, specific objectives, i.e., when "problem solving," the essential components for a new productionism are strong, long-range government policy, competent research, appropriate education of those concerned, guarantees against excessive private risk— and plenty of decentralized, individual execution. The need for increased production of food would appear to fit this model. So too would the need for workable cities, for mass transit systems to link the resources and work forces of cities and suburbs, and for the repair and rehabilitation of the broken-down rail system in the northeastern United States fit this model.

What distinguishes these problem-solving projects from opportunity-exploring ones is that the latter's ends can be less clearly defined. The current pressing search for new energy sources is an exciting example. The Energy Research and Development Administration promises to canvass possibilities ranging from the gasification of coal (which itself would create new industries) to such areas as the breeder reactor, nuclear fusion, magnetohydrodynamics, and solar energy. We do not know in what areas the effort may break through, but we can see that nothing could be more basic to further growth than the discovery of a source of cheap, plentiful energy; even alleviation of the food shortage might follow if there were cheap energy to provide the needed fertilizer for the "miracle" grains.

Similar possibilities lie in global oceanic development, which aims generally at the production of both food and mineral resources. Those involved say that this line of exploration suggests as many new dimensions as does space exploration. (In a recent advertisement, the First National City Bank reported proudly on its financing of a

Japanese-made underwater bulldozer. "Its capabilities are as broad as the ocean in which it works, from underwater earth leveling to underwater foundation construction, from harbor and channel clearing to land reclamation. Now successfully undergoing rigorous testing, it promises to usher in a new era of marine exploration and engineering.")

The important point is that when opportunities are developed successfully they can open up decades of subsequent development that "solve problems" by bursting the bounds of conventional thought. Writing in *The Economist* on potential oceanic development, Barbara Ward described the technological breakthrough succinctly: "The process becomes cumulative, the pace accelerates formidably and men are suddenly shaken awake into the realization that their whole way of life and work has been transformed."[9]

A society that concentrates on problem solving can see a role for itself only as big as the problems—and, as noted in the discussion of social achievement—new "problems" are begotten by "solutions," probably indefinitely. And hence a constant feeling of frustration accompanies achievement. But a society that is conscious of a unique and fulfilling methodology can keep a faith in growth, progress, and opportunity in dimensions yet unknown. It can absorb the value changes created by its own achievement through a kind of feedback loop—as indeed it has done in absorbing the various humanist values of affirmative action, job enrichment, pollution abatement, and so forth in less than a decade.

The business society can evaluate problems in the perspective of trade-offs and priorities, and yet at the same time it can maintain the sound growth on which so much depends. And despite pleas that it should spread its wealth out thin to soothe perceived social needs, it can with some confidence stick to the faith that its principal contribution to all social needs is large capital investment in projects that transform and extend man's conceptual view of the possible.

The promise of the future

In light of its evident record of performance of the last quarter century, why is the positive, evolutionary nature of the business society not generally perceived? The answer is that it is encountering formidable intellectual resistance on many fronts. Industry and technology stand accused (again) by the radical left of having robbed man of his soul, and the only salvation is seen to be smashing the machines and regressing to a society similar to that of Communist China.[10] Others like to see recent "progress" as an aberration, a mere blip on the radar screen of the centuries which will soon be succeeded by the old imperatives of Malthus, with men tearing at each others' throats for dwindling essentials.

Even if all other problems could be taken care of, we are still said to be caught in "the entropy trap" (Something of a semantic snare borrowed from thermodynamics), which holds that industrialization is creating waste from our terrestrial and atmospheric resources at an exponential rate that can only mean disaster for future generations. ("Every time we produce a Cadillac we do it at the cost of decreasing the number of human lives in the future."[11]) Is it really necessary to deal with the apocalyptic prophecies? Society has conquered similar recurrent arguments many times before. Moreover, the prophets themselves do not have the vision to see the mind-bending implications of such industrial-technological achievements as man's move into space and the continuing probe of the planets.

Less drastic prophecies, clustered around the Jay Forrester/Dennis Meadows Club of Rome analysis, express valid concerns about the future that are derived in most part from access to that newest projective tool, the computer.[12] They assert that the interplay of the basic elements of modern life—global population growth, pollution, food production, industrial production, and natural resource depletion—will exhaust available natural resources within 50 to 100 years and threaten the species by various forms of land, sea, and atmospheric pollution.

There have been a number of scholarly refutations of these doomsday assumptions which significantly scale down the threats in degree. I cannot pretend to evaluate the merits of this debate in this article, but capable economists have pointed out that the doomsdayers tend, generically, to ignore the regenerative and replenishing functions of technological progress. As one economist puts it, "These continuous, exponentially expanding, quality-altering, resource-creating aspects of technology... could continue to stimulate output growth at a constant rate even though labor, capital and natural resources had reached zero growth positions."[13]

Technological assesment is, of course, now a "given" in modern-day technological development—an automatic feedback loop that forestalls damaging consequences, and absorbs corrective modifications into the productive processes without destroying their positive nature. One example of such assessment is Barbara Ward's caveat on the development of ocean resources mentioned before. A wholesale competitive exploitation of the sea by the advanced nations could easily be fatal to this "prime regenerative system" of the planet, and she sternly admonished the United Nations Conference at Caracas, Venezuela to construct safeguards on a global scale. "The fundamental requirement is a system of overall environmental management in which government, international agencies and private interests can all join, provided they recognize its role in reflecting the complete interdependence of the ocean system."[14] Such cogent argument for "overall environmental management" is clearly admonitory, not apocalyptic.

The road to global unity

In truth, no society can have a "positive image" of its future without some faith in the positive consequences of its present actions. There are many. For example, idealists have looked for generations toward various forms of political federation or integration as the building blocks of "one world" of peace. In fact, the last quarter century of business development has done more to knit together rival powers in workaday understanding and similarity of goals than libraries or political ideology have ever done.

The development of the multinational corporation is a clear case in point. This expression of the business society is in its infancy, and it may have exploitive aspects that should be searched out and curbed, but at its best it can surely serve any exciting vision of constructive international development. Peter F. Drucker calls the multinational corporation "perhaps the most fruitful social innovation of the century."[15]

Raymond Vernon, in his seminal *Foreign Affairs* essay on "Economic Sovereignty at Bay," notes the rising tensions between the thrust of multinationals and the simultaneous loss of economic control by national governments, and the possibility of and explosive reaction by one or more of the advanced nations. But, he writes, in the long term "it is more than probable that the economic link between the national economies of the advanced world will become even deeper and more intimate."[16]

Walter Wriston, chairman of the National City Bank Corporation, whose Citibank has branches in 65 nations, believes that "the role of the world corporation as an agent of change may well be even more important than its demonstrated capacity to raise living standards. The pressure to develop the economy of the world into a real community must come, in part, from an increasing number of multinational firms which see the world as a whole.... The world corporation has become a new weight in an old balance. It must play a constructive role in moving the world toward the freer exchange of both ideas and the means of production so that the people of our planet may one day enjoy the fruits of a truly global society."[17]

Environmental and ecological concerns also are global in nature and must soon be reckoned with through an international agency. With shortages in petroleum, food, and other basic commodities in every day's headlines, we are constantly jarred by the sense of instant crisis—as perhaps we should be. But in the longer term one could reason that increased demands for natural resources are forcing a whole new appraisal of economic arrangements in multinational terms. Any cogent appraisal of these problems leads inevitably to the thought that we must move toward true internationalization in cataloguing and monitoring what we have and what we use.

The satellite offers the means at hand to implement global monitoring. Of course, the whole rivalry for resources could break out in blatant violations of international agreement or in Marxian imperialist wars, but the presumption of intelligent men, newly aware of the fruits of economic collaboration and growth, must be that the global society will move toward a kind of economic internationalization over the next decade.

Thus the business society again is the principal vehicle for new social values—this time on a global scale. It is a time of furious readjustment, and the adaptation process will have to take account of new weights in economic competition, internalization of social costs, pressure on finite resources, and the increased bargaining power of less developed countries (confident that they live in a business world that has ruled out recourse to military force).

The interaction of such factors surely will cause fundamental readjustments in the world business order, and they will be anything but painless. (Professor Bauer's "responsive" corporate manager will be a busy man.) But with its vision of reality, the business society can credit itself with being the prime terrestrial force for planetary integration, just at the time when man's first view of his earth from space itself has given such interpretation an almost mystical meaning.

In our time, in fact, the great opportunistic achievement of society has been the launching of man in space. The precision of satellite placement, the Apollo trips to the moon, and the constant new intelligence about the planetary system are, in sum, events so stunning in their implications for all branches of earthly thought that we will probably be decades in assimilating the new perceptions and perspectives.

In the economic sphere there is already talk of industrial production in space, once the space shuttle system is brought to maximum efficiency. President Ford has been advised that crystals of extraordinary purity grown aboard Skylab in early 1974 could be the start of a new billion-dollar industry which, among other things, would lead to computers reduced to a tenth of their present size. Ball bearings, it is said, can be produced in perfectly spherical form in the zero gravity conditions of space. Transmission of solar energy from space would not only provide an almost infinite resource but would also "solve" one large part of the problem of environmental pollution.

Recently I encountered a group of graduate economics students at Harvard who were devoting their spare time to elaborate computations aimed at justifying selective manufacture of goods in space, given a developmental governmental subsidy. I asked them whatever got them inspired to undertake such arduous work. "I guess it was reading space comics when I was a kid," said one of them sheepishly. I was glad that they had not been raised on *The Limits to Growth*.

Conclusion

One does not have to embrace space in all of its mystical aspects to catch the wider possibilities of the development of the business society. But there is a kind of parable in this epochal outreach. If the business society is to surmount the present crisis and keep the best of our system, it must build on its relevant strengths.

In my view, a simplistic fight for individual and corporate survival, even bolstered by benevolent government monetary and fiscal policies, will do little for us either materially or in terms of vision. As in war or other periods of great crisis, it is time to stress the collaborative aspects of our unique structure, and most importantly the collaboration of corporate enterprise, scholarly research, high technology, and governmental policy in a measure of directed growth. For it is in the prospect and promise of breakthrough development that Americans are at home. It is this that ensures the creation of new wealth and product, new conceptual approaches to major problems, reinforcement of individual and humanist values, and a worthy future for this unique civilization.

NOTES

1. Barbara Hubbard, in a review of "Up-wingers: A Futurist Manifesto," *The Futurist,* February 1974, p. 28.

2. Unpublished paper, Harvard Business School, 1974.

3. Peter F. Drucker, as quoted in Carl Madden, *The Clash of Culture* (Washington, National Planning Association, 1972), p. 51.

4. *Democracy in America* (New York, Vintage Books, 1945), Vol. I, pp. 450, 451; Vol. 2, p. 151.

5. Ben Wattenberg, *The Real America* (New York, Doubleday, 1974). For a less rhapsodic survey of middle-class influence see Thomas C. Cochran, *Business in American Life* (New York, McGraw-Hill, 1972). And for a sharp disagreement, attempting to prove that the American blue-collar class is degenerating into a powerful proletariat, see Andrew Levison, "The Working Class Majority," *New Yorker,* September 2, 1974.

6. See James Baughman, "New Directions in American Economic and Business History," in *American History: Retrospect and Prospect,* edited by G.A. Billias and G.N. Grob (New York, Macmillan, Free Press, 1971).

7. *Beyond the Stable State* (New York, Norton, 1973), p. 80.

8. "An Agenda for Research and Development in Corporate Responsiveness," unpublished paper, Harvard Business School, 1974.

9. "Suffering a Sea Change," June 29, 1974, p. 41.

10. Ivan Illich, *Tools for Conviviality* (New York, Harper & Row, 1973).

11. Nicholas Georgescu-Roegen, "The Entropy Law and the Economic Problem", in *Toward A Steady State Economy*, edited by Herman E. Daly (San Francisco, W.H. Freeman, 1973).

12. Dennis Meadows et al., *The Limits to Growth* (New York, New American Library, 1972), p. xi.

13. Thomas M. Humphrey, "The Dismal Science Revisited," Federal Reserve Bank of Richmond *Monthly Review,* March 1973, p. 2.

14. Barbara Ward, op. cit., p. 49.

15. *Management* (New York, Harper & Row, 1974), p. 363.

16. October 1968, pp. 110-122.

17. "The World Corporation: New Weight in an Old Balance," address before the International Industrial Conference, San Francisco, September 1973; published in *Vital Speeches,* October 15, 1973, p. 18.

John W. Gardner.
Citizen action.

The more one examines the web of influence woven by special interests and the accommodation of politicians to that influence, the less one anticipates changes from within the political system itself. It must come from citizens. They will never produce totally sanitary politics; but they can and must regain command of their own instruments of self-government.

Institutions don't overhaul themselves. They find it painful. When an institution is in need of renewal, someone must shake it up. In the case of political institutions, the shakeup must come from concerned citizens determined to create responsive government, determined to bring the parties to life, determined to cut through organizational dry rot and revitalize aging institutions.

The emergence of citizen action

It is no accident that Common Cause was launched in 1970. The time was ripe. Future historians may remember the 1970s as the decade when citizen action emerged as a revitalizing force in American society. If so, they will not report it as a new thing but as a familiar ingredient in American life that matured and came into its own.

They will note that, in the decades preceding the emergence, the American people had ignored their duties as citizens. They had allowed their instruments of self-government to fall into disrepair. They had allowed themselves to be smothered by large-scale organization and technology and all the glittering promises of modernity. They had almost forgotten the national attribute described 130 years earlier in the familiar passage from de Tocqueville.

These Americans are the most peculiar people in the world. . .in a local community in their country a citizen may conceive of some need which is not being met. What does he do? He goes across the street and discusses it with his neighbor.

Then what happens? A committee comes into existence. . .All of this is done without reference to any bureaucrat. All of this is done by private citizens on their own initiative.

The world was simpler then. As our society grew vast and complex, we became less and less sure of our capacity to act on our own initiative as citizens. Certainly, Americans in the mid-twentieth century manifested little of the confident approach to their common problems that de Tocqueville observed.

Then in the 1960s a feeling for citizen action reappeared with extraordinary vigor. It was foreshadowed in the 1950s in the civil rights movement. In the 1960s the students raised the cry of "participatory democracy." Among the poor the phrase was "community action." The peace movement, the conservation movement, the family planning movement emerged as potent elements in our national life.

Much of this activity was diffuse, erratic, and poorly organized. But little by little citizen action began to develop a more professional cutting edge. Ralph Nader demonstrated what could be accomplished by a toughminded professional approach. The civil rights movement proved that it could move history-making legislation through Congress against immensely powerful and entrenched opponents. And young civil rights lawyers were among the first to explore the full possibilities of what is now called public interest law.

The new aggressiveness and determination behind citizen action was clearly reflected in the public fight to deny Senate confirmation to Judge G. Harrold Carswell, President Nixon's nominee for the Supreme Court. When the nomination was submitted in January 1970, virtually everyone assumed that it would be accepted. The Senate had just rejected the nomination of Clement Haynsworth, and few senators wanted to enter into a second pitched battle against the massive combined strength of the administration, the Republican right wing, and the Southern bloc. But the handful of senators who were willing to oppose the nomination turned out to have a potent resource: the willing hands of many citizens. Civil rights groups led the battle. Members of the legal profession were slower to join in, but were enormously effective when they did so. Some of the most impressive contributions were those from a group of Columbia University law students whose study of Judge Carswell's published decisions revealed that he had been reversed by higher courts nearly 60 percent of the time, a third more frequently than the average of his fellow judges. The labor movement, the academic world, and other articulate segments of the electorate joined in. The firm votes against the nomination increased, first with agonizing slowness and then more rapidly. And the nomination was defeated.

Even more dramatic was the defeat of the supersonic transport (SST) in December 1970 and again in March 1971. Lined up in favor of the SST were the administration, the aviation industry, most conservatives, and most businessmen—in other words, all of the "clout" that those who call themselves political realists so reverently celebrate. Arrayed against the SST was an unlikely and not very well organized coalition of citizen groups, chiefly environmentalists. A toughminded Washingtonian can die laughing at the futility of action by earnest and well-intentioned citizens. But by March of 1971, no proponent of the SST was laughing. The SST was dead. The money-heavy lobby for the SST that operated out of downtown Washington offices was left with its pamphlets down. The citizens had won.

Such nationally publicized episodes do not capture one of the chief attributes of the new wave of citizen action, viz., that similar action is also taking place in thousands of communities and neighborhoods as citizens speak out on local issues.

What we are seeing is the beginnings of a powerful movement to call the great institutions of our society to account. The ombudsman concept is being tried in various places. Young lawyers are using litigation in ingenious ways to call private and public agencies to account. Consumerism, which is so far largely a middle-class phenomenon, is essentially the same kind of effort. All of the groping efforts at neighborhood organization are part of the same phenomenon.

The new politics and the politics of protest offer some innovative ways in which citizens can needle the great institutions of our society and demand an accounting of them. But as the movement continues, the American citizen is going to make a startling discovery. He is going to find that most of the new techniques for citizen action pale to insignificance before the enormous unused potential of the instruments of self-government that the citizen has allowed to grow rusty and out of repair. Until he turns again to those instruments, scrapes away the rust, repairs them, and resharpens them, perhaps even redesigns them, he will not regain command of his society.

The history of citizens' movements

We musn't be sentimental about what "the people" can accomplish. The resistance to change that any institution exhibits is not simply the mindless working of habit and custom. Those who enjoy power and privilege in a society preserve that power and privilege by weaving a tough protective web of custom, rules, processes, and institutional structure. Can we really expect that any citizens' movement will be strong enough and determined enough to cut through that web?

It is a crucial question, and most experienced observers would probably answer "No." There is widespread skepticism as to the impact of popular movements. But the historical record does not bear out the skepticism.

The Populist Movement in the nineteenth century altered both of the major parties before it ran out of steam. Citizens' movements led to the abolition of child labor and to the vote for women. A popular movement foisted Prohibition on the nation and a second popular movement repealed it. Relatively small groups of crusading citizens launched the labor movement, the civil rights movement, the peace movement, the conservation movement, the family planning movement. All of these welled up from the ranks of the people. None was launched by government action. Nor could they have been. But they made the government respond.

Before 1969, the organized conservation movement consisted of no more than two or three hundred thousand citizens. But they won allies among editors, among writers, among congressmen, among opinion-makers—and they pushed the environmental issue to the top of the national agenda. How long would we have had to wait for such action to emerge from the bureaucracy? Forever would be a fair estimate.

Only on the rarest occasions are significant new directions in public policy initiated by the legislature, or by the bureaucracy, or by the parties. They are initiated by the people—not "The People" taken collectively, but by vigorous and forward-looking elements within the body politic. Or they are initiated by the special interests.

The role of citizen action

Skeptics contrast the supposed impracticality of citizens' movements with the "hard realities of politics." But popular movements have proven themselves to be the hardest of realities. They have had a profound impact on the political process. The surge of citizen opinion on a given subject is always underestimated at first by politicians. But if it continues, they take it into account. Citizen opinion, massively expressed, is a form of power; and politicians are power brokers.

When we see the strength of these movements, when we see that they have often forced great issues to the attention of the bureaucracy, we begin to sense a creative force in American life that has not been fully appreciated.

In our society any group of citizens can identify a problem, offer a solution, and attempt to persuade the rest of the nation of their rightness. They nominate themselves. If the early feminists or civil rights leaders or conservationists had waited for a referendum to anoint them as the legitimate leaders of a movement, they'd still be waiting. But just as a free society gives them full rein to nominate themselves, so it reserves the right to ignore them (and thus seal their doom).

Crusading citizens' groups may not always be wise, as witness the Prohibitionists. Or they may be wise but unsuccessful in persuading their fellow citizens. For every citizens' group that changes the course of history, there are thousands, perhaps hundreds of thousands, that never create a ripple. Even of those that do make a ripple, many have a short life. They trail off into ineffectual pamphleteering, or live on as museum pieces dusted faithfully by aging followers. Or they just disappear.

The people are the soil. The movements are seeds. Some never germinate. Some die early. A few prosper and grow strong. The whole process provides the society with a superb source of new growth. It provides ample opportunity for the testing of ideas— good ideas, ordinary ideas, dismal ideas. Only the ideas with vitality survive the testing. And only the ones with a powerful popular impact will affect history. *The great virtue of a free people is to be that fertile seedbed, not, as some have supposed, to be always right or enlightened but to be the soil from which enlightenment can spring.*

The surging creative quality of popular movements gains its real significance in contrast to the limited creativity of institutions, or to put it more harshly, the tendency of *all* institutions to decay, to rigidify, and to stifle new ideas. It is not a peculiar weakness of our own society. It has been true of all human institutions since the beginning.

The hardened professionals of this world look with condescension on the undisciplined enthusiasm of citizens' movements.

But the one thing that is worse than undisciplined ardor is no ardor at all. That is one of the reasons why the individual citizen can be creative when institutions are not. How often does one see an ardent institution? The exhilaration of the crusade resides in the individual breast. The institution is by nature prudent, rational, cool, systematic, and self-preserving. It shrinks from challenge and risk. It is unbloody but bowed.

Enthusiasm is perhaps too limited a word to denote what I am talking about. The world will be changed, if it is changed at all, by men and women of exceptional vitality— vitality that has not been sapped by despair or physical deprivation, vitality that has not been drained away by the enervating climate of bureaucracy, vitality that has been released by anger or indignation.

The Spanish have a saying, "In Spain everything decays but the race." It is a universal condition. Nations decay; only the citizen, critical and loving, can bring them back to life. Institutions are weighted with the past; the individual is on the side of vitality and the future.

Is public interest lobbying legitimate?

Common Cause has described itself as "a citizens' lobby." But the idea of a citizens' lobby raises questions. One is whether the very concept of a lobby—even a lobby run by well-intentioned citizens—isn't somehow reprehensible. One distinguished American said to the founders of Common Cause: "*All lobbies should be abolished by law. In a democracy we should elect the best possible people and then expect them to follow their own best judgment without pressure from any group—even a well-motivated one.*"

What he failed to understand is that the right of any group, well-motivated or not, to try to influence government decisions is constitutionally protected in the "right to petition" clause of the First Amendment. It cannot be abolished.

From the beginning of the Republic, special-interest groups and more broadly based citizen movements have sought to influence government. Lobbying activities are carried out not only by commercial interests but by groups representing labor unions, universities, the professions, religious groups, and many others.

All experts on government accept lobbying as a legitimate part of the political process. The problem is not that it exists but that it is almost always carried on in behalf of special interests, almost never in behalf of the public interest. Everybody's organized but the people.

Interest group pluralism

There are those who recognize the legitimacy of lobbying but say it should be left to the special interests because no group of citizens, however high-minded, can take it upon themselves to say what is in the public interest. This view reflects a lingering belief in so-called interest-group pluralism. According to that doctrine, each special group pursues its own selfish concerns, but taken all together they somehow balance one another out and the public interest is served. Given the obvious dominance of special interests in our national life, that is an enormously comforting doctrine.

The only trouble is that it isn't true. Very often the public interest is not served. All the special interests clashing in the urban setting have not somehow balanced out to produce wise and far-seeing urban solutions. The public interest in clean air and water has not been served by the clash of special interests in the environmental field.

Interest-group pluralism has accounted for a good deal of our dynamism as a nation, but it has clear limitations. Let us preserve it, let us expect that it will serve us in important ways, but let us not imagine that it will do all the things that need to be done. Too often the public interest and the interests of the ordinary individual fall between the stools of the special-interest groups. We need the special-interest groups, but we also need a strong voice for the public interest. If the system were working perfectly, our instruments of self-government would

be that strong voice. When they fail to function as such, in our free society, groups of citizens make themselves heard directly. It's a tradition as old as the nation.

The concept of the public interest

Obviously, no sensible person approaches the idea of the public interest without caution. It is a tricky concept. The farmer wants higher prices for his produce and the factory worker wants cheap food. Which is in the public interest? The citizen as conservationist fights to prevent location of a new power plant in his vicinity, while the citizen as homeowner seeks more and more electric power for his appliances. Which is in the public interest?

But such perplexities simply confirm that social policy is difficult to formulate. If it were impossible for citizens to agree on *anything* that could be defined as the public interest—if there were no common ground of any sort—then there could be no Constitution, no criminal code, and no way of living together peaceably from day to day.

No citizens' movement should assume that it has some divinely inspired grasp of what is "in the public interest." It must have the courage of its convictions, but it must present those convictions in the public forum where all other groups can debate their validity. Everything it does it must do openly. And though it is a petitioner (and therefore often an adversary) in relation to the government, it must ultimately respect the public process. That is why a citizens' movement must be interested in the structure and process of government. It should not wish to substitute itself for political and governmental institutions as the *vox populi. It should want the instruments of free self-government to work. It should want the freely elected representatives of the people to represent them wisely and well.*

No particular group should identify itself as *the* citizens' lobby. Common Cause is *a* citizens' lobby taking its place among many other citizens' groups that are working in what they conceive to be the public interest.

It is a mistake to view citizen action as outside politics. It is an integral part of the political process. I have heard observers describe Common Cause as being "above politics." It is *not* above politics. It is merely nonpartisan.

The constraints on elective officials

But can a citizens' lobby be effective? The deepest skepticism on that point comes from those who believe that the election of good men and women to public office is the beginning and end of political wisdom. "If you want to change things," they say, "elect men and women who will bring about the desired changes."

The reality is considerably less simple. Often even "good" candidates begin long before election to accommodate themselves to the very forces in American life that they would have to oppose if they were to accomplish significant change. Sometimes they cannot even be nominated unless they put themselves under obligation to a corrupt political machine. Often they accept campaign gifts from powerful corporate, union, or professional groups whose interests they will later be required to weigh against the public interest. Too often, when they enter office they find themselves deeply compromised by those pre-election accommodations.

And even if they have been wise enough not to make such accommodations, they discover, upon being elected, that they are trapped in political and governmental machinery that cannot be made to work.

I think we would all agree that if we could, in any given election year, increase by 15 or 20 percent the number of good people in public office, it would be a remarkable feat—a stunning feat. Yet, I am convinced that if we were to accomplish that stunning feat it would make very little difference. Very few of the things that are really wrong with this country would be altered.

Powerful as he may seem, a President's options are limited—limited by the accommodations he made in order to get elected, limited by his desire to be re-elected (or to keep his party in power), limited by the structure and constraints of governmental institutions.

Even if Presidents were as powerful as some citizens think they are, there is no evidence that the American people will consistently—or even frequently—elect Presidents with the greatness and wisdom to initiate profound and far-reaching social changes. I have asked many experienced observers, "How often can we expect to have in the White House a man who has the intellect, character, charisma, stamina, and courage to provide truly inspired Presidential leadership?" The pessimists say once or twice in a century. The most optimistic say once in a quarter century. Clearly we cannot organize our society in such a way that we are dependent on inspired Presidential leadership, because most of the time it won't be there.

We must build creative strength in other parts of the system. And in fact that's the kind of system it was intended to be. It was never intended that we should seek a Big Daddy and lean on him. We shall save ourselves—or we won't be saved.

It is immensely important that we elect a President of superior qualifications. But we cannot put sole reliance on him nor on any of our other elected officials to bring about the deep changes in our institutions that are essential. Without an active, concerned constituency they are helpless.

Ralph Nader and Donald Ross. Toward an initiatory democracy.

This country has more problems than it should tolerate and more solutions than it uses. Few societies in the course of human history have faced such a situation: most are in the fires without the water to squelch them. Our society has the resources and the skills to keep injustice at bay and to elevate the human condition to a state of enduring compassion and creative fulfillment. How we go about using the resources and skills has consequences which extend well beyond our national borders to all the earth's people.

How do we go about this? The question has been asked and answered in many ways throughout the centuries. Somehow, the answers, even the more lasting ones, whether conforming or defiant, affect the reality of living far less than the intensity of their acceptance would seem to indicate. Take the conventional democratic creeds, for example. Many nations have adopted them, and their principles have wide popular reception. But the theories are widely separated from practice. Power and wealth remain concentrated, decisions continue to be made by the few, victims have little representation in thousands of forums which affect their rights, livelihoods, and futures. And societies like ours, which have produced much that is good, are developing new perils, stresses, and deprivations of unprecedented scope and increasing risk. As the technologies of war and economics become more powerful and pervasive, the future, to many people, becomes uncertain and fraught with fear. Past achievements are discounted or depreciated as the quality of life drifts downward in numerous ways. General economic growth produces costs which register, like the silent violence of poverty and pollution, with quiet desperation, ignored by entrenched powers, except in their rhetoric.

But the large institutions' contrived non-accountability, complex technologies, and blameworthy indifference have not gone unchallenged, especially by the young. The very magnitude of our problems has reminded them of old verities and taught them new values. The generation gap between parents and children is in part a difference in awareness and expectation levels. Parents remember the Depression and are thankful for jobs. The beneficiaries—their children—look for more meaningful work and wonder about those who still do not have jobs in an economy of plenty because of rebuffs beyond their control. Parents remember World

War II and what the enemy could have done to America; children look on the Vietnam War and other similar wars and wonder what America has done to other people and what, consequently, she is doing to herself. To parents, the noxious plume from factory smokestacks was the smell of the payroll; children view such sights as symbols of our domestic chemical warfare that is contaminating the air, water, and soil now and for many years hence. Parents have a more narrow concept of neighborhood; children view Earth as a shaky ship requiring us all to be our brother's keeper, regardless of political boundaries.

In a sense, these themes, or many like them, have distinguished the split between fathers and sons for generations; very often the resolution is that the sons become like the fathers. The important point is not that such differences involve a statistically small number of the young—historic changes, including the American Revolution, have always come through minorities—but that conditions are indeed serious, and a new definition of work is needed to deal with them.

That new kind of work is a new kind of citizenship. The word "citizenship" has a dull connotation—which is not surprising, given its treatment by civics books and the way it has been neglected. But the role of the citizen is obviously central to democracy, and it is time to face up to the burdens and liberations of citizenship.

Democratic systems are based on the principle that all power comes from the people. The administration of governmental power begins to erode this principle in practice immediately. The inequality of wealth, talent, ambition, and fortune in the society works its way into the governmental process which is supposed to be distributing even-handed justice, resources, and opportunities. Can the governmental process resist such pressures as the chief trustee of structured democratic power given it by the consent of the governed? Only to the degree to which the governed develop ways to apply their generic power in meticulous and practical ways on a continual basis. A citizenship of wholesale delegation and abdication to public and private power systems, such as prevails now, makes such periodic checks as elections little more than rituals. It permits tweedledum and tweedledee choices that put mostly indistinguishable candidates above meaningful issues and programs. It facilitates the overwhelming dominance of the pursuit of private or special interests, to the detriment of actions bringing the greatest good to the greatest number. It breeds despair, discouragement, resignation, cynicism, and all that is involved in the "You can't fight City Hall" syndrome. It constructs a society which has thousands of full-time manicurists and pastry-makers but less than a dozen citizen-specialists fighting full time against corporate water contamination or to get the government to provide food (from bulging warehouses) for millions of undernourished Americans.

Building a new way of life around citizenship action must be the program of the immediate future. The ethos that looks upon citizenship as an avocation or opportunity must be replaced with the commitment to citizenship as an obligation, a continual receiver of our time, energy, and skill. And that commitment must be transformed into a strategy of action that develops instruments of change while it focuses on what needs to be done. This is a critical point. Too often, people who are properly outraged over injustice concentrate so much on decrying the abuses and demanding the desired reforms that they never build the instruments to accomplish their objectives in a lasting manner.

There are three distinct roles through which effective citizenship activity can be channeled. First is the full-time professional citizen, who makes his career by applying his skills to a wide range of public problems. These citizens are not part of any governmental, corporate, or union institutions. Rather they are independently based, working *on* institutions to improve and reshape them or replace them with improved ways of achieving just missions. With their full-time base, they are able to mobilize and encourage part-time citizen activity.

With shorter workweeks heading toward the four-day week, part-time involvement can become an integral part of the good life for blue- and white-collar workers. Certainly many Americans desire to find the answers to two very recurrent questions: "What can I do to improve my community?" and "How do I go about doing it?" The development of the mechanics of taking a serious abuse, laying it bare before the public, proposing solutions, and generating the necessary coalitions to see these solutions through—these steps metabolize the latent will of people to contribute to their community and count as individuals rather than as cogs in large organizational wheels.

The emergence of capabilities and outlets for citizenship expression has profound application to the third form of citizenship activity—on-the-job citizenship. Consider the immense knowledge of waste, fraud, negligence, and other misdeeds which employees of corporations, governmental agencies, and other bureaucracies possess. Most of this country's abuses are secrets known to thousands of insiders, at times right down to the lowest paid worker. A list of Congressional exposures in the poverty, defense, consumer fraud, environmental, job safety, and regulatory areas over the past five years would substantiate that observation again and again. The complicity of silence, of getting along by going along, of just taking orders, of "mum's the word" has been a prime target of student activism and a prime factor leading students to exercise their moral concern. When large organizations dictate to their employees, and when their employees, in turn, put ethical standards aside and perform their work like minions—that is a classic prescription for institutional irresponsibility. The individual must have an opportunity and a right to blow the whistle on his organization—to make higher appeals to outside authorities, to professional societies, to citizen groups—rather than be forced to condone illegality, consumer hazards, oppression of the disadvantaged, seizure of public resources, and the like. The ethical whistle-blower may be guided by the Golden Rule, a refusal to aid and abet crimes, occupational standards of ethics, or a genuine sense of patriotism. To deny him or her the protections of the law and supportive groups is to permit the institutionalization of organizational tyranny throughout the society at the grass roots where it matters.

On-the-job citizenship, then, is a critical source of information, ideas, and suggestions for change. Everybody who has a job knows of some abuses which pertain to that industry, commerce, or agency. Many would like to do something about these abuses, and their numbers will grow to the extent that they believe their assistance will improve conditions and not just expose them to being called troublemakers or threaten them with losing their jobs. They must believe that if they are right there will be someone to defend them and protect their right to speak out. A GM Fisher Body inspector went public on defectively welded Chevrolets that allowed exhaust gases, including carbon monoxide, to seep into passenger compartments. He had previously reported the defects repeatedly to plant managers without avail. In 1969 GM recalled over two million such Chevrolets for correction. The inspector still works at the plant, because union and outside supporters made it difficult for GM to reward such job citizenship with dismissal.

The conventional theory—that change by an institution in the public interest requires external pressure—should not displace the potential for change when that pressure forges an alliance with people of conscience *within* the institution. When the managerial elite knows that it cannot command its employees' complete allegiance to its unsavory practices, it will be far less likely to engage in such actions. This is a built-in check against the manager's disloyalty to the institution. Here is seen the significant nexus between full-time and part-time citizens with on-the-job citizens. It is a remarkable reflection on the underdevelopment of citizenship strategies that virtually no effort has been directed toward ending these divisions with a unison of action. But then, every occupation has been given expertise and full-time practitioners except the most important occupation of all—citizenship. Until unstructured citizen power is given the tools

for impact, structured power, no matter how democratic in form, will tend toward abuse, indifference, or sloth. Such deterioration has occurred not only in supposedly democratic governments but in unions, cooperatives, motor clubs, and other membership groups. For organizations such as corporations, which are admittedly undemocratic (even toward their shareholders), the necessity for a professional citizenship is even more compelling.

How, then, can full-time, part-time, and on-the-job citizens work together on a wide, permanent, and effective scale? A number of models around the country, where young lawyers and other specialists have formed public interest firms to promote or defend citizen-consumer rights vis-à-vis government and corporate behavior, show the way. Given their tiny numbers and resources, their early impact has been tremendous. There are now a few dozen such people, but there need to be thousands, from all walks and experiences in life. What is demanded is a major redeployment of skilled manpower to make the commanding institutions in our society respond to needs which they have repudiated or neglected. This is a life's work for many Americans, and there is no reason why students cannot begin understanding precisely what is involved and how to bring it about.

It may be asked why the burden of such pioneering has to be borne by the young. The short answer is to say that this is the way it has always been. But there is a more functional reason: no other group is possessed of such flexibility, freedom, imagination, and willingness to experiment. Moreover, many students truly desire to be of service to humanity in practical, effective ways. The focused idealism of thousands of students in recent years brings a stronger realism to the instruments of student action outlined in this book. Indeed, this action program could not have been written in the fifties or early sixties. The world—especially the student world—has changed since those years.

Basic to the change is that victims of injustice are rising to a level of recurrent visibility. They are saying in many ways that a just system would allow, if not encourage victims to attain the power of alleviating their present suffering or future concerns. No longer is it possible to ignore completely the "Other America" of poverty, hunger, discrimination, and abject slums. Nor can the economic exploitation of the consumer be camouflaged by pompous references to the accumulation of goods and services in the American household. For the lines of responsibility between unsafe automobiles, shoddy merchandise, adulterated or denutritionized foods, and rigged prices with corporate behavior and governmental abdication have become far too clear. Similarly, environmental breakdowns have reached critical masses of destruction, despoilation, ugliness, and, above all, mounting health hazards through contaminated water, soil, and air. Growing protests by the most aggrieved have made more situations visible and have increased student perception of what was observed. Observation has led to participation which in turn has led to engagement. This sequence has most expressly been true for minorities and women. The aridity and seeming irrelevance of student course work has provided a backdrop for even more forceful rebounds into analyzing the way things are. Parallel with civil rights, antiwar efforts, ecology, and other campus causes, which have ebbed and flowed, the role of students within universities has become a stressful controversy which has matured many students and some faculty in a serious assessment of their relation to these institutions and to society at large.

This assessment illuminates two conditions. First, it takes too long to grow up in our culture. Extended adolescence, however it services commercial and political interests, deprives young people of their own fulfillment as citizens and of the chance to make valuable contributions to society. Second, contrary to the old edict that students should stay within their ivory tower before they go into the cold, cold world, there is every congruence between the roles of student and citizen. The old distinction will become even more artificial with the exercise and imaginative use of the eighteen- to twenty-year-old vote throughout the country.

For the first time, students will have decisive voting power in many local governments. One does not have to be a political science major to appreciate the depth of resourceful experience and responsibility afforded by such a role. The quality of electoral politics could be vastly improved, with direct impact on economic power blocs, if students use the vote intelligently and creatively around the country.

Such a happening is not a foregone conclusion, as those who fought successfully in the past for enfranchisement of other groups learned to their disappointment; but there are important reasons why this enfranchisement of the eighteen to twenty year old could be different. Over a third of the eleven and a half million people in this group are college students with a sense of identity and a geographical concentration for canvassing and voting leverage. Certainly, problems of communication are minimized, and a resurgent educational curriculum can be an intellectually demanding forum for treating the facts and programs which grow into issue-oriented politics in the students' voting capacities.

Full use of voting rights will induce a higher regard for students by older citizens, and elected and appointed officials. It is unlikely that legislators will rise on the floor of the legislature and utter the verbose ridicules wrapped in a smug authoritarian condescension that students are accustomed to hearing. From now on, legislators will pay serious attention to students. Therefore the student vote and the student citizen are intimately connected. Student Public Interest Research Groups (PIRGs) composed of full-time professional advocates and able organizers recruited by and representing students as citizens can have an enormous, constructive impact on society. It could be a new ball game, if the student players avoid the temptations of despair, dropping out, and cynicism.

There are other obstacles which students put in their own way that deserve candid appraisal by all those involved in establishing and directing student PIRGs. These are the shoals of personal piques, ego problems, envy, megalomania, resentment, deception, and other frailties which are distributed among students as they are among other people. On such shoals the best plan and the highest enthusiasm can run aground, or be worn to exhaustion by the attrition of pettiness. Even after the PIRGs are established, these frictions can continue to frustrate and weaken their missions. They will surface at every step—from recruitment to choice of subject matters to the relations with the PIRG professionals. They must be averted at every step with candor, firmness, anticipatory procedures, and a goal-oriented adhesion that reduces such interferences to nuisances. Such nuisances will serve to remind all how important are character, stamina, self-discipline, and consistency of behavior with the value espoused to the success of the PIRG idea and its repercussive impact.

Self-discipline must be emphasized in this student age of free-think and free-do. Many kinds of cop-outs come in the garb of various liberated styles which sweep over campuses. Clearly, there has to be, for the purposes discussed in this volume, a reversal of the dictum: "If you desire to do it, you should do it" to "If you should do it, you should desire to do it." Such an attitude makes for persistence and incisiveness. It forces the asking of the important questions and the pursuit of the pertinent inquiries. It develops an inner reserve that refuses to give up and that thinks of ways for causes to be continually strengthened for sustained breakthroughs. The drive for a firmly rooted *initiatory* democracy is basic to all democratic participations and institutions, but initiatory democracy does not rest on the firmaments of wealth or bureaucratic power. It rests on conviction, work, intellect, values, and a willingness to sacrifice normal indulgences for the opportunity to come to grips as never before with the requisites of a just society. It also rests on a communion with the people for whom this effort is directed.

More and more students today are realistic about power, and they reject merely nominal democratic forms which shield or legitimize abuses. The great debates of the past over where power should be placed—in private or public hands—appear sterile to them. Students are suspicious of power wherever it resides because they know how such power can corrode and corrupt regardless of what crucible—corporate, governmental, or union—contains it. Moreover, the systematic use of public power by private interests against the citizenry, including the crude manipulation of the law as an instrument of oppression, has soured many of the brightest students against the efficacy of both government and law. At the same time, however, most concerned students are averse to rigid ideological views which freeze intellects and narrow the choices of action away from adaptability and resiliency.

Such skepticism can become overextended in a form of self-paralysis. I have seen too many students downplay what other students have already accomplished in the past decade with little organization, less funds, and no support. Who began the sit-in movement in civil rights, a little over a decade ago, which led to rapid developments in the law? Four black engineering students. Who dramatized for the nation the facts and issues regarding the relentless environmental contamination in cities and rural America? Students. Who helped mobilize popular opposition to the continuance of the war in Vietnam and, at least, turned official policy toward withdrawal? Who focused attention on the need for change in university policies and obtained many of these changes? Who is enlarging the investigative tradition of the old muckrakers in the Progressive-Populist days at the turn of the century other than student teams of inquiry? Who is calling for and shaping a more relevant and empirical education that understands problems, considers solutions, and connects with people? Who poured on the pressure to get the eighteen- to twenty-year-old vote? A tiny minority of students.

Still the vast majority of their colleagues are languishing in colossal wastes of time, developing only a fraction of their potential, and woefully underpreparing themselves for the world they are entering in earnest. Student PIRGs can inspire with a large array of projects which demand the development of analytic and value training for and by students. These projects will show that knowledge and its uses are seamless webs which draw from all disciplines at a university and enrich each in a way that arranged interdisciplinary work can never do. The artificial isolations and ennui which embrace so many students will likely dissolve before the opportunity to relate education to life's quests, problems, and realities. The one imperative is for students to avoid a psychology of prejudgment in this period of their lives when most are as free to choose and act as they will ever be, given the constraints of careers and family responsibilities after graduation. The most astonishing aspect of what has to be done in this country by citizens is that it has never been tried. What students must do, in effect, is create their own careers in these undertakings.

The problems of the present and the risks of the future are deep and plain. But let it not be said that this generation refused to give up so little in order to achieve so much.

Stanley Aronowitz. On organization: a good party is hard to find.

Enormous possibilities for building a serious national movement have been opened up to the left by the temporary political disarray among America's ruling class. This crisis in governmental authority, combined with the domestic and international crisis in the U.S. economy, has created "objective" conditions that could lead to a shift of political and social forces within our country.

Until now, only the *social* crisis has been generally acknowledged—that is, the deep fissures that have appeared in the consciousness of masses of people as the compulsions of their daily lives collide with their perception that these ordinary routines of

bourgeois existence are both socially unnecessary and politically repressive. At the same time, the bankruptcy of the great institutions of social learning—family, schools, and law—has become apparent to an unprecedented degree.

Only relatively recently has it become clear that the U.S. is experiencing a *political* and an *economic* crisis as well. The details of the so-called "constitutional crisis" are well-known; less apparent is the vast turn-off to electoral politics now in process. In former years, the Republicans managed to win the support of workers and other underlying classes because of the parsimonious facade in the midst of prosperity and their manifest patrician cleanliness. These advantages, formerly used to compensate for the narrow constituency of the party, have virtually disappeared in the wake of Watergate and the seemingly rampant inflation. As for the Democrats, ordinary Americans have been treated to the most shameful display of impotent hand-wringing by the "party of the working people" in the face of its greatest opportunity since the Depression to recover from voter rejection. The lackluster quality of the 1973 municipal elections attests to the failure of the two capitalist parties to convince us that voting makes any difference.

The most telling critique of U.S. capitalism is the shortages of materials and energy that have plagued the entire economy. The fuel and materials shortages are not the result of the recent Mideast crisis. Nor do they reflect the essentially rapacious using up of natural resources that does constitute a threat to the U.S. standard of living as well as the ability of developing nations to meet their basic material needs. Rather, the "energy crisis" is a brilliant instance of the chaotic nature of capitalist production. It is yet another testament to the weakness of the profit system as an effective regulator of resource allocation. In its special report on the shortages. *Business Week* attributes the situation to corporate refusal to expand production in view of the price-control policies of the federal government and the corporations' desire to reap enormous profits on restricted output. In other words, the shortage is a polite word for the fact that key sectors of American corporations have gone on strike. In the early Seventies the rising volume of profits was invested in new "services" rather than essential production spheres because the rate of profit in such industries as car leasing was better than on many manufactured goods. We are paying for the normal laws of the capitalist marketplace in two ways: high prices on consumer goods and a cold furnace.

But none of these crises of contemporary American capitalism can, by itself, generate the environment for a new level of mass struggle that self-consciously sees its mission as the creation of new forms of popular control and social relations. On the contrary. For with the disintegration of its old institutional means of control, our rulers are turning to new social and political forms of repression. The profound meaning of Watergate is to be found in the emergence of a self-conscious and hegemonic executive branch of government, acting on behalf of the international interests of the ruling class. Nixon's assault on constitutional liberties, particularly the autonomy of the legislative and judicial branches of national government, ought not to be interpreted either as the program of an individual hungry for absolute power or as evidence of a split within the ruling class, a new elite's bid for dominance against an old financial establishment based in the traditional industries. "Eastern" capital dominates the polity under Nixon as it has under every President since the Civil War; these old groups constitute the organizing force of the major multinational corporations and show no signs of relinquishing their position. That they were able to give Nixon his "marching orders" is attested to by the character of his foreign policy, which remains fundamentally detentist with respect to old Cold War adversaries, and simultaneously aggressive with regard to national independence and socialist movements within traditional spheres of U.S. imperial power. Splits do exist—on farm policy and on the whole question of the extension of social benefits, for example. But the overwhelming Congressional approval of the huge arms appropriation

measure proposed by the Nixon administration indicates the maintenance of a remarkable degree of unity within ruling circles, just as the recent tragic coup in Chile demonstrates their capacity to recover relatively quickly from temporary setbacks. And though Nixon had to be dragged kicking and screaming into tighter wage controls (and even then retained the largely voluntary character of price constraints), the overcoming of his initial resistance to the requirements for close integration of the economy and his final capitulation represented a brilliant victory for the capitalist planners, especially in the wake of the terrible defeats they have suffered at the hands of Japan and Western Europe in recent years.

The demand that workers and the poor sacrifice their hard-won gains on the altar of the need for grain to balance the international trade deficit has been met with resistance at the grocery store, on the shop floor, and occasionally at the ballot box, as the huge support for Wallace shows. But there is no reason to assume that any of these developments points automatically in the direction of a coherent process of radicalization among the masses. It is equally possible for such protest and resistance to lead to the founding of an impressive mass authoritarian movement. An emancipatory movement must be created self-consciously: among the lessons of the past decade is that social practice must find its ideal form in new theoretical paradigms if the circularity of history is to be transcended.

The old theories have been rendered obsolete by the capacity of the system to organize its resources into an (albeit unstable) equilibrium. For example, the current economic crisis remains repressed within the framework of more or less constant rates of overall growth. Periodically, a new panic button is pushed, and monetary and diplomatic wizards are mobilized to twist arms, make concessions to capitalist partners and undertake crash programs to contain the looming breakdown. The boat is always leaking, but, thanks to restricted international competition and the complicity of the "socialist" nations, the United States has been able to get by with a little help from its "enemies."

Moreover, even if an economic crash did occur, it cannot be claimed that this would catapult radical consciousness and articulate social struggle against the system to new heights. We should have learned better from the experience of the 1930s. Capitalism lost ground in terms of production, profits and any other conceivable economic indicator, but there was never a serious threat to the power of its ideological or social institutions. In fact, the great economic crisis not only strengthened the old forms of domination but created new forms of bourgeois rule as well. And orthodox Marxism welcomed and assisted this transformation of archaic competitive capitalism into the present-day state capitalism under which we suffer. Where genuine revolutionary efforts were made, such as in Spain, China and Latin America, Western capitalist nations were absolutely unified in their determination to crush the revolts, or at least permit the most reactionary elements within the revolutionary countries to survive and counterattack. Socialism suffered an enormous defeat during this era. It failed on two fronts—not only to mount an offensive revolutionary strategy for the struggle against fascism and the economic crisis, but also—of equal and perhaps even more crucial importance—to create a self-conscious movement to transform social and sexual relations. The repression of liberatory theory and practice was a characteristic feature of the Old Left; instead, it served up a warmed-over apocalyptic political line which promised that all would be well once the single stroke of the seizure of state power has been accomplished. Thus there is little reason to rejoice now about the breakdown of order if the chances for emancipation from the social as well as economic constraints of the bourgeois order remain repressed by, and among, the revolutionaries themselves.

Mass parties and reformism

Sensing that the time has arrived to create a New Left presence on the national level, many persons have proposed the formation of a new party that is neither a vanguard of the old Leninist type nor a party of parliamentary reform that reduces its socialist programs to the status of Fourth of July orations and other patriotic appeals.

Yet the projection of a new national radical movement in terms of a mass party contains a number of ambiguities that require clarification if an effective political force is to be shaped. There is almost no evidence of a mass party in Western capitalist countries that has not deteriorated into a reformist party safely embodied within the framework of parliamentary politics. This formulation of the historical evidence holds for both the social democratic experience and the communist experience in Italy and France.

The reasons for this cannot be sought merely in the perfidy of the leadership of the left. The revolutionary intentions of the founders of the great social democratic parties of Europe and the pre-World War I United States are beyond dispute. The most right-wing of the social democrats, such as Bernstein, Guesde, and even the English Fabians, were in the minority of the socialist movement most of the time. The American socialist party's mass appeal was due to figures like Debs more than to right-wingers like John Spargo, Algernon Lee, W.E. Walling and others. In Germany, Rosa Luxemburg and Karl Kautsky shared the view that the object of social democratic politics was the replacement of capitalism by revolutionary socialism. Even Lenin admired Kautsky more than any other Western European socialist leader prior to the First World War.

To be sure, there are plenty of examples of the slide into reformism and worse, from the German social democrats voting for war credits, capitulating to the Kaiser and the liberal politicians, and opposing the Bolsheviks in 1917, to the French Communist Party's horrible position in the 1968 general strike (which was in turn only an outgrowth of the role the Party had played in French life since the 1930s). But the issues go deeper than mere "betrayals."

Reformism arises under specific social conditions. It is the political expression of that sector of the working class and the popular movement which is able to win substantial concessions within the framework of the existing advanced capitalist order. We have learned from our own history that such concessions can be made even under the most adverse economic conditions, provided the social institutions and ideologies of capitalism remain intact. Despite the militant stance of the trade unions and the old socialist left during the Thirties, their demands were essentially bourgeois. Socialist rhetoric provided efficient symbols for militant action within the system, arousing the workers spiritually even as they were seeking only modest gains.

Moreover, even if a case could have been made for the imminent economic collapse of capitalism at various times in the twentieth century, its cultural domination was never broken. As Wilhelm Reich has pointed out, the external crisis of capital did not prevent the introjection of authority within the character structure of the workers and their movements. Here culture may be said to have *overdetermined* consciousness even as the "logical" basis was being laid for its transformation. Thus, for example, in Germany the workers became part of the very system that oppressed them. Certainly it cannot be said that the mass socialist and communist parties anywhere were interested in an emancipatory project—in a movement which demands an end to the hierarchical organization of labor, which challenges bourgeois forms of leadership (forms that seem to have survived within the socialist and workers' movement even after they have suffered decay within the society at large) and which attacks the old structures of power instead of reproducing them. By the early 1930s, the social-democratization of the communist parties was nearly completed. No clearer evidence of their transformation from revolutionary tribunes to bourgeois elites can be found than in the creation of the popular-front governments in France and Spain. This was paralleled in our own country, first by the waning criticism of the Roosevelt administration and then, in the late 1930s, by the CP's full-throated support for the newly integrated state apparatus of the New Deal.

Here I dispute the claims of those who wish that the left had applied correctly the united-front principles of the Communist International. Such analyses tend to ignore the larger question of whether the communist and socialist parties could have resisted fascism by any means that did not include the struggle for fundamental social transformation. During the 1930s, particularly in Spain, the combined struggle for human liberation and against fascism was proposed as an offensive strategy by anarchists and left Marxists. This position was cruelly rejected by the popular-front parties not only with words, but with bayonets. Similarly, in May 1968 the French Communist Party spent more of its energy in attacking the militant workers and students, who insisted that the revolt was not a general strike for higher wages but a struggle to end the wage system itself, than it did in resisting the Gaullist regime. The fallacy of both the united-front and popular-front efforts at political mobilization is that they concentrate their attacks against the most right-wing elements of the ruling class—fascists and other overt authoritarians—rather than corporate or monopoly capital as such.

Parliamentary socialism

The historical lessons of the past century of parliamentary socialism can be summarized in terms of the transformation of the parties and movements from educational, agitational and cultural movements seeking to assist the self-organization of the people, into parties that project themselves as the leading force of the social struggle. The left did not heed Rosa Luxemburg's invocation to socialists:

Revolutions cannot be made at command. Nor is this at all the task of the party. Our duty is only at all times to speak out plainly without fear or trembling; that is, to hold clearly before the masses their tasks at a given historical moment, and to proclaim the political program of actions and slogans which result from the situation.

Those who wished to be the masters of society and saw themselves in the image of their bourgeois predecessors were hardly receptive to Luxemburg's argument that the chief task of socialists was the "transformation of the mass into a sure, conscious, lucid 'self leader.' "

Parliamentary socialism or reformism manifests itself as the tendency of a mass party, in seeking to win a following, to trim its sails on a host of issues. For example, communist and socialist parties have worked to protect the privileged position of skilled and professional workers instead of struggling against these conditions. Even the militant activity of radicals during the rise of the CIO failed to address squarely the fact that union agreements were signed establishing separate seniority lists, maintaining high wage differentials, and condoning the takeover of union locals by well-organized groups of skilled workers.

I should make clear that the participation of a radical group in electoral politics in the country at large or in unions or similar institutions can help to push the struggle forward at times, especially if the participation is at the local level. Similarly, struggles for immediate demands are not in *themselves* inherently reformist. Indeed, under some conditions elementary wage struggles are strikes against the state and raise revolutionary possibilities.

The mass parliamentary party is not defined by its slogans or programs, but by the social position of its professional leaders and the sectors of society it represents. The socialist movements won the support of the masses by announcing their readiness to espouse revolutionary doctrines corresponding to the felt needs of large segments of the working class. At the same time, however, left leaders were all too willing to postpone struggles for fundamental control over society in favor of incremental changes which they justified on the grounds of expediency. The socialist and communist parties became mass parties precisely because they acted like other bourgeois parties. In the day-to-day struggles of their nations they were nothing more than electoral machines and mass bases for the trade unions. In recent decades, the success of capitalist integration has been rooted precisely in the ability of capitalists to bring labor into the parliamentary system and to allow trade unions to organize the incremental demands of a minority of workers.

Lenin's analysis of the failure of social democracy pinpointed a critical feature of its leadership: they were representative of the most skilled and most privileged sectors of the working class—those whose interests were manifestly served by imperialism. The notion of the labor aristocracy was carried one step further by Marcuse, who attributed the failure of socialism in the West to the integration of the *whole* working class into a highly organized state-capitalist system able to deliver the goods and able to contain, if not overcome, its contradictions.

The implications of the idea of capitalist integration for radical strategy are clear: mass parties can only be a genuine opposition to the prevailing system when (1) the crisis of capitalist institutions reaches such a point that daily life becomes intolerable and (2) working-class and popular consciousness has reached a point where the masses see that the system can no longer meet their needs and are thus open to structural alternatives.

Unless these conditions exist, mass parliamentary parties, whatever their initial intentions, are bound to reflect the reformist possibilities of the system itself. Even when capitalism cannot satisfy the demands of the entire population, it can meet the demands of the most organized and militant sectors of the population. During the 1930s, revolutionary groups championed programs for relief and for job programs for all, but abandoned their revolutionary programs except as articles of faith. It was in consideration of this experience that the New Left chose not to build a mass party. Instead, it organized relatively loose movements around specific grievances and public issues that could dissolve after the demands were met rather than harden into oppressive bureaucracies. The call for a mass party now must respond *both* to the classical objection that mass parties under conditions of social integration inevitably become reformist *and* to the anti-bureaucratic impulse of large numbers of Americans.

What this means concretely is that the effort to build a mass "party" must contain within its own self-presentation the idea that it seeks a systemic alternative, not merely the return of our country to its basic democratic heritage. On the contrary, it would provide a critique of the myth that democratic liberties are possible within authoritarian institutional structures. It would point out that all social institutions, whether of the state (government, education, unions, etc.) or of daily life (family, work, personal relations), are organized on the principle of hierarchy. Democracy for us means the end of hierarchy. Thus, the program of the party would have as its starting point the structure of social relations, not their political manifestations. Under these circumstances, questions that have been traditionally grouped under the rubric of "culture" must have equal status with those considered of economic or political interest. The failure of the ruling class to achieve social integration is now pre-eminent in the sphere of social relations. But its economic and political ruptures are more amenable to repair as long as people still believe in the values of mobility, professional advancement and consumerism, and in the holiness of the nuclear family and of conventional sexual morality. Unless a new party offers a politics of daily existence, it will be incapable of resonating to the deep unmet needs of most Americans. Instead, it will be perceived as a left pretender to political power without a vision of a new way of life.

Here it should be pointed out that large numbers of Americans, particularly those historically excluded from participation in the mainstream of economic life, are pursuing goals that are much more closely related to the problems of basic survival. The role of a mass party is to assist these struggles without abandoning its argument that they can never be successful within the present social system. This point is not merely a matter of ideological conviction. It is vindicated by the successes of the civil rights and black movements themselves. It may be that the victories of black candidates

in major Northern cities, as well as in a significant number of metropolitan areas in the South, is a necessary prelude to the understanding that liberal reform is not sufficient. But it would constitute a massive betrayal of the black people and the poor themselves if radicals merely posed as militant champions of liberal black reformers or of drives for decent unions among the working poor. It remains painfully obvious that in the midst of the massive breakdown of the essential character of the cities, even the best-intentioned city administration cannot reverse the disintegration of urban life, cannot restore the old neighborhoods, cannot secure the economic well-being of its citizens. The cities have been bequeathed to black people cynically by corporations who have squeezed them dry. Black control of black communities is a slogan that means the ruling class has agreed to permit black public officials to administer the death of the cities, now that it has ripped the heart from them.

The role of a new mass party is to present new perspectives for the struggle to make life decent. It is our *vision* as much as our organizational resources that can make a contribution to the justified struggle of the working poor against their exclusion from the economic mainstream.

The vision of a new society is not a project confined to white, relatively well-schooled, young people. The most notable failure of the Old Left in the last 50 years was its failure of imagination. And the startling and enduring contribution of the student left of past decade was that it had such a vision. Its demise has left us without that vital element. The dreary programs of social reform within the framework of militant rhetoric have increasingly fallen on deaf ears. People have heard these things before and will only respond to fresh appeals to their own power and creativity—not to promises of deliverance.

An extra-parliamentary party

I believe the important issue for us now is to understand that the party must be pre-eminently an extra-parliamentary "party" committed first of all to mass action around popular needs. Such an organization must under no circumstances commit itself to a parliamentary road to social change. It should engage in electoral activity only when its social basis has been established through mass action, so that its identity as a revolutionary force will not be in doubt.

Similarly, the chief emphasis of such a party's workplace organizing among rank and filers must be on the autonomy of workers, their right to engage in strikes, cultural and political activity, and educational work, whether the trade unions agree or not. The main thrust of rank-and-file work cannot be union takeovers because the national unions are structurally unable to meet workers' needs. This does not preclude militants becoming stewards or committee men at the local level. I am dubious, however, about caucus movements whose aim is to capture national leadership on a program of union democracy. The record is littered with well-intentioned rank-and-file movements, even some with radical participation, that have degenerated into new bureaucracies, separated themselves from the most elementary demands of workers, become undemocratic and arbitrary, and sold out to the liberal politicians or worse. Curran, Quill, Reuther, Bridges, leaders of the Hotel Union, and hospital unionists in New York were all well-intentioned people at the beginning. Their move to conservatism was not a personal character defect or a neurosis, but a mark of the incorporation of even the most militant and democratic trade unions into the corporate consensus.

The trade unions cannot be ignored. But concentrating on working within them is ultimately self-defeating for a movement seeking the development of a radical working class. The successful working-class rank-and-file movements which have developed since 1967 have emerged despite the leadership and often in opposition to the unions themselves—the most recent example being the Chrysler sit-ins. The evidence is virtually overwhelming that young workers are not just critical of the leaders, but strain to be free of the constraints imposed by the collective-bargaining agreement itself. The union is perceived as the

property of the older, skilled workers who have the free time and the flexibility in their work assignments to capture controlling positions within the union. Moreover, it is not at all clear that the interests of the skilled and unskilled are compatible in the monopoly sectors of American industry, much less in the small, competitive sectors.

Even for those currently working in rank-and-file movements whose thrust is primarily in trade-union reform it is worthwhile to fashion a truly radical program among members who perceive the "trade" union as reactionary, but who do want forms of self-organization that can deal effectively with the onslaught of management. Without fleshing out a complete policy, it may be useful to recall four points that are objectively opposed to the deepest commitments of contemporary labor bureaucracies, irrespective of their ideological hue. Radicals should (1) advocate the right of workers to strike at any time, (2) oppose signing contracts that substitute a grievance procedure for the strike weapon, (3) oppose contracts of more than a year's duration, (4) oppose the check-off of union dues, (5) advocate rotation of officers at every level of the union and oppose full-time officials at any level, (6) oppose job classification as a basis for wage payment—that is, we should call for the abolition of pay distinctions between "skilled," "unskilled," and "professional" workers.

These points are open for debate. They are part of the long, now-forgotten tradition of revolutionary unionism that was smashed, denounced and repudiated by all trade unionists of the left as well as of the right during the 1930s. But our role is to raise the new issues, not wallow in the old ones.

The party in history

Finally, I wish to address myself to the problem of the party as a historical formation. The concept of the party as such is the creation of the radical bourgeoisie in the era of the transition from feudalism to capitalism. It represented their right to put forth their demands within the public realm independently of the old feudal state. The party became a revolutionary instrument for the establishment of the bourgeois state. The division of various sectors of the bourgeoisie into competing political parties based on the disparity of their respective interests and expectations was ensconced within a unified conception of the role of the state as the protection of the general interests of the capitalist class, and pre-eminently the protection of its property. The ninteenth-century demand of urban workers and other propertyless wage earners for the right to vote, to form political parties of their own, and to press their demands within the parliamentary sphere, was only revolutionary so long as the bourgeoisie resisted these demands. But once the right to vote was secured, mass socialist parties found that they could win substantial concessions in parliaments. The success of parliamentary socialism laid the basis for the transformation of these parties from revolutionary instruments into reformist organizations.

To be sure, none of the parliamentary socialist formations of the twentieth century renounced their revolutionary aims. The party, according to its socialist proponents, is at once an instrument for asserting the rights of the people within the capitalist order and a means for transcending that order. This contradictory role is only resolved at the moment of revolutionary change, when the party as revolutionary instrument expresses and carries out the demand of the whole working class for its self-abolition. Leaving aside the question of whether such a task can be accomplished within the context of a revolution in a single, economically backward country, there is nothing in the Marxist theory of the party that deals effectively with the tendency of all centralized organizations towards oligarchy, except the Leninist invocation to recruit to Bolshevik ranks the "most advanced elements" of the working class who, presumably, will guarantee its purity from the reformism and bureaucratic styles of work characteristic of professionals.

Even though there is much substance to the claim that the idea of a party stamps a political group with the element of serious-ness and the global objective of dealing directly with the issue of social power, the question of name and form must be examined to discover whether, in fact, the very concept of the party isn't pre-eminently designed to allow the oppressed to make their demands *within* the system. As the experience of the British Labour Party amply demonstrates, the bourgeoisie may allow a labor party to rule, provided it does so in the interest of preserving corporate domination. I am not quarreling with the need for a national movement that attempts to coordinate the activities of otherwise disparate groups. Nor can there be any dispute about the fact that the situation cries out for a revolutionary left that can present its ideas coherently to the mass of Americans. But if the term "party" is to be used at all, it must be carefully distinguished from its notorious predecessors.

The party's constituency

No mass radical party can hope to get beyond the talking stage unless it address the question of its social character—that is, situates itself in class terms. The history of opposition movements within our country is filled with instances of "people's" or "populist" parties that became effective instruments for integrating the unintegrated into the political mainstream. As progressivist and populist history shows, there were no reforms that were not incorporable by the left wing of the Democratic Party in most cases, and sometimes by the liberals among the agrarian Republicans. The McGovern victory within the Democratic Party in 1971–72 was only the latest instance of this co-optation.

The demands that are not subject to integration are those that call for self-management. A new political movement would educate and agitate for workers' self-management where decision-making is really lodged among the people. This would require a thoroughly non-hierarchical and non-authoritarian political thrust, one that raised the need, not to seize state power, but to smash it; not to control the management by workers' participation, but to abolish the managers; not to balance the professionals by parent and student control in the school, but to raise the question of who the educators are; a movement that insisted that the personal and the political are not separable.

What segments of society would make up the party's constituency? Those that have been mentioned include women, blacks, workers, students, professionals, and others. Clearly, all of these segments should be welcomed into the party. All of them have demonstrated, through their struggles against their oppression and exploitation, that their essential interests are not those of the capitalist class. None has benefited in the long run from the integration of the state and the corporations which constitute the ruling class of our country. Yet, having said that, it does not follow that the new party should place equal weight on the needs of each sector, or regard itself as a "People's Party," that is, a coalition of democratic, anti-authoritarian forces.

I want to argue for the position that a new "party" ought to give prime weight to the struggles and interests of the working class. That orientation should be present in its program as well as in the composition of its leading bodies. Thus, the question of workers' management in production and all institutions of society should be embodied in its statements, and the struggles of workers themselves to capture control over their labor, to determine the general course of working class political struggle, should be a cardinal feature of the daily struggles in which the party participates.

One of the critical tasks of the party is to assert that the working class is not just another sector of society. Its social role in the production and distribution of agricultural and industrial commodities makes it the key to social transformation, even though it would be absurd in America to argue that industrial workers can "go it alone." The existence of a mass party that recognizes the class nature of capitalist society, and is prepared to fashion a class program that can overcome it, is essential.

Within the working class all the recent evidence points to the importance of black workers' struggles as a cutting-edge of protest against both trade-union bureaucracies and companies. Black workers' movements exist in almost all basic industries, beginning with steel and auto and extending to transportation, construction, and the distributive trades. The character of black workers' movements differs from other black movements in several respects. They have been democratic—that is, the workers themselves have determined the issues and the direction of the struggles. Many have been anti-capitalistic, or at least have raised the question of workers' control over production.

Parallel movements of white workers must also be recognized. While black workers suffer special discrimination in that they are systematically barred from the skilled trades, occupy the dirtiest and heaviest jobs even among unskilled and semi-skilled workers, and have trouble entering many occupations, the critical issue is the united power of *all* workers to control production and society as a whole. The difficult question of the competition among workers themselves must be confronted by the party. For a time, for example, its capacity to attract skilled or professional older, white workers will be limited by its unwavering position for complete workers' equality, without regard to race, sex or skill.

The party has to argue within the working class for a *class* as well as a *sectoral* approach to the problems faced by blacks and women. Opposition to professionalism ought to be a key to the platform of the party. The party could raise the slogans, "equal pay for all" and "we are all equal on the production line," a phrase used by the Fiat workers in Italy. Within industrial plants the party should oppose separate seniority lists which have effectively excluded unskilled workers, both white and black, from skilled trades. The party should also oppose no-strike agreements in union contracts and management prerogatives to decide what is to be produced, by whom, by what methods, and with which work and safety standards.

Finally, the issue of the party's attitude towards trade unions, as discussed above, has to be confronted.

Although the party should welcome all who support its program, it should demand confrontation with the connection between the personal and the political, between work and extracurricular activity, between private and public life. Just as the women's movement has demanded that family life and sexual relations be considered "politics," so should the party ask that professionals examine their own relation to the life of society. No communist or socialist party has understood the pernicious role of professionalism as ideology and as political and social practice. The popular-front periods of the communist party and socialist party in the United States and elsewhere were marked by the mass recruitment of professionals and their elevation to leading positions in mass organizations (e.g., the Progressive Party, the American Labor Party, the National Negro Congress of the 1930s, etc.). There is no distinction between trade-union and party bureaucrats and doctors and lawyers; they are all professionals. And, as the record shows, the stratification and the division of labor within the movement based on categories such as sex, prestige and social class reflects the hierarchical social divisions in society as a whole.

As a social category, managerial personnel, even if not owners of industries, are professional servants of big industries and institutions and their interests are those of the owners. All "professionals," however, are not managers. Many are merely technicians working for a wage or salary who have little or no control over their own labor or the labor of others. The party should be active among technical workers such as teachers, medical workers, engineers and scientists who labor in industrial, government or university bureaucracies. It should encourage the self-organization of these groups around their social and economic interests.

One measure of a successful effort to build a mass party of social change is its capacity to attract "the best minds of our generation," in the words of Allen Ginsberg.

But intellectuals must not be regarded as an elite destined to direct the fortunes of the popular movement; rather, educators, journalists, social theorists and artistic workers must forge organic links to the base of the party and the working class. This is not to say that art or theory should be subordinate to the policies and practice of the movement. On the contrary, the independence of the intellectuals is the most precious plank in the party program in this regard. Intellectuals do not wish to exchange one set of masters for another. The experience in all Western and Eastern European countries has been that the most creative, militant and courageous intellectuals have systematically left the orthodox socialist and communist parties precisely because these parties have insisted on the subordination of their work to party doctrine. The party needs theory, good newspapers and a rich cultural life, but these cannot be purchased on the grounds of political agreement alone. The party itself must constitute a conducive atmosphere for dissent and criticism. This type of linkage is always difficult in a country and a left political movement that are profoundly anti-intellectual. Nevertheless, a party of opposition can only thrive on the originality and the strength of its social ideals and practice.

G. William Domhoff. Blueprints for a new society.

As the sixties were coming to an end, there was hope in some Left circles for imminent revolutionary change in corporate America. Then, almost as suddenly as the revolutionary enthusiasm appeared, it was gone, and the American Left was once again at a low ebb. By late 1971, the turbulent years which saw the rapid growth of a New Left already seemed like ancient history, and even in the ambiguous political landscape of 1974, any discussion of social change on a scale large enough to qualify as revolutionary still seems wildly out of place. Even so, I think such discussion is worthwhile if the Left is to be better prepared for the next time one of the inevitable consequences of corporate capitalism and imperialism—war, inflation, recession, unemployment—leads to major activist ferment.

The aspects of revolutionary change I would like to pursue concern, first, the need for what I term "blueprints" for a post-capitalist, post-corporate America and, second, the need for a new political strategy. If those who talk of revolutionary change are going to connect with the various kinds of exploitation and oppression suffered by Americans of different social strata and ethnic origins, they will have to go beyond critiques of corporate capitalism, however telling those critiques may be, and beyond ringing calls for a "new social order," however decent and humane those calls may be. They will have to help create alternative visions of United States society that are not general but specific, not vague but concrete— visions, in short, that are at the level of detail of "blue-prints" for a post-capitalist America.

I think there are three parts to a good program for large-scale change: a comprehensive critique of the present system, an alternative vision of the future, and a political plan for implementing that vision. The American Left has been good at comprehensive critiques, but not so good on visions and political strategies. Then it will have to suggest a plausible political strategy for bringing these blueprints to reality, a strategy that is appropriate to American political realities in the last quarter of the 20th century.

The basis for my suggestions is not reading and research, but observation and experience—observation on the periphery of New Left activities in the late Sixties, and experience answering questions and listening to audiences after giving speeches on the topic of "Who rules America?" or "How the power elite dominates government." As I watched and listened, I came to believe that comments like "They have a power elite in the Soviet Union, you know," or "What have you got that's better?" must be taken seriously as a clue to the underlying attitudes of most Americans toward radical criticisms and calls for social change.

Offering real choices

Rightly or wrongly, most Americans—and especially Americans over age 35—are rabidly anti-socialist, and that anti-socialism is based in good measure upon the history of the Soviet Union. Too many Americans are convinced that their choice is present-day capitalism, with all its ugliness, or a Soviet-style state socialism. Given that choice, based on fear and lack of vision, they opt for the present system. Only by talking about concrete plans will it be possible to involve people in developing their own alternative visions, thereby overcoming the paralytic anti-communism that makes it impossible to contemplate an alternative future without the fear that it will be worse than the present.

But there are other dimensions—perhaps of greater importance—to the reluctance of most Americans to consider major social change. One of them, I believe, involves the places from which so many of us came just one or two or three generations ago. For we came from something worse—the Old Country—and the United States has delivered in many ways. "Remember the Old Country!" people in audiences would warn me. "Be thankful for what you've got, young man." Thus, while we are talking about what should be morally, and about what could be, given the productive potential of the international economy, most Americans are comparing the present to the past, and being grateful. And this is not, I contend, because of the liberal apologists who constantly proclaim this inactionary doctrine, but because of the actual experiences of millions of working class families.

This point about the Old Country relates to a third factor which contributes to the need for blueprints. A great many hard-working Americans are well off enough materially that they do not seem willing to risk what they already have. Even without the fear of Soviet communism and traditional memories of the Old Country, it might be that most Americans would believe it smarter, for all their discontents, to go along with imperialism and inflation than to involve themselves in a struggle for vaguely defined goals which just might (they reason) result in something worse. Unless there is something specific to work towards—blueprints—Americans will settle for minor changes in the status quo.

It may be possible through careful studies to discover just how important each of these three factors is in helping to sustain the general corporate capitalist hegemony that exists today in the United States, but that is not my concern here. For now, I will be content with my general point that there are concrete historical reasons why many Americans seem to want a more specific alternative before they become involved in anti-capitalist political activity.

Building unity

Beyond first getting people into the mental framework where they can contemplate major political action, blueprints are needed to bind together any newly developing political movement that people might join. In other words, blueprints might be part of the answer to the difficult problem of constant divisiveness among those seeking revolutionary-scale social change. As the experience of the Sixties once again shows, it is not enough to share a common critical analysis of the capitalist system. Anti-capitalists come from such diverse social, ethnic, racial and religious backgrounds that they need something more than a common enemy to keep them together. That something more might be achieved through the conscious development of a set of long-range blueprints that would make short-run personal and stylistic differences of less importance.

The point about binding people across socio-economic, ethnic and racial chasms is closely related to another consideration— the development of detailed blueprints to neutralize certain groups of people, people who would be neither hurt nor benefited materially by large-scale social change in the United States. I think there are such groups in the middle levels of American society—teachers, government employees,

certain white-collar workers, certain skilled tradesmen, and some small businessmen and store owners. Such people might come to see that they could go along with the new society if it were to come about. I don't think they should be forced to choose sides—defined as enemies just because they won't become active supporters. Instead of a popular Sixties slogan, "If you aren't part of the solution, you're part of the problem," I think the following motto should be adopted: "If you aren't part of the problem, then you're a friend of ours."

Utopian or real

If blueprints are as important as I think they are, why has there been so little emphasis on them? I can think of several reasons, but on this question one stands out, and that is the nature of Marxism, at least as the theory has been understood by most Marxists in the United States. For the theory that in one variant or another dominates Left thinking everywhere does not put much emphasis on blueprints. If anything, in its desire to be considered "scientific," it puts down anything that seems to smack of utopian or idealistic thinking, and blueprints often get shunted into that category. Scientific marxism stresses how inexorable processes inherent in capitalism lead certain social groups into struggle, and it is out of this struggle that "consciousness" is supposed to come—meaning the inevitable realization of the necessity for social ownership of the means of production. In this view, blueprints are hardly needed. People move, step by step, into a deeper struggle, and only slowly begin to create a vision of a new and better social organization.

Now, this view may be true in some places at some times, but I don't think it is true here and now. I also think it deemphasizes the fact that the word "socialism" [is] used to embody an adequate blueprint. "Scientific" marxism, despite its denigration of utopian socialism, really did have a visionary aspect to inspire its followers. However general was the blueprint originally embodied in the idea of socialism, it was a blueprint that was sufficient for the late 19th and early 20th centuries. Now many systems call themselves socialist, some more attractive than others, and the blueprint has to be more specific.

To say that the vision of socialism has been tarnished by events leads to a second reason why blueprints are neglected in the United States. For a long time, the Soviet Union was the only blueprint entertained by the dominant American Leftists, and when things went sour there, those in and around the Communist Party were caught in a bind. They wanted to be friendly toward the Soviet Union, but they could not use the Soviet Union as an example in convincing Americans to embrace socialism. And they could not help create appropriate blueprints because they already had a blueprint that was unappealing to most Americans even before the Cold War and its hysterical propaganda. The result was a strategy which played down the need for concrete alternatives, with the hope that the Soviet Union would transcend its under-developed stages and become a full-fledged example of socialism.

But I do not want to put the whole burden on Marxism and the American Communist Party. Many New Leftists, in their attempt to be non-directive, democratic, and non-elitist, also felt that people in action would more or less gradually generate their own blueprints. "Let the People Decide" is the slogan that embodies the stance. Thus there was little or no emphasis on alternative visions in most New Left political thinking. On this score, they did not break with their predecessors on the Old Left.

I agree that the people should decide, first, whether blueprints are needed, and second, what the blueprints should be. I would only add that we are part of the people, and that it is not elitist to advocate considering whether an important next step is to develop blueprints. Indeed, if people reject a call to fashion new post-capitalist blueprints, they will have made their choice. I just hope the question gets on the agenda for discussion, and that it is not decided by appeals to Marxian theory or the experience of past revolutions.

A time to talk

So much for why we should have blueprints but don't. How should we create them? People—from all walks of life, and not just experts—should develop them, for by working on blueprints many new people could become involved in building a movement for large-scale social change. If it were mainly anti-capitalist intellectuals, labor intellectuals and students who continued to work on analyses and critiques of corporate capitalism, perhaps a wider range of people could be drawn into the process of creating blueprints to replace the system that has been analyzed and criticized.

What I have in mind is small groups of disaffected Americans in every region of the country sitting down with each other to talk about blueprints for the social institutions in which they have direct experience— whether it be factories, hospitals, schools, or agencies of one kind or another. Basing themselves on humanistic and egalitarian principles widely shared by socialists, they would discuss the kinds of organizations that would be·feasible for their work area. No doubt various kinds of experts might be catalysts and resource persons for many of these groups, but they should see themselves as political activists trying to involve people in a process, rather than as experts trying to convince people of a particular plan as to how a certain sector of the economy should be organized.

To take one example of how this process might work, consider farming and food distribution. Groups might begin by considering consumer co-ops as the basic food outlet, for this puts choice and control in local, consumer hands. They would go on to determine whether co-ops should control middlemen and producers, or whether the middlemen should be state controlled and small farmers encouraged to organize into producer co-ops. In short, they would try to develop a plan for the control of the units of a food system that would be egalitarian, flexible, and consumer-oriented.

A plan of attack

Blueprints, of course, are not enough in themselves to constitute a program for major social change. It is also necessary to have a political strategy—a plan of attack. On this score the American Left has been even weaker than on its lack of an adequate vision. It has chosen to follow strategies that have been appropriate for other times and other places, but which have been dismal failures when attempted in the United States. Partly because of a great admiration for successful revolutionary movements elsewhere, and partly because most Marxists tend to concentrate their theoretical attention on the economic "substructure" rather than mere political "superstructure," the American Left never has come to grips with the historically based realities of the American political system.[1]

My experience during the Sixties, and my reading of American political history, have led me to advocate a political strategy that involves electoral struggle within the two-party system, something that no anti-capitalist group in the 20th Century has attempted on an openly ideological basis. My plan, which leaves most Leftists gasping for breath, is to run candidates in Democratic Party primaries on the post-capitalist blueprints that are developed by the process I have just outlined. Every party election and party primary would be entered, from precinct level to the Presidency. In fact, it is essential to this approach that candidates be running at all levels on every occasion. Top-down is no good. Grass roots alone is not enough.

This strategy differs from other in-the-system attempts. It is not the old, temporary Communist Party plan of submerging ideology and supporting moderates against reactionaries and potential fascists. Instead it stresses the presentation of ideology—in the form of post-capitalist blueprints and a searing critique of corporate capitalism—as the most important part of the strategy. Nor

is this the familiar liberal or social democratic plan for supporting the "best men" or "good liberals." It calls for the encouragement of new candidates who are committed to the post-capitalist blueprints. Nor is it the newly developing strategy of single-city reform, which seems to have no avenue to national political power.

There are several merits to this plan. For one thing, it allows you to fight ideological battles instead of spending endless hours and dollars getting on the ballot and registering voters. For another, it allows you to bypass longstanding attachments to party labels on the part of the people (blue-collar and white-collar workers) you most hope to reach. But most important, it allows you to contend for working people's sympathy without helping to elect conservative Republicans, which would be the major result of third-party efforts that were very successful. In other words, it allows you to work for a long-term change in people's allegiance to the tenets of corporate capitalism without doing damage to the short-run, pocketbook issues so rightfully of concern to the middle American of blue and white collar.

Working Americans are not going to abandon the Democratic Party for a third party of the Left. They know something that American Leftists little perceive—that because of the nature of the U. S. political system, with its several constraints toward a two-party system, their only hope for change lies within the Democratic Party. With the help of their liberal friends in the ADA, working-class leaders will fight bitterly—as they did in the Henry Wallace campaign in 1948—against any third party which might diminish the chances of bread-and-butter Democrats in regular elections.

It will be objected that the major problem with this strategy is that the Democratic Party is "controlled" by the wealthy fat cats, conservative Southerners and urban machine leaders. And so it is. But these are precisely the groups who would have to be defeated by a third party anyhow. It would be necessary to break their hold on Democratic voters, who are the people any third party would have to attract. My thought is to do this within the loose structure of the

Democratic Party, where the short-run interests of the working classes are protected.

This is not a plan to wreck the Democratic Party. That is, no "rule or ruin." There would be no running on a third-party ticket if candidates lost in the primaries. Only two things are required to be a good Democrat—to register, and to support the candidate elected in the primary. No ideological credentials are required to be a part of the party, and Revolutionary Democrats would work to keep it that way. Loyalty to the party would be essential. If anyone is going to bolt, let it be the fat cats and the Southern bosses (as many of them did in 1972). The task would be to transform the Democratic Party, and the way to do that is to develop a set of blueprints which Democrats can ratify again and again by the candidates they nominate in party primaries and at party conventions. For Democratic Party ideology is what Democrats say it is—and what they say it is is determined by the people Democrats elect to attend party conventions and nominate to stand in general elections.

Given the relative openness of this process, an ideological battle fought at all levels from precinct to President could have rather dramatic results in a relatively short time. The paltry battle fought by Eugene McCarthy in 1968 first suggested this possibility, and the one-man efforts of George McGovern and George Wallace in 1972 only reinforce it. Remembering how much appeal they had running as single candidates with virtually no ideas, consider what could be accomplished by a blueprint-based effort with thousands of candidates.

The moment is ripe

As I came to believe in the soundness of this strategy between early 1970 and 1972, I repeatedly said that the year 1972 was not the time to try to implement it. I believed that the New American Movement and the Peace and Freedom Party deserved a free hand in their separate attempts to show that they could develop a Left politics which could improve upon the various unsuccessful efforts which led to the demise of the New Left between 1968 and 1970. But

neither of these political thrusts, in my opinion, has been successful. The experience of the New American Movement shows that any movement in America needs an electoral strategy; and the experience of the Peace and Freedom Party demonstrates once again that a third party will be ignored by working-class Americans and used by the conservatives—as the Republicans secretly did in California in 1972—in an attempt to divide the Democrats.

Given the failures of other Left strategies, I think the time is now ripe to give a new strategy a serious try. The idea would be to organize Revolutionary Democrats into small groups of the kind suggested earlier so that they could begin to formulate the post-capitalist blueprints on which candidates could run in 1974 and 1976. As the blueprints are developed, candidates could begin contending at all levels for precinct posts, county chairmanships and party nominations for elected government positions.

Until more Americans see the world through anti-capitalist perspectives, and believe in concrete blueprints, there is no hope for any kind of "radical" action that transcends one or another single issue that is the concern of the moment, whether that concern be nuclear testing, the Vietnam War, racism, inflation, pollution or corruption. I think the idea of presenting alternatives to corporate capitalism by running in Democratic Party elections at all levels might be a reasonable way to proceed in creating this new "consciousness." The other ways have not worked, American Leftism is again at a low point, and this particular strategy has not been tried before. True, there is more to a successful program than I have prescribed here—including the constant need to be working through a variety of means toward the neutralization of the armed forces.[2] But the idea of challenging the Democratic Party from within would be the new starting point.

So consider the following framework: Break the ideological hegemony of the corporate capitalists by bringing the struggle home to the Democratic Party. Become

Revolutionary Democrats dedicated to replacing corporate capitalism with concrete blueprints for a post-capitalist, post-corporate America.

NOTES

1. See James Weinstein's excellent *The Decline of Socialism in America, 1912-1925*, for evidence of how intoxicating the Soviet revolution of 1917 was for American Leftists. I agree with Weinstein that the Left has made no major inroads into the American underclasses since that long-ago time.

2. The shocking and bitterly ugly turn of events in Chile in September is only the most recent evidence for this basic axiom. In 1968, in a speech arguing for a continuance of nonviolent direct action, I noted that "everyone knows that any serious revolution must not only isolate the ruling social class and eliminate its economic base, but it must do away with the army that is its ultimate instrument." I then suggested the Left should oppose a standing army such as the power elite is now trying to create, and that as a movement grew in the United States, it would have to have members join the military and become advocates of "one thing and one thing only—the subservience of the military to the civilian government, the refusal to take sides in an internal political controversy."

The Weather Underground.
Against the common enemy.

This is a call to organize the people and to act. We must now apply our analysis to our particular situation, mobilize the masses and fight. Our goal for this period is to help build a mass anti-imperialist movement and to build the armed struggle, the guerrilla forces. Legal and clandestine struggle are both necessary: agitation and attack, peaceful methods and violent methods, sometimes organizing the people step-by-step, and sometimes taking a leap thru action to a new level. Mass work and armed struggle are united in revolution: each needs to support and affirm and complement the other. These are different fronts, interdependent and allied against the common enemy.

Aboveground and underground, we face the same political questions: Who do we organize? How do we bring our politics to life in practice? How do we sustain the struggle?

Our enemy is US imperialism, the enemy of all humankind. Our goal is to attack imperialism's ability to exploit and wage war against all oppressed peoples. Our final goal is the complete destruction of imperialism, the seizure of the means of production and the building of socialism. To create the conditions in which we can take the offensive, destroy the old system and build a new life, we must weaken and at least partly destroy the empire. The weakest points of empire lie in its control of the colonies, and this is why Third World liberation is leading the struggle against imperialism.

We need organization. Activists are searching for direction—some common ideas, strategy, and practice to unite around. It is frustrating and crippling to individual revolutionaries and groups to have no unified impact on history as it is being made. We all feel the need to work as part of a whole, larger than ourselves, to see our individual contributions add up to something meaningful. Organization unites, gives direction and breadth to particular political work. Activists and militants want to build something bigger, where activity leads to shared results, where masses of people can organize their strength. Anti-imperialist organization is what is needed.

We believe that communist-minded organizers can take the initiative now and lead. Move from small to large. Practice and hard work, boldness and a willingness to intervene in every struggle, big or little. There is room for lots of creativity in application and choice of work. Go to the people. Organize and mobilize. Build the struggle. Read and study. Carry your books. There is no substitute for practice in determining the revolutionary path. Conditions are developing more rapidly than is easily realized. This is not yet a program; rather it is an ideological foundation and the tools for building agitational work.

Go to the people

The US people entered the 70's weary of war, skeptical of government leaders, uncertain about the future. Masses of people have been torn away from imperial mythology, from the standard of male supremacy, from allegiance to the state. In search of more drastic solutions to the current social dislocations, people open to the possibliity of revolutionary consciousness. The 70's bring inflation, recession, unemployment, the chance of war, and crisis after crisis in the lives of millions here. We can foresee a time of food riots, unemployment councils, tenant's anti-eviction associations, neighborhood groups, anti-war organizations. The left must organize itself to understand the continuous crises of our time and mobilize the discontent into a force for freedom.

Organize poor and working people. Go to the neighborhoods, the schools, the social institutions, the work places. Agitate. Create struggle. Link up the issues that describe the system. Tell the truth.

We believe that radical teachers should work in schools in working class neighborhoods, in community or junior colleges. Radicalize other teachers, organize the parents, teach and encourage your students. Health workers can choose hospitals and clinics in poor communities. Cultural activists, street players, artists, writers should propagandize and relate to poor and working people. Community-controlled and counter-institutions should be made into insurgent bases.

Organize among youth. Organize among women. Communists should play a big role in these movements, these popular upheavals which spawned us. This is our strength. Revolutionize existing projects and movements, analyze real situations, intervene with a revolutionary anti-imperialist perspective.

Organize to survive. Support the people's right to food, adequate shelter and decent health care. Oppose HEW attacks on women and the poor. Fight to live.

Impeach Nixon and jail him for his major crimes. He is one of the top criminals of the century, a warmaker, a lifetaker. His isolation and exposed condition is the mirror-image of US defeat in Vietnam. Nixon merits the people's justice.

Politics in command

There are a thousand threads of forward motion in the social explosion of our times. A thousand threads to untangle and engage. Find a way for everyone to fight the enemy. Unite the anti-imperialists. There are some politics that are necessary for successful activity: things to carry with us in our work.

Internationalism

Revolutionaries are internationalists. Our job is to build international class consciousness, to make connections among people. A good program must synthesize—not separate—the struggles of Third World peoples with our own: to uncover the relationship between Watergate and the Vietnam War, to nourish our identification with the struggle of Cuban women rather than our distinctness, to find the commonality between the white worker and the unemployed Puerto Rican. A good program mobilizes and teaches.

The rulers scapegoat Third World people for the failures of the system. They say: "The American people are being deprived of their right to oil by the Arabs;" "Welfare mothers, not the defense budget, are responsiblé for higher taxes;" "Chilean socialism stole our copper mines." We cannot allow the maintenance of a pacified sector of privileged workers here; rather we can find ways to identify our interests with the interests of all oppressed people everywhere and sharpen the class struggle.

Liberal, anti-internationalist slogans have been put forth throughout the history of our movement: "You can only organize people around their own interest." "Don't fight other people's battles." "Support for Third World struggles is 'guilt' politics." These slogans encourage the belief that oppression is individual and must be fought by small groups distinct from and against other groups. These slogans assume that the individualism, narrowness and fear that are a major part of the socializing process here should be accepted by movement programs. They emphasize competition, a short-term sense of the struggle, and feed racism and all kinds of chauvinism. We think that organizers should oppose the liberal slogans with the communist slogan: "Fight US imperialism, the common enemy."

How to move?

Oppose nuclear war and US threat of nuclear war. Defeat nuclear sabre-rattling.

Oppose imperialist war and aggression wherever it occurs. Oppose US armed intervention. Defend Indochina from future attacks. Get the US out of the Mideast. Independence for Puerto Rico.

Also, watch for the quiet but sinister ways warfare is waged on sisters and brothers in the Third World. Expose and oppose AID programs, cultural and economic penetration, the multinational corporations, population control. Don't let them sneak around.

Oppose racism in practice. Racism is the main and most consistent weapon for holding back the revolutionary struggle. Skin color will be a brand to turn proletarians against one another until this brand is decisively rejected by white folks. The oppressed nation of Black people is the leading anti-imperialist force in our country. No doubt about it. History, continuity, militancy—even in hard times. Black and other Third World leadership has, in recent years, been the most internationalist and the most militant. Racism cuts us up, cuts us off from this leadership. All vestiges of racist thinking or action among revolutionaries must be attacked in the most forthright manner. No quarter can be given to racism in our relations with the people we are organizing. We must learn how to reject and expose the racism without rejecting the person. Represent solidarity with Third World people whenever possible.

Win a base of support for prison struggles and oppose attacks by the state on Third World revolutionaries. The greater the resistance by the people, the more widespread and successful, the greater will be the repression from the state. We can prepare for future repression by planning the next stage of advance and attack. Today people are confronted by prisons, courts, military-injustice and racism, police brutality, spying

on and controlling of civilian life, the terror of rape, discrimination, channeling and brainwashing. Does this constitute fascism or a threat of fascism? Again the main thing is the distinction between oppressor and oppressed nations. Third World people have been living under fascist conditions for generations; at the same time, the majority population feels it has some democratic rights worth defending. These contradictory perceptions reveal something that is true: fascism in the oppressor nation is the application here of the colonial policies of empire. It is selective and partial. It has always been applied to Native Americans, Black people, Puerto Ricans, Chicanos, the oppressed generally as well as those who unite with the oppressed—radicals, reds.

Fascism in this country is not a challenge to those in power by some more reactionary gang on the outside. Fascism is perpetrated on Third World people from the seats of power: the Pentagon, the Congress, the White House, the Supreme Court. In these places liberal and fascist tendencies compete, but they also connive and conspire. Our strategy must be unity against existing fascism for the liberation of all oppressed people. Imprisoned fighters face the brunt of fascist repression and are a center of our struggle. A solid bridge of communications, news, politics and support sustain sisters and brothers under brutal isolation and torture, makes a difference in the treatment of political prisoners and their chances of release. Connections maximize the impact of prison politics as an essential and leading part of our movement. Support Ruchell Magee. Defend the Attica brothers.

Like Dr. Du Bois said, "The problem of the twentieth century is the problem of the color line." It's our view that white revolutionaries should look toward building principled alliances, coalitions and working relationships with Third World people when possible. Support for self-determination can't be an excuse for failure to engage with Third World revolutionaries in day-to-day work. A new practice should develop in which we learn from, struggle with, but don't prejudge or attempt to direct Third World freedom fighters. Full understanding and support for self-determination is the basis for this kind of getting together. Win an understanding of the right of oppressed peoples to determine their own destinies.

Read Black and Third World publications. Understand the richness of the movements, the current debates, the direction and growth of struggles. Study Malcolm and George Jackson. Learn from the great teachers.

Women and revolution

The women's movement has changed the consciousness of millions of women, and the crises of US society are creating resistance and revolutionaries among women every day. This is a good time to do a lot of organizing among women, to bring the full scope of anti-imperialist and revolutionary politics into women's lives. Storm the institutions which oppress women. Direct our force against the men who control these institutions.

Support Assata Shakur, Marilyn Buck, Lolita Lebron and other women in prisons. Demonstrate to free our sisters in the Saigon jails.

It is our view that women working in revolutionary organizations with men should organize themselves into women's groups, sections, brigades, caucuses to build our solidarity, to oppose sexism, to reach out, involve, organize among women and to strive together for the full liberation of women.

Sexism within the culture of the revolutionary movement denies the full contribution of women and distorts political direction. We need an anti-sexist revolution in this country to create the basis for a new society which genuinely empowers women. The revolution must be fought for women as well as by women.

Sexism manifests itself in relationships among people, and must be fought on this level too. Men must make a continuing commitment to understanding and changing sexist ways. Criticism and self-criticism are

our tools for this struggle: fanshen, the turning over, transformation.

Militancy

A movement has no reason to exist if it doesn't fight. The system needs to be overthrown; revolutionaries must prepare for that necessity at all points along the way. Revolutionary movements must be contending for power, planning how to contend for power, or recovering from setbacks in contending for power. Certainly every movement must learn to fight correctly, sometimes retreating, sometimes advancing. But fighting the enemy must be its reason for being. We build a fighting movement.

Militancy stirs the imagination and raises the vision of victory. Militancy in a street demonstration, in a courtroom, in a rally, in a prison takeover, is recognized and respected as an uncompromising statement. It is a confrontation with the opposing system. Involving people in militant action trains and teaches. It is both an example and a strategy. Militant action is related to the understanding that the struggle is not merely for separate issues but is ultimately for power—necessarily including armed struggle to defeat the oppressive forces of state. To leave people unprepared to fight the state is to seriously mislead about the inevitable nature of what lies ahead.

Some on the left dissociate mass struggle from revolutionary violence and condemn any act of public militancy or armed struggle as adventurist. This is characteristic of oppressor-nation movements where violence is raised to a question of abstract principle, and the illusion is fostered that imperialism will decay peacefully: "Violence turns people off," "It's too early," "Violence only brings down repression."

The movement should argue for and explain armed action, develop parallel strategies, openly support the thrust and political content of revolutionary armed actions, claim and spread the message of struggles, help create the "sea" for the guerrillas to swim in. Don't talk to the FBI. Resist grand jury probes of revolutionary struggles. Laying the basis for armed struggle is also the responsibility of mass organizers.

From the very beginning of guerrilla action, mass armed capability develops. Its spontaneity will be slowly transformed into the energy of a popular armed force.

Many levels of clandestine propaganda action can be carried out which spread the consciousness of action and give people a way to learn. Spray-painting, rip-offs of corporate files, blood on the murderers. We have done these types of action ourselves, including stinkbombing a Rockefeller appearance in N.Y.C. and doing the same to the mouthpieces of the Chile junta when they travelled in the US after the murder of Allende. Build a people's militia.

A successful movement needs to keep part of its organization away from the eyes of the state. This should be part of the practice of every revolutionary. The survival and continuity of the revolutionary movement, of the activists and the supporters over a long period of time, depends on having networks and resources not exposed to computer patterns, electronic surveillance and infiltration of the repressive apparatus. The continued existence of underground organizations shows this can be done.

Building a capacity to survive over time is no substitute for militancy now in our daily work. An uncompromising, confrontational approach to political work is the best way to inspire the people, build organization, and learn to fight.

Revolution

This is a deathly culture. It beats its children and discards its old people, imprisons its rebels and drinks itself to death. It breeds and educates us to be socially irresponsible, arrogant, ignorant and anti-political. We are the most technologically advanced people in the world and the most politically and socially backward.

The quality of life of a Chinese peasant is better than ours. The Chinese have free and adequate health care, a meaningful political education, productive work, a place to live, something to eat and each has a sense of her or himself as part of a whole people's shared historical purpose. We may eat more and have more access to gadgets, but we are constantly driven by competition, insecurity, uncertainty and fear. Work is wasteful and meaningless and other people are frightening and hateful. This is no way to live.

Anti-imperialism is our cultural revolution. We must rescue ourselves from the consequences of being the base area for imperialism—the base area for war, piracy, rape and murder. In this reclamation process, we come to a better understanding of our history and ourselves. This is not for a small group but for millions of people. Much has happened in the world and in the US to move this process along. Few people really believe anymore in the great civilizing leadership role of the US. Few still think that capitalism is the best of all possible ways to meet the economic needs of the world's peoples, or that Black and Third World people are sub-human labor material destined to support the more worthwhile activities of the white supermen. Few really believe that men will go on indefinitely monopolizing power in a supremacist anti-women society. Stated simply, our strategy is to base ourselves on the trends of change, to revolutionize and push them on, and to intervene in everything.

Where do the US people look to learn about social revolution and consciousness, struggle and purpose? A decade of resistance in Vietnam demonstrated to highly "developed" Westerners that we have everything to learn from "underdeveloped" peoples. The revolutionary struggle is the social form from which will deal with the crisis of imperialism in decline. We learn from Third World people who resist US tyranny, with a unity born in a sense of collective power and purpose. We learn from our own history and examples of courage, struggles and communality which are here for us to search out and celebrate.

Our movement must discard the baggage of the oppressor society and become new women and new men, as Che taught. All forms of racism, class prejudice, and male chauvinism must be torn out by the roots. For us, proletarianization means recognizing the urgency of revolution as the only solution to our own problems and the survival of all oppressed people. It means commitment, casting our lot with the collective interest and discarding the privileges of empire. It means recognizing that revolution is a lifetime of fighting and transformation, a risky business and ultimately a decisive struggle against the forces of death.

Proletarianization is a process that is necessarily on-going. Breaking-thru to a higher level of engagement and commitment in 1968 is no guarantee that the level will be sustained in 1974. Standing still over time is sliding back. Commitment and engagement must be continually renewed.

We create the seeds of the new society in the struggle for the destruction of the empire. For our generation that has meant the birth of communalism and collective work in the most individualist, competitive society in the world. Revolution is the midwife bringing the new society into being from the old.

The culture of our communities, the people we try to become, are forged in the process of revolutionary war—the struggles for liberation. We are called on to commit ourselves to this struggle, and time is pressing. People are already dying. Lives are wasted and worn. Life itself depends on our ability to deal a swift death blow to the monster.

Fred R. Harris. Up with those who're down.

I grew up in Oklahoma during the depression years, the 1930s. Franklin Roosevelt's background was radically different from that of my sharecropping, common-labor family.

Yet we identified with Roosevelt. More than that, we revered him. I think of his voice first—on the radio. We *watched* the radio in those days. We didn't just listen. We sat around it and watched the radio, and we often heard Franklin Roosevelt's voice—reassuring, hopeful.

Later, I saw his face in newsreels—confident, determined, jolly. He was busy. He was doing things; he was changing things. And God knows we needed things done and things changed.

There was no need to waste your time telling us of any flaws in his program. We didn't want to hear it. We did not believe it. (We didn't even believe he was crippled. My mind told me he was, but I am still shocked today to see pictures that actually show it.)

We were for Franklin Roosevelt because he was for us. And he was against those who were against us. He didn't pussyfoot around about it. He called them "malefactors of great wealth." And worse.

What is happening (has happened) to the old Roosevelt Coalition? That's become the favorite parlor-game question of political writers. It was a coalition of poor and working-class blacks and whites, farmers and intellectuals. Can such groups be held together no longer?

I grew up thinking "Okie" was a derogatory word, a slur. It was a long time before I read *The Grapes of Wrath*, because everybody I knew in Oklahoma said, "Old John Steinbeck just tried to make us look bad." Years later, an Oklahoma governor started a campaign to build "Okie" into a term of pride, as Negroes had done with "black." I like that. And I wish *The Grapes of Wrath* were required reading in our schools. It would teach people something about how to keep body and soul together in hard times. We'd learn that by ourselves none of us has the power to win out.

In a lush farming valley in California, once, I campaigned for the Democratic party's candidates. "I can't understand these Okies here," a local official told me. "I remember thirty years ago they came in here and lived in old car bodies; today, they are some of the strongest supporters George Wallace has."

Had they changed? Had Democratic liberalism changed? Had the times changed? Was it a flaw in them or a failure in the appeal? During the last several years I've tried to think out more clearly the answers to those questions.

While I was wondering about Okies, a friend of mine was wondering about Italian-Americans. Monsignor Geno Baroni of the U.S. Catholic Conference, now doing ground-breaking work among white ethnics, has gone through a process similar to mine. In the early 1960s he was in the forefront of the civil rights movement in America. But, before long, some black people began to say to him, "What are you doing down here with us? We don't want you. We can run *our* affairs ourselves. White people are the majority in this country; they have the power. They can change things, not us. So why don't you leave us alone and go work with your own kind?" This hurt.

But it began to make sense, too. He became more conscious that some of his own people, Italian coal-mining families in Pennsylvania, while they loved him, derided his work with "the niggers in Washington." There was obviously something wrong with his message, or his approach, if he couldn't even convince his own family.

I had a similar realization when I served as a member of the Kerner Commission, which looked into the awful riots that ignited so many of our cities in the fearsome summer of 1967. We rightly reported that racism and black people's feelings of powerlessness were the root causes of the violence.

One year later, things were one year worse. Three years later, I served as cochairman of the Commission on the Cities in the Seventies of the National Urban Coalition. Things were *three* years worse.

"We've been talking to you politicians for five or six years, and still nothing gets done," a black woman told me in Atlanta.

She was right. Things are not better. They are worse—for both blacks and whites. Housing is worse. Health care delivery is worse—it's harder to get a doctor or to get

into a hospital. Health costs are worse—it's harder to pay for needed medical attention. Education is worse. Unemployment is worse. Crime is worse.

Ringing appeals to conscience, to join together against "the common enemies of man," have not been very effective.

A good many people unfortunately perceived the Kerner Commission message to be: "You should, out of the goodness of your heart and because of your Christian duty, pay more taxes to help poor black people in Detroit."

Their response was, "Bullshit! I've got enough troubles of my own. I'm barely making a living, and I'm already paying too much tax."

If I needed any further demonstration, this showed me that you can't have a mass movement without the masses.

As chairman of the Democratic National Committee in 1969, I had already been forced to think about that. Kevin Phillips was writing in *The Emerging Republican Majority* that the more the Democratic party worried about the problems of black people, poor people, and the people of the central cities, the more it would drive the rest of the people into the Republican party. That did not seem morally right to me, and I did not want it to be true.

It began to become clear to me that you can't appeal to black people and poor people and the people of the central cities on the basis of their own self-interest and to everybody else on the basis of morality. That kind of an appeal is the luxury of the intellectual elite—for people who are, themselves, socially and economically secure.

Instead of trying to convert people, you have to think again about why we are banded together as an organized society.

It's instructive to study the Constitution and formal governmental system of even the most unstable Latin American "republic." It may look great in print, but things haven't worked out that way. The tax laws may sound all right, but nobody pays any attention to them.

Governments are more than their basic documents. The United States Constitution is, indeed, a splendid instrument, our system of representative government a marvel.

But they work because of the social contract that underlies them—because we have, in a way, agreed to live together in the same house and to share in duties and privileges on some kind of fair—not necessarily equal—basis. That applies to *all* members of the society.

A few weeks after the terrible summer floods of 1972 in Pennsylvania, I saw HUD Secretary George Romney on television explaining why the government couldn't provide any greater and faster assistance to the wretched flood victims trying to live and rebuild. He was outraged when Governor Milton Shapp reminded him of how fast the government had come to the aid of Lockheed and Penn Central. Romney's response wasn't very persuasive: "Politics," he grouched.

Secretary Romney wound up the interview by calling on all Americans to send contributions to the Red Cross to help those who had lost their homes and belongings.

Now, nobody said those flood victims weren't deserving. Nobody said it was their own fault. Nobody said they weren't trying to help themselves. But here was their government, not thinking in terms of the *rights* of the victims, but in terms of appealing for voluntary charity to them. What kind of social contract is that?

There, exactly, is the problem with traditional liberalism, the flaw in "conscience" politics. Our society should not depend upon charity, not even charity by government. People want what's rightly theirs. It is that kind of system to which they thought they had assented.

Each American inherits our political system and history. His or her right to be a free person and to have an equal chance, economically and politically, is a part of the social contract that binds us together.

The social contract is threatening to tear apart. We see rising crime. Rising alcoholism. Rising use of narcotics. Rising violence and self-destructive behavior. Rising apathy and withdrawal. Rising anger and polarization between races and classes.

These are symptoms. Symptoms of a society in deep stress. And treating symptoms alone will not alleviate the stress.

In 1971 I visited a Chicano-run narcotics referral center in a storefront in Oakland, California. It's a neighborhood operation run by ex-addicts. That month alone, 147 people had voluntarily come in off the streets to be sent to a detoxification center.

I talked at some length with the terribly discouraged center workers. They agreed that heroin would not be so freely available except for considerable official corruption, but they said, "That's for you politicians to do something about." They uniformly made clear that the problem was much deeper.

"We're not so much interested in the supply," said one volunteer worker who had first become a heroin addict in San Quentin, where, he said, the drug was even more plentiful than on most city streets. "There's been heroin on the streets of Oakland ever since I can remember, and there will always be heroin—or something else.

"People walk in here looking for help. They go through the hell of detox and come out clean. But where can they go from there? They're back on the streets. They don't have any education. They can't get a job. They're hassled by the police.

"The first thing you know they're shooting up again, and when their habit builds back up to seventy-five or a hundred dollars a day, they're back here again looking for help.

"Man, we're not so much interested in the supply. We're interested in the *demand*. Something's gotta be done about the demand."

Similarly, most political solutions tend to deal only with the symptoms—and not the causes.

The problems of blacks and whites in America overlap to a considerable degree.

Marshall Frady wrote in *Life* magazine in 1972 about Will D. Campbell, a Yale-educated Southern Baptist preacher in Nashville, Tennessee, who'd had to do a lot of the same hard thinking that Monsignor Baroni and I had done.

"Some of my black friends like Stokely Carmichael," he told Frady, "started telling me, 'Look here, man, we pretty much got things cool and together with *our* folks. If you want to help out real bad, why don't you go to work on *your* people!' I said, 'Man, you happen to be talking about red-necks—they'll *kill* me.' And he said, 'That sort of means they're the problem then, don't it?'"

Answering that question, Campbell began to spend a good part of his time with working-class Southern whites, and he began to see a parallel. "Whatever it is that's keeping the red-neck a Kluxer and the black man a nigger—whatever's keeping them outside and poor and without any hope—is the same thing for both," he said.

In some ways it's been more damaging for the white. "In a way, see," Campbell said, "the red-neck's been the special victim of the whole system. It took his head away. The system got about everything else from the black man—his back, a portion of his spirit maybe—but it never really managed to get his head. All along, the black man's known more or less what's been going on. But the red-neck—hell, he's never known who the enemy was. If you remember anything about the course of Populism, every time the poor white began getting together in natural alliance with the equally dispossessed black, he'd be told that it meant blacks were going to ravish his wimminfolks, and the Bolsheviks were going to invade the courthouse. He's never known how he's been had."

Monsignor Baroni found the same thing with urban white ethnics. Their interests have been ignored as much as have the interests of the blacks and the Southern whites.

In America we have both a race problem *and* a class problem. And each makes the other worse.

Racism *is* a central fact of American history—of human history for that matter. It is not a passing thing. It has been with us from the first, and it's still with us. Realizing that requires a wrenching change in white thinking. White history is what we've studied. The white experience is what we've lived. But there have been blacks—and other minorities—around all the time. They are still around, and we have been made painfully aware of it.

We cannot compromise on race. That's what we've always tried, and it's morally wrong. But, in addition to that, compromise is much too costly—in blood, in money, and in self-esteem.

Economic class is also a central fact of American history—again, of human history for that matter. Income, wealth, and ownership in America—and the power that goes with them—have become increasingly concentrated in fewer and fewer hands. We cannot compromise on that issue either.

But in recent years there has come to be a growing and justified distrust of government itself, and of politicians, and of the "programmatic" approach to basic problems.

The steelworker in Gary, the small farmer in Oklahoma, the Chicano mother in Los Angeles, the old person in Miami, the native American in Arizona, the teacher in Cleveland, the garbage worker in New York—they all know that a little more housing, a little more job training, a few more food stamps, a few more summer jobs—though we need them all—will not do.

The traditional liberal approach is to look at old people who have nutritional problems and offer food stamps, or to look at old people who have housing problems and offer housing programs, or to look at old people who have health problems and offer Medicare. What most old people lack is money.

Farmers who have no economic security, black people who can't get into a building trades union, auto workers going mad with the dullness of their work—what they all lack is power.

And missing from all their lives, and the lives of many of us, is the integrating theme in our society that might give integrating worth to our existence.

When I was Democratic Chairman, back in the fall of 1969, I began to speak about "the New Populism." I didn't know yet what that meant, totally, but I knew where it was headed. I knew that the New Populism had to deal with individual rights and individual power, as opposed to concentrated economic and political power. It had to deal with the problems of economic class, as well as with the race. It had to deal with distrust of government. It had to deal with concentrated wealth and corporate power.

The New Populism—and it doesn't matter what you call it—means that most Americans are commonly exploited, but that, if we get ourselves together, we are a popular majority and can take back our government. It seeks to put America back together again—across the lines of race, age, sex, and region. Those in the coalition don't have to love each other. I wish they would. But all they have to do is recognize their common interests.

The New Populism promises a more stable, secure society of self-esteem—for the rich as well as for the not so rich. Most of us will be willing to pay and sacrifice for that promise if we can be assured that, unlike in the past, what we pay and what we give will really make a difference.

The New Populism is against bigness, against concentrated economic and political power—whether it is in government, corporations, unions, or institutions.

The choice that will dominate the 1970s is a choice between individual liberty and power or greater governmental, corporate, and institutional power.

Our national goal, simply stated, should be:

to distribute income and wealth more fairly;

to deconcentrate economic and political power; and

to make real the power and liberty of the people.

The *public* statement of this goal is vitally important. It will mean that, thereafter, governments, political parties, and politicians will regularly have to give an account of their stewardship in terms of this New Populist goal.

And the stated goal will supply some overall meaning to the work of ordinary politicians—trying to change a clause here or improve a program there. It will lend value to the way they spend their days.

This book is an attempt to update the New Populism and to give an overview of it. It doesn't try to provide an answer for everything. It doesn't, for example, say much about the critical problem of population growth—though there is strong evidence that a rise in income has more to do with a decrease in birthrate than anything else does. It doesn't attempt to deal with foreign policy—though the Ellsberg Pentagon Papers seem to indicate that a populist foreign policy, based upon the people's full knowledge and consent, would much more likely tend to be in tune with our professed ideals.

I've always believed that a senator has dual responsibilities: to work within the forum of which he is a member; and to try to change the climate within which the forum itself operates. I spent eight years in the United States Senate trying to do both. I want to spend most of my time now helping to change the public climate.

The civil rights movement, the women's movement, the ecology movement, the end-the-war movement—none of these were originated by politicians. They began as citizens' movements.

I once saw painted on a wall in a Latin American country: *"Arriba con los de abajo"*—"Up with those who are down." Not a bad slogan for a citizens' movement.

It's not a bad principle for a society.

*

Etzkowitz & Schwab—Is America Necessary—40

In this essay we will demonstrate that political science does not represent a single objective method of analyzing political issues. Rather, political science has existed from its inception as a debate between political philosophies as to how a political order should be constituted. It began as a debate between conservatives and liberals. More recently socialists have entered the academic arena to contest the principles of conservatism and liberalism and to offer a clear alternative.

Political science begins with Plato. Plato was an Athenian/Greek political philosopher who lived from 427–347 B.C. For political scientists, his major work is *The Republic*,[1] wherein his ideas about the ideal state are discussed. Speaking through Socrates, Plato maintains that the only just political system is one ruled by a Philosopher-King, an individual who allows his reason to rule his passion. Because he is reasonable, a Philosopher-King will not act fanatically, savagely, or angrily, but in the best interest of the Republic. For Plato, the term justice means doing what one is best fitted to do. A reasonable person is the one best fitted to rule. A Philosopher-King, the most reasonable of men, is the person best qualified to run political affairs. The political structure of Plato's Republic is one ruled by elites—a small group of people who know best. This is precisely the political structure that present day conservatives believe in.

Aristotle, a student of Plato, was a political philosopher who lived from 384–322 B.C. Although he agreed that a republic ruled by elites was the ideal regime, Aristotle felt that in the real world this system was not attainable.[2] The kind of person fitted to be a Philosopher-King is seldom born. Aristotle proposed an alternate political structure for the Greek city-state or *polis*. For Aristotle, the practicable regime was one that rested on the middle class, which he defined as neither the very rich nor the very poor. In his time the middle class consisted of farmers who owned their own land. It was in the interests of the middle class to have a moderate, orderly, regime that would serve the general population by protecting their property. The middle class "do not, like the poor, covet the goods of others. The best form of political society is one where power is vested in the middle class."[3]

Beyond objectivity:
conservative, liberal, and socialist politics—a paradigm

In Aristotle's system of government, or *polity,* passions would be reduced, the population would be happy, and political demands would be few. The structure of the regime was to be made up of several branches of government: legislative, executive, and judicial. The legislature consists of the middle-class population of a city-state. The judiciary would enforce laws for the common good, and would adjudicate conflicts between individuals. The magistrate—executive—would enforce laws passed by a legislature. Together the magistrate, legislature, and judiciary would ensure a "good" life for the population.[4] In the *polity* the primary arm of government was the legislature as it was the representative of the middle class. Present day liberalism, to some degree, traces its roots to Aristotelian thought. Liberals maintain that the rights of property must be respected. Nevertheless, they demand that the rights and freedoms of those who do not own property must be protected by the middle class. For Aristotle, government as representative of the middle class, is the primary institution responsible for protecting the rights of the entire population. What Aristotle called the "good life," liberals call "the pursuit of happiness."

The difference of opinion between Plato and Aristotle as to who should rule became the basic issue of debate between conservatives and liberals. The discussion of which rule was best suited for the people was renewed in the sixteenth and seventeenth centuries by British philosophers Thomas Hobbes (1588–1679) and John Locke (1632–1704). As a result of the beginning of industrialism, major owners of property in England became opposed to rule by an absolute monarch whose interests did not serve theirs.

Hobbes maintained in his book *Leviathan*[5] that people and the state were best served by a Leviathan—a leader having total executive, legislative, and judicial power over his constituents. The only right he would not have was to take another's life *violently.* This system of government would allow the two greatest benefits that political order could offer—peace and defense—to be attained. Misery, civil war, and anarchy would not take place. The Leviathan would permit a strong and powerful English state to survive and prosper. The Hobbesian argument of government by an elite is the seventeenth century equivalent of Plato's Republic, and as such represents the continuity of conservative political philosophy.

John Locke, in his *Two Treatises of Government,*[6] continues the argument put forth by Aristotle. Locke maintains that in order for property to be protected, government is necessary,[7] and that civil society—a political system based on laws—is the best society for protecting ownership. He also argues that the rights and liberties of people must be protected—no person should be denied life, liberty, or property without recourse to laws. With liberty and property protected the people will willingly support their government and civil strife will be limited. In Locke's theory, only if private property is protected can an economy prosper. For if people can not be sure that what they own will remain theirs then they will have little incentive to engage in commerce and industry to increase their own wealth and the wealth of society. Locke specified the tripartite division of government to a greater extent than any political philosopher to his time. In his political system there are two executives. The *Executive* deals with domestic matters, while the *Federative* deals with issues of war and peace. Legislative and judicial functions are united in one body. It makes the laws and sees that they are equitably carried out. Legislative and executive functions are separate, with the legislature being the supreme institution.

In essence, Locke's political system is based on protecting private property. Property is best protected by a government that is receptive to the will of the people thus insuring against revolution. With the existence of justice the temptation to resort to civil war is avoided. The protection of property and money, the base upon which capitalism is built, is, in our analysis, the core of Locke's political system.

Liberals, such as Aristotle and Locke developed their political ideas in response to conservative political thought set forth by Plato and Hobbes. In the formation of the Republic of the United States the conservative approach is represented by Alexander Hamilton and the liberal approach by Thomas Jefferson. Hamilton, Secretary of the Treasury in the Presidential administraition of George Washington stood for a strong central government protective of Eastern commercial and propertied interests.[8] He proposed the establishment of a national banking system. He also stood for limiting states rights. Jefferson, Secretary of State under George Washington, and one of the authors of the Declaration of Independence argued to uphold the interests of small farmers who owned their own land. He also stood for a weak central government, and the expansion of personal liberties. Like Locke, it is Jefferson's belief that personal freedom would aid in securing private property because civil strife would be avoided. These two positions of Hamilton and Jefferson form the terms of a political debate that carries into our own time. This argument over which is the best system of rule is carried on in political science in academic journals, by teachers in the classroom, and in professional associations.

It is our belief that Plato, Hobbes, and Hamilton formulated the basic ideas of conservatism, and Aristotle, Locke, and Jefferson were the proponents of liberalism. Political science, as an academic discipline taught in universities, derives from historical conservative and liberal political thought.

In the United States the discipline of political science was established as a separate academic entity in the 1880s. It appeared at this time as a way of making a response to criticisms and demands levelled at government. During the late nineteenth century, a grass roots movement—populism—appeared to challenge the increased control of American society by large capital, banks, railroads, and trusts.[9] Small farmers were at the mercy of railroad interests who could charge as much as they wanted to transport farm produce. High interest rates were charged by banks and alternative sources of credit were not available. Small business was being taken over by large monopolies. Workers in industry and factories were ill paid and miserably treated. Individually, small property holders and workers could do little to save themselves. As an organized group—the populist movement—they formed a new challenge to the increased control of American society by conservatives. This opposition took the form of wildcat strikes, destruction of property of large business, and refusal to pay bank debts. The Populist Party was formed in 1890 to struggle against elite control of the American political system. In its 1892 platform the Populist Party maintained that

The fruits of the toil of millions are boldly stolen to build up colossal fortunes for a few. . . . The possessors of these (fortunes) despise the republic and endanger liberty. From the same prolific womb of government injustice we breed the two great classes—tramps and millionaires.[10]

Among the responses to the Populist political challenge was the formulation and intellectual defense of the American political system through the formation in 1903 of the American Political Science Association. The Journal of the Association, the *American Political Science Review*, was started in 1906. Conservative in origin, it dealt with issues relating to constitutional forms. The Journal articulated elite conservative views and placed them in an academic context. The *Political Science Quarterly*, which originated in New York's Columbia College in 1886 was another conservative journal "devoted to the historical, statistical, and comparative study of politics."[11] Like the *American Political Science Review* it originated as a response to populist upheaval. It justified the existing political process by analyzing issues through statistics and constitutional forms. Thus, the issues raised by Plato, Hobbes, and Hamilton were now academicised in footnoted scientific journal articles produced not by a few political philosophers but by an increasing number of Ph.D.s in political science. These first two journals, from their origin, dealt primarily with domestic constitutional issues.

With America's increased involvement in foreign affairs after World War I the Council on Foreign Relations, in 1922, issued the publication *Foreign Affairs*. Its goal was "to guide American public opinion by a broad hospitality to divergent ideas. . . ."[12] In dealing with international affairs, *Foreign Affairs* was an attempt to gain public support for American intervention abroad. Through the years its writers have been leading government figures. Among them: President John Kennedy, President Richard Nixon, Secretary of Defense Robert McNamara, and Secretary of State Henry Kissinger.

Until the 1960s academic political scientists, whether conservative or liberal, conducted their discussion in the same journals. In 1968 two major journals were established: *Comparative Politics* and *Comparative Political Studies*. *Comparative Politics* began publication because its originators felt that additional journals were necessary to publish "ongoing research and communication among specialists." "Dissatisfaction has been coupled with skepticism about the value of institutional and legal analysis."[13] *Comparative Politics* was established to deal with Western and non-Western countries because of the inadequacy of traditional approaches. *Comparative Political Studies* was set up to deal with "theoretical and empirical research articles by scholars engaged in cross-nation study."[14] Two years later, in 1970, the liberal *Foreign Policy* was begun as a counterpart to the conservative *Foreign Affairs.* According to the editors of *Foreign Policy* this journal appeared in order to "redirect . . . priorities from international to domestic affairs."[15] *Foreign Policy* stands for a less expansionist foreign policy and a greater allocation of American resources to domestic problems.

In the area of domestic affairs the liberal *Annals* of the American Academy of Political and Social Science was formed in 1891 in reaction to the conservative *Political Science Quarterly.* The purpose of the *Annals* was to discuss specific proposals for public policy to ameliorate domestic problems that affected large numbers of people such as health, education, housing, and hunger. In the 1960s and 1970s additional journals, such as the conservative *The Public Interest* and the liberal *Social Policy*, were formed to deal with specific issues.

The socialist perspective was seldom represented in American academia in any social science discipline until quite recently. Socialism existed as a theoretical concept and a political movement outside of the universities. Its basic premise, as formulated by Karl Marx (1818–1883), was that politics was essentially a struggle between those who owned the means of production and those who didn't. Marx dealt with the question of how political power can be taken from elites that have it and transferred to the masses.[16] The Marxian framework in its academic form is an interdisciplinary construct in which political science, economics, sociology, and other sciences are all seen as interrelated. All deal with different aspects of the basic question: How can power be wrested from elites?

Major Marxist journals with special relevance to political science are: *Science and Society, Monthly Review,* and *Politics and Society. Science and Society* was founded in 1936 "to meet the need, increasingly evident in the United States, for a journal dedicated to the growth of Marxian scholarship. It aims to publish articles . . . illustrating the manner in which Marxism integrates various scientific disciplines."[17] In 1949 *Monthly Review* began publication. It is "devoted to analyzing, from a socialist point of view, the most significant trends in domestic and foreign affairs."[18] In 1970 *Politics and Society* was first published. It offers social scientists an alternate forum for discussing issues that could not be dealt with in traditional journals "because the leading professional social science journals continue to be obsessed with technique at the expense of imagination, significance, and readability."[19] These journals along with *Socialist Revolution, Kapital-State,* and *Radical America* are important outlets in the United States for socialist academic thought.

Political science in the 1970s is still controlled by conservatives and liberals. This is evident by the continuing predominance of conservative and liberal journals. Only in the last three decades have alternatives to the conservative and liberal journals been established. The discussion as to which political system is best for the United States is a basic issue in all of the journals we have discussed. Their issues and views are mirrored in the lectures of professors and the course offerings of universities. For example, Georgetown University, the University of Chicago, the Massachusetts Institute of Technology (MIT), and Harvard University have political science departments supportive of American foreign policy. Harvard University, Yale University, the University of Oregon are examples of colleges whose political science departments offer courses supportive of American political institutions. Harvard, Yale, New York University Law School, and St. John's University Law School offer law courses supportive of the American legal system. All of these schools are controlled by conservative or liberal political science or law faculties. Few schools offer courses with a socialist perspective. Often only a single socialist is allowed in a political science department. Antioch Law School, and the State University of New York, College at Purchase are examples of those very few institutions that do have a concentration of socialists in their social science or law departments.

It is our belief that the discipline of political science as it currently exists is rigid. Political science now represents only two aspects of a debate from which the third relevant party—socialism—is typically excluded.[20] Unless socialists are allowed into academic political science departments in large numbers to participate in these debates, political science will remain irrelevant and will have to be discarded. If the major questions regarding the nature and future of our political system are to be dealt with then all schools of thought—conservatism, liberalism, and socialism—must be represented.

NOTES

1. Plato, *The Republic*. Translated by B. Jowett. New York: Random House.

2. Aristotle, *The Politics*. Translated and introduced by Ernest Barker. New York: Oxford University Press, 1962. Note particularly, Book II, "Review of Ideal States," in which Plato's *Republic* is discussed.

3. *Ibid.* p. 182.

4. *Ibid.* p. 5.

5. Thomas Hobbes, *Leviathan*. New York: E. P. Dutton and Co., 1950.

6. John Locke, *Two Treatises of Government*, Peter Laslett, ed. Cambridge, Mass: Cambridge University Press, 1960.

7. Important here is the essay by Robert A. Goldwin, "John Locke" in Leo Strauss and Joseph Cropsey, *History of Political Philosophy*, Chicago: Rand McNally & Co., 1963.

8. See, Henry Bamford Parkes, *The American Experience*, New York: Vintage Books, 1959. Vernon L. Parrington, *The Colonial Mind, 1620–1800*, New York: Harcourt, Brace and World, 1927. Stuart Gerry Brown, *Alexander Hamilton*, New York: Washington Square Press, 1967.

9. John Hicks. *The Populist Revolt*. Lincoln: University of Nebraska Press, 1961.

10. As quoted in Samuel Eliot Morison and Henry Steele Commager, *The Growth of The American Republic*, Vol. 2, New York: Oxford University Press, 1962, p. 338.

11. *Political Science Quarterly* (Vol. I, 1886).

12. *Foreign Affairs* (Vol. I, No. 1, 1922), pp. 1–2.

13. *Comparative Politics* (Vol. 1, No. 1, 1968), pp. 1–2.

14. *Comparative Political Studies.* (Vol. 1, No. 1, 1968), p. 2.

15. *Foreign Policy.* (Vol. 1, Winter 1970–71), pp. 4–5.

16. Students should look at Karl Marx and Friedrich Engels, *The Communist Manifesto,* New York: Appleton-Century-Crofts, Inc., 1946.

17. *Science and Society* (Vol. 1, No. 1, Fall 1936), pp. 1–2.

18. *Monthly Review* (Vol. 1, No. 1, May 1949), pp. 1–2.

19. *Politics and Society* (Vol. 1, No. 1, 1970), p. 1.

20. The radical *Caucus for a New Political Science* was formed in 1967 to challenge the conservatism of American political science. It investigated and published conservative links with government, and tried to reform the discipline of political science. Though it held separate meetings within the American Political Science Association, and published fairly extensively, by the 1970s the Caucus became a relatively inactive organization. It meets only periodically and its original members do not often attend meetings. It was however the first group in political science to raise the question of whether political science was relevant. It may be reached through Alan Wolfe, Richmond Community College, Staten Island, New York.

Presently, the *Conference for a Relevant Social Science* is an organization "dedicated to enhancing radical and alternate progressive scholarship by bringing together people from all disciplines of academia and from outside of academia." This organization had its roots in the radical caucus of the Mid-West Political Science Association. The Conference can be reached through William A. Pelz, Box 198, Political Science Dept., Roosevelt University, 430 S. Michigan Avenue, Chicago, Illinois 60605.

*

Appendix

The Declaration of Independence and the Constitution are included in *Is America Necessary?* so that students will be able to compare present day American Political Institutions to the principles in these documents.

*

The Declaration of Independence

When in the Course of human events, it becomes necessary for one people to dissolve the political bands which have connected them with another, and to assume among the powers of the earth, the separate and equal station to which the Laws of Nature and of Nature's God entitle them, a decent respect to the opinions of mankind requires that they should declare the causes which impel them to the separation.

We hold these truths to be self-evident, that all men are created equal, that they are endowed by their Creator with certain unalienable Rights, that among these are Life, Liberty and the pursuit of Happiness. That to secure these rights, Governments are instituted among Men, deriving their just powers from the consent of the governed. That whenever any Form of Government becomes destructive of these ends, it is the Right of the People to alter or to abolish it, and to institute new Government, laying its foundation on such principles and organizing its powers in such form, as to them shall seem most likely to effect their established should not be changed for light and transcient causes; and accordingly all experience hath shown, that mankind are more disposed to suffer, dingly all experience hath shown, that mankind are more disposed to suffer, while evils are sufferable, than to right themselves by abolishing the forms to which they are accustomed. But when a long train of abuses and usurpations, pursuing invariably the same Object evinces a design to reduce them under absolute Despotism, it is their right, it is their duty, to throw off such Government, and to provide new Guards for their future security. Such has been the patient suffrance of these Colonies; and such is now the necessity which constrains them to alter their former Systems of Government. The history of the present King of Great Britain is a history of repeated injuries and usurpations, all having in direct object the establishment of an absolute Tyranny over these States. To prove this, let Facts be submitted to a candid world.

He has refused his Assent to Laws, the most wholesome and necessary for the public good.

He has forbidden his Governors to pass Laws of immediate and pressing importance, unless suspended in their operation till his Assent should be obtained; and when so suspended, he has utterly neglected to attend to them.

He has refused to pass other Laws for the accommodation of large districts of people, unless those people would relinquish the right of Representation in the Legislature, a right inestimable to them and formidable to tyrants only.

He has called together legislative bodies at places unusual, uncomfortable, and distant from the depository of their Public Records, for the sole purpose of fatiguing them into compliance with his measures.

He has dissolved Representative Houses repeatedly, for opposing with manly firmness his invasions on the rights of the people.

He has refused for a long time, after such dissolutions, to cause others to be elected; whereby the Legislative powers, incapable of Annihilation, have returned to the People at large for their exercise; the State remaining in the mean time exposed to all the dangers of invasion from without, and convulsions within.

He has endeavoured to prevent the population of these States; for that purpose obstructing the Laws for Naturalization of Foreigners; refusing to pass others to encourage their migrations hither, and raising the conditions of new Appropriations of Lands.

He has obstructed the Administration of Justice, by refusing his Assent to Laws for establishing Judiciary powers.

He has made Judges dependent on his Will alone, for the tenure of their offices, and the amount and payment of their salaries.

He has erected a multitude of New Offices, and sent hither swarms of Officers to harass our People, and eat out their substance.

He has kept among us, in times of peace, Standing Armies without the Consent of our legislatures.

He has affected to render the military independent of and superior to the Civil power.

He has combined with others to subject us to a jurisdiction foreign to our constitution, and unacknowledged by our laws; giving his Assent to their Acts of pretended Legislation:

For quartering large bodies of armed troops among us:

For protecting them, by a mock Trial, from Punishment for any Murders which they should commit on the Inhabitants of these States:

For cutting off our Trade with all parts of the world:

For imposing Taxes on us without our Consent:

For depriving us in many cases of the benefits of Trial by Jury:

For transporting us beyond Seas to be tried for pretended offences:

For abolishing the free System of English Laws in a neighbouring Province, establishing therein an Arbitrary government, and enlarging its Boundaries so as to render it at once an example and fit instrument for introducing the same absolute rule into these Colonies:

For taking away our Charters, abolishing our most valuable Laws, and altering fundamentally the Forms of our Governments:

For suspending our own Legislatures, and declaring themselves invested with power to legislate for us in all cases whatsoever.

He has abdicated Government here, by declaring us out of his Protection and waging War against us.

He has plundered our seas, ravaged our Coasts, burnt our towns, and destroyed the lives of our people.

He is at this time transporting large Armies of foreign Mercenaries to compleat the works of death, desolation and tyranny, already begun with circumstances of Cruelty & perfidy scarcely paralleled in the most barbarous ages, and totally unworthy the Head of a civilized nation.

He has constrained our fellow Citizens, taken Captive on the high Seas to bear Arms against their Country, to become the executioners of their friends and Brethren, or to fall themselves by their Hands.

He has excited domestic insurrections amongst us, and has endeavoured to bring on the inhabitants of our frontiers, the merciless Indian Savages, whose known rule of warfare is an undistinguished destruction of all ages, sexes and conditions.

In every stage of these Oppressions We have Petitioned for Redress in the most humble terms: Our repeated Petitions have been answered only by repeated injury. A Prince, whose character is thus marked by every act which may define a Tyrant, is unfit to be the ruler of a free people.

Nor have We been wanting in attentions to our British brethren. We have warned them from time to time of attempts by their legislature to extend an unwarrantable jurisdiction over us. We have reminded them of the circumstances of our emigration and settlement here. We have appealed to their native justice and magnanimity, and we have conjured them by the ties of our common kindred to disavow these usurpations, which would inevitably interrupt our connections and correspondence. They too have been deaf to the voice of justice and of consanguinity. We must, therefore, acquiesce in the necessity, which denounces our Separation, and hold them, as we hold the rest of mankind, Enemies in War, in Peace Friends.

We, therefore, the Representatives of the United States of America, in General Congress, Assembled, appealing to the Supreme Judge of the world for the rectitude of our intentions, do, in the Name, and by Authority of the good People of these Colonies, solemnly publish and declare, That these United Colonies are, and of Right ought to be Free and Independent States: that they are Absolved from all Allegiance to the British Crown, and that all political connection between them and the State of Great Britain, is and ought to be totally dissolved; and that as Free and Independent States, they have full Power to Levy War, conclude Peace, contract Alliances, establish Commerce, and to do all other Acts and Things which Independent States may of right do. And for the support of this Declaration, with a firm reliance on the protection of divine Providence, we mutually pledge to each other our Lives, our Fortunes and our sacred Honor.

*

Preamble

We, the people of the United States, in order to form a more perfect Union, establish justice, insure domestic tranquillity, provide for the common defense, promote the general welfare, and secure the blessings of liberty to ourselves and our posterity, do ordain and establish this CONSTITUTION *for the United States of America.*

Article 1. Legislative Department

Section 1. Congress

All legislative powers herein granted shall be vested in a Congress of the United States, which shall consist of a Senate and House of Representatives.

Section 2. House of Representatives

1. *Election and term of members.* The House of Representatives shall be composed of members chosen every second year by the people of the several states, and the electors in each state shall have the qualifications requisite for electors of the most numerous branch of the state legislature.

2. *Qualifications.* No person shall be a Representative who shall not have attained to the age of twenty-five years, and been seven years a citizen of the United States, and who shall not, when elected, be an inhabitant of that state in which he shall be chosen.

3. *Apportionment of Representatives and direct taxes.* Representatives [and direct taxes] shall be apportioned among the several states which may be included within the Union, according to their respective numbers, [which shall be determined by adding to the whole number of free persons, including those bound to service for a term of years, and excluding Indians not taxed, three-fifths of all other persons.] The actual enumeration shall be made within three years after the first meeting of the Congress of the United States, and within every subsequent term of ten years, in such manner as they shall by law direct. The number of Representatives shall not exceed 1 for every 30,000, but each state shall have at least 1 Representative; [and until such enumeration shall be made, the state of New Hampshire shall be entitled to choose 3; Massachusetts, 8; Rhode Island and Providence Plantations, 1; Connecticut, 5; New York, 6; New Jersey, 4; Pennsylvania, 8; Delaware, 1; Maryland, 6; Virginia, 10; North Carolina, 5; South Carolina, 5; and Georgia, 3.]

4. *Filling vacancies.* When vacancies happen in the representation from any state, the executive authority thereof shall issue writs of election to fill such vacancies.

5. *Officers; impeachment*. The House of Representatives shall choose their Speaker and other officers; and shall have the sole power of impeachment.

Section 3.   Senate

1. *Number of members and term of office*. The Senate of the United States shall be composed of two Senators from each state, [chosen by the legislature thereof,] for six years, and each Senator shall have one vote.

2. *Classification; filling vacancies*. [Immediately after they shall be assembled in consequence of the first election, they shall be divided as equally as may be into three classes. The seats of the Senators of the first class shall be vacated at the expiration of the second year, of the second class at the expiration of the fourth year, and of the third class at the expiration of the sixth year, so that one-third may be chosen every second year; and if vacancies happen by resignation, or otherwise, during the recess of the legislature of any state, the executive thereof may make temporary appointments until the next meeting of the legislature, which shall then fill such vacancies.]

3. *Qualifications*. No person shall be a Senator who shall not have attained to the age of thirty years, and been nine years a citizen of the United States, and who shall not, when elected, be an inhabitant of that state for which he shall be chosen.

4. *President of the Senate*. The Vice-President of the United States shall be president of the Senate, but shall have no vote, unless they be equally divided.

5. *Other officers*. The Senate shall choose their other officers, and also a president *pro tempore*, in the absence of the Vice-President, or when he shall exercise the office of President of the United States.

6. *Trial of impeachments*. The Senate shall have the sole power to try all impeachments. When sitting for that purpose, they shall be on oath or affirmation. When the President of the United States is tried, the Chief Justice shall preside; and no person shall be convicted without the concurrence of two-thirds of the members present.

7. *Penalty for conviction*. Judgment in cases of impeachment shall not extend further than to removal from office, and disqualification to hold and enjoy any office of honor, trust, or profit under the United States; but the party convicted shall nevertheless be liable and subject to indictment, trial, judgment, and punishment, according to law.

Section 4.   Elections and Meetings

1. *Holding elections*. The times, places, and manner of holding elections for Senators and Representatives shall be prescribed in each state by the legislature thereof; but the Congress may at any time by law make or alter such regulations, except as to the places of choosing Senators.

2. *Meetings*. The Congress shall assembly at least once in every year, [and such meeting shall be on the first Monday in December,] unless they shall be law appoint a different day.

3. *Journal.* Each house shall keep a journal of its proceedings, and from time to time publish the same, excepting such parts as may in their judgment require secrecy; and the yeas and nays of the members of either house on any question shall, at the desire of one-fifth of those present, be entered on the journal.

4. *Adjournment.* Neither house, during the session of Congress, shall, without the consent of the other, adjourn for more than three days, nor to any other place than that in which the two houses shall be sitting.

Section 5.   Rules of Procedure

1. *Organization.* Each house shall be the judge of the elections, returns, and qualifications of its own members, and a majority of each shall constitute a quorum to do business; but a smaller number may adjourn from day to day, and may be authorized to compel the attendance of absent members, in such manner, and under such penalties, as each house may provide.

2. *Proceedings.* Each house may determine the rules of its proceedings, punish its members for disorderly behavior, and with the concurrence of two-thirds, expel a member.

Section 6.   Privileges and Restrictions

1. *Pay and privileges.* The Senators and Representatives shall receive a compensation for their services, to be ascertained by law and paid out of the Treasury of the United States. They shall in all cases except treason, felony, and breach of the peace, be privileged from arrest during their attendance at the session of their respective houses, and in going to and returning from the same; and for any speech or debate in either house, they shall not be questioned in any other place.

2. *Restrictions.* No Senator or Representative shall, during the time for which he was elected, be appointed to any civil office under the authority of the United States, which shall have been created, or the emoluments whereof shall have been increased, during such time; and no person holding any office under the United States shall be a member of either house during his continuance in office.

Section 7.   Method of Passing Laws

1. *Revenue bills.* All bills for raising revenue shall originate in the House of Representatives; but the Senate may propose or concur with amendments as on other bills.

2. *How a bill becomes a law.* Every bill which shall have passed the House of Representatives and the Senate, shall, before it become a law, be presented to the President of the United States; if he approves, he shall sign it, but if not, he shall return it, with his objections, to that house in which it shall have originated, who shall enter the objections at large on their journal, and proceed to reconsider it. If after such reconsideration two-thirds of that house shall agree to pass the bill, it shall be sent, together with the objections, to the other house, by which it shall likewise be reconsidered, and, if approved by two-thirds of that house, it shall become a

law. But in all such cases the votes of both houses shall be determined by yeas and nays, and the names of the persons voting for and against the bill shall be entered on the journal of each house respectively. If any bill shall not be returned by the President within ten days (Sundays excepted) after it shall have been presented to him, the same shall be a law, in like manner as if he had signed it, unless the Congress by their adjournment prevent its return, in which case it shall not be a law.

3. *Presidential approval or veto.* Every order, resolution, or vote to which the concurrence of the Senate and House of Representatives may be necessary (except on a question of adjournment) shall be presented to the President of the United States; and before the same shall take effect, shall be approved by him, or being disapproved by him, shall be repassed by two-thirds of the Senate and House of Representatives, according to the rules and limitations prescribed in the case of a bill.

Section 8.   Powers Delegated to Congress

The Congress shall have power

1. To lay and collect taxes, duties, imposts, and excises, to pay the debts and provide for the common defense and general welfare of the United States; but all duties, imposts, and excises shall be uniform throughout the United States;

2. To borrow money on the credit of the United States;

3. To regulate commerce with foreign nations, and among the several states, and with the Indian tribes;

4. To establish a uniform rule of naturalization, and uniform laws on the subject of bankruptcies throughout the United States;

5. To coin money, regulate the value thereof, and of foreign coin, and fix the standard of weights and measures;

6. To provide for the punishment of counterfeiting the securities and current coin of the United States;

7. To establish post offices and post roads;

8. To promote the progress of science and useful arts by securing for limited times to authors and inventors the exclusive right to their respective writings and discoveries;

9. To constitute tribunals inferior to the Supreme Court;

10. To define and punish piracies and felonies committed on the high seas and offenses against the law of nations;

11. To declare war, [grant letters of marque and reprisal,] and make rules concerning captures on land and water;

12. To raise and support armies, but no appropriation of money to that use shall be for a longer term than two years;

13. To provide and maintain a navy;

14. To make rules for the government and regulation of the land and naval forces;

15. To provide for calling forth the militia to execute the laws of the Union, suppress insurrections, and repel invasions;

16. To provide for organizing, arming, and disciplining the militia, and for governing such part of them as may be employed in the service of the United States, reserving to the states,

respectively, the appointment of the officers, and the authority of training the militia according to the discipline prescribed by Congress;

17. To exercise exclusive legislation in all cases whatsoever, over such district (not exceeding ten miles square) as may, by cession of particular states, and the acceptance of Congress, become the seat of government of the United States, and to exercise like authority over all places purchased by the consent of the legislature of the state in which the same shall be, for the erection of forts, magazines, arsenals, dock-yards, and other needful buildings;— and

18. To make all laws which shall be necessary and proper for carrying into execution the foregoing powers, and all other powers vested by this Constitution in the government of the United States, or in any department or officer thereof.

Section 9.   Powers Denied to the Federal Government

1. [The migration or importation of such persons as any of the states now existing shall think proper to admit shall not be prohibited by the Congress prior to the year 1808; but a tax or duty may be imposed on such importation, not exceeding $10 for each person.]

2. The privilege of the writ of *habeas corpus* shall not be suspended, unless when in cases of rebellion or invasion the public safety may require it.

3. No bill of attainder or *ex post facto* law shall be passed.

4. No capitation or other direct tax shall be laid, unless in proportion to the census or enumeration herein before directed to be taken.

5. No tax or duty shall be laid on articles exported from any state.

6. No preference shall be given by any regulation of commerce or revenue to the ports of one state over those of another: nor shall vessels bound to, or from, one state, be obliged to enter, clear, or pay duties in another.

7. No money shall be drawn from the Treasury, but in consequence of appropriations made by law; and a regular statement and account of the receipts and expenditures of all public money shall be published from time to time.

8. No title of nobility shall be granted by the United States; and no person holding any office of profit or trust under them, shall, without the consent of the Congress, accept of any present, emolument, office, or title, of any kind whatever, from any king, prince, or foreign state.

Section 10.   Powers Denied to the States

1. No state shall enter into any treaty, alliance, or confederation; grant letters of marque and reprisal; coin money; emit bills of credit; make anything but gold and silver coin a tender in payment of debts; pass any bill of attainder, *ex post facto* law, or law impairing the obligation of contracts, or grant any title of nobility.

2. No state shall, without the consent of the Congress, lay any imposts or duties on imports or exports, except what may be absolutely necessary for executing its inspection laws; and the net produce of all duties and imposts, laid by any state on imports or exports, shall be for the use of the Treasury of the United States; and all such laws shall be subject to the revision and control of the Congress.

3. No state shall, without the consent of Congress, lay any duty of tonnage, keep troops, or ships of war in time of peace, enter into any agreement or compact with another state, or

with a foreign power, or engage in war, unless actually invaded, or in such imminent danger as will not admit of delay.

Article 2.   Executive Department

Section 1.   President and Vice-President

1. *Term of office.* The executive power shall be vested in a President of the United States of America. He shall hold his office during the term of four years, and together with the Vice-President, chosen for the same term, be elected as follows:

2. *Electoral system.* Each state shall appoint, in such manner as the legislature thereof may direct, a number of electors, equal to the whole number of Senators and Representatives to which the state may be entitled in the Congress; but no Senator or Representative, or person holding an office of trust or profit under the United States, shall be appointed an elector.

3. *Former method of using the electoral system.* [The electors shall meet in their respective states, and vote by ballot for two persons, of whom one at least shall not be an inhabitant of the same state with themselves. And they shall make a list of all the persons voted for, and of the number of votes for each; which list they shall sign and certify, and transmit sealed to the seat of the government of the United States, directed to the president of the Senate. The president of the Senate shall, in the presence of the Senate and House of Representatives, open all the certificates, and the votes shall then be counted. The person having the greatest number of votes shall be the President, if such number be a majority of the whole number of electors appointed; and if there be more than one who have such majority, and have an equal number of votes, then the House of Representatives shall immediately choose by ballot one of them for President; and if no person have a majority, then from the five highest on the list the said House shall in like manner choose the President. But in choosing the President the votes shall be taken by states, the representation from each state having one vote. A quorum for this purpose shall consist of a member or members from two-thirds of the states, and a majority of all the states shall be necessary to a choice. In every case, after the choice of the President, the person having the greatest number of votes of the electors shall be the Vice-President. But if there should remain two or more who have equal votes, the Senate shall choose from them by ballot the Vice-President.]

4. *Time of elections.* The Congress may determine the time of choosing the electors, and the day on which they shall give their votes; which day shall be the same throughout the United States.

5. *Qualifications for President.* No person except a natural-born citizen, [or a citizen of the United States, at the time of the adoption of this Constitution,] shall be eligible to the office of President; neither shall any person be eligible to that office who shall not have attained to the age of thirty-five years, and been fourteen years a resident within the United States.

6. *Filling vacancies.* In case of the removal of the President from office, or of his death, resignation, or inability to discharge the powers and duties of the said office, the same shall devolve on the Vice-President, and the Congress may by law provide for the case of removal, death, resignation, or inability, both of the President and Vice-President, declaring what officer

shall then act as President, and such officer shall act accordingly, until the disability be removed, or a President shall be elected.

7. *Salary.* The President shall, at stated times, receive for his services, a compensation, which shall neither be increased nor diminished during the period for which he shall have been elected, and he shall not receive within that period any other emolument from the United States, or any of them.

8. *Oath of office.* Before he enter on the execution of his office, he shall take the following oath or affirmation:—"I do solemnly swear (or affirm) that I will faithfully execute the office of President of the United States, and will to the best of my ability, preserve, protect, and defend the Constitution of the United States."

Section 2. Powers of the President

1. *Military powers.* The President shall be Commander in Chief of the Army and Navy of the United States, and of the militia of the several states, when called into the actual service of the United States; he may require the opinion, in writing, of the principal officer in each of the executive departments, upon any subject relating to the duties of their respective offices, and he shall have power to grant reprieves and pardons for offenses against the United States, except in cases of impeachment.

2. *Treaties and appointments.* He shall have power, by and with the advice and consent of the Senate, to make treaties, provided two-thirds of the Senators present concur; and he shall nominate, and by and with the advice and consent of the Senate, shall appoint ambassadors, other public ministers and consuls, judges of the Supreme Court, and all other officers of the United States, whose appointments are not herein otherwise provided for, and which shall be established by law; but the Congress may by law vest the appointment of such inferior officers, as they think proper, in the President alone, in the courts of law, or in the heads of departments.

3. *Filling vacancies.* The President shall have power to fill up all vacancies that may happen during the recess of the Senate, by granting commissions which shall expire at the end of their next session.

Section 3. Duties of the President

He shall from time to time give to the Congress information of the state of the Union, and recommend to their consideration such measures as he shall judge necessary and expedient; he may, on extraordinary occasions, convene both houses, or either of them, and in case of disagreement between them, with respect to the time of adjournment, he may adjourn them to such time as he shall think proper; he shall receive ambassadors and other public ministers; he shall take care that the laws be faithfully executed, and shall commission all the officers of the United States.

Section 4. Impeachment

The President, Vice-President, and all civil officers of the United States, shall be removed from office on impeachment for, and conviction of, treason, bribery, or other high crimes and misdemeanors.

Article 3. Judicial Department

Section 1. Federal Courts

The judicial power of the United States shall be vested in one Supreme Court, and in such inferior courts as the Congress may from time to time ordain and establish. The judges, both of the Supreme and inferior courts, shall hold their offices during good behavior, and shall, at stated times, receive for their services a compensation, which shall not be diminished during their continuance in office.

Section 2. Jurisdiction of Federal Courts

1. *General jurisdiction.* The judicial power shall extend to all cases, in law and equity, arising under this Constitution, the laws of the United States, and treaties made or which shall be made, under their authority; to all cases affecting ambassadors, other public ministers and consuls; to all cases of admiralty and maritime jurisdiction; to controversies to which the United States shall be a party; to controversies between two or more states; [between a state and citizens of another state;] between citizens of different states; between citizens of the same state claiming lands under grants of different states, and between a state, or the citizens thereof, and foreign states, citizens, or subjects.

2. *Supreme Court.* In all cases affecting ambassadors, other public ministers and consuls, and those in which a state shall be a party, the Supreme Court shall have original jurisdiction. In all the other cases before mentioned, the Supreme Court shall have appellate jurisdiction, both as to law and fact, with such exceptions, and under such regulations as the Congress shall make.

3. *Conduct of trials.* The trial of all crimes, except in cases of impeachment, shall be by jury; and such trial shall be held in the state where the said crimes shall have been committed; but when not committed within any state, the trial shall be at such place or places as the Congress may by law have directed.

Section 3. Treason

1. *Definition.* Treason against the United States shall consist only in levying war against them, or in adhering to their enemies, giving them aid and comfort. No person shall be convicted of treason unless on the testimony of two witnesses to the same overt act, or on confession in open court.

2. *Punishment.* The Congress shall have power to declare the punishment of treason, but no attainder of treason shall work corruption of blood or forfeiture except during the life of the person attainted.

Article 4.   Relations Among The States

Section 1.   Official Acts

Full faith and credit shall be given in each state to the public acts, records, and judicial proceedings of every other state. And the Congress may by general laws prescribe the manner in which such acts, records, and proceedings shall be proved, and the effect thereof.

Section 2.   Privileges of Citizens

1. *Privileges*. The citizens of each state shall be entitled to all privileges and immunities of citizens in the several states.

2. *Extradition*. A person charged in any state with treason, felony, or other crime, who shall flee from justice, and be found in another state, shall on demand of the executive authority of the state from which he fled, be delivered up, to be removed to the state having jurisdiction of the crime.

3. *Fugitive slaves*. [No person held in service or labor in one state, under the laws thereof, escaping into another, shall in consequence of any law or regulation therein, be discharged from such service or labor, but shall be delivered up on claim of the party to whom such service or labor may be due.]

Section 3.   New States and Territories

1. *Admission of new states*. New states may be admitted by the Congress into this Union; but no new state shall be formed or erected within the jurisdiction of any other state; nor any state be formed by the junction of two or more states, or parts of states, without the consent of the legislatures of the states concerned as well as of the Congress.

2. *Power of Congress over territories and other property*. The Congress shall have power to dispose of and make all needful rules and regulations respecting the territory or other property belonging to the United States; and nothing in this Constitution shall be so construed as to prejudice any claims of the United States, or of any particular state.

Section 4.   Guarantees to the States

The United States shall guarantee to every state in this Union a republican form of government, and shall protect each of them against invasion; (and on application of the legislature, or of the executive (when the legislature cannot be convened) against domestic violence.

Article 5.   Methods of Amendment

The Congress, whenever two-thirds of both houses shall deem it necessary, shall propose amendments to this Constitution, or, on the application of the legislatures of two-thirds of the several states, shall call a convention for proposing amendments, which, in either case, shall be valid to all intents and purposes, as part of this Constitution, when ratified by the legislatures of three-fourths of the several states, or by conventions in three-fourths thereof, as the one or the other mode of ratification may be proposed by the Congress; provided that [no amendments which may be made prior to the year 1808 shall in any manner affect the first and fourth clauses in the Ninth Section of the First Article; and that] no state, without its consent, shall be deprived of its equal suffrage in the Senate.

Article 6. General Provisions

1. *Public debts.* All debts contracted and engagements entered into, before the adoption of this Constitution, shall be as valid against the United States under this Constitution, as under the Confederation.

2. *The supreme law.* This Constitution, and the laws of the United States which shall be made in pursuance thereof, and all treaties made, or which shall be made, under the authority of the United States, shall be the supreme law of the land; and the judges in every state shall be bound thereby, anything in the constitution or laws of any state to the contrary notwithstanding.

3. *Oaths of office.* The Senators and Representatives before mentioned, and the members of the several state legislatures, and all executive and judicial officers, both of the United States and of the several states, shall be bound by oath or affirmation, to support this Constitution; but no religious test shall ever by required as a qualification to any office or public trust under the United States.

Article 7. Ratification

The ratification of the convention of the nine states shall be sufficient for the establishment of this Constitution between the states so ratifying the same. . . .

Amendments to the Constitution

Amendment 1. Freedom of Religion, Speech, Press, Assembly, and Petition (1791)

Congress shall make no law respecting an establishment of religion, or prohibiting the free exercise thereof; or abridging the freedom of speech, or of the press; or the right of the people peaceably to assemble, and to petition the government for a redress of grievances.

Amendment 2. Right to Keep Arms (1791)

A well-regulated militia, being necessary to the security of a free state, the right of the people to keep and bear arms shall not be infringed.

Amendment 3. Quartering of Troops (1791)

No soldier shall, in time of peace, be quartered in any house, without the consent of the owner; nor in time of war, but in a manner to be prescribed by law.

Amendment 4. Search and Seizure; Warrants (1791)

The right of the people to be secure in their persons, houses, papers, and effects, against un-reasonable searches and seizures, shall not be violated; and no warrants shall issue but upon probable cause, supported by oath or affirmation, and particularly describing the place to be searched, and the persons or things to be seized.

Amendment 5. Rights of Accused Persons (1791)

No person shall be held to answer for a capital, or otherwise infamous, crime, unless on a presentment or indictment of a grand jury, except in cases arising in the land or naval forces, or in the militia, when in actual service in time of war or public danger; nor shall any person be subject for the same offense to be twice put in jeopardy of life or limb; nor shall be compelled, in any criminal case, to be a witness against himself; nor be deprived of life, liberty, or pro-perty, without due process of law; nor shall private property be taken for public use, withour just compensation.

Amendment 6. Right to Speedy Trial (1791)

In all criminal prosecutions, the accused shall enjoy the right to a speedy and public trial, by an impartial jury of the state and district wherein the crime shall have been committed, which dis-trict shall have been previously ascertained by law, and to be informed of the nature and cause of the accusation; to be confronted with the witnesses against him; to have compulsory pro-cess for obtaining witnesses in his favor, and to have the assistance of counsel for his defense.

Amendment 7. Jury Trial in Civil Cases (1791)

In suits at common law, where the value in controversy shall exceed twenty dollars, the right of a trial by jury shall be preserved, and no fact tried by a jury shall be otherwise re-examined in any court of the United States than according to the rules of the common law.

Amendment 8.   Bail, Fines, Punishments (1791)

Excessive bail shall not be required, nor excessive fines imposed, nor cruel and unusual punishments inflicted.

Amendment 9.   Powers Reserved to the People (1791)

The enumeration in the Constitution, of certain rights, shall not be construed to deny or disparage others retained by the people.

Amendment 10.   Powers Reserved to the States (1791)

The powers not delegated to the United States by the Constitution, nor prohibited by it to the states, are reserved to the states respectively, or to the people.

Amendment 11.   Suits Against States (1798)

The judicial power of the United States shall not be construed to extend to any suit in law or equity, commenced or prosecuted against one of the United States, by citizens of another state, or by citizens or subjects of any foreign state.

Amendment 12.   Election of President and Vice-President (1804)

The electors shall meet in their respective states, and vote by ballot for President and Vice-President, one of whom, at least, shall not be an inhabitant of the same state with themselves; they shall name in their ballots the person voted for as President, and in distinct ballots the person voted for as Vice-President, and they shall make distinct lists of all persons voted for as President, and of all persons voted for as Vice-President, and of the number of votes for each, which lists they shall sign and certify, and transmit, sealed, to the seat of government of the United States, directed to the President of the Senate; the President of the Senate shall, in the presence of the Senate and House of Representatives, open *all* the certificates and the votes shall then be counted; the person having the greatest number of votes for President shall be the President, if such number be a majority of the whole number of electors appointed; and if no person have such majority, then from the persons having the highest numbers not exceeding three on the list of those voted for as President, the House of Representatives shall choose immediately, by ballot, the President. But in choosing the President, the votes shall be taken by states, the representation from each state having one vote; a quorum for this purpose shall consist of a member or members from two-thirds of the states, and a majority of all the states shall be necessary to a choice. [And if the House of Representatives shall not choose a President whenever the right of choice shall devolve upon them, before the fourth day of March next following, then the Vice-President shall act as President, as in the case of the death or other constitutional disability of the President.] The person having the greatest number of votes as Vice-President, shall be the Vice-President, if such number be a majority of the whole number of electors appointed, and if no person have a majority, then, from the two highest numbers on the list, the Senate shall choose the Vice-President; a quorum for the purpose shall consist of two-thirds of the whole number of Senators, and a majority of the whole number shall be necessary to a choice. But no person constitutionally ineligible to the office of President shall be eligible to that of Vice-President of the United States.

Amendment 13. Slavery Abolished (1865)

Section 1. Neither slavery nor involuntary servitude, except as a punishment for crime whereof the party shall have been duly convicted, shall exist within the United States, or any place subject to their jurisdiction.

Section 2. Congress shall have power to enforce this article by appropriate legislation.

Amendment 14. Rights of Citizens (1868)

Section 1. Citizenship defined. All persons born or naturalized in the United States and subject to the jurisdiction thereof, are citizens of the United States and of the state wherein they reside. No state shall make or enforce any law which shall abridge the privileges or immunities of citizens of the United States; nor shall any state deprive any person of life, liberty, or property, without due process of law; nor deny to any person within its jurisdiction the equal protection of the laws.

Section 2. Apportionment of Representatives. Representatives shall be apportioned among the several states according to their respective numbers, counting the whole number of persons in each state, excluding Indians not taxed. But when the right to vote at any election for the choice of electors for President and Vice-President of the United States, Representatives in Congress, the executive and judicial officers of a state, or the members of the legislature thereof, is denied to any of the male inhabitants of such state, being twenty-one years of age and citizens of the United States, or in any way abridged, except for participation in rebellion, or other crime, the basis of representation therein shall be reduced in the proportion which the number of such male citizens shall bear to the whole number of male citizens twenty-one years of age in such state.

Section 3. Disability for engaging in insurrection. No person shall be a Senator or Representative in Congress, or elector of President and Vice-President, or hold any office, civil or military, under the United States, or under any state, who, having previously taken an oath, as a member of Congress, or as an officer of the United States, or as a member of any state legislature, or as an executive or judicial officer of any state, to support the Constitution of the United States, shall have engaged in insurrection or rebellion against the same, or given aid or comfort to the enemies thereof. But Congress may, by vote of two-thirds of each house, remove such disability.

Section 4. Public debt. The validity of the public debt of the United States, authorized by law, including debts incurred for payment of pensions and bounties for services in suppressing insurrection or rebellion, shall not be questioned. But neither the United States nor any state shall assume or pay any debt or obligation incurred in aid of insurrection or rebellion against the United States, [or any claim for the loss or emancipation of any slave;] but all such debts, obligations, and claims shall be held illegal and void.

Section 5. Enforcement. The Congress shall have power to enforce, by appropriate legislation, the provisions of this article.

Amendment 15.   Right of Suffrage (1870)

Section 1. The right of citizens of the United States to vote shall not be denied or abridged by the United States or any state on account of race, color, or previous condition of servitude.

Section 2. The Congress shall have power to enforce this article by appropriate legislation.

Amendment 16.   Income Tax (1913)

The Congress shall have power to lay and collect taxes on incomes, from whatever source derived, without apportionment among the several states, and without regard to any census or enumeration.

Amendment 17.   Election of Senators (1913)

Section 1. Method of election. The Senate of the United States shall be composed of two Senators from each state, elected by the people thereof, for six years; and each Senator shall have one vote. The electors in each state shall have the qualifications requisite for electors of the most numerous branch of the state legislatures.

Section 2. Filling vacancies. When vacancies happen in the representation of any state in the Senate, the executive authority of such state shall issue writs of election to fill such vacancies: *Provided* that the legislature of any state may empower the executive thereof to make temporary appointments until the people fill the vacancies by election as the legislature may direct.

[*Section 3. Not retroactive.* This amendment shall not be so construed as to affect the election or term of any Senator chosen before it becomes valid as part of the Constitution.]

Amendment 18.   National Prohibition (1919)

[*Section 1.* After one year from the ratification of this article the manufacture, sale, or transportation of intoxicating liquors within, the importation thereof into, or the exportation thereof from, the United States and all territory subject to the jurisdiction thereof for beverage purposes is hereby prohibited.

Section 2. The Congress and the several states shall have concurrent power to enforce this article by appropriate legislation.

Section 3. This article shall be inoperative unless it shall have been ratified as an amendment to the Constitution by the legislatures of the several states, as provided in the Constitution, within seven years from the date of the submission hereof to the states by the Congress.]

Amendment 19. Woman Suffrage (1920)

Section 1. The right of citizens of the United States to vote shall not be denied or abridged by the United States or by any state on account of sex.

Section 2. Congress shall have power to enforce this article by appropriate legislation.

Amendment 20. "Lame Duck" Amendment (1933)

Section 1. Beginning of terms. The terms of the President and Vice-President shall end at noon on the 20th day of January, and the terms of Senators and Representatives at noon on the 3d day of January, of the years in which such terms would have ended if this article had not been ratified; and the terms of their successors shall then begin.

Section 2. Beginning of Congressional sessions. The Congress shall assemble at least once in every year and such meeting shall begin at noon on the 3d day of January, unless they shall by law appoint a different day.

Section 3. Presidential succession. If at the time fixed for the beginning of the term of the President, the President-elect shall have died, the Vice-President-elect shall become President. If a President shall not have been chosen before the time fixed for the beginning of his term, or if the President-elect shall have failed to qualify, then the Vice-President-elect shall act as President until a President shall have qualified; and the Congress may by law provide for the case wherein neither a President-elect nor a Vice-President-elect shall have qualified, declaring who shall then act as President, or the manner in which one who is to act shall be selected, and such person shall act accordingly until a President or Vice-President shall have qualified.

Section 4. Filling Presidential vacancy. The Congress may by law provide for the case of the death of any of the persons from whom the House of Representatives may choose a President whenever the right of choice shall have devolved upon them, and for the case of the death of any of the persons from whom the Senate may choose a Vice-President whenever the right of choice shall have devolved upon them.

[*Section 5. Effective date.* Sections 1 and 2 shall take effect on the 15th day of October following the ratification of this article.

Section 6. *Time limit for ratification.* This article shall be inoperative unless it shall have been ratified as an amendment to the Constitution by the legislatures of three-fourths of the several states within seven years from the date of its submission.]

Amendment 21. Repeal of Prohibition (1933)

Section 1. The eighteenth article of amendment to the Constitution of the United States is hereby repealed.

Section 2. The transportation or importation into any state, territory, or possession of the United States for delivery or use therein of intoxicating liquors, in violation of the laws thereof, is hereby prohibited.

[*Section 3.* This article shall be inoperative unless it shall have been ratified as an amendment to the Constitution by conventions in the several states, as provided in the Constitution, within seven years from the date of the submission hereof to the states by the Congress.]

Amendment 22. Two-Term Limit for Presidents (1951)

Section 1. No person shall be elected to the office of the President more than twice, and no person who has held the office of President, or acted as President, for more than two years of a term to which some other person was elected President shall be elected to the office of the President more than once. [But this Article shall not apply to any person holding the office of President when this Article was proposed by the Congress, and shall not prevent any person who may be holding the office of President, or acting as President, during the term within which this Article becomes operative from holding the office of President or acting as President during the remainder of such term.]

[*Section 2.* This article shall be inoperative unless it shall have been ratified as an amendment to the Constitution by the legislatures of three-fourths of the several states within seven years from the date of its submission to the states by the Congress.]

Amendment 23. Presidential Electors for District of Columbia (1961)

Section 1. The District constituting the seat of Government of the United States shall appoint in such manner as the Congress may direct:

A number of electors of President and Vice-President equal to the whole number of Senators and Representatives in Congress to which the District would be entitled if it were a State, but in no event more than the least populous State; they shall be in addition to those appointed by the States, but they shall be considered, for the purposes of the election of President and Vice-President, to be electors appointed by a State; and they shall meet in the District and perform such duties as provided by the twelfth article of amendment.

Section 2. The Congress shall have power to enforce this article by appropriate legislation.

Amendment 24.   Poll Tax Banned in National Elections (1964)

Section 1. The right of citizens of the United States to vote in any primary or other election for President or Vice-President, for electors for President or Vice-President, or for Senator or Representative in Congress, shall not be denied or abridged by the United States or any state by reason of failure to pay any poll tax or other tax.

Section 2. The Congress shall have the power to enforce this article by appropriate legislation.

Amendment 25.   Presidential Succession Due to Illness (1967)

Section 1. In case of the removal of the President from office or of his death or resignation, the Vice President shall become President.

Section 2. Whenever there is a vacancy in the office of the Vice President, the President shall nominate a Vice President who shall take office upon confirmation by a majority vote by both Houses of Congress.

Section 3. Whenever the President transmits to the President pro tempore of the Senate and the Speaker of the House of Representatives his written declaration that he is unable to discharge the powers and duties of his office, and until he transmits to them a written declaration to the contrary, such powers and duties shall be discharged by the Vice President as Acting President.

Section 4. Whenever the Vice President and a majority of either the principal officers of the executive departments or of such other body as Congress may by law provide, transmit to the President pro tempore of the Senate and the Speaker of the House of Representatives their written declaration that the President is unable to discharge the powers and duties of his office, the Vice President shall immediately the powers and duties of the office as Acting President.

Thereafter, when the President transmits to the President pro tempore of the Senate and the Speaker of the House of Representatives his written declaration that no inability exists, he shall resume the powers and duties of his office unless the Vice President and a majority of either the principal officers of the executive department or of such other body as Congress may by law provide, transmit within four days to the President pro tempore of the Senate and the Speaker of the House of Representatives their written declaration that the President is unable to discharge the powers and duties of his office. Thereupon Congress shall decide the issue, assembling within fourty-eight hours for that purpose if not in session. If the Congress, within twenty-one days after receipt of the latter written declaration, or, if Congress is not in session, within twenty-one days after Congress is required to assemble, determines by two-thirds vote of both Houses that the President is unable to discharge the powers and duties of his office, the Vice President shall continue to discharge the same as Acting President; otherwise, the President shall resume the powers and duties of his office.

Etzkowitz & Schwab—Is America Necessary—42

Amendment 26.   Extension of Suffrage (1971)

Section 1. The right of citizens of the United States, who are eighteen years of age or older, to vote shall not be denied or abridged by the United States or by any State on account of age.

Section 2. The Congress shall have power to enforce this article by appropriate legislation.

Proposed Amendment

Equal Rights Amendment (ERA).   No Denial of Rights on Account of Sex

Section 1. Equality of rights under the law shall not be denied or abridged by the United States or by any State on account of sex.

Section 2. The Congress shall have power to enforce, by appropriate legislation, the provisions of this article.

Section 3. This amendment shall take effect two years after the date of ratification.

NOTE

Submitted by Congress to the States for ratification on March 22, 1972. The amendment shall become part of the Constitution when ratified by the legislatures of three-fourths of the states within seven years from the date of its submission by the Congress. As of June 1, 1975, thiry-four states had ratified.

Books

Ackerman, Frank, and MacEwan, Arthur. "Inflation, Recession, and Crises." *Review of Radical Political Economics* 6, no. 1 (1974).

Adams, Nina S., and McCoy, Alfred W. *Laos: War and Revolution*. New York: Harper and Row, 1970.

Agee, Philip. *Inside The Company—CIA Diary*. New York: Stonehill Press, 1975.

Almond, Gabriel A., and Powell, G. Bingham Jr. *Comparative Politics: A Developmental Approach*. Boston: Little, Brown and Co., 1966.

Aristotle. *The Politics*. Translated & Introduced by Ernest Barker. New York: Oxford University Press, 1962.

Aronowitz, Stanley. *False Promises*. New York: McGraw-Hill Co., 1974.

Attica. Official Report of the New York State Special Commission on Attica. New York: Bantam Books, 1972.

Bell, Daniel. *The End of Ideology*. New York: The Free Press, 1960.

Bernstein, Carl, and Woodward, Bob. *All the President's Men*. New York: Simon and Schuster Pub., 1974.

Black, Jonathan, ed. *Radical Lawyers: Their Role in The Movement and in The Courts*. New York: Avon Books, 1971.

Blum, Bill. "The Oil Connection." *Liberation* 18, no. 6 (February 1974).

Blum, John Morton. *Woodrow Wilson and The Politics of Morality*. Boston: Little, Brown & Co., 1956.

Broudy, Eric. "The Trouble with Textbooks." *Teachers College Record* 77, no. 1 (September 1975).

Brown, Stuart Gerry. *Alexander Hamilton*. New York: Washington Square Press, 1967.

Brown, Stuart Gerry. *Thomas Jefferson*. New York: Twayne Pub., 1966.

Burns, James MacGregor. *The Deadlock of Democracy*. Englewood Cliffs, N.J.: Prentice-Hall, Inc., 1964.

Calleo, David P. "Business Corporations and the National State." *Social Research* (Winter 1974).

Caplovitz, David. *Consumers in Trouble: Study of Debtors in Default*. New York: The Free Press, 1974.

Charles, Joseph. *The Origins of The American Party System*. New York: Harper Torchbooks, 1961.

"Children's Flammable Sleepwear." *Consumer Reports* (February 1972).

Cirino, Robert. *Don't Blame The People*. New York: Vintage Press, 1971.

Clapp, Charles, L. *The Congressman: His Work As He Sees It*. Garden City: Anchor Books, 1964.

Cockburn, Alexander, and Ridgeway, James. "The Merchant of Sunlight, or The Saga of Schaflander And The Sunshine Boys." *The Village Voice* (April 7, 1975).

Cohen, Jules. *The Conscience of The Corporations*. Baltimore: The Johns Hopkins Press, 1971.

Cook, Fred J. *The FBI Nobody Knows*. New York: The Macmillan Co., 1964.

Cressey, Donald. *Theft of a Nation*. New York: Harper and Row, 1969.

Cummings, Milton C. Jr., and Wise, David. *Democracy Under Pressure*. New York: Harcourt Brace Jovanovich, Inc., 1971.

Curry, Leonard. "The Multinational Corruption." *The Nation* (May 24, 1975).

Dahl, Robert A. *After The Revolution?* New Haven: Yale University Press, 1974.

Dahl, Robert A. *Modern Political Analysis*. Englewood Cliffs, N.J.: Prentice-Hall, Inc., 1963.

Dahl, Robert A. *Who Governs?* New Haven: Yale University Press, 1961.

deGrazia, Alfred. *Politics For Better or Worse*. Glenview: Scott, Foresman & Co., 1973.

deSola Pool, Ithiel. "The Necessity for Social Scientists Doing Research for Governments." *Background* (no. 10, August 1966).

Dellinger, Dave. *More Power Than We Know*. Garden City: Doubleday Pub., 1975.

DiSpoldo, Nick. "How To Be A Jailhouse Lawyer." *Win Magazine* (July 10, 1975).

Doctorow, E. L. *Ragtime*. New York: Random House, 1975.

Domhoff, G. William. *Bohemian Grove*. New York: Harper Colophon Books, 1975.

Domhoff, G. William. *Fat Cats and Democrats*. Englewood Cliffs, N.J.: Prentice-Hall Co., 1972.

Dunlop, John T. "Inflation and Incomes Policies: The Political Economy of Recent U.S. Experience." *Public Policy* 23, no. 2 (Spring 1975).

Engler, Robert. *The Politics of Oil*. Chicago: The University of Chicago Press, 1969.

Epstein, Jason. *Great Conspiracy Trial*. New York: Random House, 1970.

Etzkowitz, Henry. *Is America Possible?* St. Paul: West Publishing Co., 1974.

Etzkowitz, Henry. "Sociology and Praxis: The Infant Growth Environment." *Social Theory and Practice* 3 (Spring 1971).

Etzkowitz, Henry, and Schaflander, Gerald. *Ghetto Crisis*. Boston: Little, Brown and Co., 1969.

Fairfield, Roy P., ed. *The Federalist Papers*. Garden City: Doubleday and Co., 1961.

Firestone, Shulamith. *The Dialectic of Sex*. New York: Bantam Books, 1972.

Frankfuter, Felix. *Mr. Justice Holmes and The Supreme Court*. Cambridge: Harvard University Press, 1938.

Freeman, Jo. *The Politics of Women's Liberation*. New York: David McKay Company, Inc., 1975.

Freund, Paul A. *The Supreme Court of The United States*. Cleveland: Meridian Books, 1965.

Galbraith, John K. *The Great Crash, 1929*. New York: Houghton-Mifflin Pub., 1972.

Garson, G. David. "Radical Issues in The History of The American Working Class." *Politics and Society* 3, no. 1 (Fall 1972).

Georgakas, Dan, and Surkin, Marvin. *Detroit: I Do Mind Dying*. New York: St. Martin's Press, 1975.

Gerth, H. H., and Mills, C. Wright., ed. *From Max Weber*. New York: Oxford University Press, 1958.

Granbard, Stephen. *Kissinger: Portrait of a Mind*. New York: W.W. Norton and Co., 1974.

Greenstone, David. *Labor in American Politics*. New York: Alfred Knopf Pub., 1969.

Harrington, Michael et al. *We Are Socialists of The Democratic Left*. New York: Democratic Socialist Organizing Committee, 1973.

Henderson, Hazel. "Corporate Responsibility: Politics By Other Means." *The Nation* (December 14, 1970).

Hicks, John D. *The Populist Revolt*. Lincoln: University of Nebraska Press, 1961.

Hobbes, Thomas. *Leviathan*. New York: Dutton Pub., 1950.

Hofstadter, Richard. *The American Political Tradition*. New York: Vintage Books, 1959.

Hook, Sidney. "Barbarism, Virtue, and the University." *The Public Interest* 15 (Spring 1969).

Ianni, Francis A. J. *Black Mafia: Ethnic Succession in Organized Crime*. New York: Simon and Schuster, 1974.

Inciardi, James A. *Careers in Crime*. New York: Rand McNally Co., 1975.

Isaak, Robert A., and Hummel, Ralph P. *Politics for Human Beings*. North Scituate, Mass.: Duxbury Press, 1975.

Jackson, George. *Soledad Brother*. New York: Coward McCann, Pub. 1970.

Jacobs, Harold., ed. *Weatherman*. Palo Alto, Calif.: Ramparts Press, 1970.

Joyce, R. D. *Transactional Analysis in Organizational Behavior*. New York: Pergamon Press, 1975.

Kinoy, Arthur. "A Party of the People." *Liberation* (December, 1973).

Klare, Michael T. "The Political Economy of Arms Sales: United States - Saudi Arabia." *Society*. 11, no. 6 (September-October 1974).

Lakey, George. "Manifesto for Nonviolent Revolution." *Win Magazine* (November 15, 1972).

Lamb, Karl A., ed. *Democracy, Liberalism, and Revolution*. Santa Barbara: Center for the Study of Democratic Institutions, 1971.

Lamb, Karl A. *The People, Maybe*. Belmont: Wadsworth Pub., 1971.

Leuchtenburg, William E. *Franklin D. Roosevelt and the New Deal*. New York: Harper Torchbooks, 1963.

Locke, John. *Of Civil Government: Second Treatise*. Chicago: Henry Regnery Co., 1964.

Locke, John. *Two Treatises of Government*. Edited by Peter Laslett. Cambridge: Cambridge University Press, 1960.

Lowi, Theodore J. *The End of Liberalism*. New York: Norton Pub., 1969.

Lowi, Theodore J., and Ripley, Randall B. *Legislative Politics U.S.A.* Boston: Little, Brown & Co., 1973.

Marchetti, Victor, and Marks, John D. *The CIA and the Cult of Intelligence*. New York: Alfred Knopf Pub., 1974.

Marx, Karl. *Capital: A Critique of Political Economy*. New York: Modern Library, 1936 (Trans).

Marx, Karl, and Engels, Friedrich. *The Communist Manifesto*. New York: Appleton-Century-Crofts, 1946.

McConnell, Grant. *The Modern Presidency*. New York: St. Martin's Press, 1967.

McCoy, Alfred W. et al. *The Politics of Heroin in South East Asia*. New York: Harper & Row, 1972.

Melman, Seymour. *Our Depleted Society*. New York: Holt, Rinehart & Winston, 1965.

Melman, Seymour. "Twelve Propositions on Productivity and the War Economy." *Challenge* 18, no. 1 (March/April 1975).

Mermelstein, David., ed. *The Economic Crisis Reader.* New York: Vintage Books, 1975.

Mills, C. Wright. *The Power Elite.* New York: Oxford University Press, 1956.

Morgan H. Wayne., ed. *The Guilded Age: A Reappraisal.* Syracuse: Syracuse University Press, 1963.

Morison, Samuel Eliot, and Commager, Henry Steele. *The Growth of the American Republic.* Vol. 2. New York: Oxford University Press, 1962.

Nader, Ralph; Hotchkiss, Ralf, and Dodge, Lowell. *What to Do with Your Bad Car: An Action Manual for Lemon Owners.* New York: Grossman Pub., 1971.

Orren, Karen. *Corporate Power and Social Change.* Baltimore: The Johns Hopkins Press, 1973.

Padover, Saul K. *The Genius of America.* New York: McGraw-Hill Book Co., 1960.

Parkes, Henry Banford. *The American Experience.* New York: Vintage Books, 1959.

Parrington, Vernon L. *The Colonial Mind, 1620-1800.* New York: Harcourt, Brace & World, 1927.

Parenti, Michael. "The Possibilities for Political Change." *Politics and Society* 1, no. 1 (November 1970).

Peterson, Robert W., ed. *Agnew: The Coining of a Household Word.* New York: Facts on File Pub., Co., 1972.

Petras, James. "Ideology and United States Political Scientists." *Science and Society* 29, no. 2 (1965).

Petras, James F., and LaPorte, Robert Jr. "Chile: No." *Foreign Policy* (Summer 1972).

Plato. *The Republic.* Translated by B. Jowett. New York: Random House [no date].

Puzo, Mario. *The Godfather.* New York: G. P. Putnam's Sons Co., 1969.

Rather, Dan, and Gates, Garry. *The Palace Guard.* New York: Harper & Row, 1974.

Rennie, Susan, and Grimstad, Kirsten. *New Woman's Survival Sourcebook.* New York: Alfred Knopf Pub., 1975.

Report of the President's Commission on Law Enforcement and Administration of Justice. Washington, D.C.: United States Government Printing Office, (February 1967).

Reston, James. *The Artillery of the Press.* New York: Harper and Row, 1967.

Rossiter, Clinton. *Parties and Politics in America.* Ithaca, N.Y.: Cornell University Press, 1960.

Rubenstein, Richard E. *Rebels in Eden: Mass Political Violence in the United States.* Boston: Little, Brown & Co., 1970.

Saloma, John S. III. *Congress and the New Politics.* Boston: Little, Brown and Co., 1969.

Samuelson, Robert J. "Bankrupt New York", *The New Republic* (May 10, 1975).

Savitch, H. V. "New York's Crisis and The Politics of Charter Revision." *New York Affairs* (Fall, 1975).

Schlesinger, Arthur M. Jr. *The Imperial Presidency.* New York: Houghton-Mifflin Pub., 1973.

Schuman, David. *A Preface to Politics.* Lexington, Mass.: D.C. Heath & Co., 1973.

Schwab, Peter, and Shneidman, J. Lee. *John F. Kennedy.* New York: Twayne Publishers Inc., 1974.

Shannon, David A. *The Great Depression.* Englewood Cliffs, N.J.: Prentice-Hall, Co. 1960.

Sherrill, Robert. *Why They Call it Politics.* New York: Harcourt Brace Jovanovich, Inc., 1972.

"Socialist Alternatives for America: A Bibliography." *Review of Radical Political Economics* 1 (Spring 1974).

Sorauf, Frank. *Political Parties in the American System.* Boston: Little, Brown & Co., 1964.

Staff of the *Washington Post. The Fall of a President.* New York: Dell Pub. Co., 1974.

Strauss, Leo, and Cropsey, Joseph., ed. *History of Political Philosphy.* Chicago: Rand McNally & Co., 1963.

Sullivan, Denis G. et al. *The Politics of Representation.* New York: St. Martin's Press, 1974.

Surkin, Marvin, and Wolfe, Alan. *An End to Political Science.* New York: Basic Books, 1970.

The New York Times, 11 February 1972; 15 February 1972; 12 July 1975.

The Pentagon Papers. New York: Bantam Books, 1971.

Tonsor, Stephen J. "The Conservative Element in American Liberalism." *The Review of Politics* 35, (October 1973).

Truman, Harry S. *Years of Trial and Hope: 1946-1952.* New York: Signet Pub., 1956.

Vogel, David. "The Politicization of the Corporation." *Social Policy* (May/June 1974).

Wark, Louis G. "Consumer Report/Nader Campaigns for Funds to Expand Activities of His Consumer Action Complex." *National Journal* (September 18, 1971).

Wiltse, Charles M. *The Jeffersonian Tradition in American Democracy.* New York: Hill and Wang, 1960.

Wise, David; Ross, Thomas B. *The Invisible Government.* New York: Random House, 1964.

Zeigler, Harmon. *Interest Groups in American Society.* Englewood Cliffs, N.J.: Prentice-Hall, Inc., 1964.

Foreign Policy Association, 169
  liberals' view of, 169, 170, 184–192
  RAND Corporation, 190, 191
  socialists' view of, 170, 171, 184–206
  upper social classes, 192–206
    education, 201–204
    historical development, 192–196
    Social Register, 196–198
  Washington representation, 173–184
    influence, 173–181
      coalitions, 179, 180
    information acquiring and translating, 181,
      182
    intelligence, 182
  See also Power elite.
Energy.
  multinational corporate control, 224–229
Energy Research and Development Ad-
    ministration, 572
Executive Branch. *See* Presidency.
Exxon Corporation.
  multinational energy control, 224, 225

F

FBI, 133–135, 140, 141, 150, 160–165
  Communist repression, 161–164
  conservatives' view of, 133
  historical development, 161, 162
  Hoover, J. Edgar, 161–165
  liberals' view of, 133, 134
  Morrow, Francis, 161
  organized crime, 271
  political repression, 161–164
  record keeping, 162
  socialists' view of, 134, 135, 160–165
Federal Election Campaign Act, 42
Federal Trade Commission.
    See Regulatory agencies.
Federalist Papers.
  pluralist theory, 7
  standing army, 74
  strong presidency, 64
Firestone, Shulamith.
  women's rights movement, 10
Firestone Rubber.
  multinational corporation, 210
First National City Bank
  holding company, 235
Food cooperatives, 561, 562
Foreign affairs
  presidential court, 75–78
    characteristics, 76
    recruitment, 76, 77
    structure of consensus, 77, 78
  presidential political center, 72–78
  publication, 616, 617
  See also Council on Foreign Relations,
    Presidency.

Foreign policy.
  bureaucratic-politics theory, 70–72
  Committee on Economic Development, 189,
    190
  Council on Foreign Relations, 48–50, 53, 55,
    171, 185–189
  government posts, occupational origins,
    90–98
  nuclear weapons, role of, 102–117
  Open Door policy, 70
  power elite,
    role in, 184–192
  theory, 67–70, 73
  publication, 617
  RAND Corporation, 190, 191
Foreign Policy Association, 55
Foreign service.
  · educational and social backgrounds, 90
Free Association, the, 414, 415
Freeman, Jo.
  Women's rights movement, 8, 9

G

Galbraith, John.
  military-industrial relationships, 129
  technostructure, 239, 249, 343
Gambling. *See* Crime syndication.
Gardner, John.
  public interest groups, 576–581
    See also Common cause.
General Foods.
  campaign contributions, 310
General Motors.
  defense contracts, 118
  public enterprise, 30
Georgakas, Dan.
  black auto workers, 523–536
Global Corporations. *See* Multinational
    corporations.
Government.
  conservatives' view of, 17
  decentralization, 26, 27
  demands on, revolution of, 21–28
    economic programs, 22
    financing of, 23, 24
    goals vs. resources, 24
    reform proposals, 26–28
    science and technology, 22
    social programs, 22, 23
  key positions, occupational origins, 90–98
  liberals' view of, 17
  policy, *See* Public policy.
  power elites, role of, 18, 32
  role of,
    conservatism, 6, 17
    liberalism, 17, 18
    socialism, 18
  socialists' view of, 18

value perspective of political science, 2, 3
Sweezy, Paul.
government economic intervention, 550–555

T

Television. *See* Media.
Tench, Richard.
lawyers, role of, 330–337
Tennessee Valley Authority.
public-private organization, 30
Texaco.
campaign contributions, 306
Tocqueville.
business-political relationship, 569
citizen action, 577
Equality of conditions, 21, 22, 26, 27
Truman, Harry.
inherent executive powers, 62, 63, 81
Tullock, Gordon.
government and corporation distinguished, 30
Turkus, Burton B.
organized crime, 259
Tyler, Gus.
organized crime, 259, 261, 262

U

Unemployment.
economic crisis, 539, 540, 544–549
Union Carbide.
campaign contributions, 307, 311
Union For Radical Political Economics, 538
Union Oil.
campaign contributions, 306
Unions.
black auto workers, 523–536
conservatives view of, 511, 513–519
crime syndication, 269, 270
leadership-management relationship, 511, 593
liberals' view of, 511, 519–523
socialists' view of, 511, 523–536, 593
work values, young workers, 513–519
See also Workers.
United Fruit.
multinational corporation, 210
United States Steel.
pollution, 36
price setting, 40
Universities, 413–447
College For Human Services, 560
conservatives' view of, 413, 416–427
Free Association, the, 414–415
government research programs, 413–427
NASA programs, 416–427
RANN programs, 416, 417, 427

sustaining University Program, (NASA), 417–427
liberals' view of, 413, 414, 427–434
political involvement, 413, 414
School of New Resources, 415
socialists' view of, 414, 415, 434–447
Upper class. *See* Elite clubs and associations, Power elite, Ruling class.

V

Value judgments.
role in political science, 2–4
Vietnam War.
costs of, 126
policies, 126, 127

W

War Registers' League.
socialist political group, 560, 561
Washington representation, 173–184
influence, 173–181
information acquiring and translating, 181, 182
intelligence, 182
Wealth.
income distribution, 47
Weatherman.
socialist political group, 561
Weaver, Paul.
journalism, 453–466
Weber, Max.
value perspective of political science, 3
Weidenbaum, Murray.
military-industrial relationships, 129
Wenglinsky, Martin.
television news, 467–474
Whalen, Eileen.
working women, 519–523
Wilson, James.
regulatory agencies, 349–361
Wolfe, Allan.
academia professionals, 434–447
secret police, abuses of authority, 137, 160–165
Women.
work force, 519–523
Workers.
black auto workers, 523–536
Motor City Labor League, 523, 534, 535
Revolutionary union movement, 526–536
women, 519–523
workplace, improvement, 517, 518
values, young workers, 513–519
See also Unemployment, Unions.

†